A PRACTICAL HINDI-ENGLISH DICTIONARY

[व्यावहारिक हिंदी-अंग्रेज़ी कोश]

Editors
MAHENDRA CHATURVEDI
BHOLA NATH TIWARI

National

National Publishing House
2/35 Ansari Road, Darya Ganj, New Delhi-110002 (India)

Branch
Chaura Rasta, Jaipur-302003

Thirty first Edition : 2008

Price : Rs. 275.00

Printed in India at Colourprint, Patpar Ganj Industrial Area, Delhi-110092 and published by National Publishing House, 2/35 Ansari Road, Darya Ganj, New Delhi-110002.

[ISBN 81-214-0536-X]

---

e-mail : sales@nationalpublishinghouse.com
Fax : (011) 23254407

Preface
(to the Second Edition)

The Editors have been encouraged by the spontaneous and hearty appreciation of their effort by users of the dictionary in general and by friends in particular.

The second edition is a much more improved, comprehensive and enlarged version of the first—keeping the basic framework intact. On valuable suggestions from friends in India, and esp. from friends teaching Hindi in foreign Universities, we have added some new categories of words in the dictionary and hope they will further facilitate the efforts of foreign friends trying to learn Hindi in their own universities and institutions. The new additions may be categorized as under :

1. Some mythological names which symbolise, or are characteristic of, certain traits of human personality or have given birth to idioms, sayings and proverbs current amongst Hindi-speakers (as भस्मासुर, दुर्योधन, राम, etc.). This nomenclature has enriched the language through such potential expressions and should, therefore, appropriately find a place in a general dictionary such as this.

2. Oblique forms of verbs, which do not yield to ready comprehension of the learner of Hindi, have also been incorporated in the dictionary (as किया, लिया, गया, etc.). Suggestions for the inclu-

sion of such forms had come from Hindi teachers of foreign university departments.

3. Some technical terms which have gained passage into contemporary writing.
4. Some hitherto unknown words of dialects that have been elevated to the position of recognised usages through the pen of significant writers.

Besides these categories, the dictionary has also been enlarged (and enriched) by the inclusion of numerous Hindi sayings, proverbs and idioms which would be difficult to find even in a Hindi-Hindi Dictionary. This dictionary is richer from this point of view than even the most voluminous of Hindi-Hindi dictionaries.

We have made a slight change in our system of phonetic pronunciation adopted in the first edition. In giving the phonetic pronunciations we had post-fixed an 'a' to consonant-clusters or to semi-vowels (य, व). This has now been omitted since the words that sound as ending in अ (अकारांत) are not actually so. What we hear is just plosion.

We are thankful to our friend Dr. R.K. Kohli for reading through the preface of the dictionary and suggesting improvements therein as also for some of his suggestions in general. Mention may also be made of Madhukar Chaturvedi, Km. Mukul and Rajiv Tiwari for their keen interest in, and active cooperation towards, the preparation of the press copy of the second Edition of the dictionary.

Mahendra Chaturvedi
Bhola Nath Tiwari

Dipawali, 1974.

Editorial Preface
(to the First Edition)

Those who are conversant with the pace and process of growth of reference works and lexicographical literature [part of the literature of knowledge] in Hindi will, no doubt, agree that there has been an unusual spurt of such literature in the post-Independence era. Still, measured by modern standards, there is an apalling dearth of literature dwelling on various linguistic aspects of Hindi and representing profound linguistic studies—and there is no room for controversy on this point, too. The lexicographical art in Hindi is in its primal stages and Hindi dictionaries which can match the high standards of Webster's International Dictionary or Shorter Oxford Dictionary, or bilingual dictionaries available in European languages, are yet a long way off. Dictionaries, lexicons and glossaries form a very valuable part of the literature of knowledge and their importance in any linguistic study is self-evident. It is with a deep sense of the obligation to contribute their mite to the enrichment of this rather poor field, and with full consciousness of the hazards involved, that the Editors undertook to compile a dictionary such as the present one. We have absolutely no pretensions to a pioneering work and should our endeavour prove to be of some help to the Hindi learner, the translator, and the user in general, we shall consider our efforts amply rewarded.

Dictionaries form a wide and varied genre of the literature of knowledge—one of the main categories being comprised of bilingual dictionaries. Bilingual dictionaries represent an effort to convey the meanings and significance of words, typical usages, idioms and proverbs of one language through the medium of another—which may or may not be blessed with matching verve and richness. The tradition of bilingual dictionaries can be traced back to fairly ancient times in world literature. India, too, is not without its own tradition of bilingual dictionaries although Indian languages, today, cannot claim to be as advanced or rich as some other languages of the world, such as English, French, German and Russian. And in this respect what is true of Indian languages in general is also true of Hindi.

The first bilingual dictionary in Hindi is the *Kha:liq Ba:ri:* which lists Persian (and sometimes Arabic and Turkish) equivalents of Hindi words and phrases. We can enumerate about half-a-dozen more, such as '*Lugatae Hindi*', '*Gara:ybul luga:t*', '*Alla:khuda:i:*', in this tradition. Obviously, they reflect genuine efforts on the part of immigrating Muslims to acquire fluency in the Hindi language and to understand it better. The same phenomenon was repeated when the Europeans achieved sway over the northern parts of the country and felt the imperative need to have a workable knowledge of Hindi. Hindi-English Dictionaries numbering a score and a half were compiled to fulfil this need of the times. The earliest in the series was John Fergusan's 'A Dictionary of Hindustani language' which was published in London in 1773 A.D. Among others 'A Dictionary : Hindustanee and English, Calcutta, 1808 (Taylor)', 'A Dictionary : Hindustani and English, London, 1817 (Shakespeare)', 'A Dictionary : Hindustani and English, London, 1848 (Duncan Forbes)' and 'A Dictionary of Urdu, Classical Hindi and English, London, 1884 (Platts)' deserve special mention. The last mentioned work is, undoubtedly, the best of the whole lot.

The second quarter of the present century saw another dictionary compiled by Shri R. C. Pathak (Bhargava's Standard Illustrated Dictionary of the Hindi language, Banares, 1946) which, although based essentially on Platts, represents a linguistic anachronism and betrays complete ignorance of the art of lexicography. It abounds, on the one hand, in words and meanings which never formed an essential part of standard Hindi vocabulary and ignores, on the other, numerous words and meanings that have very much been an asset to, and form an integral part of, the language. The very fact that this dictionary has gone into several editions reflects the poor state of our lexicographical equipment in the field.

In 1966, the Central Hindi Directorate of the Govt. of India, Ministry of Education, brought out a small-sized 'Hindi-English Dictionary of Common Words', comprising about five thousand entries, at the instance of the then Prime Minister, Pandit Jawaharlal Nehru. This was rather a meagre tribute to the wishes of a great and mighty man who always believed in doing things 'in a big way'. It, however, reflected an approach that was much more scientific and precision-based. With all its limitations in terms of size and selection of entries, it was a worthwhile contribution to this rather sterile field.

In fact, none of the dictionaries mentioned above incorporates all, or nearly all, the active vocabulary of modern Hindi or adopts comparatively newer lexicographical techniques. The present work is an humble effort to fulfil the twin objectives.

The main characteristics of the dictionary may be summed up as follows :

(i) It comprises almost the whole active vocabulary of modern Hindi including words of common or literary usages as also commonly prevalent technical and semi-technical terms.

(ii) An effort has been made herein to incorporate almost all current idioms, proverbs and peculiar usages of Hindi.

(iii) Each main entry is followed by its *actual* pronunciation.

(iv) While fixing the English equivalents for Hindi words, emphasis has not been laid on conglomerating all, even remotely possible, words having far-fetched affinity of meaning, but on the selection of semantically precise and exact equivalents as far as possible. It is the semantic proximity, in other words, that has mattered in the selection of words and not the numerical strength of the equivalents. In fact, we have tried to restrict the number of equivalents as far as possible.

It may, in short, be stated that an over riding emphasis on practical aspect of linguistic usages forms the keystone of its edifice. It is this factor that is sought to be reflected in the title of the dictionary viz. 'A **Practical** Hindi-English Dictionary'. We seek here to discuss, in brief, the main problems of compilation in respect of this dictionary.

Word Entries

Selection of the entries represents one of the first, and fairly ticklish, problems of compilation. It depends, most of all, on the proposed user of the dictionary—as envisaged by the compiler(s). We have focussed our attention essentially on those who are trying to learn conversational or literary Hindi, on the general user of the language and the translator of Hindi works and texts. We have not been very liberal in the inclusion of technical terms which form a very small percentage of the total entries. In fact we have, by and large, selected such words as verge on the border-line and may safely be termed as semi-technical. There is ample room for difference of opinion over the selection (or rejection) of main as well as sub-entries in a dictionary of this type and personal judgment, undoubtedly, plays a significant role in arriving at a decision in respect of all controversial entries. We have, however, taken care to ensure that words, phrases, idioms and proverbs of our active vocabulary are not left out. Apart from entries that are an aid to the comprehension of subsequent words and phrases thereunder, currency forms one of the important criteria for selection of words as main entries—though it is difficult to decide what words are more, and what others less, current without an element of subjectivity.

We have followed six different techniques of inscribing a word, phrase, idiom or proverb by way of a sub-entry under a main entry :—

1. They are in some cases written in full—especially, where the initial head-word has undergone a formal variation, inflexional or otherwise, in the sub-entry; e. g. 'अँगरेजियत' under 'अँगरेज', 'अंगांगि संबंध' under 'अंग', 'कलेजे में तीर लगना' under 'कलेजा' and so on.
2. Some of the sub-entries are preceded by a tilde (~) which means that the actual words etc. are formed by prefixing the main entry to it and that it forms an organic whole, e.g. '~च्छेद' under the head-word 'अंग' actually stands for 'अंगच्छेद' or '~ता' under 'अधिक' is actually to be read as 'अधिकता'.
3. Some others are preceded by a dash, instead of a tilde, which signifies that the main entry and the sub-entry combine to form the whole expression and yet they are written separately, e.g., '–में' under the main entry 'अधर' would denote the complete expression as 'अधर में'; '–भर' under 'कौड़ी' means 'कौड़ी भर' and '–को ग्रहण लगना' under 'चाँद' should be read as 'चाँद को ग्रहण लगना'.
4. In some cases, the reader will find a hyphen preceding a sub-entry and that should be taken to mean that the two, i.e. the main and the sub-entries form a compound and are joined together by a hyphen in usual usage. For example, '-विक्षेप' under the main entry 'अंग' should be read as 'अंग-विक्षेप', '-करकट' under 'कूड़ा' should be read as 'कूड़ा-करकट'.
5. A slanting near-vertical line (/) has been interposed in between the body of a word in certain cases which signifies that the subsequent entries are formed by prefixing the earlier portion of the word so divided. For example, we have a sub-entry as, '~रेदार' under कँगू/रा' which means that the actual sub-entry is कँगूरेदार.
6. A dot (o) preceding a sub-entry means that the latter sub-entry is formed by prefixing the whole of the sub-entry immediately before it. Thus, a dot followed by करना (viz.

o करना) under 'इधर' after -उधर is tantamount to 'इधर-उधर करना' or under 'कं/घा' and after the sub-entry '~घी' (i e. कंघी), -चोटी would denote that the word under study is 'कंघी-चोटी'.

The main entries are sometimes more than one representing prevalent variations of a word. They are grouped together alphabetically in full as one main entry (as कुमुद, कुमुदनी), or shown within bracket if the difference is confined to just one letter or so as कथ(था)कली, which denotes both the variations, viz. कथकली, कथाकली. The latter difference has also been denoted by a slanting near-vertical line as in चंगे/र,~री (which denotes two entries—चंगेर, चंगेरी).

A slanting near-vertical line interposed in between various words denotes alternatives. It just means that the words on either side of the line are alternatives and the two may be used interchangeably. For example, ~दिक्/दिश under 'चतुर्' means 'चतुर्दिक्' or 'चतुर्दिश' both, ~ष्पद/ष्पाद under चतु/ष्, 'is tantamount to 'चतुष्पद' and 'चतुष्पाद' both. The same thing holds in respect of idioms. –देना/लगाना under 'चपत' denote two sub-entries, viz. चपत देना or चपत लगाना, conveying identical meaning.

Pronunciation

The general belief amongst people is that there is exact conformity between the spoken and written forms of words in Hindi and that words are written exactly as they are spoken and spoken precisely as they are written. The truth is, however, remarkably different. 'नाना' for example is pronounced as 'नाँनाँ', 'उपन्यास' as 'उपन्न्याँस', 'बहन' as 'बैहन' and so on. It is because of this gulf between the spellings and pronunciations that we have tried to indicate the actual pronunciations of all the main entries. Some of the earlier Hindi-English dictionaries do give pronunciations, in Roman alphabet, of the words written in Devna:gri: but these are not *actual* pronunciations—they are more of transliterations of the written forms. In fact, the present dictionary is the first wherein an effort has been made to transcribe the actual pronunciations and, therefore, errors—both of omission and commission—cannot be ruled out. It would not be out of place here to recount some of the difficulties encountered in the matter of pronunciation.

1. Essentially, the written forms can only indicate the pronunciation. It is pretty difficult to reduce to exact written form the actual pronunciation of any word of any language whatsoever. Even if the effort is made, the pronunciations would need fairly advanced technical skill to be correctly comprehended because of a variety of diacritical marks and it may not be possible for all the users of the dictionary to benefit from the

additional editorial effort.

2. The editors had originally planned to make the pronunciations as accurate as possible and yet to avoid being too technical but the limitations of Hindi typography proved too much to surmount. What was possible had, therefore, to be abandoned because of the handicaps and limitations of the press. And what is now before the reader is some sort of an enforced compromise.

3. Hindi, with its variations, is the spoken language of a fairly large region of the Indian Union and we find different pronunciations in different areas of this region. Not only this, the Hindi pronunciation of a Sanskrit-knowing Hindi-speaking man of the same area differs from that of one who knows English and Urdu, while one who knows neither Sanskrit nor English and Urdu has his own peculiar style of pronunciation. Which one of these numerous variations is to be taken as the standard, and adopted ? This poses a tough problem. This preface is not the appropriate place to discuss the problem in detail, knotty as it is. Suffice it to say that we have accepted the pronunciation of *an educated original resident of Delhi as our norm.* We have, in some exceptional cases, given two variations of pronunciation when we thought it to be absolutely essential. Perhaps we thought it better to err on the right side—as the proverb goes. And yet, we have no hesitation in confessing that our notion of standard form has still been subjective. Probably there is no other way. Objectivity is impossible to achieve in the field without a thorough survey on a wide scale.

The vowel is seldom pronounced at the end of a word and, in some cases, at the end of a syllable. Thus, 'आप' is pronounced as 'आप्' and 'आवश्यकता' as 'आवश्यक्ता'. We have constantly kept the fact in view while transcribing the pronunciations. But when preceded by a compound consonant some people (esp. Sanskrit knowing people) do pronounce it, fully or partly. That is why we have retained the 'अ' in such cases. In fact, this post-compound consonantal 'अ' has not altogether disappeared in pronunciation and that is why we thought it prudent to retain it—again, perhaps, with a view to err on the right side, if at all.

5. 'ज्ञ' is variously pronounced as ज्यँ, ग्यँ, द्नँ and ग्य by Hindi-speaking people depending on the extent of their familiarity with, and fascination for, the Sanskritic style of pronunciation but the most popularly current amongst them is 'ग्य', which we have uniformly adopted.

6. ऋ, ष and the Visargas (:) had typical pronuciations in Sanskrit and though they form an integral part of the written form of the Hindi language yet, in actual practice, they are pronounced as रि, श and ह् and have, therefore, been rendered as such.

7. Although we have only one 'व' as far as the written form is concerned, in actual pronunciation it is labio dental (v) in some cases and bilabial (w) in others. This difference is not very clear in some words, yet we have kept it in view as far as possible.

8. ऐ and औ are presently pronounced in three different ways in the Hindi region. Broadly speaking, those adopting the Sanskrit tradition pronounce them as 'अई' and 'अउ' respectively, those belonging to the eastern parts and some western tract of the region pronounce them as अएँ and ओँ while in the western parts they are generally retained as base vowels ऐ and औ. (There are, of course, exceptions when they are pronounced as 'अइ' and 'अउ'). These two vowels are thus pronounced as diphthongs as well as monophthongs. We have indicated them by the symbols *ai* and *au* which should be read as base vowels 'ऐ' and 'औ' (more 'open' in comparison with 'ए' and 'ओ'). We could not work out a more approximate symbol because of typographical shortcomings and handicaps. An effort at closest possible approximation has, however, been made in all cases.

9. ऑ, क़, ख़, ग़, ज़ and फ़ have been represented by the symbols ɔ, q, ḳḥ, g̣, z and f, respectively, in words where they are so pronounced by the educated class in the Hindi region. In cases where they have been otherwise moulded into the pattern of Hindi phonetic system, they have accordingly been represented by the symbols a:, k, kh, g, j, and ph, in pronunciation.

10. A post-vowel colon (:) represents a long vowel, a horizontal line mark overhead signifies its nasalization. Considered in minutest details, each phoneme has numerous allophones but it is only the major ones that have been given in the pronunciations.

Other important points regarding the system adopted herein, for rendering the pronunciations, will become self-evident from the following charts :—

Vowels

	Front	mid	back
Close	i:, i		u:, u
Half-close	e		o
Half-open	ai	a	au
open			a:

Consonants

	bilabial	labio-dental	dental	alveo-lar	pre-palatal retroflex	palatal	soft-palatal	uvu-lar	glottal
stop	p, ph, b, bh		t, th, d, dh.		ṭ, ṭḥ, ḍ, ḍḥ		k, kh, g. gh	q	
affricate						ch, chh, j, jh			
nasal	m			n	ṇ	ṇ	ṅ		
flapped					ṛ, ṛḥ				
rolled				r					
lateral				l					
fricative		f, v		s, z		sh	ḳḥ, g̣		h
semi-vowel	w					y			

KEY TO PRONUNCIATION

		अँ	ā	ऑ	ɔ
अ	a	आँ	ā:	ऋ	ri
आ	a:	इँ	ī		
इ	i	ईं	ī:		
ई	i:	उँ	ū		
उ	u	ऊँ	ū:		
ऊ	u:	एँ	ē		
ए	e	ऐं	a̅i̅		
ऐ	ai	ओं	ō		
ओ	o	औं	a̅u̅		
औ	au				

क्	k	ख्	kh	ग्	g	घ्	gh	ङ्	ṅ
च्	ch	छ्	chh	ज्	j	झ्	jh	ञ	[illegible]
ट्	ṭ	ठ्	ṭh	ड्	ḍ	ढ्	ḍh	ण्	n
त्	t	थ्	th	द्	d	ध्	dh	न्	n
प्	p	फ्	ph	ब्	b	भ्	bh	म्	m
य्	y	र्	r	ल्	l	व्	v/w		
श्	sh	ष्	sh	स्	s	ह्	h		
क़्	q	ख़्	kh̤	ग़्	g̤				
ज़्	z	फ़्	f						
ड़्	ṛ	ढ़	ṛh						

[A colon (:) following a short vowel denotes its long form. ɔ has been used to denote a rounded a: (as in कॉलि(ले)ज). It is also rather close as compared with a:.

A horizontal line mark over the body of a vowel-symbol represents its nasalized form :—ā (अँ), ā: (आँ), ī (इँ), ī: (ईं), ū (उँ), ū: (ऊँ), ē (एँ), ā̄ī (ऐं), ō (ओं), āū (औं).]

Grammar

As far as grammatical indications are concerned, we have something to say only in respect of the gender. There is a large number of words that are used in the feminine gender in one region and in the masculine in another. The reverse is also true in an equally large number of cases. There is yet another category of words which are used sometimes in one gender and sometimes in the other. This anarchy extends to such an incredible limit that the same person uses a word in feminine gender in one context and in masculine in another. The numerous Hindi Dictionaries have only helped in perpetuating this confusion—in fact, they have contributed to make it more confounded. In all such controversial cases, we have adopted the genders that are prevalent in the western Hindi region and have been accepted as standard in grammatical works. The indication *nm, nf* stands for words that are freely used in both the genders but such cases are few, in our opinion.

Meanings

Fixation of meanings and appropriate equivalents forms the most difficult aspect of lexicographical attainments. Precise meanings and exact equivalents are much more elusive than they appear to be to a layman. The whole effort is, in fact, an exercise in approximation and the closer this approximation, the more successful the effort. Schopenhauer, in his typical philosophical manner, has rightly pointed towards the fact that the so-called synonyms in any two languages could at best be represented by two 'overlapping circles'. Nobody understands the genuineness of this remarkable expression better than a practical lexicographer. But, then, bilingual and multilingual dictionaries have been, and are being, compiled and scholars have continued to fondly indulge in this exercise in approximation. It is with the object of achieving the closest approximation between a word and its equivalent(s) and to make it (or them) distinctly intelligible that we have kept certain things in view :—

1. We have, as far as possible, adopted a strictly practical approach and have given only such meanings of words as are current and prevalent. We have generally discarded obsolescent and obsolete meanings.

2. An effort has been made to give the closest English equivalents for the various Hindi entries. We have tried to steer clear of the general tendency to collect as large a number of equivalents as possible—unscientific as it is.

3. *When the equivalents have more or less the same or proximal nuances, they are separated by a comma. But if the meanings or the shades of these meanings differ substantially, semi-colon has been used to indicate the fact of this difference.* The meanings could perhaps be numbered but that would have consumed plenty of space. The use of a semi-colon has perhaps served the purpose equally well.

4. The articles 'a', 'an' and 'the' have been appropriately prefixed to the first of the nominal meanings only.

5. A slanting near-vertical line denotes equivalents and/or interchangeability of the meanings.

The problem of finding equivalents in a bilingual dictionary becomes much more insurmountable when the cultural gap between the languages in question is wide, as in the present case. On numerous occasions, we have been faced with the predicament of failing to find an equally forceful and pithy equivalent for a simple but tricky Hindi word. Such cases may well be illustrative of the limitations of our linguistic attainments in the target language—a language with which neither of us grew in our early childhood.

With the successful (?) culmination of this rather unending task of dictionary-making in sight, we would like to express our gratitude to Shri K. L. Malik (and sons, especially his enthusiastic son Shri Surendra Malik) of M/s National Publishing House for readily agreeing to take up the project and their subsequent remarkable success in ever-concealing their exasperation and restlessness over the unforeseen delay in execution of the project under very suave and soft-spoken reminders and exhortations. But for Shri Malik's cool and composed manners, it would have become a scare for both of us. We are also very much indebted to Shri Shyam Kumar, the printer of the dictionary, whose active ways and 'voiced' personality always kept both the Editors, and perhaps also the Publisher, on the alert—fully equipped with plausible excuses for not sending the press-matter in time. We would also like to thank Shri S. P. Bajaj for his ever-readiness to do the utmost within the shortest possible time on the typing front.

Among others, we would like to make a special mention of Shri Lakshman Chaturvedi for his timely and valuable literary assistance, and of Kumari Shashi Prabha and Jyotsna for their untiring efforts towards the speedy preparation of the press copy. We would not observe the formality of expressing gratitude for their contribution because that would amount to devaluing their affectionate feelings and would sound as odd as thanking our ownselves.

And lastly, we would like to heartily thank our numerous friends, who, by their persistent enquiries regarding the delay in publication of the dictionary, made us all the more conscious of the urgency of our task and indirectly helped in the expeditious completion of the project.

अ

अ a—the first letter and the first vowel of the Devna:gri: alphabet; a prefix signifying negation or absence (of something) as असुंदर, अस्पष्ट; see अन्.

अंक aṅk (*nm*) a number, numeral, figure, digit; marks; a mark; an act (of a drama or play); lap, embrace; ~क an accountant; a marker; ~गणित (the science of) Arithmetic; —भरना, —लगाना to embrace.

अंक/न aṅkān (*nm*) stamping; plotting; marking; ~नीय worth being marked/stamped.

अंकपत्र aṅkpattr (*nm*) a mark-sheet.

अँकाई āka:i: (*nf*) an evaluation, assessment or appraisal; remuneration paid for it; marking, valuation.

अंकांतर aṅka:ntar (*nm*) act-interval.

अंकित aṅkit (*a*) marked; inscribed, written; endorsed; —करना to record; to mark.

अंकु/र aṅkur (*nm*) a sprout; an offshoot; a seed-bud; ~रित sprouted, begun to shoot forth; grown; ~रित-यौवना a female who has started showing signs of emergent youthfulness.

अँकुरना, अँकुराना ākurnā:, ākura:nā: (*v*) to sprout.

अंकुश aṅkush (*nm*) a hook, elephant-driver's iron hook; hamulus; control; —रखना to exercise control; —रहना/होना to have control over.

अँखु/आ, ~वा ākhua:, ~va: (*nm*) an eyelet; a paper-fastener.

अंग aṅg (*nm*) a limb; member; body; part; component; organ; ~च्छेद amputation; ~त्राण an armour; -प्रत्यंग each and every part of the body; -भंग mutilation of any part of the body; -भंगिमा/भंगी (fascinating or inviting) physical gesture or posture, graceful manner or carriage; ~भूत component, constituent; ~रक्षक a bodyguard; protector of person; ~रक्षा protection of person; -राग aromatic unguents and cosmetics; -विक्षेप twisting of the parts of the body for emotive expression; -संस्कार make-up; -सौष्ठव physical charm; ~हीन maimed; limbless; disabled; अंगांगि संबंध organic relationship; -अंग खिल जाना/मुस्कराना to be beaming and buoyant; -अंग ढीले हो जाना to be worn and wearied, to lose muscularity; -फूले न समाना to be in a rapture; —में अंग न समाना to be in a fit of ecstasy; —लगना (for nourishment etc.) to be manifest in the form of physical fitness or health; —लगाना to embrace.

अंगड़-खंगड़ (also अंगड़-भंगड़) aṅgaṛ khaṅgaṛ (*nm*) disorderly stuff; scraps; junk.

अँगड़ाई āgṛa:i: (*nf*) twisting for

stretching of the body for relaxation: —लेना see अँगड़ाना.

अँगड़ाना āgṛa:nā: (*v*) to twist or stretch the limbs or body for relaxation.

अंगद aṅgad (*nm*) one of the generals in the army of Lord Ra:m and the son of monkey-king बालि, —का पाँव irrevocably firm, unflinching.

अँगरखा āgarkha: (*nm*) a long loose upper garment for men.

अँगरेज āgrez (*nm*) an Englishman; अँगरेज़ियत Englishism, Anglicism.

अंगरेज़ी āgrezi: (*a*) Anglican, English; (*nf*) the English language.

अंगलेट aṅgleṭ (*nm*) build, physical frame.

अंगांगि-भाव aṅga:ṅgi bha:v (*nm*) mutual relationship of the part and the whole, organic relationship.

अंगार, अंगारा aṅga:r, aṅga:ra: (*nm*) an ember, live coal, burning charcoal; —उगलना to be fierce and fiery in speech; —बनना/होना to be red with rage, to be in a fury; —बरसना to be excessively hot (said of the weather); अंगारों पर पैर रखना to jump into hot water, to invite trouble; अंगारों पर लोटना to be in flames from within, to burn within (on account of jealousy or rage).

अंगिया āgiya: (*nf*) bodice.

अंगी aṅgi: (*a*) primary, main, dominant; —रस dominant emotion.

अंगीकार aṅgi:ka:r (*nm*) adoption; acceptance; undertaking; —करना to adopt, accept or undertake; hence अंगीकरण, अंगीकृत, अंगीकृति.

अँगीठी āgi:ṭhi: (*nf*) a grate, portable oven, fire-pot.

अंगुल aṅgul (*nm*) (measurement equal to) a finger's breadth.

अँगुली āguli: (*nf*) see उँगली.

अंगुश्त aṅgusht (*nm*) a finger.

अंगुश्ताना aṅgushta:nā: (*nm*) a metal cover for finger.

अँगूठा āgu:ṭha: (*nm*) thumb; —चूमना to flatter, to act the toady (to a person); —दिखाना to defy and deride; to evade in defiance.

अंगूठी āgu:ṭhi: (*nf*) a finger-ring.

अंगूर aṅgu:r (*nm*) grape; अंगूरी vinous; —का बाग़ vineyard —की खेती viniculture; —की फ़सल vintage; —की बेल vine; —खट्टे होना to decry something that has proved inaccessible.

अँगौछना āgauchhnā: (*v*) to wipe (the body) dry with a towel or any other piece of cloth.

अँगौछा āgauchha: (*nm*) a towel, any piece of cloth for wiping (the body) dry.

अँग्रेज़ी āgrezi: (*nf*) see अँगरेज़ी.

अंचल anchal (*nm*) the outward fringe or portion of a *sa:ri:*, etc. ; a region; frontier territory.

अंजन anjan (*nm*) collyrium an eyesalve; ~हारी a sty.

अंजर-पंजर anjar-panjar (*nm*) physical frame, skeleton; joints of the body; —ढीले होना to have the body reduced to a state of lifelessness; slackening of the joints and parts of the body (on account of excessive physical strain or sudden heavy jerk or impact)

अंजलि anjali (*nf*) the cup-shaped hollow formed by the joining of the two palms together; ~गत within one's grasp, acquired; -पुट the cup of one's palms; ~बद्ध with the palms joined together.

अंजाम anja:m (*nm*) the conclusion, end; result; completion; —देना to accomplish, to complete; —पाना to be accomplished/completed.

अंजीर anji:r (*nm*) a fig-tree; its fruit.

अंजुमन anjuman (*nf*) an association; a society.

अंझा anjha: (*nm*) intermission of work; a holiday.

अँटना āṭnā: (*v*) to be contained in; to suffice (for containment).

अंट-शंट ant-shant (*a*) absurd; incoherent, irrelevant, inconsistent; meaningless.

अंटा anta: (*nm*) a ball; pill (as of opium or *bhang*); small shell or *kauri*:; spool of thread; (somebody's) clutches; turn; ~गुड़गुड़, ~चित्त dead-drunk, excessively intoxicated; **अंटे पर चढ़ना** to fall into the clutches (of).

अंटी anti: (*nf*) fold of the loin cloth on the waist; space between any two fingers of a hand; a spool; knot; ~बाज a swindler, cheat; —पर चढ़ना to fall into hostile clutches; —मारना to swindle.

अंड and (*nm*) an egg; ~कोष testicles; ~ज born out of an egg; ~वृद्धि hydrocele.

अंड-बंड and-bānd (*a*) see **अंट-शंट**.

अंडा anda: (*nm*) an egg; **अंडे-बच्चे** the offspring; **अंडे की खातिर मुर्गी हलाल करना** to kill the hen that lays the golden eggs; **अंडे सेना** to hatch, to incubate; to sit idle.

अंडाकार (अंडाकृति) anda:ka:r (anda:kriti) (*a*) oval (shaped), egg-shaped.

अंडाणु andā:nu (*nm*) the ovum.

अंडाशय anda:shay (*nm*) the ovary.

अंडी andi: (*nf*) castor. —का तेल castor oil.

अँडुआ āṛua: (*a*) uncastrated; —बैल an uncastrated bull.

अंतःकथा antahkatha: (*nf*) an episode or event alluded to in a text.

अंतःकरण antahkarān (*nm*) the conscience, inner self.

अंतःकलह antahkalah (*nm*) internecine quarrel or warfare.

अंतःकालीन antahka:li:n (*a*) provisional.

अंतःपटल antahpaṭal (*nm*) plerome.

अंतःपुर antahpur (*nm*) the women's apartment in a royal household, harem; a thalamus.

अंतःप्रज्ञा antahpraggya: (*nf*) intuition; ~वाद intuitionism; ~श्रित intuitional; intuitionistic, intuition-based.

अंतःप्रवेश antahpravesh (*nm*) ingression.

अंतःप्रेरणा antahprernā: (*nf*) intuition; inspiration, inner urge.

अंतःशक्ति antahshakti (*nf*) potency; inherent strength.

अंतःस्थ antasth (*a*) intermediate, situated in between; (*nm*) the semi-vowels य्, र्, ल्, and व्.

अंतःस्था antastha: (*nf*) the medulla.

अंतःस्राव antahssra:v (*nm*) internal secretion.

अंत ant (*nm*) the end, termination; result, conclusion; mystery, secret; ~हीन unending, endless; —पाना to discover the secret of; —बनना to have a good end; —बिगड़ना to have a tragic finale; —भला सो भला all is well that ends well; —लेना to extort the secret.

अँतड़ी ātṛi: (*nf*) intestines; —की बात जानना to delve into the innermost secrets; —में बल पड़ना (हँसते-हँसते) to laugh into convulsions.

अंततः antatah (*adv*) lastly, finally, at last; eventually.

अंततोगत्वा antatogattva: (*adv*) at long last, lastly; eventually.

अंतरंग antarang (*a*) internal, interior; intimate; private; ~ता intimacy, intimate relationship; interiority; —वृत्त the inner circle: the inside story; —सचिव private secretary; —सभा the high command, executive.

अंतर antar (*nm*) difference; distance; interval; spacing; interior; heart; margin; —खोलना to open one's cards; to divulge one's secrets; to give vent to one's inner feelings.

अंतरक antarak (*nm*) a spacer.

अंतरण antarāṉ (*nm*) spacing; shifting; devolution; handing over.

अंतरतम antartam (*nm*) the core of the heart, heart of hearts.

अँतरा ātra: (*a*) alternative.

अंतरा antara: (*nm*) any verse of a song etc. excepting the first

अंतरात्मा antara:tmā: (*nf*) the soul, inner self, spirit.

अंतराय antara:y (*nm*) an impediment, obstacle; ~क an interruptor.

अंतराल antara:l (*nm*) an interval, intervening time or space, gap; inner space; —राज्य a buffer state.

अंतरिक्ष antariksh (*nm*) space, sky; ~गामी, ~चारी moving in the skies; —यात्री an astronaut, a space traveller; —विज्ञान meteorology.

अंतरिम antarim (*a*) interim.

अंतरीप antari:p (*nm*) a cape, headland, promontory.

अंतरीय antari:y (*nm*) the lower garment.

अंतर् antar—an allomorph of Sanskrit अंतः meaning internal, interior, inherent (as in अंतर्कथा, अंतर्गत); inter—, between two or more (as in अंतर्राष्ट्रीय, अंतर्प्रांतीय).

अंतर्कथा antarkatha: (*nf*) see अंतःकथा

अंतर्काल antarka:l (*nm*) inter-regnum.

अंतर्गत antargat (*ind.*) under, within; (*a*) included.

अंतर्ग्रह antargrah (*nm*) a planet; interior.

अंतर्ग्रहण antargrahāṉ (*nm*) ingestion.

अंतर्जात antarja:t (*a*) innate, inherent.

अंतर्जातीय antarja:ti:y (*a*) inter-caste.

अंतर्ज्ञान antargya:n (*nm*) intuition; spiritual enlightenment, self-realisation; ~वाद intuitionalism.

अंतर्ज्योति antarjyoti (*nf*) the inner light, inner flame.

अंतर्ज्वाला antarjwa:la: (*nm*) worry, languish.

अंतर्दशा antardasha: (*nf*) in Astrology, an intermediate period.

अंतर्दर्शन antardarshan (*nm*) introspection.

अंतर्दर्शी antardarshi: (*a*) introspective; (*nm*) one who can see within oneself.

अंतर्दृश्य antardrishshy (*a*) intervisible; ~ता intervisibility.

अंतर्दृष्टि antardrishṭi (*nf*) insight.

अंतर्देशीय antardeshi:y (*a*) interstate; inland.

अंतर्द्वन्द्व antardvandv (*nm*) inner/mental conflict.

अंतर्धान antardha:n (*nm*) disappearance, reduction to invisibility.

अंतर्धारा antardha:ra: (*nf*) undercurrent.

अंत/र्ध्वंस antardhvans (*nm*) sabotage; ~ध्वंसक, ~ध्वंसी saboteur.

अंतर्नली antarnalī: (*nf*) a spool.

अंतर्नियम antarniyam (*nm*) articles (of association, etc. of a company).

अंतर्निविष्ट antarnivishṭ (*a*) included; permeating within.

अंतर्निहित antarnihit (*a*) implied; understood; included.

अंतर्प्रयाण antarprayāṉ (*nm*) inward travel/march.

अंतर्प्रांतीय antarpra:nti:y (*a*) interprovincial (correct form **अंतः-प्रांतीय**).

अंतर्प्रदेशिक antarpra:deshik (*a*) inter-regional, interstate.

अंतर्बोध antarbodh (*nm*) see **अंतर्ज्ञान**.

अंतर्भाव antarbha:v (*nm*) inclusion; permeation.

अंतर्भावना antarbha:vnā: (*nf*) inner feeling; conscience.

अंतर्भूत antarbhu:t (*a*) included, involved; permeated.

अंतर्भूमि antarbhu:mi (*nf*) sub-soil.

अंतर्भेदन antarbhedān (*nm*) intrusion; probe.

अंतर्भेदी antarbhedi: (*a*) intrusive; probing.

अंतर्मना antarmanā: (*a*) introvertive.

अंतर्मुख antarmukh (*a*) introvertive; **~ता** introversion.

अंतर्मुखी antarmukhi: (*a*) introversive, introvertive.

अंतर्यामी antarya:mi: (*a*) pervading the interior or inner self; (*nm*) the Supreme Spirit.

अंतर्राष्ट्रीय antarra:shṭri:y (*a*) international; **~करण** internationalisation.

अंतर्राष्ट्रीयता antarra:shṭri:yta: (*nf*) internationalism; **~वाद** internationalism; **~वादी** (an) internationalist(ic).

अंतर्लयन antarlayān (*nm*) absorption.

अंतर्लीन antarli:n (*a*) self-engrossed, absorbed; latent.

अंतर्वती antarvati: (*a*) pregnant.

अंतर्वर्ती antarvarti: (*a*) buffer; pervading/permeating, located within, overlapping.

अंतर्वस्तु antarvastu (*nm*) the content:

अंतर्वस्त्र antarvastr (*nm*) an underwear.

अंतर्वासी antarva:si: (*a*) instaying; indoor; **—रोगी** indoor patient.

अंतर्विकार antarvika:r (*nm*) mental aberration, mental perversion.

अंतर्विराम antarvira:m (*nm*) intermission, intermittence.

अंतर्विरोध antarvirodh (*nm*) self-contradiction, inner contradiction.

अंतर्विवाह antarviva:h (*nm*) intermarriage.

अंतर्विवेक antarvivek (*nm*) the conscience, intuition.

अंतर्विषय antarvishay (*nm*) the content.

अंतर्वेग antarveg (*nm*) perturbation, mental disquiet.

अंतर्वेदना antarvednā: (*nf*) mental anguish, agony.

अंतर्वेश antarvesh (*nm*) insertion.

अंतर्व्याधि antarvya:dhi (*nf*) psychological/inner ailment.

अंतर्हित antarhit (*a*) latent, concealed; rendered invisible.

अंतस् antas (*nm*) the conscience, mind, psycne.

अंतस्तल antastal (*nm*) the heart of hearts; mind.

अंतस्ताप antasta:p (*nm*) mental agony, inner distress.

अंतस्सलिला antassalila: (*nf*) the river Saraswati: —a stream that flows unperceived.

अंतस्सार antassa:r (*nm*) the real content.

अंताक्षरी anta:kshari: (*nf*) see **अत्याक्षरी**.

अंतिम antim (*a*) last, final, ultimate, concluding/conclusive; **—चेतावनी** ultimatum, ultimate warning; **—घड़ियाँ/साँसें गिनना** lit. to count the last moments —i.e., to be on the verge of death, to be breathing one's last; **—साँस लेना** to breathe one's last.

अंतिमता antimta: (*nf*) finality; conclusiveness.

अंतिमेत्थम antimettham (*nm*) ultimatum.

अंतेवासी anteva:si: (*nm*) a resident pupil, pupil who stays in his *guru's ashram.*

अंत्य anty (*a*) the last; final; lowermost; ~**कर्म/क्रिया** the last rites; ~**ज** belonging to the lowest class/caste.

अंत्यलोप antylop (*nm*) apocope.

अंत्याक्षरी antya:kshari: (*nf*) a verse-reciting competition in which the following contestant recites a couplet beginning with the last letter of the couplet recited by the foregoing contestant and which may be carried on between competing individuals or rival teams.

अंत्यानुप्रास antya:nuppra:s (*nm*) rhyming of the terminal portions of the ultimate words in a couplet, stanza etc.

अंत्येष्टि antyeshṭi (*nf*) last/funeral rites.

अंत्र antr (*nm*) see **अँतड़ी**

अंत्रप्रदाह antrprada:h (*nm*) intestinal inflammation.

अंत्रवृद्धि antrvriddhi (*nf*) hernia.

अंदर andar (*adv*) in, inside, within; —**कर देना** to send behind the bars; hence —**हो जाना**.

अँदरसा ãdarsa: (*nm*) a kind of sweet cake.

अंदरी andari: (*a*) internal; intrinsic; inherent.

अंदरूनी andaru:nı: (*a*) internal, internecine; inward.

अंदाज़ anda:z (*nm*) an estimate, a guess; mode, style; gesture; characteristic manner; ~**न** roughly, approximately; —**लगाना** to make an estimate; to surmise.

अंदाज़ा anda:za: (*nm*) an estimate, a guess.

अंदेशा andesha: (*nm*) misgiving, misapprehension; suspicion.

अंध andh—an allomorph of **अंधा** used as the first or subsequent member in a compound word (as **अंधविश्वासी; कामांध**); see **अंधा**.

अंधकार andhka:r (*nm*) darkness; gloom; —**युग** age of darkness.

अंधकूप andhku:p (*nm*) a blind well.

अंधड़ andhaṛ (*nm*) a violent dust-storm.

अंधमति andhmati (*a*) stupid, foolish, irrational.

अंधविश्वा/स andhvishshva:s (*nm*) superstition, blind trust; ~**सी** superstitious; having blind faith.

अंधश्रद्धा andhshraddha: (*nf*) blind faith.

अंधा andha: (*a* and *nm*) blind; irrational, unenlightened; unthinking; —**कुआँ**; see **अंधकूप**; ~**कुप्प** pitch dark; black out; —**शीशा** a blind glass; —**करना** to strike blind, to turn incapable to view the realities; —**क्या चाहे दो आँखें** a blind person requires but his eyes; —**बनना** to allow oneself to be hoodwinked or cheated; to be blindfolded; —**होना** to be blinded, to be lost to realities; **अंधे की लकड़ी/लाठी** a helpless man's only support; **अंधे के आगे रोये, अपने दीदा खोये** throwing pearls before the swine; **अंधे के हाथ बटेर लगना** a prize kill by a blind man; **अंधों में काना राजा** a figure among ciphers.

अंधाधुंध andha:dhundh (*adv* and *a*) indiscreetly; indiscriminately, recklessly, at random; wild, reckless, rash; —**गोली चलाना** to fire into the brown.

अंधानुकरण andha:nukarāṉ (*nm*) blind/mechanical imitation or emulation.

अंधानुयायिता andha:nuya:ita: (*nf*) bigotry, blind following.

अंधानुयायी andha:nuya:i: (*nm*) a blind follower; (*a*) blindly following.

अंधापन andha:pan (*nm*) blindness, recklessness; folly.

अँधियारा ādhiya:ra: (*nm*) see **अंधकार**.

अँधियारी ādhiya:ri: (*a*) see **अंधकार**; (*nf*) blinkers.

अंधी andhi: (*a*) feminine form of **अंधा** (see);—**खाई** a deep dark gulf; —**खोपड़ी** a blockhead, stupid.

अंधेर andher (*nm*) outrage; wrong; anarchy, complete lawlessness or mismanagement; ~**खाता/गर्दी** pretty kettle of fish, anarchical state of affairs, complete lawlessness or mismanagement; —**नगरी** a mal-administered and lawless state or town etc.; ० **चौपट राजा** a confused ruler, a chaotic state.

अँधेरा ādhera: (*nm* and *a*) darkness; dark; —**गुप्प/घुप्प** pitch dark; black out; —**पाख** the dark half of the month; —**उजाला** prosperity and adversity;—**गहराये तो सवेरा हो** the darkest hour is that before the dawn; —**छा जाना** darkness to be thickened, to be enveloped in darkness; to be overwhelmed by gloom (due to some terrible emotional shock etc.); **अँधेरे घर का उजाला** an only son; a very handsome child; **अँधेरे मुँह** at the first dawn of the day; **अँधेरे में छलाँग लगाना** to leap into the dark; **अँधेरे में टटोलना** to grope in the dark; **अँधेरे में तीर मारना** to strike in the dark, to strike without taking an aim; **अँधेरे में रखना** to keep in dark.

अँधेरी ādheri: (*nf*) dust-storm; blinkers; —**कोठरी** a dark cell; the womb.

अँधौटी ādhauṭi: (*nf*) blinkers.

अंबर ambar (*nm*) the sky; cloth/clothes, garment; umber;—**डंबर** the crimson tinge acquired by the sky at sunset; the sky so tinged; ~**बेल** see **आकाश बेल**.

अंबार amba:r (*nm*) heap, pile, bulk; ~**खाता** a junk-house, godown.

अँबिया ābiya: (*nf*) a small unripe mango.

अंबु ambu (*nm*) water; ~**ज** a lotus flower; ~**द/धर** a cloud; ~**धि**/~**निधि** the ocean.

अंश ansh (*nm*) part; share; division; fragment; ingredient;contribution; numerator (of a fraction); degree: in Linguistics, an element; ~**कालिक** part-time: ~**दाता** a contributor; ~**दान** contribution; ~**दायी** contributory; contributor: ~**भागी** a shareholder; **अंशांशिभाव** the relationship of the part and the whole.

अंशत: anshtah (*adv*) partly; partially.

अंशांक ansha:ṅk (*nm*) a degree.

अंशावतार ansha:vta:r (*nm*) a partial incarnation.

अंशी anshi: (*nm*) the whole—having a number of parts or members.

अंशु anshu (*nf*) a ray, sunbeam; ~**माली** the sun.

अकंटक akanṭak (*a*) smooth; unobstructed; unchallenged.

अकंप akamp (*a*) unwavering, firm; hence **अकंपित, अकंप्य**.

अकठोर akaṭhor (*a*) not hard or rigid soft; weak, infirm.

अकड़ akaṛ (*nf*) stiffness, rigidity; intractability: airs; affectation, show; strut, haughtiness, conceit; ~**फूँ** airs, arrogance, arrogant behaviour; ~**बाज** haughty, arrogant, hence ~**बाज़ी** (*nf*).

अकड़ना akaṛnā: (*v*) to be stiff, rigid, intractable; to assume airs; to be affected; to be haughty or conceited; **अकड़ कर चलना** to walk with an affected air. to walk arrogantly.

अकड़ू akaṛu: (*a*) stiff-necked, self-conceited, haughty; ~**खाँ** one who is on one's high horse, thinking too much of oneself and showing off. too stiff-necked without any capability.

अकथ, अकथनीय akath, akathnI:y (*a*) ineffable, indescribable.

अकथित akathit (*a*) unsaid, untold, unexpressed, unuttered.

अकथ्य akatthy (*a*) see **अकथनीय**; not fit for utterance (for reasons of obscenity etc.).

अकबक akbak (*nf*) wish-wash; disconnected utterances, nonsense; —**करना** to indulge in wish-wash, to speak irrelevantly/nonsense; —**भूलना/मारी जाना** to be nonplussed, to be flabbergasted, to be at one's wit's end.

अकबकाना akbaka:nā: (*v*) to be flabbergasted, to make disconnected utterances, to be nonplussed.

अकरकरा akarkara: (*nm*) a medicinal plant.

अकरण akarān (*nm*) omission.

अकरणीय akarni:y (*a*) not worth doing, unfit to be done, improper; hence ~**ता** (*nf*).

अकर्तव्य akartavvy (*nm*) an improper act; (*a*) improper or unfit to be done, unworthy (act)

अकर्म akarm (*nm*) inactivity, inertia.

अकर्मक akarmāk (*a*) intransitive (verb).

अकर्मण्य akarmānny (*a*) idle, indolent; inert.

अकर्मण्यता akarmanyata: (*nf*) idleness, indolence, inertness.

अकलुष akalush (*a*) flawless; unsullied, blemishless.

अकल्पनीय akalpanI:y (*a*) unimaginable; unthinkable, inconceivable.

अकल्पित akalpit (*a*) unimagined; unthought of.

अकल्याण akalyā:n (*nm*) misfortune, disaster; ~hence ~**कर**/~**कारी** (*a*).

अकसर aksar (*adv*) see **अक्सर**.

अकसीर aksi:r (*a*) see **अक्सीर**.

अकस्मात् akasma:t (*adv*) lit. from nowhere—unexpectedly; accidentally, all of a sudden.

अकांड तांडव akā:nd tā:ndav (*nm*) much ado about nothing, unwarranted fuss.

अकांड पात akā:nd pa:t (*nm*) bathos.

अकाट्य akā:tty (*a*) irrefutable; incontrovertible, indisputable; hence ~**ता** (*nf*).

अकादेमी akā:demi: (*nf*) an academy.

अकाम akā:m (*a*) without a wish, unhaunted by desires; hence ~**ता** (*nf*).

अका/र akā:r (*nm*) the letter *a* (अ) and its sound; ~**रांत** (a word) ending in *a* (अ).

अकारण aka:rān (*adv* and *a*) without any reason or cause, without any pretext, needlessly, causelessly, wanton, causeless, groundless; unprovoked.

अकारथ aka:rath (*a* and *adv*) futile, useless, ineffectual; in vain.

अकारादि क्रम aka:ra:di kram (*nm*) alphabetical order.

अकाल aka:l (*nm*) famine; scarcity; (*a*) premature; untimely; —**कुसुम** lit. an out-of-season flower—an untimely thing; —**जरा** progeria; ~**पक्व** precocious; —**पुरुष** the Ageless One —the Supreme Being as worshipped by the Sikhs; —**प्रसव** premature delivery; —**मृत्यु** untimely demise; —**वृद्ध** prematurely aged; —**वृष्टि** untimely rains.

अकालिक aka:lik (*a*) untimely, inopportune; premature.

अकाली aka:li: (*nm*) a sect of the Sikhs; a follower of this sect.

अकिंचन akinchan (*a*) poor, pauper; destitute; ~**ता/त्व** poverty, pauperism; destitution.

अक़ीदा aqi:da: (*nm*) faith, belief.

अकीर्ति aki:rti: (*nf*) disgrace, infamy:

~कर disgraceful, resulting in infamy.

अकुंठित akunṭhit (*a*) sharp, keen; unstunted, uncramped, unrestricted.

अकुलाना akulā:nā: (*v*) to feel uneasy/restless; to be fidgety.

अकुलाहट akula:haṭ (*nf*) restlessness, uneasiness.

अकुलीन akuli:n (*a*) low-born; mean; hence ~ता (*nf*).

अकुशल akushal (*a*) unskilled; novice, amateurish; hence ~ता (*nf*).

अकूत aku:t (*a*) immeasurable, unfathomable.

अकृत akkrit (*a*) null, nullified; undone.

अकृतज्ञ akkritagy (*a*) ungrateful, thankless; hence ~ता (*nf*).

अकृती akkriti: (*a*) unskilled, inexperienced; (*nm*) a novice.

अकृतीकरण akkriti:karāṉ (*nm*) nullification; invalidation.

अकृत्रिम akrittrim (*a*) natural; genuine; unsophisticated, unaffected; hence ~ता (*nf*).

अकेला akela: (*a*) single; lonely, lonesome; solitary; (*adv*) by oneself, singly, alone; —दुकेला alone or with one or two more; —चना भाड़ नहीं फोड़ सकता a lone soldier cannot win a war; —सौ के बराबर a host in oneself; अकेला दम अकेली जान all alone, solitary.

अकेलापन akela:pan (*nm*) a feeling of loneliness, lonesomeness; solitude, solitariness.

अकेले akele (*adv*) alone, by oneself, without a companion; -अकेले all by oneself, with none to support, all alone.

अकौशल akaushal (*nm*) see अकुशल.

अक्कल दाढ़ akkal da:ṛḥ (*nf*) dens serotinus, wisdom tooth.

अक्खड़ akkhaṛ (*a*) headstrong; contumacious, rude and rough, haughty; ~ पन/~पना contumacy, headstrongness; haughtiness.

अक्तूबर aktu:bar (*nm*) (the month of) October.

अक़्द aqd (*nm*) agreement; marriage; ~नामा a marriage agreement.

अक्रम akkram (*a*) disorderly, chaotic.

अक़्ल aql (*nf*) common sense; intellect; wits; wisdom; —आना to see reason; to learn a lesson; —का अंधा a dotard, devoid of grey matter; —का घास खाना/चरना/चरने जाना to be bereft of wits, to be out of one's head; —का दुश्मन a stupid fellow; —का पुतला intellect personified; —काम न करना, —मारी जाना to be in a fix or dilemma; —कुंद होना to be at one's wit's end; —के घोड़े दौड़ाना to cudgel one's brains; to exercise one's mind in all directions, to indulge in mental gymnasium; —के पीछे डंडा/लाठी लिए फिरना to indulge in stupidity all the time, to demand a tribute to the dead; —चकराना, —चक्कर में आना/पड़ना to be nonplussed; —चरने जाना, —का चिराग़ गुल होना, —जाती रहना to lose the faculty of reasoning, to lose power of discrimination; to lose wits; —ठिकाने लगाना to set (one) right, to put to senses, to fix one in one's proper place, to cut to size; —ठिकाने होना to have learnt a lesson, to be fixed in one's proper place; —पर पत्थर/परदा पड़ना, —गुम होना to be out of one's head, to be bereft of senses or intellect, to lose one's wits; —बड़ी (या) कि भैंस knowledge predominates over mere strength; —में (तुम) उसके पासंग भी नहीं there is more wit in his little finger than in your whole body; —सठियाना to suffer senile decay, to suffer from mental paralyses; —से कोई वास्ता न होना to have nothing to do with common sense.

अक़्लमंद aqqlmānd (*a*) prudent, sagacious; intelligent; wise; sensible.

अक़्लमंदी aqqlmandi: (*nf*) prudence, sagacity; intelligence; wisdom; sensibility.

अक्लिष्ट akklisht (*a*) not intricate—easy, easily intelligible.

अक्ष aksh (*nm*) an axis.

अक्षत akshat (*a*) unimpaired, intact; (*nm*) whole grain of rice; ~ता virginity; the state of being unimpaired; ~योनि a virgin; ~वीर्य having unimpaired virility; a celebate.

अक्षम aksham (*a*) incompetent, incapable; handicapped; ~ता incompetence, incapability; handicap.

अक्षम्य akshammy (*a*) unpardonable, inexcusable.

अक्ष/य akshay (*a*) imperishable, undecaying; perennial; ~यी imperishable, undecaying; perennial.

अक्षय्य akshayy (*a*) imperishable, undecaying; perennial.

अक्षर akshar (*nm*) any letter of the alphabet, character; syllable; (*a*) imperishable, undecaying; intact; ~गणित Algebra; ~जीवी a professional author, a free-lance writer; ~माला the alphabet;–योजना (Printing) composition;—योजक compositor;–विन्यास spelling;—से भेंट न होना to be absolutely illiterate.

अक्षरचारी aksharcha:ri: (*a*) literalist (ic).

अक्षरविश्लेषण aksharvishleshān (*nm*) syllabism.

अक्षरशः aksharshah (*adv*) literally; in toto; verbatim.

अक्षरी akshari: (*nf*) spelling.

अक्षांक akshā:ṅk (*nm*) indices.

अक्षांतर akshā:ntar (*nm*) latitude.

अक्षांश akshā:nsh (*nm*) latitude.

अक्षि akshi (*nf*) an eye;—गोलक the eye-ball;—तारक the pupil;—निमेष a moment, the time taken in the twinkling of the eye;—पटल the retina;—विक्षेप a side-long glance.

अक्षुण्ण akshūnn (*a*) unimpaired, unbroken, intact; entire, complete; hence ~ता (*nf*).

अक्षुब्ध akshubdh (*a*) unperturbed; quiet.

अक्षोभ akshobh (*nm*) absence of perturbation; calmness, quiet.

अक्षौहिणी akshauhiṇi: (*nf*) in ancient military terminology, it signified a division of army consisting of 21,870 elephants, 21,870 chariots, 65,610 horses and 109,350 foot-soldiers.

अक्स aks (*nm*) a shadow, reflected image, reflection; —उतारना to photograph; to reproduce an exact image;—करना/लेना to trace.

अक्सर aksar (*adv*) often, generally, usually.

अक्सीर aksi:r (*a*) unfailing, sure; —दवा a sure/sovereign remedy.

अखंड akhaṇḍ (*a*) the whole, complete; undivided; indivisible;—पाठ non-stop recitation;—सौभाग्य the happy state of a woman survived by her husband; hence—सौभाग्यवती (*a*).

अखंडता akhāṇḍata: (*nf*) indivisibility; integrity; completeness.

अखंडनीय akhāṇḍanī:y (*a*) indivisible, infrangible, unbreakable; irrefutable; irresolvable; hence ~ता (*nf*).

अखंडित akhāṇḍit (*a*) unbroken, undivided; unimpaired; irrepudiated.

अख़बार akhba:r (*nm*) a newspaper; ~नवीस a journalist; ~नवीसी journalism; अख़बारी pertaining to news or newspaper(s); ० काग़ज़ newsprint अख़बारी भाषा journalese.

अखरना akharnā: (*v*) to make one feel sore; to be disagreeable or unpleasant.

अखरोट akhrot (*nm*) a walnut.

अख़लाक़ akhla:q (*nm*) manners, good

manners; hence ~की (*a*).

अखाड़ा akha:ṛa: (*nm*) an arena, wrestling arena; place for exercise; a congregation of *sadhus* or their abode; —**गरम होना** to have the bouts going; to have an assembly in full swing; —**जमना** an assembly to be active and enlivened; **अखाड़ेबाज** see **अखाड़िया**; **अखाड़े में आना/उतरना** to step into the arena (for a bout), to pick up the gauntlet.

अखाड़िया akha:ṛiya: (*nm* and *a*) a master fighter; skilled manoeuvrer; strategist.

अखाद्य akha:ddy (*a*) inedible; uneatable.

अखिल akhil (*a*) whole, all, entire, pan—.

अखिलेश akhilesh (*nm*) the Supreme Master, the Master of the universe.

अख़्ख़ाह akḫkḫa:h (*int*) oh ! (an exclamation of surprise or wonder in case of an unexpected appearance or meeting etc.)

अख़्तियार akḫtiya:r (*nm*) power, right, authority.

अग ag (*a*) immovable; unintelligible.

अग-जग ag-jag (*nm*) the movable and immovable taken together; the whole universe.

अगड़म-बगड़म agṛām-bagṛām (*nm*) junk, a disorderly heap of scraps.

अगणनीय agāṇani:y (*a*) innumerable; countless; hence ~ता (*nf*).

अगणित agāṉit (*a*) unnumbered, unaccounted; numberless.

अगण्य agaṉṉy (*a*) see **अगणनीय**.

अगति agati (*nf*) stagnation; inertia; hence ~क (*a*).

अगम agām (*a*) inaccessible, unattainable; incomprehensible; hence ~ता (*nf*).

अगम्य agāmmy (*a*) see **अगम**; incohabitable; **अगम्यागमन** incest; **अगम्यागामी** (an) incestuous (person).

अगम्यता agammyāta: (*nf*) inaccessibility; unintelligibility; incohabitability.

अगर agar (*ind*) if, in case; (*nm*) aloe (wood); ~चे although, though; ~बत्ती an incense stick.

अगर-मगर agar-magar (*nf*) if and but; wavering, hitch; dilly-dallying; —**करना** to dilly-dally, to vacillate, to resort to ifs and buts.

अगरु agaru (*nm*) aloe (wood).

अगर्हित agarhit (*a*) uncensured, uncondemned.

अगल-बगल agal-bagal (*adv*) on both sides; side by side; nearby.

अगला agla: (*a*) next, following; coming, approaching; the other (person).

अगवाड़ा agwa:ṛa (*nm*) the frontage, front portion.

अगवानी agwā:nɪ: (*nf*) reception, welcome (esp. one extended to a marriage party or a distinguished guest).

अगस्त agast (*nm*) (the month of) August.

अगहन agahān (*nm*) the ninth month of the Hindu calendar.

अगाऊ aga:u: (*a*) forward; advance; —**सौदे** forward trading.

अगाड़ी aga:ṛi: (*nf*) the front part; facing; the rope used for tying a horse's neck; (*adv*) in front of; in future; -**पिछाड़ी** see **आगा-पीछा**.

अगाध aga:dh (*a*) unfathomable; profound, deep; —**जल** deep/unfathomable water; hence ~ता (*nf*)

अगिनगोला agingola: (*nm*) an incendiary bomb.

अगिनबोट aginboṭ (*nf*) a steam-boat, steamer.

अगियारी agiya:ri: (*nf*) throwing or burning incense etc. into the fire.

अगुआ agua: (*nm*) a leader; pioneer,

forerunner; guide; ~ई leadership; guidance; ० करना to play first fiddle.

अगुण agūn̲ (*a*) see निर्गुण; (*nm*) see अवगुण; अगुणी having no quality/merit.

अगूढ़ agu:ṛh̤ (*a*) intelligible; apparent; simple.

अगोचर agochar (*a*) imperceptible; hence ~ता (*nf*).

अग्नि agnı (*nf*) fire; the god of fire; appetite; digestive faculty; ~कण a spark; ~ कांड arson, conflagration; ~क्रीड़ा firework; ~दाह cremating, cremation; ~ परीक्षा ordeal, severe trial; ० से गुजरा हुआ tried in the furnace; -पूजा fire-worship; -पूजक fire-worshipper; -प्रतिष्ठा summoning and worshipping the god of fire (in order to commence a religious function); —प्रवेश entry into fire; immolation; ~बाण a fire-emitting/incendiary arrow; —मंद होना to suffer from dyspepsia, to lose appetite ~वर्धक digestive; -वर्षा shelling, bombing, firing; -संस्कार cremation; ~ सात् consumed by or consigned to fire.

अग्न्यस्त्र agnyastr (*nm*) firearms.

अग्र aggr (*a*) first; foremost; chief; (*nm*) the fore-part of anything, the head; ~गण्य leading, prominent; ~गामी pioneering; pioneer, leader; ~ज/जन्मा an elder brother; ~जा an elder sister; ~त: firstly, primarily; ~ ता priority, precedence; ~दूत herald, fore-runner; —भाग front portion, front part; ~यायी pioneering, leading; ~लेख an editorial, a leading article, leader.

अग्रणी aggrani: (*a*) leading; pre-eminent, outstanding.

अग्र/धर्षण aggrdharshan̲ (*nm*) (act of) aggression; ~ धर्षी aggressive; an aggressor.

अग्रपाद aggrpa:ḍ (*nm*) fore-limb.

अग्रभूमि aggrbhu:mi (*nf*) fore-land.

अग्रवर्ती aggrvarti: (*a*) advance; located or situated ahead, forward.

अग्रसर aggrsar (*a*); —करना to forward; to move ahead; —होना to proceed, to go ahead; अग्रसारण forwarding.

अग्राम्य aggra:my (*a*) civil, civic; urbane, refined.

अग्राह्य aggra:hy (*a*) unacceptable, inadmissible; ineligible; invalid.

अग्रिम aggrım (*a*) first; foremost; chief; (*adv*) in advance; (*nm*) an advance; —प्रति an advance copy.

अग्रीकृत agri:kkrit (*a*) fronted (in Linguistics).

अघ agh (*nm*) a sin, misdeed: ~मर्षण purification. expiation/expiatory; purifying.

अघट aghaṭ (*a*) untoward, unworthy; improbable.

अघटित aghaṭit (*a*) unoceurred, not having happened.

अघाना agha:nā: (*v*) to be satiated, surfeited or satisfied (with), to have abundance (of something).

अघोरी aghori: (*a* and *nm*) filthy, uncouth and unclean (man); detestable; one who indulges in indiscriminate eating; a member of the order of mendicants called '*aghor panth*'.

अघोष aghosh (*a*) unvoiced (sound).

अचंचल achanchal (*a*) unwavering; stable, steady.

अचंभा achambha: (*nm*) wonder, surprise, astonishment; a bolt from the blue; अचंभित wonder-struck, surprised.

अचकचा/ना achkacha:nā: (*v*) to be taken aback or astonished, to be confounded/dumbfounded; ~हट

(*nf*) astonishment, a sense or state of being taken by surprise.

अचकन achkān (*nf*) a kind of tight-fitting long coat.

अचर achar (*a*) immovable; constant, invariable; (*nm*) an invariant, invariable.

अचरज acharaj (*nm*) surprise, astonishment, wonder.

अचल achal (*a*) immovable/immobile; stationary, motionless, still; firm, sessile; —संपत्ति immovable property.

अचलता achalata: (*nf*) immovability; inertia; firmness.

अचला achala: (*nf*) the earth; (*a*) see अचल.

अचाक्षुष acha:kshush (*a*) non-visual; invisible.

अचानक acha:nāk (*adv*) all of a sudden, suddenly, unexpectedly; —आ/जा लेना to take a person at advantage/by surprise.

अचार acha:r (*nm*) pickles: —डालना lit. to prepare pickles, said while aiming scoffs at unwarranted preservation or saving of a thing.

अचारी acha:ri: (*nf*) typical pickles prepared from mango parings.

अचिंतनीय achintāni:y (*a*) unthinkable, incomprehensible.

अचिंतित achintit (*a*) unplanned; unpremeditated; unexpected; unworried, unthought(of).

अचिंत्य achinty (*a*) see अचिंतनीय

अचित् achit (*a*) devoid of consciousness.

अचिर achir (*a*) prompt; without delay.

अचीन्हा achi:nhā: (*a*) unknown; unidentified.

अचूक achu:k (*a*) infallible, unfailing, unerring; sure; —दवा sure cure.

अचेत achet (*a*) devoid of consciousness; unconscious; senseless.

अचेतन achetān (*a*) unconscious; inanimate; hence ~ता (*nf*).

अचेतना achetna: (*nf*) unconsciousness; inanimation.

अचैतन्य achaitanny (*a*) unconscious; (*nm*) absence of consciousness; inanimation.

अच्छा achchha: (*a*) good; fine; excellent; pleasant; righteous; sound; genuine; (*adv*) well; correctly, granted; (*int*) all right, well done; so long; —खासा fairly good; adequate;—बुरा good and bad;—करना to cure (of an ailment);—तो यह माजरा है that accounts for the milk in the cocoanut; —लगना to have a liking (for): अच्छी कटना/गुजरना/बीतना to have good time; अच्छे-अच्छे big guns, those who matter, significant people; अच्छे-बुरे की तमीज होना to know a hawk from a handsaw; अच्छे से पाला पड़ना to encounter a difficult/unmanageable person.

अच्छाई achchha:i: (*nf*) goodness; virtue; merit; —बुराई merit and demerit; virtue and vice; good and bad.

अच्छापन achchha:pān (*nm*) goodness, positive excellence.

अच्छिन्न achchhinn (*a*) uninterrupted, unbroken; undivided.

अच्यु/त achchyut (*a*) infallible; unerring; immutable; hence ~ति (*nf*).

अछूत achhu:t (*a*) untouchable; (*nm*) an untouchable; अछूतोद्धार uplift of the untouchables.

अछूता achhu:ta: (*a*) fresh; untouched; unpolluted.

अछेद्य achheddy (*a*) impenetrable; indivisible.

अछोर achhor (*a*) without a beginning or end, unending.

अज aj (*a*) unborn, eternal.

अज़ az (*ind*) from; ~**ख़ुद** on one's own, by oneself; ~**ग़ैबी** divine; ~**तर्फ़** from; -**सरे-नौ** de novo, anew; ~**हद** very much, too much.

अजग/र ajgar (*nm*) a python, a huge snake; ~**री** phythonic, pertaining to the python; ० **वृत्ति** leisurely attitude, a sense of inertia.

अजदहा azdaha: (*nm*) see **अजगर.**

अजनबी ajnabi: (*a*) unknown, unfamiliar; alien; (*nm*) a stranger.

अजन्मा ajanmā: (*a*) see **अज.**

अजब ajab (*a*) strange. peculiar.

अज़मत azmat (*nf*) greatness, dignity,

अजर ajar (*a*) ever-young, undecaying.

अजवाइन ajwa:in (*nf*) a kind of aromatic seed — *Carum copticum.*

अजस्र ajasr (*a*) uninterrupted; continuous; —**प्रवाह** uninterrupted flow.

अजात aja:t (*a*) unborn; ~**शत्रु** one who has no enemy.

अजान aja:n (*a*) ignorant, innocent: —**में** unknowingly, unwittingly.

अज़ान aza:n (*nf*) prayer-call (by a *muazzin*) in a mosque.

अजायब/घर, ~**ख़ाना** aja:yabghar, ~k͟hā:nā: (*nm*) a museum, curio-collection centre.

अजित ajit (*a*) unconquered, undefeated.

अज़ीज़ azi:z (*a*) dear; (*nm*) a near relative, kith and kin.

अजीब aji:b (*a*) strange, peculiar, arousing a sense of wonder; **अजीबोग़रीब** unique, peculiar; amazing, baffling.

अजीर्ण aji:rṉ (*nm*) indigestion (caused by overeating)

अजूबा aju:ba: (*nm*) a curio, wonder.

अजेय ajey (*a*) invincible, unconquerable.

अज्ञ aggy (*a*) ignorant; stupid; ~**ता** ignorance; stupidity.

अज्ञात aggya:t (*a*) unknown; ~**कुल** of unknown lineage; ~**नाम**/~**नामा** of unknown name, anonymous; ~**पूर्व** unknown (before); ~**वास** secret dwelling, dwelling in an unknown place; ~**यौवना** (a girl) unaware of the emergence of youth (within her).

अज्ञा/न aggyā:n (*nm*) ignorance, paucity of knowledge; hence~**नता** (*nf*); ~**नी** ignorant, unwise; an ignoramus.

अज्ञेय aggyey (*a*) unknowable; ~**ता** unknowability; ~**वाद** agnosticism; ~**वादी** agnostic.

अटक aṭak (*nf*) obstacle, hitch; lag.

अटकना aṭaknā: (*v*) to get stuck up, to be held up.

अटकल aṭkal (*nf*) conjecture, guess; ~**बाज़** one who is given to making conjectures or guesses; hence ~**बाज़ी** (*nf*).

अटकलपच्चू aṭkalpachchu: (*a*) random; fanciful, imaginary; uncertain; (*nm*) a random guess, mere conjecture.

अटकाव aṭka:v (*nm*) hitch; hindrance, obstruction; catch-up.

अटन aṭan (*nm*) roving, going round, roaming; ~**शील** (*a*) roving, roaming, given to wandering.

अटना aṭnā: (*v*) to suffice; to be contained in.

अटपटा aṭpaṭa: (*a*) odd; absurd, incongruous; hence ~**पन** (*nm*).

अटपटाना aṭpaṭa:nā (*v*) to wobble; to become incongruous/unsteady.

अटल aṭal (*a*) firm; irrevocable; resolute, unwavering, steadfast.

अटा aṭa: (*nm*) a garret, an attic.

अटाटूट aṭa:ṭu:ṭ (*a*) immense, immeasurable; crammed full.

अटारी aṭa:ri: (*nf*) a small garret, an attic.

अटूट atu:ṭ (*a*) unbreakable; firm; incessant; immense; —**संबंध** unbreakable/firm relationship. unbreakable bond

अटेरन aṭerān (*nf*) a reel or skein of thread.

अट्ट-सट्ट aṭṭsaṭṭ (*a*) see **अंड-बंड**.

अट्टहास aṭṭha:s (*nm*) a horse-laugh, peal of loud laughter.

अट्टालिका aṭṭa:lika:(*nf*) a high palatial mansion; an attic.

अट्ठाईस aṭṭhai:s (*a*) twenty-eight; (*nm*) the number twenty-eight.

अट्ठानवे aṭṭha:nve (*a*) ninety-eight; (*nm*) the number ninety-eight.

अट्ठावन aṭṭha:vān (*a*) fifty-eight; (*nm*) the number fifty-eight.

अट्ठासी aṭṭha:si: (*a*) eighty-eight; (*nm*) the number eighty-eight.

अठ aṭh (*a*)an allomorph of **आठ** used as the first member of a compound word; ~**मा(वाँ)सा** a ceremony performed in or about the eighth month of a woman's pregnancy; a premature child born in the eighth month of pregnancy; ~**वाड़ा (रा)** a span of eight days.

अठखेली aṭhkheli: (*nf*) (usu. used in plural **अठखेलियाँ**) playfulness, frolic; merriment; **अठखेलियाँ करना** to romp and rollick, to be playful.

अठन्नी aṭhannī: (*nf*) an eight-anna coin.

अठहत्तर aṭhhattar (*a*) seventy-eight; (*nm*) the number seventy-eight.

अठारह aṭha:rah (*a*) eighteen; (*nm*) the number eighteen.

अड़ंगा aṛaṅga: (*nm*) an obstacle, obstruction, impediment; **अड़ंगेबाज** an obstructionist; **अड़ंगेबाज़ी** obstructing tactics, obstructionism; —**डालना/लगाना** to create an obstacle; —**मारना** to place an impediment; to try to topple up.

अड़ aṛ (*nf*) obstinacy, pertinacity; —**पकड़ना** to assume a pertinacious/stubborn attitude; ~**दार** unflinching, stubborn.

अड़चन aṛchān (*nf*) hindrance; hitch; difficulty.

अड़तालीस aṛta:li:s (*a*) forty-eight; (*nm*) the number forty-eight.

अड़तीस aṛti:s (*a*) thirty-eight; (*nm*) the number thirty-eight.

अड़ना aṛnā: (*v*) to stick (to a position); to insist; to halt; to be restive (as a horse).

अड़सठ aṛsaṭh (*a*) sixty-eight; (*nm*) the number sixty-eight.

अड़हुल aṛhul (*nm*) a typical reddish flower.

अड़ाअड़ी aṛa:aṛi: (*nf*) vying; rivalry.

अड़ाना aṛa:nā: (*v*) to put an obstruction; to press forward, to provoke into the forefront.

अडिग aḍig (*a*) unflinching; firm, steady; —**विश्वास** unflinching/firm faith/belief.

अड़ियल aṛiyal (*a*) inflexible; stubborn; mulish; —**टट्टू** fig, stupidly obstinate.

अड़ूसा aṛu:sa: (*nm*) a medicinal plant — *Justicia ganderussa*

अड़ो(ड़ौ)स-पड़ो(ड़ौ)स aṛo(au)s-paṛo(au)s (*nm*) neighbourhood, vicinity; **अड़ो(ड़ौ)सी-पड़ो(ड़ौ)स** neighbours.

अड्डा aḍḍa: (*nm*) a stand; base; meeting place, haunt; resort, perch; hot-bed; chopping block; —**जमाना** to stay long, —**बनाना** to turn into a frequent rendezvous/meeting place, to make a haunting place of

अढ़ैया aṛhaiya: (*nf*) a weight of two and half seers.

अणिमा aṇimā: (*nf*) atomism; infinitesimal; the first of the eight *siddhis* (see) which imparts the capacity to assume infinitesimal form; ~**दिक** the (eight) *siddhis* **अणिमा**, etc.

अणु aṇū (*nm*) a molecule: an atom; minute particle; (*a*) molecular;

atomic: ~वाद atomism; ~वादी an atomist; atomistic; ~वीक्षण (यंत्र) a microscope.

अत: atah (*ind*) hence; therefore; thus: on this account; ~परम् now onwards, hereafter.

अतएव at-ev (*ind*) hence; so, therefore.

अतप्त atapt (*a*) unheated; cool.

अतरसों atarsō (*adv*) the day prior to day-before-yesterday or next to day-after-tomorrow.

अतर्कित atarkit (*a*) unthought of; unplanned, sudden.

अतर्क्य atarky (*a*) indisputable; incontrovertible, irrefutable.

अतल atal (*a*) bottomless; fathomless; ~दर्शी having deep insight, who can see through to the bottom; ~स्पर्शी fathoming the depths, profound.

अतलांतक atlā:ntak (*nm*) the Atlantic (ocean).

अता ata: (*nm*) a gift; —करना/फ़रमाना (to be so kind as) to give away, to bestow.

अति ati—a prefix expressive of extremity, beyond, over, surpassing, extra, intense, excessive etc.; (*nf*) excess; ~कथन aggrandizement; —करना to commit an excess; to cross the limit, to go too far.

अतिकाय atika:y (*a*) huge, gigantic.

अतिकाल atika:l (*nm*) delay.

अतिक्रम, ~क्रमण atikkram, ~kkramān (*nm*) infringement; contravention, violation; hence ~क्रांत (*a*), ~क्रामक (*a*)

अति/चार aticha:r (*nm*) transgression, trespass; profanation, outrage, violation; ~चारी a trespasser; transgressing (prescribed) limits; outrageous.

अतिथि atithi (*nm*) a guest; —कलाकार guest artist; ~गृह guest-house:—धर्म duty towards a guest, rights of hospitality; ~परायण hospitable; ~परायणता hospitality;—सत्कार/सेवा hospitality; honourable treatment to a guest.

अतिथिक atithic (*a*) unhistoric.

अतिनैतिक atināitik (*a*) supermoral.

अतिपरवलय atiparvalay (*nm*) a hyperbola.

अतिपात atipa:t (*nm*) breach, violation; lapse; obstacle.

अतिपायिता atip:yita: (*nf*) alcoholism.

अतिपायी atipa:i: (*nm*) an addict, a drunkard.

अतिपुरातन atipura:tan (*a*); ~पंथी ultra conservative.

अतिप्रकृत atiprakrit (*a*) see **अतिप्राकृत**

अति/प्राकृत, ~प्राकृतिक atipra:kkrit, ~pra:kkritik (*a*) supernatural.

अति/मानव atimā:nav (*nm*) a superman; ~मानवीय superhuman.

अतिमूत्रता atimu:trata: (*nf*) polyuria.

अतिमूल्यन atimu:lyān (*nm*) overvaluation; over-assessment.

अति/रंजन atirāṇjān (*nm*) exaggeration; ~रंजित exaggerated.

अतिरंजना atiranjanā: (*nf*) exaggeration; overstatement; ~पूर्ण exaggerated.

अतिराष्ट्रीय atira:shṭri:y (*a*) chauvinistic, chauvinist.

अतिराष्ट्रीयता atira:shṭri:yata: (*nf*) chauvinism.

अतिरिक्त atirikt (*a*) additional; extra; spare; auxiliary (e.g. post); besides.

अतिरेक atirek (*nm*) plenty, abundance; surplus; excess; redundancy.

अतिलंघन atilānghān (*nm*) infringement; transgression.

अति/वाद ativa:d (*nm*) extremism; excess; ostentation; exaggeration; boastfulness; ~वादी an extremist;

extremistic; boastful; ostentatious; ~वादिता extremism; excessivism.

अतिवृष्टि ativrishṭi: (*nf*) excessive rains, unusually heavy downpour.

अतिव्याप्त ativvya:pt: (*a*) over-extended, over-extensive.

अतिव्याप्ति ativvya:pti: (*nf*) over-extension (of a rule, etc.); over-permeation; overlapping.

अतिशय atishay (*a* and *adv*) exceeding/exceedingly, excessive/excessively; ~ता plenty, abundance, (state of being in) excess.

अतिशयोक्ति atishayokti: (*nm*) exaggeration (a figure of speech); ~पूर्ण exaggerated.

अतिसामान्य atisa:mā:nny: (*a*) super-normal; too common.

अतिसार atisa:r (*nm*) dysentery.

अतिसावधान atisa:vdhā:n: (*a*) meticulous, extra-cautious.

अतिसावधानता atisa:vdhā:nta: (*nf*) meticulousness, extra-cautiousness.

अतिसूक्ष्मदर्शी atisu:kshmadarshi: (*nm* and *a*) ultramicrsocope; ultra-microscopic.

अतींद्रिय ati:ndriy: (*a*) transcendental; trans-sensuous, super-sensuous; ~ता trans-sensuous/transcendental state; ~वाद transcendentalism; hence ~वादिता (*nf*) ~वादी (*a*, *nm*).

अतीत ati:t: (*a* and *nm*) (the) past; (*adv*) beyond; ~सापेक्ष retrospective.

अतीव ati:v: (*a*) very much, too much.

अतु/ल atul: (*a*) unparalleled, unequalled; immense; also ~लनीय (*a*); ~लित (*a*); ~ल्य (*a*) out and away.

अतृप्त atript: (*a*) unsatisfied, unfulfilled, frustrated.

अतृप्ति atripti: (*nf*) non-fulfilment, non-gratification; frustration.

अत्तार atta:r: (*nm*) a perfumer; druggist, pharmaceutical chemist.

अत्यंत attyānt: (*adv* and *a*) very much, much; excessively, exceedingly.

अत्यधिक atyadhik (*a* and *adv*) very much, too much, lots of, abundant.

अत्याचार attya:cha:r (*nm*) atrocity, tyranny; excess; outrage.

अत्याचारी attya:cha:ri: (*a*) atrocious, tyrannous; excessive; outrageous; (*nm*) a tyrant, despot; —शासक a tyrant.

अत्याज्य attya:jjy (*a*) unabandonable, unforsakable; not fit to be renounced.

अत्याहारी attya:ha:ri: (*nm*) a glutton; (*a*) gluttonous.

अत्युक्ति attyukti (*nf*) a hyperbole; ~पूर्ण hyperbolic, embodying overstatement.

अत्र attr (*ind*) here; ~भवान Your Honour, Your Highness, Your Excellency, etc.

अथ ath (*nm*) the beginning, commencement; an auspicious and inceptive particle, now, then; ~च besides, moreover; —से इति तक from beginning to end.

अथक athak (*a*) untiring; unceasing; —परिश्रम untiring efforts.

अथर्व atharv ;~वेद (*nm*) the fourth and the last of the *Vedas*.

अथवा athva: (*ind*) or; that is.

अथाई atha:i: (*nf*) a centrally-located platform (used as a meeting place).

अथाह atha:h (*a*) unfathomable, bottomless; very deep.

अदंडनीय adandni:y (*a*) unpunishable, not fit to be punished; pardonable.

अदंडित adandit (*a*) unpunished; unpenalised.

अदंड्य adandy (*a*) see **अदंडनीय**.

अदक्ष adaksh (*a*) inefficient; incapable.

अदत्त adatt (*a*) not given, not gifted, not presented.

अदद adad (*nm*) a piece; number; whole number.

अदना adnā: (*a*) insignificant; low, inferior; trifling.

अदब adab (*nm*) respect; respectfulness; politeness; literature; —**क़ायदा/लिहाज़** etiquette, good manners, urbanity; courtesy and consideration.

अदबदाकर adbada:kar (*ind*) positively, without fail; deliberately.

अदबी adabi: (*a*) literary, pertaining to literature.

अदम adām (*nm*) absence; —**पैरवी** ex parte; —**मौजूदगी** in the absence of; —**सबूत** absence of proof.

अदम्य adāmmy (*a*) irrepressible; irresistible; —**उत्साह** irresistible enthusiasm.

अदरक adrak (*nf*) ginger.

अदर्शन adarshān (*nm*) ; **अदर्शनीय** (*a*) not fit to be seen; ugly.

अदल-बदल adal-badal (*nf*) exchange, interchange; modification; **अदले का बदला** eye for an eye.

अदला-बदली adala:badli: (*nf*) exchange; interchange; mutual transfer.

अदवान advā:n (*nm*) a thin rope used to keep a cot flat and firm.

अदह adah (*nm*) asbestos.

अदहन adahān (*nm*) water set to boil for the purpose of cooking food.

अदा ada: (*nf*) coquetry, blandishment; graceful manner or carriage, mien; performance; ~**कार** an actor, performer; ~**कारी** performance; —**करना** to pay; to discharge; to fulfil; to perform.

अदायगी ada:igi: (*nf*) payment; fulfilment.

अदालत ada:lat (*nf*) a court of law; —, **दीवानी** civil court; —, **फ़ौजदारी** criminal court; **अदालती** judicial; litigious; ० **जाँच** judicial enquiry; ~**बाज़** a litigant; ~**बाज़ी** litigation; litigiousness.

अदावत ada:wat (*nf*) animosity; enmity; estrangement; hostility; hence **अदावती** (*a*).

अदाह्य ada:hy (*a*) non-combustible; fire-proof; hence ~**ता** (*nf*).

अदीक्षित adi:kshit (*a*) uninitiated.

अदूरद/र्शी adu:rdarshi: (*a*) not far-sighted; unwise; hence ~**र्शिता** (*nf*).

अदूषण adu:shān (*nm*) absence of blemish; (*a*) blemishless, pure.

अदूषित adu:shit (*a*) spotless, pure, uncontaminated; untainted.

अदृढ़ addrirh (*a*) loose; non-rigid; infirm.

अदृश्य adrishy (*a*) invisible, imperceptible; not worth seeing.

अदृश्यता adrishyata: (*nf*) invisibility, imperceptibility.

अदृष्ट adrisht (*nm*) fate, fortune; (*a*) unforeseen; ~**पूर्व** unique, unprecedented; ~**वाद** fatalism; determinism; ~**वादिता** see ~**वाद**; ~**वादी** a fatalist, determinist; fatalistic, deterministic.

अदेय adey (*a*) inalienable; non-transferable, not to be handed over; not worth or fit for handing over; hence ~**ता** (*nf*).

अदेशी(य)/करण adeshi:(y)karān (*nm*) denaturalization; hence ~**कृत** (*a*).

अद्धा addha: (*nm*) one half (of anything); a half-pint bottle; half-brick; counterfoil.

अद्धी addhi: (*nf*) a kind of fine muslin-like cloth.

अद्‌भुत adbhut (*a*) marvellous, fantastic; singular; supernatural.

अद्यतन addyatān (*a*) up-to-date; modern.

अद्यावधि addya:vadhi (*ind*) up-to-date; till now.

अद्वितीय addviti:y (*a*) sui generis, unique, unparalleled; hence ~ता (*nf*).

अद्वैत addvait (*nm*) absence of duality/difference, negation of duality/difference; unity; ~वाद monism; ~वादी a monist, believer in monism; monistic.

अधःपतन adhahpatān (*nm*) downfall, fall; degradation, degeneration.

अधकचरा adhkachra: (*a*) immature; incomplete; half-baked, unassimilated; hence ~पन (*nm*).

अधकहा adhkaha: (*a*) half-expressed, semi-explicit.

अधखिला adhkhila: (*a*) semi-bloomed, half-bloom.

अधखुला adhkhula: (*a*) half-open, half-uncovered.

अधगदराया adhgadra:ya: (*a*) half-ripe, at the threshold of bloom.

अधजल adhjal (*a*) half-full of water; —गगरी छलकत जाय know little, show much; empty vessel makes much noise.

अधजला adhjala: (*a*) half-burnt.

अधन्ना adhannā: (*nm*) a half-anna coin (now out of currency).

अधपका adhpaka: (*a*) half-ripe; half-baked, half-cooked.

अधपन्ना adhpannā: (*nm*) a counterfoil.

अधम adhām (*a*) mean, base, vile; hence ~ता (*nf*).

अधमरा adhmara: (*a*) half-dead, near-dead.

अधमर्ण adhmārn̲ (*nm*) a debtor; borrower.

अधमुआ adhmua: (*a*) half-dead, near-dead.

अधर adhar (*nm*) underlip; lip; mid-air, empty space, space between earth and sky; —पान sucking/kissing of the lips; —में without support underneath; propless; —में झूलना/लटकना to hang in mid-air, to be without a prop.

अधरोष्ठ adharoshṭḥ (*nm*) the lower lip, underlip.

अध/र्म adharm (*nm*) vice; wrong; sin, sinful act; unrighteousness, immorality; ~र्मी sinful; vicious; an evildoer, a sinner.

अधाधुंध adha:dhundh (*a* and *adv*) see अंधाधुंध.

अधार्मिक adha:rmik (*a*) irreligious; unrighteous, profane; hence ~ता (*nf*).

अधिक adhik (*a*) more; much; many; plenty; surplus; abundant; ~तम maximum; ० चरता absolute variability; ~तर most; mostly; ~ता excess; plenty, abundance; —मास a leap month.

अधिकपद adhikpad (*a* and *nm*); pleonastic; pleonasm; ~त्व pleonasm; —दोष pleonasm.

अधिकरण adhikarān̲ (*nm*) locative (case); an organ, agency; instrumental; organization (as न्यायाधिकरण).

अधिकांश adhikā:nsh (*a*) more than half; most; (*nm*) a major portion; ~तः, —में mostly; generally.

अधिकाई adhika:i: (*nf*) excess.

अधिकाधिक adhika:dhik (*a*) more and more, progressively increasing; utmost.

अधिकार adhika:r (*nm*) right; authority; command; possession; occupation; entitlement; -क्षेत्र jurisdiction.

अधिकार-पत्र adhika:rpatr (*nm*) a letter of authority; charter.

अधिकारिता adhika:rita: (*nf*) locus standi.

अधिकारी adhika:ri: (*nm*) an officer; an authority; a title-holder; an owner; (*a*) vested with or possessing authority; authoritative; occupying, occupation.

अधि/कृत adhikkrit (*a*) occupied (as -क्षेत्र); authorised, vested with authority (as—प्रतिनिधि); ~कृत-सूचना authoritative information/report; ~कृति possession, occupation; ० सेना army of occupation.

अधिकेंद्र adhikēndr (*nm*) epicentrum, epicentre.

अधित्यका adhittyaka: (*nf*) upland, tableland.

अधित्याग adhittya:g (*nm*) abdication.

अधिनहन adhinahān (*nm*) annexation.

अधिनायक adhina:yak (*nm*) a dictator; supreme leader; -तंत्र dictatorship; ~त्व dictatorship; ~वाद dictatorship; ~वादी dictatorial.

अधिनिय/म adhiniyām (*nm*) an act (of legislation); ~मन enactment; ~मित enacted.

अधिनि/र्णयन adhinirn̲āyān (*nm*) adjudication; ~र्णीत adjudicated.

अधिप, ~ति adhip, ~ati (*nm*) a ruler, king, master; chief.

अधिपत्र adhipattr (*nm*) a warrant.

अधिप्राप्ति adhipra:pti (*nf*) procurement.

अधिभार adhibha:r (*nm*) surcharge.

अधिभोक्ता adhibhokta: (*nm*) an occupant.

अधिमान adhimā:n (*nm*) preference.

अधिमान्य adhimā:nny (*a*) preferable; preferential: ~ता preference, preferential treatment.

अधिमास adhimā:s (*nm*) a leap month.

अधियाना adhiyā:nā: (*v*) to bifurcate, to divide into two halves.

अधिराज adhira:j (*nm*) a sovereign, supreme ruler.

अधिराजत्व adhira:jattv (*nm*) suzerainty.

अधिराज्य adhirajjy (*nm*) a suzerain power; suzerainty.

अधिरोहण adhirohā̲n (*nm*) ascendance, ascending, climbing up.

अधिरोही adhirohi: (*a*) ascending; —क्रम an ascending order.

अधिवक्ता adhivakta: (*nm*) an advocate.

अधिवास adhiva:s (*nm*) domicile.

अधिवासी adhiva:si: (*nm*) a settler, domicile; (*a*) domiciled, settled.

अधिवेशन adhiveshān (*nm*) session; meeting.

अधिशोषण adhishoshān̲ (*nm*) absorption; —करना to absorb.

अधि/ष्ठाता adhishṭha:ta: (*nm*) a chief; (*a*) superintending, presiding; hence ~ष्ठात्री (*nf*).

अधि/ष्ठान adhisṭhā:n (*nm*) an establishment; abode, dwelling; hence ~ष्ठित (*a*).

अधिसूचना adhisu:chnā: (*nf*) a notification.

अधीक्षक adhi:kshak (*nm*) a superintendent.

अधीत adhi:t (*a*) well-read, erudite.

अधीन adhi:n (*a*) dependent; subordinate, subject to the authority of; under; ~स्थ subordinate, subservient; under.

अधीनता adhi:nta: (*nf*) subordination; subjection; dependence, subjugation.

अधीर adhi:r (*a*) restive, fidgety; impatient; petulant; nervous; ~ता impatience; petulance; nervousness.

अधुना adhunā: (*ind*) now, at present.

अधुनातन adhunā:tān (*a*) modern, up-to-date.

अधूरा adhu:ra: (*a*) incomplete, unfinished; ~पन incompleteness;

imperfection.

अधेड़ adher (*a*) middle-aged, verging on old age.

अधेला adhela: (*nm*) a half-pice coin (now out of currency).

अधोगति adhogati (*nf*) fall, downfall; degradation.

अधो/गमन adhogamān (*nm*) downfall, degradation; **~गामी** falling down, degrading, descending.

अधोमुख adhomukh (*a*) face downwards.

अधोवर्ती adhovarti: (*a*) inferior, situated or existing below or downwards.

अध्यक्ष addhyaksh (*a*) president; chairman; speaker; head; **~ता** presidentship; chairmanship; speakership; headship.

अध्ययन addhyayān (*nm*) study;**–अध्यापन** studying and teaching; **-कक्ष** study, study-room; **~शील** studious, given to reading.

अध्यवसा/य addhyavasa:y (*nm*) perseverance; enterprise, diligence; volition; **~यी** perseverant; enterprising, diligent, industrious.

अध्यात्म addhya:tm (*nm*) spiritual contemplation; **—ज्ञान** spiritual knowledge; **~परक** spiritual; hence **~परकता** (*nf*); **—योग** the discipline involved in withdrawal of senses from mundane objects and their concentration on the Supreme Being; **~वाद** spiritualism; **-विद्या/शास्त्र** metaphysics.

अध्यादेश addhya:desh (*nm*) an ordinance.

अध्या/पक addhyapa:k (*nm*) a teacher; an educator, master; **~पन** teaching, instruction; **~पिका** (*nf*); **~पकी वृत्ति** teaching profession.

अध्याप्त addhya:pt (*a*) acquired (property, etc.);**—करना** to acquire.

अध्याप्ति addhya:pti (*nf*) acquisition.

अध्याय addhya:y (*nm*) a chapter.

अध्यारो/प addhya:rop (*nm*) erroneous transference of an attribute; misprojection; hence **~पण** (*nm*); **~पित** (*a*).

अध्यास addhya:s (*nm*) misimposition; misperception.

अध्याहार addhya:ha:r (*nm*) an ellipsis.

अध्येता addhyeta: (*nm*) a student; scholar.

अनंग anāng (*nm*) see **कामदेव**.

अनंत anānt (*a*) endless, unending; eternal; infinite; (*nf*) infinity; **—चतुर्दशी** a festival celebrated on the fourteenth day of the bright fortnight of the month of **भाद्रपद** (**भादों**); hence **~ता** (*nf*).

अनंतर anāntar (*ind*) after, after wards; in the wake of.

अनंतिम anāntim (*a*) provisional.

अनंत्य ananty (*a*) see **अनंत**.

अन ān—a Hindi prefix used to impart a negative sense, as **~मेल**, **~होनी**.

अनक़रीब anqari:b (*adv*) forthwith, very soon.

अनकहा ankaha: (*a*) untold; inexplicit, implicit.

अनख anākh (*nm*) dudgeon, acerbity, petulance.

अनखाना ankhānā: (*v*) to express a sense of acerbity/petulance/dudgeon; to express resentment (by words or gestures).

अनखुला ankhula:(*a*) not open, inexposed; covered, closed.

अनगढ़ angaṛh:(*a*) crude; unwrought; unchiselled; unpolished; natural; **~पन** crudity, naturalness, absence of chiselling/polish; **—पाषाण युग** crude stone age.

अनगिन angin (*a*) see **अनगिनत**.

अनगिनत anginat (*a*) innumerable, numberless; countless.

अनगिना anginā: (*a*) unaccounted for; uncounted, unnumbered.

अनचाहा ancha:ha: (*a*) unwanted, undesired, undesirable.

अनचीता anchi:ta: (*a*) unthought of, unwanted, undesired.

अनचीन्हा anchi:nhā: (*a*) unknown, unfamiliar; strange.

अनजान anjā:n (*a*) unknown, unacquainted; ignorant.

अनजाने anja:ne (*adv*) unknowingly, unwittingly; —**में (किसी का) हित साधना** to play somebody's game; —**में किसी महापुरुष की सेवा करना** to entertain an angel unawares.

अनदेखा andekha: (*a*) unseen, unforeseen.

अनधिकार anadhika:r (*a*) unauthorised; (*nm*) want of right; —**चेष्टा** unauthorised attempt.

अनधिकारिक anadhika:rik (*a*) non-official; unauthorised.

अनधिकारी anadhika:ri: (*a*) rightless, unrightful; unauthorised; unfit, ineligible.

अनधिकृत anadhikkrit (*a*) unauthorised: unoccupied.

अनध्यवसाय anaddhyavsa:y (*nm*) akrasia; slothfulness, inactivity.

अनध्याय anaddhya:y (*nm*) an off-day; cessation of work; -**काल** vacation, intermission.

अननुकूल ananūku:l (*a*) unfavourable; not kindly/well disposed; opposed; hostile.

अनन्नास anānnā:s (*nm*) pine-apple tree or its fruit.

अनन्य ananny (*a*) identical, unique; close, intimate (as-**मित्र**); completely loyal; exclusive; —**गति** sole support; ० **क** having no other way out; ~**चित्त/मनस्क/मना** having full concentration (in), completely devoted (to); ~**ता** identity, sameness; uniqueness; exclusiveness; ~**परता** complete loyalty; ~**परायण** being exclusively devoted to one; —**भाव** sole or exclusive loyalty/devotion; ~**सामान्य** unique, typical.

अनन्यसंक्राम्य anānnyāsānkrā:mmy (*a*) inalienable, non-transferable.

अनन्याधिकार anānnyā:dhika:r (*nm*) sole/unchallenged right.

अनन्याश्रित anānnyā:shshrit (*a*) independent, not subordinate.

अनन्वय anannvay (*nm*) a meaning-based figure of speech involving comparison of an object with its own ideal (**राम के सम राम ही है**).

अनपच anpach (*nm*) see **अपच**.

अनपचा anpacha: (*a*) undigested.

अनपढ़ anparh (*a*) illiterate, unlettered.

अनपराधी anapra:dhi: (*a* and *nm*) (a) non-criminal.

अनपेक्षित anapekshit (*a*) unwanted, not required or desired.

अनबन anbān (*nm*) discord, estrangement, rift.

अनबिंधा anbīdha: (*a*) unpierced.

अनबूझ anbu:jh (*a*) see **अबूझ**.

अनब्याहा anbya:ha: (*a*) unmarried.

अनभिज्ञ anabhiggy (*a*) ignorant; unaware; unapprised; ~**ता** ignorance; unawareness.

अनभिप्रेत anabhippret (*a*) not intended/designed/implied.

अनभिव्यक्त anabhivyakt (*a*) unexpressed; implicit.

अन/भ्यास anabbhya:s (*nm*) want of practice: hence ~**भ्यासी** (*nm*); ~**भ्यस्त** unaccustomed; out of practice, having no practice.

अनभ्र anabbhr (*a*) cloudless; —**वज्रपात** a bolt from the blue; —**वृष्टि** lit. rain without a cloud—unexpected gains.

अनमना anmanā: (*a*) indisposed; out of sorts, in low spirits; absent-minded; hence ~**पन** (*nm*).

अनमिल anmil (*a*) discordant; irrelevant.

अनमेल anmel (*a*) inharmonious, discordant; dissimilar, heterogeneous; unmixed.

अनमोल anmol (*a*) invaluable, precious, priceless.

अनम्र anāmmr (*a*) disrespectful; impertinent, impudent; hence ~**ता** (*nf*).

अनर्गल anargal (*a*) unrestrained, unbarred; absurd; ~ **ता** absurdity; —**प्रलाप** unrestrained prattle, raving, incoherent prate.

अनर्जित anarjit (*a*) unearned;—**आय** unearned income.

अनर्थ anarth (*nm*) calamity; absurdity; grievous wrong; absolutely contrary meaning; ~**कर/कारी** calamitous, devastating.

अनर्ह anarh (*a*) unqualified, ineligible; ~**ता** disqualification, ineligibility.

अनल anal (*nm*) fire.

अनलहक़ analhaq—an Arabic phrase given currency by the Sufi:s in mediaeval India—meaning 'I am God; I am Truth'.

अनवच्छिन्न anvachchhinn (*a*) unbroken, continuous; hence ~**ता** (*nf*)

अनवट anvaṭ (*nf*) see **अँधौटी**.

अनवद्य anavaddy (*a*) flawelss, without a blemish; hence ~**ता** (*nf*).

अनवधान anavdhā:n (*nm*) absence of concentration, inattention, distraction; inadvertence; negligence; (*a*) distracted, inadvertent; negligent; ~ **ता** inadvertence, heedlessness.

अनवधिक anavadhik (*a*) aperiodic.

अनवरत anavarat (*a*) continuous, incessant, unremitting.

अनवरुद्ध anavruddh (*a*) unobstructed, unhampered; smooth.

अनवरोध anavrodh (*nm*) absence of obstruction; (*a*) free, smooth, unobstructed.

अनव/लंब anavlāmb (*a*) without a support, unsupported; lonely; hence; ~**लंबन** (*nm*); ~ **लंबित** (*a*).

अनवहित anavhit (*a*) inadvertent, negligent.

अनशन anshān (*nm*) fast.

अनश्वर anashshvar (*a*) immortal, immutable, imperishable; hence ~**ता** (*nf*).

अनसुना ansunā: (*a*) unheard (of); —**करना, सुना-अनसुना करना** to ignore (deliberately), not to pay any attention (to).

अनस्तित्व anastittv (*nm*) non-existence.

अन(ना)हदनाद ana(a:)hadna:d —In Indian terminology pertaining to Yog, a mysterious sound born within (without any impact between objects) and audible only to the Yogi:.

अनहोनी anhōni: (*nf*) the improbable, the impossible; (*a*) unusual; improbable, impossible.

अनाकार anā:ka:r (*a*) amorphous; shapeless.

अनाक्रमण anā:kkramān̲ (*nm*) non-aggression, non-attack; —**संधि** a non-aggression pact.

अनाक्रांत ana:kkrā:nt (*a*) unassaulted, unattacked.

अनागत ana:gat (*a*) (the) future, not come, not attained; unknown.

अना/चार anā:cha:r (*nm*) misconduct, lasciviousness, licentiousness; immorality; malpractice; wrong doing; hence ~**चरण** (*nm*); ~**चारी** lascivious, immoral, licentious; malpractitioner, wrong-doer.

अनाज ana:j (*nm*) grain, corn; –**बखरी** a corn-bin, barn.

अनाज्ञाका/री anā:gya:ka:ri: (*a*) disobedient; defiant; hence ~**रिता** (*nf*)

अनाड़ी ana:ṛi: (*a*) inexperienced, unskilful; (*nm*) a novice, tyro, bumpkin, an ignoramus; hence **~पन** (*nm*).

अनात्म ana:tm (*nm*) non-self, (something) different from spirit or soul; (*a*) corporeal, non-spiritual; **~वाद/~वादिता** materialism; **~वादी** a materialist; materialistic.

अनाथ anā:th (*nm*) an orphan; (*a*) orphan, without any protector; helpless.

अनाथालय, अनाथाश्रम anā:tha·lay, anā:tha:shshram (*nm*) an orphanage.

अनादर anā:dar (*nm*) insult; disrespect, disregard;**—करना** to insult, to disrespect.

अनादि anā:di (*a*) having no beginning, ever-existent, eternal.

अनादिष्ट anā:dishṭ (*a*) non-commissioned; undirected.

अनादृत anā:ddrit (*a*) insulted, humiliated; neglected.

अनाधिकारिक anā:dhika:rik (*a*) unofficial; unauthorised.

अनाप-शनाप ana:p-shanā:p (*a* and *nm*) slipslop, nonsense, absurd (talk), prattle, babble.

अनाम anā:m (*a*) nameless; anonymous; **~क** anonymous.

अनामिका anā:mika: (*nf*) the ring finger.

अनामिष anā:mish (*a*) vegetarian; **~भोजी** a vegetarian.

अनायास anā:ya:s (*adv*) without effort, with ease, spontaneously; suddenly.

अनार anā:r (*nm*) a pomegranate; **~दाना** dried seeds of pomegranate.

अनार्य anā:ry (*nm* and *a*) a non-Aryan; (*a*) not noble, not respectable; inferior.

अनावरण anā:varāṉ (*nm*) exposure.

अनावर्ती anā:varti: (*a*) non-recurring (as expenditure); aperiodic (as a circuit).

अनावश्यक anā:vashshyak (*a*) unnecessary; unimportant.

अनाविल anā:vil (*a*) clear, clean; healthy.

अनावृत anā:vvrit (*a*) open, uncovered.

अना/वृत्त anā:vritt (*a*) not returned; non-recurring, unrecurred, unrepeated; hence **~वृत्ति** (*nf*).

अनावृष्टि anā:vrishṭi (*nf*) drought, want of rain.

अनाश्रित anā:shshrit (*a*) independent; self-sufficient.

अनास anā:s (*a*) snub-nosed.

अनास/क्त anā:sakt (*a*) detached; unattached; **~क्त–भाव** sense of detachment/non-attachment; **~क्ति** detachment; absence of attachment.

अनास्था anā:stha: (*nf*) absence/want of faith or devotedness, faithlessness; **~वान** faithless.

अनाहत नाद anā:hat na:d—see **अनहद नाद**.

अनाहार ana:ha:r (*a*) without food.

अनाहूत anā:hu:t (*a*) uninvited, unsummoned.

अनिंदनीय anındani:y (*a*) see **अनिंद्य**.

अनिंदित anındit (*a*) uncensured; unreproached.

अनिंद्य anındy (*a*) irreproachable, flawless.

अनिच्छा anıchchha: (*nf*) reluctance, unwillingness.

अनिच्छुक anichchhuk (*a*) reluctant, unwilling.

अनित्य anitty (*a*) transient, transitory; variable; fleeting; hence **~ता** (*nf*).

अनिद्रा aniddra: (*nf*) insomnia, sleeplessness; hence **अनिद्र** (*a*).

अनिपुण anipūṉ (*a*) unskilled; inefficient; hence ~ता (*nf*).

अनिमंत्रित animāntrit (*a*) uninvited, unsolicited.

अनिमित्त animitt (*a*) without a cause, sudden.

अनिमिष, अनिमेष animish, animesh (*a*) unwinking, without a wink.

अनियंत्रित aniyāntrit (*a*) uncontrolled, unrestrained, unrestricted; arbitrary;—**शासन** absolute or arbitrary government.

अनियत anɪyat (*a*) indefinite, occasional; unallotted; erratic; casual; ~**कालिक** aperiodic; casual.

अनियम anɪyam (*nm*) lawlessness; disorder.

अनियमित anɪyamit (*a*) irregular; disorderly.

अनिर्णय anirṉāy (*nm*) indecision; uncertainty.

अनिर्दिष्ट anirdishṭ (*a*) unspecified, unprescribed.

अनिर्धार्य anirdha:ry (*a*) non-assessable; non-prescribable.

अनिर्वचनीय anirvachnɪ:y (*a*) indescribable; ineffable; hence ~ता (*nf*).

अनिल anil (*nm*) air.

अनिवार्य anɪva:ry (*a*) inevitable; unavoidable; essential, compulsory; irresistible, obligatory; mandatory.

अनिवार्यता aniva:ryta: (*nf*) inevitability.

अनिवास aniva:s (*nm*) non-residence.

अनिश्चय anishchay (*nm*) indecision, uncertainty.

अनिश्चित anishchit (*a*) uncertain, undecided; indefinite, vague; unsettled; ~ता indefiniteness; uncertainty; vagueness.

अनिष्ट anishṭ (*nm*) harm, calamity; ~**कर**,/~**कारी** । (*a*) evil, ominous; harmful, calamitous.

अनी anɪ: (*nf*) eye; point; forepeak; ~**दार** pointed, sharp.

अनीकिनी ani:kinɪ:(*nf*) corps (a body of troops).

अनीति anɪ:ti (*nf*) impropriety, inequity; high-handedness.

अनीश्वर/वाद anɪ:shshvarva:d (*nm*) atheism, agnosticism; also ~**वादिता**; ~**वादी** an atheist; agnosticist; atheistic, agnostic.

अनु anū—a prefix meaning after, afterwards, like, along with, repeatedly, towards, etc. (as **अनुयायी**, **अनुकरण**).

अनुकंपा anūkāmpa: (*nf*) kindness, compassion.

अनुकथन anūkathan (*nm*) post-statement; description.

अनु/करण anūkarāṉ (*nm*) imitation; emulation; mimicry; ~**करणीय** exemplary; imitable, worth emulating or imitating; hence ० ता (*nf*); ~**कर्ता** imitator; emulator; hence ~**कर्त्री** (*nf*); ~**क्रिया** imitation; emulation; ० **त्मक** imitative; emulative.

अनुकल्प anūkalp (*nm*) substitute.

अनुकारी anūka:ri: (*a*) imitating; emulating.

अनुकार्य anūka:ry (*nf*) imitation; emulation.

अनुकूल anūku:l (*a*) favourable; agreeable; befitting; well-disposed; conformable; ~**तम** optimum; ~**ता** favourableness, agreeability; befittingness; conformity; ~**न** conditioning; adaptation; ~**नीयता** adaptability; conformability.

अनुकृत anūkkrit (*a*) imitated; emulated.

अनुकृति anūkkriti (*nf*) an imitation; imitative shape or form; emulation.

अनुक्रम anukkrām (*nm*) sequence, succession.

अनुक्रमण anukkramāṉ (*nm*) sequence,

succession; introgression.

अनुक्रमणिका,अनुक्रमणी anūkkramāṉika:, anūkkramāṉi: (*nf*) a list of contents, an index.

अनुक्रमिक anūkkramık (*a*) successive; consecutive.

अनुक्रिया anūkkriya: (*nf*) response; ~त्मक, ~शील responsive.

अनु/गत anūgat (*a*) obedient; prone to obey or follow; (*nm*) a follower; hence ~गति obedience, following.

अनु/गमन anūgamān (*nm*) following; self-immolation by a widow; ~गामी a follower; following, obedient.

अनु/गुण anūguṉ (*a*) significant, exact, befitting; ~गुणता exactness, significance.

अनुगूँज anugū:j (*nf*) re-echo.

अनुगृहीत anūggrihi:t (*a*) obliged, grateful.

अनुग्रह anūggrah (*nm*) obligation, favour, kindness.

अनु/चर anūchar (*nm*) an attendant; a hanger-on; follower; also ~चारी (*nm*).

अनुचिंतन anūchıntān (*nm*) sympathy; continuous thinking.

अनुचित anūchit (*a*) improper; unbecoming, unseemly; wrong; —संबंध illicit relations.

अनुचिह्न anuchinh (*nm*) a trail, trace.

अनुच्छेद anūchchhed (*nm*) a paragraph; an article.

अनु/ज anūj (*nm*) a younger brother; ~जा (*nf*).

अनुजीवी anūji:vi: (*nm*) an underling, a dependant.

अनुज्ञप्ति anūggyapti (*nf*) a licence.

अनुज्ञा anūggya: (*nf*) permission; ~त्मक permissive; ~धारी a permit-holder.

अनुतट anūtaṭ (*a* and *adv*) coastwise, coastal; along the coast/bank.

अनुतप्त anūtapt (*a*) remorseful; repentant.

अनुतान anuta:n (*nf*) intonation.

अनुताप anūta:p (*nm*) remorse; repentance.

अनुत्तरदायित्व anūttarda:ittv (*nm*) irresponsibility: ~पूर्ण irresponsible.

अनुत्तरदायी anūttarda:i: (*a*) irresponsible.

अनुत्तरित anūttarit (*a*) unreplied unanswered, unresponded.

अनुत्तीर्ण anūtti:rṉ (*a*) failed; unsuccessful.

अनुत्पादक anūtpa:dak (*a*) unproductive; barren; hence ~ता (*nf*).

अनुदत्ताधिकार anūdatta:dhika:r (*nm*) franchise.

अनुदर्शन anūdarshān (*nm*) retrospection.

अनुदर्शी anūdarshi: (*a*) retrospective.

अनुदात्त anūda:tt (*a*) not sublime, lacking loftiness; ignoble; hence ~ता (*nf*).

अनुदान anūda:n (*nm*) a grant.

अनुदार anūda:r (*a*) not liberal, conservative; parochıal; parsimonious, stingy; hence ~ता (*nf*).

अनुदिन anūdin (*adv*) every day, daily.

अनुदेश anūdesh (*nm*) instruction; ~क instructor.

अनुद्विग्न anūddvign (*a*) unperturbed; composed.

अनुद्वेग anūddveg (*nm*) absence of perturbation/flurry; composure.

अनु/नय anūnāy (*nf*) persuasion, propitiation, mollification; ~नय-विनय persuasion and prayer, wooing and propitiation; hence ~नयी (*nm* and *a*).

अनु/नाद anūna:d (*nm*) resonance; echo; ~नादक resonator; ~नादी resonant; ~नादित resounded, echoed.

अनुनासिक anūnā:sik (*a*) nasal; (*nm*) a nasal sound, nasal; hence ~ता(*nf*).

अनुन्नत anūnnat (*a*) undeveloped;

not high, not prosperous.

अनुपका/र anūpka:r (*nm*) evil turn, harm; hence ~री (*nm* and *a*).

अनुप/म anūpam (*a*) matchless, unparalleled; out and away; ~मेय unparalleled; matchless.

अनुपयुक्त anūpyukt (*a*) inexpedient; unfit, unsuitable; hence ~ता (*nf*).

अनुपयो/गी anūpyogi: (*a*) useless, unavailing; ~गिता uselessness, the state of being of no utility.

अनुप/लब्ध anūplabdh (*a*) unachieved, unacquired; hence ~लब्धि (*nf*).

अनुपस्थित anūpasthit (*a*) absent.

अनुपस्थिति anūpasthiti (*nf*) absence.

अनु/पात anūpa:t (*nm*) proportion; ~पाती proportional.

अनुपान anūpā:n (*nm*) fluid vehicle in medicine.

अनुपार्जित anūpa:rjit (*a*) unearned.

अनुपालन anūpa:lan (*nm*) observance, adherence; maintenance.

अनुपूरक anūpu:rak (*a*) supplementary.

अनुपूर्ति anūpu:rti (*nf*) supplementation; compensation; subsidy.

अनुपूर्वी anūpu:rvi: (*a*) successive; consecutive.

अनुपोषण anūposhā̲n̲ (*nm*) support; maintenance.

अनुप्रयुक्त anūpprayukt (*a*) applied; -विज्ञान applied science.

अनुप्रयोग anūpprayog (*nm*) application.

अनुप्रस्थ anūpprasth (*a*) transverse.

अनुप्राणित anūpprā:n̲it (*a*) imbued, inspired, informed; —करना to imbue, to inspire, to inform.

अनुप्रास anūppra:s (*nm*) alliteration; agnomination.

अनुबंध anūbāndh (*nm*) contract; addendum; appendage; stipulation; suffix; ~कारी contracting; ० पक्ष contracting parties.

अनुबंधित anubāndhit (*a*) contracted; signed (for a contract).

अनुबद्ध anūbaddh (*a*) contracted; stipulated; —करना to annex; to enter into a contract (with).

अनुभव anūbhav (*nm*) experience; ~वाद empiricism; ~सिद्ध empirical, established by experience or perception; अनुभवातीत beyond or transcending experience, transcendental; अनुभवातीतवाद transcendentalism; अनुभवाश्रित empirical; —करना to feel; to experience.

अनुभवी anūbhavi: (*a*) experienced, veteran, seasoned.

अनुभाग anūbha:g (*nm*) section (of an office, etc.)

अनु/भाव anūbha:v (*nm*) ensuant response, suggestion (by look or gesture); hence ~भावक (*nm*); ~भावन (*nm*); ~भावी (*a*).

अनुभूत anūbhu:t (*a*) tried: experienced.

अनुभूति anūbhu:ti (*nf*) emotional experience; realisation; sensibility.

अनु/मत anūmāt (*a*) assented (to); approved; agreeable; ~मति assent, approval, leave; ० पत्र a permit, pass.

अनुमान anūmā:n (*nm*) guess, estimate, surmise; supposition; inference; ~त: approximately, about.

अनुमानित anūmā:nit (*a*) approximate; estimated.

अनुमित anūmit (*a*) inferred; estimated/guessed; concluded.

अनुमिति anūmiti (*nf*) inference: conclusion.

अनुमुद्र anūmuddr (*nm*) off-print.

अनुमेय anūmey (*a*) fit to be inferred/concluded, inferable; hence ~ता (*nf*).

अनुमो/दन anūmodān (*nm*) approval, approbation; hence ~दक (*nm*).

अनुमोदित anūmodit (*a*) approved,

approbated.

अनुयान anūyā:n (*nm*) a trailer.

अनुयायी anūya:i: (*nm*) a follower, an adherent.

अनु/रंजन anūrāṇjan (*nm*) recreation, amusement; hence **~रंजित** (*a*).

अनु/रक्त anūrakt (*a*) attached, in love (with), fond (of); **~रक्ति** attachment, dotage, fondness.

अनुरक्षक anūrakshak (*nm*) escort.

अनुरक्षण anūrakshān (*nm*) maintenance; escort.

अनुरक्षी anūrakshi: (*a* and *nm*) escort.

अनु/रणन anūranāh (*nm*) echoism; tinnitus; reverberation; hence **~रणित** (*a*).

अनुराग anūra:g (*nm*) love, affection, attachment, fondness.

अनुरागी anūra:gi: (*a*) affectionate, loving, fond.

अनुरूप anūru:p (*a*) like; fit; conformable, beseeming; according to; analogous; **~ता** accordance; analogy; conformity; fittingness; similitude;—**होना** to be in accord; to correspond/conform; to be befitting.

अनुरूपक anūru:pak (*nm*) counterpart; (*a*) resembling, having similitude.

अनुरे/खण anūrekhān (*nm*) tracing, trace; **~खित** traced.

अनु/रोध anūrodh (*nm*) solicitation; entreaty; hence **~रोधी** (*a*).

अनुर्वर anūrvar (*a*) infertile; sterile, barren; **~ता** infertility; sterility, barrenness.

अनुलिपि anūlipi (*nf*) duplicate, copy; **~करण** duplicating, copying.

अनुलोम anūlom (*nm*) descending series; direct (in Mathematics); **–विवाह** marriage of a man of higher caste with a woman of lower caste.

अनुवर्तन anūvartān (*nm*) subsequence, following; follow-up.

अनु/वर्ती anūvarti: (*a*) subsequent, following; hence **~वर्तिनी** (*nf*).

अनु/वाद anūva:d (*nm*) translation; repetition; **~वादक** a translator; **~वादित** (correct form **अनूदित**) translated; **~वाद्य** (correct form **अनूद्य**) translatable.

अनुवादी anūva:di: (*a*) musical note, other than *va:di:* and *samva:di:*.

अनु/शासन anusha:sān (*nm*) discipline; **~शासक** a disciplinarian; **~शासनबद्ध** disciplined; **~शासनिक**, **~शासनीय** disciplinary; **~शासी** disciplinarian, pertaining to discipline, disciplinary.

अनुशासित anūsha:sit (*a*) disciplined.

अनुशीलन anūshi:lan (*nm*) constant study or practice; investigation.

अनु/श्रवण anūshshravān (*nm*) monitoring; tradition; **~श्रोता** monitor.

अनु/श्रुत anushshrut (*a*) traditional; **~श्रुति** tradition.

अनुषंग anushang (*nm*) association; connection; contingency.

अनुषंगी anūshāngi: (*a*) contingent, ancillary.

अनुष्ठान anūshṭhā:n (*nm*) ritual, ceremony; religious performance; undertaking; exercise; solemnisation; **~कर्ता** a solemniser; **अनुष्ठाता** a performer of a ceremony/ritual; one who is performing an **अनुष्ठान**.

अनुसं/धान anūsāndhā:n (*nm*) research; investigation; **~धाता** a researcher; **~धित्सु** an aspirant for research.

अनुसमर्थन anūsamarthān (*nm*) ratification (of a treaty, etc).

अनुसरण anūsarān (*nm*) (the act or process of) following, pursuance.

अनुसार anūsa:r (*post*); —,**के** according to, in conformity with.

अनुसूची anūsu:chi: (*nf*) a schedule; **~बद्ध** scheduled.

अनुसेवी anūsevi: (*a*) subservient,

servile.

अनुस्यूत anūssyu:t (*a*) intertwined, interwoven.

अनुस्वार anūssva:r (*nm*) lit. after-sound—the nasal sound (in some of the Indian scripts) which is marked by a dot above the line and always follows the preceding vowel.

अनुहरण anūharān (*nm*) mimesis, mimicry, (the act or process of) mimicking.

अनुहर्ता anūharta: (*nm*) a mimic, person skilled in ludicrous imitation.

अनुहारी anūha:ri: (*a*) mimetic, pertaining to mimesis.

अनूठा anū:ṭha: (*a*) unique; unparalleled, unprecedented.

अनूढ़ा anū:ṛha: (*nf*) an unmarried woman.

अनूदित anū:dit (*a*) translated.

अनूद्य anū:ddy (*a*) translatable; fit for/worthy of translation.

अनूप anū:p (*a*) unequalled, unparalleled, singular, unique, out and away.

अनृत ànrit (*nm*) untruth; falsehood, lie.

अनेक anēk (*a*) many, numerous; several; ~ता/त्व diversity, varied character; versatility (as **प्रतिभा**); ~वाद pluralism; ~विध multifarious, of numerous types, varied.

अनेकार्थक anēka:rthak (*a*) polysemous, polysemant; ambiguous; ~ता ambiguity; polysemousness.

अनैकांतिक anaika:ntik (*a*) non-exclusive.

अनैक्य anaiky (*nm*) discord: rift, friction.

अनैच्छिक anaichchhik (*a*) involuntary, notd eliberate.

अनैतिक anaitik (*a*) immoral; deprav ed; ~ता immorality; depravity.

अनैतिहासिक anaitiha:sik (*a*) unhistorical; legendary; hence ~ता (*nf*).

अनोखा anōkha: (*a*) peculiar, queer; novel; ~पन peculiarity, queerness; novelty.

अनौचित्य anaūchity (*nm*) impropriety; indeeency.

अनौद्योगिक anaūdyogik (*a*) non-industrial.

अनौपचारिक anaūpcha:rik (*a*) informal; unofficial; unceremonious; ~ता informality; unofficial way.

अन् an—a Sanskrit prefix to words beginning with vowels, signifying negation (*e.g.*) **अनभिज्ञ, अनाचार, अनंत.**

अन्न ann (*nm*) corn, food, (usu. cooked); ~देव spirit corn.

अन्न-जल ann-jal (*nm*) bread and butter; subsistence; —उठना/छूटना (obliged) to be uprooted, to be forced to move away (from a particular place).

अन्नदाता annda:ta: (*nm*) master; patron, benefactor; one who provides subsistence; a form of address used by subjugated and subordinated people for their masters and patrons, giver of food.

अन्नप्राशन annpra:shān (*nm*) a ceremony marking the occasion when a child is administered non-liquid food (esp. **खीर**) for the first time.

अन्य anny (*a*) other, another; different; —पुरुष third person (in Grammar).

अन्यक्रामण annykrā:mān (*nm*) (act or process of) alienation.

अन्यतः annytah (*ind*) from another; from elsewhere; otherwise.

अन्यतम annytām (*a*) foremost, best.

अन्यत्र annyāttr (*ind*) elsewhere.

अन्यथा annyātha: (*adv*) otherwise; (*a*) contrary, against; ~कथन misrepresentation, false statement.

अन्यदेशीय annydeshi:y (*a*) alien,

foreign; hence ~ता (*nf*).

अन्य/मनस्क, ~मना annymānāsk, ~mānā: (*a*) out of sorts; absent-minded, mentally elsewhere; indisposed; ~मनस्कता absent-mindedness, the state of being mentally elsewhere; indisposition.

अन्यसंक्रामण annysāṅkra:mān̲ (*nm*) (act or process of) alienation; —करना to alienate.

अन्यसंक्राम्यता annysānkra:myāta: (*nf*) alienability.

अन्याय annya:y (*nm*) injustice, wrong; inequity; ~पूर्ण unjust, wrong; inequitable, —करना to give a raw deal, to do a wrong.

अन्यायी annya:yī: (*a*) unjust, inequitable; (*nm*) a wrong-doer; persecutor.

अन्याय्य annya:yy (*a*) unjust, wrongful.

अन्यार्थ annya:rth (*nm* and *a*) (having) another meaning, (imparting) a different meaning; —लेखक ghost writer.

अन्याश्रित annya:shshrit (*a*) dependent, depending on somebody else; subservient (to).

अन्यून annyū:n (*a*) not less; much.

अन्योक्ति annyokti (*nf*) an allegory; ~कार an allegorist; ~परक allegorical; —रूपक an allegory; ~वादी an allegorist; allegorical.

अन्योन्य annyōny (*a*) reciprocal; ~क्रियता interactionism; ~क्रिया interaction; ~ता reciprocity; —संबंध reciprocal relationship, reciprocity.

अन्योन्या/श्रय annyōnnya:shshray (*nm*) interdependence, reciprocity; (*a*) interdependent, reciprocal; ~श्रयवाद mutualism; ~श्रयी, ~श्रित interdependent; reciprocal.

अन्व/य annvay (*nm*) the natural order or sequence of words in a sentence; logical syntactical concordance of words in a sentence; logical connection of cause and effect or proposition and conclusion; lineage; hence ~यी (*a*).

अन्वर्थ annvarth (*a*) significant, conformable to the meaning; intelligible; hence ~ता (*nf*).

अन्वालोप annva:lop (*nm*) an envelope.

अन्वित annvit (*a*) possessed of, possessing; joined; attended; forming an orderly sequence; accompanied by, connected with; understood.

अन्वितार्थ anvita:rth (*a* and *nm*) possessing a meaning intelligible through an orderly sequence of words.

अन्विति annviti (*nf*) unity (esp. dramatic); syntactical sequence (of words).

अन्वी/क्षण annvi:kshān̲ (*nm*) investigation, thorough/microscopic examination; hence ~क्षा (*nf*); ~क्षण-यंत्र a microscope.

अन्वेष, अन्वेष/ण annvesh, ~ān̲ (*nm*) exploration, enquiry; investigation.

अन्वेषक anveshak (*nm*) an explorer, enquirer; a researcher.

अन्वेषित annveshit (*a*) explored, enquired/investigated (into).

अन्वेषी annveshi: (*nm*) see अन्वेषक.

अन्वेष्य annveshy (*a*) explorable, subject or liable to enquiry/investigation.

अपंग apaṅg (*a*) cripple(d), maimed.

अप ap—a Sanskrit prefix denoting—away, off, base, down, deterioration or inferiority; as an allomorph of आप in Hindi, it also denotes 'self' as ~काजी selfish; ~स्वार्थी selfish.

अपकरण apkarān̲ (*nm*) misfeasance; transgression.

अपकर्ता apkarta: (*nm*) an injurer, one who does damage or inflicts harm, harmer, an evil-doer.

अपक/र्म apkarm (*nm*) wrong doing, evil deed, misdeed; ~**र्मा** a wrong doer, misdoer.

अपकर्ष apkarsh (*nm*) downfall; degeneration, degradation, debasement; hence ~**क** (*nm, a*).

अपक/र्षण apkarshān (*nm*) extortion; degeneration, degradation; hence ~**र्षित** (*a*); ~**र्षी** (*a*).

अपकार apka:r (*nm*) harm, ill-turn, damage; disservice; wrong; hence ~**क** (*a*).

अपकारी apka:ri: (*a*) detrimental, hurtful/harmful, damaging; (*nm*) one who inflicts harm, one who does an evil turn.

अपकीर्ति apki:rti (*nf*) infamy, disgrace.

अपकृ/त apakkrit (*a*) (one who has been) harmed; ~**ति** see **अपकार**.

अपकें/द्र apkēndr (*a*) centrifugal; ~**द्रिक** centrifugal; ~**द्रिकता** centrifugality.

अपक्व apakkw (*a*) unripe, raw; immature.

अपक्षय apakshay (*nm*) atrophy.

अपगति apgati (*nf*) downfall, degeneration; misfortune.

अपघटन apghaṭān (*nm*) decomposition.

अपघर्षण apgharshān (*nm*) abrasion.

अपच apach (*nm*) indigestion, dyspepsia.

अप/चय apchay (*nm*) reduction; catabolism; hence ~**चित** (*a*).

अपचयन apchayān (*nm*) reduction; catabolism.

अपचार apcha:r (*nm*) evil deed; aberration.

अपचारी apcha:ri: (*a*) delinquent, aberrant.

अपटु apaṭu (*a*) inefficient, incompetent; lacking skill; hence ~**ता** (*nf*).

अपठित apaṭhit (*a*) unread; uneducated.

अपढ़ aparh (*a*) unlettered, illiterate.

अपतुष्टि aptushṭi (*nf*) appeasement.

अपतृण apattrin (*nm*) weed.

अपत्य apatty (*nm*) an offspring, child.

अपथ्य apatthy (*a*) insalubrious, unwholesome; unhealthy; (*nm*) insalubrious food/diet.

अपदस्थ apadasth (*a*) deposed, dismissed/relieved of one's post.

अपदार्थ apada:rth (*a*) insignificant, petty.

अप/धर्म apdharm (*nm*) heresy; ~**धर्मी** heretic.

अपना apnā: (*a*) one's own, pertaining to oneself; **-तेरी** (a feeling of) thine and mine, a parochial outlook; ~**पन** cordiality, (a feeling of) ownness, affinity; **-पराया** kindred and alien; **-अपना, पराया-पराया** blood is thicker than water; —**उल्लू सीधा करना** to have an axe to grind, to look for position, to serve one's own end; —**घर बदनाम करना** to foul one's own nest; —**घर भरना** to feather one's own nest; —**तोसा अपना भरोसा** everyone must stand on one's own legs; —**दही खट्टा बताना** to cry stinking fish, to condemn one's own endeavours; —**दिल खोल देना** to put (all) one's cards on the table; **अपने पाँव पर खड़े होना** to stand on one's own bottom; —**पेट काटना** to tighten one's belt; —**बोया आप काटना** as you sow so shall you reap; —**पूत सबको प्यारा** every potter praises his own pot; —**मकान कोट समान** every man's house is his castle; —**सब-कुछ एक ही दाँव पर लगा देना** to have all the eggs in one basket; **-सा मुँह लेकर रह जाना** to cut a sorry figure, to face discomfiture, to be chagrined; **अपनी-अपनी ढपली अपना-अपना राग** each one blowing one's own trumpet; **अपनी-अपनी पड़ना** to be keen each after his own interests or affairs; **अपनी करनी का फल पाना/अपनी करनी पार उतरनी** to lie in the bed one has made, to stew in one's juice; **अपनी गली में कुत्ता भी शेर** a cock on his own dunghill; **अपनी जगह डटे रहना** to stick to one's guns; **अपनी बात पर जमे रहना** to stand one's ground; **अपनी बिसात में रहना** to keep one's head; **अपनी मौत मरना** to die in one's own bed; **अपनी लगाई आग में आप जलना** to be hoist with on'e own petard; **अपने आप** by oneself, on one's own; **अपने तक रखना** to one's own check, to keep (some secret, etc.) to oneself; **अपने आप को लाट साहब समझने वाला** Jack in office; **अपने तराजू में दूसरों को तोलना** to measure other's corn by one's own bushel; **अपने मुँह मियाँ मिट्ठू बनना** self-praise is no recommendation; to indulge in self-praise; **अपने माल को सोना कहना** all his geese are swans; **अपने में मस्त रहना** to keep oneself to oneself; **अपने रंग में होना** to be in one's element; **अपने हक़ के लिए लड़ना** to fight for one's own hand.

अपनाना apnā:nā: (*v*) to (treat as one's) own; to adopt; to appropriate.

अपनिर्वचन apnirvachān (*nm*) misinterpretation.

अपभ्रंश apbhrānsh (*nm*) corrupt form of a word, corruption; one of the middle Indo-Aryan languages.

अपभ्रष्ट apbhrasht (*a*) fallen, corrupted; debased, degenerated.

अपमान apmā:n (*nm*) insult, disgrace, affront; **-लेख** libel; **-वचन** slander; **—करना** to insult; °, **खुले आम** to offer an affront (to); **—का घूँट पीना, —सहना** to pocket/swallow an insult, to eat dirt.

अपमानित apmā:nit (*a*) insulted, disgraced.

अपमिश्रण apmishrān (*nm*) adulteration; (*a*) adulterant; **—करना** to adulterate.

अपमृत्यु apmrittyu (*nf*) accidental/unnatural death.

अपयश apyash (*nm*) ill-repute, disrepute, infamy.

अपरंच aprānch (*ind*) moreover, furthermore, besides.

अपरंपार aparampa:r (*a*) boundless, infinite; hence **~ता** (*nf*).

अपर apar (*a*) other, another, different; later; latter; following; inferior.

अपरता aparta: (*nf*) distinction; sense of difference; state of being later/after.

अपरदन apradān (*nm*) erosion.

अपरदेशीय apardeshi:y (*a*) ex-territorial; extra-territorial.

अपरदेशीयता apardeshi:yta: (*nf*) exterritoriality; extra-territoriality.

अपरा apra: (*nm*) mundane or materialistic knowledge; worldly wisdom; **—विद्या** materialistic knowledge.

अपराग apra:g (*nm*) disaffection.

अपराजित apara:jit (*a*) unconquered, unvanquished.

अपराजेय apara:jey (*a*) invincible; unconquerable; hence **~ता** (*nf*).

अपराध apra:dh (*nm*) crime; offence; fault, guilt; **~विज्ञ** criminologist; **-विज्ञान** criminology; **अपराधिता** criminality.

अपराधी apra:dhi: (*a* and *nm*) (a) criminal, guilty; offending/offender.

अपरार्द्ध apara:rddh (*nm*) latter half.

अपराह्न apra:nh (*nm*) afternoon, post-midday.

अपरिग्रह apariggrah (*nm*) renunciation; possessionlessness, the state of being without any belongings; (*a*) destitute of all possessions (beyond the basic minimum).

अपरिचय aparichay (*nm*) non-introduction, non-acquaintance.

अपरिचित aparichit (*a*) unacquainted; (*nm*) a stranger.

अपरिपक्व aparipakkv (*a*) immature; unmatured, unripened; hence ~ता (*nf*).

अपरिपुष्ट aparipusht (*a*) uncorroborated; unconfirmed; hence ~ता (*nf*).

अपरिमित aparimit (*a*) measureless; limitless; enormous; infinite; indeterminate; hence ~ता (*nf*).

अपरिमेय aparimēy (*a*) immeasurable, infinite; irrational; hence ~ता (*nf*).

अपरिव/र्ती aparivarti: (*a*) steady; unchanging; invariable: hence ~र्तिता (*nf*).

अपरिवर्तनीय aparivartanı:y (*a*) unchangeable, invariable; steady; hence ~ता (*nf*).

अपरिवर्तित aparivartit (*a*) unchanged, unaltered, unmodified.

अपरिष्कार aparishka:r (*nm*) non-refinement; crudeness.

अपरिष्कृ/त aparishkrit (*a*) unrefined; crude; hence ~ति (*nf*).

अपरिहार apariha:r (*nm*) indispensation, lack of means to dispense.

अपरिहार्य apariha:ry (*a*) indispensible; inevitable, unavoidable; hence ~ता (*nf*).

अपरीक्षित apari:kshit (*a*) unexamined, untested; untried.

अपरूप apru:p (*a*) ugly; grotesque; unparalleled; hence ~ता (*nf*).

अपरोक्ष aparoksh (*a*) direct; visible, tangible; —रूप से directly, obviously.

अपर्याप्त aparya:pt (*a*) inadequate, insufficient; hence ~ता (*nf*).

अपलक apalak (*adv* and *a*) without a wink/blink, unwinking, unblinking.

अपवचन apvachān (*nm*) slander, calumny.

अप/वर्जन apvarjān (*nm*) exclusion; ~वर्जी exclusive; ~र्जिता exclusiveness.

अपवर्जित apvarjit (*a*) excluded; —करना to exclude.

अपवर्तक apvartak (*nm*) common divisor.

अपवर्तन apvartān (*nm*) abduction; regression.

अपवर्तिता apvartita: (*nf*) regression, regressiveness; abductivity.

अपवर्त्य apvarty (*nm*) factor; divisor.

अपवहन apvahān (*nm*) drift; (the act or process of) drifting.

अपवाद apva:d (*nm*) exception; slander, calumny; hence ~क, **अपवादी** (*nm*).

अपवा/रण apva:rān (*nm*) repelling, repeal, rescind; hence ~रक (*nm*); ~रित (*a*).

अपवाह apva:h (*nm*) drainage; outflow; drift; -क्षेत्र drainage area; -तंत्र drainage (system).

अपवाहिका apva:hika: (*nf*) a sink.

अपविकास apvika:s (*nm*) devolution; degeneration.

अपविचार apvicha:r (*nm*) mistrial; a mischievous/bad idea.

अपवित्र apavittr (*a*) unholy, impure; desecrated, profane; ~ता profanity; unholiness.

अपविवृति apvivriti (*nf*) misinterpretation.

अपवृद्धि apvriddhi (*nf*) excrescence.

अप/व्यय apavvyay (*nm*) wastefulness; extravagant expenditure, squandering; ~व्ययी a squanderer; wasteful, extravagant.

अपशकुन apshakūn (*nm*) ill/bad omen; inauspicious omen, an occurrence or event portending evil.

अपशब्द apshabd (*nm*) an abuse; abusive language or word, a vulgar word.

अपशिष्ट apshishṭ (*nm* and *a*) worthless residue, waste; residual.

अपसरण apsarāṉ (*nm*) divergence.

अपसामान्य apsa:mā:nny (*a*) abnormal; ~ता abnormality.

अप/सिद्धांत apsiddhā:nt (*nm*) heresy; ~सैद्धांतिक heretic.

अपसूत्र apsu:tr (*nm*) apophysis.

अपसृति apsriti (*nf*) divergence.

अपस्फीति apsphi:ti (*nf*) deflation, varicosity.

अपस्मार apasma:r (*nm*) epilepsy, eclampsia.

अपस्वर apassvar (*nm*) a discordant note; ~ता discordance.

अपस्वार्थी apswa:rthi: (*a*) selfish, concerned about own ends.

अप/हरण apaharāṉ (*nm*) abduction; kidnapping; usurpation; ~हर्ता abductor; kidnapper; usurper; ~हरण करना to abduct; to kidnap; to usurp.

अपहसित aphasit (*nm*) a guffaw, unprovoked and boisterous laughter.

अपहृत aphrit (*a*) abducted; kidnapped; usurped.

अपह्नुति apahnuti (*nf*) concealment (a figure of speech).

अपांग apā:ṅg (*nm*) the outer corner of the eye; (*a*) crippled, maimed; —दृष्टि a side-glance.

अपाच्य apa:chchy (*a*) indigestible; not worthy of or fit for cooking.

अपाठ्य apa:ṭṭhy (*a*) illegible, unreadable; worthless; hence ~ता (*nf*).

अपात्र apa:ttr (*a*) unworthy, undeserving; ineligible; ~ता unworthiness; ineligibility.

अपादान apā:dā:n (*nm*) the ablativ[e] case.

अपानद्वार apā:ndva:r (*nm*) the anus.

अपानवायु apā:nva:yu (*nf*) flatus, fou[l] wind emitted from the anus.

अपार apa:r (*a*) boundless; shoreless[;] immense; hence ~ता (*nf*).

अपारगम्य apa:rgammy (*a*) impermeable; ~ता impermeability.

अपारदर्शिता apa:rdarshita: (*nf*) opacity.

अपारदर्शी apa:rdarshi; (*a*) opaque.

अपार्थिव apa:rthiv (*a*) unearthly[;] celestial; spiritual; hence ~ता (*nf*)[.]

अपा/वरण apa:varāṉ (*nm*) exposur[e;] ~वृत exposed; hence ~वृति (*nf*).

अपाहिज apa:hij (*nm* and *a*) a cripple; crippled, disabled.

अपि api (*ind*) also; and; though[;] although; ~तु but, on the oth[er] hand.

अपील api:l (*nf*) an appeal; -अदाल[त] the court of appeal.

अपुष्ट apushṭ (*a*) unconfirmed; unnourished; stunted; hence ~त[ा] (*nf*).

अपूर्ण apu:rṉ (*a*) incomplete, unfinished; imperfect, deficien[t;] hence ~ता (*nf*); ~भूत past imperfect (tense).

अपूर्व apu:rv (*a*) unprecedente[d;] novel; unique; hence ~ता (*nf*).

अपेक्षा apeksha: (*ind*) (generally pr[e]ceded by की or the relative cas[e)] in comparison with; (*nf*) expe[c]tation, requirement; ~कृत comparatively, comparatively speaking.

अपेक्षित apekshit (*a*) expected; requ[i]site.

अपोषण aposhāṉ (*nm*) malnutritio[n.]

अपौरुषेय apaurushey (*a*) divine; n[ot] achieved by or belonging t[o] human being(s).

अप्रकट apprakat (*a*) latent, hidde[n]

invisible; hence ~ता (*nf*).

अप्रकाशित appraka:shit (*a*) unpublished; unexposed, undisclosed.

अप्रकाश्य appraka:shshy (*a*) unworthy of or unfit for publication/disclosure.

अप्रकृत apprakrit (*a*) abnormal; unnatural; hence ~ता (*nf*).

अप्रचलन apprachalān (*nm*) obsolescence; the state or circumstance of being out of currency.

अप्रचलित apprachlit (*a*) obsolete, (gone) out of currency; out of date, antiquated; hence ~ता (*nf*).

अप्रज्ञान appraggyā:n (*nm*) non-cognizance.

अप्रज्ञेय appraggyey (*a*) non-cognizable.

अप्रतिबंध appratibāndh (*a*) unconditional; non-committed.

अप्रतिबद्ध appratibaddh (*a*) uncommitted, non-committed.

अप्रतिभ appratibh (*a*) bewildered, thrown out of wits, rendered witless.

अप्रतिम appratim (*a*) matchless, unique, out and away.

अप्रतिष्ठ appratishṭh (*a*) see **अप्रतिष्ठित**.

अप्रतिष्ठा appratishṭha: (*nf*) disgrace, disrepute, ignominy.

अप्रतिष्ठित appratishṭhit (*a*) disgraced, disreputed, ignominious; unestablished.

अप्रतिहत appratihat (*a*) unhindered, unhampered; unresisted; —गति smooth movement, unhampered movement.

अप्रत्यक्ष apprattyaksh (*a*) inapparent; invisible; indirect.

अप्रत्यय apprattyay (*nm*) lack of conviction/faith; (*a*) without suffix.

अप्रत्याशित apprattya:shit (*a*) unexpected; sudden; hence ~ता (*nf*).

अप्रधान appradhā:n (*a*) secondary, subsidiary; minor; hence ~ता (*nf*).

अप्रभावी apprabha:vi: (*a*) ineffective, ineffectual.

अप्रयुक्त apprayukt (*a*) out of use, unused; obsolete (word).

अप्रयोग apprayog (*nm*) disuse.

अप्रसन्न apprasann (*a*) unhappy; displeased; out of sorts.

अप्रसन्नता apprasannata: (*nf*) unhappiness, displeasure.

अप्रसि/द्ध apprasiddh (*a*) not celebrated; obscure, little known; hence ~द्धि (*nf*).

अप्रस्तुत apprastut (*a*) indirect, accidental or extraneous; not principal, not being the main subject matter; irrelevant; (*nm*) the object of comparison (in Rhetorics); —प्रशंसा indirect description (a figure of speech); —विधान trope.

अप्रस्तुति apprastuti (*nf*) indirectness; in Rhetorics, the device of indirect description.

अप्राकृ/त, ~तिक appra:kkrit, ~tik (*a*) unnatural; abnormal; uncommon; hence ~तिकता (*nf*).

अप्राप्त appra:pt (*a*) unobtained, unachieved, unacquired; ~वय minor; of a tender age.

अप्राप्ति appra:pti (*nf*) non-attainment; non-acquisition.

अप्राप्य appra:ppy (*a*) unattainable, unobtainable; rare; hence ~ता (*nf*).

अप्रामाणिक appra:mā:ṉik (*a*) unauthoritative; inauthentic; of disputed origin.

अप्रामाणिकता appra:mā:ṉikta: (*nf*) unauthoritativeness, inauthenticity, lack/absence of authenticity or genuineness.

अप्रासंगिक appra:sāngik (*a*) irrelevant, out of context; —चर्चा irrelevant discussion/talk; hence ~ता (*nf*).

अप्रिय appriy (*a*) unpleasant, disagreeable offensive; ~ता unpleasantness, offensiveness, disagreeability; ~वादी ill-tongued, harsh-spoken.

अप्रैल aprail (*nm*) (the month of) April.

अप्सरा apsara: (*nf*) a celestial damsel, fairy; nymph.

अफरना apharna: (*v*) see **अघाना**.

अफरा aphra: (*nm*) swelling of stomach due to over-eating, indigestion or accumulation of wind.

अफ़रा-तफ़री afra:tafri: (*nf*) confusion, hurry-skurry; commotion; panic.

अफ़लातून afla:tu:n (*nm*) a person of overweening pride; boaster (based on the corrupt form of the name of one of the earliest and greatest Greek thinkers—Plato); —का नाती, —की दुम a high-hat, a boaster; an awesome person.

अफ़वा/ह afva:h (*nm*) a rumour; ~ह गर्म होना the air to be thick with rumours; ~ह फैलाना to give currency to a rumour; ~हें उड़ाना to indulge in rumour-mongering.

अफ़स/र afsar (*nm*) an officer; ~री the post, function or air of an officer; officialism; officialdom.

अफ़साना afsa:nā: (*nm*) a story, tale; ~गो a story-teller; -नवीस/निगार a story-writer.

अफ़सोस afsos (*nm*) sorrow, grief; (*int*) alas!; ~नाक sorrowful, grievous.

अफारा apha:ra: (*nm*) tympanitis.

अफ़ीम afi:m (*nf*) opium; —खाये होना to be stupidly incoherent, to be foolishly irrelevant.

अफ़ीमची afi:mchi: (*nm*) an opium-addict.

अबंध-नीति abāndh-nī:ti (*nf*) laissez faire.

अब ab (*adv*) now; —का recent, modern; — की/के this time; next time; —जाकर at long last; -तब करना to evade, to dilly-dally; -तब होना to be on the verge of death; —से now onwards, in future; —पछताये होत क्या जब चिड़िया चुग गईं खेत to cry over spilt milk, to waste one's regrets.

अबद्ध abaddh (*a*) varied; not in bondage, free.

अबरक abrak (*nm*) mica.

अबरी abri: (*nf*) marble paper; (*a*) variegated.

अबला abla: (*nf*) a member of the weaker sex—a woman.

अबाध aba:dh (*a*) without restraint: free, smooth; —गति unrestrained movement, smooth pace; hence ~ता (*nf*).

अबाधित aba:dhit (*a*) unrestricted, unrestrained; smooth.

अबाबील aba:bi:l (*nf*) a swallow.

अबी/र abi:r (*nm*) a special kind of red powder sprinkled by the Hindus on one another during the Holi festival; ~री blackish red, of the colour of **अबीर**.

अबूझ abu:jh (*a*) unintelligible; insolvable; insane.

अबे abe (*ind*) an address expressive of disrespect or intimate relationship; you fellow!; -तबे करना to use contemptuous or rude language.

अबोध abodh (*a*) innocent; ignorant; ~गम्य unintelligible; inconceivable.

अबोला abola: (*nm*) absence of speaking terms (between one person and another).

अब्द abd (*nm*) an year; ~कोश a year book.

अब्धि abdhi (*nm*) a sea, an ocean.

अब्बा abba: (*nm*) father; —जान father (a respectful term for address or for otherwise mention).

अब्राह्मण abbra:hmān (*nm*) a non-Brahman.

अभंग abhaṅg (*a*) unbroken, unimpaired.

अभक्ष्य abhakshy (*a*) uneatable, inedible; (*nm*) forbidden/uneatable food.

अभद्र abhaddr (*a*) indecent, indecorous; inauspicious; **~ता** indecency.

अभय abhay (*nm*) an assurance of safety or protection; fearlessness; (*a*) fearless, undaunted; safe; **-दान/वचन** an assurance/pledge of safety or protection.

अभागा abha:ga: (*a*) unfortunate, accursed, unlucky, ill-starred; hence **~पन** (*nm*).

अभागिन abha:gin (*a*) accursed, unlucky/unfortunate (woman).

अभागिनी abha:ginI: (*a*) see **अभागिन**.

अभाग्य abha:ggy (*nm*) misfortune, ill luck.

अभा/व abha:v (*nm*) want, dearth, deficiency, shortage, lack; **~वात्मक** negative.

अभावित abha:vit (*a*) uncontemplated, unthought of.

अभि abhi—a Sanskrit prefix denoting towards, near, over, above, repeated, excessive, etc.

अभिकथन abhikathān (*nm*) an allegation.

अभिकर्ता abhikarta: (*nm*) an agent.

अभिकल्प abhikalp (*nm*) a design; **~क** a designer.

अभिक्रिया abhikkriya: (*nf*) reaction; **~शील** reactive; **॰ता** reactivity.

अभिग्रहण abhiggrahān (*nm*) requisition.

अभिचा/र abhicha:r (*nm*) incantation, employment of spells for a malevolent purpose, sorcery, black magic; **~रक** one who practises incantation, a conjurer; **~र-क्रिया** witchcraft; sorcery; **~री** incantational, incantatory; a conjurer.

अभिजात abhija:t (*a*) aristocratic, well-born; classic; (*nm*) an aristocrat, noble; **-अभिनय** classic acting; **-कृति** a classic (work); **~तंत्र** aristocracy; **-वर्ग** aristocracy, nobility; **~वाद** classicism, aristocracy; **~वादी** a classicist; aristocrat.

अभिजात्य abhija:tty (*a*) aristocratic; classic.

अभिज्ञ abhiggy (*a*) well-conversant (with), knowing all (about something); **~ता** conversance, familiarity; knowledge.

अभिज्ञात abhiggya:t (*a*) recognised.

अभिज्ञान abhiggyā:n (*nm*) recognition; recollection; identification; anagnorisis.

अभित्रास abhittra:s (*nm*) intimidation.

अभिधा abhidha: (*nf*) denotation, the literal power or sense of a word.

अभिधान abhidhā:n (*nm*) a name; noun; nomenclature.

अभिधारणा abhidha:rnā: (*nf*) a postulate.

अभिधावन abhidha:vān (*nm*) expedition, charge.

अभिधेय abhidhey (*nm*) literal meaning.

अभिनं/दन abhināndān (*nm*) greeting, reception, a ceremonious welcome; applause; **~दन-ग्रंथ** a commemoration volume; **~दन-पत्र** an address of welcome; **~दन-भाषण** an address of welcome; **~दन-समारोह** a reception; **~दनीय** laudable, praiseworthy, fit to be greeted or welcomed; **~दित** greeted; applauded, praised.

अभिन/ति abhināti (*nf*) bias; inclination; ~त biased; inclined.

अभिनय abhināy (*nm*) acting; performing (on the stage).

अभिनव abhināv (*a*) novel, new; recent.

अभिनिवेश abhinivesh (*nm*) concentration, deliberation; perseverance.

अभिनीत abhini:t (*a*) staged, enacted.

अभि/नेता abhinēta: (*nm*) an actor; ~नेत्री an actress.

अभिनेय abhiney (*a*) actable, stageable; ~ता stageability.

अभिन्न abhinn (*a*) identical; not different; close, intimate; integral; —अंग integral part; ~ता identity; sameness, oneness; -हृदय one/united at heart, very intimate.

अभिन्यास abhinnyā:s (*nm*) lay-out.

अभि/पुष्ट abhipushṭ (*a*) affirmed; ~पुष्टि affirmance; ~पोषक affirmant; ~पोषण affirmation.

अभिप्राय abhippra:y (*nm*) intention; implication; purport; design, import, purpose.

अभिप्रेत abhippret (*a*) intended, implied; designed.

अभिप्रेरण abhipprerāṉ (*nm*) motivation; also अभिप्रेरणा (*nf*).

अभिभव abhibhav (*nm*) defeat; onslaught, attack.

अभिभावक abhibha:vak (*nm*) a guardian; ~ता/~त्व guardianship.

अभिभाषण abhibha:shāṉ (*nm*) an address (speech delivered by a dignitary).

अभिभूत abhibhu:t (*a*) overwhelmed; overpowered; overawed.

अभिमंत्रित abhimāntrit (*a*) consecrated by a मंत्र (see).

अभिमत abhimāt (*a*) favourite; desired; (*nm*) an opinion.

अभिमध्य abhimaddhy (*a*) medial.

अभिमान abhimā:n (*nm*) pride; vanity, arrogance.

अभिमानी abhimā:nı: (*a*) proud; vainglorious, arrogant.

अभिमुख abhimūkh (*ind*) directed towards, facing; disposed to, intending to.

अभि/यंता abhiyānta: (*nm*) an engineer; ~यंत्रण(ı) engineering.

अभियाचना abhiya:chnā: (*nf*) a demand.

अभियान abhiyā:n (*nm*) a campaign; an expedition; -दल an expedition.

अभियुक्त abhiyukt (*nm* and *a*) (an) accused.

अभियोक्ता abhiyokta: (*nm*) an accuser.

अभियोग abhiyog (*nm*) accusation, charge; law suit, case; indictment.

अभियोगी abhiyogi: (*nm*) an accuser

अभियोजन abhiyojān (*nm*) prosecution.

अभि/रक्षक abhirakshak (*nm*) a custodian; ~रक्षा custody.

अभिराम abhirā:m (*a*) beautiful, lovely; delightful; hence ~ता (*nf*).

अभिरुचि abhiruchi (*nf*) taste, liking.

अभिलक्षण abhilakshāṉ (*nm*) characteristic.

अभिलषित abhilashit (*a*) cherished, desired, longed for.

अभिला/षा abhila:sha: (*nf*) desire, yearning, longing, craving, wish; also ~ष(*nf*); ~षी wishing; desiring; a wisher.

अभिलिखित abhilikhit (*a*) recorded, placed on record.

अभिलेख abhilekh (*nm*) a record; transcript; -ग्रंथ a record book; ~न placing on record, making a record of; transcription.

अभिवं/दन abhivāndān (*nm*); ~दना ~nā: (*nf*) respectful salutation; ~दनीय, ~द्य deserving respectful salutation, reverend.

अभिवक्ता abhivakta: (*nm*) a pleader.

अभिवचन abhivachān (*nm*) plea; affirmation.

अभिवादन abhiva:dān (*nm*) deferential salutation; greeting.

अभिवृत्ति abhivritti (*nf*) attitude; aptitude.

अभिवृद्धि abhivriddhi (*nf*) prosperity; development; progress.

अभिवेचन abhivechan (*nm*) censorship.

अभिव्यंज/न abhivyāṇjān (*nm*) expression; **~क** expressive; **~कता** expressiveness.

अभिव्यंजना abhivyāṇjanā: (*nf*) expression; manifestation; **~वाद** expressionism.

अभि/व्यंजित abhi/vyāṇjit, **~व्यक्त** ~vyakt (*a*) expressed; manifested.

अभि/व्यक्ति abhivyakti (*nf*) expression; manifestation; **~व्यक्त** see **अभिव्यंजित**.

अभि/शंसा abhishānsa: (*nf*) incrimination, crimination; hence **~शंसन** (*nm*).

अभिशंसी abhishānsi: (*nm* and *a*) an incriminator; incriminating, incriminatory.

अभिशप्त abhishapt (*a*) cursed, accursed.

अभिशाप abhisha:p (*nm*) a curse.

अभिषिक्त abhishikt (*a*) consecrated; enthroned.

अभिषेक abhishek (*nm*) inaugurating or consecrating (by sprinkling water); inauguration of a king, royal function.

अभिसंधि abhisāndhi (*nf*) a conspiracy, plot.

अभिसमय abhisamāy (*nm*) a convention (written agreement).

अभिसरण abhisarāṉ (*nm*) going towards a point for meeting; rendezvous (of lovers); convergence.

अभिसाक्ष्य abhisa:kshy (*nm*) deposition; a statement on oath.

अभिसार abhisa:r (*nm*) meeting; rendezvous (of lovers).

अभिसारिका abhisa:rika: (*nf*) a woman who goes to meet her lover or keeps an assignation.

अभिसारी abhisa:ri: (*a*) convergent.

अभिसूचक abhisu:chak (*nm*) an index.

अभिहित abhihit (*a*) named, designated; called; **—संधि** gentlemen's agreement.

अभी abhi: (*adv*) just now, this moment; **—दम में दम है** to show fight, has fight (in him) yet.

अभीष्ट abhi:sht (*a*) desired, cherished; **—लक्ष्य** desired goal, cherished aim; **—लाभ** attainment of what is desired; **—सिद्धि** attainment of the desired objective/ thing.

अभीप्सित abhi:psit (*a*) desired, wished for, cherished.

अभुक्त abhukt (*a*) unfulfilled, ungratified; unenjoyed; unused

अभूतपूर्व abhu:tpu:rv (*a*) unprecedented; (that has) never existed before; hence **~ता** (*nf*).

अभेद abhed (*nm*) identity, oneness; hence **~ता** (*nf*).

अभेद्य abheddy (*a*) indivisible; indistinguishable; impregnable, impenetrable; hence **~ता** (*nf*).

अभोग्य abhoggy (*a*) forbidden, unworthy of being enjoyed or used.

अभौतिक abhautik (*a*) unearthly, not material or mundane, not related to or produced by the gross elements, celestial.

अभ्यंतर abbhyantar (*nm* and *a*) interior; inside.

अभ्यनुकूलन abbhyanuku:lān (*nm*) (the act or process of) adaptation.

अभ्य/र्थन, ~र्थना abbhya/rthān (*nm*), ~rthanā: (*nf*) welcome, reception; supplication, request; **~र्थनीय** deserving welcome or reception; worth requesting (for); worth supplication; **~र्थित** welcomed; supplicated, requested (for).

अभ्यर्थी abbhyarthi: (*nm*) a welcomer; suppliant; candidate.

अभ्यर्पण abbhyarpān (*nm*) surrender.

अभ्यस्त abbhyast (*a*) accustomed, habituated; habitual; trained, skilled; —**होना** to be used to; to have at one's finger tips.

अभ्याक्रमण abbhya:kkramān (*nm*) assailance;—**करना** to assail; ~**कारी** assailant; assailing.

अभ्यागत abbhya:gat (*nm*) a guest, visitor.

अभ्यारोप(ण) abbhya:rop(ān) (*nm*) indictment; —**सार** abstract of indictment.

अभ्या/स abbhya:s (*nm*) practice; exercise; habituation; ~**सी** well-up, trained; practising, carrying on practice/training.

अभ्यु/त्थान abbhyutthā:n (*nm*) rise, rising; elevation; hence ~**त्थित** (*a*).

अभ्यु/दय abbhyuday (*nm*) rise, rising (of luminaries); rising (to prosperity, happiness, etc.); advent; aggrandizement; hence ~**दित** (*a*).

अभ्र abbhr (*nm*) cloud; the sky; ~**भेदी** sky-high.

अभ्रक abbhrak (*nm*) see **अबरक**.

अमंगल amāṅgal (*nm*) inauspiciousness; evil; disaster.

अमंद amānd (*a*) not slow, quick; bright.

अमचूर amchu:r (*nm*) dried mango parings (used as spice).

अमन amān (*nm*) peace, tranquillity; -**अमान** peace and order; -**चैन** peace and happiness; ~**पसंद** peaceful, pacific, peace-loving; ~**पसंदी** pacifism, peace-lovingness, the state or mental attitude of liking peace.

अमर amar (*a*) immortal, eternal, undying; (*nm*) a god, deity; ~**बेल** parasite creeper (*Cuscuta reflexa*).

अमर/ता amarta: (*nf*) immortality; also ~**त्व** (*nm*).

अमराई amra:i: (*nf*) a mango-grove.

अमरी/का amri:ka: (*nm*) (the United States of) America; ~**की** (an) American.

अमरूद amru:d (*nm*) guava.

अमर्त्य amartty (*a*) immortal, deathless, eternal; ~**लोक** the heaven—abode of gods.

अमर्दित amardit (*a*) unvanquished, unassailed; undaunted.

अमर्या/द amarya:d (*a*) violating defined limits (of propriety); intemperate; improper; ~**दा** intemperance; affront; indignity; ~**दित** intemperate; immodest; undignified; violating defined limits (of propriety).

अमल amal (*nm*) action, execution; application; addiction; -**दरामद** formal proceedings; ~**दारी** reign, rule, authority, jurisdiction; sway; -**पानी करना** to take some intoxicating drink; to have a drinking session;—**में लाना** to execute, to implement.

अमलतास amalta:s (*nm*) *Cassia fistula* —an Indian medicinal plant used as a purgative.

अमलदारी amalda:ri: (*nf*) see **अमल** (~**दारी**).

अमला amla: (*nm*) staff; paraphernalia.

अमली amli: (*a*) practical; (*nm*) an addict;—**जामा पहनाना** to translate into action, to put into practice.

अमाँ āmā: (*ind*) man ! O !

अमांगलिक amā:ṅgalik (*a*) inauspicious, ominous, ill-foreboding.

अमात्य ama:tty (*nm*) a minister.

अमान ama:n (*nf*) assurance of protection/security.

अमानक amā:nāk (*a*) non-standard, below standard; not conforming to the prescribed standard.

अमानत amā:nāt (*nf*) something given in trust, a deposit; ~**दार** a trustee; —**में ख़यानत करना** to commit breach of trust (by grabbing the thing entrusted).

अमानती amā:nati: (*a*) deposited or given in trust.

अमानवीय amā:navi:y (*a*) inhuman, cruel; —**तत्त्व** inhuman element; abstraction; hence ~**ता** (*nf*).

अमानी amā:nɪ: (*a*) casual labour; time/daily wages; prideless, without arrogance.

अमानुषिक ama:nūshik (*a*) inhuman; beastly; cruel; hence ~**ता** (*nf*).

अमान्य amā:nny (*a*) unacceptable; not respectable; invalid; ~**ता** invalidity, non-acceptability; non-recognition.

अमालनामा amā:lnā:mā: (*nm*) a dossier.

अमावट amā:vaṭ (*nf*) dried juice of ripe mango formed into thin cakes.

अमाव/स, ~स्या amā:vas, ~sya: (*nf*), the last day of the dark fortnight.

अमिट amiṭ (*a*) indelible, ineffaceable; indestructible; —**छाप** indelible imprint.

अमित amit (*a*) unmeasured, boundless; immense, enormous.

अमिताभ amita:bh (*a*) possessing unlimited brilliance; (*nm*) a name of Lord Buddha.

अमिश्र amishshr (*a*) unmixed, unadulterated; pure.

अमिश्रित amishshrit (*a*) unmixed, unadulterated; pure; hence ~**ता** (*nf*).

अमीन amɪ:n (*nm*) a junior officer appointed for land survey and revenue collection.

अमीर ami:r (*a*) rich, wealthy; (*nm*) a rich man; a chieftain; -**ग़रीब** haves and have-nots; ~**ज़ादा** son of a rich man; an aristocrat by birth; hence ~**ज़ादी** (*nf*); **अमीराना** lordly, princely.

अमीरी ami:ri: (*nf*) richness, wealthiness.

अमुक amuk (*a*) such and such, so and so.

अमूर्त amu:rt (*a*) abstract; intangible, incorporeal; —**कला** abstract art; —**कविता** abstract poem; —**गुण** abstract quality; —**तत्त्व**/ ~**ता** abstraction; —**दृश्य-विधान/विन्यास** abstract setting; ~**वाद** abstractionism; ~**वादी** abstractionist.(*ic*)

अमूल्य amu:lly (*a*) priceless; valuable, precious.

अमृत ammrit (*nm*) nectar; -**वाणी** life-giving words; reviving/inspiring speech.

अमृतबान ammritbā:n (*nm*) a jar.

अमेय amey (*a*) immeasurable, limitless.

अमोघ amogh (*a*) unfailing, unerring; infallible.

अमौलिक amaulik (*a*) not original; not fundamental; secondary; hence ~**ता** (*nf*).

अम्माँ ammā: (*nf*) mother.

अम्ल aml (*nm*) acid; (*a*) sour; ~**ता** acidity; sourness.

अम्लान amlā:n (*a*) unwithered; bright, fresh; hence ~**ता** (*nf*).

अम्हौरी amhauri: (*nf*) prickly heat.

अयंत्रित ayāntrit (*a*) unrestricted, uncontrolled.

अयत ayat (*a*) uncontrolled; immoderate.

अयथा ayatha: (*ind*) otherwise, not as it should be.

अयथार्थ ayatha:rth (*a*) unreal, false; virtual; ~**ता** unreality.

अयश ayash (*nm*) disgrace, infamy.

अयस्क ayask (*nm*) an ore.

अयाचित aya:chit (*a*) unsolicited, unasked for.

अयाल aya:l (*nf*) mane.

अयुक्त ayukt (*a*) incompatible: illogical; absurd; unseemly; free, unjointed; **~ता** incompatibility; absurdity; the state of being free or unjointed.

अयुक्ति ayukti (*nf*) irrationality; absence of any logic or relevance, incompatibility.

अयुग्मिता ayugmīta: (*nf*) agamy.

अयोग्य ayoggy (*a*) incompetent; unworthy; unqualified; unfit; **~ता** unfitness; disqualification; inability.

अयोद्धा ayoddha: (*nm*) non-combatant.

अयोधी ayodhi: (*a*) non-combatant.

अयोनिज ayonij (*a*) non-placental.

अयौगिक ayaugik (*a*) non-compound; elemental; crude.

अरंडी arāndi: (*nf*) castor oil or plant.

अर ar (*nm*) a spoke; ray.

अरक़ araq (*nm*) see **अर्क़**.

अरक्षित arakshit (*a*) insecure; unprotected, not defended; hence **~ता** (*nf*).

अरगनी arganī: (*nf*) clothesline, a rope wire or bamboo used for hanging clothes on.

अरण्य aranny (*nm*) forest; wilderness; **~रोदन** crying in wilderness (which attracts no one), an unavailing exercise.

अरथाना arthā:nā: (*v*) to explain (the meaning of); to make explicit.

अरना arnā: (*nm*) a wild buffallo.

अरब arab (*a*) a thousand million; (*nm*) an Arab; the Arab country.

अरबी arbi: (*nf*) the Arabic language; (*a*) Arabian; pertaining to the land of Arabs.

अरमान armā:n (*nm*) aspiration, longing; **—धूल में मिलाना** to lay one's aspirations in the dust; **—निकालना** to have one's fling, to have it out; to have one's fulfilment; **—रह जाना** not to have one's aspirations materialised; **अरमानों की होली जलाना** to blast one's aspirations; **अरमानों पर पाला पड़ना** one's aspirations to be shattered.

अरविंद arvīnd (*nm*) a lotus flower.

अरवी arvi: (*nf*) a kind of taro.

अरसठ arsaṭh (*a* and *nm*) see **अड़सठ**.

अरसा arsa: (*nm*) period, duration; interval.

अरसिक arasik (*a*) dry, prosaic; inaesthetic; hence **~ता** (*nf*)

अरहर arhar (*nf*) pigeon pea, a kind of cereal or pulse—*Cajanus Indicus*.

अरा ara: (*nf*) see **अर**.

अराजक ara:jak (*a*) destitute/bereft of a ruler; anarchical; chaotic.

अराजकता ara:jakta: (*nf*) anarchy; chaos; **~वाद** anarchism; **~वादिता** anarchism; **~वादी** (an) anarchist.

अरारोट ara:roṭ (*nm*) arrow-root.

अराल ara:l (*a*) bent, slanting; crooked.

अरावल ara:val (*nm*) the vanguard.

अरि ari (*nm*) an enemy, a hostile person.

अरिष्ट arishṭ (*a* and *nm*) embodying misfortune, disastrous; misfortune, disaster.

अरीय ari:y (*a*) radial.

अरुचि aruchi (*nf*) dislike, aversion; distaste; **~कर** disgusting, loathing; unpalatable.

अरुण arūṉ (*a*) reddish-brown, ruddy; (*nm*) the dawn (personified as the charioteer of the Sun); **~चूड़/शिखा** a cock.

अरुणाचल aruṉa:chal (*nm*) the newly created (1972) eastern State of the Indian Union.

अरुणाभ arūṉa:bh (*a*) ruddy, having a reddish tinge.

अरुणिमा aruṉīmā: (*nf*) reddish brown tinge/colour.

अरुणोदय arūṉōday (*nm*) day-break,

early dawn.

अरूढ़ aru:ṛh (*a*) not established; obscure.

अरूप aru:p (*a*) formless.

अरे are (*int*) O !, a form of address (used for inferiors or juniors); **-अरे** stop this !, what is that !, why are you doing that ?

अरोचक arochak (*a*) uninteresting; boring; hence **~ता** (*nf*).

अर्क ark (*nm*) the sun; swallow wart *(Ascelpias gigantia)*.

अर्क़ arq (*nm*) essence; extract.

अर्ग/ल, ~ला argal (*nm*), ~la: (*nf*) a log for fastening a door, draw-bar.

अर्घ argh (*nm*) libation (in honour of a deity); value, price; **~दान** offering of libation; **~पात्र** a small vessel used for offering libation.

अर्घ्य arghy (*nm*) things worth offering (to a deity, etc.) as *argh* (see above).

अर्च/न, ~ना archā/n (*nm*), ~nā: (*nf*) worship, adoration; **~नीय** adorable, fit to be worshipped; **अर्चित** worshipped; adored.

अर्चा archa: (*nf*) see **अर्चन**.

अर्ज़ arz (*nf*) request, supplication; width; **~दाश्त** see **अर्दास**; **~मंद** supplicant, one making a submission/request; **~हाल** submission, appeal.

अर्जन arjān (*nm*) acquisition; earning; **~शील** acquisitive; earning; **अर्जक** acquirer; earner; **अर्जनीय** worth earning or acquiring; **अर्जित** acquired; earned; **—करना** to acquire/earn.

अर्ज़ी arzi: (*nf*) an application; petition; **~दार** an applicant; a petitioner.

अर्ज़ीदावा arzi:da:va: (*nm*) a plaint, a petition submitted by the plaintiff in a court of law.

अर्ज़ीनवीस arzi:navi:s (*nm*) a petition-writer.

अर्णव arṉāv (*nm*) a sea, an ocean.

अर्थ arth (*nm*) meaning; import, sense; wealth, money; (*ind*) for, for the sake of; **~कर/करी** profitable; **~गत** semantic, pertaining to meaning; economic; **~गर्भित** significant, pregnant with meaning; **-गौरव** profoundity of meaning; **-च्छवि/~च्छाया** nuance; **~तः** actually; from the point of view of meaning; **-पिशाच** a money-grabber; **-प्रबन्ध** financial arrangement/management; **~वत्ता** significance; **-संबंधी** economic; **~सिद्धि** fulfilment of a purpose.

अर्थक्रिया/वाद arthkriya:va:d (*nm*) pragmatism; **~वादी** a pragmatist; pragmatic.

अर्थदंड arthadāṉḍ (*nm*) a fine, penalty.

अर्थनीति arthanī:ti (*nf*) economic policy.

अर्थ-मानव arth-mā:nav (*nm*) the economic man.

अर्थमिति arthmiti (*nf*) econometrics.

अर्थवाद arthva:d (*nm*) eulogium; praise; explanation of the meaning of a precept.

अर्थवादी arthva:di: (*a* and *nm*) epideictic; eulogist.

अर्थ/विज्ञान arthviggyā:n (*nm*) semantics; **~वैज्ञानिक** semantic.

अर्थव्यवस्था arthvyavastha: (*nf*) economy; economics; economic set-up/system.

अर्थ/शास्त्र arthsha:str (*nm*) Economics; **~शास्त्री** an economist; **~शास्त्रीय** economic.

अर्थहीन arthhī:n (*a*) meaningless, absurd; moneyless.

अर्थांतर artha:ntar (*nm*) a different meaning; semantic variation.

अर्थात् artha:t (*ind*) that is, that is to say, namely (*viz.*).

अर्थालंकार artha:lāṅka:r (*nm*) meaning-based figure of speech.

अर्थी arthi: (*nf*) a bier; (*nm*) a petitioner; (*a*) desirous; suppliant.

अर्थेतर arthetar (*a*) non-pecuniary; non-semantic.

अर्दली ardali: (*nm*) an orderly, attendant.

अर्दास arda:s (*nf*) a representation; request, an entreaty.

अर्ध ardh (*a*) semi-, demi-; half; moiety; ~**विराम** semi-colon; ~**साप्ताहिक** semi-weekly, bi-weekly.

अर्धचंद्र ardhchāndr (*nm*) crescent, half-moon; **अर्धचंद्राकार** crescent-shaped; semilunar; —**देना** to push/throw out by the neck.

अर्धनारीश्वर ardhna:ri:shshwar (*nm*) Lord Shiv as envisaged in fusion with Goddess Pa:rvati:.

अर्धमागधी ardhma:gadhi: (*nf*) the form of Pra:krit (language) once current in that part of India which is now roughly covered by Awadhi:, Bagheli:, and Chhatti:sgaṛhi: dialects.

अर्ध/वृत्त ardhvritt (*nm*) semi-circle; ~**वृत्ताकार** semi-circular.

अर्धव्यास ardhvya:s (*nm*) radius.

अर्धसाप्ताहिक ardhsa:pta:hik (*a*) biweekly; semi-weekly.

अर्धांग ardhā:ṅg (*nm*) hemiplegia.

अर्धांगिनी ardhā:ṅginī: (*nf*) wife, better half.

अर्धाली ardha:li: (*nf*) two successive feet of a **चौपाई**.

अर्पण arpāṉ (*nm*) an offering; surrender(ing); assignment; cession.

अर्बुद arbud (*nm*) the number thousand million.

अर्भक arbhak (*nm*) a young one, an infant.

अर्र-बर्र arr-barr (*nf*) see **अंड-बंड**.

अर्राना arra:nā: (*v*) to crash down, to tumble down, to fall down with a violent noise.

अर्वाचीन arva:chī:n (*a*) modern, new, recent; hence ~**ता** (*nf*).

अर्श arsh (*nm*) haemorrhoids; sky, heaven; —**से फ़र्श तक** from heaven to earth.

अर्हंत arhānt (*a*) qualified; competent; (*nm*) names of Lords Jin, Buddha & Shiv.

अर्ह arh (*a*) qualified; competent.

अर्हता arhata: (*nf*) qualification; competence.

अलं/करण alaṅkarāṉ (*nm*) ornamentation, embellishment, adornment; hence, ~**कर्त्ता** (*nm*); ~**कृत** (*a*); ~**कृति** (*nf*).

अलंकार alāṅka.r (*nm*) embellishment; ornament; figure of speech; -**शास्त्र** Rhetorics; -**शास्त्री** a rhetorician; ~**शास्त्रीय** rhetoric.

अलंघनीय, अलंघ्य alāṅghnī:y, alāṅgghy (*a*) insurmountable, insuperable; inviolable; peremptory.

अलक alak (*nf*) a curl, a lock of hair; **अलकावली** locks of hair, hair-do.

अलकतरा alkatra: (*nm*) coal-tar, tar.

अलकोहल alkohal (*nm*) alcohol.

अलक्तक alaktak (*nm*) see **अलता**.

अलक्षित alakśhit (*a*) unperceived, unnoticed; unmarked.

अलक्ष्य alakshy (*a*) imperceptible; unnoticeable; latent.

अलख alakh (*a*) see **अलक्ष्य**; (*nm*) The Invisible; —**निरंजन** The Invisible; —**जगाना** to rise oneself and to arouse others in the name of The Invisible.

अलग alag (*a* and *adv*) separate, apart, aloof; distinct; -**अलग** individually; separately; distinctly; -**थलग** aloof, isolated; —**होना** to be in menses, to be away.

अलगनी alganī: (*nf*) see **अरगनी**.

अल/ग़रज algaraz (*a*) careless, negligent; ~गरजी carelessness, negligence.

अलगाना algā:nā: (*v*) to set apart, to separate; to isolate, to segregate; to disengage; to disunite.

अलगाव alga:v (*nm*) isolation, separation; breach; secession, segregation.

अलगोज़ा algoza: (*nm*) a kind of flute, flageolet.

अलगौझा algaujha: (*nm*) partition, division; separation.

अलग्न alagn (*a*) loose; untagged; unattached.

अलता alta: (*nm*) a lack-dye used by Hindu women for staining their feet red.

अलफ़ alaf; —होना said of a horse standing upright on hind legs; to be wrathful, to get restive.

अलबत्ता albatta: (*ind*) nevertheless; of course.

अलबम albām (*nm*) an album.

अलबेला albela: (*nm*) a dandy, beau; (*a*) dandy, foppish, frivolous; hence ~पन (*nm*).

अलभ्य alabbhy (*a*) rare; unattainable, unobtainable; hence ~ता (*nf*).

अलम/बरदार alāmbarda:r (*nm*) a standard-bearer; ~बरदारी standard-bearing.

अलमस्त almāst (*a*) carefree, sprightly, gay.

अलमारी alma:ri: (*nf*) an almirah, a cupboard.

अलमूनियम almū:nīyām (*nm*) aluminium.

अलम् alām (*ind*) enough!, that will do!

अलर्क alark (*nm*) a rabid dog;—रोग rabies, hydrophobia.

अललटप्पू alaltappu: (*a*) see अटकलपच्चू.

अललबछेड़ा alalbachhera: (*nm*) a young colt; an adolescent stepping into youth.

अलवान alvā:n (*nf*) a kind of woollen shawl.

अलस alas (*a*) slothful, lazy, sluggish; slackened.

अलसाना alsā:nā: (*v*) to be slack or sluggish, to feel lazy, to be overtaken by inertia.

अलसी alsi: (*nf*) linseed; —का तेल linseed oil.

अलस्सुबह alassubah (*nf*) early morning, day-break.

अलसेट alset (*nf*) (deliberate) obstruction; dilatory tactics; —डालना to create an obstruction.

अलह/दा alehda: (*a*) separate; aloof; ~दगी separation; aloofness.

अलात ala:t (*nm*) a fire-brand; -चक्र a circle caused by whirling fire-brand.

अलाप ala:p (*nm*) see आलाप; —लेना to tune the voice (for singing).

अलापना ala:pnā: (*v*) to tune the voice, to pitch or raise the voice; to sing (*on*).

अलाभ ala:bh (*nm*) disadvantage; harm; ~कर disadvantageous; harmful.

अलामत ala:māt (*nf*) sign, symptom.

अलार्म ala:rm (*nm*) alarm (of an alarm clock); —घड़ी an alarm-clock, alarm-watch.

अलाव ala:v (*nm*) a bonfire for warming up the body; camp-fire.

अलावा ala:va: (*ind*) besides, in addition to; apart from; except.

अलिंगी alingi: (*a*) asexual;— जनन asexual reproduction.

अलिंद alind (*nm*) a terrace.

अलि ali (*nm*) see भौंरा.

अलिखित alikhit (*a*) unwritten, unrecorded, unscripted.

अलिप्त alipt (*a*) unattached; indifferent; unbiased; hence ~ता (*nf*).

अलिफ़ alif (*nm*) the first letter of the

Persian alphabet;—बे न जानना not to know the ABC of.

अलीन alī:n (*nf*) a side pillar.

अलील ali:l (*a*) indisposed, ailing.

अलोना alonā: (*a*) without salt; tasteless; insipid.

अलोप alop (*a*) disappeared, vanished.

अलौकिक alaukik (*a*) unearthly, heavenly, celestial; phenomenal; transcendental, supernatural; hence ~ता (*nf*); —दृश्य feast/sight for the gods.

अल्प alp (*a*) a little, small; minute; short; few; ~कालिक short-lived; temporary; short-term; ~जनतंत्र oligarchy; ~जीवी short-lived, fugacious; ~तंत्र oligarchy; ~तम minimum, minimal; ~ता smallness, minuteness; insignificance; ~दृश्यता obscurity; ~दृष्टि short-sighted, not far-sighted; ~प्राण unaspirated; vigourless, lacking vitality; ~बुद्धि a nitwit, silly; idiot, ~भाषी taciturn; reserved; ~मत minority; ~मूल्यन under-valuation; ~वय underage; -विराम comma; ~शः by bits, in small quantities; ~संख्यक minority (group, party, community, etc.); ० वर्ग minority group; ~संख्या minority; **अल्पायु** of young age; shortlived; ephemeral; **अल्पाहार** abstemiousness, abstinence (in respect of food); **अल्पाहारी** abstemious, abstinent (in respect of food)

अल्लम-गल्लम allām-gallām (*nm*) odds and ends; all kinds of trash, edibles and inedibles; (—चीजें) cheese parings.

अल्लाह alla:h (*nm*) God; ~ताला God, the Great; ~बेली God preserve you!, Godspeed !, Adieu!;—की गाय simple, innocent and artless man, a simpleton; —को प्यारा होना to kick the bucket, to expire; **अल्लाहो अकबर** God is great !

अल्हड़ alhaṛ (*a*) carefree, having carefreeness reinforced by child-like simplicity and a touch of innocence; —अवस्था neither hay nor grass; ~पन carefree and innocent nature.

अव av—a Sanskrit prefix denoting after, downwards, smallness or diminution, decay, determination, etc

अवकरण avkarāṉ (*nm*) reduction.

अवकलन avkalān (*nm*) differentiation. —गणित differential calculus.

अवकाश avka:sh (*nm*) leisure; leave of absence; recess; ether, space; —ग्रहण करना to retire, to go into retirement; -प्राप्त retired; **अवकाशिक** spatial.

अवगत avgat (*a*) apprised; informed; —करना/रखना/होना to apprise or inform/to keep apprised or informed/to be apprised or informed; hence **अवगति** (*nf*).

अवगाहन avga:hān (*nm*) immersion, bathing; profound study, deep delve; also **अवगाह** (*nm*).

अवगुं/ठन avgūṉṭhān (*nm*) veiling, hiding; a veil; ~ठित veiled, covered with a veil, screened.

अवगुण avgūṉ (*nm*) defect, demerit, vice; fault; **अवगुणी** demeritorious, of vicious disposition.

अवचार avcha:r (*nm*) misconduct.

अवचेत/न avchetān (*nm* and *a*) (the) subconscious; ~ना sub-conscious mind.

अवच्छिन्न avachchhinn (*a*) cut off, separated.

अवच्छेद avachchhed (*nm*) cutting off, separation; a part/portion, hence ~न (*nm*); ~क (*a*).

अवज्ञा avaggya: (*nf*) contempt, disregard; defiance; insubordination, hence **अवज्ञेय** (*a*).

अवतंस avtāns (nm) crown; ornament.

अवतरण avtaraṇ (nm) descent; a passage; quotation; -चिह्न quotation marks ("   ").

अवतरित avtarit (a) descended; become incarnate; quoted.

अवतल avtal (a) concave; ~ता concavity.

अवतार avta:r (nm) an incarnation; ~वाद the theory of incarnation; —धरना/लेना to become incarnate.

अवतारी avta:ri: (a) incarnate, the source of incarnation; superhuman.

अवतीर्ण avti:rṇ (a) descended; incarnated.

अवद्य avaddy (a) faulty, having blemishes; worthless.

अवधान avdhā:n (nm) attention; concentration; alertness; hence ~ता (nf).

अवधा/रण avdha:raṇ (nm) conception; determination; ~रणा concept; hence ~रित (a); ~र्य (a).

अवधि avadhi (nf) period; time; limit; term; duration; —निर्धारित करना/बदना to set a deadline.

अवधी avdhi: (nf) a dialect of Hindi spoken in parts of eastern Uttar Pradesh.

अवधूत avdhu:t (nm) a (peculiar type of) religious mendicant; (a) rough and rugged (man).

अव/नत avnāt (a) bent; fallen; depressed; deteriorated; recessed; ~नति bending; falling, deterioration; recession; depression; demotion.

अवनमन avnāmān (nm) depression; bowing down, bending.

अवनयन avnāyān (nm) bringing down, causing fall or decline.

अवनि avāni (nf) the earth; ~पति a king, ruler.

अवपात avpa:t (nm) slump; depression.

अवपीड़न avpi:rān (nm) coercion, duress.

अवप्रेरण avpreraṇ (nm) abetment.

अवबोध avbodh (nm) understanding; hence ~क (a); ~न (nm).

अवमान, ~ना avmā:n (nm), ~ana (nf) humiliation; disrespect; indignity; contempt; hence अवमानित (a).

अवयव avayav (nm) a part, portion; member; limb; component, ingredient; a member or component part of logical argument of syllogism; अवयवी the whole consisting of members/limbs/organs.

अवयस्क avayask (a) minor; ~ता minority, the state of being a minor.

अवर avar (a) low; inferior; under; puisne; junior; ~ता juniority; inferiority.

अवरुद्ध avruddh (a) obstructed, hindered, impeded; restrained; impounded; arrested; hence ~ता (nf).

अवरोध avrodh (nm) an obstruction, hindrance, impediment; restraint; taboo; hence ~क (a), ~न (nm).

अवरोह avroh (nm) a descent; act of descending.

अवरोहण avrohaṇ (nm) descending; -क्रम descending order.

अवरोही avrohi: (a) descending, falling.

अवर्ण avarṇ (a) colourless; casteless.

अवर्णनीय, अवर्ण्य avarṇani:y, avarṇy (a) indescribable, defying description; ineffable.

अवलं/ब avlāmb (nm) support, stay; dependence; prop; ~बन dependence; support; hence~बी (a).

अवलंबित avalambit (a) supported; depended.

अवलि, अवली avali, avli: (nf) a row; range; continuous line; series;

set.

अवलेह avleh (*nm*) jelly; confection.

अवलो/क, ~कन avlo/k, ~kān (*nm*) seeing, beholding, viewing; perusal; scanning; **~कनीय, ~क्य** worth seeing; **~कित** seen, beholded; perused.

अवलोकनार्थ avalokana:rth (*ind*) for perusal, for being seen.

अवश avash (*a*) helpless, forlorn; hence **~ता** (*nf*).

अवशिष्ट avshisht (*a*) left; remaining; residuary; residual; (*nm*) residue, remnant.

अवशीत avshi:t (*a*) chilly; **~न** (the process of) chilling.

अवशेष avshesh (*nm*) remnant, remains, residue, residum; vestige; relics; (*a*) remaining, residual.

अवशोषक avshoshak (*nm*) absorbant; absorbing.

अवश्यंभा/वी avashshyāmbha:vi: (*a*) certain; inevitable; **~विता** certainty; inevitability.

अवश्य avashshy (*adv*) certainly, definitely; necessarily; **~मेव** without fail, certainly; undoubtedly.

अवसन्न avsann (*a*) despondent, dejected, dismayed; languid.

अवसन्नता avsannāta: (*nf*) languor, prostration; despondency.

अवसर avsar (*nm*) opportunity, chance; occasion; scope; **~वाद, ~वादिता** opportunism, the tendency to put expediency before principle; the mentality of time-serving; **~वादी** opportunist(ic); **—चूकना** to miss an opportunity; **—ताकना** to seek an opportunity; **—न चूकना/-हाथ से न जाने देना** to take time by the forelock; **—हाथ आना** to get a chance.

अवसाद avsa:d (*nm*) lassitude, langour; dejection; hence **~जनक** (*a*).

अवसान avsā:n (*nm*) end; terminal; termination; death; **अवसित** terminated, ended.

अवस्था avastha: (*nf*) condition, state; age; stage; phase, despondency.

अव/स्थान avsthā:n (*nm*) phase; hence **~स्थित** (*a*); **~स्थिति** (*nf*).

अवस्फी/ति avasphi:ti (*nf*) deflation; **~त** deflated.

अवहित avhit (*a*) alert; attentive; concentrative.

अवहे/लना, ~ला avhelnā:, ~la: (*nf*) neglect; disdain, contempt; hence **~लित** (*a*).

अवांछनीय avā:ṇchhanī:y (*a*) undesirable; unwelcome; hence **~ता** (*nf*).

अवांछित avā:ṇchhit (*a*) unwanted, unwelcome; undesired.

अवांतर avā:ntar (*a*) secondary; intermediate, intermediary; **—भेद** secondary classification, subdivision.

अवाक् ava:k (*a*) speechless; stunned.

अवाच्य ava:chchy (*a*) unworthy of utterance; **~ता** (*nf*).

अवाप्त avavpt (*a*) acquired.

अवाम ava:m (*nm*) the people, common man.

अवास्तव ava:stav (*a*) unreal, false.

अवास्तविक ava:stavik (*a*) unrealistic, unreal, false; hence **~ता** (*nf*).

अविकच avikach (*a*) unbloomed, unblossomed.

अविकल avikal (*a*) intact; unabridged (as—**रूपांतर**).

अविकल्प avikalp (*a*) without an alternative; certain.

अविकार avika:r (*a*) immutable, not liable to change/mutation; invariable.

अवि/कारी avika:ri: (*a*) immutable, not subject to mutation or variation; direct (form); indeclinable; **~कार्य** immutable, indeclinable.

अविकास avika:s (*nm*) aplasia, absence

of growth or development.

अविकृ/त avikkrit (*a*) unimpaired; not mutilated, not deformed; intact; ~ति immutation, indeformity.

अविगत avigat (*a*) not past; present.

अविचल avichal (*a*) steady; motionless; firm, unswerving; hence ~ता (*nf*).

अविचलन avichalān (*nm*) non-deviation; steadiness.

अविचा/री avicha:ri: (*a*) thoughtless; injudicious; ~रित not well thought out, not well considered.

अविच्छिन्न avichchhinn (*a*) uninterrupted; continuous; hence ~ता (*nf*).

अविच्छेद avichchhed (*nm*) absence of interruption, continuity; inseparable.

अविजित avijit (*a*) unconquered, unvanquished.

अवितथ avitath (*a*) exact; precise; ~ता exactitude; precision.

अवितान्य avitā:nny (*a*) inextensible; hence ~ता (*nf*).

अविदग्ध avidagdh (*a*) amateurish; puerile, stupid.

अविदित avidit (*a*) unknown.

अविद्यमान aviddyamā:n (*a*) not-existent; unreal; hence ~ता (*nf*).

अविद्या aviddya: (*nf*) nescience; superficial/mundane knowledge.

अविनय avinay (*nf*) immodesty, impertinence; hence **अविनयी, अविनीत** (*a*).

अविनश्वर avināshshvar (*a*) imperishable, indestructible; eternal; hence ~ता (*nf*).

अविनाशी avinā:shi: (*a*) immortal; indestructible, imperishable.

अविनीत avini:t (*a*) impertinent, pert, impolite, immodest; hence ~ता (*nf*).

अविभक्त avibhakt (*a*) undivided; unsplit; intact, also **अविभाजित** (*a*).

अविभाज्य avibha:jjy (*a*) inseparable; indivisible; hence ~ता (*nf*)

अविरत avirat (*a*) incessant, uninterrupted; continuous.

अविरल aviral (*a*) dense, profuse, compact; uninterrupted, incessant; continuous; hence ~ता (*nf*).

अविराम avirā:m (*a*) non-stop, without a pause, incessant; continuous; hence ~ता (*nf*).

अविलंब avilā:mb (*adv*) at once; without delay; forthwith.

अविलेय aviley (*a*) insoluble: hence ~ता (*nf*).

अविवक्षित avivakshit (*a*) intended to be stated or expressed, unimplied.

अविवाद्य aviva:ddy (*a*) indisputable; incontrovertible.

अविवाह aviva:h (*nm*) agamy.

अविवाहि/त aviva:hit (*a* and *nm*) unmarried; bachelor, celibate; hence; ~ता (*a* and *nf*).

अविवे/क avivek (*nm*) absence of reason, indiscretion; imprudence; injudiciousness; hence ~की (*a*).

अविश्वसनीय avishshvasni:y (*a*) unreliable, untrustworthy; hence ~ता (*nf*).

अविश्वस्त avishshvast (*a*) unreliable, untrustworthy; hence ~ता (*nf*).

अविश्वास avishshva:s (*nm*) distrust, disbelief; non-confidence; suspicion, doubt; -**प्रस्ताव** no-confidence motion.

अविश्वासी avishshva:si: (*a*) distrustful, suspicious; (*nm*) an unbeliever.

अविहित avihit (*a*) forbidden (by law); not prescribed.

अवृष्टि avrishti (*nf*) see **अनावृष्टि**.

अवैज्ञानिक avaiggya:nik (*a*) unscientific; unsystematic; hence ~ता (*nf*).

अवैतनिक avaitnik (*a*) honorary; —**संपादक** honorary editor; —**सलाहकार** honorary adviser.

अवैध avaidh (*a*) illegal, unlawful; illegitimate, illicit; invalid; **~जात** illicit; **~ता** illegality.

अव्यक्त avvyakt (*a*) not manifest, not apparent; imperceptible; indistinct; hence **~ता, अव्यक्ति** (*nf*); **अव्यक्तिवाद** impersonalism; **अव्यक्तिवादी** impersonalist; impersonal(istic).

अव्यय avvyay (*nm*) an indeclinable (generally used in grammatical context).

अव्ययीभाव avvyai:bha:v (*nm*) a compound word wherein the first member is an indeclinable (e.g. **यथाशक्ति, अनुरूप**).

अव्यर्थ avvyarth (*a*) unfailing; sure, effectual.

अव्यवसायी avvyavsa:i: (*a*) amateur; non-professional; **—रंगमंच** amateur theatre or stage.

अव्यव/स्था avvyavastha: (*nf*) lawlessness; disorder; disarray; chaos; **~स्थित** disorderly; chaotic; unsystematic.

अव्यवहार्य avvyavha:ry (*a*) unsociable; unusable; unactionable; impracticable; hence **~ता** (*nf*).

अव्यवहित avyavahit (*a*) contiguous, without a break/pause/gap.

अव्यवहृत avvyavhrit (*a*) unused, not tried or put into use/practice.

अव्याप्त avvya:pt (*a*) incomprehensive; of inadequate pervasion or extent; not pervaded or permeated by; uninformed (by).

अव्याप्ति avvya:pti (*nf*) non-comprehensiveness, inadequate pervasion or extent (as of a definition).

अव्यावसायिक avvya:vsa:ik (*a*) non-professional; amateur(ish); hence **~ता** (*nf*).

अव्यावहारिक avvya:vha:rik (*a*) impractical; not feasible; hence **~ता** (*nf*).

अव्युत्पन्न avvyutpānn (*a*) witless, unintelligent; not (grammatically) derived.

अव्वल avval (*a*) the first; the foremost; **~न** firstly; **—आना/रहना** to secure or obtain the first position.

अशकुन ashakun (*nm*) see **अपशकुन**.

अशक्त ashakt (*a*) weak, feeble; unable; incompetent; invalid, disabled; **~ता** disability; infirmity.

अशक्य ashakky (*a*) impossible, impracticable; unmanageable; invincible; hence **~ता** (*nf*).

अशरी/र, ~री ashari:r, ~ri: (*a*) incorporeal; immaterial; unearthly.

अशर्फ़ी asharfi: (*nf*) a gold coin; **अशर्फ़ियाँ लुटें कोयलों पर मोहर** penny wise pound foolish.

अशांत ashā:nt (*a*) restless, agitated; unquiet, disturbed, perturbed; hence **~ता** (*nf*).

अशांति ashā:nti (*nf*) unrest, disquietitude, agitation; disturbance; want of tranquillity.

अशासकीय asha:ski:y (*a*) non-official/non-governmental; private.

अशास्त्रीय asha:stri:y (*a*) contrary to the *sha:stra(s)*; unscientific; non-technical; non-classical; unprescribed; irregular.

अशिक्षित ashikshit (*a*) uneducated; unlettered, illiterate.

अशिव ashiv (*a*) inauspicious; pernicious, baleful, evil; (*nm*) the evil; hence **~ता** (*nf*).

अशिष्ट ashishṭ (*a*) ill-mannered, rude; indecent, indecorous; impolite; **~ता** indecency, impoliteness; ill manners, rudeness.

अशु/द्ध ashuddh (*a*) incorrect, erroneous, wrong; impure; **~द्धता** incorrectness; impurity; **~द्धि** an error, a mistake; ° **पत्र** errata.

अशुभ ashubh (*a*) inauspicious, ill-omened; evil; bad; (*nm*) the evil.

अशेष ashesh (*a*) all; complete, entire.

अशोक ashok (*nm*) *Jonesia asoka* (a tree); (*a*) without grief, freed from grief.

अशोभन ashobhan (*a*) unseemly, unbecoming; indecent.

अश्क ashq (*nm*) a tear.

अश्र/द्धा ashraddha: (*nf*) want of reverence; irreverence; lack of faith; ~द्धालु faithless, one lacking in reverence/veneration; an unbeliever; ~द्धेय unworthy of faith/reverence/veneration.

अश्रां/त ashshrā:nt (*a*) untired; indefatigable; hence ~ति (*nf*).

अश्राव्य ashshra:vy (*a*) inaudible, not worth listening (to); hence ~ता (*nf*).

अश्रु ashshru (*nm*) a tear; ~पात shedding of tears; ~पूर्ण tearful.

अश्रुत ashshrut (*a*) unheard (of).

अश्रुतपूर्व ashshrutpu:rv (*a*) unheard of (before); unique, novel.

अश्लिष्ट ashshlishṭ (*a*) having no pun; direct; disconnected, loose.

अश्लील ashshli:l (*a*) obscene; indecent, vulgar; ~ता obscenity, vulgarity.

अश्व ashshv (*nm*) a horse; ~मेघ (यज्ञ) the horse sacrifice—a celebrated ceremony dating back to the Vedic period, performed by a monarch desirous of becoming a **चक्रवर्ती**.

अश्वत्थ ashshvatth (*a*) the Pipal tree.

अश्वशाला ashshvsha:la: (*nf*) a stable.

अश्वसन ashshvasān (*nm*) apnoea.

अश्वारूढ़ ashshva:ru:ṛh (*a*) mounted on horse-back; riding (a horse).

अश्वारोहण ashshva:rohan̲ (*nm*) horse-ride.

अश्वारोही ashshva:rohi: (*nm*) a cavalier, horseman; (*a*) riding (a horse).

अष्ट ashṭ (*a*) eight; (*nm*) the number eight.

अष्टकोण ashṭkōn̲ (*nm*) an octagonal.

अष्टछाप ashṭchha:p—a group of eight luminaries amongst the medieval Krishna cult poets of Hindi literature (viz. Su:rda:s, Kumbhan Da:s, Parma:nand Da:s, Krishna Da:s, Chhi:tswa:mi:, Govindswa:mi:, Chaturbhuj Da:s and Nand Da:s).

अष्टमी ashṭamī: (*nf*) the eighth day of the lunar fortnight according to the Hindu calendar.

अष्टसिद्धि ashṭasiddhi (*nf*) the eight supernatural powers or faculties acquirable by the practice of *yog* (the eight usually enumerated are *anima:; mahima:, garima:, laghima:, pra:pti, praka:my; i:shitv* and *vashitv*).

असंकुल asaṅkul (*a*) uncrowded; wide open.

असंक्रामक asaṅkra:māk (a) non-infectious; —रोग non-infectious disease.

असंक्राम्य asaṅkra:mmy (*a*) inalienable; non-transferable; non-infectious; —अधिकार inalienable rights.

असंख्य asankkhy (*a*) innumerable, countless; also ~क (*a*).

असंग asaṅg (*a*) detached; uncommitted.

असंगठित asaṅgaṭhit (*a*) loose; unorganised; disunited.

असंग/त asaṅgat (*a*) incoherent; irrelevant; inconsistent; absurd; irrational, anomalous; incompatible; discordant; ~तता, ~ति incoherence; irrelevance; absurdity; irrationality; incompatibility; anomaly.

असंत asant (*a*) wicked, evil (person).

असंतुलन asantulān (*nm*) imbalance, disequilibrium.

असंतुलित asantulit (*a*) unbalanced; erratic; hence ~ता (*nf*).

असंतुष्ट asantushṭ (*a*) dissatisfied, discontented, disgruntled; malcontent; aggrieved.

असंतो/ष asantosh (*nm*) dissatisfaction; discontent; discontentment; ~**षी** insatiable, one who is temperamentally discontented, greedy.

असंदिग्ध asandigdh (*a*) indubitable; certain, definite; hence ~**ता** (*nf*).

असंपूर्ण asampu:rṉ (*a*) incomplete; imperfect; hence ~**ता** (*nf*).

असंबद्ध asambaddh (*a*) disconnected, irrelevant; incongruous; ~**ता** incoherence; irrelevancy;—**प्रलाप** irrelevant and disconnected prattle/prate, raving.

असंभव asambhav (*a*) impossible, impracticable.

असंभावित asambha:vit (*a*) unexpected; unlikely; not comprehended.

असंभा/व्य asambha:vvy (*a*) improbable; also ~**वनीय** (*a*).

असंयत asanyat (*a*) unrestrained; intemperate, immoderate.

असंय/म asanyām (*nm*) unrestraint; intemperance; absence of moderation; ~**मित** unrestrained; immoderate; ~**मी** devoid of moderation or temperance, unrestrained; fast.

असंश्लिष्ट asanshlishṭ (*a*) non-synthetic; non-composite.

असंस्कृत asanskrit (*a*) uncultured; unrefined; raw.

असंह/त asanhat (*a*) diffused, not concentrated; hence ~**ति** (*nf*).

असंहित asanhit (*a*) incompact, loose; unconnected; not concise.

असगंध asgandh (*nm*) a medicinal plant—*Physalis flexussa.*

असती asati: (*a*) unchaste, infidel (to one's husband).

असतीत्व asati:ttv (*nm*) unchastity, absence of chastity.

असत् asat (*a*) evil, bad; non-existent; illusory; ~**कार्य** evil deed, misdeed; ~**पथ** immoral path/way.

असत्त्व asattv (*nm*) vice; (*a*) weak; vicious, devoid of virtue.

असत्य asatty (*nm*) a lie, falsehood; untruth; (*a*) untrue, false; ~**ता** falsehood, untruth; ~**वादी** a liar; untrue (person).

अस/द् asad (*a*) an allomorph of **असत्** (see) as it obtains in certain compounds; ~**दाचार** misconduct, immoral conduct; ~**द्बुद्धि** vicious, evil-minded; evil genius; ~**द्भाव** non-existence; malafide; ~**द्वृत्ति** wicked(ness), vicious(ness).

असफल asaphal (*a*) unsuccessful; ~**ता** failure.

असबाब asba:b (*nm*) luggage, baggage; goods and chattles.

असभ्य asabbhy (*a*) uncivilized, uncivil; discourteous; indecent; ill-bred; rustic; ~**ता** uncivility; indecency; vulgarity; rusticity.

असमंजस asmāṉjas (*nm*) a dilemma, fix, suspense.

असमंजित asmāṉjit (*a*) maladjusted, unadjusted; uncoordinated.

असम asām (*a*) uneven; unequal; dissimilar; unmatching; (*nm*) the north-eastern Indian state of Assam.

असमत asmāt (*nf*) sanctity, chastity; ~**फ़रोश** a chastity-monger; unchaste; immoral; hence ~**फ़रोशी** (*nf*)

असमतल asāmtal (*a*) uneven; rough and rugged; hence ~**ता** (*nf*).

असमता asāmta: (*nf*) inequality; disparity; unevenness.

असमन्वय asamānvay (*nm*) incoordination, absence of coordination.

असममि/त asāmamit (*a*) asymmetrical; ~**ति** asymmetry.

असम/य asamāy (*adv* and *a*) untimely; out of season; (*nm*) time of adversity; unseasonableness; ~**योचित** inopportune, untimely.

असमर्थ asamarth (*a*) incapable, incompetent; **~ता** incapability, incompetence, incapacity, inability.

असमान asamā:n (*a*) see **असम**; **~ता** disparity, inequality; dissimilarity.

असमाप्त asamā:pt (*a*) incomplete, unfinished.

असमाहित asamā:hit (*a*) unconcentrated; wavering, flickering.

असमिया asamiyā: (*nf* and *a*) Assamese—the language and people of Assam (**असम**).

असमीचीन asamı:chı:n (*a*) improper, inappropriate; undue.

असम्म/ति asāmmāti (*nf*) non-consent; disagreement; hence **~त** (*a*).

असम्मान asāmmā:n (*nm*) disrespect; insult.

असम्मेय asāmmey (*a*) incommensurable; **~ता** incommensurability.

असर asar (*nm*) effect; influence; impression.

असल asal (*a*) real; true; original; **~का** born of (one's) real father; **—में** in fact, in reality, as a matter of fact.

असलियत asliyat (*nf*) reality; truth.

असली asli: (*a*) real; true; pure, unadulterated; **—धड़े की छूट** actual tare; **—रूप दिखाना** to show one's horns.

असवर्ण asavarn̲ (*a*) not belonging to a high caste, of low caste; not homogeneous (as sounds).

असह asah (*a*) unbearable, unendurable.

असहकार asahka:r (*nm*) non-cooperation.

असहनशील asahānshi:l (*a*) intolerant, unenduring; short-tempered; hence **~ता** (*nf*).

असहनीय asahni:y (*a*) see **असह्य** (*a*).

असहमति asahmāti (*nf*) disagreement, dissent; discordance.

असहयोग asahyog (*nm*) non-cooperation; **~वाद** the doctrine of non-cooperation; **~वादी** a follower of non-cooperative doctrine; pertaining to the doctrine of non-cooperation.

असहाय asaha:y (*a*) helpless; lonesome.

असहिष्णु asahisn̲ū (*a*) intolerant, unenduring; **~ता** intolerance, inendurance.

असह्य asahhy (*a*) intolerable, unbearable; hence **~ता** (*nf*).

असांप्रदायिक asā:mprada:ik (*a*) non-communal; non-sectarian; **~ता** non-communalism; non-sectarianism.

असा/ढ़ asa:ṛh (*nm*) the fourth month of the Hindu calendar; **~ढ़ी** pertaining to **असाढ**.

असाधारण asa:dha:rān̲ (*a*) extra-ordinary, unusual; uncommon; **~ता** extra-ordinary quality; uniqueness, unusualness.

असाधु asa:dhu (*a*) wicked, unrighteous; not standard; hence **~ता** (*nf*).

असाध्य asa:ddhy (*a*) incurable; impracticable, unfeasible; hence **~ता** (*nf*); **-साधन** performing the impracticable, achieving a miracle.

असामयिक asa:māik (*a*) untimely; inopportune; hence **~ता** (*nf*).

असामर्थ्य asa:mārtthy (*nf*) see **असमर्थता**.

असामाजिक asa:ma:jik (*a*) unsocial, anti-social; **—तत्त्व** anti-social elements; **~ता** the state of being unsocial/anti-social; unsocial/anti-social attitude.

असामान्य asa:mā:nny (*a*) uncommon; not general; particular, special; abnormal; hence **~ता** (*nf*).

असामी asa:mi: (*nm*, sometimes *nf*) a tenant; client; **victim**.

असाम्य asa:mmy (*nm*) **inequality**;

disparity; disequilibrium, imbalance.

असार asa:r (*a*) worthless; unsubstantial; unreal; illusory; immaterial; hence ~**ता** (*nf*).

असार्वजनिक asa:rvjānik (*a*) private; not public.

असावधान asa:vdhā:n (*a*) careless, uncautious; negligent; ~**ता** see **असावधानी.**

असावधानी asa:vdhā:nɪ: (*nf*) carelessness; negligence; absence of caution.

असि/द्ध asiddh (*a*) unproved; incomplete; unaccomplished; inoperative; hence ~**द्धि** (*nf*).

असीम asi:m (*a*) limitless, boundless; hence ~**ता** (*nf*).

असीमित asi:mit (*a*) unbounded, unlimited; hence ~**ता** (*nf*).

असीस asi:s (*nf*) see **आशिष.**

असुंदर asūndar (*a*) ugly; unwholesome, not beautiful; ~**ता** ugliness; absence of beauty, unwholesomeness.

असुख asukh (*nm*) non-happiness, absence of pleasure; ~**कर** conducive of non-happiness, giving no pleasure.

असुप्त asupt (*a*) not asleep, awake.

असुर asur (*nm*) a demon.

असुविधा asuvidha: (*nf*) inconvenience.

असूचित asu:chit (*a*) unadvised; unnotified.

असूझ asu:jh (*a*) invisible; where nothing can be seen or sighted.

असूया asu:ya (*nf*) envy.

असैनिक asainɪk (*a*) civil, non-military; (*nm*) a civilian.

असौंदर्य asaūdary (*nm*) absence of beauty; ugliness.

असौम्य asaummy (*a*) not amiable or gentle, unpleasant; harsh, impolite, impudent.

असौष्ठव asaushṭhav (*nm*) want of quality; ugliness.

अस्तंगत astāngat (*a*) set (as the sun); sunk; descended.

अस्त ast (*a*) set (as the sun); sunk; ~**प्राय** almost set or sunk; dying; —**होना** to set or sink; to disappear or vanish.

अस्तबल astabal (*nm*) a stable.

अस्तर astar (*nm*) the lining of a garment; inner coating of colour or varnish; base (in painting).

अस्तव्यस्त astavvyast (*a*) confused; scattered; helter-skelter;—**करना** to confuse; to scatter; to tousle;—**होना** to be scattered; to be confused, to be cluttered up with.

अस्ताचल asta:chal (*nm*) the western mountain (behind which the sun is supposed to set).

अस्ति asti (*nf*) existence; being.

अस्तित्व astittv (*nm*) existence, being, entity; ~**वाद** existentialism; ~**वादी** an existentialist; extentialistic; ~**वान** existent.

अस्तु astu (*ind*) however, well, now; be it so !

अस्तेय astey (*nm*) not stealing.

अस्त्र astr (*nm*) a weapon (esp. a missile); ~**कार** an armourer; ~**जीवी** a professional soldier; ~**विद्या** the military science; the art of using weapons; ~**शाला** an arsenal, armoury.

अस्त्र-शस्त्र astr-shastr (*nm*) armament, weaponry; arms, weapons.

अस्त्रागार astra:ga:r (*nm*) an arsenal, armoury.

अस्थायित्व astha:itv (*nm*) unstability, temporariness, the state of being provisional/tentative.

अस्थायी astha:i: (*a*) temporary, labile, unstable; provisional; —**व्यवस्था** modus vivendi; stop-gap arrangement.

अस्थि asthi (*nf*) a bone; **-पंजर** a skeleton; **~शेष** reduced to a skeleton, skeletonised.

अस्थिर asthir (*a*) unstable, unsteady; variable; vacillating; fickle, wavering; **~ता** inconstancy; unstability; unsteadiness; vacillation; also **अस्थैर्य** (*nm*).

अस्पताल aspata:l (*nm*) a hospital.

अस्पष्ट aspasht (*a*) not clear; indistinct, vague; dim, obscure; blurred; ambiguous; hence **~ता** (*nf*).

अस्पृश्य asprishshy (*a*) untouchable; **~ता** (the system and practice of) untouchability.

अस्पृष्ट asprisht (*a*) untouched.

अस्फुट asphut (*a*) indistinct, not clear; blurred; impalpable; hence **~ता** (*nf*).

अस्मिता asmita: (*nf*) ego; vanity, pride; assertion.

अस्वस्थ asswasth (*a*) unhealthy; morbid; **~ता** ill-health; morbidity.

अस्वाभाविक asswa:bha:vik(*a*) unnatural; artificial; hence **~ता** (*nf*).

अस्वी/करण, ~कार assvi:karan, ~ka:r (*nm*) non-acceptance, rejection, refusal; denial.

अस्वीकृ/त assvi:krit (*a*) unaccepted; refused, rejected; denied; **~ति** non-acceptance; refusal, rejection; denial.

अस्सी assi: (*a*) eighty; (*nm*) the number eighty.

अहं ahām (*nm*) ego; **~भाव** ego, egoism; **~वाद/~वादिता** egoism; **~वादी** egoist(ic); **-वृत्ति** ego-instinct.

अहंका/र ahānka:r (*nm*) vanity; egotism; vainglory; **~री** egotist, vainglorious.

अहंता ahānta: (*nf*) ego; egoism.

अहद ehad (*nm*) a pledge; commitment; **~नामा** an agreement.

अहदी ehdi: (*a*) slothful, lazy, indolent; hence **~पन** (*nm*).

अहबाब ahba:b (*nm*) friends and companions, dear ones (used only as the second member of the compound **दोस्त-अहबाब**).

अहम ahām (*a*) important, significant.

अहम/क़ ehmāq (*nm* and *a*) a blockhead, an idiot, a fool; most foolish; stupid; **~क़ाना** idiotic, stupid, foolish; **० हरकतें करना** to play the giddy goat.

अहमियत ehmiyāt (*nf*) importance, significance.

अहम्मन्य ahammānny(*a*) vainglorious pretentious, overweening, conceited; **~ता** vainglory, conceit, pretentiousness, overweeningness.

अहरणीय aharni:y (*a*) inviolable, unprescriptible; **—अधिकार** unprescriptible right.

अहलकार ehalka:r (*nm*) a clerk, an official (in a court of law).

अहलमद ehalmad (*nm*) a record keeper (in a court of law).

अहलेवतन ahalevatan—compatriots, countrymen.

अहस्त/क्षेप ahastakshep (*nm*) non-interference; **~क्षेप-नीति** laissez faire; **~क्षेप्य** non-cognizable: which cannot be interfered with.

अहह ahah (*int*) oh !, an exclamation expressive of surprise, sorrow, agony, etc.

अहा, अहा हा aha:, aha:ha: (*int*) an exclamation expressing surprise or delight; how excellent ! well done ! wonderful ! etc.

अहाता aha:ta: (*nm*) a compound, precincts; enclosure.

अहानिकर ahā:nikar (*a*) non-detrimental; unharmful, not injurious.

अहिंसक ahınsak (*a*) non-violent (person).

अहिंसा ahınsa: (*nf*) non-violence; **~वाद** the creed of non-violence;

~वादी a follower of the principle of non-violence; non-violent.

अहिंसात्मक ahinsa:tmak (*a*) non-violent (act, etc).

अहिंस्र ahınsr (*a*) non-violent, not fierce; harmless.

अहि ahi (*nm*) a serpent, snake; ~च्छत्रक a mushroom; ~निर्मोक slough.

अहित ahit (*nm*) harm, damage, injury; evil; ~कर harmful, injurious, detrimental.

अहितेच्छा ahitechchha: (*nf*) malevolence, malevolent intention.

अहिफेन ahiphen (*nm*) opium.

अहिवात ahiva:t (*nm*) state of a married woman ever continuing to enjoy her husband's coverture.

अहीर ahi:r (*nm*) a Hindu sub-caste.

अहेतु ahetu (*a*) without a cause or reason.

अहेतु/क, ~की ahetuk, ~ki: (*a*) without any reason or cause; without motive; unprovoked.

अहे/र aher (*nm*) see **शिकार**; ~री see **शिकारी**; a stalker.

अहैतु/क, ~की ahaituk, ~ki: (*a*) see **अहेतुक**.

अहो aho (*int.*) Oh ! O !

आ

आ a: the second letter and the second vowel of the Devna:gri: alphabet; a Sanskrit prefix used to denote the senses of upto, uptil, from, throughout, along with etc; (Imperative verb intended for youngers or juniors, etc.) come, come on, come forth;—**बैल मुझे मार** to ask for it, to ask for trouble.

आंकड़े ā:kṛe (*nm*) data; statistics, figures.

आंकना ā:knā: (*v*) to assess, to reckon; to evaluate; to appraise; to mark.

आंख ā:kh (*nf*) an eye; the eye of a needle; the sprout at the joint of a sugarcane; ~**मिचौनी** (the game of) hide and seek, blindman's buff; also ~**मिचोली**; —**आना** to suffer from ophthalmia, to have sore eyes;—**उठाकर देखना**, —**उठाना** to cast a hostile look; —**उठाकर न देखना** not to take notice, to treat with disdain; to feel ashamed or abashed; —**ऊँची न होना**, —**ऊपर न उठाना** to be unable to raise the eyes through shame, etc.;—**ओट पहाड़ ओट** out of sight, out of mind; —**का काँटा** an eye-sore; —**का काजल चुराना** to steal eyesalve out of one's eye, to be an expert thief; -**का तारा**/—**की पुतली** the apple of one's eye, iris; darling, pet, beloved; —**कान खुले रखना** to be on the alert, to be alert and agile; —**का परदा उठना** to be disillusioned, to have one's illusions shed away; —**का पानी उतर/ढल/मर जाना** blush like a dog/blue on black; to be lost to shame, to become shameless; —**की किरकिरी** an eye-sore; —**की बदी भौं के आगे** to narrate somebody's vice only to his intimate ones; —**के अंधे नाम नयनसुख** to name a dunce Plato; —**के तीर चलाना** to make eyes at, to look amorously;—**गर्म करना/सेकना** to gloat, to feast the eyes with animate beauty; to refresh, rejoice and feast the eyes; —**चढ़ना** to have heavy or drowsy eyes, to have a reddish tinge in the eyes (through anger; fever, intoxication, lack of sleep, etc.); to have the eyes upturned (as in death);—**चुराना/छिपाना** to cut indirect, to cut sublime; to avoid being sighted by, to avoid catching one's eye; —**झपकना** lit. to blink—meaning, to be heavy with sleep; to begin to fall asleep; —**टेढ़ी करना** to frown, to cast a hostile/wrathful look; —**डबडबाना** to be on the verge of tears, to have the eyes filled with tears; —**तरेरना** to look/speak daggers; to look with angry eyes;—**दिखाना** to fly in the face of; —**न ठहरना** to be dazzled (by the sight of), to be unable to fix the gaze (on);—**न लगना** not to bat an eyelid, not to sleep a wink; —**निकालना** to cast a wrathful glance; —**पड़ना** to sight per chance; —**पथराना** to have the eyes petrified, or have the vision blurred and dimmed through constant gazing; —**पसारना/फैलाना** to stare all round; to cast searchful glances all round; —**फड़कना** to feel a pulsation in the eye (according to Indian tradition pulsation in the right eye of a man and left of a woman is regarded as auspicious while the contrary is taken as a bad omen); —**फूटी पीर गई** the eye lost, the pain gone; better the eye out than suffer persistent pain; —**बचाना** to avoid being sighted;—**बदलना,—बदल लेना** to bring about a sudden change in one's favourable attitude, to withdraw favour or regard all of a sudden; —**भर कर देखना** to fill the eyes with the sight of, to cast affectionate or amorous looks to one's satisfaction;—**मारना** to cock one's eye; to make a sign with one's eye, to wink one of the eyes (as a sign of amorous intention or cofirmation of a conspiracy, etc.);—**मिलाना,—में आँख डालना** to look squarely in the face, to look straight into somebody's eyes:—**मूँदकर कूद पड़ना** a leap in the dark; —**मूँदकर विश्वास करना** to pin one's faith upon;—**मूँदकर सौदा करना** to buy a pig in a poke, —**में खून उतरना** to have one's blood up, to have the eyes reddened with extreme rage;—**लगना** to fall half asleep, to doze off;—**लड़ाना** to meet stare with stare, to interchange glances, to cast amorous glances; **आँखें खुल जाना** to be aroused from sleep; to learn a lesson; to become aware or cognizant (of); **आँखें खलना** to make conscious of things, to put somebody on the alert; **आँखें चरने जाना** not to be watchful, to be careless and negligent; **आँखें चार करना** to meet stare with stare, to interchange glances; **आँखें चार होना** to look into each other's eyes, to exchange glances; **आँखें चुराना** to avoid taking notice of; to avoid an exchange of looks; **आँखें जमाना** to stare steadily; to have the gaze fixed at something; **आँखें ठण्डी करना** to gratify the eyes, to bring cool comfort to the eyes (by seeing a pleasant object); **आँखें दिखाना/निकालना** to look (at) angrily or menacingly, to cast a threatening look; **आँखें नीची करना** to look/cast eyes downward; (out of shame, modesty, etc.); **आँखें फाड़कर** or **फाड़-फाड़कर देखना** to stare (at) with bewildered eagerness or astonishment; **आँखें फेरना** or **फेर लेना** to adopt an attitude of indifference towards someone dearly loved, to withdraw one's affection; **आँखें फोड़ना** to render blind, to ruin the sight (by strenuous study, etc.); **आँखें बन्द होना** or **मुँदना** to have the eyes shut; to die, pass away; **आँखें बचाना** to avoid being noticed, to elude the observation of; to slink away; **आँखें बदल जाना** to withdraw affection; **आँखें बिछाना** to give a very cordial welcome; **आँखें भर आना** or **डबडबाना** to have the eyes filled with tears, to be almost in tears; **आँखें लाल-पीली करना** to become livid with anger; **आँखों के आगे अँधेरा छाना** to faint (on account of a sudden fit of weakness etc.); **आँखों देखा** self-witnessed; ० **माना कानों सुना न माना** seeing is believing and hearsay is no evidence; **आँखों देखा हाल** running commentary; **आँखों पर ठीकरी रख लेना** to become cold-livered, to give a cold shoulder; to be lost to shame; **आँखों पर परदा पड़ना** to be under an illusion, not to see the obvious; **आँखों पर बिठाना/बैठना** to extend a hearty welcome, to receive and treat with utmost affection and reverence; **आँखों में खटकना** to be an eye-sore, to arouse unpleasant feelings; **आँखों में चर्बी छाना** to be blinded by pride, arrogance, lust etc.; **आँखों में धूल झोंकना/डालना** to pull wool over a person's eyes, to dust the eyes of; to throw dust in the eyes (of), to cheat; **आँखों में रात काटना** to pass the night awake, not to have a wink throughout the night; **आँखों में समाना** to fill the mind's eye, to be ever present in one's mind's eye; **—से लहू बरसना** the blood to be up.

आँगन ā:gān (*nm*) a courtyard.

आंगिक ā:ṅgik (*a*) pertaining to the body or parts thereof; performed by gesture or through physical features (a category of *abhinay*); **—अभिनय** acting through physical gestures or movement; **—व्यापार** physical action.

आँच ā:ch (*nf*) the heat of flame, fire; (fig.) harm; **—आना** to come to harm; **—खाना** to be overheated; to be heated.

आँचल ā:chal (*nm*) the extreme part of a sa:ri: enveloping the upper part of a woman's body; region.

आँजना ā:jnā: (*v*) to apply collyrium (into the eyes.)

आँत ā:t (*nf*) see **अँतड़ी**; **—उतरना** to suffer from hernia; **आँतें कुलकुलाना/कुलबुलाना** to be extremely hungry.

आंतर ā:ntar (*a*) intra.

आंतरायिक ā:ntara:ik (*a*) intermittent.

आंतरिक ā:ntarik (*a*) internal, intra; innate; **~तः** internally; hence **~ता** (*nf*).

आंतभौं/म ā:ntarbhāum (*a*) underground; subterranean; also **~मिक** (*a*).

आंत्र ā:ntr (*nm*) intestine; (*a*) intestinal.

आंदोलन ā:ndolān (*nm*) a movement, agitation, campaign; **~कर्ता ~कारी** an agitator, campaigner.

आंदोलित ā:ndolit (*a*) moved; agitated; **—होना** to be moved by intense emotion or feeling.

आँधी ā:dhi: (*nf*) a dust-storm; **—उठाना** to raise a storm; to create havoc; **—के आम** a windfall.

आँध्र a:ndhr (*nm*) the Telugu-speaking Southern state of the Indian Union —also known as **आँध्र प्रदेश**; (*a*) an inhabitant of the Andhra Pradesh.

आँय-बाँय ā:y-bā:y (*nf*) irrelevant/ridiculous talk; also-**शाँय**.

आँव ā:v (*nf*, used by some as *nm*) mucus.

आँवला ā:vla: (*nm*) the tree *Emblic myrobalan* and its fruit.

आँवाँ ā:wā: (*nm*) the potter's kiln, pottery; —का आँवाँ ही ख़राब होना to have a disgusting lot as a whole.

आंशिक ā:nshik (*a*) partial; fractional; ~ता the state or quality of being fractional.

आँसू ā:su: (*nm*) tear;—पीकर रह जाना to suppress one's tears, to hide one's sorrow;—पोंछना to console; —बहाना to shed tears.

आइंदा a:inda: (*adv*) in future; (*a*) future; ensuing;—ज़माना the future, times to come.

आइना a:inā: (*nm*) a looking glass, mirror; आइने में मुँह देखना to reflect on one's own capabilities and merits, to know oneself; ~साज़ a mirror-maker.

आइसक्रीम a:iskri:m (*nf*) ice-cream.

आई/न a:i:n (*nm*) law; legislation ~नी legal; legislative.

आक a:k (*nm*) the medicinal plant swallow wort, technically known as *Catotropis gigantea*.

आक़बत a:qbat (*nf*) transmundane existence; the other world, the future state of life;—बिगाड़ना to jeopardize one's transmundane existence.

आकर a:kar (*nm*) a mine; source; storehouse, treasury; -ग्रंथ a source book.

आकर्ण a:karn̲ (*a* and *adv*) (stretching or stretched) up to the ear.

आकर्णक a:kran̲āk (*nm*) a headphone.

आकर्षक a:karshak (*a*) attractive, charming, alluring; hence ~ता (*nf*).

आकर्षण a:karshān̲ (*nm*) attraction, charm, allurement; -शक्ति the power of gravitation; attraction.

आकर्षित a:karshit (*a*) attracted, charmed, allured.

आकर्षी a:karshi: (*a*) attractive, alluring.

आक/लन a:kalān (*nm*) reckoning, calculation; ~लित reckoned, calculated.

आकस्मिक a:kasmik (*a*) sudden, abrupt; contingent; accidental; fortuitous, casual;—छुट्टी casual leave; ~ता contingency.

आकांक्षा a:kā:ṅksha: (*nf*) aspiration.

आकां/क्षी a:kā:ṅkshi: (*a*) aspirant; ~क्षित aspired (for).

आक़ा a:ka: (*nm*) master, lord.

आका/र a:ka:r (*nm*) form, shape, size; the vowel आ (a:) and its sound; ~र -प्रकार size and shape; ~र -विज्ञान, morphology; ~र-वैज्ञानिक a morphologist; morphological; ~रांत (a word) ending in a: (आ).

आकारिकी a:ka:riki: (*nf*) morphology; ~य morphological.

आकाश a:ka:sh (*nm*) the sky; the space; ~कुसुम lit. a flower of the sky, meaning an impossibility, a fanciful thing; ~गंगा the milky way; ~गामिता levitation; sky-faring; ~गामी/चारी sky-faring; ~दीप a beacon light; ~भाषित/वचन (in theatrical language) speaking off the stage (to someone out of sight); ~मंडल the celestial sphere; ~यान aircraft;—छूना to be sky high; -पाताल एक करना to move heaven and earth, to leave no stone unturned, to put in Herculean efforts; -पाताल का अंतर as wide asunder as the sky and the nether world, a tremendous difference; —से बातें करना to be sky high, to be as lofty as the sky.

आकाशवाणी a:ka:shvā:n̲ɪ: (*nf*) an oracle; a proper name given to All India Radio.

आकाशी a:ka:shi: (*nf*) an aerial; (*a*)

celestial.

आकाशीय a:ka:shiy (*a*) pertaining to the sky; heavenly, celestial.

आकीर्ण a:ki:rṉ (*a*) crowded; full of diffusion; diffused; scattered.

आकुं/चन a:kuṇchān (*nm*) contraction; flexion; ~**चित** contracted; ० **होना** to contract.

आकुल a:kul (a) restless, uneasy; distracted; distressed.

आकुलता a:kulta: (*nf*) restlessness, uneasiness; mental distress.

आकृति a:kkriti (*nf*) shape, figure, form, structure, appearance; features; contour ~**मूलक** morphological, structural; ~**विज्ञान** morphology; ~**वैज्ञानिक** a morphologist; morphological.

आकृष्ट a:krishṭ (*a*) see **आकर्षित**.

आक्रम/ण a:kkramāṉ (*nm*) attack; aggression; incursion; invasion; ~**णकारी** invader/ invading; aggressor/ aggressive; incursionist; ~**णात्मक** offensive, aggressive.

आक्रां/त a:kkrā:nt (*a*) (one who is) attacked, invaded; ~**ता** (mistakenly used to mean) invader.

आक्रामक a:kkra:māk (*nm*) an invader; aggressor; attacker; (*a*) aggressive; ~**ता** aggressiveness, hostility.

आक्रोश a:kkrosh (*nm*) acrimony, acerbity; wrath.

आक्लांति a:kklā:nti (*nf*) boredom.

आक्षेप a:kshep (*nm*) allegation; accusation, invective; charge.

आक्सीजन a:ksi:jān (*nf*) oxygen (gas).

आखथू a:khthu: (*nm*) the sound produced during hemming and spitting; (*ind*) fie ! a condemnatory exclamation.

आख़िर a:ḳhir (*nm*) the end; (*adv*) at last, after all; ~**कार/को** eventually, after all; at long last.

आख़िरी a:ḳhiri. (*a*) last, final, ultimate;—**चाल** in bottom of bag, the last card up one's sleeve;—**दम तक काम करते रहना** to die in harness; —**दम तक जमे रहना** to die in last ditch;—**दम तक लड़ते रहना** to fight to the finish, to die game;—**वक्त में क्या खाक मुसल्माँ होंगे** death bed repentance, to make a policy change when it is too late to bear fruit.

आखेट a:kheṭ (*nm*) see **शिकार**.

आखेटक a:kheṭak (*nm*) see **शिकारी**.

आख्या/त a:kkhya:t (*a*) uttered, expressed; well-known; ~**ता** an exponent, interpreter.

आख्यान a:kkhyā:n (*nm*) telling, communication; a tale, legend; fable; description; hence ~**क** (*nm*) (diminutive).

आख्यायिका a:kkhya:ika: (*nf*) a fable, short episodic narrative.

आगंतुक a:gāntuk (*nm*) a comer, visitor.

आग a:g (*nf*) fire;—**का परकाला**,—**का पुतला** a fire-eater, fire brand, an extremely hot-tempered/hot-headed man;—**खाना अंगार हगना** to eat fire, to emit fumes;—**देना** to perform funeral rites;—**पर पानी डालना** to pacify/calm down (all infuriated persons);—**पर लोटना** to be uneasy or restless, to be consumed with jealousy, envy etc.; —**पानी/फूस का बैर** innate mutual hostility;—**फाँकना** to boast enormously, to lie grossly; ~**बबूला होना** to be inflamed, to fly in to a rage; —**बरसना** lit. shedding of fire, meaning to have scorching heat (also see—**बरसना**); (for something) to be scarce and expensive; —**बतसाना** to bombard, to cannonate (also see—**बरसना**);—**भड़काना** to stir or blow the fire (of), to fah the flame (of), to pour oil on fire;—**में कूदना** to jump into fire, to create troubles for oneself;—**में**

घी डालना to fan the flame, to pour oil on fire; to add fuel to the fire;—**में झोंकना** to thrust into the fire, to put in trouble; —**में पानी डालना** to extinguish the fire, to cause a quarrel to end; —**लगाकर तमाशा देखना** to excite a quarrel and then to enjoy it; —**लगाकर पानी को दौड़ना** lit. 'to run for water after setting fire to' —meaning, to make show of curing an evil caused by oneself; —**लगे पर कुआँ खोदना** to shut the stable door after the horse is stolen; —**से खेलना** to play with fire;—**से खेलना खतरे से खाली नहीं** it is dangerous to play with edged tools; —**होना** to be furious, to be in a rage, to have one's blood up.

आगजनी a:gzanı: (*nf*) arson.

आगत a:gat (*a*) arrived, come; occurred, happened; -**स्वागत** welcome (to a guest), warm/reception.

आगबबूला a:gbabu:la: (*a*) violently enraged, wild with rage; —**हो जाना** to flare up.

आगम a:gām (*nm*) coming near, approaching; an augment (in grammar); birth, origin; scripture; traditional doctrine or precept; collection of such doctrines; anything handed down and fixed by tradition; induction; proceeds; -**श्रुति** a tradition.

आगमन a:gamān (*nm*) arrival; approach; induction.

आगमनात्मक a:gamāna:tmāk (*a*) inductive;—**तर्कशास्त्र** inductive logic.

आगल a:gal (*nf*) a gate-bar (meant to hold its leaves shut).

आगा a:ga: (*nm*) front, frontage, the fore part of anything; face; the future, the morrow; -**पीछा** pros and cons; ० **करना** to waver, to hesitate;—**भारी होना** (vulgar) to be in the family way, to be with child.

आगाज़ a:ga:z (*nm*) beginning, start, commencement.

आगामी a:gā:mı: (*a*) next; future; coming, ensuing.

आगार a:ga:r (*nm*) a store house treasury, depository.

आगाह a:ga:h;—**करना** (*v*) to warn against or notify, to apprise (as a warning).

आगे a:ge (*adv*) ahead, in front of, before; in future; -**आगे** in future, in course of time;—**आना** to come forward, to confront; to befall; —**करना** to place at the front, to take cover (of);—**कुआँ पीछे खाई** to be on the horns of a dilemma, to be between the devil and the deep sea; —**को** in future;—**दौड़ पीछे छोड़** haste makes waste; —**नाथ न पीछे पगहा** lit. none ahead and none behind —to have no kith and kin, to have none to look after;—**पीछे** one behind the other, front and rear sooner or later; ० **कोई न होना** to be without any kith or kin;—**बढ़ना** to make progress/headway; to gain ground; —**बस न चलना** to be at the end of one's tether; —**से** in future; —**होकर लेना** to step ahead to accord a special welcome, to receive with fanfare.

आग्नेय a:gnēy (*a*) fiery; pertaining to fire; fire-emitting; fire-bearing; igneous.

आग्नेयास्त्र a:gnēya:str (*nm*) a fire-arm, fire-emitting missile.

आग्र/ह a:ggrah (*nm*) insistence, pertinacity; persistence; ~**ही** insistent, pertinacious, persistent.

आघात a:gha:t (*nm*) blow, stroke, hit; shock; impact; trauma; accent.

आघ्रा/ण a:gghrā:ṉ (*nm*) (the act or process of) smelling; ~ **त** smelt.

आचमन a:chmān (*nm*) sipping water

from the palm of the hand(for self purification); to swallow (as a liquid); to assimilate.

आच/रण a:charāṉ (*nm*) conduct; behaviour; practice; ~**रणीय** worth practising/emulating; ~**रित** practised; performed; emulated.

आचार a:cha:r(*nm*)conduct; custom, practice; ethos; behaviour; ~**भ्रष्ट** fallen, degenerated, debased; ~**वान** of good conduct, virtuous;-**विचार** manners and morals; -**व्यवहार** conduct and character; ~**हीन** characterless, immoral; hence ~**हीनता** (*nf*).

आचारक a:cha:rak (*nm*) master of ceremonies.

आचारशास्त्र a:cha:rsha:str (*nm*) ethology, ethics.

आचार–संहिता a:cha:rsānhita: (*nf*) moral code.

आचार्य a:cha:ry (*nm*) a teacher, preceptor; professor; founder or leader (of a school of thought); an initiator; hence ~**त्व** (*nm*).

आच्छद a:chchhad (*nm*) a sheath; lid, cover.

आच्छा/दन a:chchha:dān (*nm*) a covering, cover; ~**दित** covered.

आच्छेदन a:chchhedāṉ (*nm*) (the act or process of) amputation, cutting off.

आच्छिन्न a:chhinn (*a*) amputated, cut off.

आज a:j (*adv* and *nm*)today;—**मरे कल दूसरा दिन** mundane strains soon set off the blow of bereavement, unpleasant memories do not last very long.

आजकल a:jkal (*adv*) now-a-days, these days;—**करना** to put off from day to day, to dilly-dally; to defer; —**का** modern, hodiernal;—**में** in a couple of days, soon, without delay.

आजन्म a:janm (*adv*) since birth.

आजमाइ/श (*nf*) trial, test; ~**शी** on trial, experimental.

आजमाना a:zmā:nā: (*v*) to try, to (put to a) test.

आजमूदा a:zmu:da: (*a*) tried and tested.

आजाद a:za:d (*a*) independent, free; ~**ख़याल** independent-minded, open-minded; ~**तबियत** of independent temperament; open-minded; ~**मिजाज** self-willed, capricious.

आज़ादी a:za:di: (*nf*) independence freedom; ~**पसंद** freedom-loving; self-willed.

आजानुबाहु a:ja:nūba:hu (*a*) blessed with long arms (extending to the knees).

आजिज़ a:jiz (*a*) helpless; weary; meek;—**आना** to be wearied, to be fed up; **आजिज़ी** helplessness, meekness.

आजीवन a:ji:wān (*adv*) throughout life, for a whole life-time; —**कारावास** life imprisonment.

आजीविका a:ji:vika: (*nf*) livelihood; calling.

आज्ञप्ति a:ggyapti (*nf*) a decree.

आज्ञा a:ggya: (*nf*) order; -**पत्र** a writ, written order; -**पालन** obedience; -**भंग** breach of order, disobedience.

आज्ञाका/री aggya:ka:ri: (*a*) obedient; ~**रिता** obedience.

आटा a:ṭa: (*nm*) flour; (**कंगाली में**) —**गीला होना** to be plunged into yet another complication when already afflicted; **आटे के साथ घुन पिसना** to undergo an undeserved suffering on account of association; **आटे-दाल का भाव मालूम होना** to be confronted with unwelcome realities of practical life; **आटे-दाल की फ़िक्र** anxiety regarding means of sustenance; **आटे में नमक** in reasonable/

small proportions.

आठ a:ṭh (*a*) eight;(*nm*) the number eight; -**आठ आँसू रोना** to cry one's heart out, to shed floods of tears; **आठों गाँठ कुम्मैत** every inch a crook; –**पहर चौंसठ घड़ी** day in and day out.

आठैं a:ṭhaĩ (*nf*) the eighth day of a lunar fortnight.

आडंब/र a:ḍāmbaṛ (*nm*) ostentation, affectation; showing off; tinsel, hypocrisy; ~**री** ostentatious, showy; hypocrite, tinsel.

आड़ a:ṛ (*nm*) a cover, screen; a barricade; shield, strut; block;—**लेना** to take a cover.

आड़ा a:ṛa: (*a*) oblique; horizontal; transverse; –**तिरछा होना** to be provoked, to be enraged;—**वक्त** trying or difficult time; **आड़े आना/पड़ना/होना** to put impediments; **आड़े वक़्त पर काम आना** to help some dog over stile, to help one over stile, to do a good turn when one is in difficulty; **आड़े हाथों लेना** to rebuke, to put to shame by sarcasm; to tick off.

ऑडिट/र ɔḍiṭar (*nm*) an auditor; hence ~**री** (*nf*).

आड़ू a:ṛu: (*nm*) a peach.

आढ़त a:ṛhat (*nf*)commission agency; brokerage, commission.

आढ़/तिया, ~ती a:ṛhatiya:, ~ti: (*nm*) a commission agent; broker.

आढ्य a:ḍḍhy—a Sanskrit suffix denoting prosperity, plenty, abundance (as **धनाढ्य, गणाढ्य**).

आणविक ā:n̲vik (*a*) molecular.

आतंक a:tāṅk (*nm*) terror, panic; ~**वाद/वादिता** terrorism; ~**वादी** terrorist; **आतंकित** terrorised.

आतत a:tat(*a*) tense; ~**ता** tenseness.

आततायी a:tata:i: (*nm* and *a*) an oppressor; tyrant; oppressive.

आत/प a:tap (*nm*) sunlight, sun; ~**प्त** scorched, heated.

आतशक a:tshak (*nm*) syphilis.

आतिथेय a:tithey (*nm*) a host, one who extends hospitality.

आतिथ्य a:titthy (*nm*) hospitability; hospitality; -**सत्कार** hospitality.

आतिश a:tish (*nm*) fire; ~**बाज़** a fireworks manufacturer; ~**बाज़ी** fireworks; display of fireworks; pysotechnic.

आतिशी a:tishi: (*a*) pertaining to fire, fiery;—**शीशा** a magnifying glass.

आतिशय्य a:tishayy (*nm*) abundance, plenty; excess.

आती-पाती a:ti:pa:ti: (*nf*) the game of hide and seek, blind man's buff.

आतुर a:tur (*a*) rash, hasty; restless.

आतुरता a:turta: (*nf*) rashness, hastiness; restlessness.

आतुरालय a:tura:lay (*nm*) a dispensary, clinic.

आत्म a:tm (*nm*) self; (*a*) pertaining to self, one's own, personal; ~**कथा** autobiography; ~**कल्याण** one's own good; ~**केंद्रित** self-centred; ~**गत** subjective; inner; ~**गौरव** self-respect; ~**घात** suicide; ~**घातक/घाती** suicidal,self-defeating; a self-murderer; ~**चरित** an autobiography; ~**चरितात्मक** autobiographical; ~**चालित** automatic; ~ **चिंतन** self-contemplation; ~ **ज/जात** a son; ~**जा** a daughter; ~**ज्ञान** self-realisation, self-knowledge; ~**तत्त्व** the true nature of the soul or Supreme Spirit; ~**तुष्ट** self-gratified; ~**तुष्टि** self-satisfaction; ~**तृप्त** fulfilled, gratified, self-satisfied; ~**तृप्ति** self-satisfaction; self-fulfilment; -**त्याग** self-sacrifice; self-denial; ~**त्यागी** one who has made sacrifices; ~**दान** self-sacrifice; ~**दाह** self-immolation; ~**द्रोह** revolt against self; ~**निंदा** self-condemnation; -**नियंत्रण** self-restraint, self-control; -**निरीक्षण** introspection; -निर्णय self-determination; ~निर्भर self-sufficient, self-reliant; ० ता self-reliance, self-sufficiency; ~निवेदन offering oneself to a deity; self-communication; ~निष्ठ subjective;-प्रदर्शन self-display; -प्रशंसा self-praise; -बल spiritual force, psychic force; -बलिदान self-sacrifice; ~बोध see ~ज्ञान; ~भाव the self, proper or peculiar nature;-मंथन a deep introspection and analysis of one's inner self; ~मोह narcissism; -रक्षा self-defence, self-preservation; -रति self-love, amour-propre; -वंचना self-deception, self-deceit; -वध suicide; ~वाद spiritualism; ~वादी spiritualist; spiritualistic; -विजय self-conquest; -विद्या metaphysics; -विश्वास self-confidence; ~विश्वासी self-confident; -विस्मृति self-oblivion; -शासन self-rule; -श्लाघा/स्तुति self-praise; -संतोष self-satisfaction;-संघर्ष self-conflict: -संयम self-control, self-possession; -समर्पण surrender (of oneself); -सम्मान self-respect, self-regard; -सम्मोह self-delusion; -साक्षात्कार self-realisation; ~सात् assimilated; ० करना to assimilate;-साधना selfrealisation; ० वाद self-realisationism; ~सिद्धि self-realisation; -स्वीकृति confession; ~हत्या/हनन/हिंसा suicide, self-killing; -हित self-interest.

आत्मक a:tmak—a Sanskrit suffix meaning imbued with, steeped in, full of, concerned with, belonging to or forming the nature of, composed or consisting of (as रागात्मक, भावात्मक)

आत्मनेपद a:tmanepad (*nm*) in Sanskrit grammar, the form of verb which implies an action belonging or reverting to self.

आत्मसेवी a:tmsevi: (*nm* and *a*) self-seeker, self-server.

आत्मा a:tmā: (*nf*, also used as *nm* by Sanskritists) soul, spirit; —को दु:ख पहुँचाना to make one turn in one's grave; to cause grief (to); —ठंडी होना to be gratified; to be fulfilled.

आत्मानंद a:tmā:nānd (*nm*) the pleasure of self-realisation.

आत्मानुभव a:tmā:nubhav (*nm*) self-experience.

आत्मानुभूति a:tma:nubhu:ti (*nf*) self-experience, self-realisation.

आत्माभिमा/न a:tmā:bhimā:n (*nm*) self-respect; ~नी self-respecting, proud of oneself.

आत्माभिव्यंजना a:tmā:bhivyāṇjanā: (*nf*) self-expression.

आत्माभिव्यक्ति a:tmā:bhivyakti (*nf*) self-expression.

आत्मावलं/बन a:tmā:vlāmbān (*nf*) self-dependence; self-reliance; ~बी self-dependent; self-reliant.

आत्मिक a:tmik (*a*) spiritual; pertaining to self; hence ~ता (*nf*).

आत्मीकरण a:tmi:karāṉ (*nm*) assimilation.

आत्मीय a:tmi:y (*a*) pertaining to self, one's own, intimate;(*nm*) kith and kin; ~ता cordiality; intimate relationship, close affinity.

आत्मोत्कर्ष a:tmotkarsh (*nm*) eudaemonia; self-elevation.

आत्मोत्सर्ग a:tmotsarg (*nm*) self-sacrifice.

आत्मोद्धार a:tmoddha:r (*nm*) self-salvation, beatitude.

आत्मोन्नति a:tmonnāti (*nf*) self-sublimation, self-elevation.

आत्मोपजीवी a:tmōpji:vi: (*a*) self-sustaining.

आत्यंतिक a:ttyāntik (*a*) extremistic, excessive; ~ता extremism.

आदत a:dat (*nf*) habit; ~न by force of habit, as a matter of habit.

आदम a:dām (*n*) Adam (the first man

supposed to have been created on earth); ~क़द of human-size; ~खोर man-eater, cannibal; ~ ज़ाद human being, born of man.

आदमियत a:dmiyāt (*nf*) gentlemanliness; humanity; humaneness.

आदमी a:dmi: (*nm*) a man, human being; **बनना** to become humane, to be humanised; to be civil and well-mannered.

आदर a:dar (*nm*) respect, deference, esteem; ~**णीय** respectable, reverend; **भाव** respect, esteem.

आदर्श a:darsh (*nm*) an ideal, a model, norm; pattern; (*a*) ideal, model; ~**वाद/वादिता** Idealism; ~**वादी** an idealist; idealistic.

आदर्शक विज्ञान a:darshakviggya:n (*nm*) a normative science.

आदर्शलोक a:darshlok (*nm*) Utopia.

आदर्शीकरण a:darshi:karan (*nm*) idealisation.

आदर्शोक्ति a:darshokti (*nf*) a motto.

आदाता a:da:ta: (*nm*) recipient; receiver; payee; donee.

आदान a:dā:n (*nm*) receiving, taking; **-प्रदान** giving and taking exchange.

आदाब a:da:b (*nm*) manners; salutation; **-अर्ज़** salutation , greeting; **—बजा लाना** to salute humbly, to make obeissance.

आदायी a:da:i: (*a*) recipient; payee; donee.

आदि a:di (*nm*) beginning; (*ind*) etcetera; (*a*) early, initial, primordial; ~**कवि** the first-ever poet — Va:lmi:ki, the author of Sanskrit Ra:ma:yan; ~**कालीन** primitive; ~**काव्य** the Ra:ma:yan of Va:lmi:ki —the first literary creation; —**पुरुष** Brahma: —the creator of the Universe; ~**रूप** prototype.

आदिक a:dik (*ind*) etcetera.

आदितः a:ditah (*adv*) ab initio; de novo.

आदित्य a:ditty (*nm*) the sun; ~**वार** Sunday.

आदिम a:dim (*a*) primitive, early; first.

आदिल a:dil (*a*) just, equitable.

आदिवासी a:diva:si: (*nm*) an aboriginal; (*a*) aboriginal; **जनजाति/जाति** aboriginal tribe, aborigines.

आदिष्ट a:disht (*a*) commanded, commissioned.

आदी a:di: (*a*) habitual; habituated. accustomed.

आदृत a:ddrit (*a*) honoured, respected.

आदेय a:dey (*a*) worth-receiving or accepting.

आदे/श a:desh (*nm*) command; (in Grammar) substitution of one letter for another; precept; ~**शात्मक** imperative, expressing command.

आदेशिका a:deshika: (*nf*) precept.

आद्यंत a:ddyānt (*adv*) from beginning to end.

आद्य a:ddy (*a*) first, initial; primitive; archaic; **-स्वरूप** archetype.

आद्यक्षर a:ddyakshar (*nm*) initials.

आद्योपांत a:ddyopā:nt (*adv*) from beginning to end.

आधा a:dha: (*a*) half; moiety; **—तीतर आधा बटेर** intermingling of heterogeneous elements, discordant objects jumbled together; **-साझा** equal partnership; **—रह जाना/हो जाना** to be reduced to half (due to illness, tension etc); **आधी छोड़ सारी को धावे, आधी रहे न सारी पावे** he who hunts two hares leaves one and loses the other/to repeat the story of the dog and the shadow/he who grasps all, loses all.

आधान a:dhā:n (*nm*) containing; depositing; **-पात्र** a container.

आधार a:dha:r (*nm*) base; basis; foundation; data; receptacle; **-आधेय** the relationship of the container and the contained; **~भूत** fundamental; **~रेखा** base; **-वाक्य** premise; **~शिला** foundation stone; **-सामग्री** data.

आधारित a:dha:rit (*a*) based (on).

आधासीसी a:dha:si:si: (*nf*) hemicrania, pain affecting half of the forehead.

आधि a:dhi (*nf*) mental agony/suffering; **-व्याधि** mental and physical suffering.

आधिकारिक a:dhika:rik (*a*) official, authoritative; (*nm*) the main plot; hence **~ता** (*nf*).

आधिक्य a:dhikky; (*nm*) abundance, plenty; excess.

आधिदैविक a:dhidaivik (*a*) proceeding from divine or supernatural agencies.

आधिपत्य a:dhipatty (*nm*) supremacy; power.

आधिभौतिक a:dhibhautik (*a*) material; derived or produced from the primitive elements.

आधिराज्य a:dhira:jjy (*nm*) suzerainty.

आधीन a:dhi:n (*a*) see **अधीन**.

आधीनता a:dhi:nta: (*nf*) see **अधीनता**.

आधुनि/क a:dhunik (*a*) modern; **~कीकरण** modernisation, adoption of modern techniques; **~कता** modernity; **~कता-बोध** sense of modernity.

आधृत a:ddhrit (*a*) based (on).

आधेय a:dhey (*nm* and *a*) that which is contained; contained.

आध्यात्मिक a:ddhya:tmik (*a*) spiritual, pertaining to the soul or the Supreme Spirit; **~ता** spirituality.

आनंद a:nānd (*nm*) bliss, happiness; joy, pleasure, delight; **-मंगल** peace and happiness; **~मय** blissful, made up or consisting of happiness; the Supreme Spirit; **~वाद** the theory propounding the attainment of Eternal bliss as the summum bonum of life; **~वादी** a believer in he theory of **आनंदवाद**; **आनंदित** delighted, rejoiced, happy; **आनंदी** cheerful, cheery.

आन ā:n (*nf*) honour, prestige; **—की आन में** instantaneously; **-बान** honour and dignity, pomp and show; grace; **—तोड़ना** to break one's pledge/honour; **—रखना** to keep one's pledge/honour.

आनत ā:nat (*a*) bent; biassed.

आनन ā:nān (*nm*) face; mouth.

आनन-फ़ानन (में) ā:nān-fā:nān (mē) (*adv*) instantaneously, at once.

आनमन a:nāmān (*nm*) flexure: bending.

आनम्य a:nāmmy (*a*) flexure; pliant, pliable; flexible; **~ता** pliability, pliance; flexibility.

आनयन a:nayan (*nm*) to bring closer/nearer, to carry towards.

ऑनरेरी ɔ:nreri: (*a*) honorary.

आना ā:nā: (*v*) to come; (*nm*) an anna (coin); **आए दिन** every day; **-जाना** to pay visits, (to) make calls (at); **आनी-जानी** transitory, shortlived; **आया-गया** guest, visitor; **आ धमकना** to appear unannounced/all of a sudden; **आय गए की लाज** a bargain is after all a bargain; **आये सेर खाये सवा सेर** to have a large mouth but a small girdle.

आना-कानी ā:nā:kā:nɪ: (*nf*) procrastination, evasion, prevarication

आनुपूर्व्य a:nūpu:rvy (*nm*) succession, sequence.

आनुभाविक a:nubhavik (*a*) empirical based on observation and experience.

आनुमानिक a:nūmā:nik (*a*) conjectural, estimative; hence **~ता** (*nf*).

आनुरूप्य a:nuru:ppy (*nm*) consonance; conformity.

आनुवंशिक a:nuvānshik (*a*) hereditary; ~**ता** heredity.

आनुषंगिक a:nushāṅgik (*a*) contingent; accidental; hence ~**ता** (*nf*).

आन्वयिक a:nnvaik (*a*) orderly; systematic; pertaining to or related with **अन्वय**.

आप a:p (*pro*) (deferential) you (second person); pronoun used to express respect, as distinct from **तुम, तू**;—**अपने दाँव में आना** to act as a boomerang; ~**की सीख आपको मुबारक** keep your breath to cool your porridge; -**आपको** each by himself, all individually; —**काज महाकाज** achievement of one's own end is the greatest achievement; better do a thing than wish it to be done; ~**काजी** selfish; ~**बीती** the story of one's own suffering; self-experiences;—**मरे जग परलो (परलै)** after me, the deluge; the death's day is the doomsday;—**भला तो जग भला** good mind, good find; ~**रूप** your honour; incarnate;—**से आप** by itself, automatically;—**ही आप** alone, by or within one's ownself; automatically.

आपत् a:pat—used as a constituent in Sanskrit-based compounds, meaning sudden appearance of misfortune, distress. In compound, the ultimate **त्** changes into **द्** if followed by a voiced sound.

आपत्का/ल a:patka:l (*nm*) emergency, hour of distress; ~**लिक** emergent; pertaining to emergency.

आपत्ति a:patti (*nf*) objection; predicament; ~**काले मर्यादा नास्ति** necessity knows no law.

आपद a:pad (*nf*) see **आपदा**.

आपदा a:pda: (*nf*) distress, adversity.

आपद्दापन्न a:pda:pann (*a*) hazardous, involving distress.

आपद् a:pad (*nf*) see **आपत्**; ~**ग्रस्त** in distress/distressed, seized by misfortune, fallen on evil days.

आपद्धर्म a:paddharm (*nm*) a conduct permissible only in times of extreme distress.

आपस a:pas (*pro*) each other, one another; (*nm*) fellowship, kindred; —**का** one's own, of intimate circle; mutual, reciprocal; —**में** mutually, with one another; ~**वाले** kith and kin.

आपसदारी a:pasda:ri: (*nf*) reciprocity, mutual relationship.

आपसी a:psi: (*a*) mutual, reciprocal.

आपा a:pa: (*nm*) consciousness; one's own entity; ego, vanity;—**खोना** to forget or lose consciousness of real self; to become abnormal; **आपे में आना** to attain normalcy; to attain consciousness; **आपे में न रहना, आपे से बाहर होना** to be off one's chumb, to fly off the handle, to be overwhelmed by emotion, to lose self-control.

आपात a:pa:t (*nm*) an emergency; catastrophe.

आपातत: a:pa:tatah (*adv*) emergently, as a matter of emergency.

आपा/तिक, ~ती a:pa:tik, ~ti: (*a*) emergent, pertaining to emergency.

आपादमस्तक a:pa:dmastak (*adv*) from head to foot.

आपाधापी a:pa:dha:pi: (*nf*) a mad race (for self-gratification), state where each struggles for his own self-interest.

आपानगोष्ठी a:pa:ngoshṭhi: (*nf*) a drinking bout.

आपू/रित, ~र्ण a:pu:rit, ~rn (*a*) full, full to the brim; fulfilled.

आपूर्ति a:pu:rti (*nf*) fulfilment, complete gratification.

आपेक्षिक a:pekshik (*a*) comparative, relative;—**गुरुत्व** relative density; ~**ता** relativity.

आप्त a:pt (*a*) trusted, trustworthy; respected; (*nm*) authority, a credible or authoritative person; umpire; ~**काम** fulfilled, one whose wishes have all been fulfilled; gratified; ~**त्व** authority; —**प्रमाण** a trustworthy testimony; —**वचन/वाक्य** authoritative statement;—**वर्ग** inner circle; circle of friends.

आप्तोक्ति a:ptokti (*nf*) a motto.

आप्रवास a:pprva:s (*nm*) settling in a foreign country, immigration; ~**न** (the act or process) of immigration.

आप्रेषक a:ppreshak (*nm*) an addressee.

आप्रेषी a:ppreshi: (*nm*) an addressee.

आप्लावन a:ppla:vān(*nm*)inundation; immersion, complete submergence.

आप्लावित a:ppla:vit (*a*) immersed, inundated, completely submerged.

आफ़त a:fat (*nf*) distress, trouble; **आयेगी और भुगतनी पड़ेगी** there will be the device (devil) to pay; —**उठाना** to create havoc; —**का टुकड़ा/परकाला** a dare devil, a sharp astute fellow; —**का मारा** distress-stricken; —**ढाना** to work havoc; —**मचाना** to make excessive haste; to create havoc; —**मोल लेना,**—**सिर पर लेना** to ask for trouble; to invite trouble, to own unnecessary botheration.

आफ़ताब a:fta:b (*nm*) the sun.

आफ़ताबी a:fta:bi: (*nf*) a sun-shed (esp. on a window).

ऑफ़िस ɔfis (*nm*) an office.

आब a:b (*nf*) lustre, brilliance; water; -**ताब** splendour, brilliance, lustre; ~**दार** brilliant, lustrous; a servant who serves water, bearer.

आबकारी a:bka:ri: (*nf*) excise; —**महकमा** excise department.

आबदस्त a:bdast (*nm*) the post-excrement wash.

आबदाना a:bdā:nā: (*nm*) see **अन्न-जल**.

आबद्ध a:baddh (*a*) bound. tied up; —**करना** to bind.

आब/नूस a:bnu:s (*nm*) ebony; ~**सी** jet black (colour).

आबपाशी a:bpa:shi: (*nf*) irrigation; watering.

आबरू a:bru: (*nf*) honour; chastity; ~**दार** respected, honourable;—**उतारना** to debauch, to violate one's chastity; —**ख़ाक में मिलाना** to lay one's honour in the dust;—**में बट्टा लगना** one's honour to be undermined, to suffer disgrace;—**बरबाद कर देना** to give one's honour or character to the winds; —**लुटना** to be put to disgrace, to be humiliated; (a woman's) chastity to be violated, an indecent assault to be committed upon.

आबहवा a:bhava: (*nf*) climate; —**बदलना** go elsewhere for a change.

आबाद a:ba:d (*a*) inhabited, populated; prosperous; —**करना** to settle, to populate; to reclaim (barren land etc.)

आबादी a:ba:di: (*nf*) population; habitation; (signs of) prosperity.

आबालवृद्ध a:ba:lvriddh (*ind*) children and elders all.

आबियाना a:biyā:nā: (*nm*) water-rate; water-tax.

आबेहयात a:behaya:t (*nm*) nectar.

आब्दिक a:bdik (*a*) yearly, annual.

आभरण a:bharān (*nm*) ornament; decoration.

आभा a:bha: (*nf*) lustre, splendour; tint, tinge; ~**मंडल** a halo.

आभार a:bha:r (*nm*) obligation, gratitude; indebtedness; burden; —**प्रदर्शन** expression of gratitude.

आभारी a:bha:ri: (*a*) obliged; grateful; indebted.

आभास a:bha:s (*nm*) an inkling; a glimpse; semblance; fallacious appearance; phenomenon; effect.

आभासी a:bha:si: (*a*) pseudo; unreal, apparent; visual.

आभिजात्य a:bhija:tty (*nm*) aristocracy; classicism.

आभीर a:bhi:r (*nm*) name of an ancient rural region of India and its inhabitants; an ancient tribe; see **अहीर**.

आभूषण a:bhu:shān̲ (*nm*) ornament; decoration, embellishment.

आभूषित a:bhu:shit (*a*) ornamented; decorated, embellished.

आभ्यंतर a:bbhyāntar (*nm* and *a*) the interior; internal.

आभ्यंतरिक a:bbhyāntarik (*a*) internal, interior, inner; hence **~ता** (*nf*).

आमंत्रण a:māntrān̲(*nm*)an invitation, a call, solicitation; hence **आमंत्रक** (*nm*).

आमंत्रित a:māntrit (*a*) invited, solicited.

आम ā:m (*nf*) a mango; (*a*) common; general; **आदमी** the common man;—**खाने से काम रखना, पेड़ गिनने से नहीं** to be concerned with the substance rather than the source; —**जलसा** a public meeting; **~फ़हम** current; common; —**रस** mango juice; —**राय** popular opinion, public opinion;—**के आम गुठलियों के दाम** earth's joys and heaven's combined.

आमद a:mād (*nm*) arrival; approach; coming; revenue; —**व-ख़र्च** revenue and expenditure; **~रफ़्त** traffic, coming and going.

आमदनी a:madni: (*nf*) income; revenue;—**व-ख़र्च** revenue/income and expenditure.

आमना-सामना a:mnā:-sa:mnā: (*nm*) an encounter, confrontation; coming face to face.

आमने-सामने a:mnē-sa:mnē (*adv*) face to face, opposite one another, head on; vis-a-vis.

आमरण a:mārān̲ (*ind*) till death; till the end;—**अनशन** fast unto death.

आमलक a:mlak (*nm*) see **आँवला**.

आमवात a:mva:t (*nm*) rheumatism.

आमादा a:mā:da: (*a*) intent, bent upon.

आमाशय a:mā:shay (*nm*) stomach.

आमिष a:mish (*nm*) meat; flesh; **~भोजी** meat-eating; carnivorous.

आमीन् a:mi:n (*ind*) amen ! Be it so ! so let it be !

आमुख a:mukh (*nm*) the preamble.

आमुष्मिक a:mushmik (*a*) transcendental, other-worldly; hence **~ता** (*nf*).

आमूल a:mu:l (*a*) radical, fundamental; —**परिवर्तन** radical changes; **० वादी** a radicalist; radicalistic.

आमेज़ a:mez—used generally as an ultimate or intermediate member in a compound, meaning 'mixed'.

आमोद a:mod (*nm*) pleasure, joy, delight; **-प्रमोद** merriment, regaling; orgy; **-यात्रा** a pleasure-trip.

आमोदित a:modit (*a*) delighted, full of joy.

आम्र a:mmr (*nm*) a mango.

आयँत-पायँत ā:yāt-pā:yāt (*nm*) the upper and lower ends of a bedstead.

आय a:y (*nf*) income, revenue, receipt; **-व्यय** income and expenditure; **० क** budget.

आयकर a:ykar (*nm*) income-tax.

आयत a:yat (*nf*) rectangle; sentence or verse of the Qoran; (*a*) wide; long, stretched; **~लोचन** big-wide eyed; having big attractive eyes.

आयतन a:ytān (*nm*) bulk, volume.

आयताकार a:yta:ka:r (*a*) rectangular; mesomorph.

आयताकृति a:yta:kriti (*nf*) mesomorphy; rectangular shape.

आयत्त a:yatt (*a*) **dependent; tract-**

able.

आयन a:yān (*nm*) ion; movement, goings; ~मंडल/वृत्त ionosphere.

आया a:ya: (*nf*) ayah, a female attendant; (*ind*) whether, whether or not; (*v*) came; -गया (*nm*) a visitor; (*v*) forgiven and forgotten; —राम गया राम a frequent defectionist; आये थे हरि भजन को ओटन लगे कपास to set out for the church, to strand in a lurch; आये दिन every (second) day.

आयात a:ya:t (*nm*) import; ~कर्ता (an) importer; ~कारी importing; importer.

आयातित a:ya:tit (*a*) imported.

आयाम a:yā:m (*nm*) magnitude, dimension; amplitude; regulation (as in प्राणायाम).

आयास a:ya:s (*nm*) effort, exertion.

आयु a:yu (*nf*) age.

आयुक्त a:yukt (*nm*) a commissioner.

आयुध a:yudh (*nm*) armament; arms, weapons; ~जीवी a professional soldier; ~शाला armoury, arsenal.

आयुधागार a:yudha:ga:r (*nm*) an armoury, arsenal.

आयुधिक a:yudhik (*a*) pertaining to arms; (*nm*) a soldier.

आयुर् a:yur—an allomorph of आयुस् used as the first member of numerous compound words.

आयुर्बल a:yurbal (*nm*) longevity.

आयु/विज्ञान a:yurviggya:n (*nm*) Medical Science; ~वैज्ञानिक medical, pertaining to Medical Science.

आयुर्वेद a:yurved (*nm*) the Indian medicinal system; Medical Science (lit. the science of health and longevity).

आयुर्वेदिक a:yurvedic (*a*) of or pertaining to आयुर्वेद—the Indian medicinal system.

आयुष् a:yush—an allomorph of आयुस् used as the first member of compound words; ~मान having lo[ng] life; blessed with longevity (th[e] word is prefixed to the names [of] youngers to denote a wish for t[he] addressee to be blessed with long[e]vity); ~य age; life-force.

आयुस् a:yus (*nm*) age, life; long lif[e]

आयोग a:yog (*nm*) a commission [(] body of persons having authority

आयोजक a:yojak (*nm*) convene[r;] sponsor.

आयोजन a:yojān (*nm*) convenin[g;] sponsoring; organising; planning.

आयोजना a:yojanā: (*nf*) plan; plan[n]ing; –आयोग planning commission

आयोजित a:yojit (*a*) convened, a[r]ranged; sponsored.

आरंभ a:rāmbh (*nm*) start, begi[n]ning; outset; commencement; in[]ception.

आरंभिक a:rāmbhik (*a*) initial, preli[]minary; pertaining to or relate[d] with the beginning.

आरक्त a:rakt (*a*) rosy, reddish; henc[e] ~ता (*nf*).

आरक्षक a:rakshak (*nm*) police (man)

आरक्षण a:rakshāṉ (*nm*) reservation[;] guarding or protecting; police func[]tion.

आरक्षी a:rakshi: (*nm*) police (force

आरज़ू a:rzu: (*nf*) keen desire; yearn[]ing; ~मंद desirous; -मिन्नत suppli[]cation; request; beseeching; ०करन[ा] to beseech, to cajole.

आरती a:rti: (*nf*) a ceremony perform[]ed in adoration of a deity or any outstanding personage or guest by circular movement of a lighted lamp before his person; —उतारना to perform आरती.

आर-पार a:r-pa:r (*adv*) across; (*nm*) the two banks of a river; pond etc; astride.

आरभट a:rbhaṭ (*nm*) an adventurer;

adventurous man.

आरभटी a:rbhaṭi: (*nf*) sense of adventure.

आरसी a:rsi: (*nf*) a mirror, looking glass.

आरा a:ra: (*nm*) a saw; **~कश** a sawyer.

आराइश a:ra:ish (*nf*) dressing; decoration; embellishment; ornamental trees, flowers etc.

आराधक a:ra:dhak (*nm*) a worshipper, an adorer.

आरा/धना a:ra:dhnā: (*nf*) worship; adoration; also **~धन** (*nm*); **~धित** worshipped, adored.

आरा/धनीय a:ra:dhanī:y (*a*) adorable, worthy of worship.

आराध्य a:ra:dhy(*a*) adorable, worthy of worship; (*nm*) the adored one (esp. a deity).

आराम a:rā:m (*nm*) rest; comfort; relief; **~कुर्सी** an easy chair; **~गाह** resting place; rest station; **~देह** comfortable; **~पसंद** easy-going; **—करना** to rest; to cure (of an illness); **—फ़रमाना** to be resting/taking rest (said deferentially). **—से** slowly; gently; at leisure.

आरामतल/ब a:rā:mtalab (*a*) indolent; slothful, easy-going; hence **~बी**(*nf*).

आरिज़ी a:rizi: (*a*) temporary.

आरी a:ri: (*nf*) a small saw, table saw.

आरूढ़ a:ru:ṛh (*a*) mounted; ascended.

आरेख a:rekh (*nm*) a diagram; **~ण** making a diagram; drawing.

आरोग्य a:roggy (*nm*) freedom from disease, health; **-निवास** sanitorium; **~प्रद** hygienic; salubrious; **-लाभ** convalescence; **० करना** to convalesce; **~शाला** a sanitorium; nursing home; **-शास्त्र** Hygiene.

आरोप a:rop (*nm*) allegation, charge; imputation; projection; imposition; superimposition; transplantation.

आरोपण a:ropān (*nm*) imposition; superimposition; charge; mount; projection; transplantation.

आरोपित a:ropit (*a*) alleged; imposed; transplanted; projected.

आरो/ह a:roh (*nm*) ascent; **~ह-अवरोह** ascent and descent; (in music) modulation, **~ही** ascending; a rider; **~ह-क्रम** ascending order.

आरोहण a:rohan (*nm*) ascension; ascent; climb.

आर्केस्ट्रा a:rkesṭra: (*nm*) an orchestra.

आर्ट a:rṭ (*nm*) art; **-गैलरी** an art-gallery; **—पेपर** art paper.

ऑर्डर ɔrdar (*nm*) order (for supply of something); a command; **—देना** to place an order; **—बुक करना** to book an order.

ऑर्डिनेंस ɔrḍinēns (*nm*) an ordinance.

आर्त्त a:rt (*a*) aggrieved; persecuted; distressed; afflicted; **—ध्वनि/नाद/स्वर** cry of distress, pain or affliction.

आर्थिक a:rthik (*a*) economic; **—व्यवस्था** economy; economic set-up/organisation; **—स्थिति** economic condition.

आर्द्र a:rdr (*a*) wet; damp; humid; moist; tender; full of feeling; **~ता** dampness; wetness; humidity; feeling of compassion or a compassionate mental state; **~तामापी** hygrometer; **~तामिति** hygrometry; **~तालेखी** hygrograph; **~ता-विज्ञान** hygrology.

आर्मेचर a:rmechar (*nm*) armature.

आर्य a:ry (*nm*) an Aryan; (*a*) noble, of noble stock.

आर्यपुत्र a:ry:puttr (*nm*) a classical form of address or reference to respectable personages, esp. from the wife to her husband.

आर्यसत्य a:ry:satty (*nm*) the great truths in Buddhist Philosophy (four such truths are enumerated.)

आर्य/समाज a:rysama:j (*nm*) a religious order initiated by Swa:mi: Daya:nand in the latter half of the 19th century in India **~समाजी** a follower of the principles of **आर्यसमाज**.

आर्यावर्त a:rya:vart (*nm*) the land of Aryans (extending from the eastern to western sea and bounded on north and south by the Himalayas and Vindhya mountain ranges respectively).

आर्ष a:rsh (*a*) relating or belonging to, or derived from, the sages (**ऋषि**); **~काव्य-युग** the epic age; **—ग्रंथ** books composed by the ancient sages; **—प्रयोग** sacred/authoritative usages (adopted because of their source though grammatically inaccurate); **—वचन/वाक्य** a statement emanating from an authority.

आलंकारिक a:lāṅka:rik (*a*) rhetorical, pertaining to Rhetorics; ornamental; figurative, hence **~ता** (*nf*).

आलं/बन a:lāmbān (*nm*) foundation; base; (in Poetics) the object that arouses emotion; (in Rhetorics) the natural and necessary connection of a sensation which excites it; reason; cause; hence **~बित** (*a*).

आल-औलाद a:l-aula:d (*nf*) progeny.

आलक/स a:lkas (*nm*) see **आलस**; **~सी**; see **आलसी**.

आलथी-पालथी a:lthi:pa:lthi: (*nf*) a typical sedentary posture (wherein the right ankle rests on the left thigh and the left on the right thigh).

आलपिन a:lpin (*nf*) a pin.

आलम a:lām (*nm*) the world; state; **~पनाह** Protector or Master of the world; an address for kings and emperors.

आलमारी a:lma:ri: (*nf*) see **अलमारी**.

आलय a:lay (*nm*) an abode; a dwelling place; a receptacle; asylum.

आलवाल a:lwa:l (*nm*) a basin (around a tree etc.).

आलस a:las (*nm*) laziness, lethargy.

आलसी a:lsi: (*a*) lazy, lethargic; **~पन** lethargic nature, lethargy, laziness.

आलस्य a:lassy (*nm*) same as **आलस** (see).

आला a:la: (*nm*) a niche or recess; an instrument; (*a*) superior; excellent; wet, moist; **—दर्जे का** of the first order.

आलाप a:la:p (*nm*) preliminary modulation of voice before singing; a prelude to singing; slow elaboration of **राग** with or without rhythm.

आलारासी a:la:ra:si: (*a*) slow and slothful, indolent.

आलिं/गन a:liṅgān (*nm*) an embrace, embracing; clasp, clasping; hence **~गित** (*a*).

आलि/म a:lim (*a*) scholarly; learned; **~माना** scholarly, learned.

आली a:li: (*nf*) (a woman's) female friend; a row; range; (*a*) grand; excellent; **~जनाब/जाह** your Exalted Highness!; one occupying a preeminent position.

आलीशान a:li:shā:n (*a*) grand, magnificent.

आलू a:lu: (*nm*) potato; **~दम** see **दम आलू**.

आलूचा a:lu:cha: (*nm*) a kind of plum —*Prunus ovalifolia*.

आलूबुख़ारा a:lu:bukha:ra: (*nm*) dried **आलूचा** (see).

आलेख a:lekh (*nm*) a treatise; writing; plan; plot (of a graph); dictation; script; **~कार** script writer.

आले/खन a:lekhān (*nm*) writing; painting; plotting (of a graph); **~खनकला** graphic art; hence **~ख्य** (*nm*).

आलेप a:lep (*nm*) an ointment, plaster; hence ~न (*nm*).

आलोक a:lok (*nm*) light; lustre; enlightenment.

आलोकित a:lokit (*a*) lighted/lit; enlightened.

आलोचक a:lochak (*nm*) a critic.

आलोचन a:lochān (*nm*) criticism: observation.

आलोचना a:lochnā: (*nf*) criticism.

आलोचित a:lochit (*a*) criticised; reviewed.

आलोच्य a:lochchy (*a*) worth criticising; fit to be criticised; under review.

आलोड़न a:loṛān (*nm*) stirring, shaking, agitating; **-त्रिलोड़न** brooding; profound contemplation of pros and cons; **आलोड़ित** stirred; agitated; well-thought (over).

आल्हा a:lha: (*nm*) verse narrative eulogising the exploits and chivalrous deeds of A:lha: and U:dal; a ballad composed in the traditional a:lha: metre; **—गाना** to narrate one's exploits and experiences at length.

आवक a:vak (*nm*) arrivals, incoming (goods, things, etc).

आवधिक a:vdhik (*a*) periodical.

आवभगत a:vbhagat (*nf*) hospitality.

आवरक a:varak (*nm*) a covering; cover.

आवरण a:varā̲n̲ (*nm*) a cover, covering, shell; sheath; screen; lid; envelope; cladding; mask; **-परिचय** blurb; **—पृष्ठ** cover page, book jacket.

आव/र्जन a:varjān (*nm*) curb, restraint; **~र्जना** taboo; hence **~र्जित** (*a*)

आवर्त a:vart (*nm*) a whirlpool; densely populated place; recurrent; **~न** rotation; revolution; recurrence; **~नी** a rotator.

आवर्ती a:varti: (*a*) recurring; **—व्यय** recurring expenditure.

आवर्धक a:vardhak (*nm*) augmentor; magnifier; (*a*) augmenting; magnifying.

आवर्धन a:vardhān (*nm*) magnification; augmentation.

आवश्य/क a:vashshyak (*a*) necessary; essential; binding, obligatory; also **~कीय** (*a*).

आवश्यकता a:vashshyakta: (*nf*) necessity, need, requirement; **~एँ** wants, needs.

आवाँ a:vā: (*nm*) a potter's kiln; furnace; **—का आवाँ बिगड़ना** degeneration of the whole lot /clan.

आवागमन a:va:gamān (*nm*) coming and going; transmigration.

आवाज़ a:va:z (*nf*) sound, voice; report; **—उठाना/ऊँची करना** to raise the voice; **—कसना** to pass unwelcome remarks; **—देना** to call out, to hail; **—बुलंद करना** same as **—उठाना**; **—फटना** to have the voice rendered hoarse; **—भर्राना/भारी होना** to have the voice choked with emotion.

आवा-जाही a:va:ja:hi: (*nf*) see **आना-जाना**.

आवारगी a:va:rgi: (*nf*) loafing; profligacy; reckless extravagance.

आवारा a:va:ra: (*nm*) a vagabond, loafer; (*a*) vagrant, wandering, loitering; profligate.

आवारागर्द a:va:ra:gard (*a*) loafing, vagrant, loitering, (*nm*) loafer; vagabond.

आवारागर्दी a:va:ra: gardi: (*nf*) loafing; loitering, vagrancy.

आवा/स a:va:s (*nm*) residence; dwelling place; **~सी** resident.

आवाहन a:va:hān (*nm*) invocation (of a deity etc.); a call; summoning.

आविर्भाव a:virbha:v (*nm*) advent; emergence; manifestation; becoming visible.

आविर्भूत a:virbhu:t (*a*) emerged; manifested; become visible.

आविल a:vil (*a*) turbid; foul; polluted; not clear; confused: hence ~ **ता** (*nf*).

आविष्करण a:vishkaran̲ (*nm*) an invention.

आविष्कर्ता a:vishkarta: (*nm*) an inventor.

आविष्कार a:vishka:r (*nm*) an invention; ~**क** an inventor.

आविष्कृत a:vishkrit (*a*) invented.

आविष्ट a:vishṭ (*a*) possessed of an evil spirit etc.; filled by an intense emotional sentiment etc.; charged.

आवृत a:vrit (*a*) covered, enveloped, surrounded

आवृत्त a:vritt (*a*) turned round, whirled; repeated; reverted.

आवृत्ति a:vritti (*nf*) repetition; recurrence, reversion; turning round; reprint; frequency; -**सूत्र** recurrence formula.

आवेग a:veg (*nm*) impulse; passion; wave; emotion; paroxysm; ~**मूलक** impulsive; ~**शील** impulsive; impetuous; **आवेगी** paroxysmal; impulsive.

आवेगात्मक a:vega:tmak (*a*) impulsive, inspired by passion.

आवेदक a:vedak (*nm*) an applicant, a petitioner.

आवेदन a:vedān (*nm*) an application, petition; hence **आवेदनीय** (*a*); **आवेदित** (*a*); -**पत्र** an application, petition.

आवेश a:vesh (*nm*) charge; agitation; intense emotion; frenzy; wrath; hence ~**न** (*nm*).

आवे/ष्टन a:veshṭān (*nm*) enveloping, wrapping round; enclosure; ~**ष्टित** enveloped, wrapped; enclosed.

आशं/का a:shāṅka: (*nf*) apprehension; scruple; ~**कित** apprehensive; full of or filled with apprehension.

आशना a:shnā: (*a*) intimate; (*nm*) lover, beloved.

आशनाई a:shnā:i: (*nf*) intimacy; illicit love.

आशय a:shay (*nm*) intention, intent, design; purport, import, meaning; receptacle.

आशा a:sha: (*nf*) hope; ~**जनक** hopeful; promising; ~**हीन** disgusted, disappointed, hopeless; —**टूटना** to lose hope;—**पूजना** to have (one's) hope fulfilled; —**बाँधना** to have (one's) hope raised; —**की किरण फूटना** ray of hope to emerge; ~**ओं पर तुषारपात होना** to have all hopes dashed to the ground; ~**ओं पर पानी फिरना** to dash one's hope; to have (one's) hopes shattered/dashed to the ground.

आशा/तीत a:sha:ti:t (*a*) beyond hope, unexpected; ~**वादिता** optimistic attitude, optimism;

आशा/वाद a:sha:va:d (*nm*) optimism; ~**वादी** an optimist; optimistic.

आशावृत्ति a:sha:vritti (*nf*) optimistic disposition; optimism.

आशिक़ a:shiq (*nm*) a lover, an inamorato; (*a*) enamoured; -**माशूक़** the lover and beloved; ~**मिज़ाज** having the temper or disposition of a lover; given to love-making; **आशिक़ाना** befitting or peculiar to a lover; **आशिक़ी** love-making.

आशिष a:shish (*nf*) blessings, benediction.

आशीर्वचन a:shi:rvachān (*nm*) blessings, words of benediction.

आशीर्वाद a:shi:rva:d (*nm*) blessings, benediction.

आशु a:shu (*a*) prompt, quick, speedy, swift; extempore; impromptu; —**अभिनय** extempore acting; ~**कवि** an impromptu poet; ~**काव्य** extempore poetic composition; ~**गामी** fast moving; ~**तोष** one who is easily pleased; easy to please; Lord Shiv; ~**लिपि** short hand, stenography; ~**लिपिक** a stenographer,

आश्चर्य a:shchary (*nm*) wonder, surprise; astonishment; ~**चकित** surprised; bewildered, flabbergasted; ० **होना** to be struck dumb.

आश्रम a:shshrām (*nm*) hermitage; abode; one of the four stages in the life of caste Hindus (viz. brahmachary –as a student of the Vedas; Grihasth —as a householder; Va:nprasth —as abandoner of worldly things; Sannya:s—as an anchorite); ~**वासी** a hermit, inmate of an **आश्रम**.

आश्रय a:shshray (*nm*) shelter, refuge; patronage; retreat; seat; hence ~**दाता** a patron.

आश्रित a:shshrit (*a*) depending or relying on; enjoying the support of; (*nm*) a dependent, refugee; protege; hence ~**ता** (*nf*).

आश्व/स्त a:shshvast (*a*) assured; convinced; composed; ~**स्ति** composure, assurance; hence ~**स्तता** (*nf*).

आश्वासन a:shshva:sān (*nm*) assurance; guarantee.

आश्विन a:shshvin (*nm*) the seventh month of the Hindu calendar ; also called **क्वार**.

आषा/ढ़ a:sha:rh (*nm*) the fourth month of the Hindu calendar; ~**ढ़ी** pertaining to the month of ~**ढ़**; the full moon day in the month of ~**ढ़**.

आसंग a:sāṅg (*nm*) attachment; association; adhesion.

आसंजक a:sāṇjak (*a*) adhesive; ~**ता** adhesiveness, tack.

आसंजन a:sāṇjān (*nm*) adhesion.

आस a:s (*nf*) hope; expectations; support;–**टूटना** to lose hope, to be disappointed;—**तकना** to look forward hopefully;—**तोड़ना** to disappoint/despond;—**बँधाना** to extend assurances; to arouse hopes;—**पूरना** to have fulfilment of hope; to be gratified—**लगाना** to look hopefully (to).

आस-औलाद a:s-aula:d (*nf*) progeny.

आसक्त a:sakt (*a*) attached; fond addict; fascinated, charmed,

आसक्ति a:sakti (*nf*) attachment; fascination; fondness, addiction.

आस/ज्जा a:sajja: (*nf*) make-up; readiness; equipment; ~**ज्जक** make-up man.

आसत्ति a:satti (*nf*) uninterrupted sequence (of words in a sentence); proximity; juxtaposition.

आसन a:sān(*nm*)a posture; seat; saddle; stage; a small square piece of mat, carpet, deer or tiger skin used for seating;—**उखड़ना** to be dislodged; to be thrown out of gear;—**जमाना** to entrench; to stick on; to be seated firmly;—**डिगना/डोलना** to be allured or tempted; to get panicky or nervous;—**देना** to offer a seat (respectfully);–**मारना/लगाना** to sit firmly, to be firmly entrenched;— **हिलना** see—**डिगना**.

आसन्न a:sann (*a*) imminent, impending; ~**भूत** present perfect tense (in Grammar); ~**मृत्यु** one whose death is imminent, under the shadow of death.

आस-पास a:s-pa:s (*adv*) near about, in the vicinity.

आसमान a:smā:n (*nm*) the sky;—**का थूका मुँह पर पड़ता है** puff not against the wind;—**के तारे तोड़ना** to realise an impossibility;—**छूना** same as —**से बातें करना**;—**टूटना/फटना** to be struck by a calamity; —**दिखाना** (esp. in wrestling or fighting) to dash to the ground with face up—to beat all ends up; —**पर चढ़ना/उड़ना** to be too vain or proud; —**पर चढ़ाना** to exalt to the skies; to spoil (somebody) by extravagant praise/flattery;

—**पर थूकना** lit. to spit at the sky —to puff against the wind;—**पर दिमाग़ होना** to be too conceited or vain; —**में छेद करना** to achieve the impossible; to be too crafty;—**में छेद होना** to rain incessantly, to have a non-stop downpour; **में थिगली लगाना** to be too skilful/crafty;—**सिर पर उठा लेना** to create havoc, to make excessive noise or mischief;—**से गिरना/टपकना** to be attained without effort or exertion;—**से गिरकर खजूर पर (में) अटकना** to fall from the frying pan into the fire;—**से बातें करना** to vie with the sky, to rise sky-high.

आसमानी a:smā:nɪ: (*a*) azure; sky blue; pertaining to the sky.

आसरा a:sra: (*nm*) reliance; shelter.

आसव a:sav (*nm*) nourishing and intoxicating liquor prepared from yeast or ferment.

आस/वन a:savān. (*nm*) distillation; ~**वित** distilled.

आसाइश a:sa:ish (*nf*) comfort; ease.

आसान a:sā:n (*a*) easy; simple; convenient.

आसानी a:s:ani: (*nf*) convenience, easiness; -**से जीतना** to win hands down, to win in a counter;—**से पछाड़ना** to knock a person's head off, to win hands down;—**से मार गिराना** to be at one in to fits.

आसाम a:sā:m (*nm*) see **असम.**

आसामी a:sa:mɪ: (*nm*) see **असामी.**

आसार a:sa:r (*nm*) symptom, sign; breadth of a wall;—**नज़र आना** some signs to be visible.

आसीन a:si:n (*a*) seated.

आसीस a:si:s (*nm*) see **आशिष.**

आसुत a:sut (*a*) distilled.

आसुरी a:suri: (*a*) demonic, demonlike; -**माया** demonic spell/trickery; —**विद्या** demonic skill/craft.

आसूचना a:su:chnā: (*nf*) intelligence (secret information).

आस्ति a:sti (*nf*) property, estate; asset.

आस्तिक a:stik (*nm*) a theist; (*a*) devout, having a religious disposition; ~**ता** theism, devoutness.

आस्तीन a:sti:n (*nf*) a sleeve;—**का साँप** a serpent in the bosom, a foe in the guise of a friend;—**चढ़ाना** to clear the docks for action, to get ready (for a fight); to be prepared; to menace/threaten; —**चढ़ाये** with (his) buckles up; —**में साँप पालना** to cherish a serpent in the bosom.

आस्थगन a:sthagān (*nm*) deferment.

आस्थगित a:sthagit (*a*) deferred.

आस्था a:stha: (*nf*) faith, belief; -**वान** having faith (in).

आस्थान a:sthā:n (*nm*) a base.

आस्पद a:spad (*nm*) place, seat, abode; worthy (of), fit (for) (gen. used as the last member in a compound word such as **विवादास्पद, श्रद्धास्पद, घृणास्पद**); surname.

आस्य a:ssy (*nm*) fascia.

आस्वाद a:ssva:d (*nm*) flavour, relish.

आस्वा/दन a:ssva:dān (*nm*) relishing, tasting; hence ~**दित** (*a*); ~**द्य** (*a*).

आह a:h (*int*) ah!; (*nf*) a sigh indicating deep agony;—**पड़ना** to be accursed; to be afflicted by curses; —**भरना** to heave a sigh;—**लेना** to provoke the curse of.

आहट a:haṭ (*nf*) noise, sound (as of footsteps);—**लेना** to be on the qui vive (for the approaching sound of footsteps, etc).

आहत a:hat (*a*) injured, wounded; offended.

आहरण a:harāṉ (*nm*) exaction; usurpation.

आहर्ता a:harta: (*nm*) exactor; usurper.

आहा a:ha: (*int*) aha !, well done,

alas ! (an expression of astonishment, joy, sorrow, etc).

आहार a:ha:r (*nm*) food. diet, victuals; ~**विज्ञान** dietetics;—**वैज्ञानिक** a dietitian; -**विहार** routine; physical activities and dealings; hence **आहारी**; —**व्यवहार में लज्जा क्या** ? fair exchange is no robbery; eat to your heart's content so as not to repent.

आहार्य a:ha:ry (*a*) consumable, eatables; artificial (as **अभिनय**).

आहिस्ता a:hista: (*adv*) slowly, gently, softly; -**आहिस्ता** slowly; gradually, by degrees.

आहुति a:huti (*nf*) an oblation or offering (esp. to a deity); a sacrifice.

आहूत a:hu:t (*a*) invited, summoned.

आह्ला/द a:hla:d (*nm*) delight, joy, mirth; ~**दित** delighted, full of joy; ~**दी** delightful; cheerful.

आह्वान a:hva:n (*nm*) a call, summons; invocation; citation;—**करना** to summon; to invoke.

इ

इ i—the third letter and the third vowel of the Devna:gri: alphabet.

इंगला ingla: (*nf*) one of the three (**इड़ा** i.e. **इंगला, पिंगला, सुषुम्ना**) important nerves described by the *Hathyogi:s*, better known as '**इड़ा**'.

इँगलिश ɪglish (*nf*) the English language; (*a*) English.

इँगलिस्ता/न ɪglista:n (*nm*) England; ~**नी** English.

इंगलेरन ɪnglerān (*nm*) angle iron.

इंगित ingit (*nm*) an indication, hint, sign; gesture; (*a*) indicated.

इंच inch (*nm*) (an) inch.

इंचार्ज incha:rj (*a*) in-charge.

इंजन injan (*nm*) an engine.

इंजीनिय/र inji:niyar (*nm*) an engineer; ~**री** engineering.

इंजील inji:l (*nm*) the New Testament.

इंजेक्शन injekshan (*nm*) an injection.

इंटरव्यू intarvyu: (*nm*) an interview.

इंडेंट indent (*nm*) an indent.

इंडेक्स indeks (*nm*) an index.

इंतक़ाम intqa:m (*nm*) revenge.

इंतक़ाल intqa:l (*nm*) death.

इंतख़ाब intkha:b (*nm*) selection; extract (from some official record).

इंतज़ाम intzā:m (*nm*) management arrangemt.

इंतज़ार intza:r (*nm*) wait; —**करना** to wait (for).

इंतहा intaha: (*nf*) limit, extremity; ~**ई** extreme, utmost; ~**पसंद** extremistic; an extremist.

इंदराज indara:j (*nm*) an entry.

इंदीवर indi:var (*nm*) a blue lotus.

इंदु indu (*nm*) see '**चंद्रमा**'.

इंद्र indr (*nm*) the king of the gods; the god of rains; ~**जाल** magic; trickery; ~**जालिक** a magician; trickster; —**का अखाड़ा** the court of Lord Indra; an assembly wherein beautiful damsels abound;—**की परी** a fairy.

इंद्रधनुष indr:dhanush (*nm*) a rainbow.

इंद्रवधू indr:vadhu: (*nf*) a scarlet-red velvety insect (also known as बीरबहूटी).

इंद्राणी indra:ṉī: (*nf*) Lord Indra's spouse.

इंद्रायन indra:yān (*nm*) a colocynth.

इंद्रिय indriy (*nf*) sense, an organ of sense or action; the generative organ; ~गत sensual, sensuous; ~गोचर perceptible; capable of being ascertained through the senses; ~जित lit. a master of the senses—one who is in full control of his senses; -ज्ञान knowledge acquired through the senses; -निग्रह self-control; control over one's sensual pleasures or appetites; ~लोलुप one who is subserviant to sensual pleasures and appetites; -सुख sensual pleasure; ० वाद sensualism; इन्द्रियों को बस में करना to restrain one's sensual impulses, to attain self-control.

इंद्रियातीत indriya:ti:t (*a*) transcending the senses; trans-sensual.

इंद्रियार्थ indriya:rth (*nm*) an object of sense (as sound, smell etc.); anything that excites the senses.

इंद्रियास/क्ति indriya:sakti (*nf*) sensuality; attachment to sensual pleasures; hence ~क्त (*a*).

इंधन indhān (*nm*) fuel.

इंधरौड़ा indhraura: (*nm*) a fuel-store.

इंश्योरेंस inshyorens (*nm*) an insurance; -कंपनी an insurance company.

इंसा/न insā:n (*nm*) a human being, man; ~नी human, humane; —इंसान न रहे तो उससे हैवान अच्छा the more I see of men, the more I love dogs; —ग़लती का पुतला है to err is human.

इंसानियत insā:niyat (*nf*) humanity; human qualities; —का तकाजा the demand of humanity/humaneness.

इंसाफ़ insa:f (*nm*) justice, justness, equity; ~पसंद just and fair, having a keen sense of justness; hence ~पसंदी.

इंस्पेक्टर inspektar (*nm*) an inspector.

इक ik—an allomorph of एक used as the first member in numerous compound words; ~तार monotonous; uniform; ~लौता only (son); sole.

इकट्ठा ikaṭṭha: (*a*) collected, gathered; (*adv*) together, in one lot.

इकतरफ़ा iktarfa: (*a*) ex parte, unilateral; —डिग्री exparte decree.

इकतरा iktara: (*nm*) intermittent fever attacking the patient every alternate day.

इकतारा ikta:ra: (*nm*) one-stringed musical instrument.

इकतालीस ikta:li:s (*a*) forty-one; (*nm*) the number forty-one.

इकत्तीस ikatti:s (*a*) thiry-one; (*nm*) the number thirty-one.

इकन्नी ikannī: (*nf*) one-anna coin (no longer in currency).

इक़बा/ल iqba:l (*nm*) prosperity, good fortune; prestige; confession; ~ली गवाह an approver; ~ले-जुर्म pleading guilty, confession of crime.

इकमुहाँ ikmuhā: (*a*) unifacial, having one mouth.

इक़रार iqra:r (*nm*) an agreement; consent; promise; bond.

इक़रारनामा iqra:rnā:mā: (*nm*) an agreement (in writing).

इकलाई ikla:i: (*nf*) a fine variety of cotton *sa:ri:*.

इकल्ला ikalla: (*a*) alone.

इकसठ iksaṭh (*a*) sixty-one; (*nm*) the number sixty-one.

इकसार iksa:r (*a*) uniform; even.

इकहत्तर ikhattar (*a*) seventy-one; (*nm*) the number seventy-one.

इकहरा ikehra:(*a*)single, single-folded; lean and thin.

इकाई ika:i: (*nf*) a unit, the unit's place in numeration.

इका/र ika:r (*nm*) the vowel i (इ) an its sound; ~**रांत** (a word) ending in i (इ).

इकोतर ikotar (*a*) one more (than).

इक्का ikka: (*nm*) a small one-horse carriage; an ace (in the game of cards); hence **इक्की** (*nf*).

इक्का-दुक्का ikka:-dukka: (*a*) one or two, very few; rare.

इक्की(क्कि)स ikki:(i)s (*a*) tweny-one; (*nm*) the number twenty-one;—**होना** to be superior (to), to excel.

इक्यानवे ikkya:nve (*a*) ninety-one; (*nm*) the number ninety-one

इक्यावन ikkya:van (*a*) fiifty-one (*nm*) the number fifty-one.

इक्यासी ikkya:si: (*a*) eighty-one; (*nm*) the number eighty-one.

इख़राजात ikhra:ja:t (*nm*) expenses; expenditure.

इख़्तिया/र ikhtiya:r (*nm*) see **अख़्तियार**; hence ~**री** (*a*).

इच्छा ichchha: (*nf*) desire, wish; will, animus; -**पत्र** a will; -**मृत्यु** death at will;—**दबाना** to suppress a wish.

इच्छित ichchhit (*a*) desired; willed.

इच्छु ichchhu —a suffix denoting the sense of a wisher, one who wishes (as **शुभेच्छु**).

इच्छुक ichchhuk (*a*) desirous; willing.

इजरा (य) ijra: (y) (*nf*) issue (of a decree); execution.

इजलास ijla:s (*nm*) court; bench.

इज़हार izha:r(*nm*) expression, manifestation.

इजाज़त ija:zat (*nf*) permission.

इज़ाफ़ा iza:fa: (*nm*) augmentation, addition; increase.

इज़ारबंद iza:rbānd (*nm*) a lace used as belt.

इजा/रा ija:ra: (*nm*) monopoly; ~**रेदार** a monopoly-holder, monopolist; ~**रेदारी** monopoly; monopoly holding.

इज़्ज़त izzat (*nf*) prestige; honour; respect; —**उतारना/बिगाड़ना/लेना** to insult, to put to disgrace; to humiliate;—**ख़ाक/धूल/मिट्टी में मिला देना** to lay one's honour in the dust;—**खोना/गँवाना** to be disgraced, to lose one's honour or dignity; —**देना** to confer dignity or honour (on); to lose honour;—**पर आँच आना** one's honour to be in jeopardy; —**पर हाथ डालना** to try to violate the chastity/honour of;— **बेचना** to barter/sell off one's honour; —**में फ़र्क आना,—में बट्टा लगना** to have one's reputation or character sullied;—**लूटना** to make a criminal assault on; to ravish; to put to disgrace.

इज़्ज़तदार izzatda:r (*a*) respectable; reputed as honest and decent.

इठलाना ithla:nā: (*v*) to act affectedly, to assume swaggering airs.

इडा, इड़ा ida:, ira: (*nf*) see **इंगला**; the earth; speech.

इतना itnā: (*a*) this much, so much; —**बुरा नहीं जितना कहते हैं** the devil is not so black as he is painted; —**सा मुँह रह जाना** to feel small —**इतने में** in the meantime, in the meanwhile.

इतमीनान itmi:nā:n (*nm*) conviction, assurance; trust, confidence.;—**का** trustworthy.

इतर itar (*a*) other, different.

इतराना itra:nā: (*v*) to assume an air of exaltation, to behave in a self-conceited manner.

इतवार itva:r (*nm*) Sunday.

इतस्ततः itastatah (*ind*) here and there.

इति iti (*nf*) end, conclusion; (*ind*) a word denoting conclusion.

इति कृतम् iti kritam —Q.E.F.

इति/वृत्त itivritt (*nm*) a narrative; chronicle, an annal; ~**वृत्तात्मक** narrative, abounding in narration;

hence~वृत्तात्मकता (*nf*).

इति सिद्धम् iti siddham--Q.E.D.

इतिहास itiha:s (*nm*) history; ~कार a historian; ~वेत्ता a scholar of history.

इत्तफ़ा/क़ ittafa:q (*nm*) coincidence; chance; ~क़न by chance; ~क़िया chance; accidental.

इत्तला ittala: (*nm*) information; notice; ~नामा notice.

इत्तहाद ittaha:d (*nm*) unity, union.

इत्यादि, ~क ittya:di, ~k (*ind*) etcetera, so on and so forth.

इत्र ittr (*nm*) perfume; scent; essence; ~दान scent-case; ~फ़रोश a perfumer; ~साज़ a perfumer.

इदम् idām (*pro*) this; —इत्थम् it is like this.

इधर idhar (*adv*) this side, this way; here; -उधर here and there; ० करना to shilly-shally; to throw into disorder or confusion; to disarrange; -उधर की random (fact etc.); -उधर की हाँकना to beat about the bush; to gossip; —की उधर लगाना to indulge in backbiting; to create strife; —की दुनिया उधर हो जाना to have an impossibility materialised; —कुआँ उधर खाई between the devil and the deep sea, between the Scylla and the Charybdis; —या उधर this way or that; —से उधर करना to turn topy-turvy; to displace.

इन in (*pro*) these; ~को to these.

इनकम inkām (*nf*) income; -टैक्स income-tax.

इनक़लाब inqala:b (*nm*) revolution, radical change; —जिन्दाबाद long live revolution !; इनक़लाबी revolutionary.

इनकार inka:r (*nm*) refusal; denial; disavowal.

इनफ़्लुएंज़ा influenza: (*nm*) influenza.

इनाम inā:m (*nm*) prize, reward, award; -इकराम tips, gifts and presents.

इनायत inā:yat (*nf*) favour, obligation; —करना/फ़रमाना to favour, to grant.

इने-गिने ine-gine (*a*) very few, selected few.

इन्हें inhē: (*pro*) see इनको.

इफ़रात ifra:t (*nf*) abundance, plenty.

इबादत iba:dat (*nf*) adoration, worship; ~ख़ाना/गाह a place of worship, mosque.

इबार/त iba:rat (*nf*) text; writing, word; ~ती textual, pertaining to the text; written.

इब्तिदा ibtida: (*nf*) beginning, commencement.

इमदा/द imda:d (*nf*) aid, help; ~दी aided.

इमरती imarti: (*nf*) a typical indian sweet.

इमला imla: (*nf*) a dictation (matter written at somebody's instance); —लिखना to take dictation.

इमली imli: (*nf*) tamarind.

इमाम ima:m (*nm*) a religious leader.

इमामदस्ता ima:mdasta: (*nm*) an iron mortar and pounder.

इमार/त ima:rat (*nf*) building, structure; edifice; ~ती pertaining to construction, building.

इम्तहान imtaha:n (*nm*) examination, test.

इयत्ता iyatta: (*nf*) limit, boundary; quantity.

इरा ira: (*nf*) the earth; speech.

इरा/दा ira:da: (*nm*) intention, idea; ~दतन wilfully, deliberately; —छोड़देना/तर्क कर देना to throw up one's cards, to give up one's idea/plan.

इर्द-गिर्द ird-gird (*adv*) around, about, nearby.

इलज़ाम ilza:m (*nm*) allegation, accusation, charge.

इलहा/म ilha:m (*nm*) revelation; inspiration; ~**मी** inspired.

इला ila: (*nf*) see **इंगला/इड़ा**.

इला/क़ा ila:qa: (*nm*) area; sphere; district, zone, region, territory, range; locality; ~**क़ावार** areawise, zonewise; ~**केदार** an ilaqedar.

इलाज ila:j (*nm*) treatment; remedy, cure.

इलायची ila:yachi: (*nf*) cardamom; ~**दाना** sweet and small round balls of sugar containing cardamom-seeds within;—**बाँटना** lit. to distribute cardamoms—to invite to a marriage ceremony and feast (as per Muslim tradition).

इलाही ila:hi: (*int.*, *nm*) O God !; God, Almighty.

इल्तिजा iltija: (*nf*) a request, entreaty.

इल्म ilm (*nm*) knowledge, learning; **-ए-अदब** poetics; **इल्मी** academic, educational.

इल्लत illat (*nf*) botheration; malady; addiction to vice;**–पालना/-लगाना** to be addicted to (vice etc.); to own up a botheration.

इल्ली illi: (*nf*) a caterpillar.

इशा/रा isha:ra: (*nm*) sign, signal; hint, indication; gesture; ~**रेबाजी** gesticulation; winking (at); ० **करना** to tip a wink (to); to express through gestures or winks; **इशारे पर चलने वाला** a horse going well up to bridles; **इशारों पर नाचना, किसी के** to dance to the tune/pipe of.

इश्क़ ishq (*nm*) love; amour; ~**बाज़** a rake, amorously disposed, falling frequently in love; hence ~**बाज़ी** (*nf*); —**मजाज़ी** mundane love; —**हक़ीक़ी** transcendental love;—**लड़ाना** to make love; to make amorous advances.

इश्तहार ishtaha:r (*nm*) advertisement; poster.

इष्ट isht̤ (*a*) adored; favoured, favourite; ~**तम** optimum; ० **आयु** optimum age; ~**देव** a household diety; **-सिद्धि** expediency.

इस is (*pro*) this, it; —**कान से सुनना उस कान से निकाल देना** in at one ear and out at the other;—**हाथ दे उस हाथ ले** early sow, early mow.

इसपा/त ispa:t (*nm*) steel; ~**ती** made of steel, steel; ~**ती डिब्बा** all steel coach.

इसरार isra:r (*nm*) entreaty, solicitation; insistence.

इसला/म islā:m (*nm*) the religion of the Mohammedans; ~**मी** Islamic.

इसलाह isla:h (*nm*) reform; correction.

इसे ise (*pro*) to this, to it.

इस्तगा(ग़ा)सा istaga: (ga:)sa: (*nm*) prosecution, institution of criminal proceedings in a court of law.

इस्तमरारी istāmara:ri:(*a*) permanent; —**बंदोबस्त** permanent settlement.

इस्तिरी istiri: (*nf*) a smoothing iron, press.

इस्तीफ़ा isti:fa: (*nm*) resignation.

इस्तेमाल istema:l (*nm*) use; application.

इस्म ism (*nm*) name; noun; **-ए-शरीफ़** good name; **इस्मे शरीफ़, आपका** may I know your name, please ?

इह ih (*ind*) here, in this world.

इहलीला ihli:la: (*nf*) life in this world, mundane life;**–समाप्त होना** to breathe one's last, to pass away.

इह/लोक ihlok (*nm*) this world, the present world; ~**लौकिक** worldly, mundane.

ई i: —the fourth vowel and the fourth letter of the Devna:gri: alphabet.

इंगुर ɪ:gur (*nm*) cinnabar, minium.

ईंट i:ṭ (*nf*) a brick; ~**कारी** brick-work;—**का घर मिट्टी कर देना** to reduce to poverty and misery from a state of affluence and plenty; —**का जवाब पत्थर से देना** to pay back in the same coin with interest; —**मारना, गुड़ दिखाकर** to cause injury after raising high hopes;—**की मस्जिद अलग बनाना, डेढ़ या ढाई** (ironical) to blow one's own trumpet; to have peculiar/uncommon ways;—**से ईंट बजाना** to raze (a building, city etc.), to bring to ruination.

इंडुरी ɪ:ḍuri: (*nf*) a roll or ring of cloth or straw etc. used to facilitate carrying of a burden on one's head or for placing vessels or pots upon.

ईंधन ɪ:dhān (*nm*) fuel, firewood.

ईका/र i:ka:r (*nm*) the vowel i: (ई) and its sound; ~**रांत** a word ending in i: (ई).

ईख i:kh (*nf*) sugarcane.

ईजाद i:ja:d (*nf*) an invention;—**करना** to invent.

ईति i:ti (*nf*) calamity, distress, one of the six causes for crop-ruin; -**भीति** dread and distress.

ईथर i:thar (*nm*) ether.

ईद i:d (*nf*) a Muslim festival; ~**गाह** a place of assembly for offering Id-prayers;—**का चाँद होना** to be seen once in a blue moon; to make a rare appearance; —**के पीछे टर्र** a day after the fair, to kiss the hare's foot; **ईदी** pertaining to Id; a present on the occasion of Id.

ई/प्सा i:psa: (*nf*) desire, longing; ~**प्सित** desired; longed for; hence **ईप्सु** (*a*).

ईमान i:mā:n (*nm*) faith, belief; integrity; —**का सौदा** fair dealing; —**का ख़ून करना** to kill one's conscience; to barter away one's integrity; —**की कहना** to speak out the truth;—**खोना** to lose integrity; —**ठिकाने न रहना** to allow one's scruples to be thrown to the wind, to go morally astray; —**डिगना** to have one's integrity shaken; —**बिगड़ना,—में फ़र्क आना** to prove faithless; —**बेचना** to sell one's conscience; —**लाना, (पर)** to have faith in.

ईमानदार i:mā:nda:r (*a*) honest; faithful; having integrity.

ईमानदारी i:mā:nda:ri: (*nf*) honesty; faithfulness; integrity.

ईर्ष्या i:rshya: (*nf*) jealousy; ~**लु** jealous; ~**लुता** jealousness.

ईश i:sh (*nm*) God; Master; ~**कोण** the north-eastern corner; ~**ता/त्व** Godhood; mastership.

ईशान i:shā:n (*nm*);—**कोण** the north-eastern corner.

ईश्वर i:shvar (*nm*) God; ~**केंद्रवाद** theocentricism; ~**तंत्रवाद** theological determinism; -**निंदा** blasphemy; -**निषेध** denial of God, atheism: ~**निष्ठ** a theist; ~**वाद**

theism; ~वादी theist; theistic; ईश्वराधीन resting on God's will; —न करे God forbid !, Heaven forbid !

ईश्वरीय i:shvari:y (*a*) Godly, divine; —संदेश divine message.

ईषत् i:shat (*a*) a little, partly; ~विवृत partly open; ~संवृत partly close; ~स्पृष्ट partly stopped; a semi-vowel (in Grammar).

ईसबगोल i:sabgol (*nm*) a medicinal plant and its seeds.

ईसवी i:svi: (*a*) pertaining to Christ; Christian;—सन् christian era.

ईसा i:sa: (*nm*) Jesus Christ.

ईसाई i:sa:i: (*nm*) a Christian, follower of the Christian faith.

उ

उ u—the fifth letter and the fifth vowel of the Devna:gri: alphabet.

उँगली ūgli: (*nf*) a finger; —उठाना to reproach; to point a censuring finger;—करना to harass;—पकड़कर पहुँचा पकड़ना to aspire for more and more exploitation of some one, to endeavour to draw more and more benefit out of some one; —रखना to point out a flaw; —नचाना to jeer at (a person); —पर नचाना to twist or turn around one's little finger, to make somebody dance to one's tune; —लगाना to render absolutely nominal help.

उंचास uṇcha:s (*a* and *nm*) see उनंचास.

उँडेलना ūdelnā: (*y*) to pour (into).

उँह ūh (*ind*) an extralinguistic sound expressing refusal, contempt, rejection, agony etc.; pshaw !

उऋण urin̲ (*a*) debt-free;—होना to pay off a debt, to be quits; to fulfil an obligation.

उकठना ukaṭhnā: (*v*) to wither away, to dry up.

उकड़ूँ ukṛū: (*nm*) a squatting posture; —बैठना to squat.

उक/ताना ukta:nā: (*v*) to get bored or tired, to be sick (of); ~ताहट boredom, weariness.

उकसना ukas:nā: (*v*) to rise, to come up, to emerge.

उकसाना uksa:nā:(*v*) to raise; to incite, to provoke, to instigate.

उक़ाब uqa:b (*nm*) an eagle.

उका/र uka:r (*nm*) the vowel u (उ) and its sound; ~रांत a word ending in u (उ).

उकेरना ukernā: (*v*) to engrave; to carve.

उकौना ukaunā: (*nm*) the longings of a pregnant woman.

उक्त ukt (*a*) said, stated, mentioned; -प्रत्युक्त statement and counter-statement.

उक्ति ukti (*nf*) saying, statement; dictum;—वैचित्र्य ingenuity of expression.

उखड़ना ukhaṛnā: (*v*) to be uprooted, to be struck off; to be dislodged; to be dislocated; to be out of spirits, to be out of sorts; उखड़ा-उखड़ा out of sorts, in low spirits; उखड़ी-उखड़ी बात करना to talk in a disinterested and disjointed manner, to exhibit a sense of diffidence in one's utterance.

उखाड़/ना ukha:ṛnā: (*v*) to eradicate, to uproot, to dig out; to strike off; to dislocate, to dislodge; —**फेंकना** to dislodge; to root out, to eradicate.

उखाड़-पछाड़ ukha:ṛ-pachha:ṛ (*nf*) ado; indiscriminate wirepulling, pulls and pushes, manoeuvrings.

उगना ugnā: (*v*) to grow; to germinate; to spring up; to rise.

उगलना ugalnā: (*v*) to spit out; to disgorge, to eject; to talk out.

उगालदान uga:ldā:n (*nm*) a spittoon.

उगाहना uga:hnā: (*v*) to realise, to collect.

उगाही uga:hi: (*nf*) realisation, collection; the amount realised or collected.

उग्र uggr (*a*) violent, fierce; wrathful; radical; sharp; ~**वाद** radicaism, extremism; ~**वादी** an extremist, radicalist; radical-minded.

उग्रह(ण) uggrah(ān) (*nm*) de-eclipse, cessation of an eclipse.

उघड़ना ugharnā: (*v*) to be uncovered, to be exposed; to be denuded.

उघाड़ना ugha:ṛnā: (*v*) to uncover, to expose; to bare.

उचंती uchānti: (*a*) in suspense, not finally accounted for; —**खाता** suspense account.

उचकना uchaknā: (*v*) to stand on tiptoe; to be extra-curious.

उचक्का uchakkā: (*v*) a swindler, a pilferer; ~**पन** swindling, roguery.

उचटना uchaṭnā: (*v*) to withdraw from, to be weary of, to feel dejected, to be ennuied (as **जी**—); to be interrupted (as **नींद**—); to rebound (as **गोली**—).

उचाट ucha:ṭ (*a*) affected by ennui; mentally wearied; (*nm*) ennui, mental weariness.

उचित uchit (*a*) proper, right; suitable; reasonable, fair; advisable; appropriate.

उच्च uchch (*a*) high, tall; lofty; elevated; ~**ता** altitude, elevation, loftiness.

उच्चरित uchcharit (*a*) uttered, pronounced, spoken.

उच्चाकांक्षा uchcha:kā:ṅksha: (*nf*) noble/high ambition.

उच्चाटन uchcha:ṭān (*nm*) causing (a person) to quit his occupation by means of magical incantation.

उच्चार uchcha:r (*nm*) utterance, speech; pronunciation.

उच्चार/ण uchcha:rān (*nm*) pronunciation; articulation, utterance; ~**ण-स्थान** place of articulation; ~**णीय** pronouncable, utterable; also **उच्चार्य** (*a*).

उच्चारित uchcha:rit (*a*) spoken, uttered; pronounced.

उच्चित्र uchchitr (*nm*) a relief (a projected moulding or carving etc.).

उच्छ/लन uchchhalān (*nm*) rebound, act of rebounding; hence ~**लित** (*a*).

उच्छिन्न uchchhinn (*a*) cut off, uprooted.

उच्छिष्ट uchchhishṭ (*a*) leaving; remainder (esp. of food etc.), residual, waste; ~**भोजी** one who sustains on leavings.

उच्छू uchchhu: (*nf*) choking of the throat (by the stucking up of food etc.); a feeling like vomitting.

उच्छृंखल uchchhraṅkhal (*a*) licentious, unrestrained; impertinent; indisciplined, disorderly; ~**ता** licentiousness; impertinence.

उच्छेद uchchhed (*nm*) deletion; cutting off; uprooting.

उच्छेदन uchchhedān (*nm*) cutting off, rooting out, uprooting.

उच्छ्व/सन uchchhwasan (*nm*) expiration, exhalation; hence ~सित (*a*).

उच्छ्वा/स uchchhwa:s (*nm*) exhalation, aspiration; sigh; chapter (of a book), hence ~सित (*a*); ~सी (*a*).

उच्चैःश्रवा uchchaishrava: (*nm*) the mythological horse belonging to Indra—chief of the gods; (*a*) hard of hearing.

उछरना uchharnā: (*v*) to emerge (out of water or any other liquid).

उछल-कूद uchhal-ku:d (*nf*) gambol, hopping and jumping; jumping about, frisk.

उछलना uchhalnā: (*v*) to leap, to jump, to spring; to gambol; to rebound (as a ball).

उछाल uchha:l (*nf*) jump, leap; rebound; throw, toss.

उछालना uchha:lnā: (*v*) to toss, to throw up.

उछाह uchha:h (*nm*) enthusiasm; aspiration.

उछीर uchhi:r (*nf*) scantiness of crowd or assembly.

उजड़ना ujaṛnā: (*v*) to be deserted or devastated; to be ruined or destroyed.

उजड्ड ujaḍḍ (*a*) boorish, rude, uncivil, ruffian; ~पन/~पना boorishness, rudeness, incivility.

उजबक ujbak (*a*) foolish, idiotic, stupid; hence ~पन (*nm*).

उजरत ujrat (*nf*) wages, remuneration; -दर piece rate; **उजरती काम** job work, piece work.

उजला ujla: (*a*) clean: bright; white; —मुँह करना to add a feather to one's cap; to free from slander/blot or infamy.

उजागर uja:gar (*a*) brilliant; renowned; well-known; manifest.

उजाड़ uja:ṛ (*a*) deserted, desolate, devastated; barren.

उजाड़ना uja:ṛnā: (*v*) to ruin, to destroy or devastate, to render desolate.

उजाला uja:la: (*nm*) light, brightness, splendour; (*a*) bright, shining, luminous;—पाख the bright half of a month, the fifteen days of a moon's increase.

उज्ज्व/ल ujjval (*a*) bright; splendid; clear; radiant; hence ~लता (*nf*); ~लन (*nm*), ~लित (*a*).

उज्र ujjr (*nm*) objection; ~दार one who files an objection in a court of law; ~दारी an objection filed in a court of law.

उझकना ujhaknā: (*v*) to peep down, to raise oneself on tip-toe, to have a view across a wall, parapet etc.

उठँगना uṭhāgnā: (*v*) to recline against something; to assume a recumbent posture.

उठँगाना uṭhāgā:nā: (*v*) to shut the leaves of a door etc. (without bolting); to lean an object against something.

उठ/ना uṭhnā: (*v*) to raise; to get up; to be rented out; to pass away, to expire; —जाना to die; to come to an end; **उठती उम्र** the age of emergent youth; **उठती जवानी** blossoming youth; **उठते-बैठते** each and every moment; all the time; ~ना-बैठना close association intimate relationship.

उठाईगी/र, ~रा uṭha:i:gi:r, ~ra: (*nm*) a pilferer, a petty thief; ~री pilferage.

उठान uṭhā:n (*nm*) build; ascent, elevation; rise, coming up; blossoming youth.

उठाना uṭhā:nā: (*v*) to raise, to lift up; to wake up; to rent out; to bear; to remove; **उठा न रखना, बात/प्रयत्न (आदि)** to leave no stone unturned, to spare no effort; **उठा रखना** to postpone, to put off.

उड़द uṛad (*nf*) horse-bean, black gram.

उड़न uṛān—an allomorph of **उड़ना** used as the first member in compound words; ~**खटोला** a legendary flying cot; ~**छू होना** to disappear all of a sudden, to vanish; ~**झाईं** dodge, trickery; ~**दस्ता** a flying squad.

उड़/ना uṛnā: (*v*) to fly, to fade, to get dim; to vanish; to explode; —**आना** to come at a fast pace; —**चलना** to go flying or at a terrific speed; ~**ती ख़बर** an unconfirmed news, a rumour; ~**ती चिड़िया के पंख गिनना/पहचानना** to know the rook as he is seen.

उड़ाऊ uṛa:u: (*a*) extravagant, squandering; on the verge of a take off; -**खाऊ** a squanderer; squanderous; ~**पन** extravagance, squandering.

उड़ाका uṛa:ka: (*nm*) an aviator, flier.

उड़ाकू uṛa:ku: (*a*) flying, sky-going; capable of flying.

उड़ान uṛā:n (*nf*) a flight; sortie; ~**घाई** fraud, dodge; sortie; —**भरना** to make a flight; to make a flight of imagination; —**मारना** to put forth excuses; to hoodwink.

उड़ाना uṛa:nā: (*v*) to fly; to squander; to steal or kidnap; to explode, to blow away; **उड़ा देना** to blow the expense; to blow.

उड़िया uṛiya: (*nm*) the people of Orissa; (*nf*) the language of the state of Orissa (India).

उड़ीसा uṛi:sa: (*nm*) an eastern state of the Indian Union (also called **उत्कल**).

उड़ौहाँ uṛauhā: (*a*) ready to fly, on the verge of a take-off.

उड्डयन uḍḍayān (*nm*) aviation; flight; -**विभाग** department of aviation.

उड्डीन uḍḍi:n (*a*) in flight, air-borne.

उड्डीयमान uḍḍi:ymā:n (*a*) flying, air-borne.

उढ़काना uṛhka:nā: (*v*) to shut (the leaves of a door etc. without bolting).

उतना utnā: (*a*) that much, to that extent.

उतरन utrān (*nf*) second hand/old/worn-out clothes; cast-off clothing; also -**पुतरन** (*nf*).

उतरना utarnā: (*v*) to get down, to alight; to go down (as **बुख़ार**—); to come off or decay; to be dislocated (as **बाँह**—); to land, to disembark; to be off colour (as **चेहरा**—).

उतराई utra:i: (*nf*) tax for crossing a river; ferriage; unloading.

उतराना utra:nā: (*v*) to float.

उतान utā:n (*a*) supine, upright.

उतार uta:r (*nm*) descent; depreciation; fall; ebb-tide; down-gradient, falling gradient.

उतार-चढ़ाव uta:r-charha:v (*nm*) ups and downs, rise and fall, fluctuation; vicissitude, variation.

उतारन uta:rān (*nf*) see **उतरन**.

उतारना uta:rnā: (*v*) to bring down; to unload; to cause to disembark, dismount or descend; to dislocate; to copy; to take across.

उतारा uta:ra: (*nm*) the process of moving certain offerings overhead for delivering somebody possessed of an evil spirit; such offerings.

उतारू uta:ru: (*a*) bent upon, intent; dead set; ready for.

उतावला uta:vla: (*a*) rash, impatient; harum scarum.

उतावलापन uta:vla:pān (*nm*) rashness, impatience; hastiness.

उतावली uta:vli: (*nf*) haste; impatience.

उत् ut—a Sanskrit prefix denoting over, above, transgression, elevation, predominence etc.

उत्कंठा utkā<u>n</u>ṭha: (*nf*) curiosities; longing; craving; ardour.

उत्कंठित utkā<u>n</u>ṭhit (*a*) curious, keenly desirous; eager; longing (for).

उत्कट utkaṭ (*a*) excessive, keen, intense; gigantic; richly endowed with.

उत्कर्ष utkarsh (*nm*) exaltation, excellence; eminence; prosperity; hence ~क; उत्कर्षी (*a*).

उत्कल utkal (*nm*) ancient name of उड़ीसा (see).

उत्कीर्ण utki:r<u>n</u> (*a*) carved; worked out in relief; ~न inscribing in relief, engraving.

उत्कृष्ट utkrishṭ (*a*) excellent; eminent, outstanding; superior; ~ता excellence; eminence; superiority.

उत्केंद्र(क) utkendr(ak) (*a*) centrifugal; co-centric.

उत्कोच utkoch (*nm*) bribe, venality.

उत्क्रम, ~ण utkrām, ~ a<u>n</u> (*nm*) reversal.

उत्क्रांति utkrā:nti (*nf*) reversal; death.

उत्क्षिप्त utkshipt (*a*) ejected; thrown up or away.

उत्क्षेप(ण) utkshep (ā<u>n</u>) (*nm*) ejection; throwing up.

उत्खनन utkhanān (*nm*) digging; excavation.

उत्तप्त uttapt (*a*) burning; simmering; intensely excited; fermented; hence ~ता (*nf*).

उत्तम uttam (*a*) the best; excellent, good; ~ता excellence; —पुरुष first person.

उत्तमर्ण uttamar<u>n</u> (*nm*) a creditor.

उत्तर uttar (*nm*) answer, reply; north; later; —कांस्य युग late bronze age; ~जीवित survived, surviving; ~जीविता, ~जीवित्व survival, survivorship; ~जीवी, surviving; survivor; survived; —पाषाण युग neolithic age; —प्रत्युत्तर reply and counter-reply, argument.

उत्तरदान uttardā:n (*nm*) bequest, bequeathing.

उत्तरदायित्व uttarda:yitv (*nm*) responsibility; obligation; onus; accountability.

उत्तरदायी uttarda:yi: (*a*) responsible; answerable, accountable.

उत्तरप्रदेश uttarpradesh (*nm*) the biggest Indian state in terms of population, situated in the northern part of the country, lying between Delhi, Haryana, Madhya Pradesh and Bihar.

उत्तरभोगी uttarbhogi: (*nm*) a reversioner,

उत्तरवर्ती uttarvarti: (*a*) subsequent; later; northern.

उत्तराखंड uttara:khā<u>n</u>ḍ (*nm*) the northern part of India lying in proximity with the Himalayas.

उत्तराधिका/र uttara:dhika:r (*nm*) inheritance; succession, right of succession; ~री inheritor, heir, successor.

उत्तरायण uttara:yā<u>n</u> (*nm*) the summer soltice when the sun is on the north of equator.

उत्तरार्ध uttara:rdh (*a*) the latter half.

उत्तरी uttari: (*a*) northern; —ध्रुव the north pole, arctic.

उत्तरीय uttari:y (*a*) northern; (*nm*) the upper or outer garment.

उत्तरोत्तर uttarottar (*a* and *adv*) progressive, progressively; successive, successively; hence ~ता (*nf*).

उत्तल uttal (*a*) convex; ~ता convexity.

उत्तान utta:n (*a*) supine, upright.

उत्ताप utta:p (*nm*) excessive heat; ferment; distress; affliction.

उत्ताल utta:l (*a*) high; violent; plentiful; hence ~ता (*nf*).

उत्तीर्ण utti:rn̲ (*a*) passed, got through (an examination).

उत्तुंग uttuṅg (*a*) high, lofty.

उत्तेजक uttejak (*a*) provocative; exciting; stimulating; — **पदार्थ** excitant, stimulant.

उत्तेजन uttejan (*nm*) provocation; stimulation; excitement.

उत्तेजना uttejnā: (*nf*) provocation; stimulation; excitement; ~**जनक/प्रद** provocative; stimulating; exciting; ~**पूर्ण** provocative, full of provocation; **उत्तेजित** provoked; excited; stimulated; ० **करना** to provoke: to excite; to stimulate.

उत्तेजनीयता uttejni:yta: (*nf*) excitability; provocability.

उत्तोलन uttolān (*nm*) weighing; act of raising; a lever.

उत्थान utthā:n (*nm*) rise (up), act of rising; -**पतन** rise and fall; **उत्थित** risen (up).

उत्थाप/न uttha:pān (*nm*) raising up, elevating; elevation; ~**क** (*a*) elevating; (*nm*) an elevator.

उत्पत्ति utpatti (*nf*) production, produce; birth; origin.

उत्पन्न utpann (*a*) produced; born; originated; —**करना** to produce; to procreate.

उत्पल utpal (*nm*) a (blue) lotus.

उत्पाटन utpa:tān (*nm*) uprooting; exterpating.

उत्पा/त utpa:t (*nf*) mischief, confusion, nuisance; ~**ती** mischievous, miscreant; naughty.

उत्पा/द utpa:d (*nm*) product(s), yield, produce; also ~**द्य** (*nm*).

उत्पादक utpa:dak (*nm*) producer; originator; ~**ता** productivity, fecundity, fertility.

उत्पा/दन utpa:dān (*nm*) production, product, produce; out-turn, output; reproduction; ~**दित** produced; ~**दिता** productivity.

उत्पीड़क utpi:ṛak (*nm*) oppressor; (*a*) oppressive.

उत्पीड़न utpi:ṛān (*nm*) oppression; persecution; harassment.

उत्पीड़ित utpi:ṛit (*a*) oppressed; harassed; persecuted.

उत्प्रवास utprava:s (*nm*) emigration.

उत्प्रेक्षा utpreksha: (*nf*) poetical fancy (a figure of speech).

उत्प्रेरक utprerak (*nm*) a catalyser, catalytic agent.

उत्प्रेरण utpreran̲ (*nm*) catalysis, activation.

उत्प्लावक utpla:vak (*nm*) a floater.

उत्फुल्ल utphull (*a*) blossomed; delighted, in high spirits; hence ~ता (*nf*).

उत्संबोधन utsambodhān̲ (*nm*) apostrophe.

उत्स uts (*nm*) a fountain; spring, source.

उत्सर्ग utsarg (*nm*) sacrifice, abandonment.

उत्सर्जन utsarjān (*nm*) excretion; emission, abandoning.

उत्सव utsav (*nm*) festival, celebration; festivity.

उत्साह utsa:h (*nm*) enthusiasm, zeal; ~**पूर्ण** full of beans, in high spirits, as keen as mustard; —**भंग करना** to demoralise; ~**वर्धक** encouraging; ~**वर्धन** encouragement; —**की लहर दौड़ना** a wave of enthusiasm to spread out, to be infected by a sense of enthusiasm.

उत्साही utsa:hi: (*a*) enthusiastic; (*nm*) an enthusiast.

उत्सुक utsuk (*a*) curious, eager, keen; ~**ता** curiosity, eagerness, anxiousness.

उथल-पुथल uthal-puthal (*nf*) upheaval, turmoil; —**मचाना** to cause an upheaval.

उथला uthla: (*a*) shallow; ~**पन** shallowness.

उदंत udānt (*nm*) news, report.

उदधि udadhi (*nm*) ocean, sea.

उदय uday (*nm*) rising; rise, ascent; emergence; (*fig.*) prosperity.

उदयाचल udaya:chal (*nm*) the mythological mountain from behind which the sun is supposed to rise.

उदयास्त udaya:st (*nm*) rise and fall, ascent and descent; rising and setting.

उदर udar (*nm*) abdomen, stomach; **-वृद्धि** dropsy; **~स्थ** devoured, swallowed, eaten; abdominal; **उदरीय** abdominal.

उदात्त uda:tt (*a*) sublime, lofty; acute (accent); hence **~ ता** (*nf*).

उदार uda:r (*a*) generous, liberal; magnificent; **~ चेता**, **~ मनस्क**, **~मना** noble-minded, magnanimous, open-minded; **~हृदय** liberal, noble-minded, open-minded; hence **~हृदयता** (*nf*).

उदारता uda:rta: (*nf*) magnanimity, generosity; liberality; **~वाद** liberalism; **~वादी** liberal; a liberalist.

उदास uda:s (*a*) sad, dejected, gloomy.

उदासना uda:snā: (*v*) to wrinkle up (the bedding, bedsheet, etc.).

उदासी uda:si: (*nf*) sadness, dejection, melancholy.

उदासीन uda:si:n (*a*) indifferent; disinterested, non-chalant; **~ ता** indifference; disinterestedness; non-chalance.

उदा/हरण uda:harān (*nm*) an example, instance; illustration; **~हृत** illustrated; exemplified.

उदाहरणात्मक uda:harāna:tmāk (*a*) exemplary; illustrative.

उदाहरणार्थ uda:harāna:rth (*ind*) for instance, for example, e.g.

उदित udit (*a*) risen, ascended; emerged.

उदी/ची udi:chi: (*nf*) the north (direction); **~च्य** belonging to the north, northern; an inhabitant of the north.

उदीयमान udi:ymā:n (*a*) rising, ascending.

उद्गम udgām (*nm*) origin, fountainhead, source; rising, coming up; **~न** rising, coming up.

उद्गार udga:r (*nm*) (expression of) inner feelings/sentiments.

उद्गीत udgi:t (*nm*) an anthem.

उद्घा/टन udgha:ṭān (*nm*) inauguration, release; uncovering; hence **~टित** (*a*).

उद्घोष udghosh (*nm*) proclamation.

उद्घोषक udghoshak (*nm*) a proclaimer; herald, announcer.

उद्घोषण udghoshan (*nm*), **~णा** na: (*nf*) proclamation, announcement.

उद्दंड uddānd, (*a*) contumelious, insolent, impertinent; rude; rebellious; hence **~ता** (*nf*).

उद्दाम uddā:m (*a*) unrestrained, unbound; violent, impetuous; hence **~ता** (*nf*).

उद्दिष्ट uddishṭ (*a*) aimed at, directed; desired, intended for.

उद्दीपक uddi:pak (*nm*) stimulant; (*a*) stimulating; exciting.

उद्दी/पन uddi:pān (*nm*) stimulus, stimulation; provocation; incandescence; **~पित** see **~प्त**.

उद्दीप्त uddi:pt (*a*) stimulated; provoked; incandescent.

उद्दीप्ति uddi:pti (*nf*) incandescence; stimulation.

उद्देश्य uddeshy (*nm*) object; purpose; motive; subject(in Grammar); end; **~वाद** teleology.

उद्धत uddhat (*a*) contumacious; haughty; ill-behaved; boorish; impudent; hence **~ता** (*nf*); **~मना** contumacious, haughty. impudent.

उद्धरण uddharān̲ (*nm*) quotation; citation; extract, extraction.

उद्धार uddha:r (*nm*) deliverance, salvation; redemption, riddance; restoration; uplift.

उद्धारक uddha:rak (*nm*) deliverer, saviour; redeemer; uplifter.

उद्धृत uddhrit (*a*) quoted, cited.

उद्बुद्ध udbuddh (*a*) awakened, alerted.

उद्बोधक udbodhak (*nm*) a teacher; one who awakens (through one's teachings).

उद्बोधन udbodhān (*nm*) awakening.

उद्भट udbhaṭ (*a*) powerful, extraordinary, eminent.

उद्भव udbhav (*nm*) birth; origin; coming into existence.

उद्भावक udbha:vak (*nm*) an originator; one who conceives an idea; inventor.

उद्भावन udbha:vān (*nm*) origination; imagination; invention; vision, conception.

उद्भावना udbha:vanā: (*nf*) idea, concept; imagination.

उद्भास udbha:s (*nm*) illumination, lustre; appearance.

उद्भासित udbha:sit (*a*) appeared, come forth; illuminated.

उद्भिज्ज udbhijj (*a*) sprouting from beneath the ground; (*nm*) vegetation.

उद्भूत udbhu:t (*a*) produced; born; emerged.

उद्भ्रांत udbhrā:nt (*a*) wandering; bewildered.

उद्यत uddyat (*a*) ready, prepared; hence ~**ता** (*nf*).

उद्यम uddyām (*nm*) enterprise; venture; exertion; diligence, ~**कर्ता** an entrepreneur.

उद्यमी uddyamī: (*nm*) an entrepreneur; (*a*) enterprising; diligent.

उद्यान uddyā:n (*a*) a garden; ~**विद्या** horticulture, gardening.

उद्यापन uddya:pān (*nm*) closing ceremony (of a religious performance).

उद्योग uddyog (*nm*) industry; labour, effort; –**धंधा** industry; ~**पति** an industrialist; ~**वाद** industrialism; **उद्योगी** industrious.

उद्योगी/करण uddyogi:karān̲ (*nm*) industrialisation; hence ~**कृत** (*a*).

उद्रेक uddrek (*nm*) overflow; abundance, preponderance, excess.

उद्विग्न uddvign (*a*) restless, troubled, unquiet; hence ~**ता** (*nf*).

उद्वे/ग uddveg (*nm*) restlessness, uneasiness, unquiet; hence ~ **गी** (*a*).

उद्वे/लन uddvelān (*nm*) turmoil; agitation; ~**लित** agitated, worked up.

उधड़ना udharṇā: (*v*) to be unsewn; to be ripped/opened out; to be untwisted; to be unrolled; to be unravelled; to be excoriated.

उधर udhar (*adv*) on that side, that way; —**से** from the other side, from that side; —**ही उधर** keeping away, excluding the speaker.

उधार udha:r (*nm*) borrowing; credit; loan; debt; —**खाता** credit account; —**खाना** to subsist on borrowings; —**खाए फिरना** bent on something, to be only too ready for something; ~**दाता** a lender.

उधेड़/ना udherṇā: (*v*) to unsew; to unravel; to open up; to unroll, to untwist; to excoriate; — **कर रख देना** to excoriate thoroughly, to inflict a thorough beating; to expose thoroughly, to uncover each and every secret.

उधेड़बुन udherbun (*nf*) lit. unpicking and weaving—hence, a process of indecisive, uneasy and constant reflection.

उनंचास unāṇcha:s (*a*) forty-nine; (*nm*) the number forty-nine.

उन un (*pvo*) those, the oblique plural form of **वह** (see); **उन्हीं पैरों लौट जाना** (said of person) to return without a stop/even a moment's pause.

उनचास uncha:s (*a*) see **उनंचास**.

उनताली(लि)स unta:li:(li)s (*a*) thirty-nine; (*nm*) the number thirty-nine.

उनती(ति)स, उनत्तीस unti:(ti)ṣ, unatti:s (*a*) twenty-nine; (*nm*) the number twenty-nine.

उनमना unmānā: (*a*) see **अनमना**.

उनवान unvā:n (*nm*) heading; title.

उनसठ unsaṭh (*a*) fifty-nine; (*nm*) the number fifty-nine.

उनहत्तर unhattar (*a*) sixty-nine; (*nm*) the number sixty-nine.

उनासी una:si: (*a*) see **उन्यासी**.

उनींदा unī:da: (*a*) sleepy, drowsy; dozing.

उन्नत unnāt (*a*) elevated; high; developed; lofty; improved.

उन्नति unnāti (*nf*) progress, rise; promotion; improvement, betterment; development.

उन्नतोदर unnātodar (*a*) convex.

उन्नमन unnamān (*nm*) (the act of) bending upwards; lifting up, raising; increase.

उन्नयन unnayān (*nm*) progress; development; uplift; elevation; **~वाद** meliorism.

उन्नाब unna:b (*nm*) the jujube tree and its fruit—*Rhamnus zizyphus*.

उन्नायक unnā:yak (*nm*) champion (of a cause); exponent; uplifter.

उन्निद्र unnidr (*a*) insomnolent; **—रोग** insomnia.

उन्नीस unni:s (*a*) nineteen; (*nm*) the number nineteen; **—बीस होना** to be slightly better or worse/more or less/superior or inferior; to be almost equal; **—होना** to be inferior, to be lower in rank, quality etc.

उन्मज्जन unmajjān (*nm*) emergence.

उन्मत्त unmātt (*a*) intoxicated; wild; crazy; hence **~ता** (*nf*); **—प्रलाप** mad/delirious utterances, disjointed and irrelevant talk, raving; **—होना** to be in a frenzy; to be hysterical; to run amuck.

उन्मद unmad (*a*) see **उन्मत्त**.

उन्माद unma:d (*nm*) hysteria, insanity; lunacy; mania; intoxication; rabidity; frenzy, intense passion; hence **~क** (*a*); **~ग्रस्त**(*a*); **~न** (*nm*); **उन्मादी** insane; frenzied; hysterical.

उन्मी/लन unmī:lān (*nm*) opening (of eyes); blooming; hence **~लित** (*a*).

उन्मु/क्त unmukt (*a*) liberated, free; unrestricted unrestrained; open; hence **~क्तता** (*nf*); **~क्ति** immunity; liberation; absence of restriction.

उन्मुख unmukh (*a*) inclined, disposed (towards); intent.

उन्मूलन unmu:lān (*nm*) uprooting, rooting out; abolition; extermination, extirpation; **—करना** to abolish; to exterminate; to root out.

उन्मेष unmesh (*nm*) opening; blooming.

उन्मोचन unmochān (*nm*) discharge; liberation.

उन्यासी unnyā:si: (*a*) seventy-nine; (*nm*) the number seventy-nine.

उप up—a Sanskrit prefix denoting proximity, commencement, diminution, subordination, secondary character, etc.

उपकथा upkatha: (*nf*) a sub-plot, side plot.

उपकर upkar (*nm*) a cess.

उपकरण upkaran̲ (*nm*) appliance; equipment, apparatus.

उपकर्ता upkarta: (*nm*) a benefactor

—one who does a good turn to a person, cause or institution etc.

उपकार upka:r (*nm*) beneficence, benefaction; good; —मानना to feel grateful, to express gratitude.

उपकारक upka:rak (*nm*) benefactor; (*a*) beneficial, beneficient; favourable.

उपकारी upka:ri: (*a*) beneficial; favourable; helping, obliging; (*nm*) a benefactor.

उपकुलपति upkulpati (*nm*) (formerly used to mean) Vice-Chancellor (now the word कुलपति is used to mean Vice-Chancellor).

उपकृत upakkrit (*a*) obliged, grateful.

उपक्रम upakkram (*nm*) preparation, a beginning; prelude; —करना to undertake, to set about (doing something).

उपखंड upkhā̱ṇḍ (*nm*) sub-clause, sub-part.

उपगम upgām (*nm*) approach, access.

उपग्रह upaggrah (*nm*) satellite, secondary planet.

उपचय upchay (*nm*) accumulation; increase.

उपचर्या upcharya: (*nf*) nursing.

उपचा/र upcha:r (*nm*) treatment, remedy; attending (upon); formality; seasoning; ~रक a male nurse; ~रिका a nurse.

उपज upaj (*nf*) produce, product; crop, harvest, yield, out-turn.

उपजना upajnā: (*v*) to be produced; to be born; to grow; to spring up.

उपजाऊ upja:u: (*a*) fertile, productive; ~पन fertility, productivity.

उपजात upja:t (*nm*) a bye-product.

उपजाति upja:ti (*nf*) a sub-caste.

उपजाना upja:nā: (*v*) to (cause to) grow; to produce.

उपजिह्वा upjihwa: (*nf*) epiglottis.

उपजीविका upji:vika: (*nf*) an occupation.

उपजीव्य upji:vvy (*a*) affording or serving for livelihood/subsistence, that on which one rests or depends.

उपटना upaṭnā: (*v*) to be uprooted; to be torn off; to fall off.

उपत्यका upattyaka: (*nf*) a valley, low-lying land.

उपदंश updānsh (*nm*) syphilis.

उपदान updā:n (*nm*) a subsidy.

उपदेव(ता) updev (ta:) (*nm*) a demi-god.

उपदेश updesh (*nm*) precept, sermon; preaching, teaching; ~वाद didacticism; ~वादी didactician; didactic; उपदेशात्मक didactic; hence उपदिष्ट (*a*).

उपदेशक updeshak (*nm*) a preceptor, sermoniser.

उपदेष्टा updeshṭa: (*nm*) see उपदेशक.

उपद्रव upaddrav (*nm*) riot, disturbance: mischief; tumult, kick-up.

उपद्रवी upaddravi: (*a*) riotous, rowdy; mischievous; naughty; (*nm*) a rioter, rowdy.

उपद्वीप upaddvi:p (*nm*) an islet, isle.

उपधान updhā:n (*nm*) a pillow, bolster.

उपधारा updha:ra: (*nf*) a sub-clause.

उपनगर upnagar (*nm*) a suburb.

उपनदी upnadi: (*nf*) a rivulet.

उपनयन upnayān (*nm*) a ceremony marking the investiture of the sacred thread (यज्ञोपवीत or जनेऊ).

उपनाम upnā:m (*nm*) pen name, nom de plume; nickname, alias.

उपना/यक upna:yak (*nm*) a side-hero; ~यिका a side-heroine.

उपनियम upniyām (*nm*) a bye-law; sub-rule.

उपनिवेश upnivesh (*nm*) a colony; settlement; ~ वाद colonialism; ~वादी colonialist (ic); उपनिवेशिक colonial.

उपनिवेशी upniveshi: (*nm*) a coloniser;

(*a*) colonial; ~य colonial.

उपनिषद् upnishad (*nm*) sacred ancient books of the Hindus.

उपन्या/स upānnyā:s (*nm*) a novel; ~सकार a novelist; ~सिका a novelette.

उपपति upapati (*nm*) a paramour.

उपपत्ति upapatti (*nf*) proof, evidence.

उपपत्नी upapatni: (*nf*) a mistress, keep, hetaera.

उपप्रमेय upappramey (*nm*) a corollary.

उपबन्ध upbāndh (*nm*) a provision, proviso.

उपभवन upbhavān (*nm*) an annexe, a supplementary building.

उपभाषा upbha:sha: (*nf*) a sub-language; dialect.

उपभुक्त upbhukt (*a*) consumed; used.

उपभेद upbhed (*nm*) a sub-division; sub-classification.

उपभोक्ता upbhokta: (*nm*) a consumer; user.

उपभो/ग upbhog (*nm*) enjoyment/enjoying; consuming/consumption; using; hence ~गी (*nm*); ~ग्या (*a*).

उपभोज्य upbhojjy (*a* and *nm*) consumable(s), consumptible(s); worth-enjoying.

उपमंत्री upmāntri: (*nm*) a Deputy Minister.

उपमति upmāti (*nf*) acquiescence.

उपमहाद्वीप upmaha:dvi:p (*nm*) a sub-continent.

उपमा upmā: (*nf*) a simile; comparison.

उपमान upmā:n (*nm*) the object of comparison as 'कमल' in मुखकमल —lotus like face. (cf. उपमेय).

उपमित upmit (*a*) compared; illustrated by comparison.

उपमेय upmey (*nm*) the subject of comparison, that which is compared (with); (*a*) comparable (with).

उपयुक्त upyukt (*a*) proper, suitable, appropriate; used; ~ता expediency; suitability, appropriateness.

उपयोक्ता upyokta: (*nm*) a user.

उपयोग upyog (*nm*) use, utilisation, utility; exploitation; ~कर्त्ता a usufructuary; consumer.

उपयोगिता upyogita: (*nf*) usefulness, utility; ~वाद utilitarianism; ~वादी utilitarian; utilitarianist (ic).

उपयोगी upyogi: (*a*) useful; helpful; serviceable; ~करण processing; rendering serviceable.

उपरत uprat (*a*) detached, disinterested.

उपरांत uprā:nt (*adv*) after, afterwards.

उपराष्ट्रपति upra:shṭrapati (*nm*) Vice-President.

उपरि upari (*int*) above.

उपरिलिखित uparilikhit (*a*) above-given, above-mentioned.

उपरूप upru:p (*nm*) an allomorph.

उपरूपक upru:pak (*nm*) a secondary or lower category of *ru:pak* (see) which has eighteen different types.

उपरोक्त uprokt (*a*) see उपर्युक्त.

उपर्युक्त uparyukt (*a*) aforesaid, above-mentioned, said above.

उपल upal (*nm*) hail.

उपलक्ष/ण uplakshāṉ (*nm*) a characteristic; the act of implying something that has not been expressed or made explicit; metonymy; ~णा implication.

उपलक्षित uplakshit (*a*) implied, conveyed through implication.

उपलक्ष्य uplakshy (*nm*); —में on account of; to celebrate.

उपलब्ध uplabdh (*a*) available; acquired; hence ~ता (*nf*).

उपलब्धि uplabdhi (*nf*) achievement; accomplishment, attainment.

उपलभ्य uplabbhy (*a*) available; ~**ता** availability.

उपला upla: (*nm*) a cow-dung cake.

उपल्ला upalla: (*nm*) the upper portion or fold; (*a*) upper.

उपवन upvān (*nm*) a garden, park, parkland.

उपवाक्य upvā:kky (*nm*) a clause.

उपवा/स upvā:s (*nm*) fast; ~**सी** one who observes a fast.

उपविभाग upvibhā:g (*nm*) sub-division; a subordinate department.

उपव्यवसाय upvyavsa:y (*nm*) an avocation.

उपश/मन upshamān (*nm*) abatement; subsidence; hence ~**मित** (*a*).

उपशाखा upsha:kha; (*nf*) sub-branch, subsidiary branch.

उपशिक्षक upshikshak (*nm*) a tutor.

उपशीर्षक upshi:rshak (*nm*) a subheading; sub-title.

उपसंगी upsāṅgi: (*a*) subsidiary, auxiliary.

उपसंपादक upsāmpā:dak (*nm*) a subeditor.

उपसंहार upsānha:r (*nm*) an epilogue; conclusion, concluding chapter (of a book); —**खंड** apodosis; —**करना** to conclude, to say by way of conclusion.

उपसभापति upsabha:pati (*nm*) Vice-President, Vice-Chairman.

उपसमिति upsamiti (*nf*) a sub-committee.

उपसर्ग upsarg (*nm*) a prefix.

उपसाधक upsa:dhak (*a*) accessory.

उपस्कर upaskar (*nm*) equipment, apparatus.

उपस्त्री upastri: (*nf*) a keep, mistress.

उपस्थ upasth (*nm*) buttock (s); male or female genitals.

उपस्थापन upastha:pān (*nm*) presentation; representation (on the stage etc.).

उपस्थित upasthit (*a*) present;—**होना** to be present; to attend

उपस्थिति upasthiti (*nf*) presence, attendance, roll-call.

उपहसित uphasit (*nm*) a loud derisive laughter.

उपहा/र upha:r (*nm*) a present, gift; ~ **री** one who presents (a gift).

उपहास upha:s (*nm*) derision, ridicule, mockery;—**करना** to deride, to ridicule; -**चित्र** a caricature.

उपहासास्पद upha:sa:spad (*a*) ridiculous, absurd, worth being laughed at; hence ~**ता** (*nf*).

उपहास्य upha:ssy (*a*) ridiculous, fit to be laughed at.

उपांग upā:ṅg (*nm*) an accessory organ, a minor limb or member of the body; sub-division.

उपांत upā:nt (*nm*) a border; edge, margin; proximity to the end, edge or margin; vicinity, proximity.

उपांतिक upā:ntik (*a*) proximate/proximal, near, marginal.

उपां/तिम, ~**त्य** upā:ntim, ~tty (*a*) last but one, penultimate.

उपाकर्म upa:karm (*nm*) a ritual performed on *pu:rṉima:* in the month of *Shra:vaṉ* as a pre-requisite to the commencement of the recitation of the Vedas.

उपाख्यान upa:kkhyā:n (*nm*) an episode, a subordinate tale or story; anecdote.

उपाटना upa:ṭnā: (*v*) to uproot; to tear off; to fell, to cause to fall off.

उपादान upa:dā:n (*nm*) material (cause); ingredient;—**कारण** the material cause.

उपादेय upa:dey (*a*) useful, of utility, beneficial; hence~**ता** (*nf*).

उपाधि upa:dhi (*nf*) degree; qualification; title; attribute; botheration; ~धारी a title-holder; a degree-holder.

उपाध्यक्ष upa:ddhyaksh (*nm*) Vice-President; Vice-Chairman; Deputy Speaker.

उपापचय, ~न upa:pchay, ~ān (*nm*) metabolism.

उपाय upa:y (*nm*) way, measure; device; cure, remedy.

उपायोजन upa:yojān (*nm*) attachment.

उपा/र्जन upa:rjān (*nm*) earning; acquisition, acquirement; ~र्जित earned; acquired; ० रुचि acquired interest.

उपालंभ upa:lambh (*nm*) complaint; reproach.

उपास upa:s (*nm*) see **उपवास**.

उपासक upa:sak (*nm*) a worshipper; an adorer.

उपासना upa:snā: (*nf*) worship, adoration; —पद्धति cult; technique of worship.

उपासित upa:sit (*a*) adored, worshipped.

उपास्थि upa:sthi (*nf*) cartilage.

उपास्य upa:ssy (*a*) adorable, worthy of worship, fit to be revered or honoured.

उपाहार upa:ha:r (*nm*) refreshment; -कक्ष/गृह refreshment room/house.

उपेक्षणीय upekshnī:y (*a*) negligible, fit to be ignored/neglected/discarded; hence ~ता (*nf*)

उपेक्षा upeksha: (*nf*) negligence; neglect, disregard; ~कारी negligent; —करना to ignore, to disregard, to brush aside.

उपेक्षित upekshit (*a*) neglected, ignored; discarded, disregarded.

उपोद्घात upodgha:t (*nm*) exordium, prolegomenon.

उफ़ uf (*int*) ah!;—न करना to endure quietly, not to utter a sigh or syllable (in face of unbearable agony).

उफनना uphannā: (*v*) to boil over; to effervesce; to fume or froth.

उफान uphā:n (*nm*) effervescence; ebullience, ebullition.

उबकाई ubka:i: (*nf*) nausea, a feeling of vomitting.

उबट/न ubṭān (*nm*) a cosmetic paste rubbed over the body for cleaning and softening of the skin; hence ~ना (*v*).

उबरना ubarnā: (*v*) to be liberated; to get rid of, to be free; to be salvaged.

उबल/ना ubalnā: (*v*) to boil, to simmer; —पड़ना to infuriate into a torrent of invectives, to give unrestrained vent to one's rage.

उबाना uba:nā: (*v*) to bore, to cause to be fed up.

उबारना uba:rnā: (*v*) to liberate, to emancipate, to rid, to salvage.

उबाल uba:l (*nm*) boiling, seething, simmering.

उबालना uba:lnā: (*v*) to boil; to cause to simmer; to heat till a liquid boils.

उबासी uba:si: (*nf*) a yawn;—आना (*nf*) to yawn.

उभय ubhay (*a*) both; the two; ~चर an amphibian; amphibious; ~तः on both sides; in both cases; in both manners; ~तोमुख having a face at each of the two sides, double-faced; ~निष्ठ common to both; loyal to both; hence ~निष्ठता (*nf*); —पक्ष the two sides/parties/aspects; hence ~पक्षता (*nf*); ~भावी ambivalent; ~मुख ambivert; ०ता ambiversion;—लिंग common gender; ~विधि of both types; ~वृत्ति ambivalence; **उभयात्मक** made up of the two, covering both.

उभरना ubharnā: (*v*) to emerge; to protrude or project; to bulge out.

उभार ubha:r (*nm*) a bulge, bulging; projection or protrusion; bossing;

~दार bulging, protruding.

उभारना ubha:rnā: (*v*) to incite or instigate, to provoke; to raise; to (cause to) protrude; (*nm*) incitement.

उमंग umāṅg: (*nf*) aspiration; gusto, zeal; -भरा in high spirits, as keen as mustard.

उमँगना umāgnā: (*v*) to be ebullient; to feel an inner upsurge, to be in a gusto.

उमड़ना umaṛnā: (*v*) to surge; to overflow, to flood, to burst with; to gust, to gather thick; -घुमड़ना to gather thick (as बादल); to concentrate.

उम/दा umda: (*a*) nice, fine, excellent; ~दगी/~दापन excellence, fineness, nicety.

उमस umās (*nf*) sultriness, sultry weather; -भरा sultry, stuffy.

उमा umā: (*nf*) the goddess Pa:rvati: —Lord Shiv's spouse.

उमेठना umeṭhnā: (*v*) to twist, to wring; to wind; to pull, (as कान).

उम्दा umda: (*a*) see उमदा.

उम्मीद ummı:d (*nf*) hope, expectation; —बर आना to have a wish fulfilled, to have a wish realised; उम्मीदों पर पानी फेरना to lash all hopes to the ground.

उम्मीदवा/र ummı:dva:r (*nm*) a candidate; ~री candidature.

उम्र ummr (*nf*) age; lifetime; —का पैमाना/प्याला भर जाना to approach one's end, to complete the days of one's life; —क़ैद life imprisonment; —क़ैदी prisoner for life; —ढलना to age, to be on the wane; ~दराज़ होना to have a long life; —भर throughout life; —भर का life-long.

उर ur (*nm*) see हृदय.

उरद urad (*nf*) a kind of pulse; black gram, *Dolichos pilosus*.

उरु uru (*nm*) thigh.

उरूज uru:j (*nm*) ascendancy, rise; —पर होना to be in the ascendancy.

उरेहना urehnā: (*v*) to draw (as चित्र); to paint; (*nm*) etching.

उरोज uroj (*nm*) the female breast.

उर्दू urdu: (*nf*) the Urdu language; ~दाँ a scholar of Urdu.

उर्फ़ urf (*ind*) alias.

उर्मि urmi (*nf*) a wave, ripple; ~ल wavy, undulating; hence ~लता(*nf*).

उर्वर urvar (*a*) fertile, productive; ~ता fertility, productivity, fecundity; उर्वरा (*a* and *nf*) fertile.

उर्वरक urvarak (*nm*) fertiliser.

उर्स urs (*nm*) the celebration organised to observe the day of a muslim saint's demise.

उलछारना ulchha:rnā: (*v*) to throw up.

उलझन uljhān (*nf*) complication; entanglement; perplexity;—में होना to be in the cart, to be in a fix.

उलझना ulajhnā: (*v*) to be entangled, to be involved or ravelled up; to become complicated; to be entwined (as रस्सी); to catch a crab; to cross swords with.

उलझाना uljha:nā: (*v*) to entangle, to complicate; to involve, to entwine.

उलझाव uljha:v (*nm*) entanglement; involvement; complication.

उलटना ulaṭnā: (*v*) to overturn or be overturned, to capsize; to reverse or be reversed; to subvert; to turn over.

उलट-पलट/पुलट ulaṭ-palaṭ/pulaṭ (*nm*) shuffling; disarray, disarrangement; reversal; (*a*) topsy-turvy, in disarray; over-turned.

उलट-फेर ulaṭ-pher (*nm*) shuffling, upsetting; changes; vicissitudes.

उलटवाँ ualṭvā: (*a*) reversible.

उलटवाँसी ulaṭvā:si: (*nf*) a form of expression which abounds in apparently curious, untenable and abnormal statements and incidents.

उलटा ulṭa: (*a*) reverse/reversed; topsy-turvy; opposite, contrary; overturned; inverted; —चलाना to back-drive, to drive backward; —चोर कोतवाल को डाँटे the case of a thief threatening the policeman; –जमाना strange/preposterous times; —तवा jet black, coal-black; —पाठ पढ़ाना to misguide, to mislead; -पुलटा topsy-tuvy, deranged; confused, higgledy piggledy; -सीधा absurd, irrelevant; hurriedly performed; उलटे छुरे से मूँड़ना/हलाल करना to fleece, to strip, somebody of money by befooling him; —ढंग से कामकरना to skin an eel by the tail; उलटे बाँस बरेली को carrying coal to New Castle.

उलटी ulṭi: (*nf*) vomit, vomitting; (*a*) upside down; topsy-turvy; backwards; see उलटा; —खोपड़ी का a block-head; a pervert; —गंगा बहाना to put the cart before the horse, to act contrary to customary practices;–पट्टी पढ़ाना to poison the mind of, to mislead; —बात करना to put the cart before the horse; —माला जपना/फेरना to invoke a curse upon; —समझ perverted/erroneous understanding, perversion; -सीधी सुनाना to scold roundly; to revile; -सीधी हरकतें करना to cut papers; —हवा बहना the setting in of contrary wind, to put contrary customs and manners into practice; उलटे पैरों लौटना to return without a (moment's) pause.

उलफ़त ulfat (*nf*) love, attachment.

उलाँघना ulā:ghnā: (*v*) to cross over, to transgress; to disobey.

उलार ula:r (*a*) too weighty at the back (used for a carriage etc.)

उलाहना ula:hnā: (*nm*) complaint; twitting, reproach.

उलीचना uli:chnā: (*v*) to drain out, to empty (something full of water or other liquid) with the help of some device (or with the palms of the two hands put together).

उलूक ulu:k (*nm*) see उल्लू.

उल्का ulka: (*nf*) a falling star, meteor; flame; firebrand; ~धारी a torch-bearer; ~पात the falling of a meteor; disaster, devastation.

उल्था ultha: (*nm*) rendering into another language, a free translation; interpretation.

उल्लंघन ullāṅghān (*nm*) violation; contravention; ~कर्ता a violator, one who contravenes.

उल्लसित ullasit (*a*) joyous, full of delight and joy.

उल्लास ulla:s (*nm*) joy, delight, merriment; a chapter (of a book); revelry; elation; hence ~पूर्ण/~मय (*a*).

उल्लिखित ullikhit (*a*) referred, mentioned; written, inscribed.

उल्लू ullu: (*nm*) an owl; an idiot, a fool; –का पठ्ठा an absolute dullard; —बनाना to befool, to make a fool of, to give one a flap with a fox-tail; to dupe; —बोलना to be deserted/ruined; —सीधा करना to serve one's own ends, to jockey for position.

उल्लेख ullekh (*nm*) mention, reference; citation, quotation; —करना to refer, to mention; to cite.

उल्ले/खनीय ullekhnɪ:y (*a*) remarkable; worthy of being mentioned; also ~ख्य; hence ~ खनीयता (*nf*).

उषा usha: (*nf*) the dawn.

उष्ण ushn̲ (*a*) hot; warm; —कटिबंध tropical region or belt, tropics; ~ता warmth, heat.

उष्णीष ushn̲ɪ:sh (*nm*) a turban; crown.

उष्मा ushma: (*nf*) see **ऊष्मा**.

उस us (*pro*) oblique singular form of **वह; उसे/~को** to him.

उसनना usannā: (*v*) to knead (into a dough); to boil.

उसाँस usā:s (*nf*) a sigh.

उसारा usa:ra: (*nm*) a shed; verandah.

उसू/ल usu:l (*nm*) a principle; **~ली** pertaining to principles; theoretical; **॰ तौर पर** in principle, as a matter of principle.

उसूलन usu:lan—as a matter of principle, in principle.

उस्तरा ustara: (*nm*) a razor (blade).

उस्ता/द usta:d (*nm*) a teacher; master; (*a*) cunning, tricky; **~ दी** tutorship, teaching; cunningness, cleverness; **~द होना** to be skilled/crafty; to be an expert; **~दी दिखाना** (to try) to be clever/cunning

ऊ

ऊ u:—the sixth vowel and the sixth letter of the Devna:gri: alphabet.

ऊँघ ū:gh (*nf*) drowsiness, sleepiness; **—लेना** to have a nap.

ऊँघना ū:ghnā: (*v*) to doze; to nap; to be sleepy/drowsy.

ऊँच-नीच ū:ch-nɪ:ch (*nm*) pros and cons; good and evil; ups and downs; high and low; an untoward incident; **—से वाकिफ़ होना** to know the ropes.

ऊँचा ū:cha: (*a*) high, lofty, elevated; **-नीचा** uneven; pros and cons; **—बोल** arrogant utterance, tall talk; **— सुनना** to be hard of hearing; **ऊँची उड़ान** far-fetched imagination, too high a flight; **ऊँची जगह** high office/position; **ऊँची दुकान फीका पकवान** great cry, little wool/great boast, little roast; **ऊँचे दाम** exorbitant/high price; **ऊँचे इरादे होना** flying at a higher game; **ऊँचे दर्जे का** belonging to the high class; of a high order; **ऊँचे-नीचे पाँव पड़ना** to stumble; to go astray; to make mistakes.

ऊँचाई ū:cha:i: (*nf*) height, altitude, elevation; loftiness.

ऊँछना ū:chhnā: (*v*) see **ऐंछना** .

ऊँट ū:ṭ (*nm*) a camel; **~गाड़ी** a camel-driven cart; **~वान** a camel driver; **(देखिए) —किस करवट बैठता है** (let's) wait and watch/see how things turn out; **—की कोई कल सीधी नहीं होती** to be unsymmetrical through and through/all round; **—की चोरी और झुके-झुके/निहुरे-निहुरे** to try to conceal the conspicuous; **—के मुँह में जीरा** a drop in the ocean; **—चढ़े कुत्ता काटे** misfortune has long arms for the unlucky; **—निगल जायें दुम से परहेज करें** to challenge a lion and fear a lamb; **—मक्का को ही भागता है** water finds its own level.

ऊँहूँ ū:hū: (*ind*) no, never !; that won't be !, not at all !.

ऊका/र u:ka:r (*nm*) the letter u: (**ऊ**) and its sound; **~रांत** (a word) ending in u: (**ऊ**).

ऊख u:kh (*nm*) see **ईख** .

ऊखल u:khal (*nm*) see **ओखली** .

ऊजड़ u:jaṛ (*a*) deserted, desolate.

ऊटपटाँग u:tpaṭā:g (*a*) slipslop, absurd, ridiculous, incoherent.

ऊत u:t (*a*) idiotic, doltish; ~**पन**/~**पना** stupidity, doltishness.

ऊतक u:tak (*nm*) a tissue.

ऊदबिलाव u:dbila:w (*nm*) an otter.

ऊदा u:da: (*a*) violet.

ऊध/म u:dham (*nm*) hurly-burly, uproar; mischief; a kick- up; ~**मी** mischievous, naughty; hence ~**मीपन** (*nm*).

ऊन u:n (*nf*, also *nm*) wool; (*a*) less (than), small; –**की दून मारना** to exaggerate no end.

ऊनी u:nī: (*a*) woollen, woolly.

ऊपर u:par (*adv*) on, upon; above; upward; over; —**की आमदनी** extra income; —**की** superficial **से** externally, superficially; —**वाला** the Almighty; —**होना** to be senior in status or office.

ऊपरी u:pari: (*a*) upper; superficial, artificial, showy.

ऊब u:b (*nf*) boredom, tedium, monotony.

ऊबड़-खाबड़ u:baṛ-kha:baṛ (*a*) uneven; rough and rugged.

ऊबना u:bnā: (*v*) to be bored, to feel irked.

ऊभ-चूभ u:bh-chu:bh (*nf*) floating and sinking, submerging and emerging; prolonged indecisive deliberation.

ऊर्ज/स्वी u:rjasswi: (*a*) energetic, vigorous, full of vigour and vitality; ~**स्वित** (*a*); ~**स्विता** (*nf*) vigorousness, vitality, energy.

ऊर्जा u:rja: (*nf*) energy; vigour and vitality, ~**विज्ञान** energetics.

ऊर्जित u:rjit (*a*) energetic, full of energy.

ऊर्णनाभ u:rn̲na:bh (*nm*) a spider.

ऊर्ध्व u:rdhw (*a*) vertical; upward; —**गति** vertical/upward movement; emancipation, salvation; ~**गामी** moving vertically; attaining salvation; ~**दृष्टि** ambitious; looking beyond the world; ~**लोक** the heaven, other world; —**बिंदु** the zenith.

ऊर्ध्वाधर u:rdhva:dhar (*a*) vertical.

ऊर्मि u:rmī (*nf*) see **उर्मि**.

ऊर्मिमाला u:rmīma:la: (*nf*) undulation; (a series of) waves.

ऊर्मिल u:rmil (*a*) wavy; undulating/undulatory.

ऊलजलूल u:l-jalu:l (*a*) slob, slipslop, irrelevant, absurd, ridiculous; hence ~**पन** (*nm*).

ऊष्मक u:shmāk (*nm*) a heater.

ऊष्मसह u:shmāsah (*a*) heatproof.

ऊष्मा u:shmā: (*nf*) heat; warmth.

ऊष्माधारिता u:shmā:dha:rita: (*nf*) thermal capacity.

ऊष्मीय u:shmi:y (*a*) thermal.

ऊसर u:sar (*a* and *nm*) barren or fallow (land); —**की खेती** literally, tilling a barren land —wasting one's industry, undertaking an impossible task.

ऊहा u:ha: (*nf*) flight of imagination; far-fetched imagination, exaggerative comprehension; ~**पोह** reflection on pros and cons (of a problem); indecisive reflection.

ऋ

ऋ ri—the seventh vowel and the seventh letter of the Devna:gri: alphabet. In Hindi, however, ऋ is used in writing only तत्सम words, and is not accepted as a vowel within the Hindi phonetic set-up.

ऋका/र rika:r (*nm*) the letter ऋ (ri) and its sound; ~रांत (a word) ending in ऋ (ri).

ऋक्थ rikth (*nm*) inheritance, legacy; ~भागी an inheritor.

ऋग्वे/द rigved (*nm*) the earliest of the four Vedas ; ~दी well-versed in, and acting according to, the Rigved.

ऋचा richa: (*nf*) a Vedic hymn.

ऋजु riju (*a*) straight; simple; not crooked; ~ता straightness; simplicity, sincerity.

ऋण rin (*nm*) a debt; loan; minus; ~ग्रस्त indebted; ०ता indebtedness; ~त्रय the three debts (देवऋण, ऋषिऋण, पितृऋण i.e. those of the gods, the preceptor and the parents); ~दाता a creditor; ~पत्र bond; security; ~मुक्त debt-free, free from debt; ~मुक्ति/शुद्धि/शोध repayment of a debt.

ऋणात्मक rina:tmāk (*a*) negative; pertaining to or concerning a debt.

ऋणाधार rina:dha:r (*nm*) a security.

ऋणी rinī: (*a*) indebted; (*nm*) a debtor.

ऋत rit (*nm*) truth; righteousness; divine law.

ऋतु ritu (*nf*) season; ~काल the period of menstrual discharge, the period of menses; ~मती a woman in her menses; ~विज्ञान meteorology; ~सह weather-proof.

ऋद्धि riddhi (*nf*) prosperity, accomplishment; -सिद्धि wealth and prosperity.

ऋषि rishi (*nm*) a sage, seer; preceptor; ~कल्प saintly.

ए

ए e—the seventh vowel and the seventh letter of the present day Devna:gri: alphabet. [If ऋ (ri), and also लृ (lri), are taken into account ए becomes theninth]; o!, a vocative particle; (just) listen !

एँड़ा-बेंड़ा ēra:-bēra: (*a*) topsy-turvy. incoherent; unsystematic.

एंबुलेंस embulens (*nf*) an ambulance.

एक ek (*a*) one, a, single, alone; (*nm*) the number one; -आध one or two, a few; -एक each and every; one at a time; ०करके one by one; ~चित्त resolute, determined; like-minded; ~च्छत्र having absolute authority, autocratic; ~जान completely identified (with one another); in complete union; ~तंत्र autocracy; ~तंत्रीय autocratic; ० राज्य autocratic rule; ~तंत्रीय शासन-प्रणाली autocratic system of government; ~तल्ला one-storeyed; ~ तान intent; harmonic; ~तानता harmoniousness, harmony; ~तारा a monochord; one-stringed instrument; ~ताल having perfect rhythm; ~धर्मा/धर्मी having common attribute or characteristic; ~निष्ठ devoted to or having faith in one; hence ~निष्ठता; ~पक्षीय unilateral; hence ~पक्षीयता; -ब-एक all of a sudden; ~बारगी all at once; ~मंजिला see ~तल्ला; ~मति/मता unanimous, having complete concord; ~मुश्त in one lot, in a lump sum; ~रस monotonous; constant; ० ता monotony; ~रूप uniform; ० ता uniformity; ~विध uniform, homogeneous; ० ता uniformity, homogeneity; —अनार सौ बीमार one post, a hundred candidates;—आँख न भाना to have absolutely no liking (for somebody or something) ; to have extreme/complete aversion (to); —आँख से सबको देखना to treat one and all alike; एक कौड़ी दाँत से पकड़ना lit. to hold each shell with one's teeth —his money comes from him like drops of blood, to be excessively stingy/parsimonious; -एक पल भारी/पहाड़ होना each moment to weigh heavily on the mind; —ओर कुआँ, दूसरी ओर खाई between the devil and the deep sea, between Scylla and the Charybdis; —के दस-दस करना to earn enormous profits, to reap a bumper harvest of profits; —और एक ग्यारह होते हैं lit. one and one make eleven' —strength lies in union; —की चार लगाना to level exaggerated charges (against somebody); to multiply accusations; —की दस सुनाना to pay back with interest, to pay back ten to one in the same coin; —चना भाड़ नहीं फोड़ सकता a lone soldier cannot win a battle;—चुप सौ को हराये patient men win the day;—जान एक जिगर united in soul and heart; true, sincere and in complete mutual harmony; —तवे की रोटी, क्या मोटी क्या छोटी those cast in the same mould are almost equal in all respects, members of the same family enjoy equal status; —तीर से दो शिकार to kill two birds with one stone; —थैली के चट्टे-बट्टे birds of the same feather/flock, cast in the same mould; -न-एक one or the other; –न चलना all efforts to prove in vain/ of no avail; —नजर सौ नसीहत a lone example is better than a hundred precepts; —न सुनना/मानना to turn a deaf ear; —पंथ दो काज to kill two birds with one stone; —परहेज सौ इलाज diet cures more than doctors; —पाँव से खड़े रहना to be ever ready to serve, to carry out commands; —फूँक में उड़ा देना to brush aside, to blow up into thin air; —मछली पूरे/सारे तालाब को गन्दा कर देती है one dirty fish infects the whole mass of water; —म्यान में दो तलवारें two of a trade seldom agree; —लाठी से हाँकना to rule all men with the same rod; —से दो भले two heads are better than one; —स्वर से unanimously; —हाथ से ताली नहीं बजती it takes two to make a quarrel; –ही रट लगाये रहना, –ही राग

अलापना to harp on the same string.

एकक ekak (*nm*) a unit.

एककालिक ekka:lik (*a*) synchronic, synchronizing.

एकटक ektak (*adv*) without blinking, without a wink.

एकड़ ekaṛ (*nf*) an acre.

एक/तंत्र ektāntr (*nm*) autocracy; ~तंत्रवादी an autocrat; autocratic; ~तंत्रात्मक, ~तंत्रीय autocratic.

एकतरफ़ा ektarfa: (*a*) unilateral; one way; one-sided; —डिग्री an ex-parte decree; —फ़ैसला a unilateral decision, an ex-parte judgment.

एकता ekta: (*nf*) oneness; unity, solidarity.

एकत्र ekattr (*a*) together, in one place, collected.

एकत्रीकरण ekatri:karan̲ (*nm*) collections; collecting together, accumulation.

एकत्रित ekattrit (*a*) collected, accumulated, gathered.

एकत्व ekattv (*nm*) see एकता; ~वाद monism; ~वादी monist (ic).

एकदम ekdām (*ind*) suddenly, in one breath; completely; (*a*) perfect.

एकदेशीय ekdeshi:y (*a*) belonging to one and the same country; localized, restricted in extent or scope.

एकपक्षीय ekpakshi:y (*a*) unilateral, ex-parte; hence ~ता (*nf*).

एकपत्नी/त्व ekpatni:ttv (*mn*) monogamy; -प्रथा monogamy; ~वादी a monogamist; ~वाद monogamy.

एकपार्श्विक ekpa:rshvik (*a*) unilateral; one-sided.

एकबारगी ekba:rgi: (*adv*) all at once, all of a sudden.

एकभाषिक ekbha:shik (*a*) monolingual (for a dictionary, books, etc.).

एकभाषी ekbha:shi: (*a*) monolingual (for men).

एकमत ekmāt (*a*) having complete accord; unanimous.

एकमात्र ekmā:ttr (*a*) sole; solitary; the only one.

एकमुश्त ekmusht (*a* and *adv*) lump (sum); in a lump, lot.

एकरंगा ekrañga: (*a*) monochrome; not diverse.

एकरूप ekru:p (*a*) uniform.

एकरूपता ekru:pta (*nf*) uniformity.

एकल ekal (*a*) single; alone, solitary.

एकलिंगिता eklingita: (*nf*) unisexualism.

एकलिंगी eklingi: (*a*) unisexual.

एकवचन ekvachān (*a*) singular (number).

एक/वाद ekva:d (*nm*) monism; ~वादी monist(ic).

एकविवाह ekviva:h (*nm*) monogamy.

एकसदनी eksadni: (*a*) unicameral.

एकसम eksām (*a*) uniform; even.

एकसर eksar (*a*) even; fully stretched/unfolded.

एकसार eksa:r (*a*) even, uniform; smooth.

एकसूत्र eksu:ttr (*a*) coordinated; well knit; —करना to string together, to unify, to harmonise into a whole.

एकसूत्रता eksu:ttrata: (*nf*) coordination; the state of being well-knit.

एकस्व ekassv (*nm*) patent.

एकस्वदाता ekassvada:ta: (*mn*) a patentor.

एकस्वरता ekassvarta: (*nf*) monotony: the state of having one voice.

एकस्वी ekassvi: (*nm*) a patentee.

एकांकी ekā:ṅki: (*a* and *nm*) one act (play); ~कार a one-act playwright.

एकांगी ekā:ṅgi: (*a*) partial; biassed; one-sided.

एकांत ekā:nt (*a*) exclusive; (*mn*) solitude; seclusion; ~वास residing in solitude/seclusion; ~वासी

recluse, one who resides in seclusion.

एकांतता ekā:ntata: (*nf*) privacy; seclusion, secludedness.

एकांतर ekā:ntar (*a*) alternate.

एकांतरण ekā:ntarāṉ (*nm*) alternation.

एकांतिक ekā:ntik (*a*) exclusive; absolute, private.

एका eka: (*nm*) oneness; unity, solidarity.

एका/एक eka:ek (*adv*) suddenly, unexpectedly, all at once; also ~**एकी**.

एकाकार eka:ka:r (*a*) identical; fused; merged (into one).

एकाकी eka:ki: (*a*) lonely, solitary; single; ~**पन** (a feeling of) loneliness; hence ~**पना** (*nf*).

एकाग्र eka:ggr (*a*) concentrated on the same point, intent, resolute; ~**चित्त** closely attentive, having full concentration.

एकाग्रता eka:ggrata: (*nf*) concentration (of mind), resoluteness.

एकात्म eka:tm (*a*) forming one identity, identical, integrated (into one); ~**क** monistic; ~**वाद** monopsyohism.

एकादशी eka:dashi: (*nf*) the eleventh day of either fortnight of a lunar month.

एकाध eka:dh (*a*) one or two, a few.

एकाधिक eka:dhik (*a*) more than one; several.

एकाधिका/र eka:dhika:r (*nm*) monopoly; ~**री** a monopolist.

एकाधिपति eka:dhipati (*nm*) an absolute ruler; exclusive master.

एकाधिपत्य eka:dhipatty (*nm*) exclusive sway, absolute mastery; autocracy.

एका/र eka:r (*nm*) the vowel e (**ए**) and its sound; ~**रांत** (a word) ending in e (**ए**).

एकार्थक eka:rthak (*a*) univocal.

एकाश्मक eka:shmāk (*a*) monolithic.

एकी/करण eki:karāṉ (*nm*) integration; amalgamation; ~**कृत** integrated; united; also ~**भवन** (*nm*); ~**भूत** (*a*).

एकेडमी ekeḍamı: (*nf*) an academy.

एकेश्वरवा/द ekeshshvarva:d (*nm*) monotheism; ~**दी** a monotheist; monotheistic.

एकोन्माद ekonmā:d (*nm*) monomania.

एक्का ekka: (*nm*) see **इक्का**.

एक्सरे eksre (*nm*) an x-ray; —**विभाग** x-ray department.

एजेंट ejenṭ (*nm*) an agent.

एजेंसी ejensi· (*nf*) an agency.

एटर्नी eṭarnı: (*nm*) an attorney; —**जनरल** attorney general.

एटलस eṭlas (*nm*) an atlas.

एडवोकेट eḍvokeṭ (*nm*) an advocate.

एडिट/र eḍiṭar (*nm*) an editor; ~ **री** editorship; an editor's work or office.

एडिशन eḍishān (*nm*) an edition.

एड़ eṛ (*nf*) spur; stroke of the heel; —**लगाना** to strike with the heel or apply the spur; to urge.

एड़ी eṛi: (*nf*) heel; **एड़ियाँ रगड़ना** to run about under the stress of circumstances; -**चोटी का जोर लगाना/पसीना एक करना** to leave no stone unturned, to put in all possible efforts; —**से चोटी तक** from head to foot.

एतदर्थ etadarth (*ind*) ad hoc; —**समिति** an ad hoc committee.

एतबा/र etba:r (*nm*) confidence, trust, belief; ~**री** trustworthy.

एतमाद etmā:d (*nm*) trust, faith.

एतराज etra:z (*nm*) objection, exception.

एतावत eta:vat (*a*) so much, this much; —**मात्र** only this much, thus far and no more.

एनेमल enemal (*nm*) enamel.

एफ़िडेविट efiḍeviṭ (*nm*) an affidavit.

एरंड erāṉḍ (*nm*) castor; —**फल** regma.

एलची elchi: (*nm*) an envoy, emissary.

एलबम elbām (*nm*) an album.

एलान elā:n (*nm*) an announcement, a declaration.

एलार्म ela:rm (*nm*) alarm; **—घड़ी** an alarm clock; **—चेन** an alarm chain.

एवं evām (*ind*) and; as also; **—अस्तु** (**एवमस्तु**) Be it so!, Thus may it be!

एवज़ evaz (*nm*) substitution; **—में** in lieu of, in exchange of.

एवज़ी evzi: (*nm*) substitute; (*a*) officiating, acting; relieving.

एषणा eshṉā: (*nf*) wish, strong desire.

एषणीय eshaṉi:y (*a*) covetable, worth-desiring (for); hence **~ता** (*nf*).

एसिड esiḍ (*nm*) an acid.

एसेंबली esembli: (*nf*) an assembly.

एहतियात ehtiya:t (*nm*) precaution; **~न** by way of precaution; **एहतियाती** precautionary; **॰ कार्यवाही** precautionary measure.

एहसान ehsā:n (*nm*) obligation; beneficence; **~फ़रामोश** ungrateful; **—जताना** to remind (one) of the favours conferred, to burden a person with obligation, to do a good turn and to make it a burden for the obliged; **—मानना** to feel obliged.

एहसानमंद ehsā:nmānd (*a*) grateful; obliged; hence **—होना**.

एहसास ehsa:s (*nm*) feeling.

ऐ

ऐ ai—the eighth vowel and the eighth letter of modern Devna:gri: alphabet. (If **ऋ** (ri) and **ऌ** (lri) are also to be taken into account, it becomes the tenth); O!, a vocative; just listen!

ऐंचना a͞ichna: (*v*) to pull; to draw; to drag; to snatch.

ऐंचाताना a͞icha:ta:nā: (*a*) squint-eyed.

ऐंचातानी a͞icha:ta:nɪ: (*nf*) manipulation and manoeuvring, tugging and pulling, struggle inspired by selfish motives.

ऐंछना a͞ichhnā: (*v*) to comb (hair).

ऐंठ a͞iṭḥ (*nf*) twist, twine, ply; torque; convolution; stiffness; conceit; perk; **—दिखाना** to continue one's emotional upsurge within one self; stiff/perky, conceited.

ऐंठन a͞iṭḥān (*nf*) convolution, twist; torsion, contortion.

ऐंठना a͞iṭḥnā: (*v*) to twist; to contort; to extort; to warp; to fleece; to cramp; to be conceited/perky; to stiffen.

ऐंठू a͞iṭḥu: (*a*) perky; arrogant, conceited.

ऐंड़ाना a͞iṛa:nā: (*v*) to stretch one's limbs to relax, to have it easy.

ऐंद्रजालिक aindrja:lik (*nm*) a sorcerer, magician; hypnotist; (*a*) pertaining to sorcery, magical.

ऐंद्रिय a͞indriy (*a*) sensual, pertaining to senses; also **~क** (*a*).

ऐकमत्य aikmāty (*nm*) unanimity

complete accord.

ऐकांतिक aikā:ntik (*a*) exclusive, without exception; hence ~ता (*nf*).

ऐकात्म्य aika:tmy (*nm*) identity, oneness.

ऐका/र aika:r (*nm*) the vowel ai (ऐ) and its sound; ~रांत (a word) ending in ai (ऐ).

ऐक्ट aikṭ (*nm*) an act (of a legislature or of a play).

ऐक्टर aikṭar (*nm*) an actor.

ऐक्ट्रेस aikṭres (*nf*) an actress.

ऐक्य aikky (*nm*) unity; identity, oneness.

ऐच्छिक aichchhik (*a*) optional, voluntary; —विषय an optional subject.

ऐडमिरल aiḍmiral (*nm*) an admiral.

ऐडवांस aiḍvā:ns (*nm*) an advance.

ऐडवोकेट aiḍvokeṭ (*nm*) an advocate.

ऐतिहासिक aitiha:sik (*a*) historic, historical; ~ता historicity; historical genuineness; —युग historic age.

ऐतिह्य aitihy (*nm*) tradition.

ऐन ain (*a*) exact, just; —वक्त पर in the nick of time, just then, just in time, at the eleventh hour.

ऐनक aināk (*nf*) spectacles.

ऐब aib (*nm*) defect; vice; ~दार defective, having lapses or demerits; hence ~दारी (*nf*).

ऐबी aibi: (*a*) defective, faulty; having defective limbs; vicious.

ऐयार aiya:r (*a*) shrewd, wily, sly; (*nm*) a shrewd person, skilled manipulator having the requisites of a gifted detective.

ऐयारी aiya:ri: (*nf*) wiliness, shrewdness; job or profession of an ऐयार.

ऐयाश aiya:sh (*a* and *nm*) (a) debauch, lewd; one addicted to luxurious life.

ऐयाशी aiya:shi: (*nf*) debauchery, lewdness, lechery; living in luxury.

ऐरा-ग़ैरा aira:-gaira: (*a*) inferior, trifling; alien, having no status; —नत्थू ख़ैरा, —पँच कल्यानी Tom, Dick and Harry, Tag-rag and bobtail; ० होना to follow in the crowd of nobodies.

ऐरावत aira:vat (*nm*) the mythological elephant of Indra, Chief of gods.

ऐलान ailā:n (*nm*) see एलान.

ऐश aish (*nm*) sensuous pleasure, enjoyment, luxury; ~परस्त wedded/given to sensual enjoyment/pleasure, luxury-loving; hence ~परस्ती; ~पसन्द luxurious, luxury-loving; -ओ-आराम luxury, luxury and comfort; -ओ-इशरत luxury and sensual pleasure/enjoyment; —उड़ाना/लूटना to revel in pleasure/with sensual enjoyment.

ऐश्वर्य aishvary (*nm*) opulence; prosperity, glory and grandeur; ~वान/शाली opulent; prosperous.

ऐसा aisa: (*a*) such, of this type; -वैसा trifling, of no consequence; insignificant; ऐसी (की) तैसी an abusive expression (directed towards something or someone); down (with him); —० करना/० में जाने देना damn it, let it go to hell, to damn with feint praise.

ऐसे aise (*adv* and *a*) in this way, thus; (*a*) such, of this type.

ऐहलौकिक aihlaukik (*a*) mundane, worldly, earthly; secular, terrestrial; ~ता mundaneness, worldliness; ० परक secular, mundane.

ऐहिक aihik (*a*) mundane, worldly, secular; ~ता mundaneness, worldliness; secularity.

ओ

ओ o—the ninth vowel and the ninth letter of modern Devna:gri: alphabet. (If ऋ & लृ are to be taken into account, it becomes the eleventh); O !, a vocative particle.

ओंकार oṅka:r (*nm*) the sacred and mystical syllable *om* (ॐ).

ओक ok (*nm*) the hollow of a palm/the two palms formed into a cup (as for drinking water).

ओकना oknā: (*v*) to vomit.

ओकाई oka:ɪ: (*nf*) nausea, feeling of vomitting.

ओका/र oka:r (*nm*) the vowel and the sound O (ओ); ~रांत (a word) ending in ओ (O).

ओखली okhli: (*nf*) a mortar (for pounding grain in); —में सिर देना to be ready to undertake risks and face ordeals deliberately, to take up a difficult challenge; —में सिर दिया तो मूसलों से क्या डरना over shoes over boots.

ओघ ogh (*nm*) aggregate, multitude, collection.

ओछा ochha: (*a*) petty, mean, low, trifling; small; shallow; ~पन pettiness, meanness, smallness; shallowness; —वार करना to hit below the belt.

ओज oj (*nm*) vigour and virility; lustre, splendour; ~स्वी vigorous and virile, brilliant; hence ~स्विता (*nf*.)

ओझल ojhal (*a*) out of sight; evanescent; —होना to get out of sight.

ओझा ojha: (*nm*) an exorcist, one who cures by the magic of charms.

ओट oṭ (*nm*) a cover, shelter; —लेना to take shelter/cover.

ओटना oṭnā: (*v*) to gin; to boil (a liquid) for long.

ओटा oṭa: (*nm*) a small raised chair-like platform.

ओठ oṭh (*nm*) a lip; —चबाना to be in fury/rage; —फड़कना throbbing of the lips signifying suppressed rage; ओठों पर on the verge of being uttered,.

ओढ़ना oṛhnā: (*v*) to cover (the body) with; to own up; (*nm*) covering, covering sheet, etc.; -बिछौना covering and bedding, total belongings/possessions; ओढ़े कि बिछाये (said of a thing when it is) utterly insufficient; of no avail.

ओढ़नी oṛhnɪ: (*nf*) a woman's mantle; —बदलना (for women) to become intimate friends.

ओत-प्रोत otapprot (*a*) full of, inspired/permeated by/infused with.

ओफ़ of (*ind*) Oh !; Ah me !, an expression of pain, grief, wonder, etc.

ओम् ōm (*nm*) the sacred word prefixed and suffixed to the Veda mantras symbolising God Almighty.

ओर or (*nm*) side, direction; beginning

ओर-छोर or-chhor (*nm*) the beginning and the end; the two ends; —न

होना to have neither a beginning nor an end, stretched endlessly, to have an immeasurable expanse.

ओरी ori: (*nf*) eaves, projecting edges of a thatching.

ओलती olti: (*nf*) eaves.

ओला ola: (*nm*) a hailstone, hail.

ओवरकोट ovarkoṭ (*nm*) an overcoat.

ओवरसिय/र ovarsiyar (*nm*) an overseer; ~री and overseer's position or job.

ओषधि oshadhi (*nf*) a medicinal herb; medicine.

ओष्ठ oshṭh (*nm*) see ओठ.

ओष्ठ्य oshṭhy (*a*) labial; —वर्ण a labial letter.

ओस os (*nf*) dew; —का मोती lit. a pearl of dew, i. e. something very shortlived; —चाटने से प्यास नहीं बुझती dew drops can scarcely quench one's thirst; —पड़ना to lose luster/brilliance.

ओसर osar (*nf*) a young cow or buffalo yet to reproduce.

ओसाना osā:nā: (*v*) to winnow.

ओसा/रा osa:ra: (*nm*) a verandah or shed; also ~री (*nf*).

ओह oh (*int*) oh ! an exclamation of sorrow or wonder, etc.

ओह/दा ohda:(*nm*) post; designation; rank, status; ~दे के एतबार से ex-officio, by virtue of an office.

ओहदेदा/र ohdeda:r (*nm*) an officer; an office-bearer; ~री an office; official position.

ओहो oho (*ind*) alas ! an expression of regret.

औ

औ au —the tenth vowel and the tenth letter of the Devna:gri: alphabet (exclusive of ऋ and ऌ which are not accepted as Hindi vowels by modern phoneticians).

औंठ a͞uth (*nf*) border; rim (of a utensil); —उठाना to reclaim waste land.

औंड़ा a͞uṛa: (*a*) deep; ~ई depth.

औं/धा a͞udha: (*a*) upside down, inverted, overturned, with the face downwards; ~धी खोपड़ी perverted, stupid; blockhead; ~धे मुँह procumbent; prostrate; face downwards.

औंधाना a͞udha:nā: (*v*) to turn upside down; to overturn

औंस auns (*nm*) (an) ounce.

औक़ात auqa:t (*nf*) status; capability; —,बाज at times; —का ध्यान होना, अपनी to be aware of one's status.

औका/र auka:r (*nm*) the letter au (औ) and its sound; ~रांत (a word) ending in au (औ).

औघड़ aughaṛ (*nm*) a carefree and unsophisticated man; an uncouth person; (*a*) carefree; difficult (to deal with).

औचक auchak (*ind*) all of a sudden, abruptly.

औचित्य auchitty (*nm*) propriety, appropriateness; validity.

औचित्य-स्थापन auchitty-stha:pān (*nm*) rationalisation; establishment of the propriety (of).

औज़ार auza:r (*nm*) an instrument.

औटना auṭnā: (*v*) to continue to boil (for a long time) with a slow fire.

औट/पाय auṭpa:y (*nm*) mischief, mischievous activity; ~**पाई** mischievous, naughty (person).

औटाना auṭa:nā: (*v*) to (cause to) boil (with a slow fire) for a long time.

औढर auḍhar (*a*) easily propitiated, easy to please; —**दानी** a bountiful giver, one who gives away with a free hand.

औत्सुक्य autsukky (*nm*) see **उत्सुकता**.

औदार्य auda:ry (*nm*) see **उदारता**.

औदीच्य audi:chchy (*a*) pertaining to or belonging to the north.

औद्धत्य auddhatty (*nm*) incivility, impertinence, rudeness, haughtiness.

औद्योगिक auddyogik (*a*) industrial; ~ **ता** industrialism; —**युग** industrial age.

औद्योगी/करण auddyogi:karāṉ (*nm*) industrialisation; ~**कृत** industrialised.

औने-पौने āunē-paunē (*a*) at a discount, below par, at a lesser price; —**करना** to sell out at a discount.

औपचारिक aupcha:rik (*a*) formal; ceremonial; ~**ता** formality; ceremoniality.

औपनिवेशिक aupniveshik (*a*) colonial, pertaining to a dominion; —**राज** a dominion; —**दर्जा** dominion status.

औपन्यासिक aupannyā:sik (*a*) pertaining to, or of the nature of, a novel; (*nm*) a novelist.

और aur (*conj*) and; (*adv*) more; else; other; —**का और** something other than, something entirely different; —**तो और** other things apart, leaving other things, let alone other considerations.

औरत aurat (*nf*) a woman; wife.

औरस auras (*a*) legitimate (child); ~**ता** legitimacy.

और्जिकी aurjiki: (*nf*) energetics.

औलाद aula:d (*nf*) a progeny, an offspring.

औलिया auliya: (*nm*) a muslim saint or sage.

औषध aushadh (*nm*) a medicine, drug.

औषधालय aushadha:lay (*nm*) a dispensary.

औषधीय aushadhi:y (*a*) medicinal, medical.

औषधोपचार aushadhopcha:r (*nm*) medical treatment.

औसत ausat (*a*) average; (*nf*; also *nm*) the average; mean; ~ **न** on an average.

औसान ausā:n (*nm*) wits, presence of mind; —**खता होना** to be like a duck in thunderstorm, to lose wits, to be demoralised; —**भुलाना** to unnerve, to put in a quandry.

औसाना ausa:nā: (*v*) to winnow.

क

क ka—the first consonant and the first member of the first pentad (i.e. **कवर्ग**) of the Devna:gri: alphabet; **—ख ग** alphabet; ABC, rudiments of any subject; o **जानना** to know the ABC (of any subject).

कंकड़ kāṅkaṛ (*nm*) a gravel, pebble; small piece of stone; **-पत्थर** lit. pebble and stone—i.e. trash, rubbish; **कंकड़ी** a small piece of gravel.

कंकण kāṅkāṉ (*nm*) a bracelet.

कंकरीट kāṅkri:ṭ (*nm*) concrete—a mixture of gravel, lime, cement and sand; **—का** strong; unbreakable.

कँकरीला kākri:la: (*a*) strewn with gravels, gravelly.

कंकाल kāṅka:l (*nm*) a skeleton, bare physical frame; **~शेष** reduced to/turned into a skeleton.

कंकालिनी kāṅka:lini: (*a* and *nf*) (*a*) quarrelsome (woman).

कँखवारी kākhva:ri: (*nf*) an armpit-boil.

कंखौरी kākhauri: (*nf*) see **कँखवारी**.

कंगन kāṅgān (*nm*) see **कंकण**; also **कँगना**.

कँगनी kāgni: (*nf*) cornice, horizontal moulded projection crowning a building, etc.

कंगारू kāṅga:ru: (*nm*) a kangaroo.

कंगाल kāṅga:l (*nm*) a pauper, poor man; (*a*) penniless, impecunious; **—बाँका** a penniless dandy; **—,घोर** poor as a church-mouse.

कंगाली kāṅga:li: (*nf*) penury, poverty; pauperism, pauperdom; **—में आटा गीला** yet another misery for an already miserable man, yet another stroke for the stricken.

कँगू/रा kāgu:ra: (*nm*) niched battlement (of a castle); an ornamental cornice; turret; **~रेदार** having niched battlement, turreted.

कं/घा kaṅgha: (*nm*) a comb; comb-shaped appliance for weaving; **~घी** a small comb; **० चोटी** make-up, dressing up.

कंचन kāṇchān (*nm*) gold; **-काया** golden (physical) frame, beautiful figure.

कंचुक kānchuk (*nm*) brassieres; armour.

कंचुकी kāṇchuki: (*nf*) brassieres; a sentinel of the royal household, a door-keeper.

कंज kaṇj (*nm*) lotus.

कंजर kāṇjar (*nm*) a nomadic tribe (or a member thereof); (*a*) low-born; shabby; hence **~पन/पना** (*nm*).

कं/जा kāṇja: (*a*) having greyish blue eyes; **~जी** greyish blue.

कंजूस kāṇju:s (*a*) miserly, miser, niggardly, parsimonious; **-मक्खी-चूस होना** to skin a flint.

कंजूसी kāṇju:si: (*nf*) miserliness, parsimony, niggardliness.

कंटक kāṉṯak (*nm*) see **काँटा**; **—होना** to be an obstacle; to be troublesome.

कँटिया kāṭiya: (*nf*) a fishing hook; a small nail.

कँटीला kāṭi:la: (*a*) thorny, prickly;

hence ~पन (*nm*).

कंठ kāṉṭḥ (*nm*) the throat; neck; larynx, voice-box ; -संगीत vocal music; ~स्थ memorised, committed to memory; ~हार a necklace; —करना to memorize; —खुलना to become vocal; —फूटना to make an utterance, to start speaking; —बैठना to develop a sore throat; the voice to turn hoarse; —मिलाकर in one voice, in tune, (with); —सींचना to take in a few drops of water; —होना to be memorised, to be committed to memory.

कंठाग्र kaṉṭḥa:gr (*a*) committed to memory, on the tip of tongue.

कंठी kaṉṭḥi: (*nf*) a string of small beads (of तुलसी etc.) donned esp. by Vaishṉavas as a matter of faith; ~धारी one who dons a कंठी; —छूना to swear by the कंठी; —तोड़ना to renounce the वैष्णव faith (and take to wine and meat etc.); —बांधना/लेना to be initiated in the वैष्णव faith, to become a वैष्णव.

कंठ्य kāṉṭḥy (*a*) guttural; —ध्वनि/—वर्ण a guttural sound.

कंडक्टर/र kāṉḍaktar (*nm*) a conductor; ~री the post or job of a conductor.

कंडरा kāṉḍara: (*nm*) a tendon.

कंडा kāṉḍa: (*nm*) a cowdung cake; —होना to become very lean and thin; the body to be stiffened—to die; to become hard and stiff.

कंडिका kāṉḍika: (*nf*) a para/paragraph.

कंडी kāṉḍi: (*nf*) a basket.

कंडील kāṉḍi:l (*nf*) a lamp (made of paper clay or mica).

कंथा kāntha: (*nm*) a patch-work garment; ~धारी an ascetic.

कंद kānd (*nm*) an esculent tuber-root; sugar candy; an edible root (radish, etc.)

कंदरा kāndara: (*nf*) a cave, cavern.

कंदील kandi:l (*nf*) see कंडील.

कंधा kāndha: (*nm*) a shoulder; —डाल देना to lose heart, to be demoralised; to shun responsibilities;—देना to be a coffin-bearer (of), to lend a shoulder in carrying a dead body; कंधे से कंधा छिलना to be over-crowded (so as to have shoulders rubbing with one another); कंधे से कंधा मिलाना to stand shoulder to shoulder with somebody, to lend full cooperation; कंधों पर आना (responsibility etc.) to devolve on, to be shouldered by; कंधों पर उठाना to shoulder (responsibility etc.); to give a rousing welcome.

कंप kāmp (*nm*) see कंपन.

कंपन kāmpān (*nm*) tremor; quivering, trembling; shivering; vibration.

कंपनी kāmpanɪ: (*nf*) a company.

कंपाउंड/र kāmpa:ūṉḍar (*nm*) a compounder; hence ~री (*nf*).

कंपायमान kāmpa:ymā:n (*a*) tremulous/trembling; quivering; shivering; wavering.

कंपित kampit (*a*) trembled; quivered, shivered; wavered.

कंबल kāmbal (*nm*) a blanket, rug.

ककहरा kakehra: (*nm*) alphabet, ABC (of something).

कका/र kaka:r (*nm*) the consonant क् (k) and its sound; ~रांत (a word) ending in क् (k).

ककड़ी kakṛi: (*nf*) a kind of cucumber.

ककैया kakaiya: (*nf*) a kind of small and strong brick.

कक्का kakka: (*nm*) uncle.

कक्ष kaksh (*nm*) a room, chamber; armpit; side, flank.

कक्षा kaksha: (*nf*) class, class-room;

orbit.

कखौरी kakhauri: (*nf*) an armpit-boil; also **कँखवारी, कँखौरी.**

कगार kaga:r (*nm*) a precipice, scarp.

कचक/च kachkach (*nf*) an altercation; a chattering/clattering noise; **~चाना** to altercate; to chatter; to make clattering noise.

कचनार kachna:r (*nm*) the tree *Bauhinia variegata* (its buds are used as vegetable and its flowers in medical prescriptions); **—की कली** a bud of **कचनार.**

कचरा kachra: (*nm*) refuse, rubbish; sweepings; debris; breezing.

कचरी kachri: (*nf*) *Cucumis madraspatanus* (a small fruit of the melon family).

कचहरी kachehri: (*nf*) a court of justice, court of law;**—में जाना** to take recourse to legal processes.

कचाई kacha:i: (*nf*) rawness; imperfection; inexperience.

कचायँध kachā:yādh (*nf*) (the smell or touch of) rawness.

कचालू kacha:lu: (*nm*) the esculent root *Arum colocasia*; **—करना/बनाना** to give a sound thrashing.

कचूमर kachu:mar (*nm*) anything well-crushed; **—करना/निकालना** to make mincemeat of a person, to crush, to pound thoroughly; to render (something) unserviceable by careless handling.

कचोट kachoṭ (*nf*) a lingering agony; smarting pain; **~ना** to experience a lingering agony; to be smarted.

कचौरी kachauri: (*nf*) a cake made of flour stuffed with bruised pulse or boiled potato etc. fried in ghee or oil.

कच्चा kachcha: (*a*) uncooked; unboiled; raw, unripe; green; crude; incomplete, unfinished; rough; imperfect, immature; inauthentic; doubtful; vague; weak; built of mud-bricks; provisional; not fast (as sleep, colour); **—अ(आ)सामी** a temporary cultivator; one who is not sincere in one's dealings; an unsteady man; **—करना** to put to shame, to abash; to baste; **—काग़ज़** a provisional document; **—खा जाना** lit. to swallow up unroasted—it denotes an angry outburst; **—खिलाड़ी** an inexperienced strategist; **—घड़ा** unbaked earthen pot; an impressionable mind;**—चबा जाना** see**—खा जाना**; **—चिट्ठा** bonafide detailed account, inside story, real tale; **-पक्का** half-cooked; half-baked; **—पड़ना** to prove unavailing/ineffective; **—माल** raw material;**—रंग** not fast colour, colour that will wash out; **—हाथ** an untrained hand ; **कच्ची उम्र** immature age, impressionable age; **कच्ची कली** a budding beauty; **कच्ची गोली खेलना** lit. to 'play with mud marbles'—to act in an inexperienced manner; not to hold all strings under control; **कच्ची गोली नहीं खेलना** to be nobody's fool, to have learnt the tricks of the trade; **कच्ची जबान** loose talk; 'slander, reviling utterance, abuse; **कच्ची नींद में जगाना** to awaken when one has not had full sleep; **कच्ची-पक्की** unconfirmed; **कच्ची-पक्की कहना** to scold roundly, to take to task; **कच्ची बही** a rough account book; **कच्ची बात** loose talk; unconfirmed report; **कच्ची रसोई** articles of food not prepared or fried in ghee (as rice, pulses, etc.).

कच्छप kachchhap (*nm*) tortoise, turtle; **—अवतार** the second incarnation of Lord Vishṉū.

कछा/र kachha:r (*nm*) alluvial land, moist low-lying land by a river; **~री भूमि** alluvion,

कछुआ kachhua: (*nm*) a turtle, tortoise; **-धर्म** tortoise-like conduct—to keep to oneself, to be averse to external contact.

कज kaj (*nf*) a defect, flaw.

कजली kajli: (*nf*) a typical folk-song (sung during the rainy season); a black-eyed cow; also **कजरी**.

क़ज़ा qaza: (*nf*) death; destiny; **—आना** to fall under the shadow of death.

क़ज़िया qazia: (*nm*) quarrel; wrangle.

कटक kaṭak (*nm*) a cantonment; an army.

कटकटाना kaṭkaṭa:nā: (*v*) to gnash; to produce a snapping or cracking sound.

कटखना kaṭkhanā: (*a*) snappish, prone to bite; of aggressive disposition.

कटन kaṭān (*nf*) incision; marks of cutting; off-cut; erosion.

कटना kaṭna: (*v*) to be cut, to be wounded (by a blade etc.); to die in battle; to be destroyed; to pass away time; to complete (a journey, etc.); to be ashamed; to be disconnected; to be deprived of; to be made to part with; **कट मरना** to battle to death; **कटनी** harvesting; **कटा-कटा रहना** to keep away (from), to avoid contact or coming face to face (with); to keep a distance; **कटे पर नमक छिड़कना** to add insult to injury; **कटा-कटी/कटा-मरी** quarrelling; violent hostilities, bloodshed.

कटपीस kaṭpi:s (*nm*) cutpiece (cloth).

कटरा kaṭra: (*nm*) an enclosed yard (for residential purposes or turned into a market place); a buffalo calf.

कटवाँ kaṭwā: (*a*) cut or ripped up, split up; deducted; **—ब्याज** simple interest (on actual capital).

कटहरा kaṭehra: (*nm*) see **कठघरा**.

कटहल kaṭhal (*nm*) the jack tree or its fruit.

कटाई kaṭa:i: (*nf*) harvesting; cutting; cutting charges.

कटाकटी kaṭa:kaṭi: (*nf*) bloodshed, bloody encounter; hostilities.

कटाक्ष kaṭa:ksh (*nf*) a side-glance, ogling; leer, taunt, taunting remark;**—करना** to make a taunting/oblique remark.

कटा-फटा kaṭa:phaṭa: (*a*) cut and torn; mutilated.

कटा/र kaṭa:r (*nf*) a dagger, poniard; **~री** a stiletto, small dagger.

कटाव kaṭa:w (*nm*) erosion; recess; trim, trimming.

कटि kaṭi (*nf*) loin, waist; lumbar, **~बंध** a girdle, belt; zone; **~बंधीय** zonal; **~बद्ध** girt up; ready, resolved.

कटु kaṭu (*a*) bitter, vitriolic; unpleasant; **~ता** bitterness; unpleasantness.

कटूक्ति kaṭu:kti (*nf*) a bitter utterance, caustic/unpleasant remark.

कटोरदान kaṭordā:n (*nm*) a tiffin-carrier.

कटो/रा kaṭora: (*nm*) a big bowl; **~री** a small bowl.

कटौती kaṭauti: (*nf*) rebate, discount; deduction; reduction; cut;**—प्रस्ताव** a cut-motion.

कट्टर kaṭṭar (*a*) strict; obdurate; dogmatic; fanatic; rabid; **~ता** obduracy; dogmatism, bigotry; fanaticism;**~पंथी** a diehard, religioner; dogmatic; fanatic, bigot; **~पन** (*nm*) see **कट्टरता**.

कठघ/रा kaṭhghara: (*nm*) a bar, dock; wooden enclosure/palisade;**~रे में खड़ा करना** to bring into the dock, to bring before the bar.

कठपुतली kaṭhputli: (*nf*) a puppet; an underling; **—होना, किसी के हाथ में**

to be a puppet in somebody's hand, to dance to the tune of.

कठबैद kaṭhbaid (*nm*) a quack.

कठमुल्ला kaṭhmulla: (*nm*) a bigot, fanatic; quack religious leader; hence ~पन (*nm*).

कठि/न kaṭhin (*a*) difficult, arduous; tough; stiff, hard; severe; ~नता/नाई difficulty.

कठोर kaṭhor (*a*) hard; severe, stern, stringent; rough; cruel; rigid, rigorous; ~ता hardness; stringency; cruelty; severity, rigidity, rigour/rigorousness; ०वाद rigourism; ~हृदय heartless, hard-hearted, cruel; hence ~हृदयता (*nf*).

कड़क kaṛak (*nf*) crack, thunder, sudden sharp noise; vigorousness; (*a*) strong; vigorous.

कड़कड़ाना kaṛkaṛa:nā: (*v*) to crack/crackle (as oil etc. when boiling); to break with a cracking sound; to decrepitate.

कड़कड़ाहट kaṛkaṛa:haṭ (*nf*) crackling sound, thundering sound; decrepitation.

कड़कना kaṛaknā: (*v*) to crackle; to thunder; to break up with a crack.

कड़की kaṛaki: (*nm*) indigence, extreme scarcity, poverty; –का जमाना hard days; –में होना to be hard up, to be tight.

कड़वा kaṛwa: (*a*) bitter; unpleasant; ~ना to get bitter; to become averse, to feel sore; to have a burning sensation (as in the eyes); –तेल mustard oil; hence ~पन (*nm*); ~हट bitterness; unpleasantness; कड़वी जबान bitter vitriolic speech/tongue.

कड़ा kaṛa: (*a*) hard; strict; stiff; harsh, cruel; arduous; sharp; rigid; strong; (*nm*) a bangle, metal ring; ~ई/~पन stiffness; hardness; harshness; strictness; sharpness; rigidity; –मिज़ाज stiff/harsh/stern nature; –पड़ना to adopt a stiff attitude, to become stern; hence कड़ी (*fem.*).

कड़ा/का kaṛa:ka: (*nm*) a loud crack; going without food, a rigid fast; ~ के का severe (as जाड़ा); sharp.

कड़ा/ह kaṛa:h (*nm*) a big boiling pan, frying pan; cauldron; ~ही (diminutive, *nf*).

कड़ी kaṛi: (*nf*) a small beam; rafter, joist; link; line of a song; (*a*) see कड़ा; –कार्यवाही करना, (किसी के ख़िलाफ़) to crack down upon, to take strong action (against).

कड़ुआ kaṛua: (*a*) see कड़वा; –तेल mustard oil.

कढ़ाई kaṛha:i: (*nf*) embroidery; the process or act of embroidering; a huge frying pan.

कढ़ी kaṛhi: (*nf*) curry, a preparation consisting of gram flour dressed with spices and sour milk (*i.e. dahi:*); –का उबाल momentary excitement; –में कंकड़ी/कोयला a pebble in the pudding.

कण kāṉ (*nm*) a particle; an iota, very small quantity; granule, grain; –कण में in each and every particle, everywhere.

कणिका kāṉika: (*nf*) an atom, a particle (as of sand); grain, granule.

क़तई qatai: (*adv* and *a*) wholly, entirely; finally; certainly; final, conclusive.

कतरन katran (*nf*) cutting, off-cut, scrim; parings.

कतरना katarnā: (*v*) to clip, to chip; to cut; to pare; to scrim.

कतरनी katarnī: (*nf*) scissors; nippers; –चलाना to wag one's tongue, to be too gabby.

कतर-ब्योंत katar-byōt (*nf*) contrivance, manipulation, adjustment and readjustment; –करना to manipulate, to contrive.

क़तरा qatra: (*nm*) a drop; fragment; cutting.

कतराना katra:nā: (*v*) to slink away (from); to go out of the way (of·), to avoid an encounter or coming face to face.

कतवार katwa:r (*nm*) sweepings, dregs; rubbish, refuse; a spinner; ~ख़ाना a refuse-bin.

क़ता qata: (*nm*) breaking, cutting; a portion; ~ताल्लुक़ breaking off relation (with).

कताई kata:i: (*nf*) (the act of or wages paid for) spinning.

क़तार qata:r (*nf*) a line, row; series; –बाँधना to make / stand in a row.

कतिपय katipay (*a*) some, a few; several.

कत्तल kattal (*nf*) a chip, piece; chipping/cutting.

कत्थई katthai: (*a*) catechu-coloured.

कत्थक katthak (*nm*) a Hindu tribe specialising in dancing and singing; a kind of classical system of dancing; –नृत्य a typical classical dance.

कत्था kattha: (*nm*) catechu *Terra japonica.*

क़त्ल qatl (*nm*) murder; slaughter; –ए-आम general massacre.

कथ(था)कली kath(tha:)kali: (*nf*) a typical classical Indian dance style.

कथक्कड़ kathakkar̤ (*nm*) a professional story-teller, one who recites old traditional tales.

कथन kathān (*nm*) saying, statement, utterance; speech.

कथनी kathnı: (*nf*) anything said or uttered; speech; –और करनी profession and practice; –से करनी भली brag is a good dog but hold-fast is better.

कथनीय kathnı:y (*a*) worth saying or narrating; describable; hence ~ता (*nf*).

कथरी kathri: (*nf*) a patch-work bedding.

कथांतर kathā:ntar (*nm*) a side-story, subsidiary plot.

कथा katha: (*nf*) a story, tale, fable; narrative; religious discourse; –चित्र a feature film; ~नायक the hero, main character; ~मुख lead, introductory part of the story; ~वस्तु the plot; –वार्ता religious discourse and discussion; conversation on a variety of topics; ~सार a synopsis.

कथानक katha:nāk (*nm*) the plot.

कथित kathit (*a*) said; told, mentioned; narrated.

कथोपकथन kathopkathān (*nm*) dialogue (in a literary work).

कथ्य katthy (*nm*) content, subject-matter; (*a*) worthsaying.

कदंब kadāmb (*nm*) the tree *Nauclea cadamba.*

क़द qad (*nm*) size; height; –काठी stature; figure and frame; क़दोक़ामत stature, figure and frame.

कदन्न kadānn (*nm*) coarse grain.

कदम kadām (*nm*) see कदंब; see क़दम.

क़दम qadām (*nm*) step, pace; foot-step; ~चा foot-rest in a latrine; –ब-क़दम step by step; in the foot-steps of; slowly; ~बोसी kissing the feet (as a mark of deep respect or for flattering); –उखड़ना to be swept off one's feet; –उठाना to march apace, to make progress; –चूमना see ~बोसी (करना); –बढ़ाना to march forward; to step up one's pace.

क़दर qadar (*nf*) extreme, absolute; see क़द्र.

कदर्थना kadarthanā: (*nf*) harassment; humiliation.

कदाकार kada:ka:r (*a*) ludicrous, absurd, ugly (in form).

कदाचा/र kada:cha:r (*nm*) misbehaviour, misconduct; corruption; ~री delinquent; wicked, corrupt.

कदाचित् kada:chit (*adv*) perhaps, possibly, may be.

कदापि kada:pi (*adv*) ever; –नहीं never.

कदाशय kada:shay (*nm*) malafide intent; (*a*) malafide, ill-meaning.

क़दी/म, ~मी qadi:/m, ~mɪ: (*a*) old, ancient.

क़द्दावर qadda:var (*a*) tall and towering, possessing an imposing stature.

कद्दू kaddu: (*nm*) pumpkin; gourd; ~कश an implement for turning a gourd, pumpkin, etc. into parings.

क़द्र qaddr (*nf*) worth, merit; estimation, appreciation; ~दाँ, ~दान a connoisseur, just appreciator; patron; ~दानी just appreciation of somebody's merits; patronage.

कन kān (*nm*) see कण; an allomorph of कान used as the first member of compound words; ~कटा ear-cropt, earless; ~कौवा a big kite; ~खजूरा a centipede; ~टोप a cap which covers the ears; hood; ~पटी temple; ~पेड़ा glandular swelling at the root of the ear; ~बतियाँ whispering into the ears, whispering talk; ~मैलिया one whose profession is to remove wax from the ears.

कनक kanāk (*nm*) see गेहूँ; see सोना; see धतूरा.

कनखी kankhi: (*nf*) an ogle, a leer, side-glance; a sign with an eye; –मारना to eye amorously; to cast a side glance; to sign with an eye; कनखियों से देखना to cast a side glance, to look in an oblique manner, to ogle.

कनगुरिया kānguria: (*nf*) the little finger.

कनर/स kānras (*nm*) a taste for musical or melodious voice; an ardent love for sweet talks; hence ~सिया (*nm*).

कनस्तर kanāstar (*nm*) a canister.

क़नात qana:t (*nf*) awning, curtain; can screen.

कनिष्ठ kanishṭḥ (*a*) the youngest, junior most; hence ~ता (*nf*).

कनिष्ठिका kanishṭḥika: (*nf*) the little finger.

कनी kanɪ: (*nf*) a particle; broken piece of rice; diamond dust; drop; –चाटना to commit suicide by an intake of diamond dust.

कनीज़ kanɪ:z (*nf*) a slave girl, handmaid.

कनेर kaner (*nf*) oleander—the plant or the flower.

कनौड़ा kanauṛa: (*a*) obliged, grateful; ashamed, disgraced; (*nm*) a slave, person under extreme obligation.

कनौती kanauti: (*nf*) the pointed end of a beast's ear; –बदलना to prick up the ears (said of a horse); to assume a cautious posture.

कन्ना kannā: (*nm*) edge, border; that part of the kite to which the string is tied; –ढीला होना to get demoralised; to fall into disarray; कन्ने से उड़ना/कटना to come clean out from, to be cut off at the parts where it is tied (said of a kite); to be clean-swept, to be thoroughly beaten.

कन्नी kannɪ: (*nf*) border; the ends of a kite, edge; trowel; –काटना to slink away, to evade, to fight shy of.

कन्या kannyā: (*nf*) a virgin; daughter;

girl; (राशि) virgo; ~रासी possessing an effeminate disposition or temper; weakling; ~दान giving away a daughter in marriage.

कन्हैया kanhaiya:(*nm*) a corrupt form of कृष्ण (see); a charming child or boy.

कपट kapaṭ (*nm*) fraud, ruse, guile; artifice; trickery; hypocrisy; dissimulation; –करना to defraud, to beguile; –चाल fraudulent act; hypocritic idea, trickery; ~पूर्ण fraudulent, hypocritical; –साक्ष्य spurious testimony; कपटाचार dissimulation, artificial/hypocritical behaviour or conduct; कपटी dissimulator, crafty, fraudulent.

कपड़ kapaṛ —an allomorph of कपड़ा used as the first member in compound words; ~छन thoroughly strained or sifted (through a piece of cloth).

कपड़ा kapṛa: (*nm*) cloth; clothing; fabric; textile; –लत्ता clothings; articles of apparel; clothes; कपड़े उतार लेना to deprive of all belongings; to fleece; कपड़े रँगना or रँगाना (figuratively) to take to an ascetic's attire; to renounce the world.

कपाट kapa:ṭ (*nm*) (the leaves of) a door; shutter; sluice; valve.

कपाटिका kapa:ṭika: (*nf*) a valve.

कपाल kapa:l (*nm*) the skull, head, cranium; destiny; a begging bowl; –क्रिया the ceremony of breaking the skull of a corpse before setting fire to the funeral pyre (a son or one of the nearest relatives performs the ceremony); –संधि a treaty on equal terms; –संश्रय a buffer state.

कपास kapa:s (*nf*) cotton; cotton-plant.

कपि kapi (*nm*) a monkey.

कपिला kapila: (*nf*) a white or grey-coloured cow, harmless cow; gentle woman; a harmless person.

कपूत kapu:t (*nm*) an unworthy or wicked son, an undutiful son; (*a*) degenerate; disobedient.

कपूर kapu:r (*nm*) camphor.

कपोल kapol (*nm*) cheek; –कल्पना a cock and bull story, tale of a tube; fancy, fantastic imagination; ~कल्पित false, fantastic, fabricated.

कप्तान kaptā:n (*nm*) a captain.

कफ kaph (*nm*) phlegm, mucus; ~कर phlegmatic; ~नाशक antiphlegmatic.

कफ़ kaf (*nm*) a cuff.

कफ़न kafān (*nm*) shroud, pall; ~खसोट/चोर penny-pincher; penny pinching, stingy, cheese-paring; –को कौड़ी न रखना to spend every penny (of one's earnings); –को कौड़ी न होना to be penniless; –फाड़कर उठना to rise from the grave; –फाड़कर चिल्लाना to shriek out unexpectedly; –सिर से बाँधना to be ready to risk life or court death; to engage in a perilous venture.

कबंध kabāndh (*nm*) a torso.

कब kab (*adv*) when, at what time; –कब how often; rarely; –का since long, long back.

कबड्डी kabaḍḍi: (*nf*) a typical outdoor Indian game.

कबरा kabra: (*a*) spotted, mottled.

कबरी kabri: (*nf*) entwined hair formed into a braid; (*a*) feminine variant of कबरा (see).

कबाड़ kaba:ṛ (*nm*) junk, scrap; any disorderly stuff; ~खाना a junk-store, junk-house.

कबाड़ा kaba:ṛa: (*nm*); –करना to spoil; ruin, to undo; –होना to be spoiled; to be ruined, to be undone.

कबाड़िया, कबाड़ी kaba:ṛia:, kaba:ṛi:

(*nm*) a junk dealer; one engaged in a low occupation.

कबाब kaba:b (*nm*) roasted meat, roast; collops or small pieces of meat, roasted on a skewer or spit; **–में हड्डी होना** to be a skeleton at the feast, to be like a fly in the ointment, to be an unpalatable ingredient in a delicious dish; to be an unwelcome intruder; **–होना, (जल-भुनकर)** to burn with rage, to be enraged.

क़बाला qaba:la: (*nm*) a transfer/sale deed.

क़बीला kabi:la (*nm*) a tribe.

कबीर kabi:r (*nm*) a great mediaeval Hindi poet; a type of peculiar folk songs (sp. prevalent in U.P. and Bihar) abounding in obscene language.

कबूतर kabu:tar (*nm*) a pigeon; **~ख़ाना** a pigeon house, pigeon hole; dovecot; **~बाज़** one who rears sporting pigeons; **~बाज़ी** rearing of sporting pigeons.

क़बूल qabu:l (*nm*) agreement, consent; admission; confession; **–करना** to admit; to confess; **–कर लेना, साफ़-साफ़** to make a clean breast of.

क़बूलना qabu:lnā: (*v*) to agree; to admit; to concede; to confess.

क़ब्ज़ qabz (*nm*) constipation.

क़ब्ज़ा qabza: (*nm*) possession, occupation; a handle, grip; hinge; **~दार** hinged; one who holds possession, one who is in occupation (of), occupying; **क़ब्ज़े पर हाथ रखना** to get ready to strike/hit.

क़ब्ज़ियत, क़ब्ज़ी qabziyat, qabzi: (*nf*) constipation.

क़ब्र qabbr (*nf*) a grave; **–खोदना** to devise ways and means for ruination/destruction; **–में पाँव लटकाए होना** to be on the brink of the grave, to have one foot in the grave, to be on the verge of death; **–से उठ आना** to escape death, to get a fresh lease of life.

क़ब्रिस्तान qabrista:n (*nm*) a graveyard, cemetery.

क़ब्ल qabbl (*ind*) prior to, before.

कभी kabhi: (*ind*) sometime; ever; **–कभी** sometimes, now and then, occasionally.

कमंडल kamāndal (*nm*) the pot used by mendicants.

कमंद kamānd (*nf*) a rope-ladder used for scaling a building; a noose for entangling wild animals etc.

कम kām (*a*) little, few, scanty; less; short, small; deficient; (*adv*) rarely; seldom; **~अक़्ल** stupid, foolish, unwise; **~असल** crossbreed, hybrid; base; **–उम्र** young, young in age; **–क़ीमत** cheap, low-priced; **~ख़र्च** thrifty, frugal, economical; **~ख़र्ची** thrift, frugality, econony; **~ख़्वाब** brocade, silk wrought with gold and silver flowers; **~तर** smaller; lesser; **~तरीन** smallest; least; **~नसीब** unfortunate; hence **~नसीबी**; **–ख़र्च बाला नशीन** economical and yet of a superior quality; low cost, great show.

कमची kamchi: (*nf*) a strip of wood or bamboo, slender stick

कमज़ोर kāmzor (*a*) weak, feeble; ineffectual.

कमज़ोरी kāmzori: (*nf*) weakness, feebleness; deficiency; debility.

कमती kāmti: (*a*) less, scanty; (*nf*) lack, deficiency, scarcity.

कमनीय kāmni:y (*a*) lovely, beautiful; pretty; hence **~ता** (*nf*).

कमबख़्त kāmbakht (*a*) unfortunate, ill-fated, unlucky.

कमबख़्ती kāmbakhti: (*nf*) misfortune, ill-luck, adversity; **–का मारा** fallen in adversity, accursed, ill-fated.

कमर kamar (*nf*) waist, loins, girdle; the middle part of something; ~**कोट** a parapet, protection wall; ~**तोड़** lit. that which breaks the back—arduous, stringent; unbearable; ~**पट्टी** a belt; ~**बंद** a girdle; –**कसना** to gird up one's loins; to brace oneself up, to be all set for action; –**झुकना** to become old/feeble; –**टूटना** to be rendered hopeless; to be demoralised, to lose all self-confidence; –**तोड़ना** to break one's back; –**बाँधना** to get ready for, to resolve; –**सीधी करना** to relax for a while.

कमरख kāmrakh (*nm*) a sour and pungently tasty fruit; fruit of *Averrhoa carambola*.

कमरा kamra: (*nm*) a room, chamber.

कमल kamal (*nm*) a lotus flower and its plant; –**ककड़ी** the root of lotus; ~**गट्टा** the seed of lotus; ~**नाल** the lotus-stalk.

कमलिनी kamalinı: (*nf*) a small lotus.

कमली kamli: (*nf*) a small blanket.

कमसि/न kamsin (*a*) tenderly young, of tender age; hence –**नी** (*nf*).

कमाई kama:i: (*nf*) earnings; –**हुई (देह)** built up (body–through exercise etc.), strong and muscular.

कमाऊ kama:u: (*a*) earning (a livelihood).

कमान kamā:n (*nf*) a bow; an arch, a curve; command.

कमाना kamā:nā: (*v*) to earn; to merit; to process (leather etc.); to clean (w.c. etc.)

कमानी kamā:nı: (*nf*) a spring; the truss worn by people suffering from hernia; ~**दार** fitted with a spring.

कमाल kama:l (*nm*) a miracle, wonder; excellence; miraculous perfection; –**करना** to work wonders, to perform a miracle.

कमासुत kama:sut (*a*) earning; worthy.

कमिश्न/र kamıshnar (*nm*) a commissioner; ~**री** a territory administered by a commissioner; office of a commissioner.

कमी kamı: (*nf*) deficiency; shortage, paucity, lack, want, scarcity, scantiness; abatement; defect; failing; reduction.

कमीज़ kamı:z (*nf*) a shirt.

कमीन kamı:n (*a*) mean; low-born; hence ~**पन**, ~**पना** (*nm*).

कमीनदार kamında:r (*nm*) a sniper.

कमीना kamı:nā: (*a*) mean, wicked, vile; ~**पन** meanness, wickedness.

कमीशन kamı:shān (*nm*) commission (body of persons having authority or warrant conferring authority in the army etc.); discount.

कमेटी kameṭi: (*nf*) a committee.

कमेरा kamera: (*nm*) a workman, worker.

क़याम qayā:m (*nm*) stay, halt, halting.

क़यामत qayā:māt (*nf*) the day of judgment, the day of resurrection; annihilation, destruction; –**की घड़ी** a moment of extreme crisis; –**बरपा करना** to bring about a devastating crisis; to raise a commotion, to create a stir.

क़यास qaya:s (*nm*) guess, conjecture.

करं/ड karāṉḏ (*nm*) hive; a bamboo basket; ~**डी** a kind of pseudo-silken cloth.

कर kar (*nm*) a hand; ray; the trunk of an elephant; tax, duty, custom; tribute; as a suffix it imparts the sense of an agency (e.g. **सुखकर**–that which gives pleasure); ~**तल**

palm (of a hand); ०ध्वनि clapping, also **करताल**; ~द, ~दाता tributory; tax-paying or tax-payer; ~देय taxable; –निर्धारण tax-assessment; ~मुक्त tax-free; –संपुट open palms placed side by side in a hollowed position.

करकट karkaṭ (*nm*) used as the second member in the compound कूड़ा– meaning—dregs; rubbish, sweepings.

करकना karaknā: (*v*) to produce a painful sensation, to produce an itch (as when some alien matter falls into the eye).

करघा kargha: (*nm*) a weaver's loom.

करछी, करछुल, करछुली karchhi:, karchhul, karchhuli: (*nf*) a ladle.

करण karaṉ (*nm*) articulation; articulator; instrumental case; an organ; instrument; function; doing

करणीय karṉi:y (*a*) worth doing.

करत/ब kartab (*nm*) a feat; performance; exploits; skill; acrobatics, jugglery; ~बी manoeuverer, skilful, dexterous.

करता karta: (*nm*) see **कर्त्ता**.

करतार karta:r (*nm*) the Creator, the Master.

करतूत kartu:t (*nf*) misdeed, evil deed, doing.

करधनी kardhanı: (*nf*) a girdle (of gold, silver or yarn etc.).

करनफूल karānphu:l (*nm*) see **कर्णफूल**.

करना karnā: (*v*) to do; to perform; to complete; to act; to execute; to commit; to hire; to have as man or wife; to run or set up (as दुकान–); to practise (as वकालत–); to solve (as सवाल–); to cohabit; **करै कोई भरै कोई** to bark up a wrong tree.

करनी karnı: (*nf*) doing, deed; a mason's trowel.

कर/ब, ~बी karab, karbi: (*nf*) the stalk of *jua:r* and *ba:jra*: used as fodder.

करम karām (*nm*) deed, doings; act, work, action; destiny, fate; mercy; ~जली an abusive term for a woman or girl meaning luckless/of ill-luck/unfortunate; –ठोकना to lament over one's lot; –फूटना to have a stroke of ill luck, to fall into adversity; to be widowed.

करमकल्ला karāmkalla: (*nm*) cabbage.

करमुहाँ karmūhā: (*a*) a word of abuse meaning one having a blackened face; ill-famed, infamous.

करवट karwaṭ (*nf*) lying on one side, the position of lying or sleeping on the side; a bank; –बदलना/लेना to turn from one side to the other or to change sides while lying; to adopt a new course; –बदलते रात बीतना to spend a restless night.

कराधान kara:dhā:n (*nm*) taxation.

करामात kara:mā:t (*nf*) a miracle, thaumaturgy; feat.

करामाती kara:mā:ti: (*a*) working wonders, miraculous; (*nm*) thaumaturgist.

करार kara:r (*nm*) a river-bank, precipice; see **क़रार**.

क़रार qara:r (*nm*) an agreement, a contract; commitment, undertaking; ~नामा a written agreement; article (as of an association).

करारा kara:ra: (*a*) crisp; hard; strong, stout, sturdy; forceful; hence ~पन (*nm*).

कराल kara:l (*a*) terrifying, formidable; hence ~ता (*nf*)

कराह kara:h (*nf*) a groan, moan.

कराहना kara:hnā: (*v*) to groan, to moan, to cry in pain.

करिश्मा karishmā: (*nm*) a miracle, miraculous feat, magic.

क़रीना qari:nā: (*nm*) orderliness;

method; symmetrical techniques; ~नेदार orderly, methodical.

क़रीब qari:b (*adv*) near, close by; about, approximately, almost; -क़रीब almost; ~न approximately, almost; क़रीबी close, near.

करील kari:l (*nm*) a thorny leafless shrub—*Capparis aphylla*; shoot of a bamboo.

करुण karu̱n (*a*) touching; pathetic, tragic; ~हृदय merciful, compassionate.

करुणा karu̱nā: (*nf*) pity, compassion, pathos; benignity; tenderness of feelings; ~कर/ ~निधान/ ~निधि attributes of God–The Merciful; ~मय tender-hearted, abounding in compassion.

करेला karela: (*nm*) bitter gourd—*Momordica charantia*; –और नीम चढ़ा a bad man in a bad company; hence करेली (diminutive, *nf*).

करैत karait (*nm*) a venomous black snake.

करैला karaila: (*nm*) see करेला; hence ~ली (diminutive, *nf*).

करोड़ karoṛ (*a* and *nm*) ten million; ~पति a multi-millionaire.

करौंदा karaũda: (*nm*) the corinda–*Carissa carandas*, a small acid fruit.

करौली karauli: (*nf*) a poniard, small dagger.

कर्क kark (*nm*); –राशि cancer—the sign of zodiac; –रेखा tropic of cancer.

कर्कश karkash (*a*) hard, harsh, screechy; hoarse; hence ~ता (*nf*).

कर्कशा karkasha: (*a*) termagant, shrew; quarrelsome; (*nf*) quarrelsome/shrewish woman.

कर्ज़ karz (*nm*) loan; debt; ~दार a debtor; ~दारी indebtedness; –खाना to live on loans; to be indebted.

कर्ज़ा karza: (*nm*) see कर्ज़.

कर्ण karṉ (*nm*) an ear; helm; rudder (of a boat); hypotenuse; ~कटु discordant, disagreeable, harsh (sound); ~गोचर audible; ~धार helmsman, one who steers (a boat); ~पाली the lobe of the ear; ~मूल the root of the ear; a disease resulting in swelling at the root of the ear, parotitis; ~शूल ear-ache; ~स्राव running of the ear, discharge of ichorous matter from the ear.

कर्णफूल karṉphu:l (*nm*) an ornament worn in the ear.

कर्णातीत karṉā:ti:t (*a*) ultrasonic.

कर्त्तन kartan (*nm*) cutting, chopping; trimming.

कर्त्तव्य kartavvy (*nm*) duty; (*a*) proper/fit to be done, what ought to be done; ~च्युत fallen/deviated from duty; ~निष्ठ/परायण dutiful; hence ~निष्ठता/परायणता (*nf*); ~मूढ़/विमूढ़ perplexed as to the proper course of action, placed in a dilemmatic state.

कर्त्ता karta: (*nm*) doer; the Creator; subject (in Grammar); head of a joint Hindu family; author; –धर्ता all in all, the active or the managing member of a social, political or any other unit.

कर्तृ kartri—an allomorph of the word कर्त्ता used as the first member in compound words; ~प्रधान वाक्य (a sentence) wherein the subject dominates; ~वाचक a term that denotes the subject; ~वाच्य the active voice.

कर्तृत्व kartrittv (*nm*) the act or property of being an agent, agency; doing; achievement.

कर्दम kardām (*nm*) mud, slime; sin.

कर्नल karnāl (*nm*) a colonel.

कर्बुर karbur (*a*) variegated, spotted.

कर्म karm (*nm*) deed; action; any religious action or rites; fate; object; ~कर a worker; ~कांड the body of religious ceremonies commanded by Hindu law or convention; the cult of religious rituals; ~कांडी a ritualist, specialist in the field of religious rituals; one who performs such rituals; ~कार a wage earner, workman; worker; ~कारक the objective case; –कौशल workmanship; ~चारिवर्ग retinue, body of employees; ~चारी an employee, an official, a worker, servant, member of the staff; ०वृंद staff; ~धारय a kind of compound word; ~निष्ठ dutiful; one who performs rituals as a matter of duty; ~प्रधान (वाक्य) (a sentence) wherein the object dominates; ~फल the outcome of one's deeds; ~बंधन the bondage resulting from one's deeds, the bond of birth and death; ~भोग experiencing or facing the consequences of action; ~योग the philosophy of the discipline of detached action, unmindful of results; hence ~योगी (*nm*); ~वाच्य the passive voice; ~वाद the theory that one has to face the consequences of one's action—good or bad; hence ~वादी; ~वीर one who fulfils one's duties enthusiastically, a hero whose actions are marked by deep enthusiasm; ~शाला a workshop; ~शील industrious; ~हीन unlucky, unfortunate.

कर्मठ karmāṭh (*a*) diligent, assiduous, active and energetic (person); ~ता diligence, hard work, assiduousness.

कर्मणा karmāṉā: (*adv*) by deed, by action.

कर्मण्य karmāṉṉy (*a*) industrious, hard working; active; ~ता activity, industriousness,

कर्मण्यतावाद karmāṉṉyata:va:d (*nm*) activism.

कर्मी karmı: (*nm*) a member of a crew; worker.

कर्मेंद्रिय karmēndriy (*nf*) an organ of action (the hand, the foot, etc.).

कर्षण karshāṉ (*nm*) traction; extraction.

कलंक kalāṅk (*nm*) blemish; stigma; slur, disgrace; –का टीका a blot, mark of disgrace; –धोना to wash off a stigma; –लगाना to stigmatize, to cause a stigma to be attached with.

कलंकित kalāṅkit (*a*) disgraced; blemished.

कलंकी kalāṅki: (*nm*) (one who is) disgraced, stigmatic.

कलंगी kalāgi: (*nf*) see कलगी.

क़लंदर qalāndar (*nm*) a monkey or bear dancer; a kind of Mohammedan recluse; a carefree type of man.

कल kal (*a*) sweet; soft and tender; gentle; low and weak (tone); (*nm* and *adv*) tomorrow; yesterday; (*nf*) peace, tranquillity, comfort; a machine or its parts; ~कंठ one blessed with sweet and soft voice; having a pleasing tone or note; ~कल sweet and soft sound (of a flowing stream or spring); ०ध्वनि sweet and gentle sound; –का too small (as लड़का); of recent past, of recent origin; pertaining to the future (as कल की कल पर है); ~दार a rupee coin: –उमेंठना/ऐंठना/घुमाना to incite a person to perform or to desist from an act; to give a sudden turn to one's line of thinking; –के छोकरे babes and sucklings; –दबाना to make somebody act, to cause to act; –बेकल होना to be ill at ease. to lose physical or mental normalcy, to be disturbed or disquieted; –हाथ में होना to exercise complete control, to have full sway (over).

कल–used as a first member of compound words, meaning black; ~मुहाँ lit. black-faced—disgraced, branded with a stigma.

क़लई qalai: (*nf*) whitewash; tin; tin plating; stone lime, coating; show; external grandeur; ~गर a tinman, tinner of pots and pans; ~दार tin-plated; –उघड़ना/खुलना to be exposed, to be unmasked.

कलक kalak (*nm*) keen regret, remorse, penitence.

कलक्टर kalakṭar (*nm*) a collector.

कलगी kalagi: (*nf*) a plume, crest; aigrette; a gem-studded ornament fixed in the turban; the comb(of a cock).

कलछी kalchhi: (*nf*) a long-handed ladle.

कलन kalān (*nm*) calculus; calculation.

कलपना kalapnā: (*v*) to lament, to bemoan or bewail.

कलफ़ kalaf (*nm*) starch; ~दार starched.

कलम, क़लम kalam, qalām (*nf*) a pen; a painter's brush; a school or style of painting; graft; cutting, chopping; the growth of hair on man's temples; ~क़साई a hack-writer; one who practises butchery through one's pen, one who misdirects or propagates ignorance through one's writings; ~कारी engraving, painting with a brush; ~दान a pen and ink case; pentray, penstand; ~बंद penned, put into black and white, reduced to writing, written; ० करना to write down, to record in writing; hence कलमबंदी (*nf*); –करना to chop off, to cut; to prune; –का धनी a master of the art of writing; –घसीटना to scrible; –घिसना to write insignificant things/ineffectively; –चलाना to write; चूमना lit. to kiss one's pen —to immensely like an expression, to be all praise for (one's writing); –तोड़ना to work wonders in (one's) writing; to write amazingly well; –फेरना to strike out or delete what is written; –में जादू होना to work wonders with the pen; –में ज़ोर होना to wield the pen effectively.

कलमा kalmā: (*nm*) the basic statement or confession of Mohammedan faith; –पढ़ना to repeat the Muslim confession of faith; to embrace Islam; –पढ़ाना to initiate (somebody) into Islam.

क़लमी qalamı: (*a*) grafted; crystallised; –आम grafted mango; –शोरा saltpetre.

कलवार kalwa:r (*nm*) a caste amongst the Hindus who formerly used to deal in liquor; a wine merchant.

कलश kalash (*nm*) a pitcher, an urn; a dome, pinnacle.

कलसा kalsa: (*nm*) a metal pitcher; hence कलसी (diminutive, *nf*).

कलह kaleh (*nm*) quarrel, scramble, strife, broil; dispute; ~प्रिय quarrelsome; ० ता quarrelsomeness; कलही quarrelsome.

कलाँ kaḷā: (*a*) large, larger; big, bigger; elder.

कला kala: (*nf*) art, craft, skill; a portion, division; a digit or one sixteenth of the moon's diameter; sport, play; degree; very minute division of time; ~कार an artist; ~कृति a work of art, an artistic creation; –कौशल artistic skill; artifice; ~जंग a somersault, a trick in the art of wrestling; ~धर, ~निधि the moon; ~परक artistic;

~बाज an acrobat; ~बाज़ी acrobatics, acrobatic feat, taking a somersault; ~वंत an artiste, possessed of artistic skill; ~वादी aesthetic; a believer in art for art's sake; ~विलासी a dilettante.

कलाई kala:i: (*nm*) wrist; –घड़ी a wrist watch.

कलाकंद kala:kānd (*nm*) a kind of sweetmeat.

कलाबत्तू kala:battu: (*nm*) silk thread covered with gold or silver; silk and silver or gold thread twisted together; gold or silver thread.

कलार kala:r (*nm*) see कलवार.

कलावा kala:va: (*nm*) a red thread (tied on the wrist by the Hindus on auspicious occasions).

कलि kali, ~युग, ~yug (*nm*) the *kali* age, the fourth and the last age of the universe according to the Hindu mythology; (fig.) the age of vice; hence ~युगी of or belonging to कलियुग.

कलिका kalika:(*nf*) a bud.

कलिया qalia: (*nm*) meat-curry.

कली kali: (*nf*) a bud; gusset, a piece put in a garment; a maiden who has yet to attain youth, an unblossomed maiden.

कलीसा kali:sa: (*nm*) a Christian church.

कलुष kalush (*nm*) turbidity, impurity; sin; (*a*) turbid, impure; sinful, wicked.

कलुषित kalushit (*a*) sinful, profane; filthy.

कलूटा kalu:ṭa: (*a*) blacky, dark-complexioned.

कलेंडर kalēn̲dar (*nm*) a calendar.

कलेजा kaleja: (*nm*) liver; heart; courage; –उछलना to have the heart throb out of excitement; –कड़ा करना to pull oneself together; to steel one's heart; to prepare oneself for a shock/hardship, etc; –काँपना to be terrified; to be struck with extreme terror; –छलनी होना to be afflicted by taunts and sarcastic remarks; –जलना to suffer extreme agony, to be heart-sore; –जलाना to put to agony, to torment; –टूटना to lose all hope, to be completely demoralised; –ठंडा/तर होना to be fulfilled or gratified, to be assuaged (on account of an adversary's distress); –थाम कर रोना to weep bitterly; –थाम के रह जाना to repress grief, not to let one's grief be manifested; –धक-धक करना to have a violent heart-throb (on account of fear, apprehension, etc.); –धक से हो जाना to be dumbfounded; to receive a violent shock; –धड़कना the heart to palpitate (through anxiety, fear, apprehension); –निकाल कर रख देना to express one's inner hurt feelings; to express/expose oneself without reservation; to surrender one's all; to give away what is best or dearest; –पकना to be deeply wounded; to be fed up of enduring affliction; –पत्थर का करना to become stone-hearted; to get ready to face the worst eventuality; –फटना to have the heart rent by deep sorrow; –बल्लियों/बाँसों उछलना to be full of excitement through joy; –मुँह को आना to have one's heart in one's mouth, to be restless on account of grief; कलेजे का टुकड़ा core of one's heart; something or somebody dearest to one's heart; कलेजे पर चोट लगना suffer a heavy emotional shock or blow; कलेजे पर छुरी चलाना to experience a deep emotional shock; कलेजे पर साँप लोटना to be struck with jealousy, to be under a sense of deep grief (on recollection of some unwelcome event): to repine; **कलेजे पर हाथ रखना** to have a statement endorsed by one's conscience; **कलेजे में आग लगना** the heart to burn through jealousy; to have a sense of love aroused in the heart; **कलेजे में खटकना** to prick, to keep on pinching; **कलेजे में तीर लगना** to be deeply wounded emotionally; **कलेजे से लगाना** to embrace fondly, to caress.

कलेवर kalevar (*nm*) physical structure, external build-up; size.

कलेवा kalewa: (*nm*) breakfast.

कलोल kalol (*nm*) fun and frolic, sport.

कलौंजी kalaũji: (*nf*) nigella; stuffed vegetable.

कल्प kalp (*nm*) era; having the manner or form of, similar to, resembling, almost like (**ऋषिकल्प** like a sage; **पितृकल्प** like father).

कल्पतरु kalptaru (*nm*) a mythological tree or plant that is supposed to grant all desires.

कल्पना kalpanā: (*nf*) imagination; fiction; supposition, assumption; **–चित्र** imaginary picture; **~प्रवण** imaginative; hence **~प्रवणता** (*nf*); **~प्रसूत** imaginary, fictional; invented; **–लोक** in an imaginary/phantastic world; **–लोक में होना** to be in the clouds, to be in a world of phantasy; **–शक्ति** imagination, imaginative faculty; **–सृष्टि** a mental creation, imaginative creation.

कल्पनातीत kalpanā:ti:t (*a*) unimaginable, beyond imagination; incomprehensible.

कल्पनीय kalpnī:y (*a*) imaginable; worth imagining; hence **~ता** (*nf*).

कल्पलता kalplata: (*nf*) a mythological creeper supposed to possess the power to grant all wishes.

कल्पवृक्ष kalpvriksh (*nm*) see **कल्प-तरु**.

कल्पित kalpit (*a*) imaginary; virtual; fictitious; **–नाम** nom de plume; **–स्वर्ग** cockaigne, el Doredo.

कल्मष kalmāsh (*nm*) sin; impurity, filth.

कल्याण kallyā:n̲ (*nm*) welfare, benediction; **~कारी** propitious, auspicious; good, beneficial; **–राज्य** welfare state.

कल्ला kalla: (*nm*) a sprout; interior part of the cheek; **–फूटना** to sprout.

कल्लोल kallol (*nf*) play, sport, frolic.

कवक kavak (*nm*) fungus.

कवच (*nm*) armour, amulet; shell; **~धर/धारी** armoured; **कवचित** armoured.

कवयित्री kavaitri: (*nf*) a poetess.

कवरी kavari: (*nf*) a fillet or braid of hair.

कव/र्ग kavarg (*nm*) the *ka*-pentad of five soft-palatal consonants in the Devna:gri: script, viz. **क, ख, ग, घ, ङ**; **~र्गीय** belonging to the *ka*-pentad.

कव/ल (*nm*) a morsel, mouthful; **~लित** devoured, swallowed, eaten.

क़वायद qava:yad (*nf*) exercise, drill.

कवि kavi (*nm*) a poet; **–कर्म** poetic function, composition/creation; **–प्रसिद्धि** poetic convention; **~राज** a physician; a king of poets; **~वर** a leading poet, an excellent poet; **–समय** age-old traditional description.

कविता kavita: (*nf*) poetry; a poem.

कवित्त kavitt (*nm*) a class of a particular meter in Hindi poetry, esp. *Braj*; poetry, in general (arch.).

कवित्व kavittv (*nm*) poetic content or quality; **–शक्ति** poetic faculty/power.

क़व्वाली qavva:li: (*nf*) a form of group vocal music and song.

कश kash (*nm*) a whip, lash; drawing, pulling; whiff, puff, inhalation; a suffix used to denote one who pulls or lifts, e.g., **मेहनतकश**; ~**मकश** struggle; divergent pulling, wrangling; –**खींचना/लगाना/लेना** to have a puff.

कशिश kashish (*nf*) attraction.

कशीदा kashi:da: (*nm*) ornamental needlework, embroidery; ~**कारी** embroidery.

कशेरुक kasheruk (*nm*) vertebral column; spine; (*a*) vertebrate.

कषाय (*a*) ruddle-coloured; astringent.

कष्ट kasht̤ (*nm*) suffering, pain; hardship; distress; ~**कर/कारक** troublesome, painful, distressing; –**कल्पना** far-fetched imagination; ~**दायक**/~**प्रद** see **कष्टकर**; ~**साध्य** difficult; troublesome; onerous.

कस kas (*nm*) assay, test; strength, power; ~**दार** strong, sturdy; –**बल** strength, power.

कस kas—an allomorph of **काँसा** used as the first member in compound words; ~**कुट** an alloy of copper and zinc; ~**हँड़ी (कसेंड़ी)** a huge bronze pitcher.

कसक kasak (*nf*) smarting pain, aching sensation; internal pain; lingering agony; –**निकालना/मिटाना** to assuage pain; to derive relief by retaliation.

कसकना kasaknā: (*v*) to have an aching sensation/lingering agony.

कसना kasnā: (*v*) to tighten, to frap; to fasten; to bind; to gird up, to brace; to test (on a touchstone), to assay; to reduce to thin shreds (with the help of an implement, e.g. pumpkin, cucumber, etc.).

क़सबा qasba: (*nm*) a township, small town.

कसबी kasbi: (*nf*) a prostitute, harlot adulterous woman.

क़सम qasām (*nf*) an oath, swearing; –**उतारना** to set free of the bonds of oath; to perform an act nominally; –**खाना** to swear, to take an oath; –**खाने को** nominally; –**तोड़ना** to violate an oath; –**दिलाना** to administer an oath (to); to make one swear; to put under an oath; –**देना** to put on oath; –**लेना** to swear, to take an oath.

कसमसाना kasməsā:nā: (*v*) to fidget, to be restless; to wriggle; to bestir oneself.

कसमसाहट kasmasa:hat̤ (*nf*) fidgeting, restlessness, uneasiness; wriggling; bestirring.

क़समिया qasamīyā: (*adv*) on oath, bound by oath.

कसर kasar (*nf*) deficiency; loss; drawback; lacuna, shortcoming; (in Mathematics) a fraction;–**करना/रखना** to be wanting (in), to fail (to); –**खाना/उठाना** to suffer loss or damage; –**देना** to inflict loss (on); –**न उठा रखना** to leave no avenue unexplored, to leave no stone unturned; –**निकलना** to be compensated; to be avenged; –**निकालना** to make up the loss; to avenge, to be quits (with).

कसर/त kasrat (*nf* physical exercise; abundance, plenty; ~**ती** athletic, built-up by physical exercise (as body).

क़साई qasa:i: (*nm*) a butcher; (*a*) cruel, pitiless; ~**खाना/घर** butchery, slaughter house; –**के खूँटे (से) बँधना** to get wedded to a merciless man; to be entrusted to a cruel fellow; –**के खूँटे (से) बाँधना** to hand over to a merciless person/butcher.

कसा-कसाया kasa:kasa:ya: (*a*) ready-packed; ready; saddled; muscular.

कसाकसी kasa:kasi: (*nf*) tension; antagonism.

कसार kasa:r (*nm*) wheat flour fried in *ghee* and mixed with sugar.

कसा/ला kasa:la: (*nm*) toil, labour; ~**ले का** requiring great toil and pains; oppressive and laborious (business).

कसाव kasa:v (*nm*) tightness; stiffness; the quality of being well-knit; terse (language style); muscularity; hence ~**दार** (*a*).

कसावट kasa:vaṭ (*nf*) tightness; terseness; muscularity.

क़सीदा qasi:da: (*nm*) a special variety of eulogical poetic composition in Urdu/Persian.

क़सूर qasu:r (*nm*) fault; guilt; ~**वार** a guilty person.

कसेरा kasera: (*nm*) a particular Hindu community manufacturing and dealing in bronzeware.

कसैला kasaila: (*a*) astringent; hence ~**पन** (*nm*).

कसौटी kasauṭi: (*nf*) a touchstone; test, criterion;–**पर कसना, किसी को** to put a person through his facings.

कस्तूरी kastu:ri: (*nf*) musk; –**मृग** a musk-deer.

क़स्द qasd (*nm*) resolution, will; ~**न** deliberately, wilfully.

क़स्साब qassa:b (*nm*) a butcher; ~**खाना** butchery.

क़हक़हा qahqaha: (*nm*) a burst/peal of laughter; –**लगाना** to laugh boisterously.

क़हत qahat (*nm*) famine; utter scarcity; ~**ज़दा** famine-struck.

कहना kehnā: (*v*) to say, to state, to tell, to utter; (*nm*) saying, utterance, order; advice; **कहते न बनना** to be beyond description, not to be able to narrate/describe; –**कुछ करना कुछ** double dealing; –**सुनना** persuasion, inducement; wrangling; **कहने को** virtually, nominally; **कहने में आना** to be misled, to be induced; to veer round; **कहने में होना** to be under (somebody's) commands, to be under the spell (of); –**कहने से कुम्हार/धोबी गधे पर नहीं चढ़ता** you can take a horse to the water but you cannot make him drink; **कह-बदकर** with explicit resolution, challengingly; **कहें खेत की, सुनें खलिहान की** to talk of chalk and to hear of cheese.

कहनावत kehnā:vat (*nf*) saying.

कहनी-अनकहनी kehnɪ: ānkehnɪ: (*nf*) vituperation, unpleasant utterance.

क़हर qahar (*nm*) calamity; divine wrath/affliction; –**ढाना**/–**बरपा करना** to cause a devastation/calamity.

क़हवा qehwa: (*nm*) coffee; ~**खाना/घर** coffee house.

कहाँ kahā: (*adv*) where; –**अमुक, कहाँ अमुक** the one being no match to the other, a world of difference between the two; –**का कहाँ** carried afar; stretched too remote; –**राजा भोज कहाँ गंगू तेली** the one not fit even to hold a candle to the other.

कहा kaha: (*nm*) saying; advice, order; –**सुना** verbal impropriety, harsh words; –**सुनी** altercation, verbal duel.

कहानी kaha:nɪ: (*nf*) a (short) story; tale; –**कला** the art of story-telling; ~**कार** a story-writer, story teller; –**गढ़ना** to fabricate tales, to tell tales.

कहार kaha:r (*nm*) a Hindu community earning its livelihood by supplying/carrying water, bearing palanquin and washing utensils, etc.; a member of this community; utensil cleaner.

कहावत kaha:vat (*nf*) a saying, proverb.

कहीं kahɪ: (*ind*) somewhere; any where; lest; –**कहीं** in some cases/

places; –का of some unknown origin; excessive; extreme; –का न रखना to cause one's undoing; to cause one's devastation; –का न रहना to be undone; to suffer a total devastation; –की ईंट कहीं का रोड़ा, भानुमती ने कुनबा जोड़ा queer combination of heterogeneous elements; the creation of a whole with heterogeneous parts; –बूढ़े तोते भी पढ़ते हैं? Can you teach an old woman to dance?

काँख kā:kh (*nf*) an armpit.

काँखना kā:khnā: (*v*) to grunt, to groan; to cough.

काँच kā:ch (*nm*) glass; intestinum rectum; the end of the lower garment (*dhoti:*) which is tucked to the waist at the back; –निकलना a disorder in which the intestinum rectum is prolapsed.

काँजी kā:ji: (*nf*) a kind of sour gruel vinegar made by steeping mustard seed, etc. in water and letting the liquor ferment.

काँजी हाउस kā:ji:ha:us (*nm*) a cattle pond.

काँटा kā:ṭa: (*nm*) a thorn, spicule; fork; hook; fishing hook; prong; balance; the tongue of a balance; hands of a watch; the process of testing the correctness of a multiplication sum; bone of fish; obstacle; –निकलना to have an obstacle removed; to be relieved of a lingering agony; –होना to be reduced to a skeleton, to wither away; to act as an obstacle; काँटे की तौल exact in weight; काँटे बिछाना to pave somebody's way with thorns; काँटे बोना to sow seeds of distress or misfortune; काँटों का ताज lit. a crown studded with thorns –an authority difficult to wield; काँटों की सेज a bed of thorns; काँटों पर लोटना to writhe in pain; to be overawed by jealousy; काँटों में घसीटना to embarrass (by undue exaltation/praise/respect).

काँटी kā:ṭi: (*nf*) a bait.

कांटेदार kā:ṭeda:r (*a*) thorny; prickly, spiky.

कांड kā:n̲ḍ (*nm*) untoward or unseemly/incident; even sectional division; chapter; shaft; –करना to cause an untoward or unseemly/incident.

कांत kā:nt (*nm*) husband; (*a*) lovely, pleasant; pleasing.

कांता kā:nta: (*nf*) wife; sweetheart; (*a*) beloved; lovely; –सम्मित उपदेश a curtain lecture.

कांतार kā:nta:r (*nm*) a dense forest.

कांति kā:nti (*nf*) brightness, lustre, splendour, gloss; loveliness; ~मय/मान bright, lustrous, glossy.

काँपना kā:pnā: (*v*) to tremble; to quiver; to shiver.

कांफ्रेंस kā:nfreṇs (*nf*) a conference.

काँव-काँव kā:v-kā:v (*nf*) crowing; unpleasant sound/words.

काँसा kā:sa: (*nm*) bronze; ~गर bronzesmith.

कांस्टेबल kā:nsṭebal (*nm*) a constable.

कांस्य kā:nsy (*nm*) see काँसा; –पदक a bronze medal; –युग the bronze age.

का ka:–a post-position expressive of genitive case—of, belonging to, pertaining to, related with; in some dialects of Hindi 'का' is interrogative pronoun standing for क्या ?; –बरखा जब कृषी सुखाने after meat, mustard; after death, the doctor.

काइयाँ kā:ɪyā: (*a*) cunning, shrewd, crafty (man); hence ~पन (*nm*).

काई ka:i: (*nf*) moss; algae; –छुड़ाना to rub out the moss, filth, etc; –सी फटना to be scattered, to go helter-skelter.

काउंटर ka:unṭar (*nm*) a counter.

काक ka:k (*nm*) a crow; cunning fellow; ~**तालीय** chance; ० **न्याय** a chance happening; ~**पद** a caret.

काका ka:ka: (*nm*) a paternal uncle. hence **काकी** (*nf*).

काकु ka:ku: (*nm*) a peculiar tone; (resulting from distress or fear or anger etc.); sarcasm; an oblique unwelcome remark.

काग ka:g: (*nm*) a crow; cork.

कागज ka:gaz (*nm*) paper; –**पत्र** documents; papers; –**काला करना** to waste both paper and ink, –**की नाव** a house of cards, a transitory thing; –**के घोड़े दौड़ाना** to indulge in a vain and unproductive effort

कागजात ka:gza:t (*nm*) papers, documents.

कागजी kagzi: (*a*) made of paper; documentary, written; (*e.g.* –**सबूत**); having a thin rind (*e.g.*) – **बादाम**); academic action limited merely to paper; delicate; (*nm*) a paper merchant; –**कार्यवाही** action in writing; –**सबूत** documentary/written evidence; –**घोड़े दौड़ाना** to indulge in mere paper transactions, to confine to sheer paper/academic actions; to accomplish projects on paper alone.

काज ka:j (*nm*) a button hole; work; ceremony; –**सरना** to have a work accomplished.

काजल ka:jal (*nm*) collyrium; soot; –**की कोठरी** an abode of evil: a place or affair which imparts a stain on one's character by association.

क़ाज़ी qa:zi: (*nm*) a Muslim judge or magistrate; one who performs the ceremony of *nika:h* in a Muslim marriage; –**कि मुल्ला ?**, (**आप कौन हैं ?**) What is your locus standi ? How dare you interfere ? What business have you to intrude? –**जी दुबले (क्यों), शहर के अँदेशे** to be worried about affairs that are not one's concern.

काजू ka:ju: (*nm*) cashewnut.

काट ka:ṭ (*nm*) a cut, (act of) cutting; section; rebuttal; counter; erosion; incision; dissection; –**करना** to rebut; to counter; –**छाँट** cropping, trimming, pruning; abridgement; additions and alterations; –**पीट** cutting and over-writing, mutilation (of writing etc.).

काट/ना ka:ṭnā: (*v*) to cut; to chip; to chop; to bite; to trim; to prune; to shear; to reap; to mow; to interrupt (*e.g.* **बात**~**ना**); to fell (*e.g.* **पेड़**~**ना**); to pass/mark (*e.g.*) **वक्त**~**ना**); to while away; to fleece; to divide a number leaving no remainder; –**खाना** to bite; to sting; **काटने दौड़ना** to snap/bite one's nose up, to answer snappishly, to fly into a rage, to fret and fume; **काटे खाना** to be snappish, to look spark daggers; arouse a feeling of desolation; **काटो तो ख़ून नहीं** to be in a blue funk, to be stupefied, to be paralysed by sudden fear/apprehension etc.

काठ ka:ṭh (*nm*) wood; timber; a block; (*fig.*) wooden, feelingless person; –**कबाड़** lumber, useless or cumberous material; –**का कलेजा होना** to be hard-hearted, to be heartless; –**का उल्लू** a beetle-brain, an absolute blockhead; –**की हँडिया दुबारा नहीं चढ़ती** it is a silly fish that is caught with the same bait –**की हांडी** a means for dupery; –**मार जाना** to be stunned; –**में पाँव देना** to put one's legs in the stocks to take to a troublesome course –**होना** to be petrified.

काठी ka:ṭhi: (*nf*) a saddle; frame; structure.

काढ़ना karhnā: (*v*) to embroider; to extricate; to draw; to comb (hair).

काढ़ा ka:ṛha: (*nm*) a decoction.

कातना ka:tnā: (*v*) to spin.

कातिक ka:tik (*nm*) the eighth month of the Hindu calendar; also **कार्तिक**.

कातिब ka:tib (*nm*) a scribe; calligraphist.

क़ाति/ल qa:til (*nm*) a murderer; **~लाना** murderous.

कान kā:n (*nm*) an ear; **–उमेठना/ऐंठना** to twist somebody's ear/ears by way of punishment; **–कतरना/काटना** to outwit, to prove more than a match; to excel, to surpass; **–का कच्चा** easily misguided; too credulous; **–खड़े करना** to prick up the ears; to get alert; **–खड़े होना** to be alarmed; **–खाना** to, pester, to dig into the ears (of); **–खोलकर (सुनना)** to listen attentively, to pay heed to; **–खोलना** to put on the alert; **–दबाना** not to protest; **–देना, –देकर सुनना** to incline one's ear to, to heed (somebody's words); **–धरना** to lend ear, to listen attentively; **–न देना** to turn a deaf ear; **–न हिलाना** not to budge in protest; **–पकड़कर निकाल देना** to force out with disdain, to turn out disrespectfully; **–पकड़ना** to cry 'enough', to vow never to do a thing again, to express contrition (for); **–पकना** the ears to become sore (through persistent unwelcome talk etc.); **–पर जूँ न रेंगना** to turn a deaf ear to, to be utterly heedless, to be very negligent or careless; **–पर हाथ धरना** to express ignorance; to pretend not to hear; **–फटना** to be inflicted by a deafening noise; **–फूँकना** to initiate; to tutor; **–फूटना** to become deaf; to be deafened; **–फोड़ना** to deafen (by excessive noise); **–बंद/बहरे कर लेना** to turn a deaf ear (to); **–बजना** to fancy that one hears a sound when there is none; **–बहना** to have pus oozing/flowing out of the ear; **–भरना** to poison the ear (of), to excite dissension by talebearing; **–मरोड़ना/मलना** to twist the ear (by way of warning or punishment); **–में उँगली दिए रहना** to refuse to be attentive, to be heedless; **–में (कोई बात) डाल देना** to apprise somebody (of something); **–में तेल डालना** to be inattentive or negligent; **–लगाकर सुनना** to listen attentively, to pay heed to (what somebody is saying); **कानों-कान खबर न होना** to have a veil of absolute secrecy, not to allow a secret to be divulged.

काना ka:nā: (*a*) one-eyed; (a fruit) partly eaten away by insects; having slight obliquity (as **कपड़ा**); hence **कानी**; **कानी उँगली** the little finger; **कानी के ब्याह में सौ-सौ जोखिम/जोखों** a one-eyed girl's way to matrimonial bliss is strewn with a hundred hazards, there is many a slip between the cup and the lip; **कानी कौड़ी भी पास न होना** to be extremely indigent, to be without a penny; **काने को काना कहना** to call a blind as blind (to utter an unwelcome truth).

कानाफूसी ka:na:phu:si: (*nf*) whisper, below one's breath; **–करना** to speak in whispers, to whisper.

क़ानून qa:nū:n (*nm*) law; **–और व्यवस्था** law and order; **-छाँटना/~दाँ** a legalist, jurist, one who knows law; **–बघारना** to be too much of a legalist, to talk law and nothing but law; to impose one's own interpretations on everything.

क़ानूनन qa:nū:nān (*adv*) legally,

lawfully, by law.

क़ानूनगो qa:nu:ngo (*nm*) a land-record officer.

क़ानूनियत qa:nu:niat (*nf*) legality.

क़ानूनी qa:nu:nī: (*a*) legal, lawful; –**कार्यवाही/चाराजोई** legal proceedings.

कापालिक ka:pa:lik (*nm*) a follower of the *va:m-ma:rgi: shaiv* sect, who carries human skull (*kapa:l*) in his hand, eats meat and drinks all sorts of intoxicants.

कापी, कॉपी ka:pi:, kɔpi: (*nf*) an exercise book; a copy; ~**राइट** copyright.

क़ाफ़िया qa:fiya: (*mn*) rhyme; –**तंग करना** to harass, to put into a tight corner, to persecute.

काफ़िर ka:fir (*nm*) a disbeliever (in the tenets of Islam); an atheist; (*a*) infidel; merciless.

काफ़िला qa:fila: (*nm*) a caravan, convoy.

काफ़ी ka:fi: (*a*) enough; sufficient, adequate; (*nf*) coffee.

काफ़ूर ka:fu:r (*nm*) camphor; –**होना** to vanish, to disappear.

काबला ka:bla: (*nm*) a bolt.

क़ाबलियत qa:bliyat (*nf*) ability, capability, competence.

काबा ka:ba: (*nm*) a square building at Mecca where Mohammedans from all over the world go for pilgrimage.

क़ाबिज़ qa:biz (*a*) possessing, occupying; constipative; (*nm*) a possessor.

क़ाबिल qa:bil (*a*) able; worthy; capable, competent; –**ए –तारीफ़** praiseworthy.

काबुल ka:bul (*nm*) the capital of Afghanistan; –**में भी गधे होते हैं** even paradise has its share of fools.

क़ाबू qa:bu: (*nm*) control; hold; –**से बाहर होना** to take bit between teeth, to get out of hand.

काम kā:m (*nm*) work, task; job, employment; performance; function; passion, lust; desire, needlework; embroidery; –**कला** the art of love; –**कुंठा** sex complex; –**केलि/क्रीड़ा** amorous sport, dalliance; ~**चार** a caprice; ~**चारी** capricious; ~**देव** Cupid–god of love; ~**बाण** the fire of passion, the flowery arrows of Cupid; –**भावना** amoristic sentiment; –**मद** oestrus; ~**मूढ़** overwhelmed by passion; –**वासना** libido, sexual craving; –**वृत्ति** sexual instinct; –**आना** to be of avail or of servive; to come into use; to come to one's rescue; to help; to be killed or slain (in battle); –**करना** to prove effective, to do the trick; to succeed; –**को काम सिखाता है** it is work that makes a workman, practice makes a man perfect; –**चलाना** to manage, to do with, to keep the work going, –**तमाम करना** to put an end to; to destroy, to undo; to kill; –**देखो, अपना** mind your own business; –**निकालना** to have the work accomplished; –**पड़ना** to have to do with, to have business with; –**प्यारा होता है, चाम नही** handsome is that handsome does; –**बनना** to have a purpose served; –**बिगाड़ना** to make a mess of a business; to put a spoke in one's wheel; to foil; –**में जुटे रहना** to be busy as a bee; –**में लाना** to turn to account, to bring into play; –**लगना** to get busy, to have a pressing engagement; to get employed; –**से काम रखना** to mind one's (own) business; –**होना** to have one's purpose served; to have to do a job.

कामकाज ka:m ka:j (*nm*) business, work; –**में आलसी भोजन में हुशियार** the cats love fish but fear to wet their paws,

कामकाजी kā:mka:ji: (*a*) busy; active, industrious.

कामगार kā:mga:r (*nm*) a worker, labourer, labour.

कामचलाऊ kā:mchala:u: (*a*) workable, serviceable; caretaker (government); (answering as a) makeshift, stop-gap.

काम/चोर kā:mchor (*a*) malingerer, shirker: hence ~चोरी (*nf*).

कामदानी kā:mdā:nı: (*nf*) embroidered work.

कामदार kā:mda:r (*a*) embroidered; (*nm*) an agent; employee.

कामदी kā:madi: (*nf*) a comedy, farcical dramatic representation; ~कार a comedy writer.

कामदेव ka:mdev (*nm*) Cupid--the god of love.

काम-धंधा kā:mdhāndha: (*nm*) work; occupation; business.

काम-धाम kā:mdhā:m (*nm*) work; business; occupation.

कामना kā:mnā: (*nf*) desire; lust, passion.

कामया/ब kā:mya:b (*a*) successful; ~बी success.

कामांध kā:mā:ndh (*a*) passion-blind, overwhelmed by lust; hence ~ता (*nf*).

कामाग्नि ka:ma:gnı (*nf*) the fire of passion, excessive passion.

कामातुर ka:ma:tur (*a*) passion-blind, blinded by lust; hence ~ता (*nf*).

कामार्त ka:ma:rt (*a*) love-lorn, obsessed by love; hence ~ता (*nf*).

कामिनी ka:mını: (*nf*) a (lustful) woman; beautiful lady.

कामी ka:mı: (*a*) sexually crazy, libidinous, amorous.

कामुक ka:mūk (*a*) amorous, salacious, libidinous; sensual.

कामुकता ka:mūkta: (*nf*) sexuality; libidinousness, amorousness, salaciousness.

कामोत्कंठा ka:motkāṉṯha: (*nf*) sexual craving, sexual urge.

कामो/त्तेजक, ~द्दीपक ka:mottejak, ~ddi:pak (*a*) passion-arousing, exciting, aphrodisiac.

कामो/न्माद ka:monmā:d (*nm*) crotomania, sex-craze; ~न्मादी sex-crazy.

काम्य ka:mmy (*a*) desirable, covetable; worthy; hence ~ता (*nf*).

कायचिकित्सा ka:ychikitsa: (*nf*) medicine; medical science.

क़ायदा qa:yda: (*nm*) a rule; practice; primer; —क़ानून rules and regulations.

क़ायम qa:yām (*a*) firm; established; located; ~मिज़ाज composed, calm and composed; ~मुकाम officiating; —करना to establish.

कायर ka:yar (*a*) coward, timid; ~ता cowardice, timidity.

क़ायल qa:yal (*a*) acknowledging, extending recognition (to); consenting; convinced; —करना to bring home to; to convince (by argument); to silence; —होना to be convinced; to yield, to be silenced.

काया ka:ya: (*nf*) the body, person; soma; ~कल्प rejuvenation; ~न्तरण metamorphosis, metamorphism; ~पलट metamorphosis.

कायिक ka:yik (*a*) somatic, physical, bodily, —व्यापार physical action.

कार ka:r –a suffix denoting a doer, performer, e.g. ग्रथंकार, चित्रकार; or a particular sound as भकार, मकार; (*nf*) a motor car.

कारआमद ka:r–a:mad (*a*) effective, useful.

कारक ka:rak (*nm*) a case (in Grammar); factor; a suffix denoting the factor responsible for a result, e.g. हानिकारक.

कारकुन ka:rkūn (*nm*) an agent;

employee.

कारख़ा/ना ka:rkha:nā:(*nm*) a factory, workshop; mill; ~**नेदार** owner of a factory/workshop/mill.

कारगर ka:rgar (*a*) effective.

कारगुज़ारी ka:rguza:ri: (*nf*) an achievement, attainment.

कारचोबी ka:rchobi: (*nf*) embroidery.

कारण ka:rā<u>n</u> (*nm*) reason, cause; agency, instrument; ~**ता** causation; causality; –**शरीर** causal body –the original embryo or source of the body existing with the Universal Impersonal Spirit; **कारणात्मक** causal.

कारतू/स ka:rtu:s (*nm*) a cartridge; ~**सी** carrrying firing cartridges.

कारनामा ka:rna:ma: (*nm*) a feat, laudable deed; deed, doing.

कारनिस ka:rnɪs (*nf*) cornice.

कारपोरेशन ka:rporeshān (*nm*) corporation.

कारबार ka:rba:r (*nm*) see **कारोबार**.

कारवाँ ka:rvā: (*nm*) a caravan.

कारसा/ज़ ka:rsa:z (*a*) working wonders, dexterous, adroit, efficient; trickster; ~**ज़ी** working of wonders; dexterousness, adroitness; trickery.

कारा ka:ra: (*nf*) a prison.

कारा/गार, ~**गृह** ka:ra:ga:r, ~grih (*nm*) a prison; jail.

कारावास ka:ra:va:s (*nm*) imprisonment; captivity.

कारिंदा ka:rɪnda: (*nm*) a work agent, an agent.

कारिका ka:rika: (*nf*) versified interpretation, commentary in verse.

कारिस्तानी ka:rista:nɪ: (*nf*) doing; trickery, craftiness; misdeed.

कारी ka:ri: –a suffix denoting performance of an act or a doer, e.g. **कल्याणकारी**.

कारीग/र ka:ri:gar (*nm*) an artisan, craftsman; mechanic; tradesman, workman; ~**री** craftsmanship; workmanship.

कारूँ ka:rū: (*nm*) a cousin of Moses who was very rich and niggardly; –**का ख़ज़ाना** immense wealth, immearsurable treasure.

कारोबा/र ka:roba:r (*nm*) business; occupation; ~**री** busy; pertaining to business; owning or having a business.

कार्टून ka:rṭū:n (*nm*) a cartoon; ~**कार** a cartoonist.

कार्ड ka:rḍ (*nm*) a card.

कार्तिक ka:rtik (*nm*) see **कातिक**.

कार्बन ka:rbān (*nm*) carbon.

कार्मिक ka:rmɪk (*nm*) workman; labour; personnel.

कार्य ka:ry (*nm*) job; task, work; action; function; religious function; ceremony; role; transaction; denouement (in a drama); effect; –**कारण भाव** causality, the relationship of cause and effect; –**काल** term (of office); ~**भार** workload; charge (of office); ~**भारी** in-charge; –**विवरण** details of business/transaction; –**व्यापार** action; –**सिद्धि** success, fulfilment of a job.

कार्यकर्ता ka:rykarta: (*nm*) a worker; an employee.

कार्यकुशल ka:rykushal (*a*) efficient; ~**ता** efficiency.

कार्यक्रम ka:rykkram (*nm*) programme; schedule, ~**ण** programming, scheduling.

कार्यक्षम ka:rykkshām (*a*) potential competent; ~**ता** potentiality; competence.

कार्यत: ka:rytah (*ind*) de facto.

कार्यपालिका ka:rypa:lika: (*nf*) the executive.

कार्य-प्रणाली ka:rypra<u>n</u>a:li: (*nf*) modus operandi.

कार्य-भंग ka:rybhāṅg (*nm*) breakdown.

कार्यवाहक ka:ryva:hak (*a*) acting; officiating.

कार्यवाही ka:ryva:hi: (*nf*) action; proceedings.

कार्यवृत्त ka:ryvritt (*nm*) minutes (of a meeting etc.).

कार्यसाधक ka:rysa:dhak (*a*) effective; expedient; ~**ता** expediency.

कार्यसूची ka:rysu:chi: (*nf*) the agenda (of a meeting).

कार्यांग ka:ryā:ṅg (*nm*) the executive (wing).

कार्यान्वय ka:rya:nnvay (*nm*) execution, implementation.

कार्यान्वित ka:rya:nnvit (*a*) executed, implemented; –**करना** to execute;

कार्यान्विति ka:rya:nviti (*nf*) execution, implementation.

कार्याल/य ka:rya:lay (*nm*) an office, bureau; ~**यीय** official.

कार्यावली ka:rya:vali: (*nf*) the agenda.

कार्योत्तर ka:ryottar (*a*) post facto, ex post facto.

काल ka:l (*nm*) time; period; age, era; tense (in Grammar); end, death; famine; calamity; season; ~**कूट** a very deadly poison; –**कोठरी** a death cell; –**देवता** the death - God; –**पुरुष** time personified; –**बली** all–powerful Death; –**आना** the end to come; –**कवलित होना/के गाल में समाना/के मुँह में जाना** to be devoured by Death, to give up the ghost; –**सा लगना** to be as unwelcome as Death; –**सिर पर खड़ा होना/नाचना** to be at Death's door.

कालकोठरी ka:lkoṭhri: (*nf*) a death cell, solitary cell, blackhole.

कालक्रम ka:lkkrām (*nm*) chronology; passage of time; ~**विज्ञान** chronology.

कालचक्र ka:lchakkr (*nm*) the wheel of time.

कालजयी ka:ljayi: (*a*) that which transcends time; immortal.

कालत्रय ka:lttray (*nm*) the three times –past, present and future taken together.

काल-दोष ka:ldosh (*nm*) anachronism.

कालधर्म ka:ldharm (*nm*) death; timely duty.

का(काॅ)लर ka:(ɔ)lar (*nm*) a collar.

कालांतर ka:lā:ntar (*nm*) time interval; –**में** (*adv*) in course of time, with the passage of time.

काला ka:la: (*a*) black; dark; strained; –**कलूटा** jet black; –**क़ानून** black law; –**कौआ** as black as a crow; –**चोर** unknown/untraced person; –**ज़ीरा** carum; –**धन** black money; –**नमक** a kind of rock-salt; –**नाग** a cobra; a venomous/wicked person; –**पानी** life imprisonment; the Andamans where Indians sentenced for life were deported during the British regime; –**बाज़ार** black market; –**भुजंग** pitch dark; –**मुँह करना** to be gone; to acquire a bad name; **काली करतूत** evil doings; **काली खाँसी** whooping cough; **काले के आगे चिराग़ नहीं जलता** nothing sustains in an encounter with the devil; **काले कारनामे** evil deeds; **काले कोसों** very far.

कालातीत ka:la:ti:t (*a*) not bound by time; timeless; time-barred.

कालानुक्रमण ka:la:nūkkramāṉ (*nm*) seriation.

कालावधि kala:vadhi (*nf*) period (of time).

कालिक ka:lik (*a*) periodical; seasonal.

कालिका ka:lika: (*nf*) see **काली**.

कालिख ka:likh (*nf*) soot, blackness; stain, stigma; –**पुतना/लगना** to be stigmatised, to come to disgrace, to have one's reputation sullied.

कालिमा ka:limā: (*nf*) blackness;

stigma; blemish.

काली ka:li: (*a*) black, dark complexioned; (*nf*) an epithet of goddess Durga:; –**छाया** an ominous shadow (foreboding ill); –**ज़बान** Cassandra, prophet of ill, an ill-omened tongue; –**मिर्च** pepper; –**मां के गोरे बच्चे** a black hen laying white eggs.

कालीन ka:lɪ:n —a suffix denoting relationship in time e.g. **समकालीन तत्कालीन**.

क़ालीन qa:li:n (*nm*) a carpet.

कालेज, कॉलिज ka:lej, kɔlij (*nm*) a college.

कालोचित ka:lochit (*a*) expedient; in accordance with the times; ~**ता** expediency, accordance with the times.

कालौंच ka:lãuch (*nf*) blackness, sootiness.

काल्पनिक ka:lpanɪk (*a*) imaginary, fictitious; utopian; hence ~**ता** (*nf*).

काव्य ka:vvy (*nm*) poetry; –**कला** the art of poetry; ~**कार** a poet; –**कृति** a poetic work; –**पाठ** recitation; -**मर्मज्ञ**/ –**मर्मी** a connoisseur of poetry; hence –**मर्मज्ञता**; **काव्यात्मक** poetic; hence **काव्यात्मकता** (*nf*).

काश ka:sh (*ind*) Had God willed thus !

काशीफल ka:shi:phal (*nm*) squash gourd.

काश्त ka:sht (*nf*) cultivation, farming; holding; ~**कार** a cultivator, farmer, tenant; ~**कारी** cultivation, farming.

काष्ठ ka:shṭh (*nm*) wood; –**कला** woodcraft; ~**वत्** as dead as wood, motionless.

काहि/ल ka:hil (*a*) slothful, lazy, indolent; ~**ली** laziness, lethargy, indolence.

काही ka:hi: (*a*) blackish green, of the colour of moss; jealous.

किंकर्त्तव्य kinkartavvy: –**मीमांसक** causist; –**मीमांसा** causistry; –**विमूढ़** in a fog, caught in a dilemma, placed on the horns of a dilemma; hence ~**विमूढ़ता** (*nf*).

किंचित् kiṇchit (*a*) little, somewhat, slight.

किण्वन kiṉvān (*nm*) fermentation, brewing.

किंतु kɪntu (*ind*) but; –**परंतु** ifs and buts; ०**करना** to dilly-dally, to be evasive.

किंवदंती kɪmvadānti: (*nf*) rumour, hearsay, tradition.

किंवा kɪmva: (*ind*) or, otherwise.

कि ki (*ind*) that; for.

किकियाना kikia:nā: (*v*) to scream, to shriek, to screech; to shout in angry tones.

किचकिच kichkich (*nf*) altercation, quarrel; useless prattling.

किचकिचाना kichkicha:nā: (*v*) to gnash in anger.

किचपिच kichpich (*nf*) crowdedness, excessive throng.

किटकिटाना kiṭkiṭa:nā: (*v*) to gnash in anger, to produce a gritty sound.

कितना kitnā: (*a*) how much; **कितने पानी में हैं, (आप)** where you stand.

कितने kitnē (*a*) how many.

क़िता qita: (*nm*) a plot of land, piece; number.

किताब kita:b (*nf*) a book; ~**ख़ाना** a library; –**चाटना** to read through, assimilate a book thoroughly. **किताबी** bookish; pertaining to books; ०**कीड़ा** a bookworm, a voracious reader; **किताबी ज्ञान** bookish knowledge.

किधर kidhar (*adv*) where, whither.

किन kɪn (*pro*) an oblique plural form of **कौन** (see).

किनका kīnka: (*nm*) a small particle, granule; (*pro*) of whom ?

किनार kinā:r (*nf*) see **किनारी**; ~**दार** having a border, bordered; having an edge.

किनारा kina:ra: (*nm*) bank; shore; edge, border, verge; ~**कशी** the act of drawing away; –**करना/कसना** to draw afar; **किनारे लगना** to arrive at the destination; **किनारे होना** to step aside, to dissociate.

किनारी kina:ri: (*nf*) border; edge.

किन्नर kɪnnar (*nm*) a mythical being with human figures and a head of horse or with a horse's body and the head of a man; a race celebrated as musicians.

किफ़ायत kifa:yat(*nf*) economy, thrift, frugality; ~**शार** spendthrift, frugal, thrifty; ~**शारी** thrift, frugality, economy; **किफ़ायती** economical, thrifty.

कियत्ता kiyatta: (*nf*) quorum; extent.

किया kiya: (*v*) did —past-participle form (mas. singular) of the verb **करना**; **किया –कराया/धरा** taken to a successful conclusion, accomplished; ०**मिट्टी में मिलाना** to undo what has been achieved/accomplished; **किये का फल भोगना** to drink as one has brewed; **किये कराये/धरे पर पानी फेरना** to mar all one's efforts, to undo what has been achieved.

किरंटा kirā̃ṉṯa: (*nm*) (used derogatorily for) a Christian.

किरकिरा kirkira: (*a*) impaired, marred, spoilt; sandy, gritty; –**करना, मजा** to mar the pleasure (of); –**होना** to have one's pleasure (out of something) marred.

किरकिराना kirkira:nā: (*v*) to grate, to be gritty; to have an itching sensation in the eye caused by a foreign matter.

किरकिराहट kirkira:haṭ (*nf*) a grating noise.

किरकिरी kirkiri: (*nf*) a particle of foreign matter fallen in the eye; humiliation, disgrace; –**होना** to suffer humiliation/disgrace.

किरच kirach (*nf*) a bayonet.

किरचा kircha: (*nm*) small particles; splinters.

किरण kirāṉ (*nf*) a ray, beam; –**फूटना** a ray to shoot forth.

किरमिच kirmɪch (*nf*) canvas.

किरमिजी kirmīji: (*a*) crimson (colour).

किरात kira:ṭ (*nm*) an ancient Indian tribe.

किराना kira:nā: (*nm*) grocery.

किरानी kira:nɪ: (*nm*) a clerk.

किराया kira:ya: (*nm*) rent, hire; fare; **किराये पर चढ़ाना/देना to rent** out; **किराये पर चलाना** to hire out.

किरायेदा/र kira:yeda:r (*nm*) a tenant; ~**री** tenancy.

किरिच kirich (*nf*) see **किरच**.

किलक kilak (*nf*) a joyful outcry.

किलकना kilaknā: (*v*) to produce a joyful outcry.

किलकारना kilka:rnā: (*v*) to shriek joyfully.

किलकारी kilka:ri: (*nf*) joyful shriek/outcry; –**मारना** see **किलकारना**.

किलबिलाना kilbila:na: (*v*) to crawl; to wriggle.

क़ि/ला qila: (*nm*) a fort, castle; ~**लेबंदी** fortification; **क़िलेदार** garrison commander; **क़िलेदारी** the charge of a fort; the position of a **क़िलेदार**; ~**ला फ़तह/सर करना** to conquer an enemy, to achieve a victory; to accomplish a gigantic task.

किलो kilo (*nm*) kilo (gram); ~**ग्राम** a kilogram; ~**मीटर** a kilometre; ~**लीटर** a kilolitre.

क़िल्लत qillat (*nf*) difficulty, botheration; paucity, scarcity, dearth; –**पालना** to own up a botheration.

किल्ली killi: (*nf*) a small peg; key; -**घुमाना** to direct an operation; to manoeuvre; to beguile; (**किसी की**) –**हाथ में होना** to have sway or control (over someone).

किवाड़ kiva:r (*nf*) door leaf, shutter; –**देना** to shut the door.

किशमि/श kishmish (*nf*) raisin; ~**शी** raisin-coloured; of raisin.

किशोर kishor (*a*) adolescent; youthful; –**अवस्था** adolescent age; ~**ता** adolescence; youthfulness; hence **किशोरी** (*nf*).

किश्त kisht (*nf*) a checkmate (in the game of chess).

किश्ती kishti: (*nf*) a boat, ferry.

किस kis (*pro*) oblique singular form of **कौन** (see); –**खेत की मूली हो,** (**तुम** etc.) What are you worth ? What do I care for you ? –**गिनती में हो** ? What do you count for ? Who reckons with you ? –**चिड़िया का नाम है** ? Who the hell is that ? –**मुँह से** to have the cheek to.

किसा/न kisa:n (*nm*) a farmer, peasant; ~**नी** farming; of or pertaining to a peasant; ~**न चाहे वर्षा कुम्हार चाहे सूखा** donkey means one thing and the driver another.

किसी kisi: (*pro*) oblique singular form of **कोई** (see); –**तीसरे को भेद न देना** between you and me and the bedpost; –**पर जाना** to resemble; –**बात को पक्का करना** to make assurance double sure; –**से निपटना** to have bone to pick with someone.

क़िस्त qist (*nf*) an instalment; ~**बंदी** fixation of instalments; –**बाँधना** fixation of instalments; ~**वार** by/in instalments; –**क़िस्तों में** in instalments.

क़िस्म qism (*nf*) type; kind; quality; variety; –**क़िस्म का** of different kinds/types/varieties/qualities.

क़िस्मत qismat (*nf*) fate, fortune, lot, luck; ~**वर** lucky, fortunate; –**आजमाना** to take one's chance, to chance one's arm, to try one's luck; –**का खेल** irony of fate; –**चक्कर/फेर** (a stroke of) ill luck; –**का धनी** lucky, fortunate; –**का लिखा** the decree of fate, dictates of destiny; –**का हेठा** one who is humbled by fortune, not a favourite of Dame Luck; –**अपने हाथ में होती है** every man is the architect of his own fate; –**किसी को तख्त देती है, किसी को तख़्ता** fortune to one is mother, to an other is stepmother; –**खुलना/चमकना/जागना/फिरना** to have a favourable turn of fortune, to have an advent of good luck; –**पलटना/उलटना** to have a turn of fortune, to have a sudden change in the course of one's luck; –**फूटना** to fall into adversity, to have a stroke of ill luck; –**लड़ना** to have a run of good luck; –**लड़ाना** to test/try one's luck; –**सो जाना** fortune to turn its back upon.

क़िस्सा qissa: (*nm*) a story, tale; quarrel, dispute; –**कहानी** fiction, tales; ~**गो** a tale-teller; –**कोताह करना** to present in short; to say in brief; –**ख़त्म/तमाम करना** to put a stop to the quarrel; to put an end to; to wind up (the matter).

क़िस्से/बाज़ qisseba:z (*nm*) a tale-teller, an idle talker; ~**बाज़ी** mess, imbroglio; complication.

की kɪ: (*v*) did – feminine plural form of **किया.**

की ki:–*feminine* form of **का** and **किया.**

कीकर ki:kar (*nm*) see **बबूल.**

कीच ki:ch (*nf*) mud, slime; sewage.

कीचड़ ki:chaṛ (*nm*) mud, slime, sewage, sludge; mattery discharge which collects in the corner of the eye; –**उछालना** to fling dirt, to indulge in denunciatory remarks (about); to cast aspersions on one's character; to indulge in character assassination; –में फँसना to get involved in a mess, to get embroiled in a fussy affair.

कीजिए ki:jie (*v*) please do, honorofic imperative form of the verb 'करना'; ~गा same as कीजिए but relating to the future.

कीट ki:ṭ (*nm*) an insect, a worm; ~विज्ञान entomology; ~वैज्ञानिक entomologist; entomological.

कीटाणु ki:ṭā:ṇū (*nm*) a germ; ~नाशक insecticide; –युद्ध germ-warfare.

कीड़ा ki:ṛa: (*nm*) an insect, a worm; –काटना to get restless; –लगना to be eaten up by worms; कीड़े पड़ना worms to breed (in), to get rot, to suffer physical disintegration; to suffer consequences of sins.

कीना ki:nā: (*nm*) rancour, grudge; self-dignity; ~वर/कीनेवाला one who is meticulous in preserving (one's) self-dignity; rancorous.

कीप ki:p (*nf*) a funnel.

क़ीमत qi:mat (*nf*) price; cost; value.

क़ीमती qi:mti: (*a*) precious; costly, valuable.

क़ीमा qi:ma: (*nm*) minced meat; –करना to mince.

कीमिया ki:mia: (*nf*) alchemy; ~गर/~साज an alchemist; ~गरी/ ~साजी (the practice of) alchemy.

कीर्तन ki:rtān (*nm*) devotional singing/song; ~कार the performer of कीर्तन; also कीर्तनिया.

कीर्ति ki:rti (*nf*) reputation, fame, renown, glory; ~मान enjoying reputation, renowned; record; ०स्थापित करना to establish a record; ~शाली reputed, famous, renowned; ~शेष surviving by virtue of glory; dead, late; ~स्तंभ a column built to commemorate a triumphal event, a pillar/tower of triumph.

कील ki:l (*nf*) a nail; pin; peg; toggle; wedge, spike, spline; core (of a boil); a gold or silver pin worn by women on one side of the nose; –काँटा tools and accoutrements; -काँटे से लैस/दुरुस्त tip-top, in full attire; in complete readiness; to be fully equipped.

कीलक ki:lak (*nm*) a pivot; rivet; cuneus.

कीलना ki:lnā: (*v*) to drive a nail into; to spell-bind; to charm, to breathe a spell or incantation over; to render ineffective.

कीश ki:sh (*nm*) a monkey.

कीली ki:li: (*nf*) an axis, a pillar.

कुँआ/रा kūa:ra: (*a*) bachelor, unmarried; ~री virgin, unmarried (girl).

कुंकुम kūnkum (*nf*) saffron; rouge.

कुंचित kuṇchit (*a*) curved; curled, curly.

कुंज kuṇj (*nf*) a grove, bower, arbour.

कुँजड़ा kūjṛa: (*nm*) a vegetable vendor; green-grocer; कुंजड़ों की तरह लड़ना to quarrel like low-bred people, to quarrel over trifles.

कुंजी kūṇji: (*nf*) a key (for a lock/for a difficult text or book etc.); –हाथ में होना to possess the key to.

कुंठा kūṇṯha: (*nf*) frustration; complex; ~ग्रस्त frustrated, obsessed by frustration; complexed.

कुंठित kūṇṯhit (*a*) blunt; frustrated; stunted; ~बुद्धि not of sharp intellect, dullard.

कुंड kūṇḏ (*nm*) a reservoir; pool; cistern.

कुंड/ल kūṇḏal (*nm*) a large-sized ear-ring; ~लाकार circular, ring-like.

कुंडलिनी kūṇḏalini: (*nf*) the serpent

force of the *hathyogi:*.

कुंडली kūṇḍli: (*nf*) a coil; horoscope; **कुंडलित** coiled; circular, spiral; serpentine.

कुंडा kunḍa: (*nm*) a large earthen bowl/pot; **–करना** to devastate, to undo, to ruin.

कुंडी kūṇḍi: (*nf*) a hasp; an iron-chain fixed in a door (for locking purposes); see **कुंडी**; **–खटखटाना/खड़खड़ाना** to rattle the chain (signifying a request to open the door); **–लगाना** to bolt, to fasten the door-chain.

कुंद kūnd (*nm*) a kind of flower; (*a*) obtuse; blunt; slow; **~ज़ेहन** dull, obtuse.

कुंदन kundan (*nm*) purified and glittering gold; **–की तरह दमकना** to shine like purified gold.

कुंदा kūnda: (*nm*) the butt (end of a gun); log; block of wood; handle (of an instrument).

कुंभ kumbh (*nm*) a pitcher, pot (of clay); Aquarius, sign of the zodiac; a sacred festival of the Hindus which falls after every twelve years; **~क** in *pra:ṇa:ya:m*, the phase of stopping the breath by shutting the mouth and closing the nostrils with the fingers of the right hand; **~कार** a potter.

कुँवर kūwar (*nm*) a prince; son.

कु ku—a Sanskrit perfix meaning deterioration, depreciation, deficiency, want, littleness, hindrance, reproach, contempt, guilt; **~कृत्य** see **कुकर्म**; **~ख्यात** notorious, infamous; **~ख्याति** notoriety, infamy; **~गति** bad plight, state of affliction; **~चैला** dirty, filthy (used only as the latter member of the compound **मैला-कुचैला**); **~जोग** mischance, adverse circumstance, ill luck; **~टेक** obduracy; addiction, a bad habit; **~डौल** ugly, having disproportionate physical build, possessing unsymmetrical physical frame; **~ढंगा** absurd; lacking proportion or symmetry; inappropriate; **~ढब** undesirable manner/ill practice; evil way; **~दर्शन** ominous; ugly, grotesque; **~दिन** unfavourable times, adversity; **~दृष्टि** ominous glance, a glance resulting in ill-luck; **~धातु** a base metal; iron; **~धान्य** ill-earned foodgrains; **~नाम** infamy, disrepute; notorious; **~पंथ/यश** immoral/evil course; **०गामी** following an immoral/evil course, morally degenerate; **~पुत्र** an undutiful son, bad son; **~बेला** late hour; too late; **~भाव** ill-will, rancour, jealousy; **~मंत्र** evil counsel, misleading advise; **~योग** see **~जोग**; **~राह** evil course, the path of sin; uneven path; **~राही** one who follows the path of degeneration; a sinner; **~वृत्ति** evil tendency; evil calling; bad mentality; ill-disposition.

कुआँ kuā: (*nm*) a well; **–खोदना** to dig a well; (*fig.*) to endeavour to harm somebody; to make an effort for one's own needs; **कुएँ का मेंढक** frog of a well—one having too limited experience or a narrow outlook; a know-little; **–प्यासे के पास नहीं जाता, प्यासा कुएँ पर जाता है** the mountain will not come to Mahomet, Mahomet will go to the mountain; **कुएँ पर से प्यासा आना** to reach the destination and yet return frustrated; **कुएँ में धकेलना** to ruin the life of, (*esp.*) used for a girl when she is married off to an undeserving person or in an undesirable family; **कुएँ में बाँस डालना** to make a frantic search;

कुएँ में भाँग पड़ना all (in a family etc.) to go off their heads.

कुकरे kukre (*nm*) (used in plu.) trachoma.

कुक/र्म kukarm (*nm*) evil deed, misdeed, sin; ~र्मी evil doer, sinner.

कुकुर kukur (*nm*) a dog; –खाँसी whooping cough; ~मुत्ता a mushroom.

कुकृत्य kukritty (*nm*) see कुकर्म.

कुक्कुट kukkuṭ (*nm*) a cock; –पालन poultry-farming.

कुक्षि kukshi (*nf*) the womb.

कुख्या/त kukkhya:t (*a*) notorious, infamous, of ill repute; ~ति notoiety, infamy.

कुगति kugati (*nf*) bad plight; state of affliction.

कुच kuch (*nm*) the female breast; ~मंडल the female breasts.

कुच/क्र kuchakkr (*nm*) a conspiracy, plot; ~क्री conspirator, plotter.

कुचलना kuchalna: (*v*) to crush, to trample (over).

कुचला kuchla: (*nm*) strychnine.

कुचा/ल kucha:l (*nm*) misconduct; aberration, evil course; ~ली corrupt, aberrant.

कुचेष्टा kucheshṭa: (*nf*) misdemeanour, condemnable activity.

कुछ kuchh (*pro* and *a*) some, a few; something; –एक some; –कुछ somewhat; to some degree; –कर देना to overwhelm by magical or demonological charm; –कर बैठना to take a wrong step; to do something wrong; –कहना to say harsh/unpleasant words; –का कुछ something altogether different, something just the contrary; –गुड़ ढीला कुछ बनिया, –सोना खोटा, कुछ सुनार to have some deficiency at either end; –न चलना to have no say; –न पूछिए to be simply indescribable; –न गिनना/न समझना to consider as utterly insignificant, to count for nothing; –न सूझना to be in a fog, to be at a loss; –पल्ले न पड़ना not to be able to make head or tail of; –भी हो come what may!; –समझना to assume airs; –होकर रहना something unusual to be bound to happen; –होना to be significant; something unusual to be imminent.

कुछेक kuchhek (*pro.*) a few, some, several.

कुजाति kuja:ti (*nf*) an inferior or low caste; low breed.

कुटनी kuṭnī: (*nf*) bawd, procuress.

कुटाई kuṭa:i: (*nf*) ramming, pounding; thrashing.

कुटिल kuṭil (*a*) crooked; curved, tortuous; perverse; ~ता crookedness; curvature; perversity; tortuosity.

कुटी kuṭi: (*nf*) a cottage, hut hermitage; cut grass and weeds (for cattle to eat).

कुटीर kuṭi:r (*nm*) cottage, –उद्योग cottage industry.

कुटुं/ब kuṭumb (*nm*) a family, household; ~बी a member of the family, kinsman: a householder; ~ब चलाना/पालना to maintain a family, to run a household.

कुटेव kuṭev (*nf*) evil/bad habit, addiction.

कुट्टी kuṭṭi: (*nf*) see खुद्दी; cut grass and weeds.

कुठला kuṭhla: (*nm*) a small earthen granary, barn.

कुठाँव kuṭhā:v (*nm*) wrong or forbidden place or point; undesirable or delicate place or point; –मारना to hit below the belt; to make an unbearable stroke.

कुठा/र kuṭha:r (*nm*) a kind of axe or hatchet; ~राघात a violent stroke.

कुठौर kuṭhaur (*nm*) see कुठाँव.

कुढं/ग kuḍhang (*nm*) ill manner,

evil way; ~गी ill-mannered, aberrant.

कुढ़न kuṛhan (*nf*) fretting, repining; grudge.

कुढ़/ना kuṛhnā: (*v*) to fret or grieve, to begrudge, to repine; –कुढ़ कर मरना to fret out one's life.

कुतरना kutarna: (*v*) to nibble; to gnaw.

कुत/र्क kutark (*nm*) sophistry, fallacious/false reasoning, argument for argument's sake; perverse argumentation; ~र्की sophistical; one who indulges in perverse argumentation.

कुतिया kutia: (*nf*) a bitch; an abusive term for a woman.

कुतुबनुमा qutubnumā: (*nm*) a compass.

कुतूह/ल kutu:hal (*nm*) curiosity, inquisitiveness; wonder; ~ली curious, inquisitive.

कु/त्ता kutta: (*nm*) a dog; (in mechanics) detent; a worthless fellow, flunkey, ~त्ते का काटना, पागल to run amuck, to go berserk; कुत्ते की दुम कभी सीधी नहीं होती, कुत्ते की पूँछ टेढ़ी की टेढ़ी natural characteristics persist forever, a leopard never changes its stripes; curst cows have short horns; कुत्ते की जिंदगी जीना to live a dog's life; कुत्ते की नींद dog-sleep; कुत्ते की मौत मरना to die a dog's miserable death; कुत्ते के भौंकने से हाथी नहीं डरता the dog barks while the elephant passes by; कुत्ते तक को नहीं दुत्कार सकता not to be able to say go to a goose.

कुत्सा kutsa: (*nf*) vileness, evil/vile feeling.

कुत्सित kutsit (*a*) contemptible, despicable; vile.

कुदकना kudaknā: (*a*) to hop.

क़ुदरत qudrat (*nf*) (the) nature; –का खेल the feats of nature.

क़ुदरती qudrati: (*a*) natural; original, spontaneous.

कुदान kuda:n (*nf*) a jump; –भरना to take a jump.

कुदा/ल kuda:l (*nm*) a pick-axe: ~ली a small pick-axe.

कुनकुना kunkunā: (*a*) lukewarm, tepid; hence ~पन (*nm*).

कुनबा kunba: (*nm*) family, kinsfolk; ~परस्त nepotist; devoted to the family; ~परस्ती nepotism; devotion to the family.

कुनैन kunāin (*nf*) quinine.

कुपं/थ kupanth (*nm*) evil/immoral course; ~थी immoral, one who takes to an evil course, aberrant.

कुपच kupach (*nm*) dyspepsia, indigestion.

कुपढ़ kupaṛh (*a*) illiterate, uneducated.

कुपथ kupath (*nm*) evil/immoral course; ~गामी one who takes to an evil/immoral course.

कुपथ्य kupatthy (*nf*) unwholesome/unsalubrious food; consuming unwholesome or unsalubrious food.

कुपात्र kupa:tr (*a* and *nm*) (an) undeserving (person), unworthy (fellow).

कुपित kupit (*a*) enraged, angry, irate.

कुपोषण kuposhan̲ (*nm*) malnutrition.

कुप्पा kuppa: (*nm*) a big flask; –सा मुँह करना/फुलाना to get sulky, to begrudge; –होना to be inflated (with joy); to become plump.

कुप्पी kuppi: (*nf*) a funnel; small flask; small metallic lamp.

कुप्रबंध kupprabandh (*nm*) mismanagement, maladministration.

कुप्रशासन kupprasha:san (*nm*) maladministration.

कुफ़्र kufr (*nm*) blasphemy, heresy; a belief that defies Islam; –तोड़ना

to break the resolution (of), to get to veer round; to overcome the obstinacy (of).

कुब/ड़ा kubṛa: (*a*) hunch-backed; bent; ~ड़े को लात a blessing in disguise.

कुबुद्धि kubuddhi (*a*) wicked, vicious, depraved; (*nf*) wickedness, viciousness, depravity.

कुबोल kubol (*nm*) unpleasant/ominous words.

कुमक kumāk (*nf*) reinforcement, relief; –भेजना to send reinforcement.

कुमति kumāti (*nf*) perversity; base intellect; disunity.

कुमार kuma:r (*a*) bachelor; –व्रत celibacy; –व्रती a celibate.

कुमारिका kuma:rika: (*a*) see कुमारी.

कुमारी kuma:ri: (*a*) virgin, maiden; unmarried; (*nf*) a virgin/maiden; cape; –कन्या a virgin girl.

कुमार्ग kuma:rg (*nm*) evil/undesirable course; ~गामी taking an evil course.

कुमुद, कुमुदिनी kumud (*nm*), kumudinı; (*nf*) a lily (flower).

कुम्मैत kummāit (*a*) bay-coloured, bay; (*nm*) a bay horse; –, आठ गांठ guileful through and through.

कुम्ह/ड़ा kumhṛa: (*nm*) field pumpkin, ash gourd; ~ड़े की बतिया a feeble and fragile person.

कम्हलाना kumhla:nā: (*v*) to fade; to wither; to shrivel; to lose lustre.

कुम्हार kumha:r (*nm*) a potter.

कुरकुरा kurkura: (*a*) crisp.

कुरचना kurachna: (*nf*) malformation.

कुरता kurta: (*nm*) a lose-fitting upper garment.

कुरती kurti: (*nf*) a blouse (for women); jacket; jerkin.

क़ुरान qurā:n (*nf*) the sacred book of the Mohammedans (said to be inspired by God); –उठाना, –पर हाथ रखना to swear by the Qoran.

कुरीति kuri:ti (*nf*) condemnable/evil practice or custom.

कुरूप kuru:p (*a*) ugly, unsightly, hideous; hence ~ता (*nf*).

कुरेदना kurednā: (*v*) to rake; to scoop.

क़ुर्क़ qurq (*a*) attached; distrained; –करना to attach; to distrain; –अमीन a baillif, a court-official empowered to attach property of the person against whom a decree has to be executed.

क़ुर्की qurqi: (*nf*) attachment; distraint.

क़ुर्बान qurbā:n (*a*) sacrificed; –जाना to be sacrificed; –होना to sacrifice oneself over (somebody).

क़ुर्बानी qurbā:nı: (*nf*) sacrifice; –देना to make a sacrifice.

कुर्सी kursi: (*nf*) a chair; plinth (of a building); a position of authority; authority; –तोड़ना to idle away time on a chair, to occupy a chair idly; –देना to receive with respect, to honour (by offering a chair); –पर बैठना to occupy a chair/position, to wield power/authority; –मिलना to get a portion of authority.

कुल kul (*a*) total; aggregate; entire; lineage, pedigree; family; –कलंक a slur on the fair name of a family; ~गुरु the family priest; ~देव/देवता Penates, the family-deity; ~नाम surname: ~पति Vice-chancellor (of a University); head of a family; –परम्परा a family tradition; –पुरुष man of a respectable family; –पुरोहित family priest; –मर्यादा dignity of a family; –वधू woman of a dignified family; –का दीपक lit. light of the family; a son who brings honour to the family;

—का नाम डुबाना to bring disgrace to the family; —में कलंक/दाग़ लगाना to cause the family to be stigmatised, to cause a slur on the family.

कुलक्षणी kulakshāṉi: (*nf*) an ominous woman; woman of evil disposition.

कुलटा kulṭa: (*nf* and *a*) (an) unchaste (woman), (a) lewd (woman); a trollop; hence ~पन (*nm*).

कुलफा kulpha: (*nm*) a kind of green leafy vegetable.

कुलफ़ी kulfi: (*nf*) ice-cream frozen in a conical mould.

कुलबुलाना kulbula:nā: (*v*) to wriggle; to creep; to be restless.

कुलबुलाहट kulbula:haṭ (*nf*) wriggling; creeping; restlessness.

कुल/वंत kulvānt (*a*) well-born, belonging to a noble family, genteel; ~वंती of noble descent, chaste and faithful (woman).

कुलाँच kulā:ch (*nf*) a leap; bound; somersault; hence ~ना (*v*); ~भरना to take a leap/jump, to hop.

कुलाँट kulā:ṭ (*nf*) see कुलाँच.

कुलाधिपति kula:dhipati (*nm*) Chancellor (of a University).

कुलाध्यक्ष kula:dhyakksh (*nm*) Visitor (of a University).

कुला/बा kula:ba: (*nm*) a hinge; hook; ~बे मिलाना, ज़मीन-आसमान के to try to bring heaven and earth together; to build castles in the air, to indulge in fantastic planning.

कुलिया kulia: (*nf*) a small earthen crucible; —में गुड़ फोड़ना to perform a task very secretly, not to let others have even an inkling of one's doings.

क़ुली quli: (*nm*) a coolie; —कबाड़ी a rag-tag, person commanding no respect; low-born (person).

कुलीन kuli:n (*a*) belonging to higher castes, aristocratic, noble, of noble descent; —तंत्र (caste) aristocracy; ~ता nobility, noble descent, caste aristocracy.

कुल्ला kulla: (*nm*) gargle, rinsing the mouth; sprout; also कुल्ली (*nf*).

कुल्हड़ kulhaṛ (*nm*) a small earthen bowl.

कुल्हा/ड़ा kulha:ṛa: (*nm*) a large axe; ~ड़ी a small axe.

कुवचन kuvachān (*nm*) filthy/unpleasant words; abusive language.

कुवासना kuva:snā: (*nf*) sinful/immoral desire; evil mental impression.

कुविचा/र kuvicha:r (*nm*) a bad/evil idea, an indiscreet idea; ~री indiscreet, imprudent.

कुव्यवहार kuvvyavaha:r (*nm*) bad behaviour, misbehaviour.

क़ुव्वत quvvat (*nf*) strength, power, energy, vitality.

कुश kush (*nm*) a sort of sacrificial grass—*Doa cynosuroides.*

कुशल kushal (*a*) skilful, skilled, deft, proficient, dexterous; (*nf*) well-being, happiness; —क्षेम well-being, happiness; —प्रश्न inquiry after the health and welfare (of a person); —मंगल welfare, well-being.

कुशलता kushalta: (*nf*) dexterity, skill, deftness; well-being.

कुशाग्र kusha:ggr (*a*) sharp; pointed; ~ता perspicacity; sharpness; ~बुद्धि sharp, of keen intelligence perspicacious.

कुशासन kusha:san (*nm*) bad government, maladministration.

कुश्क kushk (*nm*) a kiosk.

कुश्तमकुश्ता kushtāmkushta: (*nm*) juxtaposed wrestling, interlocking encounter.

कुश्ता kushta: (*nm*) nutritive and retentive calx prepared by chemical processes.

कुश्ती kushti: (*nf*) wrestling; –खाना to lose a wrestling bout; –मारना to win a wrestling bout; –लड़ना to wrestle, to have a wrestling bout.

कुष्ट kushṭ (*nm*) leprosy; –निवारण eradication of leprosy; –पीड़ित suffering from leprosy, leprous.

कुसंग, ~ति kusāṅg (*nm*), ~ti (*nf*) bad company, evil association.

कुसंस्का/र kusānska:r (*nm*) unwholesome or evil mental impression/ways; hence ~री (*a*).

कुसमंजन kusamaṇjan (*nm*) maladjustment.

कुसमय kusamay (*nm*) inopportune time; period of adversity.

कुसुम kusum (*nm*) a flower.

क़ुसूर qusu:r (*nm*) fault, omission; default; ~मंद/वार defaulter; at fault.

कुहक kuhak (*nf*) cooing, twittering (of a cuckoo); warbling; melodious notes.

कुहकना kuhaknā: (*v*) to coo; to twitter, to warble.

कुहनी kuhnı: (*nf*) an elbow; a hanger.

कुहर kuhr (*nm*) a meatus, a channel or passage (in the body).

कुहरा kuhra: (*nm*) fog, mist.

कुहराम kuhrā:m (*nm*) uproar, havoc, tumult; loud lamentation, bewailing; –मचना an uproar/tumult to be raised, havoc to be created/caused.

कुहासा kuha:sa: (*nm*) mist, fog.

कुहासिया kuha:siya: (*nm*) fogman.

कुहुक kuhuk (*nf*) cooing; twittering, warbling.

कूँचा kū:cha: (*nm*) a broom.

कूँची kū:chi: (*nf*) a brush, a small broom; –फेरना to undo, to reduce to naught.

कूँड़ kū:ṛ: (*nf*) a furrow; ~दार furrowed.

कूँ/ड़ा kū:ṛa: (*nm*) a large shallow earthen bowl; basin; hence ~ड़ी fem. (diminutive).

कूक ku:k (*nf*) cooing; warbling.

कूकना ku:knā: (*v*) to coo; to warble; to wind (a watch etc.).

कूच ku:ch (*nm*) march, departure; –करना to march, to depart. –का डंका बजाना to commence a march; –बोलना to (order a) march.

कूचा ku:cha: (*nm*) a lane, bylane.

कूज, ~न ku:j (*nf*), ~an (*nm*) warbling.

कूजना ku:jnā: (*v*) to warble.

कूट ku:ṭ (*nm*) a hill-top; enigmatical verse; (*a*) counterfeit; forged; false; pseudo; ~कर्म deceptive act; forgery; ~कार a fraudulent person, forger; codifier; –काव्य enigmatical poetry; ~नीति diplomacy; underhand manoeuvring; ~नीतिज्ञ a diplomat, diplomatist; manoeuvrer; hence ~नीतिज्ञता; –योजना a plot, an intrigue; –युद्ध deceptive warfare; –लिपि code-script; –लेख code-writing; forged document; –साक्षी perjury, false witness; –साक्ष्य false evidence, forged testimony.

कूटना ku:ṭnā: (*v*) to pound, to pestle; to crush; to beat; to thrash; कूट-कूट कर भरा होना to be full of; to be imbued with.

कूड़ा ku:ṛa: (*nm*) rubbish; sweepings, refuge; trash; –करकट scourings, waste materials, rubbish, midden; ~खाना rubbish dump; कूड़ेदान a dust-bin; –करना to spoil, to mar; कूड़े के भी दिन फिरते हैं every dog has his day.

कूढ़ ku:ṛh (*a*) stupid, dull-headed; ~मग्ज a dullard, nincompoop.

कूत ku:t (*nf*) estimate, assessment.

कूतना ku:tnā: (*v*) to appraise; to assess, to estimate

कूद ku:d (*nf*) a leap, jump; –फाँद gambols.

कूदना ku:dnā: (*v*) to jump; to skip;

to leap.

कूप ku:p (*nm*) a well; a deep pit; –**मंडूक** lit. frog of a well–a know-little, one confined within narrow limits of experience and knowledge.

कूपन ku:pān (*nm*) a coupon.

कूबड़ ku:baṛ (*nm*) a hump, hunch.

कूल ku:l (*nm*) a bank.

कूल्हा ku:lha: (*nm*) haunch, hip; **कूल्हे मटकाना** to make a flirtatious swinging of the hips.

क़ूवत qu:vat (*nf*) see '**क़ुव्वत**'.

कृतकार्य kritaka:ryy (*a*) successful; fulfilled; one who has accomplished his assignment; hence ~**ता** (*nf*).

कृतकृत्य kritkritty (*a*) fulfilled, gratified; hence ~**ता** (*nf*).

कृतघ्न kritaghn (*a*) ungrateful, thankless; ~**ता** ungratefulness, thanklessness.

कृतज्ञ kritaggy (*a*) grateful, indebted, obliged; ~**ता** gratefulness, indebtedness, thankfulness.

कृताकृत krita:krit (*a*) complete as well as incomplete; partially complete; acts of commission and omission,

कृतार्थ krita:rth (*a*) gratified; obliged; hence ~**ता** (*nf*).

कृति kriti (*nf*) a work (esp. of art or literature), composition, performance; deed; ~**कार** the author, the creator.

कृतित्व krititt̄v (*nm*) accomplishment, achievement; creation.

कृती kriti: (*a* an *nm*) creative; one who has laudable achievements to his credit, accomplished.

कृत्य kritty (*nm*) performance; duty; function.

कृत्रिम krittrim (*a*) artificial; synthetical; pseudo; spurious; fictitious; sham; affected; laboured; –**गर्भाधान** artificial insemination ; ~**ता** artificiality, sham, affectedness.

कृदं/त kridānt (*nm*) participle; ~**तज** derived or created from a participle; ~**ती** pertaining to, or related with, a participle.

कृपण kripāṉ (*a*) miser, stingy, parsimonious, niggardly; ~**ता** stinginess, niggardliness, parsimoniousness.

कृपया kripaya: (*ind*) kindly, please.

कृपा kripa: (*nf*) kindness; favour; grace; kindly disposition; favourable attitude; –**कटाक्ष** kindly/favourable look or disposition; ~**कांक्षी** seeking favour; -**दृष्टि** see –**कटाक्ष**; –**पात्र** deserving favour; favourite; ~**मूर्ति** His/Your Grace; –**सिंधु** lit. ocean of kindness—an epithet of God.

कृपाण kripā:ṉ (*nm*) a dagger, sword.

कृपालु kripa:lu (*a*) kind, compassionate, benign; ~**ता** kindness, compassion, benignity.

कृमि krimı (*nm*) a worm, an insect; ~**नाशक** an insecticide; –**रोग** helminthiasis; ~**विज्ञान** helminthology.

कृश krish (*a*) lean, thin; feeble, emaciated; ~**काय** lean and thin; ~**ता** leanness, thinness, slenderness; **कृशांग** lean and thin, feeble; hence **कृशांगी** (*nf* and *a*).

कृषक krishak (*nm*) a farmer, peasant; cultivator; –**दास** a serf; ०**प्रथा** serfdom.

कृषि krishi (*nf*) agriculture; farming, cultivation; –**कर्म** farming, cultivation; ~**कार** farmer, cultivator; ~**जीवी** a professional farmer, one who earns his livelihood through farming; –**विज्ञान/शास्त्र** (science of) Agriculture.

कृष्ण krishṉ (*a*) black; dark; (*nm*) Lord Krishṉā; –**पक्ष** the dark half of the month, the fortnight of the waning moon.

केंचुआ kēchua: (*nm*) an earthworm.

केंचुली kēchuli: (*nf*) the slough (of a snake); **–छोड़ना** to cast off the slough; to assume one's true colours; **–बदलना** to take on a new slough; to metamorphose, to assume new colours.

केंद्र kendr (*nm*) (the) centre; **~गामी** centripetal, directed towards the centre; **~स्थ** centrally located, central; **केंद्रापसारी** centrifugal; **केंद्राभिमुख/केंद्राभिसारी** centripetal.

केंद्र/क kendrak (*nm*) a nucleus; centroid; **~कीय** nuclear.

केंद्रित kendrit (*a*) concentrated; centred; hence **~ता** (*nf*).

केन्द्री/करण kendri:karan̲ (*nm*) centralisation; concentration; **~कृत** centralised; concentrated.

केंद्रीभूत kendri:bhu:t (*a*) centralised; concentrated.

केंद्रीय kendri:y (*a*) central.

के ke—plural and oblique form of **का** (see); **–अनुरूप** as per, according to; **–अनुसार** according to; **–लिए** for, for the sake of.

केकड़ा kekṛa: (*nm*) a crab.

केतकी ketki: (*nf*) pandanus, screw pine.

केतली ketli: (*nf*) a kettle.

केतु ketu (*nm*) the descending node of moon, comet; a mythological demon whose head (Ra:hu) was severed by Lord Vishṇu and the torso was later known as **केतु**; a banner.

केर/ल keral (*nm*) Kerala –a southern state of the Indian Union; **~ली** Keralite.

केला kela: (*nm*) a banana, a plantain tree.

केलि keli (*nf*) amorous sport, amorous dalliance; fun and frolic; sexual intercourse.

केवट kevaṭ (*nm*) a boatman.

केवड़ा kevaṛa: (*nm*) pandanus, screw-pine; fragrant pandanus water; **–जल** fragrant pandanus water.

केवल keval (*a* and *ind*) only, mere; merely; simply.

केश kesh (*nm*) the hair; **~कलाप** hair-do; **~पाश** the ringlets of the hair; **~बंध** the hair-ribbon; **–रचना/विन्यास** hair-do.

केशिका keshika: (*nf*) capillary; **~त्व** capillarity.

केस/र kesar (*nf*) saffron; **~रिया** saffron (coloured); **०बाना** donning of saffron robes (for sacrifice).

केसरी kesri: (*nm*) a lion.

क़ैंची qāichi: (*nf*) scissors; shears; a trick applied in wrestling; **–करना** to cut or clip with scissors; **–बाँधना** to apply the trick called **क़ैंची**; **-सी ज़बान चलना** to talk nineteen to the dozen.

कैंटीन kāin̲ṭi:n: (*nf*) a canteen.

कैं/ड़ा kāiṛa: (*nm*) established standard or size; norm; scale; **~ड़े का आदमी** a man of certain standard; **~ड़ेबाज़** cunning.

कैंप kaimp (*nm*) a camp.

कैंसर kainsar (*nm*) cancer.

कैंसिल kainsil (*a*) cancelled; **–करना** to cancel.

क़ै qai (*nf*) vomit, vomitting; **–करना** to vomit.

कै kai (*pro.*) colloquial variant of **कितने** (see).

कैथ kaith (*nm*) the wood apple–*Feronia elephantum*.

कैथी kaithi: (*nf*) an earlier offshoot of the Devna:gri: alphabet.

क़ैद qaid (*nf*) imprisonment, confinement, incarceration; bondage; **~ख़ाना** a prison, jail; **–,सख़्त** rigorous imprisonment; **–,सादा** simple imprisonment; **–काटना/भोगना** to suffer imprisonment, to be in jail.

क़ैदी qaidi: (*nm*) a prisoner.

कैफ़ियत kaifiyat (*nf*) description; account; remarks; **–का खाना** the remarks column; **–तलब करना** to call for an explanation; **–देना** to explain; to give/submit an explanation.

कैमरा kaimra: (*nm*) a camera; **~मैन** a cameraman.

कैरट kairaṭ (*nm*) carat.

कैवल्य kaivally (*nm*) the Ultimate Realisation, Eternal Emancipation, Perfect Liberation.

कैसा kaisa: (*a*) of what condition or kind; what sort of; (*adv*) how.

कैसे kaise (*adv*) how, in what way; what type of.

कोंक/ण koṅkāṉ (*nm*) in the Indian Union, the region lying west of Sahya:dri, administratively a part of Maha:ra:shṭra; **~णी** the language spoken in Koṅkāṉ; a person belonging to **कोंकण**.

कोंचना kōchnā: (*v*) to prod; to goad; to coax; **कोंचा-काँची** prodding, goading; coaxing.

कोंपल kōpal (*nf*) a new and tender leaf (just sprouting).

को ko—a postposition denoting accusitive and dative case; to; for; on the point of; towards.

कोई koi: (*pro*) any, anybody; a few; some one; **–कोई** some; **–न कोई** someone or the other; **–कसर उठा न रखना** to ring the changes; to leave no stone unturned; **–सूरत नज़र नहीं आती** bad is the best.

कोक kok (*nm*) see **चकवा**.

कोकशास्त्र koksha:str (*nm*) a treatise on sex by an ancient Indian sexologist Koka:; the science of sex.

कोकि/ल, ~ला kokil (*nm*), kokila: (*nf*) see **कोयल**; **~कंठ/~कंठी** sweet-spoken as a cuckoo; **~बैनी** same is **~कंठी**.

कोकीन koki:n (*nf*) cocaine; **~बाज़** a cocaine addict.

कोख kokh (*nf*) womb; **~जली** a barren woman; **–उजड़ना** a woman's only child to die; **–बंद होना**, **–मारी जाना** to become barren.

कोचवान kochva:n (*nm*) a buggy-driver.

कोचीन kochi:n (*nm*) a former princely state in South India.

कोट koṭ (*nm*) a coat; citadel, castle; **~पाल** the governor of a citadel.

कोटर koṭar (*nm*) a cavitation, cavity, hollow of a tree; cinus.

कोटा koṭa: (*nm*) quota.

कोटि koṭi (*nf*) degree, rank; quality; category; ten million; the end of a bow; **~क** same as **कोटि**; **~श**: ten million times; o**धन्यवाद** many many thanks.

कोठरी koṭhri: (*nf*) a cabin; closet; cell; small room.

कोठा koṭha: (*nm*) a big room (esp. in the upper storey); an extensive chamber; a warehouse; the stomach; square (of a chess-board etc.); **–बिगड़ना** to suffer from indigestion; **–साफ़ होना** to have clearance of the bowels; **कोठे पर बैठना** to turn into a prostitute; **कोठेवाली** a prostitute.

कोठा/र koṭha:r (*nm*) a store-house; warehouse; barn; **~री** the keeper of a store-house.

कोठी koṭhi: (*nf*) a bungalow, mansion; a banking firm.

कोड़ा koṛa: (*nm*) a whip lash, scourge.

कोड़ी koṛi: (*nf*) a score, an aggregate of twenty.

कोढ़ koṛh (*nm*) leprosy, leprosis; (*fig.*) heinous evil; **–में खाज** aggravation of a calamity (by the onslaught of another); **–चूना/टपकना** oozing out of leprous matter.

कोढ़ी korhi: (*nm*) a leper; thoroughly indolent man; **–मरे संगाती चाहे** a drowning man seeks a companion.

को/ण kon (*nm*) an angle; a corner; **~णिक/~णीय** angular.

कोतल kotal (*nm*) a majestic horse; (*a*) spare and saddled (horse).

कोतवाल kotwa:l (*nm*) the police officer-in-charge of a **कोतवाली**.

कोतवाली kotwa:li: (*nf*) city's main police-station.

कोताही kota:hi: (*nf*) deficiency, dearth, want; decrease.

कोदों kodō (*nm*) a kind of cheap coarse grain; **–देकर पढ़ना** to have free and (by implication) unavailing education; to remain illiterate.

कोना konā: (*nf*) a corner, nook; **–अँतरा** corners and recesses; **–कोना छान मारना** to search high and low, to see every nook and corner; **कोने-कोने से** from every nook and corner, from all the length and breadth of; **कोने झाँकना** to feel abashed.

कोप kop (*nm*) fury, anger, wrath; **–पात्र/भाजन** target of anger, victim of wrath.

कोफ़्त koft (*nf*) ennui, tedium.

कोफ़्ता kofta: (*nm*) pounded meat or grated and boiled vegetable made into balls and cooked in soup.

कोमल komal (*a*) soft; tender; delicate; slender; a flat note in music; **~ता** softness; tenderness, delicacy.

कोयल koyal (*nf*) a cuckoo.

कोय/ला koyla: (*nm*) coal, charcoal; **~ले की दलाली में हाथ काले** evil association must leave its impress.

कोया koya: (*nm*) the eye-ball or its corner; cocoon; ripe pulp of a jackfruit.

कोर kor (*nf*) edge; flange; border; **–कसर** deficiency; defect, drawback, flaw; **~दार** flanged; **–दबना** to be under the pressure of.

कोरक korak (*nm*) a bud.

कोरनिश kornish (*nf*) salutation with the head and body bowing down; **–बजाना** to make deferential salutation.

कोरम korām (*nm*) quorum.

कोरस koras (*nm*) chorus.

कोरा kora: (*a*) blank; unused, untouched; unwashed; brand new; fresh; unlettered; **~पन** freshness; newness; virginity; **–आदर्शवादी** a don Quixote; **–जवाब** flat refusal; **–मूर्ख** thoroughly stupid; **–लौटना** to return empty-handed; **कोरी कल्पना** cock and bull story; **कोरी बातें** empty talks.

कोरी kori: (*nm*) a Hindu weaver; (*a*) feminine form of **कोरा** (see).

कोर्ट मार्शल kort ma:rshal (*nm*) court martial.

कोर्स kors (*nm*) course.

कोलाहल kola:hal (*nm*) noise, uproar, clamour, tumult.

कोल्हू kolhu: (*nm*) a crusher; **–काटकर मुँगली (री) बनाना** to suffer a greater loss for smaller gain; **–का बैल** a galley slave, drudge.

कोश kosh (*nm*) a dictionary; lexicon; a sheath; covering; shell; ball; testicles; **–कला** the art of lexicography; **~कार** a lexicographer; **~विज्ञान** lexicology, the science of lexicography; **–वृद्धि** hydrocele.

कोशिका koshika: (*nf*) (in Biology) a cell.

कोशिश koshish (*nf*) effort, endeavour.

को/ष kosh (*nm*) a treasure, fund; **~षागार** treasury; **~षाध्यक्ष** treasurer.

कोष्ठ koshth (*nm*) an apartment, a chamber; stomach; bracket; **~बद्धता** constipation; **~शुद्धि** purgation.

कोष्ठक koshthak (*nm*) a bracket;

~बद्ध bracketed.

को/स kos (*nm*) a measurement of distance equivalent to two miles; ~सों miles away; ~सों,काले very far.

कोसना kosnā: (*v*) to curse, to impricate; –,पानी पी-पीकर to indulge in utter damnation, to shower curses upon.

कोहनी kohni: (*nf*) an elbow; –मारना to elbow.

कोहेनूर kohenu:r (*nm*) lit. mountain of light—world famous historical diamond which was cut into two; still adorning the crown of the British kings and queens.

कौंध kaudh (*nf*) a flash; sudden trail of brilliant light.

कौंधना kaudhnā: (*v*) to flash; to glitter.

कौंधा kaundha: (*nm*) a flash; momentary glitter.

कौआ kau:a: (*nm*) a crow; harsh-spoken or cunning fellow; jet black man; uvula; –जब बोले तब काँव lit. a crow would always be harsh-spoken—a harsh spoken man would always utter harsh words; –चला हंस की चाल every ass thinks himself worthy to stand with the king's horses; –धोने से बगला नहीं होता a crow is never the whiter for washing herself often.

कौटुंबिक kauṭumbik (*a*) familial, pertaining to the household.

कौड़ी kauṛi: (*nf*) a cowrie, –small shell; –कफ़न को न होना to be too indigent, to be penniless; –का, दो not worth a farthing, utterly unworthy; –,कानी/फूटी a bad cowrie, a disfigured cowrie; –भी न होना not to have even a farthing, to have no money whatever; –काम का नहीं of absolutely no avail; utterly insignificant; –के तीन-तीन dirt/damn cheap; –के मोल dirt/damn cheap, almost free; –के मोल न पूछना to consider as worthless/as of no avail; –के मोल बिकना to go very cheap; to lose all respect; –कौड़ी को मुहताज utterly indigent; –ग़लत पड़ना to misfire, to hit off the mark; –कौड़ी चुकाना to pay off every farthing; –कौड़ी जोड़ना to save up every farthing; to be very miserly; –कौड़ी दाँत से पकड़ना to be a stickler for every penny, to look twice at a penny; –कौड़ी भरना to repay to the last farthing; –कौड़ी से माया जुड़ती है penny and penny laid up will be many; –भर very little, very meagre in quantity.

कौतु/क kautuk (*nm*) curiosity; amazement: fun, fun and frolic; spectacle; ~की frolicsome.

कौतूहल kautu:hal (*nm*) see कुतूहल.

कौन kaun (*pr.*) who; –सा what, which; ० मुँह दिखाना not to be in a position to show up through shame, to keep away for shame; -सा मुँह लेकर (how) to muster courage to.

कौपीन kaupi:n (*nm*) a privity cover, piece of cloth worn by ascetics over the privities.

क़ौम quam (*nf*) a nation; community; caste; ~परस्त national, nationalistic; ~परस्ती nationalism; क़ौमियत nationality; nationalism.

क़ौमी qaumi: (*a*) national; –तराना national song.

कौमार्य kauma:ry (*nm*) virginity; bachelorhood; –भंग करना to break the virginity, to have first sexual intercourse; –व्रत vow to ever remain a bachelor/virgin, celibacy; ~व्रती committed to be a celibate.

कौर kaur (*nm*) morsel; –छीनना, मुँह का to rob somebody of his share, to deprive somebody of his subsistence.

कौरव kaurav (*nm*) the descendants of king Kuru, representing the vanquished party amongst the belligerents in the great Indian war –Maha:bha:rat.

कौल **qual** (*nm*) promise; agreement; contract; statement, dictum; –करार mutual promise; –का पक्का true to one's word; –देना to make a firm promise; –हारना to pledge (one's) word (to).

कौशल kaushal (*nm*) skill, dexterity, adroitness.

कौशेय kaushey (*a*) silky; silken.

क्या kya: (*pro*) what; –कहने/खूब excellent! well-done! Bravo!;–खाकर/मुँह लेकर how dare ! how can (you) muster courage to.

क्यारी kya:ri: (*nf*) bed (of a garden or field).

क्यों kyō (*ind*) why; ~कर how; ~कि because; since; –न हो! why not; excellent ! it's but natural !.

क्रंदन krāndān (*nm*) lamentation, weeping and wailing, bewailing.

क्रम kram (*nm*) order; system; method; rank; sequence; ~गुणित factorial; ~बंधन marshalling; putting into order; ~बद्ध orderly; systematic; hence ~बद्धता; –भंग disarrangement, disarray, disorder; ~विकास evolution, steady growth; –सूची a catalogue; –से respectively; ~हीन irregular; unsystematic; disorderly.

क्रमश: kramshah (*adv*) respectively; in order; by degrees.

क्रमांक kramā:ṅk (*nm*) roll number.

क्रमानुसार kramā:nusa:r (*adv*) respectively, in order, turn by turn.

क्रमिक kramık: (*a*) ṣerial, successive, turn by turn; hence ~ता (*nf*).

क्रय kray (*nm*) purchase, buying; –विक्रय purchase and sale, buying and selling.

क्रांत/दर्शी krā:ntdarshi: (*a*) a seer, visionary, gifted with preternatural vision; hence ~दर्शिता (*nf*).

क्रांति krā:nti (*nf*) a revolution; ~कारी revolutionary; ~दूत (one) heralding a revolution.

क्रिकेट krikeṭ (*nf*) (the game of) cricket.

क्रियमाण kriyamā:n̲ (*a*) being performed/done, in progress.

क्रिया kriya: (*nf*) action, act; function; a religious performance; verb; last rites;–,अकर्मक intransitive verb; –कर्म last rites, funeral rites; ~कलाप activity; ~कल्प technique; –कौशल manipulation; ~त्मक functional, operative, practical; verbal; ~पद a verb; ~वाची verbal; ~वाद activism; ~विशेषण adverb; —सकर्मक transitive verb; —,करना to perform the last rites.

क्रियात्मक kriya:tmāk (*a*) functional, active; verbal; hence ~ता (*nf*).

क्रियान्वि/ति kriya:nviti (*nf*) implementation, translation into action; ~त implemented.

क्रियाविधि kriya:vidhi (*nf*) procedure, methodology.

क्रियाशील kriya:shi:l (*a*) active, functional; hence ~ता (*nf*).

क्रिस्ता/न kristā:n (*nm*) a christian; ~नी christian.

क्रीड़ा kri:ṛa: (*nf*) play, game, sport, dalliance; fun; –कौतुक fun and frolic.

क्रीत kri:t (*a*) bought, purchased; –दास a paid-for slave.

क्रुद्ध kruddh (*a*) angry, infuriated, enraged, wrathful.

क्रूर kru:r (*a*) cruel, unkind, merciless, ruthless; ~कर्मा cruel, ruthless.

क्रूरता kru:rta: (*nf*) cruelty, ruthlessness, mercilessness.

क्रेय krey (*a*) purchaseable; worth-buying.

क्रोध krodh (*nm*) anger, wrath, fury, rage; ~**वश** out of anger, possessed by fury; –**पी जाना** to subdue (one's) anger.

क्रोधित krodhit (*a*) angry, rageful, wrathful, enraged.

क्रोधी krodhi: (*a*) short-tempered, hot-tempered; irascible.

क्रौंच kraunch (*nm*) a kind of curlew.

क्लब klab (*nm*) a club.

क्ल/र्क klark (*nm*) a clerk; ~ **र्की** a clerical job; position of a clerk.

क्लांत klā:nt (*a*) weary, tired; exhausted; languid.

क्लांति klā:nti (*nf*) weariness, tiredness; exhaustion; languor.

क्लास kla:s (*nf*) a class (of students).

क्लिष्ट klishṭ (*a*) difficult, incomprehensible; far-fetched; –**कल्पना** far-fetched imagination; hence ~**ता** (*nf*).

क्लीव kli:v (*a*) impotent, unmanly; timid; ~**ता** impotency, unmanliness; timidness.

क्लेश klesh (*nm*) anguish; affliction; pain; misery; ~**कर** painful, irksome; ~**दायक/दायी** painful, troublesome, imparting misery.

क्लैव्य klaivvy (*nm*) **क्लीवता**.

क्वचित kvachit (*ind*) rare, rarely.

क्वथ/न kvathan (*nm*) boiling; ~**नांक** boiling point.

क्वार kva:r (*nm*) the seventh month of the Hindu calendar (**आश्विन**).

क्वार्टर kva:rṭar (*nm*) a quarter.

क्षण kshān (*nm*) a moment, an instant; –**क्षण** each and every moment; ~**जीवी** evanescent, transient; ~**भंगुर** momentary, transitory; hence ~**भंगुरता** (*nf*).

क्षणिक kshānik (*a*) momentary, transient, fleeting, transitory; ~**जीवी** ephemeral; ~**वाद** momentaryism, the Buddhist philosophy which lays down that things die i.e. change, every moment.

क्षत kshat (*a*) injured, wounded, hurt;–**विक्षत** wounded/torn all over.

क्षति kshati (*nf*) loss; harm; injury; detriment; wastage, damage; ~**ग्रस्त** put to loss/harm; injured; ~**पूरक** compensatory.

क्षतिपूर्ति kshatipu:rti (*nf*) compensation; reparation; indemnity; –**बंध** indemnity bond.

क्षत्रप kshattrap (*nm*) a satrap.

क्षत्राणी kshattrā:ṇi: (*nf*) a woman of the *kshattriy* caste; brave woman.

क्षत्रिय kshattriy (*nm*) the second i.e. the warrior or the regal caste in the traditional Hindu caste-hierarchy; ~**त्व** the attribute of the *kshattriy* caste, heroism.

क्षमता kshamta: (*nf*) efficiency, competence, capacity; power.

क्षमा kshamā: (*nf*) condonation, remission; forgiveness, pardon; –**याचना** begging pardon, seeking forgiveness; ~**शील** tolerant, readily forgiving; hence ~**शीलता** (*nf*).

क्षम्य kshammy (*a*) pardonable, forgiveable.

क्षय kshay (*nm*) decay, decadence, loss; waste; tuberculosis; –**रोग** tuberculosis; ~**शील** decadent, prone to wane away, dwindling.

क्षयी kshayi: (*a*) decadent, waning, dwindling.

क्षात्र ksha:ttr (*a*) pertaining to or typical of a *kshattriy* (see); –**तेज** the brilliance or heroism typical of a *kshattriy*, martialling acumen; –**धर्म** the duty or function of a *kshattriy*; martialling duty.

क्षार ksha:r (*nm*) an alkali; –**गुण** alkaline property; –**भूमि** barren land.

क्षा/लन ksha:lān (*nm*) washing, cleaning; ~**लित** washed, cleaned.
क्षिति kshiti (*nf*) the earth; land.
क्षितिज kshitij (*nm*) the horizon.
क्षि/प्त kshipt (*a*) thrown, projected; interpolated; ~**प्तांश** interpolation, interpolated text.
क्षिप्र kshippr (*a*) quick, nimble; ~**ता** quickness, nimbleness.
क्षीण kshī:n̲ (*a*) feeble, weak, slender; delicate; languid; impaired; emaciated; ~**काय** lean and thin, attenuated, emaciated, languid; ~**ता** impairment; emaciation; leanness, thinness; langour; ~**रक्त** anaemic; ~**वीर्य** enfeebled, impaired, exhausted, dissipated.
क्षीयमाण kshi:yma:n̲ (*a*) waning, dwindling, declining.
क्षुद्र kshuddr (*a*) small; mean, base, petty; wicked; contemptible.
क्षुद्रता kshuddrata: (*nf*) smallness; meanness, baseness, pettiness, wickedness; contemptibility.
क्षुधा kshudha: (*nf*) appetite, hunger; ~**र्त/**–**पीड़ित** hungry, famished.
क्षुब्ध kshubdh (*a*) agitated; excited, unquiet.
क्षेत्र kshettr (*nm*) field, ground, range; region, area; ~**मिति** mensuration.
क्षेत्रफल kshettrphal (*nm*) area.
क्षेत्राधिकार kshettra:dhika:r (*nm*) jurisdiction.
क्षेत्रिक kshettrik (*a*) territorial, zonal, regional.
क्षेत्रीय kshettri:y (*a*) territorial, zonal, regional.
क्षेप/क kshepak (*nm*) interpolation; ~**कांश** interpolation, interpolated passages.
क्षेपण kshepān̲ (*nm*) interpolation; projection.
क्षेम kshēm (*nf*) welfare, well-being.
क्षैतिज kshaitij (*a*) horizontal; ~**तः** horizontally.
क्षोभ kshobh (*nm*) agitation; excitement, commotion; fret.
क्षौर kshaur (*nm*) hair-cutting, shaving; –**कर्म** hair-cutting, shaving

ख

ख kha—the second consonant and the second member of the first pentad (i.e. **कवर्ग**) of the Devna:gri: alphabet; (*nm*) used in Sanskrit compound words to mean the sky (as **खग, खगोल**, etc).
खँखार khākha:r (*nm*) expectoration, hawking.
खँखारना khākha:rnā: (*v*) to expectorate, to hawk.
खँगालना khāga:lnā: (*v*) to rinse, to clean out; to probe (as **पूरी किताब खँगालने पर दो चार नये शब्द मिलेंगे**).
खँजड़ी, खंजड़ी khājṛi:, khanjṛi: (*nf*) a timbrel.
खंजन khañjan (*nm*) a wagtail—*Motacilla alba*; in literature, it is frequently used as an **उपमान** for playful gay eyes (**खंजन-नयन**).
खंजर khañjar (*nm*) a dagger, poniard.
खंड khand̲ (*nm*) a portion, part, fragment, piece, bit; scrap; lump;

chunk; section; clause; block; segment; canto; volume; factor; region; division; –कथा a small narrative/tale; ~काव्य a long episodic poem (not fulfilling the requirements of an epic), a near-epic poem, epicoid; –खंड broken/turned into pieces; fragmented; –प्रलय partial deluge; –वाक्य a clause.

खंडन khandān (*nm*) refutation, rebuttal, repudiation; denial; –मंडन repudiation and vindication; discussion for and against; खंडनात्मक repudiative, causing or embodying refutation/rebuttal/denial.

खंडश: khandshah (*adv*) sectionwise; clausewise; portion-wise; division-wise; piecemeal.

खँड(ड़)सारी khād(r)sa:ri: (*nf*) an indigenous form of sugar, unprocessed sugar.

खँडहर khādhar (*nm*) ruins; a dilapidated building; –कर/बना देना to cause ruin/devasation, to dilapidate.

खंडित khandit (*a*) broken; fragmented; split; repudiated; –व्यक्तित्व split personality; खंडिता a woman whose husband or lover has let her down/been guilty of infidelity; also ० नायिका.

खंदक khandak (*nm*) a moat, ditch, trench.

खंबा khamba: (*nm*) see खंभा.

खंभा khambha: (*nm*) a pillar, column; post, pole.

खखार khakha:r (*nm*) see खँखार.

खखारना khakha:rna (*v*) see खँखारना.

खग khag (*nm*) a bird.

खगो/ल khagol (*nm*) Astronomy; ~ल–विज्ञान Astronomy; astronomical science; ~लीय astronomical; celestial.

खग्रास khaggra:s (*nm*) complete/whole eclipse.

खचाखच khacha:khach (*a* and *adv*) overcrowded, packed to full; absolutely (full); –भरा होना to be packed to full.

खचित khachit (*a*) studded; inlaid, engraved.

खच्चर khacchar (*nm*) a mule.

खच्चरी khachchari: (*nf*) a janet.

खज़ांची khaza:nchi: (*nm*) a treasurer, cashier.

खज़ाना khaza:nā: (*nm*) treasure; treasury; repository; –अफ़सर treasury officer.

खजूर khaju:r (*nf*) date, date-palm; a kind of sweetmeat.

खट khaṭ (*nf*) sound produced by the impact of one object on another, sound of knocking, rap; –खट rapping, rap-trap; knocking; broil, quarrel.

खटक khaṭak (*nf*) an apprehension, misgiving; a lurking hitch (in the mind); pinch.

खटकना khaṭaknā: (*v*) to click; to pinch, to offend; to raise apprehensions or misgivings; to/be an eye-sore (to); to have a wrangling, to become estranged (with).

खटका khaṭkā: (*nm*) an apprehension, doubt; click; catch.

खटकाना khaṭka:nā: (*v*) to knock, to rap; to cause to wrangle, to cause estrangement.

खटखटाना khaṭkhaṭa:nā: (*v*) to tap; to keep on reminding.

खटना khaṭnā: (*v*) to toil, to labour hard.

खटपट khaṭpaṭ (*nf*) wrangling, squabbling, estrangement.

खटपाटी khaṭpa:ṭi: (*nf*) one side of a bedstead; –लेना to become sulky, to lie repining in bed.

खटमल khaṭmal (*nm*) a bed-bug.

खटमिट्ठा, खटमीठा khaṭmiṭṭha:, khaṭmi:ṭha: (*a*) having a mixed taste of sour and sweet.

खटराग khaṭra:g (*nm*) mess, ado; entanglement; botheration.

खटाई khaṭa:i: (*nf*) a powder prepared from dried up (raw) mango parings [used as spice]; sourness, tartness; **–में डालना** to throw cold water on; to keep in a state of suspense, to shilly-shally; **–में पड़ना** to be kept in abeyance; to keep on dragging (some job or assignment).

खटाखट khaṭa:khaṭ (*nf*) rap, constant clicking; tapping noise; (*adv*) quickly, briskly.

खटाना khaṭa:nā: (*v*) to get sour.

खटास khaṭa:s (*nf*) a touch of sourness/tartness, rancidity.

खटीक khaṭi:k (*nm*) a low caste in the Hindu caste-hierarchy (whose main occupation is fruit-selling, pig-keeping and poultry farming etc.)

खटोला khaṭola: (*nm*) a small cot (meant for children).

खट्टा khaṭṭa: (*a*) sour, tart; **–चूक** very sour; **–मिट्ठा** sorrel.

खट्टिक khaṭṭik (*nm*) see **खटीक**.

खड़कना khaṛaknā: (*v*) to rattle; to clatter; to click; to tingle.

खड़खड़ाना khaṛkhaṛa:nā: (*v*) to rustle; to clatter, to rattle.

खड़खड़ाहट khaṛkhaṛa:haṭ (*nf*) rustling; clattering, rattling, cluttering.

खड़ा khaṛa: (*a*) standing, erect; upright, straight; vertical; steep, high; stationary; unreaped (as **खड़ा खेत**); whole, entire; **खड़े-खड़े** at once, there and then, instantly; standing a long while; **–होना** to stand (for election etc.)

खड़ाऊँ khaṛa:ū: (*nf*) a wooden sandal.

खड़िया khaṛiya: (*nf*) chalk, gypsum.

खड़ी khaṛi: (*a*) feminine form of **खड़ा**; **–चढ़ाई** steep ascent; **–तैराकी** upright swimming; **–पाई** sign of full stop; a small vertical straight line which forms a part of a number of Devna:gri: characters (e.g. प, त, श, स); **–बोली** standard modern form of Hindi which has been adopted as the official language of the Indian Union and which has become synonymous with Hindi; **–हुंडी** an outstanding bill of exchange.

खड्ग khaḍg (*nm*) a sword; **–कोश** a sheath; **~हस्त** with a sword in hand, ready to strike.

खड्ड khaḍḍ (*nm*) a deep pit, gorge.

ख़त ḳhat (*nm*) a letter; line; handwriting; **ख़तो-किताबत** correspondence; **–खींचना** to draw a line; **–करना** a line to be drawn; **–होना** a breach/ crack to develop.

ख़तना ḳhatnā: (*nm*) circumcision (of the foreskin of male organ); **–करना** to circumcise (the foreskin of the male organ); to convert to Islam.

ख़तरनाक ḳhatarnā:k (*a*) dangerous, hazardous, risky.

ख़त/रा ḳhatra: (*nm*) danger, hazard, risk; **~रे की घंटी** a danger signal; **~रे से खेलना** to play with fire, to risk hazards.

ख़ता ḳhata: (*nf*) fault; guilt; error; **~वार** guilty; **–करना** to commit a mistake/fault.

खतियाना khatiya:na: (*v*) to enter into the ledger, to make an entry, to post; to draw a line of demarcation.

खतौनी khatauni: (*nf*) a patwari's register containing details of tenants' holdings.

खत्ता khatta: (*nm*) a barn; ditch, pit.

खत्ती khatti: (*nf*) a barn, subterranean grain store.

ख़त्म ḳhatm (*a*) ended; completed; concluded; **–करना** to do away with;

to complete/conclude.

खत्री khattri: (*nm*) a caste among the Hindus.

खदान khada:n (*nf*) a quarry; mine; deep ditch formed by mining operations.

खदिर khadir (*nm*) catechu; cutch.

खदेड़/ना khaderṇā: (*v*) to rout; to drive away, to chase out; **–देना** to put to flight.

खद्दर khaddar (*nm*) hand-spun coarse cloth; **~धारी** one who dons clothes made of **खद्दर**.

खन khān (*nm*) a storey; moment; jingling sound (as produced by a coin by its impact on hard surface).

खनक khanāk (*nf*) a jingle/clink, jingling or clinking sound.

खनकना khanaknā: (*v*) to jingle/clink, to produce a jingling/clinking sound.

खनकार khanka:r (*nf*) a jingle/clink, jingling/clinking sound; hence **~ना** (*v*).

खनखनाना khankhanā:nā: (*v*) see **खनकना**.

खनन khanān (*nm*) mining, digging; **–कार्य** mining/digging operations.

खनिक khanik (*nm*) a miner, mine worker.

खनिकर्म khanikarm (*nm*) mining (work or operation).

खनिज khanij (*a*) mineral; **–पदार्थ** minerals; **–विज्ञान** Mineralogy.

खपच्ची khapachchi: (*nf*) a bamboo-sliver, splinter, vertically rent piece of bamboo.

खपत khapat (*nf*) consumption; sale.

खपना knapnā: (*v*) to be consumed; to be sold; to be destroyed/ruined.

खपरा khapra: (*nm*) a cupel; round broken earthenware piece; an earthen roofing tile.

खपरैल khaprail (*nf*) a tiled shed.

खप्पर khappar (*nm*) a cupel; begging bowl, cranial bowl.

ख़फ़गी ḳhafgi: (*nf*) displeasure, anger.

ख़फ़ा ḳhafa: (*a*) displeased, angry.

ख़फ़ीफ़ ḳhafi:f (*a*) petty, small, trivial; undignified.

ख़फ़ीफ़ा ḳhafi:fa: (*nm*) a court of small causes.

ख़बर ḳhabar (*nf*) news, information; **–उड़ना** news to be in the air/afloat; **–गर्म होना** news to go allround; **–लेना** to call/haul over the coals, to give it hot, to take to task, to settle accounts (with); to enquire (about).

ख़बर/दार ḳhabarda:r (*a*) cautious, watchful; **~दारी** cautiousness, watchfulness.

ख़बीस ḳhabi:s (*a*) stingy; filthy (fellow).

ख़ब्त ḳhabt (*nm*) craze, mania, fad, eccentricity; **–सवार होना** to be crazy (about).

ख़ब्ती ḳhabti: (*nf*) a maniac, an eccentric; (*a*) crazy, faddish.

ख़ब्तुलहवास ḳhabtulhava:s (*a*) absent-minded, eccentric (person).

ख़म ḳham (*nm*) a kink; bend; curl; curve; **~दार** curved; curly; **–खाना** to get curved; to be vanquished; **–ठोकना** lit. to slap the arms—to assume a challenging posture, to challenge to a dual; **–देना** to joggle, to impart a curve.

ख़मियाज़ा ḳhamiya:za: (*nm*) retribution, punishment; loss; **–उठाना** to reap the fruit (of), to suffer retribution.

ख़मीर ḳhami:r (*nm*) yeast, leaven; **–उठाना** to leaven, to ferment.

ख़यानत ḳhaya:nat (*nf*) defalcation, perfidy, breach of trust.

ख़रगोश ḳhargosh (*nm*) a rabbit, hare; **–का दिल** a timid heart.

ख़रदिमा/ग़ ḳhardima:g (*a*) hot-headed, ill-tempered; **~ग़ी** hot-headedness; ill-temper.

खरपतवार kharpatwa:r (*nm*) weed.

खरपात kharpa:t (*nm*) see **खरपतवार**.

खरबू/ज़ा ḳharbu:za: (*nm*) a musk melon; ~**ज़े को देखकर ख़रबूज़ा रंग बदलता है** association inevitably breeds affinity.

खरल kharal (*nm*) a mortar; –**करना** to pestle.

खरहरा kharehra: (*nm*) a currycomb.

खरहा kharha: (*nm*) a hare, rabbit.

खरा khara: (*a*) pure, genuine; straightforward; upright; honest; plain-speaking; overhot (e. g. **खरा तवा, खरी आँच**); crisp; –**आसामी** a good paymaster; a straightforward person; –**उतरना** to hold water, to bear examination; –**कहैया** a plain-speaking man; –**खेल** genuine straightforward dealings; –**खेल फ़र्रुखा़बादी** straightforward undaunted dealings/conduct, calling a spade a spade; –**खोटा** good and bad, genuine and spurious; –**दाम अच्छा काम** good wages good work; –**परखना** to distinguish good from bad, to discriminate between good and bad; –**सिक्का** a good coin.

ख़रा/द ḳhara:d (*nm*) a lathe; ~**दिया** a turner; –**पर चढ़ाना** to turn on a lathe; to reform.

ख़रादना ḳhara:dnā: (*v*) to turn on a lathe.

ख़राब ḳhara:b (*a*) bad; spoiled; wicked; defective, faulty; depraved, miserable; –**करना** to cause the fall of, to deprave; to spoil.

ख़राबी ḳhara:bi: (*nf*) badness, wickedness; defect, fault; demerit.

ख़रामा-ख़रामा ḳhara:ma:-ḳhara:ma: (*adv*) slowly, with (graceful) ease.

ख़राश ḳhara:sh (*nm*) scratch; irritation (esp. in the throat).

खरी khari: (*a*) feminine form of **खरा** (see); chalk; oil cake; –**खोटी** harsh and unpalatable, relentless (words); –**खरी सुनाना** to call a spade a spade, to tell one some home-truths, to speak out unpalatable truths; –**खोटी सुनाना** to send one away with a flea in one's ear, to give a bit of one's mind, to take to tasks; –**मजूरी, चोखा काम** good wages, good work

ख़रीता ḳhari:ta: (*nm*) a pouch, small silk bag (in which letters for important men were enclosed).

ख़रीद ḳhari:d (*nf*) purchase, buying; –**फ़रोख़्त** purchase and sale, buying and selling; –**करना** to purchase, to make purchases.

ख़रीदना ḳhari:dnā: (*v*) to buy, to purchase.

ख़रीदा/र ḳhari:da:r (*nm*) a buyer, vendee; ~**री** buying, purchasing.

ख़रीफ़ ḳhari:f (*nf*) the kharif crop.

खरोंच kharōch (*nf*) scratch, bruise.

खरोंचना kharōchnā: (*v*) to scratch, to bruise.

ख़रोष्ठी kharoshṭhi: (*nf*) an ancient script which was prevalent in north-west frontier of India roughly between 4th century B.C. and 3rd century A.D.

ख़र्च ḳharch (*nm*) expenditure, expense; cost; –**उठाना** to bear the expenses; –**तोड़ना** to reduce expenditure (on); –**निकलना** expenditure to be (re) covered.

ख़र्चा ḳharcha: (*nm*) expenditure, expense; cost, outlay; –**पड़ना** to cost; to have to spend; –**बाँधना** to cause recurring expenditure.

ख़र्चीला ḳharchi:la: (*a*) spendthrift, extravagant; expensive, costly; uneconomdical.

खर्रा kharra: (*nm*) a long sheet, roll (of paper); lengthy account.

खर्रा/टा kharra:ṭa: (*nm*) snore; ~**टे भरना/मारना/लेना** to drive pigs to the market, to snore while asleep; to be fast asleep.

खल khal (*a*) wicked, vile, mischievous; (*nm*) a mortar; villain; ~नायक a villian; ~नायिका a vamp.

खलना khalnā: (*v*) to feel offended/bad, to take ill, to be displeasing.

खलबली khalbali: (*nf*) agitation, commotion; –पैदा होना/–मचना a commotion to be caused.

ख़लल k̤h̤alal (*nm*) interruption, disturbance, obstruction.

ख़लास k̤h̤ala:s (*a*) discharged; emptied; released.

ख़लासी k̤h̤ala:si: (*nm*) a seaman, khallasi, porter.

खलिहान khaliha:n (*nm*) a barn; threshing floor.

खली khali: (*nf*) oil cake.

ख़लीफ़ा k̤h̤ali:fa: (*nm*) a caliph; veteran wrestler; ~ओं के कान काटना to prove more than a match to veterans, to outdo the veterans.

ख़ल्क k̤h̤alq (*nm*) creation, world.

खल्वाट khalva:ṭ (*a*) bald; ~ता baldness.

ख/वा khava: (*nm*) the end of the shoulder (farther from the neck), the root of the arm; ~वे से खवा छिलना to have a jumbling and jostling crowd, to have shoulders rubbing with one another, to be overcrowded.

ख़स k̤h̤as (*nm*) fragrant root of a typical grass used for cooling purposes; its essence; –की टट्टी a screen made of the fragrant roots of ख़स and used for cooling purposes during the summers.

ख़सम k̤h̤asam (*nm*) husband; master; ~खानी/पीटी widowed, a malediction meaning may you be widowed;–करना to take a husband.

खसरा khasra:. (*nm*) measles.

ख़सरा k̤h̤asra: (*nm*) a patwari's survey-book (containing an account of the number, area etc. of each field or plot of land).

ख़सख़स k̤h̤ask̤h̤as (*nm*) poppy seed.

ख़सलत k̤h̤aslat (*nf*) nature, disposition.

ख़सी (ख़स्सी) k̤h̤asi: (khassi:)(*a*) castrated, rendered impotent; (*nm*) a (castrated) he-goat; –करना to castrate.

खसोट khasoṭ (*nf*) snatching, seizing quickly or unexpectedly.

खसोटना khasoṭnā: (*v*) to snatch, to seize quickly or unexpectedly.

ख़स्ता k̤h̤asta: (*a*) crisp; brittle; ~हाल afflicted, in distress, ragged; brittle, fragile, worn out; hence ~हाली (*nf*); –कचौड़ी a kind of crisp कचौड़ी; –हो जाना/~हाल हो जाना to go to grass; to become brittle.

खाँ/च, ~चा khā:ch (*nf*), ~a: (*nm*) a groove, recess, slit, vallecula; a big basket; coop.

खाँचेदार khā:cheda:r (*a*) vallecular; slitting, having slit(s).

खाँड़ khā:ṛ (*nf*) unrefined sugar.

खाँडा/(ड़ा) khā:ḍ(ṛ)a: (*nm*) a big broad sword; –बजना fighting to ensue/commence.

खाँप khā:p (*nf*) a slice (of some fruits).

खाँसना khāsnā: (*v*) to cough.

खाँसी khā:si: (*nf*) cough.

खाई kha:i: (*nf*) ditch, trench, moat; entrenchment; –पाटना to bridge a gulf (between two or more parties); –होना to have a gulf/distance beween.

खाऊ kha:u: (*a*) voracious, gluttonous; bribee; –उड़ाऊ extravagant, wasteful, squanderer; –मीत/यार selfish, self-serving; –वीर gluttonous.

ख़ाक k̤h̤a:k (*nf*) ashes; dirt and dust; anything trivial, precious little; nothing whatever; ~सार lowest of the low; humble, (this) humble petitioner (used with reference to oneself while talking in humble terms); –उड़ना to be ruined; –करना to reduce to ashes, to devastate; –का पुतला a mortal being made of dust; –छानना to beat the air; to wander al round; –डालना to bury; to bury the hatchet; to conceal (an affair or anything disgraceful); –बरसना to be in ruins, to be in doldrums; –में मिलना to fall to the ground, to be reduced to dust or ashes; –सिर पर उड़ाना to mourn, to be in mourning.

ख़ाका k̤ha:ka: (*nm*) sketch, outline; map, layout; –खींचना to make a fun (of) to pull one's leg.

ख़ाकी k̤ha:ki: (*a*) dull yellow-coloured, dust-coloured.

खाज kha:j (*nf*) scabbies, mange.

खाट kha:ṭ (*nf*) a cot, bedstead; –खटोला household effects; –तोड़ना to keep on lying idle; –पर पड़ना to be bed-ridden; –से उतारा जाना to be on the verge of death; –सेना to be confined to bed through prolonged illness; –से लगना to be reduced to skeleton, to be emaciated.

खाड़ी kha:ṛi: (*nf*) a bay.

खात kha:t (*nm*) fovea, fossa.

खाता kha:ta: (*nm*) ledger; account; –खोलना to open an account; –डालना to commence dealings (with); खाते में डालना to debit to the account (of).

ख़ातिर k̤ha:tir (*nf*) hospitality; (*ind*) for, for, the sake of; ~जमा assurance; –रखना to rest assured; ~दार hospitable, one who extends hospitality; ~दारी hospitality, warm reception,

ख़ातिरी k̤ha:tiri: (*nf*) hospitality.

ख़ातून k̤hā:tu:n (*nf*) a lady.

खाद kha:d (*nf*) manure, fertilizer.

खादर kha:dar (*nm*) alluvial land, moor.

खादी kha:di: (*nf*) see खद्दर; ~धारी see खद्दरधारी.

खाद्य kha:ddy (*nm*) food; (*a*) eatable; –अखाद्य eatable and non-eatable, edible and inedible; good and/or bad food.

खान kha:n (*nf*) mine; quarry; receptacle, store-house; an abridged form of खाना used as the first member in compound words (खान-पान).

ख़ान k̤ha:n (*nm*) a chieftain muslim chief; an honorific used with Afghan Muslim names; also a form of address to them.

ख़ान/दान k̤ha:ndā:n (*nm*) family, kinsfolk; ~दानी familial; traditional; belonging to a high or noble family; ० आदमी descendant of a noble family.

खान-पान kha:n-pā:n (*nm*) (mode and manner of) eating and drinking; living; social relationship.

ख़ानसामा k̤ha:nsa:mā: (*nm*) a house-steward; head of the kitchen and pantry.

खाना kha:na (*v*) to eat; to live on (e.g. साँप हवा खाता है); to corrode; to misappropriate (e.g. पैसा खाना); to sting (as by a venomous insect); to destroy; to squander, to take a bribe; (*nm*) food, meal; खाओ तो ठेंगे से न खाओ तो ठेंगे से Hobson's choice; खा जाना to devour; to ruin; to squander; to misappropriate; खाता-पीता well-to-do, fairly prosperous; –कमाना to exert to earn one's livelihood; –पीना to enjoy; to take bribe; खाते-खाते पेट फट जाना to burst buttons with food; खाने के लाले पड़ना

to be hard up for each meal; –दौड़ना to react violently/offensively, to be easily irritated; to cause grief (by raking up past memories); खाने-पीने से सुखी well-to-do, well-off.

ख़ाना k̤ha:nā: (*nm*) a shelf; column; compartment; abode; chest or case; –आबाद(रहो) may you prosper; prosperous; –आबादी prosperity, flourishing as a householder; ~ख़राब ruined; without home and hearth, wandering; ~ख़राबी ruination; state of being homeless; ~तलाशी search, house-search; ~बर्बाद squandered, one who ruins one's own home; ~बर्बादी ruination.

ख़ानापूरी k̤ha:nā:pu:ri: (*nf*) to complete the formalities.

ख़ानाबदो/श k̤ha:na:badosh (*nm*) a nomad, an idle wanderer; ~शी nomadism.

ख़ामी k̤ha:mɪ: (*nf*) defect, drawback, flaw.

ख़ामोश k̤ha:mosh (*a*) silent.

ख़ामोशी k̤ha:moshi: (*nf*) silence.

खार kha:r (*nm*) a rainy rivulet.

ख़ार k̤ha:r (*nm*) a thorn; animosity, rancour; –खाना to nurse a spirit of rancour (against), to have a sense of animosity; to be in readiness to take revenge.

खारा kha:ra: (*a*) brackish; saline, salty; ~पन salinity; brakishness; hence खारी.

ख़ारिज k̤ha:rij (*a*) dismissed; rejected; –करना to dismiss, to reject; to strike off (a name).

ख़ारिश k̤ha:rish (*nm*) scabbies, itch, mange.

खाल kha:l (*nf*) skin; hide; –उड़ाना to flay bare; to give a good thrashing; –उतारना to desquamate, to skin; to flay; –उधेड़ना to beat black and blue, to give one gyp; –खींचकर भूसा भर देना to inflict severe physical punishment; –खींचना to peel off the skin, to flay.

ख़ालसा k̤ha:lsa: (*nm*) the sikh community; a sikh; –दीवान a religious assembly of the sikhs.

ख़ाला k̤ha:la: (*nf*) mother's sister; –का घर an easy undertaking, a simple job; also ~जी का घर.

ख़ालिक़ k̤ha:liq (*nm*) the creator.

ख़ालिस k̤ha:lis (*a*) pure; unmixed, unadulterated; hence ~पन (*nm*).

ख़ाली k̤ha:li: (*a*) empty, vacant; unoccupied; blank; unemployed; unaccented beat (in music); ineffective (e.g. वार–जाना) fallow; only; mere (e.g. –बात); only; –करना to vacate, to empty; to evacuate; –जगह vacancy; –जाना (वार) to miss the mark; –जेब empty pocket, penniless; –पेट empty stomach; –बैठना to be idle, to be unemployed; –हाथ empty-handed; unarmed; –हाथ लौटना to draw a blank, to return empty-handed, to fail in one's mission.

ख़ाविंद k̤ha:vind (*nm*) husband, man; –बीवी man and wife.

ख़ास k̤ha:s (*a*) special; particular; peculiar; proper (e.g. ख़ास दिल्ली का रहने वाला); important; chief: own (e.g. मेरा ख़ास आदमी); ~कर particularly; –ख़ास selected (few); ~गी private; ख़ासमख़ास very special; very intimate, ख़ासियत speciality, characteristic; ख़ासुलख़ास very intimate; very dear one; ख़ासोआम all people, the big and the small.

ख़ासा k̤ha:sa: (*a*) fairly good, ample.

ख़ासियत k̤ha:siyat (*nf*) characteristic; peculiarity; speciality; distinctive quality; natural disposition.

खिंचना khɪchnā: (*v*) to be pulled; to be tightened; to be expanded; to be attracted towards (–, की ओर);

to be extracted, to be removed; to be drawn (apart); to be repelled; खिंचे-खिंचे रहना to keep a distance (mentally/physically), to keep aloof.

खिंचाई khicha:i: (*nf*) the act or process of pulling/drawing/tightening/expanding / extracting / removing; leg-pulling.

खिंचाव khīcha:v (*nm*) strain; stretch; draught; attraction.

खिंडना khīḍnā: (*v*) to spill; to be spilled.

खिचड़ी khichṛi: (*nf*) a preparation of rice and pulse boiled together; a mixture, medley; hotch-potch; the festival known as मकर संक्रांति; (*a*) mixed; –अलग पकाना, अपनी to blow one's own trumpet, to go one's own queer way; –भाषा a hotch-potch language; –खाते पहुँचा उतरना to be incredibly delicate; –पकाना to hatch a plot, to conspire; –होना, (बालों का) to have a sprinkling of grey hair amongst black.

ख़िज़ाँ khizā: (*nf*) the autumn, fall; (*fig.*) period of decay, adversity.

ख़िज़ाब khiza:b (*nm*) a hair-dye.

खिझाना khijha:na: (*v*) to tease, to vex; to assail playfully or maliciously.

खिड़की khiṛki: (*nf*) a window; ~दार having window(s), ventilated; –खोलना (दिमाग़ की) lit. to open the window—to let in fresh air (of ideas etc.).

ख़िताब khita:b (*nm*) a title; –देना to onfer a title (on).

ख़ित्ता khi:tta: (*nm*) a tract of land.

ख़िदमत khidmat (*nf*) service; lackeying; ~गार a servant; lackey; ~गारी service, lackeying; –बजाना to serve, to be at the service of.

ख़िन्न khinn (*a*) gloomy, glum, depressed; sad; ~ता glumness, sadness, depression.

ख़िराज khira:j (*nm*) a tribute.

खिलंदरा khilandra: (*a*) playful, buoyant.

खिलखिलाना khilkhila:nā: (*v*) to burst into laughter; to laugh heartily.

खिलखिलाहट khilkhila:haṭ (*nf*) a guffaw, burst of laughter.

खिलना khilnā: (*v*) to blossom, to bloom; to blow; to be delighted; to split up, to be rent asunder; to befit.

खिलवाड़ khilwa:ṛ (*nm*) frolic, fun and frolic, pastime; –करना to play with, to treat lightly.

खिलाड़ी khila:ṛi: (*nm*) a player, sportsman; (*a*) playful, frolicsome; –,कच्चा inexperienced player; –,पक्का/सधा हुआ experienced/balanced player; ~पन sportsmanship, playfulness.

खिलाना khila:nā: (*v*) to feed; to entertain to a meal; to administer (as medicine etc.); made to blossom/bloom/blow up/play.

ख़िलाफ़ khila:f (*a*) against, opposed; adversely disposed; ~वर्ज़ी defiance; violation, transgression; –होना to be opposed (to), to be adversely disposed.

ख़िलाफ़त khila:fat (*nf*) pertaining to a calif; opposition (a wrongly coined equivalent for मुख़ालिफ़त —see).

खिलौना khilaunā: (*nm*) a toy, plaything; –बनाना to make a plaything of; –होना to be a plaything in the hands of.

खिल्ली khilli: (*nf*) derision, making fun, ridiculing: ~बाज़ a wag, derider, one who holds others to ridicule; –उड़ाना to make fun/game of, to poke fun at, to deride, to ridicule.

खिसकना khisaḳnā: (*v*) to move slowly; to move farther, to slip away.

खिसिया/ना khisiya:nā: (*v*) to feel piqued/disparaged/embarrassed; to be in an impotent rage; **~नी बिल्ली खंभा नोचे** a thrashed army resorts to rampage.

खिसियाहट khisiya:haṭ (*nf*) a sense or feeling of pique; impotent rage.

खींचना khi:chnā: (*v*) to pull; to pull one's leg; to draw; to tighten; to expand; to extract; to attract; to drag; **खींच-तान** tussel; tugging; twisting (e.g. meaning of a word or statement); **खींचा-तानी** manipulation, tussel and tugging; twisting and distorting, far-fetching.

खीझ (खीज) khi:jh (khi:j) (*nf*) grouch, vexation, fret.

खीझ(ज)ना khi:jh (j)nā: (*v*) to grouch to fret, to be irritated/vexed.

खीर khi:r (*nf*) a sweetened preparation of rice and milk boiled together; a typical sweet Indian dish.

खीरा khi:ra: (*nm*) a cucumber.

खील khi:l (*nm*) parched paddy; **–खील होना** to be shattered (to pieces); to split up.

खी/स khi:s (*nf*) grinning; **~सें काढ़ना/निकालना/निपोरना** to wear a grin; to sing.

खुंदक khundak (*nf*) a feeling of rancour/ill-will; offence; **–खाना** to take offence; to nurse a feeling of ill-will/rancour.

खुंभी khumbhi: (*nf*) mushroom.

खुजलाना khujla:nā: (*v*) to experience an itching sensation, to itch; to scratch.

खुजलाहट khujla:haṭ (*nf*) itch; itchiness, itching sensation.

खुजली khujli: (*nf*) itch, itchiness, itching sensation; scabbies.

खुजाना khuja:nā: (*v*) to itch; to scratch.

खुटकना (*v*) to tap.

खुट्टी khuṭṭi: (*nf*) severance of mutual cordial terms (amongst children); cutting off the bond of friendship; **–करना** to severe speaking terms, abandon friendly relation.

खुड्डी khuḍḍi: (*nf*) an improvised structure (of bricks etc.) to sit on for the discharge of faeces; hollow space or the foot-rest improvised for the purpose; hollow between two teeth.

ख़ुद ḳhud (*pro*) self; (*adv.*) of one's own accord, voluntarily, **~इख़्तियार** independent; **~इख़्तियारी** independence; **~काश्त** direct cultivation; **~कुशी** suicide; **~परस्त** self-centred, self-aggrandising; **~परस्ती** self-aggrandisement; **–ब-ख़ुद** on one's own, self, by itself; **~मुख़्तार** autonomous; **~मुख़्तारी** autonomy.

ख़ुदग़र/ज ḳhudgaraz (*a*) selfish, self-seeking; **~ज़ी** selfishness, self-seeking temperament.

खुदरा khudra: (*a*) retail (goods); small coins.

ख़ुदा ḳhuda: (*nm*) God; the Lord; **~ई** Providence; Godhood; Creation; **~परस्त** devout, God-worshipping; **~परस्ती** devoutness; **~वंद, ~वंदा** God Almighty; O Lord, O Master; **–का ग़ज़ब** Divine wrath; **–की मार** Divine vangeance; **–की राह में** in the name of God; **–को प्यारा होना** to kick the bucket, to expire; **–ख़ुदा करके** at long last, with immense difficulty; **–ख़ैर करे!** May God secure !; **–गंजे को नाख़ून नहीं देता** those who would destroy, find themselves disarmed; **–न करे!** God forbid!; **~या** Oh God; **–हाफ़िज़!** good-bye ! adieu; so long!

खुदाई khuda:i: (*nf*) engraving,

carving; digging, excavation; charges in respect thereof.

ख़ुदी k̤hudi: (*nf*) ego, vanity.

ख़ुद्दा/र k̤hudda:r (*a*) self-respecting; ~री self-respect.

ख़ुनकी k̤hunki (*nf*) a touch of cold, slight cold.

ख़ुन/स khuna:s (*nf*) rancour, spite; ~सी rancorous, spiteful.

ख़ुफ़िया k̤hufiya: (*a*) detective, secret; (*nm*) a detective spy: –पुलिस secret police.

ख़ुबा(मा)नी k̤hub(m)a:ni: (*nf*) an apricot.

ख़ुमा/र k̤huma:r (*nm*) hang-over (of a drink); slight intoxication; drowsiness (resulting from inadequate sleep etc.); also ~री(*nf*); ~र उतरना hang-over to be on the decline.

खुरंट khurant̤ (*nm*) scale, dry incrustation formed over a healing wound; –पड़ना a scale to be formed, drying up of a wound.

खुर khur (*nm*) hoof.

खुरचन khurchan (*nf*) scrape, scrapings; a kind of sweetened milk-product.

खुरचना khurachnā: (*v*) to scrape, to erase.

खुरजी khurji: (*nf*) a long double haversack.

खुरदरा khurdara: (*a*) rough, coarse; scabrous; hence ~पन (*nm*).

खुरपा khurpa: (*nm*) a big scraping instrument.

खुरपी khurpi: (*nf*) a kind of small scraping instrument.

ख़ुरमा k̤hurma: (*nm*) a date-fruit; a kind of sweetmeat.

ख़ुराक k̤hura:q (*nf*) dose; diet; nutritive diet; ration.

ख़ुराफ़ा/त k̤hurā:fa:t (*nf*) smut, indecent act or smutty speech; mischief; disgraceful deed; ~ती mischievous: evildoer; one who indulges in smutty talk.

ख़ुर्द k̤hurd (*a*) mirco—; small (in size, extent, etc.).

ख़ुर्दबीन k̤hurdbi:n (*nf*) a microscope.

खुर्राट khurrā:t̤ (*a*) cunning, clever.

खुलना khulnā: (*v*) to be untied; to be uncovered; to be unravelled, to be exposed; to be unfolded (as भेद); to be dispersed (as बादल); to be laid aside (as पाबंदी etc.); to start (as गाड़ी etc.); to be set up (as दुकान etc.); to be restored (as भूख खुलना); to become favourable (as भाग्य खुलना); to acquire fullness or depth (as रंग खुलना); खुलकर openly, frankly; खुलकर खेलना to indulge in misdeeds openly; खुलता रंग light appealing colour.

खुला khula: (*a*) open; lose; untied; uncovered; exposed; unrestricted; frank, hearty; spacious; fair (as मौसम); overt; –हाथ bounteous, spending profusely/liberally; –हुआ exposed; open; खुली छूट देना to give a free hand; खुली तबियत hearty; खुली मुट्ठी होना to be open-handed, to be generous; खुले आम/ख़ज़ाने/बाजार/मैदान openly, publicly; unhesitatingly; खुले दरवाज़े न शर्माना open door invites a saint; खुले दिल का open-hearted, hearty; खुले दिल से heartily, liberally.

खुलाव khula:v (*nm*) exposure; expanse; openness.

ख़ुलासा k̤hula:sa: (*nm*) summary, gist; abstract; essence; (*a*) clear, brief.

खुल्लमखुल्ला khullām:khulla: (*adv*) publicly, openly, unreservedly.

ख़ुश k̤hush (*a*) happy, pleased; good; ~ख़त good hand-writing; one who possesses a good handwriting; ~गप्पी (exchange of) pleasantries, pleasant chat; ~गवार pleasant; ~ज़ायका tasty; delicious; ~दिल jovial, merry, cheerful;

~दिली cheerfulness, joviality; ~नवीस calligraphist; ~नवीसी calligraphy; ~नुमा pleasant; pleasant-looking, good-looking; ख़ुशामदीद welcome; ख़ुशियाँ मनाना to kick up one's heels.

ख़ुशकिस्म/त k̤hushkismat (*a*) fortunate; lucky; ~ती good fortune, good luck.

ख़ुशख़बरी k̤hushk̤habri: (*nf*) good news.

ख़ुशनसी/ब k̤hushnasi:b (*a*) fortunate, lucky; ~बी good fortune, good luck.

ख़ुशबू k̤hushbu: (*nf*) fragrance, aroma; perfume, scent; ~दार fragrant, aromatic, perfumed, scented.

ख़ुशमिज़ाज k̤hushmiza:j (*a*) cheerful, gay, good-tempered; hence ~मिज़ाजी (*nf*).

ख़ुशहा/ल k̤hushha:l (*a*) prosperous. well-to-do, flourishing; ~ली prosperity, well-being.

ख़ुशाम/द k̤husha:mad (*nf*) flattery; ~दी flattering; (*nm*) a flatterer, sycophant; ०टट्टू a professional flatterer/sycophant.

ख़ुशी k̤hushi: (*nf*) joy, delight, happiness; ख़ुशियाँ rejoicing, gaiety; –का सौदा a matter of choice, a matter of free will; –ख़ुशी happily, cheerfully; –से नाच उठना/–से पाँव ज़मीन पर न पड़ना to tread on air; to dance with joy, to be overwhelmed with joy; –से फूल उठना/–से फूले न समाना to exult, to be in exultation, to tread on air.

ख़ुश्क k̤hushk (*a*) dry; withered.

ख़ुश्की k̤hushki: (*nf*) dryness; drought; (dry) land; dandruff; –की राह/से by land.

खुसुर-फुसुर khusur-phusur (*nf*) whispering; (*adv*) in whispers, in very low tones.

ख़ुसूसियत k̤husu:siyat (*nf*) plural form of ख़ासियत (see).

ख़ूँख़्वा/र k̤hū:k̤ha:r (*a*) ferocious, murderous; hence ~री (*nf*).

खूँट khū:ṭ (*nm*) a corner; corner-stone; direction.

खूँटा khū:ṭa: (*nm*) a stake; peg; –गाड़ना to establish oneself; to fix one's tether; खूँटे के बल कूदना/–के बल बंदर नाचे to venture beyond one's tether on extraneous strength.

खूँटी khū:ṭi: (*nf*) a small peg; spike; stump (of a tree, etc.); root of the hair; ear of a stringed musical instrument.

खूँदना khū:dnā: (*v*) to trample (over).

ख़ूँरेज़ी k̤hū:rezi: (*nf*) bloodshed.

ख़ून k̤hu:n (*nm*) blood; murder; -ख़च्चर/ख़राबा bloodshed; massacre; –उतरना, आँखों में to be filled with fury; –उबलना/खौलना the blood to boil, to be in a bloody rage; –करना to murder, to kill; to squander lavishly; –का जोश blood-affection; –का दौरा blood-circulation; –का प्यासा blood-thirsty, sworn enemy; –का बदला blood for blood, revenge for blood; –की नदी बहाना to shed a stream of blood; –की होली a carnival of bloodshed; –के आँसू बहाना/रोना to be in a terrible throe; –के घूँट पीना to suppress one's fury; –खौलना the blood to boil, to be in a bloody rage; –गर्दन पर होना to be blood-guilty/blood-stained; –चूसना to suck the blood of; to exploit; –जमना one's blood to freeze; –ठंडा होना the blood to freeze; to be lost to the sense of self-respect; to be bereft of passion; –पसीना एक करना to toil in the sweat of one's brow; –पसीने की कमाई hard-earned money; –पानी होना to lose all sense of self-respect; –पीना to cause non-stop harassment; –बहाना to shed blood; to cause bloodshed; –,मुँह (को) लगना to get addicted to, to cultivate a taste for the unsavoury; –में होना (कोई गुण या अवगुण आदि) to run in the blood, to be a family trait; –लगाकर शहीद बनना/शहीदों में दाख़िल होना to feign sacrifice, to manage to be lauded as a martyr; –सफ़ेद होना to lack natural affection; to become inhumane; –सिर पर चढ़कर बोलता है murderous hands must one day be exposed; –सिर पर सवार होना to be in a murderous mood, to run amuck, to be in a frenzied thirst for blood; –सूखना to be mortally scared, to be unnerved; –से हाथ रँगना to stain one's hands with blood.

ूनी k̤hu:nī: (*nm*) a murderer, an assassin; (*a*) blood-thirsty, ferocious; involving bloodshed.

ूब k̤hu:b (*a*) very much, in plenty/abundance; good, beautiful; (*adv*) very (as ख़ूब अच्छा); (*inter.*) excellent! very good !.

ूबसूरत k̤hu:bsu:rat (*a*) beautiful, pretty; handsome; comely.

ूबसूरती k̤hu:bsu:rti: (*nf*) beauty, prettiness; handsomeness.

ूबी k̤hu:bi: (*nf*) merit; characteristic quality; speciality.

ूसट khu:saṭ (*a*) decrepit, haggard.

ेड़ा kheṛa: (*nm*) a hamlet, small village.

ेत khet (*nm*) a field, farm; –आना see –खेत रहना; –पर चढ़े किसानी it is the harvest that proves the farmer; –बदना to fix a bout, to have it out; –रहना to be killed in action, to bite the dust.

ेतिहर khetihar (*nm*) a farmer, cultivator.

ेती kheti: (*nf*) farming, cultivation; agriculture; –बारी(ड़ी) agriculture, agricultural undertaking.

खेद khed (*nm*) regret; sorrow; ~जनक regrettable; ~प्रकाश apology, expression of regret.

खेना khenā: (*v*) to row.

खेप khep (*nf*) a trip; quantity or number transported in one lot.

खेमा k̤hemā: (*nm*) a tent, camp; –डालना to encamp; खेमे में होना, किसी के to be in the camp of.

खेल khel (*nm*) play, game, sport; show; -कूद sports; fun and frolic; –करना to frolic; –के दिन age of merriment; boyhood; –खिलाना to give a long rope; –ख़त्म होना the game to be up; –खेलना to make a crafty move; –खेल में in a trice, without any effort; –बनाना to have a business accomplished; –,बना बनाया near-accomplished job; –बिगड़ना a person's apple-cart to be upset; to have a game or business spoilt; –बिगाड़ना to upset a person's apple-cart; –समझना to consider damn easy; to look through one's game.

खेलना khelnā: (*v*) to play; to stage (e.g. नाटक); –खाना to eat, drink and be merry; खेलने-खाने के दिन the age to eat, drink and be merry; खेला-खाया well-versed in the ways of life; खेली-खाई having diverse experiences of life; well-up in sexual experiences.

खेवट kheyaṭ (*nm*) the register of mutations, land-record of shares; a rower, boatman.

खेवनहार khevanha:r (*nm*) a rower, boatman.

खेवा kheva: (*nm*) ferry-toll; ferry-trip

खेवाई kheva:i: (*nf*) ferry-toll; ferrying; –भी देना और बह भी जाना to foot the bill and get nil.

खेस khes (*nm*) a thick cotton sheet.

खेह kheh (*nf*) ash, dirt and dust; –**खाना** to be in a miserable plight; to knock about from pole to post.

खैर khair (*nm*) catechu.

ख़ैर k̤hair (*nf*) well-being; welfare; (*ind*) well, all-right; ~**ख़्वाह** a well-wisher; well-wishing: ~**ख़्वाही** well-wishing, benevolence; ~**सल्ला** does not matter (e.g. **काम हो जाये तो ठीक नहीं तो ख़ैरसल्ला**).

ख़ैरात k̤haira:t (*nf*) charity, alms; ~**ख़ाना** alms-house; **ख़ैराती** charitable; ०**अस्पताल/दवाख़ाना** charitable hospital/dispensary.

ख़ैरियत k̤hairiyat (*nf*) welfare; safety.

खोंचा khoṇcha: (*nm*) see **खोमचा**.

खोंसना khōsnā: (*v*) to tuck in; to insert; to thrust (into).

खोखला khokhla: (*a*) hollow; ~**पन** hollowness.

खोखा khokha: (*nm*) a stall, kiosk.

खोज khoj (*nf*) search, quest, investigation; discovery; exploration; –**ख़बर लेना** to enquire about one's welfare; –**मिटाना** to wipe out all traces (of); to efface the footprints (of).

खोजना khojnā: (*v*) to seek, to search; to explore; to investigate; to discover.

ख़ोजा k̤hoja: (*nm*) a eunuch (esp. one employed to be in attendance in a royal harem); a trading Muslim community.

खोट khoṭ (*nf*) a defect, flaw, blemish; alloy.

खोटा khoṭa: (*a*) defective, faulty; false, counterfeit; spurious; adulterated, malicious; -**खरा** good and bad; inferior and superior; genuine and spurious; –**माल** inferior goods; –**सिक्का** a counterfeit coin; ०**चलाना** to chant horses: **खोटी-खरी सुनाना** to heap reproaches on, to chide.

खोदना khodnā: (*v*) to dig; to engrave; to excavate; **खोद-खोदकर पूछना** to make a searching enquiry

खोना khonā: (*v*) to lose; to squander; **खो जाना** to be lost (*lit.* as well as *fig.*—e.g. lost in thinking etc.) **खोया-खोया रहना या खोया-खोया-सा रहना** to be in the dumps, to look lost, to be absent-minded.

खोपड़ा khopṛa: (*nm*) the skull; a coconut kernel;–**खोलना** to break the skull open.

खोपड़ी khopṛi: (*nf*) the skull; –**खुजलाना** to be bent on getting a thrashing; –**चाटना** see **भेजा खाना चाटना**; –**पर सवार होना** to hang on; –**फोड़ना** to break the skull (of); –**रँगना/लाल करना** to strike one's skull, to cause blood to ooze; to break one's skull.

खोमचा k̤hōmcha: (*nm*) a vendor's or pedlar's selling basket.

खोया khoya: (*nm*) a typical milk product thickened and dehydrated by boiling; (*v*) past participle of the verb '**खोना**'.

खोल khol (*nm*) a cover; sheath; shell (casting); holster.

खोलना kholnā: (*v*) to open; to unfold; to untie; to detach; to unravel; to unroll; to unfasten; **खोलकर** frankly, without mincing words.

खोसना khosnā: (*v*) to snatch.

खोह khoh (*nf*) a cave, cavern; an abyss.

ख़ौफ़ k̤hauf (*nm*) fear, dread; ~**ज़दा** terrorized, scared, fear-stricken; ~**नाक** dreadful, terrible; –**खाना** to be scared of, to fear.

खौलना khaulnā: (*v*) to boil; to effervesce.

ख्यात khya:t (*a*) reputed, celebrated, famous; historical; ~**गर्हित** notorious; infamous.

ख्याति khya:ti (*nf*) fame, reputation

renown; –प्राप्त reputed, famous.

याल khya:l (*nm*) an idea, thought; view; opinion; one of the principal forms of modern Hindustani classical vocal music; –में न लाना not to take into account; –में समाना to be ever present in memory; –रखना to attend to, to look after; –से उतरना to slip out of memory/mind; to forget; to become indifferent (to).

याली khya:li: (*a*) imaginary, fancied; assumed; –पुलाव पकाना to build castles in the air, to indulge in absurd fancies.

ष्ट khri:sht (*nm*) (Jesus) Christ.

ख़्रीष्टाब्द khri:shta:bd (*nm*) the Christian era.

ख़्रीष्टीय khri:shti:y (*a*) Christian, pertaining to Christ.

ख़्वा/ब kha:b (*nm*) a dream; ~बी pertaining to or existing in dreams; imaginary; ~बों की or ~बी दुनिया world of dreams, imaginary world.

ख़्वारी khwa:ri: (*nf*) insult; embarassment.

ख़्वाहमख़्वाह khā:mkhā (*ind.*) uselessly, for no rhyme or reason, without any purpose.

ख़्वाहिश kha:hish (*nf*) wish, strong desire; ~मंद desirous, solicitous.

---

ga—the third consonant and the third member of the first pentad (i.e. कवर्ग) of the Devna:gri: alphabet; a Sanskirt suffix denoting a mover (as खग).

गा ganga: (*nm*) the Ganges (considered to be the most sacred river by the Hindus); –जमुनी made up of two colours or two metals (like gold and silver); ~जल sacred water of the Ganges; ~जली a metal goblet to preserve the holy water of the Ganges; ०उठाना to swear by the water of the Ganges; –नहाना to accomplish a difficult task; to achieve a destination.

ज ganj (*nf*) baldness; (*nm*) a market place.

जफ़ा ganjfa: (*nm*) see गंजीफ़ा.

जा ganja: (*a*) bald, baldheaded; hence ~पन (*nm*).

गंजी ganji: (*nf*) a male under-garment for the upper part.

गंजीफ़ा ganji:fa: (*nm*) a pack or game of cards.

गँजेड़ी gājeri: (*a*) a *gā:ja:*- addict.

गँठ gāth—an allomorph of गाँठ used as the first member of a number of compound words; ~कटा a pickpocket; ~जोड़ alliance; line-up; ~बंधन wedding; intimate relationship, alliance.

गँड़त/रा gārtara: (*nm*), ~री (*nf*) a thick baby diaper.

गंडा gānda: (*nm*) a knotted black string (tied round the neck as a charm); a coloured ring on the neck of certain birds like parrot; –तावीज conjuring; ० करना securing against evil spirits or charms.

गँड़ा(डा)सा gāra:(da:)sa: (*nm*) a chopper (with a broad blade).

गँडेरी gāḍeri: (*nf*) a small horizontally cut segment/piece of a peeled sugarcane.

गंतव्य gāntavvy (*nm*) the destination.

गंद gānd (*nf*) filth; morbidity.

गंदगी gāndgi: (*nf*) dirtiness, filthiness, filth; morbidity.

गँदला gādla: (*a*) muddy (as water).

गंदा gānda: (*a*) dirty, filthy; morbid.

गंदु/म gāndum (*nm*) wheat; **~मी** wheatish (colour).

गंध gandh (*nf*) smell, odour; **~वह/~वाह** air; **~हर** deodorant; **~हीन** odourless; **~युक्त** odoriferous/odorous.

गंध/क gandhak (*nm*) sulphur; **~क का तेज़ाब/~काम्ल** sulphuric acid; **~की** sulphury, sulphurous.

गंधर्व gandharv (*nm*) mythological community of celestial musicians; a caste of singers; **-विद्या** music; **–विवाह** one of the eight recognized types of marriages prescribed by the Hindu law-giver **मनु**, e. i-ling mutual pledge between he lover and the beloved in the presence of respectable people.

गंधी gāndhi: (*nm*) a perfumer, perfume-manufacturer.

गंभीर gambhi:r (*a*) serious, grave; sober; grim; reserved; deep; profound.

गंभीरता gambhi:rta: (*nf*) seriousness; gravity; sobriety; reservedness; depth; profundity.

गँवाऊ gāva:u: (*a*) squandering, wasteful.

गँवा/ना gāva:nā: (*v*) to lose; to waste; to squander; **–बैठना** to let slip through one's fingers, to suffer a (total) loss.

गँवार gāva:r (*a*) uncivilised; rustic, stupid; **~पन/~पना** uncivilised manners; rusticity; rudeness; stupidity; vulgarity; **–को अतर सुँघाना** pearls before the swine; **–गन्ना न भेली दे** penny wise pound foolish to give away the finished product in a bid to save the raw material.

गँवारू gāva:ru: (*a*) rustic; rude; vulgar; slang (language, etc.).

गऊ gau: (*nf*) a cow; (*a*) meek gentle.

गगन gagan (*nm*) the sky, firmament; **~चर** sky-going; moving in the sky, a bird; **~चुंबी/स्पर्शी** sky-high skyscraping.

गगरी gagri: (*nf*) a small earthen pot.

गच gach (*nf*) mortar, plaster, stucco; heaviness (in the stomach); **~कार** stucco; **–बैठना** the stomach to be heavy and constipative.

गच्चा gachcha: (*nm*) a pitfall; hazard; **–खाना** to be hoodwinked, defrauded; to be subjected to a pitfall; **–देना** or **गच्चे में डालना** to deceive, to hoodwink, to defraud.

गज gaj (*nm*) an elephant; **~गति** graceful carefree gait (like that of an elephant); **~गामिनी** (a woman) blessed with a graceful carefree gait (like that of an elephant); **-निमीलिका** looking through one's fingers, connivance; feigned ignorance; **~स्नान** unavailing activity.

गज़ gaz (*nm*) a yard; yardstick.

गज़क gazak (*nm*) a sweetmeat prepared from sesame seed and sugar.

गज़ट gazaṭ (*nm*) a gazette.

ग़ज़ब gazab (*nf*) a calamity; fury; wrath; tyranny, outrage; **–का** extremely amazing, wonderful; **–, ख़ुदा का** divine wrath/fury; **–टूटना** to be shattered by a calamity, to be in deep distress; **–ढाना** to commit an outrage/atrocity, to be outrageous/atrocious; **~नाक** amazing, wonderful.

गजर gajar (*nm*) the chimes (gene

aily rung after every four hours); morning-bells; ~दम very early in the morning.

गजरा gajra: (*nm*) a thick flower-garland; bracelet.

ग़ज़ल gazal (*nf*) a popular poetic form of Urdu; ~गो a composer of *gazals*; hence ~गोई (*nf*).

गज़ेटियर gazeṭiar (*nm*) a gazetteer.

गट gaṭ (*nf*) the sound produced while swallowing or gulping a liquid; ~गट same as गट; quikly, all at once; –से quickly, all at once.

गटकना gaṭaknā: (*v*) to swallow, to gulp.

गटागट gaṭa:gaṭ (*adv.*) see गटगट.

गटापारचा gaṭa:pa:rcha: (*nm*) gutta-percha.

गट्टा gaṭṭa: (*nm*) plug; sprag; wrist-joint; ankle; a joint or knot.

गट्ठर gaṭṭhar (*nm*) a large bundle, bale; package.

गट्ठा gaṭṭha: (*nm*) a bundle, package; bulb (of onion or garlic etc.)

गठजोड़ gaṭhjoṛ (*nm*) see गँठ (~जोड़).

गठन gaṭhan (*nf*) build, structure, construction; composition.

गठना gaṭhnā: (*v*) to be tied/closed together; to be compact in texture; to be intimate; गठा बदन well-built/muscular body.

गठबंधन gaṭhbandhan (*nm*) see गँठ (~बंधन).

गठरी gaṭhri: (*nf*) a bundle, package.

गठिया gaṭhiya: (*nf*) gout, rheumatism.

गठीला gaṭhi:la: (*a*) compact; well-built; muscular (body); knotty; nodose; ~पन knottiness, compactness; nodosity.

गड़गड़ाना gaṛgaṛa:nā: (*v*) to gurgle; to rumble, to produce a thundering sound.

गड़गड़ाहट gaṛgaṛa:haṭ (*nf*) gurgling, rumbling or thundering sound

गड़ना gaṛnā: (*v*) to be buried; to penetrate; to be fixed, to stick into; to be pierced; गड़ जाना, शर्म से to be thoroughly ashamed; गड़ा धन buried/underground treasure; गड़े मुर्दे उखाड़ना to dig up things buried deep, to rake up the long lost past.

गड़प gaṛap (*nf*) a plashing sound; swallowing; –करना to swallow; –से all at once; with a splashing sound; –होना to be drowned, to be swallowed by the waves.

गड़पना gaṛapnā: (*v*) to swallow; to usurp.

गड़बड़ gaṛbaṛ (*nf*) muddle, mess; confusion, disorder, disquiet; ~झाला a pretty kettle of fish, medley, confusion, disorder.

गड़बड़ाना gaṛbaṛa:nā: (*v*) to be confused/confounded; to be spoilt; to confuse, to spoil; to stumble.

गड़बड़ी gaṛbaṛi: (*nf*) see गड़बड़.

गडमड gaḍmaḍ (*nf*) confusion, medley; jumble, a jumbled mass; scramble.

गड़रिया gaṛariya: (*nm*) a shepherd.

गड़ारी gaṛa:ri: (*nf*) a pulley; spool, reel; ~दार having circlets or rings.

गड्ड gaḍḍ (*nm*) a heap, mass; medley; ~मड्ड see गडमड.

गड्डी gaḍḍi: (*nf*) a pack; bundle.

गड्ढा gaḍḍha: (*nm*) a pit, ditch; hollow; loss; –खोदना to create pitfalls; –भरना to make up (the loss); गड्ढे में गिरना to be in distress, to suffer a grievous loss.

गढ़ंत gaṛhant (*a*) imaginary, fancied; (*nf*) forging.

गढ़ gaṛh (*nm*) a fort, castle, citadel; stronghold; ~पति a fort-commander; –जीतना/तोड़ना to achieve a resounding victory, to accomplish a difficult job.

गढ़त gaṛhat (*nf*) structure, figure and features, build; mould.

गढ़ना garḥnā: (*v*) to forge; to fabricate; to mould, to form, to fashion; to carve (as a statue).

गढ़ा garḥa: (*nm*) see **गड्ढा**.

गढ़ाई garḥa:i: (*nf*) moulding, fashioning; malleating; dressing; malleating/dressing charges.

गढ़ी garḥi: (*nf*) a keep, fortress.

गण gān (*nm*) a community, union, group; a body (signifiying collectivity, as **सदस्य**~); an attendant, agent; totem; ~**पति** chief of a **गण** (community); see **गणेश**.

गणक gānak (*nm*) a scorer, reckoner.

गण-चिह्न gānchinh (*nm*) a totem.

गणतंत्र gāntāntr (*nm*) a Republic; republican system of government; –**दिवस** republic day.

गणतंत्रात्मक gāntāntra:tmak (*a*) republican; pertaining or belonging to **गणतंत्र**.

गणतंत्रीय gānta:ntri:y (*a*) Republican, pertaining or belonging to **गणतन्त्र**.

गणतांत्रिक gānta:ntrik (*a*) republican; pertaining or belonging to **गणतंत्र**.

गणना gānnā: (*nf*) counting; calculation, reckoning; ~**कार** an enumerator, a reckoner.

गणनीय gānani:y (*a*) worth reckoning/counting.

गणपूर्ति gānpu:rti (*nf*) quorum.

गणराज्य gānra:jjy (*nm*) a republic, republican state.

गणिका gānika: (*nf*) a prostitute, harlot.

गणित gānit (*nm*) Mathematics; ~**ज्ञ** a mathematician; –**विद्या** mathematical science; **गणितीय** mathematical; ० **सांख्यिकी** mathematical Statistics.

गणेश gānesh (*nm*) a popular Hindu deity believed to be the god of wisdom symbolising auspiciousness.

गण्य gānny (*a*) see **गणनीय**; ~**मान्य** distinguished, of outstanding merit

गत gat (*a*) past, gone; dead; devoid of; pertaining to, in respect of; condition, plight; appearance; a musical time or measure; an air, a tune; –**का** worthwhile, conforming to a standard; ~**काल** past; ~**प्राण** dead; lifeless; ~**प्राय** almost past; –**मास** ultimo: –**बजाना** to play an air/a musical tune; –**बनाना** to reduce to a miserable plight; to give a thorough beating.

गतांक gata:ṅk (*nm*) the last issue (of a paper, magazine, etc.)

गतानुगत gata:nugat (*nm*) an adherent to a custom or tradition; unquestioning follower.

गतानुगतिक gata:nugatik (*a*) tradition-bound, traditional; ~**ता** traditionality, unquestioning adherence to tradition.

गति gati (*nf*) motion, movement; speed; state, condition, plight; shape, appearance; access, approach, pass; destiny, salvation; ~**ज** kinetic; ०**ऊर्जा** kinetic energy; ~**बोधक** kinesthetic; ~**भंग** being out of tune/rhythm; ataxia; ~**भ्रंश** abasia; ~**मात्रा** momentum; ~**मूलक** kinetic; ~**विज्ञान** dynamics; ~**विधि** activity, goings; developments; ~**विभ्रम** ataxia; ~**संवेदना** kinesthesis; ~**शील** dynamic; ~**शीलता** dynamism; kinesis; activity; ~**हीन** inert, inactive, static; ~**हीनता** inertness; inactivity, statism; –**होना** to have a go, to have knowledge of, to have been initiated into.

गति/मान gatimā:n (*a*) active, dynamic, moving; ~**मत्ता** dynamism; activity.

गत्ता gatta: (*nm*) strawboard; cardboard.

ग़दर gadar (*nm*) a rebellion, mutiny;

—मचाना to create a havoc/row.

गतिशील gatishi:l (*a*) dynamic, active; ~ता dynamism, activity; kinesis.

गत्यात्मक gattya:tmāk (*a*) dynamic, pertaining to activity or movement; hence ~ता (*nf*).

गदराना gadra:nā: (*v*) to be half-ripe; to attain the state of youthful bloom.

गदहा gadaha: (*nm*) see गधा.

गदा gada: (*nf*) a club; ~धारी one who wields a गदा (club).

गदागद gada:gad (*ind*) in quick succession, one quickly after the other.

गदेला gadela: (*nm*) a thick cushion; pad.

गदेली gadeli: (*nm*) the palm (of the hand).

गद्गद gadgad (*a*) overwhelmed (by ecstatic emotion), in ecstasy; ~कंठ (emotionally) choked throat; —स्वर (emotionally) chocked voice.

गद्दर gaddar (*a*) half-ripe; hence ~ पन (*nf*).

गद्दा gadda: (*nm*) a bed-cushion; cushion; pack saddle.

ग़द्दा/र gadda:r (*nm* and *a*) (a) traitor; traitorous; treacherous; ~री traitorousness, treachery.

गद्दी gaddi: (*nf*) a cushion; throne; seat; pack-saddle; pad, lay; ~नशीन installed on the throne, coronated; ~नशीनी coronation; —पर बैठना to ascend the throne, to be enthroned; —से उतारना to be dethroned/deposed.

गद्य gaddy (*nm*) prose; —काव्य prose-poetry; गद्यात्मक prosaic.

गधा gadha: (*nm*) an ass, a donkey; a damn fool, stupid fellow; ~पन folly, stupidity; ०करना to make an ass of oneself; to commit follies; —पीटने से घोड़ा नहीं होता the Etheopian never changes his skin; गधे को अंगूरी बाग honey is not for donkey's mouth; गधे को खिलाया, न पाप न पुण्य kindness is lost upon an ungrateful man; गधे को बाप बनाना flatter a fool for expediency; गधे पर चढ़ाना to humiliate, to insult; गधे पर बस न चला कुम्हारी के कान उमेठ दिये to bark up a wrong-tree; गधे से हल चलवाना to cause complete ruination (of); to raze to the ground.

ग़नीमत gani:māt (*nf*) a redeeming feature, consoling factor.

गन्ना gannā: (*nm*) a sugarcane.

गप gap (*nf*) a gossip, hearsay; ~शप gossip, tittle-tattle; chit-chat; —उड़ाना to rumour; to set afloat a rumour; —मारना to indulge in boastful gossip; to brag and boast.

गपकना gapaknā: (*v*) to swallow hastily, to gulp, to gobble; to catch (as a ball).

गपड़चौथ gaparchauth (*nf*) mess and medley, confusion and disorder, confoundedness.

गपागप gapa:gap (*ind*) (eating) hastily, quickly.

गपोड़ gapoṛ (*nm*) a gossiper; chatterer; ~बाज़ a gossiper, tall-talker; ~बाज़ीgossiping; chattering.

गप्प gapp (*nf*) see गप.

गप्पी gappi: (*nm*) a gossiper, chatterer; (*a*) boastful, indulging in gossips.

गफ़ gaf (*a*) compact, dense, densely woven.

ग़फ़लत gaflat (*nf*) negligence, carelessness; swoon, unconscious state; ~ज़दा unconscious; negligent, careless; —की नींद deep/sound sleep, carefree sleep; caused by unconsciousness.

ग़बन gabān (*nm*) embezzlement; —करना to embezzle.

गबरू gabru: (*a*) youthful, young;

(*nm*) bridegroom.

गबरून gabrū:n (*nf*) a kind of coarse chequered cloth.

ग़म gam (*nm*) grief, woe; tolerance; ~**ख़ोर** tolerant, enduring; ~**ख़ोरी** tolerance, endurance; ~**गीन** gloomy, full of sorrow; ~**ज़दा** grieved; sorrow-stricken, afflicted; ~**नाक** sorrowful, woeful; –**खाना** to be tolerant, to endure; –**ग़लत करना** to comfort/solace oneself; to drown (one's) sorrows in an intoxicant.

गमक gamāk (*nf*) fragrance; a kind of musical ornamentation; the sound of a drum.

गमकना gamaknā: (*v*) to emit fragrance; to resound.

गमतख़ाना gamatk̤h̤a:nā: (*nm*) a bilge.

गमतरी gamtari: (*nf*) a bilge.

गमन gamān (*nm*) the act of going; locomotion; sexual intercourse.

गमनागमन gamna:gamān (*nm*) coming and going, traffic.

गमला gamla: (*nm*) a flower-pot.

ग़मी gamı: (*nf*) death; mourning, the period of mourning.

गम्य gammy (*a*) accessible, approachable, attainable; hence ~**ता** (*nf*).

गम्या gammyā: (*a*) fit for coition; cohabitable (woman).

गया gaya: (*v*) went—past participle form of the verb '**जाना**'; –**गुज़रा बीता** good for nothing, inferior, insignificant.

ग़रक़ garaq (*a*) immersed, submerged.

गरगज gargaj (*nm*) battlement.

गरचे garche—though, even though.

गरज garaj (*nf*) thunder; roar; fulmination.

ग़रज़ garaz (*nf*) concern; interestedness, interested motive; need; (*adv*) in short, briefly speaking, ~**मंद** needy; desirous (of); having an interested motive (in); ~**मंदी** interestedness, the state of being needy/concerned; –**का आशना** a self seeker; –**का बावला** a slave to one's purpose, purpose-server; –**बावली होती है** a self-seeker has no moral code; **गरजी यार किसके, दम लगाई खिसके** the dinner over, away go the guests; **ग़रज़े कि** in brief, in a nut-shell.

गरजना garajnā: (*v*) to thunder, to roar, to fulminate, to speak loudly.

गरदन gardān (*nf*) the neck; –**उड़ाना/काटना** to behead, to chop off one's head; to decollate, to cut the throat; to put to tremendous harm; –**झुकाना** to yield; to be ashamed; –**न उठाना** not to utter a word in protest; to endure everything; –**नापना** to catch hold of one's neck; to insult; –**नीची होना** the head to hang down through shame; –**पकड़ना** to catch hold of the neck, to hold by the neck; to insult; –**पर छुरी चलाना/फेरना** to submit (somebody) to grave injustice, to cut the throat (of); –**पर जुआ रखना** to assign a difficult job; –**पर सवार होना** to have complete sway; to subjugate (somebody), to keep on pestering; –**फँसना** to be embroiled in a mess; to be involved in a difficulty, to be in somebody's grip; –**मरोड़ना** to throttle; to twist or wring the neck (of); –**मारना** to behead; –**में हाथ देना** to hold by the neck, to humiliate.

गरदनियाँ gardaniyā: (*nf*) a hold by the neck to push out; –**देना** to hold the neck for forcing out, to push by the neck.

गरदान gardā:n (*nf*) declension and conjugation.

गरम garām (*a*) hot; warm; burning; fiery; zealous; ardent; woollen (cloth); –ख़बर hot news; –बाज़ारी boom; –मिज़ाज hot-tempered, fiery; –व सर्द उठाना/देखना/सहना to go through all sorts of prosperity and adversity in life, to have had a chequered career; to go through a chequered coarse of good and bad experiences; –होना to fly into a rage, to get infuriated.

गरमागरम garmā:garām (*a*) hot, heated; fresh (as news).

गरमागरमी garmā:garmī: (*nf*) excitement, heated exchange.

गरमाना garma:nā: (*v*) to warm up; to be excited, to fly into a rage.

गरमाहट garma:haṭ (*nf*) warmth, heat; also **गर्माव**.

गरमी garmī: (*nf*) heat, warmth; summer; passion; anger, violence; ardour; syphilis; –निकलना to be relieved of one's passion; to have one's vanity struck out; to be knocked down.

गरांडील garā:ṉḍi:l (*a*) robust, huge and hefty, of imposing stature.

ग़रारा gara:ra: (*nm*) gargle; loose female pyjamas.

गरारी gara:ri: (*nf*) a pulley.

गरिमा garimā: (*nf*) dignity, grace; gravity; hence ~मंडित, ~मय (*a*).

गरिष्ठ garishṭḥ (*a*) heavy (esp. food), indigestible; hence ~ता (*nf*).

ग़रीब gari:b (*a*) poor; meek; humble; ~ख़ाना humble dwelling (i.e. my humble home—said out of modesty); –ग़ुरबा the poor, the poverty-stricken (class); ~निवाज़ kind to the poor, supporting the poor; ~परवर sustaining the poor, merciful to the poor; your exalted self !; –की जोरू सब की भाभी a poor beauty finds more lovers than husbands; –की हाय a poor man's curses.

ग़रीबाना gari:ba:nā: (*a*) befitting a poor man, in a humble/meek fashion.

ग़रीबी gari:bi: (*nf*) poverty, penury.

गरुड़ garuṛ (*nm*) aquila, a large mythological eagle-like bird believed to be the vehicle of Lord Vishṉū.

ग़रूर garu:r (*nm*) vanity, pride, haughtiness.

गरेबान garebā:n (*nm*) part of the garment resting on the fore-par of the neck; –चाक करना to go crazy, to tear one's collar to pieces (out of craziness); –में मुँह डालना to introspect, to have a realisation of one's sins/deeds.

ग़रेरी gareri: (*nf*) a pulley.

गर्जन garjān (*nm*) a roar, bellowing; thunderous sound; a loud rebuke; –तर्जन a loud rebuke, fretting and fuming.

गर्जना garjanā: (*nf*) a roar, bellowing; thunderous sound.

गर्जित garjit (*a*) roared, roaring.

गर्त gart (*nm*) a pit; recess.

गर्तिका gartika: (*nf*) a fovea.

गर्द gard (*nf*) dirt, dust; ~ख़ोर dust-absorbing; –ग़ुबार dust and dirt; –बैठ जाना the dust to be settled.

गर्दन gardān (*nf*) the neck; ~तोड़ बुख़ार cerebrospinal fever.

गर्दभ gardabh (*nm*) see **गधा**.

गर्दिश gardish (*nf*) distress, trouble; vicissitudes (of fortune); circulation; revolution.

गर्भ garbh (*nm*) the womb; pregnancy; foetus; the interior; -कोश the womb; ~क्षय abortion; ~गृह naos; -धारण conception; -निरोधक a contraceptive; ~पात miscarriage; ~पातक abortifacient; ~वती pregnant; ~स्थ inside the womb; ~स्राव abortion; ~स्रावक abortifacient.

गर्भाधान garbha:dhā:n (*nm*) impregnation; insemination.

गर्भाशय garbha:shay (*nm*) the womb.

गर्भिणी garbhinī: (*a*) pregnant.

गर्भित garbhit (*a*) impregnated; involved (as a sentence).

गर्म garm (*a*) see **गरम.**

गर्मजोशी garmjoshi: (*nf*) warmth, cordiality; **–से मिलना** to greet with cordiality, to receive warmly.

गर्माना garma:nā: (*v*) see **गरमाना.**

गर्मी garmī: (*nf*) see **गरमी.**

गर्व garv (*nm*) pride; elation.

गर्वि/त garvit (*a*) elated; conceited, proud; hence **~ता** feminine form.

गर्वीला garvi:la: (*a*) see **गर्वित.**

गर्हणा garhaṇā: (*nf*) censure, reproach, condemnation.

गर्हणीय garhāṇi:y (*a*) censurable, condemnable.

गर्हित garhit (*a*) wicked, vile, contemptible.

गल gal—an allomorph of '**गला**' and '**गाल**' used as the first member in compound words; **~गंड** a disease resulting in the inflammation of throat-glands; **~बहियाँ** embracement with arms thrown around each other's neck; **~मुच्छ** hooked moustache, long curled whiskers; **~सुआ** a disease resulting in the inflammation of jaw-gums and consequent fever.

गलगाजना galga:jnā: (*v*) to vociferate; to be ebulliently loud; to be noisily boastful.

गलतंस galtans (*nm*) childless deceased; **–हो जाना** to have no descendant.

ग़लत galat (*a*) wrong: incorrect, untrue; erroneous; improper; **–जगह पर** in the wrong box; in an awkward position; **–मोहरे पर हाथ रखना** to back the wrong horse.

ग़लतफ़हमी galatfehmī: (*nf*) misunderstanding, misgiving.

ग़लतबयानी galatbaya:nī: (*nf*) misstatement, false statement.

ग़लती galati: (*nf*) mistake, error; fault; **–किससे नहीं होती** Homer sometimes nods.

ग़लतुल-आम galatul-a:m(*nm*) a wrong usage adopted in a language by virtue of its wide currency; also **ग़लतुल-आमफ़हम.**

गलना galnā: (*v*) to melt; to decay; to rot; to be boiled or cooked till softened; to be frost-bitten.

गला gala: (*nm*) neck; throat; gullet; voice; collar (of a garment); neck of a pot; **गलेबाज़** one gifted with a sweet voice, one who exploits one's vocal gifts (poet etc.); **गलेबाज़ी** exploitation of one's vocal gifts; indulgence in vocal feats; **–कटना** to be beheaded; to suffer a heavy loss; to be deprived of one's due; **–खुलना** to re-attain normalcy of voice; **–घोटना** to throttle, to strangle; **–छुड़ाना** to liberate or to be liberated; to (get) rid of; **–तर करना** to moisten the throat (by a few drops of cold water, etc.); **–दबाना** to throttle; to choke; to exercise undue pressure; **–पकड़ना** to catch hold by the neck; to harass, (some eatable) to produce irritation in the throat; **–पड़ना/बैठना** to develop a sore throat/hoarse voice; **–फँसना** to get entangled or embroiled (in an untoward affair); to get into a mess; **–फाड़ना** to vociferate, to bellow; **–भर आना** to have the throat choked through emotion;. **–भर्राना** see **–भर आना**; **–रुँधना** see **–भर आना**; **–रेतना** to slaughter; to torture to slow death; **गले तक डूबना** to be submerged chin deep; **–गले का हार** extremely dear and intimate; one who constantly hangs upon, a constant companion; **गले के नीचे उतरना** to be swallowed; to comprehend and be convinced; गले न उतरना to stick in one's gizard, to be more than one can stomach; गले पड़ना to become an encumbrance, to be obliged to endure; गले पड़ा ढोल बजाना to hold the baby, to assume an undesired responsibility; गले पर छुरी फेरना to put to gross injustice; to inflict grave injury; गले बाँधना या मढ़ना to pass the baby, to pass the buck to, to make a dupe of (person); to hang to somebody's neck, to impose, to enforce acceptance; गले मिलना to embrace, to hug; गले में अटकना not to be swallowed or gulped; not to be palatable or welcome; गले लगाना to embrace, to hug.

गलित galit (*a*) melted; decayed; over-ripened; oozing; worne out; –कुष्ट oozing leprosy; –यौवना a woman whose youth has decayed.

गलियारा galiya:ra: (*nm*) a gallery; corridor.

गली gali: (*nf*) a lane, alley, alleyways; –कूचा lanes and bylanes.

ग़लीचा gali:cha: (*nm*) a carpet.

ग़लीज़ gali:z (*a*) dirty, filthy.

गल्प galp (*nf*) a tale; story.

ग़ल्ला galla: (*nm*) grain, corn; a shopkeeper's sale proceeds for the day the cash box; herd, flock.

गवरमेंट gavarmenṭ (*nf*) the government.

गवर्न/र gavarnar (*nm*) governor; ~री the office or function of a governor; gubernatorial.

गवाँना gavā:nā: (*v*) to lose; to waste; to suffer detriment.

गवाक्ष gava:ksh (*nm*) an oriel, spyhole, bull's eye.

गवारा gava:ra: (*a*) agreeable, acceptable, tolerable; –करना to tolerate, to stand.

गवाह gava:h (*nm*) a witness; deponent.

गवाही gava:hi: (*nf*) evidence, testimony.

गवेषणा gaveshn̲ā: (*nf*) research, investigation.

गवैया gavaiya: (*nm*) a singer.

ग़श gash (*nm*) swoon, fainting fit; –आना/खाना to faint, to swoon.

गश्त gasht (*nf*) patrol, beat; –लगाना to patrol.

गश्ती gashti: (*a*) patrol, patrolling; circular; –चिट्ठी circular letter.

गस्सा gassa: (*nm*) a morsel.

गहकना geheknā: (*v*) to be exhilarated, to be buoyant.

गहगड्ड gehgaḍḍ (*a*) very strong (intoxicating beverage, as भाँग).

गहगहाना gehgaha:nā: (*v*) to be exultant, to be buoyant.

गहन gahan (*a*) deep; intricate; impregnable; obscure; mysterious, dense; inaccesible; ~ता depth; intricacy; impregnability; obscurity; mysteriousness; density; inaccessiblity.

गहना gehnā: (*nm*) ornament; (*v*) to catch; गहने jewellery; ०रखना to pawn, to mortgage.

गहमागहमी gehmā:gehmi: (*nf*) hustle and bustle, fanfare, intense activity

गहरा gehra: (*a*) deep; profound; intimate, close (as गहरी दोस्ती); bold (as–रंग) secretive; grave (as–संकट); sound (as गहरी नींद); intricate, unintelligible (as गहरी चाल); strong (as गहरी भाँग); –अ(ा)सामी a well-todo guy; a rich prey; –पेट undivulging nature/disposition, secretive temperament; –हाथ मारना to reap a rich harvest; to inflict a severe stroke; गहरी चाल चलना to play a deep game; गहरी छनना to take a strong dose of *bhā:g*; to be extremely intimate/friendly; **गहरी पैठ** profound understanding (of); **गहरी साँस भरना** to heave a deep sigh; **गहरे पानी पैठना** to delve deep (into).

गहराई gehra:i: (*nf*) depth; profundity; **–नापना** to sound; to fathom, to assess the depth.

गहराना gehra:nā: (*v*) to deepen; to become more dense; to be overcast (with).

गहाई gaha:i: (*nf*) threshing.

गह्वर gahvar (*nm*) a recess; cave; chasm.

गाँजा gā:jā: (*nm*) the hemp plant or its leaves.

गाँठ gā:ṭḥ (*nf*) a knot; tie; node; knob; bale; bundle; joint; hardened or enlarged gland; bulb; complex; rancour; **~कट** a pickpocket; **~दार** knotty; **–कटना** to have one's pocket picked; **–कतरना/काटना** to pick pocket; **–करना** to pocket, to misappropriate; **–का** belonging to oneself, being exclusively one's own; **०पूरा** beforehand with the world, having a full purse; **–का पूरा आँख का अंधा** having a full purse and an empty head, a nitwit with a fat purse; **–खोलना** to remove misunderstanding or prejudice; to open one's purse; **–जोड़ना** to tie the nuptial knot; to splice; **–पड़ना** to create bad blood, to harbour ill feeling towards; to have estranged relation; **–बाँधना** to make a note of, to keep in mind; **–से जाना** to be lost, to suffer loss or detriment.

गाँठना gāṭḥnā: (*v*) to cobble; to stitch; to interlock; to bring (somebody) to one's side, to win over; to have complete sway.

गाँ/ड gā:ḍ (*nf*) the anus; **~डू** catamite, passive partner in sodomy; timid, cowardly.

गांधर्व gā:ndharv (*a*) pertaining to or related with the *gandharv* community or country.

गांधी gā:ndhi: (*nm*) the great Indian leader Mohanda:s Karamchand Ga:ndhi:, father of the Indian Nation, popularly so known because of his membership of the Gujarati Vaishya community called Ga:ndhi:); **–टोपी** a typical *khaddar* boat-shaped cap; **–दर्शन** the Gandhian philosophy; **~वाद** Gandhism; **~वादी** a Gandhite, a follower of Gandhian ideology; Gandhian.

गांभीर्य gā:mbhi:ry (*nm*) depth, profundity, gravity; solemnity.

गाँव gā:v (*nm*) a village.

गाँस gā:s (*nf*) a loop; an obstruction.

गाँसना gā:snā: (*v*) to chinse; to intertwine.

गाँसी gā:si: (*nf*) an intertwined knot; the head of an arrow or any other pointed weapon.

गाइड ga:iḍ (*nm*) a guide.

गाउन ga:ūn (*nm*) a gown.

गागर ga:gar (*nf*) an earthen pitcher; **–में सागर भरना** to express too much in too few words, frugal in words fathomless in meaning.

गाज ga:j (*nf*) a thunder-bolt, lightning; **–गिरना/पड़ना** to be thunderstruck, to be afflicted by a calamity.

गाजर ga:jar (*nf*) carrot; **–मूली** petty things.

गाजी ga:zi: (*nm*) a crusader (amongst the Muslims).

गाटर ga:ṭar (*nm*) a girder.

गाड़ना gaṛ:na: (*v*) to bury; to lay; to implant; to fix; to sink; to drive (as **कील–**); to pitch (as **तंबू–**); to cover.

गाड़ी ga:ṛi: (*nf*) a cart, coach, cab; vehicle, carriage; train; ~**वान** a cart/coach-driver, cabman.

गा/ढ़ा ga:ṛha: (*a*) thick; dense; close as (**गाढ़ी दोस्ती**); deep; concentrated (as –**द्रव**); strong (as **गाढ़ी चाय**); (*nm*) a thick coarse cloth; ~**ढ़ा वक्त** times of crisis, trying times; ~**ढ़ी कमाई** hard-earned money; ~**ढ़ी छनना** to be very thick; to take a strong intoxicant (as **भाँग**); ~**ढ़े दिन** times of crisis, difficult days; ~**ढ़े पसीने की कमाई** hard-earned money ०**करना** to earn an honest penny; ~**ढ़े में** in a crisis.

गात ga:t (*nm*) body, person.

गात्र ga:ttr (*nm*) body, person.

गाथा ga:tha: (*nf*) a tale; narrative; ballad; ~**कार** author of a narrative tale.

गाद ga:d (*nf*) sediment, dregs, lees.

गाध ga:dh (*a*) shallow, fathomable.

गान gā:n (*nm*) a song; singing; –**वाद्य** music—vocal and instrumental; ~**विद्या** music.

गाना gā:nā: (*v*) to sing, to chant; (*nm*) a song; –**बजाना** singing and playing of musical instruments; celebration, festivity.

ग़ाफ़िल g̣a:fil (*a*) negligent, unaware; unconscious.

गाभिन ga:bhin (*a*) pregnant (used for animals).

गाय ga:y (*nf*) a cow; (*a*) meek and humble. harmless; –**मरी खर कौने काम** a day after the fair, to kiss the hare's foot.

गाय/क ga:yak (*nm*) a singer; musician; vocalist; ~**की** singing, vocal music; traditional style (in music); ~**क –वृंद** chorus.

गायन ga:yan (*nm*) singing; vocal music.

ग़ायब g̣a:yab (*a*) vanished, disappeared; lost; –**करना** to make off (with); to cause to disappear; –**होना** to disappear, to vanish.

ग़ार g̣:ar (*nm*) ditch, pit; cave.

ग़ारत g̣a:rat (*a*) devastated, destroyed.

गारद ga:rad (*nf*) a guard (of soldiers); watch; –**बिठाना** to deploy a guard.

गारा ga:ra: (*nm*) mud, mortar.

गार्हस्थ्य ga:rhasthy (*nm*) the phase of the householder in life; –**धर्म** the duties enjoined upon a householder.

गाल ga:l (*nm*) cheek; –**पिचकाना** to become emaciated; –**फुलाना** to sulk; to get into a sullky mood; –**बजाना** to boast, to brag.

गाला ga:la: (*nm*) a ball of carded cotton.

ग़ालिब g̣a:lib (*a*) predominant, overpowering, overwhelming; –**करना**, **रौब** to dominate, prevail over, overwhelm.

ग़ालिबन g̣a:libān (*ind.*) perhaps, probably.

गाली ga:li: (*nf*) an abuse, invective; abusive songs sung by women as part of (marriage) celebrations; –**गलौज/गुफ़तार** billingsgate, violent invectives; (exchange of) abusive terms; –**खाना** to endure abusive/foul language; –**देना** to abuse, to call names; –**गालियों पर उतरना** to stoop to the use of abusive language.

गावतकिया ga:vtakiya: (*nm*) a bolster, large stuffed pillow.

गावदी ga:vdi: (*a*) stupid, doltish, blockheaded; (*nm*) a nitwit, dolt.

गावदुम ga:vdum (*a*) tapering, conical.

गाह/क ga:hak (*nm*) a customer, purchaser; client; ~**की** buying.

गाहना ga:hnā: (*v*) to thresh; to chinse.

गिचपिच gichpich (*a*) clumsy;

crowded; (*nf*) crowding.

गिटपिट gitpiṭ (*nf*) unintelligible chattering; **–बोली/भाषा** the English language; **–करना** to speak in English/unintelligible language.

गिटार giṭa:r (*nm*) guitar (a musical instrument).

गिट्टक giṭṭak (*nf*) a wedge.

गिट्टी giṭṭi: (*nf*) grit, roadstone.

गिड़गिड़ाना girgira:nā: (*v*) to entreat, to beseech, to implore humbly, to grovel in the dust.

गिड़गिड़ाहट girgira:haṭ (*nf*) humble entreaty, beseeching.

गिद्ध giddh: (*nm*) a vulture; **–दृष्टि** long-sighted, capability to view from a great distance.

गिनती ginti: (*nf*) counting; calculation; reckoning; number; **–के** counted few; **–में आना** to be of some significance or worth; **–में होना** to be recognised, to be reckoned with, to be significant; **–होना** to be reckoned.

गिनना ginnā: (*v*) to count, to enumerate; **गिन-गिनकर** making a thorough count; **०क़दम रखना** to proceed very cautiously; to walk gracefully; **गिन-गिनकर गालियाँ देना** to let loose a volley of abuses; **गिने-गिनाये** exact(ly); in a limited number; **गिने-चुने** a few; selected few.

गिनाना ginā:nā: (*v*) to enumerate, to count over, to count (so as to satisfy somebody).

गिन्नी ginnī (*nf*) a guinea (a British gold coin).

गिरगिट girgiṭ: (*nm*) chameleon; a turn-coat; **–की तरह रंग बदलना** to turn cat in pan, to change colours, to make frequent somersaults.

गिरजा(घर) girja:(ghar) (*nm*) a church, cathedral.

गिरदावर girda:var (*nm*) a petty land revenue official (also called (**गिरदावर क़ानूनगो**).

गिरना girnā: (*v*) to fall, to come down, to collapse; to drop; to stumble, to tumble; to decrease (e.g. **भाव**--); to be degraded: to be spilt; to be afflicted by a disease; **गिरकर सौदा करना** to strike a bargain at a discount; **गिरता-पड़ता** in a tottering manner; **गिरती हालत** worsening condition.

गिरफ़्तार girafta:r (*a*) arrested, captured, apprehended.

गिरफ़्तारी girafta:ri: (*nf*) arrest, capture, apprehension.

गिरमिटिया girmiṭiya: (*nm*) contracted native labour (during the British regime).

गिरवी girvi: (*nf* and *a*) mortgage(d), pawn(ed); pledge(d); **~दार** mortgagee; **~नामा** a deed of mortage; **–रखना** to pawn/pledge/mortgage.

गिरस्ती girasti: (*nf*) see **गृहस्थी**.

गिरह girah (*nf*) a knot; joint; fold in the loin-cloth used for safe keeping of money; somersault; a measure – one sixteenth part of a yard; **~कट** a pick-pocket; **~दार** knotted, knotty; **~बाज (कबूतर)** a somersault pigeon; **–काटना** to pick pocket; [for other usages and idioms, **गिरह** is synonymous with **गाँठ** (which please see)].

गिराना gira:nā: (*v*) to fell, to cause to fall, to pull down; to spill; to drop; to demolish; to abuse; to lower; to decrease; to degrade; **गिरे हुए को उठाना** to set a man on his feet.

गिराव gira:v (*nm*) see **गिरावट**.

गिरावट gira:vaṭ (*nf*) fall, downfall, degradation; slump; decrease.

गिरि giri (*nm*) a mountain, hill; **~राज** the Himalayas.

गिरिपीठ giripi:ṭh (*nm*) foothill.

गिरी giri: (*nf*) kernel.
गिरोह giroh (*nm*) a gang, group, band; –बनाना/बाँधना to form a band/group.
गिर्द gird (*ind.*) around, all round.
गिलट gilaṭ (*nf*) nickel; nickel-coat.
गिलहरी gilehri: (*nf*) a squirrel.
गिला gila: (*nm*) complaint; reproach; –शिकवा informal complaint and reproach.
गिलाफ़ gila:f (*nm*) cover, pillow-cover; case.
गिलास gila:s (*nm*) a tumbler.
गिलोय giloy (*nf*) a medicinal creeper (very bitter in taste).
गिलौरी gilauri: (*nf*) a stuffed and folded betel-leaf.
गिल्टी gilṭi: (*nf*) gland, hard glandular swelling.
गिल्ली gilli: (*nf*) a toggle; –डंडा the game of tip-cat; ०खेलना to play the game of tip-cat; to play away one's time.
गीत gi:t (*nm*) a song, a lyrical poem; ~काव्य lyrical poetry; –गाना to sing a song; to shower praises upon, to eulogize.
गीता gi:ta: (*nf*) the Bhagwadgi:ta: which contains the celebrated discourse of Lord Krishṉā directed to Arjun, the stupefied hero of the Maha:bha:rat.
गीति gi:ti (*nf*) a lyric; ~काव्य lyrical poetry; ~तत्त्व lyrical element; ~नाट्य/रूपक a lyrical play.
गीदड़ gi:daṛ (*nm*) a jackal; (*fig.*) a timid man; hence ~पन timidness, cowardice; –भभकी a mere/false threat, bluff(ing).
गीधना gi:dhnā: (*v*) to acquire a predatory habit; to become habituated or used to undue advantages.
गीला gi:la: (*a*) moist, wet; ~पन wetness.
गुंजक gūṇjak (*nm*) a buzzer.
गुंजन gūṇjan (*nm*) buzzing, humming (sound).
गुंजाइश gūṇja:ish (*nf*) scope, capacity; accommodation.
गुंजायमान gūṇja:ymā:n (*a*) humming, buzzing.
गुंजार gūṇja:r (*nm*) humming, buzzing as of a blck bee).
गुंजारना gūṇja:rnā: (*v*) to buzz, to hum.
गुंठन gūṉṭhan (*nm*) a veil.
गुंड/ई gūṉḏai: (*nf*) scoundrelism, rascality, roguery, hooliganism; also ~पन (*nm*).
गुंडा gūṉḏa: (*nm* and *a*) (a) rogue, scoundrel, hoodlum, hooligan; ~गर्दी hooliganism, rowdyism; hence ~पन (*nm*).
गुँथना gūthnā: (*v*) to be threaded; to be stitched; to be plaited; to be interlocked.
गुँधना gūdhnā: (*v*) to be kneaded.
गुंफ gūmph (*nm*) a string (of words); cluster.
गुंफन gūmphān (*nm*) stringing.
गुंबद gūmbad (*nm*) a dome, vault.
गुइयाँ guīyā: (*nm*) a chum, close friend; partner (in a game).
गु/च्छा guchchha: (*nm*) a bunch, cluster; tuft; ~च्छेदार tufty.
गुज़र guzar (*nf*) maintenance; living; passing of time; –बसर maintenance; livelihood; –करना/–बसर करना to subsist; to maintain (oneself); –जाना to pass away; to cross; –होना to subsist, to sustain.
गुज़रना guzarnā: (*v*) to pass; to pass away; to cross over.
गुज़ारना guza:rnā: (*v*) to pass time.
गुज़ारा guza:ra: (*nm*) subsistence; livelihood; –करना to keep the pot boiling, to make both ends meet.
गुजारिश guza:rish (*nf*) submission, supplication.

गुज्जी gujji: (*nf*) a dowel.

गुट guṭ (*nm*) a block, faction, clique; group; ~**बंदी** groupism, factionalism ; ~**बाज़** a factionalist, one who forms a clique; ~**बाज़ी** see ~**बंदी**.

गुटका guṭka: (*nm*) a manual, handbook; puncheon; skid, scotch.

गुटरगूँ guṭargū: (*nf*) cooing of (a pigeon).

गुटिका guṭika: (*nf*) a tablet; pill.

गुट्ट guṭṭ (*nm*) see **गुट**.

गुट्ठल guṭṭhal (*a*) (a fruit, etc.) having a stone within, stony; blunt.

गुट्ठी guṭṭhi: (*nf*) the stone (of a fruit, etc.).

गुठली guṭhli: (*nf*) the stone (of a fruit etc.); ~**दार** stony.

गुड़ guṛ (*nm*) jaggery; –**खाना गुलगुले से परहेज़ करना/बैर** to swallow a camel, to strain at a gnat; –**गोबर करना** to make a hash of, to mar a happy occasion; to undo all that has been done; –**दिखाकर ढेला मारना** to commence with a caress and conclude with a stab; –**न दे गुड़ जैसी बात करे/कह दे** a good word costs nothing; –**भरा हँसिया** a sugar-coated quinine pill; –**से मरे तो ज़हर क्यों दे**? why administer quinine, should sweet stuff serve the purpose ?

गुड़गुड़ guṛguṛ (*nm*) a bubbling noise (such as produced while smoking a hooqah or by movement of air through the intestines).

गुड़गुड़ाना guṛguṛa:na: (*v*) to produce a bubbling noise.

गुड़गुड़ाहट guṛguṛa:haṭ (*nf*) a bubbling noise.

गुड़गुड़ी guṛguṛi: (*nf*) a hubble-bubble.

गुड़हल guṛhal (*nm*) the plant *Bassia latifolia* and its flower.

गुड़ाई guṛa:i: (*nf*) hoeing; thrashing; beating; charges therefor.

गुड़िया guṛiya: (*nf*) a doll; ~**यों का खेल** a childish/non-serious affair.

गुड्डा guḍḍa: (*nm*) a big doll (in male attire); a large kite; **गुड्डे-गुड़ियों का खेल** a childish affair.

गुड्डी guḍḍi: (*nf*) a kite; a female child.

गुण guṉ (*nm*) quality; attribute, property; virtue; merit; chief quality of all existing beings (viz. **सत्त्व, रजस्, तमस्**); a cord; ~**क** a multiplier; ~**कारक/कारी** effective (as **ओषधि**); beneficial; ~**गान** a panegyric, encomium; o**करना/गाना** to chant the praises of, to eulogize, to extol, to narrate the virtues of; ~**ग्राहक** a connoisseur; o**ता** appreciation; quality of a connoisseur; ~**ज्ञ** a connoisseur; appreciator of merit; –**त्रय** the three *gunas* (**सत्त्व, रजस्** and **तमस्**); –**दोष** merits and demerits; merits; ~**धर्म** property; ~**भेदक** qualitative; ~**वाचक/वाची** attributive; ~**वान** meritorious; possessing good qualities; ~**हीन** devoid of merit or quality; hence ~**हीनता** (*nf*).

गुणन guṉān (*nm*) multiplication; –**चिह्न** sign of multiplication; ~**फल** product of multiplication.

गुणा guṉā: (*nm*) multiplication; –**करना** to multiply.

गुणाढ्य guṉa:ḍḍhy (*a*) gifted, of many gifts, possessing many virtues.

गुणातीत guṉa:ti:t (*a*) transcendental, freed from or beyond all properties.

गुणात्मक guṉa:tmāk (*a*) qualitative.

गुणानुवाद guṉā:nuva:d (*nm*) encomium, eulogy, singing praises (of).

गुणान्वित guṉā:nvit (*a*) meritorious, virtuous.

गुणावस्था guṉa:vastha: (*nf*) quality.

गुणित gunit (*nm*) multiple; (*a*) multiplied by, times.

गुणी guni: (*a*) meritorious, possessing merits; adept in (some) art.

गुण्य gunny (*nm*) multiplicand.

गुत्थमगुत्था gutthamguttha: (*nf*) a scuffle, brawl, close combat.

गुत्थी gutthi: (*nf*) a knot, entanglement; riddle, enigma; **–सुलझाना** to cut the gordian knot.

गुथना guthnā: (*v*) to interweave, to entwine; to interlock; to braid, to plait.

गुदकार gudka:r (*a*) fleshy, plump, pulpy.

गुदगुदा gudguda: (*a*) soft; plump, fleshy; hence **~पन** (*nm*).

गुदगुदाना gudguda:nā: (*v*) to tickle, to titillate.

गुदगुदाहट gudguda:haṭ (*nf*) titillation, tickling (sensation).

गुदगुदी gudgudi: (*nf*) see **गुदगुदाहट**.

गुदड़ी gudṛi: (*nf*) pallet, rags, tattered garment; **–का लाल** a diamond in rags (a precious thing in most shabby quarters).

गुदना gudnā: (*nm*) tattoo; (*v*) to be tattooed.

गुदा guda: (*nf*) the anus; **~भंजन/मैथुन** act of sodomy; (*fig.*) undoing.

गुनगुना gūngūnā: (*a*) lukewarm, tepid; hence **~पन** (*nm*).

गुनगुनाना gūngūnā:nā: (*v*) to hum; to sing to oneself in subdued tones.

गुनना gunnā: (*v*) to ponder (over); to assimilate.

गुनहगार gunehga:r (*a*) guilty, sinful; (*nm*) sinner.

गुना gunā:—a suffix denoting times or fold (as **तिगुना**—three times or threefold).

गुनाह gunā:h (*nm*) sin; fault, guilt; **~गार** see **गुनहगार**; **–और बेलज्जत** game not worth the candle.

गुनिया guniyā: (*nf*) a try-square.

गुप्त gupt (*a*) hidden, secret, latent; confidential; **~घात** assassination; **~घाती** an assassin; **~ता** secrecy; **–दान** anonymous donation; **–धन** hidden treasure.

गुप्त/चर guptachar (*nm*) detective, spy; **~चर्या** espionage.

गुप्ती gupti: (*nf*) a sword-stick.

गुफा gupha: (*nf*) a cave, cavern; **~वासी** cave-dwelling; caveman.

गुफ़्तगू guftgu: (*nf*) talk, conversation, chit-chat.

गुबरैला gubraila: (*nm*) a beetle, scarab.

गुबार guba:r (*nm*) dirt, dust; affliction; spite; **–निकालना** to blow off steam, to give vent to one's sense of affliction/wrath.

गुब्बारा gubba:ra: (*nm*) a balloon.

गुम gum (*a*) lost; missing; **–चोट** inner injury; **~नाम** anonymous; **~राह** misled, (led) astray; **~शुदा** missing; **~सुम** quiet, mute, taciturn.

गुमटी gumṭi: (*nf*) a watch tower; monkey island.

गुमड़ीदार gumṛi:da:r (*a*) muricate.

गुमान gumā:n (*nm*) pride, vanity; surmise, guess.

गुमाश्ता gumā:shta: (*nm*) an agent, representative, manager; **~गीरी** office or function of an agent/representative.

गुर gur (*nm*) formula; device; **–समझ लेना** to get the hang/knack of.

गुरगा gurga: (*nm*) see **गुर्गा**.

गुरदा gurda: (*nm*) kidney; courage.

गुरिया guriya: (*nf*) a small bead (of a rosary).

गुरिल्ला gurilla: (*nm*) guerilla; **–दस्ता** a guerilla squad; **–युद्ध** guerilla warfare.

गुरु guru (*nm*) a teacher; mentor; preceptor, spiritual guide; jupiter (ironically) a knave fellow; (*a*) grave; heavy; difficult; long (syllable); ~कुल in olden times in India, a residential teaching institution, run by an outstanding scholar; ~ग्रन्थ साहब the sacred book of the Sikhs; ~घंटाल knave and cunning (fellow); ~जन elderly people; ~दक्षिणा the fee or honorarium voluntarily paid by the disciple to his preceptor at the conclusion of his studies; ~भाई brother by virtue of preceptorial affinity, a fellow disciple; ~मंत्र an initiatory *mantr* from a spiritual guide.

गुरुआई gurua:i: (*nf*) the profession or function of a *guru* (preceptor); heaviness.

गुरुआनी gurua:ni: (*nf*) *guru's* wife.

गुरुडम gurudām (*nf*) gurudom—effort to create an intellectual dominion by self-aggrandisement.

गुरुता guruta: (*nf*) the office or position of a *guru*; eminence; gravity; heaviness.

गुरुत्व guruttv (*nm*) see गुरुता; –केंद्र the centre of gravity.

गुरुत्वाकर्षण guruttva:karshān (*nm*) gravitation; –नियम law of gravitation.

गुरुद्वारा gurudva:ra: (*nm*) a sikh temple.

गुरुमुखी gurumukhi: (*nf*) a differently developed form of ancient *Devna:gri*: script, which is now used for writing Punja:bi:.

गुरुवार guruva:r (*nm*) Thursday.

गुरुघंटाल guru:ghanta:l (*a* and *nm*) knave, astute, crafty (fellow).

गुर्गा gurga: (*nm*) a henchman; an agent; hence ~पन (*nm*).

गुर्ज gurz (*nm*) a mace, club.

गुर्दा gurda: (*nm*) see गुरदा.

गुर्राना gurra:nā: (*v*) to growl, to snarl, to gnarl.

गुर्राहट gurra:haṭ (*nf*) a snarl, gnar

गुल gul (*nm*) a flower; snuff (of candle etc); the ashy substanc on the front of a lighted cigarett etc; print; ~कारी embroidery ~ज़ार a garden; gay, bustling wit life; ~दस्ता a bouquet; ~दान flower vase; ~बदन soft and deli cate (like a flower); ~शन small garden; –करना to snuff ou to put out; –खिलना to have stra nge or funny things to happen c come to light; hence causativ –खिलाना; –होना to be snuffed out to be put out.

गुलकंद gulkand (*nm*) a conserv prepared from rose-leaves.

गुलखैरा gulkhaira: (*nm*) a hollyhock

गुलगपाड़ा gulgapa:ṛa: (*nm*) an uproa tumult, din.

गुलगुला gulgula: (*a*) soft; henc ~पन (*nm*); (*nm*) a kind of swee preparation.

गुलगुलाना gulgula:nā: (*v*) see गुदगुदान

गुलगुली gulguli: (*nf*) see गुदगुदी.

गुलचा gulcha: (*nm*) a light stroke o the fist (on the cheek).

गुलछर्रे gulchharre (*nm*) merry-mak ing, revelry; –उड़ाना to live lik fighing cocks, to enjoy freely, to indulge in riotous merry-making to revel with abandon.

गुलज़ार gulza:r (*nm* and *a*) see गुल (~ज़ार).

गुलमेंहदी gulmēhdi: (*nf*) touch-me not, the balsam plant and its flowe

गुलाब gula:b (*nm*) rose; ~जल rose water; ~जामुन a delicious sweet-meat preparation; ~पाश a vase for sprinkling rose-water.

गुलाबी gula:bi: (*a*) rosy; mild (as जाड़ा).

गुला/म gulā:m (*nm*) a slave; ~मी slavery, servility, bondage; –होना to eat out of one's hand.

लाल gula:l (*nf*) coloured farinaceous powder which the Hindus apply on one another's face and/or forehead during the Holi: festival.
लूबंद gulu:band (*nm*) a muffler; an ornament worn around the neck.
लेल gulel (*nf*) a stone bow pellet bow; ~ची a pellet bowman, stone bowman.
ल्फ gulph (*nm*) an ankle.
ल्म gulm (*nm*) a cluster of plants; a kind of shrub; (in olden times) division of an army.
ल्लक gullak (*nm*) a till, an earthen cash-box.
ल्ली gulli: (*nf*) see गिल्ली; –डंडा see गिल्ली-डंडा; ०खेलना see गिल्ली-डंडा खेलना.
सल gusal (*nm*) a bath.
सलख़ाना gusalkha:nā: (*nm*) a bath, bath-room.
स्ताख़ gusta:kh (*a*) impertinent, impudent.
स्ताख़ी gusta:khi: (*a*) impertinence, impudence.
स्सा gussa: (*nm*) anger, rage, fury; गुस्सेबाज़ irascible, choleric; –उतारना/निकालना to give vent to one's rage; –करना to put a person's back up; –ठंडा होना one's anger to subside; –थूक देना to be pacified, to forgive and forget; –दिलाना to set a person's back up; –पी जाना to restrain oneself; –भड़क उठना to blaze up, to burst out in anger; –हवा हो जाना one's anger to evaporate/disappear.
स्सैल gussail (*a*) irascible, choleric, hot-headed.
हना guhnā: (*v*) to thread, to string; to weave; to braid, to plait.
हा guha: (*nf*) cave; cavity; cavitation; ~मानव the caveman.
हार guha:r (*nf*) an humble appeal (for justice, protection, etc.).

गुह्य guhy (*a*) occult; secret.
गूँ/गा gũ:ga: (*a*) dumb, mute; (*nm*) a dumb person; ~गे का गुड़ an experience that defies expression.
गूँज gũ:j (*nf*) an echo, a reverberation.
गूँजना gũ:jnā: (*v*) to echo, to resound.
गूँथना gũ:thnā: (*v*) to braid, to plait.
गूँधना gũ:dhnā: (*v*) to knead.
गू gu: (*nm*) faeces; –का चोथ (चोंत) an ugly inert man; –मूत human excreta; –में घसीटना to subject (somebody) to grave humiliation and embarrassment; –में ढेला फेंकना to provoke a wily tongue.
गूगल gu:gal (*nm*) Indian bdellium, a fragrant gum resin used as a perfume and medicament.
गूढ़ gu:ṛh (*a*) occult, mysterious; abstruse; obscure.
गूढ़ता gu:ṛhta: (*nf*) occultation, mysteriousness; abstruseness; obscurity.
गूढ़ोक्ति gu:ṛhokti (*nf*) equivocation; a subtle remark.
गूदड़ gu:daṛ (*nm*) rags, tattered clothes.
गू/दा gu:da: (*nm*) flesh (of fruits and vegetables, etc.) pulp; ~देदार fleshy; pulpy.
गूलर gu:lar (*nm*) a kind of wild fig tree; –का फूल a non-existent object, rare find.
गृध्र griddhr (*nm*) a vulture; (*a*) greedy; –दृष्टि long-sighted; one gifted with a capability to see remote things.
गृह grih (*nm*) a residence; –उद्योग cottage industry; –कलह internecine quarrels; –प्रबंध household management: –प्रवेश house-warming ceremony; ~युद्ध civil war; ~लक्ष्मी (a deferential term for) a housewife; ~स्वामिनी mistress of the household; ~स्वामी master of

the household.

गृहस्थ grihasth (*nm*) a householder.

गृहस्थाश्रम grihastha:shshram (*nm*) the position or phase of the householder (the second of the four phases of life viz. *Brahmachary*, *grihasth*, *va:nprasth* and *Sannya:s* prescribed by the ancient Hindu savants).

गृहस्थी grihasthi: (*nf*) household; family.

गृहिणी grihiṇi: (*nf*) wife, housewife.

गृहीत grihi:t (*nm*) postulate; (*a*) assumed; accepted.

गेंडली genḍli: (*nf*) coil, things arranged in concentric circles; coiled rope, cloth, etc. for carrying heavy utensils on the head.

गेंद gēd (*nf*) a ball; **–बल्ला** ball and bat.

गेंदा gēda: (*nm*) marigold (plant and its flower).

गेटिस geṭis (*nf*) garter.

गेरुआ gerua: (*a*) ochrous, of the colour of red ochre, russet; **–बाना** ochre-coloured dress, the dress of a Hindu *Sannyā:si:*.

गेरू geru: (*nm*) red ochre, ochre, ruddle.

गेहुँअन gehūān (*nm*) see **गोहुअन**.

गेहुँआ gehūā: (*a*) wheat-coloured, wheatish.

गेहूँ gēhū: (*nm*) wheat; **–के साथ घुन भी पिस जाता है** when bulls fight, crops suffer.

गैंडा gaĩḍa: (*nm*) a rhinoceros.

गैंती gaĩti: (*nf*) a pick, pick-axe.

ग़ैबी gaibi: (*a*) divine, other-worldly; unknown.

ग़ैर gair (*nm* and *a*) stranger, other; (prefix) non-, un-, in-; **-अदायगी** non-payment; **-इंसाफ़ी** inequity, injustice; **-क़ानूनी** illegal, unlawful; **-ज़रूरी** unnecessary; unimportant; **-जिम्मेदार** irresponsible; **-मनक़ूला** immovable (property); **-मामूली** extraordinary; **-मुनासिब** unfair; unreasonable; **-मुमकिन** impossible; **-मौरूसी** non-inherited; acquired; **-वाजिब** unreasonable, improper; **-सरकारी** non-governmental; unofficial; private; **-हाज़िर** absent; **-हाज़िरी** absence.

ग़ैरत gairat (*nf*) sense of honour, self-respect; **~मंद** having a sense of honour, self-respecting; **–मरना** to lose all sense of self-respect.

गैरिक gairik (*a*) ochrous, russet, of the colour of red ochre.

गैलन gailan (*nm*) gallon (a measure).

गैलरी gailari: (*nf*) a gallery.

गैस gais (*nf*) a gas.

गोंठ gōṭh: (*nm*) everted rim.

गोंठना gōṭhnā: (*v*) to stitch in a rather crude manner; to skirt the edges; to encircle.

गोंड़ा gōṛa: (*nm*) a cattle pen (an enclosure meant for domestic animals).

गोंद gōd (*nm*) gum, wood gum; **~दानी** a gum bottle; **गोंदीला** gummy.

गोंदा gōda: (*nm*) pise.

गो go (*nf*) a cow; a sense (of perception etc.); **~घात** cow-slaughter; **~घाती** a butcher; killer of the cow; **~चारण** tending the cows (at a pasture); **०काव्य** pastoral poetry; **~दान** the gifting away of a cow; **~धन** cattle wealth; **~धूलि** dusk, evening; **०बेला** dusk, evening; **~**[illegible] a cowherd; **~पद** hoof of a cow; the imprint of a cow-hoof; **~पाल**[illegible] tending the cows; **~पुच्छ** cow's tail; any tapering structure; **~मांस** beef; **~रक्षा** cow-protection; **~र**[illegible] cow-milk, buttermilk, etc; **~व**[illegible] cow-slaughter; **~संवर्धन** cow-breeding; **~हत्या** cow-slaughter.

गो go (*ind*) although, though; **~कि**

though, although.

गोखरू gokhru: (*nm*) a medicinal plant and its thorny fruit; corn (on one's feet); caltrop.

गोचर gochar (*a*) perceptible, experienced through the senses; hence **~ता** (*nf*).

गोट goṭ (*nm*) gold or silver lace, brocade; a piece (in games like *chaupaṛ*, etc.); a picnic party; **–जमना/बैठना** to achieve success in (one's) manipulation.

गो/टा goṭa: (*nm*) gold or silver lace, edging; **~टेदार** brocaded; fitted with gold or silver lace.

गोटी goṭi: (*nf*) a piece (in games like *chaupaṛ* etc.) —see **गोट**; small round stone or pebble; **–जमना/बैठना** see **गोट** (**जमना/बैठना**).

गोड़ goṛ (*nm*) a leg.

गोड़ना goṛnā: (*v*) to hoe; to dig; to upturn (the soil).

गोड़ाई goṛa:i: (*nf*) see **गुड़ाई**.

गोत got (*nm*) see **गोत्र**.

ग़ोता g̠ota: (*nm*) dive; dip; **~ख़ोर** a diver; **~मार** diver; submarine; **–खाना** to suffer a dip; to be deceived; to suffer at somebody's hand; **–देना** to enforce a dip, to cause a dip; to deceive; **–मारना** to dip, to dive, to have a plunge; to give a slip; **–लगाना** to have a dip (in a river).

गोत्र gottr (*nm*) lineage.

गोद god (*nf*) lap; **–का** in the lap; very young; **–देना** to give away for adoption; **–भरना** to be blessed with motherhood; to fill the lap of a woman with auspicious articles (like cocoanut, etc.); **–लेना** to adopt (a child); **–सूनी होना** to lose the only child.

गोदना godnā: (*v*) to tattoo, to pick; to prick; to puncture; to goad; (*nm*) a tattoo-mark.

गोदाम godā:m (*nm*) a godown, warehouse.

गोदी godi: (*nf*) lap; a dock, dockyard.

गोपन gopān (*nm*) concealment, hiding; **~शील** secretive, of undivulging nature; **~शीलता** secretiveness; **गोपनीय** secret; confidential; **०ता** secrecy.

गोपिका gopika: (*nf*) see **गोपी**.

गोपी gopi: (*nf*) a cowherd's wife.

गोबर gobar (*nm*) cow-dung; dung; **–गणेश** a beetle-brain; a plump fool, nitwit, an inert blockhead; **–का चोथ (चोंत)** a good-for-nothing fellow; an indolent fool; an utterly ineffective man.

गोभी gobhi: (*nf*) cauliflower; **—,बंद** cabbage.

गोया goya: (*ind*) as if; **–कि** as if.

गोरखधंधा gorakhdhandha: (*nm*) a labyrinth; labyrinthine affair, complicated riddle.

गोरखा gorkha: (*nm*) an inhabitant of Nepal, a Gorkha.

गोरखाली gorkha:li: (*nf*) Gorkhali—the language of Nepal.

गोरा gora: (*a*) white, fair-skinned; (*nm*) a whiteman; an European; hence **~पन** (*nm*)

गोरिल्ला gorilla: (*nm*) a gorilla.

गोरी gori: (*a*) fair-comple (*nf*) a beautiful damsel.

गोलंदा/ज़ golānda:z (*nm*) a gunner, marksman; **~ज़ी** gunnery, marksmanship; cannonading.

गोलंबर golāmbar (*nm*) a dome-like structure, cupola.

गोल gol (*a*) round; circular; globular; (*nm*) a goal (in games); misappropriation; mess, confusion; gang; **~गप्पा** a small cake-like Indian preparation taken with spiced water; corpulent, chubby; **–गोल** equivocal; fat; round; **~मटोल**

equivocal; vague; fat, corpulent; ~मापी spherometer; ~माल mess, confusion; ~मोल vague, ambiguous; hotch-potch; ०उत्तर देना to fence with question/questioner; ०बातें करना to double and twist; –करना to evade, to avoid, not to implement; –बाँधना to form into a gang.

गोलक golak (*nm*) see गुल्लक; ball (as eye-ball नेत्र~).

गोला gola: (*nm*) a ball; cannon-ball; a bomb shell; kernel of a cocoanut; sphere; globe; a large round beam (of wood); colic; ~ई roundness, rotundity, sphericity; curvature, ~बारी shelling, bombardment; –बारूद ammunition.

गोलाकार gola:ka:r (*a*) round; globular; circular.

गोलार्ध gola:rdh (*nm*) hemisphere.

गोली goli: (*nf*) a bullet; pill; tablet, ball; (*nm*) goalkeeper; –खाना to be hit by a bullet; –चलना firing to take place; –मारना to shoot; to ignore, to damn, to let go.

गोलीय goli:y (*a*) spherical; rotund.

गोल्फ़ golf (*nm*) golf.

गोशाला gosha:la: (*nf*) a cow-shed, cow-tending centre.

गोश्त gosht (*nm*) flesh, meat; ~ख़ोर a meat-eater; —,गाय का beef; —,भेड़/बकरी का mutton; —,सुअर का pork; —, हिरन का venison.

गोष्ठी goshṭhi: (*nf*) a seminar; discussion.

गोह goh (*nf*) iguana.

गोहुअन gohuān (*nm*) a (wheatish complexioned) deadly snake.

गौ gau (*nf*) see गो.

गौण gaun̠ (*a*) secondary, subsidiary; auxiliary; minor; hence ~ता (*nf*).

गौना gaunā: (*nm*) the ceremony of the bride's going to her husband's home after a post-marriage interval.

गौर gaur (*a*) fair-skinned, fair, white; ~वर्ण fair-complexioned.

ग़ौर gaur (*nm*) reflection, deliberation, consideration, close attention; ~तलब worth considering/reflecting on, requiring close attention; –करना to take note of; to ponder, to deliberate, to think attentively; –होना to be thought of attentively, to be pondered over.

गौरव gaurav (*nm*) pride, glory, honour; heaviness; –ग्रंथ a classic (work); ~मय glorious; hence ~मयी feminine form of ~मय; ~शाली glorious, dignified.

गौरवान्वित gaurava:nvit (*a*) filled/crowned with glory, glorified.

गौरी gauri: (*nf*) the goddess Pa:rvati:—Shiv's spouse; ~शंकर the Mount Everest.

गौरैया gauraiya: (*nf*) a sparrow, hen-sparrow.

गौशाला gausha:la: (*nf*) a cowshed, habitat for cows; cow-tending centre.

ग्यारह gya:rah (*a*) eleven; (*nm*) the number eleven.

ग्रांडील gra:nḍi:l (*a*) see गरांडील.

ग्रंथ grānth (*nm*) a book; voluminous book; ~कार a writer, author (of a book); ~माला a series of books; –रचना writing of a book; ~विज्ञान (the science of) bibliography; ~विज्ञानी a bibliographer; –विमोचन formal releasing of a book; ~सूची bibliography; a list of books; ०कार a bibliographer.

ग्रंथि granthi (*nf*) a knot; complex; ~ल knotty, complicated.

ग्रंथिका granthika: (*nf*) a booklet.

ग्रसना grasnā: (*v*) to swallow, to make a morsel of, to seize, to capture.

ग्रस्त grast (*a*) caught (into), possessed by, involved in; eclipsed.

ग्र/ह grah (*nm*) a planet; ~ह-ग्रस्त planet-stricken; ~ह-शांति countering of evil planetary effects; ~हीय planetary.

ग्रह/ण grahān (*nm*) eclipse; taking, catching, seizing; hence ~णीय (*a*).

ग्रा/म gra:m (*nm*) a village; gamut; gramme (a weight); as a suffix it means multitude, collection; ~मीण rural, uncivil; ~म्य rural, uncivil; hence ~मीणता, ~म्यता; ~म्यत्व vulgarity.

ग्रास gra:s (*nm*) a morsel; victim; eclipsed part (of Sun or Moon).

ग्राह gra:h (*nm*) a crocodile.

ग्राहक gra:hak (*nm*) a customer, client; -वर्ग clientele; –टूटना a customer to be veered away/to be alienated.

ग्राही gra:hi: —a suffix denoting one who catches/takes/seizes.

ग्राह्य gra:hy (*a*) worth taking, acceptable; hence ~ता (*nf*).

ग्रीक gri:k (*nf*) Greek (language).

ग्रीवा gri:va: (*nf*) the neck.

ग्रीष्म gri:shm (*nm*) the summer; –काल summer season; ~कालीन pertaining to or of the summer season, summer.

ग्रेजुएट grejuet (*nm*) a graduate.

ग्लानि gla:nı (*nf*) remorse, repentance.

ग्वा/ला gwa:la: (*nm*) a milkman, cowkeeper; ~लिन a milkwoman.

घ

घ gha—the fourth consonant and the fourth member of the first pentad (i.e. कवर्ग) of the Devna:gri: alphabet.

घँघोलना ghāgholnā: (*v*) to mash; to mix by stirring; to make turbid (by mixing).

घंटा ghanta: (*nm*) a bell; gong; clock; an hour; ~घर a clock-tower.

घंटी ghanti: (*nf*) a small bell, tintinnabulum; the ringing of a bell; ovula.

घट ghat (*nm*) a pitcher; the physical frame/body; nominal form of the verb घटना used as the first member of the compound घटबढ़ fluctuation, variation; ०होना to fluctuate; to vary; to be slightly more or less; –घट में समाना to permeate each and every body/through all and sundry.

घटक ghatak (*nm*) a factor, component/constituent/ingredient.

घटती ghatti: (*nf*) decline; decrease; descent; diminution.

घटना ghatnā: (*nf*) an incident, event; incidence, occurrence; phenomenon; (*v*) to happen; to be subtracted; to decrease, to lessen; –क्रम series of events; –चक्र march of events; –बढ़ना to fluctuate, to vary; ~स्थल the site/scene of an incident/occurrence.

घटनावली ghatnā:vali: -(*nf*) a series of incidents.

घटवार ghatva:r (*nm*) a wharf-owner,

wharfinger.

घटा ghaṭa: (*nf*) a dark cloud; mass of dark clouds; **–उठना** emergence of thick dark clouds; **–घिरना/छाना** gathering of thick dark clouds.

घटाटोप ghaṭa:ṭop (*nm*) gathering of dense clouds in the sky; a covering used for carriage etc.

घटाना ghaṭa:nā: (*v*) to reduce; to subtract; to deduct; to diminish; to lessen/decrease; to apply.

घटाव ghata:w (*nm*) reduction, decrease; diminution.

घटिका ghaṭika: (*nf*) a time-interval of 24 minutes; also called **घड़ी**.

घटित ghaṭit (*a*) happened; applied.

घटिया ghaṭiya: (*a*) inferior, of low quality or standard; cheap; shoddy; hence **~पन** (*nm*).

घ/ट्टा, ~ट्ठा ghaṭṭa:, ~ṭṭha: (*nm*) corn, callosity; cork, plug.

घड़घड़ा/ना ghaṛghaṛa:nā: (*v*) to rattle; to rumble; to thunder; **~हट** rattle; rumble; thunder.

घ/ड़ा ghaṛa: (*nm*) a pitcher, pot; **~ड़ों पानी पड़ना** to be flushed with shame, to suffer extreme humiliation.

घड़िया ghaṛiya: (*nf*) a crucible.

घड़ियाल ghaṛiya:l (*nm*) an alligator; a crocodile.

घड़ी ghaṛi: (*nf*) a watch, time-piece; moment; a time interval of 24 minutes; **–घड़ी** every moment; repeatedly, time and again; **–भर को** for a while; **–में** in a trice; **~साज़** a horologist, watch-maker; **~साज़ी** horology, watch maker's work/profession; **घड़ियाँ गिनना** to count every passing moment restlessly; to await keenly; **–टलना** the appointed time to pass away; to miss the opportune moment.

घड़ौंची ghaṛauchi: (*nf*) a pitcher-stand.

घन ghān (*nm*) a hammer, sledge-hammer; cube; cloud; (*a*) dense; solid; **~घोर** very dense; terrible, profound; **~चक्कर** a blockhead; dolt; **~फल** cube; **~मूल** cube-root; **–की चोट** a heavy shattering stroke, hammer stroke.

घनघना/ना ghānghanā:nā: (*v*) to produce a deep ringing sound (as of a gong); hence **~हट** (*nf*).

घनता ghanata: (*nf*) density; solidity; compactness.

घनत्व ghanatv (*nm*) see **घनता**.

घना ghanā: (*a*) dense, thick; intensive (as cultivation); compact; **~पन** denseness; compactness.

घनाभ ghanā:bh (*nm*) a cuboid.

घनिष्ठ ghanishṭh (*a*) close; closest, most intimate; **~ता** closeness; intimacy; rapport.

घनीभूत ghanī:bhu:t (*a*) condensed; concentrated; solidified; profound.

घप/ला ghapla: (*nm*) bungling; mess; confusion; disorder, pretty kettle of fish; **~लेबाज़** a bungler, one who creates a mess; hence **~लेबाज़ी**; /**~ला करना** to make hay of.

घबड़ा(रा)/ना ghabṛa:(ra:)nā: (*v*) to be nervous, to lose nerve; to be non-plussed; to get panicky; **–जाना** to be in flap; to be panicky/nervous.

घबड़ा(रा)हट ghabṛa:(ra:)haṭ (*nf*) nervousness; restlessness; panic.

घमंड ghamāṉḍ (*nm*) conceit; vanity.

घमंडी ghamāṉḍi: (*a*) conceited; vain; **–का सिर नीचा** pride goeth before a fall.

घमासान ghamā:sā:n (*a*) fierce; **–युद्ध/लड़ाई** fierce fight or battle.

घमौरी ghamauri: (*nf*) prickly heat.

घर ghar (*nm*) home; house, residence; apartment, room; compartment; native place. homeland; office (as **तारघर, डाकघर**); square or cell (in a chess-board); –गृहस्थी household; family; –घर each and every house; –घाट hearth and home; ~घुसना/घुस्सू one who always keeps within the bounds of the female apartment; an effeminate man; ~जँवाई one who lives with, and is subordinated to, one's in-laws: ~जोत self-cultivation, self-tillage; –द्वार household effects; home and hearth: –पीछे per household; ~बार househol d; ~बारी a householder, family-man; ~वाला husband, the master of the household; ~वाली wife, the mistress of the household; –आबाद करना to marry/remarry; to build up a family; to enter or re-enter the householder's stage; –उजड़ना ruination of a household/family; the demise of one's wife; –करना to create a room for oneself; to build up a household; –का a near one; one's own, internal; ०अच्छा well-to-do; –का आँगन होना a house to be completely razed; to suffer ruination; –का उजाला beloved of the whole family; glamour of the family; –का काटने को दौड़ना, –का काटे खाना the house to arouse a feeling of desolation and disgust; –का घर the entire family; –का चिराग़ see –का उजाला; –का जोगी जोगना आन गाँव का सिद्ध a prophet is not honoured in his own land; –का न घाट का belonging neither here nor there; –का नाम डुबोना to bring disgrace to the fair name of the family; –का भेदी one who knows the secrets of the house; ०लंका ढाए traitors prove to be the worst enemies; –का मर्द/शेर a hero within one's own fourwalls; household hero; –की आधी भली बाहर सारी नाहिं dry bread at home is more welcome than sweetmeat elsewhere; –की खेती easily procurable, easy to procure; –की मुर्गी दाल बराबर what is easy to procure, does not score; –के घर रहना to be even in a bargain; –चलाना to run a household; –जमाना to establish a household; –देख लेना to get habituated; to become a habitual visitor, to make profitable visits; –फूँक तमाशा देखना to ruin one's household for the sake of an idle pleasure; –फोड़ना to spell internecine. quarrel in a household; –बिगाड़ना to bring ruin on a household; –बैठना to become a/(somebody's)mistress; to be out of employment; the house to crash down; –बैठे without moving out; without a stroke of work; –भरना to amass wealth; to achieve prosperity; –भाँय-भाँय करना the house to be desolated; –में गंगा आना to achieve one's purpose without a stroke of work; to gain divine visit without effort; –में डालना to take as a mistress; –में दिया जला कर तब मस्जिद में दिया जलाना self-insterest is the first law of nature; –में भूँजी-भाँग न होना to carry off meat from the graves, to be as poor as the church mouse; –में सूत न कपास जुलाहे से लट्ठम-लट्ठा count not your chickens till they are hatched; –सिर पर उठाना to make a terrible noise or create a commotion; to kick up a row in the house; –से पाँव निकालना to transcend the bounds of one's home; to undermine the honour of the family; –से बेघर करना to turn a householder into a homeless being

घरघरा/ना gharghara:nā: (*v*) to produce a whirring sound; to snort; hence ~ हट (*nf*).

घराती ghara:ti: (*nm*, member of

the bridal party (in a marriage).

घराना ghara:nā: (*nm*) a family, clan.

घरू gharu: (*a*) domestic; familial; private.

घरेलू gharelu: (*a*) domestic; private.

घरौंदा gharauda: (*nm*) a toy-house.

घर्घर gharghar (*nf*) rumble; gurgle; snorting sound.

घ/र्षण gharshān (*nm*) friction; clash; ~र्षित clashed; in clash, in friction.

घलुआ ghalua: (*nm*) that which a buyer gets over and above the quantity paid for; a tip in kind to a buyer.

घसखोदा ghaskhoda: (*nm*) a grass-cutter; petty person; ignoramus.

घसियारा ghasiya:ra: (*nm*) a grass-cutter; hay-trusser; a inadept.

घसीट ghasi:ṭ (*nf*) scribble; scrawl.

घसीटना ghasi:ṭnā: (*v*) to drag; to trail; to scribble; to scrawl.

घहराना ghehra:nā: (*v*) to thicken (as clouds); to thunder; to gurgle.

घाई gha:i: (*nf*) the intervening space in between two fingers.

घाघ gha:gh (*nm* and *a*) cunning, shrewd (person).

घाघरा gha:ghra: (*nm*) a petticoat; skirt from waist to ankle.

घाट gha:ṭ (*nm*) wharf, quay; berth; ferry, bank; ~बंदी embargo; –शुल्क ferriage; –का पत्थर a public property; –घाट का पानी पीना to wander from pillar to post; to gather varied experience; –लगना to reach ashore; to find a foothold.

घाटा gha:ṭa: (*nm*) loss; deficit; –खाना to suffer a loss; घाटे का सौदा a losing proposition; घाटे का बजट a deficit budget.

घाटिया gha:ṭiya: (*nm*) a *Bra:hman* on a bathing bank who applies sandalwood paste on bathers' foreheads.

घाटी gha:ṭi: (*nf*) a valley; mountain pass.

घात gha:t (*nf*) ambush, ambuscade; killing; slaughter; stroke; power degree; –पर चढ़ना, –में आना to fall into one's clutches; –में फिरना to mark time for an ambuscade: –में बैठना to wait for an ambuscade; –में रहना to be upon the catch, to ambuscade; to look for a tactical opportunity to strike; –लगाना to lie in ambush; घातें बताना to play tricks; to impart lessons in trickery.

घातक gha:tak (*a*) lethal; fatal; ruinous; (*nm*) a killer; murderer.

घातांक gha:tāṅk (*nm*) index.

घा/ता gha:ta: (*nm*); ~ते में over and above what is paid for, free; without effort or spending; by trickery.

घाती gha:ti: (*nm*) a killer, assassin; slaughterer; trickster; (*a*) cunning and crafty.

घान ghā:n (*nm*) a lot; quantity of oilseed, wheat, etc. ground or pressed in one lot; things cooked or fried in one lot.

घाम ghā:m (*nm*) sunshine; heat of the sun.

घामड़ ghā:maṛ (*nm*) an idiot, a blockhead, dullard; (*a*) idiotic, dull.

घायल gha:yal (*a*) wounded, injured; hurt; –की गति घायल जाने its the sufferer alone who knows the pain.

घालना gha:lnā: (*v*) to strike; to thrust; to destroy; to place; to pour(into).

घाव gha:w (*nm*) a wound; an injury; –खाना to be wounded/injured, to receive an injury, –पर नमक छिड़कना to add insult to injury; –पुरना/भरना a wound to heal up; –हरा होना a wound to revive.

घास gha:s (*nf*) grass: –पात rubbish; weed and straw: worthless food;

–फूस rubbish; weed and straw; –काटना/खोदना/छीलना to undertake a petty/worthless job; to idle away one's time; –खाना said of one who betrays some sort of stupidity; to be bereft of wits or senses.

घासले/ट gha:sleṭ (*nm*) vegetable oil; inferior stuff; (*a*) trash; ~टी worthless; inferior, trash; cheap; ०साहित्य gutter/trash literature, cheap literature.

घिग्घी ghigghi: (*nf*); –बँधना to have the throat choked (out of fear or emotional upsurge); to be so stunned as to become tongue-tied.

घिघियाना ghighiya:nā: (*v*) to grovel in the dust, to show up the teeth, to beg for mercy; to supplicate; to falter in speech (due to fear or emotional upsurge).

घिचपिच ghichpich (*a*) crowded; clumsy; illegible; (*nf*) congestion; clumsiness.

घिन ghın (*nf*) abhorrence, odiousness; nausea; –आना one's gorge to rise at.

घिनौना ghināūnā: (*a*) abominable; loathsome; odious; nauseating; hence ~पन (*nm*).

घिया ghiya: (*nf*) bottle gourd; ~कश a grater.

घिरनी ghirnı: (*nf*) a pulley.

घिराई ghira:i: (*nf*) the act of surrounding or encircling, the act of keeping a watch on grazing cattle; the fee or charge for so doing.

घिराव ghira:v (*nm*) *gherao*—the act of surrouding a person or persons in authority to press acceptance of certain demands.

घिर्री ghirri: (*nf*) a sheave; pulley.

घिसटना ghisaṭnā: (*v*) intrasitive form of the verb घसीटना (see); घिसट-घिसट कर मरना to die by inches.

घिसघिस ghisghis (*nf*) higgling; drudgery; dull routine work; dilatoriness; dilly-dallying.

घिसना ghisnā: (*v*) to rub; to be worn out/to wear out; to be impaired/to impair; घिसा-पिटा hackneyed; worn out.

घिसाई ghisa:i: (*nf*) the work of or charges paid for rubbing or smoothening; hard labour; abrasion; wear.

घिस्सा ghissa: (*nm*) friction; a powerful hard rub (on the body); attrition; dodge.

घी ghi: (*nm*) *ghee*; –के चिराग़/दिए जलाना lit. to light up *ghee* lamps –to celebrate (the fulfilment of some cherished desire) by fanfare/merry-making/festivity; –खिचड़ी/शक्कर होना to be hand in glove with; to be in intimate association; to become inseparably united; –दूध की नदी बहना to be very prosperous and affluent.

घुँघची ghūghchi: (*nf*) a small red and black seed of *Abrus precatorius.*

घुंघराले ghūghra:le (*a*) curly (plural form of घुँघराला—the singular from is seldom used).

घुँघरू ghūghru: (*nm*) a set of small jingling bells (worn around the ankles, esp. during a dance performance); –बाँधना to take to a dancing career; to take lessons in dancing (from a guru).

घुंडी ghūṇḍi: (*nf*) a knob; nipple; switch; ball-shaped button of cloth; ~दार knobby.

घुइयाँ ghuıyā: (*nf*) arum—a kind of Indian vegetable.

घुग्घू ghugghu: (*nm*) an owl; a fool, stupid fellow.

घुटना ghuṭnā: (*v*) to be suffocated; to experience suffocation; to be clean-shaven; (*nm*) a knee; घुट-घुट कर जान देना to fret out one's life, to be gradually suffocated to death; घुटने टेकना to knuckle down/under, to yield; to accept subordination; घुटनों के बल चलना to move on all fours (as a child); घुटनों में सिर देना to be engrossed in some worry/thought; घुटा हुआ cunning and clever; clean-shaven.

घुटन्ना ghuṭannā: (*nm*) knickers, half-pants.

घुटाई ghuṭa:i: (*nf*) levigation and its charges; work of and charges for levigation; surfacing; cramming.

घुट्टी ghuṭṭi: (*nf*) digestive medicine or tonic given to infants; –में पड़ना to become habituated (to) from the very infancy; something to become a part of one's nature.

घुड़ ghuṛ—an allomorph of घोड़ा used as the first member in compound words; ~चढ़ी a ceremonial horse-riding of the bridegroom (to the bride's house) forming a part of the marriage celebrations; a ceremonial horse-riding; ~दौड़ horse-race; ~मुहाँ horse-faced, one having a horse-like oblong face; ~सवार a horse-rider; a cavalier; ~साल a horse-stable.

घुड़कना ghuṛaknā: (*v*) to brow-beat, to (administer a short and sharp) reprimand.

घुड़की ghuṛki: (*nf*) a hollow threat; brow-beating, a sharp reprimand/rebuff; bluff.

घुणाक्षर न्याय ghuṇā:kshar nya:y (*nm*) fortuitous and unexpected manner, happy chance.

घुन ghūn (*nm*) a weevil, wood-worm; –लगना to be in the grip of canker; to suffer internal decay.

घुनना ghunnā: (*v*) to be eaten by wood-worm, to be weevilled; to rot

घुन्ना ghūnnā: (*a*) perversely reticent; rancorously secretive.

घुप्प ghupp (*a*); –अँधेरा pitch dark, total black-out.

घुमक्कड़ ghumākkaṛ (*a*) fond of/in the habit of wandering about, roving; (*nm*) a rover; wanderer.

घुमड़ना ghumaṛnā: (*v*) to gather up (as clouds or sentiments); to converge and concentrate.

घुमरी ghumri: (*nf*) see घुमेरी.

घुमाना ghumā:nā: (*v*) to revolve; to roll; to swirl round; to circulate; to spin; to turn; to brandish (as a sword); to take round; to beguile; to give a twist; घुमा-फिरा कर बात करना to beat about the bush.

घुमेरी ghumēri: (*nf*) giddiness, vertigo; –आना to feel giddy.

घुमाव ghuma:v (*nm*) a turning; curvature; twist; ~दार winding, circuitous; curved.

घुरघुराना ghurghura:nā: (*v*) to produce a snorting sound; hence घरघुर and घुरघुराहट (*nf*).

घुलनशील ghulānshi:l (*a*) soluble; ~ता solubility.

घुल/ना ghulnā: (*v*) to be dissolved; to be liquefied; to be mixed; to languish; to suffer decadence or to waste away; to become lean and thin; –घुलकर काँटा होना to be reduced to a skeleton; -घुलकर जान देना/मरना to fret out one's life, to eat one's heart out; to waste oneself away to death; -घुलकर बातें करना to have a tete-tete, to have a flow of soul.

घुसना ghusnā: (*v*) to enter; to pierce; to penetrate; to thrust into; to intrude.

घुसपैठ ghuspaiṭh (*nf*) intrusion; infiltration; access; घुसपैठिया an intruder; infiltrator; –करना to intrude; to infiltrate.

घुसेड़ना ghuserṇā: (*v*) to thrust into; to pierce; to penetrate.

घूँ/सा ghu:sa: (*nm*) fist; fist-blow; ~सेबाज a boxer; ~सेबाज़ी fisticuffs, boxing; ~सों का क्या उधार let not the revenge of fistblows be deferred until the morrow; have forthright dealings where you must.

घूँघट ghu:ghaṭ (*nm*) face-veil; veil; –उलटना to unveil; to remove the veil; –करना/काढ़ना/निकालना to veil, to have a veil on.

घूँघर ghu:ghar (*nm*) curl (of hair); ~वाले curly.

घूँट ghu:ṭ (*nm*) a draught, gulp, sip.

घूमना ghu:mnā: (*v*) to take a walk, to stroll; to wander; to gyrate; to revolve; to whirl; to turn; to return; to roll; to spin; to waggle; to swim (as head); घूम-फिर कर वहीं पहुँचना to come full circle.

घूरना ghu:rnā: (*v*) to stare (at); to gloat; to frown (at).

घूरा ghu:ra: (*nm*) midden, heap of refuse/sweepings; घूरे के भी दिन फिरते हैं every dog has his day.

घूर्ण ghu:rn (*nm*) moments; rotation.

घूर्णन ghu:rnāṇ (*nm*) rotation; घूर्णित rotated.

घूस ghu:s (*nf*) bribe, illegal gratification; a bandicoot rat; ~ख़ोर bribee; ~ख़ोरी bribery;–खाना to accept bribe;–देना to bribe.

घृणा ghrinā: (*nf*) hatred, scorn, abhorrence; loathing.

घृणास्पद ghrinā:spad (*a*) hateful, abhorrent; loathsome, despicable.

घृणित ghrinit (*a*) abominable; abhorred, heinous.

घृण्य ghrinny (*a*) see घृणास्पद.

घृत ghrit (*nm*) *ghee*.

घेंटी ghēṭi: (*nf*) an unripe pod (of grain etc.)

घेर gher (*nm*) circumference; –घार hemming in; encirclement; ~दार skirted; loose; having a wide circumference.

घेरना ghernā: (*v*) to besiege; to encircle; to hem in; to blockade; to confine.

घेरा ghera: (*nm*) a siege; an encirclement, enclosure, cordon; fence; skirt; girth; circumference; rim; -डालना to besiege, to surround; ~बंदी encirclement; siege; blockade.

घोंघा ghōgha: (*nm*) shell; snail; couch; oyster; ~बसंत an idiot, a nincompoop.

घोंटना ghōṭnā: (*v*) see घोटना.

घोंपना ghōpnā: (*v*) to pierce, to penetrate.

घोंसला ghōsla: (*nm*) a nest.

घोखना ghokhnā: (*v*) to cram up, to commit to memory.

घोटना ghoṭnā: (*v*) to cram up, to commit to memory; to levigate; to choke; to strangle (e.g. गला घोटना); to smoothen; to shave.

घोटा ghoṭa: (*nm*); –लगाना to cram up; to levigate thoroughly.

घोटाला ghoṭa:la (*nm*) bungling; confusion, mess; disorder.

घोटू ghoṭu: (*nm*) a crammer, an adept in the art of cramming up.

घोड़ा ghoṛa: (*nm*) a horse; hammer of a gun; ~गाड़ी a horse-carriage; –कसना to saddle a horse; –चढ़ाना to cock a gun; –पालूँ और पैदल चलूँ what! keep a dog and bark myself; –फेरना/सधाना to break a horse (to the rein); –बेचकर सोना to go into a deep carefree sleep.

घोड़ी ghoṛi: (*nf*) a mare; high wooden stand; –चढ़ना see घुड़ (~चड़ी).

घोर ghor (*a*) awful; formidable; terrible; dense, thick; deep; sharp.

घोल ghol (*nm*) a solution; myrrh.

घोलना gholnā: (*v*) to dissolve; to mix; –घोलकर पी जाना to assimilate thoroughly; to acquire expertise; to gulp in.

घोष ghosh (*v*) voiced; (*nm*) sound; voiced sound; a habitation.

घोषणा ghoshna: (*nf*) a declaration, proclamation.

घोषित ghoshit (*a*) declared, proclaimed.

घोसी ghosi: (*nm*) a milkman.

ङ

ङ ṅa—the fifth (and nasal) consonant and the ultimate member of the first pentad (i.e. **कवर्ग**) of the Devna:gri: alphabet. No word in use in Sanskrit or Hindi begins with this letter. It is usually found as the first member of a conjunct consonant preceded by a vowel but in reformed Devana:gri: script it has been replaced by a dot even in such cases (as **गंगा**, and not **गङ्गा**, is the correct accepted form).

च

च cha—the first letter of the second pentad (i.e. **चवर्ग**) of the Devna:gri: alphabet; a click sound produced by the impact of the tongue on the hard palate as an expression of pity, disgust, etc., what a pity! How sad! How bad! etc., also **च् ··· च्···**

चंग chāṅg (*nf*) a typical brand of paper kite; (*nm*) a musical instrument like a small timbrel; **–पर चढ़ाना** to instigate, topuff up; to inflate (so as to veer somebody round to a particular course of action).

चंगा chāṅga: (*a*) healed, recovered; good, sound, **–भला** hale and hearty, in good health; **–करना** to cure, to restore to normal health; **–होना** to recover; to be restored to normal health.

चंगुल chāṅgul (*nm*) claw, clutch talon; grasp; **–में पड़ना/फँसना** to fall into the clutches (of), to be in the cruel grasp (of); **–से बचना** to be spared from the clutches of, to get out of the clutches of.

चंगे/र, ~री chāṅg/er, ~eri: (*nf*) a small shallow basket; a small swinging cot (for babies).

चंचरीक chāṇchari:k (*nm*) a buzzing bee.

चंचल chāṇchal (*a*) unsteady, transient; inconstant; fickle; flickering; quivering, shaking; fidgety, restless; skittish; playful; coquettish; nimble; ~**चित्त** unsteady, fickle, fidgety, restless (person).

चंचलता chāṇchalta: (*nf*) unsteadiness; inconstancy; transience; fickleness; flicker, shakiness; restlessness, fidgetiness; skittishness; playfulness, coquettishness; nimbleness.

चंचला chāṇchala: (*nf*) an epithet of Lakshmi: (the goddess of wealth); lightning; (*a*) unsteady, fickle; transient.

चंचु chāṇchu (*nf*) beak; bill; ~**प्रवेश** smattering knowledge (of a subject), mere elementary study.

चँचोरना chāchornā: (*v*) see **चिचोरना.**

चंट chāṇṭ (*a*) cunning, clever, wily; ~**पन** cunningness, cleverness, wiliness.

चंड chāṇḍ (*a*) fierce, furious; violent; powerful; hence ~**ता** (*nf*).

चंडाल chāṇḍa:l (*nm*) a sub-caste amongst the *shu:dras* taken to be the lowest in the traditional Hindu caste hierarchy; (*a*) low-born; wretched, wicked, depraved; cruel.

चंडी chāṇḍi: (*nf*) the goddess **दुर्गा**; a quarrelsome defiant woman; a woman of violent nature.

चंडू chāṇḍu: (*nf*) an intoxicating drug made of opium; ~**खाना** a place of assembly for *chandu*: smokers; a rumour-manufacturing centre; ~**बाज** a *chandu*:-addict; rumour-monger; ~**खाने की गप** an unfounded rumour/gossip, frivolous talk.

चंडूल chāṇḍu:l (*nm*) a kind of lark; an ugly repulsive person.

चंद chānd (*nm*) the moon; (*a*) a few, some; ~**रोजा** lasting only a few days; transient.

चंदन chāndān (*nm*) sandalwood, sanders; ~**सार** sandalwood paste; ~**हार** see **चंद्रहार**.

चँदराना chādra:nā: (*v*) to make enquiry with a feigned air of ignorance; to feign ignorance.

चंदरोजा chandroza: (*a*) short-lived, transient, transitory, perishable.

चंदा chānda: (*nm*) the moon; subscription; contribution; donation; –**इकट्ठा करना** to raise a fund by contribution/donation; –**करना** to contribute, to subscribe; –**देना** to subscribe, to contribute; –**मामा** moon—the maternal uncle (said to humour the children); –**सा** as beautiful as the moon (esp. used for face).

चँदावल chāda:val (*nm*) rear guard.

चँदिया chādiya: (*nf*) the cranium, the middle part of the skull; the last small bread prepared from remaining dough (insufficient for a full-size bread).

चँदोवा chādova: (*nm*) a small canopy

चंद्र chandr (*nm*) the moon; crescent; ~**कला** lunar crescent; a digit of the moon (sixteenth part of the circumference); ~**कांत** moonstone; ~**ग्रहण** lunar eclipse; ~**बिंदु** the nasal sign represented by a crescent with a dot over it (ँ), as distinct from **अनुस्वार** represented by a dot above the top (ं); ~**बिंब** the lunar disc; ~**मंडल** the halo of the moon; ~**मुखी** a woman blessed with a moon-like face; ~**लोक** the sphere or heaven of the moon; ~**वंश** the lunar race—one of the two major *kshatriya* dynasties that flourished in ancient India; ~**वंशी** belonging to the lunar dynasty (**चन्द्रवंश**); ~**वदन** blessed with a moon-like face; ~वदनी a beauty blessed with a moon-like face; ~वार Monday; ~विंदु see चंद्रबिंदु; ~शेखर Lord Shiv—whose head is said to be ever adorned by the presence of the lunar crescent; ~ हार a kind of broad necklace.

चंद्रमा chāndramā: (*nm*) the moon.

चंद्रिका chāndrika: (*nf*) the moonlight, moonshine.

चंद्रिकोत्सव chāndrikotsav (*nm*) the festival of the autumnal full moon.

चंद्रोदय chāndroday (*nm*) rise of the moon.

चंपई chāmpai: (*a*) having the tint of the *champa*: flower, having a yellowish white or light yellow tinge.

चंपक chāmpak (*nm*) see चंपा.

चंपत chāmpat (*a*) vanished, disappeared; absconded; –बनना/होना to turn tails, to take to one's heels, to run away.

चंपा chāmpa: (*nm*) the tree *Michelia champaca* and its pleasant fragrant light yellow or yellowish white flower; ~कली buds of चंपा; a necklace studded with stones resembling buds of the *champa*:.

चंपी chāmpi: (*nf*) massage; shampoo; –करना to massage; to shampoo; to try to propitiate.

चंपू chāmpu: (*nm*) a literary composition with alternation of prose and verse.

चँवर chāvar (*nm*) a whisk, a flapper made of the tale of a yak—*Bos grunnieus* (used for flapping away flies, etc.); –डुलाना to wave a चँवर to and fro (as a mark of respect to one who is attended upon); to serve deferentially; ~ढार one who wields a चँवर.

चक chak (*nm*) a holding, plot of land; discus, a kind of a circular toy played with a string; ~डोरी the string of the toy discus; the discus and string; ~फेरी round, circumambulation.

चकई chakai: (*nf*) a discus-shaped whirling toy; a female ruddy goose.

चकती chakti: (*nf*) a patch; soapcake.

चकत्ता chakatta: (*nm*) rash, a blotch on the skin, any round scar or mark (on the skin); used in Braj Bhasha poetry to denote the moghul Emperor Aurangzeb—a descendant of चगताई, son of Chengiz Khan.

चकनाचूर chaknā:chu:r (*a*) shattered (to pieces); broken into fragments; wearied; despirited; –करना to shatter, to dash to the ground (as अरमान–, सपने–).

चकबंदी chakbāndi: (*nf*) consolidation of holdings.

चकमक chakmāk (*nm*) flint.

चकमा chakmā: (*nm*) hoodwinking, dodge; stunt; trick, trickery; –खाना to suffer a dodge, to be tricked/hoodwinked; –देकर ऐंठ लेना to do one down/brown; –देना to dodge, to play a trick, to hoodwink.

चकमे/बाज़ chakmēba:z (*nm*) a dodger, trickster, fraudulent person; hence ~बाज़ी (*nf*).

चकरा/ना chakara:nā: (*v*) to feel dizzy; to whirl, to revolve; to lose one's head/wits, to be confounded/astounded; –जाना to lose one's head/wits.

चकला chakla: (*nm*) a brothel; pastry-board, circular wooden or stony board for spreading dough into a bread; चकलेदार the owner of a brothel: –चलाना to run/own a brothel.

चकल्लस chakallas (*nm*) fun, jocularity, drollery; ~बाज़ one who indulges in drollery/fun making; ~बाज़ी drollery, fun, indulgence in fun; hence –करना.

चक/वा chakva: (*nm*) a ruddy goose; ~वी a female ruddy goose.

चकाचक chaka:chak (*a*) fully satisfied; (*adv*) to the full, to the fullest satisfaction; to the brim/full; –घुटना to prepare/have a strong doze of भाँग; to have very intimate relationship.

चकाचौंध chaka:chaũdh (*nm*) dazzle, dazzlement, dazzling effect; brilliance, brilliant display.

चकित chakit (*a*) amazed, surprised, flabbergasted, wonder-struck.

चकोतरा chakotra: (*nm*) a shaddock, a variety of lemon bigger than the usual size —*Citrus decumana*.

चकोर chakor (*nm*) the Indian red-legged partridge (fabled to subsist upon moon-beams and to eat embers); hence चकोरी (*nf*).

चक्कर chakkar (*nm*) circle; ring, whirl; twirl; spin; rotation; round; revolution; circumambulation; vertigo, giddiness; confusion; trick, fraud; ~दार circuitous; round about; spiral; –आना to suffer from vertigo, to feel giddy; –काटना/लगाना to take rounds, to revolve, to whirl; to swirl; –खाना to go round, to revolve; to take a circuitous route; to be non-plussed, to be confounded; –चलाना to launch a tricky move; –मारना to whirl round; to wander about; –में आना/पड़ना to be taken in (by); to be in a mess; to suffer harassment; to be dodged; –में डालना to em broil/involve in a mess; to dodge.

चक्का chakka: (*nm*) a wheel; sphere; an orderly heap (of bricks, stone slabs, etc.); chunk.

चक्की chakki: (*nf*) a quern; mill; grinding mill; kneepan; cake (e.g. soapcake); –का पाट mill-stone; –के पाटों के बीच पड़ना/पिसना to be sandwiched between two afflictions; –पीसना to grind; to put in rigorous work; to be under imprisonment; –में पिसना to be constantly in harness.

चक्र chakkr (*nm*) a wheel; cycle; circle; disc, discus; discus-shaped missile; ~गति circular motion; ~ण spin(ning); ~धर armed with a discus-shaped missile; an epithet of Lord Vishnu; ~वर्ती universal; (an emperor) ruling over a vast empire; ~वात a whirlwind, cyclone; ~वृद्धि compound (interest); ~व्यूह a circular array of troops; impregnable battle-array (as practised in ancient Indian military strategy); –चलाना see चक्कर (–चलाना).

चक्रवाक chakrava:k (*nm*) see चकवा.

चक्राकार chakkra:ka:r (*a*) circular; wheel-shaped.

चक्रीय chakkri:y (*a*) rotational, whirling, circular.

चक्षु chakshu (*nm*) an eye; ~गोचर visible, perceptible; tangible; ~रिन्द्रिय the eye—organ of seeing; –विषय the object of vision, visible object; ~श्रवा a snake.

चख chakh (*nf*) altercation, noisy dispute; ~चख verbal altercation; chatter, noisy exchanges, discordant discussion; ०करना/मचाना to create a row/havoc, to cause an altercation, to enter into a heated discussion.

चखना chakhnā: (*v*) to taste, to relish.

चचा chacha: (*nm*) paternal uncle; ~ज़ाद born of paternal uncle; –होना to excel, to surpass (in cleverness, tricks, etc.), to be ahead of.

चचिया chachiya: (*a*) pertaining to or related with paternal uncle (e.g. **–ससुर** uncle-in-law; **–सास** aunt-in-law).

चचेरा chachera: (*a*) of, pertaining to, or related with, paternal uncle; **–भाई** first cousin (brother); **–चचेरी बहन** first cousin (sister).

चचोड़ना chachorṇā: (*v*) see **चिचोरना**.

चट chaṭ (*adv*) instantly, instantaneously, at once; (*nf*) snap/snapping; crack, breaking or cracking sound; **~चट** repeated cracking/snapping sounds; **~पट** very promptly, immediately, with utmost urgency; **~शाला** a nursery school; **~सार** a nursery school; **–से** instantly, instantaneously; **–कर जाना** to polish off, to consume hurriedly and entirely; **–मँगनी पट ब्याह** to propose this moment, to marry the very next; to implement a proposal without delay.

चटक chaṭak (*nf*) glitter, splendour, brilliance; agility; crack; sprain; a sparrow; (*a*) bright, brilliant, loud (colour); **~दार** brilliant; gaudy, loud; **–मटक** gaud/gaudiness; coquetry; ornamentation, glitter.

चटकना chaṭaknā: (*v*) to crack, to crackle, to produce a snapping/cracking sound; to crack with a report; to burst or open (as a bud); to cause to snap.

चटकनी chaṭkanī: (*nf*) see **चटखनी**.

चटकाना chaṭka:nā: (*v*) to snap; to cause to crack or crackle.

चटकारा chaṭka:ra: (*nm*) see **चटख़ारा**.

चटकीला chaṭki:la: (*a*) brilliant, bright; loud, glittering; gaudy; hence **~पन** (*nm*).

चटखनी chaṭkhanī: (*nf*) a latch, bolt, tower bolt.

चटख़ा/रा chaṭkha:ra: (*nm*) a clack of the tongue with the palate (expressive of relishing experience); **~रे भरना/लेना** to express relishing of or desire for (delicious food or talk etc.).

चटचटाना chaṭchaṭa:nā: (*v*) to produce a cracking or snapping sound; to burn with a crackling noise

चटनी chaṭnī: (*nf*) sauce indigenous sauce; **–करना/बनाना** to transform into pulp, to beat up thoroughly.

चटप/टा chaṭpaṭa: (*a*) pungent, spicy; **~टापन** pungency spiciness; hence **~टी** (fem. form); **० बातें** spicy talk.

चटाई chaṭa:i: (*nf*) a mat; the act or process of licking; **–नाप** two-dimensional measurement.

चटाक chaṭa:k (*nm*)a crackling sound (comparatively louder and more lasting than **चट**); smack; **–पटाक** promptly, swiftly.

चटाका chaṭa:ka: (*nm*) a smack, crackling report.

चटाचट chaṭa:chaṭ (*nf*) a repeated crackle or smack; (*adv*) with a repeated crackling or smacking report.

चटाना chaṭa:nā: (*v*) to cause to lick; to bribe; —,**धूल** to throw aground, to fell; —,**रुपया** to bribe, to give monetary gratification.

चटियल chaṭiyal (*a*) bare, barren.

चटुल chaṭul (*a*) fickle, unsteady; flippant, swift moving; hence **~ता** (*nf*).

चटोर/चटोरा chaṭor/chaṭora: (*a*) gastroume, greedy of delicious dishes; **~पन** gastroumy, greediness for delicious dishes.

चट्टान chaṭṭā:n (*nf*) a rock, cliff; **–की तरह** solid like a rock, firm and resolute.

चट्टा-बट्टा chaṭṭa:-baṭṭa: (*nm*) a set of toys or other implements (in a conjurer's bag); –चट्टे-बट्टे, एक ही थैली के chips of the same block, birds of the same feather.

चट्टी chaṭṭi: (*nf*) slipper(s); loss, damage; a halting place (esp. on hilly-routes); –देना to inflict a loss/damage; –लगना to suffer a loss/damage.

चड्डी chaḍḍi: (*nf*) a scanty underwear (esp. for children); ride; back-ride; –गाँठना to have a back-ride; –लेना to have a ride; to ride on the back (of).

चढ़त charhat (*nf*) offering(s) to a deity, priest, etc.

चढ़ता charhta: (*a*) rising; growing; increasing; blooming; hence चढ़ती (fem. form); –चढ़ती जवानी में in the flower of one's age, in the prime of youth; –चढ़ते सूर्य को नमस्कार/प्रणाम करना see चढ़ना.

चढ़/ना charhnā: (*v*) to go up; to ascend; to be ascendant; to climb; to rise; to mount; to ride; to be offered (to a deity etc.); to launch an attack, to charge; to be recorded; to take possession of (as by an evil spirit); to be placed on fire for cooking; to be in spate, to be in a tide; to increase, to be on the increase; to be covered by something; (said of a man) to enter into sexual union, to overpower into sexual act; –उतर कर बात करना to make a harsh and unwelcome utterance, to talk arrogantly; –कर superior, excelling; ~ते सूर्य को नमस्कार/प्रणाम करना to climb on the bandwagon, to bow to the rising sun, to strive to be on the winning side; –दौड़ना to launch an invasion, to charge; –बनना to have a run of good luck, to enjoy a lucky spell; –बैठना to ride on; to overpower; to trample down.

चढ़ाई charha:i: (*nf*) ascent, bank, climb; rise; invasion; –करना to invade; to climb (an ascent).

चढ़ा-उतरी charha:utri: (*nf*) fluctuation, repeated ascents and descents.

चढ़ा-ऊपरी charha:u:pari: (*nf*) see चढ़ा-चढ़ी.

चढ़ा-चढ़ी charha:charhi: (*nf*) (spirit of) rivalry, competitive bid(ding).

चढ़ाना charha:nā: (*v*) to cause to go up or rise; to offer; to put on; to mount; to record; to place on fire for cooking; to cover; to load; to brace; to tighten; to string (a bow); to anoint, to apply a paste or liquid (on the body); to fix (a bayonet); to drink off/up; to provoke/incite; to puff up (through exaggerated praise); to inject, to infuse.

चढ़ाव charha:w(*nm*) ascent, acclivity; rise (in prices, etc.); ornamental gift for the bride (from the bridegroom's side); upstream; swelling (of a river, etc.).

चढ़ावा charha:wa: (*nm*) oblation, offering (to a deity, etc.), ornamental gift presented to the bride (from the bridegroom's side).

चतुर chatur (*a*) clever, shrewd; wise; skilful, skilled; ~ता/पन cleverness, shrewdness; wisdom; skill.

चतुराई chatura:i: (*nf*) cleverness; wisdom; skill, dexterity.

चतु/र् chatur—used as the first member of Sanskrit compound words being an allomorph of चतुः, meaning four; ~रंग quadripartite, consisting of four members or parts; ~रंगिणी quadripartite, comprised of four members or parts; (used esp. to denote an army comprised of four arms or departments, viz; elephants, cavalry, chariots and the infantry); a complete army; ~राश्रम the four stages in a man's life (see आश्रम); ~र्थ the fourth; ~र्थांश quadrant; quarter, one-fourth (part); ~र्थाश्रम the fourth आश्रम i.e. संन्यास–the stage of the anchorite; ~र्थी the fourth day of a lunar fortnight; ~र्दश the fourteenth day of a lunar fortnight; ~र्दिक्/दिश all round, on all the four sides; ~र्धाम the four sacred places of pilgrimage of the Hindus (viz. पुरी, बदरिकाश्रम, द्वारका, रामेश्वर); ~र्भुज a quadrangle; quadrilateral; an epithet of Lord Vishnu having four arms; ~र्मास the four months of the rainy season extending from the twelfth day of the moonlit half of आषाढ़ to that of कार्तिक; ~र्मुख four-faced; the Creator-god ब्रह्मा; all round. four-sided; ~र्मुखी all round, four-sided; ~र्युग the four *yugas* (viz. सत, त्रेता, द्वापर, कलि); ~र्वर्ग the four human pursuits [viz. virtue (धर्म), wealth (अर्थ) sensual pleasures (काम) and salvation (मोक्ष)]; ~र्वर्ण the four main castes of the Hindus (viz. ब्राह्मण, क्षत्रिय, वैश्य and शूद्र); ~र्वाद्य quartet; ~र्विध of four types, four-fold; ~र्वेद the four *Vedas*. (viz. ऋक्, साम, यजुर् and अथर्व); ~र्वेदी a scholar well-versed in the four *Vedas*; a subcaste of the Bra:hmāṉs.

चतु/ष् chatush—an allomorph of चतुः used as the first member of Sanskrit compound words meaning four; ~ष्कोण four-cornered; a quadrangle; ~ष्कोणीय quadrangular; ~ष्पथ a road-crossing; ~ष्पद/ष्पाद four-footed; a quadruped.

चतुष्टय chatushṭay (*nm*) an aggregate of four (things, persons, etc.).

चतु/स् chatus—used as the first member of Sanskirt compound words being an allomorph of चतु —meaning four; ~स्सूत्री four point(ed); four-stringed.

चद्दर chaddar (*nf*) see चादर.

चनकटा chankaṭa: (*nm*) a slap.

चना chanā: (*nm*) gram; -चबैना parched gram and allied grains poor people's diet.

चनार chana:r (*nm*) a kind of tal beautiful tree (generally found in the hills).

चपकन chapkān (*nm*) a peculiar long tight coat.

चपटा chapṭa: (*a*) flat; ~पन flatness

चपटी chapṭi: (*nf*) homosexual act between two females.

चपड़-चपड़ chapaṛ:chapaṛ (*nf*) lap offensive sound made during chewing; tattle, unavailing and unending prattle; –करना to continue to prattle.

चपड़ा chapṛa: (*nm*) shellac.

चपत chapat (*nm*) a slap; (*nf*) loss damage; –झाड़ना to slap; –देना/लगाना to inflict a loss; to damage to slap; –पड़ना/बैठना/लगना to be slapped; to sustain a loss/ damage; –रसीद करना to (give a) slap.

चपती chapti: (*nf*) a fillet.

चपनी chapnı: (*nf*) a knee-cap.

चपरकनाती chapārkana:ti: (*a*) stupid foolish; of no consequence; (*nm*) a riff-raff.

चपरगट्टू chaparagaṭṭu: (*a* and *nm*) (*a*) blockhead, duffer, nincompoop

चपरास chapra:s (*nf*) a breast plate a plate worn on belt (as a mark of office) by peons ete.; (in wrestling) a violent stroke of the left foot on the right of the adversary and vice-versa.

चपरासी chapra:si: (*nm*) a peon ~गीरी a peon's function or office

चपल chapal (*a*) unsteady; wavering

flippant; tremulous; restless; quick; nimble; hoity-toity.

चपलता chapalta: (*nf*) unsteadiness; flippancy; tremulousness, restlessness; quickness; nimbleness.

चपला chapla: (*nf*) the goddess of wealth—*Lakshmi*:; lightning; (*a*) feminine form of **चपल** (see).

चपाती chapa:ti: (*nf*) a thin bread of the Indian style.

चपेट chapeṭ (*nf*) striking range; stroke (of misfortune etc.); involvement; a sudden involving blow or accident; **–में आना** to be embroiled in a blow or accident; to sustain injury/loss; to be struck; **–लगना** to sustain injury or loss, to get embroiled in an accident or a blow, to suffer a stroke.

चपेटा chapeṭa: (*nm*) see **चपेट**

चप्पल chappal (*nf*) slipper(s) (open at the front), sandal.

चप्पा chappa: (*nm*) a hand-breadth, a measure of four fingers; a span, small piece of land: **–चप्पा** every span of land, every inch of ground; every nook and corner; **० छान मारना** to make a thorough search, to scan every inch of land, to search every nook and corner.

चप्पू chappu: (*nm*) an oar.

चबाई chaba:i: (*nm*) a backbiter.

चबाना chaba:nā: (*v*) to chew; to munch; to masticate; **चबा-चबाकर बोलना** (to speak) haltingly and with a munching action.

चबा/उ, ~व chaba:u, ~w (*nm*) backbiting; **–चिट्ठा** systematic and frequent backbiting, indulgence in the act of talking ill of others.

चबूतरा chabu:tra: (*nm*) a raised platform; stoop.

चबे(बै)ना chabe(ai)nā: (*nm*) miscellaneous parched grains (mixed together).

चमक chamāk (*nf*) flash; brilliance, lustre, shine; gloss; glare; radiance; a localised flash of pain; **–दमक** glitter; brilliance; pomp and show; **~दार** shining, brilliant, glittering, glossy; **–उठना** to shine forth; to cut a dash, to make a brilliant show; to be provoked all of a sudden, to flare up.

चमकना chamāknā: (*v*) to shine, to glitter, to sparkle; to flash; to flare, to flare up, to get angry; to have a localised flash of pain.

चमकीला chamki:la: (*a*) shining, glossy; radiant, brilliant, bright; lustrous, luminous; hence **~पन** (*nm*).

चमगादड़ chamga:daṛ (*nm*) a bat; vampire; (fig.) one who manages to keep in two opposite camps.

चमचमाना chamchamā:nā: (*v*) to shine, to glitter, to be glossy; to sparkle.

चमचा chamcha: (*nm*) a large spoon; flunkey, flatterer; **~गीरी** cheap flattery, sycophancy.

चमटी chamṭi: (*nf*) a guide stick.

चम/ड़ा chamṛa: (*nm*) leather; hide; skin; **~ड़ा कमाना** to tan, to cure; **~ड़े का सिक्का** a false coin, worthless article.

चमड़ी chamṛi: (*nf*) skin; **–उधेड़ना** to beat bare; to flay, to skin; **–जाये पर दमड़ी न जाये** to suffer a flaying, to save a penny; to be excessively stingy; **–का, मोटी** thick-skinned; **—,गोरी** fair-complexioned; **–पर मरना** to fall for external beauty.

चमत्का/र chamatka:r (*nm*) a marvel, miracle; wonder; thaumaturgy; spectacle; **~रिक** thaumaturgic, marvellous, miraculous; spectacular; hence **~रिकता**; **~री** miraculous; one who performs miracles, a thaumaturge.

चमत्कृ/त chamatkrit (*a*) ast ounded,

astonished, wonder-struck; ~ति a miraculous performance, marvel; spectacle; spectacular show, thaumaturgy.

चमन chamān (*nm*) a small garden; parterre, bed of a garden; a place full of life and luxury.

चमरी chamri: (*nf*) a chumrey; a yak (*mas*. **चमर**); see **चँवर**.

चमरौधा chamraudha: (*nm*) an indigenous type of sturdy shoe.

चमाचम chamā:chām (*adv*) with a shine/gloss, brilliantly, brightly.

चमा/र chamā:r (*nm*) a cobbler, shoe-maker; a scheduled caste amongst the Hindus traditionally living by shoe-making; a lowly person; ~**रिन/री** feminine form of **चमार**.

चमू chamū: (*nf*) a division of an army; ~**नायक/पति** an army-commander, a general.

चमेली chameli: (*nf*) (a kind of) jasmine (plant and its flower); –**का तेल** jasmine oil.

चम्मच chammach (*nm*) a spoon.

चयन chayān (*nm*) selection; picking up; compiling; –**समिति** selection committee.

चयनिका chayanika: (*nf*) an anthology, a selection/collection of choicest or representative writings.

चर char (*nm*) a spy, secret messenger, emissary; a variable; (*a*) moving; unsteady; variable; hence ~**ता** see **चरता**.

चरकटा charkaṭa: (*nm*) a chaff-cutter; riff-raff, an insignificant person.

चरका charka: (*nm*) fraud, swindle, rigging; –**खाना** to be swindled/defrauded; –**देना** to defraud, to swindle; –**लगना** to be defrauded/swindled.

चरख charakh (*nm*) a large revolving wheel.

चरखा charkha: (*nm*) a spinning wheel; hyena.

चरखी charkhi: (*nf*) a reel, spool pulley; sheave; see **चरख**; tourbillion, revolving firework; a catherine wheel.

चरचराना charchara:nā: (*v*) to crackle to make a sputtering noise; to produce a painful sensation as by the drying up of a wound.

चरचराहट charchara:haṭ (*nf*) crackle sputtering noise; painful sensation as by the drying up of a wound.

चरण charāṉ (*nm*) a foot (also of a verse); step; quarter; phase; -**कमल, पद्म** lotus-like feet; -**चिह्न** footprint ~**तल** sole of the foot; ~**धूलि/~रज** dust of the feet (of); to be no match to, to be too inferior for comparison; -**सुश्रूषा/सेवा** obsequious attendance; reverential service ~**सेवी** an obsequious attendant one who renders reverential service; –**चाँपना/चूमना** to press/lick the feet of, to be extremely servile/submissive, to keep on flattering; –**छूना** to touch one's feet (as a traditional mark of respect) –**धोकर पीना** to be very reverential and respectful; **चरणों में अर्पित करना/चढ़ाना** to make a respectful offering to; to surrender with deference.

चरणामृत charṉā:mmrit (*nm*) foot ambrosia, the water in which the idol of a deity has been bathed or the feet of a revered person have been washed (considered to be a sacred drink).

चरणोदक charṉodak (*nm*) see **चरणामृत**.

चरता charta: (*nf*) variability; unsteadiness; mobility; (*a*) grazing.

चरना charnā: (*v*) to graze.

चरपरा charpara: (*a*) piquant; hot

of pungent taste; ~पन/~हट piquancy, pungency/hotness (of taste).

चरबा charba: (*nm*) tracing paper; copy, sketch.

चरबी charbi: (*nf*) fat, fats and oils; grease; tallow; ~दार greasy; fatty; –चढ़ना to grow fat; to become arrogant; –छाना, आँखों में to grow mad with passion, to be neglectful (on account of arrogance, carelessness, etc.) of others.

चरम charām (*a*) absolute; ultimate; last, final; extreme: –लक्ष्य ultimate aim; –सीमा extreme; extreme limit.

चरमर charmar (*nf*) a creaking sound (as of new boots); squeak.

चरमराना charmara:nā: (*v*) to creak; to squeak.

चरमराहट charmara:haṭ (*nf*) a creaking or squeaking sound; creak; squeak.

चरवाहा charva:ha: (*nm*) a herdsman, grazier.

चरस charas (*nm*) an intoxicating drug prepared from the flowers of hemp; a huge leather bucket.

चरसा charsa: (*nm*) a huge leather bucket.

चराई chara:i: (*nf*) grazing, pasturage; the rent or wages paid for grazing (one's cow, buffalo, etc).

चरागाह chara:ga:h (*nm*) pasture, pasture land, meadow, graziery.

चराचर chara:char (*a*) movable and immovable, animate and inanimate; (*nm*) the entire creation.

चराना chara:nā: (*v*) to (cause to) graze; to befool, to hoodwink.

चरित charit (*nm*) biography; doings, goings; ~कार/-लेखक a biographer; -नायक the hero or the main character (of a literary work); -रूपक biographical feature.

चरितार्थ charita:rth (*a*) validated/vindicated; proven correct; gratified; –होना to attain one's object or end; to prove valid, to be vindicated; to aquire a meaning.

चरितार्थता charita:rthata: (*nf*) significance, meaningfulness; fulfilment, success; validity.

चरितावली charita:vali: (*nf*) a collection of biographies; biography.

चरित्र charitr (*nm*) character; -चित्रण/निर्माण characterisation, portrayal; -दोष flaws of character; ~वान (a man) of sound character; -हत्या character assassination; ~हीन profligate, deprave, characterless.

चरित्रांकन charitrā:ṅkān (*nm*) characterisation; portrayal, delineation.

चरी chari: (*nf*) green plants used for cattle-fodder; graziery.

चर्ख charkh (*nm*) see चरख.

चर्खा charkha: (*nm*) see चरखा.

चर्खी charkhi: (*nf*) see चरखी.

चर्च church (*nm*) a church.

चर्चक charchak (*nm*) one who mentions or discusses.

चर्चा charcha: (*nf*) mention; discussion; rumour; –होना to take air, to be talked about.

चर्चित charchit (*a*) discussed; mentioned; smeared, anointed.

चर्बी charbi: (*nf*) see चरबी.

चर्म charm (*nm*) leather; skin; hide; ~कार a cobbler; shoe-maker; tanner; ~मय leathery, coraceous.

चर्या charya: (*nf*) routine; goings, conduct; performance (of rites and ceremonies).

चर्राना charra:nā: (*v*) to crack/creak/crackle; to make a cracking/creaking/crackling sound; to smart on account of tension (as of skin); to have an intense urge (esp. in शौक–).

चर्वं/ण charvān (*nm*) masticating, masticational chewing; relishing; also ~णा (*nf*).

चर्वित charvit (*a*) masticated, chewed; -चर्वण chewing the chewed; tedious reiteration.

चल chal (*a*) unsteady; transient; inconstant; variable; movable, mobile (as पुस्तकालय); –अर्थ currency; -चलाव the verge of departure/death; ~चित्त fickle-minded, unsteady; ~चित्र a movie; motion picture, cinema, cinematograph; -विचल unsteady, inconstant; –संपत्ति movable property.

चलता chalata: (*nm*) mobility; unsteadiness; (*a*) mobile, moving; current, in use; flourishing (as चलती दुकान); cursory (e.g. चलती निगाह); cunning, clever; workable; temporary; light (as चलती चीज) ; –खाता current account; –पुरज़ा cunning; clever; -फिरता mobile; –सिक्का a current coin; –करना to dispose of; to tell off, to send away; –फिरता नज़र आना to be making a move, to be moving off; –बनना to turn tails; to slip away; चलती का नाम गाड़ी nothing succeeds like success; चलती रक़म a clever/cunning fellow; चलती सीढ़ी excalator; चलते usage typical to the Biharis—because of, due to, owing to; चलते चलते incidentally, casually, in passing; चलते-चलाते by the way, without prior deliberation.

चलताऊ chalta:u: (*a*) workable; serviceable; casual/temporary; about to go or depart; moribund; –डेरा being on the verge of death or departure.

चलतू chaltu: (*a*) workable, temporary.

चलन chalān (*nm*) vogue; usage; custom; conduct; –कलन Differential Calculus; –समीकरण differential equation; ~सार durable; current.

चलना chalnā: (*v*) to walk; to move, to proceed; to be in vogue/use/currency; to last; to flow; to be initiated/started (as बात-), to be pressed into; used (as लाठी–); to blow (as हवा–); to be thrown (as तीर–); to be effective; to go off (as बंदूक–); to be operated (as मशीन–); to be filed (as मुक़दमा–); to pass (as सिक्का–); चल निकलना to be consolidated; to get going, to make a progress; to flourish; चल पड़ना (काम आदि) to catch on; चल बसना to pass away, to expire; चलते घोड़े को एड़ लगाना to spur a willing horse.

चलनी chalnī: (*nf*) a sieve; (*a*) durable

चलाऊ chala:u: (*a*) durable, lasting.

चलाचल chala:chal (*a*) mobile and immobile; movable and immovable; transient; –संपत्ति movable and immovable property.

चलाचली chala:chali: (*nf*) (verge of) departure; time of departure; readiness for departure.

चलाना chala:nā: (*v*) to cause to walk; to move; to drive; to guile, to pass (as सिक्का–); to operate (as मशीन–); to manipulate (as क्रेन–); to initiate (as चर्चा–); to throw/fire (as गोला, गोली–); to file (as मुक़दमा–).

चलायमान chala:ymā:n (*a*) moving; fickle, wavering; unsteady.

चलार्थ chala:rth (*nm*) currency.

चलित chalit (*a*) moved, wavered, unsteady.

चवन्नी chavannī: (*nf*) a twenty-five paisa (four anna) coin; ~वाले low-class prople.

चवर्ग chavarg (*nm*) the 'cha' pentad

of five palatal consonants in the Devna:gri: script viz. च, छ, ज, झ and ञ.

चवालीस chava:li:s (*a*) forty-four; (*nm*) the number forty-four.

चश्म chashm (*nf*) an eye; ~दीद witnessed; seen; °गवाह an eye-witness; ~पोशी connivance; -ए-बद evil eye; malicious glance; °दूर may not an evil glance be cast upon you !, avaunt malicious glances !

चश्मा chashmā: (*nm*) spectacles, glasses; fountain, spring; –,धूप का/–,धूपी goggles; –,रंगीन coloured glasses.

चसका chaska: (*nm*) proclivity, addiction; compelling habituation; –,पड़ना/लगना (used in denunciatory sense) to get addicted/habituated/used to (some degenerating habit), to develop an irresistible proclivity for.

चस्पाँ chaspā: (*a*) affixed, stuck; fitting; applicable.

चहक chehak (*nf*) chirping, warbling.

चहकना chehaknā: (*v*) to chirp, to warble; to be merrily talkative.

चहकार chehka:r (*nf*) see चहक.

चहचहाना chehcheha:nā: (*v*) to chirp, to warble.

चहबच्चा chahbachcha: (*nm*) a catch-pit; subterranean store-pit.

चहलक़दमी chehalqadmɪ: (*nf*) stroll, leisurely walk, ramble.

चहल-पहल chehalpehal (*nf*) hustle and bustle; commotion: gaiety, merriment.

चहारदीवारी chaha:rdi:va:ri: (*nf*) the four-walls, boundary.

चहेता chaheta: (*a*) beloved; favourite.

चांचल्य chā:nchally (*nm*) see चंचलता.

चाँटा chāṭa: (*nm*) a slap; –जड़ना/देना/लगाना/रसीद करना to (give a) slap.

चांडाल chā:nḍa:l (*nm*) see चंडाल; –चौकड़ी a swindling/nuisance making quartet/foursome.

चाँद chā:d (*nm*) the moon; the bull's eye; (*nf*) the crown (of); the head; ~तारा a kind of fine muslin; a kite bearing the figures of the crescent aud the star; ~मारी shooting practice; range; °का मैदान shooting range; –का टुकड़ा a beauty; –को गहन (ग्रहण) लगना to have a blot in a beauty; –गंजी करना to boot to baldness, to thrash bald; –गंजी होना to become bald-headed; –पर थूकना/धूल उड़ाना to slander the unassailable (and have one's own image sullied); –में भी दाग़ है every bean has its black, no one is without his faults; -सा मुखड़ा a face as lovely as the moon, lovely face.

चाँदना chād:nā: (*nm*) light; –होना to have light, to be lighted; to dawn, to have the day-break.

चाँदनी chā:dnɪ: (*nf*) the moonlight; a large white sheet of cloth; bed-sheet, canopy; –खिलना/छिटकना moonlight to spread all over.

चाँदा chā:da: (*nm*) a protractor.

चाँदी chā:di: (*nf*) silver; –कटना to be minting money; –का जूता/की जूती monetary temptation; bribe; –के टुकड़े rupee coins; money in general; –के दिन pleasant/delightful days; –बनाना to mint money, to earn fabulously; –होना to have fabulous earnings; to have all round gains.

चांद्र cha:ndr (*a*) lunar, pertaining to the moon; –मास lunar month; –वत्सर/वर्ष lunar year.

चांद्रायण cha:ndra:yan (*nm*) a typical fast observed by the Hindus and related to the waning and waxing of the moon.

चाँपना cha:pnā: (*v*) to press.

चाक cha:k (*nm*) chalk; the potter's wheel; (*a*) torn; split; –**करना** to tear apart.

चाक़-चौबंद cha:q-chaubānd (*a*) smart; alert and agile.

चाकर cha:kar (*nm*) a servant; menial atten ant.

चाकरी cha:kri: (*nf*) service, attendance; –**करना** to fetch and carry; –**बजाना** to be in servile attendace.

चाक़ू cha:qu: (*nm*) a knife; –**घोंपना/भोंकना** to stab with a knife.

चाक्षुष cha:kshush (*a*) visual, pertaining to the eye.

चाखना cha:khnā: (*v*) to taste, to relish.

चा/चा cha:cha: (*nm*) paternal uncle; ~**ची** paternal uncle's wife, aunt.

चाट cha:ṭ (*nf*) a spicy preparation of cut fruits, vegetables, etc.; habit, compelling habituation, irresistibile proclivity; –**पड़ना/लगना** see **चसका पड़ना/लगना**.

चाटना cha:ṭnā: (*v*) to lick; **चाट जाना** to consume the whole, to polish. off; to be inflicted by; ०,**धूप का** to be sun-struck.

चाटु cha:ṭu (*nm*) flattery, adulation, false praise.

चाटु/कार cha:tuka:r (*a*) a flatterer, sycophant; adulator; ~**कारिता**, ~**कारी** flattery, sycophancy, adulation.

चाटूक्ति cha:ṭu:kti (*nf*) a flattering statement, flattery.

चातक cha:tak (*nm*) an Indian bird —*Cuculus melanoleucus*.

चातुरी cha:turi: (*nf*) cleverness, ingeniousness, tact; dexterity.

चातुर्मा/स, ~ **सिक** cha:turmā:s, ~sik (*a* and *nm*) pertaining to the rainy season; the rainy season; comprised of four months; also ~**स्य** (*nm*).

चातुर्य cha:tury (*nm*) cleverness, ingeniousness, tact; dexterity.

चातुर्वर्ण्य cha:turvarny (*a*) pertaining to the four castes as prescribed under the ancient Indian social system (viz. **ब्राह्मण, क्षत्रिय, वैश्य, शूद्र**); –**व्यवस्था** the (four) caste-system (as practised in the Indian tradition.

चादर cha:dar (*nf*) a sheet; plate; bedsheet, bed-cover; cover-let; an upper cover garment used by women; ~**बंदी** sheeting; –**उतारना** to expose, to put to shame; –**ओढ़ाना/डालना** to have a widow as wife; –**के बाहर (पाँव फैलाना)** to go beyond one's means; –**तानकर सोना** to have a carefree sleep; –**देखकर पाँव फैलाना** to cut one's coat according to the cloth; –**फैलाना** to send the cap/hat round.

चादरा cha:dra: (*nm*) a coverlet, an overall clothes-covering sheet (used by women).

चाप cha:p (*nf*) arc; pressure; a bow; (foot) sound/blow.

चापलूस cha:plu:s (*a*) flattering, sycophantic, adulatoring.

चापलूसी cha:plu:si: (*nf*) flattery, sycophancy, adulation; –**करना** to butter up, –**से काम निकालना** to coax thing out of a person, to coax fire to light, to coax key in to lock.

चापल्य cha:pally (*nm*) see **चपलता**.

चाबना cha:bnā: (*v*) see **चबाना**.

चाबी cha:bi: (*nf*) a key; spline; –**घुमाना** to tutor, to make some body dance to one's tune; –**देना** to wind (a watch etc.); –**हाथ में होना** to be under the sway of, to be dominated by.

चाबुक cha:buk (*nm*) a whip, flog, lash; ~**सवार** an ace horse-rider; a horse-trainer; –**घुमाना** to threat to flog.

ाभी cha:bhi: (*nf*) see **चाबी**.

ाम chā:m (*nm*) skin; hide; **—के दाम** lit. a leather coin—meaning a coin having no worth; earnings through immoral traffic in women.

ाय cha:y (*nf*) tea; **~घर** a tea-house, canteen; **~दानी** a tea-pot; **-पानी** breakfast; tea; tea and snacks, light refreshment; **—पर बुलाना** to invite for tea.

ार cha:r (*a*) four; several, a few; (*nm*) the number four; spying; **~कर्म** spying; intelligence work; **~ख़ाना** chequered cloth; **~दीवार** fence walls, four walls; **~दीवारी** boundary, four walls; **—धाम** see **चतुर्धाम** under **चतुर्**; **—पदार्थ** the four achievements for which man aspires (viz. **धर्म, अर्थ, काम, मोक्ष**); **—अक्षर पढ़ना** to gain smattering knowledge, to learn a modicum of (something); **—आँखें करना** to exchange glances, to meet eye with eye; to come face to face; **—आँखें होना** to be face to face, to see each other; **—आदमी** people in general; representatives of the community; **—क़दम** a short distance; **—क़दम आगे होना** to be superior to, to excel, to be more than a match; to be ahead of; **—के कंधे/कंधों पर चढ़ना** to be taken in a coffin, to perform the last journey; **—के कान पड़ना** to become public, to become known; **—चाँद लगना** to have a feather added to one's cap; to become more charming than ever; **—दिन का** short-lived, transient; **—दिन का मेहमान** having a fleeting existence, faced with imminent death, destined to die shortly; **—दिन की चाँदनी** a fleeting existence; a nine days' wonder, a limited period of merry-making; **—पैसे कमाना** to make some earning; **चारों ओर अँधेरा** bad to be the best; **चारों ख़ाने चित्त गिरना** lit. to fall at full stretch to be beaten all ends up; to be thoroughly vanquished; to be down and out; to set one's foot on the neck of; to lose one's wits; **चारों चूल बराबर** all square; fit all round; **चारों फूटना** to suffer total blindness; to lose one's mental as well as physical vision.

चारण cha:rān (*nm*) a wandering minstrel, bard; grazing; a sub-caste of Ra:jastha:n Bra:hmans; **—काव्य** bardic poetry.

चारपाई cha:rpa:i: (*nf*) a bedstead, bed, cot; **—पकड़ लेना** to be bed-ridden, to be confined to bed; **—पर पड़ना** to be confined to bed, to be taken ill; **—सेना** to suffer a prolonged illness, to be bed-ridden for long; **—से लगना** to be reduced to a skeleton.

चार सौ बी/स cha:r sau bi:s (*a*) fraudulent; deceitful; (*nm*) a fraud, forgerer; **~सी** fraud, forgery; criminal deception.

चारा cha:ra: (*nm*) fodder, forage, feed; bait, lure; remedy; means; **—और भूसा** fodder and forage; **—डालना/फेंकना** to bait, to entice through temptation; **—न होना, और कोई** to have no other way out.

चाराजोई cha:ra joi: (*nf*) measures, proceedings; **—, क़ानूनी** legal measures/proceedings.

चारित्र्य cha:rittry (*nm*) character; **~हीन** having no character, characterless, depraved; hence **~हीनता** (*nf*).

चारी cha:ri:—used as a suffix meaning 'faring', 'going' (e.g. **समुद्रचारी** seafaring); (*nf*) a dance posture, gesture.

चारु cha:ru (*a*) beautiful, appealing,

attractive, charming; hence ~ता (*nf*), ~त्व (*nm*).

चार्ज cha:rj (*nm*) a charge; ~शीट a charge-sheet; –करना to charge (in electricity); –देना to hand over charge; –लेना to take charge.

चार्ट cha:rṭ (*nm*) a chart.

चार्टर cha:rṭar (*nm*) a charter.

चाल cha:l (*nf*) gait; speed; march; motion; movement; move; trick; device; custom; a huge building inhabited by a large number of tenant families; -चलन conduct; -ढाल ways, bearing, demeanour; ~बाज crafty, cunning, tricky; a trickster; ~बाजी craftiness; cunningness; trickery; –चलना to play a trick; to make a (deft) move; –चूकना to miss the target, to make an unsuccessful move; a trick to misfire; –में आना to fall into one's trap; to be a victim to one's trick.

चालक cha:lak (*a*) a driver; conductor; hence ~ता (*nf*).

चालन cha:lān (*nm*) operation, working; driving; conduction.

चाला cha:la: (*nm*) departure; auspicious day or time (for commencing a journey); –न होना the occasion (time, day) to be inauspicious for undertaking a journey.

चालाक cha:la:k (*a*) cunning, clever, crafty; –कौआ (fig.) a crafty crow, cunning fellow.

चालाकी cha:la:ki: (*nf*) cunningness, craftiness.

चालान cha:lā:n (*nm*) a challan, invoice; prosecution; ~दार an invoice-holder; -बही an invoice book; –करना to challan, to register a case (against).

चाली/स cha:lɪ:s (*a*) forty; (*nm*) the number forty; ~सवाँ fortieth; a ritual observed on the fortieth day after death; ~सा an aggregate of forty (verses, etc.); a ritual observed on the fortieth day after demise.

चालू cha:lu: (*a*) current; running; prevalent; tenable; commonplace; moving, in motion; cunning, unscrupulous (e.g. –आदमी); –औरत a woman of easy virtue; unscrupulous woman; –करना to bring into play; to bring into operation; –हालत में in running condition.

चाव chā:v (*nm*) fondness, eagerness.

चावल cha:val (*nm*) rice.

चाशनी cha:shnɪ: (*nf*) treacle; a viscous state of syrup; –घुलना, (मन में) to be happy (within); to be sweetened; –देना to give a touch of, to reinforce with; –सी sweet like syrup.

चाह cha:h (*nf*) liking, love, craving; desire; will; a well; –से राह बनती है where there is a will, there is a way.

चाहत cha:hat (*nf*) liking, love, fondness.

चाह/ना cha:hnā: (*v*) to wish, to want; to like, to love, to be fond of; to crave for, to desire; to require; ~ने वाला a lover.

चाहिए cha:hie—the precative form of the aorist of चाहना, used as a phrase, meaning—is necessary, is needful or requisite, is proper or right; it behoves; should or ought or must (be).

चाहे cha:he (*ind*) either...or; or...or; even though/though......yet/still; –कितना (भी) however great/much; –कुछ भी/–कोई whichever, whoever; –जो हो for better for worse, come what may, whatever happens.

चिंघाड़ chɪngha:ṛ (*nm*) trumpet (of an elephant); a roar (in rage).

चिंघाड़ना chɪngha:ṛnā: (*v*) to trumpet (as an elephant); to roar (in rage).

चिंतक chīntak (*nm*) thinker, contemplator; philosopher.

चिंतन chīntān (*nm*) thinking: reflection, contemplation; musing; ~मनन contemplation and reflection; thinking and deliberating; ~शील thoughtful, contemplative; hence ~शीलता (*nf*).

चिंतना chīntanā: (*nf*) thinking; thought; contemplation.

चिंतनीय chīntanī:y (*a*) worth thinking of; contemplatable; thinkable; doubtful; causing anxiety/concern.

चिंता chīnta: (*nf*) worry, concern; anxiety; care; ~जनक causing anxiety/concern; ~धारा ideology; ~मग्न engrossed in worry/anxiety; worried; musing; ~मुक्त free of worry/anxiety; ~रहित carefree, having no worry; ~शील given to worrying, ever worried; ~खाये जाना/मारे डालना worry to be eating up, worry to be taking its toll; ~में डूबना/-उतराना to be engrossed in constant worry; —चिता समान grief is the canker of heart, care killed the cat.

चिंताकुल chīnta:kul (*a*) perturbed/disturbed by anxiety, worried, concerned; hence ~ता (*nf*).

चिंतातुर chīnta:tur (*a*) see चिंताकुल.

चिंतामणि chinta:māṇi (*nf*) a fabulous mythological gem supposed to grant all desires.

चिंतित chīntit (*a*) perturbed, worried, anxious; concerned.

चिंत्य chīnty (*a*) causing concern/anxiety/worry; doubtful; questionable.

चिंदी chīndi: (*nf*) shred, scrap.

चिंपांजी chīmpā:nzi: (*nm*) a chimpanzee.

चिया chīyā: (*nm*) see चिया.

चिउड़ा chiura: (*nm*) rice parched and beaten flat.

चिक chik (*nf*) a screen of bamboo parings or reed, bamboo curtain.

चिकन chikān (*nm*) embroidered fine muslin.

चिकना chiknā: (*a*) smooth; glossy; oily or greasy; slippery; -चुपड़ा well made up; looking smart and attractive; full of flattery, flattering (as चिकनी-चुपड़ी बातें); —घड़ा like water off duck's back; incorrigible, unabashing (person), shameless; —देखकर फिसल पड़ना to fall for the slightest temptation; चिकनी मिट्टी marl, clay; चिकनी-चुपड़ी बातें करना to curry favour.

चिकनाई chiknā:i (*nf*) smoothness; greasiness; fat; lubricant.

चिकनाना chiknā:nā: (*v*) to smoothen; to lubricate; to tallow; to put on fat.

चिकनापन chiknā:pān (*nm*) smoothness; greasiness; glossiness.

चिकनाहट chikna:haṭ (*nf*) greasiness; glossiness; smoothness; fattiness.

चिकारा chika:ra: (*nm*) a kind of violin.

चिकित्सक chikitsak (*nm*) a physician, medical practitioner.

चिकित्सा chikitsa: (*nf*) treatment; remedy; medication, therapy; (*a*) medical therapeutic; -पद्धति system of medicine; line of treatment; -व्यवसाय medical practice; -व्यवसायी medical practitioner; -शास्त्र medicine, medical science.

चिकित्सालय chikitsa:lay (*nm*) a hospital, dispensary.

चिकित्सीय chikitsī:y (*a*) therapeutic, medicinal, medical.

चिकुर chikur (*nm*) the hair (on the head).

चिकोटी chikoṭi: (*nf*) pinch; tweak; twitch; —काटना/भरना to pinch.

चिक्कण chikkāṇ (*a*) see चिकना; hence

~ता (nf).

चिक्कार chikka:r (nf) scream, trumpet (as of an elephant); hence **चिक्कारना** (v).

चिचियाना chichiya:nā: (v) to scream, to shriek, to squeak.

चिचोरना chichornā: (v) to suck (as bone etc.) by holding between the teeth.

चिट chiṭ (nf) a chit.

चिटकना chiṭaknā: (v) to crack; to crackle.

चिट्टा chiṭṭa: (a) white, fair.

चिट्ठा chiṭṭha: (nm) account book; day book; detailed list; muster roll; account of doings.

चिट्ठी chiṭṭhi: (nf) a letter; -पत्री correspondence; letter, etc.; ~रसाँ/ ~रसा a postman; –डालना to post a letter.

चिड़चिड़ा chirchira: (a) grouch, irritable, irascible, petulant, peevish; hence ~ना (v); ~हट see **चिड़चिड़ापन**.

चिड़चिड़ापन chirchira:pān (nm) irritability, irascibility, petulance; peevishness.

चिड़िया chiṛiya: (nf) a bird; shuttlecock (in the game of Badminton); the club (in a suite of cards); ~खाना/घर a zoo; an aviary; –का दूध a non-existent commodity; an impossibility; –उड़ जाना the bird to fly off, the victim to get out of reach; –का पूत भी न होना none at all to be present; –फँसाना to entrap a bird (a beauty or a man of wealth); –मरी राजा को स्वाद न आया it may be death to one and not even fun to another; –हाथ से निकल जाना see –उड़ जाना; चिड़ियों की मौत गँवारों की हँसी it may be fun to you but it is death to frogs.

चिड़ीमार chiri:mā:r (nm) a fowler, bird-catcher.

चिढ़ chiṛh (nf) irritation, huff, strong aversion; a teasing nickname.

चिढ़ना chiṛhnā: (v) to be irritated, to be teased; to (take) huff; to have a strong aversion.

चिढ़ाना chiṛha:nā: (v) to tease, to cause irritation, to mock, to jeer (at), to huff.

चित chit (a) supine; (lying) flat on the back; (nm) mind, heart; head (of a coin); ~चोर alluring, appealing (person); he who steals away one's heart; –करना to throw flat on the back; to overpower, to vanquish; –कर देना to bowl over, to overpower, to vanquish; –पट करना to decide this way or that (by throw of a coin); – भी मेरी पट भी मेरी (अंटा मेरे बाप का) heads I win, tails you lose; –होना to be overpowered, to be vanquished; to fall on the back.

चितकबरा chitkabra: (a) variegated; spotted; piebald, mottled; ~पन variegation; spottedness; piedness.

चितला chitla: (a) see **चितकबरा**.

चितवन chitvan (nf) (compelling) glance, (fascinating) look; ogle; –,तिरछी oblique glance, ogling.

चिता chita: (nf) funeral pyre; –पर चढ़ना to immolate oneself.

चिति chiti: (nf) consciousness.

चितेरा chitera: (nm) a painter.

चित् chit (nm) consciousness; (a) conscious.

चित्त chitt (nm) mind, heart; (a) supine, flat on the back; ~वृत्ति mentality, mental disposition/ attitude; -शुद्धि mental purification; –उचटना to feel ennuied, to be out of spirits/sorts, to become averse/ disinclined (to somebody, place or thing); –करना/कर देना see चित करना /कर देना; –चढ़ना to take to heart;

to develop a fondness/fascination (for); –चुराना to steal (away) one's heart, to enchant; ~चोर see चित (~चोर); –देना to heed, to pay attention; –पर चढ़ना to be constantly present in the mind, to be impressed on the mind; –बँटना to be distracted; –भी मेरी पट्ट भी मेरी see under चित; –में चुभना to prick; to appeal; –में बसना/समाना to be ever present in one's mind; to be in love with; –देना/–लगाना to pay heed to, to concentrate on; –से उतरना to lose favour with, to be deprived of the graces (of).

चित्ताकर्षक chitta:karshak (*a*) attractive, charming, alluring, fascinating; hence ~ता (*nf*).

चित्ती chitti: (*nf*) a speck, spot; ~दार spotted, specked.

चित्र chittr (*nm*) picture; painting; illustration; figure; (still) film; -कर्म painting; -कला (art of) painting; ~कार a painter; an artist; ~कारिता painting; ~कारी (the profession or work of) painting; ~पट screen, cinema film; ~फलक canvas; ~लिपि pictograph, pictorial script; ~लेख pictograph; pictorial writing; ~लेखक a painter; an artist; ~लेखन painting; -विचित्र mottled; variegated; picturesque; ~शाला a picture-gallery; -संग्रह an album; ~सारी a picture-gallery.

चित्रण chittrān (*nm*) portrayal, delineation; painting, drawing.

चित्रवल्लरी chittrvallari: (*nf*) a frieze.

चित्रमय chittrmāy (*a*) pictorial; illustrated; hence ~ता (*nf*).

चित्रवत् chittrvat (*a*) still; picturelike.

चित्रसारी chittrsa:ri: (*nf*) a picture gallery; an inner apartment for amorous enjoyment.

चित्रांकन chitra:ṅkan (*nm*) delineation, portrayal.

चित्राक्षर chittra:kshar (*nm*) an ideogram.

चित्राक्षरी chittra:kshari: (*nf*) acrostic (poetry).

चित्रात्मक chitra:tmak (*a*) pictorial, (stated or described) in pictures.

चित्राधार chittra:dha:r (*nm*) a portrait-stand.

चित्रालेख chittra:lekh (*nm*) the scenario (of a film etc.), screen play.

चित्रित chittrit (*a*) portrayed; painted, pictured; drawn.

चिथड़ा chitḥa: (*nm*) a rag, shred, tatter; –लगाना to be in tatters; चिथड़े-चिथड़े हो जाना to be torn to shreds, to be tattered, to be turned into rags.

चिनक chināk (*nf*) smarting pain; painful twitching sensation; hence ~ना (*v*).

चिनगारी chinga:ri: (*nf*) a spark; –छोड़ना to make an incendiary remark; to emit/give out sparks.

चिनाई china:i: (*nf*) brick-laying, bilge and cantline.

चिनार chinā:r (*nm*) see चनार.

चिन्मय chinmay (*a*) conscious, pervaded or permeated by consciousness; (*nm*) All Consciousness, Pure Consciousness; hence ~ता (*nf*).

चिन्ह chinh (*nm*) see चिह्न.

चिप/कना chipaknā: (*v*) to adhere; to stick, to cling; (*a*) adhesive; clinging/hanging (on); ~के रहना to keep on clinging.

चिपकवाँ chipakvā: (*a*) applique; adhesive, sticky.

चिपकाना chipka:nā: (*v*) to paste; to stick; to cause to cling; to embrace; to put into an employment.

चिपकू chipku: (*a* and *nm*) hanger-on.

चिपचिपा chipchipa: (*a*) sticky, greasy; adhesive; viscid; ~ना to be sticky/

greasy/viscid; ~हट stickiness, greasiness; adhesiveness; viscidity.

चिपटना chipaṭnā: (*v*) to cling; to hang on; to embrace; to hold fast.

चिप्पी chippi: (*nf*) label, paster.

चिबुक chibuk (*nm*) the chin.

चिमटना chimāṭnā: (*v*) to cling to, to hang on; to embrace; to hold fast.

चिमटा chimṭa: (*nm*) tongs; pincers; **–गाड़ना** (for a mendicant) to bivouac, to make a halt.

चिमटाना chimṭa:nā: (*v*) to embrace; to paste; to stick to.

चिमटी chimṭi: (*nf*) forceps, tweezer, pincers.

चिमनी chimnī: (*nf*) a chimney; flue-pipe.

चिया chiya: (*nm*) the seed (stone) of tamarind fruit.

चिरंजीव chirāṇji:v (*a*) (one) blessed with longevity; a benedictory epithet prefixed with the names of youngers; (*int.*) may you live long !; (*nm*) son.

चिरंजीवी chirāṇji:vi: (*a*) long-living; blessed with long life; immortal.

चिरंतन chirāntan (*a*) lasting, everlasting, perpetual; hence **~ता** (*nf*).

चिर chir (*a*) long-lasting; lasting; perpetual; (*ind.*) existing for a long time, ever; **~कांक्षित** long-desired; long-cherished; **~काल** long time; **~कालिक** long-existent; perpetual; old; chronic (as **–रोग**); **~कुमार** a chronic bachelor; celibate; **~जीवी** blessed with long life, long-living; immortal; **~नवीन** ever-new; ever-fresh; ever-green; **~निद्रा** sleep that knows no breaking, perpetual sleep; death; **०मग्न** dead; **~नूतन** see **नवीन**; **~परिचित** long known; **~पोषित** long-cherished; **~प्रचलित** time-honoured; long-current; long-prevalent; **~प्रतीक्षित** long-awaited; **~प्रसिद्ध** long-reputed, famous for a long time; **~रोगी** a chronic patien[t] **~वियोग** long separation; **~विस्मृ[त]** long-forgotten; long gone int[o] oblivion; **~शत्रु** perpetual enemy **०ता** perpetual animosity; **~शां[ति]** perpetual/enduring peace; **~सं[गी]** lifelong companion; **~स्थ** long lasting; perpetual, permanent enduring; quality or state of exis[t]ing for/lasting long; **~स्थायित[्व]** endurance, permanency; **~स्थाय[ी]** enduring; perpetual, permanent **~स्मरणीय** memorable; wort[h] remembering (for long).

चिरकना chiraknā: (*v*) to have [a] (slight) outflow of loose faeces.

चिरकुट chirkuṭ (*nm*) tattered cloth rag.

चिरना chirnā: (*v*) to be torn; to b[e] split; to be sawed; to be dissected **चिरा-फटा** lacerate.

चिरवाई chirva:i: (*nf*) sawing; tear ing, splitting; wages for sawing splitting/tearing.

चिराई chira:i: (*nf*) see **चिरवाई**.

चिराग़ chira:g (*nm*) a lamp; light **–गुल करना** to put out the lamp **–गुल, पगड़ी ग़ायब** twitch the eyelids gone are your belongings; **–गुल होना** a lamp to be put out; ligh[t] to be gone; **–जले** at dusk, at the time when lamps are lit; **–ठंड करना** see **–गुल करना**; **–तले अँधेर** nearer the church, farther from heaven; **–दिखाना** to illuminate one's path; **–बढ़ाना** to put out the lamp; **–लेकर ढूँढ़ना** to search every nook and corner; to make a thorough search; **–से चिराग़ जलता है** one lamp kindles another.

चिरायँध chirā:yādh (*nf*) the smell emitted by burning leather, hair, etc.

चिरायता chira:yta: (*nm*) chirata, wormwood — *Gentiana charetta*.

a plant used in medicine.

चिरायु chira:yu (*a*) blessed with long life, long living; **–हो !** may you live long !

चिराव chira:v (*nm*) splitting; sawing; tearing; dissecting, dissection; split fuel wood.

चिरौंजी chirāũji: (*nf*) the tree *Chironjia sapada* and its edible nut.

चिरौं(रौ)टा chirāũ(au)ṭa: (*nm*) a young male sparrow.

चिरौरी chirauri: (*nf*) an humble entreaty, supplication; **–करना** to make an humble entreaty, to supplicate.

चिलक chilak (*nf*) a painful twitching sensation, twitch; smarting pain.

चिलकना chilaknā: (*v*) to make a twitching sensation, to twitch; to smart.

चिलगोजा chilgoza: (*nm*) the nut of the pine tree.

चिलचिलाना chilchila:nā: (*v*) to shine scorchingly; **चिलचिलाती धूप** scorching sun/heat.

चिलबिल्ला chilbilla: (*a*) naughty, mischievous.

चिलम chilām (*nf*) an earthen or metallic vessel on the top of a hubble-bubble for containing fire and tobacco; **~बरदार** a servant who prepares the **चिलम**; a flunkey; **~बरदारी** the act or office of a **~बरदार**; flunkeyism; servitude; **–चढ़ाना/भरना** to fill or prepare a **चिलम**, to dance attendance upon; **–पीना** to smoke a **चिलम**; **–फूँकना** to smoke a **चिलम** heavily.

चिलमची chilāmchi: (*nf*) a (wash) basin.

चिलमन chilmān (*nf*) a bamboo-curtain.

चिल्लपों chillapō (*nf*) clamour, confused cries, hullabaloo.

चिल्लर chillar (*nm*) change (small coins).

चिल्ला chilla: (*nm*) a bow-string; (*a*) biting; **–जाड़ा** biting cold; the coldest part of the winter (said to continue for 40 days).

चिल्लाना chilla:nā: (*v*) to cry, to shout, to squeak.

चिल्लाहट chilla:haṭ (*nf*) an outcry, shouting and screaming, clamorous cries.

चिहुँकना chihũknā: (*v*) to start, to wince.

चिह्न chinh (*nm*) sign; mark, marking, brand; trait, trace; **–छोड़ना** to leave traces behind.

चिह्नित chinhit (*a*) signed; marked, branded.

चीं chī: (*nf*) warbling; chirp(ing); **-चपड़** jabber; protest explicitly; (expression of) resentment; **-चीं** chirping; warbling; chattering; **–बोलना** to cry 'enough'; to confess helplessness; to concede victory, to own defeat.

चींटा chī:ṭa: (*nm*) a big black ant.

चींटी chī:ṭi: (*nf*) an ant; **–की चाल** very slow movement; **–के पर निकलना** to be heading for trouble/death; to outgrow oneself.

चींथना chī:thnā: (*v*) to reduce to tatters, to tear to pieces; to spoil by scribbling.

ची chi: — a suffix which imparts the meaning of one who keeps or uses, e.g. **तोपची, अफ़ीमची**; or act as diminutive e.g. **संदूकची**.

चीकट chi:kaṭ (*a*) dirty; greasy and dirty; (dirty) residue (of greasy substances).

चीकू chi:ku: (*nm*) sapodilla.

चीख chi:kḥ (*nf*) scream, shriek; screech, squeak; **-पुकार** shriek and scream, hubbub; loud supplication; **–निकलना** to let out a sudden shriek/screech; **–मारना** to scream, to squeak, to screech.

चीखना chi:ḳḥnā: (*v*) to scream, to shriek, to squeak, to screech.

चीज़ chi:z (*nf*) a thing, an article; item, object; a commodity; an ornament; a wonderful or precious thing; **-बस्त** belongings, articles, goods and chattles.

चीड़ chi:ṛ (*nm*) a pine tree; **-वन** a pine forest.

चीतल chi:tal (*nm*) a white-spotted antelope.

चीता chi:ta: (*nm*) a leopard; panther; (*a*) liked, longed for (as **मनचीता**).

चीत्कार chi:tka:r (*nf*) a sudden scream/screech, loud shriek.

चीथ/ड़ा chi:thṛa: (*nm*) rag, tatters; **~ड़े लपेटना** to be dressed in rags, to put on tattered clothes.

चीथना chi:thnā: (*v*) to rend, to tear to pieces/tatters; to spoil by scribbling.

चीना chi:nā: (*nm*) millet; a Chinese; (*a*) belonging to China.

चीनी chi:nī: (*nf*) sugar; a Chinese; (*a*) Chinese; pertaining or belonging to China; **–मिट्टी** clay.

चीमड़ chi:maṛ (*a*) tough, hardy; stiff; tenacious; **~पन/~पना** toughness, hardness; stiffness; tenacity.

चीर chi:r (*nm*) a strip of cloth, feminine mantle; (*nf*) slit, cut, cleavage; **-फाड़** surgical operation; dissection.

चीरना chi:rnā: (*v*) to saw; to rend; to cleave; to tear; to dissect, to cut open; to incise.

चीरा chi:ra: (*nm*) incision, a surgical operation; **–लगाना** to incise, to cut open; to perform an operation.

चील chi:l (*nf*) a kite; **–झपट्टा** a sudden (kite-like) swoop, a snap; a boy's game; **–के घोंसले में मांस कहाँ** lit. to look for meat in a kite's nest—to seek for something in a quarter where it is bound to be used up.

चीवर chi:var (*nm*) a mendicant tattered dress.

चीस chi:s (*nf*) a smart, smarting rankling pain (as in a wound, etc

चुंगी chūngi: (*nf*) octroi, terminal tax; **–की चौकी /~घर** octroi-post.

चुंधा chūndha: (*a*) possessing sma half-shut eyes; purblind, dim sighted.

चुँधियाना chūdhiya:nā: (*v*) to b dazzled.

चुंबक chūmbak (*nm*) a magnet; **~त** magnetism; **~न** magnetisation **चुंबकीय** magnetic.

चुंबन chūmban (*nm*) a kiss, kissing

चुंबित chūmbit (*a*) kissed; touched.

चुंबी chūmbi: (*a*) a suffix meanin touching or kissing (e.g. **गगनचुंबी**

चुआना chua:nā: (*v*) to (cause tc drip; to percolate.

चुकंदर chukāndar (*nm*) beet, suga beet—*Beta vulgaris*.

चुकटी chukṭi: (*nf*) handful, palm ful; **–भर** handful, palmful.

चुकता chukta: (*a*) settled; paid up paid in full.

चुकना chuknā: (*v*) to be finished spent up/exhausted/completed; t be paid off in full; to be settled

चुकाई chuka:i: (*nf*) settlemen paying off.

चुकाना chuka:nā: (*v*) to settle; t pay off, to defray.

चुक्क chukk (*a*) extremely sour— often used as the second membe in the compound **खट्टा-चुक्क**.

चुखाना chukha:nā: (*a*) to suckle, t give suck to.

चुगद chugad (*nm*) lit. an owl; a nit wit; (*a*) slow-witted, stupid; henc **~पन** (*nm*).

चुगना chugnā: (*v*) to pick; to pec

food with the beak).

ल chugal (*nm*) a back-biter; ~ख़ोर a back-biter; ~ख़ोरी (the act r habit of) back-biting.

ली chugli: (*nf*) back-biting, peaking ill of (somebody in his/er absence); complaint;–करना/ाना/लगाना to backbite, to speak ll of; to complain, to level an ccusation.

गा chugga: (*nm*) pickings (of irds).

ाना chucha:nā: (*v*) to drip, to rickle.

ुवाना chuchuva:nā: (*v*) see चुचाना.

ट्की chuṭki: (*nf*) a pinch, snapping with the finger; –काटना to pinch; -बजाते (में) in a trice; in a moment; -बजाना to snap the fingers; –भर a pinchful; very small quantity; -भरना to make a caustic remark; -लेना to make a sarcastic remark, o taunt; चुटकियों में in a trice; ~उड़ाना to accomplish (a work) in no time; to treat like a joke, to joke away.

टकु/ला chuṭkula: (*nm*) an anecdote; a joke, pleasantry; ~ला छोड़ना to let off a squib; to utter a pleasantry; ~लेबाज one who narrates too many anecdotes; ~लेबाजी adecdotage; narration of anecdotes, narration of incidents in a lighter vein.

टिया chuṭiya: (*nf*) a lock of hair on the top of the head (kept by traditionalist Hindus); braid; –हाथ में होना to be under one's thumb, to be under complete control (of).

टीला chuṭi:la: (*a*) wounded, hurt; incisive; penetrating, causing mental upheaval; three-stranded cotton or silken braid with tassels used for hair-do.

ुड़ैल churail (*nf*) a witch; shrew.

ुदक्कड़ chudakkaṛ (*a*) addicted to venery; libidinous; (*nm*) a womanizer; a past-master in the sexual act.

चुदना chudnā: (*v*) to be subject to sexual intercourse (by a male).

चुदाई chuda:i: (*nf*) the act or process of copulation (by a male), performance of sexual act by man.

चुनचुना chūnchunā: (*a*) causing a typical burning sensation (by touch).

चुनचुना/ना chūnchūnā:nā: (*v*) to cause a burning sensation; ~हट a typical burning sensation.

चुनना chunnā: (*v*) to select, to choose; to pick; to elect.

चुनरी chunri: (*nf*) a thin cloth with red ground and white or some other type of specks; a particoloured cloth sheet or *sa:ri:*.

चुनाँचे chunāche (*ind*) thus, therefore, as a result.

चुनाव chuna:v (*nm*) election; selection; -क्षेत्र constituency; -मंडल electorate; –लड़ना to fight/contest an election.

चुनिंदा chunında: (*a*) selected, chosen; choicest.

चुनौती chunauti: (*nf*) a challenge; –देना to throw a challenge; –स्वीकार करना to accept a challenge.

चुन्नट chunnaṭ (*nf*) a rumple, crease; ~दार rumpled, creased.

चुन्नी chunnı: (*nf*) a woman's small-sized upper covering or mantle.

चुप chup (*a*) silent, quiet; –रहना to keep quiet, to keep breath to cool porridge; –साधना to assume silence, not to utter a word.

चुप/का chupka: (*a*) silent, quiet; still; ~की quietitude, silence; ~के से silently, quietly; stealthily; without making a fuss.

चुप/चाप chupcha:p (*adv*) silently, quietly; stealthily; clandestinely; ~चुपाते quietly, silently.

चुपड़ना chuparnā: (*v*) to besmear, to annoint, to apply a greasy substance.

चुपड़ा chupra: (*a*) besmeared, anointed; greasy; **चुपड़ी** (feminine form); **०और दो-दो** you cannot eat your cake and have it too.

चुप्पा chuppa (*a*) taciturn; secretive.

चुप्पी chuppi: (*nf*) silence; **–छाना** pindrop silence to prevail; **–तोड़ना** to break the ice; **–साधना** to assume silence, not to utter a word, to be mute, to keep breath to cool one's porridge.

चुभन chubhān (*nf*) pricking, pricking sensation, lingering or haunting pain (physical or mental).

चुभना chubhnā: (*v*) to be pricked/pinched/punctured; to feel bad, to have a pricking sensation within; **चुभती हुई बात** a prickly/piercing remark.

चुभाना chubha:nā: (*v*) to prick/pinch/puncture; to pierce slightly.

चुभोना chubhona: (*v*) see **चुभाना**.

चुमकारना chumka:rnā: (*v*) to produce a kissing sound; to fondle, to caress.

चुम्मा chumma: (*nm*) a kiss; **–लेना** to kiss, to plant a kiss.

चुरकुट churkuṭ (*a*) pulverized, reduced to powder or pieces.

चुरट churaṭ (*nm*) a cheroot.

चुरमुर churmur (*nf*) the sound produced by the cracking of a crisp or brittle substance.

चुरमुरा churmura: (*a*) crisp, brittle, fragile.

चुराना chura:nā (*v*) to steal, to pinch.

चुल chul (*nf*) titillation, prurience; wantonness; sexual passion; **–उठना** to have a titillating sensation, to be passionate, to have a sex urge; **–मिटाना** to satisfy one's passion or sexual urge.

चुलबुला chulbula: (*a*) playful; fidget restless; frolicsome; **~पन** playful ness; fidgetiness, restlessness frolicsomeness; also **~हट** (*nf*).

चुलबुलाना chulbula:nā: (*v*) to be play ful/fidgety/restless/frolicsome.

चुल्लू chullu: (*nm*) the hollow cu formed by joining the fringes o the two palms together; the up turned hollow palm (of a singl hand); a handful/palmful (o liquid); **–भर** a handful, meagr quantity; **०पानी में डूब मरना** lit. t be drowned in a palmful of wate —to be ashamed beyond reprieve to die through shame; **–में उल्लू हो जाना** to lose self-control even o slight intoxication.

चुसकी chuski: (*nf*) a sip, suck.

चुस्त chust (*a*) active, smart, agile tight; narrow; **-चालाक** sharp and smart; **-दुरुस्त** agile and active.

चुस्ती chusti: (*nf*) agility, alertness smartness.

चुहचुहा/ना chuhchuha:nā (*v*) see **चह-चहाना**; to be full of juiciness; **~ते** juicy, provocative.

चुहल chuhal (*nf*) jollity, joviality, jocundity; **~बाज** jolly, jovial, jocund; **~बाजी** jollity, joviality, jocundity.

चुहिया chuhiya: (*nf*) a female mouse

चूँ chū: (*nf*) chirping, twitter; squeaking; creaking; a slight or low noise; **-चूँ** chirping, twitter; **०का मुरब्बा** an incoherent mass of heterogeneous stuff; **–न करना** not to make the slightest protest, to utter no sound.

चूँकि chū:ki (*ind.*) because, as.

चूक chu:k (*nf*) lapse, slip, omission; error; fault; default; (*a*) extremely sour (used in this sense as the second member of the com-

pound खट्टा-चूक); –जाना to catch a crab.
चूकना chu:knā: (*v*) to miss, to fail; to err; to make a lapse, to default.
चूची chu:chi: (*nf*) a nipple, teat; female breast.
चूचुक chu:chuk (*nm*) a nipple, teat.
चूज़ा chu:za: (*nm*) a chicken.
चूड़ांत chu:ṛā:nt (*nm*) extreme; (*a*) extreme; excessive.
चूड़ा chu:ṛa: (*nm*) a lock of hair on on top of the head; a large-sized broad bangle; (*a*) the best, most eminent; ~कर्म the ceremony of tonsure; ~मणि a jewel worn on top of the head; the best; most excellent (of).
चूड़ी chu:ṛi: (*nf*) a bangle; ring; pucker; ~दार puckered; चूड़ियाँ तोड़ना to break a woman's bangles —an act symbolizing widowhood; to be turned into a widow; चूड़ियाँ पहनना to don female attire; to become effeminate; (for a widow) to remarry; चूड़ियाँ पहनाना to marry a widow.
चूत chu:t (*nf*) the female genital organ, vagina.
चूतड़ chu:taṛ (*nm*) the buttock, rump, bum; –दिखाना to turn tail; –पीटना/बजाना to slap the rump with joy, to be overjoyed, to express extreme joy.
चूतिया chu:tiya: (*nm* and *a*) dolt (ish), stupid, blockhead, nincompoop; ~खाता/~चक्कर a doltish affair; stupid involvement; ~पन/~पंती (~पंथी) doltishness, stupidity.
चून chū:n (*nm*) flour, wheat-meal.
चूना chū:nā: (*v*) to leak; to drop; to ooze (*as* कोढ़); (*nm*) lime; ~दानी a small lime-case; a watch that does not record correct time; –लगाना, (के) to dupe, to bamboozle
चूमना chū:mnā: (*v*) to kiss, to lip; -चाटना to kiss and caress.
चूमा chū:ma: (*nm*) kiss, kissing; -चाटी kissing and caressing.
चूर chu:r (*nm*) filings, powder; (*a*) pulverized; steeped in (as नशे में–); crushed; exhausted; besotted; -चूर करना to pulverize; to crush thoroughly; to break into atoms.
चूरन chu:rān (*nm*) a powder; digestive powder.
चूरमा chu:rmā: (*nm*) a kind of sweetmeat made from crumbled bread or bread-crumbs mixed with ghee and sugar.
चूरा chu:ra: (*nm*) a powder; filings; small fragments; (saw) dust.
चूर्ण churn̲ (*nm*) powder, pulverized or powdered substance; digestive powder.
चूर्णित churn̲it (*a*) crushed, pulverized, reduced to powder.
चूल chu:l (*nf*) tenon; pivot; mortise; joint; ~दार pivoted, tenoned; –बैठना to fit in; –से चूल मिलना to have complete adjustment, to have a harmonious relationship; चूलें ढीली होना lit. the joints to become loose or dislocated; to be tired out, to be wearied, to be exhausted.
चूल्हा chu:lha: (*nm*) a fire-place, hearth; -चक्की routine household chores; –न्यौतना to invite the whole family; –फूँकना to keep busy in cooking work; चूल्हे में जाना/पड़ना to be damned, to go to hell, to go to pot; चूल्हे से निकलकर भट्टी में (पड़ना) from the frying pan into the fire.
चूषण chu:shān̲ (*nm*) suction, sucking.
चूसना chu:snā: (*v*) to suck, to suck dry; to sip; to drink in; to exploit; to exhaust.
चूहा chu:ha: (*nm*) a rat, mouse; चूहेदानी a rat-trap; चूहों का डंड पेलना,

पेट में to be extremely hungry, to be starved; चूहों की मौत बिल्ली का खेल it may be fun to you but it is death to the frogs.

चें chē (*nf*) chirping, twitter; -चें chirrup; jabber, idle noisy talk; –बोलना to utter a cry of helplessness; to concede victory, to own defeat.

चेंप chēp (*nm*) the acidic viscous substance ejaculated from the mango fruit as its nipple is removed; stickiness, viscosity; ~दार containing चेंप, sticky.

चेक chek (*nm*) a cheque; chequered cloth; –काटना to issue a cheque.

चेचक chechak (*nf*) small-pox.

चेत chet (*nm*) consciousness; senses.

चेतन chetān (*a*) animate; conscious; (*nm*) the conscious (mind); the animate (world); ~वाद animatism.

चेतना chetnā: (*nf*) consciousness, awareness; animation; (*v*) to become conscious/animated; to become alert; to be provoked; -प्रवाह stream of consciousness.

चेतावनी cheta:vanī: (*nf*) a warning; an alarm; –,अंतिम an ultimatum, final warning.

चेन chēn (*nf*) a chain.

चेरी cheri: (*nf*) a female attendant, maid servant.

चे/ला chela: (*nf*) a pupil, disciple; hence ~ली (*nf*).

चेष्टा cheshṭa: (*nf*) effort, endeavour; movement; demeanour; gesture.

चेहरा chehra: (*nm*) face, countenance; mask; front; -मोहरा lineament; –उतरना to be downcast, to be in low spirits; –खिंचा होना to appear in a tense mood, tension to be writ on the face; –खिल उठना the face to glow up/to brighten up, to cheer up; –पीला पड़/हो जाना to turn pale, to lose lustre;–फक हो जाना to grow lustreless, to be put out of countenance; –सफ़ेद हो जाना to grow anaemic; to lose lustre; चेहरे का रंग उड़ जाना/का रंग फक हो जाना to get out of countenance, to lose facial lustre; चेहरे पर बारह बजना to have a face as long as a fiddle; चेहरे पर शिकन न आना to maintain complete composure, to show no facial signs of tension, to be absolutely unruffled; चेहरे पर हवाइयाँ उड़ना to be struck with panic; to lose colour, to be despirited; चेहरे से बदमाशी टपकना to have the gallows in one's face; चेहरे से मनहूसियत टपकना to have a sinister appearance.

चेहल्लुम chehallum (*nf*) (among Muslims) the rites observed on the fortieth day after death; the mourning observed on the fortieth day of the death of the martyrs of Karbala:.

चैत chait (*nm*) the opening month of the year according to the Hindu calendar.

चैतन्य chaitanny (*a*) conscious; sensitive; alert and awake; (*nm*) consciousness; spirit.

चैती chaiti: (*a*) pertaining to, or related with, चैत (see); (*nf*) the *Chait*-harvest.

चैत्य chaitty (*nm*) a monastery, (esp. Buddhist) shrine.

चैत्र chaittr (*nm*) see चैत.

चैन chain̐ (*nm*) relief; rest; tranquillity, calm and quiet; –की छानना/बंसी बजाना to be in clover, to be in absolute ease and luxury, to enjoy oneself thoroughly; –पड़ना to feel relieved; to feel a sense of relief; –से कटना/से गुज़रना to live easefully, to have an easy time.

चोंगा chōga: (*nm*) a (telephone) receiver; cylindrical tinpot.

चोंच chōch (*nf*) beak; bill; dolt; **चोंचें होना, (दो-दो)** to have a wordy duel, to exchange word volleys.

चोंच/ला chōchla: (*nm*) affectation, airs; coquetry, dalliance; **~लेबाज** a coquette; coquettish; **~लेबाजी** coquettishness, indulgence in coquetry; **~ले सहना** to put up with somebody's affected/coquettish conduct.

चोंप chōp (*nm*) see **चेंप**.

चोआ choa: (*nm*) a mixture of four perfumes (viz. sandal, agallochum, saffron and musk).

चोकर chokar (*nm*) bran.

चोखा chokha: (*a*) fine, good; genuine; (*nm*) mash made of boiled or roasted vegetables; **–दाम, चोखा काम** good wages, good work.

चोग़ा choga: (*nm*) a gown, toga.

चोट **choṭ** (*nf*) an injury; blow; stroke; hurt; **-चपेट/फेंट** wound, injury, bruise; **–उभरना** resurgence of an injury; **–करना** to strike a blow; to launch an attack; **–खाना** to recieve a blow; to be wounded; **--पर चोट पड़ना** to suffer one blow after another; **चोटें चलना** to measure swords, to exchange blows.

चोटिल choṭil (*a*) wounded, struck.

चोटी choṭi: (*nf*) an apex; crown; braid; a lock of hair on top of the head (kept by traditionalist Hindus); **~दार/वाला** possessing a **चोटी**; **–करना** to braid, to arrange hair in braids; **–का** superb, of the highest order; **–का पसीना एड़ी तक आना** to labour hard, to work to perspiration; **–दबना** or **हाथ में होना** to be under one's thumb, to be in the clutches (of), to be under complete control (of).

चोट्टा choṭṭa: (*nm*) a petty thief, pilferer; hence **चोट्टी** (feminine form); **चोट्टी कुतिया जलेबियों की रखवाली** to set a fox to keep the geese.

चोथ choth (*nm*) a lump of human/animal faeces/stool; extremely inert and inactive person.

चोदना chodnā: (*v*) to copulate(with), (for a man) to have sexual intercourse.

चोदू chodu: (*nm*) an adept in the art of copulation (with woman), one addicted to venery; one who indulges in excessive sexual intercourse.

चोप chop (*nm*) see **चेंप**; zest, aspiration.

चोब chob (*nm*) a tent-pin; gold or silver-plated club; drum-stick; **~दार** a gatekeeper/watchman.

चोबा choba: (*nm*) a nail; see **चोब**.

चोर (*nm*) a thief; pilferer; burglar; **-कर्म** stealing; theft; **-खिड़की** a small secret exit; **-गढ़ा** a hidden pit; **-गली** a secret lane, back lane; **-चकार** a thief or a swindler; **-दरवाज़ा/द्वार** a trap-door; secret door-way; back door; **-बाजार** black-market; **-बाज़ारिया** black-marketeer; **~बाज़ारी** black-marketing; **-महल** a back-stairs lodge; **-रास्ता** a back-stairs pathway; **-सीढ़ी** back stairs; **–का दिल आधा** a thief has no guts; **–की दाढ़ी में तिनका** a guilty conscience cannot shed off its alarmed stance; **–के घर छिछोरा** one thief robs another; **–चोर को पहचानता है** a thief knows a thief as a wolf knows a wolf; **–का साथी गिरहकट** a thief will have another for company, birds of the same feather flock together; **-चोर मौसेरे भाई** dogs don't eat dogs, there is honour among thieves; **–चोरी से जाये पर हेरा-फेरी से न जाये** a snake must still hiss, even if he does not bite; **–से कहो**

चोरी कर और साहु से कहो जागता रह to run with the hare and hunt with the hounds, to play a double game.

चोरी chori: (*nf*) theft, burglary, pilferage; –का काम/–की बात an underhand affair/a secret information; -चोरी clandestinely, stealthily; -छिपे stealthily, surreptitiously; –से stealthily, clandestinely; –का गुड़ मीठा forbidden fruits are sweet; –का माल कुछ धर्मखाते बाकी हलाल cheating the devil and sharing a part of ill-begotten gains with the church;–का माल पचाना to whip the devil round the stump; to enjoy the fruits of evil doing; –का माल लेने वाला भी चोर the receiver of stolen goods is as bad as a thief, abetment of a crime is as bad as its commission.

चोला chola: (*nm*) a long robe, gown; appearance; physical frame, body; –बदलना to effect a metamorphosis, to change one's appearance; to change the physical frame; to be reborn.

चोली choli: (*nf*) brassieres; bodice; -दामन का साथ close by jowl, a perpetual association, an everlasting bond.

चौंक/ना chaūknā: (*v*) to be startled/started; to be alarmed; –उठना to jump out of one's skin.

चौंतीस chaūti:s (*a*) thirty-four; (*nm*) the number thirty-four.

चौंध chaūdh (*nf*) dazzling effect, dazzlement; blink.

चौंधियाना chaudhiya:nā: (*v*) to be dazzled, to suffer a dazzling effect.

चौंसठ chaūsaṭḥ (*a*) sixty-four; (*nm*) the number sixty-four.

चौ chau—an allomorph of चतु: (चार) used as the first member in compound Hindi words; ~आई (वाई) from all the four directions, blowing all round (as हवा); ~कड़ी a quartet; bound, leap; ०भरना to bounce, to proceed by leaps and bounds, to be buoyant; ~कड़ी भूलना to have one's senses benumbed; to be put out of countenance, to be non-plussed/bewildered; ~कस cautious, alert, watchful; in order, intact; ~कसी cautiousness, vigilance; ~कोन quadrangular, quadrilateral, four-sided; ~कोना quadrangular; four-sided: ~कोर quadrilateral, quadrangular, four-sided; ~खंड four-storeyed; ~खट threshold; door-frame, door-sill; ०न झाँकना never to cross over somebody's threshold, never to visit somebody's house; ~खटा frame, framework; ~खना four-storeyed; ~खाना chequered cloth; ~खूँट the four quarters; all round; ~खूँटा quadrangular; four-cornered; ~गड्डा quartet, foursome, a set of four; ~गिर्द all round; ~गुना fourfold, four times; ~तरफ़ा all round, from all the four quarters; ~ताल a typical musical mode; ~दस the fourteenth day of the lunar fortnight; ~पट razed, ruined, undone; ०चरण a person whose presence casts an ominous spell causing ruination; ~पाई a typical Hindi poetic metre; ~पाया a quadruped; livestock; ~पाल a rural meeting place; a verandah used as drawing room in village houses; ~पेजी quarto; ~बारा an assembly room with a number of doors and windows; ~मंजिला four-storeyed; ~मासा the rainy season; four months comprising the rainy season extending from आषाढ़ to क्वार; ~मुहाँ/मुखा four-faced; all round; ~मुखी all round;

versatile; ~मुहानी a quadrivial, juncture of four streams or pathways; ~रंगा four-coloured; of four kinds; ~रस even, plane; squared off; ~रस्ता/राहा crossing; crossroads; ~लड़ा four-stringed; ~हद्दी boundary.

चौक chauk (*nm*) a crossing; square; market place; see **सीमंत** (-**संस्कार**).

चौकन्ना chaukannā: (*a*) alert, vigilant; –**होना** to prick up/cock one's ears.

चौका chauka: (*nm*) the sanctified space in the kitchen where tradition-loving Hindus take their meals; kitchen; a rectangular slab of stone; a set of four; -**बरतन** cleansing of the kitchen utensils; –**अलग करना** to establish a separate household; –**उठाना** to wind up the lunching/dining activity (for the day).

चौकी chauki: (*nf*) a post, check post; low square or rectangular seat.

चौकीदा/र chauki:da:r (*nm*) a watchman, guard; ~**री** watch, guard; the office or function of a watchman or the wages paid therefor.

चौगान chaugā:n (*nm*) a game akin to polo; the field where this game is played.

चौड़ा chaura: (*a*) broad, wide; ~**ई** breadth, width; -**चकला** expansive; weighty and well-built.

चौतरा chautra: (*nm*) see **चबूतरा**.

चौथ chauth (*nf*) the fourth day of the lunar fortnight; a cess (levied by the Mara:ṭha:s on other neighbouring states); –**का चाँद** lit. the moon of the fourth—an object to be shunned (as it is said to result in slanderous accusations being levelled against one who happens to see it).

चौथा chautha: (*a*) the fourth (in succession); (*nm*) (the rituals observed on) the fourth day of (somebody's) death; ~**पन** the old age, the last phase of life (that of a **संन्यासी**—an anchorite).

चौथाई chautha:i: (*a*) one-fourth.

चौथी chauthi: (*nf*) the formal function observed on the fourth day of the marriage celebrations; (*a*) see **चौथा**.

चौदह chaudeh (*a*) fourteen; (*nm*) the number fourteen.

चौधरी chaudhri: (*nm*) the headman of a clan or community, chief, chieftain; ~**पन**/~**पना** supremacy: leadership.

चौपड़ chaupar (*nf*) a game played with oblong dice (3 in number) or with *kauri:s* (on a cloth or board having two transverse bars in the form of a cross); the board or the cloth (as mentioned above).

चौपन्ना chaupannā: (*nm*) a pamphlet.

चौपहिया chaupahi:ya: (*a*) four-wheeled; (*nm*) a four-wheeler; railway wagon.

चौबच्चा chaubachcha: (*nm*) a catchpit.

चौबीस chaubi:s (*a*) twenty-four; (*nm*) the number twenty-four.

चौरा chaura: (*nm*) an altar; a raised platform forming part of a religious or ritualistic installation.

चौरानवे chaurā:nve (*a*) ninety-four; (*nm*) the number ninety-four.

चौरासी chaura:si: (*a*) eighty-four; (*nm*) the number eighty-four.

चौर्य chaury (*nm*) theft, stealing; -**कर्म**/-**वृत्ति** theft, stealing, pilferage.

चौवन chau:ān (*a*) fifty-four; (*nm*) the number fifty-four.

चौवालीस chauva:li:s (*a* and *nm*) see **चवालीस**.

चौसर chausar (*nf*) see **चौपड़**.

चौहत्तर chauhattar (*a*) seventy-four;

(*nm*) the number seventy-four.

चौहरा chauhra: (*a*) fourfold; quadruplicate; ~**ना** to make fourfold

च्यु/त chyut (*a*) fallen (from), deprived (of), banished; deviated (from); strayed; ~**ति** lapse, default; eclipsis, banishment; fall.

छ

छ chha–the second letter of the second pentad (i.e. **चवर्ग**) of the Devna:gri: alphabet; an allomorph of **छह** used as the first member in a number of Hindi compound words; ~**कड़ी** a group or set of six; ~**गुना** six times; six-fold; ~**माही** six-monthly, half-yearly.

छंगा chhāṅga: (*a*) having six fingers (in one or each of the palms or toes).

छँगु/नी, ~**ली** chhāguni:, ~li: (*nf*) the little finger.

छँटना chhāṭnā: (*v*) to be sorted; to be thinned (as **भीड़**) or diffused (as **बादल**); to be trimmed or reduced (as **मुटापा, बादी**); **छँटा हुआ** (it carries a derogatory sense) out and out, of the first order; a rascal, rogue, of blackest/deepest dye.

छँटनी chhāṭni: (*nf*) retrenchment; weeding out.

छँटाई chhāṭa:i: (*nf*) the work or wages for sorting/pruning/trimming; assortment; reduction, retrenchment.

छंद chhānd (*nm*) metre, measure; -**बंद** scheming, manoeuvering; trickery; -**बंध** the bonds of metre (in a poetic composition); ~**बद्ध** see **छंदोबद्ध**; ~**शास्त्र** prosody.

छंदोबद्ध chhāndobaddh (*a*) metrical, cast in a metrical form; hence ~**ता** (*nf*).

छंदोभंग chhāndobhang (*nm*) metrical flaw, breach of metrical arrangement.

छ: chh/ai, ~e, ~ah (*a* and *nm*) see **छह**.

छकड़ा chhakṛa: (*nm*) a carrier bullock cart; a worn out vehicle; –**हो जाना** (a vehicle etc.) to be worn out, to become unserviceable.

छकना chhaknā: (*v*) to be gratified, to be full to be cloyed; to be teased/harassed; to be outwitted.

छकाना chaka:nā: (*v*) to gratify, to cloy; to tease/harass; to outwit.

छक्का chhakka: (*nm*) a set of six; sixer (in cricket); the sixth in a pack of cards; the six (at dice, etc.); -**पंजा** manoeuvrings, tactical moves; **छक्के छूटना** to lose the six senses, to be at one's wit's end; to be demoralised, **छक्के छुड़ाना** to give one his gruel, to smite hip and thigh, to out-manoeuvre, to demoralise, to force out of gear.

छछूँदर chhachhū:dar (*nf*) a mole, shrew; –**छोड़ना** to let off a squib.

छज्जा chhajja: (*nm*) a balcony; terrace; drip stone; hood; **छज्जेदार** having a terrace or a balcony;

broad-brimmed; hooded.

छटपटा/ना chhaṭpaṭa:nā: (*v*) to writhe in pain, to be restless, to toss and tumble about; to long/yearn impatiently; hence ~**हट** (*nf*).

छटाँक chhaṭā:k (*nf*) one-sixteenth of a seer (**सेर**) .

छटा chhaṭa: (*nf*) refulgence, splendour, lustre; beauty.

छठ chhaṭh (*nf*) the sixth day of the lunar fortnight.

छठा chhaṭha: (*a*) the sixth (in order); **छठे कान में पड़ना** to be passed on to a third person, to be likely to become public; **छठे-छमासे** once in a blue moon, rarely.

छठी chhaṭhi: (*nf*) the ceremony performed on the sixth day of child-birth; **–का दूध याद आना** to be put/forced in a very tight corner, to be in a terrible predicament.

छड़ chhaṛ (*nf*) a rod, bar.

छड़ा chhaṛa: (*a*) unmarried; with no encumbrance; all by oneself, alone.

छड़ी chhaṛi: (*nf*) a stick, cane; ~**दार** striped; ~**बरदार** a watchman, guard.

छत chhat (*nf*) the ceiling; roof.

छतनार chhatna:r (*a*) (said of tree, plants, etc.) diffused, giving diffused shade; sparse.

छतरी chhatri: (*nf*) an umbrella; a pigeon-umbrella; parachute; kiosk; pavilion; turret; a cenotaph in honour of a Hindu national or religious leader or (in olden days) a big feudal lord, etc.; ~**दार** fitted with an umbrella, canopied, covered; ~**धारी** carrying an umbrella; equipped with a parachute; ०**सैनिक** a parachuter.

छत्ता chhatta: (*nm*) a beehive; archway, corridor; ~**धानी** beehive.

छत्ती/स chhatti:s (*a*) thirty-six; (*nm*) the number thirty-six; ~**सा** a shrewd/crafty person; ~**सी** shrewdness/craftiness; ~**स होना** to be estranged.

छत्र chattr (*nm*) an umbrella; a cenotaph in honour of some outstanding personality; ~**च्छाया** patronage, protection; ~**धर/धारी** an umbrella-bearer; one over whose head an umbrella is borne as a mark of dignity and authority; ~**पति** a king, ruler; **छत्राकार** peltate.

छदाम chhadā:m (*nm*) one-fourth of a pice, a very small coin (of olden times).

छद्म chhadm (*a*) pseudo-, disguised, deceptive; hypocritical; (*nm*) dissimulation; hypocrisy; stratagem; ~**नाम** pseudonym; ~**रूपी** pseudomorph; ~**वेश** disguise; ~**वेशी** disguised, in disguise.

छन chhān (*nm*) a moment, an instant; (*nf*) the hissing sound produced when a drop of water falls on a hot plate; tinkling/jingling sound (as of a **घुँघरू**); **-छन** jingling; tinkling or hissing sound; **–भर** a moment, an instant; **–भर भी न लगाना** not to take a moment's time.

छनक chhanāk (*nf*) jingling, tinkling or hissing sound; **-मनक** jingle (of ornaments); ornamental make-up, foppishness.

छनकना chhanaknā: (*v*) to jingle/tinkle; to evaporate instantly with a hissing sound; to be reduced in quantity by being heated.

छनना chhannā: (*v*) intransitive verbal form of **छानना** (see); **–,खूब/गहरी/गाढ़ी** to be in intimate relationship; **–,गहरी/गाढ़ी** to have a strong dose of **भंग**.

छनाछन chhanā:chhan (*adv*) with a jingling-tinkling sound.

छन्ना chhannā: (*nm*) a filter; a piece

of tattered cloth.

छप chhap (*nf*) a splashing sound, splash; **-छप** splatter; (with) a recurrent splashing sound; also **छपाछप**.

छपकना chhapaknā: (*v*) to splash, to splatter.

छपछपा/ना chhapchhapa:nā: (*v*) to splash, to splatter; hence ~**हट** (*nf*).

छपना chhapnā: (*v*)) to be printed or stamped; **छपते-छपते** stop press.

छपर chhapar—a variant of **छप्पर** used as the first member in some Hindi compounds; ~**खट** a bedstead fitted with mosquito-net bars; ~**बंदी** thatching; wages paid for thatching work.

छपाई chhapa:i: (*nf*) printing; cost of printing.

छपाका chhapa:ka: (*nm*) a (violent) splash (produced by the impact of something on water).

छप्पन chhappān (*a*) fifty-six; (*nm*) the number fifty-six; ~**छुरी** a smart dashing sharp woman; **–प्रकार के व्यंजन** (fifty-six, i.e.) numerous dishes of delicacies.

छप्पय chhappay (*nm*) an important Hindi poetic metre running into six lines, a hexametre.

छप्पर chhappar (*nm*) a thatch, thatched roof; ~**बंदी** see **छपरबंदी**; **–पर फूस न होना** not to have even a thatched roof to live under; to be extremely poverty-stricken; **–फाड़ कर देना** to bestow an unexpectedly large fortune, to give as a huge windfall.

छबीला chhabi:la: (*a*) spruce; foppish; dandy; hence ~**पन** (*nm*); **छबीली** (*fem.* form).

छब्बीस chhabbi:s (*a*) twenty-six; (*nm*) the number twenty-six.

छमछम chhamchhām (*nf*) tinkling (sound), tinkle.

छमकना chhamāknā: (*v*) to make a clinking sound; to show off.

छमछमाना chhamchhamā:nā: (*v*) to move with a succession of clinking sounds.

छमाछम chhamā:chhām (*nf*) the sound of incessant downpour etc.

छरहरा chharehra: (*a*) slim and smart; of spare frame; hence ~**पन** (*nm*).

छरीदा chhari:da: (*a*) with no encumbrances, all by oneself; without bag or baggage.

छर्रा chharra: (*nm*) a buck shot.

छल chhal (*nm*) guile, deception; trick; ruse; sham; **-कपट** dodge and duplicity; ~**घात** assassination; ~**घाती** an assassin; **-छंद** guile and wile; ~**छंदी** fraudulent, deceitful; **-छिद्र** guile and wile; **-बल से** by hook or crook, by fair means or foul; fraudulently.

छलकना chhalaknā: (*v*) to overflow; to spill out from a full vessel (during movement).

छलछलाना chhalchhala:nā: (*v*) to have the eyes filled with tears; to be on the verge of flowing out/dripping.

छलना chhalnā: (*v*) to cheat, to deceive; to delude, to dodge; to wile/beguile; (*nf*) sham, will-o-th'-wisp, illusion.

छलनी chhalnī: (*nf*) a sieve; strainer; **–कर देना** to batter, to riddle; **–हो जाना** to be battered/riddled; **–में पानी भरना** to square the circle; to attempt to do the impossible.

छलाँग chhalā:g (*nf*) a leap, bound; –, **अंधी** a leap in the dark; **–मारना** to leap, to bound.

छलावा chhala:va: (*nm*) an illusion; apparition. will-o-th'-wisp, jack-o'-lantern.

छलिया chhaliya: (*a* and *nm*) (a) cheat, fraudulent; deceitful (person).

छली chhali: (*a*) cheat, fraudulent, deceitful.

छल्ला chhalla: (*nm*) a ring, ringlet, stirrup; washer; eye-curl; **छल्लेदार** ringed; curly.

छवि chhavi (*nf*) pretty features; features; splendour, beauty; winsomeness; photograph; **~कार** a photographer.

छह chhai, chhe, chhah (*a*) six; (*nm*) the number six; **—और तीन का संबंध होना** to be mutually estranged, to have mutually opposed stances.

छहराना chhehra:nā: (*v*) to sprinkle; to spray, to shed all round.

छाँट chhā:ṭ (*nf*) selection; (mode of) cutting.

छाँटन chhā:ṭān (*nf*) parings, cuttings; prunings.

छाँटना chhā:ṭna: (*v*) to select, to sort out; to cut, to trim/prune; to cast out, to knock off; to reduce; to retrench; to chop; to boast (knowledge of); to talk in high-flown terms (e.g. –,क़ानून).

छाँव chhā:v (*nf*) shade; shadow.

छाँह chhā:h (*nf*) shade; shadow; **~दार** shady; shadowy; **—तक न छू पाना** to be much less in excellence, to be no match at all to; **—देना** to provide shelter/patronage to; **—न छूने देना** to allow no proximity, to keep at a distance; **—में बैठना** to enjoy the patronage of, to be under the protection of; **—से बचना** to keep away from, to evade even the shadow of.

छाक chha:k (*nf*) mid-day meals (for outdoor workers).

छागल chha:gal (*nm*) a hircine; (*nf*) a canvas water-bag; silver anklet.

छाछ chha:chh (*nf*) butter-milk.

छाजन chha:jan (*nf*) a covering, thatching; eczema.

छाता chha:ta: (*nm*) an umbrella; **~धारी** parachute (troop); a parachutist.

छाती chha:ti: (*nf*) breast; chest; bosom; spirit; **—उठना/उभरना** (said of female breasts) to protrude, youthful curves to be formed; **—उमगना** to be affected by an emotional upsurge; **—उमड़ना** to be overwhelmed by affectionate/tragic feelings; **—कठोर होना** to be unfeeling, to be heartless; **—कड़ी करना** to acquire control over feelings; to restrain oneself; **—कूटना** see **—पीटना**; **—गज भर की होना** to have a heart of steel; to be puffed up with joy; **—छलनी होना** the heart to be battered; **—जलना** to have a heart-sore, to be under the spell of grief; to be in the grip of a terrible jealousy; **—जुड़ाना** see **—ठंडी करना**; **—ठंडी करना** to relieve oneself of one's heart-burning, to assuage one's feelings; **—ठंडी होना** to be relieved of heart-burning; to be assuaged; **—ठुकना** to feel assured; **—ठोक कर कहना** to make an utterance with complete assurance; to take a pledge; **—तानना** to confront without fear/with complete self-assurance; **—धकधक करना/—धड़कना** to have one's heart in one's mouth; **—धुकुर-पुकुर होना** the heart to palpitate through apprehension; **—निकालकर चलना** to stalk, to strut; **—पकना** to feel very sore, to be fed up; **—पत्थर की करना** to mould one's heart to face the worst; **—पर चढ़ना** to overpower; to nag, to keep on pestering; **—पर धर/लाद कर ले जाना** to carry along (one's belongings) in one's post-mortem journey; to care too much for worldly belongings; **—पर पत्थर रखना** to endure patiently; to still the heaving of the heart; **—पर**

बाल होना to have a high morale/fortitude; to be firm-worded; –पर मूँग दलना to indulge in an activity designed to inflict pain on somebody, to be calculatively painsgiving; –पर सवार होना to put one's foot on the neck of; to thoroughly subdue; –पर साँप लोटना to burn with jealousy, to be green with envy, to be tormented by envy; –पर से बोझ उतरना to be relieved of a mental botheration/worry/burden; –पर हाथ रखकर कहना to speak with a clear conscience; –पीटना to lament; to beat the breast (as an expression of mourning); –फटना the heart to rend with grief; to be overwhelmed by grief; –फाड़कर with very hard labour, working rigorously; –फुलाना to be swollen by pride, to assume airs; –वज्र करना to mould one's heart into steel; –सराहना to praise the courage of; –सुलगना see –जलना; –से लगाना to embrace, to fondle.

छात्र chha:tr (*nm*) a student; -अनुशासन student discipline; -अनुशासनहीनता student indiscipline; -आंदोलन student agitation; student movement; ~त्व studentship; -नेता a student leader; ~वृत्ति scholarship.

छात्रालय chha:ttra:lay (*nm*) see छात्रावास.

छात्रावास chha:ttra:va:s (*nm*) a (student) hostel, boarding house.

छादन chha:dān (*nf*) a covering, shed.

छान/ना chhā:nnā: (*v*) to filter; to strain; to percolate; to sieve; to drink *bhang*; to screen; -फटक investigation; enquiry, sorting and sifting.

छानबीन chhā:nbi:n (*nf*) screening, investigation, scrutiny, probe.

छानबे chhā:nbe (*a* and *nm*) see छियानबे.

छाना chha:nā: (*v*) to cover, to thatch; to overwhelm, to shadow; to overspread; छा जाना to overwhelm, to dominate.

छाप chha:p (*nf*) a print, an imprint; impression; stamp; mark; trademark; brand; –छोड़ना to leave a mark, to impress.

छापना chha:pnā: (*v*) to print; to publish; to mark.

छापा chha:pa: (*nm*) an imprint; a stamp; raid; ~मार guerilla; a raider; ०युद्ध guerilla warfare; –मारना to (conduct a) raid.

छापाखाना chha:pa:kḥa:nā: (*nm*) a printing press.

छायांकन chha:ya:ṅkan (*nm*) photography.

छाया chha:ya: (*nf*) a shadow; shade; image; reflection; influence; resemblance; protection; phantom; adumbration; –और प्रकाश light and shade; ~कार photographer; -चित्र a silhouette; ~देह intangible form; ~नुवाद shadow translation, a translation carrying only an overall impression of the original; ~लोक abstract/unreal/intangible world; ~वाद a romantic movement in early modern Hindi poetry; –छूना to pursue the unreal; –की तरह साथ रहना to shadow constantly; –न छू पाना to be nowhere near, to be far behind in excellence; –से दूर रहना to keep away (from), to evade the shadow (of).

छायामय chha:ya:may (*a*) shadowy; shady.

छार chha:r (*nf*) ash; dust, powder; small fragments; -छार होना to be reduced to small fragments; –होना to be reduced to ashes; to be ruined.

छाल chha:l (*nf*) bark.

छाला chha:la: (*nm*) a blister, burn; **छाले पड़ना/होना** to have blisters.

छालिया chha:liya: (*nf*) betelnut, betelnut parings.

छाली chha:li: (*nf*) cream of boiled milk; betelnut or its parings.

छावनी chha:vnī: (*nf*) cantonment, temporary or permanent troop lodging.

छिंगुनी chhīgunī: (*nf*) see **छँगुनी**.

छिः-छिः chhih-chhih (*int*) fie !, pish !, tut ! (*nf*) infantile faeces.

छिछड़ा chhichhṛa: (*nm*) waste meat fragments, waste fibrous; fragments in a soup.

छिछला chhichhla: (*a*) shallow; **~पन** shallowness.

छिछोर/पन, ~पना chhichhorpān, ~panā: (*nm*) frivolity, triviality, pettiness.

छिछोरा chhichhora: (*a*) frivolous, trivial, petty; **~पन** see **छिछोरपन**.

छिटकना chhiṭaknā: (*v*) to be scattered; to be spread; to be diffused all round.

छिड़कना chhiṛaknā: (*v*) to sprinkle or spray; to water (by sprinkling); to asperse (with).

छिड़काव chhiṛka:v (*nm*) sprinkling or spraying; watering (by sprinkling); aspersing.

छिड़ना chhiṛnā: (*v*) to be commenced, to begin, to start; to break out (as **युद्ध**); to be teased/harassed.

छितराना chhitra:nā: (*v*) to disperse, to scatter; to be dispersed/scattered.

छितराव chhitra:v (*nm*) sparseness, diffusedness.

छिदना chhidnā: (*v*) to be pierced; to be perforated; to be bored.

छिदरा chhidra: (*a*) bored, perforated; thinned; **~ना** to be thinned; to be perforated.

छिद्र chhiddr (*nm*) pore; bore; slot, aperture, opening; defect, flaw; **~दर्शी** a fault-finder; fault-finding.

छिद्रान्वे/षण chhiddra:nnveshaṉ (*nm*) fault-finding; **~षी** a fault-finder; fault-finding; **~षण करना** to pick holes in, to find fault with.

छिद्रित chhiddrit (*a*) bored; perforated.

छिद्रिल chhiddril (*a*) having bores/perforation, perforated.

छिनकना chhinaknā: (*v*) to blow out the nose, to spurt mucus out of the nose.

छिनना chhinanā: (*v*) to be seized (from), to be wrested/snatched away.

छिनाल chhina:l (*a* and *nf*) sluttish; dissolute; a woman of easy virtue, trollop; hence **~पन** (*nm*).

छिनाला chhina:la: (*nm*) sluttishness, dissoluteness; immoral sex-indulgence.

छिन्न chhinn (*a*) incised; rent; cut off; chopped off; **-भिन्न** cut; broken; scattered, shattered; **~मूल** cut up from the root, uprooted.

छिपकली chhipkali: (*nf*) a lizard; a hateful creature.

छिपना chhipnā: (*v*) to hide, to lurk; to set; to be covered; **छिपा रुस्तम** a dark horse; pseudo-gentleman; **छिपे-छिपे** stealthily, clandestinely.

छिपाना chhipa:nā: (*v*) to hide, to conceal; to cover/screen; to disguise.

छिपाव chhipa:v (*nm*) concealment; secrecy; hiding; reservation.

छियानबे(वे) chhiyā:nbe(ve) (*a*) ninety-six; (*nm*) the number ninety-six.

छियालीस chhiya:li:s (*a*) forty-six; (*nm*) the number forty-six.

छियासी chhiya:si: (*a*) eighty-six; (*nm* the number eighty-six.

छिलका chhilka: (*nm*) the peel, ski husk; bark; shell.

छिलना chhilnā: (v) to be bruised or scratched; to be excoriated; to be peeled; the skin to be taken off.

छिलाई chhila:i: (nf) the act or process of excoriating/peeling/ taking off the skin; the charges paid therefor.

छिह(य)त्तर chhiha(ya)ttar (a) seventy-six; (nm) the number seventy-six.

छींक chhī:k (nf) a sneeze, sternutation; —होना occurrence of a sneeze (portending evil).

छींकना chhī:knā: (v) to sneeze, to sternutate; छींकते नाक कटना to be over-penalised for a petty fault.

छींका chhī:ka: (nm) a hanging pot-rest; —टूटना to have a windfall, to have an unexpected fortune.

छींट chhī:ṭ (nf) chintz.

छींटा chhī:ṭa: (nm) a sprinkle; splash; bespattering; slight shower (of rain); aspersion, ironical remark; ~कशी (casting of) aspersion, ironical utterance; —फेंकना to cast aspersion, to ridicule.

छी chhi: (int) fie !, pish!; tut!; (nf) infantile faeces; —छी करना to condemn; to express disgust or contempt; to discharge faeces (as by a child).

छीछालेद(दा)र chhi:chha:leda(da:)r (nf) humiliation; embarrassment; disgrace; muck; mess.

छीज chhi:j (nf) decay, wearing away; wastage; loss.

छीजन chhi:jān (nf) decay, wearing away; wastage; leakage, reduction; loss.

छीजना chhi:jnā: (v) to decay; to wear away; to dwindle, to reduce; to be wasted.

छीनना chhi:nnā: (v) to snatch, to grab, to seize; छीना-झपटी grabbing and scrambling, scramble.

छीलन chhi:lān (nm) scrappings; shavings; chippings.

छीलना chhi:lnā: (v) to scrap; to scratch; to shave; to chip; to peel; to take off the skin; to bruise.

छुआछूत chhua:chhu:t (nf) untouchability; consideration of touchability and untouchability.

छुईमुई chhui:mui: (nf) touch-me-not—Mimosa pudica; a kid-glove, an over-sensitive/over-dainty/over-delicate person.

छुट chhuṭ—an allomorph of छोटा used as the first member in several compound words; ~पन (~पना) smallness, pettiness; boyhood, childhood; young age; ~पुट stray; minor; ~भैया a petty person, jackstraw.

छुटकारा chhuṭka:ra: (nm) riddance; acquittal, release, liberation.

छुटाई chhuṭa:i: (nf) see छोटाई.

छुटौती chhuṭauti: (nf) a ransom.

छुट्टा chhuṭṭa: (a) loose. not tied, not in a lump or group or company etc.; free; in small denomination (change etc); (nm) small change.

छुट्टी chhuṭṭi: (nf) leave; holiday; release; permission to leave; —करना to call it a day; to dismiss (from service etc); to destroy; —मनाना to celebrate a holiday.

छुड़ाई chhuṛa:i: (nf) release; a ransom.

छुड़ाना chhuṛa:nā: (v) to get released; to cause to set free; to cause to give up; to take delivery; to discharge; to remove.

छुतहा chhutaha: (a) contagious, carrying contagion; —अस्पताल contagious diseases hospital; —रोग a contagious disease.

छुरा chhura: (nm) a razor; dagger; छुरेबाज़ी infliction or exchange of dagger-blow(s).

छुरी chhuri: (nf) a knife; small

ıagger; -कटारी रहना या होना to be ıt dagger's drawn; -चलाना to ɪpeak daggers; to inflict blows; -तेज़ करना to sharpen the knife; o get ready to strike; -फेरना to ːut with a dagger.

ुारा chhuha:ra: (*nm*) a date-palm.

छा chhū:chha: (*a*) empty; unsubs-antial; -पड़ना to prove ineffec-ive; to grow ineffectual.

chhu: (*nf*) sudden outblow of ı gush of air from the mouth (as luring incantation, conjuration, ːnchantment, magic, etc); ~मंतर ın incantation; a charm; hey ɔresto !; -करना to exorcise, to ɔronounce an incantation and ɔlow upon; to cause to disappear, o vanish; -बनना to disappear, to vanish (said of animate objects); ~मंतर होना (said of person, pain, ːtc.) to disappear forthwith, to vanish.

ट chhu:ṭ (*nf*) rebate, discount; llowance; concession; riddance; ·elease; remission; exemption; ·elaxation; liberty.

टना chhu:ṭnā: (*v*) to be left behind ɔr out; to lag; to be dismissed/ lischarged or released; to get rid ɔf; to be abandoned; छूटा (हुआ) साँड़ lit. a freely moving bull—a ·obust carefree man without ːncumbrances.

त chhu:t (*nf*) contagion; conta-mination; -की बीमारी contagious lisease.

ना chhu:nā: (*v*) to touch; to feel.

कना chheknā: (*v*) to discriminate ıgainst; to leave out; to obstruct.

कानुप्रास chheka:nuppra:s (*nm*) ːompound alliteration.

ड़ chheṛ (*nf*) teasing, offending; ɔricks, pranks.

ड़खानी chheṛkḫa:nɪ: (*nf*) act of teasing or provoking; offensive activity; raillery; pranks.

छेड़छाड़ chheṛchha:ṛ (*nf*) provoca-tion; molestation; teasing; pricks and pranks.

छेड़ना chheṛnā: (*v*) to tease, to irri-tate; to meddle; to disturb, to stir up; to commence (a work).

छेद chhed (*nm*) a hole, bore; per-foration; opening; incision, punc-ture; ~दार perforated; bored; hav-ing hole(s)/opening(s).

छेदना chhednā: (*v*) to bore, to make a hole; to perforate, to pierce; to incise.

छेना chhenā: (*nm*) a kind of cheese.

छेनी chhenɪ: (*nm*) a chisel.

छैल chhail—an allomorph of छैला (see).

छैला chhaila: (*nm*) a dandy, foppish person; (*a*) dandical, foppish; also छैल-चिकनिया; छैल-छबीला; hence ~पन (*nm*).

छोकरा chhokra: (*nm*) a lad, boy.

छोटा chhoṭa: (*a*) small; little; short; young(er); petty; subordinate; junior; insignificant; -आदमी a small man, petty person; common man; ~पन smallness, pettiness; -बड़ा young and old; rich and poor; -मोटा petty, minor, insignificant, ordinary; -गिनना to consider as insignificant, to consider to be of no consequence; -बनाना to humi-liate, to debase; -मुँह बड़ी बात proud words from a week stomach; छोटे से ही सब बड़े होते हैं lads will be men.

छोटाई chhoṭa:i: (*nf*) smallness, pettiness; shortness; juniority.

छोटी chhoṭi: (*a*) feminine form of छोटा; -जाति low(er) cast; -बात petty utterance; petty matter; -हाजिरी breakfast.

छोड़ना chhoṛnā: (*v*) to leave; to abandon; to omit; to release; to entrust to; to assign to (as किसी पर); छोड़ने जाना to go to see off.

छोर chhor (*nm*) the end, fag end; extremity; edge.

छोरा chhora: (*nm*) a lad.

छोलदारी chholda:ri: (*nf*) a small tent.

छोह chhoh (*nf*) affection; compassion.

छौंक chhau̅k (*nf*) seasoning (pu vegetable, etc.) with boiled gh oil and spices; –भी न होना to utterly insufficient/inadequate.

छौंकना chhau̅knā: (*v*) to season (छौंक).

छौना chhaunā: (*nm*) a young on

ज ja—the third letter of the second pentad (i.e. चवर्ग) of the Devna:gri: alphabet; a suffix denoting the sense of born of (as जलज, अंडज, वातज, etc.).

जंकशन jaṅkshān (*nm*) a (railway) junction.

जंग jaṅg (*nf*) a war, battle, fight; ~बाज a war-monger; ~बाजी war-mongering.

जंग zaṅg (*nm*) rust; ~दार rusted, rust-eaten; –लगना to get rusted, to be eaten up by rust; to turn in-effective (by disuse).

जंगम jaṅgām (*a*) moving; movable; –संपत्ति movable property.

जंगल jaṅgal (*nm*) a forest, wood; wilderness; –में मंगल a paradise in wilderness; –में मोर नाचा किसने देखा wood in a wilderness, moss in a mountain and wit in a poor man's breast are little thought of.

जं(जँ)गला jaṅ(jā)gla: (*nm*) grating; railing; fence/fencing; balustrade; a grille or bar-fitted window.

जंगली jaṅgli: (*a*) savage; wild; beastly: –जानवर a wild beast; savage.

जंगी jaṅgi: (*a*) martial, relating war; huge, large; –जवान a gigar youngman; –जहाज a man of w battleship; –बेड़ा a naval fle –लाट commander-in-chief (un British rule).

जंघा jaṅgha: (*nf*) a thigh.

जँचना jāchnā: (*v*) to be examined be valued; to appeal; to lo attractive/befitting.

जंजाल jan̤ja:l (*nm*) botheration; e anglement; embarrassment; car trouble; fuss;(*nf*) a small cann

जंजाली jan̤ja:li: (*a*) fussy; troub some, occasioning botheration.

जंजीर zanji:r (*nf*) a chain; shack

जंतर jantar (*nm*) an amulet, philt -मंतर an observatory; witchcra conjuring

जंतरी jantri: (*nf*) an almanac.

जंतु jantu (*nm*) a creature, an anim

जंबुद्वीप jambudwi:p (*nm*) the na of one of the seven ancient con nental divisions of the world; central part of the above divisi including India. [According some it is an ancient name

India].

बूर jambu:r (*nm*) pliers.

बूरा jambu:ra: (*nm*) claw bar, pliers.

भाई jābha:i: (*nf*) yawning, a yawn; –लेना to yawn.

भाना jābha:nā: (*v*) to yawn.

ई jai: (*nf*) oat; new shoots of barley.

ई/फ़ zai:f (*a*) old; weak, infirm; ~फ़ी senility; weakness; infirmity.

क jak (*nf*) obstinacy; mania, incessant insistence.

कड़ jakaṛ (*nf*) grip, tight grasp, firm hold; ~न inflexibility, immobility; ~बंदी firm hold.

कड़ना jakaṛnā: (*v*) to grasp, to hold firmly; to tighten.

कात jaka:t (*nf*) octroi, octroi-duty; ~घर octroi post; जकाती octroi collector.

का/र jaka:r (*nm*) the letter ज (ja) and its sound; ~रांत (a word) ending in ज् (j).

ख़ी/रा zakḥi:ra: (*nm*) stock, store; hoard; ~रेबाज a hoarder; ~रेबाज़ी hoarding.

ख़्म zakḥm (*nm*) a wound, cut, injury; ulcer; -ए-जिगर an emotional wound; –ताजा/हरा होना an old wound to be revived; –पर नमक़ छिड़कना to afflict the afflicted; to add insult to injury.

ख़्मी zakḥmı: (*a*) wounded, hurt, injured.

जग jag (*nm*) the world, universe; people; ~प्रसिद्ध world renowned: ~बीती others' tales/experiences; ~हँसाई popular ridicule/mockery; open calumny.

जगजगाना jagjaga:nā: (*v*) see जगमगाना.

जगत jagat (*nm*) the world, universe; (*nf*) a raised circular curb (around a well); ~गुरू (जगद्गुरू) a title of certain Hindu scholarly priests (4 in number); preceptor of the universe; ~पति master of the universe–God; ~पिता Creator of the universe; ~प्रसिद्ध world renowned, of world fame.

जगती jagti: (*nf*) the world; earth; mankind.

जगदीश jagdi:sh (*nm*) the Lord of the World, Lord Vishṉū.

जगदीश्वर jagdi:shvar (*nm*) see जगदीश.

जगना jagnā: (*v*) to wake up, to awaken; to be aroused.

जगन्नियंता jagānnıyānta: (*nm*) the Almighty, the Controller of the world.

जगमग jagmag (*a*) refulgent, shining, glittering, glimmering; also जगजग

जगमगाना jagmaga:nā: (*v*) to be refulgent, to glitter, to shine, to gleam.

जगमगाहट jagmaga:haṭ (*nf*) refulgence, glitter, shine, gleam, glimmer.

जगर-मगर jagar-magar (*a*) see जगमग.

जगराता jagra:ta: (*nm*) see रत(~जगा)

जगह jageh (*nf*) place; space, quarter; post; -जगह everywhere.

जगात jaga:t (*nf*) see जकात.

जगाना jaga:nā: (*v*) to wake up, to awaken; to arouse.

जगार jaga:r (*nf*) wake; state of being or keeping awake.

जघन्य jaghānny (*a*) low; detestable, abominable; heinous; hence ~ता (*nf*).

जच्चा zachcha: (*nf*) a woman in post-delivery confinement; ~ख़ाना/घर maternity home; -बच्चा the new-born and the mother in confinement.

ज/ज jaj (*nm*) a judge; ~जी a judge's court; judgeship; the post or function of a judge.

जजमा/न jajmā:n (*nm*) see यजमान; ~नी see यजमानी.

जज़िया jaziya: (*nm*) a levy imposed

by Emperor Aurangzeb on the non-Muslims.

जज़ीरा jazi:ra: (*nm*) an island.

जज़्ब jazb (*a*) absorbed; assimilated.

जज़्बा jazba: (*nm*) an emotion, feeling; passion; (~त plural); ~ती emotional; **जज़्बात को भड़काना** to fan the flame of passion, to blow the coals.

जटा jaṭa: (*nf*) mated or tangled hair; fibrous root; ~**जूट** matted hair rolled up over the head; ~**धारी** wearing matted hair rolled up; an ascetic.

जटित jaṭit (*a*) studded, imbedded with.

जटिल jaṭil (*a*) intricate, complicated; inaccessible; ~**ता** intricacy, complication.

जठ/र jaṭhar (*nm*) the stomach; ~**राग्नि** digestive fire of the stomach; ~**रानल** same as **जठराग्नि**.

जड़ jaṛ (*nf*) root; (*a*) inanimate, immovable, inert; idiot, stupid; **-चेतन** the animate and the inanimate; **—जगत** the inanimate world; **—पदार्थ** matter; ~**बुद्धि/मति** idiot; stupid; ~**बुद्धिता** idiocy; ~**वाद/**~**वादिता** materialism; ~**वादी** a materialist; materialistic; **—उखाड़ना** to root out, to strike at the root; to destroy completely; **—काट कर तने को पानी देना** to cut the root and water the leaves; **—काटना/खोदना** to undermine, to eat into the vitals of; to inflict heavy damage; **—जमना/पकड़ना** to strike deep roots; to establish; to consolidate (oneself); **-पेड़/मूल से** root and branch; thoroughly; **—हिला देना** to cause a thorough shake-up, to shake the foundation (of).

जड़त jaṛat (*nf*) inlay, insetting.

जड़ता jaṛta: (*nf*) inertia, torpor; insensibility; idiocy, stupidity; stupefaction.

जड़त्व jaṛattv (*nm*) see **जड़ता**.

जड़ना jaṛnā: (*v*) to stud; to inlay; to fix, to set; to mount (as a **तसवीर**); to put in; to lay on (as **तमाचा**).

जड़ाई jaṛa:i: (*nf*) the act or process of setting/inlaying; the wages or charges paid for setting/inlaying.

जड़ाऊ jaṛa:u: (*a*) studded or inset with jewels.

जड़ात्मवा/द jaṛa:tmva:d (*nm*) animism; ~**दी** an animist; animistic.

जड़ावर jaṛa:war (*nf*) warm clothings.

जड़िमा jaṛimā: (*nf*) stupor, torpor; insensibility; stupidity.

जड़िया jaṛiya: (*nm*) a setter (of jewels etc.); an expert in insetting.

जड़ी jaṛi: (*nf*) a simple, medicinal root; **-बूटी** medicinal herbs, simples.

जड़ीभूत jaṛi:bhu:t (*a*) stupefied, rendered inert and inactive.

जताना jata:nā: (*v*) to apprise, to make known; to warn.

जत्था jattha: (*nm*) a band; gang; flock; ~**बंदी** formation into groups or bands; **जत्थेदार** a group-leader (amongst sikhs).

ज़द zad (*nf*) striking range, range.

ज़दा zada: —a suffix used to mean afflicted by (as **ग़मज़दा, मुसीबतज़दा**).

जद्दोजहद jaddojehad (*nf*) struggle, hard endeavour.

जन jān (*nm*) people; public; folk; **-आंदोलन** popular movement; ~**गणना** census; **-जन** each and every person; **-जागरण** renaissance, popular awakening; ~**जीवन** public life; public living; ~**तंत्र** democracy; ~**तंत्रवाद** democracy; ~**तंत्रीय** democratic(al); ~**तांत्रिक** democratic(al); **-धन** men and money; ~**पद** rural region; ~**पदीय** regional; **-प्रवाद** popular/public rumour; ~**प्रिय** popular; ~**मत**

public opinion; ०संग्रह referendum; plebiscite; -मन/मानस popular mind, people's mind; ~रंजन popular, pleasing to the people, of popular gratification; ~वासा a temporary dwelling for a marriage party; ~शक्ति manpower; ~श्रुति tradition; rumour; ~संख्या population; ~समाज community at large; ~समुदाय crowd; community; ~समूह crowd; ~साधारण the common man; community at large; the masses; -सेवक public man; public servant; ~सेवा public service; ~हित public welfare/interest; ~हीन desolate; uninhabited; secluded, lonely.

न zan (*nf*) a woman; a suffix meaning one or that which inflicts or strikes (as राहज़न — one who strikes on the way i.e. one who waylays).

नक janāk (*nm*) father; procreator, originator; used as a suffix to mean causing or bringing forth (as खेदजनक, निराशाजनक).

नख़ा zankha: (*nm*) a eunuch, womanly man.

न/जाति janja:ti (*nf*) a tribe; ~जातीय tribal.

नता janta: (*nm*) the public, people, masses; -जनार्दन the people symbolising God.

नन janān (*nm*) procreation, procreating; generation, generating; production, producing; -क्षमता potency, generating/productive/procreative power.

नना jannā: (*v*) to (re)produce; to give birth (to), to bear.

ननायक janna:yak (*nm*) a popular hero, leader of the people.

ननी janni: (*nf*) mother, progenitrix.

ननेंद्रिय jananēndriy (*nf*) sex organ, genitals.

जनवरी janwari: (*nf*) (the month of) January.

जनांतिक janā:ntik (*nm*) aside (in a drama).

जना jana: (*a*) produced; procreated: (*nm*) person, individual (as कितने जने आयेंगे ?).

जनाकीर्ण jana:ki:rn̲ (*a*) crowded; thickly populated; hence ~ता (*nf*).

जनाज़ा jana:za: (*nm*) the corpse wrapped in a coffin-cloth; bier (with the corpse laid on it).

ज़नानख़ाना zanā:nkh̲a:nā: (*nm*) the harem, seraglio; zenana, female apartment.

ज़नाना zana:nā: (*a*) female, feminine; impotent; (*nm*) female apartment; a eunuch; ~पन effeminacy; impotence; hence ज़नानी; –राज petticoat rule/government.

जनाब jana:b (*a* and *nm*) mister; (*int*) Sir !, Your Excellency !; –आली Sir, Your Honour !, Your Excellency !; जनाबे मन Sir, respected Sir!

जनित janit (*a*) produced/generated (by); caused (by), procreated (by).

जनेऊ janeu: (*nm*) the sacred or sacrificial thread worn by the Hindu:s.

जनोपयोगी janopyogi: (*a*) of public utility; –सेवाएँ public utility services.

जन्नत jannāt (*nf*) paradise, heaven; –की हूर a celestial damsel/beauty.

जन्म janm (*nm*) birth; origin; genesis; ~कुंडली a short horoscope; ~गत by or relating to birth; innate; inborn; ~तिथि date of birth; ~दाता progenitor; father; originator; -दर birth-rate; -दिन/दिवस birth-day; ~नाम christian name; ~पत्र/पत्रिका/पत्री a horoscope; ~भूमि motherland; -मरण birth and death; ~स्थान birth-place; –गँवाना to waste one's life.

जन्मजात janmāja:t (*a*) congenital; inherent, innate.

जन्मना janmanā: (*ind*) by birth; (*v*) to be born.

जन्मांतर janmā:ntar (*nm*) another birth; ~**वाद** doctrine of rebirth; hence ~**वादी** (*a* and *nm*).

जन्मांध janmā:ndh (*a*) blind since birth, born blind; hence ~**ता** (*nf*).

जन्माष्टमी janmā:shṭmi: (*nf*) the eighth day of the dark half of the month of **भादों** when Lord Krinhṉā is supposed to have been born.

जन्मोत्तर janmottar (*a*) post-natal, after birth.

जन्मोत्सव janmotsav (*nm*) birth-day celebration

जन्य janny (*a*) born, produced/generated; used as a suffix meaning —generated by or born of (as **युद्ध-जन्य, परिस्थितिजन्य**).

जप jap (*nm*) adoration by way of repeating passages from scriptures, sacred formulae or a deity's name, etc.; -**तप** worship, adoration; devotion; ~**माला** a rosary.

जप/ना japnā: (*v*) to murmur or to utter quiet prayers; to repeat reverentially (God's name as a sacred formula); ~**नीय** worth repeating by way of adoration.

जपित japit (*a*) whispered (sound).

जफ़ा jafa: (*nf*) excess; tyranny.

जब jab (*adv*) when; —**कभी** whenever; sometimes; ~**कि** when; whenever, at whatever time; -**तब** sometime; at times; imminent; —**अपनी उतरी तो दूसरे की उतारते क्या देर ?** beware of him who regards not his reputation; —**उतर गई लोई तो क्या करेगा कोई** the shameless dread no society; —**तक गंगा (जमना) को धारा बहती है** as long as the Ganges (and the Jamuna) flows (flow), for all times to come —**तक जहरमुहरा आएगा, सांप का काटा मर जाएगा** the steed will die till the grass grows; —**तक सांस तब तक आस** as long as there is life there is hope.

जबड़ा jabṛa: (*nm*) a jaw; ~**तोड़** jaw breaking; a jaw-breaker (said of a word difficult to pronounce).

जबर zabar (*a*) strong; huge; —**मारे और रोने न दे** the mighty hits and permits no bewailing.

जबरद/स्त zabardast (*a*) strong, powerful; vigorous, violent; high-handed; ~**स्ती** high-handedness injustice; by force, forcibly.

जबरन zabrān (*adv*) by force, forcibly.

जबह zabeh (*nm*) slaughtering, slaughter; —**करना** to slaughter.

जबान zabā:n (*nf*) tongue; language ~**दराज** loquacious, sharp-tongued ~**दराजी** loquaciousness, wagging of one's tongue; ~**दाँ** expert of a language; ~**दानी** linguistic expertise; —**का कडुआ(वा)** bitter-tongued; —**का तेज़** sharp-tongued; —**का मीठा** honey-tongued; sweet-tongued —**का शेर** bold only in speech; —**के नीचे जबान होना** to be double-tongued; —**काँटा होना** the tongue to become senseless through thirst, to be very thirsty; —**काटना** to express a sense of surprise/repentance (through holding the tongue between the teeth); to render mute, speechless; —**कैंची-सी चलना** the tongue to run on wheels; to talk nineteen to the dozen; —**को लगाम जरूरी है** a bridle for the tongue is a necessary piece of furniture; —**को लगाम देना** to stop one's gab, to hold one's tongue; —**खल्क नक़्क़ारे ख़ुदा** public voice is God's voice —**खींचना** to pull out somebody's tongue (said as a threat of punishment); to quieten; –खुलना to find one's tongue; to speak out; to talk with one's tongue in one's cheek; –खोलना to speak out; –चलना to have a fluent tongue; to have an impudent tongue; –चलाना to wag one's tongue, to be too talkative; –डालना to interfere by speech; to dishonour one's word; –तलवार से ज़्यादा तेज़ होती है the tongue cuts deeper than steel; –थामना to hold the tongue; –दबाकर कहना to utter in whispers; to say implicitly; –दिखाना to put out the tongue; –देना to pledge one's word (to), to make a commitment; –न होना, मुँह में to be too meek to speak, to be very reticent; –निकालना to pull out the tongue of (said of a threat of punishment); –पकड़ना to cavil (at); to hush up; –पर आना to be on tongue's the tip; to be on the verge of speaking out; –पर चढ़ना to be on the tongue (of), to be subject of talk; to be on the tip of one's tongue, to have or know a thing by heart; –पर मुहर होना not to be in a state to speak out, to be speechless; –पर लाना to utter; to mention; –पलटना to go back on one's word; –पर (में) ताला लगना to be stricken dumb, to be rendered speechless; –पर होना to be on the tip of the tongue; to be a subject of talk; –बंद करना to silence, to render speechless; –बंद होना to be tongue-tied; to be cornered (in an argument); –बदलना see –पलटना; –बिगड़ना to become abusive-tongued/scurrilous; to become subservient to tongue-tastes; –बुरी होना to be ill-tongued; –मुँह में रखना to hold one's tongue; –में खुजली होना to feel like quarrelling; –में लगाम न होना to lose control on one's tongue; not to have a civil tongue in one's head; –लड़ाना to enter into argument, to contort verbally; –सँभाल कर बोलना to keep a civil tongue in one's head; –सँभालना to hold one's tongue; –हारना to be committed: to have pledged one's word –हिलाना to speak out, to make an utterance.

ज़बानी zaba:nı: (*a*) oral, verbal; unwritten; (*adv*) orally, verbally; –जमा-खर्च sweet nothings, superficial utterances; tall talk.

ज़ब्त zabt (*a*) forfeited, confiscated, impounded; (*nm*) forbearance, restraint; ~शुदा forfeited, confiscated; ज़ब्ती confiscation, forfeiture; –करना to exercise restraint; to confiscate.

जमघट jamghaṭ (*nm*) crowded assembly; multitude.

जमना jamnā: (*v*) to freeze; to solidify, to become firm or hard; to clot; to be established/settled; to settle; to have a prolonged sitting, to sit for long; to be fixed; to take root; to be effective; (*nf*) the river यमुना; जमे रहना to nail colours to mast, to refuse to climb down, to stick to one's guns.

जमा jamā: (*a*) collected, deposited; (*nm*) deposit; credit; accumulation; sum-total; -खर्च debit and credit; receipts and disbursements; ~ख़ातिर reassurance; ०रखना to rest assured; -जथा accumulations, accumulated wealth; -पूँजी total accumulation; ~मार one who misappropriates; a bad debtor; dishonest; -खर्च करना to account for debts and credits; to prepare the accounts; –मारना to misappropriate.

जमाई jama:i: (*nm*) a son-in-law;–राजा

a son-in-law (said in affection).

जमात jamā:t (*nf*) a class (in a school), assembly; group.

जमादा/र jamā:da:r (*nm*) a jamadar, head of a group; sweeper; ~री profession of a jamadar; acting as head of a group.

ज़मानत zamā:nāt (*nf*) surety; bail; security; guarantee; ~दार a guarantor, surety; ~नामा surety-bond.

ज़मानती zamā:nati: (*a*) bailable; guaranteeing; (*nm*) a surety, guarantor.

जमाना jamā:nā: (*v*) transitive verbal form of जमना (see).

ज़माना zamā:na: (*nm*) time(s), age, period; present-day world; fortunate times; ~साज़ a temporizer; time-server; ~साज़ी temporization; time-serving mentality; –उलटना times to turn radically, a perverted era to dawn; –छानना to make a thorough search; –देखना to acquire wide experience; –देखे होना to be widely experienced; to have undergone all sorts of experiences; –पलटना/बदलना the tide to take a turn; –बीत जाना/लद जाना good old days to be over, the golden times to be past; ज़माने का मारा हुआ beaten in the struggle of life, done for; ज़माने का रुख देखना to have/keep an ear to the ground, to watch which way the wind blows; ज़माने की गर्दिश temporal vicissitudes; ज़माने की हवा लगना to be affected by the (changing) times, to adopt (oneself) according to the wind of times; –के साथ क़दम मिलाकर चलना to go with the tide/times.

जमाल jama:l (*nm*) glory; elegance, prettiness.

जमालगोटा jama:lgoṭa: (*nm*) a purgative nut—*Croten tiglium.*

जमाव jama:v (*nm*) assembly, gathering; setting up, concentration; accumulation.

जमावड़ा jama:vṛa: (*nm*) assembly, gathering; concentration; accumulation.

ज़मीं zamı: (*nf*) see ज़मीन.

ज़मींकंद zamı:kānd (*nm*) a vegetable—elephant's foot.

ज़मींदार zamı:da:r (*nm*) a landlord; cultivator.

ज़मींदारी jamı:da:ri: (*nf*) zamindari, landlordism; landed estate; cultivation.

ज़मींदोज़ zamı:doz (*a*) subterranean, subearthen.

ज़मीन zamı:n (*nf*) the earth; land, ground; ground work; background; -आसमान एक करना to leave no stone unturned, to make all possible efforts; -आसमान का फ़र्क as wide asunder as heaven and earth, world of/fundamental difference; -आसमान के कुलाबे मिलाना to speak of heaven and earth in one breath; to speak in hyperboles; to try one's level best; –का पाँव तले से खिसक जाना to be stunned out of wits; –चटाना/दिखाना to fell/throw flat; –चूमना to lie prostrate; to be felled by face; –तैयार करना to prepare the ground (for); –नापना to wander in search of employment; –पर पाँव/पैर न पड़ना to feel inflated, to be puffed up with pride; –में गड़ जाना to be bashfully embarrassed, to be deeply ashamed/sheepish.

ज़मीर zami:r (*nm*) the conscience; inner self; ~फ़रोश conscience-seller; hence ~फ़रोशी (*nf*).

जमुना jamunā. (*nf*) the river *yamuna:.*

जम्हाई jamha:i: (*nf*) yawning; -लेना to yawn.

जम्हाना jamhā:nā: (*v*) to yawn.

जयंती jayānti: (*nf*) (birth) anniversary; jubilee.

जय jay (*nf*) conquest, victory; triumph; (*a*) used as a suffix in compound words meaning, one who has achieved a victory or has triumphed over (e.g. **मृत्युंजय, धनंजय,** etc). (*int*) bravo ! hurrah ! ; ~**घोष** applause, applausive shouts, cheering approbation; ~**ध्वज** banner of victory; ~**ध्वनि** see ~**घोष**; -**पराजय** victory and defeat; ~**माल/माला** a bay, garland symbolic of triumph; garland put by the bride round the neck of the bridegroom; ~**लक्ष्मी/श्री** victory.

जयकार jayka:r (*nm*) applause, applausive shouts, cheers hailing victory.

जयजयकार jayjayka:r (*nf*) triumphal cheers, applausive shouts, applause hailing a victory.

जयिष्णु jayishnū (*a*) one who conquers/achieves victory, ever-victorious.

जयी jayi: (*a*) winner, victorious; (*nm*) a conqueror.

ज़र zar (*nm*) wealth, riches, gold; ~**ख़रीद** purchased, bought; ~**ख़ेज़** fertile; ~**ख़ेज़ी** fertility; ~**दोज़** embroidered (with gold); ~**दोज़ी** (golden) embroidery.

ज़रदा zarda: (*nm*) scented and specially prepared tobacoo; a special dish of rice treated with saffron.

ज़रदुश्त zardusht (*nm*) the founder of the fire-worshipping 'Pa:rasi:' religion and author of the scripture 'Zend Avesta'.

जरनैल jarnail (*nm*) a generla.

ज़रब zarab (*nm*) trauma; blow; stroke; crack; multiplication; -**तकसीम** multiplication and division; –**आना** to develop a crack, to be injured; –**देना** to inflict a blow/stroke; to multiply.

जरसी jarsi: (*nf*) a jersey.

जरा jara: (*nf*) old age, senility; ~**ग्रस्त** aged, decrepit; ~**जीर्ण** age-worn, decrepit.

ज़रा zara: (*a*) a little, a bit, slight; (*adv*) for a while; slightly; just (as –**ठहरो** just wait); please, kindly (as –**मेरे साथ चलो**); -**ज़रा** in bits; petty, trivial; -**ज़रा-सी बात पर तुनक उठने वाला** like a hen with one chicken, absurdly fussy; -**सा** some; small, a small quantity.

जरायमपेशा jara:yāmpesha: (*a*) criminal, of criminal profession; –**कबीला** a criminal tribe.

जरायु jara:yu (*nm*) placenta; ~**ज** placental.

जरासीम jara:si:m (*nm*) germs.

ज़रि/या zariya: (*nm*) means; medium, instrument; ~**ये**, **के** through, through the agency of.

ज़रीया zari:ya: (*nm*) see **ज़रिया**.

ज़री zari: (*nf*) gold brocade, gold lace.

जरीब jari:b (*nm*) a land-measuring chain.

ज़रूर zaru:r (*adv*) certainly, undoubtedly, positively; without fail; -**ज़रूर** positively; without fail.

ज़रूरत zaru:rat (*nf*) necessity, importance; need, requirement; ~**न** because of a need; ~**मंद** needy.

ज़रूरियात zaru:riya:t (*nf*) necessities; requirements, needs.

ज़रूरी zaru:ri: (*a*) important; necessary, needful; compulsory; indispensable.

ज़र्क-बर्क़ zark-barq (*a*) brilliant, gaudy, gaudily made-up; (*nf*) brilliance, gaudiness.

जर्ज/र jarjar (*a*) decrepit, worn out; crushed, senescent; ~**रता** senescence, decrepitude; ~**रित** worn out; decrepit crushed, decayed;

~रीभूत worn out, crushed, decrepit.

ज़र्द zard (*a*) pale, yellow; –पड़ना to turn pale, to be off colour; to become anaemic.

ज़र्दा zarda: (*nm*) see ज़रदा.

ज़र्दी zardi: (*nf*) paleness, yellowness; the yellow (part).

जर्मन सिल्वर jarmān silvar (*nm*) an alloy used for making utensils.

ज़र्रा zarra: (*nm*) an atom; a particle: -ज़र्रा each and every particle; –भर a minute particle; a very small quantity; insignificantly small.

जर्रा/ह jarra:h (*nm*) a (traditionally trained) surgeon, one who dresses wounds; ~ही surgery, dressing of wounds.

जल jal (*nm*) water, aqua; hydro-; -अपघटन hydrolysis; ~कपाट sluice; ~कर water-tax; ~कल a water pipe; °विभाग waterworks; ~कुंभी a typical water plant; ~कुक्कुट a water-fowl; ~कूप a water-well; ~कृषि water-culture; ~केलि water-gambol, aquatic sport; ~घड़ी a water-clock; ~चर/चारी aquatic (animal, etc.); -चादर a sheet of water; -जंतु aquatic creatures; ~ज/जात aqueous; lotus; ~डमरूमध्य a strait; -त्रास hydrophobia; -थल water and land; °एक होना a deluge to set in, water to submerge all visible land; ~द a cloud; ~दस्यु a pirate; ~धर a cloud; ~धारा a water current; ~धि an ocean; ~पत्ती a water-cress; ~पथ waterways; -परी a siren, mermaid; -प्रपात a watefall, cataract; -प्रलय cataclysm, deluge; -प्रवाह a torrent/current of water; -प्लावन inundation; -भीति hydrophobia; -मंडल hydrosphere; ~मग्न submerged by or immersed under water; ~मय submerged in water; watery, hydrous; ~मार्ग channel, waterways; water-course; -यात्रा a voyage; ~यान a ship, vessel; boat; -युद्ध naval war; ~राशि body or accumulation of water; ~लेख hydrography; -विज्ञान/विद्या hydrology; ~विद्युत hydro-electric; -संत्रास hydrophobia; -संधि a strait; -समाधि watery grave, to go deep into water for ending up one's life; ~सर्वेक्षण hydrography; ~सह waterproof; -सेना the navy, naval force; -स्तंभ a column of water; lighthouse; -स्तंभन the skill of keeping under water for prolonged spells; -स्तर water level; ~स्थल land and water; ~स्थलीय amphibious; -स्रोत source of water; water current; ~हीन water-free; without water; जलाक्रांत waterlogged; जलागार a reservoir; –बिनु मीन a fish out of water.

जलज़ला zalzala: (*nm*) an earthquake.

जलन jalān (*nf*) a burning sensation; jealousy.

जल/ना jalnā: (*v*) to burn; to be inflamed/kindled; to be scorched; to feel jealous, to envy; –कर out of jealousy, inspired by jealousy; -भुनकर कबाब/कोयला/ख़ाक/राख होना to burn with rage or envy; –मरना to burn oneself out of jealousy; to immolate oneself; ~ती आग में कूदना to knowingly burn one's fingers; ~ती आग में घी/तेल डालना to add fuel to the fire, to fan the flame; जला कर राख कर देना to lay to the ashes; जला-जलाकर मारना to inflict a slow painful death, to tease to death; जला-भुना fretting and fuming; जली-कटी सुनाना to make caustic and stinging remarks; जले को जलाना to insult the already afflicted; जले पर नमक छिड़कना to add insult to injury; जले फफोले

फोड़ना to give vent to one's accumulated rage; to burst forth with invectives.

जलपान jalpā:n (*nm*) light refreshment; breakfast; at home; -गृह a refreshment room.

जलवायु jalva:yu (*nf*) climate; ~विज्ञान climatology; ~वैज्ञानिक a climatologist.

जलसा jalsa: (*nm*) a meeting, function; festivity; social gathering; –, आम a public meeting.

जलाना jala:nā: (*v*) to light, to kindle; to burn, to scorch; to excite envy, to provoke jealousy.

जलार्णव jala:rn̲av (*nm*) an ocean.

जलाल jala:l (*nm*) glory, splendour; pre-eminence; awe, awefulness.

ज़लालत zala:lat (*nf*) meanness, wretchedness; disgrace.

जलावत/न jala:vatān (*nm*) exile; (*a*) exiled; ~नी exile.

जलावन jala:van (*nm*) fuel.

जलावर्त jala:vartt (*nm*) a whirlpool.

जलाशय jala:shay (*nm*) a reservoir; a body of water.

ज़लील zali:l (*a*) mean, wretched, contemptible; disgraced, insulted; –करना to crop one's feathers, to humiliate.

जलूस jalu:s (*nm*) a procession; –निकालना to take out (in) a procession.

जलेबी jalebi: (*nf*) a kind of sweetmeat; a kind of firework that shoots up like spiral.

जलोढ़ jalor̤h (*a*) alluvial; –मिट्टी alluvial soil.

जलोढ़क jalor̤hak (*nm*) alluvium.

जलोदर jalodar (*nm*) dropsy, ascites.

जलौका jalauka: (*nf*) see जोंक.

जल्द jald (*adv*) quickly; swiftly; hurriedly; instantly; ~बाज़ hasty, impetuous; rash; a tear-away; ~बाज़ी hastiness, impetuousity, rashness; --में सौदा करना to clap up a bargain.

जल्दी jaldi: (*nf*) hurry, haste; (*adv*) quickly, urgently, immediately; –का काम शैतान का haste makes waste.

जल्प jalp (*nm*) sophistry.

जल्लाद jalla:d (*nm*) a slaughterer; butcher; (*a*) cruel or merciless (person).

जवाँ javā: (*a*) young, youthful; an allomorph of जवान used as the first member in some compound words; ~मर्द heroic; gallant; manly; ~मर्दी heroism, bravery; manliness, gallantry.

जवान jawā:n (*a*) young/youthful; (*nm*) a youth; soldier.

जवानी java:nı: (*nf*) youth, young age, youthfulness; –उतरना/ढलना youth to be on the decline; to age; –का आलम the time of youthful frolic or adventure; –की नींद uninterrupted carefree sleep; –चढ़ना youth to make appearance, youth to be on the ascendance; to be affected by youthful lust; –दीवानी है youth knows no bounds; –फट पड़ना youthfulness to make appearance all over, youth to be in its fullest bloom; –में माँझा ढीला young age, old ways; what is youth but its vitality and vigour.

जवाब java:b (*nm*) reply, answer; response; counter-move; ~तलब करना to call for an explanation, to bring to book; ~तलबी (seeking of) an explanation; ~दार responsible, accountable; hence ~दारी (*nf*); ~दावा written statement filed by the defendant: counter-statment; ~देह responsible, answerable, accountable; ~देही responsibility, accountability; obligation;

-सवाल question and answer, cross-questioning; –देना to give a reply to; to remove from service; to break/collapse.

जवाबी java:bi: (*a*) counter; (in the nature of or requiring a) reply; –कार्ड a reply card; –तार a reply-paid telegram.

जवा/हर jawa:har (*nm*) a jewel; ~हिरात jewellery.

जश्न jashn (*nm*) festivity, merriment, festive celebration.

जस्त, जस्ता jast, jasta: (*nm*) zinc.

जहन्नुम jehnnūm (*nm*) the hell, inferno; ~रसीद consigned to hell; –में जाना or –रसीद होना to go to hell, to be damned.

ज़हमत zehmāt (*nf*) trouble, botheration; –मोल लेना to own a botheration, to create trouble for oneself, to invite trouble.

ज़हर zehar (*nm*) poison, venom; anything bitter or disagreeable; (*a*) disagreeable, unpalatable; ~दार poisonous, venomous; ~बाद a carbuncle; septic; ~मोहरा bezoar; –उगलना to make venomous utterances; to speak spitefully; –उगलना, कलम से to dip one's pen in gall; –कर देना to make (an eatable) unpalatably bitter; –का घूँट a bitter disagreeable phenomenon, a mouthful of poison; ०पीकर रह जाना to stand/suppress unbearable rage, to tolerate insult/humiliation; –की पुड़िया one who incites quarrels or factions, a stormy petrel; –चढ़ना poison to spread within the system; –में बुझाना to treat with poison; to impart a poisonous sting (to words); –लगना to be most unwelcome.

ज़हरी, ~ला zehri:, ~la: (*a*) full of venom; venomous, poisonous.

जहाँ jahā:—an allomorph of 'जहान' (see) used as the first member in several compound words; ~दीदा one who has seen the world, experienced (person); ~पनाह the protector of the world; an honorofic used for kings and emperors, (*adv*) where, wherever; –तक as far as; -तहाँ here and there; everywhere, all round; –का तहाँ at the original place; –चाह वहाँ राह where there is a will there is way, he who has a mind to beat a dog will easily find a stick; –धुआँ वहाँ आग no smoke without fire; –सौ वहाँ सवा सौ over shoes over boots; –सत्यानाश वहाँ सवा सत्यानाश as well risk much as little.

जहाज़ jaha:z (*nm*) a vessel, ship; ~रानी shipping, navigation; –का जहाज़ quite a ship, a ship itself; –का पंछी one who has but one habitat; forlorn.

जहाज़ी jaha:zi: (*a*) naval, nautical; (*nm*) a mariner, sailor; –डाकू a pirate.

जहान jahā:n (*nm*) the world; the people.

जहालत jaha:lat (*nf*) illiteracy, incivility, boorishness.

ज़हीन zahi:n (*a*) sharp, intelligent.

ज़हे किस्मत zahe kismat—its my fortune, fortunate am I !

जहेज़ jahez (*nm*) dowry; -प्रथा the dowry system.

जाँ jā:—an allomorph of जान used as the first member in compound words; ~निसार one who can sacrifice one's life, devoted; ~बाज़ venturesome, one who can risk one's life; ~बाज़ी the quality that distinguishes a जाँबाज़, venturesomeness

जाँगलू jā:glu: (*a*) incivil; boorish, rustic; wild.

जाँघ jā:gh (*nf*) a thigh.

जाँघिया jā:ghiya: (*nm*) a lower underwear, short drawers.

जाँच jā:ch (*nf*) an investigation, examination; test; scanning; enquiry; -पड़ताल investigation, enquiry; -परख test, scanning, examination.

जाँचना jā:chnā: (*v*) to investigate; to verify; to test; to evaluate.

जांतव jā:ntav (*a*) pertaining/relating to or born of a जंतु (see).

जाँता jā:ta: (*nm*) a quern, stone handmill.

जाकड़ ja:kaṛ (*nm*) on approval (purchases); –का माल goods/articles on approval.

जाकेट jakeṭ (*nf*) a jacket.

जाको ja:ko (*pro*) in Braj Bhasha, the counterpart of जिसको (whom); –राखे साइयाँ मार सकै ना कोय every bullet has its billet.

जागतिक ja:gtik (*a*) worldly, earthly, mundane.

जागना ja:gnā: (*v*) to rise, to wake up; to be alert; to be on the ascendance (as नसीब–); to brighten up (as लौ–); जागते को कौन जगाये a nod is as good as a wink to a blind horse.

जागरण ja:grān̲ (*nm*) awakening, wakefulness, vigil; sitting through the night in religious or festive collective singing.

जागरित ja:grit (*a*) awakened, risen, woken up.

जागरूक ja:gru:k (*a*) alert, vigilant, wakeful; ~ता wakefulness, vigilance, alertness.

जागीर ja:gi:r (*nf*) property, landed property, land etc. given by the government as a reward, jaghir; ~दार the holder of a जागीर, a fief, jaghirdar; ~दारी feudalism; jaghirdari.

जागीरी ja:gi:ri: (*nf*) pertaining to or related with landed property.

जागृति ja:ggriti (*nf*) an awakening.

जाजम ja:jam (*nf*) see जाज़िम.

जाज़िम ja:zim (*nf*) a multi-coloured floor sheet.

जाज्वल्यमान jajvallymā:n (*a*) shining; resplendent; refulgent, luminous.

जाट ja:ṭ (*nm*) a sub-caste of the Hindu community mostly inhabiting western Uttar Pradesh, the Punjab, Rajasthan and Haryana States of the Indian Union; –मरा तब जानिए जब तेरहवीं/सत्रहवीं हो जाये do not halloo till you are out of the wood.

जाड़ा ja:ṛa: (*nf*) cold; winter; –खाना to be struck by cold; –लगना to feel cold.

जात ja:t (*a*) born; manifest; (*nf*) caste; ~कर्म/क्रिया the fourth of the sixteen major संस्कारs of the Hindus performed after the childbirth; -पाँत caste, caste and community; ~मृत still-born.

ज़ात za:t (*nf*) self; person; individual, individuality; breed; characteristic quality; -पाँत caste and community.

जातक ja:tak (*nm*) the new-born; (astrological calculation of) nativity; see जातकर्म; the collection of the tales of Lord Buddha's previous births.

जाति ja:ti (*nf*) caste; community; race; sect; genus; type; kind; breed; ~गत racial; communal, sectarian; ~च्युत expelled from the community; ~तत्त्व ethnological content; °विज्ञान ethnology, ~धर्म generic property; caste-characteristic; conduct peculiar to a caste/community; -पाँति caste and community; -बहिष्कार ex-communication; -बहिष्कृत ex-communicated;

-भ्रष्ट fallen from one's caste/community; ~वाचक (संज्ञा) common (noun); ~वाद casteism, racism/racialism; communalism; ~विज्ञान ethnology; ethnography; raciology; ~हीन belonging to a low-caste; –से निकालना to excommunicate.

ज़ाती za:ti: (*a*) personal, individual; –तौर पर personally, personally speaking.

जातीय ja:ti:y (*a*) racial; communal; generic; –अल्पसंख्यक racial minority; –एकता racial unity; –घृणा racial hatred; –पृथग्वासन apartheid; –भेद-भाव racial discrimination.

जातीयता ja:ti:yta: (*nf*) raciality; communality/communalism.

जादू ja:du: (*nm*) magic, juggling; charm; spell; -टोना sorcery, witchcraft; voodooism; –उतरना the charm to be dispelled, to be disenchanted; –करना to cast a spell on, to practise magic; to bewitch; to conjure; –चलना to come under the spell (of), to be spell-bound; –वह जो सिर पर चढ़ कर बोले magic manifests itself in procuring quiet obeisance; the means that achieve the end are the best means.

जादूग/र ja:du:gar (*nm*) a magician; juggler; sorcerer, conjurer; ~रनी (*nf*); ~री magic, sorcery; jugglery, witchcraft.

जान jā:n (*nf*) life, animation; stamina, vitality; energy; essence; spirit; sweetheart; darling; -ए-मन darling!, sweetheart!; -जोखिम risk of life; ~दार having vitality; lively, animate; -बीमा life-insurance; ~लेवा deadly; mortal; -व-माल life and property/belongings; –आना to be revived; to have a lease of life; –आफ़त में होना to be at a dead lift; –आँखों में आ जाना to be on the verge of death;–ओठों पर आना to have life hanging by a feeble thread; to be in a mortal agony; –का गाहक/ग्राहक bent on causing one's end; –का नुकसान loss of life; –की अमान guarantee of life; –की ख़ैर surety of life; –की ख़ैर मनाना to endeavour or pray for the safety of life; –की पड़ना to be worried about the security of one's life; –की बाज़ी लगाना (I) would give my ears, to stake one's life, to be ready to make any sacrifice; –के लाले पड़ना to be under the shadow of death, to be in an irretrievably risky position; –खपाना to put in arduous work, to labour hard; –खाना to pester constantly; –चुराना see जी चुराना; –छिड़कना to be deeply in love (with), to be ready to stake life for; –छुड़ाना to get rid of, to skulk from; –छूटना to get rid of; –देना to sacrifice; to be in passionate love (with); –निकलना to become lifeless, to be in great agony; –पर आना; –पर आ बनना to be exposed to imminent danger, to be exposed to imminent risk of life; –पर खेलना to stake one's life, to put one's life in peril; –पर नौबत आना see –पर आ बनना; –बचाना to save the life of; to shirk/skulk/funk; to save one's carcass; –बची लाखों पाए security of life represents the greatest achievement; Dutch comfort; –भारी होना to be weary of life, to feel life to be a burden; –मुट्ठी में होना to have a person cold, to have him at one's mercy; –में जान आना to feel relieved, to feel comforted; –लड़ाना to exert to the utmost, to strain every nerve; –लेना to kill to inflict grave suffering; to put to arduous labour; –सूखना to be scared out of wits; to be stunned; –से जाना to pass away; to lose life; –से बेज़ार होना to be fed up of life; –से मारना to kill; –से मार डालना to kill, to deprive of life; –से हाथ धो बैठना to lose one's life, to have to abandon one's life; –हथेली पर लिए फिरना to be ever ready to stake one's life; –है तो जहान है no life, no pleasure; the world lives as long as you live.

जानका/र ja:nka:r (*a*) knowing, knowledgeable, conversant; (*nm*) one who knows; ~री knowledge, acquaintance; brief.

जानना ja:nnā: (*v*) to know, to become aware of; to perceive; जानकर knowingly, deliberately, wilfully; ०अनजान बनना to feign ignorance; जानने वाले acquaintance; जान-बूझकर knowingly, deliberately, wilfully; ०आग में कूदना/कुएँ में पड़ना to deliberately jump into fire to deliberately risk a hazard to life; ०मक्खी निगलना to connive at; जाने-अनजाने wittingly or unwittingly, knowingly or unknowingly.

जानपद ja:npad (*a*) pertaining, belonging to, or related with, a जनपद.

जान-पहचान ja:n-pehchā:n (*nf*) acquaintance; ०वाले acquaintances.

जानवर ja:nwar (*nm*) an animal, beast.

जानशी/न ja:nashı:n (*nm*) successor, heir; ~नी succession, inheritance.

जाना ja:nā: (*v*) to go, to depart; to lose (as मेरा क्या जाता है ?); to flow (as ख़ून जा रहा है); जाते रहना to pass away; to continue to go; जा धमकना to appear on the scene all of a sudden; जा निकलना to arrive by chance; जाने देना to let go; to pardon; जा लेना to catch up, to overtake.

जानिब ja:nib (*nf*) side, direction; ~दार a partisan, supporter; ~दारी taking of sides, adoption of a partisan attitude.

जानी ja:nı: (*a*) pertaining to, or aiming at, life; beloved, darling; –दुश्मन a deadly enemy, sworn enemy.

जाप ja:p (*nm*) see जप.

जापा ja:pa: (*nm*) delivery, child birth; ~घर maternity home.

ज़ाफ़रा/न zā:frā:n (*nm*) saffron; ~नी saffron (coloured).

जा-बेजा ja:beja: (*a*) indiscriminate; proper and improper, good and bad; (*adv*) at the opportune or inopportune moment/time/place etc., indiscriminately.

ज़ाब्ता za:bta: (*nm*) rule, regulation; –दीवानी code of civil procedure; –फ़ौजदारी code of criminal procedure.

जाम ja:m (*a*) jammed; (*nm*) jam; a peg; –कर देना to jam, to jam up; –चलना to have a drinking spree; –पर जाम चलना to take peg after peg, to have a drinking spree.

जामदानी ja:mdā:nı: (*nf*) a kind of flower-woven fine cloth.

जामन ja:mān (*nm*) rennet – the small quantity of curd used for coagulating milk.

जा/मा ja:mā: (*nm*) attire, clothing; a long gown worn by the bridegroom; ~मे में फूले न समाना to be puffed up/swollen with joy; ~मे से बाहर होना to be unable to contain oneself (out of joy or rage); to transcend one's limits.

जामाता ja:mā:ta: (*nm*) a son-in-law.

ज़ामिन za:min (*nm*) a surety, guarantor.

जामु/न ja:mun (*nf*) jambo, a black plum (the tree and its fruit); ~नी of the colour of जामुन, bluish black.

ज़ाय/क़ा za:yqa: (*nm*) taste, relish; ~क़ेदार delicious, tasty; ~क़ा बिगड़ना to have one's (sense of) taste impaired.

जायज़ ja:yaz (*a*) suitable; proper; befitting; legitimate.

जायज़ा ja:yza: (*nm*) a scrutiny; survey.

ज़ायद za:yad (*a*) cxtra; additional.

जायदाद ja:yda:d (*nf*) property; –ग़ैर-मनक़ूला immovable property; –मनक़ूला movable property.

जाफ़री ja:fri: (*nf*) a trellis.

जायफल ja:yphal (*nm*) a nutmeg –*Myristica moschata*.

जाया ja:ya: (*nf*) spouse, wife; (*a*) born (of).

ज़ाया za:ya: (*a*) waste, ruined; –करना to waste, to ruin; –जाना to be wasted/ruined.

जार ja:r (*nm*) an adulterer, a paramour; –कर्म adultery, adulterous activity; ~ज संतान a bastard, adulterine, illegitimate; born on the wrong side of the blanket; ~जता illegitimacy; जारिणी an adulteress.

ज़ार za:r (*a*); -ज़ार रोना to weep bitterly.

जारी ja:ri: (*a*) continued; current, running; issued; in force; –करना to issue, to enforce; to commence; –रखना to continue, to keep up.

जाल ja:l (*nm*) a net, network; mesh; snare; plot; ~साज a conspirer; forgerer, deceitful; ~साज़ी plotting; conspiracy; forgery; –डालना/फेंकना to cast a net; –फैलाना to lay a trap; –में फँसना to be caught in a trap, to be trapped.

जालक ja:lak (*nm*) a ploxus; lattice.

जाला ja:la: (*nm*) a cobweb; net; flake; cataract; जाले साफ़ करना to blow away the cobwebs.

जालिका ja:lika: (*nf*) a plexus.

ज़ालिम za:lim (*a*) cruel, atrocious tyrannical; (*nm*) a tyrant.

ज़ालिमाना za:limā:nā: (*a*) atrocious tyrannical.

जालिया ja:liya: (*a*) see जाल (~साज

जाली ja:li: (*a*) forged, counterfeit (*nm*) mesh; hammock; muzzle grating; ~दार meshed, fitted with grating.

जावित्री ja:vittri: (*nf*) mace.

जासू/स jasu:s (*nm*) a spy, detective ~सी espionage, spying, intelligenc work; detective.

ज़ाहि/र za:hir (*a*) apparent; obvious evident; ~रा apparently; ०तौर प apparently; obviously; evidently

जाहिल ja:hil (*a*) illiterate; uncivil boorish.

ज़िंदगानी zindga:nı: (*nf*) life.

ज़िंदगी zindagi: (*nf*) life; liveliness –भर all one's life, throughou life; –के आख़िरी दिन गिनना/–के दिन पूरे करना to pass time somehow to count the last days of life –बसर करना to spend life; to carry on anyhow; –भारी होना life to hang heavy; –में मौत का मज़ा चखना to know death in life, to undergo tremendous hardships in life; –से बेज़ार होना to be fed up/tired of life.

ज़िंदा zında: (*a*) alive, living; not dead; ~दिल sprightly, lively, cheerful; ~दिली sprightliness, liveliness, cheerfulness; ~बाद ! long live !; –लाश spiritless, dead alive.

जिंस jıns (*nf*) commodity; cereals; ~वार commoditywise; ~वारी commoditywise classification.

ज़िक्र zikkr (*nm*) mention, reference.

जिगर jigar (*nm*) the liver; heart courage; –का टुकड़ा a son; very dear one; –के टुकड़े होना lit. the liver to be torn asunder—to be shattered by a grave shock; –था

कर बैठ जाना to be rent by unbearable agony; to keep in readiness for a shock; –होना to have courage, to be courageous.

जिगरा jigra: (*nm*) courage.

जिगरी jigri: (*a*) pertaining to the liver; beloved, dear; very intimate; –दोस्त bosom friend, very intimate friend.

जिच zich (*nf*) checkmate; stalemate; –करना to checkmate; to be placed in a stalemate; –होना to be checkmated; to be in a stalemate.

जिजीवि/षा jiji:visha: (*nf*) the life instinct, will to live; ~षु willing to live, having the will to live.

जिज्ञासा jiggya:sa: (*nf*) curiosity, inquisitiveness; spirit of learning.

जिज्ञासु jiggya:su (*a*) curious, inquisitive; willing to learn; (*nm*) a learner.

जिठानी jiṭha:nī: (*nf*) husband's elder brother's wife.

जित jit—an adjectival suffix/prefix used in Sanskrit words meaning 'one who has conquered' (e.g. जितकोप, इन्द्रजित); ~कोप/क्रोध one who has conquered or subdued the feeling of anger/wrath; ~शत्रु a conqueror of enemies; ~श्रम tireless, one who has conquered the sense of fatigue.

जित/ना jitna: (*a*) as much as; ~ने as many (as); ~ना गुड़ डालोगे उतना ही मीठा होगा the more the sugar, the sweeter the beverage; ~नी लंबी चादर हो उतने पैर फैलाओ cut your coat according to your size.

जितात्मा jita:tmā: (*a* and *nm*) (one) in full control of oneself; a self-conqueror.

जिताना jita:nā: (*v*) to cause to win to achieve victory.

जितेंद्रिय jitendriy (*a* and *nm*) (one) in full control of one's senses; a conqueror of senses, an ascetic; hence ~ता (*nf*).

ज़िद zid (*nf*) obstinacy, stubbornness; insistence; –करना to insist; –पर आना to adopt an inflexible attitude, to strike a stubborn posture.

ज़िद्दी ziddi: (*a*) obstinate, stubborn, inflexible; insistent; hence ~पना (*nm*).

जिधर jidhar (*adv*) wherever, in whichever direction; -जिधर in whatever directions.

जिन jin (*nm*) lord Buddha; the Jain Ti:rthankars (see); (*pro*) the plural form of जिस.

ज़िना zinā: (*nm*) adultery: ~कार an adulterer; adulterous; ~कारी adultery; –बिल-जब्र rape.

जिन्न jinn (*nm*) a jinnee, according to Mohammedan demonology one of the lower type of spirits; –सवार होना to be possessed by a jinnee, to be under a satanic influence.

ज़ि/म्मा zimmā: (*nm*) responsibility, charge, obligation; ~म्मेदार, ~म्मेवार responsible, answerable; ~म्मेदारी, ~म्मेवारी responsibility, obligation; ०निभाना to deliver the goods; ~म्मा लेना to take or own the responsibility (of), to undertake.

ज़ियाफत ziya:fat (*nf*) a feast.

ज़ियार/त ziya:rat (*nf*) a pilgrimage; ~ती a pilgrim; pertaining to pilgrimage.

जिरगा jirga: (*nm*) an assembly; a representative body of the frontie Paṭha:ns.

जिरह jireh (*nf*) cross-examination, cross-questioning; –करना to cross-examine, to cross-question.

ज़िरहबक्तर zirahbaktar (*nm*) armour

जिराफ़ jira:f (*nm*) a giraffe.

ज़िला zila: (*nm*) a district; –अदालत the district court; –अफ़सर a collector; –कचहरी see –अदालत; –जज the district judge; -जेल the district jail; –बोर्ड the district board; –मजिस्ट्रेट the district magistrate.

ज़िलाधीश zila:dhi:sh (*nm*) the district magistrate.

जिलाना jila:nā: (*v*) to (cause to) revive, to restore to life; to cause to live.

जिल्द jild (*nf*) binding (of a book); cover; skin; ~दार bound; ~बंद bound (book); ~बंदी book-binding work; –,बिना unbound; ~साज़ a bookbinder; ~साज़ी book-binding.

ज़िल्लत zillat (*nf*) humiliation, insult; –उठाना to suffer humiliation, to put up with insult.

जिस jis (*pro*) an oblique form of जो (see); –कल बैठाये बैठना to dance to the tune of; ~का पल्ला भारी उसी से कर यारी to come down on the right side of the fence; ~की खाना उसी की बजाना he that pays the piper calls the tune; –गाँव जाना नहीं उसका रास्ता क्या पूछना ? to evince no interest in the course one does not have to follow; ~ने दर्द दिया उसी से दवा लेना to take hair of the dog that bit you; –पत्तल में खाना उसी में छेद करना to fell the tree that gives you shelter, to cut the hand that feeds.

जिस्म jism (*nm*) body; physique.

जिस्मानी jismā:nī: (*a*) physical, bodily; –ताक़त physical force.

जिहाद jiha:d (*nm*) crusade; –बोलना to launch a crusade.

जिहादी jiha:di: (*nm*) a crusader; (*a*) crusading.

जिह्वा jivha: (*nf*) the tongue, lingua; ~मूल the root of the tongue; ~ग्र the front of the tongue; -नोक the tip of the tongue; ~मध्य the middle of the tongue; ~लोलुप see चटोरा; –पर होना to be on the tip of the tongue.

जी ji: (*nm*) mind; heart; (*ind*) an honorofic suffix; yes !, yes, sir ! –आ जाना, (किसी पर) the heart to be set on (somebody or something), to fall in love with, to be fascinated by; –उकताना to be fed up (of), to be weary (of), to get disgusted (with); –उचटना to be ennuied, to get disinterested; not to be able to concentrate (on); –उड़ा जाना to feel nervously restless; –ऊबना/ऊब जाना to be fed up, to be browned off; –कड़ा करना to muster courage, to prepare oneself for any eventuality; –करना to set heart on, to long (for); –काँपना to feel scared; –का बोझ हलका होना to be relieved of a worry or apprehension; to feel soothed; –की अमान माँगना to seek or request pardon; to preface a discourse with excuses; –की जी में रहना (a wish or longing) not to have a chance for expression or materialisation; –को मारना to repress a longing; to practise self-denial; –खट्टा होना to be disenchanted/disgusted; to set (person's) teeth on the edge; –खोलकर freely, without any restraint or stint; to one's heart's content; –घबराना to feel nervous, to be uneasy; –चाहना to desire, to long (for); –चाहे if you feel like, if you so desire; –चुराना to shirk (work); to cast a spell (upon), to charm, to captivate; –छोटा करना to lose heart, to be discouraged; –जलना to be grieved, to have a sore heart; –जलाना to get in one's hair, to wound/grieve, to plague; –जान heart and soul, passionately, whole-heartedly; –जान से कोशिश करना to knuckle down to i

–जान से जुट जाना to blaze away; –जान से क़ुर्बान devoted heart and soul; –जान से फ़िदा होना to be passionately in love with, to be infatuated by; –टूट जाना to be frustrated/disheartened; –डूबना to sink, to faint; –तरसना to long or yearn (for); –तोड़ कोशिश करना to try heart and soul, to knuckle down to it; –दहलना to be scared out of wits; –दुखाना to grieve, to cause grief (to); –धक-धक करना see –धड़कना; –धड़कना the heart to palpitate, to have a palpitation, to shudder; –पानी होना the heart to be moved by compassion; –पिघल जाना to be deeply moved by pity; –फटना see दिल फटना; –फिरना to be disgusted with, to feel repelled from; –बहलाना to recreate, to divert the mind, to amuse so as to dissipate reflection; –बैठना see दिल बैठना; –भर आना (lit.) the heart to be full, to be touched with compassion or be deeply moved; –भर कर to one's heart's content, to the top of one's bent; –भरना to be satiated, to be fed up; –मतलाना/मिचलाना to feel nausea, to feel like vomitting; –में आना to occur in one's mind; to have a fancy (for); –में घर करना, –में बसना to find a place in the heart (of), to create a profound sense of endearment (in); –में जलना to be consumed with jealousy or envy, to eat one's heart out; –में बैठना to be impressed or fixed in the mind; –रखना to appease; to please; –लगना to feel quite oneself; ०लगना (किसी काम आदि में) to be able to concentrate on, to be absorbed in; ०(किसी जगह आदि पर) to feel easy; to feel quite at home; –लगाना to set one's heart (on); to concentrate (on); to fall in love (with); –ललचाना to hanker after, to feel allured; –लुभाना to allure or entice, to captivate the heart of; –लोट-पोट होना to pant for; to be passionately charmed (by); –से उतर जाना to lose the favour or regard of, to fall in the esteem of; –से जाना to lose one's life; –हारना to lose spirits, to be disheartened/discouraged; ~हुज़ूर a yes-man, sycophant; ~हुज़ूरी करना to chime in, to play a sycophant.

जीजा ji:ja: (*nm*) elder sister's husband.

जीजी ji:ji: (*nf*) an elder sister.

ज़ीट zi:ṭ (*nf*) boasting, bragging; –मारना to brag, to boast.

जीत ji:t (*nf*) victory, success; -हार victory and defeat, success and failure; –मुट्ठी में होना to have the game in one's hands.

जीतना ji:tnā: (*v*) to win, to conquer; to prevail upon; to master.

जीता ji:ta: (*a*) living, alive; won; -जागता living, lively; up and kicking; जीती बाजी a battle already won; जीती मक्खी निगलना to wilfully commit or connive in a wrong; जीते जी during the life-time of; as long as one is living or is in existence; ०मर जाना to suffer death in life, to endure extreme misery or anguish; जीते रहो ! may you live long !

ज़ीन zi:n (*nf*) a saddle; a kind of thick suiting (cloth); ~साज a saddle maker; ~साजी saddle-making.

जीना ji:nā: (*v*) to live, to be alive; जी उठना to be revived, to be infused with new life; –दूभर करना to make it too hot for, to make life hell; –दूभर या भारी हो जाना the life to become a burden or an impossibility, life to become too hot; **जीने का मज़ा** pleasure of life.

ज़ीना zi:nā: (*nm*) a staircase, ladder.

जीभ ji:bh (*nf*) tongue, lingua; **–ऐंठ जाना** the tongue to be twisted; to be on the verge of death; **–का कड़ुआ मन का उजला** one's bark to be worse than one's bite; **–का चटख़ारे लेना** to have an inkling for dainties; **–काटना** see **ज़बान काटना**; **–के तले जीभ होना** to be double-tongued; **–खींच लेना** see **–निकालना**; **–चलना** to talk too much, to be gabby; to talk grandly or largely; **–निकालना** lit. to pull out the tongue—to inflict heavy punishment; to quieten for ever; **–हिलाना** to speak out; **–पर सरस्वती बसना/विराजना/होना**; **–पर सरस्वती का वास होना** to have the gift of the gab, to make utterances that eventually prove true.

जीभी ji:bhi: (*nf*) a tongue-cleaner.

जीमना ji:mnā: (*v*) to feast, to fare sumptuously.

जीरा zi:ra: (*nm*) cumin seed; chipping.

जीर्ण ji:rṉ (*a*) time-worn, decayed, decrepit; old, chronic; **–ज्वर** chronic fever; hence **~ता** (*nf*); **–वस्त्र** worn-out/tattered cloth; **-शीर्ण** tattered, worn and torn.

जीर्णोद्धार ji:rṉoddha:r (*nm*) resurrection, resuscitation.

जीवंत ji:vānt (*a*) lively, living, animated, life-like; hence **~ता** (*nf*).

जीव ji:v (*nm*) a creature, living being; life; soul; **~घाती** destroyer of life, killer; murderous; **-जंतु** creatures; tiny creatures; **-जगत** the animate world; **~दान** sacrifice of life; **~धारी** living being, organism; **~भौतिकी** biophysics; **~रसायन** biochemistry; **~लोक** mortal world; **~वाद** vitalism, animism; **~वासिकी** bionomics, bionomy; **~विज्ञान** biology; **~विष** toxin; **~वैज्ञानिक** a biologist; biological; **-हत्या/हिंसा** destruction of life; **~हीन** lifeless.

जीवट ji:vaṭ (*nm*) courage; spirit, adventure; endurance; hence **~दार**, **–का आदमी** having the heart of oak

जीवन ji:vān (*nm*) life; animation; existence; **-क्रम** the journey of life; living; **~चरित** biography; **~चरितकार** a biographer; **~चर्या** living; routine of life; **-दान** sacrifice of life; (commitment) to spare somebody's life; **~धन** the basic wealth of life; a woman's husband; **-नैया/नौका** the ship of life; **-मरण** life and death; **०चक्र** the life and death-cycle; **-वृत्त/वृत्तांत** biography, bio-data; **-शक्ति** elan vital, vitality; **-संघर्ष** struggle for life; struggle for existence; **-संध्या** the evening of one's life—the last phase of life; **-स्तर** standard of living; **~हीन** lifeless; insipid; **~हेतु** livelihood; the basis of existence; **–भार होना** life to become a burden.

जीवनी ji:vnī: (*nf*) biography; **~कार** a biographer.

जीवन्मु/क्त ji:vānmukt (*a*) freed from worldly bonds in life, liberated; **~क्ति** freedom from worldly bonds in life, liberation.

जीवन्मृत ji:vānmrit (*a*) living dead, experiencing death in life.

जीवांकिकी ji:vā:ṅkiki: (*nf*) Biometry.

जीवाणु ji:vā:ṉū (*nm*) bacteria; microbe.

जीवाधार jiva:dha:r (*nm*) vitals; basis of life.

जीविका ji:vika: (*nf*) livelihood; subsistence; **–चलाना** to earn one's livelihood, to make both ends meet.

जीवित ji:vit (*a*) alive, living; (*nm*)

ssence.

वी ji:vi: (*nm*) a living organism; . suffix meaning living or subsisting by or for, e.g. **चिरजीवी, श्रमजीवी, द्धिजीवी.**

वोपयोगितावा/द jivopyogita:va:d(*nm*) biologism; hence ~**दी** (*nm* and *a*).

व्यता ji:vyta: (*nf*) viability.

बिश jumbish (*nf*) activity, movement.

आ jua: (*nm*) gambling; yoke; -**खाना/घर** a gambling den, gambling house; **—कंधे से उतार फेंकना** to throw off the yoke, to free/liberate oneself from; **—रखना/धरना** to put yoke upon; to cause to work hard.

आरी jua:ri: (*nm*) a gambler.

काम zuka:m (*nm*) cold, catarrh; **बिगड़ना** the rheum to become thick and clotted, the defluxion from the head to be suddenly stopped.

jug (*nm*) see **युग**; **-जुग** for ages, for ever; **-जुग जियो** ! (a benediction from an elderly person) May you live for ages !

त jugat (*nf*) a skilful device/measure, contrivance; **-भिड़ाना/ड़ाना** to manipulate, to contrive.

नू jugnū: (*nm*) a fire-fly, glow-worm.

ल jugal (*nm* and *a*) pair, couple, the two, duet; **—जोड़ी** a matching pair.

लबंदी jugalbandi: (*nf*) a duet (of two musical instruments).

ाड़ juga:ṛ (*nf*) way, device, measure, manoeuvre; **—करना** to manage, manoeuvre, to find a way (to achieve); **—बैठाना/भिड़ाना/लगाना/ड़ाना** to manage, to manoevure, to find a way out.

ाल juga:l (*nm*) a cud.

ाली juga:li: (*nf*) rumination; **—करना** to ruminate.

जुगुप्सा jugupsa: (*nf*) disgust, intense aversion: hence ~**जनक**, ~**मूलक** (*a*).

जुज़ juz (*nm*) a part, portion; forme of a book; (*ind*) without; ~**बंदी** the sewing of the individual formes of a book, putting the parts together.

जुझा/र, ~**रू** jujha:r, ~ru: (*a* and *nm*) (a) combatant; warrior.

जुट juṭ (*nm*) pair; batch.

जुटना juṭnā: (*v*) to be engaged (in a work) in full force; to unite; to assemble, to flock.

जुटाना juṭa:nā: (*v*) to gather; to procure; to cause to work in full force.

जुठारना juṭha:rnā: (*v*) to defile by tasting a little (of victuals etc.) or by using (clothes etc.); to have the first relish; to render second-hand.

जुड़ना juṛnā: (*v*) to be attached/added/jointed/linked; to be procured or collected.

जुड़नार juṛna:r (*nf*) fittings.

जुड़वाँ juṛwā: (*a* and *nm*) twin/twins.

जुतना jutnā: (*v*) to be tilled/ploughed; to be yoked, to be harnessed to work.

जुताई juta:i: (*nf*) (the act or process of) ploughing; tillage.

जुतियाना jutiya:nā: (*v*) to strike with a shoe; to humiliate.

जुदा juda: (*a*) separate; disunited; **-जुदा** different; severally.

जुदाई juda:i: (*nf*) separation.

जुनून junū:n (*nm*) craziness, madness, insanity; mania.

जुन्हाई junha:i: (*nf*) the moonlight.

जुमला jumla: (*nm*) a sentence; (*a*) all, total.

जुमा jumā: (*nm*) Friday; **-जुमा आठ दिन** a very limited span of time, only a few days; **जुमेरात** Thursday.

जुर्म jurm (*nm*) crime; offence; **–साबित करना** to bring charge home to a person.

जुर्माना jurmā:nā: (*nm*) a fine, penalty.

जुर्रत jurrat (*nf*) courage; audacity, effrontery, cheek; **–होना** to have the cheek.

जुर्राब jurra:b (*nf*) socks, stocking.

जुल jul (*nm*) duplicity, trickery, guile; **~बाज** a cheat, trickster; **~बाज़ी** duplicity, cheating, knavery; **–देना** to cheat, to deceive, to practise fraud.

जुलाई jula:i: (*nf*) (the month of) July.

जुलाब jula:b (*nm*) a purgative.

जुलाहा jula:ha: (*nm*) a weaver.

जुलूस julu:s (*nm*) a procession.

ज़ुल्फ़ zulf (*nm*) (curled) lock of hair.

ज़ुल्म zulm (*nm*) oppression, tyranny, outrage; **~पसंद** a tyrant; tyrannical; oppressive; **ज़ुल्मो-सितम** oppression and repression; **–ढाना** to commit outrage, to oppress; to indulge in oppressive measures.

ज़ुल्मी zulmı: (*a*) tyrant, tyranni l; oppressive.

जुहार juha:r (*nf*) a typical term of salutation (usually prevalent in Ra:jastha:n).

जुही juhi: (*nf*) a kind of Jasmine—*Jasminum anriculatum*.

जूँ jū: (*nf*) a louse; **–न रेंगना, कान पर** see **कान पर जूँ न रेंगना**.

जूझना ju:jhnā: (*v*) to fight hard, to struggle; to combat; **जूझ जाना** to die fighting.

जूट ju:ṭ (*nm*) jute; matted hair.

जूठन ju:ṭhān (*nf*) leavings (of food, drink, etc.).

जूठा ju:ṭha: (*a*) defiled by eating, drinking or using otherwise.

जूड़ा juṛa: (*nm*) a bun-shaped hair-do.

जूड़ी ju:ṛi: (*nf*) ague, malarial fever.

जूतमपैज़ार ju:tampaiza:r (*nf*) a shoe-fight, exchange of shoe-blows, mutual application of sh strokes in a quarrel; general sc ffle.

जूता ju:ta: (*nf*) a shoe, footwea **–उठाना** to raise a shoe in order beat, to be ready to give a sh blow; **०,(किसी का)** to do meni chores; **–चलना** exchange of sho blows, mutual hitting by shoe **–चलवाना** to set people together the ears; **जूते की नोक पर रखना** care a fig/tuppence for; **जूते चाट** to lick somebody's shoe; to servilely flattering; **जूते पड़ना/बरस** to be beaten by shoes, to be or struck repeatedly by shoe **जूते खाना** to be beaten by shoe **जूते मारना/लगाना** to give a sho beating; to humiliate; to retalia in an insulting manner; **जूते ख़बर लेना** to apply the shoe, inflict a shoe-beating; **जूते से पू करना** to resort to shoe-beatin to beat with shoes; **जूते से ब करना** to apply the shoe, straightaway resort to the appl cation of shoe force; **जूते की नो पर मारना** to treat (somebody) wi contempt, to consider (somebod as absolutely of no significanc to care a fig (for).

जूती ju:ti: (*nf*) a typical light sho ladies footwear; **–की नोक पर** ca a fig for; **–के बराबर समझना** to tre with utter contempt, to consid as absolutely of no value; **जूति उठाना** to dance attendance upon, do menial chores for; **जूतियाँ चटक फिरना** to roam about aimless **जूतियाँ बगल में दबाना** to slink aw or slip off quietly; **जूतियाँ सीधी कर** to perform menial chores; cringe to, to behave obsequious **जूतियाँ सिर पर रखना** lit. to car somebody's shoes over the head to flatter survilely; जूतियों की बदौलत/जूतियों के तुफ़ैल से through the bounteous grace of, through the magnanimous pleasure of.

जून ju:n (*nm*) (the month of) June; time (as दो जून की रोटी); half a day.

जूरी ju:ri: (*nf*) the jury; -अदालत the court of the jury.

जूही ju:hi: (*nf*) see जुही.

जेठ jeṭh (*nm*) the third month of the Hindu lunar calendar; elder brother of a woman's husband.

जेठा jeṭha: (*a*) elder; senior.

जेठानी jeṭha:nī: (*nf*) see जिठानी.

जेब jeb (*nf*) a pocket; ~कट/कतरा a pickpocket; ~ख़र्च pocket-expenses, pocket money; ~घड़ी pocket watch; –कटना pocket to be picked; –कतरना to pick pocket; –खाली होना to have no money in one's pocket, to be penniless; –गरम होना to have a full pocket; to receive a bribe; –भारी होना to have plenty of money; –में रहना to be far ahead in excellence, to be very very superior.

जेबी jebi: (*a*) pertaining to, or fit for keeping in, a pocket, pocket–;(*nf*) a pouch.

ज़ेब्रा zebra: (*nm*) a zebbra.

ज़ेर zer (*ind*) under; below; (*a*) subdued, subjugated; -तजवीज़ under consideration; ~बार under a heavy burden, indebted; -साया under the protection (of); –हिरासत in/under custody; –करना to subdue, to subjugate; –होना to be subdued/subjugated; ज़ेरे-ग़ौर under consideration.

जेल jel (*nf*) a prison, jail/gaol; –काटना to suffer imprisonment, to be put behind the bars; –की रोटियाँ तोड़ना to suffer imprisonment; to be in jail; –की हवा खाना to suffer imprisonment, to go behind the bars.

जेलख़ाना jelkḥa:nā: (*nm*) a prison-house, jail/gaol.

जेलर jelar (*nm*) a jailor/gaoler.

जेली jeli: (*nm*) a prisoner; (*nf*) jelly.

जेवनार jevna:r (*nf*) a feast.

ज़ेवर zevar (*nm*) an ornament; (*pl.*) jewellery.

ज़ेवरात zevra:t (*nm*) plural of ज़ेवर.

ज़ेहन zehan (*nf*) intellect; memory, mind; ~दार intelligent, sharp, –में आना to occur (in the mind); –में बैठना to follow/understand; to take to one's heart; ज़ेहनियत mentality, nature.

जै jai (*nf*) see जय.

ज़ैतून zaitu:n (*nm*) olive (tree and its fruit).

जैन jain (*nm*) a follower of Jainism–a religious order; a Jain.

जैनेरल jaineral (*nm*) a general (of an army).

जैव jaiv (*a*) biological; ~विज्ञान Biology; ~वैज्ञानिक a biologist, biological.

जैसा jaisa: (*a*) similar to, like, resembling; (*adv*) as, like, such as; –करोगे वैसा भरोगे as you sow so shall you reap; –पिता वैसा पूत/-बाप वैसा बेटा like father like son; –पेड़ वैसा फल like wood, like arrows; जैसी (feminine form); ०करनी वैसी भरनी to lie in the bed one has made, to drink as one has brewed; जैसे का तैसा as it was, the self-same; intact; जैसे को तैसा tit for tat, to pay one in his own coin; a R wland for an Oliver, measure for measure.

जैसे jaise (*adv*) as, as if; according as; (*ind*) for example; for instance; as; जैसे-तैसे somehow; somehow or other; catch as catch can;

जैसे मुँह में जबान न हो to look as if butter would not melt in his mouth; –नागनाथ वैसे साँपनाथ nothing to choose between; –ही as soon as, no sooner than; –बने as well as possible, in any possible manner; by hook or by crook; –सोना और पीतल as like as chalk and cheese; also see जैसा.

जोंक jōk (*nf*) a leech; (fig) a blood-sucker, parasite; –की तरह चिपकना to hang on irresistibly.

जो jo (*pro*) who; which; what; that; (*ind*) if; –गरजते है वे बरसते नहीं barking dogs seldom bite; –जागत है सो पावत है it is the early bird that catches the worm, –पीछे रह जाये जहन्नुम जाये devil take the hindmost; –भी हो however; at any rate; –मिले सो हलाल all is grist that comes to his mill; –होगा सो देखा जायेगा to go bald-headed; –हो सो हो come what may.

जोख jokh (*nf*) lit. it means weighing, used only in the compound नाप-जोख (see).

जोखिम jokhim (*nm*) risk, danger; enterprise; –का काम a risky or hazardous job; –उठाना/लेना to take a risk, to run a hazard; –में on thin ice, on dangerous ground; –में डटे रहना to stand in the breach; –मोल लेना to go (in) off the deep end, to take risks.

जोखों jokhō (*nm*) see जोखिम.

जोगिन jogin (*nf*) a female ascetic/ mendicant.

जोगिनी jogini: (*nf*) see जोगी.

जोगिया jogiya: (*a*) saffron, saffron-coloured; –कपड़े/बाना/वस्त्र saffron robes—as donned by a mendicant; –बाना धारण करना to take to mendicancy/asceticism.

जोगी jogi: (*nm*) an ascetic, a mendicant; –बनना to renounce the world.

जोड़ joṛ (*nm*) sum, total; addition, union; joint; articulation; splice; seam; a patch; match; -जोड़ each and every joint; -तोड़ ad libitum; manipulation, machination, contrivance; ~दार jointed, having joints; ~पट्टी fish plate; –का matching, equal to; –का तोड़ a match, counter; –बदना to fix a a bout; -बाक़ी debit and credit; addition and subtraction; ०बराबर होना to be quits, to have no debit and no credit; –मिलना to be equal/matching; to tally.

जोड़ना joṛnā: (*v*) to add, to sum up; to link; to unite; to connect; to attach; to collect, to accumulate; to weld; to bind; to cement; to set (a bone etc.); to assemble; to save up; जोड़-जोड़कर धरना to save up little by little; जोड़-बटोरकर by collecting together.

जोड़ा joṛa: (*nm*) a pair, couple; suit.

जोड़ी joṛi: (*nf*) a pair, couple; a pair of clubs; –का matching, of equal status; ~दार a match; comrade; matching.

जोत jot (*nf*) tillage, holding; flame; ~दार a land-holder, tiller; –से जोत जले one flame kindles another.

जोतना jotnā: (*v*) to plough, to till; to yoke; to harness to work.

जोबन jobān (*nm*) blooming youth; youthful charm; full bloom; puberty; youthful breasts; –ढलना to take the bloom off; –पर आना/ होना to be in full bloom; –लूटना to enjoy the youthful charm of a woman; to commit outrage.

ज़ोम zom (*nm*) fervour; vigour; zeal; pride; –में होना to be in full vigour.

ज़ोर zor (*nm*) strength, force, power; stress, strain: emphasis; support; influence; -आज़माई trial of strength; -ज़बरदस्ती coercion, duress; force; -ज़ुल्म oppression and injustice; ~दार powerful, strong, forceful; influential; hence ~दारी (*nf*); -शोर zest, enthusiasm; fast tempo; gusto; ०से चालू रखना to keep the pot boiling, to keep things moving at full speed; —का powerful, forceful, violent; vigorous; —आज़माना to chance one's arm; —चलना to have sway (over); —डालना to put pressure (on), to influence, to insist; —देकर with emphasis or force; —देना to strengthen; to emphasise; —पकड़ना to acquire momentum/strength; —पर होना to be in full swing, to be in speed; —बाँधना to acquire momentum/force; —मारना to make (frantic) efforts; ज़ोरों से with emphasis; in full force/swing.

ज़ोरावर zora:var (*a*) powerful, strong.

ज़ोरू joru: (*nf*) wife; -जाँता household, household effects; —का गुलाम an uxorious husband, obedient; hen-pecked husband; ०होना to live under the cat's foot, to be under petticoat government; —न जाँता अल्ला मियाँ से नाता no household, no worldly cares.

जोश josh (*nm*) enthusiasm; excitement, fervour, passion; zeal; -व-ख़रोश fervour and frenzy; —खाना to boil; to be excited; to be agitated; —ठंडा पड़ना passion/excitement to subside, all fervour/zeal to disappear; —मारना to be agitated; to be in a passion; —में आना to be provoked/excited; जोशे जाम Dutch courage (courage induced by drinking), pot-valour.

जोशाँदा joshā:da: (*nm*) a medicinal decoction (used as a remedy for cough and cold).

जोशीला joshila: (*v*) spirited, enthusiastic, zealous; vigorous; hence ~पन (*nm*).

जोहना johnā: (*v*) to await; to look for.

जौ jau (*nm*) barley: —भर a grain/particle.

जौहर jauhar (*nm*) valour; skill or skilful manipulation; a mediaeval Rajput custom wherein the women performed self-immolation to save their honour; —दिखाना to prove one's mettle/valour.

जौहरी jauhari: (*nm*) a jeweller; a connoisseur.

ज्ञ gya—a Sanskrit suffix meaning 'one who knows or realises' as गुणज्ञ, बहुज्ञ, कृतज्ञ.

ज्ञात gya:t (*a*) known; comprehended; ~यौवना traditionally, a heroine conscious of her blooming youth.

ज्ञातव्य gya:tavvy (*a*) knowable, worth knowing.

ज्ञाता gya:ta: (*nm* and *a*) (one) who knows; a scholar; learned (person).

ज्ञान gya:n (*nm*) knowledge, learning; sense; ~गम्य knowable, perceptible; intelligible, ~गोचर knowable, perceptible; ~चक्षु the inner vision; one who is blessed with intellect; ~दाता a preceptor, giver of knowledge; ~पिपासा thirst for knowledge; hence ~पिपासु (*nm*); ~मीमांसा epistemology; ~वान learned, scholarly; -साधन medium or means of perception or acquisition of knowledge; -साधना pursuit of knowledge.

ज्ञानमय gya:nmay (*a*) full of knowledge; knowledge incarnate.

ज्ञानी gya:nɪ: (*a*) wise; learned, knowledgeable, well-informed; one who has attained self-realisation; -ध्यानी devoted to meditation/spiritual pursuits.

ज्ञानेंद्रिय gya:nēndriy (*nf*) the (five) senses of perception, viz. the eye, the ear, the nose, the tongue and the skin.

ज्ञानोदय gya:noday (*nm*) the advent/emergence of knowledge.

ज्ञापक gya:pak (*nm*) memo; informant; (*a*) informative; indicative.

ज्ञापन gya:pān (*nm*) memorandum; proclaiming, making known; hence **ज्ञापित** (*a*).

ज्ञेय gyey (*a*) knowable; worth knowing; hence **~ता** (*nf*).

ज्या jya: (*nf*) a bow-string.

ज्यादती zya:dati: (*nf*) excess, high-handedness, injustice.

ज्यादा zya:da: (*a*) more; many; much; plenty; **~तर** mostly, in most cases.

ज्यामि/ति jya:miti (*nf*) Geometry; **~तीय** geometrical.

ज्येष्ठ jyeshṭh (*a*) the eldest (brother, son, etc.), the senior-most; senior, elder; hence **~ता** (*nf*); (*nm*) the third month of the Hindu calendar

ज्यों jyō (*ind*) as, as if; **-ज्यों** as; **-त्यों** somehow, by manipulation; **–हीं** as soon as; **–का त्यों** as it was (before), intact.

ज्योति jyoti (*nf*) light; flame; lustre; vision; **~मंडल** the planetary system; **~र्मिति** photometery; **~र्विद्या/ज्योतिःशास्त्र** Astronomy; astronomical science; uranography; **~र्विद** an astronomer; uranographer.

ज्योतिर्मय jyotirmay (*a*) resplendent luminous, bright; **~ता** resplendence, luminosity, brightness.

ज्योतिष jyotish (*nf*) Astrology; **-विद्या/शास्त्र** Astrology.

ज्योतिषी jyotishi: (*nm*) an astrologer

ज्योति/ष्मान jyotishmā:n (*a*) luminous, lustrous; radiant, resplendent; hence **~ष्मती** (*fem*).

ज्योत्स्ना jyotsnā: (*nf*) the moonlight.

ज्यौंनार jyāuna:r (*nm*) see **जेवनार**.

ज्वर jvar (*nm*) fever, pyrexia; **~ग्रस्त** down with fever; **–चढ़ना** to run temperature; to feel uneasy.

ज्वलंत jvalānt (*a*) blazing, burning; conspicuous; striking; hence **~ता** (*nf*).

ज्वलन jvalān (*nm*) inflammation; combustion, burning; **~शील** inflammable, combustible.

ज्वलित jvalit (*a*) inflamed, burnt; set ablaze.

ज्वार jva:r (*nm*) flood tide; (great) millet; **-भाटा** flood tide and ebb tide; vicissitudes.

ज्वाला jva:la: (*nf*) flame, blaze.

ज्वालामुखी jva:la:mukhi: (*nm*) a volcano; (*a*) volcanic; **–पर्वत** volcanic mountain, a volcano.

झ

झ jha—the fourth letter of the second pentad (i.e. **चवर्ग**) of the Devna:gri: alphabet.

झंकार jhāṅka:r (*nf*) tinkling, jingling; clinking sound; chirr.

झंकारना jhāṅka:rnā: (*v*) to produce tinkling/jingling/clinking sound, to tinkle/jingle/clink; to chirr

झंकृत jhāṅkrit (*a*) tinkled, jingled, clinked; chirred; set tinkling/jingling.

झंखाड़ jhāṅkha:ṛ (*nm*) leafless thick thorny bush; a cluster of thorny bushes.

झंझ/ट jhāṇjhaṭ (*nm*) botheration; mess, trouble, imbroglio; ~**टी** quarrelsome; trouble-maker; ~**ट मोल लेना** to ask for/wilfully own a botheration, to embroil oneself in a mess.

झँझरी jhājhri: (*nf*) lattice; ~**दार** latticed; ~**नुमा** like lattice, of the shape of lattice.

झंझा jhāṇjha: (*nm*) a gale, storm; ~**वात** (*nm*) see **झंझा**.

झँझोड़ना jhājhoṛnā: (*v*) to jerk violently; to hold with the teeth and give a jerk.

झंडा jhāṇḍa: (*nm*) a flag, banner, standard; ensign; –**जहाज** a flagship; ~**बरदार** a standard-bearer; –**उठाना** to hold a banner aloft; to take up a cause; –**के नीचे** under the banner of, under the leadership of; –**खड़ा करना** to invoke people to fight for a cause; to establish a record; –**गाड़ना** to come off with flying colours; to achieve a victory; to set up a flag, to plant a standard; –**झुकाना** to lower a flag, to be in mourning; –**फहराना** to hoist a flag; to come out with flying colours; **झंडे तले जमा होना, एक**– to gather under one banner, to fight under the same leadership or for one cause.

झंडी jhāṇḍi: (*nf*) a bunting, small flag; ~**दार** fitted with buntings or small flags; –**दिखाना** to give a slip; to give a signal.

झँपना jhāpnā: (*v*) to be closed (as (**आँखें**); to cover; to conceal.

झक jhak (*nf*) a whim; craze; (*a*) clean, tidy; ~**मक** clean, neat and tidy.

झकझक jhakjhak (*nf*) wrangling, higgling; altercation, wordy quarrel.

झकझोरना jhakjhornā: (*v*) to shake or jerk violently, to shake off.

झकझोरा jhakjhora: (*nm*) a violent jerk.

झकाझक jhaka:jhak (*a*) spotlessly clean, shiningly tidy, clean and tidy.

झका/र jhaka:r (*nm*) the letter **झ** (jha) and its sound; ~**रांत** (word) ending in **झ्** (jh).

झकोर jhakor (*nm*) see **झकोरा**.

झकोरना jhakornā: (*v*) (the air) to flow gustily (through the trees); to blast through.

झकोरा jhakora: (*nm*) a blast, gust, whiff.

झक्कड़ jhakkaṛ (*nm*) a storm, hurricane.

झक्की jhakki: (*a*) crazy, whimsical; whacky; given to prattling (out of indignation/discontentment); hence ~**पन** (*nm*).

झख jhakh (*nf*) a fish; craze, whim; –**मार कर** left with no alternative, under compulsion; –**मारना** to be a fool for one's pains, to be engaged in a fruitless work.

झगड़ना jhagaṛnā: (*a*) to quarrel, to altercate, to scramble.

झगड़ा jhagra: (*nm*) a quarrel, dispute; altercation; scramble; fray; -**झंटा**/-**टंटा** argumentation and altercation, dispute, quarrel; –**खड़ा करना** to kick up a row/dust; –**खत्म करना** to bury the hatchet, to be done with it; –**छेड़ना** to assume the aggressive; –**मोल लेना** to trail one's coat tails; to get embroiled in a quarrel/dispute; to fasten quarrel upon; to pick a quarrel/altercation; **झगड़े की जड़** apple of discord, bone of contention.

झगड़ालू jhagṛa:lu: (*a*) quarrelsome, disputatious, pugnacious; hence ~पन (*nm*).

झट jhaṭ (*adv*) instantly, at once.

झटकना jhaṭaknā: (*v*) to jerk off, to twitch; to wrest, to snatch; to extort; to obtain by force or fraud.

झटका jhaṭka: (*nm*) a jerk, jolt, shock; lurch; beheading (an animal) with one stroke; the meat of an animal so beheaded.

झटकारना jhaṭka:rnā: (*a*) to twitch; to shake or knock off (as dust or crumples from a bedsheet, etc.); to clean.

झटपट jhaṭpaṭ (*adv*) instantaneously, quickly, promptly.

झड़ना jhaṛnā: (*v*) to be shed off; to lrop or fall; to be discharged (as semen).

झड़प jhaṛap (*nf*) a skirmish, snap flght; altercation.

झड़पा-झड़पी jharpa:jharpi: (*nf*) an altercation; a brawl.

झड़ी jhaṛi (*nf*) incessant downpour; non-stop shower; –**लगना** to have an incessant downpour.

झनक jhanāk (*nf*) tinkling, clinking, clink-clank; hence ~**ना** (*v*).

झनकार jhanka:r (*nf*) (see) **झंकार**

झनकारना jhanka:rnā: (*v*) see **झंकारना**.

झनझनाना jhanjhana:nā: (*v*) to be benumbed or cramped; to be infused with a sharp benumbing sensation; to clang, to tinkle, to jingle.

झनझनाहट jhanjhana:haṭ (*nf*) a sharp sensation of numbness; tinnitus; disaesthesia; tinkling/jingling/clinking clanking sound.

झन्नाना jhannā:nā: (*v*) to be benumbed; to make torpid/insensible.

झन्नाहट jhanna:haṭ (*nf*) see **झन्नाना**.

झप jhap; –**होना** to be suddenly closed (eyes); to be rendered visionless all of a sudden; also ~**ना**.

झपकना jhapaknā: (*v*) to blink, to wink; to twinkle.

झपकी jhapki: (*nf*) a nap, short sleep; blink; –**लेना** to have a nap.

झपटना jhapaṭnā: (*v*) to make a sudden swoop, to pounce (upon), to dash; to snatch, to grab.

झपट्टा jhapaṭṭa: (*nm*) a swoop, pounce; –**मारना** to swoop, to (make a) pounce.

झपेट jhapeṭ (*nf*) (striking) range; stroke; swoop; –**में आना** to come into the striking range of; to be struck (by).

झपेटा jhapeṭa: (*nm*) see **झपेट**.

झबरा jhabra: (*a*) shaggy, having wildly abundant hair all over.

झबरीला jhabri:la: (*a*) see **झबरा**.

झब्बा jhabba: (*nm*) a tassel; **झब्बेदार** tasselled, fitted with tassel(s).

झमकना jhamaknā: (*v*) to flounce, to make an agitated, coyous or violent motion.

झमझमाना jnamjhamā:nā: (*v*) to produce a tinkling sound; to glisten; to (impart a) shine.

झमेला jhamela: (*nm*) a mess; botheration; imbroglio.

झरना jharnā: (*nm*) a spring, cascade, fall: (*v*) to flow forth, to spring; to fall; to trickle.

झरोखा jharokha: (*nm*) an oriel, oriel window, network of airholes/apertures; mesh.

झलक jhalak (*nf*) a glimpse; semblance; adumbration; –**दिखाना** to show a glimpse; –**मारना** to have a semblance of.

झलकना jhalaknā: (*v*) to show up faintly or imperfectly; to be reflected; to carry a semblance of.

झलमल jhalmal (*nf*) glitter, gleam, bright tremulous light, twinkle.

झलमलाना jhalmala:nā: (*v*) to gleam,

to glitter; to be aglow with a tremulous light, to twinkle.

झलाई jhala:i: (*nm*) welding; welding charges; ~**गर** a welder; –**करना** to to weld.

झल्लरी jhallari: (*nf*) fimbria.

झल्लाना jhalla:nā: (*v*) to shout peevishly; to be irritated, to fret and fume; hence **झल्लाहट** (*nf*) tantrums.

झाँई jhā:ɪ: (*nf*) a shadow; reflection; darkness; a dark facial freckle; –**आना** to be dazed; to be stupefied; –**मारना** to show a semblance of.

झाँकना jhā:knā: (*v*) to peep in or out, to peer; –**भी नहीं, किसी के यहाँ** to have absolutely nothing to do, to have no contact at all.

झाँकी jhā:ki: (*nf*) a glimpse; tableau; scene.

झाँझ jhā:jh (*nf*) a sistrum; hollow tinkling anklet.

झाँट jhā:ṭ (*nf*) pubes, the hairy growth around the genitals.

झाँप jhā:p (*nf*) a weather-shed; shade, covering.

झाँपना jhā:pnā: (*v*) to cover; to shade.

झाँय-झाँय jhā:yjhā:y (*nf*) sound produced by violent flow of air in a desolate tract of land; –**करना** (air) to produce a frightful sound in its flow through desolateness; to altercate, to enter into a heated argument, altercation, wordy quarrel.

झाँवाँ jhā:vā: (*nm*) pumic (stone), strigil.

झाँसा jhā:sa: (*nm*) wheedling; hoodwinking, dodge; -**पट्टी** wheedling, trickery; pettifogging; **झाँसेबाज** a wheedler, pettifogger; **झाँसेबाजी** wheedling trickery, habitual pettifogging; –**देना** to dodge, to play a trick on; **झाँसे में आना (आसानी से)** to be caught with chaff, to rise to the fly, to be taken in by a hoax.

झाऊ jha:u: (*nm*) a tamarisk tree—*Tamarix Indica.*

झाग jha:g (*nm*) foam; lather; scum; froth; ~**दार** foamy; frothy; lathery; scummy.

झाड़ jha:ṛ (*nm*) a bush, shrub; small tree; .chandelier; (*nf*) reprimand, scolding; ~**खंड** a forest track; brambles; -**झंखाड़** bushes and shrubs, abatis; ~**दार** bushy, shrub by; -**फ़ानूस** chandelier; ~**बंध** abatis; –**पिलाना** to administer a reprimand, to scold severely.

झाड़न jha:ṛān (*nf*) a duster; whisk; sweepings.

झाड़/ना jha:ṛnā: (*v*) to sweep, to brush, to clean; to chide, to reprimand; to extort; to grab; to shake or knock off; to hocus-pocus; -**पोंछ** brushing and cleaning; cleansing; -**फूँक** hocus-pocus; -**बुहार** sweeping and cleaning.

झाड़ी jha:ṛi: (*nf*) a bush, thicket.

झाड़ू jha:ṛu: (*nm*) a broom, besom; ~**कश**/~**बरदार** a sweeper; –**फिरना** to be swept off; to be clean-swept; everything to be ruined/undone; –**मारना** to damn a thing, to be done with it.

झापड़ jha:paṛ (*nm*) a full-blooded slap; –**रसीद करना** to slap violently.

झाबर jha:bar (*nm*) a moor.

झाबा jha:ba: (*nm*) a pannier.

झाम jhā:m (*nm*) a dredger, grabbing crane.

झामक jha:māk (*nm*) see **झाँवाँ**.

झारी jha:ri: (*nf*) a ewer with a slender neck and a spout fitted into it.

झाल jha:l (*nm*) a solder; soldering/welding.

झालना jha:lnā: (*v*) to solder, to weld.

झालर jha:lar (*nf*) festoon; frill, fringe; ~**दार** fimbriate, frilled, fitted with festoons.

झाला jha:la: (*nm*) a rhythmic pattern of instrumental music.

झिंझरी jhījhri: (*nf*) a lattice, grating.

झिझक jhijhak (*nf*) hesitation, hitch; shyness; **–खोलना** to break the ice, to shed off one's hesitation/shyness.

झिझकना jhijhaknā: (*v*) to hesitate; to feel shy.

झिड़कना jhiṛaknā: (*v*) to tick off, to snap, to snub.

झिड़की jhiṛki: (*nf*) ticking off, snap, a snub; **–देना** to tick off, to snub.

झिपना jhipnā: (*v*) to be shut/closed (as **आँखें**) per force.

झिरझिरा jhirjhira: (*a*) thinned/thin; threadbare; hence **~पन** (*nm*).

झिरी jhiri: (*nf*) slit, recess; fissure, cleft; chink.

झिलमिल jhilmil (*nf*) twinkle/twinkling; shimmer/shimmering; flicker/flickering.

झिलमिलाना jhilmila:nā: (*v*) to twinkle; to shimmer; to flicker.

झिलमिलाहट jhilmila:haṭ (*nf*) twinkle; shimmer; flicker.

झिलमिली jhilmili: (*nf*) venetian shutters, persiennes.

झिल्ली jhilli: (*nf*) a membrane; film; pellicle; a kind of cricket; **~दार** membranous; covered with a film/pellicle.

झींकना jhī:knā: (*v*) to repine; to fret; to grumble/grouse.

झींखना jhī:khnā: (*v*) see **झींकना**

झींगा jhī:ga: (*nf*) a prawn.

झींगुर jhī:gur (*nm*) (an insect) cricket.

झीना jhī:nā: (*a*) thinned/thin, threadbare; hence **~पन** (*nm*).

झील jhi:l (*nf*) a lake.

झुंझना jhūjhnā: (*nm*) see **झुनझुना**.

झुंझला/ना jhūjhla:nā: (*v*) to get irritated/petulant/peeved/annoyed; to be peeved, to fret; **–कर बोलना** to snap/bite one's nose off.

झुंझलाहट jhūjhla:haṭ (*nf*) irritation, irascibility, peevishness, petulance; annoyance.

झुंड jhūṇḍ (*nm*) a flock, herd; clump, cluster; **–के झुंड** swarms, hordes.

झुकना jhuknā: (*v*) to bow; to droop; to stoop; to bend; to yield; to lean (towards); to be tilted.

झुकाना jhuka:nā: (*v*) to bend; to cause to stoop, to force to yield; to cause to lean (towards); to tilt.

झुकाव jhuka:v (*nm*) inclination, bent, bias; leaning; curvature; flexion; trend; tilt.

झुटपुटा jhuṭpuṭa: (*nm*) twilight, the morning or evening hour when the sunlight is very faint.

झुठलाना jhuṭhla:nā: (*v*) to belie, to falsify; to give a lie to.

झुठाई jhuṭha:i: (*nf*) falsehood, untruth.

झुनझुना jhuṇjhunā: (*nm*) a child's rattle, rattling toy.

झुनझुनाना jhuṇjhunā:nā: (*v*) to produce a rattle/rattling sound.

झुमका jhumka: (*nm*) pendant (of an ear-ring etc.)

झुरझुरी jhurjhuri: (*nf*) a shivering sensation, shivering.

झुरमुट jhurmūṭ (*nm*) an abatis, a cluster of shrubs, grove; **~दार** full of shrubs, shrubby.

झुर्री jhurri: (*nf*) wrinkle, crinkle, fold; **~दार** wrinkled, crinkled, rugose.

झुलना jhulnā: (*v*) see **झूला**.

झुलसन jhulsān (*nf*) a sensation of burning; a slight burn, scorch, singe; charring.

झुलसना jhulasnā: (*v*) to be scorched, to be singed; to be effected with a burning sensation; to be charred

झुलाना jhula:nā: (*v*) to swing, to rock; to keep in suspense/uncertainty.

झूँझल jhū:jhal (*nf*) see झुँझलाहट.

झूठ jhu:ṭh (*a*) false, untrue, incorrect; (*nm*) falsehood, lie, untruth; ~मूठ falsely; without any rhyme or reason; just for fun; ०का sham, false; -सच partly true and partly false, a mixture of fact and fiction; —का पुतला falsehood personified, a habitual liar; —का पुल बाँधना lit. to build a bridge of lies —to tell one lie after another; —सच जोड़ना/लगाना to add fabrication to fact; to make false complaints.

झूठन jhu:ṭhan (*nf*) see जूठन.

झूठा jhu:ṭha: (*a*) false; fictitious; untrue; sham; mock; feigned; (*nm*) a liar; —पड़ना to prove false; to be rendered ineffective; झूठे का मुँह काला a liar is damned to ultimate exposure; झूठे को घर/क़ब्र तक पहुँचाना to expose a lie and humiliate the liar; to call off one's bluff, to prick a bubble; झूठे पर ख़ुदा की लानत the liar be damned; झूठों का बादशाह/सरदार a king of liars, a liar par excellence.

झूमना jhu:mnā: (*v*) to swing in a gay mood or intoxication; to sway to and fro.

झूल jhu:l (*nm*) a long loose overcover (for a horse, an elephant, etc.).

झूलना jhu:lnā: (*v*) to swing; to oscillate; to dangle; to linger in suspense; (*nm*) see झूला.

झूला jhu:la: (*nm*) a swing; suspended scaffold; cradle.

झेंपना jhēpnā: (*v*) to blush; to feel abashed/shy; to be put out of countenance.

झेंपू jhēpu: (*a*) bashful, temperamentally shy, prone to feel abashed; hence ~पन (*nm*).

झेलना jhelnā: (*v*) to bear, to endure, to suffer.

झोंक jhōk (*nf*) impulse, impulsive sway; swing; craze; tantrums; —में in a mood of craze, in an impulsive sway.

झोंकना jhōknā: (*v*) to throw in; to thrust in; to pour in.

झों/का jhōka: (*nm*) a blast, puff, whiff, gust, jet; ~केदार gusty, whiffy, puffy.

झोंटा jhōṭa: (*nm*) a thick lock of dishevelled hair; a push (given to a swing).

झोंपड़ा jhōpṛa: (*nm*) a shanty, hut.

झोंपड़ी jhōpṛi: (*nf*) a hut, small cottage; —में रहकर महलों के ख्वाब देखना to live in a shanty and dream of plenty, to live on earth and dream of heaven.

झोल jhol (*nm*) bagginess; sagging looseness; rumple, pucker; soup; broth; a fine coating of a metal; ~दार baggy; sagging; loose; rumpled, puckered; soupy.

झोला jhola: (*nm*) a bag, kit, haversack, knapsack.

झोली jholi: (*nf*) a small bag; any cloth stretched out to collect something; begging bag; —फैलाना to beg; to seek a favour; —में डालना to give away, to donate.

झौंरा jhaura: (*nm*) a foliage, cluster (of leaves, etc.).

ञ ṇa—the fifth and final (nasal) letter of the second pentad (i.e. चवर्ग) of the Devna:gri: alphabet

ट ṭa—the first letter of the third pentad (i.e. टवर्ग) of the Devna:gri: alphabet.

टंक tāṅk (*nm*) a coin; typing; ~लिपि typescript; ~विज्ञान numismatics; ~शाला see टकसाल.

टंकक ṭāṅkak (*nm*) a typist.

टंकण tāṅkān̲ (*nm*) typing; soldering; mintage.

टँकाई ṭāka:i: (*nf*) (the work of or wages for) stitching/studding/soldering; mintage.

टंकार ṭāṅka:r (*nf*) the twang (of a bow); tinkling sound; hence ~ना (*v*).

टंकी ṭāṅki: (*nf*) a tank; cistern; reservoir.

टँगड़ी ṭāgṛi: (*nf*) a leg-trick (in wrestling); ~बाज़ an obstructionist, one habituated to create obstacles; hence ~बाज़ी; –अड़ाना to butt in, to intermeddle; to create or cause an obstacle/obstruction; –मारना to apply a leg-trick; (fig.) to create obstruction.

टं/टा ṭān̲ṭa: (*nm*) wrangling; altercation; quarrel; encumbrance; botheration; used as the second member in the compound झगड़ा-टंटा (see); ~टेबाज़ querulous; prone to wrangle or altercate; hence ~बाज़ी (*nf*).

टक ṭak (*nf*) a stare, gaze; –बाँधना to stare intently; –लगाना to wait impatiently.

टकटकी ṭakṭaki: (*nf*) a gaze, stare, fixed look; –बाँधना see -टक बाँधना; –लगाना see टक लगाना.

टकटोह(र)ना ṭakṭoh(r)nā: (*v*) to grope; to make a preliminary survey, to reconnoitre; to seek to know one's mind by letting off a feeler.

टकराना ṭakra:nā: (*v*) to clash; to collide; to knock (against), to dash (against); to encounter.

टकसाल ṭaksa:l (*nf*) a mint.

टकसाली ṭaksali: (*a*) genuine (coin, etc.); standard (as speech); (*nm*) mint-master; -प्रयोग standard usage; –बोली standard speech; –भाषा standard language.

टका ṭaka: (*nm*) an out-of-currency Indian copper coin worth half an *anna* (equivalent roughly to current three paise); –पास न होना to be penniless; -सा जवाब देना to refuse point-blank, to say a flat 'no'; -सा मुँह लेकर रह जाना to be ticked off into a sense of humiliation, to feel humiliated; टके का inconsequential, negligible; worthless; -टके को न पूछना to consider as of no consequence/worthless; to reckon as a non-entity.

टका/र ṭaka:r (*nm*) the letter ट (ṭa) and its sound; ~कांत (word) ending in ट् (ṭ).

टकोरना ṭakornā: (*v*) to strike a drum or as a drum; to tap, to twang.

टक्कर ṭakkar (*nf*) a collision; clash; impact; confrontation; –का matching; equivalent; –खाना to bump against, to collide against; to go bumping; –झेलना to stand a loss; to endure a blow; –लेना to set one's face against; टक्करें मारना/मारते फिरना to toss/tumble about, to have confrontation with.

टखना ṭakhnā: (*nm*) an ankle; fetlock.

टटका ṭaṭka: (*a*) fresh.

टटपुँजिया ṭaṭpūjiya: (*a*) see टुटपुँजिया.

टटोलना ṭaṭolnā: (*v*) to feel; to give a feeler, to sound; to grope; to probe; to reconnoitre.

टट्टर ṭaṭṭar (*nm*) a large bamboo or wickerwork frame.

टट्टी ṭaṭṭi: (*nf*) a screen (made of bamboo parings or reed, etc.) latrine; stool, faeces; –की आड़/ओट में शिकार खेलना to indulge in clandestine activities, to attack from behind a cover, to sabotage.

टट्टू ṭaṭṭu: (*nm*) a pony.

टन ṭan (*nm*) (a measure of weight) ton; (*nf*) a tinkling/twanging sound; ~टन ding-dong; ting, peal.

टनटना/ना ṭanṭana:nā: (*v*) to peal, to ring; to tinkle; to twang; ~हट pealing/ringing/tinkling/twanging sound.

टना/का ṭanā:ka: (*nm*) a twang, sharp ring; ~केदार sharp ringing (e.g. voice); strong, powerful, scorching; ~के की strong; scorching.

टनाटन ṭanā:ṭan (*a* and *nf*) continuous twanging (sound).

टप ṭap (*nf*) the sound made by dripping liquid or falling fruits, etc.; the hood of a tonga, etc.; ~टप patter, pattering sound; –से instantly; with a patter.

टपकना ṭapaknā: (*v*) to drip; to leak; to drop; to dribble.

टपका ṭapka: (*a*) fallen (from the tree); टपके का (a fruit that has) fallen by itself (from the tree)—e.g. टपके का आम.

टपाटप ṭapa:ṭap (*adv*) with successive tapping, producing successive tapping sound, patteringly.

टप्पा ṭappa: (*nm*) a form of light classical Hindustani music employing very quick movements; bound (as of a ball, etc. –see टिप्पा).

टब ṭab (*nm*) a tub.

टमटम ṭāmṭām (*nf*) a tumtum, tandem, an open horse-carriage.

टमाटर ṭamā:ṭar (*nm*) a tomato; –की तरह लाल होना to be ruddy, to be tomato-red.

टरकना ṭaraknā: (*v*) to slip away, to slink off; to go slowly.

टरकाना ṭarkā:nā: (*v*) to put off, to tell off; to evade; to dispose of summarily.

टरटराना ṭarṭara:nā: (*v*) to prattle angrily or through discontentment to prate; to blab, to clatter.

टर्रटर्र ṭarraṭarr (*nf*) a croak, a deep

hoarse sound; angry or discontented prattle.

टर्रा ṭarra: (*a*) harsh-spoken (person), haughty, grumbling (person).

टर्राना ṭarra:nā: (*v*) to croak; to grumble haughtily.

टलना ṭalnā: (*v*) to be averted; to be postponed; to slip or slink away; to make off; to get out of the way; **टल जाना** to pass off, to blow over; to move away (said of an undesirable element); to be averted.

टल्लेबाज़ ṭalleba:z (*a*) evasive, given to evasiveness, (one) who tries to put off a thing (on some pretext).

टल्लेबाज़ी ṭalleba:zi: (*nf*) evasion, evasiveness, putting off (on one pretext or another).

टवर्ग ṭavarg (*nm*) the third pentad of the Devna:gri: alphabet incorporating the letters **ट,ठ,ड,ढ,** and **ण**.

टशन ṭashan (*nm*) a favourable superstitious act/remedy.

टस ṭas; **–से मस न होना** not to budge an inch; to stay unimpressed/unmoved.

टसर ṭasar (*nf*) tussore (a kind of cloth).

टसु/आ ṭasua: (*nm*) tear; **~ए बहाना** to shed tears, to cry.

टहनी ṭehnī: (*nf*) a twig, sprig.

टहल ṭehel (*nm*) drudgery, menial service; **–बजाना** to dance attendance (upon); to render menial service to.

टहलना ṭehelnā: (*v*) to stroll, to ramble, to saunter; to slip off.

टहलुआ ṭehelua: (*nm*) a drudge, menial servant.

टाँकना ṭā:knā: (*v*) to stud; to stitch; to cobble; to solder; to jot down.

टाँका ṭā:ka: (*nm*) a stitch; solder; **–मारना** to apply a stitch; **–लगाना** to solder.

टाँकी ṭā:ki: (*nf*) a chisel; a small piece cut or scooped out (of a melon, etc. to examine its quality).

टाँग ṭā:g (*nf*) a leg; **–अड़ाना** to butt in, to horn in, to intermeddle; **–खींचना** to pull one's leg; **–तले से निकलना** to accept defeat, to yield, to concede supremacy; **–तोड़ना** (ironical) to attain unprecedented excellence, to give/reduce to a bad shape/miserable plight (as **अँग्रेज़ी की टाँग तोड़ना**); **–पसार कर सोना** to spend a carefree time, to sleep carefreely, to be at complete ease.

टाँगना ṭā:gnā: (*v*) to hang; to suspend; to keep in suspense.

टाँट ṭā:ṭ (*nf*) the skull, bare head.

टाँड ṭā:ḍ (*nf*) a projecting shelf (in a wall), whatnot.

टाँडा ṭā:ḍa: (*nm*) a train or line of cattle etc.; unmanageable paraphernalia; trade-caravan; **–लादे फिरना** to go about with an unmanageable paraphernalia.

टाँय-टाँय ṭā:y-ṭā:y (*nf*) prattling, a sequence of hoarse sounds; **–फिस** much ado about nothing, ending up in smoke; a flash in the pan.

टाइप ṭa:ip (*nm*) type; typing; a typewriter; **~राइटर** a typewriter.

टाइपिस्ट ṭa:ipisṭ (*nm*) a typist.

टाइम ṭa:im (*nm*) time; **-टेबुल** timetable; **~पीस** a time-piece.

टाई ṭa:i: (*nf*) a necktie.

टाउनहॉल ṭa:unhɔll (*nm*) the town-hall.

टाट ṭa:ṭ (*nm*) a sack cloth; floor-mat; **–उलटना** to go bankrupt; **–पर मूँज की बखिया** a tag on a rag; **–बाहर होना** to be outcaste; **–में पाट की बखिया** a silk patch on a rag.

टाप ṭa:p (*nf*) tramp (of a horse); hoof; (*nm*) hood (of a tonga, etc.).

टाप/ना ṭa:pnā: (*v*) to leap or spring over; to be left helpless; to be left in a lurch; **~ते रह जाना** to be left in a lurch.

टापू ṭa:pu: (*nm*) an island.

टायर ṭa:yar (*nm*) a tyre.

टारपीडो ṭa:rpi:ḍo (*nm*) a torpedo.

टार्च ṭa:rch (*nm*) a torch.

टाल ṭa:l (*nf*) a stock, heap; a (fuel) shop; prevarication; postponement, deferment; evasion, avoidance; ~**मटोल** prevarication, putting off (on some pretext); avoidance, evasion; ०**करना** to drag one's feet; to gain time.

टालना ṭa:lnā: (*v*) to postpone, to put off; to procrastinate; to avert, to avoid/evade; **टाल जाना (किसी प्रश्न का उत्तर)** to fence with a question/questioner.

टिंचर ṭinchar (*nm*) tincture iodine.

टिंडा ṭinḍa: (*nm*) a kind of green vegetable—*Diospyros melanoxylon*.

टिकट ṭikaṭ (*nm*) a ticket; stamp; –**खिड़की** the ticket-window, booking counter; ~**घर** booking office; –**बाबू** a booking clerk.

टिकटिक ṭikṭik (*nf*) ticking sound (as that of a watch).

टिकटिकाना ṭikṭika:nā: (*v*) see **तिकतिकाना**.

टिकठी ṭikṭhi: (*nf*) a bier; stretcher; gallows; mantelpiece.

टिकना ṭiknā: (*v*) to last; to stay; to tarry; to stand (one's ground).

टिकाऊ ṭika:u: (*a*) durable, lasting; abiding; ~**पन** durability; abiding quality.

टिकिया ṭikiya: (*nf*) a small cake; tablet; pill.

टिकुली ṭikuli: (*nf*) a spangle; small glittering object gummed on the forehead by Indian women as ornamentation.

टिचन ṭichān (*a*) ready; fit; –**होना** to be/get ready.

टिटकारना ṭiṭka:rnā: (*v*) to make a ticking sound (esp. in urging an animal to pace ahead).

टिटहरी ṭiṭahri: (*nf*) a pewit, lapwing; sand-piper.

टिड्डा ṭiḍḍa: (*nm*) a grasshopper.

टिड्डी ṭiḍḍi: (*nf*) a locust; –**दल** locust swarm; ०**की तरह आना** to gather like a locust swarm.

टिप्पणी ṭippaṇi: (*nf*) a note; annotation; comment, observation; critical remark.

टिप्पस ṭippas (*nf*) manipulation, contrivance, manoeuvre to achieve an end; –**भिड़ाना/लड़ाना** to manipulate/to manoeuvre.

टिप्पा ṭippa: (*nm*) a rebound; bounce; **टिप्पेदार** bounding, bumping (ball etc.); –**खाना** to rebound.

टिब्बा ṭibba: (*nm*) see **टीबा**.

टिमटिमा/ना ṭimṭimā:nā: (*v*) to twinkle, to glimmer, to flicker, to scintillate; hence ~**हट** (*nf*).

टिमाक ṭimā:k (*nm*) foppishness, ostentation, showy make-up; ~**दार** ostentatious, used to showy make-up; made-up.

टीका ṭi:ka: (*nm*) vaccination; inoculation; a commentary (on a book, etc.); annotation; a small mark (of vermilion, sandalpaste, etc.) over the forehead; an ornament worn by a woman whose husband is alive; a pre-marriage ceremony; -**टिप्पणी** (adverse) comments, criticism.

टीकाकार ṭika:kā:r (*nm*) a commentator; an annotator.

टीन ṭi:n (*nm*) a can, tin; ~**बंद** canned, tinned.

टीप ṭi:p (*nf*) an entry; jotting down; pointing (in masonry); tapping; high pitch (in music); ~**कारी** pointing (in masonry); -**टाप** finishing touches, pointing, tip-topping.

टीपना ṭi:pnā: (*v*) to enter; to record, to jot down; to point; to copy.

टीबा ṭi:ba: (*nm*) a dune; undoing; –करना to undo, to bring ruination; –होना to be undone, to be ruined.

टीम ṭi:m (*nf*) a team (homogeneous group).

टीमटाम ṭi:mṭa:m (*nm*) showing off; dressing; ostentation; finishing touches.

टीला ṭi:la: (*nm*) a mount, mound, hillock, hummock.

टीस ṭi:s (*nf*) smarting pain, acute throbbing pain; lingering (mental) agony.

टीसना ṭi:snā: (*v*) to smart, to throb with pain; to suffer from a throbbing agony.

टुँड़ी ṭũṛi: (*nf*) the navel.

टुकड़ ṭukar—an allomorph of टुकड़ा used as the first member in compound words; ~खोर/तोड़ lit. one who thrives on leavings –a sponge.

टुक/ड़ा ṭukṛa: (*nm*) a piece, fragment; part; splinter; (fig) leavings; ~ड़े तोड़ना to sponge on; ~ड़े-टुकड़े करना to cut into pieces; ~ड़े-टुकड़े के लिए तरसना to be starved for every bit; ~ड़ों पर पलना, (किसी के) to thrive on leavings.

टुकड़ी ṭukṛi: (*nf*) a detachment (of troops); group; stone slab.

टुकुर-टुकुर ṭukur-ṭukur (*adv*) with a stare, with a fixed look.

टुच्चा ṭuchcha: (*a*) lowly, mean; petty; (*nm*) a skunk; hence ~पन (*nm*).

टुटपुँजिया ṭuṭpũjiya: (*a*) of meagre means/resources, bankrupt.

टुल्ल ṭull (*a*) heavily drunk, overdrunk; out of senses.

टूक ṭu:k (*nm*) a piece, fragment, part; -टूक होना to be broken into pieces, to be shattered.

टूटना ṭu:ṭnā: (*v*) to break, to be broken; to be fractured; to be shattered; to have twitching pain (as देह–); to be on the wane; to be dissolved (as साझेदारी–); to fail (as बैंक–); टूट-फूट wear and tear, breakage, breach; damage; टूटा-फूटा broken; damaged; decrepit, worn out; टूट पड़ना to attack; to pounce; to come down suddenly on; to jump upon, to pounce upon, to come down on; to fly at (upon); टूटी-फूटी broken, imperfect (as ०भाषा).

टूर्नामेंट ṭu:rnā:mēn̲ṭ (*nm*) a tournament.

टें ṭẽ (*nf*) screech of a parrot; -टें babbling, prating; –होना, –बोल जाना to collapse, to crash down.

टेंट ṭẽṭ (*nf*) a fold in the loin cloth; ripe fruit of करील tree; pupilary bulge of the eye; ~दार having a pupilary bulge in the eye.

टेंटी ṭẽṭi: (*nf*) ripe fruit of the करील tree.

टेंटुआ ṭẽṭua: (*nm*) the throttle, the throat; –दबाना/मसकना to throttle; not to allow to speak freely.

टेंडर ṭẽn̲ḍar (*nm*) a tender.

टेक ṭek (*nf*) a prop, stay, support; refrain, burden of a song; resolve; ~बंदी strutting; –निबाहना/निभाना/पूरी करना to fulfil one's resolve; –पकड़ना to stick resolutely to one's resolve.

टेकना ṭeknā: (*v*) to lean; to support; to rest; to prop, to set down

टेकरी ṭekri: (*nf*) a knoll, hummock.

टेट ṭet (*nf*) see टेंट.

टेढ़ ṭeṛh (*nf*) a curve, bend, curvature; crookedness; ~दार having a curve/bend.

टेढ़ा ṭeṛha: (*a*) curved; bent; oblique; skew; difficult; intricate; ~ई/पन curvature; bend; obliquity; intricacy; skewness; –मामला an intricate case/affair; -मेढ़ा crooked/

zigzag, irregular; –पड़ना to become difficult; to assume a rigid attitude; टेढ़ी आँख/नज़र से देखना to cast an angry glance, to look wrathfully; टेढ़ी खीर a hard nut to crack, difficult job, टेढ़ी-सीधी कहना/सुनाना to scold roundly, to reproach.

ना ṭenā: (*v*) to sharpen, to whet; to twist and to taper off to a point (as मूँछ).

निस ṭenis (*nf*) (the game of) tennis.

र ṭer (*nf*) a call; loud appeal/summon.

रना ṭernā: (*v*) to call, to summon.

लीप्रिंटर ṭeli:printer (*nm*) a teleprinter.

लीफ़ोन ṭelifōn (*nm*) a telephone.

लीविज़न ṭeli:vizān (*nm*) a television.

व ṭev (*nf*) habit, wont, settled tendency; –पड़ना to fall into the habit (of), to acquire the habit of.

सुआ ṭesua: (*nm*) see टसुआ.

सू ṭesu: (*nm*) the tree *Butea frondosa* and its flower.

क ṭāṅk (*nm*) a tank; ~बेधी/मार anti-tank; ॰गोला an anti-tank shell/bomb; ~बेधी/मार तोप an anti-tank gun.

स ṭaiks (*nm*) a tax.

सी ṭaiksi: (*nf*) a (car) taxi.

टा ṭōṭa: (*nm*) one-handed person.

टी ṭōṭi: (*nf*) a tap; nozzle; (water) faucet; spout, spigot; ~दार spouted, fitted with a tap/nozzle/spigot.

क ṭok (*nf*) an interruption; questioning, interrogation; -टाक interruption and intervention.

कन ṭokān (*nm*) a token.

कना ṭoknā: (*v*) to interrupt; to question, to interrogate.

करा ṭokra: (*nm*) a large basket, coop; hence टोकरी (*nf*).

टका ṭoṭka: (*nm*) a superstitious remedy, sorcerous act, magical charm; an amulet.

टोटा ṭoṭa: (*nm*) a loss, damage; want, scarcity; butt-end (of a cigarette, etc.); rench; –पड़ना/होना to be/become scarce.

टोड़ी ṭoṛi: (*a*) sycophant; detestable; disgusting.

टोना ṭonā: (*nm*) magic, spell; sorcerous act; (*v*) to touch, to feel; -टोटका sorcerous act, supersititious remedy; witchcraft, black art; hence टोनहाई (*nf*).

टोप ṭop (*nm*) a hat; helmet.

टोपा ṭopa: (*nm*) a large-sized headwear (worn during winters).

टोपी ṭopi: (*nf*) a cap; cover; cowl; percussion cap; ~दार capped, cowled; percussion– (as a gun); –उछालना to expose publicly, to cause public disgrace; –उतारना to insult/humiliate.

टोल ṭol (*nm*) a band, batch; group; –बनाना to form a group.

टोला ṭola: (*nm*) a quarter/zone of a town or village.

टोली ṭoli: (*nf*) a team, batch, band, group, troop, troupe.

टोह ṭoh (*nf*) search, reconnaissance; sounding; whereabout; –में रहना to be in constant search, to keep track of; –लगाना to sound, to reconnoitre to take up the trace of.

टोहना ṭohnā: (*v*) to sound; to reconnoitre, to take up the trace of

टोहिया ṭohiya: (*nm*) a reconnoiterer; tracer; sounding person.

ट्यूब ṭyu:b (*nf*) a tube.

ट्यूबवेल ṭyu:bvel (*nm*) a tube-well.

ट्रंक ṭraṅk (*nm*) a trunk, box.

ट्रक ṭrak (*nf*) a truck.

ट्रस्ट ṭrasṭ (*nf*) a trust; ट्रस्टी a trustee.

ट्राम ṭra:m (*nf*) a tram car.

ट्रेडमार्क ṭredma:rk (*nm*) a trademark.

ट्रेन ṭren (*nf*) a railway train.

ट्रेनिंग ṭrenɪng (*nf*) training; **–देना** to impart training, to train.

ट्रैक्टर ṭraikṭar (*nm*) a tractor.

ठ

ठ ṭha—the second letter of the third pentad (i.e. **टवर्ग**) of the Devna:gri: alphabet.

ठंड ṭhāṉḍ (*nf*) cold; coldness, chilliness.

ठंडक ṭhāṉḍak (*nf*) coolness; **–पड़ना** to feel cooled; to feel comforted/gratified.

ठंडा ṭhāṉḍa: (*a*) cool; cold; bleak; dull; insipid, lifeless; unresponsive; unfeeling; **~पन** frigidity, unresponsiveness; **–स्वभाव** cool/dispassionate temperament; **–स्वर** dispassionate voice, dispassionate manner of speech; **ठंडे-ठंडे** quietly; before it is too late; while it is cool; **–करके खाओ** blow first, sip afterwards; act in haste, have a nasty taste; **–करना** to pacify; to put out, to extinguish; **–पड़ना** to be pacified, to be subdued or tamed; to lose all passion or warmth; to be extinguished; to be assuaged; **–पड़ना, जोश** to draw/pull in one's horns; **–होना** to be put out/extinguished, to pass away; to be unresponsive/frigid; **ठंडी साँस लेना** to heave a sigh; **ठंडे दिमाग़/दिल से** coolly, dispassionately.

ठक ṭhak (*nf*) a rap; (*a*) aghast, baffled; **~ठक** rap, tap; knock; **–हो जाना to be aghast/stunned/baffled.**

ठकठकाना ṭhakṭhaka:nā: (*v*) to knock; to produce a sequence of rappin[g] or tapping sounds.

ठका/र ṭhaka:r (*nm*) the letter **ठ** (ṭha) and its sound; **~रांत** (word) ending in **ठ्** (ṭh).

ठकुरसुहाती ṭhakursuha:ti: (*nf*) flattery, likeable talk, utterance i[n] one's master's voice.

ठकुराई ṭhakura:i: (*nf*) supremacy[,] nobility; haughtiness; lordliness.

ठग ṭhag (*nm*) a thug, cheat, an impostor; **~ई/पन/हाई** (the practice o[r] act of) cheating/thuggery/dupery.

ठगना ṭhagnā: (*v*) to cheat, to dupe[,] to defraud; **ठगा-सा** aghast, completely lost/non-plussed.

ठगी ṭhagi: (*nf*) thuggery, the ac[t] or practice of duping or cheating.

ठट्ठ ṭhaṭṭh (*nm*) throng, millin[g] crowd; huge heap;**–के ठट्ठ** throngs[,] huge heaps.

ठट्ठा ṭhaṭṭha: (*nm*) fun, humour[,] joke, jest, wagging; **ठट्ठेबाज़** a wag given to joke and jest; hence **ठट्ठेबाज़ी**; **–मारना/लगाना** to burst out laughing.

ठठ ṭhaṭh (*nm*) see **ठट्ठ**.

ठठरी ṭhaṭhri: (*nf*) a skeleton; bier[,] skin and bone; **–बँधना** to be reduced to a skeleton.

ठठाना ṭhaṭha:nā: (*v*) see **ठट्ठा** (**–मारना**).

ठठेरा ṭhaṭhera: (*nm*) a tinker, brazi[er]; **ठठेरे-ठठेरे बदलाई** a bargain betwee[n] two equals; diamond cuts diamond.

ठनक ṭhanāk (*nf*) a deep ringing sound as of a drum-beat; hence **~ना** (*v*).

ठनठन ṭhānṭhān (*nf*) metallic ringing sound; clink; **~गोपाल** a have-nothing, a pauper.

ठनठनाना ṭhānṭhānā:nā: (*v*) to produce a **ठनठन**/clinking sound.

ठनना ṭhannā: (*v*) to be resolved; hostilities to ensue, (fighting) to be launched; **ठनी रहना** to live a cat and dog life.

ठनाका ṭhanā:ka: (*nm*) a short sharp metallic ring, clink.

ठनाठन ṭhanā:ṭhān (*nf*) see **ठनठन**; coins, money.

ठप ṭhap (*adv*) at a standstill; reduced to a state of inactivity; closed; **–कर देना** to freeze out.

ठप्पा ṭhappa: (*nm*) a stamp; mould; die; matrix, impression; **–लगाना** to be branded/typed; **ठप्पेदार** stamped, bearing a stamp.

ठर्रा ṭharra: (*nm*) country liquor.

ठस ṭhas (*a*) nitwit, dull; thick, compact, dense; (a coin) of dull sound; **–दिमाग़** a nitwit, dullard.

ठसक ṭhasak (*nf*) uppishness; perkiness; swagger, affectation; **~दार** uppish, perky; swaggering.

ठस/का ṭhaska: (*nm*) see **ठसक**; a sense of ego; hacking sound of cough; **~के से रहना** to keep one's sense of self-respect/ego intact/conspicuous.

ठसाठस ṭhasa:ṭhas (*a*) stuffed full, crowded, packed, cram-full; (*adv*) fully, crowdedly.

ठस्सा ṭhassa: (*nm*) a hacking sound of cough (caused by obstruction in the wind or food-pipe etc.).

ठहरना ṭhehrnā: (*v*) to stop, to halt, to pause; to stay, to wait; to stabilise; **ठहर-ठहर कर** by fits and starts, spasmodically.

ठहराव ṭhehra:v (*nm*) stability; settlement; pause.

ठहाका ṭhaha:ka: (*nm*) peal/explosion of laughter; **–लगाना** to burst into laughter, to laugh aloud; **ठहाकेदार** accompanied by peal/explosion of laughter.

ठाँय ṭhā:y (*nf*) the sound of gunfire; **-ठाँय** persistent sound of gunfire.

ठाँव ṭhā:v (*nf*) a place, opportune place.

ठाँसना ṭhā:snā: (*v*) to cram full; to stuff full; to thrust.

ठाकुर ṭha:kur (*nm*) a lord, master; God; God's idol; (title for a) **क्षत्रिय**; **~द्वारा** a temple; **~बाड़ी** a temple.

ठाट ṭha:ṭ (*nm*) pomp, splendour, magnificence; **-बाट** pomp and show.

ठाठ ṭha:ṭh (*nm*) pomp, splendour, magnificence; a pattern of musical composition; concourse; **~दार** magnificent, splendid, pompous; accompanied by fanfare/pomp and show; **-बाट** pomp and show; **ठाठें मारना** to flow in abundance, to form a concourse.

ठानना ṭha:nnā: (*v*) to resolve, to determine; to launch.

ठाला ṭha:la: (*a*) idle; out of employment; unoccupied; (*nm*) scarcity; shortage.

ठिका/ना ṭhika:nā: (*nm*) the destination; place, abode; station; trust; a small estate; **~नेदार** owner of an estate; **~ने आना** to veer round, to come to the proper course; **~ने का** appropriate; trustworthy; reasonably good; to the point; **~ने की बात** a rational or logical utterance/proposal/remark, etc.; **~ने न रहना** not to be in proper shape/form/state/frame; **~ने पहुँचाना** (to cause) to reach the destination; ~ने लगना to be settled. to find an employment; to be put to death; ~ने लगाना to give one his gruel, to put to proper use; to find an employment/a station; to put to death.

ठिगना ṭhignā: (*a*) short, short-statured, dwarfish; hence ~पन (*nm*).

ठिठकना ṭhiṭhaknā: (*v*) to hesitate, to waver, to pause and ponder; to stop short; to stand amazed.

ठिठुरना ṭhiṭhurnā: (*v*) to be chilled, to shiver with cold.

ठिठोली ṭhiṭholi: (*nf*) persiflage, banter, jesting, jocularity; —करना to banter, to rally, to make fun, to crack jokes; hence ठिठोलिया (*a* and *nm*).

ठि/या ṭhiya: (*nm*) a fixed place (of habitation or activity); station; seat; ~येदार one owning/in possession of a ठिया.

ठीक ṭhi:k (*a*) right, correct, exact; proper; true; (*adv*) all right; precisely, accurately; -ठाक regularly, properly; shipshape; all right; regular; so-so; ०होना to be well; to be quite oneself; ~मठीक just, exact(ly), precise(ly); —उतरना/निकलना to prove correct, to be vindicated; —कर देना to bring to senses, to fix in one's proper place; to repair; —होना to recover; to be correct; to come to senses.

ठीक/रा ṭhi:kra: (*nm*) a shard, potsherd; a broken piece of earthenware; a worthless thing; trite; ~रा समझना to consider as of no worth; ~री (*nf*).

ठी/का ṭhi:ka: (*nm*) a contract; ~केदार see ठेकेदार under ठेका.

ठुकराना ṭhukra:nā: (*v*) to kick off to knock away; to treat/reject contemptuously.

ठुकाई ṭhuka:i: (*nf*) beating; tamping.

ठुड्डी ṭhuḍḍi: (*nf*) see ठोड़ी.

ठुनकना ṭhunāknā: (*v*) to whimper.

ठुमकना ṭhumāknā: (*v*) to walk with a jerky, mincing or wanton gait; rhythmic footwork in dancing, to move the feet alternately in a rhythmic manner (preparatory to dancing); hence ठुमक (*nf*); ठुमका (*nm*).

ठुमरी ṭhumri: (*nf*) a style of classical Indian music.

ठुर्री ṭhurri: (*nf*) semi-parched grain.

ठूँठ ṭhū:ṭh (*nm*) a stump, stub; deadwood.

ठूँठा ṭhū:ṭha: (*a*) stubby; leafless (tree, etc.)

ठूँसना ṭhū:snā: (*v*) to stuff full, to cram; to glut; to thrust forcibly.

ठूँसा ṭhū:sa: (*nm*) a forceful fist-blow.

ठेंगा ṭhẽga: (*nm*) the thumb (used only to show contempt or defiance); bludgeon; —दिखाना lit. to show the thumb—to express a contemptuous or defiant refusal; to disappoint; ठेंगे पर नचाना to make somebody dance to his tune; ठेंगे से care a fig !, not to care two hoots.

ठेका ṭheka: (*nm*) a contract; halting place; rhythmic percussion or stress (in music); ठेकेदार a contractor; —लेना to own responsibility; to hold aloft the banner of; to be in possession of.

ठेठ ṭheṭh (*a*) pure, genuine, unadulterated, unsophisticated; proper; typical.

ठेलना ṭhelnā: (*v*) to thrust, to shove, to push forward, to propel, to thrust with force.

ठेलमठेल ṭhelāmṭhel (*nf*) hustle and bustle; jostling.

ठेला ṭhela: (*nm*) a trolly; cart; truck; barrow: stroke; thrust, violent push; –देना to thrust/push forward.

ठेस ṭhes (*nf*) a knock in the sole (causing lingering pain); (emotional) shock; –लगना/पहुँचना to receive a setback/shock.

ठोंग ṭhōg (*nf*) a peck.

ठोंगा ṭhōga: (*nm*) a large envelope.

ठोकना ṭhoknā: (*v*) to dust one's coat; to beat; to hammer; to drive into (as a nail); to tamp; –बजाना to make a thorough assessment, to test thoroughly; ठोक-पीट कर thoroughly; by thrashing; ०वैद्यराज/हकीम बनाना to beat into an expert, to coerce into acting a sham expert.

ठोकर ṭhokar (*nf*) a kick, stroke; percussion; stumbling toe; front portion of the threshold; –खाना to stumble; to be knocked; to suffer a loss (on account of negligence, etc); –खाते फिरना to be kicked about, to suffer kicks; to wander aimlessly; –मारना to kick off; to treat with contempt; –लगना to suffer a kick of adversity; to be knocked down.

ठोड़ी ṭhoṛi: (*nf*) the chin; –छूना/में हाथ डालना/में हाथ लगाना to cajole, to entreat; to try to humour.

ठोर ṭhor (*nm*) see **ठोंग**.

ठोस ṭhos (*a*) solid; sound; ~पन solidity.

ठौर ṭhaur (*nm*) a place; -ठाँव/ठिकाना whereabout, habitat; -कुठौर out of place; indiscriminately; in vital parts; –हो जाना to die then and there/instantaneously.

ड

ड ḍa the third letter of the third pentad (i.e. टवर्ग) of the Devna:gri: alphabet.

डंक ḍaṅk (*nm*) a sting; the tip of a nib or pen; ~दार having a sting; stinged; –तोड़ना to deprive of the sting/venomousness; –मारना to make a caustic/stinging remark.

डंका ḍaṅka: (*nm*) a kettle-drum; –बजना to be renowned; to exercise sway over; to achieve fame all over; –बजना, लड़ाई का hostilities to commence/be launched; the battle to be initiated;–पीटना/–बजाना to make a public pronouncement; to make public; डंके की चोट (पर) कहना to proclaim from house-top, to announce publicly without fear.

डंगर ḍāṅgar (*nm*) cattle; quadruped.

डंठल ḍāṉṭhal (*nm*) a stalk; stem.

डंड ḍāṉḍ (*nm*) an athletic exercise (in which both the hands are placed on the ground and then the semi-stretched body is bent down so as almost to touch the ground with the breast); muscular arm; penalty, fine; –पेलना to take exercise in the form of डंड (see); to take it absolutely easy, to be completely carefree.

डंडा ḍāṉḍa: (*nm*) a staff, stick, wand; -डोली a children's play; –दिखाना to extend a threat of physical violence, to threaten; डंडे का राज

club law; डंडे के ज़ोर से by the dint of might, by resorting to the rod; डंके के ज़ोर पर शासन चलाना to rule with a rod of iron; डंडे खाना to be beaten with a stick; डंडे बजाना to loaf about; to idle away time.

डंडी ḍa̲n̲ḍi: (*nf*) the beam of a scale; handle (as of an umbrella); penis; –**मारना** to give short weight.

डँसना ḍāsnā: (*v*) to sting; to bite.

डकार ḍaka:r (*nf*) a belch; eructation; (*nm*) the letter ड (ḍa) and its sound; –**न लेना** to appropriate another's due and not to let out any sign of it, to quietly assimilate another's due; –**जाना/लेना** to appropriate and assimilate another's due; to swallow.

डकारना ḍāka:rnā: (*v*) to belch, to eructate; to polish off (an eatable); to swallow; to misappropriate.

डकारांत ḍaka:rā:nt (*a*) (word) ending in ḍ (ड्).

डकैत ḍakait (*nm*) a dacoit, bandit.

डकैती ḍakaiti: (*nf*) a dacoity, banditry.

डकौत ḍakaut (*nm*) a sub-caste of Hindus who subsist on alms asked for on saturdays and claim skill in fortune telling; an individual of this caste.

डग ḍag (*nm*) a pace, step, stride; foot; –**भरना** to take a step, to stride, to step ahead; –**मारना** to pace/stride ahead, to go at a quicker pace.

डगमग ḍagmag (*a*) faltering, staggering; rolling; unsteady.

डगमगा/ना ḍagmaga:nā: (*v*) to falter, to stagger; to roll; to shimmy; ~**हट** faltering; staggering; rolling, shimmy.

डगर ḍagar (*nf*) a path, track, course.

डटना ḍaṭnā: (*v*) to stay/stand firm; to take a stand/position; to be determined; **डट जाना** to put one's foot down; **डटे रहना** to hold one's ground.

डट्टा ḍaṭṭa: (*nm*) a cork, spigot; plug.

डढ़ियल ḍaṛhiyal (*a*) bearded, sporting a bread.

डपट ḍapaṭ (*nf*) a sharp rebuke, reprimand; see **डाँट**–.

डपटना ḍapaṭnā: (*v*) to administer a sharp rebuke, to reprimand.

डपोरसंख ḍaporsaṅkh (*nm*) see **ढपोरसंख**.

डफ़ ḍaf (*nf*) a tambourine.

डफ़ली ḍafli: (*nf*) a kind of small tambourine.

डबडबाना ḍabḍaba:nā: (*v*) to be tearful (said of eyes).

डबल ḍabal (*a*) double; an old one-paisa coin; –**रोटी** a bread.

डब्बा ḍabba: (*nm*) a tiny box; chest; railway wagon; compartment; –**गुल होना** to come to a naught/an end; to be spent up.

डमरू ḍamru: (*nm*) a leather-covered musical percussion instrument, narrow in the middle and wider at the ends; ~**मध्य** a narrow strip of land or water connecting two expanses of water or two tracts of land respectively.

डर ḍar (*nm*) fear, fright, dread; –**जमना/-बैठना, (मन में)** a fear to go deep into one's mind.

डरना ḍarnā: (*v*) to fear/dread, to be afraid/frightened.

डरपोक ḍarpok (*a*) coward(ly); timid; hence ~**पन** (*nm*).

डराना ḍara:nā: (*v*) to frighten, to terrify.

डरावना ḍara:vnā: (*v*) fearful, dreadful; terrible, horrible.

डरावा ḍara:va: (*nm*) a scare, bugbear; deterrent.

डला ḍala: (*nm*) a lump, clod, small solid mass; big wickerwork basket.

डलिया ḍaliya: (*nf*) a small open basket; diminutive of **डला** (see).

डली ḍali: (*nf*) a small fragment, small lump.

डसना ḍasnā: (*v*) see **डँसना**.

डाँगर ḍā:gar (*nm*) see **डंगर**.

डाँट ḍā:t (*nf*) scolding, reprimand, sharp rebuke; **-डपट** rebuke and reproof; **–पड़ना** to get a rebuke/reprimand; to call/haul over the coals; **-फटकार** rebuke and reprimand; **–पिलाना/लगाना (बुजुर्गाना)** to talk to one like a Dutch uncle; **–में रखना** to keep under control.

डाँटना ḍā:ṭnā: (*v*) to scold, to rebuke sharply, to chide.

डाँड़ ḍā:ṛ (*nm*) a jib; an oar; fine, penalty; **–भरना** to have to pay a penalty, to have to suffer a fine; **–लगना** to be fined, a penalty to be imposed.

डाँड़ना ḍa:ṛnā: (*v*) to penalise/fine.

डाँड़ामेड़ी ḍā:ṛa:mēṛi: (*nf*) a demarcation wall; wordy duel.

डाँड़ी ḍā:ṛi. (*nf*) see **डंडी**; a dandy (a chair-like carriage used in hilly districts for carrying up passengers).

डाँस ḍā:s (*nm*) a kind of large-sized mosquito.

डाइन ḍa:in (*nf*) a witch; hag, sorceress; a scold; **–भी सात घर छोड़कर खाती है** a wise fox will never rob his neighbour's hen-roost.

डाइनामाइट ḍa:inā:ma:iṭ (*nm*) dynamite.

डाई ḍa:i: (*nf*) a die.

डाक ḍa:k (*nf*) mail, post, dak; **-खर्च** postage; **~खाना** a post office; **-गाड़ी** a mail train; **~घर** a post office; **-बँगला** a dak bungalow, a rest house for officials, etc.; **-भार** postage; **-व्यय** postage.

डाका ḍa:ka: (*nm*) a dacoity; **~जनी** commitment of (a series of) dacoities; **–डालना** to rob, to commit a dacoity; **–डालना, इज्जत पर** to rob one of one's honour; to make an assualt on one's modesty.

डाकिनी ḍa:kinī: (*nf*) a lamia, hell-cat, hag.

डाकिया ḍa:kiya: (*nm*) a postman.

डाकू ḍa:ku: (*nm*) a dacoit, bandit.

डाक्टर ḍa:kṭar (*nm*) a doctor, medical practitioner.

डाक्टरी ḍa:kṭari: (*nf*) the medical practice/professoin.

डाट ḍa:t (*nf*) a cork, spigot, plug; stopper; bung; archway; keystone; **~दार** stoppered, having a cork or plug.

डाढ़ ḍa:ṛh (*nf*) a molar or grinding tooth.

डाढ़ी ḍa:ṛhi: (*nf*) a beard, growth of hair on the face; **~जार** lit. one whose beard is burnt —a term of abuse generally used by women; **~दार** bearded; **–बनाना** to shave; **–रखना** to grow a beard.

डाबर ḍa:bar (*nm*) a pit; sullage; (*a*) dirty.

डाभ ḍa:bh (*nm*) see **अंकुर**; raw cocoanut.

डामर ḍa:mar (*nm*) tar, pitch, asphalt bitumen.

डायनमो ḍa:inamō (*nm*) dynamo.

डायरी ḍa:iri: (*nm*) a diary.

डायरेक्टर ḍa:irekṭar (*nm*) a director.

डाल ḍa:l (*nf*) a branch.

डालना ḍa:lnā: (*v*) to put in; to pour, to drop; to thrust; **डाल देना** to abandon, to cast off; to thrust in.

डॉलर ḍɔlar (*nm*) a dollar.

डाली ḍa:li: (*nf*) a branch; basket; basketful of fruits, sweets, etc. given as a present.

डावाँडोल ḍa:vā:ḍol (*a*) wavering; fluctuating; unsteady, fickle; wobbly; **–हालत में होना** to be in doldrums.

डा/ह ḍa:h (*nm*) jealousy, envy, ~**ही** jealous, envious.

डिंगल ḍiṅgal (*nf*) the mediaeval poetic language of the bards of Ra:jastha:n.

डिंगी ḍiṅgi: (*nf*) a dinghy, jolly-boat.

डिंब ḍimb (*nm*) embryo; -**ग्रंथि** ovary.

डिंभ ḍimbh (*nm*) a larva.

डिक्टेट/र ḍikṭeṭar (*nm*) a dictator; ~**री** dictatorship; dictatorial.

डिगना ḍignā: (*v*) to deviate; to swerve; to be shaken; **डिग जाना** –, **उसूल से** to run away from one's own guns; –, (**कौल से**) to eat one's words.

डिगरी ḍigri: (*nf*) a decree; degree; ~**दार** a decree-holder; –**इजरा करना** to issue a decree; –**तामील करना** to execute a decree; –**होना** a decree to be granted (in favour of)

डिज़ाइन ḍiza:in (*nm*) a design.

डिठौना ḍiṭhaunā: (*nm*) a black sooty mark on the face (supposedly to guard against an evil glance).

डिपो ḍipo (*nf*) a depot.

डिप्टी ḍipṭi: (*nm*) a deputy; –**कलक्टर** a deputy collector.

डिबिया ḍibiya: (*nf*) a tiny box, case or casket.

डिब्बा ḍibba: (*nm*) see **डब्बा**; ~**बंद** canned, tinned; hence ~**बंदी** (*nf*).

डिब्बी ḍibbi: (*nf*) see **डिबिया**.

डिमाई ḍima:i: (*nf*) demy—a measure of printing paper (18″×22″).

डिमारच ḍima:rach (*nm*) see **डैमरेज**.

डींग ḍi:g (*nf*) vaunt bragging, braggadocio, boasting hot air; ~**मार** braggart, braggadocio; –**मारना/हाँकना** to brag, to boast, to vomit.

डीज़ल ḍi:zal (*nm*) diesel (oil).

डील ḍi:l (*nm*) stature, size, physique; ~**डौल** stature; physique.

डुगडुगी ḍugḍugi: (*nf*) a small kettle-drum, tom-tom; see **डमरू**; proclamation by drum-beat; –**पीटना/बजाना** to make a proclamation.

डुग्गी ḍuggi: (*nf*) see **डुगडुगी**.

डुबकी ḍubki: (*nf*) a dip; –**मारना/लगाना** to take a dip; to keep out of sight for a long time, to disappear.

डुबाना ḍuba:nā: (*v*) to drown; to immerse, to submerge; to dip; to sully, to disgrace (as **नाम**–).

डुबाव ḍuba:v (*nm*) depth of water sufficient to be drowned, drowning.

डुबोना ḍubona: (*v*) see **डुबाना**.

डूँडा ḍū:ḍa: (*a*) single-horned (bull, cow, etc.), empty; unequipped; without ornaments.

डूबना ḍu:bnā: (*v*) to be drowned, to sink; to plunge, to be immersed/submerged; to set (as **सूरज**–); to be sullied or disgraced; **डूबते को तिनके का सहारा** a drowning man catches at a straw; **डूब मरना** to drown out of disgrace; **डूबती नैया पार लगाना** to resurrect a sinking boat/ship; **डूबा हुआ, (आपादमस्तक/चोटी तक)** over head and ears.

डेक ḍek (*nm*) the deck.

डेग ḍeg (*nf*) see **देग**.

डेढ़ ḍeṛh (*a*) one and a half; –**ईंट की मस्जिद चु(चि)नना**, –**चावल की खिचड़ी पकाना** to blow one's lone trumpet; –**पसली का** of a scanty frame, lean and thin.

डेरा ḍera: (*nm*) a camp; encampment; billet, abode; temporary abode; (*a*) left (as –**हाथ**); -**डंडा** belongings, household effects; –**उखाड़ना/उठाना** to get ready for departure, to decamp; –**डालना** to encamp, to come to stay.

डेरी ḍeri: (*nf*) a dairy; –**फ़ार्म** a dairy farm.

डेला ḍela: (*nm*) an eye-ball; a lump (of clay); a clod (of earth).

डेल्टा ḍelṭa: (*nm*) a delta.
डेवढ़ा ḍevṛha: (*a*) see **ड्योढ़ा**.
डेस्क ḍesk (*nm*) a desk.
डैना ḍainā: (*nm*) a wing (of a bird), pinion; **डैनेदार** winged, pinioned.
डैमरेज ḍaimrej (*nm*) demurrage.
डैलिया ḍailiya: (*nm*) dahlia—plant and its flower.
डैश ḍaish (*nm*) a dash.
डोंगा ḍōga: (*nm*) a large canoe, serving bowl.
डोंगी ḍōgi: (*nf*) see **डिंगी**.
डोंडी ḍōḍi: (*nf*) a tiny tom-tom; proclamation; **–पीटना/बजाना** to proclaim by beat of drum, to proclaim from house-tops.
डोम ḍōm (*nm*) a low caste in the traditional Hindu caste hierarchy.
डोर ḍor (*nf*) a string; thread.
डोरा ḍora: (*nm*) a thread, sewing or stitching thread; **डोरे डालना** to set one's cap at, to entice, to allure.
डोरिया ḍoriya: (*nm*) a kind of thin striped cloth.
डोरी ḍori: (*nf*) a string; lanyard.
डोल ḍol (*nm*) a round shallow pail (usually of iron); skip; **~ची** a small pail; wickerwork basket.
डोलना ḍolnā: (*v*) to swing, to oscillate; to rove about, to ramble, to wobble; to be tilted sideways.
डोला ḍola: (*nm*) a litter; a kind of sedan (for women); hence **डोली** (*nf*).
डौल ḍaul (*nm*) shape, form; appearance; a method/manner; device; opportunity, **-डाल** device, measure; chance, opportunity; **–लगाना** to find some way out.
डौली ḍauli: (*nm*) a field ridge.
ड्यूटी ḍyu:ṭi: (*nf*) duty, binding force of what is right; payment to public revenue levied on import, export etc.
ड्योढ़ा ḍyoṛha: (*a*) one and half-times.
ड्योढ़ी ḍyoṛhi: (*nf*) the threshold; vestibule; **~वान** a gate-keeper; watchman.
ड्रम ḍram (*nm*) a drum.
ड्राइंग ḍra:ɪng (*nf*) drawing; **–रूम** drawing room.
ड्राइव/र ḍra:ivar (*nm*) a driver; **~री** the job or position of a driver.
ड्रामा ḍra:mā: (*nm*) a drama.
ड्रिल ḍril (*nm*) drill, exercise.
ड्रेस ḍres (*nf*) dress.

ढ

ढ ḍha—the fourth letter of the third pentad (i.e. **टवर्ग**) of the Devna:gri: alphabet.
ढंग ḍhang (*nm*) manner, method, mode, way; demeanour; tact.
ढँढोरना ḍhãḍhornā: (*v*) to make a thorough search, to probe into each and every item.
ढँढोरा ḍhãḍhora: (*nm*) proclamation by beat of drum; proclamation; **–पीटना** to proclaim aloud; **ढँढोरची** a drummer, proclaimer.
ढकना ḍhaknā: (*v*) to cover; to conceal; (*nm*) see **ढक्कन**.

ढका/र ḍhaka:r (*nm*) the letter ढ (ḍha) and its sound; ~रांत (word) ending in ढ् (ḍh).

ढकेलना ḍhakelnā: (*v*) see धकेलना.

ढकोसना ḍhakosnā: (*v*) to ingurgitate (a liquid), to drink in large quantities (said in anger or sarcasm).

ढकोस/ला ḍhakosla: (*nm*) hypocrisy; humbug, sham; ~लेबाज़ a hypocrite, humbug; hence ~लेबाज़ी (*nf*).

ढक्कन ḍhakkān (*nm*) a lid, cover, buckler.

ढचरा ḍhachra: (*nm*) a skeleton, worn out framework (of a vehicle, etc.).

ढनमनाना ḍhanmānā:nā: (*v*) to stumble about, to roll.

ढपली ḍhapli: (*nf*) see डफ़ली.

ढपोरसं(शं)ख ḍhapors(sh)aṅkh (*nm*) a talk-tall give-nothing person, babbler, pratter.

ढब ḍhab (*nm*) manner, ways, conduct; fashion.

ढरकना ḍharaknā: (*v*) to roll/trickle down; to flow down.

ढर्रा ḍharra: (*nm*) way(s); path; method; style, fashion.

ढलकना ḍhalaknā: (*v*) see ढरकना.

ढलना ḍhalnā: (*v*) to be moulded/cast; to be poured out, to spill; to age; to set (as सूरज–); to be on the decline/decrease; ढलती उम्र advanced age, the phase of aging; ढलती जवानी withering/fading/dwindling youth.

ढलवाँ ḍhalvā: (*a*) cast; inclined, sloping; slanting; steep; –लोहा pig iron.

ढलाई ḍhala:i: (*nf*) moulding, casting; minting; ~खाना a foundry; ~गर a caster; ~घर a foundry, mintage.

ढलान ḍhalā:n (*nf*) a slope, descent, ramp.

ढलैया ḍhalaiya: (*nm*) a founder.

ढहना ḍhehnā: (*v*) to crash down; to fall/tumble down; to be razed/destroyed.

ढाँचा ḍhā:cha: (*nm*) frame, framework; skeleton; carcass; ~बंदी carcassing; fitting into a framework.

ढाई ḍha:i: (*a*) two and a half; –दिन की बादशाहत a transitory ascendance, short-lived authority.

ढाक ḍha:k (*nm*) the tree *Butea frondosa*; –के तीन पात for ever in straits, always in a tight position; sticking to an unwelcome convention/custom.

ढाटा ḍha:ṭa: (*nm*) a strip of cloth tied over the beard to keep it in good trim (used sometimes by the *Sikhs*) or around the face (generally used by dacoits to conceal their identity).

ढाढ़स ḍha:ṛhas (*nm*) solace, consolation; –देना/बँधाना to console, to comfort.

ढाना ḍha:nā: (*v*) to demolish, to dismantle, to pull down, to raze to the ground; to heap on

ढाबा ḍha:ba: (*nm*) a small commonplace hotel; thatched roofing of a hut.

ढाल ḍha:l (*nf*) a shield; slope, declivity, falling gradient; pitch, ramp; –बनाना to act as a defence/safeguard.

ढालना ḍha:lnā: (*v*) pour out (as liquor); to mould or cast; to found

ढालू ḍha:lu: (*a*) sloping, declivious, descending.

ढिंढोरा ḍhinḍhora: (*nm*) see ढँढोरा.

ढिठाई ḍhiṭha:i: (*nf*) contumeliousness, archness, pertness; impudence/audacity; (generally born out of the other person's indulgence).

ढिबरी ḍhibri: (*nf*) a nut socket; small earthen or tin lamp, –ढीली

होना to be crazy/whimsical, some mental screw to be loose.

ढिलाई ḍhila:i: (*nf*) sluggishness, laxity; flexibility; softness; infirmity; relaxation; leniency; flabbiness.

ढीठ ḍhi:ṭh (*a*) contumelious, arch, pert; impudent; audacious; hence ~पन/~पना (*nm*).

ढील ḍhi:l (*nf*) lavity; sluggishness; leniency; relaxation; –देना to allow relaxation; to be lenient; to let go, to give a long handle/rope.

ढीलना ḍhi:lnā: (*v*) to let go; to free; to untie; to relax; to loosen.

ढीला ḍhi:la: (*a*) loose; slack, sluggish; soft; infirm; flabby; -ढाला loose; flabby; sluggish; ~पन see ढिलाई; –करना to loosen; to soften; to force to give up a rigid posture; –पड़ना to soften, to mellow down; to get sluggish; to slacken; –होना to sotfen, to mellow down.

ढुलकना ḍhulaknā: (*v*) to roll down, to trickle down; to spill.

ढुलमुल ḍhulmul (*v*) vacillating; wavering; fickle/fickle-minded; unsteady; ~पन vacillation; fickleness/fickle-mindedness, unsteadiness; ~यक़ीन fickle-minded, wavering.

ढुलाई ḍhula:i: (*nf*) cartage, transportation (charges); haulage.

ढूँढना ḍhū:ḍhnā: (*v*) to seek, to search; to trace.

ढूह ḍhu:h (*nm*) a mound, hummock; heap.

ढेंकली ḍhēkli: (*nf*) a water-lifting appliance.

ढेर ḍher (*nm*) a heap; pile, accumulation; bulk, lot; (*a*) plenty, abundant; –करना to kill; to strike down; –हो जाना to die, to pass away; to be struck down.

ढेरी ḍheri: (*nf*) see ढेर (*nm*).

ढेला ḍhela: (*nm*) a clod; lump (of earth); brickbat.

ढोंग ḍhōg (*nm*) hypocrisy; fraud; imposture; ~बाज़ a hypocrite, an impostor; ~बाज़ी hypocritic/fraudulent practices, imposture.

ढोंगी ḍhōgi: (*a* and *nm*) impostorous, hypocritical, fraudulent; an impostor, hypocrite.

ढोना ḍhonā: (*v*) to transport, to cart, to haul, to carry; to bear (on head or shoulder, etc.).

ढोर ḍhor (*nm*) cattle; -डंगर cattle, livestock.

ढोल ḍhol (*nm*) a tomtom, large drum; barrel; -ढमक्का hustle and bustle; –की पोल खोलना to call a person's bluff, to make one show one's cards, to prick the bubble; –पीटना to publicise, to proclaim aloud.

ढोल/क ḍholak (*nf*) a small drum played on both the ends; ~किया a drummer, one who plays on a ढोलक.

ढोला ḍhola: (*nm*) centring; a popular folk narrative sung in parts of Uttar Pradesh.

ढोली ḍholi: (*nf*) a pack/bundle of betel leaves.

ढौरी ḍhauri: (*nf*) a sense of vying, emulative ardour; –लगाना to arouse a sense of vying.

ण

ण ṉā—the ultimate nasal letter of the third pentad (i.e. **टवर्ग**) of the Devna:gri: alphabet.

त

त ta—the first letter of the fourth pentad (i.e. **तवर्ग**) of Devna:gri: alphabet.

तंग tāṅg (*a*) narrow; scarce; troubled; harassed; girth, belt of a horse; **~दस्त** short of money, scarcity-stricken; **~दस्ती** state of penury, scarcity of money, poverty; **~दिल** hide-bound, small hearted; hence **~दिली** (*nf*); **~हाल** tight, distressed, in great straits; **~हाली** narrow circumstances, straits, tightness; **–आना** to be tired (of), to be fed up; to be browned off; **–करना** to trouble, to harass, to victimize.

तंगी tāṅgi: (*nf*) scarcity, poverty, tightness.

तंडुल tāṇḍul (*nm*) rice.

तंतु tāntu (*nm*) a thread, fibre; filament; tendril; cord or string of a musical instrument; **~क** a fibril; **~मय** fibrous; **-वाद्य** stringed musical instrument; **~वाय** a weaver; spider.

तंत्र tāntr (*nm*) a system; technique; a string gut; a body of mystical formulae or practices (for the attainment of super-human powers); incantation; **-मंत्र** hocus-pocus, voodooism, spell and incantation; **-साधना** tantra-practices for the attainment of a desired goal or super-human faculties.

तंत्रज्ञ tāntragy (*nm*) one who has attained expertise in **तंत्र** (see).

तंत्रि/का tāntrika: (*nf*) a nerve; **~का-तंत्र** nervous system; **~कीय** nervous.

तंत्री tāntri: (*nf*) a practitioner of enchantments; a stringed musical instrument—a lyre.

तंदुरुस्त tāndurust (*a*) healthy.

तंदुरुस्ती tāndurusti: (*nf*) health(iness); **–हजार नियामत** a sound health is a thousand blessings.

तंदू/र tāndu:r (*nm*) an oven; **~री** fired or prepared in, or pertaining to, an oven.

तंद्रा tāndra: (*nf*) drowse, drowsiness; somnolence, dormancy; **~लु** drowsy.

तंद्रिल tāndril (*a*) drowsy; **~ता** drowsiness.

तंबाकू tāmba:ku: (*nm*) tobacco.

तंबीह tāmbi:h (*nf*) an admonition, a gentle reproof; **–देना** to admonish, to reprove; ~न as a matter of warning/reproof.

तंबू tāmbu: (*nm*) a tent, marquee.

तंबूर tāmbu:r (*nm*) a tambour.

तंबूरा tāmbu:ra: (*nm*) a four-stringed drone.

तंबोली tāmboli: (*nm*) see तमोली.

तक tak (*ind*) to, upto; till, until; by.

तक़दीर taqdi:r (*nf*) luck, lot, fate, fortune; –आज़माना to try one's luck; –ऊँची जगह लड़ना to be related (matrimonially) to a rich family, to turn out to be lucky in matrimony; –का खेल wonders wrought by Luck; –का धनी/सिकंदर blessed with a lucky lot, favoured by Dame Luck; –का पलटा खाना (one's) luck to take a turn; –का लिखा नहीं मिटता what is lotted cannot be blotted; –का हेठा having a wretched lot; –खुलना/जागना to be in luck, to be in the ascendant; –खोटी होना to have a bad/an ill-luck; –ठोकना to curse one's ill-luck; –फूटना to be out of luck, to be under the spell of ill-luck; –लड़ना to be favoured by luck, to get a lucky chance; –से तदबीर बड़ी है its effort that counts more in life than mere luck.

तक़दीरी taqdi:ri: (*a*) pertaining or related to luck/fate.

तकना taknā: (*v*) see ताकना.

तकनी/क takni:k (*nf*) technique; ~की technical; ०जानकारी technical know-how.

तक़रार takra:r (*nf*) an altercation, wrangling, quarrel.

तक़रीबन taqri:bān (*ind*) approximately, nearly.

तक़रीर taqri:r (*nf*) a speech, lecture.

तकला takla: (*nm*) the spindle (of a spinning wheel).

तकली takli: (*nf*) a small तकला (see); bobbin of cotton.

तकलीफ़ takli:f (*nf*) trouble, distress; ailment; –में होना to be in trouble/distress.

तकल्लुफ़ takalluf (*nm*) formality; meticulous observance of propriety or etiquette; –करना/में पड़ना to be formal, to observe formality, to stand upon ceremony.

तक़सीम taqsi:m (*nf*) division; distribution.

तक़ाज़ा taqa:za: (*nm*) dun, dunning; demand (of payment, one's due, etc.).

तका/र taka:r (*nm*) the letter ta (त) and its sound; ~रांत (word) ending in त् (t).

तक़ावी taqa:vi: (*nf*) taccavi (loan), advance of money to cultivators.

तकिया takiya: (*nm*) a pillow, bolster, cushion, abode of a Mohammedan hermit.

तकियाकलाम takiya:kala:m (*nm*) a prop word, an expletive.

तकुआ takua: (*nm*) a distaff, large-sized needle; chopper, spindle (of a spinning wheel).

तक्र takkr (*nm*) butter-milk.

तक्षक takshak (*nm*) a kind of deadly serpent.

तख़मीना takḥmi:nā: (*nm*) an estimate, assessment, valuation; –लगाना to make an estimate.

तख़लिया takḥliya: (*nm*) solitude, a state of being all alone.

तख़ल्लुस takḥallus (*nm*) pen-name.

तख़्त ṭakḥt (*nm*) a wooden structure of planks; throne; ~नशीन enthroned, installed on the throne; ~नशीनी enthronement, accession to the throne; –का तख़्ता हो जाना to have prosperity turned into absolute adversity, to be undone; –या तख़्ता to win the horse or lose the saddle; तख़्ते-ताऊस the celebrated peacock throne of the Indian

Moghal Emperor, Shahjahan, which was taken away by Na:dirsha:h of Iran when he invaded and plundered Delhi in 1739 A.D.

तख़्ता takhta: (*nm*) a plank; board; –**उलटना/पलटना** to bring about a coup; to suffer a coup; to fall/throw into adversity.

तख़्ती takhti: (*nf*) a small wooden plate; small board to write on.

तगड़ा tagra: (*a*) strong, powerful, robust; hence ~**पन** (*nm*); –**पड़ना** to prove more than a match, to prove stronger; to take a strong stand.

तगा taga: (*nm*) thread.

तगा/दा taga:da: (*nm*) see **तक़ाज़ा**; ~**दगीर** one who calls for the recovery of his due.

तगार(ड़) taga:r(r) (*nm*) a reservoir for mixing lime and mortar; a big hollow utensil.

तचना tachnā: (*v*) to be heated/boiled (as milk); to be parched/scorched.

तज़किरा tazkira: (*nm*) mention; discussion.

तजना tajnā: (*v*) to abandon, to give up; to quit, to leave.

तजवीज़ tajvi:z (*nf*) a proposal; suggestion; scheme.

तजुर/बा tajurba: (*nm*) (an) experience; experiment; ~**बेकार** experienced (person); hence ~**बेकारी** (*nf*).

तज्जनित tajjanit (*a*) born thereof, resulting therefrom.

तज्जन्य tajjany (*a*) possible therefrom; born thereof.

तट tat (*nm*) a bank; coast, shore.

तटवर्ती tatvarti: (*a*) riverian; littoral; coastal, situated or located on the coast/bank.

तटस्थ tatāsth (*a*) neutral; objective; indifferent; situated on a bank/coast; ~**ता** neutrality; objectivity; indifference, being situated on a bank/coast etc.; **तटस्थित** see **तटवर्ती**; **तटस्थीकरण** neutralisation the act or process of imparting objectivity/indifference; –**रहना** to sit on the fence, to be non-aligned not to take sides.

तटी tati: (*nf*) a river; bank.

तटीय tati:y (*a*) coastal; riverian pertaining to a bank; –**व्यापार** coastal trade.

तड़ tar (*nf*) a crack, crackling noise (as of a slap); –**से** with a crack or snap.

तड़क tarak (*nf*) the act or process of cracking; a crack mark; snap split; fissure; -**भड़क** ostentation tawdry/tawdriness, pompousness.

तड़कना taraknā: (*v*) to split with a crack, to crack, to crackle; to snap

तड़का tarka: (*nm*) day-break, dawn; cracking noise; a snap; seasoning heated oil or ghee in which spices and onion, etc. are well-stirred and browned (to be administered as a relish to pulses, etc.)

तड़तड़ा/ना tartara:nā: (*v*) to produce a cracking/crackling noise; to break with a crack; hence ~**ह**(*nf*).

तड़प tarap (*nf*) tossing or rolling about in agony; yearning; smart restlessness, restivity; crack.

तड़पना tarapnā: (*v*) to toss or roll about restlessly or uneasily; to writhe in pain; to yearn (for) to smart; to crack; to be restive restless.

तड़फड़ा/ना tarphara:nā: (*v*) to (be in a) throe, to writhe in pain; hence ~**हट** (*nf*).

तड़ाक tara:k (*nf*) a cracking sound snap, loud report, sound of stroke or blow; -**फड़ाक** at once swiftly; –**से** with a loud report

–से जबाब देना to answer back unhesitatingly/insolently, to retort.

ड़ाका tara:ka: (*nm*) a loud report; crack, snap.

ड़ातड़ tara:tar (*adv*) with successive reports; with promptitude, instantaneously; –जवाब देना to answer back in quick succession/unhesitatingly/insolently; –पड़ना to be hit in quick succession.

ड़ित tarit (*nf*) the lightning; –संवाद a flash.

ड़ी tari: (*nf*) braggadocio; ascendancy, overbearing conduct, overbearingness; show of superiority; ~बाज़ braggadocio; braggart; making a show of superiority; hence ~बाज़ी; –देना to indulge in empty vaunting, to try to subdue, to hoodwink; –मारना to give oneself airs; to do the grand; –में आना to be taken in; to yield to braggadocio.

तिम्मा tatimma: (*nm*) an appendix, a supplement.

ते/या tataiya: (*nf*) a wasp; ~या काटना/ ~ये लगना to feel uneasy/restive.

त् tat (*pro*) that; ~पश्चात् thereafter; ~पुरुष (in Grammar) a variety of समास.

त्का/ल tatka:l (*adv*) forthwith, immediately, there and then; ~लिक immediate, of the/that time, contemporaneous; ~लीन belonging to that time, contemporaneous, contemporary.

त्क्षण tatkshān (*adv*) that very moment, instantaneously.

त्ताथेइ tatta:thei (*nf*) a dancing strain.

त्त्व tattv (*nm*) an element; essence; principle; substance; factor; phenomenon; truth, reality; ~ज्ञ a metaphysician, one who has realised the Supreme Truth; -ज्ञान metaphysical knowledge, the realisation of the Supreme Truth; ~ज्ञानी see ~ज्ञ; -दर्शन realisation of the Supreme Truth; ~दर्शी one who realises the Supreme Truth; one who can perceive the Truth; -दृष्टि vision, truth-probing vision, insight; ~निष्ठ wedded to truth/essence; ~मीमांसक metaphysicist; -मीमांसा Metaphysics; elementism; ~मीमांसीय metaphysical; ~विद् see ~ज्ञ; -विद्या Metaphysics; ~वेत्ता see ~ज्ञ; -शास्त्र see -विद्या.

तत्त्वत: tattvtah (*ind*) essentially, in essence, in reality.

तत्त्वांतरण tattva:ntarā:n (*nm*) transmutation.

तत्त्वावधान tattva:vdha:n (*nm*) auspices, aegis; –में, के under the auspices/aegis of.

तत्पर tatpar (*a*) ready; devoted; ~ता readiness; devotedness.

तत्पाती tatpa:ti: (*a*) fugacious.

तत्र tattr (*adv*) there, in that place; ~भवान His/Her Majesty, His/Her Excellency; His/Her Highness.

तत्सम tatsam (*nm* and *a*) lit. same as that—a word of Sanskrit origin used as such in later languages.

तथा tatha: (*ind*) and; so.

तथाकथित tatha:kathit (*a*) so-called.

तथागत tatha:gat (*nm*) a name of Lord Buddha.

तथापि tatha:pi (*ind*) even so; still, yet, inspite of that.

तथास्तु tatha:stu (*ind*) Be it so !

तथ्य tatthy (*nm*) reality; fact, factum; ~निष्ठ factual, realistic; hence ~निष्ठता/ ~निष्ठा (*nf*); ~परायण see ~निष्ठ; hence ~परायणता (*nf*); ~भाषी/वादी one who speaks the fact, true.

तथ्यत: tatthytah (*ind*) ***de facto, ipso facto***.

तदनंतर tadnāntar (*adv*) thereafter, thereupon, consequently.

तदनुभूति tadanubhu:ti (*nf*) empathy.

तदनुरू/प tadanuru:p (*a*) identical; corresponding to, according to (that); ~**पी** corresponding.

तदनुसार tadanusa:r (*ind*) accordingly, according to that, corresponding.

तदपि tadapi (*ind*) still, even then.

तदबीर tadbi:r (*nf*) effort; means; device, contrivance.

तदर्थ tadarth (*a*) ad hoc; –**समिति** ad hoc committee.

तदुपरांत taduparā:nt (*ind*) consequently, thereafter.

तद् tad—an allomorph of **तत्** (meaning 'that') used in compounds; ~**आकार** / (**तदाकार**) / ~**रूप** (**तद्रूप**) identical, having identical form; ~**रूपता** (**तद्रूपता**) identity, sameness, formal correspondence.

तद्भव (*nm* and a) lit. evolved or born therefrom—words of Sanskrit origin which have assumed, a'd are used in, a modified form later languages.

तन tān (*nm*) body; –**की तपन बुझाना** to quench the thirst of one's physical needs, to attain physical gratification; –**बदन की सुध न रहना** to transcend one's physical being, to be beyond oneself; –**बदन में आग लगना** to get one's goat; -**मन से** wholeheartedly, with all physical and mental resources; -**मन-धन से** with all physical, mental and material resources; -**मन से सेवा करना** to serve somebody hand and foot.

तनक़ीह tanqi:h (*nf*) an issue; –**लगाना** to frame issues.

तनख़्वाह tankẖa:h (*nf*) pay, salary; ~**दार** paid, salaried.

तनज़ेब tanzeb (*nf*) superfine muslin.

तनज़्ज़ुली tanazzuli: (*nf*) demotion; decline, fall.

तनतनाना tāntanā:nā: (*v*) to snap at to be in a fury, to be wrathfully outspoken.

तनना tannā: (*v*) to be pulled tight to be stretched full; to be pitched: to be upright; to run into a temper to assume an air of affectation; to assume an uncompromising, unyielding posture; **तने रहना** to be ever in temper, to sulk, to be cross.

तन/य tanay (*nm*) a son; hence ~**या** (*nf*) a daughter.

तनहा tanha: (*a*) alone, lonely, solitary; ~**ई** loneliness, solitude.

तना tanā: (*nf*) a stem, trunk; bole.

तनातनी tanā:tanī: (*nf*) a state of (mutual) tension, tenseness.

तनाव tana:v (*nm*) tension, tenseness, strain; tautness; –**की**/~**पूर्ण स्थिति** tense situation.

तनिक tanik (*a*) a little, slight; –**अच्छा/आगे** a cut above.

तनी tani: (*nf*) a string or fastening of a garment; ~**दार** stringed, with a string around.

तनु tanu (*a*) lean, tenuous, thin, slender; dilute.

तनु/ज tanuj (*nm*) a son; hence ~**जा** (*nf*) a daughter.

तनुता tanuta: (*nf*) tenuousness, tenuity; leanness; delicacy; dilution.

तनू/करण tanū:karān̲ (*nm*) attenuation, dilution; hence ~**कृत** (*a*).

तन्मय tānmay (*a*) identified (with); fully engrossed/absorbed (in); ~**ता** complete identification; trance.

तन्यता tannyāta: (*nf*) tensility.

तन्वंगी tannvāṅgi: (*a*) tenuous, slim; delicate, of delicate frame; slender.

तन्वी tannvi (*a*) see **तन्वंगी**.

तप tap (*nm*) devout austerity, asceticism, self-mortification, penance.

तपकन tapkān (*nf*) throbbing agony;

smarting pain; hence **तपकना** (*v*).

तपन tapān (*nm*) heat; anguish; tingle, burning sensation (within or without).

तपना tapnā: (*v*) to be heated; to burn with pain or grief; to practise self-mortification.

तपश्चर्या tapashcharya: (*nf*) see **तपस्या**.

तपस्या tapassya: (*nf*) penance, self-mortification; asceticism.

तपस्वी tapassvi: (*nm* and *a*) an ascetic, devoutly austere (person), one who practises self-mortification; hence **तपस्विनी** (*fem*).

तपाक tapa:k (*nm*) warmth; apparent cordiality; promptitude; **–से** with open arms, cordially; with promptitude, instantaneously.

तपिश tapish (*nm*) heat; mental anguish, affliction.

तपेदिक़ tapediq (*nf*) tuberculosis.

तपो tapo—an allomorph of **तपस्** (see **तप**) used in compounds; **~धन** lit. one whose sole capital is **तप(स्या)** (see)–an ascetic; **~निष्ठ** (one) devoted to penance; **~बल** the power acquired through penance; **~भंग** (causing) breach of ascetic practices; **~मय** pertaining or given to penance or self-mortification; **~वन** an ascetic's grove, a grove where ascetics perform their religious ascetic activities; **~व्रत** devoted/devotion to self-mortification.

तप्त tapt (*a*) heated, warmed up; afflicted.

तफ़्तीश tafti:sh (*nf*) an investigation, probe.

तफ़रीह tafri:h (*nf*) recreation, regalement, fun; **~न** for fun/recreation.

तफ़सील tafsi:l (*nf*) details; particulars.

तब tab (*adv*) then, at that time; afterwards, thereafter, thereupon; consequently; **–भी** even then, even so, in spite of this.

तबक़ा tabqa: (*nm*) a class; status.

तबदील tabdi:l (*nf*) change, alteration; exchange; (*a*) changed, altered; exchanged; **–आबोहवा** change of climate.

तबदीली tabdi:li: (*nf*) change, alteration; transfer.

तबलची tabalchi: (*nm*) a tabla-player.

तबला tabla: (*nm*) small tambourine—a percussion musical instrument; **~वादक** a *tabla*-player; **~वादन** the act or process of playing on the *tabla*; **–खनकना/ठनकना** the *tabla* to be played upon; a musical/dancing session to be in progress.

तबादिला taba:dila: (*nm*) transfer.

तबाह taba:h (*a*) ruined, destroyed; **–होना** to come to grief, to meet with disaster.

तबाही taba:hi: (*nf*) ruination, ruin, destruction; **–मचाना** to spell ruination, to cause destruction/havoc.

तबि(बी)यत tabi(bi:)yat (*nf*) the state of (physical or mental) health; temperament, disposition; nature; **~दार** large-hearted; hearty; of impulsive disposition; of keen sensibilities; **–आना** to fall in love with, to fall for; **–का साफ़** a man of good faith, bonafide / clean / hearty person; **–गिरना** condition to become worse; **–झक होना** see **–साफ़ होना**; **–बिगड़ना** to become indisposed, to feel sick; to be excited by; **–भर जाना** to feel satiated, to be cloyed with; **–मचलना** to go wayward; **–लगना** to feel at home; **–साफ़ होना** to come to senses, to be restored to one's true being, to be **taught**

a lesson, to be cut to size.

तबेला tabela: (*nm*) a stable.

तभी tabhi: (*adv*) at that moment, just at that time, just then; for this reason.

तमंचा tamāṇcha: (*nm*) a pistol, revolver; **–तानना** to aim a pistol at.

तम tām (*nm*) darkness; gloom; (fig.) ignorance.

तमकना tamaknā: (*v*) to snap; to fly into a rage.

तमग़ा tamga: (*nm*) a medal.

तमतमा/ना tamtamā:nā: (*v*) the face to redden (with rage or heat); hence **~हट** (*nf*).

तमन्ना tamannā: (*nf*) an aspiration, a longing.

तमस् tamas (*nm*) the third of the three qualities incidental to creation or the state of humanity, viz. the quality of darkness or ignorance; darkness; ignorance.

तमस्सुक tamassuk (*nm*) a promissory note.

तमाचा tamā:cha: (*nm*) a slap; **–खाना** to be slapped; **–जड़ना** to plant a slap (on).

तमाम tamā:m (*a*) all; whole, entire.

तमाल tama:l (*nm*) a big evergreen tree —*Xanthocymus pictorius*.

तमाशबी/न tama:shbī:n (*nm*) lit. a show-seer, an onlooker, a spectator; having a superficial mentality; **~नी** lit. show-seeing, the centring of interest on mere show aspect or entertainment; entertainment by show-seeing.

तमाशा tama:sha: (*nm*) a show, spectacle; entertainment; **~ई** see **तमाशबीन**.

तमिल tamil (*nf*) the oldest of the four major south Indian languages belonging to the Dravidian family; **~नाडु** the South-Indian state of Tamilna:du.

तमिस्रा tamiṣra: (*nf*) darkness; dark night.

तमीज़ tami:z (*nf*) etiquette, decorum; discrimination; **~दार** mannerly, decorous; having proper etiquette; **–करना** to discriminate, to distinguish (between).

तमोगुण tamogūṉ (*nm*) one of the three qualities (viz. **सतोगुण, रजोगुण, तमोगुण**) incidental to creation or the state of humanity, the quality of darkness or ignorance.

तमोगुणी tamogūṉī: (*a*) person in whom **तमोगुण** (see) predominates.

तमोमय tamōmay (*a*) one in whom the element of **तमस्** (see) is predominant; dark; abounding in ignorance; wrathful.

तमोली tamoli: (*nm*) a betel-seller.

तय tay (*a*) decided, settled; fixed; covered; **–करना** to decide, to settle; to cover (as **रास्ता**).

तरंग tarāṅg (*nf*) a wave, ripple; whim, caprice; **–में होना** to be on the top of the world, to be in a light and pleasant mood.

तरंगायित tarāṅga:yit (*a*) wavy, ripply; in a light and pleasant mood; fanciful.

तरंगित tarāṅgit (*a*) waved, rippled, full of waves/ripples; fleeting, unsteady; (in a) fanciful (mood).

तरंगी tarāṅgi: (*a*) whimsical, capricious; fanciful; unsteady.

तर tar (*a*) wet, soaked; damp, dank; fresh; a suffix used to denote comparative degree (as **उच्चतर, महत्तर, बेहतर**); rich (as food etc.—**तर माल**); **-ब-तर** soaked, drenched; **-ओ-ताज़ा** freshed, refresh, revived; **–करना** to soak, to drench; to refresh.

तरकश tarkash (*nm*) a quiver; **~बंद** equipped with a quiver.

तरकारी tarka:ri: (*nf*) a vegetable (green or cooked).

तरकीब tarki:b (*nf*) way, means; tact, contrivance, device; –**भिड़ाना/लड़ाना** to find a way out, to work out a strategy; –**से काम लेना** to handle tactfully/with gloves.

तरक़्क़ी taraqqi: (*nf*) progress; advancement, improvement; promotion; an increment; ~**पसंद** progressive.

तरजी/ह tarji:h (*nf*) preference; priority; ~**ही** preferential; deserving priority.

तरजुमा tarjumā: (*nm*) translation; ~**न** a translator; ~**नी** translation.

तरणि taraṉi (*nm*) the sun; (*nf*) a boat.

तरतीब tarti:b (*nf*) an order, arrangement; ~**वार** in (proper) order; –**देना** to impart an order, to set in order.

तरद्दुद taraddud (*nf*) botheration; headache, concern.

तरना tarnā: (*v*) to cross (over); to attain salvation; to fulfil an obligation.

तरन्नुम tarannūm (*nm*) modulation, rhythm.

तरफ़ taraf (*nf*) side; direction; (*adv*) towards; ~**दार** partisan; partial; supporter; ~**दारी** the act of taking a side, backing; partisanship, partiality.

तरबू/ज(जा) tarbu:z(a:) (*nm*) a watermelon.

तरमीम tarmi:m (*nf*) an amendment, a modification.

तरल taral (*a*) fluid; fickle, unsteady; (*nm*) a liquid; ~**क** a thinner; –**पदार्थ** a liquid.

तरलता taralta: (*nf*) fluidity; fickleness.

तरस taras (*nf*) compassion, pity; –**खाना** to pity.

तरसना tarasnā: (*v*) to pine for, to crave or long for.

तरह tareh (*nf*) kind, sort; method way; likeness; allowance; –**का** like, resembling; –**देना** to be lenient; to over-look, to pass over, not to take due notice.

तराई tara:i: (*nf*) foothill; curing (of concrete etc.); constant wetting/drenching.

तराज़ू tara:zu: (*nf*) a balance, scales.

तराना tara:nā: (*nm*) a song, rhythmic musical composition using syllables.

तराबोर tara:bor (*a*) drenched, soaked.

तरावट tara:vaṭ (*nf*) coolness: freshness, dampness; verdure.

तराश tara:sh (*nf*) cut, trim; mould. structure.

तराशना tara:shnā: (*v*) to cut, to trim; to chisel; to pare; to fashion.

तरी tari: (*nf*) coolness; dampness; freshness, verdure; curry; wealthiness, richness; –**होना** to be moneyed/wealthy.

तरी/क़ा tari:qa: (*nm*) a method; mode way, manner; technique; tact; ~**क़े का** of a proper type/mould; reasonably good.

तरीन tari:n–a suffix denoting superlative degree as **बेहतरीन** (the best), **कमतरीन** (the lowest), etc.

तरु taru (*nm*) a tree.

तरुण taruṉ (*a*)young, youthful; (*nm*) a youth, youngman; hence **तरुणी** (*nf*).

तरुणाई taruṉa:i: (*nf*) youth, young age.

तरुणिमा taruṉimā: (*nf*) see **तरुणाई**.

तरेड़ tareṛ (*nm*) a crack; crevice, shake.

तरेरना tarernā: (*v*);–,**आँखें** to cast an admonishing glance, to look obliquely.

तर्क tark (*nm*) an argument, plea, contention; reason, reasoning; logic; abandonment, relinquishment; **-वितर्क** argumentation for and against, discussion; **–शृंखला** chain of argument; **~संगत** logical; legitimate, justifiable, rational/reasonable; **~संगति** justification; rationality/reasonableness; logicality; **~हीन** illogical, irrational, unreasoning; **–करना** to argue, to contend; to abandon, to relinquish.

तर्कना tarknā: (*nf*) reasoning, arguing; **~वाद** rationalism.

तर्कबुद्धि tarkbuddhi (*nf*) reason, reasoning faculty; discursive intellect, **~वाद** rationalism; hence **~वादी** (*a, nm*).

तर्कविद्या tarkaviddya: (*nf*) (the science of) Logic.

तर्क/शास्त्र tarkasha:str (*nm*) (the science of) Logic; **~शास्त्री** a logician; **~शास्त्रीय** logical, pertaining to Logic.

तर्काभास tarka:bha:s (*nm*) fallacy, fallacious argument.

तर्कु tarku (*nm*) see **तकुआ**.

तर्क्य tarky (*a*) debatable, worth arguing about, disputable.

तर्ज tarz (*nf*) tune (in music); style, fashion; mode.

तर्ज/न, ~ना tarjan (*nm*), ~nā: (*nf*) rebuke, reproof, snubbing.

तर्जनी tarjanī: (*nf*) the fore-finger, trigger-finger.

तर्जुमा tarjumā: (*nm*) see **तरजुमा**.

तर्पण tarpān̲ (*nm*) gratification; libation of water to deceased ancestors or the manes.

तर्रार tarra:r (*a*) used as the second member in the compound **तेज-तर्रार** (see).

तल tal (*nm*) the bottom; under part; surface, floor; **~स्पर्शी** going deep, profound.

तलक talak (*ind*) to, upto, till, until; even.

तल/ख talakḥ (*a*) bitter; acrid; **~खी** bitterness; acridity.

तलछट talchhaṭ (*nf*) the sediment, dregs.

तलना talnā: (*v*) to fry.

तलफ़्फ़ुज़ talaffuz (*nm*) pronunciation.

तलब talab (*nf*) an urge, craving; salary, wages; **~गार** desirous (of), seeking; **~नामा** summons; **–करना** to summon, to send for; **–होना** to feel the urge for.

तलबाना talba:nā: (*nm*) summon-charges, fee paid for the service of summons.

तलबी talbi: (*nf*) summons, order to appear before.

तल/वा talva: (*nf*) sole of the foot; **~वे चाटना** to fawn upon, to lick the boots of, to indulge in servile flattery; **~वे चाटने वाला** king Charles' spaniel; **~वे सहलाना** to flatter, to blandish, to indulge in servile flattery.

तलवार talwa:r (*nf*) a sword, sabre; **–का धनी** a heroic swordsman; **–की आँच** the flash/fierceness of the sword; **–की धार** most hazardous path; **–के घाट उतारना** to put to the sword, to put to death; **–के ज़ोर से** through blood and iron, through relentless use of force; **–खींच लेना/घुमाना** to unsheath/brandish a sword; **–सूँतना** to brandish a sword; **–से मक्खी मारना** to break butterfly on wheel.

तलहटी talehṭi: (*nf*) foothill; submountain region.

तला tala: (*nm*) the bottom; sole (of a shoe); base; floor; keel (of a boat); lower/under side.

तलाक़ tala:q (*nm*) divorce; **~नामा** agreement for divorce; **~शुदा**

divorced.

तलाश tala:sh (*nf*) search, quest.

तलाशना tala:shnā: (*v*) to search, to go in quest (of),

तलाशी tala:shi: (*nf*) search; –देना to allow/cause to be searched; –लेना to make/carry out a search.

तली tali: (*nf*) the bottom; sole (of a shoe).

तले tale (*ind*) below; under; beneath; –ऊपर one over the other; one succeeding the other; –की दुनिया ऊपर होना the world to be turned upside down; the world to undergo radical changes.

तल्ख़ talkh̤ (*a*) see तलख़; तल्ख़ी see तलख़ी.

तल्ला talla: (*nm*) a storey; floor, sole (of a shoe etc.).

तल्लीन talli:n (*a*) immersed (in); deeply involved (in); identified with; engrossed (in); ~ता deep involvement; concentration; the state of being one with.

तवक़्क़ो tavaqqo (*nf*) expectation; –रखना to expect; –होना, किसी से to be expected of (somebody).

तवज्जो tavajjo (*nf*) heed, attention; –दिलाना to draw attention to; –देना to pay heed/attention to.

तवा tava: (*nm*) a griddle, an iron plate for baking bread; a gramophone record; small plate or shard in a चिलम on which tobacco is placed; a chest shield (used by warriors); –सिर से बाँधना to be ready to face blows/hardships; तवे की बूँद a drop over the frying pan, (something) destined to disappear instantly.

तवाज़ा tava:za: (*nf*) see ख़ातिर.

तवायफ़ tava:yaf (*nf*) a prostitute, harlot, dancing girl.

तवारीख़ tava:ri:kh̤ (*nf*) plural form of तारीख़–date; history.

तवालत tava:lat (*nf*) botheration, trouble; –मोल लेना to ask for/own up trouble.

तशरीफ़ tashri:f (*nf*) a term signifying honour and respect, seldom used except with verbs like रखना, लाना, ले जाना; welcome appearance, advent, coming; –का टोकरा said in a lighter jocular vein—(one's) being; –रखना to be seated; –लाना to grace (an occasion or a place) by coming, to come; –ले जाना to depart, to go.

तश्तरी tashtari: (*nf*) a plate; tray; ~, उड़न flying saucer.

तसकीन taski:n (*nf*) solace, consolation; satisfaction.

तसदीक़ tasdi:q (*nf*) verification; attestation; confirmation; –करना to verify, to attest; to confirm.

तसफ़िया tasfiya: (*nm*) a settlement, reconciliation.

तसबीह tasbi:h (*nf*) a rosary.

तसमा tasmā: (*nm*) a leather-strap; tab.

तसला tasla: (*nm*) a shallow pan.

तसलीम tasli:m (*nf*) admission, confession; salutation, greeting, responsive greeting; –करना to admit, to confess.

तसल्ली tasalli: (*nf*) satisfaction; patience; consolation; ~बख़्श satisfactory; –देना to console; –रखना to have patience; –से patiently.

तसवीर tasvi:r (*nm*) a picture, portrait; image.

तसव्वुफ़ tasavvut (*nm*) Sufism; Spiritualism.

तसू tasu: (*nm*) a unit of measure (esp. used in the context of building work).

तस्कर taskar (*nm*) a smuggler; ~वृत्ति smuggling, a smuggler's profession

तस्करी taskari: (*nf*) the act, process

or practice of smuggling.

तह teh (*nf*) a layer; fold; bottom; ~**ख़ाना** a basement, subterranean/underground vault, cell/cellar; **-ब-तह** one fold/layer over the other; **-ए-दिल से** from the core of the heart, earnestly; **–तक पहुँचना** to get to the bottom of; **–में जाना** to go behind somebody's words, to delve deep into.

तहक़ी/क़, ~क़ात tehqi:q, ~a:t (*nf*) an enquiry, investigation, probe.

तहज़ीब tehzi:b (*nf*) civilization; manners; ~**याफ़्ता** civilised.

तहत tehat (*ind.*) under.

तहबंद tehband (*nm*) a long strip (often striped) of cotton or silk worn by man round the waist, a sarong; (*a*) folded, arranged in folds/layers.

तहबंदी tehbandi: (*nf*) folding, arrangement in layers; flake.

तहमद tehmad (*nm*) see **तहबंद** (*nm*).

तहरी tehri: (*nf*) a preparation of rice cooked with vegetables etc.

तहरी/र tehri:r (*nf*) writing; anything written; ~**री** written; ०**सबूत** documentary evidence.

तहलका tehalka: (*nm*) turmoil, commotion, agitation, havoc, schemozzle; **–मचाना** to cause a commotion/havoc.

तहस-नहस tehas-nehas (*a*) ruined, devastated, destroyed; **–करना** to ruin; to devastate, to destroy.

तहसील tehsi:l (*nf*) tehsil—an administrative sub-division of a district; the office or court of a *tehsildar*.

तहसील/दार tehsilda:r (*nm*) a tahsildar—revenue officer in command of a *tehsil;* sub-collector of revenue; ~**दारी** the office or function of a tehsildar.

तहाँ tahā: (*adv*) there, at that place.

तहाना taha:nā: (*v*) to arrange in folds, to fold up; to wrap.

ताँगा tā:ga: (*nm*) a tonga; ~**वाला** a tonga-driver.

तांडव tā:ṉḍav (*nm*) a violent (manly) dance-form; the mythological annihilatory dance of Lord Shiv; also **–नृत्य**.

ताँत tā:t (*nf*) a string gut, catgut.

ताँता tā:ta: (*nm*) a series, succession, train; influx; **–टूटना** the chain to be broken; **–बँधना/लगना** to have an unbroken chain; a non-stop influx.

तांत्रि/क tā:ntrik (*nm*) a practitioner of **तंत्र**; (*a*) pertaining to **तंत्र**; ~**कीय** pertaining to or related with a **तांत्रिक** or **तंत्रविद्या**.

ताँबा tā:ba: (*nm*) copper.

तांबूल tā:mbu:l (*nm*) a betel.

ता ta: (*ind*) till, until, upto; a suffix used to form abstract nouns from adjectives (as **सुंदरता, मधुरता** etc.); ~**उम्र** throughout life; ~**ज़िंदगी** till the end of life.

ताई ta:i: (*nf*) father's elder brother's (**ताऊ**'s) wife.

ताईद ta:i:d (*nf*) support; **–करना** to second, to support.

ताऊ ta:u: (*nm*) father's elder brother.

ताऊन ta:u:n (*nm*) plague; epidemic.

ताक ta:k (*nf*) look out; nominal form of the verb **ताकना** (see); **-झाँक** see under **ताकना**.

ताक़ ta:q (*nm*) a niche; **–पर धरना/रखना** to set aside (for later use), to defer.

ताक़त ta:qat (*nf*) power, force, strength, might; **–आज़माई** trial of strength.

ताक़त/वर ta:qatvar (*a*) powerful, strong, mighty; hence ~**वरी** (*nf*).

ताकना ta:knā: (*v*) to stare, to gaze, to watch intently; to view; **ताक-झाँक** casting of stealthy glances, viewing unnoticed; **ताक में रहना** to be on the look out, to watch for; **ताक लगाना** to ambush, to watch for opportune moment.

ताकि ta:ki (*ind*) so that, in order that.

ताक़ीद ta:qi:d (*nf*) an instruction; caution.

तागा ta:ga: (*nm*) thread.

ताज ta:j (*nm*) crown; diadem; **~दार** crowned; king; **~पोशी** enthronement, installation on the throne.

ताजगी ta:zgi: (*nf*) freshness; newness.

ताजा ta:za: (*a*) fresh; new; recent; **~दम** fresh; **–समाचार** late news.

ताजि/या ta:ziya: (*nm*) a replica of the shrines of Hasan and Hussain (taken out in a procession on the occasion of Muharram); **~ए-ठंडे होना** lit. the burying of the **ताजिया** —the tide of plenty to ebb out; all enthusiasm to subside.

ताजीरात ta:zi:ra:t (*nm*); **-ए-हिन्द** the Indian Penal Code.

ताज्जुब ta:jjub (*nm*) wonder, astonishment.

ताड़ ta:ṛ (*nm*) the palmyra tree, palm, toddy tree; **~पत्र** palmyra leaf.

ताड़ना ta:ṛnā: (*nf*) admonition, rebuke; punishment; (*v*) to admonish; to guess, to smell, to perceive the reality in a flash.

ताड़ी ta:ṛi: (*nf*) toddy, fermented juice of palm tree.

तात ta:t (*nm*) any venerable person; father; an address to anyone who is dear and younger.

ताताथेई ta:ta:thei: (*nf*) see **तत्ताथेई**.

तातील ta:ti:l (*nf*) a holiday; vacation.

तात्कालिक ta:tka:lik (*a*) instantaneous; immediate; pertaining to a certain period of time or moment.

तात्त्विक ta:ttvik (*a*) elemental, elementary, fundamental; essential; substantial; hence **~ता** (*nf*).

तात्पर्य ta:tpary (*nm*) purport, meaning; design; spirit.

तादात्म्य ta:da:tmy (*nm*) identity; identification, unity, oneness.

तादाद ta:da:d (*nf*) number, count.

तादृश ta:ddrish (*a*) like that, such like; hence **~ता** (*nf*).

तान tā:n (*nf*) a musical note; fast rhythmic movement; tone; stay; **~ता** tonicity; **–छेड़ना** to strike up a melodious tune; to commence a disagreeable talk/an unending talk.

तानना tā:nnā: (*v*) to stretch, to spread; to tighten; to erect; to brandish (a sword, stick, etc.); **तानकर सोना, (लंबी)** to enjoy a carefree sleep.

तानपूरा ta:npu:ra: (*nm*) an accompanying stringed instrument.

ताना tā:nā: (*nm*) a taunt, sarcasm, gibe; the warp; **-बाना** warp and woof; the whole structure; **~रीरी** discordant note, useless talk; **–देना/–मारना** to taunt, to gibe.

तानाशा/ह tā:nā:sha:h (*nm*) a dictator; **~ही** dictatorship; dictatorial conduct.

ताने/बाज ta:neba:z (*nm*) one who makes taunting/sarcastic remarks; **~बाजी** taunting, sarcasm, ironical utterances.

ताप ta:p (*nm*) heat; temperature; pyrexia, fever; affliction, mental agony; (*a*) thermal; **~क्रम** temperature scale; **~ग्राही** thermoreceptor; **-तरंग** heat-wave; **~त्रय** the triple affliction i.e. physical (**दैहिक**), divine (**दैविक**) and mundane (**भौतिक**); **~मान** temperature; **०चित्र** temperature map; **~मापी** a thermometer; **~मिति** thermometry; **~लेखी** thermometrograph, thermograph; ~सह thermostabile; ~हर / ~हारी causing to counter an affliction; causing temperature to go down.

तापक ta:pak (*nm*) a heater.

तापना ta:pnā: (*v*) to heat or to warm oneself or something.

तापस ta:pas (*nm*) see तपस्वी.

तापीय ta:pi:y (*a*) thermal.

ताफ़्ता ta:fta: (*nm*) a kind of fine glossy silken cloth.

ताब ta:b (*nf*) courage, cheek; —न लाना not to have the courage/cheek to; —लाना to muster courage to.

ताबड़तोड़ ta:baṛtoṛ (*adv*) in rapid succession, non-stop, incessantly; forthwith.

ताबूत ta:bu:t (*nm*) a coffin.

ताबे ta:be (*a*) subservient, subordinate; ~दार obedient, servile attendant; ~दारी servility, servitude.

तामचीनी tā:mchi:nī: (*nf*) enamelware; enamel.

तामझाम ta:mjha:m (*nm*) originally, an open sedate chair or palanquin—paraphernalia.

तामलो(ले)ट ta:mlo(e)ṭ (*nm*) a wide metal tumbler (gen. used in the latrine).

तामस ta:mās (*nm*) see तमोगुण.

तामसिक tā:msik (*a*) pertaining to, related with or inspired by तमोगुण (see).

तामी/र ta:mi:r (*nf*) construction, building work; ~री structural, pertaining to construction.

तामील ta:mī:l (*nf*) carrying out, implementation (of an order); service (of summons etc.).

ताम्र tā:mmr (*nm*) copper; ~कार a coppersmith; -पट्ट a copper plate (used in olden times for documentation or inscription of edicts etc.); -पत्र see -पट्ट; -पात्र copperware; -युग aenolithic; -पाषाण युग chalcolithic.

ताया ta:ya: (*nm*) see ताऊ.

तार ta:r (*nm*) a wire; thread; fibre; chord; string; telegram; series, non-stop sequence; order; (*a*) high pitched; ~कश a wire-maker; ~कशी a kind of needlework; soft lustrous thread used for needlework; —स्वर high-pitched note; -कुतार होना things to go astray/out of order, disorder to prevail; -तार करना to shred; to reduce to shreds; -तार होना to be reduced to shreds; —न टूटना sequence not to be broken, order to be retained; —बिगड़ना things to get confused/disturbed, to go into disarray.

तारक ta:rak (*nm*) a star; asterisk; -चिह्न asterisk mark.

तारकीय ta:rki:y (*a*) stellar.

तारकोल ta:rkol (*nm*) tar, coal-tar, tarmac.

तारघर ta:rghar (*nm*) a telegraph office.

तारतम्य ta:rtammy (*nm*) harmony, harmonious relationship (of things); sequence, ascending or descending order.

तारत्व ta:rattv (*nm*) pitch (of sound notes); loudness.

तारना ta:rnā: (*v*) to cause to cross over; to deliver, to free from bondage.

तारपीन ta:rpī:n (*nm*) turpentine; —का तेल turpentine oil.

तारांकित ta:rā:ṅkit (*a*) starred; —प्रश्न starred question.

तारा ta:ra: (*nm*) a star: pupil (of the eye); ~कार stellate; ~कृति stellate; ~गण congregation of stars; ~मंडल constellation; तारे गिनना lit. to count the stars—to keep awake the whole night; not to have a blink throughout the night; तारे

तोड़ लाना to achieve the impossible, to perform a miracle; **तारे दिखाई दे जाना** lit. to see stars fleeting before the eye -to come face-to-face with a hard realisation; to be overpowered by a hardship; to be stunned helpless; **तारों की छाँह में** in the small hours of the morning, prior to day-break.

तारिका ta:rika: (*nf*) a small star; cine-actress.

तारीख़ ta:ri:kh (*nf*) a date; an appointed day; history; **~वार** datewise; **तारीख़ी** historical; **–टलना** a date; to be postponed; **–डालना** to date, to give a date; **–पड़ना** a date to be fixed.

तारीफ़ ta:ri:f (*nf*) praise; definition, description; introduction; **–?,आपकी** may I know your name ? may I have the privilege of your introduction ?; **–के पुल बाँधना** to sing the praises of, to shower encomiums on.

तारु/ण्य ta:ru̲n̲ny (*nm*) youth, youthfulness; young age, age of puberty; **~ण्यागम** advent of youth; puberty.

तार्किक ta:rkik (*a*) logical; (*nm*) a logician.

ताल ta:l (*nm*) a pond, pool, tank; a musical measure; rhythm, rhythmic cycle; see **ताड़**; slapping with the palm the inner side of the thigh as a gesture of challenge or defiance; **~ता** rhythmicity; **-पत्र** palm leaf; palmyra leaf; **~बद्ध** rhythmic(al); **०ता** rhythmicity; **-बेताल** inharmonious; discordant, out of tune; **~मखाना** the seed of *Solanum Indicum*; **~वन** a palmyra forest; **~वृंत** palm-leaf; **–ठोकना** to slap the inner side of the thigh as a gesture of defiance or challenge (in wrestling); **–देना** to chime, to correspond to a musical note with snapping, clapping or footwork; **–पर नाचना, (किसी की)** to dance to the tune of; **–से बेताल होना** to slip out of tune, to strike a discordant note.

तालमेल ta:lmel (*nm*) co-ordination; concordance, harmony, agreement; **–खाना** to be in agreement; to be well co-ordinated; **–बिठाना** to co-ordinate, to bring into harmony.

तालव्य ta:lavvy (*a*) palatal (sound etc.).

ताला ta:la: (*nm*) a lock; **~बंदी** a lock-out; **–जड़ना/ठोकना/मारना** to lock.

तालाब ta:la:b (*nm*) a tank, pool,

तालिका ta:lika: (*nf*) a list; key; table, schedule; **~बद्ध करना** to arrange in a tabular form.

तालिब ta:lib (*nm*) a pupil; (*a*) desirous (of); **~इल्म** a student, pupil, seeker after knowledge.

ताली ta:li: (*nf*) a key; clapping (of hands); **–एक हाथ से नहीं बजती** it takes two to make a quarrel; **–पिट जाना** to get the goose, to get hissed on the stage; kentisth fire; **–पीटना** lit. to clap—by way of derision; to mock at; **–बजना** lit. to have clapping—by way of approbation, to be applauded; to have clapping by way of derision or condemnation.

ताली/म ta:li:m (*nf*) education; **~मी** educational, academic.

ता/लु, ~लू ta:lu, ~lu: (*nm*) the palate; **–चटकना/सूखना** lit. the palate to be dried up—to be very thirsty; **–से जीभ न लगाना** never to be quiet, to go on chattering.

ताव ta:v (*nm*) heat; huffiness, rage, anger; overflow of passion; tempo; sheet (of paper); **–आना** to run into a temper, to be infuriated; to be adequately heated; **–खाना** to take a huff, to get up steam;

—बिलाना to set one's/another's bristles; —न खाना to keep one's hair on; —पर होना to be in a state of readiness, to be ready for handling; to be in a tempo; to be in fury, to be infuriated; to be overheated; to have a stroke of heat; —में in a huff; —में आना to set another's/one's bristles.

तावान ta:vā:n (*nm*) penalty, damage, recompense.

तावीज़ ta:vi:z (*nm*) an amulet, talisman.

ताश ta:sh (*nm*, also *nf*) playing cards; —की गड्डी a pack of cards.

तासीर ta:si:r (*nf*) effect; property.

तास्सु/ब ta:ssub (*nm*) bigotry, fanaticism, religious prejudice; ~बी fanatic, bigot.

ताहम ta:hām (*ind*) even so, in spite of this.

ति ti—an allomorph of तीन used in compounds, e.g. तिगुना/तिकोना, etc.

तिकड़/म tikṛām (*nf*) manoeuvre, manipulation; expedient measures; unfair means; ~मी manoeuvring, manipulating; (*nm*) an adept in manoeuvring/manipulation; —भिड़ाना/लड़ाना to manipulate, to make a manoeuvring effort.

तिकड़ी tikṛi: (*nf*) a trio, a group of three.

तिकोन tikōn (*nf*) a triangle; (*a*) triangular, three-cornered.

तिकोना tikonā: (*a*) triangular, three-cornered.

तिक्की tikki: (*nf*) a playing card having three pips.

तिक्त tikt (*a*) acrid; pungent; ~ता acridity; pungency.

तिखूँटा tikhū:ṭa: (*a*) having three ends or corners.

तिगुना tiguna: (*a*) three times, three-fold, triple.

तिग्गी tiggi: (*nf*) see तिक्की.

तिजार/त tija:rat (*nf*) commerce, trade; ~ती commercial.

तिजारी tija:ri: (*nf*) tertian ague, intermittent fever occurring every third day.

तिजोरी tijori: (*nf*) an iron safe/chest.

तिड़ी tiṛi: (*nf*) see तिक्की; cheating, swindling; ~बाज़ a swindler; ~बाज़ी swindling; -बिड़ी helter-skelter, disequilibrium; —करना to swindle; to cause to disappear, to make away with; —भूल जाना to be thrown out of wits, to be non-plussed; —होना to flee; -बिड़ी होना to be scattered, to be thrown helter-skelter; to be thrown in a state of disequilibrium.

तितर-बितर titaṛ-bitar (*a*) scattered; dispersed; diffused.

तितली titli: (*nf*) a butterfly; (fig.) glamour girl.

तिति/क्षा titiksha: (*nf*) endurance, patience; hence ~क्षु (*a*).

तितिम्मा titimmā: (*nm*) a supplement; an appendix.

तिथि tithi: (*nf*) a date; ~त dated.

तिदरी tidari: (*nf*) a three-door verandah.

तिनका tinka: (*nm*) a straw; —तोड़ना lit. to break a straw—to safeguard a dear one against an evil eye; -दाँतों में दबाना/पकड़ना to beg for mercy; —तक न टालना/तोड़ना/हिलाना not to lift/stir even a finger, not to do a hand's turn; तिनके का सहारा, डूबते को a drowning man catches at a straw; तिनके का सहारा लेना to hang on by the eyelids; तिनके की ओट पहाड़ lit. a hill hidden behind a straw—a big secret hidden under an apparent trifle.

तिपाई tipa:i (*nf*) a tripod.

तिबारा tiba:ra: (*ind*) for the third time; (*nm*) a three-door verandah.

तिब्ब tibb (*nm*) the Yunani system

of medicine.

तिब्ब/त tibbat(*nm*)Tibet; ~ती Tibetan.

तिब्बिया tibbiya: (*a*) pertaining to तिब्ब (see).

तिमाही tima:hi: (*a*) quarterly.

तिमिर timir (*nm*) darkness; ~मय dark, full of darkness.

तिरंगा tirãnga: (*a*) tri-coloured; (*nm*) the tri-colour flag; –झंडा tri-coloured flag.

तिरकट tirkaṭ (*nm*) foresail; foreyard.

तिरखान tirkhā:n (*nm*) a carpenter.

तिरछा tirchha: (*a*) slanting; oblique; skew; ~पन slant, obliquinty, skewness, तिरछी नजर slanting glance, amorous look.

तिरछाव tirchha:v (*nm*) slant, obliquity, skewness.

तिरछौहाँ tirchhãuhā: (*a*) having slight slant, slandicular.

तिरता tirta: (*a*) afloat.

तिरना tirnā: (*v*) to float.

तिरपाल tirpa:l (*nf*) tarpaulin; dodger, awning.

तिर/स्कार tiraska:r (*nm*) contempt, slight, opprobrium; disregard, disrespect; ~स्कृत disregarded, insulted; reproached; condemned.

तिरानबे tira:nbe (*a*) ninety-three; (*nm*) the number ninety-three.

तिरासी tira:si (*a*) eighty-three; (*nm*) the number eighty-three.

तिराहा tira:ha: (*nm*) a junction of three roads/paths.

तिरिया tiriya: (*nf*) a woman; –चरित्तर a woman's wiles/mysterious ways.

तिरेसठ tiresaṭh (*a*) sixty-three; (*nm*) the number sixty-three.

तिरोधान tirodhā:n (*nm*) disappearance, ceasing to be visible.

तिरोभाव tirobha:v (*nm*) see तिरोधान.

तिरोभूत tirobhu:t (*a*) see तिरोहित.

तिरोहित tirohit (*a*) disappeared, vanished; rendered/become invisible.

तिरौंदा tirāuda: (*nm*) a float.

तिर्यक् tiryak (*a*) slanting, oblique; crooked; (ग्) –योनि the aves; –रूप an oblique form.

तिलंगा tilãnga: (*nm*) a native soldier.

तिल til (*nf*) sesamum (plant and its seed); a mole; pupil (of the eye); small particle; the least bit; ~कुट a kind of sweetmeat prepared from तिल and sugar or gur; ~चट्टा a cockroach; –का ताड़ करना to make a mountain of a mole; –की ओट पहाड़ a mountain hidden underneath a mole-hill; –तिल करके by small bits; by inches; –धरने की जगह न होना to be packed full, not to have an iota of space; –भर just a bit; –भर का अंतर within an ace of, hair's breadth; तिलों में तेल न होना to be dry and stingy; to yield nothing worthwhile.

तिलक tilak (*nm*) an ornamental or religious mark over the forehead (signifying installation on the throne or engagement etc.); a vermilion or sandal mark (over the forehead); the most eminent member (of a class, clan, dynasty, etc. as रघुकुलतिलक); commentary (of a text).

तिलमि/लाना tilmila:nā: (*v*) to be in the grip of impotent anger; to writhe in agitation, to be painfully restless; to be dazzled; hence ~लाहट (*nf*); ~ली (*nf*).

तिल/स्म tilasm (*nm*) magic, magical spell; talisman; ~स्मी magical; miraculous; talismanic; ~स्म तोड़ना to break a magical spell, to expose the reality underneath a magical proposition, to expose a myth.

तिलहन tilhān (*nm*) oilseed.

तिलांजलि tilā:ṇjali (*nf*) originally—a handful of water mixed with sesamum seeds offered to the manes or deceased ancestors—now, bidding a final good-bye, giving up, abandonment; **–देना** to bid good-bye, to give up, to abandon.

तिला tila: (*nm*) an aphrodisiac oil/ointment; drawn gold.

तिल्ली tilli: (*nf*) spleen; niger; a fanlight.

तिवारी tiva:ri: (*nm*) a sub-caste of the Bra:hmaṉs.

तिस tis (*pro*) the singular oblique form of **सो**; **–पर** then, after that, even so; moreover, besides.

तिहत्तर tihattar (*a*) seventy-three; (*nm*) the number seventy-three.

तिहरा tihra: (*a*) triple, triplicate; threefold.

तिहाई tiha:i; (*a*) one-third.

तीक्ष्ण tikshṉ (*a*) sharp; keen; pungent; intelligent; penetrating; **~दृष्टि** (endowed with) keen/penetrating vision; of keen obser vation; **~बुद्धि** nimble-witted, keenly intelligent; keen intelligence.

तीक्ष्णता tikshṉāta: (*nf*) sharpness, keenness, pungency; intelligence; penetration.

तीखा ti:kha: (*a*) sharp; pungent; harsh; high-pitched; **~पन** sharpness; pungency; harshness; high pitchedness; **तीखे नाक-नक़्श/नैन-नक़्श** sharp (facial) features.

तीज ti:j (*nf*) the third day of the fortnight (in a lunar calendar); a festival held on the third day of the lunar fortnight in the month of **सावन**.

तीतर ti:tar (*nm*) a partridge.

तीन ti:n (*a*) three; (*nm*) the number three; **-चार** three or four; **-पाँच** tricks, foul play; squabble; **–तिलंगे** three musketeers; **–और छह का रिश्ता** heading towards opposite directions, perpetual opponents; **-तेरह होना** to dissipate, to go into disarray, to be scattered; **-पाँच करना** to squabble; to dilly-dally; to play tricks, to dodge; **–में न तेरह में** a small fry; (a person) of no significance, not taken into account at all; to be on the fence; **–लोक से मथुरा न्यारी** to have no parallel, to be unique.

तीमारदा/र ti:ma:rda:r (*nm*) an attendant; a person attending on a patient; **~री** attending on or nursing (a patient).

तीरंदा/ज ti:rānda:z (*nm*) an archer; **~जी** archery, skill in shooting arrows.

तीर ti:r (*nm*) an arrow; a shaft; bank, shore; **~वर्ती/स्थ** situated on the bank/shore, coastal; **–कमान से निकल चुका है** lit. the arrow is shot—the die is cast, what is done cannot be undone; **–की तरह जाना** to make a beehive to, to go straight at full speed; **–ठिकाने/निशाने पर बैठना/लगना** to hit the mark; **–या तुक्का** see **लगे तो तीर नहीं तो तुक्का**.

तीर्थंकर ti:rthāṅkar (*nm*) the twenty-four leading religious preceptors of Jainism, the last of them being Lord Maha:vi:r.

तीर्थ ti:rth (*nm*) a place of pilgrimage; sacred place; **-यात्रा** pilgrimage; **~यात्री** a pilgrim; **~राज** an epithet of Praya:g (Allahabad)—considered to be the most pre-eminent of all the places of pilgrimage.

तीर्थाटन ti:rtha:ṭan (*nm*) pilgrimage.

तीली ti:li: (*nf*) a spoke; matchstick

तीव्र ti:vvr (*a*) fast; pungent; high high pitched; sharp; violent intense, vehement; virulent; ardent; bright; strong; ~बुद्धि bright, sharp, of keen intellect.

तीव्रता ti:vvrata: (*nf*) fastness; pungency; high-pitchedess; sharpness; violence; intensity; virulence.

तीस ti:s (*a*) thirty; (*nm*) the number thirty; ~मार खाँ a sham hero; तीसों दिन all the time, ever.

तीसरा ti:sra: (*a*) (the) third; –पहर afternoon; तीसरे thirdly.

तीसी ti:si: (*nm*) linseed.

तुंग tuṅg (*a*) high; tall; ~ता altitude, height.

तुंगिमा tuṅgimā: (*nf*) the state or quality of being high/tall; height.

तुंड tuṇḍ (*nm*) trunk (of an elephant); snout.

तुंद tund (*nf*) belly.

तुंदिल tundil (*a*) paunchy, pot-bellied; hence ~ता (*nf*).

तुंदी tundi: (*nf*) the navel.

तुंदैला tūdaila: (*a*) paunchy, abdominous, having a big bulging belly.

तुंबा tumba: (*nm*) a gourd; a pot made out of scooped gourd; hence तुंबी (*nf*).

तुक tuk (*nf*) rhyme; sense; harmony; ~बंदी rhyming, improvising verses; –बैठना to rhyme; to harmonise, to co-ordinate; –में तुक मिलाना to chime in, to sing in the same strain, to attune (to somebody else); –होना (बातचीत आदि में) to be rational, to make a sense.

तुकांत tuka:nt (*a*) rhyming, having terminal alliteration.

तुक्कड़/ड़ tukkaṛ (*nm*) a poetaster, mere versifier; hence ~ड़ी (*nf*).

तुक्का tukka: (*nm*) a blunt arrow; unsure means; vain bid; –भिड़ाना/लगाना to make a conjecture; to make an unsure bid, to take a chance; –लगना to accomplish just by chance.

तुक्तक tuktak (*nm*) a limerick.

तुख्म tukhm (*nm*) a seed; sperm; –तासीर सोहबते असर the seed must have its effect and company must mould all men.

तुच्छ tuchchh (*a*) petty, trivial, trifle; frivolous; contemptible; insignificant; ~ता pettiness; triviality; insignificance; frivolity.

तुझ tujh (*pro*) oblique form of तू (see); तुझे to/for thee, to/for you.

तुड़ाई tuṛa:i: (*nf*) the act of or charges for breaking/plucking.

तुड़ाना tuṛa:nā: (*v*) to (cause to) break/pluck; to change (a coin or a currency note) into smaller denominations; to (be in readiness to) run away.

तुतला tutla: (*a* and *nm*) see तोतला.

तुतला/ना tutla:nā: (*v*) to lisp, to babble, to stutter; ~हट lisping, babbling, stuttering.

तुतली tutli: (*a* and *nm*) see तोतला.

तुनकना tunaknā: (*v*) to be pettish/petulant.

तुनकमिज़ा/ज tunakmiza:j (*a*) easily irritated, pettish, petulant; fastidious; ~जी pettishness, petulance; fastidiousness.

तुपक tupak (*nf*) a small gun; ~ची a gunner.

तुफ़ैल tufail (*nm*) cause; means; intervention; –से through, by means of; through the grace of.

तुम tum (*pro*) you.

तुमुल tumul (*a*) tumultous, uproarious; hence ~ता (*nf*).

तुम्हारा tumha:ra: (*pro*) possessive form of तुम—your, yours.

तुम्हीं tumhī: (*pro*) you alone, you and only you.

तुम्हें tumhē (*pro*) to you, unto you.

तुरंग turāṅg (*nm*) a horse; also ~म.

तुरंत turānt (*adv*) at once, quickly, forthwith; immediately, instantly;

soon.

तुरई turai: (*nf*) see तुरही; see तोरई.

तुरत turat (*adv*) see तुरंत; –दान महा कल्याण he gives twice who gives in a trice; the sooner done, the better.

तुरपना turapnā: (*v*) to stitch (lengthwise) by hand; to oversew; to botch; to overcast.

तुरपाई turpa:i: (*nf*) (lengthwise) hand-stitching; whip stitching; botch.

तुरमची turamchi: (*nm*) a trumpeter.

तुरही turahi: (*nf*) a bugle, trumpet.

तुरीय turi:y (*nm*) according to the *Veda:nt*, a stage where the individual self is united with the Universal Self; also –अवस्था.

तुरुप turup (*nm*) a trump; –का पत्ता a trump card; –चाल moving the trump card, sure move.

तुर्क turk (*nm*) a Turk.

तुर्किस्ता/न turkista:n (*nm*) Turkey; hence ~नी (*a*).

तुर्की turki: (*a*) turkish; (*nf*) the Turkish language; -ब-तुर्की जवाब देना to give as good as one gets, to give as sharp a retort.

तुर्रा turra: (*nm*) forelock, an ornamental tassel fitted on the turban; crest; –यह (है) कि what is more, over and above this, moreover, apart from this.

तुर्श tursh (*a*) sour; acidic; (fig.) unpleasant.

तुर्शी turshi: (*nf*) sourness; acidity; (fig.) unpleasantness.

तुल/ना tulnā: (*nf*) comparison; (*v*) to be weighed; to be bent upon; hence ~नीय (*a*); ~ना करना, किसी से to compare with, to make a comparative assessment.

तुलनात्मक tulna:tmāk (*v*) comparative; –अध्ययन comparative study; hence ~ता (*nf*).

तुलवाई tulwa:i: (*nf*) the act of, or wages paid for, weighing.

तुलसी tulsi: (*nf*) the holy basil pla[nt] —*Ocymum sanctum*; –दल/पत्र basil leaf; –वन a basil grove.

तुला tula: (*nf*) a balance, pair [o]f scales; the sign of Libra—sevent[h] sign of the zodiac; ~दंड the bea[m] of a balance; ~दान a gift of gol[d] silver or grain etc. equivalent t[o] the weight of the donor; –हु[आ] dead set, bent upon.

तुलाई tula:i: (*nf*) see तुलवाई.

तुल्य tully (*a*) equivalent; lik[e]; ~काल/कालीय contemporaneou[s], synchronous; ~कालत्व synchronis[m]; ~रूप resembling, of like appea[r]ance; ~वृत्ति co-professional.

तुल्यता tullyata: (*nf*) equivalenc[e], parity; likeness, similarity.

तुषार tusha:r (*nm*) frost; ~कण sno[w] flakes; ~पात frost-fall; ०होना li[t.] to be frost-hit—to be liquidate[d], to be razed; ~सह frost-proo[f]; तुषाराहत frost-bitten.

तुष्ट tushṭ (*a*) satisfied, gratifie[d], contented.

तुष्टि tushṭi (*nf*) satisfaction, grat[i]fication; contentment.

तुष्टीकरण ṭushṭi:karaṉ (*nm*) appeas[e]ment; –नीति policy of appeas[e]ment.

तुहिन tuhin (*nm*) frost, snow; –क[ण] snow-flakes.

तूँबी tū:bi: (*nf*) see तुंबा; a float.

तू tu: (*pro*) thou; you; -तू मैं-मैं lo[w] level altercation, squabblin[g]; -तड़ाक boorish/uncivil languag[e]; ०पर उतर आना to stoop to booris[h] uncivil language; –मेरी डफली ब[जा] मैं तेरा राग अलापूँ claw me an[d] I'll claw thee.

तूणीर tū:ṉi:r (*nm*) a quiver (for kee[p]ing arrows).

तूतिया tu:tiya: (*nf*) blue vitriol, su[l]phate of copper.

तूती tu:ti: (*nf*) a rosefinch; **–बोलना** to command overweening influence, to have unquestioned sway/mastery.

तूफ़ान tu:fā:n (*nm*) a storm, tempest, hurricane; typhoon; **–खड़ा करना/–बरपा करना/मचाना** to work havoc, to unleash a storm.

तूफ़ानी tu:fa:nı: (*a*) stormy, tempestuous, violent and vehement; **–दस्ता** flying squad; **–दौरा** whirlwind tour.

तूमना tū:mnā: (*v*) to card (cotton) with fingers.

तूमा/र, ~ल tu:ma:r, ~l (*nm*) fuss; magnifying a point beyond due limits; **–बाँधना** to create a fuss, to magnify a point beyond all reasonable limits, to stretch things too far.

तूरा/न tu:rā:n (*nm*) the middle-Asian Tartar country; **~नी** pertaining to **तूरान**; an inhabitant/language of **तूरान**.

तूर्य tu:ry (*nm*) a trumpet; **~नाद** sounding of trumpet(s).

तूल tu:l (*nm*) length; prolixity; cotton; **-अर्ज़** length and breadth; **-तबील** long and huge; **–देना** to magnify, to make prolix; to overstretch a point; to carry too far; **–पकड़ना** to take a violent turn, to be over-stretched, to go too far.

तूलिका tu:lika: (*nf*) a painter's brush.

तूस tu:s (*nm*) the husk; a kind of fine wool.

तृण trin̲ (*nm*) a straw; **~मय** made of straw; **~वत्** as insignificant as a straw, trifling; **~शय्या** straw-bedding.

तृणावर्त trin̲a:vart (*nm*) a hurricane.

तृतीय triti:y (*a*) (the) third; **~क** tertiary.

तृतीयांश triti:ya:nsh (*nm*) one third (portion).

तृतीया triti:ya: (*a*) (the) third; (*nf*) the third day of the lunar fortnight.

तृप्त tript (*a*) contended; gratified, fulfilled.

तृप्ति tripti (*nf*) contentment; gratification, fulfilment.

तृषा trisha: (*nf*) thirst; **~लु** thirsty.

तृषित trishit (*a*) thirsty.

तृष्णा trishn̲ā: (*nf*) thirst; greed; longing, craving; **–का अंत नहीं होता** craving knows no end; the eye is bigger than the belly.

तेंदुआ tēdua: (*nm*) a leopard.

तेईस tei:s (*a*) twenty-three; (*nm*) the number twenty-three.

तेग teg (*nm*) a sword; cutlass, scimitar; **–तलवार** sword and scimitar.

तेज tej (*nm*) glow; splendour, brilliance, refulgence; awe; **~स्विता** see **तेजस्विता**; **~स्वी** see **तेजस्वी**.

तेज़ tez (*a*) sharp; sharp-pointed; dear, costly; acute; keen; penetrating (as **–नज़र**); acrid, pungent; corrosive, caustic; violent, fiery; swift, quick (as **–रफ़्तार**), fleet; smart; intelligent, nimble-witted; **-तर्रार** fiery and fierce, caustic-tongued; sharp and smart; **~दिमाग़** sharp, intelligent; **~मिज़ाज** short-tempered; petulant; **~रफ़्तार** swift fast-moving.

तेजड़िया tejaṛiya: (*nm*) a bull (in speculation).

तेज/वंत, ~वान tejvant, ~vā:n (*a*) see **तेजस्वी**.

तेजस्विता tejasvita: (*nf*) brilliance, luminosity, glow; impressiveness, imposingness.

तेजस्वी tejasvi: (*a*) brilliant, luminous, glowing; impressive, imposing.

तेज़ा/ब teza:b (*nm*) an acid; **~बी** acidic; treated with acid.

तेज़ी tezi: (*nf*) sharpness; boom; dearness; keenness; acridity, pungency; quickness, swiftness; smartness; intelligence; -**मंदी** straddle.

तेजोमय tejomay (*a*) brilliant, refulgent, luminous; glowing; resplendent; hence ~**ता** (*nf*).

तेतालीस teta:li:s (*a*) forty-three; (*nm*) the number forty-three.

तेतीस teti:s (*a*) thirty-three; (*nm*) the number thirty-three.

तेते tete (*pro*) In Braj Bha:sha:, it means **उतने** –to that extent; –**पाँव पसारिए जेती लंबी सौर** cut your coat according to the cloth.

तेरस teras (*nf*) the thirteenth day of the lunar fortnight.

तेरह terah (*a*) thirteen; (*nm*) the number thirteen.

तेर/हीं, ~ही tera/hĩ:, ~hi: (*nf*) the thirteenth day after death; the rituals performed on the thirteenth day signifying the end of the post-mortem rituals.

तेरा tera: (*pro*) possessive form o **तू**—thy, thine, your(s); -**सा/तेरी-सी** favourable to you, serving your interest.

तेल tel (*nm*) oil; petrol; –**चढ़ाना** to perform to ceremony of pre-marital oil anointment; –**देखो तेल की धार देखो** see which way the cat jumps/wind blows; –**निकालना** lit. to extract oil out of, to tire out, to make one work till one perspires profusely.

तेलहन telhan (*nm*) see **तिलहन**.

तेलिया teliya: (*a*) oily; (*nm*) see **तेली**.

तेली teli: (*nm*) an oilman; a Hindu sub-caste which subsists on oil-extraction and sale; –**का बैल** lit. an oilman's ox—a toiling wretch, one condemned to a slog.

तेवर tevar (*nm*) an eye-brow; a frown; stance: –**चढ़ाना** to frown. to scowl; –**बदलना** to scowl, to frown; to strike an adverse posture, to assume an angry look; -**तेवरों में बल पड़ना** to fly into a rage, to assume an angry look.

तैंतालिस taĩta:lis (*a* and *nm*) see **तेतालीस**.

तैंतिस taitis (*a* and *nm*) see **तेतीस**.

तैथि/क taithik (*a*) chronological; ~**की** chronology.

तैना/त taina:t (*a*) deployed, posted; appointed; ~**ती** posting, deployment; appointment.

तैयार taiya:r (*a*) ready, willing; ready-made; prepared; finished, ripened, matured; in bloom, blooming; robust; fat; –**माल** manufactured goods.

तैयारी taiya:ri: (*nf*) readiness; preparation/preparedness; ground work; robustness; bloom; practice; –**पर होना** to be in form; –**पर होना, पूरी** to be in the best of form; hence **तैयारियाँ** (plural form).

तैरना tairnā: (*v*) to swim; to float.

तैरा/क taira:k (*a*) an expert swimmer; ~**की** (the art of) swimming.

तैलंगाना tailānga:nā: (*nm*) a southern region of the Indian union, presently part of the state of **आंध्रप्रदेश**.

तैल tail (*nm*) oil; ~**चित्र** an oil painting; ~**पोत** an oil tanker; ~**रंग** oil colour; **तैलाक्त** anointed or smeared with oil.

तैश taish (*nm*) provocation; rage, wrath; –**खाना**,–**में आना** to take a huff; to get one's dander up; to be provoked; to fly into a rage; –**में होना** to be in a huff, to be in a state of provocation

तैसा taisa: (*a*) like that, similar to that.

तोंद tõd (*nf*) paunch, potbelly; –**पिचकना** lit. the paunch to be deflated–to lose corpulence/fat, all air to blow out.

तोंदीला tōdi:la: (*a*) see **तुंदैला**.

तो to (*ind*) then; therefore; moreover; an emphatic particle (*e.g.* **मैं तो जाऊँगा**); at any rate, however; at least; **–भी** even so, even then, in spite of this/that; nevertheless, nonetheless, still.

तोड़ tor(*nm*) antidote; counter, counter-measure; breach/break; whey; forceful current of water (in a river etc.); **-फोड़** sabotage; breakage; destruction; **०की कार्यवाही** sabotaging activity, sabotage; **-फोड़ करने वाला** a saboteur; **-मरोड़** mutilation.

तोड़ना tornā: (*v*) to break; to violate; to fracture; to pluck; to disband; to twist, to demolish; to snap; to change (into coins or currency notes of smaller denomination); to reduce; to win over, to cause to defect.

तोड़ा tora: (*nm*) scarcity; deficiency; name of an ornament worn round the wrist; rhythmic structure in instrumental music; a long narrow meshwork bag (used in olden times for carrying cash tied round the waist); match-lock (of a gun); **तोड़ेदार** fitted with a match-lock; **०बंदूक** a match-lock gun.

तोतला totla: (*a*) lisping; (*nm*) (one) who lisps; hence **तोतली** (*fem.*).

तोता tota: (*nm*) a parrot; **~चश्म** lit. parrot-eyed – capable of shifting to cool indifference from cordiality; **~चश्मी** the attribute or attitude of a **~चश्म**; **~परी** a variety of mango; **~रटंत** see **तोते की तरह रटना**; **–पालना** to get addicted to an evil; to allow a malady to get aggravated; **तोते की तरह आँखें फेरना** to give one the cut direct, to forget the past cordiality, to assume cool indifference; **तोते की तरह पढ़ाना** to teach over and over again; **तोते की तरह रटना** to repeat unintelligently, to cram up; to continue to harp on the same note.

तोप top (*nf*) a gun, cannon; **~खाना** artillery; **~ची** a gunner; **–विद्या** gunnery; **~दम करना** to blow off with a gun.

तोबड़ा tobra: (*nm*) a nose bag; face as a whole; **–फुलाना** to become glum/sulky.

तोबा toba: (*nf*) vowing to sin no more, vowing never to repeat (an act); **–करना** to cry 'enough', to vow to do no more, to vow never to repeat; **–तोड़ना** to break a pledge, to violate a vow; **–बुलवाना** to apply pressure/harass till one yields.

तोय toy (*nm*) water.

तोरई torai: (*nf*) the cucurbitaceous plant and its vegetable—*Luffa acutangula*.

तोरण torāṉ (*nm*) a pylon; an arched gateway; festoons.

तोल tol (*nf*) weight; **-माप** weights and measures.

तोलना tolnā: (*v*) to weigh; to balance; to assess or to gauge; **तोलकर बोलो** think/weigh before you speak.

तोला tola: (*nm*) an Indian unit of weight—one eightieth of a seer.

तोशक toshak (*nf*) cushioned mattress.

तोष tosh (*nm*) appeasement; gratification.

तोहफ़ा tohfa: (*nm*) a present, gift.

तोहम/त tohmāt (*nf*) slander, false accusation; **~ती** a slanderer.

तौंसना tausnā: (*v*) to be scorched.

तौंसा tausa: (*nm*) scorching heat.

तौक़ tauq (*nm*) a neck-ring; (*fig.*) a

yoke; –, गुलामी की the yoke of slavery.

तौर taur (*nm*) mode, method, way; -तरीक़ा ways, technique; -तरीक़े manners.

तौल taul (*nf*) see तोल.

तौलना taulnā: (*v*) see तोलना.

तौलिया tauliya: (*nf*, also *nm*) a towel.

तौही/न tauhi:n (*nf*) insult, disrespect; humiliation; contempt; ~ने-अदालत contempt of court.

त्यक्त tyakt (*a*) abandoned; renounced; forsaken; sacrificed, abnegated; hence त्यक्ता (*fem.*) an abandoned (woman).

त्यजन tyajān (*nm*) abandoning; renouncing, forsaking; sacrificing, abnegating.

त्याग tya:g (*nm*) abandonment; relinquishment, renunciation forsaking; sacrifice, abnegation; -पत्र (letter of) resignation; ~मय full of sacrifice/renunciation; ~शील sacrificing, renunciative, prone to forsake/abnegate/sacrifice; hence ~शीलता (*nf*).

त्यागना tya:gnā: (*v*) to abandon, to give up, to relinquish, to renounce; to resign, to abnegate, to forsake, to sacrifice.

त्यागी tya:gi: (*nm*) one who has made sacrifices, renouncer; a recluse.

त्याज्य tya:jjy (*a*) abandonable, renounceable, fit to be forsaken/given up, worth forsakng/giving up.

त्योहा/र tyoha:r (*nm*) see त्यौहार; ~री see त्यौहारी.

त्यों tyaū (*ind*) thus; like that, so, in like manner; -त्यों so, in the same manner/measure.

त्यौरस tyauras (*nm*) the year before last; the year after next.

त्यौरी tyauri: (*nf*) wrinkles of the forehead; contracted eyebrows; –चढ़ाना to wrinkle up one's forehead—to scowl, to frown; –में बल पड़ना the forehead to be wrinkled up, to be in a temper/rage/furious mood.

त्यौहा/र tyauha:r (*nm*) a festal day, festival; festivity; ~री a festal gift (in cash or kind).

त्रय tray (*a*) three; (*nm*) the number three.

त्रयी trai: (*nf*) a trio, trinity; (*a*) trimerous.

त्रयोदश trayodash (*a*) thirteen; thirteenth; (*nm*) the number thirteen.

त्रयोदशी trayodashi: (*nf*) the thirteenth day of the lunar fortnight.

त्रसित trasit (*a*) frightened, scared, terrified.

त्रस्त trast (*a*) frightened, scared, terrified.

त्राण trā:n̲ (*nm*) protection; means of protection, defence; shelter; salvation; ~कर्ता protector, saviour; ~कारी protector/protecting; saviour/saving; ~दाता see त्राता.

त्राता tra:ta: (*nm*) a saviour, protector.

त्रास tra:s (*nf*) fear, fright, scare, terror, dread; ~क/कर/कारी fearful; frightening, frightful, terrifying.

त्रास/द, ~दायी tra:sad, ~da:i: (*a*) frightening, terrifying, dreadful.

त्रासदी tra:sadi: (*nf*) a (dramatic) tragedy; ~कार author of a tragedy; ~य tragic.

त्रासन tra:sān (*nm*) (the act or process of) frightening/scaring/terrifying.

त्रासिक tra:sik (*a*) tragic; frightening; –कामदी a tragi-comedy.

त्राहि, ~माम tra:hi, ~mā:m (*ind*) protect me !, save me !; deliver me !; –त्राहि करना to repeatedly call for mercy or deliverance;

–त्राहि मचना to be resounded with calls of 'save me ! deliver me !'; a disastrous chaos to be let loose.

त्रि tri (*a*) three; ~क a trio, trinity; ~काल the three times—past, present, future; ०ज्ञ omniscient, knowing the three times (see त्रिकाल); ~कालदर्शी a seer, sage, one gifted with a vision to see through the past, present and future alike; also ~कालदर्शक; hence ~कालदर्शिता (*nf*); ~कुटी the interval between the eye-brows and the junction of the forehead and the nose; ~कोण a triangle; ०मिति (the science of) trigonometry; ~कोणिक/ ~कोणीय triangular; ~गुण the set of three *guṇas* (सत्व, रज, तम); threefold, three times; possessing the three *guṇas*; ~गुणातीत transcending the three *guṇas*; ~गुणात्मक possessing the three *guṇas*; ~गुणित multiplied by three; three times; ~जगत see ~लोक; ~ज्या radius; ~ताप the three तापs (physical, mundane, divine); ~त्व a trilogy; ~देव the trinity of ब्रह्मा, विष्णु and महेश; ~दोष disorder of the three humours, viz. wind (वात), bile (पित्त) and phlegm (कफ); ~धा in three ways; in three parts; ~पक्षीय trilateral; representing three sides/parties/aspects; ~पथ a tri-junction; the three paths for the Supreme Realisation—knowledge (ज्ञान), action (कर्म) and devotion (भक्ति); ~पाठी a sub-caste of the Bra:hmans; ~पुंड/पुंड्र a mark of sandal-paste or ash over the forehead comprised of three horizontal or crescent-shaped lines; ~पुटी a set of three; ~फला a mixture of three myrobalans viz. myrobalan (हड़); belleric myrobalan (बहेड़ा) and emblic myrobalan (आँवला); ~बली see ~वली; ~भुज a triangle; ~भुजाकार triangular (shaped); ~भुवन the three worlds viz. this world (मृत्युलोक), the other world (आकाश), and the nether world (पाताल); ~मूर्ति see ~देव; ~लोक the three worlds; see ~भुवन; ~लोचन the three eyed—Lord Shiv; ~वली the three skin-folds about the navel—a source of feminine charm; ~विध of three kinds; ~वेणी the confluence of the three rivers (in Praya:g) —the Gāṅga:, the Yamunā: and the (invisible) Saraswati: ; ~वेदी a sub-caste of the Bra:hmaṇs; ~शंकु an ancient Indian King of the Solar dynasty (according to Hindu mythology the sage Vishwa:mittr, through his spiritual powers, tried to send him physically to the kingdom of Heavens. Indra, the king of gods, refused him entry into his world and sent him tumbling down. He is thus said to be tucked up in between the heaven and the earth); neither here nor there, hanging in space; ~शूल a trident; ०धर/०धारी (the) trident-bearer—an epithet of Lord Shiv; ~सूत्री trisomic, three-point.

त्रिया triya: (*nf*) a woman; -चरित्र wiles/mysterious ways of a woman.

त्रुटि truṭi (*nf*) an error, mistake; defect, deficiency; ~पूर्ण erroneous, defective; ~त broken.

त्रेता treta: (*nm*) the second of the four ages according the Hindu mythology—the silver age.

त्रैकालिक traika:lik (*a*) pertaining to त्रिकाल (see under त्रि); of all times.

त्रैमासिक traimā:sik (*a*) quarterly, three-monthly.

त्रैलोक्य trailokky (*a*) pertaining to

or of the three worlds (लोक).

त्रैवार्षिक traiva:rshik (*a*) triennial.

त्वक् tvak (*nm*) the skin; bark.

त्वचा tvacha: (*nf*) the skin.

त्वदीय tvadi:y (*a*) yours.

त्वरण tvarā<u>n</u> (*nm*) acceleration; speeding up.

त्वरणीय tvara<u>n</u>i:y (*a*) acceleratable; worth speeding up; urgent.

त्वरा tvara: (*nf*) haste; quickness; urgency; —**लिपि** shorthand.

त्वरित tvarit (*a*) quick, swift; (*adv*) quickly, swiftly.

थ

थ tha—the second letter of the fourth pentad (i.e. **तवर्ग**) of the Devna:gri: alphabet.

थंब, थंबा thāmb, thāmba: (*nm*) a pillar.

थकन thakān (*nf*) see **थकान**.

थकना thaknā: (*v*) to be tired/wearied/fatigued; **थका-माँदा** dead beat, worn and wearied, tired out, jaded; **थका-हारा** see **थका-माँदा**; **थक कर चूर होना** to be dead tired, to be extremely wearied; **थक जाना** to be tired/wearied/jaded; to be fed up; to be exhausted.

थकान thakā:n (*nf*) weariness, fatigue, tiredness; exhaustion; —**उतारना** to relax after exertion/exhaustion.

थका/र thaka:r (*nm*) the letter **थ्** (th) and its sound; ~**रांत** word ending in **थ्** (th).

थकाव(ह)ट thaka:v(h)aṭ (*nf*) see **थकान**.

थकित thakit (*a*) tired, wearied, fatigued; exhausted.

थकौहाँ thakaūhā: (*a*) somewhat tired; looking wearied/exhausted/fatigued.

थक्का thakka: (*nm*) a clot; lump.

थन thān (*nm*) the udder; ~**दुहा** fresh from the udders, just milked.

थपकना thapaknā: (*v*) to pat (as a child to sleep), to strike gently with the palm; to tap.

थपकी thapki: (*nf*) pat; tap; —**देकर सुलाना** to pat to sleep (as a child); —**देना** to pat.

थपड़ी thapṛi: (*nf*) a clap; clapping; —**पीटना/बजाना** to clap.

थपथपाना thapthapa:nā: (*v*) to pat, to strike gently with the palm; to tap; —,**पीठ** to back; to pat the back with approbation.

थपथपाहट thapthapa:haṭ (*nf*) a sequence of pats or gentle strokes of palm, constant tapping.

थपथपी thapthapi: (*nf*) see **थपकी**.

थपेड़ा thapeṛa: (*nm*) a violent blow/stroke; buffet; dash (as of violent waves).

थप्पड़ thappaṛ (*nm*) a slap; buffet; spank; —**जड़ना**/—**रसीद करना**/—**लगाना** to (implant a) slap (on the cheek).

थमना thamnā: (*v*) to stop; to come to a standstill; to wait; to be supported by or propped up.

थमा(म्हा)ना thamā:(mhā:)nā: (*v*) to hand over, to entrust; to recline.

थरथर tharthar (*a*) trembling(ly),

shuddering(ly), quivering(ly).

थरथराना tharthara:nā: (*v*) to tremble, to shudder, to quiver.

थरथ/राहट tharthara:haṭ (*nf*) trembling, shuddering, quivering.

थरथरी tharthari: (*nf*) see **थरथराहट**.

थरहरी tharehri: (*nf*) see **थरथरी**.

थर्मस tharmās (*nm*) a thermos flask.

थर्मामीटर tharmā:mi:ṭar (*nm*) a thermometer; **–लगाना** to take the temperature (of a person).

थर्रा/ना tharra:nā: (*v*) to shudder, to tremble with terror; hence **~हट** (*nf*).

थल thal (*nm*) land; place; **~चर/-चारी** terrestrial (animal); **–सेना** the army; **थलीय** land, pertaining to the land.

थलथ/ल, ~ला thaltha/l, ~la: (*a*) flabby; flaccid: **~लापन** flabbiness, flaccidity.

थहराना thehra:nā: (*v*) see **थर्राना**; to become still, to settle down; to form a precipitate.

थहाना thaha:nā: (*v*) to fathom, to sound; to go to the bottom of.

थाँवला thā:vla: (*nm*) see **थाला**.

था tha: (*v*) was.

थाक tha:k (*nf*) stick(ing).

थाती tha:ti: (*nf*) a trust, anything entrusted to somebody; a charge.

थान thā:n (*nm*) a long piece of cloth of standard size; a raised platform where a deity's image is installed, deity's abode; stall (of an animal); position

थाना tha:nā: (*nm*) a police station.

थाने/दार tha:nēda:r (*nm*) a police sub-inspector; **~री** the office or function/job of a sub-inspector of police.

थाप tha:p (*nf*) pat, tap; a palm-stroke over a percussion instrument; see **थापा**; **–देना** to commence playing a percussion instrument (esp. **तबला**)

थापना tha:pnā: (*nm*) installation (of a deity etc.); (*v*) to install. to pat into cakes (as cow-dung etc.).

था/पा tha:pa: (*nm*) a palm-imprint; **~पे देना** to apply the palm-imprints (with turmeric).

थापी tha:pi: (*nf*) a mallet; tamper; a wooden patting device (used by masons, etc.).

थाम thā:m (*nm*) a strut; used as the second member in the compound **रोक-थाम** (see).

थामना tha:mnā: (*v*) to (cause to) stop; to hold; to grasp; to prop; to support; to restrain; to resist.

थाल tha:l (*nm*) a large flat metallic plate slightly edged up; basin.

थाला tha:la: (*nm*) a basin (dug round a tree or plant for holding water).

थाली tha:li: (*nf*) a smaller form of **थाल** (see); **–का बैंगन** fickle-minded, wavering (person); **–में घी इधर-उधर/बिखरा-बिखरा** as broad as it is long.

थाह tha:h (*nf*) depth; estimate of depth; **–पाना** to get at the truth; to probe the depth of; **–लेना** to assess the depth of; to unearth the reality.

थाहना tha:hnā: (*v*) to fathom, to sound, to estimate the depth (of).

थिएटर thieṭar (*nm*) a theatre (hall).

थिगली thigli: (*nf*) a patch (for mending cloth); **–लगाना** to patch. to mend with a patch.

थिर thir (*a*) stable; static; tranquil; hence **~ता** (*nf*).

थिरक thirak (*nf*) rhythmic vibration of body parts (in dancing), nimble footwork (in dancing); also **–न** (*nf*).

थिरकना thiraknā: (*v*) to make the body parts vibrate rhythmically;

to move the feet nimbly in a dance sequence.

थिरना thirnā: (*v*) to settle down (the sediment of a liquid); to become still and tranquil.

थिराना thira:nā: (*v*) see **थिरना**.

थुक्का-फ़जीहत thukka-faji:hat (*nf*) reproach and reproof, censure and condemnation; altercation.

थुड़ी thuṛi: (*nf*) a word expressing contemptuous indignation; **-थुड़ी करना** to express censure and condemnation, to express contemptuous indignation; **-थुड़ी होना** to suffer indignation, to be subjected to shameful disgrace.

थुथना thuthnā: (*nm*) a nozzle.

थुलथु/ल, ~ला thulthu/l, ~la: (*a*) see **थलथल**.

थू thu: (*nm*) the sound made in spitting; (*ind*) an expression of indigation and contempt; shame ! fie ! pish !; **-थू करना** see **थुड़ी-थुड़ी करना**; **-थू होना** see **-थुड़ी-थुड़ी होना**.

थूक thu:k (*nm*) spittle, sputum; saliva; **–देना** to kick at; to spit at; **–से सत्तू नहीं सनता** you cannot make horn of a pig's tail; **–से** or **थूकों सत्तू सानना** to try to make a silk purse out of a sow's ears, to try overmuch with meagre means; to be stupidly tight-fisted.

थूक/ना thu:knā: (*v*) to spit; to reproach and reprove; to treat with contempt; **–कर चाटना** to eat one's own words; **~ना भी नहीं/~ने भी न आना** to lift up the heel against, to treat with utmost contempt.

थूथन thuthān (*nm*) see **थूथनी**.

थूथनी thu:thnɪ: (*nf*) the snout (of an animal); muzzle.

थूनी thu:nɪ: (*nf*) a small post; prop; pillar.

थेई-थेई thei:-thei: (*nf*) a prop expression to mark time in dance or musical recital.

थैला thaila: (*nm*) a bag, sack, haversack, wallet.

थैली thaili: (*nf*) a money bag; small bag; pouch; pocket; **–(का मुँह) खोलना** to open the strings of the purse, to spend liberally; **~वाले** capitalists, moneyed people.

थोक thok (*nm*) whole lot, wholesale; bulk; a heap, mass; locality; **–का भाव** wholesale price; **~फ़रोश/विक्रेता** a wholesale dealer, wholesaler; **–में** in large numbers; in wholesale.

थोड़ा thoṛa: (*a*) a little, some, meagre, scanty; short; **-बहुत** some, somewhat, a little; **-सा** a bit, a little; **–कहा बहुत समझना** a word to the wise should be enough; **थोड़े** a few, some; **॰ही** little indeed; not at all; never.

थोथा thotha: (*a*) hollow, empty, worthless; unsubstantial; **~पन** hollowness, emptiness; **–चना बाजे घना** an empty vessel makes much noise.

थोपना thopnā: (*v*) to impose, to thrust upon; to implant; to plaster.

थोबड़ा thobṛa: (*nm*) the snout (of an animal); **–फुलाना** to sulk, to go into a sulky mood/posture.

द da—the third letter of the fourth pentad (i.e. **तवर्ग**) of the Devna:gri: alphabet; a suffix added to impart the meaning of, or to denote, a giver (as **जलद**– giver of water, a cloud).

दंग dāṅg (*a*) wonder-struck, astonished, flabbergasted; **–रह जाना** to be wonder-struck/astonished/flabbergasted.

दंगई dāṅgai: (*a*) turbulent; rowdy; riotous, pugnacious; (*nm*) a rioter, rowdy.

दंगल dāṅgal: (*nm*) a wrestling tournament/bouts; wrestling arena; tumultuous assembly; **–जुड़ना** tumultuous elements to assemble; **–मारना** to win a wrestling bout; **–में उतरना** to step into the (wrestling) arena; **–लड़ना** to participate in a wrestling bout.

दंगली dāṅgli: (*a*) fit to wrestle/fight; an adept in, or given to, wrestling/fighting; (*nm*) a (keen) wrestler/fighter.

दंगा dāṅga: (*nm*) a riot; disturbance; tumultuous quarrel, fracas; **~ई** a rioter; **दंगेबाज़** riotous, pugnacious; quarrelsome; lawless, rebellious; **दंगेबाज़ी** rioting; riotousness; outbreak of lawlessness, disturbance of peace.

दंड dān̲ḍ (*nm*) punishment; penalty fine; a staff, rod; beam, shaft; stalk; a measure of time (about 24 minutes); see **डंड**; **~नायक** a magistrate; **-नीति** the rule of force, the rule of inflicting punishment to attain a sway over one's foes and criminals; **~पाल** a watchman, gatekeeper; **-प्रणाम** prostrating oneself in reverence; **-भय** fear of punishment; **-विधान/विधि** criminal law; penal code; **~शास्त्र** penalogy; **–भरना** to make amends; to pay the penalty.

दंडनीय dān̲ḍni:y (*a*) punishable, deserving punishment; hence **~ता** (*nf*).

दंडवत् dān̲ḍavat (*nm*) prostration, prostrating oneself in reverence, deferential salutation (directed towards elders or holy persons); **–करना** to kiss the ground.

दंडात्मक dān̲ḍa:tmāk (*a*) penal, involving punishment.

दंडादेश dān̲ḍa:desh (*nm*) condemnation (in a court of law).

दंडाधिकारी dān̲ḍa:dhika:ri: (*nm*) a magistrate.

दंडित dān̲ḍit (*a*) punished, penalised.

दंड्य dan̲ḍy (*a*) see **दंडनीय**.

दंत dānt (*nm*) a tooth; **~कथा** a legend; tradition; an anecdote; **~क्षत** dental marks (as might appear on cheeks, lips, etc. in the wake of amorous sport, sexual indulgence; **~चिकित्सक** a dentist; dental surgeon; **-चिकित्सा** dentistry; treatment of dental ailments; **~मूल** a fang, root of the tooth; **~मूलीय** (sounds) uttered from the root of the teeth; **~हीन** edentate.

दंतावली dānta:vali: (*nf*) the row of teeth, denture.

दंती danti: (*a* and *nm*) tusky; having tusks/teeth; an elephant.

दंतुर dāntur (*a*) tusky, having long or projected teeth.

दँतुली dãtuli: (*nf*) a denticle, small growing tooth as in children.

दंतोष्ठ्य dāntoshṭhy (*a*) labio-dental (sound).

दंत्य dānty (*a*) dental (sound); pertaining to the teeth/a tooth.

दंदान dāndā:n (*nm*) a tooth; **~साज़** a dentist; **~साज़ी** dentistry, one who fixes a denture.

दंदा/ना dāndā:nā: (*nm*) a tooth; jag; **~नेदार** toothed; jagged.

दंपति dāmpati (*nm*) a (married) couple, husband and wife.

दंभ dāmbh (*nm*) conceit, vainglory, vanity.

दंभी dāmbhi: (*a*) conceited, vainglorious, vain.

दँवरी dãvri: (*nf*) (the process of) trampling of reaped harvest by bullocks for separating corn from chaff.

दंश dānsh (*nm*) a sting; bite, biting; **~न** stinging, biting; **दंशित** bitten, stung.

दई dai: (*nm*) providence; fate, destiny; see **दैया**; **~जार** unfortunate, ill-fated (a term of abuse used generally by women); **-दई** O God! O God; O God, save me!; **~मारा** ill-fated; damned by Providence.

दक/न dakān (*nm*) the south; south India, Deccan; **~नी** southern/pertaining to Deccan; see **दक्खिनी**.

दक़ियानू/स daqiya:nū:s (*a*) conservative (person); **~सी** (an old fogey) conservative (person, idea, thinking); conservatism; **~सीपन** conservatism, conservative conduct.

दक्खि/न dakkhin (*nm*) the south; **~नी** southern, pertaining to the south; South Indian form and style of Hindi; also called **०हिंदी**.

दक्ष daksh (*a*) efficient, expert; **~ता** efficiency, expertness.

दक्षिण dakshin̲ (*nm*) the south; right; favourably disposed; (in poetical jargon) attribute of a hero (**नायक**) who keeps all his heroines in good humour; **–पंथ** right; **~पंथी** rightist; **–होना** to be favourably disposed.

दक्षिणा dakshin̲ā: (*nf*) honorarium (paid in olden days to a preceptor by his pupil at the successful conclusion of his student career); reward to priest, etc.; remuneration; **~पथ** the southern region of India.

दक्षिणाभिमुख dakshin̲ā:bhimukh (*a*) facing the south.

दक्षिणायन dakshin̲ā:yan (*nm*) the movement of the sun to the south of the equator; the period of six months called the winter solstice; (*a*) gone south.

दक्षिणावर्त्त dakshin̲ā:vart (*a*) clockwise; **–गति** clockwise movement.

दक्षिणी dakshin̲i: (*a*) southern; (*nm*) a southerner.

दख़लंदा/ज़ dak̲halanda:z (*a*) one who interferes/intrudes/meddles, an interferer, a meddler; **~ज़ी** interference, intrusion, meddling.

दख़ल dak̲hal (*nm*) interference; interruption; occupation; authority, authoritative knowledge, go (in a subject); **–करना** to occupy; **–देना** to interrupt, to interfere; **–होना** to have a say, to have knowledge of; **~कार** an occupant; **~कारी** occupying.

दग़ा daga: (*nf*) treachery; deception, perfidy; **~बाज़** treacherous; deceitful, perfidious; **~बाज़ी** treacherousness, deceitfulness, perfidiousness; –देना/दे जाना to turn one's coat, to deceive.

दगीला, दगैल dagi:la:, dagail (*v*) stained; specked; blemished; stigmatic.

दग्ध dagdh (*a*) burnt, scorched.

दचक dachak (*nf*) a jerk (experienced while travelling in or on a vehicle); a bump; jerking; shock.

दचकना dachaknā: (*v*) to bump; to suffer a jerk (as in or on a vehicle), to undergo a sequence of jerks or shocks.

दच/का dachka: (*nm*) a bump, jerk; shock; (also fig.); blow; ~केदार bumpy, jerky.

दढ़ियल darhiyal (*a*) bearded.

दतुवन, दतौन datuvān, datāūn (*nf*) see दातौन.

दत्त datt (*a*) given, assigned; (*nm*) data.

दत्तक dattak (*a*) adopted; (*nm*) an adopted son; also –पुत्र; ~ग्राही adopter; दत्तकी पिता adoptive father; दत्तकी माता adoptive mother; –ग्रहण करना/लेना to adopt (a son).

दत्तचित्त dattachitt (*a*) deeply/fully attentive, concentrated, having concentration; –होकर सुनना to be all ears.

ददिया dadiya: (*a*) grand-paternal; grand-maternal (as –ससुर, –सास).

ददोरा dadora: (*nm*) a rash, a bump or swelling (caused by insect-bite or bad state of blood).

दद्रु daddru (*nm*) ring-worm.

दधि dadhi (*nf*) curd, coagulated milk; ~मंथन churning of curd.

दनदनाना dāndanā:nā: (*v*) to go as fast as a shot; to shoot along or forth; to resound.

दनादन danā:dān (*adv*) resoundingly; non-stop, incessantly.

दनुज danuj (*nm*) a demon; hence ~ता (*nf*).

दन्न dann (*nf*) a thunderous sound as produced by a gun-fire; –से in full speed, with a thunderous sound.

दफ़ती dafti: (*nf*) card-board, paste-board, mill-board.

दफ़न dafān (*nm*) burial/entombment; –करना to bury; to entomb.

दफ़नाना dafnā:nā: (*v*) to bury; to entomb.

दफ़रा dafra: (*nm*) a fender.

दफ़राना dafra:nā: (*v*) to fend, to fend off.

दफ़ा dafa: (*nm*) time (as in counting the number of times, e.g. तीन दफ़ा three times, दस दफ़ा ten times); section (in a code of law); warding off, removing; ~दार a dafadar—a small army officer; ~दारी, the office or function of a दफ़ादार; –करना to ward off; to bury; –लगना to be accused under a particular section of the penal code; –हो ! be damned ! go to hell; get away; –होना to move off; to get off.

दफ़्तर daftar (*nm*) an office; –का वक्त office time; office hours.

दफ़्तरी daftari: (*nm*) a daftary; a book-binder; (*a*) official.

दफ़्ती dafti: (*nf*) see दफ़ती.

दबंग dabāng (*a*) overbearing, strong-headed, dauntless; of commanding presence; hence ~पन (*nm*).

दबकना dabaknā: (*v*) see दुबकना.

दबदबा dabdaba: (*nm*) awe; sway; overwhelming/commanding influence; –जमाना to attain overwhelming influence, to have complete sway; hence –होना.

दबना dabnā: (*v*) to be pressed; to yield; to submit, to act in a submissive manner; to be subdued, to be repressed; to be tamed; to give way; to be covered; to be concealed; to be hushed up; to cool down; दबी आवाज़ subdued tone; दबी ज़बान से कहना to speak in a subdued tone, to say in a hushed manner; दबे-दबाए रहना to lie subdued, to be tamed; दबे पाँव (walking) quietly/stealthily; दबे स्वर से (में) in a subdued/hushed manner; in whispers.

दबाऊ daba:u: (*a*) weighty by the head.

दबाना dabā:nā: (*v*) to press, to press down; to suppress, to cause to yield/submit, to coerce; to cow down, to subdue; to hush up; to cool down; to cover.

दबाव daba:v (*nm*) pressure, duress; suppression, compression; compulsion, coercion; stress/strain; –डालना to influence; to coerce; to exercise pressure; –में आ कर काम करना to act under coercion/duress.

दबिश dabish (*nf*) beat, round (as of a police patrol).

दबीज़ dabi:z (*a*) thick, strong; firm.

दबैल dabail (*a*) meek; submissive; under subjection or control.

दबोचना dabochanā: (*v*) to pounce, to swoop down upon, to seize suddenly.

दब्बू dabbu: (*a*) tame; of meek or submissive nature; ~पन/पना submissiveness; tameness; meekness.

दम dām (*nm*) breath; life, stamina; mettle; endurance; moment; trick; trickery; –आलू (cooked vegetable of) whole potato; -ख़म stamina, vigour, strength; ~दार strong and sturdy; vigorous; having abundant stamina; -दिलासा vain consolation; ०देना to rouse vain hopes; to extend false consolation; ~पट्टी pettifogging; simulation; ~बाज a pettifogger, sham, humbug; ~बाज़ी hoodwinking, pettifogging; ~साज़ a vocal accompanyist o a singer; hence ~साज़ी (*nf*) –अटकना the breath to be choked normal process of respiration to be disturbed;–उखाड़ना to be out of breath; to lose stamina; to be exhausted; –ओठों पर आना to be on the verge of death, to be mortally afflicted; –के दम में instantaneously, there and then; –खींचना to withhold the breath; to become still; –ख़ुश्क होना to get the wind up; –घुटना to be suffocated; –घोटना to strangle, to suffocate; –टूटना to run short of breath, to be out of breath; to be exhausted; –तोड़ना to kick the bucket, to breathe the last, to give up the ghost, to pass away; –देना to cheat, to hoodwink; to incite; –न होना to have no guts/courage; to have no strength; –निकलना to pass away; to be exhausted; –फूलना to breathe short, to become breathless; –बढ़ाना to practise holding of the breath, to increase one's stamina; –बाँधना to be breathless in attention, to be very attentive; –भर a moment, an instant; ०को for a moment/instant; –भरना to get out of breath, to be exhausted; to champion the cause of; to sing the praises (of); to boast; to have faith (in); –भर में in a moment; –मारना to have an instant's rest, to rest a while; to give oneself airs; to take a puff (of hashish etc. through a cigarette, *hookah*, etc); –में दम रहना/होना, जब तक as long as life exists; till one is alive; –लगा घटने ख़ैरात लगी बँटने the devil sick would be a monk; –लगाना to smoke, to take a puff at हुक्का or चिलम

(see); –लेना see –मारना; –साधना to be still; to practise holding the breath, to try to gain control over the process of respiration; to keep mum; –सूखना to be mortally scared, to be terrified; to be at once's wit's end; –होना to have the cheek/guts to; to have stamina/strength.

दमक damāk (*nf*) flash; brilliance; glimmer, glow.

दमकना damaknā: (*v*) to flash; to glimmer, to glitter, to glow.

दमकल damkal (*nm*) the fire-brigade; a fire-engine.

दमड़ी damṛi: (*nf*) an obsolete Indian coin worth one-eighth of a pice; –की बुढ़िया टका सिर मुँड़ाई a game not worth the candle, the horse eating its head off; –की मुर्गी टका ज़बहकराई a penny for the bill and a pound for the tip; –के तीन-तीन damn cheap, of no worth; –भी न होना, पास में to be penniless.

दमदमा dāmdamā: (*nm*) a raised sand-bag cover (in gun-fight); report of the booming of guns; a huge kettle-drum; tumult.

दमन damān (*nm*) suppression, repression; subjugation, control; ~कारी suppressive; repressive; a suppressor; –चक्र a series of suppressive/repressive acts; ~शील suppressive/repressive; hence ~शीलता; दमनीय suppressible/repressible; fit to be kept under subjugation/control; hence दमनीयता (*nf*).

दमा damā: (*nm*) asthma, aasmus.

दमाद dama:d (*nm*) see दामाद.

दमित damıt (*a*) suppressed, repressed; subjugated; –इच्छाएँ suppressed desires.

दयनीय daynı:y (*a*) pitaible, inspiring pity; hence ~ता (*nf*).

दया daya: (*nf*) pity; mercy, compassion; ~दृष्टि kindly attitude, kindness; ०रखना to continue to be kind, to be compassionate; ~निधान/निधि/सागर/सिंधु abode of compassion, compassionate, merciful; –पात्र deserving mercy/compassion; ~वीर a hero with a deeply compassionate heart; one imbued with deep compassion; ~शील kindly, kind-hearted, merciful; hence –शीलता (*nf*).

दयानत daya:nāt (*nf*) honesty; genuineness, truthfulness; ~दार honest; truthful, genuine; ~दारी honesty; genuineness, truthfulness.

दयामय daya:may (*a*) filled with or full of compassion, merciful, kind; hence ~ता (*nf*).

दयार्द्र daya:rdr (*a*) moved by compassion, compassionate, tender-hearted; hence ~ता (*nf*).

दयालु daya:lu (*a*) kind, kind-hearted, generous; hence ~ता (*nf*).

दया/वंत, ~वान daya:vānt, ~vā:n (*a*) see दयालु.

दर dar (*nf*) rate; (*nm*) door; pass; (*ind*) in, within; ~असल (में) in reality, in fact, as a matter of fact; ~किनार apart, on one side; leave alone; ~गुज़र separate; excluded; ०करना to pass over, to ignore; -दर door to door, place to place; ~परदा stealthily, clandestinely, under cover; –दर की ख़ाक छानना, –दर की ठोकरें खाना, –दर मारे-मारे फिरना to be tossed about from pillar to post, to knock at one door after another; ~हक़ीक़त in fact, in reality; ~हाल these days, now-a-days; ~गुज़र करना to exclude; to leave aside; to give up.

दरकना daraknā: (*v*) to be cracked; to be split; to be rent.

दरकार darka:r (*nf*) necessity, need; (*a*) necessary, needed.

दरकूच darku:ch (*ind*) moving on and on, moving on from one halt to another.

दरख़्त darakht (*nm*) a tree.

दरख़्वास्त darkhva:st (*nf*) application, petition; request; **–करना** to request; **–देना** to submit an application.

दरगाह darga:h (*nf*) a shrine; holy place; tomb (of a saint which is a pilgrimage spot and a place of worship).

दरज daraj (*nf*) a cleft, fissure, crack; **~बंदी** torching; filling up the cracks.

दरदरा dardara: (*a*) coarsely ground, not well-ground, granulated; grating under the teeth; hence **~हट** (*nf*).

दरदराना dardara:nā: (*v*) to grind coarsely; to grate under the teeth; to produce a sound as by grating under the teeth.

दरपेश darpesh (*adv*) in front, face to face; **–आना** to encounter, to be con- fronted with; to come face to face.

दरबा darba: (*nm*) a coop, pigeon-hole.

दरबा/न darba:n (*nm*) a gatekeeper, of a watchman; **~नी** the duties or job watchman/gatekeeper.

दरबार darba:r (*nm*) a royal court; hall of audience; **-ए-आम** hall of public audience; **-ए-ख़ास** hall of private audience; **~दारी** courtiership, presence or attendance at a court; enduring long obsequious sittings; **०करना** to be assiduous at court; to dance attendance (on); to be obsequious; **–जोड़ना/–लगाना** to assemble a set of courtiers/ sycophants; to convene a court/ an assembly.

दरबारी darba:ri: (*nm*) a courtier; a sycophant; (*a*) of court.

दरमिया/न darmiyā:n (*nm*) the middle (*ind*) during, in between, within, among; **~ना** middle; intermediary.

दरवाज़ा darva:za: (*nm*) a door; door leaves; **–खटखटाना** to knock at the door (of); to seek entry; **–खुला रखना** to keep the door open; **–झाँकना** to call at; to come for help; **–बंद करना** to close the doors, to have no contact whatever.

दरवेश darvesh (*nm*) a dervish, a Muslim mendicant.

दराँती darā:ti: (*nf*) a sickle; scythe.

दराज़ dara:z (*nf*) a drawer (of a table, etc.); see **दरज**; (*a*) long, prolonged.

दराबी dara:bi: (*nf*) a pully-block.

दरार dara:r (*nf*) a crevice, slit; crack, fissure; breach, rift; **~दार** creviced; cracked; **–पड़ना** to crack up, to be creviced; a rift to be created.

दरिंदा darında: (*nm*) a beast, beast of prey; carnivorous beast.

दरिद्र dariddr (*a*) poor, pauper; shabby; of low qualities; wretched; (*nm*) poverty, miseries, miserable plight, wretched state; **~ता** poverty, pauperdom, pauperism; miserable plight; **~नारायण** the have-not, the poor; **–दूर होना** all miseries to be gone.

दरिद्री dariddri: (*a*) poor, miserable, wretched; shabby; greedy (of eating).

दरिया dariya: (*nn*) a river; **~ई** riverine; **०घोडा** a river horse, hippopotamus; **~दिल** liberal, large-hearted; **~दिली** liberality, large-heartedness.

दरियाफ़्त dariya:ft (*nm*) an enquiry; **–करना** to make an enquiry.

दरी dari: (*nf*) a cotton carpet; a

cavern, cave, grotto.

दरीबा dari:ba: (*nm*) a (betel) market.

दरेसी daresi: (*nf*) dressing; a flattened tract of land.

दरोग़हल्फ़ी daroghalfi: (*nf*) false testimony (made on oath).

दरोगा daroga: (*nm*) see दारोगा.

दर्ज darj (*a*) recorded, entered; (*nf*) see दरज; –करना to record, to enter (into the records etc.).

दर्ज/न darjān (*nm*) a dozen; ~नों dozens.

दर्जा darja: (*nm*) a class; degree; rank; gradation; status; category; quality; order; ~बंदी classification, categorization.

दर्जी darzi: (*nf*) a tailor; –की सुई a hack-worker; ~खाना a tailor-shop; ~गीरी tailoring (work).

दर्द dard (*nm*) pain, ache; affliction; ~नाक painful, tragic, piteous; ~मंद compassionate, sympathetic; hence ~मंदी (*nf*); –दिल heart-ache, mental agony, anguish.

दर्प darp (*nm*) arrogance, haughtiness; दर्पित, दर्पी arrogant, haughty.

दर्पण darpān (*nm*) a looking glass, mirror.

दर्रा darra: (*nm*) a (mountain) pass.

दर्शक darshak (*nm*) an onlooker, a spectator; visitor; -कक्ष visitors' chamber, auditorium; ~गण audience; assembly of spectators; -दीर्घा visitors' gallery.

दर्शन darshān (*nm*) sight, view; appearance (a term used to express a sense of deference); philosophy; –मेला seeing and meeting, assemblage; –शास्त्र philosophy; ~शास्त्री a philosopher; –करना to have a view (of a revered person or a sacred place); –दुर्लभ होना (often ironical) to be seen rarely, one's appearance to be rare; –देना to grace by making an appearance; –पाना to obtain a glimpse of, to have a view of.

दर्शनीय darshanɪ:y (*a*) worth-seeing; beautiful; hence ~ता (*nf*).

दर्शनी हुंडी darshanɪ: Hūndi:' (*nm*) a sight bill.

दर्शाना darsha:nā: (*v*) to show; to display, to exhibit.

दर्शित darshit (*a*) shown; displayed exhibited; appeared.

दर्शी darshi:—a suffix meaning he who can see or that which can help see, e.g, दूर~, क्रांत~, सूक्ष्म~, त्रिकाल~; (*a*) seeing, viewing.

दल dal (*nm*) a party; group; team; troop; swarm; herd; petal; leaf; thickness of layers etc.; used in compound words as the second member to denote multitude; टिड्डी-दल, सैनिक-दल; ~दार of thick layer, pulpy; ~पति chief or leader of a team/group etc; ~बंदी groupism, group politics; -बल an army of followers and supporters; ०सहित in full force; –बदल defection; ०की राजनीति politics of defection; ~बदलू a defectionist; –बादल mass of clouds; –बाँधना to form a gang.

दलदल daldal (*nm*) marsh, mire, fen, swamp, bog; –में फँसना to be bogged down, to be caught in a mire.

दलद/ला daldala: (*a*) boggy, marshy, swampy, quaggy; hence ~ली (*nf*).

दलना dalnā: (*v*) to grind coarsely, to mill; to crush; to destroy.

दलाल dala:l (*nm*) an agent; a broker, middleman; tout.

दलाली dala:li: (*nf*) middlemanship, touting; brokerage (the work and commission of a broker); –खाना to earn brokerage; to live on touting.

दलित dalit (*a*) downtrodden; depressed; ~वर्ग a depressed class.

दलिया daliya: (*nf*) mash, hominy; porridge.

दलील dali:l (*nf*) a plea, an argument.

दलेल dalel (*nf*) penalty parade; **–बोलना** to order penalty parade (to be performed by).

दवा dava: (*nf*) medicine, drug; cure; **~ख़ाना** a dispensary, clinic; **–दारू** medical treatment; medicine; **~फ़रोश** a druggist; **–करना** to be treated (for some ailment); **–न होना, कोई** to have no cure (for).

दवाई dava:i: (*nf*) see **दवा**.

दवात dava:t (*nf*) an inkpot.

दवामी dava:mi: (*a*) permanent; **–पट्टा** permanent lease; **–बंदोबस्त** permanent settlement (of land).

दश dash (*a*) ten; (*nm*) the number ten; **~कंठ/कंधर/ग्रीव/मुख/मौलि/शिर/शीर्ष/शीश** attributes of the demon king **रावण**; **~रथ** famous king of Ayodhya:, father of **राम**.

दशक dashak (*nm*) a decade, decennium.

दशम dashām (*a*) the tenth.

दशमलव dashāmlav (*nm*) decimal; **-पद्धति/प्रणाली** the decimal system.

दशमांश dashamā:nsh (*nm*) one tenth (part).

दशमी dashmi: (*nf*) the tenth day of each lunar fortnight.

दशहरा dashehra: (*nm*) a prominent Hindu festival celebrated on the tenth day of the month of **क्वार** to remember the victory of **राम** over **रावण**, symbolizing the conquest of good over evil.

दशांग dasha:ng (*nm*) incense composed of ten ingredients used in performing a **हवन** (see)

दशा dasha: (*nf*) condition, state; plight; **–बिगड़ना** condition to take a turn for the worse; **–सुधरना** condition to improve.

दशानन dasha:nān (*nm*) see **दशकंठ** under **दश**.

दशानुकू/ल dasha:nūku:l (*nm*) acclimatisation; also **~लन**; **~लित** acclimatised.

दशानुव/र्तन dasha:nūvartān (*nm*) acclimatisation; **~र्तित** acclimatised.

दशा/ब्द, **~ब्दी** dasha:bd (*nm*) ~bdi: (*nf*) decade, decennium.

दशावतार dasha:vta:r (*nm*) the ten incarnations of Lord vishn̲ū viz **मत्स्य, कच्छप, वराह, नृसिंह, वामन परशुराम, राम, कृष्ण, बुद्ध** and **कल्कि**.

दशी dashi: (*nf*) a decade, decennium.

दस das (*a*) ten; (*nm*) the number ten; **–लाख** a million; **–नंबरी** a notorious criminal; **दसों दिशाओं में** all round, all over, everywhere.

दसवाँ dasvā: (*a*) the tenth; (*nm*) the rituals performed on the tenth day after death.

दस्तंदा/ज़ dastanda:z (*nm*) an interferer, meddler; **~ज़ी** interference, meddling.

दस्त dast (*nm*) loose stool(s); stool; hand; **-ब-दस्त** hand in hand, from hand to hand; **~बस्ता** with folded hands; **~याब** acquired, obtained, achieved; hence **~याबी** (*nf*); **–आना/लगना** to have loose motions; to suffer from diarrhoea.

दस्तक dastak (*nf*) a knock or rap (with the palm at the door); **–देना** to knock at the door.

दस्तकार dastka:r (*nm*) an artisan, craftsman, tradesman.

दस्तकारी dastaka:ri: (*nf*) artisanship, handicraft, tradesmanship; craft, trade.

दस्तख़त dastaḳḥat (*nm*) signature; **–करना** to sign.

दस्तख़ती dastaḳḥati: (*a*) signed, bearing signature; **–दस्तावेज़** signed document.

स्तगीर dastagi:r (*nm*) one who extends a helping hand, a helper, helping hand; supporter.

स्तबंद dastaband (*nm*) a wrist ornament worn by women.

स्तबरदा/र dastabarda:r (*a*) (one who has) desisted from/moved his hands off/relinquished; ~र होना to wash one's hands off, to give up; ~री relinquishment (of a claim etc.), abandonment, giving up.

स्तरख्वान dastarḳhā;n (*nm*) a dining table-cloth to place dishes etc. on; –बिछाना (to lay the cloth) to make preparation for serving meals.

स्ता dasta: (*nm*) a squad (of troops, police, etc.); handle; haft; sleeve hafting; quire (of loose sheets of paper); bouquet (of flowers etc.); a pounder.

स्ताना dasta:nā: (*nm*) a hand-glove.

स्तावर dasta:var (*a*) laxative, purgative.

स्तावे/ज dasta:vez (*nm*) a document; deed; ~जी documentary.

स्ती dasti: (*a*) pertaining to hand, manual; carried or delivered by hand (as –चिट्ठी); handle; handkerchief.

स्तूर dastu:r (*nm*) a custom; practice; constitution.

स्तूरी dastu:ri: (*nf*) customary discount, commission; routine.

स्यु dassyu (*nm*) a robber, dacoit, bandit; -वृत्ति robbery, banditry, dacoity.

ह dah (*nm*) a deep pool; in a river the spot where the water is exceptionally deep.

हकना dehaknā: (*v*) to blaze, to burn with a red hot flame; to be very hot.

हक़ा/न dehqā:n (*nm*) a peasant; villager; (*a*) boorish, rustic, unlettered; ~नीयत rusticity, boorishness; ~नी rustic, boorish.

दहन dehān (*nm*) burning, combustion; ~शील combustible; ~शीलता combustibility.

दहलना dehalnā: (*v*) to be terrorised/terror-stricken; to tremble (with fear); to be terribly alarmed.

दहला dehla: (*nm*) a playing card with ten pips.

दहलीज dehli:z (*nf*) threshold; entrance; –का कुत्ता a sponger; one subsisting on leavings; a parasite); –झाँकना to call at somebody's with a selfish motive; –न फाँदना to be confined within the four walls; never to cross out the threshold.

दहशत dehshat (*nf*) terror; panic; –खाना to be terrorised, to be panic-stricken.

दहाई daha:i: (*nf*) the figure ten; the place of tens (in numeration).

दहाड़ daha:ṛ (*nf*) roar of a lion; a roar; –मारना to roar; to cry aloud.

दहाड़ना daha:ṛnā: (*v*) to roar; to cry or shout aloud.

दहाना daha:nā: (*nm*) the mouth (of a river).

दही dahi: (*nm*) curd, coagulated milk.

दहेड़ी daheṛi: (*nf*) a curd-pot.

दहेज dahej (*nm*) dowry; –प्रथा the dowry system.

दांडिक dā:ṇḍik (*a*) penal, punitive.

दाँत dā:t (*nm*) a tooth; –काटी रोटी intimate friendship, close relationship; –काढ़ना to whine; to crinch; –किचकिचाना/कटकटाना/किटकिटाना to grind the teeth (through cold, wrath, etc.);–किरकिरे होना to accept defeat; –खट्टे करना to make one lick the dust, to set the teeth on edge; to force the enemy into a tight corner; –गाड़ना to fix a covetous eye on something; –झाड़ना to knock out the teeth; -तोड़ना lit. to knock off the teeth —to humble, to deprive of the sting; to render powerless; –दिखाना see –निपोरना; –निपोरना to whine, to crinch; to show meekness/humbleness; –पीसना to gnash the teeth (in anger etc.), to be in a fury; –फाड़ना to grin; –बजना the teeth to chatter (through chill or cold); –बैठना/लगना the teeth to be clinched (as in lock-jaw etc.); –से (पैसा) पकड़ना to be extremely stingy; –होना, (किसी चीज़) पर lit. the teeth to be fixed on—to have the procurement (of someone or something) as a target; दाँतों तले उँगली दबाना lit. to bite the finger in astonishment etc.—to stand amazed; to be aghast; दाँतों में तिनका दबाना to express complete sub-mission, to yield unconditionally.

दांत dā:nt (*a*) subdued, supressed, subjugated.

दाँता dā:ta: (*nm*) a notch, cog or tooth (of a saw etc.), sprocket; dent; ~किलकिल wrangle, wrangling, altercation; दाँतेदार jagged, notched, cogged; dented.

दाँती dā:ti: (*nf*) row of teeth; –पीसना to gnash (the teeth); –बजना see दाँत बजना.

दांपतिक dā:mpatik (*a*) conjugal; –संबंध conjugal relationship.

दांपत्य dā:mpatty (*a*) conjugal, marital; (*nm*) conjugal relations; conjugal functions.

दाँय dā:y (*nf*) see दँवरी.

दाँव dā:v (*nm*) see दाव.

दाइँ dā:ı: (*a*) right, right hand.

दाई da:i: (*nf*) a midwife; nurse; ~गीरी midwifery; –को दूध पिलाना to teach one's grandmother to suck eggs; –से पेट छिपाना lit. to hide the stomach from the midwife—to keep a secret from one who is bound to know it.

दाक्षिणात्य da:kshina:tty (*a*) southern (*nm*) a southerner.

दाक्षिण्य da:kshinny (*nm*) skill; favourable disposition, favourableness.

दाख़िल da:k̤hil (*a*) entered; admitted –ख़ारिज mutation of names in land-records; –दफ़्तर filed; –करना to admit; to deposit; to submit; to file; –होना to be admitted/deposited/submitted/filed.

दाख़िला dak̤hila: (*nm*) admission; entry.

दाग da:g (*nm*) cremation, setting on fire; –देना to cremate, to set on fire; to brand (a bull etc.)

दाग़ dag (*nm*) a speck; stain, scar, mark; stigma, blemish; ~दार specked; scarred, marked, branded stained; blemished; stigmatic; ~बे dagbel—a dig mark symbolising commencement of a construction work (building, road, etc.); ०डालना to commence construction (work); ~बेल पड़ना construction (work) to be commenced; –लगाना to blemish, to sully the reputation (of), to stigmatise.

दागना da:gnā: (*v*) to burn, to ignite; to fire; to cauterise; to brand (a bull etc.).

दाग़ी da:gi: (*a*) stained, specked; scarred, marked; branded; stigmatised, blemished; damaged (fruit).

दाघ da:gh (*nm*) heat, burning.

दाड़िम da:ṛim (*nm*) pomegranate (tree and its fruit).

दाढ़ da:ṛh (*nm*) a jaw-tooth; grinder.

दाढ़ी darhi: (*nf*) beard; ~जार lit. beard-burnt—a term of abuse usually used by women; be damned !; –को हाथ लगाना to make entreaties; –पकना (the beard) to grow grey, to grow old; –बनाना to shave (the beard); –रखना to grow a beard.

दातव्य da:tavvy (*a*) donative, charitable; worth giving; (somebody's) due; –औषधालय a charitable dispensary.

दाता da:ta. (*nm*) a giver, donor, benefactor, a liberal or generous man; –से सूम भला जो फटक के (ठावें) देय जवाब a point-blank refusal is better than an uneasy suspense.

दाति da:ti (*nf*) delivery.

दातौ(तू)न da:tau(tu:)n (*nf*) a fibrous twig used for brushing teeth.

दातृत्व da:trittv (*nm*) munificence, bounteousness, generosity.

दात्री da:tri: (*nf*) feminine of दाता (see).

दाद da:d (*nf*) ring worm, shingles; vocal appreciation; praise; –देना to give due praise; to express vocal appreciation.

दादरा da:dra: (*nm*) a particular style of singing.

दादा da:da: (*nm*) (paternal) grandfather; elder brother; a word of respect used for elders; a gangster, hoodlum, leader of a gang; a cock of the walk; दादी (paternal) grandmother; ~गीरी hooliganism, gangsterism; the act of leading a gang.

दान dā:n (*nm*) donation; charity, alms; a religious gift (in cash or kind); a suffix used to denote a stand, container or pot etc. (e.g. कलमदान, पीकदान, शमादान); the fluid that flows from the temples of an elephant while in rut; -दक्षिणा alms and donations; -धर्म religious practices, charity and munificence; ~पत्र a gift-deed; ~पात्र a donating box; (one) deserving alms; ~लीला a famous sport of Lord Krishṉā wherein he realised toll from the milk-maids; ~वीर a hero characterized by generous disposition; bountiful, munificent; hence ~वीरता; ~शील generous, bountiful, munificent; °ता generous disposition, bounteousness, munificence; –की बछिया के दाँत गिनना to look a gift horse in the mouth; –देना to donate, to give in alms.

दान/व da:nav (*nm*) a demon; giant; hence ~वी (*nf*); ~वीय demonic; giant-like.

दाना da:nā: (*nm*) grain, parched grain; corn; seed; food; a bead; pustule; pimple, piece; grainy diet of animals; (*a*) wise; –पानी livelihood; food and drink; °उठना see अन्न-जल उठना; दाने-दाने का तरसना to be in the clutches of starvation, to starve; दाने-दाने को मुहताज starving, poverty-stricken.

दानी da:nɪ: (*a* and *nm*) generous/munificent (person); -दान करे भंडारी का पेट पिराय/फूले the owner makes a gift, the treasurer feels the pinch of it.

दानेदार da:nēda:r (*a*) granular; granulated.

दाब da:b (*nf*) pressure; strain; impression; दाबानुकूलित pressurised.

दाबड़ा da:bṛa: (*nm*) a buffer.

दाबना da:bnā: (*v*) to press; to press down; to keep in check.

दाम dā:m (*nm*) price; value; a rope; one of the four policies (as specified in ancient Indian diplomacy) for conquest over the enemy—the policy of monetary gratification; –करावे काम money makes the mare go.

दामन da:mān (*nm*) skirt of a garment; the extreme end of a *sa:ri:* etc.; ~गीर an adherent, dependant; claimant; –पकड़ना to seek the protection of, to become an adherent or follower (of); –फैलाना to beg; to supplicate; –में दाग लगना a have a broken feather in one's wing, to suffer a moral fall.

दामाद da:ma:d (*nm*) a son-in-law.

दामिनी da:mini: (*nf*) the lightning.

दामी damī: (*a*) costly, highly priced.

दायँ dā:y (*nf*) see **दँवरी**.

दाय da:y (*nm*) heritage, inheritance; ~भाग inheritance, apportionment of inherited property etc.; ~भागी an inheritor.

दायक da:yak (*nm*) a donator; a suffix meaning a giver (e.g. फलदायक, लाभदायक).

दायजा da:yja: (*nm*) dowry; presents

दायमी da:ymi: (*a*) permanent; perennial.

दायर da:yar (*a*) filed (a law-suit, case, etc); –करना to file (a law suit).

दायरा da:yra: (*nm*) a circle; ring range.

दायाँ da:yā: (*a*) right; –हाथ (one's) right hand (man), closest or most reliable supporter/associate.

दाया da:ya: (*nf*) see **दाई**.

दायागत da:ya:gat (*a*) inherited; paternal.

दायाद da:ya:d (*nm*) an heir.

दायाधिका/र da:ya:dhika:r (*nm*) inheritance; heritage; ~री an inheritor, heir.

दायि/ता, ~त्व da:ita: (*nf*), ~ttv (*nm*) liability; responsibility; obligation; vouchment.

दायी da:yi:—a suffix meaning a giver or giving (as उत्तरदायी, फलदायी).

दार da:r—a suffix meaning a person having/owning/possessing (e.g. दुकानदार, खरीदार).

दारा da:ra: (*nf*) wife.

दारिद्र्य da:ridry (*nm*) poverty, indigence.

दारी da:ri: (*nf*) see छिनार; a term of abuse for a female.

दारुण da:rūṉ (*a*) awful; horrible; severe; heart-rending; hence ~ता (*nf*).

दारू da:ru: (*nf*) liquor; medical treatment; medicine (as in दवा-दारू).

दारोग़ा da:roga: (*nm*) a sub-inspector (of police); a superintending official (as in a municipality).

दारोमदार da:romda:r (*nm*) full responsibility; complete dependence.

दार्शनिक da:rshanīk (*nm*) a philosopher; (*a*) philosophical; hence ~ता (*nf*).

दाल da:l (*nf*) pulse; ~मोंठ (ट) a kind of fried and spiced preparation with pulse as one of the ingredients; –गलना a manoeuvre/tricky measure to succeed; a (guileful) move to pay; –दलिया pot-luck, poor diet; ०करना to enforce a decision either way, to decide this way or that way ०होना to be decided once for all; to be ruined; –न गलना to cut no ice, to effect little; –भात में मूसलचंद an unwelcome intruder; –में काला होना to have something fishy; –रोटी चलना to maintain ones elf somehow, just to manage a living.

दालचीनी da:lchi:nī: (*nf*) ceylon cinnamon, cinnamon.

दालान da:lā:n (*nm*) a yard; verandah

दाव da:v (*nm*) stake; opportunity, chance; sleight; a trick (in wrestling); strategy; time(s); turn (in games etc); -पेच tricks, strategical moves, manoeuvres; –में आना (आसानी से) to be caught with chaff.

दा/व da:v (*nm*) forest wood; ~वाग्नि/.

~वानल forest fire.

दावत da:vat (*nm*) feast, banquet; invitation; ~नामा an invitation (letter); –देना to invite; to invite for lunch or dinner.

दावा da:va: (*nm*) a claim; suit; –करना to make a claim; to suit; –दायर करना to file a suit, to launch legal proceedings.

दावात da:va:t (*nf*) an inkport.

दावेदा/र da:veda:r (*nm*) a claimant, hence ~री (*nf*).

दाशरथि da:shrathi (*nm*) son of दशरथ; Ra:m (the eldest son of दशरथ).

दास da:s (*nm*) a slave; servant, serf; thrall; –भाव thraldom, the attitude of slavery, servility; ~वाद slavocracy; ~वादी a slavocract; slavocratic; –प्रथा (practice/system of) slavery, serfdom.

दास/ता, ~त्व da:sta: (*nf*), ~attv (*nm*) servility, servile disposition, slavery, bondage; thraldom, serfdom; ~ता की बेड़ी bonds/fetters of slavery.

दासानुदास da:sa:nūda:s (*nm*) slave of a slave, very humble slave.

दासी da:si: (*nf*) a maid-servant; a slave girl.

दास्ताँ, दास्तान da:stā:, da:stā:n (*nf*) a tale, narrative; account.

दास्य da:ssy (*a*) servile, slavish; humble; (*nm*) servitude, one of the nine types of devotion (भक्ति –see) wherein the devotee considers himself to be a humble servant of his Master; –भाव see दास भाव (under दास).

दाह da:h (*nm*) burning, heat; inflammation; mental agony; cremation; scald; ~कर्म/क्रिया/संस्कार cremation.

दाहक da:hak (*a*) incendiary; causing burns, inflammatory; agonising; ~ता inflammatory or incendiary property or character.

दाहि/ना da:hinā: (*a*) right; ~ना हाथ (one's) right hand, most reliable associate; ~नी आँख फड़कना lit. throbbing of the right eye (considered a good omen for a man and a bad one for a woman); ~ने to (wards) the right; ~ने होना to be favourably disposed.

दाही da:hi: (*a*) see दाहक.

दाह्य da:hy (*a*) inflammable, combustible; hence ~ता (*nf*).

दिक diq (*nm*) tuberculosis; (*a*) vexed, harassed; fed up; –करना to harass.

दिक् dik (*nf*) direction; quarter; space; ~काल see दिक्काल; ~चक्र the aggregate of all directions; ~पाल the ten protecting dieties of all the ten directions; ~शूल see दिशाशूल; ~स्थापन orientation; ~स्थिति bearing.

दिक़्क़त diqqat (*nf*) difficulty; trouble; ~तलब troublesome; difficult.

दिक्का/ल dikka:l (*nm*) space and time; ~लातीत transcending space and time, transcendental.

दिक्सूचक diksu:chak (*nm*) a compass.

दिखना dikhnā: (*v*) to be visible/seen/sighted/viewed.

दिखरावनी dikhra:vnı: (*nf*) the act or process of seeing the newly-wed bride for the first time; the presents made or cash paid on the occasion.

दिखाऊ dikha:u: (*a*) presentable; worth-seeing; ostensible, showy.

दिखावट dikha:vaṭ (*nf*) show, display; ostentation.

दिखावटी dikha:vṭi: (*a*) artificial; showy, ostensible; ostentatious.

दिखावा dikha:va: (*nm*) show, ostentation, display.

दिगंबर digāmbar (*a*) lit. clad in or covered by space—unclad; stark naked; (*nm*) an epithet of lord Shiv; a sect of Jainism.

दि/ग् dig—an allomorph of दिक्; –गंत the end of space; the horizon; —गंतर the interval space between two directions; ~गंतव्यापी extending to the end of, or all, space, permeating the horizons, gone far and wide; ~ग्गज one of the eight elephants mythologically supposed to support the earth in tact in the eight different directions; a giant or pre-eminent person (in any field of activity); ~ग्दर्शक यंत्र a compass; ~ग्दिगंत (में) all over, (in) all directions; ~ग्भ्रम/ग्भ्रांति loss of bearings, directional confusion; ~ग्भ्रमित/ग्भ्रांत one who has lost his bearings, strayed, gone astray; ~ग्वसन/ग्वस्त्र see दिगंबर; ~ग्विजय universal conquest, subjugation of many realms in all directions; ~ग्विजयी a conqueror of many realms or the world; ~व्यापी/~व्याप्त permeating all space, spreading in all directions; gone far and wide.

दिग्दर्शक digdarshāk (*nm*) a director (of a stage performance, film, etc.); ~त्व directorship.

दिग्दर्शन digdarshān (*nm*) direction, the act or process of directing; general introduction (of a subject etc.)

दिङ् diṅ —an allomorph of दिक्; ~नाग see दिग्गज (in दिग्); ~नाथ see दिक्पाल (in दिक्); ~मंडल see दिक्चक्र (in दिक्); ~मात्र mere indication; ~मूढ़ see दिग्भ्रांत (in दिग्); ~मोह see दिग्भ्रम (in दिग्).

दिठौना diṭhaunā: (*nm*) an evil-countering black mark, a black mark or artificial mole (put on the forehead or the cheek, esp. of a child) to ward off the influence of a malignant eye/an evil glance.

दिन din (*nm*) a day (comprised of twenty-four hours from sunrise to sunrise); a day (extending from sunrise to sunset), day-time; time(s); ~कर/मणि the sun; –दशा (adveristy or favourableness of) times; ०खराब होना to be under a cloud, to fall on bad days; –दिन/-ब-दिन day by day, from day to day, daily, with the passage of time; ~मान duration of the day; time interval between sunrise and sunset; -रात/रैन day and night, always, all the time; ~शेष evening; दिनांत the close of the day, sunset; दिनांध day-blind; ०ता day-blindness; दिनागम day-break, morning; दिनारंभ day-break, beginning of the day; –कटना to be marking time, to be dragging out one's days; to be passing a life of pain and sorrow; –काटना to drag out one's days, to maintain oneself somehow; to survive hardship; –को तारे दिखना, –को तारे नज़र आना to have the stars dance before one's eyes (by a blow etc.); to be thoroughly beaten up; –को तारे दिखाना to make stars dance before one's eyes (by a blow etc.); to beat up thoroughly; to put in a very tight corner; –को दिन रात को रात न समझना to be completely lost in work; to take no notice of the passage of time; –को रात कहना to reverse the truth; –गँवाना to waste time, to while away time; –गिनना to pass uneventful days, to keep on waiting from day to day; –चढ़ना the day to be far advanced, the sun to have gone up in the sky; to pass beyond the time (of menstruation); –चढ़े late in the morning, when the day is far advanced; –छिपना the sun to set; –ढलना the day to come to a close; the sun to start declining; –ढले at eventide, late in the afternoon; –दहाड़े in broad daylight; –दूना रात चौगुना बढ़ना to grow by leaps and bounds; –धरना to appoint a day (for some auspicious ceremony etc.); –पहाड़ होना the time to hang heavy; –पूरे करना to mark time; to pass one's days somehow; –पूरे होना to be gone full time; to have completed the period of gestation; –फिरना/बहुरना the times to take a favourable turn, prosperous phase of life to commence; -भर all day, through out the day; –भारी होना see –पहाड़ होना; –लगना to give oneself airs; to become vain; –लद जाना (one's) heydays to be gone/past; –से while yet day, during the daytime; दिनों का फेर run of (good) luck to be changed.

दिनचर्या dincharya: (*nf*) daily routine.

दिनां/क dinā:ṅk (*nm*) date; ~कित dated.

दिनेश dinesh (*nm*) the sun.

दिप/ना dipnā: (*v*) to glow, to glitter, to shine; also ~दिपाना.

दिमाग़ dima:g (*nm*) the brain, mind intellect; conceit; ~दार intelligent; conceited; ~दारी intelligence; conceitedness; -आसमान पर चढ़ाना to turn one's head; –आसमान पर होना to have a swollen head, to think no end of oneself, to be very much conceited; –करना to put on airs, to be conceited; –की खिड़कियाँ खुली होना to have an open mind/head; –खपाना to tax one's mind; –खाना/चाटना to pester with constant babble, to tire out somebody by continuous chatter, to inflict continuous prate on somebody; –खाली करना to beat or rack the brain; –चढ़ना to get inflated by conceit; –ठंडा होना to be restord to normalcy, to come to senses; –न मिलना to be unable to fathom the conceit (of); to be too fastidious to make adjustments; –पर ज़ोर डालना to tax one's brain; –फिर जाना one's head to be turned, to have a swollen head; –बिगाड़नी be turn one's head, to make one dizzy; –में आना to take to one's head; –में खलल होना something to be psychologically wrong, not to be in mental equilibrium; –में ठूँसना to hammer (an idea etc.) into somebody's head; –में बैठ जाना to go to one's head; –लड़ाना to exercise or tax one's brain; –सातवें आसमान पर होना to be too conceited/vainglorious, to think no end of oneself.

दिमाग़ी dima:gi: (*a*) mental, pertaining to the brain or mind; intellectual; –ऐयाशी mental indulgence; –तनाव mental tension; –दिवालियापन intellectual bankruptcy; –लड़ाई intellectual conflict.

दिया diya: (*nm*) a lamp, an earthen lamp; (*v*) past tense form of देना –gave; (*a*) given; –बढ़ाना to put out a lamp; ~बत्ती lights, lamp, etc.; ~बत्ती करना to make the lights, to light up the lamp.

दियासलाई diya:sala:i: (*nf*) a matchstick; a matchbox, safety match; –दिखाना/–लगाना to put on fire; to damn, to be done with it.

दियानत diya:nat (*nm*) see दयानत; ~दार see दयानतदार; ~दारी see दयानतदारी.

दिल dil—(*nm*) the heart; courage; spirit; will; ~कश attractive, alluring, charming; hence ~कशी (*nf*); ~खुश pleasant; ~गीर heart-sick, out of heart; ~गीरी gloominess, unhappiness; ~जमई conviction; assurance; ~जला full of grudge; bitter; ~जोई consolation, solace; ~दार beloved; generous, bountiful; courageous; hence~दारी (*nf*); ~पसंद favourite, to one's liking; ~फ़रेब alluring; ~फेंक of romantic disposition, flirtacious, frivolous; ~बर beloved; hence~बरी (*nf*); ~बस्तगी entertainment; ~रुबा tempting; beloved; ~रुबाई the act or process of tempting; ~शाद happy; ~सोज़ sympathetic; ~सोज़ी sympathy; –अटकना to take a fancy; to feel drawn towards; –आना to catch the fancy of, to take a fancy for; -ओ-दिमाग़ पर छाये रहना to get a person on the brain; –कड़ा करना to summon up courage; not to get unnerved; –का खोटा ill-meaning, ill-intentioned; not clean at heart; –का गवाही देना to conform to the dictates of conscience; to feel in one's bones; –का ग़ुब्बार/बुख़ार/–की भड़ाँस निकालना to get things off one's chest; to let out one's steam, to give free vent to one's grudge; –का बादशाह a king at heart; –की आग बुझाना to have one's passions fulfilled; –की कली खिलना to be in exultation, to be frisky; –की दिल में रहना to have a wish remain unfulfilled; an aspiration to wither away by non-fulfilment; –की फाँस a lingering agony; –की बात the inner truth/feelings; ०बताना to show one's cards, to keep no reservation; –के फफोले फूटना to have the heart purged of all wrathful emotions; to have it out till pacified; –को करार होना to feel contended; –को ठेस पहुँचाना to tread on one's kibes; –को लगाना to take a thing to heart; –खट्टा होना to develop a sense of aversion; to feel repulsed; –खोल कर ख़र्च करना to dip into one's purse; to spend freely; –खोल कर रख देना/ –खोल देना to place one's card's on the table: –चुराना to lure one's heart away; –छलनी होना iron to enter into one's soul; –छूती बात कहना to touch the right cord; –छोटा करना to feel dejected; –जमना to be intent on; to feel assured/convinced; –जलना to be sore at heart; –टटोलना to look within; –टटोलना, किसी का to feel out; –डूबना to have the heart sinking; –तोड़ना to break one's heart; –दहलना to be scared out of wits; to have the heart in one's boots; –दुखाना to cause mental agony/trouble; –देना to fall in love with, to lose one's heart to; –धड़कना heart to palpitate; to be unnerved; –पक जाना to be fed up of enduring affliction, to be fed up of sarcasm; –पर नक़्श होना to leave an indelible imprint on the mind; –पर साँप लोटना see कलेजे पर साँप लोटना; –पसीजना to feel moved; –फट जाना, –फटना to develop a sense of aversion; –फटा जाना the heart to be rent, to be extremely restless; –बढ़ना to be encouraged, to gain self-confidence, to become generous/bountiful; –बढ़ाना to encourage, to back up; –बाग़-बाग़ होना to be overwhelmed by joy; to be extremely delighted; –बुझना to feel dejected, to be disheartened, to be in low spirits; –बैठा जाना the heart to be sinking; –भर आना to be moved by compassion; –मज़बूत करना to pull oneself together; –मिलना the minds to be in complete harmony, to be mutually tied by bonds of harmony; –में आना an idea to occur, to feel like; –में गाँठ/गिरह पड़ना to nurse a hostile feeling, to have dissension created (in between), to have a fissure developed between; –में घर/जगह करना to be taken to heart; to find a place in one's inmost feelings; –में न रखना to wear one's heart upon one's sleeve; –में फफोले पड़ना to suffer intense mental torture; to be heart-rent; –में फ़र्क आना to have animus, to develop a mental reservation; –में बसना/समाना to be ever-present within; –में मैल आना malicious feeling to creep up, to develop a some mental reservation; –लगना see जी लगना; –लगाना see जी लगाना; –से heartily, from to core of one's heart; –से उतरना to no longer occupy a venerable place in one's heart; to be out of favour; –से दूर करना to forget; –से निकाल देना to forget and forgive; –से हट जाना to be out of favour; to be repulsed; to have a sense of repulsion; –ही दिल में in the heart of hearts; दिलोजान से heart and soul, from the core of (one's) heart.

दिलच/स्प dilchasp (*a*) interesting; ~स्पी interest; ०लेना to take interest.

दिलाना dila:nā: (*v*) to cause to be given/handed over.

दिला/वर dila:var (*a*) bold, brave, courageous; ~वरी boldness, bravery, courageousness.

दिलासा dila:sa: (*nm*) consolation, solace; assurance; –देना to console; to comfort; to assure.

दिली dili: (*a*) heart-felt, hearty, cordial; sincere.

दिले/र diler (*a*) courageous, daring, brave; volorous; ~री courage, bravery, daring, valour.

दिल्लगी dillagi: (*nf*) jest, joke, fun; humour; ~बाज़ funny; humoursome; jocular; ~बाज़ी jocularity, funmaking.

दिल्ला dilla: (*nm*) a panel of a door or window; ~बंदी panelling; दिल्लेदार panelled.

दिल्ली dilli: (*nf*) Delhi—the capital city of India; –दूर है lit. Delhi is still a far cry—fulfilment of a dream/mission is still far off; –में बारह बरस रह कर भी भाड़ झोंका to be in the midst of all opportunities and yet to avail of none.

दिवंगत divāṅgat (*a*) late, deceased.

दिवस divas (*nm*) a day; –निशि day and night.

दिवांध divā:ndh (*a*) day-blind; ~ता day-blindness.

दिवा diva: (*nm*) a day; ~कर the sun; -रात्रि day and night; ~स्वप्न a day-dream; ०देखना to day-dream; to build castles in the air.

दीवाना di:va:nā: (*a*) see दिवाना.

दिवालख़ोर dival:khor (*nm*) a lame duck.

दिवाला diva:la: (*nm*) bankruptcy, insolvency; –निकलना/पिटना to become a bankrupt/insolvent.

दिवालिया diva:liya: (*nm*) a bankrupt; an insolvent.

दिवाली diva:li: (*nf*) a Hindu festival celebrated on the day of the new moon of कार्तिक, when lamps are lit on house-tops etc. symbolising the conquest of light over darkness and of good over evil; (fig.) times of merriment.

दिव्य divvy (*a*) divine, celestial; charming, beautiful; brilliant; ~चक्षु gifted with divine vision, charming-eyed; blind; ~दृष्टि divine insight; penetrating vision; –पुरुष divine person; ~मूर्ति divine being/figure; hence दिव्यता, दिव्यत्व.

दिव्यांगना divvya:ṅganā: (*nf*) a celestial dame; nymph.

दिशा disha: (*nf*) a direction; line; **दिशांतरण** redirection; –**निर्देश** guidance, direction.

दिशाशूल disha:shu:l (*nm*) any inauspicious planetary conjunction forbidding departure from or to certain directions on certain specified days.

दिसंबर disāmbar (*nm*) (the month of) December.

दिसाव/र disa:var (*nm*) another country/region; foreign mart; ~**री** imported; belonging to another region or country.

दीं dī: (*v*) gave—feminine plural past tense form of **देना**.

दी di: (*v*) gave—feminine singular past tense form of **देना**; (*nf*) abbreviated form of **दीदी** – elder sister.

दीक्षक di:kshak (*nm*) an initiator; a preceptor.

दीक्षण di:kshāṉ (*nm*) (the process or act of) initiation.

दीक्षांत di:kshā:nt (*nm*) the end of preceptorial period, the conclusion of a phase of education; –(**अभि**)**भाषण** a convocation address; –**समारोह** convocation.

दीक्षा di:ksha: (*nf*) initiation; ~**गुरु** the initiator, preceptor.

दीक्षित di:kshit (*a*) initiated.

दीखना di:khnā: (*v*) to be visible/seen.

दीगर di:gar (*a*) another; different.

दीजिए di:jie (*v*) honorofic imperative form of the verb **देना** –please give; ~**गा** interchangeable with **दीजिए** in practical usage but has a distinctness in as far as it points to a s'ightly more remote future.

दी/दा di:da: (*nm*) an eye; vision; ~**दावर** a connoisseur, one who can appreciate; ~**दे निकालना** to stare, to cast an angry look; ~**दे फाड़ना** to stare, to gaze; ~**दे लगना** to be attentive; to concentrate (in some work); ~**दे लड़ाना** to exchange amorous glances; ~**दे का पानी ढल जाना** to be lost to shame.

दीदार di:da:r (*nm*) sight, view, appearance; seeing.

दीदी di:di: (*nf*) (a form of address for) an elder sister.

दीन di:n (*a*) poor, miserable, humble, arousing a sense of compassion; (*nm*) religion; -**ईमान** religion and morality; ~**दयालु** kind and considerate to the poor; an epithet of God; ~**दार** religious-minded, devout; –**दुनिया** this world and the other world; –**धर्म** religion and morality; ~**बंधु** a helper of the poor, compassionate; an epithet of God; ~**वत्सल** see ~**दयालु**.

दीनानाथ di:nā:nā:th (*nm*) Lord/Protector of the poor; an epithet of God.

दीनार di:na:r (*nm*) an ancient gold-coin, once current in Asian and European countries.

दीप di:p (*nm*) an earthen lamp; the most eminent person of a family or clan; ~**गृह** a light-house; ~**दान** offering of a lamp to a deity for adoration; ~**माला/मालिका** a row of lamps; the **दिवाली** festival; ~**वर्ति/वर्तिका** the wick of a lamp; ~**शिखा** the flame of a lamp; ~**स्तंभ** a lamp-post; –**से दीप जले** one lamp kindles another.

दीपक di:pak (*nm*) a lamp; –**बुझना** the light to go out; one's lineage to come to an end.

दीपकाकार, दीपाकार di:paka:ka:r, di:pa:ka:r (*a*) resembling the shape or structure of a **दीपक** or

दीप.

दीपाधार di:pa:dha:r (*nm*) a lamp-stand.

दीपावली di:pa:vali: (*nf*) see दिवाली.

दीपित di:pit (*a*) see दीप्त.

दीप्त di:pt (*a*) radiant; luminous, brilliant, bright.

दीप्ति di:pti (*nf*) lustre, splendour, luminosity, brilliance, flash; ~भ्रम photism; ~मान radiant, lustrous, brilliant, shining; –रेखा a trace.

दीबाचा di:ba:cha: (*nm*) a preface.

दीमक di:māk (*nf*) termite, white ant; –लगना to be termite-infested/termite-eaten.

दीया di:ya: (*nm*) see दिया.

दीर्घ di:rgh (*a*) long; large; wide; tall, huge; deep; ~काय tall, gigantic; ~कालिक sustained; chronic; ~जीवी long-living, blessed with longevity; ~ता length; largeness; width; hugeness; –निःश्वास a deep sigh; ~लोचन wide-eyed; ~वत् oblong; ~वृत्त ellipse; ~वृत्ताकार elliptical; ~सूत्रता dilatoriness, procrastination; ~सूत्री a slow-coach; procrastinator; dilatory; –स्वर long vowel.

दीर्घा di:rgha: (*nf*) a gallery.

दीर्घाकार di:rgha:ka:r (*a*) gigantic, huge, colossal.

दीर्घायु di:rgha:yu (*a*) long-lived, long-living, blessed with long life; (*nf*) longevity; ~ष्य see दीर्घायु.

दीर्घावकाश di:rgha:vka:sh (*nm*) long vacation.

दीर्घावधि dirgha:vadhi (*a* and *nf*) long term.

दीवट di:vaṭ (*nf*) a lamp-stand.

दीवा di:va: (*nm*) see दिया.

दीवान di:vā:n (*nm*) a Chief Minister (in a royal court), dewan; a couch without back-rest; a royal court; a collection of poems; -ए-आम a public hall of audience; ~ख़ाना a drawing room, a hall of audience; -ए-ख़ास a hall of private audience.

दीवानगी di:va:ngi: (*nf*) craziness, madness.

दीवाना di:va:nā: (*a*) mad, crazy, insane; ~पन madness, craziness, insanity.

दीवानी di:va:nī: (*nf*) a civil court; the office of a दीवान (see); (*a*) civil (law etc., as opposed to criminal); feminine form of दीवाना; –क़ानून civil law, civic law.

दीवार di:va:r (*nf*) a wall; –खड़ी करना, के बीच to create a gulf (between), to raise a barrier (between); –ढह जाना barriers to be razed; (दीवार) दीवारों के भी कान होते हैं walls also have ears; –बनना to act as a barrier, to cause separation between.

दीवाल di:va:l (*nf*) see दीवार.

दीवाली di:va:li: (*nf*) see दिवाली.

दुंद dūnd (*nm*) see द्वंद्व.

दुंदुभि dūndubhi: (*nf*) a (huge) kettle-drum, drum.

दुंदुभी dūndubhi: (*nf*) see दुंदुभि.

दुंबा dūmba: (*nm*) a kind of ram which has a round, flat and tuft-like tail-end; unusually fat; –हो जाना to grow too fat.

दुः duh—a Sanskrit prefix signifying bad, evil, badly, wicked, wickedly, wrong, difficult, hard, contemptible, etc.

दुःख du(k)kh (*nm*) sorrow; unhappiness; suffering, grief, distress; ~कर distressing, grievous, bringing sorrow and suffering in its wake; ~त्रय the three sorrows viz. physical, mundane and divine; ~द painful, grievous/sorrowful; dolorous; ~दायक/~दायी painful, causing grief/sorrow; distressing, agonising; -द्वंद्व distress and affliction; ~प्रद see दुःखद; ~साध्य difficult, that which can be attained or achieved through sorrow/suffering; -सुख में through thick and thin; ०शरीक होना to cast one's lot with, to stand through thick and thin; –उठाना to endure suffering/sorrow; to undergo hardships; –का पहाड़ टूटना grave calamity to befall; to be in terrible distress; –देखना to pass through a suffering; –देना to grieve, to inflict grief/sorrow/suffering (on), to trouble; –पहुँचना to feel sorry, to be grieved/distressed, to feel unhappy; –पाना to endure suffering/sorrow, to suffer, to undergo hardships; –बँटाना to share one's sorrow, to minimize sorrow through sympathy; –मानना to be sorry, to be sorrowful, to be unhappy; –में सुमिरन सब करैं सुख में करै न कोय the devil sick would be a monk.

दुःखमय du(k)khmay (*a*) full of sorrow, tragic, unhappy, dolorous, filled with grief.

दुःखांत du(k)khā:nt (*a*) tragic, culminating in a tragedy, resulting in grief; also ~क; –नाटक a tragedy.

दुःखांतिका du(k)khā:ntika: (*nf*) a tragedy, tragic play/drama.

दुःखातीत du(k)kha:ti:t (*a*) impassible, transcending sorrow and suffering.

दुःखात्मक du(k)khā:tmāk (*a*) tragic; sorrowful, lugubrious, full of suffering; hence ~ता (*nf*).

दुःखार्त्त du(k)kha:rt (*a*) grief-stricken, overpowered by sorrow/suffering; hence ~ता (*nf*).

दुःखि/त du(k)khit (*a*) unhappy, sorrowful; grief-stricken, woeful; hence ~ता (fem.)

दुःखी dukkhi: (*a*) sorrowful, sad, unhappy; grief-stricken, afflicted, woeful.

दुःशील dushshi:l (*a*) insolent, impudent, impertinent, ill-bred, wicked; hence ~ता (*nf*).

दुःसह dussah (*a*) intolerable, unbearable, unendurable; hence ~ता (*nf*).

दुःसाध्य dussa:dhy (*a*) difficult, arduous, hard to accomplish; hence ~ता (*nf*).

दुःसाहस dussa:has (*nm*) audacity, effrontery, cheek.

दुःसाह/सी dussa:hasi: (*a*) obtrusive, audacious, cheeky; ~सिक audacious, cheeky (act etc.).

दुःस्वप्न dusswapn (*nm*) a nightmare, an incubus.

दुःस्वभाव dusswabha:v (*a*) ill-tempered; ill-natured.

दु du—an allomorph of दो used as the first member in numerous compound words; ~अन्नी a two-anna coin; ~अम्ली see राज; ~आब (~आबा) a tract of land lying in between two rivers; ~गाना a duet; ~गुना double; two-fold; ~चित्ता double-minded; irresolute, uncertain; ~तरफ़ा bilateral, two-sided; ~तल्ला double-storeyed; ~धारा double-edged; ~धारी double-edged; ~नाली double-barrelled; ~पट्टा a rochet, scarf, an overall cover cloth; ~पलिया having two folds, double-folded; a kind of cap; ~पहर noon, mid-day; ~पहरिया a small plant that grows red flowers; ~पहरी see पहर; ~फ़सली growing in both the crops—*rabi:* and *khari:f*, indefinite, uncertain; ~बारा a second time, once again; ~विधा uncertainty; suspense; ~भाषिया an interpreter; ~मंज़िला double-storeyed; ~माही bimonthly; ~मुँहा double-mouthed, double-tongued; ~रंगा two-coloured; duplex, treacherous, equivocal; ~राज diarchy; ~राजी diarchical government, diarchical system; ~रुखा double-sided; bilateral; ~लड़ा double-stringed (necklace etc.); ~लत्ती two-legged kick, kick with the two hind legs (as by a horse or an ass); ~शाला a double shawl; shawl; ~सूती a kind of thick cloth with double warp and woof; ~हत्था double-handed; fitted with two hands; ~हत्थी a double-handed stroke; ~हरा see दुहरा; ~हाजू married a second time.

आ dua: (*nf*) prayer, blessings; –सलाम slight acquaintance, nodding acquaintance; exchange of greetings; ०में फ़र्क आना even the superficial relations to be spoiled, to be completely estranged; –करना to pray for; –देना to wish well, to bless; –माँगना to pray for (somebody's well-being); –लगना to have one's prayer answered/blessings fulfilled.

कड़ा dukra: (*nm*) a pair; fitted in twos; one fourth of a pice.

कड़ी dukri: (*nf*) duo, a set of two; a playing card having two pips; carriage drawn by two horses.

कान dukā:n (*nf*) a shop; ~दार a shopkeeper; ~दारी shopkeeping; the work or job of a shopkeeper; higgling; –उठाना a shop/business to be closed for good; –जमाना to firmly establish a business/shop; –बढ़ाना to close the shop (for the day).

काल duka:l (*nm*) famine; scarcity.

कूल duku:l (*nm*) a fine overall cloth.

केला dukela: (*a*) not alone, accompanied by another.

क्की dukki: (*nf*) a playing card with two pips.

खंडा dukhā̃nda: (*a*) double-storeyed.

ख dukh (*nm*) see दुःख.

दुखड़ा dukhra: (*nm*) saga of sufferings, tale of woes; –रोना to narrate one's tale of woes, to describe the saga of one's sufferings.

दुखना dukhnā: (*v*) to ache; to suffer pain.

दुखाना dukha:nā: (*v*) to inflict sorrow/grief/suffering; to cause pain; to grieve, to torment.

दुखित dukhit (*a*) see दु:खित.

दुखिया dukhiya: (*a*) suffering, in distress/grief, afflicted with sorrows.

दुखिया/रा dukhiya:ra: (*a*) in the grip of sufferings, grieved, afflicted, in distress; ~री feminine adjectival form of दुखियारा.

दुखी dukhi: (*a*) see दु:खी.

दुगाना duga:nā: (*nm*) a duel.

दुग्ध dugdh (*nm*) milk; -पान taking milk; ~शाला a dairy.

दुत dut (*ind*) avaunt !, be gone !

दुतकार dutka:r (*nf*) a sharp indignant snub, snub, contemptuous reprimand.

दुतकारना dutka:rnā: (*v*) to administer a sharp snub, to snap, to reproach indignantly.

दुद्धी duddhi: (*nf*) euphorbia, a milky medicinal grass.

दुध dudh—an allomorph of दूध used as the first member in certain compounds; ~मुँहा suckling, still feeding on mother's milk; an infant; a know-nothing; ~हँड़ी an earthen pot for imparting slow heat to milk.

दुधा/र, ~रू dudha:r, ~ru: (*a*) milch; yielding much milk; –गाय की लातें भी सहनी पड़ती हैं if you will enjoy fire, you must put up with the smoke.

दुधैल dudhail: (*a*) with a generous yield of milk.

दुनिया duniyā: (*nf*) the world; people; ~ई worldly, mundane; ~दार

worldly, worldly-wise; absorbed in worldly affairs; ~दारी worldliness; worldly wisdom; worldly affairs; ~साज़ adept in worldly dealings, tactful, cunning; ~साज़ी superficial dealings, tactfulness, cunningness; –उजड़ना to lose one's all, to be in the grip of a disaster; –की हवा लगना to veer round to worldly ways; to acquire worldly wiles; –के परदे पर on the face of the earth; –देखना to gather varied experience; –देखे होना to have known the world; –भर का unparalleled/unmatched in the world; the greatest; –से उठ जाना/ –से कूच कर जाना to disappear from the face of the earth; to pass away.

दुनियावी duniya:vi: (*a*) worldly, mundane.

दुबकना dubaknā: (*v*) to be crouched, to be hidden, to be concealed, to lurk.

दुबला dubla: (*a*) lean, thin, weak; -पतला lean and thin, scrawny; hence ~पन (*nm*).

दुबिधा dubidha: (*nf*) a dilemma, fix; ~ग्रस्त on the horns of a dilemma, in a fix, in two minds; –में दोऊ गये माया मिली न राम if you run after two hares, you will catch neither.

दुबे dube (*nm*) a sub-caste of Brahmans.

दुम dūm (*nf*) tail; hind-most part (of an animal); a hanger-on, one who is a constant close follower; ~दार tailed, having a tail; –के पीछे फिरना to follow closely; –दबाकर भागना to turn tails; –दबा जाना to be scared away; –बने फिरना/रहना to be a hanger-on, to always hang on; –होना (said ironically) to be a symbol of (as ईमानदार की दुम); to be an apology for; –हिलाना to wag the tail like a dog, to flatter.

दुरंगी durangi: (*a*) see दु(~रंगी) -चाल चलने वाला Jack of both sides, a double-dealer.

दुरंत durānt (*a*) proving detrimental in the end; difficult to get through or to comprehend; violent; hence ~ता (*nf*).

दुर dur (*ind*) stand off !; be gone ! –दुर an utterance meant to drive off a dog.

दुरतिक्रम duratikkrām (*a*) difficult to cross over, inaccesible, insurmountable, inviolable.

दुरदुराना durdura:nā: (*v*) to drive off indignantly; to express contempt.

दुरना durnā: (*v*) to hide (oneself) to get out of sight.

दुरन्वय duravnay (*a*) difficult to follow/co-ordinate, incomprehensible

दुरभिसंधि durabhisāndhi (*nf*) a conspiracy, collusion, secret plot ~कर्त्ता a conspirer, plotter.

दुरमुट durmūṭ (*nm*) a (hand) rammer beater, punner.

दुरवस्था duravastha: (*nf*) predicament, miserable plight, pitiable state.

दुराकृति dura:kkriti (*nf*) ugly; deformed, deshaped.

दुराग्रह dura:ggrah (*nm*) contumacy pertinacity; importunity, obduracy *mise en demure*.

दुराग्रही dura:ggrahi: (*a*) contumacious, pertinacious; importunate mulish, obdurate.

दुरा/चरण, ~चार dura:/charāṇ ~cha:r (*nm*) misconduct, malfeasance, wickedness; immorality depravity.

दुराचा/री dura:cha:ri: (*a*) wicked malfeasant; immoral, licentious depraved; hence ~रिता (*nf*).

दुरात्मा dura:tmā: (*a*) wicked, vicious

vile.

दुराराध्य dura:ra:ddhy (*a*) fastidious, difficult to propitiate; hence ~ता (*nf*).

दुराव dura:v (*nm*) concealment; reservation; -छिपाव concealment and reservation.

दुराशय dura:shay (*a*) malafide, malevolent; ill-meaning; ~ता malafide, malevolence.

दुराशा dura:sha: (*nf*) hope against hope, false hope.

दुरुपयोग durupyog (*nm*) misuse, misusage, misapplication.

दुरु/स्त durust (*a*) proper, fit, correct, all right; ~स्ती correction, mending; refitting; ~स्त करना to mend; to put to one's proper place, to teach a lesson.

दुरूह duru:h (*a*) obscure, abstruse, unintelligible; ~ता obscurity, abstrusencess; unintelligibility.

दुर् dur—an allomorph of दु: (see) (as दुर्वह, दुर्व्यसन, etc.).

दुर्गंध durgandh (*nf*) bad odour, disagreeable smell, stench, stink.

दुर्ग durg (*nm*) a fort, castle; citadel; ~पति master of a fort, fort commander; ~पाल protector of the fort, fort-guard.

दुर्गति durgati (*nf*) predicament; misery, miserable state; distress; –करना/–बनाना to force into a miserable plight; to give a good thrashing.

दुर्गम durgām (*a*) difficult, difficult of access/approach, inaccessible; hence ~ता (*nf*).

दुर्गमनीय durgamanɪ:y (*a*) see दुर्गम.

दुर्गा durga: (*nf*) the spouse of Shiv, symbolising primaeval energy worshipped in different forms; a heroic woman-destroyer of sinners; a shrew.

दुर्गु/ण durgun̲ (*nm*) defect; fault, flaw; vice; ~णी vicious, having faults or defects.

दुर्ग्राह्य durgra:hy (*a*) untenable, difficult to accept/hold/adopt; hence ~ता (*nf*).

दुर्घटना durghaṭnā: (*nf*) an accident, mishap, tragic incident; ~ग्रस्त ill-fated, that has suffered an accident, involved in a mishap; –स्थल place/venue of an accident/a mishap.

दुर्जन durjān (*nm*) a wicked person, rascal, scoundrel; ~ता wickedness, rascality.

दुर्जय durjay (*a*) difficult to overcome or subdue, indomitable, impregnable.

दुर्जेय durjey (*a*) inconquerable; hence ~ता (*nf*).

दुर्ज्ञेय durgyey (*a*) impalpable, difficult to know/understand, incomprehensible, unintelligible; hence ~ता (*nf*).

दुर्दम durdām (*a*) indomitable; irrepressible; unyielding; difficult to subdue.

दुर्द/मनीय, ~म्य durdamni:y, ~mmy (*a*) see दुर्दम; hence ~मनीयता, ~म्यता (*nf*).

दुर्दशा durdasha: (*nf*) predicament, miserable plight, misery.

दुर्दांत durdā:nt (*a*) see दुर्दम; hence ~ता (*nf*).

दुर्दिन durdɪn (*nm*) adverse times; bad weather (overcast with clouds).

दुर्दैव durdaiv (*nm*) misfortune, ill-luck.

दुर्धर्ष durdharsh (*a*) invincible, indomitable, difficult to subdue; hence ~ता (*nf*).

दुर्नम्य durnāmmy (*a*) inflexible, rigid; stiff; ~ता inflexibility; rigidity; stiffness.

दुर्नि/वार, ~वार्य durni/va:r, ~va:ry (*a*) unrestrainable, irrepresible; inevitable.

दुर्नीति durnı:ti (*nf*) impolicy, impolitic conduct; vice.

दुर्ब/ल durbal (*a*) weak, feeble; powerless; emaciated; imbecile; **~लता** weakness, feebleness; emaciation, debility; imbecility; **~लमनस्क** feeble-minded; **~लेच्छा** velleity, weak will.

दुर्बुद्धि durbuddhi (*a*) evil-minded, perverse; foolish, stupid.

दुर्बोध durbodh (*a*) abstruse, obscure; unintelligible; hence **~ता** (*nf*).

दुर्भर durbhar (*a*) onerous, arduous; hence **~ता** (*nf*).

दुर्भाग्य durbha:ggy (*nm*) misfortune, ill-luck; tragedy.

दुर्भाव durbha:v (*nm*) malice, malevolence, ill-will.

दुर्भावना durbha:vnā: (*nf*) see **दुर्भाव**.

दुर्भिक्ष durbhiksh (*nm*) famine; scarcity, paucity.

दुर्भेद्य durbheddy (*a*) invulnerable, impregnable.

दुर्योधन duryodhan (*nm*) the villain of the great ancient Indian war—Maha:Bha:rat, head of the *kauravas*; **–की जाँघ** the Achilles' heel, the weakest point.

दुर्लंघ्य durlāṅghy (*a*) impassable; inviolable, insurmountable; hence **~ता** (*nf*).

दुर्लभ durlabh (*a*) rare, scarce; unattainable; unavailable; excellent; unique; **~ता** rarity, scarcity; unavailability; excellence.

दुर्वचन durvachān (*nm*) scurrility, scurrilous words; abuse; (*a*) scurrilous, foul-tongued.

दुर्वह durvah (*a*) unbearable; difficult to carry.

दुर्वासना durva:snā: (*nf*) malevolence, malicious disposition, malafide intention.

दुर्विनि/योग, ~योजन durvini/yog, ~yojān (*nm*) misappropriation.

दुर्विनीत durvinı:t (*a*) impudent, defiant, ill-mannered.

दुर्विपाक durvipa:k (*nm*) tragic end; accident, evil consequence.

दुर्वृ/त्त durvritt (*a*) misbehaved; vile, wicked; hence **~त्ति** (*nf*).

दुर्व्यवस्था durvyavastha: (*nf*) maladministration; maladjustment, mismanagement; chaos.

दुर्व्यवहार durvyavha:r (*nm*) misbehaviour, misconduct, ill-treatment.

दुर्व्यसन durvyasān (*nm*) addiction; vice, dissipation.

दुलकी dulki: (*nf*) trot, trotting, **–चलना** to trot (as a horse).

दुलखना dulakhnā: (*v*) to reject; not to accede to (a request etc.).

दुलत्ती dulatti: (*nf*) a kick (by an ass or a horse) with the two hind legs.

दुलराना dulra:nā: (*v*) to fondle, to caress, to pet.

दुलहन dulhan (*nf*) bride; **–की तरह सजी हुई** got up to kill, fascinatingly dressed.

दुलारा dula:ra: (*a*) beloved, darling (child), dear.

दुविधा duvidha: (*nf*) a dilemma, fix; **~ग्रस्त** see **दुबिधा (~ग्रस्त)**; **–में दोऊ गये माया मिली न राम** see **दुविधा**.

दुश/वार dushva:r (*a*) difficult: **~वारी** difficulty.

दुशाला dusha:la (*nm*) see **दु (~शाला)**.

दुश्चक्र dushchakkr (*nm*) a vicious circle.

दुश्चरित्र dushcharitr (*nm*) misconduct, malfeasance; depravity, profligacy; (*a*) deprave, degenerate; malfeasant; profligate; hence **~ता** (*nf*).

दुश्म/न dushmān (*nm*) enemy, foe; **~नी** enmity, animus, hostility; **~नी मोल लेना** to antagonise for nothing, to invite hostility.

दुष्कर dushkar (*a*) difficult, hard,

arduous; hence ~ता (*nf*).

दुष्क/र्म dushkarm (*nm*) a misdeed; sin, vice, wrong; ~र्मा/~र्मी mis-doer, wrong-doer; sinful, wicked.

दुष्काल dushka:l (*nm*) hard time; time of scarcity; famine.

दुष्कीर्ति dushki:rti (*nf*) infamy, dis-repute, ill-reputation.

दुष्कृ/ति dushkriti (*nf*) see **दुष्कृत्य**; ~ती sinner, a sinful man, wrong-doer.

दुष्कृत्य dushkritty (*nm*) tort, evil deed, misdeed; sin, vicious act.

दुष्ट dusht (*a*) wicked, vile; knave; bad; malevolent; faulty; (*nm*) a scoundrel, rascal, scamp; ~बुद्धि wicked, vile, vicious, mischiev-ous.

दुष्टता dushṭata: (*nf*) wickedness, viciousness, knavery; mischievous-ness; malevolence.

दुष्टात्मा dushṭa:tmā: (*a*) see **दुरात्मा**.

दुष्परिग्रह dushparigrah (*a*) difficult to subdue/domesticate/tame.

दुष्प्रकृति dnshprakriti (*nf*) ill-temper, evil nature; (*a*) ill-tempered, evil-natured, churlish; base, mean, wicked.

दुष्प्रयोग dushprayog (*nm*) misuse, misapplication; acyron.

दुष्प्रवृत्ति dnshpravritti (*nf*) ill-trend, unwholesome tendency; mean mentality.

दुष्प्राप्य dushpra:ppy (*a*) rare, scarce; difficult to achieve or attain.

दुसराना dusra:nā: (*v*) to repeat, to say or do over again.

दुसह dusah (*a*) see **दुःसह**.

दुस्तर dustar (*a*) difficult to cross, impassable; insurmountable, in-superable.

दुह/त्ती, ~त्थी, duhatti:, ~tthi: (*nm*) a blow or stroke with the two palms joined together.

दुहना duhnā: (*v*) to milk; to squeeze, to exploit.

दुहनी duhnı: (*nf*) a milking pot.

दुहरा duhra: (*a*) two-fold, double-folded; double, dual.

दुहराना duhra:nā: (*v*) to repeat, to say or do over again; to revise.

दुहाई duha:i: (*nf*) an outcry or en-treaty for help/mercy/justice; plaint; oath; loud proclamation; process of or wages paid for milk ing (a cow etc.); –देना to appeal in the name of.

दुहिता duhita: (*nf*) a daughter.

दूज du:j (*nf*) the second day of each lunar fortnight; –का चाँद one who makes a rare appearance, seen only once in a blue moon.

दूत du:t (*nm*) a messenger, courier; legate; an emissary, envoy; -कर्म (the job of) message-carrying; envoyship.

दूतावास du:ta:va:s (*nm*) an embassy, legation.

दूती du:ti: (*nf*) a procuress, bawd.

दूध du:dh (*nm*) milk; juicy sub-stance of certain plants; -पूत men and money; ~वाला a milk-man, milk-vendor; –उतरना milk to desend into the udder or breasts; –का जला छाछ फूँक-फूँक कर पीता है a burnt child dreads fire, once caught twice shy; –का दूध और पानी का पानी sifting of true from the false/just from unjust; –का धोया pure, unsullied, blemish-less; –की मक्खी an unwanted and inconsequential entity, an insigni-ficant person; ०की तरह निकाल फेंकना to discard as unwanted and inconsequential;–के दाँत calf's milk teeth; ०न टूटना to be too young and raw;–को दूध और पानी को पानी कहना to call a spade a spade, to say what is true without fear or favour; –छुड़ाना to wean; ~पीता

बच्चा a suckling; an innocent fellow; –फटना (milk) to decompose into its watery and substantial content; दूधों नहाना पूतों फलना to prosper in men and money.

दूधिया du:dhiya: (*a*) milky; milk-white; with a substantial quantity of milk; juicy; tender, green; (*nm*) a milk-vendor; an opal (also –पत्थर).

दून dū:n (*a*) double; (*nm*) a valley; –की लेना/की हाँकना to boast, to brag, to talk tall.

दूना du:nā: (*a*) double.

दूब du:b (*nf*) a kind of green/lawn grass.

दूबदू du:badu: (*ind*) face to face; in straight fight/contest, in direct clash.

दूभर du:bhar (*a*) difficult, onerous; arduous; –करना to make it too hot.

दूरंदेश du:randesh (*a*) far-sighted, prudent, sagacious.

दूरंदेशी du:randeshi: (*nf*) far-sightedness, prudence, sagacity.

दूर du:r (*adv* and *a*) far off, far away, away; distant; remote; ~गामी far-reaching; ~ग्राही teleceptor; ~चित्र telephoto; ~दर्शक prescient, prudent, far-seeing; a telescope; ०यंत्र a telescope; ~दर्शन television; ~दर्शिता far-sightedness, prudence, sagacity; ~दर्शी far-sighted, prudent, sagacious; ~दृष्टि farsight; farsightedness; ~बीन a telescope; ~भाष a telephone; ~मुद्रक a teleprinter; ~वर्ती distant, remote; ~वीक्षण a telescope; ०यंत्र a telescope; ~संचार telecommunication; ~संवेद्य telesthetic; ~स्थ/~स्थित remote, distant, located/situated far away; outlying; –करना to reject, to condemn; to ward off, to remove; –का situated far away; remote; far-fetched; –की कहना to make a remarkable utterance, to make an utterance with far-reaching implications, to make a prudent remark; –की कौड़ी far-fetched imagination, fantastic idea; –की बात a far cry; far-fetched remark; very subtle remark; –की सोचना to visualise future course of events; to be sagacious, to be prescient; –के ढोल सुहावने far fowls have fair feathers; –क्यों जाइये ! why go far, take a ready example; –से नमस्कार/सलाम करना to give wide berth to, to avoid, to steer clear of.

दूरान्वय du:ra:nnvay (*nm*) maladjustment / misplacement /enjambment (of sentence parts).

दूरारूढ़ du:ra:ru:ṛh (*a*) carried too far; far-fetched; –कल्पना far-fetched imagination, fantastic idea.

दूरी du:ri: (*nf*) distance, remoteness; range.

दूर्वा du:rva: (*nf*) see दूब.

दूल्हा du:lha: (*nm*) a bridegroom; husband.

दूषण du:shān (*nm*) contamination, pollution, stigma; defect, flaw.

दूषित du:shit (*a*) contaminated, polluted; stigmatic; defective; defiled; corrupted; vitiated, sullied; vicious.

दूसरा du:sra: (*a*) second; other, another; next; दूसरों का मुँह ताकना to look to others for help; दूसरों की ताल/ताली पर नाचना to dance to some other's tune; दूसरों के लिए काँटे बिछाना to seek to strew others' path with thorns; दूसरों के हाथ बिक जाना to be sold out to another.

दृग drig (*nm*) an eye.

दृढ़ driṛh (*a*) firm, resolute, strong-willed; strong; tough; hard; rigid, tenacious; ~चेता strong-willed, resolute; ~निश्चय determined, firm. of unbending resolution/firm determination; ~प्रतिज्ञ/व्रत upholding one's pledge, true to one's word; ~संकल्प resolute, determined.

दृढ़ता drirhta: (nf) firmness, resoluteness; toughness; strength; rigidity; tenacity.

दृढ़त्व drirhattv (nm) see दृढ़ता.

दृढ़ोक्ति drirhokti (nf) an assertion, averment.

दृप्त dript (a) arrogant; overbearing; presumptuous; intoxicated with pride.

दृश्य drishshy (nm) a scene; sight, spectacle, view; (a) visible, spectacular; –घटना a phenomenon; ~लेख a panorama; scenario; –श्राव्य audiovisual.

दृश्यता drishshyata: (nf) visibility; visual character; range.

दृश्यमान drishshyamā:n (a) visible, -perceptible, tangible; apparent, obvious; hence ~ता (nf).

दृश्यांतर drishshya:ntar (nm) wipe; change-scene.

दृश्यावली drishshya:vali: (nf) a scenery; panorama.

दृष्टकूट drishṭakuṭ: (nm) an enigmatic composition.

दृष्ट/वाद drishṭava:d (nm) empiricism; ~वादी an empiricist; empirical.

दृष्टांत drishṭā:nt (nm) an instance; illustration (a figure of speech); precedent; –कथा a parable.

दृष्टि drishṭi (nf) sight; view; vision; glance; ~कोण viewpoint, point of view; ~क्षीणता asthenopia; ~गत seen, viewed, perceived; ~गोचर visible, perceptible; apparent; ~दोष visual deficiency/defect, misperception; ~पटल the retina; ~पथ visual range; ~परक visible, visual; ~पात glance, glancing, viewing; ~बंध

set (in theatre, etc.); ~भ्रम optical illusion; ~मूलक visual; pertaining to one's sight/view; ~लेख scenario; ~लेखक a scenarist; –वैषम्य astigmatism; ~हीन blind; ~पात करना to view, to glance; –देना to give an insight (into); –फेरना to withdraw one's favour; –बचाना to evade, to avoid being sighted; –रखना to keep a watch on, to keep under observation.

देख/ना dekhnā: (v) to see, to look; to view; to perceive; to observe; to read; to correct; to consider; to experience; –कर जलना, (किसी को) to look through green glasses; ~ते बनना a sight worth seeing, a sight for the gods to see; –न सकना not to stand the very sight of; –लेना (as देख लेंगे) to face the music.

देख-भाल dekh-bha:l (nf) care; maintenance; supervision.

देख-रेख dekh-rekh (nf) supervision, guidance, care.

देखा-देखी dekha:-dekhi: (adv) in emulation/imitation of, inspired by the example of.

देग deg (nf) a cauldron.

देगची degchi: (nf) a small cauldron.

देदीप्यमान dedi:pyamā:n (a) brilliant, lustrous, resplendent, radiant; ~ता brilliance, lustre, resplendence, radiance.

देन den (nf) contribution; gift; giving; ~गी charge, payment due; ~दार a debtor; ~दारी payment due; indebtedness; -लेन give and take; exchange; banking business; ~हार a giver.

दे/ना denā: (v) to give; to grant; to confer, to bestow; to entrust, to assign; to yield, to surrender; used freely and frequently as an auxiliary verb, as कर दिया, चल दिया, दे

दिया, etc.; –मारना to fell; (as in wrestling) to throw flat; to say crudely.

देय dey (*a*) worth giving; payable; due; hence ~ता (*nf*).

देर der (*nf*) delay; lag; -सवेर sooner or later; –आयद दुरुस्त आयद better late than never.

देरी deri: (*nf*) delay; lag.

देव dev (*nm*) a god, deity; a respectable person; a giant, demon; ~ऋण the debt of the gods; ~कन्या a celestial maiden, nymph; ~कार्य a religious rite or sacrifice performed for propitiating a deity; ~कुल pantheon; ~गण gods in their totality, divine community; ~गृह a temple; the abode of a deity; ~चर्या worship, adoration; ~त्रयी the divine trio of Brahma:, Vishn̲ū, Mahesh; ~दारु a pine tree, cedar; ~दासी a temple dancer, a dancing girl dedicated to a deity; ~दूत an angel, a prophet, divine messenger; ~नदी the river of gods—the Gaṅga:; -प्रतिमा the idol of a deity; ~बाला a nymph, a celestial damsel; ~भाषा Sanskrit—the language of gods; ~मूर्ति the idol of a deity; ~यान a celestial plane; ~वाणी see ~भाषा; ~सभा the assembly of gods; ~स्थान a temple.

देवता devta: (*nm*) a god, deity; divine being; –कूच कर जाना to be dumb-founded, to be terribly nervous.

देवत्व devatv (*nm*) godhood; godliness, divinity.

देवनागरी devna:gri: (*nf*) the script which evolved in India during the post-Gupta era and ultimately developed into a systematic and scientific instrument of writing during the 10th and 11th centuries A.D. Scholars have attributed, though not conclusively various reasons for its nomenclature. It is the script, at present adopted for writing Hindi: and Mara:ṭhi: in their respective areas and for Sanskrit all over India; –अक्षर Dev:na:gri: character(s); –वर्णमाला the Devna:gri: alphabet

देवर devar (*nm*) husband's younger brother.

देवरानी devra:ni: (*nf*) husband's younger brother's wife.

देवांगना devā:ṅganā: (*nf*) a god's spouse; celestial damsel.

देवाधिदेव deva:dhidev (*nm*) the god of gods, Lord Shiv (also Vishn̲ū)

देवाल deva:l (*nm*) one who gives; one who owes; one who wants to repay (a loan etc.); a seller.

देवालय deva:lay (*nm*) a temple, seat of a deity.

देवी devi: (*nf*) a goddess; the goddess Durga: ; (deferential term for a) lady; –दिन काटें पंडा परचा (परिचय) माँगें a deity in trouble has to prove himself even to a devotee.

देश desh (*nm*) a country; land; native home; region; space; –काल time and space; native land (as देश काल का समाचार सुनाओ); ०दोष anachronism; ~ज native; local; a word evolved indigenously, indigenous; -दर्शन seeing the land/country; -देशांतर one's own and other lands; -दोष anachronism; –धर्म religion/morals/conduct befitting or prevailing in a country; ~भक्त a patriot; ~भक्ति patriotism; ०पूर्ण patriotic; ~भक्ति-भाव patriotic sentiment; –भाषा native language; language current in a country; -विदेश native and alien lands.

देश/द्रोह desh(d)droh (*nm*) treason

disloyalty to the country; ~द्रोह, घोर high treason; ~द्रोहात्मक treasonable, treasonous; ~द्रोही a traitor, one who is disloyal to the country; –निर्वासन/निष्कासन exile, expatriation, banishment from the country.

देशनिकाला deshnika:la: (*nm*) expatriation; exile, banishment.

देशांतर deshā:ntar (*nm*) terrestrial longitude, longitude; another/foreign country; ~गमन migration; transmigration; ~ण migration; transmigration.

देशाचार desha:cha:r (*nm*) native custom/practice/usage.

देशाटन desha:ṭān (*nm*) going round the country; going from one country to another.

देशी deshi: (*a*) native; indigenous, local.

देशीकरण deshi:karān̲ (*nm*) naturalisation.

देशीय deshi:y (*a*) see **देशी**.

देशीयकरण deshi:yakarān̲ (*nm*) see **देशीकरण**.

देस des (*nm*) see **देश**; ~वाल co-native, co-patriot.

देसाव/र desa:var (*nm*) a foreign country; an export-centre, marketing centre; ~री of or belonging to a foreign country/export centre; imported; ०माल imported goods/stuff; brought from a marketing centre.

देसी desi: (*a*) indigenous, native, country-made.

देह deh (*nf*) body, person; physique; soma; ~त्याग voluntary end of life, abandonment of the physical form; -धर्म physical/bodily functions; corporeal requirements; ~धर्मी somatic; ~धारी possessing a physical form/body; corporeal; ~पात death; ~विज्ञान somatology; ~सार somaplasm; –को लगना to nourish the body; –चुराना (said of a woman) to conceal one's youthfulness/physical charm; –छोड़ना to die; –टूटना to feel pain in the body(due to strain, exhaustion, exertion or fever); –ढलना physical decay/decline to set in; to become loose and lustreless; to lose muscularity; –धरना to be born; to acquire a physical form; –धरे को दंड है सब काहू को होय its the way of all flesh; –में आग लगना to get infuriated/enraged.

देह/क़ान dehqā:n (*nm*) a villager, rustic fellow; (*a*) rustic, rural; ~क़ानियत rusticity; incivility; ~क़ानी rustic, rural.

देहरी dehri: (*nf*) the threshold, doorsill, doorstep; –पार करना to cross the doorstep.

देहली dehli: (*nf*) see **देहरी**.

देहांत dehā:nt (*nm*) death, demise.

देहाकृति deha:kkriti (*nf*) physical form; somatotype.

देहा/त deha:t (*nm*) countryside; village; ~ती a villager; rustic; rural; hence ~तीपन (*nm*).

देहातीत deha:ti:t (*a*) transcendental, incorporeal, beyond physical limitations; ~वाद transcendentalism.

देहात्म deha:tm (*nm*) the body and soul; ~वाद a philosophic principle that identifies body with the soul, materialism; ~वादी a materialist; materialistic.

देहावसान deha:vsā:n (*nm*) death, demise.

दैत्य daitty (*nm*) a demon, giant, ogre.

दैत्याकार daittya:ka:r (*a*) giant-sized, ogrish.

दैनंदि/न daināndın (*a* and *adv*) daily, diurnal, from day to day, day by day; ~नी a diary.

दैनि/क dainik (*a*) daily; (*nm*) daily newspaper; ~की a diary.

दैन्य dainny (*nm*) meekness, humbleness; poverty, indigence.

दैया daiya: (*nf*) (a proclamation of utter helplessness) oh God! Gosh! Goodness gracious!; also –रे दैया.

दैर्घ्य dairghy (*nm*) length; expanse.

दैव daiv (*nm*) fate, fortune, destiny; ~कृत supernatural, vis major; ~गति accident; course of events as inspired by Divine Will; –दुर्विपाक misfortune; irony of fate; ~योग chance, accident; ~वश by chance, accidentally; ~वशात् by chance, accidentally; ~वाणी an oracle; Sanskrit—the speech of gods; ~वाद fatalism; ~वादी a fatalist; fatalistic; ~हीन unfortunate, unlucky; ill-fated; -दैव आलसी पुकारा its the indolent alone who shout for a divine prop, its the do-nothings who wait for a miracle.

दैवात् daiva:t (*adv*) by chance, accidentally.

दैविक daivik (*a*) divine, godly, pertaining to or inspired by god(s).

दैवी daivi: (*a*) divine, ethereal, celestial.

दैहिक daihik (*a*) physical, somatic, corporeal; material.

दोंचना dōchnā: (*v*) to pound, to crush; to give a beating/thrashing.

दो do (*a*) two; (*nm*) the number two; (for compounds also see दु~); ~अमली diarchy; dual administration; ~आब, ~आबा doab, a tract of country lying between two rivers; the territory lying between the rivers गंगा and यमुना; ~एक one or two, a few; ~गला a bastard, crossbred; illegitimate; -चार a few, several; -टूक decisive, categorical, crystal clear (statement, talk, etc.); ०फ़ैसला करना the door must either be shut or open; to arrive at a conclusive decision; ~पहर midday; noon; ~पहरी midday, noon; ~फ़सली yielding two crops a year; मुँहा see दु(~मुँहा); ~रुखा double-faced; having two faces or aspects; ~साला biennial, of two years; –की चार सुनाना to pay in the same coin along with interest; –कौड़ी का worth nothing, inconsequential; –घोड़ों पर सवारी करना to ride two horses at a time; -चार a few; ०होना to be confronted with; -दो हाथ करना to try out comparative strength; –दिन का of recent origin, comparatively young or new; transitory; –दिन का मेहमान one whose days are numbered, with a short lease of life;–मुल्लाओं में मुर्ग़ी हराम too many cooks spoil the broth; –नावों पर पैर रखना to ride two horses at a time; –रोटी कमाना to earn one's livelihood, to make both ends meet; –शब्द a few words; –सिर होना to be ready to face death; to invite one's doom, to tread the path of sure doom.

दोज़/ख़ dozakh (*nm*) the hell, inferno; ~ख़ी hellish, infernal.

दोना donā: (*nm*) a cup formed by folding up large-sized leaves of certain trees (as ढाक, बड़, etc.).

दोनों donō (*a*) both, the two; –वक़्त मिलना to become dusk; –हाथ लड्डू होना to have victory on the one hand and conquest on the other; –हाथों से लुटाना to burn the candle at both ends.

दोयम doyam (*a*) number two, the second.

दोलक dolak (*nm*) an oscillator; a rocker.

दोलन dolān (*nm*) oscillation; rocking.

दोलायमान dola:ymā:n (*a*) oscillating; rocking; wavering, unsteady, fickle.

दोलायित dola:it (*a*) see **दोलित**.

दोलित dolit (*a*) oscillated; rocked; wavered, unsteady.

दोष dosh (*nm*) a fault; flaw, guilt; defect; demerit; blame; disorder (of the humours of the body); **~कारी** harmful, damaging; creating disorder; **~त्रय** see **त्रिदोष**; **-दृष्टि** a fault-finding eye; **-पत्र** a charge sheet; **~पूर्ण/युक्त** defective; faulty; guilty; **–देना** to accuse; to make an accusation; **–मढ़ना** to level a charge against; **–सिद्ध कर देना** to bring home to, to substantiate a charge.

दोषारोप, ~ण dosha:rop, ~āṉ (*nm*) charging, accusation.

दोषी doshi: (*a* and *nm*) (the) guilty; culprit.

दोस्त dost (*nm*) a friend; **~नवाज़** a cherisher of friends, kindly disposed towards friends; hence **~नवाज़ी** (*nf*).

दोस्ताना dosta:nā: (*nm*) friendship, friendliness; (*a*) friendly, worthy of a friend.

दोस्ती dosti: (*nf*) friendship; **–गाँठना** to make friends with an ulterior motive.

दोहद dohad (*nm*) the longings of a pregnant woman.

दोहन dohān (*nm*) milking; exploitation.

दोह/रा dohra: (*a*) double, two-folded; equivocal; stoutish (as **बदन**); **~रा साधन** two strings to one bow; **~री चाल चलना** to play a double game; **~री बात** an equivoque, ambiguous utterance.

दोहराना dohra:nā: (*v*) to revise, to recapitulate; to repeat, to reiterate; to make two-fold.

दोहा doha: (*nm*) a typical Hindi poetic metre; a couplet.

दौंचना daũchnā (*v*) see **दोंचना**.

दौंची daũchi: (*nf*) a road-dint.

दौड़ dauṛ (*nf*) a race; run, running; **-धूप** endeavour, running about; all out effort; **–मारना/लगाना** to make a dash; to make a long and hurried journey; to run about (for fulfilment of some objective).

दौड़ना dauṛnā: (*v*) to run, to run about; to rush.

दौड़ादौड़ी dauṛa:dauṛi: (*nf*) haste, hastiness, urgency; all out effort.

दौर daur (*nm*) a phase; stage; round; **-दौरा** sway, dominance; **–चलना** to have one round after another; **–पर दौर चलना** one round to continue after another, to have round after round.

दौरा daura: (*nm*) a tour; fit; **–आना/पड़ना** to have a fit; **–करना** to (undertake a) tour; **–सुपुर्द करना** to commit to the sessions; **दौरे पर रहना/होना** to be out on a tour.

दौरान daurā:n:; **इसी—** in the meanwhile; during this period; **के—** during.

दौर्बल्य daurbally (*nm*) weakness; infirmity, debility.

दौर्मनस्य daurmānassy (*nm*) ill-will, malevolence.

दौलत daulat (*nm*) riches, wealth; **~खाना** (euphemistically) residence; **~मंद** rich, wealthy, opulent, moneyed; **~मंदी** richness, wealthiness; opulence; **–से इज्ज़त भली** a good name is better than a golden girdle.

दौवारिक dauva:rik (*nm*) a door-keeper, gateman.

दौहि/त्र dauhittr (*nm*) daughter's son, grandson; hence **~त्री** (*nf*).

द्युति dyuti (*nf*) radiance, lustre, brilliance, glow; **~मंत/मान** radiant, lustrous, brilliant, bright.

द्यूत dyu:t (*nm*) gambling; **~कर/कार**

a gambler; -क्रीड़ा gambling: –मंडल/समाज a team of gamblers; -वृत्ति gambling profession; urge to gamble.

द्योतक dyotak (*a*) illustrative (of), expressive (of), exemplifying/signifying.

द्योतन dyotān (*nm*) illustration expression, exemplification/signification.

द्योतित dyotit (*a*) illustrated, expressed, signified; lighted, illuminated.

द्रव drav (*nm*) a liquid, fluid; ~चालित hydraulic; ~ता/त्व fluidity; liquidity; ~शील melting, prone to melt away; ~स्थैतिक hydrostatic; ~स्थैतिकी hydrostatics.

द्रवण dravāṉ (*nm*) melting, flowing; ~शील melting, prone to melt/flow; hence –शीलता (*nf*).

द्रविड़ dravir̤ (*a*) Dravidian, (*nm*); the Dravidian country; a Dravidian; –देश the Dravidian country; –प्राणायाम lit. catching the nose for holding the breath (प्राणायाम) by bringing the right hand over the head —a round about way of doing a thing; making a detour.

द्रविण draviṉ (*nm*) wealth, prosperity.

द्रवित dravit (*a*) melted; moved (by emotion).

द्रवीभूत dravi:bhu:t (*a*) melted; moved (by emotion).

द्रव्य dravvy (*nm*) substance, matter; money; (*a*) material, substantial; -संचय amassing / accumulating wealth.

द्रव्यमय dravvyamay (*a*) substantial, material; full of or abounding in wealth.

द्रव्यमान dravvyamā:n (*nm*) a mass; (*a*) wealthy; material.

द्रव्यार्जन dravvya:rjān (*nm*) earning; money-earning.

द्रष्टव्य drashṭavvy (*a*) worth-seeing; pleasing (to see); notable, worth taking a note of.

द्रष्टा drashṭa: (*nm*) a seer, visionis sage; spectator.

द्रावक dra:vak (*a*) moving, touchin melting, liquefying; (*nm*) a thinn

द्राविड़ dra:vir̤ (*a* and *nm*) see द्रवि hence द्राविड़ी (*nf*).

द्रुत drut (*a*) fast, fast moving, quic swift; moved; melted; ~गति/गा fast moving; quick, lightlegged.

द्रुति druti (*nf*) fastness, swiftnes molten/melted state; moved stat

द्रुम drum (*nm*) a tree.

द्रोणी droṉi: (*nf*) a basin; troug

द्रोह droh (*nm*) malice, rancou rebellion, hostility; ~बुद्धि malicio malevolent; rebellious; hostile.

द्रोही drohi: (*a*) malicious, rancorou malignant; rebellious; insubordi nate, hostile.

द्रौपदी draupadi: (*nf*) wife of th Pa:ṉdavas in the great epi Maha:bha:rat; –का चीर (a proces etc.) that knows no end; –क बटलोई a blessed utensil that feed one and all.

द्वंद्व dwāndw (*nm*) conflict, quarrel duel; uproar; hubbub; a pair couple; copulative compound, a compound wherein the member if uncompounded would be in th same case and connected by th conjunction 'and' (as राम-लक्ष्मण, माता-पिता); ~मूलक conflictional, pertaining to or arising out of a conflict; duelistic; -युद्ध a duel.

द्वंद्वात्मक dwāndwa:tmāk (*a*) dialec tical; conflictional; duelistic –भौतिकवाद dialectical materialism

द्वंद्वी dwāndwi: (*a*) quarrelsome prone to enter into conflict.

द्वय dway (*a*) two; (*nm*) pair, couple

द्वादश dwa:dash (*a*) twelve; twelfth (*nm*) the number twelve.

द्वादशी dwa:dashi: (*nf*) the twelfth

day of each lunar fortnight.

ापर dwa:par (*nm*) the third of the four *yugas* or ages according to the Hindu mythology, the age of transition from good (सतयुग and त्रेता) to the age of vice (कलियुग).

ाभा dwa:bha: (*nf*) twilight.

ार dwa:r (*nm*) a door; doorway; gate; exit; –कपाट leaves of the door; ~चार one of the ceremonies held at the bride's door during the marriage; ~पाल/पालक a door-keeper, watchman; ~पूजा a ceremony wherein the adoration of the bridegroom is performed at the doorstep of the bride's house and forms part of the marriage proceedings; –खुलना the door to open; an avenue to open up; –खुला रखना to keep the door open (for negotiation, etc.); –पर दस्तक देना to knock at the door; to be imminent; –पर होना to be on the threshold of; –बंद करना to shut the door (for negotiation, etc.).

ारा dwa:ra: (*ind*) by, through, through the medium/agency of.

ाराचार dwa:ra:cha:r (*nm*) see द्वारचार (under द्वार).

: dwi (*a*) two; ~कर्मक (a verb) having two objects; ~गु a kind of compound (word) wherein the first member is a numerical; ~गुण double; twice; ~गुणित doubled; ~ज/जन्मा/जाति lit. twice-born—a Bra:hman; the three higher castes (i.e. ब्राह्मण, क्षत्रिय, वैश्य) in the traditional Hindu hierarchical society; the moon; aves; ~जिह्व lit. double-tongued—a snake; backbiter; ~दली/दलीय bipartite; having two leaves or petals; ~धातु bimetallic; an alloy; ~पक्ष/पक्षीय bilateral, bipartite; ~पद/पाद bipodal, bifooted, having two legs or feet; –भाषिक/भाषी bilingual; –मासिक bimonthly, brought out every two months; ~लिंगी bisexual; ~वचन the dual (number), signifying two; ~विध of two kinds or types; ~विधा dilemma, suspense; uncertainty; ~वेदी a subdivision of the Bra:hmān community; ~समत्रिभुज isosceles triangle; ~साप्ताहिक biweekly.

द्वितीय dwiti:y (*a*) the second; –आश्रम the second or the householder's stage in an individual's life; ~क second; secondary.

द्वितीया dwiti:ya: (*nf*) the second day of each lunar fortnight.

द्वित्व dwittw (*nm*) duplication; repetition; –व्यंजन double consonant.

द्विधा dwidha: (*ind*) in two ways, in two parts; (*nf*) dilemma, uncertainty; ~ग्रस्त in two minds, in a dilemma.

द्विधार्थक dwidha:rthak (*a*) ambiguous, equivocal; ~ता ambiguity, equivocation.

द्विरागमन dwira:gamān (*nm*) see गौना.

द्विरु/क्त dwirukt (*a*) twice mentioned; duplicate; redundant; ~क्ति duplication, mentioning twice, redundance.

द्वीप dwi:p (*nm*) an island; –समूह (group of) islands.

द्वेष dwesh (*nm*) malice: aversion, repugnance; ill-will; malevolence; dislike, disaffection.

द्वेषी dweshi: (*a*) malicious, malevolent, harbouring ill-will/disaffection/dislike.

द्वैत dwait (*nm*) duality, dualism; discrimination, ~वाद/~वादिता dualism; –वादी dualist(ic).

द्वैध dwaidh (*a*) of two types; discriminatory; hence ~ता (*nf*); –शासन-प्रणाली diarchical system of government.

द्वैधवत्तिक dwaidhvattik (*a*) ambivalent.

द्व्यर्थ, ~क dwyarth, ~ak (*a*) ambiguous, equivocal; **~ता** ambiguity, eqivocation.

ध

ध dha—the fourth and penultimate letter of the fourth pentad (i.e. **तवर्ग**) of the Devna:gri: alphabet.

धं/धा dhāndha: (*nm*) vocation, occupation; business; work; **~धे से लगना** to get busy, to get down to work.

धँसना dhāsnā: (*v*) to sink: to penetrate into, to enter into; to get stuck into; to descend.

धँसान dhāsa:n (*nf*) a quagmire, boggy land; descent, slope, subsidence; process or act of descending.

धँसाना dhāsa:nā: (*v*) to thrust; to penetrate, to cause to enter/descend; to countersink.

धँसाव dhāsa:v (*nm*) **धँसान**.

धक dhak (*nf*) palpitation; sudden suspension of normal heart-throb; **~धक/पक** enhanced heart-throb, palpitation; **–से रह जाना** to be stunned, to be paralysed (through fear or astonishment), to stand aghast; **–होना, मन में** to be stunned, to be aghast.

धकधका/ना dhakdhaka:nā: (*v*) the heart to throb violently (through fear, panic, etc.), to palpitate: hence **~हट** (*nf*).

धकधकी dhakdhaki: (*nf*) see **धुकधुकी**.

धकापेल dhaka:pel (*nf*) indiscriminate shoving, shoving and pushing; jostling; (*adv*) vigorously, vehemently, non-stop; **–चलना** to go at full speed, to speed unhindered, **–मचाना** to create a commotion/havoc; to do things in very quick succession.

धका/र dhaka:r (*nm*) the letter **ध** (dha) and its sound; **~रांत** (word) ending in **ध्** (dh).

धकियाना dhakiya:nā: (*v*) to shove, to push about; to thrust ahead.

धकेलना dhakelnā: (*v*) to shove, to push.

धक्कमधक्का dhakkāmdhakka: (*nm*) jostling, shoving and pushing; rush.

धक्का dhakka: (*nm*) a push; shove; shock; setback; stroke, buffet, jostle, jolt, impact; **~मुक्की** jostling, shoving and pushing; elbowing; **–खाना** to receive a shock; to suffer a set-back; to be kicked and knocked; **–देना** to push; to give a push/impetus/support; **–लगना** to be shocked; to get a setback; to get a push/prop/support (as **थोड़ा धक्का लग जाये तो काम चल पड़े**); **–धक्के खाना** to be tossed about; to suffer indignities, to suffer kicks and knocks.

धज dhaj (*nf*) air, demeanour; mien, appearance, look; **–बनाना** to put on a queer/unusual appearance.

धजा dhaja: (*nf*) see **धज**.

धज्जी dhajji: (*nf*) a shred, strip, tatter; lath; ~**बंदी** lathing; **धज्जियाँ उड़ना** to be reduced to shreds, to be tattered, to be torn to pieces; **धज्जियाँ उड़ाना** to knock the bottom out of, to tatter, to tear into pieces.

धड़ंग dharaṅg (*a*) used as the second member in the compound **नंग-धड़ंग** —meanning completely/stark naked.

धड़ dhaṛ (*nm*) a torso, trunk, fuselage; rattling/banging sound; ~**धड़** (with) a quick succession of rattling sounds; –**से** with a rattling/banging noise; without hitch; instanly.

धड़क dhaṛak (*nf*) hitch, hesitation.

धड़कन dhaṛkān (*nf*) throbbing, palpitation; pulsation; –**बढ़ना** to become nervous/restless.

धड़कना dhaṛaknā: (*v*) to throb, to palpitate, to pulsate.

धड़का dhaṛka: (*nm*) a throb, palpitation, pulsation; apprehension; doubt.

धड़धड़ा/ना dhaṛdhaṛa:nā: (*v*) to make a rattling or banging sound; to rap-tap or knock (at a door); to walk heavily and briskly; hence ~**हट** (*nf*).

धड़/ल्ला dhaṛalla: (*nm*); ~**ल्ले का** dauntless, fearless, overbearing; headstrong, strong; ~**ल्लेदार** (**आदमी**) dauntless; unyielding, headstrong, strong; ~**ल्ले से** dauntlessly, fearlessly, with a bang.

ध/ड़ा dhaṛa: (*nm*) tare; counterbalance, counter-balancing weight; speculation; faction; ~**ड़ेबंदी** counterpoise; counterbalancing; factionalism; ~**ड़ेबाज़** factionalist; ~**ड़ेबाज़ी** factionalism; ~**ड़ा उठाना** to assess the weight; ~**ड़ा करना** to counter-poise; to counterbalance; to weigh; ~**ड़ा लगाना** to speculate. to stake (money) in speculation.

धड़ा/का dhaṛa:ka: (*nm*) an explosion, crash; a loud report; ~**के से** with a loud report, with a rattle; quickly, swiftly.

धड़ाधड़ dhaṛa:dhaṛ (*adv*) in a quick succession, one after the other; incessantly.

धड़ाम dhaṛā:m (*nf*) thud, crash, loud report (of a falling body); –**से** with a crash/loud report/thud; instantaneously.

धड़ी dhaṛi: (*nf*) a measure of weight equivalent to five seers; ~, **कच्ची** a weight of five seers; ~, **पक्की** a weight of ten seers.

ध/त dhat (*nf*) a mania, craze; ~**ती** addicted to, crazy, having an inveterate habit.

धता dhata: (*nm*) (the act of) driving away, putting off, evasion; –**देना**/–**बताना** to tell off,/drive away

धतूरा dhatu:ra: (*nm*) the *Datura alba*, the thorn apple which is a powerful narcotic; –**खाए फिरना** to go about crazily.

धत् dhat (*ind*) be off !, stand away !; you naughty !; –**तेरे की** damn it !, Gosh !, what a surprise !, how done it !.

धधकना dhadhaknā: (*v*) to blaze, to flare up, to burn intensely.

धन dhān (*nm*) wealth, riches, money; additional number; (*prep.*) plus; (*a*) positive (as an electric charge or a number); ~**कुबेर** a man as rich as the god of wealth; **चिह्न** plus sign; ~**तेरस** the thirteenth day of the dark fortnight of the month of **कार्तिक** (when the Hindu:s commence the adoration of **लक्ष्मी** —the goddess of wealth and purchase new household utensils; -जन money and men; -जन की हानि loss of men and money; -दौलत wealth and affluence, riches; -धान्य all-round prosperity, affluence; ~पति *kuber*—the god of wealth; ~पिशाच avaricious, cruelly stingy, overniggardly; -मद money-intoxication, purse-pride; ~मत्त lit. intoxicated with wealth —purse-proud; ~मूल capital; ~वंत wealthy, rich; moneyed; -वाद a money-suit; ~वान wealthy, rich; -विधेयक a money bill; ~शाली wealthy, rich; ~हीन poor, moneyless, indigent; —के सिर सेहरा the writ of fate never changes; —बरसना to have a shower of riches, to get money in huge quantities, to have affluence all round; —सब को अंधा कर देय gold is the dust that blinds all eyes; —सब गुण का मूल है money creates qualities that never were; —से धन आता है money begets money.

धनाढ्य dhanaḍḍhy (*a*) rich, prosperous, wealthy, moneyed; hence ~ता (*nf*).

धनात्मक dhanā:tmāk (*a*) positive (as an electric charge etc,); pertaining to money; plus; hence ~ता (*nf*).

धनादेश dhanā:desh (*nm*) a draft (issued by a bank); money order.

धनार्थी dhanā:rthi: (*a*) desirous of money, money-seeking.

धनिक dhanik (*a*) opulent, wealthy, rich, moneyed; (*nm*) a wealthy person.

धनिया dhanīyā: (*nm*) coriander.

धनी dhanı: (*a*) rich, opulent, moneyed; effective; (*nm*) master; owner; —,कलम का one who wields his pen effectively, a richly creative author; —, बात का one whose utterances are effective, one who sticks to his word; -मानी eminent, affluent and effective; magnate.

धनु dhanū (*nf*) a bow.

धनु/र्धर, ~र्धारी dhanurdhar, ~rdha:ri: (*a*) wielding a bow/arch; (*nm*) a bowman, an archer.

धनुर्विद्या dhanurviddya: (*nf*) archery, the art and science of archery; bowmanship.

धनुर्वेद dhanurved (*nm*) the part of यजुर्वेद which deals with the art and science of archery; the art and science of archery.

धनुष dhanush (*nm*) a bow, an arch.

धने/श, ~श्वर dhanesh, ~shvar (*nm*) see धनपति (under धन).

धन्नासेठ dhannā:seṭh (*nm*) an opulent and affluent/money-proud man; -का नाती one who considers oneself as a V.I.P., self-conceited/money-proud (man).

धन्य dhanny (*a*) blessed, worth felicitation, fortunate; (*int.*) well done !, bravo !, blessings on you!, how fortunate !; ~ता blessedness.

धन्यवाद dhannyāva:d (*nm*) thanksgiving; an expression of gratitude; (*int.*) thanks !, thank you !

धन्वंतरि dhanvāntari (*nm*) the mythical physician of the gods, an expert physician (esp. in आयुर्वेद).

धन्वा dhannva: (*a*) wielding an arch.

धप dhap (*nf*) a thud; persistence; unending repetition of a demand; hence ~धप (*nf*); —धरना to persist, to go on repeating one's demand persistently.

धबधब dhubdhab (*nf*) a sequence of thuds (produced by the impact of a heavy and soft thing falling on some surface).

धब्बा dhabba: (*nm*) a blemish, blot, slur; stain, taint; speck; —लगना to have a blot, to be blemished; to be infamized.

धम dhām (*nf*) ā thud, report resulting from the fall of a heavy object or its movement on the ground; ~धम recurrence of the sound of धम; –से with a report or thud.

धमक dhamāk (*nf*) the vibrations caused by the impact or movement of a heavy object on a suface; thumping sound; the report of moving footsteps; stamping sound; throbbing sound, pulsation; **–लगना** to be affected by an impact.

धमकना dhamaknā: (*v*) to fall with a thud; –,**आ/जा** to make a sudden swift appearance here/there.

धमकाना dhamka:nā: (*v*) to threaten, to intimidate.

धमकी dhamki: (*nf*) a threat, bluster; **–देना** to threaten, to intimidate; **–में आना** to yield to a threat, to be intimidated.

धमधमा/ना dhāmdhamā:nā: (*v*) to produce a sequence of thuds/thumping sounds/stamping sounds; hence **~हट** (*nf*).

धमधूसर dhamdhu:sar (*a*) disproportionately corpulent; flabby and flaccid.

धमनी dhamnī: (*nf*) an artery.

धमाका dhamā:ka: (*nm*) a loud report, explosion, burst.

धमाचौकड़ी dhamā:chaukṛi: (*nf*) a row; tumult, turmoil; gambol; frolic; **–करना/–मचाना** to blow great guns, to be very boisterous/windy.

धमाधम dhamā:dhām (*adv*) with a constant thumping sound.

धमार dhama:r (*nm*) a form of classical music; a kind of rhythmic cycle of fourteen beats; gambol, row.

धर dhar—a Sanskrit suffix meaning he who or that which bears/carries/holds/sustains (e.g. **जलधर**, **भूधर**, etc.); (*nm*) nominal form of **धरना**; **-पकड़** mass arrests, searching and arrests, apprehensions, combing operations.

धरण dharāṉ (*nm*) the act of holding/bearing.

धर/णि, ~णी dharāṉi, ~ṉī: (*nf*) the earth; **~णीधर** a mountain.

धरती dharti: (*nf*) the earth; world; **–का फूल** a mushroom; **–का लाल** son of the soil; **–पर पाँव न पड़ना** see **ज़मीन (पर पाँव न पड़ना)**; **–से उठ जाना** to pass away.

धरन dharān (*nf*) a beam.

धरना dharnā: (*v*) to hold; to place; to put; to arrest, to apprehend; to take as husband/wife, to pawn, to pledge; (*nm*) picketing, sitting doggedly to enforce compliance of a demand; **धरा-ढका** kept in reserve, safely set aside for late use; **धर दबाना** to pounce upon, to force into a tight corner; **धरा रह जाना** to prove of no avail; not to be utilised.

धरनी dharnī: (*nf*) a beam; stand; the earth.

धरा dhara: (*nf*) the earth.

धराऊ dhara:u: (*a*) preservable (valuables, etc.); preserved for special occasions.

धरात/ल dhara:tal (*nm*) surface; surface of the earth; **~लीय** superficial, pertaining to the surface.

धराधिपति dhara:dhipati (*nm*) a king, ruler.

धराशायी dhara:sha:i: (*a*) fallen, fallen aground, razed (to the ground); **–करना** to fell, to raze to the ground; to vanquish.

धरित्री dharittri: (*nf*) the earth.

धरोहर dharohar (*nf*) a trust (in cash or kind); deposit.

धर्म dharm (*nm*) religion; faith; justice; duty; righteousness; property, attribute; -ईमान righteousness and integrity; -कर्म religious act/rite; –काँटा an accurate balance installed for public benefit (in a market); -कार्य religious rites/functions; -खाता charity account: ~गुरु religious teacher; –ग्रंथ a scripture; -चक्र the wheel of religious instruction as propounded by Lord Buddha; ~चर्या observation of religious duties/functions; -चिंतन/चिंता religious contemplation; ~च्युत fallen or deviated from duty/religion; -जिज्ञासा religious inquisitiveness; ~ज्ञ conversant with (the nature of) religion; -ज्ञान knowledge of religion, religious scholarship/learning; -तंत्र theocracy; ~तंत्रीय theocratic; ~त: according to religion, from the religious point of view; -दर्शन theology; philosophy of religion; –द्रोह profanity, infidelity to religion, heresy; ~द्रोही heretic, profane, irreligious, a traitor to one's religion, renegade; ~धुरीण staunchly devout, leading in piety; ~ध्वज/ध्वजी a religious hypocrite, pietist; pietical; carrying aloft the banner of religion; -नियम jus sacrum; ~निष्ठ pious, devout, religious-minded; ~निष्ठता/~निष्ठा piety, devoutness, religiosity; -निरपेक्ष secular; irrespective of religious consideration: ०ता secularism; ~निरपेक्ष राज्य a secular state; ~पर/परायण religious, religious-minded, devout; ~परता/परायणता religiosity, devoutness; –परिवर्तन (religious) conversion; ~पीठ religious seat; –पुस्तक see –ग्रंथ; -प्रचार religious propaganda/propagation; -प्रचारक a missionary; -प्रवचन religious discourse; ~प्राण devoted/dedicated to religion, extremely religious; -बुद्धि pious, religiously discreet; piety, religious discretion;~भीरु religion-fearing; profane, fallen from religion/duty; –भ्रष्ट gone astray from the path of religion; ~मय imbued/infused with a sense of religion, wedded to religion; -मार्ग the path of virtue, -मीमांसा religious investigation/reflection; –युद्ध crusade; righteous/principled fighting; -रक्षक a protector of religion; -रक्षा protection of religion; ~रत devoted to religion; dutiful; -रति love of religion; ~वान see ~निष्ठ; ~वीर a dauntless fighter for religion; ~व्रत a religious pledge, duty-binding; ~व्रती pledged to religion; duty-bound; ~शाला a hospice, a free-of-charge public lodging; –शास्त्र theology; theological jurisprudence; ~शास्त्री a theologian, theologist; ~शास्त्रीय theological; ~शील religious (by nature) endowed with a religious inclination; ~संकट a dilemma; -संधि a concordat; -संहिता a code of religious conduct; -सुधार reformation; ~स्व endowment; -ईमान बेच खाना to thrive at the cost of righteousness and virtue; –की बात कहना to say what is true and just; –बदलना to be converted to another faith, to change one's religion; –बिगाड़ना/लेना to cause religious dereliction; to violate the chastity of; –रखना to protect one's religion; –से डिगना to deviate from the path of righteousness/virtue, to undergo a religious dereliction.

धर्मांतर dharmā:ntar (*nm*) another religion.

धर्मांध dharmā:ndh (*a*) frenzied (in

religious matters), fanatic(al); ~ता fanaticism, religious frenzy.

धर्माचरण dharma:charā<u>n</u> (*nm*) religious conduct, acting according to the tenets of religion.

धर्माचार्य dharma:cha:ry (*nm*) a religious preceptor.

धर्मातिक्रमण dharma:tikkramā<u>n</u> (*nm*) violation/defiance of religious tenets; transgression of the bounds of religion.

धर्मात्मा dharma:tmā: (*a*) devout, religious; hence ~पन (*nm*).

धर्मादा dharma:da: (*nm*) endowment; charity; –खाता charity account.

धर्मादेश dharma:desh (*nm*) (religious) commandment.

धर्माधर्म dharma:dharm (*nm*) religion and irreligion; virtue and vice.

धर्माधिष्ठाता dharma:dhishṭha:ta: (*nm*) a religious leader, chief of a religious sect.

धर्मार्थ dharma:rth (*a*) charitable; –औषधालय a charitable dispensary; –न्यास a charitable trust.

धर्मावतार dharma:wta:r (*nm*) a term of address to a virtuous man or a dispenser of justice; justice/religion incarnate; a very virtuous man.

धर्माश्रित dharma:shshrit (*a*) based or dependent on or supported by religion or justice.

धर्मासन dharma:san (*nm*) seat of justice/religion.

धर्मिष्ठ dharmishṭh (*a*) extremely devout/religious/virtuous; hence ~ता (*nf*).

धर्मी dharmī: (*a*) religious, virtuous, pious.

धर्मोपदेश dharmopdesh (*nm*) religious discourse/precept/teachings; ~क religious preceptor/teacher.

धव/ल dhaval (*a*) white; clear; bright; beautiful; ~लता whiteness; clearness; brightness; ~लित whitened; cleared; brightened.

धवलिमा dhavalimā: (*nf*) whiteness; clearness; brightness.

धसक dhasak (*nf*) pungent smell emitted by dry tobacco leaf, chillies, etc. (which causes constant sneezing or coughing); depression; sinking, lowering (as a reaction of impact of heavy weight).

धसकन dhaskān (*nf*) depression, sinking, lowering.

धसकना dhasaknā: (*v*) to be depressed, to sink, to go low, to move downwards.

धसका dhaska: (*nm*) bronchitis, dry cough; coughing reaction caused by the blocking of the windpipe.

धसमसाना dhasmasa:nā: (*v*) to sink, to move downwards, to be swallowed by the earth.

धाँध/ली dhā:dhli: (*nf*) chaos, chaotic state; arbitrary conduct, arbitrariness; highhandedness, outrage; ~लेबाज one who indulges in highhandedness, of outrageous character; hence ~लेबाजी (*nf*).

धाँस dhā:s (*nf*) offensive/pungent smell causing constant sneezing or coughing.

धाक dha:k (*nf*) commanding/overwhelming influence, sway; awe; –जमना/बँधना to command overwhelming influence, to hold sway; –बैठना to have overwhelming influence/sway; –बैठाना to establish overwhelming influence / sway; –होना to be held in, or regarded with, awe.

धाकड़ dha:kaṛ (*a*) dauntless; daring, dashing; headstrong; hence ~पन (*nm*).

धागा dha:ga: (*nm*) a thread.

धाड़ dha:ṛ; –**मारना**, –**मारकर रोना** to cry aloud/wildly, to lament loudly.

धातु dha:tu (*nf*) a metal; constituent elements (of the body); semen; root; ~**कर्म** metallurgy; ~**कर्मी** metallurgist; -**क्षय** elemental/vital decay; ~**नाशक** causing elemental decay, vitality–exhausting; -**पुष्टि** vitalisation of the semen; -**युग** metal age, metallikum; ~**वर्द्धक** vitality–raising, augmenting vitality; ~**वाद** alchemy; ~**वादी** an alchemist; -**विज्ञान/विद्या** metallurgy; ~**शोधन** metallurgical operation.

धातुमय dha:tumay (*a*) metallic; abounding in metal(s).

धात्री dha:ttri: (*nf*) a wet-nurse, foster-mother; midwife; –**कर्म** a wet-nurse's job or profession; -**विद्या** midwifery.

धात्वर्थ dha:ttvarth (*nm*) root meaning.

धात्विक dha:ttvik (*a*) metallic; (*nm*) a metallurgist.

धात्वीय dha:ttvi:y (*a*) metallic.

धान dhā:n (*nm*) paddy; –**का खेत** a paddy-field.

धानी dha:nı: (*a*) light green; (*nf*) a receptacle; stand, cupboard.

धानुक dhā:nuk (*nm*) a low caste (in the Hindu caste system).

धान्य dha:nny (*nm*) crop; -**कोष** a barn, granary.

धान्यागार dha:nnyā:ga:r (*nm*) a barn, granary.

धाबा dha:ba: (*nm*) see **ढाबा**.

धाम dhā:m (*nm*) residence, abode; seat of a diety; the four chief pilgrimage centres (of the Hindus).

धाम (मि) न dha:mā(ı)n (*nf*) a typical Indian snake (said to have the venom stored in its tail).

धायँ dhā̧:y (*nf*) sound of a gun shot; -**धायँ** a sequence of gunshots; –**करना** to fire a gun.

धाय dha:y (*nf*) see **धात्री**.

धार dha:r (*nf*) an edge; sharp edge; sharpness; current; flow; jet; an adjectival suffix meaning one who holds or supports (as **कर्णधार**). ~**दार** sharp; –**धरना** to sharpen (as a knife, sword, etc); –**बँधना** to flow non-stop; to flow out in a jet; –**के संग तैरना** to swim with the flowing side, to go afloat with the current; to take to an easy course.

धारक dha:rak (*nm*) see **धारणकर्त्ता** (under **धारण**); bearer.

धारण dha:rā̱n (*nm*) holding; wielding; supporting, maintenance/maintaining; wearing; assumption; retention; ~**कर्ता** one who holds/maintains/wields/wears; -**क्षमता/शक्ति** retentiveness, power of retention; capacity.

धारणा dha:rṉā: (*nf*) an impression; concept, notion, idea; (power of) retention (also -**शक्ति**).

धारणीय dha:raṉı:y (*a*) worth retaining/remembering/wearing/holding

धारयि/ता dha:raita: (*nm*) see **धारणकर्त्ता** (under **धारण**); hence ~**त्री** (*nf*).

धारा dha:ra: (*nf*) current, stream; flow (of water etc.), eddy; section (of law); clause (of a bill); ~**प्रवाह** fluent, non-stop, incessant; ~**वाहिक/वाही** serial; serialised; -**सभा** a legislative assembly, legislature; ~**सार (वर्षा)** incessant and heavy (downpour).

धारित dha:rit (*a*) held; maintained; wielded; worn.

धारिता dha:rita: (*nf*) retentiveness; capacity.

धारी dha:ri: (*nf*) a stripe; line; an adjectival suffix meaning one who or that which holds/supports/possesses/maintains/wears; ~**दार** striped, striate.

धारोष्ण dha:roshṉ (*a*) (milk) fresh from the udders, just milked.

धार्मिक dha:rmɪk (*a*) religious, religious-minded; pertaining to a religion or following the tenets of a faith, **–कृत्य** religious rite; **~ता** religiosity, piety.

धावक dha:vak (*nm*) a runner.

धावन dha:vān (*nm*) (the act or process of) running; run; **–पथ** runway.

धावल्य dha:vally (*nm*) see **धवलता**.

धावा dha:va: (*nm*) a raid, charge, attack, assault; **–करना** to attack, to raid; **–बोलना** to launch an attack/expedition; **–मारना** to cover a long distance, to make a long march; **–होना** to be raided/attacked.

धिक् dhik—an interjectional word denoting censure, contempt, aversion, etc.; shame ! fie !

धिक्कार dhikka:r (*nm*) censure; curse; opprobrium, condemnation.

धिक्कारना dhikka:rnā: (*v*) to censure; to curse; to condemn, to reproach.

धींगरा dhɪ:gra: (*nm*) an indolent and impish person; a robust rogue.

धींगाधींगी dhɪ:ga:dhɪ:gi: (*nf*) violent or forcible self-imposing technique or effort, high-handedness, high-handed ways.

धींगामुश्ती dhɪ:ga:mushti: (*nf*) see **धींगाधींगी**; a scuffle.

धीमा dhi:mā: (*a*) slow; dull; mild; low; gentle; **~पन** slowness; mildness; gentleness; hence **धीमी** (*fem.*)

धीया dhi:ya: (*nf*) a daughter.

धीर dhi:r (*a*) patient; resolute, firm, steady; slow; (*nm*) consolation, solace; patience; **~चेता** of steady mind, firm and resolute; **~प्रशांत** (a category of hero in traditional Indian poetics) whose characteristic is quiet gallantry; quietly gallant; **~ललित** (a category of traditional Indian poetical hero) whose personality is characterised by steady gallantry and frolicsomeness;**–बँधाना** to console; **–धीरा सो गँभीरा** still waters run deep.

धीरज dhi:raj (*nm*) patience; fortitude; composure; **–छूटना** to lose patience; **–देना/–बँधाना** to console.

धीर/ता, ~त्व dhi:r/ta: (*nf*), ~attv (*nm*) composure; patience; fortitude.

धीरे dhi:re (*adv*) slowly; gently, mildly; **-धीरे** by slow degrees, by and by, gradually; **–से** slowly, quietly, stealthily.

धीरोदात्त dhiroda:tt (*a*) (a category of hero in traditional Indian poetics) characterized by quiet gallantry and loftiness of conduct.

धीरोद्धत dhi:roddhat (*a*) (a category of hero in traditional Indian poetics) characterized by carefree composure and insolence of conduct.

धीवर dhi:var (*nm*) a low caste (in traditional Hindu social order) subsisting by fishing and sailing etc.

धुंध dhūndh (*nf*) mist, fog; haze; **–छा जाना, आँखों के आगे** to have one's vision blurred.

धुंधकारी dhūndhka:ri: (*a*) mischievous, naughty; tumult-raising.

धुँधलका dhūdhalka: (*nm*) twilight, darkishness, duskiness; haziness; **–छा जाना** to be(come) dusky.

धुँधला dhūndhla: (*a*) hazy, dim, misty, foggy; faded; blurred, vague; **~पन** haziness, dimness, mistiness; fogginess; vagueness; blur; fadedness; **–करना** to dim; to turn vague; to make hazy; to blur.

धुँधलाना dhūdhla:nā: (*v*) to be dimmed; to be turned vague; to become hazy; to be blurred/to blur; to fade.

धुंधाना dhūdha:nā: (*v*) to emit smoke/fumes; to fume.

धुंधुआना dhūdhua:nā: (*v*) see **धुंधाना**.

धुआं dhūā: (*nm*) smoke; fume; ~**कश** a chimney; ~**दार/धुएंदार** smoky; ~**धार** fiery; violent; eloquent; torrential; non-stop; ~**सा** a chimney; –**देना** to emit fumes/smoke; –**निकालना** to fret and fume; –**होना** to turn black; – **वहाँ आग, जहाँ** where there is smoke, there is fire; **धुएं के बादल उड़ाना** to indulge in tall talk, to talk through one's hat.

धुआंयध dhuā:yādh (*nf*) smokiness, smack of smoke; a touch of smoke (in eatables, etc).

धुआंना dhūā:nā: (*v*) to be smokey, to smudge, to be disflavoured by smoke; to acquire a touch of smokiness.

धुकड़-पुकड़ dhukaṛ-pukaṛ (*nf*) pit(a) pat; palpitation; suspense; –**लगी रहना** to be in a constant suspense; to be apprehensively uneasy.

धुकधुकी dhukdhuki: (*nf*) throbbing (of the heart); suspense; –**बंद होना** the heart-throb to stop.

धुकपुकी dhukpuki: (*nf*) see **धुकधुकी**.

धुकुड़-पुकुड़ dhukuṛ-pukuṛ (*nf*) see **धुकड़-पुकड़**.

धुत्त dhutt (*a*) stupefied (by liquor); besotted (with); steeped (in); –**होना** to be dead drunk; to go off one's head.

धुन dhūn (*nf*) assiduity, perseverence; mania, fad; ardour; tune, keynote; –**का पक्का** persevering; assiduous; resolute; –**लगी रहना** to follow (something) resolutely, to be constantly after; –**लगी रहना, किसी की** to get a person on the brain; –**सवार होना** to concentrate feverishly on something, to be in the grip of an ardent desire.

धुनकी dhunki: (*nf*) a cotton-carding bow.

धुनना dhunnā: (*v*) to card or comb as (cotton); to beat thoroughly; to go on repeating; –, **सिर** lit. to beat the head with the palms —to repent, to lament, to wail.

धुनाई dhuna:i: (*nf*) carding; beating, thrashing.

धुनिया dhunıyā: (*nm*) a cotton-carder

धुनी dhunı: (*a*) persevering; assiduous; resolute, having the quality of constant and steadfast pursuit of an aim.

धुप्पल dhuppal (*nm*) bluff, bluffing; ~**बाज** a bluffer; ~**बाजी** bluffing.

धुमैला dhumaila: (*a*) smoky, of the colour of smoke.

धुरंधर dhurāndhar (*a*) pre-eminent (as a scholar), leading, par-excellence, of the top-most grade; (*nm*) a pastmaster.

धुर dhur (*a*) extreme, remotest; (*nm*) extremity; –**से** from the outset; from the extreme point; –**ऊपर** at the uppermost extreme.

धुरा dhura: (*nm*) axle, axis; shaft.

धुरी dhuri: (*nf*) axis, axle; pivot; –**होना** to be the pivot, to be at the centre, to enjoy the key position.

धुरीण dhurı:n—an adjectival suffix meaning leading, outstanding, foremost (as **धर्मधुरीण**).

धुर्रा dhurra: (*nm*) powder, dust; rustic, incivil; axle, axis; **धुर्रे उड़ाना** to tear to pieces, to ruin, to devastate.

धुलना dhulnā: (*v*) to be washed, to be cleansed; to be undone.

धुलाई dhula:i: (*nf*) the act or process of washing, a wash; washing charges.

धुस्सा dhussa: (*nm*) a kind of coarse and thick blanket.

धूधू dhu:dhu: (*nf*) frou-frou of flaming fire; **–करके जलना** to burn with flames rising high.

धूनी dhu:nı: (*nf*)fumigation; burning of incense; the fire lit by a Hindu mendicant to inhale smoke for penance or for keeping warm; **–जगाना/रमाना** to activise/keep alive the **धूनी**; to fumigate; to turn into an ascetic.

धूप dhu:p (*nf*) the sun; sunshine; incense, gum benzoin; **~घड़ी** a sundial; **–चढ़ना** the sun to rise high in the sky, to be nearing midday; **-छाँह** sun and shade; a kind of cloth with a sun and shade touch; (fig.) happiness and sorrow; **~दान** an incensory; a thurible; thurification, incensing; **~दानी/पात्र** an incensory, a thurible; **~दार** sunny; **-दीप** accessories for worship—incense (–stick) and lamp; **~बत्ती** an incense-stick; **~स्नान** basking; **–खाना** to bask in the sun; to be heat-struck; to be sun-treated; **–दिखाना** to put or spread in the sun; **–देना** to burn incense (for religious performance); to spread out in the sun (as clothes etc.); **–में बाल सफ़ेद होना** to age without experience; to be old and yet devoid of wisdom; **–लेना/–सेकना** to bask in the sun.

धूम dhū:m (*nm*) smoke; fume; (*nf*) fanfare, tumult, bustle, pomp; ado; eceat; boom; **~कर** a smoker; **~केतु** a comet; **-धड़क्का/~धाम** hustle and bustle, fanfare, tumult, eclat; pomp; **~धाम से** with fanfare, with great pomp and eclat; in a tumultuous manner; **~पान** smoking; **~यान** a railway train; **–मचना/होना** to have great fanfare, a tumult to be raised/created; to be or become famous or notorious.

धूमायमान dha:ma:ymā:n (*a*) fumigated, rendered smoky, filled with or full of smoke or fume.

धूमिल dhu:mil (*a*) vague; blurred; fumigated; hence **~ता** (*nf*).

धूम्र dhu:mmr (*nm*) smoke; fume; (*a*) smoke-coloured; **~पान** smoking; **~वर्ण** smoke-coloured.

धूर्त dhu:rt (*a*) knave, cunning, crooked; rascal; **~ता** knavery, cunningness, crookedness; rascality, humbuggery.

धूल dhu:l (*nf*) dust, dirt, **–उड़ना** to be devastated/ruined; **–की रस्सी बटना** to attempt an impossibility, to labour in vain; **–चटाना** to humble to the dust, to knock down; to inflict a conclusive defeat; **–चाटना** to eat dirt, to eat crow; **–झाड़ना, –झाड़कर खड़े हो जाना** lit. to dust off—to dust off the humiliation of defeat; **–झोंकना, आँखों में** to throw dust in the eyes of, to pull wool over somebody's eyes; **–फाँकना** to wander without a job; **–में मिलना** to be ruined, to be devastated; **–में लट्ठ मारना** to strike in vain, to make a vain bid; to make a random effort.

धूलि dhu:li (*nf*) dust; dirt; **~धूसर/~धूसरित** steeped in dust, dusty.

धूसर dhu:sar (*a*) dusty; dust-coloured.

धूसरित dhu:sarit (*a*) filled or strewn with dust; turned dusty.

धृति dhriti (*nf*) fortitude, steadiness; **~मान** steady, fortitudinous.

धृष्ट dhrishṭ (*a*) contumelious, impudent, insolent; obtrusive; impertinent; **~ता** impudence, insolence; obtrusiveness, impertinence.

धेनु dhenū (*nf*) a (milch) cow.

धेला dhela: (*nm*) a half-pice coin

(now out of currency); –करना to undo, to reduce to naught; –पास न होना to be penniless, to be extremely indigent.

धेली dheli: (*nf*) a half-rupee coin.

धैर्य dhairy (*nm*) patience; fortitude, endurance; -परीक्षा test of one's endurance/patience; –धरना/रखना to hold one's horse; –बँधाना to console.

धोखा dhokha: (*nm*) deception, deceit; fraud, cheating, guile; subterfuge; a scarecrow; -धड़ी beguilement; cheating, deceit; humbuggery; धोखेबाज a cheat, swindler; shyster; deceitful, guileful; fraudulent; धोखेबाज़ी fraud, deception, cheating; humbuggery; –खाना to suffer deceipt, to be taken in, to be deceived/beguiled/cheated, to be hoodwinked; –देना to play false; to deceive, to cheat, to hoodwink, to beguile; धोखे की टट्टी a Trojan horse, a camouflage, false screen, a fraudulent device; धोखे में आना/पड़ना to be taken in, to be deceived/cheated.

धोती dhoti: (*nf*) *dhoti*: —loin cloth worn by the Hndus; –ढीली होना to be demoralised; to be scared out of wits; –बिगाड़ना to be terribly scared, to have a run of loose motions.

धो/ना dhonā: (*v*) to wash; to launder; to cleanse; to undo; –कर पी जाना to leave no trace of, to eradicate the entity of; –देना to wash off, to undo; –बहाना to wash off; to nullify.

धोब dhob (*nm*) a laundry—batch of clothes sent to or from a launderer in one lot; washing; wash.

धोबी dhobi: (*nm*) a washerman, launderer; -घाट a laundering venue (by the side of a river or a tank); ~पछाड़ a wrestling trick wherein the rival wrestler is thrown over the shoulder (as a washerman dashes down a cloth); -पाट see -पछाड़; a washerman's board or stone (to strike the cloth against); –का कुत्ता, न घर का न घाट का neither fish nor fowl, a rolling stone gathers no moss; one who rides two boats is sure to be overthrown.

धोरे dhore (*ind*) near, close by.

धोवन dhowān (*nm*) a wash; water in which anything has been washed.

धौंकना dhāuknā: (*v*) to blow with bellows etc,; to fan a fire.

धौंकनी dhāuknī: (*nf*) bellows, blower; blow-pipe; –चलना to have palpitation.

धौंस dhāus (*nf*) bluster, coercive stance; awesome demeanour; ~पट्टी see धौंस; –जताना/जमाना/दिखाना to menace, to bluster; –देना to bluster into subdual; –में लेना to take in by bluster; to cause to yield by bluster; –सहना to bear with the blustering of.

धौंसा dhāusa: (*nm*) a huge kettle-drum; –बजना to be lauded all round.

धौंसिया dhāusiya: (*nm*) a kettle-drummer; blusterer.

धौरा dhaura: (*a*) white, fair; (*nm*) a betelnut piece.

धौल dhaul (*nm*) a hand-blow, buffet -धक्कड़ scuffle, row; exchange of blows; -धक्का a blow, push; -धापड़/धप्पा scuffle, exchange of blows, row; –देना to give a (hand blow.

धौला dhaula: (*a*) white; fair.

ध्यान dhyā:n (*nm*) attention, heed; meditation; contemplation; concentration of mind; ~गम्य perceivable or perceived only through contemplation/meditation, realised through contemplation/meditation; ~तत्पर/निष्ठ/पर/परायण/मग्न/रत absorbed or engrossed in contemplation/meditation; contemplative; meditative; –योग meditation-based योग; ~साध्य achievable or achieved through contemplation/meditation; ~स्थ engrossed or steeped in meditation; meditating, contemplating; –आना to remember, to recall; –छूटना to have one's meditation interrupted; to lose the concentration of mind; –देना to heed, to pay attention; to contemplate or meditate; –धरना to meditate or contemplate; –बँधना to have the mind concentrated upon; –में न लाना to ignore, not to mind; –लगाना to concentrate (upon), to meditate; –से उतरना to forget, to lose the memory of.

ध्यानाभ्यास dhya:nābbhya:s (*nm*) practice of meditation/contemplation/concentration.

ध्यानावस्था dhya:nā:vastha: (*nf*) state of meditation/contemplation; –में होना to be in meditation.

ध्यानावस्थित dhya:nā:vasthit (*a*) engrossed or absorbed in meditation/contemplation.

ध्यानी dhya:nī: (*a*) meditative; given to meditation/contemplation; –ज्ञानी given to meditation and contemplation.

ध्येय dhyey (*nm*) an aim, end; –वाद tendenciousness, a theory or attitude in literature which inspires the artist to so organise his composition as to strive for the achievement of a definite end; ~वादी tendencious.

ध्रुपद dhrupad (*nm*) a form of classical Indian music.

ध्रुव dhruv (*nm*) a pole; the polar star; (*a*) fixed, firm; permanent; –तारा the polar star; ~दर्शक a compass; –वृत्त the meridian line; –सत्य eternal truth.

ध्रुवता, ~त्व dhruv/ta: (*nf*), ~attv (*nm*) polartity; fixedness firmness; permanency.

ध्रुवाणु dhruva:n̲ū (*nm*) a polocyte.

ध्वंस dhvāns (*nm*) ruination; destruction, devastation; ~क destructive, devastating; a destroyer, devastator, one who spells ruination; ~न ruination, destruction; devastation.

ध्वंसावशेष dhwansa:vashesh (*nm*) remains, ruins.

ध्वज dhvaj (*nm*) a flag, banner, ensign, colours; -दंड a flagstaff; -पोत a flagship.

ध्वजा dhvaja: (*nf*) a flag, standard, ensign, banner; colours; ~धारी a standard-bearer; ~रोपण implantation of a flag; ~रोहण hoisting of a flag.

ध्वजोत्तोलन dhvajottolān (*nm*) see ध्वजा(~रोहण).

ध्वनन dhvanān (*nm*) sounding; suggestion (in Poetics).

ध्वनि dhvanı (*nf*) sound; suggestion (in Poetics); suggested meaning; ~की Phonetics; ~ग्राम a phoneme; ०विज्ञान phonemics; -परिवर्तन/विकार sound-change; -विज्ञान phonetics; phonology.

ध्वनित dhvanıt (*a*) sounded; suggested (meaning in Poetics).

ध्वन्यर्थ dhvannyarth (*nm*) suggested meaning; hence ~ता (*nf*).

ध्वन्यात्मक dhvannyā:tmāk (*a*) phonetic; phonolgical; suggestive, suggestion-based (poetry etc.); hence ~ता (*nf*).

ध्वस्त dhvast (*a*) ruined; destroyed, devastated; hence ~ता (*nf*).

ध्वानिक dhva:nık (*a*) acoustic; (*nm*)

acousticist; ~ता acoustics, acousticity.

ध्वानिकी dhva:nīki: (*nf*) acoustics; ~य acoustic.

न

न nā—the last letter of the fourth pentad (i.e. तवर्ग) of the Devna:gri: alphabet; (*ind.*) no, not; a typical conversational particle used for laying emphasis or ascertaining the other person's reaction (as चलो–; पत्र लिखोगे– ?); isn't it !; –तो,– neither...nor; –करना to say 'no', to refuse; to decline; to deny; –आए की खुशी न गए का दुःख if rich be not elected, if poor be not dejected; –इधर –उधर sitting on the fence; –घर का –घाट का neither fish nor fowl, neither here nor there; –नौ मन तेल/सोना होगा –राधा नाचेगी if the sky falls, we shall gather larks; –कुछ से कुछ भला something is better than nothing, better are small fish than an empty dish; –खाये –खाने दे dog in the manger; –खुदा ही मिला –विसाले सनम he who hunts two hares leaves one and loses the other, like a donkey between two heaps of hay; –जाये मांदन न पाये रफ़्तन up a gum-tree, at the end of one's wits; –तीतर –बटेर neither fish/flesh nor fowl, neither hawk nor buzzard; –बाबा आयें –घंटा बाजे no priest, no mass; –रहेगा बाँस –बजेगी बाँसुरी no root, no fruit; –सावन सूखे –भादों हरे ever drunk ever dry.

नंग-धड़ंग nāṅg-dhaṛāṅg (*a*) stark naked, completely nude.

नंगा nāṅga: (*a*) naked, nude; bare, uncovered; exposed; leafless; shameless; wicked; ~झोली (री) a thorough personal search; –नाच brazen/shameless performance, act or display; ~पन nakedness, nudeness; shamelessness; wickedness; –बुच्चा/बूचा indigent and deformed; –भूखा poverty-stricken, indigent and afflicted; –,मादरजाद stark-naked, naked as one is born; –लुच्चा mean and wicked; depraved and degenerate; नंगे पाँव bare-footed; –करना to denude, to strip (of clothes); to expose; to uncover, to bare; –हो जाना to show the cloven foot/hoof.

नंद nānd (*nf*) see ननद; (*nm*) traditionally speaking, the chief of the clan of गोपs of Gokul, who adopted कृष्ण as his son.

नंदकिशोर nāndkishor (*nm*) an epithet of कृष्ण (being the adopted son of नंद).

नंदकुमार nāndkuma:r (*nm*) see नंदकिशोर.

नंदन nāndan (*nm*) one who delights; a son; the mythological garden of इंद्र —the chief of gods; –कानन/–वन the mythological garden of Indra —the cheif of gods.

नंदलाल nāndla:l (*nm*) see नंदकिशोर.

नंदित nāndit (*a*) delighted; pleased.

नंदिनी nāndinī: (*nf*) a daughter.

नंदोई nāndoi: (*nm*) see **ननदोई**.

नंबर nāmbar (*nm*) number; marks; counting; ~**दार** a headman, village-head; ~**वार** one by one; turnwise; –**एक का** of the first order (used in derogatory senses only as –**एक का बेवकूफ़/चालाक/धोखेबाज़** etc.).

नंबरी nāmbari: (*a*) notorious; the mark of authority; of one hundred (as **नोट**); bearing a number, numbered; of the first order.

नई nai: (*a*) new; fem. of **नया** (see); –**आवती** fresh receipt; –**नवेली** young and new; –**निकोर** brand new.

नक nāk—an allomorph of **नाक** used as the first member in compound words; ~**कटा** nose-clipt, noseless, a person whose nose has been chopped off; shameless, brazen-faced; ~**चढ़ा** fastidious, peevish, irate; ~**पिच्चू** snub-nosed; ~**वानी** harassing, plaguing.

नकटा nākṭa: (*nm*) see **नक** (~**कटा**); –**जीए बुरे हवाल** he that hath ill name is half-hanged.

नकटी nākṭi: (*nf*) feminine form of **नकटा** (see); snot, nasal mucus.

नक़द naqad (*a*) cash, hard cash; (*nm*) cash, ready money; money in (the form of) coins; (*adv*) in cash; –**का व्यवहार** cash transaction; –**नारायण** lit. money—that is god; almighty cash/money.

नक़दी naqdi: (*nm*) see **नक़द**; (*a*) hand cash; –**चिट्ठा** a cash book.

नक़ब naqab (*nf*) burglary, house-breaking; ~**ज़न** a burglar; ~**ज़नी** burglary; –**लगाना** to burgle, to commit burglary.

नक़ल naqal (*nf*) a copy, duplicate; imitation; mimicking, mimicry; ~**ची** a mimicker; an imitator; one who copies; ~**नवीस** a copyist; ~**नवीसी** the office or work of a copyist; copying; –**करना** to play the ape, to imitate; –**के लिए भी अक़्ल चाहिए** even imitation has to be accomplished with a touch of intelligence; –**को अक्ल क्या** why use your wits for imitation !; –**ही सच्ची ख़ुशामद है** imitation is the sincerest flattery.

नक़ली naqli: (*a*) counterfeit, false; artificial; fabricated, fictitious; sham; spurious; impostorous.

नक़्शा naqsha: (*nm*) a map, chart, plan; pomp and show; ~**नवीस** a draftsman; ~**नवीसी** draftsmanship; **नक़्शे** symptoms; prospects; pomp and show; showing off; **नक़्शेबाज़** one who shows off a lot; **नक़्शेबाज़ी** showing off, blazonry.

नकसीर naksi:r (*nf*) spistaxis, nose-bleed; –**आना**/–**फूटना** the nose to start bleeding.

नक़ाब naqa:b (*nf*) a mask; veil; visor, vizard; –**पोश** (*a*) masked (man), wearing a mask; –**उलटना** to expose (somebody), to uncover the real man.

नका/र naka:r (*nm*) the letter **न** (na) and its sound; (*nm*) decline; refusal; negation; denial; ~**रांत** (a word)ending in **न्** (n).

नकारना naka:rnā: (*v*) to refuse, to decline; to negate; to deny; to dishonour (as a **चेक**—).

नकारात्मक naka:ra:tmāk (*a*) negative, implying refusal/denial/decline; hence ~**ता** (*nf*).

नक़्क़ाशना naqa:shnā: (*v*) to engrave; to carve; to sculpture.

नकियाना nakiya:nā: (*v*) to speak through the nose; to pester, to vex.

नकेल nakel (*nf*) a nose-string, nose-halter (of ox, bear or camel which serves as rein); wooden or iron pin fixed in camel's nose; a caves-son; –**डालना** to tame, to bring under absolute control; (किसी को) –हाथ में होना to lean a person on the hip, to exercise complete command over, to have the power to direct (somebody) at will.

नक्का nakka: (*nm*) the eye of a needle.

नक़्क़ारख़ा/ना naqqa:rḳḥa:nā: (*nm*) the kettle-drum chamber; ~ने में तूती की आवाज़ (कौन सुनता है) (who would listen to) a cry in wilderness.

नक़्क़ारची naqqa:rchi: (*nm*) a kettle-drummer, one who plays on/beats a kettle-drum.

नक़्क़ा/रा naqqa:ra: (*nm*) a huge kettle-drum; ~रा बजाकर, ~रे की चोट पर lit. by beat of drum, meaning —with a public proclamation; publicly, openly; ~रा बजाते फिरना to go about declaring openly, to proclaim by beat of drum, to blazon all round.

नक़्क़ाल naqqa:l (*nm*) a cheat; imitator; a mimic, mimicker.

नक़्क़ाश naqqa:sh (*nm*) an engraver; a carver.

नक़्क़ाशी naqqa:shi: (*nf*) engraving, carving; etching; designing; ~दार engraved; carved; etched; carrying designs.

नक्की nakki:; —करना, हिसाब to clear off, to pay in full, to be quits.

नक्कू nakku: (*a*) long-nosed (person); (a person) who thinks too much of himself; non-conforming, a butt for accusing fingers; notorious for non-conformist initiatives; fastidious; –बनना to take a non-conformist initiative, to cause accusing fingers to be raised by non-conformist conduct.

नक़्द naqd (*a* and *nm*) see नक़द.

नक़्दी naqdi: (*nm*) नक़दी.

नक़्श naqsh (*a*) engraved; imprinted; (*nm*) features; -ए-क़दम पर in the footsteps of, emulating;–, तीखे sharp features; ~दार imprinted, carrying an imprint; –होना to be imprinted; to create an impression.

नक़्शा naqsha: (*nm*) see नक़शा; ~नवीस, ~नवीसी see under नक़शा.

नक्षत्र nakshattr (*nm*) a star; a constellation, an asterism in the moon's path comprised of 27 or 28 stars; ~धारी born under a lucky star, destined to rise high; ~लोक the sky; ~वान lucky, fortunate; ~विद an astrologist; ~विद्या Astrology.

नख nakh (*nm*) nail; (*nf*) a fruit akin to the pear in shape, size and taste; ~क्षत bruises caused by the nails (in amorous sport); ~शिख top to bottom, the entire physical frame; ~शिख-वर्णन elaborate description of physical charms; –से शिख तक from top to bottom, from head to heel.

नख़रा naḳḥra: (*nm*) coquetry; flirtatious airs, airs and graces; –तिल्ला coquetry, coquette; नख़रेबाज़ coquetish; नख़रेबाज़ी coquette, coquetry; नख़रे दिखाना, नख़रे करना to coquet.

नख़लिस्तान naḳḥlista:n (*nm*) an oasis.

नख़ास naḳḥa:s (*nm*) a market-place; cattle-sale market; horse-market.

नग nag (*nm*) a gem, jewel, precious stone; a piece, number; an item; a mountain; ~पति the Himalayas.

नगण्य nagāṉṉy (*a*) trifle, trifling, trite; insignificant; worthless; inappreciable; hence ~ता (*nf*).

नगद nagad (*a* and *nm*) see नक़द.

नगदी nagdi: (*nm*) hard cash.

नग़मा nagmā: (*nm*) a song; melody.

नगर nagar (*nm*) a city; town; –का urban; -निगम municipal corporation; ~पालिका municipality, municipal committee; ~पिता city father, municipal councillor; -प्रमुख the mayor; -प्रांत urban area; a suburb;

skirt of a city; -रक्षा civil defence; -राज्य a city state; -वधू a prostitute; ~वासी a citizen; townfolk.

नगरी nagri: (*nf*) a big city.

नगा/ड़ा naga:ṛa: (*nm*) a big kettle-drum, timbal, tomtom; ~ड़े की चोट पर openly, publicly.

नगीना nagi:nā: (*nm*) a gem, jewel; ~गर/साज a gem-smith, one who studs or insets a gem (in an ornament etc.); –जड़ना to stud or inset a jewel/gem.

नग्न nagn (*a*) nude, naked; uncovered; ~ता nudeness, nakedness; shamelessness, wickedness; –नृत्य a show of shamelessness, a brazen performance/act/display.

नचाना nacha:nā: (*v*) to cause/make somebody to dance (to one's tune), to cause to act at will; to move the pupil(s) of the eye(s); (as आँख–); to harass; to tease.

नज़दीक nazdi:k (*adv*) near, close, in the vicinity; –के close to/by, near; नज़दीकी near, close (as रिश्तेदार).

नज़र nazar (*nf*) sight; eyesight, vision; look, glance; attention; gift, present, offering; influence cast by an evil eye; ~बंद in detention, under watch; an internee, detenu; ~बंदी detention, internment; ~अंदाज़ करना to brush aside, to take no notice of, to overlook, to ignore, to disregard; –आना to come in sight or view; to see, to appear; –करना to present, to offer; to look, to see; –गड़ाना to gaze at, to look with a fixed gaze/intently; –चुराना to evade being sighted, to avoid an exchange of looks;–दौड़ाना to look round, to have a hurried look around; –न उठना not to be in a position to look straight, to be downcast through shame; –पड़ना to spot, to sight; –पर चढ़ना to catch the fancy of, to have a liking for, to be attracted (towards); to appear pretty; –फिसलना to be dazzled, not to be able to fix the eyes at one point; –बचाना to try to evade, to avoid being sighted/spotted; –बदलना one's favours to be withdrawn; one's attitude to undergo a change; to assume a different posture; –लगना to be afflicted by an evil eye, to be struck by an ominous glance; नज़रें चार होना to catch each other's eye, to exchange glances; नज़रें मिलना to look into each other's eyes, to catch each other's eyes; नज़रेसानी revision; नज़रों में चढ़ना to be in good books of, to go up in the esteem of; नज़रों से गिरना to be deep in one's black books, to be in bad books of; नज़रों से दूर दिल से दूर far from eye, far from heart, out of sight out of mind.

नज़राना nazra:nā: (*nm*) a present, gift.

नज़रिया nazariya: (*nm*) point of view, viewpoint; angle.

नज़ला nazla: (*nm*) catarrh, cold: –गिरना to suffer from bad cold; to be a victim of somebody's wrath.

नज़ाकत naza:kat (*nf*) delicacy, tenderness, grace; –दिखाना to make two bites of a cherry.

नजात naja:t (*nf*) salvation, liberation, riddance; –मिलना to be freed/liberated.

नज़ारत naza:rat (*nf*) the position or office of a *na:zir*.

नज़ारा naza:ra: (*nm*) a scene, view; spectacle, sight; –है, क्या what a sight !

नज़ीर nazi:r (*nf*) a precedent; an example, instance; –पेश करना to cite a precedent.

नजूमी naju:mi: (*nm*) an astrologer.

नज़ूल naju:l (*nm*) the improvement trust.

नज़्म nazm (*nf*) a poem; verse.

नट naṭ (*nm*) an acrobat; a particular low-caste amongst the Hindus who earn their livelihood through acrobatic performances; a member of this caste; a rope-dancer, funambulist, tumbler; an actor; **~नागर** Lord Krishṉā; **~राज** Lord Shiv; **~वर** Lord Krishṉā;. hence **नटिनी** (*nf*).

नटख/ट naṭkhaṭ (*a*) naughtiness, mischievous; **~टपना/~टपन** naughtiness, mischievousness; also **~टी** (*nf*).

नटना naṭnā: (*v*) to go back on one's words, to refuse; to negate, to say 'no'.

नटी naṭi: (*nf*) feminine form of **नट** (see); an actress: the stage manager's spouse.

नत nat (*a*) bent, tilted, curved; bowed; humble(d); **~मस्तक** having the head bowed down (through modesty, shame, etc.); respectful.

नति nati (*nf*) inclination, bias; bend; modesty.

नतिनी natini: (*nf*) a grand-daughter.

नतीजा nati:ja: (*nm*) the result; consequence; conclusion.

नत्थी natthi: (*a*) attached; annexed; appended, tagged; **–करना** to tag; to attach; to annex.

नथ nath (*nf*) a nose-ring; nose-rope (for bullocks, etc.); **–उतारना** in feudal times, a ceremony amongst prostitutes when a young girl stepped into the family profession and was surrendered to a wealthy customer for the first time in return for enormous reward or consideration.

नथ/ना nathnā: (*nm*) a nostril, nares; **~ने फुलाना** to be in rage, to be infuriated; **~ने सिकोड़ना** to express dislike or disgust through shrinkage of the nostrils.

नथनी nathni: (*nf*) a small **नथ** (see).

नद nad (*nm*) a big river.

नदारद nada:rad (*a*) missing, not present; disappeared, vanished; absent.

नदी nadi: (*nf*) a river; **-घाटी** river valley; **-तल** the river bed; **-नाव संयोग** a chance meeting; **-पात्र** the river basin; **~मुख** embouchure, mouth of a river; **–बहाना, ख़ून की** to shed a stream of blood, to cause immense bloodshed.

नदीश nadi:sh (*nm*) the ocean, sea.

ननद nanād (*nf*) sister-in-law, husband's sister.

ननदोई nandoi: (*nm*) brother-in-law, the husband of a woman's **ननद** (see).

ननसाल nansa:l (*nf*) mother's paternal home.

ननिहाल naniha:l (*nf*) see **ननसाल**.

ननु-नच nanū-nach (*ind.*) if and but, hitch; **–,बिना** without questioning, without any ifs and buts, without any hitch.

नन्हाँ nannhā: (*a*) tiny; small; wee; to young.

नपा napa: (*a*) measured; **-तुला** precisely assessed; precise; **नपी-तुली बात कहना** to speak by the card.

नपाई napa:i: (*nf*) measurement, the process of and charges paid for measuring.

नपुंसक napunsak (*nm*) a eunuch; an impotent person; a coward; (*a*) impotant; cowardly, unmanly; **~ता/त्व** impotence; unmanliness; cowardice; **–लिंग** neuter gender.

नफ़रत nafrat (*nf*) hatred, dislike; contempt, abomination; **~अंगेज** contemptible, hateful, abominable, despicable.

नफ़री nafri: (*nf*) daily wage (of a

labourer); a work-day, man-day.

नफ़ा nafa: (*nm*) profit; gain; advantage; -नुकसान समझना to know which side one's bread is buttered; to know one's good and bad; –खाना to profit through (some act), to reap the advantage of.

नफ़ासत nafa:sat (*nf*) nicety, fineness; sophistication; ~पसन्द dainty; one who has a liking for exquisiteness and excellence; cox-comb; hence ~पसंदी (*nf*).

नफ़ी nafi: (*nf*) minus; negation.

नफ़ी/री nafi:ri: (*nf*) a clarionet; ~रची/~रीबाज़ a clarionet-player.

नफ़ीस nafi:s (*a*) nice, fine, excellent, exquisite, dainty.

नफ़्स nafs (*nm*) soul, self; passion; ~परस्त selfish; wanton; debauch; ~परस्ती selfishness; wantonness; debauchery.

नबी nabi: (*nm*) a prophet, a divine messenger.

नब्ज़ nabz (*nf*) pulse (of the hand); –छूटना, –न रहना the pulse beat to stop; –टटोलना/देखना to feel the pulse; –पहचानना/–से वाक़िफ़ होना to know through and through, to have one's hand on the pulse of, to be apprised of the mental working of.

नब्बाज़ nabba:z (*nm*) a pulse-specialist, an expert in diagnosing through check-up of the pulse-beat.

नब्बे nabbe (*a*) ninety; (*nm*) the number ninety.

नभ nabh (*nm*) the sky; firmament; ether; ~गामी/चर/चारी sky-faring.

नभश्चर nabhashchar (*nm*) see नभचर (under नभ).

नभोगति nabhogati (*nf*) movement in the sky.

नभोगामी nabhoga:mı: (*a*) see नभ (~गामी).

नभोमणि nabhomāni (*nm*) the sun.

नमः nāmāh (*nm*) deferential salutation, bowing.

नम nām (*a*) moist; humid, damp; –होना, आँखें eyes to get wet, tears to show up in the eyes.

नमक nāmāk (*nm*) salt; table salt; (touch of) prettiness; ~ख़्वार loyal, loyal servant; hence ~ख़्वारी; ~दान/दानी salt-cellar; ~हराम ungrateful, disloyal; faithless, unfaithful; ~हरामी ungratefulness, ingratitude; disloyalty; faithlessness; ~हलाल one who serves the master loyally; loyal, grateful, faithful; ~हलाली rendering loyal service to the master, gratefulness, gratitude, loyalty; –(का हक़) अदा करना to discharge (one's) obligation to the master, to make any sacrifice to preserve one's loyalty; –खाना, किसी का to have subsisted on somebody's patronage, (and therefore to be under a debt of gratitude);–छिड़कना, कटे पर/घाव पर/जले पर to add insult to injury, to inflict one affliction upon another; –फूटकर निकलना to get punishment for disloyalty/ingratitude/infidelity; -मिर्च लगाना to exaggerate (things); to put forth a hyperbolic description; –होना, चेहरे पर to have pretty looks.

नमकी/न nāmki:n (*a*) salty, salted; saltish, saline; pretty, beautiful; (*nm*) a salty dish of snacks; ~नी prettiness, pretty looks.

नमदा nāmda: (*nm*) felt; coarse woollen blanket.

नमन nāmān (*nm*) deferential salutation, bowing; flexure; dip; –करना to bow, to salute deferentially.

नमना nāmnā: (*v*) to bow, to salute, to make obeisance.

नमनीय nāmnı:y (*a*) worth salutation/

bowing down to; respectable, adorable; elastic; plastic; flexible; hence ~ता (*nf*).

नमस्कार nāmaska:r (*nm*) salutation, a term of greeting; adieu !, so long; –करना to salute, to greet; to say good bye; ०, दूर से keep away, not to have anything to do with.

नमस्ते nāmaste (*nf*) lit. salutation to you; see नमस्कार.

नमाज़ nāma:z (*nf*) a formal prayer (by the muslims); ~गाह a mosque, venue for the muslims to offer their prayers; –अदा करना/पढ़ना to offer prayers.

नमाज़ी nāma:zi: (*a*) meticulously regular in नमाज़ (see); a devout, muslom.

नमी nāmī: (*nf*) humidity; dampness; moisture; ~दार humid; damp; moist.

नमूदार namū:da:r (*a*) manifest; apparent; –होना to appear, to make appearance, to be manifest.

नमूना namū:nā: (*nm*) a sample; specimen, model; design; type; pattern; –होना to be a peculiar specimen; to be strange.

नम्य nāmmy (*a*) see ~नमनीय; ~ता plasticity; elasticity; flexibility.

नम्र nāmmr (*a*) modest, humble; polite; meek, submissive; ~ता modesty, humility, politeness; meekness, submissiveness; –निवेदन humble submission.

नय nay (*nm*) policy; ~शास्त्र political science.

नयन nāyān (*nm*) an eye; –कोर extreme end of the eye; ~गोचर visible, tangible; ~छद/पंट an eyelid; ~जल/वारि/सलिल tear(s); ~पथ the visual range; –विषय a visual object.

नयनाभिराम naynā:bhira:m (*a*) charming, beautiful, attractive; hence ~ता (*nf*).

नया naya: (*a*) new, novel; fresh; unused; green; recent; modern; raw; inexperienced; young; ~पन newness, novelty; originality; unacquainted; not known; –गुल खिलाना (said derisively) to do something unusual and unseemly; to give a novel and peculiar turn to events; –नौकर तीरंदाज़ a new broom sweeps clean; –नौ दिन पुराना सौ दिन while the new perishes, the old endures; –मुल्ला अल्ला ही अल्ला पुकारता है, –मुल्ला दिन में दस बार नमाज़ पढ़ता है the newer the initiate, the more rigid his approach; –शिकार फँसना to get at a game; नई राह निकालना to break fresh ground; नए सिरे से *ab initio*, afresh.

नयाचार naya:cha:r (*nm*) protocol; -प्रमुख chief of protocol; –विभाग the protocol department.

नर nar (*nm*) a man; male; (*a*) male; ~कपाल human skull; ~केसरी/केहरी/शार्दूल a lion-hearted/lion-like man; incarnation of Lord Vishnū; see नृसिंह; ~त्व manhood; ~नाथ a king; -नारी man and woman; ~पति a king; ~पशु a beastly man; ~पिशाच a devilish man, cruel man, atrocious; ~पुंगव foremost amongst men; an outstanding man; ~बलि human sacrifice; ~भक्षी a man-eater; cannibal; ~मेध human sacrifice, killing of man; ०यज्ञ a sacrifice (यज्ञ) involving killing of a human being; ~लोक this world; -वध slaughter of human being(s); ~सिंह see नृसिंह; -हत्या see नरवध; ~हरि see नृसिंह; –चेती नहीं होत है प्रभु चेती तत्काल man doth what he can and God what He will.

नरक narak (*nm*) the hell, inferno; a place of great torture or agony; a place unfit for human habitation;

–कुंड an inferno; a hell-pool (wherein evil souls are supposed to be dipped or dropped for torture); ~गामी hell-going, heading for the hell; ~पाल Yamra:j—Lord of the hell; -यातना infernal agony, damnation; ~वास living in hell, infernal stay, a stay involving great torture and agony; –का कीड़ा a hellish creature, low sinful man; –भोगना to suffer (the agonies of) hell, to undergo immense suffering; –में पड़ना to go to hell.

र/कट, ~कुल nar/kaṭ, ~kul (*nm*) reed.

रगि/स nargis (*nf*) the narcissus plant and its flowers; ~सी a kind of cloth on which narcissus flowers are imprinted; like a narcissus flower, as beautiful as a narcissus flower (as—आँखें).

रम narām (*a*) soft, gentle; delicate; pliant, flexible; kind, merciful; moderate; ~दिल soft/kind hearted; –पंथ moderate course; ~पंथी moderate; –,कभी, कभी गरम to blow hot and cold; –पड़ना to soften down.

रमा narmā: (*nm*) a kind of cotton.

रमाना narmā:nā: (*v*) to soften, to become gentle, to mellow, to become moderate.

रमी narmı: (*nf*) softness; gentleness; delicacy; kindness; moderateness.

रसों narsō (*adv*) two days after tomorrow; two days before yesterday.

राधम nara:dhām (*nm*) the meanest of men; vile/depraved person.

राधिप nara:dhip (*nm*) a king.

राधिपति nara:dhipati (*nm*) a king.

रेंद्र narēndr (*nm*) a king.

रेश naresh (*nm*) a king.

रेश्वर nareshwar (*nm*) a king.

रोत्तम narottām (*nm*) the foremost/best of men; an excellent man.

नर्क nark (*nm*) see नरक.

नर्कट narkaṭ (*nm*) see नरकट.

नर्कुल narkul (*nm*) see नर/कट, ~कुल.

नर्गि/स nargis (*nf*) see नरगिस; ~सी see नरगिसी (under नरगिस).

नर्तक nartak (*nm*) a dancer; -दल a troupe of dancers.

नर्तकी nartaki: (*nf*) a female dancer, dancing girl; ~,राज a court dancer.

न/र्तन nartān (*nm*) dancing, dance; ~र्तित dancing; danced.

न/र्म narm (*a*) see नरम; ~र्मी see नरमी.

नर्स nars (*nf*) a nurse.

नल nal (*nm*) a pipe; tap, hydrant; one of the leading monkey-warriors of Ram's army that fought the demon-king Ra:vān̲; ~का a pipe, hydrant; ~कूप a tube-well.

नलिका nalika: (*nf*) a tubule; tube, pipe; ~कार tubular.

नलिन nalin (*nm*) a lotus.

नलिनी nalinı: (*nf*) a lotus; lily.

नली nali: (*nf*) a tube; tubule; pipe, spout; barrel (of a gun).

नवंबर navāmbar (*nm*) (the month of) November.

नव nav (*a*) new, novel, neo–; young; fresh; recent; modern; nine; (*nm*) the number nine; ~ ग्रह the nine planets according to Indian astronomy, viz. सूर्य, चंद्र, मंगल, बुध, गुरु, शुक्र, शनि, राहु, केतु; ~जात newly born, nascent, neo-natal; ~ता/~त्व newness, novelty; ~धा of nine ways/kinds; ninefold; ० भक्ति the nine ways of भक्ति (see) viz. श्रवण, कीर्तन, स्मरण, पादसेवन, अर्चन, वंदन, दास्य, सख्य, आत्मनिवेदन; ~निधि the nine treasures of कुबेर (the god of riches), viz. पद्म, महापद्म, शंख, मकर, कच्छप, मुकुंद, कुंद, नील, खर्व; ~नीत butter; ~पाषाण युग neolithic age; ~मानववाद neo-humanism; ~मार्क्सवाद neo-Marxism; ~युवक a young man; youth; ~युवती a young woman; ~युवा see ~युवक; ~यौवना a woman in the prime of youth, a woman in youthful bloom; ~रत्न nine great men of a king's court; the nine gems viz. pearl (मोती), diamond (हीरा) etc.; ~रस the nine रसs (see) in literature according to Indian poetics, viz. शृंगार, हास्य, करुण, रौद्र, वीर, भयानक, वीभत्स, अद्भुत, शांत; ~रात्र the nine days and nights in चैत्र and आश्विन from प्रतिपदा to नवमी when special worship of goddess दुर्गा is performed; ~वधू newly-wed bride; young bride; ~शब्दघटन neologism; ~शिक्षित neo-literate; ~साक्षर neo-literate.

नवमी navmī: (*nf*) the ninth day of each lunar fortnight.

नवल naval (*a*) new, novel, neo–; fresh; young; recent; ~किशोर an epithet of Lord Krishn̲ā; young man; hence ~ता (*nf*).

नवाँ navā: (*a*) the ninth (in order).

नवागंतुक nava:gantuk (*nm*) a newcomer.

नवागत nava:gat (*a*) recently arrived; (*nm*) a newcomer, a guest; hence नवागता (*nf*).

नवाचार nava:cha:r (*nm*) an innovation.

नवाज़िश nava:zish (*nf*) kindness.

नवाना nava:nā: (*v*) to bend; to humiliate; to cause to yield.

नवान्न nava:nn (*nm*) new corn (of a harvest).

नवाह्न nava:nnh (*nm*) a nine-day performance; aggregate of nine days (of some religious observance).

नवाब nava:b (*nm*) a Nawab, Muslim noble or ruler; title of some Muslim rulers; a man living with great pomp and show; ~ज़ादा son of a नवाब; ~ज़ादी daughter of a नवाब; नवाबी pertaining to a नवाब; Nawab-like; the position of a नवाब; conduct similar to that of a नवाब; ०ठाठ/०ठाठ-बाट luxurious and lavish living (comparable to that of a Nawab); नवाबी करना to live a lordly life; to conduct oneself in the manner of a Nawab.

नवासा nawa:sa: (*nm*) a daughter's son.

नवासी nawa:si: (*a*) eighty-nine; (*nm*) the number eighty-nine; (*nf*) a daughter's daughter.

नवी/करण navi:karān̲ (*nm*) renewal, renovation, rejuvenation; ~कृत renewed, renovated, rejuvenated.

नवीन navi:n (*a*) new, novel, neo-modern; recent; fresh; youthful; young; ~तम latest; most modern; up-to-date; ~तर newer, more modern; नवीनीकरण rejuvenation, renewal.

नवीनता navi:nta: (*nf*) novelty, newness; freshness; ~शून्य/हीन hackneyed, stale,

नवीयन navi:yān (*nm*) renewal; renovation, rejuvenation.

नवी/स navi:s (*nm*) a writer, scribe; ~सी the work or profession of writing/scribing.

नवे/ला navela: (*a*) youthful, young, of young age; ~ली (a lady) of young age; a young/youthful woman.

नवो/ढा, ~ढ़ा navo/ḍha:, ~ṛha: (*nf*) a new bride; (*a*) newly-wed, (woman).

नव्य navvy (*a*) new, novel, neo-; modern; recent; hence ~ता (*nf*).

नशा nasha: (*nm*) intoxication; inebriation; ~खोर an inebriate, one addicted to intoxicants; ~खोरी addiction to intoxicants. consuming alcohol as an addiction; inebriation; -पानी some intoxicating drink; ~बंदी prohibition; –उतरना

to be deintoxicated; the effect of intoxication to end; to regain normalcy after a state of intoxication to come to senses; pride or vanity to be knocked off; –काफ़ूर होना see –हिरण होना; –चढ़ना/छाना to get inebriated, to be intoxicated, to take a drop too much, to be under a spell of intoxication; –जमना to be inebriated, to have the full effect of intoxication; intoxication to attain its fullness; –मिट्टी होना the fun of intoxication to be lost/spoilt; –हिरण होना to be deintoxicated; to be shocked/stunned back to senses, to come to senses (from an abnormal state of intoxication); नशे की हालत होना में to have a drop in one's eyes; नशे में चूर/धुत हो जाना to drink till all is blue.

शीं, नशीन nashi:, nashi:n—a suffix denoting one who sits (e.g. पर्दानशीन, तख़्तनशीन).

शी/ला nashi:la: (*a*) intoxicating; inebrient; hence ~ली feminine form.

शेबा/ज़ nasheba:z (*nm* and *a*) (an) addict, habitual drunkard, (one) addicted to an intoxicant; inebriate; hence ~ज़ी (*nf*).

श्तर nashtar (*nm*) a lancet; surgical knife; –लगाना to operate upon; to lance.

श्वर nashshvar (*a*) perishable, destructible; transient; hence ~ता (*nf*).

ष्ट nashṭ (*a*) destroyed, perished, annihilated; destructed, ruined; ~दृष्टि one who has lost his eyesight, rendered blind; ~बुद्धि/~मति stupid, off one's head; -भ्रष्ट destroyed; ruined, destructed; ~स्मृति one who has lost his memory; –करना to destroy perish, to destruct; to annihilate; to ruin, to demolish; to deform; to waste; to mar; to spoil; to raze.

नस nās (*nf*) a vein, sinew; nerve; ~बंदी vasectomy; -नस ढीली होना to be unnerved; to be demoralised; -नस पहचानना/-नस से वाकिफ़ होना to know through and through; -नस फड़क उठना the whole being to thrill in excitement; to be thrilled; -नस में all over the body, in one's whole being; -नस में बिजली दौड़ना to be electrified, to be suddenly excited and stimulated; -नस में होना bred in the bone.

नसर nasar (*nf*) prose (writing).

नसल nasal (*nf*) breed, pedigree, genealogy; –सुधारना to breed.

नसवार naswa:r (*nm*) snuff.

नसीब nasi:b (*nm*) fate, luck, fortune; destiny; –आज़माना to try one's luck; –का खेल miracles wrought by luck, freaks of fortune; –का खोटा unfortunate; –का मारा struck by ill-luck, rendered helpless by misfortune; –का लिखा lot; dictates of destiny; –खुल जाना/चमकना/जागना/सीधा होना to be in luck, fortune to smile on someone, to be favoured by Dame Luck; –टेढ़ा होना to be hard of luck, to be out of luck, to have a wretched lot; to be frowned upon by Dame Luck; –पलटना luck to undergo a change; to be lucky, a run of good-luck to commence; –फूटना/सो जाना to be struck by ill-luck, to be under a spell of misfortune; –लड़ना to prove lucky to be favoured by Dame Luck; –होना to attain, to achieve to obtain/get, to have

नसीबा nasi:ba: (*nm*) see नसीब.

नसीहत nasi:hat: (*nf*) teaching, precept; counselling; preaching; **–करना/देना** to preach; to counsel; to impart a teaching.

नसे(सै)नी nase(ai)nɪ: (*nf*) a ladder; staircase, stairway.

नस्ल nasl (*nf*) see **नसल**.

नहन्नी nehannɪ: (*nf*) see **नहरनी**.

नह/र nehar (*nf*) a canal, channel; waterway; **~री** pertaining or belonging to a **नहर**, canal.

नहरनी neharnɪ: (*nf*) a nail-cutter, nail-paring instrument.

नह/ला nehla: (*nm*) the nine in playing cards, a playing card with nine pips; **~ले पर दहला** to go one better, to outdo an adversary.

नहलाई nehla:i: (*nf*) the act, process of, or wages paid for, bathing.

नहलवाना nehalwa:nā: (*v*) to (cause to) bathe, to give a bath.

नहलाना nehla:nā: (*v*) to give a bath.

नहाना naha:nā: (*v*) to bathe, to take a bath; **-धोना** lit. bathing and washing—bathing; bathing and other incidental acts; to bathe and perform other incidental acts.

नहीं nāhɪ: (*ind*) no, not; **–तो** otherwise, or else; if not; lest; but for; no, certainly not.

नहूसत nahu:sat (*nf*) inauspiciousness; unluckiness.

नाँघना nā:ghnā: (*v*) see **लाँघना**.

नाँद nā:d (*nf*) a manger; tub, trough.

नांदी nā:ndi: (*nm*) a benedictory prologue (in Indian dramaturgy); the mythological bull – vehicle of Lord Shiv; **~कर** one who recites the **नांदी**; **~पाठ** recitation of the **नांदी**.

नाँवाँ nā:vā: (*nm*) money; cash.

ना nā: (*ind*) a word denoting negation, no; **~इंसाफ़** unjust; **~इंसाफ़ी** injustice; **~इत्तिफ़ाकी** disagreement; **~उम्मीद** hopeless; disappointed, despaired; **~उम्मीदी** hopelessness; disappointment, despair; **~क़दरा/क़द्र** a non-connoisseur, one who does not appreciate merit; **~क़दरी/~क़द्री** non-appreciation, neglect, disregard; **~काफ़ी** inadequate, insufficient; **~क़ाबिल** unworthy; unqualified; incapable; undeserving, not fit for, not worth; **~क़ाबिलियत** incapability, inability; unworthiness; **~काम** fruitless, ineffective; disabled; unsuccessful; **०लौटना** to draw blank; **~कामयाब** unsuccessful; failed; **~कामयाबी** failure; **~कामी** failure; ineffectiveness; **~कारा** useless, worthless; unserviceable, good for nothing; a bad egg; idle; **०कर देना** to clip one's wings, to make ineffective unserviceable; **~क़िस** inferior; wicked, worthless; defective; **~खुदा** see **नाखुदा**; **~खुश** unhappy; displeased; annoyed; **~खुशी** unhappiness, displeasure; annoyance; **~ख्वांदा** illiterate, unlettered; **~गवार** intolerable, unbearable; **०गुज़रना** to be unbearable; a sense of displeasure to be aroused; to feel offended; **~गहानी** accident, accidental occurrence; **~चाक़ी** discord, estrangement, estranged feelings; **~चीज़** a small fry; worthless, insignificant, petty, trifling; **~जायज़** improper; undue; illegitimate; **~तजर्बेकार** inexperienced; a novice; **~तजर्बेकारी** cack of experience; **~तमाम** incomplete; **~तवाँ** feeble, weak; **~तवानी** feebleness, weakness; **~दान** ignorant, stupid, nincompoop; **० की दोस्ती जी का जंजाल** befriend a fool and suffer a thousand falls; **नादान दोस्त से दाना दुश्मन अच्छा** better have a sensible foe than a foolish friend; ~दानी ignorance; stupidity; ~देहंद a habitual defaulter in due payment; -नुकर roundabout denial; hesitant refusal; ~पसंद not likeable, not to one's liking, repulsive; hence ~पसंदगी; ~पाक polluted; unholy; unchaste; uncouth; ~पाकी pollutedness; unholiness; absence of chastity, uncouthness; ~पायदार not durable; not lasting; not firm or steady; ~पायदारी lack or want of durability, temporariness; absence of firmness/steadiness; ~पैद rare, scarce; ~फ़रमाँ disobedient; defiant; ~फ़रमानी disobedience; defiance; ~बालिग़ minor, under-age; ~बालिग़ी the state or condition of being minor/under-age, minority; ~मंज़ूर rejected; disapproved; ~मंज़ूरी disapproval; rejection; ~मर्द impotent, emasculate; coward; ~मर्दी impotence, emasculation; cowardice; ~माक़ूल unworthy, undeserving; unfit, improper; ~मालूम unknown, unidentified; ~मुआफ़िक unfavourable, unsuitable, not suited; ~मुनासिब improper; undue; unbecoming; ~मुमकिन impossible; ~मुराद frustrated, ill-fated; hence ~मुरादी; ~मेहरबान unkindly, not favourably disposed; ~मौज़ूं incompatible, not befitting; incongruous; ~याब unique, rare; precious; hence ~याबी; ~वाकफ़ियत ignorance, the state of not being in know of, not knowing, not being apprised; ~वाकिफ़ not knowing, not apprised (of); ignorant; a stranger; hence ~वाकफ़ियत; ~वाजिब improper, undue, not befitting; ~शाद unhappy, gloomy; ~शुक्रगुज़ार/~शुक्रा ungrateful, thankless; ~शुक्रगुज़ारी ungratefulness, thanklessness; ~साज indisposed; ~साज़ी indisposition; ~हमवार uneven, rough and rugged.

नाइट्रोजन na:itrojān (*nf*) the nitrogen gas.

नाईं nā:ɪ: (*ind*) like, as, in the manner of.

नाई na:i: (*nm*) a barber, a low caste in the traditional Hindu social order subsisting on hair-cutting, shaving, etc.; -तेली-धोबी the butcher, the baker, the candlestickmaker.

नाक nā:k (*nf*) the nose; (a symbol of) prestige; honour; pre-eminent person (in a class or group); (*nm*) the heaven; a kind of crocodile; used as a suffix to mean 'full of/impregnated with' as ख़तरनाक, शर्मनाक; -नक़्श facial features, facial cut; ~वाला honourable; having a prestige; -ऊँची होना to be honourable; to acquire added status/respect; social standing to be enhanced; -कटना to lose face, to have one's fair name tarnished, to be faced with humiliation; one's honour to be sullied; -काटना to inflict humiliation; to defame; to disgrace, to dishonour; to outwit, to prove more than a match; -का बाल very intimate, in the closest of counsels; -की सीध में just in front, as the crow flies; -के नीचे under the very nose of, in the very presence of; -के सुर में बोलना to speak in a nasalised voice, to speak through the nose; -घिसना see -रगड़ना; -चढ़ाना lit. to stretch the nostrils upwards— to express indignation/contempt; -छिड़कना see ~सिनकना; -जाना to lose one's honour, prestige/honour to be sullied, one's reputation to be tarnished; --चाहे इधर से पकड़ो, चाहे उधर से different courses for identical destination; to try both possible alternatives, to try either way; –तक खाना to cram one's stomatch full, to over-eat; –पर गुस्सा होना to be very petulant, to be very short-tempered; –पर मक्खी न बैठने देना to have no obligations whatever, to be quits with all, to allow none to acquire an upper hand; –पर मारना to pay off readily (so as to keep one's image unsullied); –फटना lit. the nose to be split up—foul smell to be unbearable; to be extra-fastidious; to have a clip on one's shoulder; –बचाना to have kept one's name intact, to safeguard one's honour; –बहना the nose to be running; -भौं चढ़ाना/सिकोड़ना lit. to turn up the nose and knit the brows—to frown, to express indignation; to cock one's nose –में दम करना to set (somebody's) teeth on edge, to make it too hot for; to pester, to plague, to harass; –में दम होना to be plagued, to be fed up; things to become too hot, to have the teeth see on edge; –में नकेल डालना to have complete control over, to be in a position to make one dance to his tune; –रखना to save or preserve one's honour, to have a good name unsullied; –रगड़ना to beseech very humbly; to eat humble pie; –सिकोड़ना lit. to turn up the nose—to express contempt or disapproval; –सिनकना to blow the nose; –से आगे न देख पाना not to see beyond one's nose; to be short-sighted/unwise; नाकों चने चबवाना to tor ment, to cause excessive harassment.

नाक-नक़्शा nā:k-naqsha: (*nm*) features, facial cut.

नाका nā:ka: (*nm*) the entrance or extremity (of a road etc.), a check-post; eye (of a needle); a kind of crocodile.

नाका(के)बंदी nā:ka:(ke)bāndi: (*nf*) blockade, barring of entry and exit.

नाक्षत्र nā:kshattr (*a*) pertaining to or related with नक्षत्र (see).

नाख na:kh (*nf*) a fruit akin to the pear in shape, size and taste.

नाख़ुदा nā:ḳhuda: (*nm*) captain of a ship; (*a*) atheist(ic).

नाख़ू/न nā:ḳhū:n (*nm*) a nail; ~नतराश a nail cutter; ~नी of the breadth of a nail—of very small breadth; nail-coloured.

नाग na:g (*nm*) a cobra, snake; an elephant; (*a*) treacherous, venomous; –देवता serpent god; ~लोक the world of snakes—पाताल, the nether world.

नागपंचमी na:gpāṇchmi: (*nf*) a Hindu festival celebrated on the fifth day of the moonlit fortnight of the month of सावन.

नागफनी na:gphani: (*nf*) a cactus, prickly pear.

नागर na:gar (*a*) urban; civil, civic, civilian; wise; (*nm*) a civilian; a subcaste of Bra:hmans of Gujarat; Na:gri:(Devna:gri:) letters/alphabet also –अक्षर; ~ता civility; urbanity.

नागराक्षर na:gara:kshar (*nm*) a Devna:gri: character/letter.

नागराज na:gra:j (*nm*) the mythological king of snakes called शेषनाग; a huge snake.

नागरिक na:grik (*a*) civil; civilian; urbane; (*nm*) a citizen; civilian; –अधिकार civilian rights, citizenship rights; ~ता citizenship; civility.

नागरी na:gri: (*a*) (fem. form of

नागर)—the Devna:gri: script.

ागरीकरण na:gri:karān (*nm*) urbanisation; transcription into Devna:gri: letters.

ागहानी na:gha:nı: (*a*) sudden, accidental.

ागा na:ga: (*nm*) a Shaivite sect (whose members go about nude); a member of this sect; a tribe inhabiting the north-east frontier in the hill state of Assam (in India); ~लैंड the small north-east frontier state of the Indian Union.

ाग़ा na:ga: (*nf*) absence from work.

ागिन na:gin (*nf*) a she-cobra, female snake; (*a*) venomous (woman).

ाच nā:ch (*nf*) dance; -कूद festivity, dancing and fun-making; -गाना dance and music; ~घर a dancing hall; -रंग merry-making, entertainment; –उठना to dance through joy; to burst forth into a dance; –नचाना to lead person a pretty dance, to make somebody dance to one's tune; to cause harassment, to harass; –न जाने आँगन टेढ़ा a bad workman quarrels with his tools.

ाच/ना nā:chnā: (*v*) to dance; to run about; ~ना -गाना dancing and singing, merry-making; ~ने वाली a dancing girl.

ाज na:j (*nm*) see अनाज.

ाज़ na:z (*nm*) coquetry; airs; feigned air, pride, vanity; -नख़रा coquettishness, alluring gestures; ~नीं/नीन a delicate beauty; ~बरदार one who dances attendance upon; who puts with or endures the coquettish conduct of another; hence ~बरदारी; -ओ-अदा see –नख़रा; -ओ-नियाज़ amorous goings-on; –उठाना to endure the coquettish/alluring gestures of.

नाज़िम na:zim (*nm*) manager, organiser.

नाज़िर na:zir (*nm*) a court-official, supervisor.

नाज़िल na:zil; –होना to befall, to come down upon; to be struck by.

नाज़ी na:zi: (*nm*) see नात्सी.

नाज़ुक na:zuk (*a*) delicate, frail, tender; critical; ~ख़याल (of) subtle or tender ideas; ~दिमाग़ of a delicate temper; touchy; ~दिल soft-hearted, kind; ~बदन of a delicate frame, of a frail constitution; ~मिज़ाज touchy, irascible; of sensitive disposition; –हालत में होना to hang by a thread, to be in a precarious condition.

नाटक nā:ṭak (*nm*) a drama; play; ~कार a dramatist, playwright; ~शाला a theatre; –करना to stage a play; –रचना to create a (dramatic) scene; to author a play/drama; नाटकीकरण dramatization.

नाटकीय nā:ṭaki:y (*a*) dramatic; histrionic; ~ता dramatic element/character; –प्रभाव stage effect,

नाटना nā:ṭnā: (*v*) to decline; to refuse; to deny.

नाटा nā:ṭa: (*a*) short,short-statured, dwarfish.

नाटिका nā:ṭika: (*nf*) diminutive of नाटक—a short play.

नाट्य nā:ṭṭy (*a*) dramatic; histrionic; ~कला dramatic art, histrionics; ~कार a dramatist, playwright; an actor; a performer (of a play); ~शाला a theatre; -शास्त्र dramaturgy; ~शास्त्री dramaturgist; ~शिल्प stagecraft, the art of theatre; hence ~शिल्पी (*nm*).

नाट्याचार्य nā:ṭṭya:cha:ry (*nm*) a master of the dramatic/histrionic art, dramaturgist.

नाट्योचित nā:ṭṭyochit (*a*) befitting a drama; dramatic, histrionic.

नाठ nā:ṭh (*nf*) ruination, destruction.

नाड़ा na:ṛa: (*nm*) trousers' string, tape inserted in the upper part of the trousers for binding it round the waist.

नाड़िका na:ṛika: (*nf*) a vein.

नाड़ी na:ṛi: (*nf*) pulse; vein; artery; **-परीक्षा** feeling of the pulse (by a physician); **-संस्थान** the whole system of arteries and veins; **–देखना** to feel the pulse of; **–पहचानना** to be aware of the pulse vibrations of to know thoroughly well.

नाता nā:ta: (*nm*) relation; connection; **–जोड़ना** to establish relationship with, to have links with; **–तोड़ना** to break off.

ना/ती nā:ti: (*nm*) a grandson; hence **~तिन** (*nf*).

नाते nā:te (*nm*) relations, connections; (*adv*) by virtue of; for the sake of, for; because of; **-के** as, by virtue of being; **-रिश्ते** relationship, relations and connections.

नातेदा/र nā:teda:r (*nm*) a relative, kinsfolk; **~री** relationship; **~र-रिश्तेदार** kith and kin, body of relatives.

नात्सी na:tsi: (*nm*) a Nazi; **-दल** the Nazi party; **~वाद** Nazism; **~वादी** a Nazi; Nazist, Nazistic.

नाथ nā:th (*nm*) a master, husband; nose-rope (of a bullock etc.); a member of the mediaeval religious sect called the **नाथपंथ**; **~पंथ** a mystical mediaeval religious sect; **– पंथी** an adherent of the **~पंथ**.

नाथना nā:thnā: (*v*) to pierce the nostril (of); to bring under control, to hold sway; to string (into one).

नाद na:d (*nm*) a sound, musical sound; noise; (*nf*) see **नाँद**.

नादा/न na:da:n (*a*) see **ना** (**~दान**) **~नी** see **ना** (**~दानी**); **~न की दोस्ती जी का जंजाल** befriend a fool and suffer a thousand falls; **~न दोस्त से दाना दुश्मन अच्छा** better have a sensible foe than a foolish friend.

नादित na:dit (*a*) sounded; voiced.

नादिम na:dim (*a*) ashamed, filled with shame.

नादिया na:diya: (*nm*) see **नांदी**; a show-bull used by some quack astrologers to obey specific commands and make certain answers etc.

नादिरशा/ह na:dirsha:h (*nm*) a tyrant tyrannous dictator (a usage based on the name of the cruel Persian invader who stormed Delhi and ordered a general massacre in the year 1738); king stork, an oppressively active ruler; **~ही** tyranny, high-handedness; tyrannous; **०हुक्म** a tyrannous command to be obeyed forthwith.

नान nā:n (*nf*) a kind of thick oven-cooked bread.

नानख़ताई nā:nkḥata:i: (*nf*) a kind of sweatmeat.

नानबाई nā:nba:i: (*nm*) a bread-seller.

नाना nā:nā: (*nm*) maternal grandfather; (*a*) varied, diverse, manifold; miscellaneous.

नानाविध nā:nā:vidh (*a*) varied, variegated, multifarious; miscellaneous; hence **~ता** (*nf*).

नानिहाल na:niha:l (*nf*—also *nm* in some parts of the Hindi-speaking area) see **ननिहाल**.

नानी nā:nī: (*nf*) maternal grandmother; **–का घर** an easy job, a place of fun and frolic; **–के आगे ननसाल का बखान** to teach one's grandmother to suck eggs, a novice instructing an expert; –मर जाना to be in a predicament; to feel lost; to be demoralised, to be non-plussed.

नाप nā:p (*nm*) measure, measurement; -जोख/तोल measure and weight, measurement; assessment.

नापना nā:pnā: (*v*) to measure.

नापित nā:pit (*nm*) a barber.

नाफ़ nā:f (*nf*) the navel; –चलना the navel to be dislocated.

नाबदान nā:bdā:n (*nm*) a drain, gutter; –का कीड़ा a despicable creature; –में मुँह मारना to indulge in a despicable act, to stoop too low.

ना/भि, ~भी na:/bhi, ~bhi: (*nf*) the navel; umbilicus, hub; -केंद्र the focal point, focus; -मूल the part of the abdomen just below the navel.

नाभि/क na:bhik (*nm*) the nucleus; ~कीय nuclear; ०ऊर्जा nuclear energy; ०विज्ञान nuclear science.

नाभिका nā:bhika: (*nf*) see नाभि.

नाम nā:m (*nm*) name; title; appellation; renown, fame; ~करण baptism; naming; nomenclature; ०संस्कार the ceremony of naming a child, baptismal ceremony; -कीर्तन constant repetition of God's name; -ग्राम whereabouts, the name and address; ~चीं renowned, well-known; ~ज़द nominated; ~ज़दगी nomination; ~तंत्र nomenclature; ~दार well-known, famous; ~धातु nominal verb/root; -धाम name and address, whereabouts; ~धारी named, known by the name of; ~धेय bearing the name of, known as; -निर्देश mention or reference of the name (of); -निशान trace; vestige; ~पट्ट a name-plate; signboard; –पत्र a label; -पत्रांकन labelling; -पद्धति (system of) nomenclature; ~मात्र को only in name, nominal; ~मात्रवाद nominalism; ~माला a string of names; a collection of nomenclature; ~रासी name-sake; ~रूप name and form; ०वाद nominalism; ~लेवा a survivor, one who remembers (a deceased); ~वर renowned, famous; ~वरी renown, fame; ~शेष deceased, late, one who has survived only through name; ~हीन nameless, unnamed; –आसमान पर होना to be very famous, to be held in high esteem; –उछलना to become a byword (amongst people); to be disgraced; –उछालना to bandy one's name about; to bring disgrace upon; –उजागर करना to bring name/credit to; (ironically) to tarnish the reputation of; –उठ जाना even the memory to be lost, to have no survivor whosoever; –कटना one's name to be struck off (the rolls); –कमाना to set the world on fire, to earn a name, to acquire renown; –करना to earn a name, to become famous; –का only in name; nominal; –, (किसी के) addressed to (somebody), meant for; in favour of (somebody); debited to the name of, recorded in the name of; –का डंका पिटना/ –की धूम मचना to become known far and wide, to be held in high esteem all over; to become a byword; –का भूखा yearning for fame/renown; –की माला जपना to remember every moment, to have somebody in one's thoughts all the time; –के लिए for the sake of name, without any practical use or meaning, nominal; –को see –के लिए; –को/पर थूकना to spit at/on; to treat with ignonimity;

–को रोना to repine for another's misdeed; –चमकना one's name to shine forth, to acquire glory; –चलना to continue to be remembered; to live through one's progeny; –डालना to debit to the name of; to be recorded opposite the name of; –डुबाना to tarnish the fair name (of); to lose one's reputation/honour; to bring disgrace or infamy; –तक न रहने देना to wipe of the very name of, to leave no vestiges of; –धरना to name; to assign an offensive name; –धराना to bring a bad name; –न लेना never to make a mention of; to keep miles away from; –नहीं not even a trace of; that defies description; –निकलना to become a byword; to become notorious; to become celebrated; –पड़ना to be debited to the name of; to be recorded against the name of; –पर, (किसी के) in the name of; for the sake of; –पर कलंक/धब्बा/बट्टा लगना one's fair name to be tarnished/sullied; –पैदा करना to earn name and fame; –बड़े दर्शन थोड़े great/much cry little wool; –बढ़ाना to enhance the reputation/glory of; –बिकना to be a draw; to have numerous fans; –मिटना a name to be wiped off; to have not even the trace of a name left; –रखना to save or protect the honour/prestige of; –रह जाना to live only in name; to live through good deeds; –रोशन करना to bring name and fame to; to bring good name to; –लगना to be branded (an accused); –लिखना to enrol; –लेना to remember (with gratitude etc.), to make an approbative mention of, to praise; ~लेवा पानी देवा न रहना to be survived by none at all, to have no successor whatever (even for the performance of post-death rites).

नामक nā:māk (*a*) named, bearing the name (of).

नामत: nā:mtah (*ind*) by name.

नामन nā:mān (*nm*) nomination, naming.

नामां/कन nā:mā:ṅkān (*nm*) nomination; inscription of name; ~कित nominated, the name inscribed on.

नामांतर nā:mā:ntar (*nm*) alias, another name.

नामा nā:mā: – an adjectival suffix meaning named or bearing a name (as ख्यातनामा); used as a suffix to mean a book (as शाहनामा), document or deed (as हलफ़नामा), set (as सवालनामा–questionnaire); see नाँवाँ; ~निगार a correspondent; ~बर a letter-bearer; messenger.

नामावली nā:mā:vali: (*nf*) a nominal roll; list of names; nomenclature.

नामिका nā:mɪka: (*nf*) a panel (of names).

नामित nā:mit (*a*) named; nominated.

नामी nā:mɪ: (*a*) famous, reputed, renowned, eminent; named, bearing the name (of); -गिरामी famous, reputed, eminent.

नामोनिशान na:mōnishā:n (*nm*) trace, vestige; –बाकी न रहना to have no trace left, to be completely annihilated/devastated, to be erased out of existence/memory.

नाम्ना na:mnā: (*ind*) through/by name (as –परिचय होना to know by name).

नायक na:yak (*nm*) a hero; leader, chief; a military official of a low rank; ~त्व leadership; hegemony.

नाय/ब na:yab (*a*) deputy; (*nm*) a deputy, an assistant; ~बी the office or job of a नायब.

नायाब na:ya b (*a*) see ना(~याब).

नायिका na:yika: (*nf*) a heroine; procuress; -भेद in Indian Poetics, the study of the different categories and sub-categories of heroines/female characters.

नारंगी na:rāṅgi: (*nf*) an orange.

नारकीय na:rki:y (*a*) hellish, infernal; of or befitting the hell; hence ~ता (*nf*).

नारद na:rad (*nm*) a celestial sage in Indian mythology (who caused internecine quarrels amongst the various gods and goddesses by tale-bearing); one who causes quarrels amongst people; also~जी/~मुनि; नारदी कला/विद्या the art of causing quarrels by tale-bearing.

ना/रा na:ra: (*nm*) a slogan; ~रेबाज़ a slogan-monger; ~रेबाज़ी slogan-mongering.

नारा/ज़ na:ra:z (*a*) angry, enraged; displeased; ~ज़गी/ ~ज़ी anger, rage; displeasure.

नारायण na:ra:yāṉ (*nm*) God, Lord Vishṉu.

नारिकेल na:rikel (*nm*) the cocoanut tree and its fruit.

नारियल na:riyal (*nm*) see नारिकेल.

नारी na:ri: (*nf*) a woman; (*a*) female; -उपासना geneolatory; -द्वेष misogymy.

नाल na:l (*nm*) a shaft; peduncle, stalk (as of a lotus); a horse-shoe; heavy stone-ring used in weight-lifting exercise; barrel; tube; a woodpipe used for administering medicine etc. to the cattle; blow-pipe; the navel string; the gullet; a weaver's spindle; (*nf*) commission realised by a gambling den-owner from the gambling party; ~कटाई process or act of cutting of the navel-string (of a new-born) or the remuneration therefor; -गड़ी होना, (कहीं पर) to be as dear as the motherland, to have immense liking for; ~बंद a farrier; ~बंदी the profession of a farrier; the work of fixing horse-shoes.

नाला na:la: (*nm*) a rivulet; water-course, culvert; big drain, gutter,

नालाय/क़ na:la:yaq (*a*) unworthy, worthless; unfit; incompetent; ~क़ी unworthiness, worthlessness, unfitness; incompetence.

नालिका na:lika: (*nf*) a flume; small tube.

नालिश na:lish (*nf*) a law-suit; suit; plaint; -करना/ठोकना/दागना to file a law-suit, to lodge a complaint (in a court of law).

नाली na:li: (*nf*) a drain, drain-pipe; sewer, scupper; -का कीड़ा most contemptible/despicable creature.

नाव na:v (*nf*) a boat, ferry; -घाट a ferry, wharf; -डूबना one's boat to sink; -पार लगाना to enable/cause to cross over; -मँझधार में होना to be in mid-stream.

नावक na:vak (*nm*) a sailor, boatman; deadly small arrow.

नावाधिकरण nā:va:dhi:karāṉ (*nm*) admiralty.

नाविक na:vik (*nm*) a sailor, seaman, boatman.

नाश nā:sh (*nm*) destruction, ruination, devastation; waste; ~क/कारी destructive, devastating; killing; wasteful; ~वाद nihilism; ~वादी a nihilist; nihilistic; ~वान/शील perishable, destructible; ephemeral, transitory; also नाश्य; -करना to destroy; to spoil, to ruin.

नाशपाती nā:shpa:ti: (*nf*) a pear, pyris.

नाशी na:shi: -used as a suffix to mean he who or that which causes annihilation/devastation/ruin (as सत्यानाशी, सर्वनाशी).

नाश्ता na:shta: (*nm*) breakfast; light refreshment; **-पानी** breakfast, light refreshment.

नास nā:s (*nm*) snuff; **~दानी** a snuff-box.

नासम/झ nā.samajh (*a*) unintelligent, dull of understanding; stupid; also **~झदार;~झदारी/ ~झी** lack of intelligence; stupidity.

नासा nā:sa: (*nf*) the nose; **~पुट** a nostril; **~रंध्र** nares.

नासिका nā:sika: (*nf*) the nose; **-विवर** nasal cavity.

नासिक्य nā:sikky (*a*) nasal.

नासूर nā:su:r (*nm*) sinus; **-होना** to have a perpetual painful ailment.

नास्तिक nā:stik (*nm*) an atheist, unbeliever; **~ता** atheism, disbelief (in the existence of God); **-दर्शन** atheistic philosophy.

नास्ति/वाद nā:stiva:d (*nm*) cynicism; atheism; **~वादी** a cynicist; atheist.

नाहक़ nā:haq (*adv*) in vain, for nothing, to no purpose;, without rhyme or reason.

नाहर na:har (*nm*) a lion; **-नर** a lion-like man.

नाहरू na:hru: (*nm*) the Guinea-worm—*Filaria medinesis*.

निंदक nındak (*nm*) one who speaks ill (of somebody); a blamer, slanderer, censurer, calumniator.

निंदनीय nındani:y (*a*) condemnable; blamable, reprehensible, deserving or liable to reproof or blame.

निंदा nında: (*nf*) ill-speaking, censure, condemnation; **-प्रस्ताव** censure motion; **-स्तुति** censure and praise, speaking ill or well (of somebody).

निंदासा nıda:sa: (*a*) sleepy, drowsy.

निंदित nındit (*a*) spoken ill of; condemned, censured; blamed.

निंद्य nındy (*a*) see **निंदनीय**.

निंब nımb (*nm*) see **नीम**.

नि: nih—a Sanskrit prefix meaning out, away from, free from, without, destitute of or imparting the sense of a strengthening particle (i.e. thoroughly, entirely, etc).

नि:श्रेयस nishshreyas (*nm*) the summum bonum, highest good.

नि.श्वसन nishshvasān (*nm*) (the act or process of) expiration, breathing out.

नि.श्वास nishshva:s (*nm*) expiration, breathing out.

नि.स्पंद nisspānd (*a*) still, motionless; hence **~ता** (*nf*).

नि.स्पृह nissprih (*a*) selfless, having no selfish motives; content(ed); hence **~ता** (*nf*).

नि:स्राव nishsra:v (*nm*) outflow, oozing out.

नि.स्वार्थ nissva:rth (*a*) unselfish, selfless; **~ता** unselfishness, selflessness.

नि ni—a Sanskrit prefix either to verbs or to nouns meaning down, back, in, into, within and also negation and privation (e.g. **निचय, निनाद, निधन**, etc.)

निआमत nia:mat (*nf*) see **नियामत**.

निकट nikaṭ (*adv* and *a*) near, close, proximate; **~दृष्टि** myopia, short sight; **~दृष्टिमत्ता** short-sightedness; **~पूर्व** near East; **~वर्ती** adjacent; near, close, proximal; **-संबंध** close relation/relationship; **-संबंधी** near relation; **~स्थ** close, near, proximal; **०अवयव** immediate constituent, hence **~स्थता** (*nf*).

निकटता nikaṭta: (*nf*) proximity, closeness, nearness.

निकम्मा nikāmmā: (*a*) inert, idle, indolent; without employment; worthless, useless, good for nothing **~पन** inertness, idleness, indolence; worthlessness, uselessness.

निकर nikar (*nm*) heap, pile, bundle; multitude, flock; shorts half-pants.

निकल nikal (*nf*) nickel; **–चढ़ाना** to plate with nickel.

निकलना nikalnā: (*v*) to come/get out; to emerge; to rise (as **सूरज**); to ooze out; to proceed; to emanate; to appear; to be extracted, (as **अर्क़**); to be deduced (as **निष्कर्ष**); to be solved (as **सवाल**); to issue or be issued (as **हुक्म**); to be published (as **पत्रिका**, **किताब**); to slink away; **निकल जाना** to go away/out; to be lost, to be wasted; to elope (with).

निकष nikash (*nm*) a touchstone; criterion.

निकाई nika:i: (*nf*) goodness, excellence; dragged work.

निकाय nika:y (*nm*) a body; system.

निकालना nika:lnā: (*v*) to take out; to bring out; to oust; to expel; to extract; to draw; to dismiss; to discharge; to issue; to deduce; to solve; to publish.

निका/स nika:s (*nm*) an outlet, exit, vent; source; origin; discharge; out-turn, yield; **~सी** clearance; outturn; output, produce; transit-duty; income.

निकाह nika:h (*nm*) marriage, marriage ceremony; **~नामा** marriage-agreement.

निकुंज nikūṇj (*nm*) an arbour, a bower.

निकृष्ट nikrishṭ (*a*) inferior, inferior-most; low, base, vile; hence **~ता** (*nf*).

निकेत,~न niket,~ān (*nm*) a house, residence; abode.

निक्षिप्त nikshipt (*a*) thrown; deposited; **–उपवाक्य** parenthetical clause.

निक्षेप nikshep (*nm*) throwing; depositing; deposit.

निखट्टू nikhaṭṭu: (*a* and *nm*) indolent, idle; without employment, worthless; unearning; an idler, a drone: hence **~पन** (*nm*).

निखरना nikharnā: (*v*) to be cleansed/brightened up; to become clear/elegant/crystallised; to be settled/stabilised.

निखार nikha:r (*nm*) brightness; lustre elegance; **–पर होना** to have ever-growing lustre/brightness, to be brightening up.

निखालिस nikha:lis (*a*) pure; unadulterated.

निखिल nikhil (*a*) all, whole, pan.

निगति nigati (*nf*) anagnorisis, denouement.

निगम nigām (*nm*) the Vedas or any portion thereof; a corporation.

निग/मन nigamān (*nm*) deduction; **~मित** deduced; incorporated.

निगमागम nigamā:gām (*nm*) the Vedas and other (Hindu) scriptures.

निगरानी nigra:nī: (*nf*) supervision; guard, watch; **–करना** to watch; to guard; **–रखना** to keep a watch/a guard.

निगलना nigalnā: (*v*) to swallow; to gulp.

निगह nigeh (*nf*) see **निगाह**; **~बान** a guard, watch; **~बानी** guarding, watching.

निगाह niga:h (*nf*) look, glance; sight, vision; **–दौड़ाना** to cast a hurried glance, to see through hurriedly; **–फिरना** to have a change of attitude (from good to bad); **–रखना** to keep an eye on, to keep a guard/watch; **–से उतर जाना/गिर जाना** to suffer devaluation in the eyes of, to be lowered in one's esteem; **–से चूकना** to pass through oversight; **निगाहें चार होना** to look into each other's eyes, to exchange glances.

निगुरा nigura: (*a*) without a mentor/preceptor; uninitiated.

निगूढ़ nigu:ṛh (*a*) secret, latent, hidden; obscure, abstruse; unintelligible; hence ~ता (*nf*).

निगूढ़ार्थ nigu:ṛha:rth (*a*) having a secret meaning, obscure, abstruse; (*nm*) secret meaning.

निगेटिव nigeṭiv (*nm*) a negative.

निगोड़ा nigoṛa: (*a*) worthless; indolent, idle; an abusive term used by women for persons who are idle and indolent; (*nm*) an idler.

निग्रह niggrah (*nm*) restraint; self-repression; subdual; ~वाद rigorism; hence ~वादी (*a*, *nm*).

निग्रही niggrahi: (*a* and *nm*) (one) who exercises restraint or self-repression.

निघंटु nighāṉṭu (*nm*) a classical Sanskrit name for a glossary; a Vedic lexicon.

निघटना nighaṭnā: (*v*) to be exhausted; to be finished.

निचय nichay (*nm*) accumulation, collection; a digest.

निचला nichla: (*a*) lower; situated below, low-lying.

निचाई nicha:i: (*nf*) lowness; depth, declivity, see नीचता.

निचोड़ nichoṛ (*nm*) essence; gist, substance, sum and substance.

निचोड़ना nichoṛnā: (*v*) to squeeze; to wring; to extract.

निचौहाँ nichāuhā: (*a*) slightly low-lying; lowish; bent downwards.

निछावर nichha:var (*nf*) see न्योछावर.

निज nij (*a*) own, one's own; –करके particularly; personally; –का personal, one's own; ~ता/ ~त्व characteristic, characteristic quality; personal element; ~स्व (one's) due.

निज़ाम nizā:m (*nm*) management, administration; order; –बदलना to change the established order.

निजी niji: (*a*) one's own, personal, individual; private; unofficial; –तौर पर in a personal capacity, individually; –उद्योग private industries; –क्षेत्र private sector; –सहायक personal assistant.

निठल्ला niṭhalla: (*a*) idle, indolent, lazy; lolling; without any employment; (*nm*) an idler; ~पन indolence, laziness; unemployment; lolling.

निठुर niṭhur (*a*) cruel, ruthless; obdurate; ~ता cruelty, ruthlessness; obduracy.

निठुराई niṭhura:i: (*nf*) see निठुर (~ता).

निडर niḍar (*a*) fearless, daring, dauntless; intrepid; ~ता/ ~पन/ ~पना fearlessness, dauntlessness; intrepidness.

निढाल niḍha:l (*a*) languid, wearied; spiritless, down and out.

नितंब nitāmb (*nm*) buttocks, hips.

नितंबिनी nitāmbini: (*nf*) a woman having shapely hips.

नित nit (*adv*) every day, daily; –नित day-by-day, every day.

नितांत nita:nt (*a*) excessive; absolute; complete.

नित्य nitty (*a*) excessive; eternal; essential; invarable; (*adv*) constantly; always; daily; –कर्म/कृत्य/क्रिया daily chores; ~चर्या routine; –नियम eternal rule; -नैमित्तिक regular and casual (chores); ~प्रति every day; daily; -भाव permanence; eternity; invariability.

नित्य/ता, ~त्व nittya/ta:, (*nf*) ~ttv (*nm*) permanence; eternity; invariability.

नित्यश: nittyshah (*adv*) every day, daily; always.

निथार nitha:r (*nm*) decantation.

निथारना nitha:rnā: (*v*) to decant.

निदरना nidarnā: (*v*) to insult; to humiliate; to neglect.

निदर्श/न nidarshān (*nm*) illustration, exemplification; example, type; hence ~क (*nm*).

निदान nidā:n (*nm*) diagnosis; (*adv*) at last; consequently; ~**गृह**/~**शाला** a clinic; ~**शास्त्र** ltiology.

निदेश nidesh (*nm*) direction; directive; ~**न** direction.

निदेश/क nideshak (*nm*) a director ~**कीय** directional.

निदेशात्मक nidesha:tmāk (*a*) directive; directional.

निदेशालय nidesha:lay (*nm*) a directorate.

निद्रा niddra: (*nf*) sleep; slumber; –**देवी** Somnus; goddess of sleep; ०**की गोद में/शरण में जाना** lit. to be consigned to the care of Somnus (the goddess of sleep)—to go to sleep; –**रोग** narcolepsy; ~**विज्ञान** hypnology.

निद्राचा/र niddra:cha:r (*nm*) somnambulism; sleep-walk, sleep-walking; ~**री** a somnambulist; sleep-walker.

निद्रालस niddra:las (*a*) slumberous, sleepy, overwhelmed by sleep; hence ~**ता** (*nf*).

निद्रालु niddra:lu (*a*) slumberous, somnolent; ~**ता** slumberousness, somnolence.

निधड़क nidharak (*adv*) unhesitatingly; fearlessly, boldly.

निधन nidhān (*nm*) death, passing away; ~**कारी** fatal, killing.

निधान nidhā:n (*nm*) abode, repository; substratum.

निधानी nidhā:nī: (*nf*) a shelf.

निधि nidhi (*nf*) a treasure; fund.

निनाद ninā:d (*nm*) a sound; reverberation, humming, resonance.

निनादित nina:dit (*a*) filled with sound, reverberated, resonant (with).

निन्यानबे ninnyā:nbe (*a*) ninety-nine; (*nm*) the number ninety-nine; –**का चक्कर/फेर** craze for augmenting one's wealth, keen concentration on swelling one's savings; involvement in a predicament.

निपंग nipāng (*a*) crippled, invalid; worthless.

निपट nipat (*adv*) extremely absolutely; exceedingly; –**गँवार** absolutely boorish/rustic.

निपटना nipaṭnā: (*v*) to be settled; to be decided; to be finished; to be disposed of; to be relieved; to settle score with; to face; hence **निपटाना**; **निपट लेना** to face the music, to have it out.

निपटान nipṭā:n (*nm*) disposal.

निपटारा nipṭa:ra: (*nm*) disposal; settlement; reconciliation; conclusion, termination.

निपाठ nipa:ṭḥ (*nm*) a recitation; –**करना** to recite.

निपात nipa:t (*nm*) a particle.

निपुण nipūṉ (*a*) skilful, expert; dexterous; efficient; ~**ता** skill, expertise; dexterity; efficiency.

निपू/ता nipu:ta: (*a*) childless, issueless; barren; hence ~**ती** (fem. form).

निबंध nibāndh (*nm*) an essay; ~**कार**/**लेखक** an essayist; -**संग्रह** a collection of essays; **निबंधावली** a series/collection of essays.

निब nib (*nf*) a nib.

निबटना nibaṭnā: (*v*) see **निपटना**; hence **निबटाना**.

निबटारा nibṭa:ra: (*nm*) see **निपटारा**.

निबद्ध nibaddh (*a*) tied; joined or fastened together; intertwined; composed.

निबल nibal (*a*) weak, feeble; invalid; hence ~**ता** (*nf*); –**की लुगाई सब गाँव की भौजाई** a weakling's wife attracts all eyes.

निबाह niba:h (*nm*) subsistence, sustenance; maintenance; accommodation; carrying on, pulling on; fulfilment (as of **ज़िम्मेदारी**).

निबाहना niba:hna: (*v*) to subsist, to sustain; to accommodate; to maintain; to carry on; to pull on; to perform; to fulfil; to accomplish.

निबिड़ nibiṛ (*adv*) impervious; dense, thick; hence ~**ता** (*nf*); –**वन** a thick/dense forest.

निबौरी nibauri: (*nm*) the fruit of the *neem* tree.

निभना nibhnā: (*v*) to be carried on; to be pulled on; to be accommodated; to be accomplished; to pass; to subsist, to sustain.

निभाना nibha:nā: (*v*) to carry on; to pull on, to accommodate; to fulfil; to accomplish; to perform; maintain.

निभाव nibha:v (*nm*) see **निबाह**.

निभृत nibhrit (*a*) lonely, solitary, secret.

निमंत्रण nimāntrān̲ (*nm*) an invitation; -**पत्र** (a letter of) invitation; invitation card.

निमंत्रित nimāntrit (*v*) invited.

निमग्न nimagn (*a*) sunken; submerged; absorbed; engrossed; hence ~**ता** (*nf*).

निम/ज्जन nimajjān (*nm*) a dip; submersion; immersion; ~**ज्जित** submerged, immersed; sunken.

निमटना nimaṭnā: (*v*) see **निपटना**; hence **निमटाना**.

निमित्त nimitt (*nm*) a cause, reason; factor; purpose, motive; (*ind*) for the sake of, on account of; –**कारण** instrumental/efficient cause; –**मात्र** only an instrument; only instrumental.

निमिष nimish (*nm*) twinkling of an eye, blink, nictitation, time taken in the twinkling of an eye; –**मात्र में** in the twinkling of any eye, in no time.

निमीलन nimi:lān (*nm*) closing/twinkling of any eye.

निमीलित nimi:lit (*a*) closed (eyes), shut.

निमेष nimesh (*nm*) see **निमिष**.

निमोनिया nimōniyā: (*nm*) pneumonia.

निम्न nimn (*a*) low; mean; depressed; sunken; following, given below; ~**तम** lowest, lowermost; minimum; ~**तर** lower; ~**ता** lowness; ~**लिखित** undermentioned, the following, mentioned below; ~**स्थ** low-lying, situated/located below.

निम्नांकित nimnā:ṅkit (*a*) the following, under-mentioned, mentioned below.

निम्नोक्त nimnokt (*a*) cited below, as (stated) hereunder.

नियंता niyānta: (*nm*) a controller; ruler.

नियंत्रक niyāntrak (*nm*) a controller.

नियंत्रण niyāntrān̲ (*nm*) control; restraint; ~**कर्ता** controller.

नियंत्रित niyāntrit (*a*) controlled; restrained.

नियत niyat (*a*) fixed; given, prescribed; decided; allotted; constant, invariable, unchanging; ~**त्ववाद** determinism.

नियतन niyatan (*nm*) allotment, fixation.

नियताप्ति niyata:pti (*nf*) (in a drama) anagnorisis, denouement.

नियति niyati (*nf*) destiny, fate; luck; ~**वाद** fatalism determination; ~**वादी** fatalist(ic), determinist (ic); —**का खेल** vicissitudes of destiny, wonders wrought by destiny; –**नटी** the reigning queen of destiny.

नियम niyam̐ (*nm*) a rule, canon; law; principle; ~**त:** as a matter of rule/law; ~**निष्ठ** an adherent to rule/law, a rule-abiding person; ~**निष्ठता/निष्ठा** adherence to rules; formalism; ~**बद्ध** bound by rule(s); regulated; hence ~**बद्धता** (*nf*); -**विरुद्ध** contrary to rule, unfair; violating a law; -**विरोध** defiance/breach of law; -**विरोधी** against the law; a law defier/breaker –**भंग करना** to violate/defy a rule.

नियमन niyamān (*nm*) regulation.

नियमानुकूल niyamā:nuku:l (*a*) conforming to or in accordance with a rule, regular; ~**ता** conformation to rule; ~**न** regularisation.

नियमानुसार niyamā:nusa:r (*adv*) according to rule/law.

नियमावली niyamā:vali: (*nf*) rules, rules and regulations.

नियमित niyamit (*a*) regular; regulated; regularised; ~**ता** regularity; –**करना** to regularise; to regulate.

नियाज़ niya:z (*nm*) supplication; desire; acquaintance; favour; inclination; –**हासिल करना** to acquire the favour of; to attain one's desire.

निया/मक niya:māk (*nm*) a regulator; controller; (*a*) regulative; hence ~**मिका** (*nf*).

नियामत niya:māt (*nf*) a rare gift; divine blessing.

नियुक्त niyukt (*a*) appointed; employed; posted.

नियुक्ति niyukti (*nf*) appointment; employment; posting.

नियोक्ता niyokta: (*nm*) one who appoints, an appointing authority; employer.

नियोग niyog (*nm*) an ancient Aryan practice according to which a childless widow or woman was permitted to have sexual intercourse with a person other than her husband to beget a child.

नियोजक niyojak (*nm*) an employer; one who appoints; appointing authority.

नियोजन niyojān (*nm*) employment; appointment.

नियोजित niyojit (*a*) employed; appointed.

निरंक nirāṅk (*a*) blank; unmarked; –**चैक** a blank cheque.

निरंकुश nirāṅkush (*a*) despotic; uncontrolled, unrestrained; absolute; unruly; ~**ता** despotism; absolutism; –**शासक** a tyrant, despot; –**शासन** tyranny, despotic rule.

निरंजन nirāṇjan (*nm*) God (who is beyond the spell of **माया** or the range of worldly flaws and defects), The Transcendental.

निरंतर nirāntar (*a*) continuous; uninterrupted, incessant, non-stop; perpetual; (*adv*) continuously; uninterruptedly, incessantly; ~**ता** continuity; non-interruption.

निरंध nirāndh (*a*) absolutely blind; hence ~**ता** (*nf*).

निरक्षर nirakshar (*a*) illiterate, unlettered, uneducated; ignorant, foolish; ~**ता** illiteracy, the state or position of being unlettered; –**भट्टाचार्य** an absolutely illiterate fellow, unlettered person.

निरख/ना nirakhnā: (*v*) to see, to look, to view; to inspect; -**परख** judgment, close examination; hence ~**ना -परखना** (*v*).

निरगुन nirgun (*a*) see **निर्गुण**.

निरगुनिया nirguniyā: (*nm*) one who follows the **निर्गुण पंथ**; (*a*) see **निरगुनी**.

निरगुनी nirgunī: (*a*) appreciating or recognizing no merits; ungrateful.

निर/त nirat (*a*) engaged; absorbed, engrossed; hence ~**ति** (*nf*).

निरनुनासिक niranunā:sik (*a*) non-nasal, not pronounced with a nasal touch; hence ~**ता** (*nf*).

निरनुमोदन niranūmodan (*nm*) disapproval.

निरन्न nirann (*a*) without (having taken any) food; devoid of/without cereals; (*adv*) fasting, without taking any food or cereals.

निरपरा/ध, ~धी nirapara:dh, ~dhi: (*a*) innocent; guiltless, faultless;

hence ~धिता (*nf*).

निरपवाद nirapva:d (*a*) without (any) exception, with no exception.

निरपेक्ष nirapeksh (*a*) absolute; indifferent; without expectation, unconcerned; –आदर्शवाद absolute idealism; –आर्द्रता absolute humidity; –इकाई/एकक absolute unit; –गुट non-aligned; –घनत्व absolute density; –दीप्ति absolute brilliance; –मात्रक-पद्धति absolute system of units; –विचलन absolute deviation; –शासक an absolute ruler; –सत्य absolute truth; –सममिति absolute symmetry; –हस्तांतरण absolute conveyance/handing over.

निरपेक्षता nirpekshata: (*nf*) absoluteness; the state of being unconcerned; -, गुट non-alignment; ~वाद absolutism; ~वादी absolutist; hence निरपेक्षित (*a*).

निरबं/स nirbān/s, ~सी si: (*a*) issueless, childless; having no progeny.

निरभिमा/न, ~नी nirabhimā:n, ~nī: (*a*) prideless, not proud; humble.

निरभिलाष nirabhila:sh (*a*) undesirous, having no wish or desire; detached.

निरभ्र nirabbhr (*a*) cloudless; clear (sky); hence ~ता (*nf*).

निरमोही nirmohi: (*a*) see निर्मोही.

निरर्थक nirarthak (*a*) meaningless; vain; useless, fruitless, pointless; insignificant, worthless; empty; futile; ~ता meaninglessness; fruitlessness, uselessness, worthlessness; insignificance; futility; –पुनरुक्ति palilogy.

निरवकाश niravka:sh (*a*) without time/holiday/scope/recess/space.

निरवधि niravadhi (*a*) endless, limitless; timeless; continuous, immense.

निरवयव niravyav (*a*) limbless, without limbs or parts; shapeless; inorganic.

निरवलंब niravlāmb (*a*) without prop or support, helpless; ~ता helplessness.

निरसन nirasān (*nm*) cancellation; repealing, throwing away.

निरस्त nirast (*a*) cancelled; repealed; thrown away.

निरस्त्र nirastr (*a*) unarmed; disarmed.

निरस्त्री/करण nirastri:karān (*nm*) disarmament; ~करण-सम्मेलन disarmament conference; ~कृत disarmed.

निरहंकार nirahāṅka:r (*a*) prideless, free from egotism/vanity/conceit.

निरा nira: (*a*) pure; absolute; entire, complete; mere; much; (*adv*) entirely, completely; merely; very much.

निराई nira:i: (*nf*) weeding, work of or wages paid for weeding.

निराकर/ण nira:karān (*nm*) abrogation, annulment, removal, act or process of dispelling (as of भ्रम/भय); ~णीय abrogable: worth being annulled.

निराकार nira:ka:r (*a*) shapeless, formless; incorporeal; (*nm*) The Formless (God).

निराकुल nira:kul (*a*) unperturbed, undeterred; calm, quiet.

निराकृत nira:kkrit (*a*) abrogated; annulled; removed; dispelled.

निराकृति nira:kkriti (*nf*) abrogation; annulment; removal; dispelling.

निरा/दर nira:dar (*nm*) disrespect, disgrace, dishonour, insult; ~दृत insulted, dishonoured, humiliated.

निराधार nira:dha:r (*a*) baseless; groundless, unfounded; without prop or support; false; hollow.

निराना nira:nā: (*v*) to weed.

निरापद nira:pad (*a*) secure, safe; protected; without trouble; ~ता security, safety; ~वाद tutiorism.

निरामिष nira:mish (*a*) vegetarian; —भोजन vegetarian food; ~भोजी a vegetarian.

ररायुध nira:yudh (*a*) armless; unarmed; defenceless.

रालंब nirā:lamb (*a*) destitute, having no shelter/support; helpless.

राला nira:la: (*a*) unique, peculiar; uncommon; strange; ~पन uniqueness, peculiarity.

रावरण nira:varāṇ (*a*) uncovered, without covering; open, exposed.

रावृत nira:vvrit (*a*) uncovered; open, exposed.

राश nira:sh (*a*) frustrated, disappointed, desperate, disheartened; despaired, dejected, hopeless.

राशा nira:sha: (*nf*) frustration; espair, disappointment; dejection, espondency; hopelessness; pessiism; ~वाद/~वादिता pessimism; ~वादी a pessimist; pessimistic.

राश्रय nira:shshray (*a*) destitute, elterless, forlorn, helpless; ence ~ता (*nf*).

हार nira:ha:r (*a* and *adv*) without food; fasting.

क्षक niri:kshak (*nm*) an inspecr; invigilator.

क्षण niri:kshāṇ (*nm*) inspection; vigilation.

क्षित niri:kshit (*a*) inspected; vigilated.

श्वरवा/द niri:shshvarva:d (*nm*) eism; ~दी an atheist; atheistic.

ह niri:h (*a*) innocent; harmless; nple; desiring nothing; ~ता ocence; harmlessness; simpliy; the state of having no sire.

क्त nirukti (*nf*) etymology; mology or exposition of Vedic rds, etymological explanation or exposition (of words).

निरुत्तर niruttar (*a*) silenced, rendered wordless; unable to answer back; hence ~ता (*nf*).

निरुत्सा/ह nirutsa:h (*a*) spiritless; devoid of enthusiasm; ~हित disheartened, discouraged; demoralised.

निरुद्देश्य niruddeshy (*a* and *adv*) aimless(ly), without purpose.

निरुद्यमी niruddyamī: (*a*) non-industrious; inert, dull; lazy.

निरुप/म nirupām (*a*) unequalled, unparalleled; peerless, matchless.

निरुपाधि nirupa:dhi (*a*) categorical; unconditional; without an attribute.

निरुपाय nirupa:y (*a*) helpless; resourceless; hence ~ता (*nf*).

निरूढ़ niru:ṛḥ (*a*) stylised; fixed by usage; current.

निरूपक niru:pak (*a* and *nm*) representing; one who or that which explains/demonstrates/characterises/portrays/determines.

निरूपण niru:pāṇ (*nm*) representation; portrayal; characterisation; explanation; demonstration.

निरूपित niru:pit (*a*) represented; portrayed; characterised; explained; demonstrated.

निरो/ग, ~गी niro/g, ~gi: (*a*) free from disease, healthy; in sound health.

निरोध nirodh (*nm*) restraint, control; obstruction; restriction; detention; hence ~क (*a*)

निर्ख nirḳḥ (*nm*) rate; quotation.

निर्गंध nirgāndh (*a*) odourless; without any smell,

निर्गम nirgām (*nm*) outlet, exit, egress; ~न exit, egression; departure; o मार्ग exit; egress.

निर्गुण nirgūṇ (*a*) without attributes or qualities, without सत, रज and तम गुणs; an epithet of God who is beyond the three गुणs (see); –ब्रह्म the Supreme Soul unlimited by the three गुणs.

निर्गुणिया nirgūniyā: (*a*) believing in the निर्गुण ब्रह्म; see निरगुनिया (*nm*); a devotee of the निर्गुण ब्रह्म.

निर्जन nirjān (*a*) lonely, solitary; desolate, deserted; uninhabited; ~ता loneliness, desolation; the state of being deserted or uninhabited.

निर्जर nirjar (*a*) ever-young, blessed with perennial youth.

निर्ज/ल nirjal (*a*) anhydrous; without water; dry; ~लीय non-aqueous; ~ल व्रत a fast wherein taking of even water is forbidden.

निर्जला nirjala: (*a*) see निर्जल; –एकादशी the eleventh day of the bright fortnight of the month of ज्येष्ठ on which day Hindus, especially women, observe complete fast and do not take even water.

निर्जीव nirji:v (*a*) lifeless; inanimate; dead; spiritless; insipid; inorganic; hence, ~ता (*nf*).

निर्झ/र nirjhar (*nm*) a fall, cataract, spring, stream, torrent; ~रिणी a stream, rivutet; ~री see निर्झरिणी.

निर्णय nirnay (*nm*) a judgment, decision, conclusion; ~कर्ता a judge, referee, umpire.

निर्णयात्मक nirnaya:tmak (*a*) decisive, conclusive.

निर्णायक nirnā:yak (*nm*) a judge, referee, umpire; (*a*) decisive/deciding; concluding.

निर्णीत nirnī:t (*a*) judged; decided; concluded.

निर्णेता nirnēta: (*nm*) a judge; referee.

निर्दय nirday (*a*) ruthless, merciless, cruel, heartless (person or act); ~ता ruthlessness; o से mercilessly, ruthlessly.

निर्दयी nirdai: (*a* and *nm*) ruthles cruel, heartless (person).

निर्दल nirdal (*a*) without leave non-party, independent.

निर्दलन nirdalān (*nm*) annihilatio ruination, destruction, devasta tion.

निर्दलीय nirdali:y (*a*) non-part independent.

निर्दि/ष्ट nirdisht (*a*) specified, expl cit, expressed; directed; referre (to), pointed out, mentione alluded; hence ~ष्टता (*nf*); ~ specification.

निर्दे/श nirdesh (*nm*) specificatio mention; reference; direction; ~ director, directing; ~शन directio guidance; ~शांक coordinates.

निर्दोष nirdosh (*a*) faultless, flawles guiltless; inculpable; innocent.

निर्दो/षी nirdoshi: (*a*) see निर्दो ~षिता innocence, faultlessnes flawlessness.

निर्द्वंद्व nirdvāndv (*a*) carefree, witho any inner conflict; hence ~ता (*n*

निर्धन nirdhān (*a*) poor; moneyle indigent, impoverished; destitu ~ता poverty; indigence; destit tion.

निर्धा/रण nirdha:rān (*nm*) fixatio determining; laying down, pre cribing; assessment; ~रणीय fix ble, which can be assessed/dete mined; ~रित fixed; prescrib determined; o करना to assess; fix; to prescribe; to determi ~र्य see ~रणीय.

निर्निमेष nirnimēsh (*a* and *adv*) winking; with fixed look.

निर्नैतिक nirnāitik (*a*) amoral; ~ amorality.

निर्बंध nirbāndh (*a*) free, withe binding/restriction; uninhibit unbound; hence ~ता (*nf*).

निर्बल nirbal (*a*) weak, feeble; powerless; frail, fragile; ~ता weakness; feebleness; powerlessness; frailty, fragility;—के बल राम God helps those who have none to help.

निर्बाध nirba:dh (*a*) free; smooth; without binding/restriction; unobstructed; ~ता freedom; smoothness; absence of restriction/obstruction; –रूप से without any obstruction/hindrance/restriction/binding.

निर्बीजित nirbi:jit (*a*) sterilised; rendered unproductive/barren.

निर्बुद्धि nirbuddhi (*a*) stupid, foolish; blockheaded.

निर्भय nirbhay (*a*) fearless, dauntless, undaunted; daring; ~ता fearlessness, dauntlessness.

निर्भर nirbhar (*a*) dependent; based (on); subject or subordinate (to), depending (on), relying (on); ~ता dependence; subjection/subordination; reliance; –होना to depend, to be dependent; to rely; to base; to be subject or subordinate (to).

निर्भीक nirbhi:k (*a*) fearless, dauntless, undaunted; ~ता fearlessness, dauntlessness.

निर्भ्रम nirbhrām (*a*) having no doubt/illusion; unambiguous, cate: gorical, unequivocal.

निर्भ्रांत nirbhra:nt (*a*) see **निर्भ्रम**.

निर्मम nirmām (*a*) cruel, heartless, ruthless; dry; unfeeling; ~ता cruelty, heartlessness, ruthlessness.

निर्मल nirmal (*a*) clean; clear; pure; unsullied, spotless, stainless; ~ता cleanness; clearness; purity; stainlessness.

निर्मा/ण nirmā:ṇ (*nm*) construction; creation; manufacture; ~ण-कार्य construction work; ~ण-विद्या architecture; ~णशाला a workshop, factory; ~णात्मक formative; constructive; manufacturing; ~णावस्था formative/constructive stage.

निर्माणाधीन nirmā:ṇā:dhi:n (*a*) under construction.

निर्माणी nirma:ṇī: (*nf*) a factory, manufacturing unit.

निर्माता nirmā:ta: (*nm*) a constructor, producer (as of a film etc.); builder; creator.

निर्मि/त nirmit (*a*) constructed, built; produced; created; ~ति structure, construction; creation.

निर्मुक्ति nirmukti (*nf*) absolution; freedom, acquittal.

निर्मूल nirmu:l (*a*) baseless, groundless, unfounded, rootless; perfectly uprooted/destroyed/ruined; hence ~ता (*nf*).

निर्मोक nirmok (*nm*) moult, slough (of a snake); the upper surface of the skin.

निर्मोह nirmoh (*a*) disillusioned; unattached; callous.

निर्मोही nirmohi: (*a*) see **निर्मोह**; heartless, stone-hearted, having no affection and attachment.

निर्यात nirya:t (*nm*) export; -कर/शुल्क export duty; -व्यापार export trade.

निर्योग्य niryogy (*a*) disabled; ~ता disability.

निर्लज्ज nirlajj (*a*) shameless, lost to shame, brazen-faced; impudent, immodest; ~ता shamelessness; immodesty; impudence, effrontery.

निर्लिप्त nirlipt (*a*) detached; uninvolved; indifferent; hence ~ता (*nf*).

निर्लेप nirlep (*a*) see **निर्लिप्त**.

निर्लोभ nirlobh (*a*) not greedy, unavaricious; (*nm*) loss of greediness.

निर्वंश nirvānsh (*a*) non-proligerous, having no progeny/lineage, with no filial continuity.

निर्वच/न nirvachān (*nm*) interpretation; explanation; etymology; (*a*) speechless; ~नीय fit to be explained/interpreted.

निर्वनीकरण nirvanī:karāṉ (*nm*) deforestation.

निर्वस/न nirvasan (*a*) nude, naked; with no clothes on; uncovered; hence ~ना—fem. form.

निर्वहण nirvahāṉ (*nm*) see निर्वाह; discharge; the catastrophe (in a drama).

निर्वाचक nirva:chak (*nm*) an elector; -गण/मंडल/समूह electorate; -नामावली/सूची electoral roll.

निर्वाचन nirva:chān (*nm*) election; -क्षेत्र constituency.

निर्वाचित nirva:chit (*a*) elected.

निर्वाण nirvā:ṉ (*nm*) salvation, liberation (from existence; used in Buddhist Philosophy as a technical term); extinction; –प्राप्त करना to achieve salvation.

निर्वात nirva:t (*nm*) vacuum; (*a*) devoid of air, airless.

निर्वाप(ण) nirva:p(āṉ) (*nm*) extinction, extinguishing.

निर्वा/सन nirva:san (*nm*) expulsion; exile, expatriation, banishment; ~सित expelled; exiled, expatriated, banished.

निर्वाह nirva:h (*nm*) maintenance, subsistence; sustenance; accomplishment, adjustment; -भत्ता maintenance allowance.

निर्विकल्प nirvikalp (*a*) resolute, unwavering, concentrated, having no alternative.

निर्विकार nirvika:r (*a*) immutable, invariable; passionless; hence ~ता (*nf*).

निर्विघ्न nirvighn (*a*) uninterrupted, unobstructed; smooth; (*adv*) freely, unobstructedly; smoothly.

निर्विरोध nirvirodh (*a* and *adv*) unanimous(ly); unopposed, uncontested.

निर्विवाद nirviva:d (*a*) incontrovertible; indisputable, irrefutable.

निर्विशेष nirvishesh (*a*) without distinction, having no attributes; invariable; (*nm*) the Transcendental Reality.

निर्वीर्य nirvi:ry (*a*) impotent; unmanly; vigourless; spiritless; (*nm*) a weakling.

निर्वेग nirveg (*a*) with no dash/passion; calm, quiet.

निर्वेद nirved (*nm*) disregard of worldly objects, resignation.

निर्व्याज nirvya:j (*a*) honest, sincere; genuine; hence ~ता (*nf*).

निर्व्याधि nirvya:dhi (*a*) free from maladies; healthy.

निलय nilay (*nm*) abode, habitat; dwelling (place), nacelle.

निवल nival (*a*) net; –लाभ net gain; –हानि net loss.

निवार(ड़) niva:r(ṛ) (*nf*) wide and compact cotton tape used for a bedstead.

निवारक niva:rak (*a*) preventive; preclusive; deterrent.

निवा/रण niva:rāṉ (*nm*) prevention, preclusion; redress; deterrence, determent; ~र्य preventible, fit to be precluded; also ~रणीय (*a*).

निवाला niva:la: (*nm*) a morsel.

निवास niva:s (*nm*) residence, abode, habitation, lodging, dwelling; -स्थल quarter, habitat; -स्थान house, residence.

निवासी niva:si: (*a*) inhabitant; resident; inmate; native.

निविड़ niviṛ (*a*) thick, dense; impervious; ~ता thickness, density; imperviousness.

निविदा nivida: (*nm*) a tender; -सूचना tender notice.

निविष्ट nivishṭ (*a*) concentrated; penetrated.

निवृत्त nivritt (*a*) disencumbered; retired; freed; liberated; unoccupied; finished, completed, terminated.

निवृत्ति nivritti (*nf*) disencumberance, retirement; resignation (from mundane activity); freedom, liberation; absence of occupation; completion, finishing, termination.

निवेदक nivedak (*nm*) supplicant, applicant; one who makes a request/submission.

निवेदन nivedān (*nm*) supplication; request; submission; application; –**करना** to submit, to make an humble submission; hence **निवेदित** (*a*).

निवेरना nivernā: (*v*) to settle; to thrash out.

निवेश nivesh (*nm*) investment; concentration, penetration; encampment, habitation; hence **निवेशित** (*a*).

निशांध nishā:ndh (*a*) night-blind; ~**ता** night-blindness.

निशा nisha: (*nf*) night; ~**कर** the moon; ~**चर** a demon; evil spirit; ~**चरी** demonic; o **वृत्ति** demonic spirit; ~**नाथ** the moon.

निशाख़ातिर nisha:k̤ha:tir (*nf*) assurance, conviction; –**रखना** to rest assured.

निशान nishā:n (*nm*) a sign, mark; landmark; marking; scar; an impression; standard, flag; an emblem; a clue, trace; ~**देही** identification; demarcation; ~**बरदार** a standard-bearer; ~**बरदारी** carrying aloft of a standard.

निशाना nisha:nā: (*nm*) a target, butt; mark, aim; –**बनाना** to make a butt of, to aim at; –**बाँधना** to draw a bead on, to take an aim; –**मारना/लगाना** to strike, to hit a target; –**साधना** to take an aim.

निशानी nishā:nī: (*nf*) a memento, keepsake, token, mark mark of identification, sign; trace.

निशाने/बाज़ nisha:neba:z (*nm*) a marksman, expert/crack shot; ~**बाज़ी** marksmanship.

निशास्ता nisha:sta: (*nm*) wheat-starch.

निशि nishi (*nf*) night; ~**कर** the moon; ~**चर** a demon, evil spirit; ~**दिन** day and night; ~**वासर** see ~**दिन**.

निशीथ nishi:th (*nf*) night, midnight.

निश्च/य nishchay (*nm*) determination, resolution; settlement; decision; certainty; (*a*) definite; certain; positive; (*adv*) definitely, certainly; positively; ~**यात्मक** positive; definite, decisive, certain; hence ~**यात्मकता** (*nf*).

निश्चर nishchar (*a*) see **निश्चल**; (*nm*) an invariant; hence ~**ता** (*nf*).

निश्चल nishchal (*a*) steady; unwavering; quiet; quiescent; immovable; immobile; stationary; hence ~**ता** (*nf*).

निश्चायक nishcha:yak (*a*) decisive; positive.

निश्चिंत nishchint (*a*) carefree, (self-) assured; convinced; unconcerned; hence ~**ता** (*nf*).

निश्चित nishchit (*a*) definite, certain, sure; ascertained, positive, definite; hence ~**ता** (*nf*).

निश्चेतक nishchetak (*a*) anaesthetic.

निश्चेष्ट nishchesht (*a*) still, motionless; inert, quiet; unconscious; hence ~**ता** (*nf*).

निश्छल nishchhal (*a*) straightforward; honest; uncanny, without wiles, guileless; hence ~**ता** (*nf*).

निश्वास nishshva:s (*nm*) exhalation; sigh.

निश्शंक nishshānk (*a*) unhesitating; unapprehensive; dauntless, intrepid, fearless; hence ~ता (*nf*).

निषंग nishāṅg (*nm*) a quiver.

निषि/द्ध nishiddh (*a*) tabooed; prohibited, forbidden, banned; ~द्धि a taboo; prohibition, ban.

निषेचन nishechān (*nm*) insemination.

निषेध nishedh (*nm*) a taboo; prohibition, ban, negation; ~वाद negativism; ~वादी negativistic; a negativist; -विधि negative rule, forbidding rule; -वृत्ति negativism, negativitic attitude; hence ~क (*nm*); ~न (*nm*).

निषेधाज्ञा nishedha:gya: (*nf*) injunction; stay order.

निषेधात्मक nishedha:tmāk (*a*) negative, prohibitive, forbidding; hence ~ता (*nf*).

निषेधाधिकार nishedha:dhika:r (*nm*) veto power; –का प्रयोग करना to veto, to exercise veto.

निष्कंटक nishkāṉṭak (*a*) unobstructed, smooth; secure; –राज्य/शासन smooth/secure/uninterrupted government.

निष्कंप nishkāmp (*a*) unwavering, unquivering, untremulous, unflickering, steady; hence ~ता (*nf*).

निष्कपट nishkapaṭ (*a*) straightforward, honest, ingenuous, uncanny, guileless, unwily; hence ~ता (*nf*).

निष्कर्ष nishkarsh (*nm*) conclusion, inference; extract, epitome; ~ण extraction; –निकालना to draw an inference, to arrive at a conclusion.

निष्कलंक nishkalāṅk (*a*) immaculate, spotless, stainless; without a blemish, pure; chaste; hence ~ता (*nf*).

निष्कलुष nishkalush (*a*) sinless, flawless, immaculate, clean; hence ~ता (*nf*).

निष्काम nishkā:m (*a*) without attachment, disinterested, free from desires/wishes, desireless, unselfish; ~ता state of being without attachment, disinterestedness, unselfishness.

निष्का/सन nishka:sān (*nm*) expulsion; ejectment; ~सित expelled; ejected.

निष्कृति nishkriti (*nf*) salvation, riddance, redemption.

निष्क्रमण nishkramāṉ (*nm*) exit; evacuation; withdrawal.

निष्क्रांत nishkrā:nt (*a* and *nm*) (an) evacuee.

निष्क्रिय nishkriy (*a*) inactive, inert; idle, non-working; passive; ~ता inactivity, inaction, inertia; idleness, passivity; --प्रतिरोध passive resistance.

निष्ठ nishṭḥ (*a*) trusting, having faith; usually used as an adjectival suffix meaning having faith/trust (in); devotion, affection; readiness, (for), or allegiance (to), engrossed (in), well-disposed (towards), etc. (as सत्यनिष्ठ, यथार्थनिष्ठ, कर्मनिष्ठ, etc.); ~ता used as a nominal suffix meaning the quality or state of having faith/trust in or allegiance to (as सत्यनिष्ठता, न्यायनिष्ठता, etc.).

निष्ठा nishṭḥa: (*nf*) allegiance; loyalty; faith; fidelity; devotion; ~वान loyal; faithful; fidel; devoted; ~हीन disloyal; faithless; infidel.

निष्ठुर nishṭḥur (*a*) ruthless; merciless, brutal; cruel, harsh; ~ता ruthlessness, mercilessness; brutality, cruelty; harshness.

निष्णात nishṉa:t (*a*) adept, expert; skilled.

निष्पंद nishpānd (*a*) steady; unwavering, unquivering, unflickering; hence ~ता (*nf*).

निष्पक्ष nishpaksh (*a*) objective; neutral, unbiassed; ~ता objectivity; neutrality, unbiassedness.

निष्पत्ति nishpatti (*nf*) attainment,

accomplishment, achievement; consummation; perfection; ~वाद perfectionism.

निष्पन्न nishpann (*a*) accomplished, concluded successfully, achieved consummation.

निष्पादन nishpa:dān (*nm*) execution; attaining, accomplishing, achieving; hence **निष्पादित** (*a*) **निष्पाद्य** (*a*).

निष्पाप nishpa:p (*a*) sinless, immaculate; innocent.

निष्प्रभ nishprabh (*a*) lustreless; devoid of glitter/shine; put out of countenance, disconcerted; hence ~ता (*nf*).

निष्प्रभाव nishprabha:v (*a*) ineffective; nullified, invalidated; defunct.

निष्प्रयोजन nishprayojān (*a* and *adv*) aimless(ly), without a purpose or object; hence ~ता (*nf*).

निष्फल nishphal (*a*) unavailing; ineffective, infructuous, inefficacious; vain; hence ~ता (*nf*).

निसबत nisbat (*nf*) connection; attachment, relationship; comparison; (*adv*) about; –, की as compared with.

निसर्ग nisarg (*nm*) nature; ~ज natural; innate, inborn; spontaneous; ~तः spontaneously, naturally; ~सिद्ध natural; spontaneous; innate, inborn.

निसार nisa:r (*a*) sacrificed; –करना to sacrifice.

निस्तत्त्व nistattv (*a*) worthess; unsubstantial, immaterial; having no content.

निस्तब्ध nistabdh (*a*) still; without motion or noise; quiet; hence ~ता (*nf*).

निस्तार nista:r (*nm*) quittance, riddance; redemption; emancipation.

निस्तेज nistej (*a*) lustreless, pallid; lifeless; spiritless; insipid.

निस्पंद nispānd (*a*) see **निष्पंद**.

निस्पृह nisprih (*a*) see **निःस्पृह**.

निस्यंद nisyānd (*a* and *nm*) filtrate; ~क a filter; ~न filtration.

निस्संको/च nissāṅkoch (*a*) unhesitating; inhesitant; (*adv*) unhesitatingly, without hesitation; hence ~ची (*a* and *nm*).

निस्संग nissāṅg (*a*) unattached; indifferent; hence ~ता (*nf*).

निस्संतान nissāntā:n (*a*) childless, issueless.

निस्सत्त्व nissattv (*a*) unsubstantial; worthless.

निस्सरण nissarāṇ (*nm*) going out or forth; outflow; -मार्ग exit, outlet.

निस्सहाय nissaha:y (*a*) helpless; ~ता helplessness.

निस्सार nissa:r (*a*) unsubstantial, illusory; worthless; hence ~ता(*nf*).

निस्सारण nissa:rān (*nm*) extraction, causing to flow or go out.

निस्सीम nissi:m (*a*) limitless, boundless; infinite; ~ता limitlessness; infinity.

निस्स्वार्थ nissva:rth (*a*) selfless, unselfish; ~ता selflessness; unselfishness.

निहंग nihāṅg (*a*) naked; shameless; alone; –लाड़ला spoilt love.

निहत्था nihattha: (*a*) unarmed; –करना to disarm; to cut the claws of; –होना to be disarmed

निहाई niha:i: (*nf*) an anvil.

निहानी nihā:nī: (*nf*) a compressor.

निहायत niha:yat (*adv*) extremely, excessively, absolutely, very much.

निहारना niha:rnā: (*v*) to see, to look at, to behold.

निहाल niha:l (*adv*) fulfilled, gratified; delighted.

निहित nihit (*a*) inherent, implied; vested; –स्वार्थ vested interest.

निहितार्थ nihita:rth (*nm*) implication; implied meaning.

निहोरना nihornā: (*v*) to entreat;

to supplicate.

निहोरा nihora: (*nm*) an entreaty; supplication; **निहोरे करना** to entreat; to supplicate.

नींद nī:d (*nf*) sleep, slumber; **–आना** to feel like sleeping, to be sleepy; **– उचटना** sleep to be dissipated, to have one's sleep broken abruptly; **–उड़ना** one's sleep to vanish, not to be able even to wink; **–, कुंभकर्ण की** long lasting sleep without rocking;**–खुलना/टूटना** to be awakened from one's sleep; **–,गहरी** sound sleep, sleep like a log; **–भर सोना** to have one's fill of sleep;**–लेना** to have a sleep/nap; **–हराम करना** to disturb one's sleep, not to allow one to sleep in peace.

नींबू nī:bu: (*nm*) see **नीबू**.

नींव nī:v (*nf*) foundation; base, ground; **–का पत्थर** foundation stone; **–जमाना** to consolidate, to establish on a firm footing; **–डालना** to lay the foundation (of); **–पड़ना** the foundation to be laid; **–देना** to provide with a base/foundation.

नीच nī:ch (*a*) mean, base, vile; inferior; low, lowly; **-ऊँच** low or/and high, good or/and bad, proper or/and improper; **–कमाई** ill-earned money; immoral profession; **–कुल** low family, low clan; **०का** low-born; **–जाति** low caste; **~पन/~पना** see **नीचता**.

नीचता nī:chta: (*nf*) meanness, baseness, vileness;inferiority; lowliness.

नीचा nī:cha: (*a*) mean, base, vile; low; deep; **~ई** lowness;depth; **~न** same as **नीचाई**; **–काम** mean act; work undertaken by low castes, menial work; **–खाना** to suffer a defeat, to be put to humiliation; **–दिखाना** to humble to the dust, to beat one into fits; to insult/humiliate; to overpower, to inflict a defeat; **नीची निगाह से देखना** to treat as low or inferior; to think as of no significance.

नीचे nī:che (*adv*) below; beneath; under, down; **–ऊपर** in succession, one immediately below or after the other; turned upside down, topsy-turvy; **–का पाट भारी** grey mare is better horse, wear the breeches (said of a wife dominating over her husband); **–की साँस नीचे और ऊपर की साँस ऊपर रह जाना** to hold/catch one's breath;**–गिरना** to fall; to be felled; to be morally degraded; **–से ऊपर तक** from head ;o foot; from top to bottom.

नीड़ ni:ṛ (*nm*) a nest;**–का पंछी** homesick (person).

नीति nī:ti (*nf*) policy; expediency; morality, eth.cs; **–काव्य** didactic poetry; **~कुशल/चतुर/निपुण** politic; sagacious; **~मत्ता** adherence to ethical laws; **~मान** one who knows and follows ethical laws, just and fair; **-विद्या/शास्त्र** ethics, the science of morality.

नीतिज्ञ ni:tigy (*a*) sagacious, politic; hence **~ता** (*nf*).

नीबू nī:bu: (*nm*) a lemon.

नीम nī:m (*nm*) the margosa tree;(*a*) half, semi; **~आस्तीन** half-sleeve; **~जाँ** half-dead; **~पुख़्ता** semi-ripe; half-consolidated; **~रज़ा** half-consent, connivance;**~हकीम** a quack; **०ख़तरा-ए-जान** a little knowledge is a dangerous thing.

नीमचक nī:mchak (*nm*) the wooden platform of a well upon which the brick-work or masonry rests as a foundation.

नीयत nī:yat (*nf*) motive; intention; **–डाँवाडोल होना/डिगना/बदलना/बद होना/बिगड़ना/बुरी होना/में फ़र्क आना** toundergo a change of intention, to be lured into ill intention, the motive to turn malafide, to be swept off the ground of honesty; –बाँधना to make a firm resolve; –लगी रहना to keep concentrating upon.

नीर ni:r (*nm*) water; -क्षीर -विवेक (power of) discrimination between the substantial/genuine and the unsubstantial/sham; ~ज a lotus flower; ~द/धर a cloud; ~निधि the ocean, sea; —बहाना to shed tears.

नीरम ni:rām (*nm*) ballast.

नीरव ni:rav (*a*) quiet, calm; still; ~ता quietude, calmness; stillness.

नीरस ni:ras (*a*) sapless, juiceless; dry; flat; stodgy; insipid; prosaic; uninteresting; hence ~ता (*nf*).

नीरा ni:ra: (*nm*) unfermented palm juice (a refreshing and stimulating beverage).

नीरो/ग ni:rog (*a*) free from disease; hale, healthy; also ~गी (*a*).

नील ni:l (*nm*) indigo, the plant and the dye; ten billions; (*a*) blue; (in mediaeval usage) also black; ~कंठ the blue-necked jay: Coracias Indica; an epithet of Lord Shiv; –कमल blue lotus; ~गाय a species of deer; –निलय the sky; ~मणि a sapphire; –लोहित reddish blue, purple; नीलांजन blue vitriol; –पड़ना to be beaten blue, to be belaboured; to develop a blue scar (on the skin etc.).

नीलम ni:lām (*nm*) a sapphire.

नीला ni:la: (*a*) blue, azure; –थोथा copper sulphate; ~पन blueness; -सा bluish; –करना lit. to beat blue, to belabour; -पीला होना to be in a terrible temper, to be enraged/infuriated.

नीलाम ni:la:m (*nm*) auction, public sale; ~कर्ता auctioneer; ~घर an auction house; auctioneering agency; –पर चढ़ाना to be brought to the hammer; to sell by inch of candle; –में बोली बोलना to bid.

नीलामी ni:la:mī: (*nf*) auction, public sale; –पर चढ़ाना to auction.

नीवी ni:vi: (*nf*) a waist-cord.

नीहार ni:ha:r (*nm*) mist, fog; –जल dew.

नीहारिका ni:ha:rika: (*nf*) a nebula.

नुकता nukta: (*nm*) a defect; flaw, fault; deficiency; ~चीं a fault-finder, critic; ~चीनी fault-finding, criticism.

नुक़ता nuqta: (*nm*) a point, dot; blot, patch.

नुकती nukti: (*nf*) a kind of sweetened tiny pills of gram floor fried in ghee.

नुक़सान nuqsā:n (*nm*) (*a*) loss, damage; harm; disadvantage; ~देह harmful, disadvantageous; –उठाना to suffer a loss/damage; –देना to inflict a loss; –पर नुक़सान उठाना to throw the helve after the hatchet; –पहुँचना to be harmed, to suffer a loss; –भरना to recompense, to make good the loss.

नुकीला nuki:la: (*a*) pointed, sharp; ~पन pointedness, sharpness; hence नुकीली (fem. form).

नुक्कड़ nukkaṛ (*nm*) corner, bulging or protruding corner; end; turning point (of a road etc.).

नुक़्स nuqs (*nm*) defect; fault, flaw; deficiency; ~दार defective; faulty; deficient; –निकालना to find fault.

नुनखरा nūnkhara: (*a*) saltish, saline, brackish; ~पन saltishness, brackishness.

नुमा numā: —an adjectival suffix which imparts such meanings as manifesting, showing, exhibiting; like, resembling, etc. to the words it is appended to (e.g. रहनुमा,

खुशनुमा).

नुमाइंदगी numa:īndgi: (*nf*) representation: delegacy.

नुमाइंदा numa:īnda: (*nm*) a representative; delegate.

नुमाइ/श numa:ish (*nf*) an exhibition, a show; display; ~शी showy, ostentatious; meant for display.

नुमायाँ numā:yā: (*a*) manifest; glaring, apparent, obvious; –होना to appear, to be manifest.

नुसख़ा nuskḥa: (*nm*) a prescription, recipe; formula; –बाँधना to dispense (as a prescription); –लिखना to give a prescription.

नूतन nu:tan (*a*) new, novel; ~ता newness, novelty.

नूपुर nu:pur (*nm*) an anklet; -ध्वनि melodious sound of an anklet.

नूर nu:r (*nm*) light; lustre; resplendence; ~चश्म beloved son.

नृ nri (*nm*) used in compound words—meaning man; ~केशरी an incarnation of Lord Vishnū; possessing the valour of a lion, lion-like man; ~पशु a beastly man; ~सिंह see ~केशरी; ~हरि see ~केशरी.

नृत्य nritty (*nm*) dance, dancing; a dance performance; -कला the art of dancing; -गुरू dance-teacher; -नाट्य ballet; -प्रतियोगिता dance competition; ~शाला a dancing hall; -समारोह a dance festival.

नृप nrip (*nm*) a king, monarch.

नृपति nripati (*nm*) see नृप.

नृपोचित nripochit (*a*) befitting a king, kingly, monarchical, majestic.

नृशंस nrishans (*a*) atrocious; savage, cruel.

नृशंसता nrishansata: (*nf*) atrociousness, savagery, cruelty.

ने ne—a postposition denoting the subjective case.

नेक nek (*a*) good, virtuous; –अख़्लाक well behaved; –ख़्याल well-meaning, good; ~चलन of good conduct; ~चलनी good conduct; ~ज़ात of good breed, well-bred; ~तर better; ~तरीन best; ~दिल virtuous, gentle; ~नाम reputed, well-known, having a good name; ~नामी reputtation, good name; ~नीयत well-intentioned, genuine, honest; ~नीयती good faith, goodness of intention, genuineness, honesty; –पाक virtuous; ~बख़्त fortunate, lucky, blest; ~बख़्ती fortune, luck, happy lot.

नेकी neki: (*nf*) goodness; virtue, piety; -बदी good and bad/evil; –और पूछ-पूछ why seek the permission of one you are doing a good turn to ?; do a good turn but why embarrass your beneficiary ?; –कर और कुएँ/दरिया में डाल to cast your bread upon the water, do a good turn and forget it, be beneficient but do not publicise your deed.

नेग neg (*nm*) conventional due, customary presents and gifts on festive occasions (to those relatives and dependents who are entitled by virtue of their relationship); ~चार, ~जोग see नेग.

नेज़ा neza: (*nm*) a javelin, lance; ~बरदार a javelin-bearer, lancer.

नेता neta: (*nm*) a leader; pioneer, ~गीरी leadership used in a derogatory sense.

नेति neti—a Sanskrit expression (meaning 'there is no end') used by philosophers to underline the view that He (God) defies all description.

नेतृत्व netrittv (*nm*) leadership; –शक्ति faculty of leadership; –करना to lead; –देना to provide leadership,

नेत्र nettr (*nm*) an eye; ~क an eye-piece; -जल tear(s); -रोग eye diseases; ~विज्ञान ophthalmology; ~वैज्ञानिक ophthalmologist;

~ विहीन blind.

नेपथ्य nepatthy (*nm*) back of the stage, green room; -संगीत playback music.

नेपा/ल nepa:l (*nm*) a sovereign Hindu state situated in the north of India; ~ ली an inhabitant of Nepal; pertaining to Nepal; the Nepalese language.

नेफ़ा nefa: (*nm*) the stitched hollow strip in the upper part of trousers etc. wherein a cord is passed for binding round the waist; abbreviated nomenclature for the North Eastern Frontier Agency of the Indian union (NEFA).

नेम nēm (*nm*) routine; rule (of religious conduct); religious practice; custom; –धरम religious practice, custom; religious practices and customs.

नेमत nēmāt (*nf*) see नियामत.

नेवला nevla: (*nm*) a mongoose, an ichneumon.

नेस्त nest (*a*) naught, non-existent; ~ नाबूद completely destroyed/devastated; in ruins.

नेस्ती nesti: (*a*) ominous; lazy; ~ पन ominousness; laziness.

नेह neh (*nm*) *tadbhav*-form of Sanskrit स्नेह (see).

नैकट्य naikaṭṭy (*nm*) nearness, proximity.

नैचा naicha: (*nm*) the pipes of a hubble-bubble tied together.

नैज naij (*a*) personal, one's own.

नैतिक naitik (*a*) moral, ethical; –अंतर्बोध synderesis; ~ ता morality; –भावना moral sense.

नैत्यिक naittyik (*a*) routine; usual.

नैन nāīn (*nm*) an eye; ~ नक़्श facial features/cut; ~ सुख a typical fine cotton cloth; –अघाना eyes to be gratified (through the sight of a beautiful object); –उलझना to catch a fancy for, to fall for.

नैपुण्य naipūnny (*nm*) dexterity, skillfulness, adroitness.

नैमित्तिक naimittik (*a*) casual; occasional, accidental; hence ~ ता (*nf*).

नैरंतर्य nairāntary (*nm*) continuity, uninterruptedness.

नैराश्य naira:shshy (*nm*) frustration; disappointment, despair; –भावना sense of frustration/despair.

नैवेद्य naivedy (*nm*) oblation, offerings made to a deity.

नैष्ठिक naishṭhik (*a*) faithful; inspired by religious faith; hence ~ ता (*nf*); –ब्रह्मचारी one who faithfully observes strict celibacy from the sacred thread ceremony till the end while residing at the preceptor's hermitage.

नैसर्गिक naisargik (*a*) natural, spontaneous; ~ ता naturalness, spontaneity.

नैहर naihar (*nm*) a woman's paternal home/village/city.

नोक nōk (*nf*) point; tip; end; forepart; -झोंक mutual repartee, pleasantry, mock altercation; ~ दार pointed; sharp.

नोच nōch—abstract nominal form of the verb नोचना, rarely used except in the compound -खसोट grabbing, pinching and snatching.

नोचना nōchnā: (*v*) to pinch; to scratch; to pluck.

नोट noṭ (*nm*) a note, currency note; ~ बुक a notebook; –करना to make a note of, to note (down).

नोटिस noṭis (*nm*) a notice; –देना to serve a notice.

नोद nod (*nm*) a thrust.

नोदन nodān (*nm*) propulsion; -शक्ति propelling force; –करना to propel.

नोन nōn (*nm*) salt; -तेल-लकड़ी daily household needs/necessaries; ०की चिंता होना to be worried about daily household needs.

नोनी nonī: (*nf*) butter.

नोश nosh (*nm*) nectar, delicious drink—not in usage in Hindi as such except in the idioms–करना, –फ़रमाना used in respectful speech meaning to eat/to drink.

नौ nau (*a*) nine; new, fresh; (*nm*) the number nine; a boat ship; -अधिकरण the admiralty; ~कर्ण a rudder; ~घाट ferry; ~चालन navigation, shipping; ~जवान a youngman, in the prime of youth; ~जवानी prime of youth, young age; ~निहाल the growing/rising generation, youth; child; ~परिवहन navigation, shipping; ~बहार spring; new bloom; ~बेड़ा navy, naval fleet; ~रोज़ the new year's day (according to the Pa:rsi: system) a day of festivity; ~रोहण embarkation; shipment; ~लखा costing nine lacs of rupees; very precious; ~वहन shipping; ~विधि naval law; ~सिखिया greenhorn; a novice, learner, fresher; ~सेना navy, naval force; ~सेनाध्यक्ष naval chief; ~सैन्यवाद navalism; ~सेवा navy, naval service; –दिन चले अढ़ाई कोस to be very slow in movement, to make a movement that is as good as no movement; –नगद न तेरह उधार a bird in hand is better than two in the bush; -दो ग्यारह होना to turn tails, to make good one's escape, to show a clean pair of heels.

नौकर naukar (*nm*) a servant; an employee; -चाकर the whole retinue of servants/attendants/employees; domestics; ~शाह a bureaucrat; ~शाही bureaucracy; bureaucratic; hence नौकरानी (*nf*).

नौकराना naukra:nā: (*a*) servile; befitting, pertaining or belonging to a servant; (*nm*) wages.

नौकरी naukri: (*nf*) a service, job; an employment; –बजाना to render service, to dance attendance(upon); ~पेशा (people) in-service; ०वर्ग in-service class; –से जवाब मिलना to set the boot, to be fired,

नौका nauka: (*nf*) a boat, ferry.

नौज nauj (*ind*) lest; God forbid; no matter.

नौबत naubat (*nf*) state of affairs; condition; turn; a kettledrum; ~ख़ाना drum-house; -ब-नौबत turn by turn; –आना to come to such a pass, to come to a miserable plight; –बजना drums to be beaten, festivity to commence; –बजाकर openly; with beat of drums.

नौशा nausha: (*nm*) the bridegroom.

नौसादर nausa:dar (*nm*) sal-ammoniac, ammonium chloride.

न्यस्त nyast (*a*) deposited, trusted, vested; abandoned.

न्यागमन nya:gamān (*nm*) devolution.

न्याय nya:y (*nm*) justice; fairness; a popular maxim or apposite illustration (as घुणाक्षर न्याय); logic; ~कर्ता a judge, one who sits in judgment; ~निष्ठ; just, fair, equitable. ~निष्ठता justness, fairness, equitability; -पथ just/fair/equitable course; ~पर just, fair, equitable; ~परता justness, fairness, equitability; ~परायण just, fair, equitable; ~परायणता justness, fairness, equitability; ~पालिका see न्यायांग; ~पीठ bench; ~प्रिय just, fair, equitable; hence ~प्रियता (*nf*); ~वादी an attorney; just/fair/equitable in utterance; ~शास्त्र jurisprudence; ~शास्त्री jurisprudent; ~शील see ~पर; ~संगत just, fair, equitable; -सभा a court of law; bench.

न्यायतः nya:ytah (*ind*) legally; justly speaking, for the sake of justice.

न्यायमूर्ति nya:ymu:rti (*a*) justice (so and so).

याांग nya:yā:ṅg (*nm*) the judiciary.
ायाधिकरण nya:ya:dhikarān (*nm*) a tribunal.
ायाधिवक्ता nya:ya:dhivakta: (*nm*) the judge-advocate.
ायाधीश nya:ya:dhi:sh (*nm*) a judge; Justice.
यालय nya:ya:lay (*nm*) a court of law; judicature.
ायासन nya:ya:sān (*nm*) the seat of justice.
ायिक nya:yik (*a*) judicial, juridical.
ायी nya:yi: (*a*) just, justly, equitable.
ायोचित nya:yochit (*a*) just, equitable, fair.
ाय्य nya:yy (*a*) see न्यायोचित.
ारा nya:ra: (*a*) separate(d); staying away (from a joint family); unique, novel; distinct; hence ~पन (*nm*).
ास nya:s (*nm*) a trust; deposit; arrangement; ~धारी a trustee.
न्यासी nyā:si: (*nm*) a trustee.
न्यून nyu:n (*a*) less; lacking, deficient; low, inferior; small; –कोण acute angle; ~तम minimum, minimal; ~तर lesser, less than, smaller; hence ~ता (*nf*); –मूल्यांकन under-valuation.
न्यूनाधिक nyū:nā:dhik (*a*) more or less.
न्यो(यौ)छावर nyo(yau)chha:var (*nf*) a propitiatory offering; coins or currency notes scattered or gifted away on festive occasions (as birth-day etc.) and marriages (to ward off troubles and tribulations from the person concerned; sacrifice; –होना to offer to make a sacrifice (for someone).
न्यो(यौ)तना nyō(āu)tnā: (*v*) to invite.
न्यो(यौ)ता nyō(āu)ta: (*nm*) an invitation; –देना to extend an invitation.

प

प pa—the first letter of the fifth and ultimate pentad (i.e. पवर्ग) of the Devna:gri: alphabet; a Sanskrit suffix meaning drinking/one who drinks (as मद्यप); guarding, protecting (as गोप); ruling (as नृप); (in music) the fifth note of the gamut.
पंक pāṅk (*nm*) mud, slush; mire, bog, quagmire.
पंकज paṅkaj (*nm*) a lotus (flower).
पंकिल paṅkil (*a*) muddy; slushy; boggy; ~ता muddiness, bogginess; quagginess.
पंक्चर paṅkchar (*nm*) a puncture; –करना to puncture; –जोड़ना mend a puncture.
पंक्ति paṅkti (*nf*) a line; row; file; rank; queue; ~बद्ध arranged in a line or row; queued up; hence ०ता (*nf*); –बनाना to fall in
पंक्तिका paṅktika: (*nf*) diminutive of पंक्ति (see).
पंख paṅkh (*nm*) wing; pinion, feather; blade; –कतरना/काटना see पर–(कतरना); –जमना/निकलना lit. to grow wings–to take to risky ways; to give oneself airs; –परेवा बना

डालना to invest a trifle with undue importance, to make fuss, to over-stretch a point; –लगना to move at a very fast pace; to take to risky ways.

पंखड़ी paṅkhṛi: (*nf*) a petal; blade.

पंखा paṅkha: (*nm*) a fan; –करना/–झलना to fan; –चलाना to switch on the fan.

पंखिका paṅkhi:ka: (*nf*) a finlet.

पंखीं paṅkhi: (*nf*) a small fan; (*nm*) a bird.

पंखु/ड़ी, ~री paṅkhuṛi:, ~ri: (*nf*) see पंखड़ी.

पंग/त, ~ति paṅgat, ~ti (*nf*) a row; a row of invitees taking meals en masse, community feast; –बैठना to be seated in a row for community feasting; –से बाहर करना to excommunicate.

पंगु paṅgu (*a*) lame (crippled by defect in a foot or leg); ~ता, ~त्व lameness; ~ल lame; –हो जाना to be incapacitated, to be rendered helpless.

पँच pach—an allomorph of पंच (five) used in a number of compound words; ~मेल a mixture of five; a mixture of five kinds of sweetmeat; ~रंगा five-coloured; ~लड़ा consisting of five strings; ~हरा quintuplicate.

पंच paṇch (*a*) five; (*nm*) the number five; an arbitrator or a body of arbiters or jury; the headman of a caste or village; ~क a set or aggregate of five; in Astrology, a coincidence of five stars wherein commencement of an auspicious ceremony is prohibited; ~कर्म the five actions of the body as propounded under the Indian medicinal system; ~कोण a pentagon; ~कोश according to the Veda:nt, the five covering shells of the soul viz. अन्नमय कोश, प्राणमय कोश, मनोमय कोश, विज्ञानमय कोश and आनंदमय कोश; ~खना five-storeyed; ~गव्य the five products of the cow, viz. milk, curd (coagulated milk), butter and the liquid and solid excreta (गोबर and गोमूत्र); ~गुण five-times; the five attributes of sound (शब्द), touch (स्पर्श), form (रूप), taste (रस) and smell (गंध); ~तत्त्व the five essential elements viz, earth, water, fire, air and ether; ~त्व the transformation of the five elements of the body (पंचभूत) to their respec- five original forms; death; o को प्राप्त होना lit. to be transformed into the five original elements—to expire; ~दश fifteen; ~देव the five major gods of the Hindu:s—Vishṇū, Shiv, Gaṇēsh, Su:ry, Durga:; ~नद having five rivers; the province of Punjab in pre-partition India; ~नामा the mutualy written agreement between the contending parties; to appoint an arbitrator or a body of arbitrators; ~पात्र the five vessels of adoration collectively; a vessel used for offering water to the idol; ~प्राण the five vital airs of the body; -फ़ैसला arbitration, the award of a court of arbitration; ~भूत the five elements viz. earth, fire, water, air and ether; ~भूतात्मा a human being made up of the पंचभूत; ~मकार in religious rites of the Va:m-ma:rgi:s, the five essentials each beginning with the letter 'म' viz. मद्य (wine), मांस (human flesh), मत्स्य (fish), मुद्रा (gesticulation) and मैथुन (copulation); –महायज्ञ the five great sacrifices specified for the Hindus viz. the worship of the spirits (भूतयज्ञ); the worship of progenitors (पितृयज्ञ); the worship of gods

(देवयज्ञ); the worship of the Vedas (ब्रह्मयज्ञ), and the worship of mankind (नृयज्ञ); ~लौह an alloy of five metals, viz. gold, silver, copper, tin and lead; ~वटी the aggregate of the five trees (पीपल, बेल, बड़, हड़ and अशोक); the venue of Ram's stay in Daṇḍaka:-rāṇṇy while in banishment; ~वर्षीय quinquennial; ~शील the five basic principles of international conduct designed to achieve and consolidate world peace, first enunciated by Free India's first Prime Minister, Paṇḍit Jawa:harla:l Nehru:—(1) respect for each other's sovereignty and territorial integrity; (2) assurance of mutual non-aggression; (3) non-interference in each other's internal affairs; (4) equality and co-operation for mutual benefit; (5) peaceful co-existence; –की दुहाई appeal to the arbitrators (for help); –परमेश्वर taking the arbitrator as representing God; –बदना/मानना to agree on an arbitrator/mediator.

पंच/म pāṇchām (*a*) fifth; (*nm*) the fifth note of Indian musical scale; one of the musical modes; ~मांग fifth column; ~मांगी a fifth columnist; ~माक्षर the fifth and nasal letter of each pentad viz. ङ, ञ, ण, न, म.

पंचमी pāṇchmī: (*nf*) the fifth day of each lunar fortnight.

पंचर panchar (*nm*) see पंक्चर.

पंचांग pāṇchā:ng (*a*) having five members/parts/sub-divisions; (*nm*) a calendar, analmanac, ephemeris.

पंचाग्नि pāṇcha:gnī (*nf*) a collection of five fires (one each of the east, west, north, and south, the sun overhead being the fifth) amidst which Hindu devotees perform penance, five mystic fires supposed to be present in human body; —तपना to undertake the severest penance.

पंचाट pāṇcha:ṭ (*nm*) an award, arbitral award.

पंचामृत pāṇcha:mrit (*nm*) a mixture of milk, curd, sugar, ghee and honey.

पंचायत pāṇcha:yat (*nf*) a village assembly; arbitration or a body of arbitrators; an assembly of elected representatives; (a gathering for) gossip-mongering; ~घर the seat of the पंचायत; –जोड़ना/बटोरना to cause a gossip gathering, to assemble a team of gossip-mongers; to assemble a body of arbitrators; –बैठाना to submit a dispute to the पंचायत for settlement; to assemble a body of arbitrators.

पंचायती pāṇcha:yati: (*a*) pertaining or belonging to the community as a whole, common, public; run by elected representatives; –राज्य rule by elected representatives; a republic.

पंचेंद्रिय pāṇchēndriy (*nf*) the five organs of sense (the eye, ear, nose, tongue, and skin or of action (the hand, foot, larynx, anus and the genital organ).

पंछी pāṇchhi: (*nm*) a bird.

पं/ज pāṇj (*a*) five; ~जाब the Paṇja:b –land of five rivers, a northern state of the Indian Union.

पंजर pāṇjar (*nm*) a skeleton, frame; cage; –बँधना to be reduced to a skeleton.

पंजा pāṇja: (*nm*) a claw, paw, forefoot; five fingers or toes; an aggregate of five; playing card having five pips; –फैलाना/बढ़ाना to extend one's hand for gaining control (over); to extend the scope of influence; पंजे में firmly under control; पंजों के बल चलना to walk on the toes, to walk unnoticed/stealthily.

पंजा/ब pānja:b (*nm*) a northern state of the Indian Union; the erstwhile land of the five rivers (viz. सतलुज, व्यास, रावी, चनाब, जेहलम); ~बी the language of the Panja:b; an inhabitant of the Panja:b; pertaining to the Pānja:b.

पंजिका pānjika: (*nf*) a word by word commentary, detailed commentary; an almanac.

पंजी pānji: (*nf*) a register; ~करण/~यन registration; ~यित/~कृत registered.

पँजीरी, पंजीरी pāji:ri:, pānji:ri: (*nf*) a typical preparation of wheat flour fried in ghee and sugar mixed with ground coriander seeds and dry ginger administered to puerperal women or distributed as प्रसाद (see).

पंजुम pānjūm (*a*) the fifth.

पंडा pānda: (*nm*) a Hindu: priest helping devout pilgrims in the performance of religious rites on holy river banks; ~गीरी the function or profession of a पंडा.

पंडाल pānda:l (*nm*) a huge pavilion, marquee.

पंडित pāndit (*nm*) a Bra:hmān (by caste); a scholar, learned person; one well-versed in scriptures and performance of religious rites; -मंडली/सभा an assembly of scholars; a learned assembly; ~राज a pre-eminent scholar, king of scholars; ~वादी a pedant, pedagogue.

पंडितम्मन्य pānditmmānny (*nm*) a pedant, one who over-rates oneself as a scholar and is proud of it; ~ता pedantry, pedantic conceit.

पंडिताई pāndita:i: (*nf*) scholarship; erudition; the function or profession of a *pandit*; –छाँटना to make a show of or to exhibit one's scholarship/erudition.

पंडिताऊ pāndita:u: (*a*) pedantic; bookish, academic; befitting a *pandit*; hence ~पन (*nm*).

पंथ pānth (*nm*) a path, road; creed, sect, cult; religious order (as कबीर-पंथ, दादूपंथ); the sikh panth; –दिखाना to guide, to lead on correct lines; –देखना/निहारना to wait, to keep in wait for; –पर लाना/लगाना to veer round to the correct course, to lead to right lines.

पंथी pānthi: (*nm*) a traveller; an adherent or follower of a sect.

पंद्रह pāndreh (*a*) fifteen; (*nm*) the number fifteen.

पंप pāmp (*nm*) a pump; a kind of shoe.

पँवारा pāwa:ra: (*nm*) a saga of heroic deeds; boring detailed narrative; –करना/गाना to render into wearying details.

पंसारी pānsa:ri: (*nm*) a grocer.

पँसेरी, पंसेरी pāseri:, panseri: (*nf*) a five-seer weight; –में पाँच सेर की भूल करना to make a total error.

पकड़ pakar (*nf*) hold; grip; catch-up; seizure, grasp; understanding; a hug; -धकड़ apprehensions, seizures, (round) of arrests; –जाना to be arrested/apprehended; –ढीली होना the grip to be loosened; –मजबूत होना the grip to be tight(ened); –में आना to be held; to fall into the clutches (of).

पक/ड़ना pakarnā: (*v*) to catch (hold of); to hold; to grasp, to seize apprehend; ~ड़ा-धकड़ी see पकड़-धकड़.

पकना paknā: (*v*) to ripen; to be cooked; to mature; to supporate (as फोड़ा–); to turn grey (as बाल–); पका-आम on the last leg of one's worldly journey.

पकवान pakwā:n (*nm*) dressed foods; a fried delicacy.

पकाई paka:i: (*nf*) seasoning; curing; maturity, ripening.

पकाना paka:nā: (*v*) to ripen; to cook; to bake; to season; to cure.

पकौ/ड़ा pakauṛa: (*nm*) a fried saltish vegetable-stuffed gram-flour preparation; hence ~ड़ी diminutive (*nf*).

पक्का pakka: (*a*) ripe; strong, lasting, permanent; firm; net; expert; confirmed; fried in ghee (as –खाना); boiled; –गाना a classical song; –करना to ensure fully, to get final confirmation.

पक्व pakkv (*a*) ripe; boiled; mature; strong; hence ~ता (*nf*).

पक्ष paksh (*nm*) side; party; flank; aspect; a fortnight; a wing; ~क an aerofoil; ~कार a party; ~ग्रहण taking a side; ~धर a supporter; partisan, partial; ~पोषण advocacy, championing of a cause; -विपक्ष pros and cons; ~सार a brief; ~हीन wingless; –लेना, किसी का to side with.

पक्ष/पात pakshpa:t (*nm*) partiality; favouritism; ~पातिता partisanship, partiality; ~पाती partial, partisan.

पक्षांतर pakshā:ntar (*nm*) another fortnight; the other side/party; transposition.

पक्षांतरण pakshā:ntarāṇ (*nm*) transposition; –करना to transpose.

पक्षाघात paksha:gha:t (*nm*) hemiparesis, paralysis.

पक्षी pakshi: (*nm*) a bird; aves; -पालन aviculture; -विज्ञान ornicology.

पक्षीय pakshi:y (*a*) pertaining to a side/party/wing; as a suffix it means related to a wing (as दक्षिण-पक्षीय right-winged).

पक्ष्म pakshm (*nm*) an eye-lash.

पख pakh (*nm*) a fin; ~युक्त having fins.

पख़ pakẖ (*nf*) an obstacle, hindrance; condition; defect, flaw; –निकालना to point a flaw, to sight a defect; –लगाना to impose a condition; to create an obstacle.

पखवाड़ा(रा) pakhwa:ṛ(r)a: (*nm*) a fortnight.

पखारना pakha:rnā: (*v*) to cleanse, to wash clean.

पखाव/ज pakha:waj (*nf*) a kind of drum; ~जी one who plays a पखावज.

पखेरू pakheru: (*nm*) a bird.

पग pag (*nm*) a foot; step; pace; ~चाप/~ध्वनि (sound of) footsteps; ~तल foot, sole of the foot; -पग पर at every step.

पगडंडी pagḍanḍi: (*nf*) a footway, track.

पगड़ी pagṛi: (*nf*) a turban; gratification in cash for letting out a house or shop; –उछालना to heap insults on; to humiliate; –उतारना to disgrace, to insult; to fleece; –बदलना to make friends; –पैरों पर रखना to beg for protection/mercy/help.

पगना pagnā: (*v*) to be impregnated with syrup; to be soaked in love/devotion.

पगला pagla: (*a*) mad, crazy, amuck; hence पगली (feminine form).

पगहा pagaha: (*nm*) a tether; —, आगे नाथ न पीछे to have neither home nor hearth, to be without any near and dear ones.

पगार paga:r (*nf*) wages, salary.

पगुराना pagura:nā: (*v*) to ruminate, to chew the cud.

पगोडा pagoḍa: (*nm*) a pagoda.

Buddhist monastery.

पच pach –an allomorph of **पाँच**; ~**कल्यानी** cunning; wicked; ~**खना** five-storeyed; ~**गुना** five times; five-fold; ~**मेल** a mixture of five ingredients; five different sweet-meats mixed together; ~**रंगा** multi-coloured; five-coloured; ~**लड़ा** a five-stringed necklace.

पच/ड़ा pachṛa: (*nm*) mess, muddle; trouble; ~**ड़ा खड़ा करना** to create a mess/muddle, to cause unnecessary trouble; ~**ड़ा ले बैठना** to begin a long drawn and monotonous narrative; ~**ड़े में पड़ना** to get embroiled/involved in a mess/muddle.

पचना pachnā: (*v*) to be digested; to be assimilated; **पच मरना** to toil hard.

पचपन pachpān (*a*) fifty-five; (*nm*) the number fifty-five.

पचहत्तर pachattar (*a*) seventy-five; (*nm*) the number seventy-five.

पचहरा pachehra: (*a*) five-fold; having five layers.

पचास pacha:s (*a*) fifty; (*nm*) the number fifty.

पचासी pacha:si: (*a*) eighty-five; (*nm*) the number eighty-five.

पचीस pachi:si: (*a*) twenty-five; (*nm*) the number twenty-five.

पचीसी pachi:si: (*nf*) a collection or aggregate of twenty-five.

पच्चर(ड़) pachchar(ṛ) (*nm*) a wedge; packing piece; quoin; –**अड़ाना** to create an obstacle/impediment; –**ठोकना** to wedge; to harass.

पच्ची/कार pachchi:ka:r (*nm*) mosaic work expert, inlay work specialist; ~**कारी** mosaic work; inlay work; –**हो जाना, किसी में** to be merged (with), to be identified (with).

पच्चीस pachchi:s (*a* and *nm*) see **पचीस**.

पछताना pachhta:nā: (*v*) to repent; to rue, to be full of remorse, to be penitent; **पछताये होत का जब चिड़िया चुग गई खेत**, **अब** its no use crying over spilt milk.

पछताव pachhta:v (*nm*) see **पछतावा**.

पछतावा pachhta:va: (*nm*) repentance, remorse; penitence.

पछत्तर pachhattar (*a* and *nm*) see **पचहत्तर**.

पछाड़ pachha:ṛ (*nf*) a dashdown, violent fall on the back, sudden fall, falling back in a swoon; –**खाना** to be dashed down; to fall back in a swoon, to fall in grief; –**देना** see **पछाड़ना**.

पछाड़ना pachha:ṛnā: (*v*) to dash/knock down, to cause a fall, to throw down; to overcome, to overpower.

पछिया pachhiya: (*nf*) the butt (of a gun).

पछीत pachhi:t (*nf*) the rear wall or part of a house.

पछुवा pachhuva: (*a* and *nf*) westerly (wind); west wind.

पछोरना pachhornā: (*v*) to winnow (with a **सूप**).

पजरना pajarnā: (*v*) to be scorched/charred, to be burnt; to blaze.

पजामा paja:mā: (*nm*) pyjamas.

पजावा paja:va: (*nm*) a brick kiln.

पटंगा paṭanga: (*nm*) a fall; dash-down, throw; set-back; –**खाना** to suffer a set-back; –**देना** to throw down, to fell, to dash down; to cause a serious set-back.

पट paṭ (*nm*) a garment, piece of cloth covering; screen; an allomorph of **पट्ट** meaning favourite, principal (as **पटरानी**); a door leaf; tail (of a coin); sound of falling or breaking or beating; septa; groomed lock of hair; (*a*) lying flat, upside down; ineffective, waste (land); effaced, wiped out; ~कथा screen play; ~कार a fabric worker; weaver; ~पट recurrent sound of पट; ~मंडप pavilion; ~रानी the queen consort, the principal wife of a king; –उघड़ना/खुलना the door leaves to (be thrown) open; –पड़ना to lie face downwards; (a venture) to come to a standstill; to be slackened/closed down; –बंद होना the door leaves to be shut; –होना to come to a nought, to be ruined.

पटक paṭak (*nf*) a throw, fall, dash(ing) down.

पटकना paṭaknā: (*v*) to dash down, to throw down, to enforce a violent fall; –, किसी के ऊपर/किसी के सिर पर to entrust to an unwilling person, to thrust upon.

पटकनी paṭaknī: (*nf*) a knock/dash down, a fall; set-back; –देना to dash/knock down, to enforce a violent fall, to throw down.

पटका paṭka: (*nm*) a cincture, girdle; cloth-belt; –बांधना to gird up the loins (for), to get ready for.

पटतर paṭtar (*a*) equal, bearing a similarity or an equivalence (to); matching; (*nm*) comparison, equivalence; match.

पटना paṭnā: (*v*) to be covered; to be filled (with); to be quits, to be repaid in full (as कर्ज); to be taken in; to be veered round, to yield to persuasion; to live in harmony.

पटपर paṭpar (*a*) flat, plane (ground); hollow, grainless (as green pea).

पटरा paṭra: (*nm*) a plank; harrow; –कर देना to devastate, tospell ruination; to demolish; to raze to the ground; –फेरना to devastate, to raze to the ground; –बैठना (business etc.) to crash, to be undone/ruined; –होना to be ruined/undone.

पटरी paṭri: (*nf*) rail; trackway; pavement; a ruler, wooden strip; –खाना to have harmonious relationship, to carry on smoothly; –जमाना to establish a rapport (with); to have things going smooth; –न बैठना not to be able to draw horses together; –पर लाना to veer round, to bring round; –बैठना to have harmonious relations, to have rapport; to have an identity of purpose, to pull together.

पट/ल paṭal (*nm*) a table; film; screen; board; layer; ~लिका lamella.

पटवा paṭwa: (*nm*) one who strings beads, pearls, etc., a craftsman engaged in the entwining of ornaments with silk; hence ~गीरी (*nf*).

पटवारी paṭwa:ri: (*nm*) a patwari, the village official who maintains land records; ~गीरी the office or function of a पटवारी.

पटसन paṭsan (*nm*) jute; –उद्योग jute industry; –मिल a jute mill.

प/टा paṭa: (*nm*) a scimitar; cudgel; seating plank or board; ~टेबाज a fencer, one who wields a foil or cudgel with skill; ~टेबाजी fencing, playing with foils/cudgels.

पटाक paṭa:k (*nf*) report of a cracking sound; (*ind*) forthwith, at once, without a moment's hesitation; –से instantaneously; forthwith.

पटाका paṭa:ka: (*nm*) a cracker; an explosive stuff; the report of a cracker; explosion; the sound of 'पट'.

पटाक्षेप paṭa:kshep (*nm*) ringing down of the curtain, curtain-fall; closing of an affair.

पटाखा paṭa:k͟ha: (*nm*) a cracker, any explosive stuff, the report of a cracker; explosion, the sound of पट.

पटाना paṭa:nā: (*v*) to settle; to conclude; to persuade; to cause to veer round, to bring round; to repay in full; to seduce.

पटापट paṭa:paṭ (*nf*) continuous sound of **पट-पट**; (*adv*) with successive sounds of **पट-पट**; briskly, swiftly.

पटाव paṭa:v (*nm*) the work of covering; covered place; covering, roofing.

पटिया paṭiya: (*nf*) a wooden or stone slab; flagstone; neighbouring area.

पटु paṭu (*a*) ingenious, skilled, dexterous; efficient; clever; hence **~ता** (*nf*); **~त्व** (*nm*).

पटुआ paṭua: (*nm*) jute.

पटुली paṭuli: (*nf*) the frontage folds of a *dhoti*: or *sa:ri*: tucked in near the navel and flowing downwards therefrom; a narrow board used for a seat on a swing.

पटेला paṭela: (*nm*) a flat boat; tablet, a land-levelling appliance.

पट्ट paṭṭ (*nm*) a plate; tablet; tail (of a coin); royal grant or order (written on a copper plate etc.); (*a*) face downwards; **~महिषी**/**~रानी** the queen consort, the principal queen; **–शिष्य** favourite/dovout student; staunch follower; **–स्वर** dialtone.

पट्टन paṭṭān (*nm*) a city, town, port.

पट्टा paṭṭa: (*nm*) a title deed; lease, lease deed, tenure; dog-collar; a plank; **~कर्ता** a lessor; **~कार** ligulate; **~दाता** a lessor; **~देय** leasable; **~दार** a lessee; **पट्टेदार** a lessee; **पट्टेदारी** tenancy, tenure, lease-hold; **पट्टे पर** on lease, on lease-hold; **–बांधना** to domesticate, to tame; enslave; **–लिखना** to execute a bond.

पट्टिका paṭṭika: (*nf*) a plate.

पट्टी paṭṭi: (*nf*) a bandage; band, batten; strap; strip; belt, fillet; shelf; plate, wooden plate (for beginners to write on); misguidance; co-share (in landed property); **~दार** co-sharer, partner; banded; **~दारी** co-share; partnership; **–पढ़ाना** to tutor; to misguide; to persuade for selfish motives; to give a lesson so as to veer round to one's own line; **–पुजना** a ceremony marking the commencement of one's education, to be initiated, to commence one's education; **–में आना** to be taken in, to succumb to tricky words.

पट्टू paṭṭu: (*nm*) a variety of coarse woollen cloth.

पट्ठा paṭṭha: (*nm*) a robust young man; young one, offspring; nerve sinew; wrestling apprentice/pupil.

पठन paṭhān (*nm*) reading; study; **-पाठन** reading and studying; **~शील** given to reading, studious.

पठनीय paṭhnī:y (*a*) readable; worth reading; intelligible; hence **~ता** (*nf*).

पठार paṭha:r (*a*) a plateau.

पठित paṭhit (*a*) read, studied; scholarly.

पठौनी paṭhaunī: (*nf*) presents sent on special occasions (to relatives, esp. sister, daughter, etc.).

पड़(र)ता paṛ(r)ta: (*nm*) purchase or manufacturing cost; real value; (suitability of) price; rate; margin of profit; **–आना** the price to suit/to be convenient; **–खाना**/**–पड़ना** the price to be suitable/convenient, to have adequate margin (of profit); **–फैलाना/बैठाना** to work out the cost; to fix the sale price after working out the cost.

पड़ताल parta:l (*nf*) checking up, testing; survey; investigation; collation; re-measurement (of a field etc.); re-vetting; hence ~ना (*v*).

पड़ना paṛnā: (*v*) to fall; to fall down; to drop; to lie (down); to occur; to befall; to be involved; to be hit.

पड़वा paṛva: (*nf*) the first day of each lunar fortnight (also **प्रतिपदा**).

पड़ा paṛa: (*nm*) he-calf of a buffalo; hence **पड़िया** (*nf*); **पड़िया के ताऊ** a fool, nincompoop.

पड़ाव paṛa:v (*nm*) a halt; halting place; bivouac; encampment, camp; —**डालना** to bivouac; to camp; to make a halt.

पड़ो(ड़ौ)स paṛo(ṛau)s (*nm*) neighbourhood; vicinity, proximity.

पड़ो(ड़ौ)सी paṛo(ṛau)si: (*nm*) a neighbour.

पढ़त paṛhat (*nf*) reading.

पढ़ना paṛhnā: (*v*) to read; to study; to recite; -**लिखना** to study, to read and write; **पढ़ा-लिखा** learned, scholarly; **पढ़े न लिखे नाम विद्यासागर** an ignorant man keeping great fuss, a nincompoop bearing the name Plato.

पढ़ाई paṛha:i: (*nf*) study; education, learning; -**लिखाई** studies.

पढ़ाना paṛha:nā: (*v*) to teach, to instruct, to educate; to tutor.

पण pāṇ (*nm*) a bet; ~**न** marketing, selling; traffic.

पण्य pāṇṇy (*nm*) a commodity; merchandise; (*a*) marketable; ~**ता** marketability; -**योग्यता** marketability; ~**शाला** an emporium.

पतंग pataṅg (*nf*) a paper kite; (*nm*) the sun; ~**बाज़** a kite-flier; ~**बाज़ी** kite-flying.

पतंगा pataṅga: (*nm*) a moth, an insect.

पत pat—an allomorph of **पत्ता** used as the first member of compound words; (*nf*) honour, dignity; ~**झड़/झर** the fall, autumn; defoliation; -**उठ जाना** to lose credit, to be trusted no more; -**उतारना** to disgrace; to compromise the honour of; to humiliate; -**रखना** to maintain the dignity of, to preserve the honour of.

पतन patan (*nm*) fall, downfall; decline; degeneration; ~**शील** tending to fall, degenerating/falling, decaying; hence ~**शीलता** (*nf*).

पतनोन्मुख patanōnmukh (*a*) falling, tending to fall, degenerating; hence ~**ता** (*nf*).

पतला patla: (*a*) thin, slender, tenuous; fine; flimsy, dilute(d); narrow; ~**पन** thinness; slenderness, tenuousness; fineness; flimsiness, dilution; narrowness; -**दुबला** lean and thin; emaciated; -**पड़ना** to be mellowed down; to be afflicted; to be diluted; -**मूतना** to yield, to admit being inferior; **पतली आवाज़** tanyphonia.

पतलून patlu:n (*nf*) a pantaloon; trousers; ~**नुमा** resembling/looking like a pantaloon/trousers

पतवार patwa:r (*nf*) rudder, helm; a large oar used for a rudder; -**थामना** to take the helm, to assume captaincy of the ship of, to guide the course of.

पता pata: (*nm*) an address; whereabouts; information, knowledge; **पते की कहना** to put the axe in the helve, to hit the right nail on the head; **पते की बात** a remarkable/revealing utterance.

पताका pata:ka: (*nf*) a flag, banner; pennant; streamer; -**फहराना** to hoist one's banner; to make a conquest, to establish one's command; to achieve a distinction.

पति pati (*nm*) husband, master;

~देव/-देवता husband (said in deference); -धर्म duty towards the husband; duty of the husband (towards his wife); -पत्नी husband and wife, a couple; ~भक्ति devotion to the husband; ~व्रत exclusive devotion/dedication/fidelity to the husband; ~व्रता a faithful wife, virtuous wife; -सेवा dedication to the husband; –के इशारों पर चलना/को उँगलियों पर नचाना a grey mare is better horse.

पतित patit (*a*) fallen, depraved; hence पतिता (fem. form); ~पावन a saviour of the fallen; hence ~पावनी (fem. form).

पतियाना patiya:nā: (*v*) to trust, to believe, to have faith (in).

पतियारा patiya:ra: (*nm*) trust, belief, faith.

पतीला pati:la: (*nm*) a huge cooking brass-kettle.

पतीली pati:li: (*nf*) diminutive of पतीला.

पतुरिया paturia: (*nf*) a prostitute, concubine, a woman of easy virtue.

पतोहू patohu: (*nf*) a daughter-in-law.

पत्तन pattān (*nm*) a town, city; port city.

पत्तल pattal (*nf*) a plate made up by tagging broad tree leaves together (for serving food); food served on a pattal; –के खाने वाले, एक lit. having meals in the same plate—very intimate, in intimate relationship; –चाटना to survive on leavings, to be humiliatingly servile to; –पड़ना the *pattals* to be arranged; –परसना to serve meals (on a *pattal*); –में खाना, किसी की to take meals together; to develop intimate relationship; –में खाना, उसी में छेद करना, जिस to blow off the roof that provides shelter; to cut off the hand that feeds; to be foolishly ungrateful; –लगना the food to be served on the *pattal*.

पत्ता patta: (*nm*) a leaf; playing card; –कटना to be told off, to be thrown out of, to be sacked, to be fired; hence –काटना; –खड़कना a rustle of leaves to be produced some apprehension to be caused; –न हिलना everything around to be still, to have not the slightest movement of the air; –पड़ना to have a run of good cards; –पत्ते को देखना, जड़ न देखना to care for the leaves and ignore the root; पत्ते पर कुलाँच खाना to somersault, to make a sudden change of one's stand; पत्ते फेंटना to reshuffle the cards; पत्तेबाज a card-sharpner; a fraudulent man; पत्तेबाजी card-sharpening; fraud; पत्ते लगाना card-sharpening.

पत्ती patti: (*nf*) a small leaf; foliage; share; flats; a narrow metal-sheet paring; lamination; ~दार leafy; a share-holder, partner; laminated; hence ~दारी (*nf*).

पत्थर patthar (*nm*) stone; (*fig.*) hard-hearted; heartless, unfeeling (person); –की खान a quarry; ~चटा a kind of grass; a kind of snake; stingy (person); ~फोड़ा (said ironically) a stone-dresser; ~बाज one who pelts/throws stones (at); ~बाजी pelting of stones, stone-throwing; –का कलेजा/दिल/हृदय stony heart, unfeeling heart; –की छाती unmoving heart; unwavering will; –की लकीर indelible mark; unfading/invariable truth; –पड़ना to be damned, to be ruined/undone; pouring down of hails; –पड़े (an abusive term) be you damned/doomed!; –पर दूब जमना lit. emergence of grass on stony surface—an impossible phenomenon to occur; –पसीजना/पानी होना/पिघलना blood out of a stone, pity from the pitiless; a stony heart to be moved; –मारे भी न मरना to be disgraced and still alive; to live in disgrace; -सा खींच मारना/फेंक मारना to say (something) bluntly; to be bluntly frank, to be insultingly curt; –हो जाना to be petrified, to be devoid of sensation/sensibility; to become insensitive; to become heartless/unfeeling.

पत्नी patnī: (*nf*) wife; a man's spouse; ~व्रत (vow to be) loyal (to one's wife); ~त्व wifehood, the position or function of a wife; –के रूप में ग्रहण करना to take as (one's) wife.

पत्र pattr (*nm*) a letter; paper; note; leaf; ~क leaflet, handbill, plate; ~दल lamina; -पुष्प token honorarium; token of hospitality; ~वाहक bearer of a letter; -व्यवहार correspondence, exchange of letters, etc; -संग्रह collection of letters.

पत्र/कार pattraka:r (*nm*) a journalist; pressman; -शैली journalese, journalistic style; ~कारिता journalism.

पत्रा pattra: (*nm*) an almanac.

पत्राचार pattra:cha:r (*nm*) correspondence; exchange of letters, etc; -पाठ्यक्रम correspondence courses.

पत्रिका pattrika: (*nf*) a magazine; journal; horoscope.

पत्री pattri: (*nf*) a horoscope; a letter (used in this sense generally as the second memeber in the compound चिट्ठी-पत्री).

पथ path (*nm*) a path, way, course, route; -कर toll; ~गामी a traveller, wayfarer; ~दर्शक/प्रदर्शक a guide; leader; -प्रदर्शन guidance.

पथर pathar—an allomorph of पत्थर used as the first member in compound words (as पथरचटा see पत्थर ~चटा).

पथराना pathra:nā: (*v*) to petrify; to deaden; to harden (into stone); to be rendered insensitive (as आँखें पथराना).

पथराव pathra:v (*nm*) pelting with stones, stoning.

पथरी pathri: (*nf*) a whetstone; gallstone; calculi.

पथरीला pathri:la: (*a*) stony; littered with stones; lithic; hence ~पन (*nm*).

पथि/क pathik (*nm*) a traveller, wayfarer; ~का siding.

पथी pathi: (*nm*) see पथिक.

पथ्य patthy (*nf*) diet, medically prescribed or salubrious diet (for one who is recuperating after illness); (*a*) salubrious, wholesome; –मिलना to be given medically prescribed diet after recovery from an illness; –लेना to take light and medically prescribed food after an illness; –से रहना to avoid forbidden food; to take only prescribed diet.

पथ्यापथ्य patthya:patthy (*a*) wholesome and unwholesome (diet); (*nf*) diet–salubrious or otherwise (according to prescription).

पद pad (*nm*) an office, status; a rank; a versified composition (esp. eulogizing God or His sport); foot (of a measure or verse); (foot) step; expression; term, word in its particular context; articles (like an umbrella, shoes, clothes, utensils) given away for the gratification of the soul of a deceased; -कंज/कमल lotus-like feet; ~क्रम order of official precedence; word-order in a sentence; ~गति gait;

~चारी a pedestrian; ~चिह्न a footstep, footmark; trace, trail; ~चिह्नों पर चलना to follow in the footsteps of; to emulate; ~च्छेद parsing; ~च्युत dismissed, discharged from office; ~तल sole; foot; -त्याग renunciation/abandonment of an office; ~त्राण footwear; shoe; ~दलित trodden under foot, down-trodden; trampled; ~नाम designation; ~न्यास diction; disposition of words; -पंकज/पद्म see पदकमल; -पद पर at every step; ~बंध a phrase; -योजना diction, word disposition, arrangement of words; -रचना arrangement of words, diction; literary composition; morphological construction; ~रज dust of the feet (of a revered person); ~विग्रह/विच्छेद analysis of a compound word; ~शैया diction, typical arrangement of words in a literary composition; -संज्ञा official title, designation; -सोपान hierarchy; ~सोपानिक hierarchical; -स्थापना posting.

पदक padak (*nm*) a medal, medallion; badge.

पदवी padvi: (*nf*) a title; status; rank; degree.

पदाक्रांत pada:kkrā:nt (*a*) trampled under foot, in complete subjugation.

पदाघात pada:gha:t (*nm*) a kick; stroke with one's foot.

पदाति pada:ti (*nm*) an infantryman; footman, pedestrian.

पदातिक pada:tik (*nm*) see पदाति.

पदातिका pada:tika: (*nf*) the infantry.

पदाधिकारी pada:dhika:ri: (*nm*) an office-bearer; official.

पदाना pada:nā: (*v*) to tire out, to cause to field for long spells (in games); to harass, to cause to labour hard.

पदान्वय pada:nvay (*nm*) paraphrase, paraphrasing.

पदारविंद pada:rvind (*nm*) lotus-like (tender and soft) feet.

पदार्थ pada:rth (*nm*) meaning of a term; matter, substance; an object; article.

पदार्पण pada:rpāṇ (*nm*) advent; arrival, stepping in.

पदावधि pada:vadhi (*nf*) term of office, tenure.

पदावनत pada:vanat (*a*) demoted, reverted, fallen in rank or status.

पदावनति pada:vanāti (*nf*) demotion, reversion, fall in rank or status.

पदावली pada:vali: (*nf*) expression; diction; a collection of *padas* (versified composition esp. eulogizing the Lord or His sport).

पदासीन pada:si:n (*a*) holding office, in office.

पदिक padik (*nm*) a foot-soldier, an infantryman.

पदी padi: (*nf*) a series of steps.

पदेन paden (*a*) ex-officio.

पदोदक padodak (*nm*) water collected after a foot-wash, water in which the feet of the idol of a deity or some revered person have been washed (considered to be sacred).

पदोन्नत padonnat (*a*) promoted, risen in rank or status.

पदोन्नति padonnati (*nf*) promotion, rise in rank or status.

पद्धति paddhati (*nf*) method, system; process; custom.

पद्म padm (*nm*) a lotus-flower and its plant; -पत्र a lotus-leaf; -कोश a lotus-cell; ~नाभि an epithet of Lord Vishṇū (from whose navel the primordial lotus is said to have shot forth. Mythologically, it was this lotus on which ब्रह्मा is supposed to have come into being); -नाल a lotus stalk; ~नेत्र (having) lotus-like eyes.

पद्मासन padmā:san (*nm*) a sedentary Yogic posture wherein the practitioner sits upright with legs crossed over the thighs.

पद्मिनी padminī: (*nf*) an exceptionally charming woman (the first of the kinds specified by ancient Indian sexologists); a lotus.

पद्य paddy (*nm*) verse; poetry; ~बद्ध versified; ~मय abounding in verse; versified; hence ~बद्धता; ~मयता (*nf*).

पद्यकार paddyka:r (*nm*) a versifier; poetaster.

पद्यात्मक paddya:tmāk (*a*) poetic, composed in poetic form.

पधराना padhra:nā: (*v*) to be installed with honour; to seat reverentially.

पधारना padha:rna: (*v*) a deferential usage —to grace (a place or occasion) by coming, to arrive (at); to depart.

पन pan—a suffix added to common and attributive nouns to form abstract nouns (e.g. लड़कपन); a variant of पानी, पान, पण्य and पाँच in compound formations; ~गाड़ी a water-cart; ~घट the periphery of a well etc. where water is drawn; ~चक्की a water-mill; ~छन्ना a strip of wet cloth generally tied on a fresh cut; ~डुब्बी a submarine; ~धौंकनी water-bellows; ~बदरा rain and sunshine; ~बाड़ी a betel-enclosure, a betel-garden; ~वाड़ी a betel-seller; ~सारी one who sells commodities as spices, dry fruits, etc.; ~साला a water-kiosk, stand where water is stored and distributed to travellers; of five years; ~सुइया a small dinghy; ~सेरी a five-seer weight; ~हार/हारा a water-bearer.

पनपना panapnā: (*v*) to be revived/recovered, to flourish, to thrive, to prosper; -बढ़ना to be born and bred.

पनहाँ panahā: (*nm*) a shoe; breadth of a cloth piece; hence पनहीं diminutive (*nf*) of पनहाँ.

पना panā: —a suffix added to common nouns and adjectives to form abstract nouns e.g. बचपना, सुअरपना, हरामीपना; (*nm*) a typical beverage prepared from mango juice or mango flesh with the addition of tamarind and cumin seed etc.; breadth of a cloth piece.

पनारी(ली) pana:ri:(li:) (*nf*) diminutive of पनाला; ~दार corrugated; ०चादर a corrugated sheet.

पनाला pana:la: (*nm*) a gutter, drain.

पनाह pana:h (*nf*) shelter, refuge; ~घर (place of) shelter, refuge; -देना to provide shelter, to take under one's care; -माँगना to seek shelter; to evade confrontation or association with; to concede victory and submit; -लेना to find shelter, to take refuge.

पनि panī—an allomorph of पानी used as the first member in certain compounds; ~हार a water-bearer; ~हारिन/हारी a female water-bearer.

पनिया panīyā: (*a*) aquatic, hydrous; (*nm*) water; ~ना to run with water; to get wet, to be softened/priming.

पनिहा panihā: (*a*) aquatic, hydrous; (*nm*) a water-snake.

पनीर panī:r (*nm*) cheese.

पनीरी pani:ri: (*nf*) a sapling; (*a*) (of) cheese, pertaining to or made of cheese.

पनीला panī:la: (*a*) watery, sodden; hence ~पन (*nm*).

पन्न/ग pannag (*nm*) a snake; ~गारि lit. enemy of snakes —Garuṛ, the divine eagle, vehicle of Vishnū.

पन्ना pannā: (*nm*) an emerald, leaf of a book, page, folio; see पना; पन्ने उलटना/पलटना to skip over the pages (of a book); to glance through; पन्ने रँगना to write page after page; to waste both ink and paper.

पन्नी pannī: (*nf*) a fine metallic leaf; tin-foil, gold or silver plated multi-coloured paper; ~साज a professional manufacturer of पन्नी; ~साजी the profession of manufacturing पन्नी.

पपड़ियाना papaṛiya:nā: (*v*) to encrustate, to form crusts on the surface, to be withered and dried up.

पपड़ी papṛi: (*nf*) a thin crust, incrustation/encrustation, scurf, scale, scab; flake; thin cakes of wheat, gram, etc.; ~दार incrusted, encrusted; scurfy, scaled, scabby; flaky; ~ला see ~दार.

पपीता papi:ta: (*nm*) papaya.

पपीहरा papi:hara: (*nm*) see पपीहा.

पपीहा papi:ha: (*nm*) a typical species of Cuckoo (which finds usual mention in Indian love-songs as exemplifying the ideal of lovelorn beings)—*Cucculus nelanoleucus*.

पपोटा papoṭa: (*nm*) an eye-lid.

पब्लिक pablik (*nf*) public.

पय pay (*nm*) milk; water; ~स्विनी a river, stream.

पया/म payā:m (*nm*) a message; ~मी a messenger.

पयाल paya:l (*nm*) coarse straw (used as fodder).

पयो payo—an allomorph of पयस् meaning milk/water; ~द a cloud; ~धर a cloud; female breasts; ~धि/निधि an ocean, a sea; ~व्रत fasting with only milk as diet.

परंतप parāntap (*a*) scaring or causing affliction to the enemy.

परंतु parāntu (*ind*) but; however; ~क a proviso.

परंपरा parāmpara: (*nf*) tradition; ~गत traditional; orthodox; ~निष्ठ traditional; orthodox; ~निष्ठता traditionalism; orthodoxy; ~वाद traditionalism; orthodoxy; ~वादिता traditionalism; orthodoxy; ~वादी a traditionalist; traditional; orthodox.

परंपरित parāmparit (*a*) traditional; tradition-bound.

परंपरीण parāmpari:ṇ (*a*) traditional; inherited, communicated through heredity.

परः parah—an allomorph of परस् used as the first member in compound words, ultra; ~पुरुष higher than man; superman; ~शत more than a hundred; ~श्व the day after tomorrow.

पर par (*ind*) but; yet; even so, even then; on; at; after; (*a*) opposite, inimical; other; alien; higher; (*nm*) a wing; feather; plume; ~कटा wing-clipped; ~काज other's job, other's interest; ~काजी serving others' interest; benevolent/benignant; ~काय another's body/person; ०प्रवेश entering into another's body through *yoga*; ~कृति another's performance/deed; ~क्राम्य negotiable; ~जन belonging to others; not our own (people); ~जाति another caste, not our own caste; ~तंत्र see परतंत्र; ~तंत्रता see परतंत्रता; ~दार another man's wife; ~द्रोही/द्वेषी cynical, jealous of or hostile to all others;

~धन another's wealth; ~धर्म another's religion; ~नाम allonym; ~निर्भरता dependence; ~पक्ष the other side; the opponent's case/argumentation; -पार the other bank/coast, across; ~पीड़क a sadist, causing harassment/affliction to others; ~पुरुष other person, a man other than a woman's husband; stranger; ~बस dependent on others; under other's control/sway; ~भाषा another language; ~भृत nursed and brought up by another; a cuckoo; ~रति alloeroticism; ~लेख allograph; ~वश see परवश; ~वशता see परवशता; ~वाद a rumour; slander; ~वादी a rumour-monger; slanderer; ~साल last year; next year; ~सुखवाद altruism, altruistic hedonism; ~सुखवादी altruistic; ~स्त्री another man's wife; ~स्व another's property/money/due; ०हरण anusurpation, depriving somebody of his due/property/money; ~हित other's interest/good; –आना/उगना see –निकलना; –कट जाना to be rendered ineffective/inefficacious, to be incapacitated; –कतरना see –कैंच करना; –काट देना to render ineffective/inefficacious; to incapacitate; –कैंच करना to clip the wings; to render ineffective/inefficacious/inactive; –जमना to grow wings; (fig.) to manifest one's mischievous self, to take to mischief; –निकलना/लगना to ride for a fall, to grow wings; to take to mischievous deeds; –फड़फड़ाना to make a desperate effort (to get free or to achieve any other objective); –बाँध देना to render helpless/inactive,

परकार parka:r (*nf*) callipers; a compass.

परकाला parka:la: (*nm*) a staircase; threshold, (glass) piece; spark; —, आफ़त का calamity personified; trouble-maker, mischief-monger.

परकी/करण paraki:karān (*nm*) alienation; ~कृत alienated.

परकीया paraki:ya: (*nf*) (in traditional Indian Poetics) one of the three types of heroines (viz. स्वकीया, परकीया, सामान्या)—an adulteress, a woman carrying on a love affair out of wedlock; (*a*) devoted to another (person), adulterous.

परकोटा parkota: (*nm*) a rampart; precincts, boundary.

परख parakh (*nf*) test, examination; probation; judgment/judging; distinguishing faculty; –होना to have an eye for, to have a due sense of.

परख/चा parkhacha: (*nm*) a shred, fragment, piece; ~चे उड़ाना to reduce to pieces, to shred.

पर/खना parakhnā: (*v*) to test, to examine; to judge; ~खाई the job of testing/judging (something or somebody); the charges paid for testing/judging (something); ~खा जाना to go through one's facings, to be tested.

परगना paraganā: (*nm*) an administrative sub-division comprising a number of villages; -हाकिम administrative head of a परगना,

परचना parachnā: (*v*) to get thick, to establish a rapport, to get to know well; to get habituated.

परचा parcha: (*nm*) a piece of paper; question paper, a chit; introduction; a newspaper; proof; leaflet, a handbill; –देना to give a proof, to introduce; –माँगना to call for or seek a proof; to ask somebody to disclose his real identity.

परचू/न parchu:n (*nm*) provisions

grocery; (*a*) retail; ~नी a grocer; dealer in provisions; retail-seller.

परछत्ती parchhatti: (*nf*) a large-sized plank fixed in a wall of a room for storing things over; a small thatch over mud-walls.

परछाईं parchha:ī: (*nf*) a shadow; reflection; –से डरना to be scared of a shadow; –से डरना, किसी की to be terribly scared of (somebody); —पड़ना to fall within the range of adverse influence of; –से दूर रहना, किसी की to keep far away from, to keep out of the orbit of influence of, to maintain a safe distance.

पर/जीवी parji:vi: (*nm*) a parasite; (*a*) parasitic; heterotrophic; ~जीविता parasitism; heterotrophy.

परतंत्र partāntr (*a*) dependent; slave; subordinate(d), subjugated; heteronomous; ~ता dependence; slavery; subordination; subjugation; heteronomy.

परत parat (*nf*) a layer; fold; tuck; lagging; film; lamination; ~दार layered; folded; laminated; ~बंदी lamination, laminate.

परती parti: (*nf*) fallow land; uncultivated/waste land; (*a*) uncultivated, fallow.

परदा parda: (*nm*) a curtain; screen; veil; privacy; (ear) drum; surface (as दुनिया का परदा); ~दार maintaining a veil (of secrecy); concealing (oneself) under a veil; ~दारी concealment of a secret; concealment of one's failing; ~नशीन veiled, maintaining a veil; hence ~नशीनी (*nf*); –उठाना/खोलना to expose (a secret); to uncover, to unearth, to reveal, to remove the veil of secrecy; –करना to observe a veil (said of a woman), to keep (oneself under) a veil; –डालना to conceal; to veil; to ring down a curtain; –पड़ना, आँख पर to be blinded, not to see the manifest; –पड़ना, बुद्धि पर to act foolishly, to behave like a stupid fellow; ~फ़ाश करना to expose, to lay bare, to unearth, to tear the veil of secrecy; ~फ़ाश होना to be exposed, to be laid bare, to be unearthed, the veil of secrecy to be torn; –रखना, किसी का to save the honour of; not to let out somebody's secret; to maintain a veil over somebody's failing; –रखना to keep out of somebody's sight; to keep on evading; परदे के पीछे clandestine(ly), stealthily; परदे में रखना to keep behind a curtain; to keep under a veil; (for women) not to move out of the house, not to mix freely.

पर/दादा parda:da: (*nm*) (paternal) great-grandfather; ~दादी (paternal) great-grandmother.

परदारा parda:ra: (*nf*) another's woman/wife.

पर/देश pardesh (*nm*) another country, a country other than one's native land, foreign country; ~देशी an alien, foreigner, stranger.

पर/नाना parnā:nā: (*nm*) (maternal) great-grandfather; ~नानी (maternal) great-grandmother.

पर/नाला parna:la: (*nm*) a gutter, kennel, drain pipe; ~नाली (*nf*) diminutive of परनाला.

परपट parpaṭ (*a*) flat; (*nm*) level ground.

परपो/ता parpota: (*nm*) great-grandson; hence ~ती (*nf*).

परबल parbal (*nm*) see परवल.

परबी parbi: (*nf*) a festal ~~day,~~ festival.

परम parām (*a*) extreme; ultimate; absolute; supreme; best; utmost;

(*nm*) the Supreme Being, God; –अग्रता absolute priority; –गति liberation, salvation; –गहन extremely complicated/incomprehensible; too deep; too difficult; insurmountable; –तत्त्व the Essential Element, the Supreme Being; –ताप absolute temperature; –पद the highest seat, liberation, salvation; –पावन His Holiness; extremely holy, of supreme holiness; –पिता the Creator of all, God; –पुरुष God; –पुरुषार्थ highest Good, summum bonum; –ब्रह्म God; –भट्टारक an ancient honorofic title or form of address to an Emperor; –महामान्य His Exalted Highness; –मापक्रम absolute scale; ~हंस the supreme amongst the संन्यासीs; a liberated soul, one who has attained transcendental existence.

परमाणु parmā:ṇū (*nm*) an atom; -बम an atom-bomb; -भट्टी a nuclear reactor; -युद्ध atomic warfare; ~वाद atomism; atomic theory; ~वादी an atomist; atomistic; -सिद्धान्त atomic theory.

परमाण्विकी paramā:ṇviki: (*nf*) atomistics.

परमाण्वीय paramā:ṇvi:y (*a*) atomic; –सिद्धान्त atomic theory.

परमा/त्मा parmā:tmā: (*nm*) God, the Supreme Self/Being/Spirit; ~त्म तत्त्व the Universal Soul, the Supreme Spirit/Being; ~त्मा की कृपा से by the grace of God.

परमादेश paramā:desh (*nm*) mandamus.

परमाधिकार paramā:dhika:r (*nm*) prerogative.

परमानंद parama:nānd (*nm*) the beatitude, the ultimate pleasure/supreme bliss/blessedness; God.

परमार्थ paramā:rth (*nm*) the ultimate end, the highest good, summum bonum; universal good; spiritual knowledge, salvation; ~वाद belief in the attainment of the summum bonum, faith in the attainment of spiritual knowledge; hence ~वादिता (*nf*); ~वादी (*a, nm*).

परमार्थी paramā:rthi: (*a* and *nm*) (one) devoted to universal good/ultimate salvation.

परमिट parmiṭ (*nm*) a permit.

परमुखापेक्षिता paramukha:pekshita: (*nf*) dependence, tendency/proneness to depend on others.

परमुखापेक्षी paramukha:pekshi: (*a*) dependent, prone to depend on others.

परमेश्वर parmeshwar (*nm*) God, the Almighty.

परमेश्वरी parmeshwari: (*nf*) see दुर्गा a shrew, quarrelsome woman.

परराष्ट्र parara:shṭr (*nm*) another country, foreign land; -मंत्रालय the Ministry of External/Foreign Affairs; -मंत्री the Minister for External Affairs, Foreign Minister; परराष्ट्रीय of, pertaining to or related with another nation, alien, foreign.

परला parla: (*a*) of the other side, of that side; —सिरा the other end; परले दर्जे/सिरे का of blackest/deepest dye, of the first order (often in derogatory contexts, as परले सिरे का बेईमान/बेवकूफ़ etc.); hence परली (fem. form).

परलोक parlok (*nm*) the other world, after world, next world; heavenly paradise; ~गमन death, dying, going to the next world; demise; ~वासी late; dead; –की चिंता करना to care for the other world, to do something to brighten one's other-worldly prospects; –बनना/सुधरना the way to the next world to be paved (by good deeds); –बनाना/सुधारना to ensure a good deal in post-mortem existence; –बिगाड़ना to spoil one's other-worldly prospects; –सिधारना to leave for one's heavenly abode, to expire.

परवर Parwar—a Persian suffix meaning one who fosters/nurtures as **बंदापरवर, ग़रीबपरवर**.

परवरदिगार parvardiga:r (*nm*) the Almighty, He Who nurtures/fosters/protects the world.

परवरिश parvarish (*nf*) upbringing, fostering; nurture; patronising.

परवर्ती parvarti: (*a*) later, subsequent.

परवल parval (*nm*) a kind of vegetable—*Trichosanthes dioeca.*

परवल/य parvalay (*nm*) a parabola; ~यिक parabolic.

परवश parvash (*a*) dependent; subservient, under another's control; ~ता dependence; subservience, under another's sway.

परवा parwa: (*nf*) see **परवाह**; the first day of each lunar fortnight.

परवाज़ parwa:z (*nf*) flight.

परवान parvā:n (*nm*) yard, foreyard; authentic; true; –चढ़ना to achieve fulfilment, to prosper, to flourish/thrive; to be married.

परवाना parwā:nā: (*nm*) a warrant, an order; a moth; (fig.) a dedicated lover; -गिरफ़्तारी a warrant of arrest; -तलाशी a search-warrant; -राहदारी a passport; –होना, (किसी पर) to sacrifice oneself (for somebody); to be fascinated; –बनना, किसी का to fall passionately in love with.

परवाह parva:h (*nf*) concern; care, heed.

परशु parashu (*nm*) a battle axe; ~धर one who wields a **परशु**; see ~राम; ~राम the great son of the seer Jamdagni, and a sworn enemy of the *kshatriyas*, who annihilated the *kshatriyas* twenty-one times and ultimately suffered a defeat at the hands of **राम**.

परसना parasnā: (*v*) to serve food; to touch, to feel (by touch).

परसर्ग parsarg (*nm*) a postposition (i.e. **ने, को, से, में, पर**).

परसा parsa: (*nm*) see **परशु**.

परसों parsō (*ind*) the day after tomorrow; the day before yesterday.

परस्त parast—a Persian substantive used as a suffix in word-formations, meaning a worshipper, an adorer; e.g. **बुतपरस्त, वतनपरस्त**; hence **परस्ती (वतनपरस्ती)**.

परस्पर paraspar (*ind*) mutual; reciprocal; ~ता mutuality; reciprocity; -संबंध mutual relations.

परहित parahit (*nm*) benefaction, beneficence, benevolence; -निष्ठा altruism; ~वाद altruism; hence ~वादिता (*nf*); ~वादी an altruist; altruistic.

परहे/ज़ parhez (*nm*) abstinence; avoidance; regimen; keeping aloof; ~ज़गार abstinent, abstainer, one who keeps aloof; ~ज़गारी abstinency, keeping aloof; ~ज़ी one who practises abstinence; pertaining to or related with abstinence; ~ज़ करना to abstain from; ~ज़ होना to be refraining from/abstaining from; not to be taking/using/consuming (a thing etc.) through abstinence.

परां(व)ठा parā:(v)ṭha: (*nm*) a typical Indian pancake-like preparation from kneaded floor fried in *ghee*.

परा para: –a Sanskrit prefix to nouns and verbs meaning away, off; aside; along; on; ultra; transcendental; (*a*) the best; ~मनोविज्ञान Parapsychology; ~विद्या Spiritualism, Metaphysics; ~शक्ति transcendental power; ~शक्तिवाद transcendentalism.

पराकाष्ठा para:ka:shṭha: (nf) climax; culminating point, extremity; extreme.

पराकोटि para:koṭi (nf) see पराकाष्ठा.

पराक्रम para:kkram (nm) heroism, gallantry, valiance, bravery.

पराक्रमी para:kkramī: (a) heroic, gallant, valiant, brave; (nm) a hero, gallant/valiant/brave person.

पराग para:g (nm) the pollen (of a flower); -कण/केसर pollen grain, pollen containing fine filament (of a flower).

पराङ्मुख para:nmukh (a) turning the back upon, averse from, hostile to, regardless of, shunning.

पराजय para:jay (nf) defeat, ~वाद/ ~वादिता defeatism; ~वादी (a) defeatist; ०मनोवृत्ति defeatist mentality.

पराजित para:jit (a) defeated, vanquished; overthrown.

पराठा para:ṭha: (nm) see परौंठा.

परात para:t (nf) a large shallow circular metallic vessel (often used for kneading flour).

परात्पर para:tpar (a) transcendental; beyond all; hence ~ता (nf); (nm) the Almighty.

पराधीन para:dhi:n (a) dependent; subject; subjugated; in bondage; ~ता dependence; bondage; subjection; subjugation; -सपनेहुँ सुख नाहीं bondage is the very antithesis of happiness, those who are in bondage know no happiness.

परानुभूति para:nubhu:ti (nf) empathy; another's experience; ~त experienced by another.

परान्न para:nn (nm) another's food; ~भोजी subsisting on food provi-

ded by somebody else; leading a parasitic life.

पराभव para:bhav (nm) defeat, overthrow; ruin; humiliation.

परा/भूत para:bhu:t (a) defeated, overthrown; ruined; humiliated; ~भूति see पराभव.

परामर्श para:marsh (nm) counsel; advice; consultation; ~दाता an adviser, a counsel; ~दात्री समिति an advisory committee; परामर्शीय advisory, consultative; ०मत advisory opinion; -करना to lay/put heads together; -देना to advise.

परायण para:yaṇ (a) attached to; devoted to; used as a suffix meaning attached/devoted/dedicated to (e.g. धर्मपरायण, नीतिपरायण, etc.); hence ~ता (nf).

परायत्त para:yatt (a) see पराधीन; ~ता see पराधीनता.

पराया para:ya: (a) pertaining or belonging to another, not one's own, alien, foreign; ~पन of or belonging to another; the state or sense of being alien/foreign/not one's own; hence पराई (fem); -पराया अपना अपना blood is thicker than water; to resort to double standards; पराई आग में हाथ तापना/ सेकना to fish in troubled water.

परार्थ para:rth (nm) altruism, benevolence, beneficence; ~पर/ परायण benevolent, beneficent; altruistic; ~परता / ~परायणता altruism; ~वाद altruism; hence ~वादिता (nf); ~वादी an altruist; altruistic; परार्थी an altruist, a benevolent man.

परावर्तक para:vartak (nm) a reflector; (a) reflecting, causing reflection; ~ता reflectance.

परावर्तन para:vartān (nm) reflection; regression; withdrawal; return; —, पूर्ण total reflection.

पराश्रय para:shshray (*nm*) dependence on another; subjugation, subjection.

पराश्रव्य para:shshravy (*a*) ultrasonic.

पराश्रित para:shshrit (*a*) dependent (on others), under subjugation/subjection; hence ~ता (*nf*).

परास para:s (*nf*) range.

परास्त para:st (*a*) defeated, vanquished; overthrown; —भाव a sense of defeat.

पराहं para:hām (*nm*) the super-ego.

परिंदा parinda: (*nm*) a bird; –पर न मार सके, (जहाँ) where even a bird would have no access.

परि pari–a Sanskrit suffix imparting the sense of round, around, about, round about; fully, abundantly, richly; against; in the direction of; beyond; more than; outside of, etc.

परिकक्ष parikaksh (*nm*) a shell.

परिकथा parikatha: (*nf*) a tale, narrative.

परिकर parikar (*nm*) in traditional Rhetorics, a figure of speech; coterie, circle.

परिकर्म parikarm (*nm*) make-up.

परिकर्मी parikarmī: (*nm*) a make-up man; an attendant.

परि/कलन parikalān (*nm*) calculation; ~कलित calculated.

परि/कल्पना parikalpanā: (*nf*) a hypothesis; fabrication; ~कल्पित hypothetical; fabricated.

परि/क्रमण parikkramān (*nm*) the act or process of revolving, revolution; going round; hence ~क्रांत (*a*).

परिक्रमा parikkramā: (*nf*) revolution; going round; –करना to go round the idol of a deity or a holy place etc.

परिक्रय parikkray (*nm*) a ransom; barter, exchange.

परिक्षा/लन pariksha:lān (*nm*) cleaning thoroughly, cleansing, washing; hence ~लित (*a*).

परिखा parikha: (*nf*) a moat, trench or fosse around a town or fort.

परि/गणन pariganān (*nm*) (the act or process of) enumeration; calculating, assessing; hence ~गणनीय (*a*); ~गणित (*a*).

परिगणना pariganana: (*nf*) enumeration, calculation, assessment.

परिग्रह pariggrah (*nm*) possessions; family, retinue; encircling; engulfing; seizing, apprehension.

परिग्रहण pariggrahān (*nm*) seizing, engulfing.

परिचय parichay (*nm*) introduction; acquaintance, familiarity; -पंक्ति a legend; -पत्र a letter of introduction; –कराना/देना to introduce; to familiarize.

परिचर parichar (*nm*) an attendant; a servant.

परिचर्चा paricharcha: (*nf*) a symposium.

परिचर्या paricharya: (*nf*) attendance, attending on a patient; nursing.

परिचायक paricha:yak (*a*) introductory, illustrative (of); (*nm*) one who or that which introduces, familiarizes.

परिचा/रक paricha:rak (*nm*) an attendant, a male nurse; ~रिका a female attendant, nurse.

परि/चालक paricha:lak (*nm*) an operator; a steersman, navigator controller; ~चालन operation operating; steering, navigation ~चालित operated; steered, navigated, controlled.

परिचित parichit (*a*) introduced acquainted; familiar; (*nm*) a acquaintance.

परिच्छद parichchhad (*nm*) a cove

covering; clothing.

परिच्छेद parichchhed (*nm*) a chapter; section.

परिजन parijan (*nm*) body of dependents, kith and kin.

परिज्ञात pariggya:t (*a*) well-known, known thoroughly; ascertained.

परिज्ञा/न pariggya:n (*nm*) thorough knowledge, deep insight, mastery (over a subject); ascertainment; ~त see **परिज्ञात**.

परिणत pārinat (*a*) changed, transformed; culminated; having reached the point of culmination.

परिणति parinati (*nf*) transformation, culmination; form.

परिणय parinay (*nm*) wedding, marriage; -**सूत्र** wedlock, bonds of marriage; **०में बँधना** to enter into wedlock.

परिणाम parinā:m (*nm*) result, outcome; consequence; conclusion; effect; magnitude; ~**स्वरूप** as a result of, with the result; consequently; ~**दर्शी** foresighted, one who knows the ultimate result; ~**वाद** the doctrine of evaluation, the doctrine which propounds that the effect is hidden in the cause and that, therefore, cause is nothing but non-manifest effect; hence ~**वादिता** (*nf*); ~**वादी** an adherent of **परिणामवाद**; –**भुगतना/भोगना** to suffer/face the consequences of.

परिणामी parinā:mī: (*a*) resultant; ever-transforming.

परिणी/त parini:t (*a*) wedded, married; ~**ता** married (woman).

परितः paritah (*ind*) about; around.

परितप्त paritapt (*a*) hot; heated; afflicted; anguished, in deep anguish; see **परिताप**.

परिताप parita:p (*nm*) heat; affliction; anguish.

परि/तुष्ट paritusht (*a*) gratified, fulfilled; fully satisfied; ~**तुष्टि** gratification; fulfilment, satisfaction.

परि/तृप्त paritript (*a*) satiated; thoroughly satisfied; fulfilled, gratified; ~**तृप्ति** satiation; thorough satisfaction, fulfilment, gratification.

परितोष paritosh (*nm*) satisfaction; fulfilment, gratification; hence **परितोषी** (*a*).

परि/त्यक्त parittyakt (*a*) abandoned; given up; forsaken, renounced sacrificed; ~**त्यक्ता** (an) abandoned (woman); ~**त्यक्ती** abandonee.

परि/त्याग parittya:g (*nm*) abandonment/abandon, giving up; sacrifice, renunciation; ~**त्यागी** an abandoner; one who makes a sacrifice, one who renounces.

परि/त्राण parittrā:n (*nm*) protection; deliverance; salvation; ~**त्राता** a protector; deliverer.

परिदर्शन paridarshān (*nm*) a panoramic view, an all-round view.

परिदृश्य pariddrishy (*nm*) a landscape; panorama.

परिधान paridhā:n (*nm*) clothes; clothing, cladding.

परि/धि paridhi (*nf*) circumference; periphery; boundary; ~**धिगत** peripheral; ~**धीय** peripheral, pertaining to or related with the circumference/periphery.

परिनिर्वाण parinirvā:n (*nm*) final beatitude, complete liberation/salvation.

परिनिवृत्ति parinivritti (*nf*) liberation, salvation.

परिनिष्ठित parinishthit (*a*) standard; –**प्रयोग** standard usage; –**भाषा** standard language.

परि/पक्व paripakv (*a*) ripe; mature; fully developed; ~**पक्वता** ripeness maturity; full development

~पक्वावस्था the state of being fully developed.

परिपत्र paripattr (*nm*) a circular; circular letter.

परिपथ paripath (*nm*) a circuit; -, विद्युत् electric circuit.

परिपाक paripa:k (*nm*) (achievement of) perfection; complete assimilation; maturity, maturing.

परिपाटी paripa:ṭi: (*nf*) a convention; tradition; ~गत/बद्ध conventional; traditional, tradition-bound; –पर चलना to follow the convention/tradition.

परिपार्श्व paripa:rshv (*nm*) perspective; flank; vicinity; ~गत of/in perspective; –में around, in the vicinity; ~वर्ती existing in perspective, flanking.

परि/पालन paripa:lan (*nm*) execution, implementation; maintenance; ~पालक one who executes/implements/maintains; hence ~पालनीय (*a*); ~पालित (*a*).

परि/पीड़न paripi:ṛān (*nm*) oppression, tyranny; atrocity; ~पीड़क an oppressor, tyrant; atrocious.

परिपुष्ट paripushṭ (*a*) well-built, well-nourished, stout and sturdy; corroborated; confirmed.

परि/पूरक paripu:rak (*a*) supplementary; causing or helping in the attainment of completion/perfection.

परिपूरित paripu:rit (*a*) supplemented; fully accomplished/completed/perfected; full (of), infused or informed (by).

परिपूर्ण paripu:rn̤ (*a*) perfect; complete; self-contained; full (of); infused by or imbued with.

परिपूर्ति paripu:rti (*nf*) perfection; completion; abundant supply; gratification, satisfaction.

परिपृच्छा pariprichchha: (*nf*) an enquiry, questioning.

परि/पोष pariposh (*nm*) (adequate) nourishment; nurture; corroboration; confirmation; hence ~पोषण (*nm*); ~पोषित (*a*).

परिपोषी pariposhi: (*a*) nourishing; corroborative, confirmative.

परिप्रश्न pariprashn (*nm*) a probing question; interrogation.

परिप्रेक्ष्य paripreksby (*nm*) perspective; –में, इस (आदि) in this perspective.

परि/प्लावित paripla:vit (*a*) inundated (with), submerged, immersed; overwhelmed/swayed by.

परिप्लुत pariplut (*a*) see परिप्लावित.

परि/बंध paribāndh (*nm*) a bound; unrelenting grasp; ~बंधन unrelenting grasp; hence ~बद्ध (*a*).

परि/बोध paribodh (*nm*) appreciation; warning; ~बोधन act or process of appreciation/warning.

परि/भाषा paribha:sha: (*nf*) definition; ~भाषागत/~परक definitional; ~भाषित defined; –में बाँधना to define.

परिभू paribhu: (*a* and *nm*) all-embracing, permeating all-round; God, the Almighty.

परि/भ्रम paribbhrām (*nm*) wandering; rotating; confusion; ~भ्रमण wandering; rotation; stroll; jaunt.

परिमंडल parimāṇḍal (*nm*) a circle, globe, orbit; halo.

परिमल parimal (*nm*) fragrance, aroma.

परिमा parimā: (*nf*) periphery; rim, magnitude.

परिमाण parimā:n̤ (*nm*) quantity; volume; ~वाचक quantitative; –की दृष्टि से quantitatively.

परिमाप parimā:p (*nm*) perimeter; dimension.

परि/मार्जन parima:rjān (*nm*) cleansing, purging; refinement; hence

~मार्जनीय (*a*); ~मार्जनीयता (*nf*).

परिमार्जित parima:rjit (*a*) cleansed, purged; refined.

परिमित parimit (*a*) finite; measured; limited; ~ता limitation; finiteness.

परिमेय parimey (*a*) measurable; fit to be or worth being limited; rational; hence ~ता (*nf*).

परिरंभ parirāmbh (*nm*) embrace, embracing, hugging; hence ~ण (*nm*).

परि/रक्षण parirakshāṉ (*nm*) preservation; custody; shielding; ~रक्षक preserving, shielding; a custodian; preserver, one who shields; ~रक्षी preservative; shielding, custodial.

परि/वर्जन parivarjān (*nm*) abandonment, forsaking; ~वर्जनीय abandonable, worth being and fit for forsaking.

परिवर्जना parivarjanā: (*nf*) an inhibition.

परिवर्जित parivarjit (*a*) abandoned; forsaken, given up.

परिवर्त parivart (*nm*) revolution; interchange; change.

परि/वर्तन parivartān (*nm*) change; alteration; variation; interchange; ~वर्तनवादी radical, supporting constant change; ~वर्तनीय changeable; alterable; variable; interchangeable; ~वर्तित changed, altered; undergone variation; interchanged; ~वर्तितता variability; changeability.

परिवर्ती parivarti: (*a*) changing, undergoing alteration; variable; unsteady.

परि/वर्धन parivardhan (*nm*) development, growth; enlargement; ~वर्धनीय fit to grow/develop, fit to be enlarged, worth being enlarged; developable; ~वर्धित developed; grown; enlarged.

परि/वहन parivahān (*nm*) transportation; ~वहनीय transportable.

परि/वाद pariva:d (*nm*) complaint; scandal; calumny; hence ~वादक (*nm*).

परिवादी pariva:di: (*nm*) complainant; scandal-monger; calumniator; (*a*) complaining; calumnious; scandalous.

परिवार pariva:r (*nm*) a family; household; –चलाना to run a family/household; –टूटना a family to break-up.

परि/वीक्षण parivi:kshāṉ (*nm*) probation; ~वीक्षा probation; ~वीक्षाधीन a probationer; on probation.

परि/वृत parivrit (*a*) surrounded; enveloped; ~वृति surrounding, enveloping.

परि/वृत्त parivritt (*a*) revolved; changed; hence ~वृत्ति (*nf*).

परिवेश parivesh (*nm*) environment; enclosure; precincts.

परि/वेष्टन pariveshṭān (*nm*) enclosing; wrapping; surrounding; a wrapper; ~वेष्टित enclosed; wrapped; surrounded.

परिव्यय parivvyay (*nm*) expenditure; outlay; disbursement.

परिव्रज्या parivvrajya: (*nf*) wandering from place to place; leading the life of a religious mendicant; abandonment of the world.

परिव्राजक parivvra:jak (*nm*) a wandering religious mendicant; an ascetic.

परिशिष्ट parishishṭ (*nm*) an addendum; a supplement; (*a*) remaining, left over.

परिशीलन parishi:lān (*nm*) study, critical study.

परि/शुद्ध parishuddh (*a*) accurate; precise; absolute; pure; ~शुद्धता/~शुद्धि accuracy; precision; absoluteness; purity.

परि/शोधन parishodhan (*nm*) revision; purification; rectification, rectifying; ~**शोधित** revised; purified; rectified.

परि/श्रम parishshrām (*nm*) labour, industry, hard work, exertion, diligence; ~**श्रमशील** tending to labour/work hard, industrious, disposed to exert; hence ~**श्रमशीलता**(*nf*); ~**श्रमी** laborious, industrious, painstaking; hardworking, diligent; –**कभी व्यर्थ नहीं जाता** industry must bring its reward, hard work is never wasted.

परि/श्रान्त parishshra:nt (*a*) wearied, tired, fatigued; worn out; exhausted; ~**श्रान्ति** weariness, fatigue; exhaustion.

परिष/द् parishad (*nf*) a council; an association; hence ~**दीय** pertaining to or related with a council/an association.

परि/ष्कार parishka:r (*nm*) refinement; purification; finish; finesse; ~**ष्कृत** refined; purified; ~**ष्कृति** refinement; purification; finesse.

परिसंपत्ति parisāmpatti (*nf*) assets.

परिसंबंध parisambāndh (*nm*) articulation.

परिसंवाद parisamva:d (*nm*) a symposium.

परिसज्जा parisajja: (*nf*) finish; finishing touches; make-up; embellishment.

परिसमापन parisama:pan (*nm*) completion; conclusion.

परिसमा/प्त parisama:pt (*a*) completed; concluded; ~**प्ति** completion; conclusion.

परिसर parisar (*nm*) premises; enclave.

परि/सीमा parisi:mā: (*nf*) boundary, extreme limit; line of demarcation; precincts; ~**सीमन** limitation; demarcation.

परिस्तान paristā:n (*nm*) a fairyland; a place where pretty damsels hover all around; an enchanting world of beauty.

परिस्थिति paristhiti (*nf*) circumstance(s); ~**गत** circumstantial; -**विज्ञान** ecology; ~**सिद्ध** circumstantial, accomplished through circumstances; –**का दास होना** to be a slave of (one's) circumstances; –**का मारा हुआ** struck by adversity, downed/afflicted by circumstances; –**से ऊपर उठना** to rise above the circumstances; –**से जूझना** to struggle with adverse circumstances.

परिस्फुट parisphuṭ (*a*) manifest; defined; evident; hence ~**ता** (*nf*).

परिहार pariha:r (*nm*) avoidance; abstaining, refraining (from); forestalling; rectifying (a flaw, error).

परिहार्य pariha:ry (*a*) avoidable, that can be abstained/refrained (from); capable of being forestalled/rectified; hence ~**ता** (*nf*).

परिहा/स pariha:s (*nm*) joke; humour; ~**सप्रिय** humour-loving, humorous; ~**सात्मक** jocular, humorous.

परिहित parihit (*a*) past participle form of **परिधान**—clad, clothed.

परी pari: (*nf*) a fairy, nymph; dream girl, beautiful damsel; ~**खाना** an abode of fairies; ~**जाद** born of a fairy; ~**लोक** a fairyland, an abode of pretty women.

परीक्षक pari:kshak (*nm*) an examiner; -**प्रतिवेदन** examiner's report.

परीक्षण pari:kshān (*nm*) act or process of examination, examining; test/testing; trial.

परीक्षा pari:ksha: (*nf*) an examination, test; trial; -**काल** the hour of examination; examination days; -**पद्धति/प्रणाली** examination system;

-भवन examination hall; -शुल्क examination fee; -का माध्यम medium of examination; -सुधार examination reform.

परीक्षार्थी pariksha:rthi: (*nm*) an examinee.

परीक्षित pari:kshit (*a*) examined; tested; tried.

परीक्ष्य pari:kshy (*a*) fit to be or worth being examined/tested/tried.

परीशान pari:sha:n (*a*) see **परेशान**.

परुष parush (*a*) hard, harsh, severe; unpleasant; rough; unkind, cruel, pitiless; hard-hearted; –**वचन** harsh/rough words, unpleasant utterance; hence **परुषा** (feminine form) see **पुरुष**; a shrew.

परुष/ता, ~**त्व** parushta:, ~atv (*nf*) hardness, harshness, severity; cruelty; pitilessness, hard-heartedness.

परुषोक्ति parushokti (*nf*) harsh/rough words, cruel/unpleasant utterance.

परे pare (*ind*) beyond; across; above; on the other side; afar; afterwards; outside; –**करना** to ask to keep away; to ask for keeping a distance; –**बिठाना** to outwit; to outmanoeuvre, to defeat/vanquish.

परेड pared (*nf*) parade; –**करना** to be wearied out, to have to undertake a tiring job; –**कराना** to entrust tiring jobs; to cause to run about; –**का मैदान** parade ground.

परेवा pareva: (*nm*) a pigeon; fast-flying bird.

परेशान pareshā:n (*a*) bothered; worried; troubled; harassed; ~**हाल** afflicted, in a troubled state; hence; ~**हाली** (*nf*).

परेशानी paresha:nī: (*nf*) botheration; worry; trouble; harassment.

परोक्ष paroksh (*a*) indirect; implicit; invisible, imperceptible; latent; secret; ~**त**: indirectly, in an indirect, implicit manner; hence ~**ता** (*nf*).

परोक्षार्थ paroksha:rth (*nm*) implication, indirect/implied meaning.

परोप/कार paropka:r (*nm*) beneficence, benevolence; charity; altruism; ~**कारिता** beneficence; altruism; ~**कारी** beneficent, benevolent; charitable; altruistic; an altruist.

परोपजी/वी paropji:vi: (*a*) parasitic; (*nm*) a parasite; hence ~**जीविता** (*nf*).

परोपदेश paropdesh (*nm*) teaching imparted to others, precept meant for others.

परोसना parosnā: (*v*) to serve food; **परोसी हुई थाली को लात मारना** to kick the table when the meal has been served.

परोसा parosa: (*nm*) (a) dish of food sent for an invitee who has failed to turn up to participate in a banquet/feast.

पर्चम parcham (*nm*) a banner, standard.

पर्चा parcha: (*nm*) see **परचा**.

पर्ची parchi: (*nf*) a slip/piece of paper; –**काटना** to issue a slip/permit; to mark for a kill; to prepare the ground for eventual kill.

पर्जन्य parjanny (*nm*) a cloud.

पर्ण parn (*nm*) a leaf; -**कुटी** a bower, hut made up of leaves; -**भोजन** (an ascetic) subsistence on leaves; –**शब्द** frou-frou (of leaves); ~**शाला** a hut made up of leaves; ~**शैया** bedding made up of leaves.

पर्दा parda: (*nm*) see **परदा**

पर्यंक paryāṅk (*nm*) a bed, bedstead.

पर्यंत paryānt (*ind*) till; upto; until; unto

पर्यटक paryaṭak (*nm*) a tourist; -**दल**

touring party/team, group of tourists.

पर्यटन paryaṭan (*nm*) touring; tourism; -दल touring party/team.

पर्यवसान paryavasa:n (*nm*) culmination; conclusion, termination.

पर्यवसित paryavasit (*a*) culminated; concluded, terminated.

पर्यसन paryasan (*nm*) throwing out/off; expulsion; exclusioı

पर्यस्त paryast (*a*) thrown out/off; expelled, excluded.

पर्याप्त parya:pt (*a*) enough, sufficient; ample, adequate; hence ~ता (*nf*).

पर्याय parya:y (*nm*) a synonym, synonymous/equivalent word; -कोश a dictionary of synonyms; ~त्व synonymity; ~वाचक/वाची synonymous; ०शब्द a synonym, synonymous word; –विज्ञान synonymy.

पर्या/लोचन, ~लोचना parya:lochān/ (*nm*), ~lochanā: (*nf*) thorough review; critical study, investigation.

पर्युषण paryushāṇ (*nm*) adoration, worship.

पर्व parv (*nm*) festival; festal day; a day or occasion for performance of religious rites; a chapter; -काल festal day/occasion.

पर्वत parvat (*nm*) a mountain; hill; high heap or dump; –देवी/परी an oread; ~माला a mountain range; ~राज Himalayas, the king of mountains; ~वासी inhabiting, or belonging to, the hills; -विज्ञान orography; orology; -श्रेणी mountain range, sierra; -पृष्ठ a ridge.

पर्वतारोहण parvata:rohan (*nm*) mountaineering.

पर्वतारोही parvata:rohi: (*nm*) a mountaineer; -दल a team of mountaineers, mountaineering team.

पर्वतीय parvati:y (*a*) hilly; mountainous; pertaining or belonging to the hills/mountain.

पर्वरिश parvarish (*nf*) see **परवरिश.**

पर्वाना parva:nā: (*nm*) see **परवाना.**

पलँग/पलंग palāg, palāng (*nm*) a bed, bedstead; ~तोड़ indolent, slothful; inert (person); sexually stimulating; ~पोश a bed-sheet; –को लात मारकर खड़ा होना to recover from a long confinement; to rise after a long spell of inactivity; –लगाना to spread the bedding; to get the bed ready.

पल pal (*nm*) a measure of time equivalent to twenty-four seconds; –भर (को) for a while, for a moment; ०में in a moment, instantaneously; –में तोला पल में माशा to chop and change, to play fast and loose.

पलक palak (*nf*) an eyelid; –झपकते/गिरते in a blink, in no time; –न मारना not to sleep a wink, not to bat an eyelid; –पसीजना to have tearful eyes; to be moved by compassion; –बिछाना to extend a respectful welcome; –पाँवड़े बिछाना to extend a red carpet welcome, to give a deferential welcome; –भाँजना to wink (at); –मारना to wink (at); to have a wink; –मारते in a blink or within a moment, in no time; –लगना to have a short nap/sleep, to go asleep; –से पलक न लगना to lie wide awake, to have no sleep; –से ज़मीन झाड़ना, –से तिनके चुनना to serve reverentially; पलकें भारी होना the eyes to be heavy through sleep, to feel sleepy; पलकों पर बिठाना/रखना/लेना to accord a most cordial welcome, to receive with immense cordiality.

पलटन palṭān (*nf*) a platoon; a force; –की पलटन large numbers; in force.

पलटना palaṭnā: (*v*) to turn back, to return; to alter; to overturn; to overthrow; to convert; to upset; to reverse.

पलटनिया palṭaniyā: (*a*) belonging to the army; strong and sturdy.

पलटा palṭa: (*nm*) a turn; change; return; relapse (as after illness); –खाना to take a turn; to make a somersault; to suffer a relapse; पलट में in return, in exchange.

पलड़ा palṛa: (*nm*) a balance-pan; –ऊँचा होना to have an upper hand; to be in an advantageous position; –भारी होना to have a stronger case, to be in a stronger position; to have an advantage over; to gain an upper hand.

पलथी palthī: (*nf*) see पालथी

पलना palnā: (*nm*) a cradle; (*v*) to be brought up, to be reared/fostered; to be nourished.

पलस्तर palastar (*nm*) plaster; –करना to plaster; –ढीला करना to thrash; to weary out of countenance; –ढीला होना to be thrashed, to be wearied out of countenance; –बिगड़ना see –ढीला होना; –बिगाड़ना see –ढीला करना.

पलायक pala:yak (*nm*) one who escapes; a fugitive.

पलायन pala:yān (*nm*) escape, fleeing; ~वाद escapism; hence ~वादिता (*nf*); ~वादी (an) escapist.

पलायमान pala:ymā:n (*a*) escaping, fleeing, on the run.

पलायित pala:it (*a*) escaped; fugitive; left abruptly.

पलाश pala:sh (*nm*) the tree *Butea fondosa* and its purple-coloured flower; –वन a forest of पलाश.

पलास pala:s (*nm*)see पलाश; (*nf*)pliers.

पलित palit (*a*) aged, old, grey-haired; greyed (hair).

पली/ता pali:ta: (*nm*) a wick; an ignitor; guncotton; ~ता दिखाना/~ता लगाना to ignite, to burn; ~ते में आग लगाना the fat to be in fire.

पलीद pali:d (*a*) (rendered) impure, contaminated, unclean; vitiated, polluted; –करना to pollute; –करना, मिट्टी to cause disgrace to be heaped on, to subject to disgraceful embarrassment.

पलेट paleṭ (*nf*) a pleat; plat; ~दार pleated.

पलेटन paleṭan (*nf*) a platten.

पलेथन palethan (*nm*) dry flour applied on both sides of dough while rolling it into a cake; –पकाना to contrive the ruin (of); –निकालना to thrash severely, to beat to a pulp or mash.

पलेनर palenar (*nm*) a planer, planing machine.

पल्लव pallav (*nm*) a new tender leaf; ~ग्राहिता superficiality; smattering knowledge; ~ग्राही a smatterer; smattering, superficial; ~ग्राही ज्ञान/पांडित्य smattering knowledge, superficial scholarship; hence ~न (*nm*).

पल्लवित pallavit (*a*) having/growing new leaves; flourishing; thriving; expanded; prospered; -पुष्पित flourished and thrived; prospered all round.

पल्ला palla: (*nm*) the hem/border/extreme end of a cover garment; side; leaf; flap; facet; scale/pan of a balance; see पटला; परला; पल्लेदार a porter, grain-porter; पल्लेदारी portage, grain-porting; charges paid for carrying bags of grain; –छुटना to be rid of; to attain riddance; –छुड़ाना to get rid of; –झाड़ना to completely dissociate, to get out of (an altercation; mess, etc.); –झुकना to prove more than a match; to acquire an upper hand; –पकड़ना to seek the support of; to be under the benevolent protection of; –पसारना to beg of (somebody); to seek favours from, to make an humble appeal for being granted a favour; –भारी होना to have an upper hand; to be in a position of strength, to prove stronger; पल्ले पड़ना to be condemned to possess/have, to have the misfortune of owning/being in possession of; to have to obtain; पल्ले बँधना to be married/wedded to (an undesirable person); to be entrusted to; पल्ले बाँधना to make a note of, always to remember; to thrust on; to marry off; –से बाँधना to thrust on, to marry off.

पल्ली palli: (*nf*) a village; hamlet; see परली (under परला).

पल्लू pallu: (*nm*) extremity of a female garment (*sa:ri:*) used as a head-cover.

पवन pavan (*nm*) air, breeze; wind; –चक्की a wind-mill; –संघात a jet blast of wind.

पवमान pawmā:n (*nm*) see पवन.

पवर्ग pavarg (*nm*) the fifth pentad of the Devna:gri: script beginning with the letter प and ending with म.

पवाड़ा pava:ṛa: (*nm*) a long boring narrative, dry unending tale.

पवित्र pavittr (*a*) holy, sacred; pure; ~ता holiness, sanctity, purity; –करना, घर आदि को (said out of reverence) to impart sanctity (by paying a visit), to come (e.g. आज मेरे घर को पवित्र कीजिए).

पवित्रात्मा pavittra:tmā: (*nm*) (a) holy person; noble.

पवित्रित pavittrit (*a*) sanctified; purified.

पवित्रीकरण pavittri:karān (*nm*) sanctification; purification.

पशम pashām (*nm*) pubes; very fine soft wool; —उखाड़ना to be able to cause no injury/loss; to be able to do just nothing; —न उखाड़ पाना to be absolutely ineffective; to be able to cause no harm/loss/injury; –न समझना to consider just insignificant, to consider as of absolutely no consequence; to attach no importance at all; –पर मारना to care a fig (for); to take as absolutely inconsequential.

पशमीना pashmī:nā: (*nm*) very fine soft wool; superfine woollen cloth made of this wool.

पशु pashu (*nm*) an animal; beast; cattle; a savage brute; ~चर्या beastly/savage conduct; sensual gratification; ~पति(नाथ) an epithet of Lord Shiv; ~पाल/पालक a cattle-breeder; ~पालन cattle-breeding; ~बल brute force, mere physical strength; -बलि animal sacrifice; -भाव beastliness, savagery; ~वत् beastly, savage, brutal; resembling an animal.

पशुता pashuta: (*nf*) beastliness; savagery, brutality, savage conduct.

पशुत्व pashuttv (*nm*) see पशुता.

पशेमा/न pashemā:n (*a*) ashamed; remorseful/repentant; hence ~नी (*nf*).

पश्च pashch (*a*) latter; later; following; back; western; –स्वर a back vowel.

पश्चात् pashcha:t (*ind*) after, afterwards; behind.

पश्चात्ता/प pashcha:tta:p (*nm*) remorse,

repentance, compunction; ~पी remorseful, repentant, compunctious; ~प की आग में जलना to suffer within through a sense of remorse/repentance.

पश्चाद् pashcha:d—an allomorph of पश्चात् (see); ~भाग the latter portion, the remaining part; ~वर्ती following; subsequent, situated/located behind.

पश्चार्द्ध pashcha:rddh (*nm*) the latter/later half.

पश्चि/म pashchim (*nm*) west; (*a*) western; ~मार्द्ध the latter/later/western half; ~मी western; ~मोत्तर west-northern.

पश्म pashm (*nm*) see पशम.

पश्मीना pashmī:nā: (*nf*) see पशमीना.

पसं/द pasānd (*nf*) liking; choice; taste; ~दगी liking, choice; ~दीदा liked, chosen.

पसर pasar (*nm*) see पसा.

पसरना pasarnā: (*v*) to stretch full; to lie dishevelled/stretched; to be inert.

पसली pasli: (*nf*) a rib; –फड़क उठना to be thrilled, to throb with emotion; पसलियां ढीली करना to beat hollow, to give a severe thrashing.

पसा pasa: (*nm*) the two handfuls; as much as can be held in both hands joined in a cup-like structure.

पसाना pasa:nā: (*v*) to pour off the watery content of boiled rice; to pour off superfluous water.

पसार pasa:r (*nm*) expanse; diffusiveness/diffusion.

पसारना pasa:rnā: (*v*) to spread; to expand; to stretch; to diffuse all round.

पसावन pasa:vān (*nm*) the watery content of boiled rice,

पसिंजर pasinjar (*nm*) a passenger; (*nf*) passenger train.

पसीजना pasi:jnā: (*v*) to perspire; to ooze; to be moved by pity/compassion; to deliquesce.

पसीना pasi:nā: (*nm*) sweat, perspiration; –आना to perspire; to have cold feet; –छूटना to have cold feet; –निकालना to tire out, to cause to be wearied; –बहाना to labour hard, to make strenuous effort; पसीने की कमाई hard-earned money, money earned by the sweat of one's brow; पसीने की जगह ख़ून बहाना, किसी के to be ready to make sacrifices for the sake of, to shed blood out of loyalty (to someone) पसीने-पसीने होना to perspire profusely.

पसोपेश pasopesh (*nm*) a dilemma; fix; hesitation; –में पड़ना to make two bites at a cherry, to be in a fix, to be in a state of uncertainty; to hesitate.

पस्त past (*adj*) wearied, weary, worn out, defeated, dejected; ~क़िस्मत luckless, unfortunate; having a wretched lot; ~हिम्मत demoralised; ~हिम्मती demoralisation; ~हौसला demoralised; dejected; –करना to defeat; to weary (somebody) out; to demoralise; –होना to be vanquished, to be wearied out; to be demoralised.

पस्ती pasti: (*nf*) state of being wearied/worn out; demoralisation; sense of defeat/dejection.

पहचान pehchā:n (*nf*) acquaintance; familiarity; recognition; identification; identity; identification mark; -चिह्न identification mark; -पत्र identity card.

पहचानना pehchā:nnā: (*v*) to recognize; to distinguish, to discriminate; to identify.

पहनना pehnnā: (*v*) to wear (as clothes); to put on (as clothes, watch, ornaments, etc.); -ओढ़ना to dress up decently; to live well.

पहनाना pehnā:nā: (*v*) to cause to wear/put on; to clothe.

पहनावा pehna:va: (*nm*) dress; clothing; manner of dressing up.

पहर pehar (*nm*) a measure of time equal to three hours; —, आठों throughout the day, day in and day out; दो~ midday, noon; तीसरे– afternoon.

पहरा pehra: (*nm*) a guard; watch; पहरेदार guard, sentry, watchman; पहरेदारी watchmanship, guarding; –देना to guard, to keep a watch; –बदलना to (have a) change (of) guard; –बैठाना to institute a guard, to deploy a guard; पहरे पर होना to be on guard (duty), to be on watch and ward duty; पहरे में देना to entrust under a guard; to assign to the custody of; पहरे में रखना to keep under watch; to keep in custody; पहरे में होना to be under custody/watch.

पहरी pehri: (*nm*) a guard, watchman, sentry.

पहरुआ pehrua: (*nm*) a guard, watchman, sentry.

पहल pehal (*nf*) initiative; ~क़दमी initiative; ०करना to take an initiative; —करना to break ground, to take an initiative.

पहल/वान pehalva:n (*nm*) a wrestler; hefty-sturdy man; ~वानी wrestling; the job or profession of wrestling; wrestling acumen.

पहला pehla: (*a*) first; foremost; most important; primary.

पहलू pehlu: (*nm*) side; aspect; flank, facet; ~दार multi-faceted; having many sides/aspects; –आबाद होना to have the beloved by one's side; to be in sweet company; –दबाना to exert pressure on the flank; –बचाना to avoid confrontation/clash, to steer clear of; –में बैठना to sit in close proximity; to be seated in a compromising pose; –में रहना to be in close proximity, to be at close quarters.

पहले pehle (*ind*) first (of all); in the beginning; in olden times; originally; before; beforehand; -पहल first of all; for the first time; –अपने पीछे पराये blood is thicker than water, charity begins at home; –आत्मा फिर परमात्मा self before service; –स्वार्थ तब परमार्थ self before service, to serve one's own interests before serving others.

पहलौटा pehlauṭa: (*a*) first-born, the eldest of all (one's children).

पहलौटी pehlauṭi: (*nf*) first born (girl); the first delivery.

पहाड़ paha:ṛ (*nm*) a mountain, hill; a huge heap; –उठाना to perform a very ardous task; –टल जाना the hump to be over the worst to be over; –टालना (said ironically) to achieve a feat, to perform a miraculous task; –टूटना, –टूट पड़ना to be hit by a calamity; to be in the throes of a crisis; -सा दिन (said when time hangs heavy on one's mind) a day that seems to have no end, a long-long day; –से टक्कर लेना to kick against the pricks, to cross swords with a giant; to defy a colossus; –होना to be agonising, to be too heavy, to seem to be unending.

पहाड़ा paha:ṛa: (*nm*) a multiplication table; –याद करना to memorize a multiplication table.

पहाड़ी paha:ṛi: (*a*) mountainous; hilly; pertaining or belonging to the hills/mountain; (*nf*) a hillock; mount; ridge; (*nm*) a highlander.

पहि/या pahiya: (*nm*) a wheel; **~येदार** wheeled, moving on wheels; **~ये लगना, पाँव में** to go/move very fast (as if on wheels).

पहुँच pahūch (*nf*) reach; access; arrival, intimation of arrival; receipt.

पहुँचना pahūchnā: (*v*) to reach; to arrive; **पहुँचा हुआ** accomplished; perfect; (one who has) attained perfection; guileful/vile person.

पहुँचा pahūcha: (*nm*) the wrist; **–पकड़ना** to try to take undue advantage; to make advances; to hold back.

पहुँचाना pahūcha:nā: (*v*) to (cause to) reach; to carry; to transmit; to convey; to lead.

पहुँची pahūchi: (*nf*) a wrist-ornament (worn by women).

पहुनाई pahuna:i: (*nf*) guestship; the state of being a guest; entertainment, hospitality; **–करना** to go about as a guest, stay as a guest (at a relative's house).

पहेली paheli: (*nf*) a riddle, puzzle; **–बुझाना** to talk in riddles, to make an enigmatical utterance; **–बूझना** to solve a riddle.

पाँख pā:kh (*nf*) see **पख**.

पाँखी pā:khi: (*nf*) a bird.

पाँखुरी pā:khuri: (*nf*) see **पखुड़ी**.

पाँच pā:ch (*a*) five; (*nm*) the number five; **पाँचों (उँगलियाँ) घी में होना** to live on the fat of the land, to have one's bread buttered on both sides; to attain the utmost/highest advantage, to thrive on all fronts; **पाँचों उँगलियाँ बराबर नहीं होतीं** all are not equal, all of a clan are not alike; **पाँचों सवारों में नाम लिखाना** to count/consider oneself amongst the privileged few.

पाँचवाँ pā:chvā: (*a*) fifth.

पांडव pāṇḍav (*nm*) the five valiant sons of King Pa:ṇḍu, and the heroes of the Maha:bha:rat (**युधिष्ठिर, भीम, अर्जुन, नकुल, सहदेव**).

पांडित्य pa:ṇḍitty (*nm*) scholarship, learning; erudition; **-प्रदर्शन** making a show/exhibition of scholarship.

पांडु pa:ṇḍu (*a*) yellow; yellowish white; pallid; hence **~ता** (*nf*); (*nm*) jaundice (a disease); an ancient king of Hastinā:pur and the father of the valiant heroes of the great war of Maha:bha:rat.

पांडु/लिपि pa:ṇḍulipi (*nf*) a manuscript; also, **~लेख**; **~लिपिविज्ञान** papynology

पांडुर pa:ṇḍur (*a*) yellow; yellowish white; pallidus; **~ता** etiolation, pallor.

पाँडे, पांडे, पांडेय pā:ḍe, pā:ṇḍe, pā:ṇḍey (*nm*) a sub-caste of the Bra:hmāṇs.

पाँत, पाँति pā:t, pā:ti (*nf*) a row; line; row of invitees in a feast; **–से डालना** to excommunicate.

पाँय pā:y (*nm*) see **पाँव**.

पाँयचा pā:ycha: (*nm*) a foot-rest.

पाँव pā:w (*nm*) foot; leg; **~पोश** a foot-rug; **–अड़ाना** to put one's foot; to hinder; to create hindrance; **–उखड़ना** to be swayed away/off, to be dislodged, to lose one's hold, to lose ground, to be routed; **उठना, की ओर** to automatically proceed towards; **–ऊँचे-नीचे पड़ना** not to be able to balance oneself out of intoxicaton); to go astray, to move in a wayward fashion; to be infused with a sense of fear; to feel unsteady; **–की जंजीर** fetters, something that holds back; **–की**

जूती समझना to treat with utter disdain/contempt; -की धूल होना to be a fool to, to be nothing in comparison with; -के नीचे से धरती खिसक जाना see -तले की धरती खिसकना; -चलना, दबे to walk stealthily, to tiptoe; -जमना to be well entrenched, to have one's position consolidated; to be firmly lodged; -जमाना to find one's feet, to entrench oneself, to consolidate one's position, to acquire a firm footing; -डगमगाना to feel uncertain/unsteady, to wobble, to waver; -डिगना to feel shaky, to waver, to wobble, to slip; to make a lapse; -तले की धरती खिसकना to develop cold feet, to be funky; to be dumbfounded/flabbergasted; -तोड़कर बैठना to lose all one's mobility; to just stick to one's point, not to go/move anywhere; -थर्राना see -काँपना; -पकड़ना to yield, to surrender oneself to somebody's mercy; to touch one's feet humbly; -पड़ना to make humble entreaties, to request humbly; -पर पाँव रखकर बैठना to be absolutely indolent, to do nothing, to idle away one's time; -पर पाँव रखना to follow in somebody's footsteps, to follow somebody without the least deviation; -पूजना to worship one's feet: -फटना to suffer from chilblains; -फूंक-फूंक कर रखना to tread as on eggs, to advance every step with utmost care; -फैला कर सोना to enjoy a carefree sleep; to lead a carefree life; -भारी होना to be in the family way; -में पहिये लगना to move very fast (as if on wheels), to race ahead; see also पैर.

पाँवड़ा pā:wṛa: (*nm*) a foot-rug, red carpet.

पाँवड़ी(री) pā:wṛi:(ri:) (*nf*) wooden sandals.

पाँसा pā:sa: (*nm*) a die, dice; उलटना/पलटना a scheme to misfire; a chance/order or situation to be topsyturvied; to topsyturvy a situation/chance/order, etc.; -फेंकना to cast the die; to make a strategic move; -सीधा पड़ना to succeed in one's move, to be favoured by luck.

पाइका pa:ika: (*nm*) a special (printing) type which is 1/6th of an inch in breadth.

पाइप pa:ip (*nm*) a pipe.

पाई pa:i: (*nf*) a pie, the smallest Indian copper coin equivalent to one-third of the old paisa (now no longer in currency); a small vertical line used in writing or printing the Devna:gri: characters; a full stop punctuation mark (।) used in Devna:gri: writing; -पाई चुकाना to repay/pay off every penny; -पाई वसूल करना to recover every penny.

पाउंड pa:unḍ (*nm*) pound; sterling pound.

पाउडर pa:uḍar (*nm*) powder; face; powder; -पोतना to (put up a crude) make-up (said derisively).

पाएदार pa:eda:r (*a*) see पायदार.

पाएदान pa:eda:n (*nm*) see पायदान.

पाक pa:k (*a*) holy, sacred; pure; clean; (*nm*) Pakistan; cooking; maturation; -कला the art of cooking; -क्रिया cooking; ~दामन see पाकदामन; ~दिल clean-hearted, pure and simple; ~नीयत genuine, earnest, honest; ~विद्या/शास्त्र cookery, the science of cooking; ~शाला a kitchen; -संबंधी culinary; -साफ़ clean; pure; upright; with no selfish motive; —करना, झगड़ा to put a stop to a quarrel; to complete an arduous work/a difficult task.

पाकड़ pa:kaṛ (*nm*) the citron-leaved Indian fig tree.

पाकदाम/न pa:kda:mān (*a*) chaste; morally unassailable; virtuous; hence ~नी (*nf*).

पॉकिट, पाकेट pokiṭ, pa:keṭ (*nf*) a pocket; ~मार a pick-pocket; ~मारी pick-pocketing; –गरम करना to bribe; to accept bribe; –मारना to pick-pocket.

पाक्षपातिक pa:kshapa:tik (*a*) partisan, partial; (*nm*) a partisan, one who takes sides.

पाक्षिक pa:kshik (*a*) fortnightly, biweekly.

पाखंड pa:khāṇḍ (*nm*) hypocrisy; pretence, pretension, sham, dissimulation; –करना to be pretentious, to indulge in hypocritical conduct, to dissimulate; –फैलाना to contrive plans for deception; to indulge in hypocritical intrigues, to put up a show, to prepare the stage for dissimulatory acts.

पाखंडी pa:khāṇḍi: (*a*) hypocritical, pretentious, sham, dissimulating; (*nm*) a hypocrite, dissimulator.

पाखाना pa:kḫa:nā: (*nm*) privy, latrine; faeces; human excrement, stool.

पाग pa:g (*nm*) anything which is boiled in sugar-syrup; (*nf*) a long-winding narrow turban.

पागना pa:gnā: (*v*) to dip or boil in sugar-syrup; to sweeten (by being permeated with sugar-syrup).

पागल pa:gal (*a*) mad, insane; lunatic; deranged; crazy; bedlamite, rabid; (*nm*) a lunatic, maniac, mad person; –कुत्ता a rabid dog; ~खाना a bedlam, lunatic asylum; ~पन/~पना lunacy; insanity, madness; craziness, mania; –करना to madden, to turn crazy; –होना to be crazy; to run amuck.

पागुर pa:gur (*nm*) (the act or process of) chewing the cud; –करना to chew the cud, to ruminate.

पाचक pa:chak (*a*) digestive; (*nm*) a digestive powder or medicine etc; ~ता (*nf*) digestive power/quality, digestiveness.

पाचन pa:chān (*nm*) digestion; -शक्ति digestion, digestive power.

पाचनीय pa:chanī:y (*a*) digestible, that can be digested; hence ~ता (*nf*).

पाच्य pa:chchy (*a*) digestible; that can be easily digested; hence ~ता (*nf*).

पाजामा pa:ja:mā: (*nm*) see **पायजामा**.

पाजी pa:ji: (*a*) wicked, vile; depraved; mean; base; (*nm*) a rascal, scoundrel; ~पन/~पना wickedness, vileness, scoundrelism; rascality.

पाज़ेब pa:zeb (*nm*) an ornament worn round the ankles.

पाटंबर pa:ṭāmbar (*nm*) a silken cloth.

पाट pa:ṭ (*nm*) jute; span; width, breadth (as of a river, etc.); a grindstone, mill-stone; a tow; plank; a slab of stone on which a washerman washes his clothes.

पाटन pa:ṭān (*nf*) city; roof, roofing over a building.

पाटना pa:tnā: (*v*) to dump; to roof; to cover with earth etc.; to fill; to heap, to pile up; to bridge, to connect.

पाटल pa:ṭal (*nm*) a typical ochre-coloured flower and its tree; (*a*) rose-red, ochrous.

पाटव pa:ṭav (*nm*) see **पटु** (~ता).

पाटी pa:ṭi: (*nf*) a thin wooden board on which children are taught to write the alphabet; each side piece of a bedstead; a kind of mat (e.g. शीतलपाटी); parting of the locks of hair on the head; method, way; series; line; –पढ़ना to receive elementary instruction/lesson/education; to be initiated/instigated.

पाठ pa:ṭḥ (*nm*) a lesson; text; recital/recitation; reading, study; ~चर्या syllabus; -भेद different reading, varying version, variant; ~विज्ञान textual criticism; -शोधन emendation, correction/rectification (of the text); -संशोधन emendation; –पढ़ाना to teach lesson; to initiate; to instigate someone into vile ways; –पढ़ाना, उलटा to misinstruct, to instigate into vile ways; –सीखना to learn a lesson from.

पाठक pa:ṭḥak (*nm*) a reader; a subcaste of the Bra:hmāṉs.

पाठन pa:ṭḥān (*nm*) reading; teaching.

पाठशा/ला pa:ṭḥsha:la: (*nf*) a school; ~लीय pertaining to the school.

पाठान्तर pa:ṭḥā:ntar (*nm*) version; variant text, variation of text.

पाठा pa:ṭḥa: (*nm*) a strong youngman; a stout young animal.

पाठालोचन pa:ṭḥa:lochan (*nm*) textual criticism.

पाठी pa:ṭḥi:—used as a suffix conveying the sense of a reader or scholar as वेदपाठी, मंत्रपाठी.

पाठ्य pa:ṭṭḥy (*a*) readable, worth reading; pertaining to a text/lesson,l egible; ~क्रम curriculum; course, syllabus; ~चर्या syllabus; –पुस्तक a text-book.

पाड़ pa:ṛ (*nf*) staging, builder's staging; the border of a *dhoti*: *ṣa:ri:*, etc; scaffold; –बाँधना to put up a scaffold/staging.

[illegible]ा/ड़ा pa:ṛa: (*nm*) a part or locality of a city or town; male young of a [illegible]alo; ~ड़ी female young buffalo.

पाणि pa:ṉī (*nm*) a hand; ~ग्रहण marriage, wedding; ०संस्कार the wedding ritual/ceremony; ~गृहीत married (man); ~गृहीता married (woman); ~तल palm (of the hand).

पाणि/नि pa:ṉīnī (*nm*) the celebrated pioneering Grammarian of ancient India whose famous work is entitled अष्टाध्यायी; ~नीय Pa:ṉīnian, pertaining to पाणिनि, his grammatical school or his technique of linguistic analysis.

पात pa:t (*nm*) ~~fall,~~ falling; a leaf; –झरना shedding of (tree) leaves.

पात/क pa:tak (*nm*) a sin; misdeed; ~की a sinner; an evil-doer; sinful.

पाताल pa:ta:l (*nm*) the nether-most world; –लोक the nether-most world (as referred to in the Pura:ṉas), the farthest of the seven nether-worlds.

पातिव्रत pa:tivrat (*nm*) chastity (of a woman), (woman's) loyalty/fidelity (to the husband).

पाती pa:ti: (*nf*) a letter, leaf.

पात्र pa:ttr (*nm*) utensil; pot; vessel, container; character (in a play, drama, etc.); a deserving person; hence पात्री (*nf*); —, का worthy/deserving of; eligible (for); ~ता/त्व state of deserving; worthiness; eligibility; -निर्धारण casting (in a play etc.); -वर्ग/-सूची cast (in a play etc.); पात्रीय pertaining to a पात्र.

पाथना pa:thnā: (*v*) to turn into cakes, to make cow-dung into cakes for fuel.

पाथर pa:thar (*nm*) see पत्थर.

पाथेय pa:they (*nm*) provisions for a journey.

पाद pa:d (*nm*) a foot; leg; foot of a meter; foul wind (discharged from the posterior opening); quadrant;

one-fourth part; ~तल sole of the foot; foot; ~क्षेप footwork; ~पद्म lotus-like feet; –पूर्त्ति completion of the foot of a verse; –प्रहार a kick, knock; ~बंध fetters; ~मूल lower part of the foot; foothill; ~हत kicked; knocked down; ~हीन without feet; footless.

पादना pa:dnā: (*v*) to break wind, to discharge foul wind (through the posterior opening).

पादप pa:dap (*nm*) tree; plant.

पादरी pa:dri: (*nm*) a clergy, clergyman, christian priest; a missionary.

पादाक्रांत pa:da:kkrā:nt (*a*) crushed under the feet, trampled over; kicked.

पादाग्र pa:da:ggr (*nm*) the front of the foot.

पादाघात pa:da:gha:t (*nm*) kick/kicking.

पादाति, ~क pa:da:ti, ~k (*nm*) an infantryman, a foot-soldier; pedestrian.

पादुका pa:duka: (*nf*) a sandal, wooden sandal.

पादोदक pa:dodak (*nm*) the water with which the feet of a revered person or an idol of God have been washed.

पाधा pa:dha: (*nm*) a Hindu priest.

पान pa:n (*nm*) betel, betel-leaf; (the act or process of) drinking (water or any other liquid); ~दान a metallic box in which betel-leaves, lime, catechu, etc. are kept, betel-leaf receptacle; –पत्ता insignificant/meagre offering or presents; –का बीड़ा seasoned and folded betel-leaf; –फेरना to shuffle and reshuffle the betel-leaves; –लगाना to season a betel-leaf for chewing, to apply lime, catechu, etc. on a betel-leaf and fold it.

पाना pa:nā: (*a*) to get, to obtain; to acquire, to attain, to achieve; to be able to reach; to regain; to eat; (*nm*) a spanner.

पानागार pa:nā:ga:r (*nm*) a bar, liquor-house; a tavern.

पानी pa:nī: (*nm*) water, aqua; rain; essence; liquid substance; valour; lustre, brightness; climate; breed; honour; sense of self-respect; thin coating/plating; ~दार respectable, honourable; lustrous; possessing a sense of self-respect; of a good breed (as घोड़ा); ~देवा son or a near relative who is supposed to offer a libation of water to a deceased; a son; ~पाँड़े/वाला a waterman; –आना to start raining, rain to commence; to be watery; –आना, मुँह में the mouth to water; –उतरना to develop cataract (in the eye); to suffer from hydrocele; to be disgraced, to be dishonoured; –उतारना to disgrace, to dishonour, to humiliate; –कर देना to appease to the fullest satisfaction; to soften, to move; –का बताशा see गोल (~गप्पा); –का बुलबुला (as uncertain as) a water-bubble, transitory, having a momentary existence; –की तरह बहाना to make/play ducks and drakes of/with, to squander away; –के मोल damn/extremely cheap; almost free; –को भी न पूछना to completely neglect a visitor, to treat a visitor with contempt; –जाना to be disgraced, to suffer humiliation; to water; –जाना, आँखों का to become shameless; to be lost to shame; –टूटना to run short of water (as a well etc.); to have the level of water much too reduced; –दिखाना to (show) water (to); to bring (a pail of) water for drinking purposes (for a horse, cattle, etc.); –देना to offer a libation of water to one's manes; to water (plant etc.), to irrigate; —देना और जड़ काटना to have a handkerchief in one hand and sword in the other; –न माँगना to die instantly; to succumb instantaneously; –पड़ना to rain; –पड़ना, घड़ों see under घड़ा; –पर नींव रखना lit. to lay the foundation on a mass of water—to initiate a plan on fluid premises; –पानी होना to go hot and cold, to be overwhelmed with shame, to be put out of countenance; –पीकर जाति पूछना to put the cart before the horse, to consider the pros and cons after performing an act; –पी-पीकर कोसना to heap curses upon; to lash out with a torrent of curses; –फिर जाना to fall to the ground, to be undone, to be ruined/dissipated/destroyed; –फेरना to undo, to dissipate, to destroy, to ruin; –बचाना/रखना to safeguard the honour of; not to allow one's honour to be sullied/compromised/undermined; –बदलना to go for a change of climate; –भर आना, मुँह में watering of the mouth to be salivated; –भरना to draw/fetch water; not fit to hold a candle to, to be much inferior to; to be no match to, to be a pygmy as compared with; –मरना water to go on being absorbed (by a wall etc. causing it to be weakened); to be lost to shame; –में आग लगाना lit. to cause fire in water —to cause the impossible to happen; –में रहकर मगर से बैर to live in Rome and clash with the Pope; –लगना to be affected adversely; to assume pretentious ways; water to be accumulated at some place; water to cause a smarting pain (in decaying teeth); –लेना to disgrace, to dishonour; –से पतला thinner than water; –से पहले पुल/पाड़ बाँधना to devise plans too much in advance against a contingency; to make preparation to counter an unseen crisis.

पानेवाला pa:newa:la: (*nm*) a payee; recipient.

पाप pa:p (*nm*) a sin, vice; evil; evil deed; –कर्म sin, sinful deed; ~कर्मा a sinner; ~घ्न/नाशक/नाशी countering a sin, destroying (the effect of) a sin; ~दृष्टि sinful eye; greedy eye; ~बुद्धि sinful, villainous, depraved; sinning mentality; ~मय abounding in sins, sinful; sinning; ~मुक्त free from sins, liberated from sins; unsinning; ~मोचन liberation/riddance from sins; –उदय होना committed sins to bring forth their evil results; to get the return for accumulated sins; –कटना to get rid of sins/evil or unwarranted man or job etc; a botheration to come to an end; –कमाना/बटोरना to commit sinful acts, to accumulate sins (which are bound to have their repercussions in due course); –का घड़ा भरना (one's) sinful deeds to reach the extremity, the vessel of sins to be full to the brim, he that swims in sins sinks in sorrow; –की गठरी the burden of one's sins; –मोल लेना to knowingly own a botheration or commit sinful acts; –लगना to earn sins, to load oneself with the commission of sinful acts.

पापड़ pa:paṛ (*nm*) salted (spiced)

crisp thin cake made of ground pulse or sago etc; --बेलना to go through fire and water, to be in hard circumstances; to pass one's days in calamitous conditions; to endure hardships.

पापड़ी pa:pṛi: (*nf*) a kind of sweet; small round thin salted and crisp cakes made of ground flour or *maida:*.

पापलीन pa:plī:n (*nm*) poplin (cloth); (a) immersed in sinful acts.

पापा pa:pa: (*nm*) papa, father.

पापाचा/र pa:pa:cha:r (*nm*) sinful conduct/living; ~री a sinner; sinning (person); hence ~रिणी (*nf*).

पापात्मा pa:pa:tmā: (*a*) sinful, unholy; (*nm*) a sinner, an evil doer.

पापिष्ठ pa:pishṭḥ (*a*) sinning, committing sinful acts; (*nm*) a sinner; great sinner.

पापी pa:pi: (*a*) sinning, sinful; immoral; (*nm*) a sinner; –से घृणा मत करो, पाप से डरो Hate the sin and not the sinner.

पाबंद pa:bānd (*a*) bound, obliged; restricted; under control; –, वक्त का punctual; –होना to be bound/obliged by.

पाबंदी pa:bāndi: (*nf*) binding, obligation; restriction, control, ban; –, वक्त की punctuality; –लगाना to impose a restriction.

पामर pa:mār (*a*) low, wicked, mean, base; sinful; hence ~ता (*nf*).

पामा pa:mā: (*nm*) eczema.

पामा/ल pa:mā:l (*a*) trampled, trodden over; hence ~ली (*nf*).

पायँ pā:y (*nm*) foot; ~चा one of the two legs of pyjamas or pants; ~ता the lower part of a bedstead.

पाँयत pā:yat (*nm*) symbol of the person going to commence a journey kept at a place in the direction of the projected journey at an auspicious moment and restored to the person concerned when he actually starts; see पायँता (under पायँ).

पायंदाज pa:yānda:z (*nm*) a foot-rug, a thick mat for dusting the feet.

पायजामा pa:yja:mā: (*nm*) pyjamas, trousers.

पायज़ेब pa:yzeb (*nm*) an ornament for ankles, an anklet.

पायताबा pa:yta:ba: (*nm*) a thin leather cut piece inserted into the shoe etc. for the foot to comfortably rest on; stocking.

पायदान pa:ydā:n (*nm*) a foot-rest; foot-board.

पायदा/र pa:yda:r (*a*) lasting, durable; firm, strong; ~री durability, lastingness; firmness.

पाय(इ)रिया pa:y(i)riya: (*nm*) pyorrhoea.

पायल pa:yal (*nm*) an anklet.

पाया pa:ya: (*nm*) leg (of a furniture etc); post, pillar; prop, support; –बुलंद होना to be up-posted/upgraded; to thrive/prosper; पायेदार see पायदार; पाये का आदमी a steady dependable man, a man of strength of character.

पायी pa:i: —a suffix used to denote one who or that which drinks/absorbs/sucks, e.g. स्तनपायी, विषपायी.

पारंग/त pa:rāṅgat (*a*) adept, expert; well-versed, well-conversant; learned (in a subject); hence ~तता, ~ति (*nf*).

पारंपरिक pa:rāmparik (*a*) traditional; hereditary; ~ता traditionality; hereditariness.

पारंपरीण pa:rampari:n (*a*) traditional; hereditary.

पारंपरीय pa:rāmpari:y (*a*) traditional, hereditary.

पार pa:r (*nm*) the other coast/bank/side, extremity; limit; conclusion; end; (*adv*) across, on the other side/bank/coast; (*adj.*) past, last; next; ~**गमन** transmission; ~**गमनीयता** transmissibility; ~**गम्य** pervious; o **ता** perviousness; ~**गामी** going through; pervading, pervasive; ~**साल** last year; next year; —**उतरना** to cross over (a river or difficulty etc.), to ferry over, to finish; to accomplish; to get rid of some dilemma, etc.; –**करना** to pinch; to kidnap; to seduce; to cross through/over; to (cause to) cross; to salvage; to pass by; to overtake; –**पड़ना** to contend with successfully, to see things through; –**पाना** to be able to measure the depth or expanse of; to reach the end (of); to equal (in struggle etc.) or to defeat; –**लगना, बेड़ा** see –**उतरना**; –**होना** see –**उतरना**.

पारखी pa:rkhi: (*nm*) a connoisseur; one who can well appreciate merits (of); taster; hence ~**पन** (*nm*).

पारण pa:rāṇ (*nm*) the first meal taken after a fast; passage; –**करना** to take the first meal after a fast; to pass.

पारतंत्र्य pa:rtāntry (*nm*) see **परतंत्रता**.

पारद pa:rad (*nm*) mercury.

पार/दर्शक pa:rdarshak (*a*) transparent; ~**दर्शकता** transparency, transparence; ~**दर्शिता** transparency; ~**दर्शितामापी** diaphanometer; ~**दर्शी** transparent.

पारपत्र pa:rpattr (*nm*) a passport.

पार/भासक; ~**भासी** pa:rbha:sak; ~bha:si: (*a*) translucent; ~**भासकता** translucence.

पारमार्थिक pa:rma:rthik (*a*) transcendental, ultra-mundane; pertaining to spiritual objects; benevolent, beneficent; hence ~**ता** (*nf*).

पारलौकिक pa:rlaukik (*a*) ultra-mundane, transcendental, relating to the other/next world; hence ~**ता** (*nf*).

पारश्वसन pa:rshwasān (*nm*) transpiration.

पारस pa:ras (*nm*) the mythical (philosopher's) stone which is said to convert iron into gold by mere touch; an object of unusual merits; also–**पत्थर** (*nm*); ~**मणि** (*nf*).

पारसा pa:rsa: (*a*) chaste (woman), of moral purity, of unimpeachable character; hence ~**ई** (*nf*).

पारसी pa:rsi: (*a* and *nm*) a member of the Parsi community; Zoroastrian; —**धर्म** Zoroastrianism.

पारस्परिक pa:rasparik (*a*) reciprocal, mutual; ~**ता** mutuality, reciprocity.

पारांध pa:rā:ndh (*a*) opaque; ~**ता** opacity.

पारा pa:ra: (*nm*) mercury; –**उतरना** to be pacified, to calm/cool down; –**गरम होना/चढ़ना** to get infuriated, to fly into a rage; –**पिलाना** to fill a thing with mercury so as to make it very heavy.

पारायण pa:ra:yāṇ (*nm*) thorough reading, reading a book from beginning to end.

पारावत pa:ra:wat (*nm*) a pigeon.

पारावार pa:ra:wa:r (*nm*) an ocean, a sea; limit; (both) shores; –**न होना** knowing no end, to be limitless (as **खुशी का**–).

पारिजात pa:rija:t (*nm*) the coral tree —*Erythrina Indica*; the name of one of the five trees said to exist in paradise.

पारित pa:rit (*a*) passed; –**करना** to pass (a bill, resolution, etc.)

पारितोषिक pa:ritoshik (*nm*) a reward, prize; –**वितरण** prize distribution.

पारिपार्श्विक pa:ripa:rshwik (*a*) horizontal; –**विकास** horizontal development.

पारिभाषिक pa:ribha:shik (*a*) technical; definitional, pertaining to definition; hence ~**ता** (*nf*); –**शब्द** a technical term; –**शब्दावली** technical terminology.

पारिवारिक pa:riva:rik (*a*) familial; pertaining to a family; hence ~**ता** (*nf*); –**वर्गीकरण** genealogical classification (oft he languages of the world).

पारिश्रमिक pa:rishsramik (*nm*) remuneration.

पारिषद pa:rishad (*nm*) a councillor, senator; (a) pertaining to **परिषद्**.

पारिस्थिति/की pa:risthitiki: (*nf*) ecology; ~**कीय** ecological.

पारी pa:ri: (*nf*) shift; turn; –**पारी** by turns; o **से** alternatively; turn by turn; –**का बुखार** alternating fever, fever attacking every alternate day.

पारेन्द्रिय pa:rendriy (*a*) extra-sensual; –**ज्ञान** telepathy.

पारेष/ण pa:reshān (*nm*) (the act or process of) transmission; ~**क** transmitter.

पार्क pa:rk (*nm*) a park; –**करना** to park (a vehicle, etc.)

पार्टी parṭi: (*nf*) a party.

पार्थक्य pa:rthakky (*nm*) separation; distinction, differentiation; secession; ~**वाद** separatism; ~**वादी** separatist(ic); secessionist(ic).

पार्थि/व pa:rthiv (*a*) terrestrial, earthly; material; worldly, mundane; hence ~**वता** (*nf*); ~**वेतर** ultramundane, other-worldly; ~**व शरीर** material frame, mundane being.

पार्लियामेंट pa:rlia:menṭ (*nf*) parliament.

पार्वतिक pa:rvatik (*a*) orographic, mountainous, hilly; pertaining/belonging to **पर्वत** (see).

पार्वती pa:rvati: (*nf*) the spouse of Lord Shiv, an epithet of Goddess **दुर्गा**; ~**कुमार/नंदन** Ganesh and Ka:rtikey —the two sons of **पार्वती**.

पार्वतीय pa:rvati:y (*a*) mountainous, hilly, orographic; pertaining to the mountains/hills.

पार्वतेय pa:rvatey (*a*) born of a mountain/hill; mountainous, hilly.

पार्वत्य pa:rvatty (*a*) mountainous, hilly, of or belonging to mountains or hills.

पार्श्व pa:rshv (*nm*) side; flank; facet; armpit; vicinity, proximity, neighbourhood; ~**गायक** playback singer; hence ~**गायिका** (*nf*); ~**चित्र** a profile; –**छवि** a profile; ~**वर्ती** lateral; proximate, situated in the vicinity/neighbourhood; –**संगीत** background/side music, playback.

पार्श्विक pa:rshvik (*a*) lateral; pertaining to a **पार्श्व**; –**विकृति** lateral strain; –**व्यंजन** lateral consonant; **पार्श्विका** a profile.

पार्षद pa:rshad (*nm*) a councillor, senator; courtier; an attendant.

पार्ष्णि pa:rshṇī (*nf*) a rear guard (of an army).

पार्सल pa:rsal (*nf*) a parcel.

पाल pa:l (*nf*) a sail; the layers of straw, leaves, etc, between which unripe mangoes (and some other fruits) are ripened within doors; a suffix denoting a protector, maintainer, manager administrator, etc. (as **राज्यपाल, लेखपाल** etc.); —**का पका** ripened in **पाल**; ~**घर** sail-loft; —**में डालना** to keep fruits under layers of straw etc. to ripen.

पालक pa:lak (*nm*) a protector; one who or that which keeps/maintains/sustains/nourishes; spinach, spinage.

पालकी pa:lki: (*nf*) a palanquin; sedan chair.

पालतू pa:ltu: (*a*) tame/tamed; domestic/domesticated; –**बना लेना** to tame, to domesticate.

पालथी pa:lthi: (*nf*) a cross-legged sitting posture; –**मारकर बैठना/लगाना** to sit with legs crossed over each other.

पालन pa:lān (*nm*) abiding by; observance; upbringing; nourishing, fostering; tending; maintenance; -**पोषण** upbringing; nourishing/providing nourishment, fostering; nurture/nurturing; mothering, bringing up, cherishing; ~**हार** one who tends/rears/fosters/brings up; God; –**करना** to abide by; to observe; to nurture, to mother, to foster, to bring up.

पालना pa:lnā: (*v*) to bring up, to rear; to nurture; to foster; to feed, to mother; to tame, to domesticate; (*nm*) a (swinging) cradle/crib; **पाला-पोसा** brought up, nourished, reared.

पाला pa:la: (*nm*) frost; side; concern; (*a*) reared, nurtured, brought up, fostered, tended; cherished; –**पड़ना** to be frost-hit; to be devastated, to suffer destruction; –**पड़ना, किसी से** to have to contend with; to be confronted with (a difficult person etc.); to face a difficult person in hostility and defiance; –**मारना** to be frost-hit, to be frost-bitten.

पालागन pa:la:gān (*nm*) deferential salutation; touching the feet of somebody out of reverence.

पालि pa:li (*nf*) a middle Indo-Aryan language used by the Buddha for his teachings and by his followers in subsequent Buddhist scriptures.

पालित pa:lit (*a*) brought up, nourished, nurtured, fostered; cherished; observed; adhered to; maintained, sustained; hence **पालिता** (*nf*); –**पोषित** reared and tended, fostered, cherished and nourished.

पा(ॉ)लिश pa:(ɔ)lish (*nf*) polish; –**करना** to polish.

पा(ॉ)लिसी pa:(ɔ)lisi: (*nf*) policy; an insurance policy; ~**बाज** cunning, shrewd(person); diplomatic; ~**बाजी** cunningness, shrewdness; shrewd diplomacy.

पाली pa:li: (*nf*) turn; shift; see **पालि**.

पाले pa:le; –**पड़ना, किसी के** to fall in the cruel clutches of, to be under the control of (somebody).

पाव pa:w (*nm*) one-fourth of a seer; (*a*) one-fourth; quarter; foot; ~**दान** a pedal; footstep; tradle of machine; ~**रोटी** a bread.

पावक pa:vak (*nm*) the fire.

पावती pa:vti: (*nf*) a receipt; –**देना** to acknowledge receipt.

पावन pa:vān (*a*) holy, sacred; immaculate; pure; a suffix denoting one who or that which purifies (as **पतितपावन**); ~**ता** holiness, sanctity; immaculation; purification, purity.

पावना pā:vnā: (*nm*) money due to be realised (as **देना**–); (*a*) due.

पावनी pa:vanī: (*a*) that which purifies/sanctifies (as पतितपावनी).

पावर pa:war (*nm*) power (as हार्स-पावर); electric power (as ~लूम); –स्टेशन a power station; –हाउस a power house.

पावस pa:vas (*nf*) the rainy season.

पावा pa:wa: (*nm*) foot (of a chair etc.).

पाश pa:sh (*nm*) a bond, tie; noose; snare, trap; fetter; chain; mass; lock (as केश~); an instrument used for sprinkling/spraying (as गुलाबपाश); ~बंध a bond; snare; ~बद्ध in bond, snared, in fetters.

पाशक pa:shak (*nm*) a dice/die; as a suffix it means a bond, snare.

पाशव pa·shav (*a*) beastly, beast-like; brutal, savage, belonging/pertaining to beasts/animals.

पाशविक pa:shvik (*a*) brutal, beastly, beast-like, savage; hence ~ता (*nf*).

पाश्चात्य pa:shcha:tty (*a*) western, belonging to the west.

पाषंड pa:shānḍ (*nm*) see पाखंड.

पाषाण pa:shā:ṇ (*nm*) stone; –युग the stone age; ~हृदय hard-hearted, stone-hearted, cruel, merciless, ruthless; unfeeling; hence ~हृदयता (*nf*).

पासंग pa:sāṅg (*nm*) a counter-weight, make-weight, something placed on one pan of a scale to counter-balance the other; –न होना to be a fool to, to be nothing in comparison with.

पास pa:s (*nm*) a pass; (*adv*) near by, in the neighbourhood of; (*a*) passed, not failed; -का near; close by, proximal, located in the vicinity/neighbourhood;–पास near, side by side; close by; ~वान a neighbour; an attendant; a watchman/guard; hence ~वानी (*nf*); –जाना to go near; to be intimate; to cohabit with; –तक न फटकना not to go anywhere near, to keep absolutely aloof, to keep at an arm's length (from); –होना to get through; to pass.

पासपोर्ट pa:sporṭ (*nm*) a passport.

पास/बाँ pa:sbā: (*nm*) a protector; guard, watchman; ~बानी protection, guarding, keeping a watch.

पासा pa:sa: (*nm*) a dice; die; –पड़ना the die to be cast favourably, to be favoured by luck, to have a spell of good luck;—पलटना the tide to be turned, to have a changed run of luck; –फेंकना to cast the die; to try one's luck; –सीधा पड़ना the die to be cast favourably, one's effort to succeed.

पासी pa:si: (*nm*) a low caste amongst the Hindus.

पाहन pa:hān (*nm*) a stone.

पाहि pa:hi (*int*) save me ! protect me !; also पाहिमाम, पाहिमाम !

पाही pa:hi: (*nf*) a far-flung place, remote location.

पाहुन pa:hun (*nm*) a guest.

पाहुना pahunā: (*nm*) a guest; पाहुने आना to come as a guest.

पाहुर pa:hur (*nm*) a present, offering (to relatives).

पिंग pīṅg (*a*) reddish brown.

पिंगल piṅgal (*nm*) prosody; (*a*) yellow, tawny; ~शास्त्र (the science of) prosody; ~शास्त्री a prosodist: ~शास्त्रीय prosodical.

पिंगला pīṅgala: (*nf*) one of the three main canals of the body (the other two being इडा and सुषुम्ना) as described by the Haṭhyogi:s); an exceptionally pretty damsel.

पिंज/ड़ा, ~रा pījṛa:, ~ra: (*nm*) a cage, trap; ~रापोल a cow-pan; ~रे का पंछी a caged bird; a person in bondage.

पिंजर pīnjar (*nm*) a cage; skeleton, physical frame.

पिंड pīnḍ (*nm*) a body/the body; lump (of anything); a ball, round mass; chunk; ~**ज** viviparous; ~**दान** oblation of cooked rice to the manes; –**छूटना** to get rid of; –**देना** to offer oblation to the manes; –**पड़ना** to pester, to go on pestering; to cause continuous harassment.

पिंडली pīḍli: (*nf*) the calf (of a leg); back of the shank.

पिंडा pinḍa: (*nf*) a body; lump of cooked rice for oblation to the manes; a rounded mass; ball.

पिंडाकार pīnḍa:ka:r (*a*) nodular, round; resembling a rounded mass.

पिंडारी pīnḍa:ri: (*nf*) an ancient tribe inhabiting the southern part of India.

पिंडी pīnḍi: (*nf*) a small lump; small round mass of anything; round skein of thread; a crook.

पि/क pik (*nm*) (the Indian) cuckoo; hence ~**की** (*nf*).

पिघलना pighalnā: (*v*) to melt, to be liquefied; to thaw; to fuse; to flow; to be moved by passion/emotion; to become compassionate (towards somebody); to soften.

पिघलाव pighla:w (*nm*) melting, liquefying; (lit. and fig.) softening

पिचक pichak (*nf*) a dent; contraction, deflation.

पिचकना pichaknā: (*v*) to be dented; to be contracted/deflated.

पिचकारी pichka:ri: (*nf*) a syringe; flit gun.

पिचपिचा pichpicha: (*a*) sticky; adhesively watery.

पिच्छल pichchhal (*a*) slippery, slipperily smooth.

पिछ pichh—an allomorph of **पीछा** used as the first member in several compound words; ~**लगा/लगू/लग्गू** a hanger-on, lackey; satellite; ~**होना**, **का** to play second fiddle (to); ~**लगी** hanging on, lackeying, dancing attendance on.

पिछड़ना pichharṇā: (*v*) to lag, to lag behind, to be left behind, to be defeated, to be vanquished.

पिछड़ा pichhṛa: (*a*) backward; defeated, vanquished; ~**पन** backwardness; –**हुआ** backward; defeated.

पिछला pichhla: (*a*) hind, rear, hinder; back, back portion/part; latter; past; last.

पिछवा/ड़ा pichhwa:ṛa: (*nm*) a backyard, rear or hinder part; ~**ड़े** in the backyard, at the rear.

पिछाड़ी pichha:ṛi: (*nf*) a tether, a tethering rope; rear portion; hind part; –**दबाना** to follow closely on the heel of, to go on chasing.

पिटक piṭak (*nm*) a small box/basket; collection of Buddhist scriptures [**त्रिपिटक**].

पिटना piṭnā: (*v*) to be beatēn, to be thrashed; to flop (as a **फ़िल्म**).

पिटाई piṭa:i: (*nf*) beating; thrashing; defeat; work or wages for beating/thrashing.

पिटा/रा piṭa:ra: (*nm*) a large basket; wickerwork pannier; big box/chest; hence diminutive ~**री** (*nf*).

पिट्ठू piṭṭhu: (*a* and *nm*) a lackey; toady, sycophant; a playmate; a turn played in lieu of an imaginary playmate in games; ~**पन** lackeying, acting servilely.

पिठौरी piṭhauri: (*nf*) a salty dish prepared by boiling flour-balls in pulse.

पिढ़ई pirhai: (*nf*) diminutive of **पीढ़ा** (see).

पितर pitar (*nm*) manes, deceased ancestors.

पितराइँध pitrā:idh (*nf*) acrid taste caused by the reaction (on cooked vegetables etc.) of brassware, brassiness of taste.

पितराना pitra:nā: (*v*) to acquire a brassiness of taste, to get an acrid taste through reaction (on coooked vegetables etc.) of brassware.

पिता pita: (*nm*) father, procreator, progenitor.

पिताम/ह pita:mah (*nm*) grandfather; ~**ही** grandmother.

पितिया pitiya: (*nm*) uncle; –**ससुर** brother of father-in-law; hence **सास**.

पितृ pittri (*nm*) the base Sanskrit noun meaning father; paternal ancestor (in Hindi, this uninflected form is used only in compounds); ~**ऋण** one of the three debts on a man (the other two being **देवऋण** and **ऋषिऋण**) from which he is freed when he begets a son; ~**कल्प/तुल्य** like a father; a father-figure; respected, revered; ~**कुल** paternal family, people of father's or ancestor's family; ~**गण** manes, deceased forefathers; ~**घात** patricide; ~**घाती** a patricide; ~**तंत्र** patriarchy; patriarchal system; ~**त्व** fatherhood; paternity; ~**दान** oblation to the manes/deceased forefathers; ~**पक्ष** the dark fortnight of the month of **आश्विन** when oblations are offered to the manes for their spiritual gratification; paternal side; -**परंपरा** ancestry, paternal tradition; ~**भक्त** devoted to one's father; loyal to one's father; ~**भक्ति** filial devotion; ~**भूमि** fatherland; ~**लोक** the world of manes or deceased ancestors; ~**वंश** paternal family; –**विसर्जन** the rites performed on the fifteenth day of the dark fortnight of the month of **आश्विन** which marks farewell to the manes; ~**श्राद्ध** the **श्राद्ध** (see) performed for the gratification of the manes; ~**सत्तात्मक** patriarchal; o **युग** patriarchal age; ~**हंता** a patricide; ~**हत्या** patricide.

पितृव्य pittrivvy (*nm*) an uncle.

पित्त pitt (*nm*) bile, gall; bilious humour; ~**कर** bilious; –**ज्वर** bilious fever; ~**दाह** bilious fever; ~**नाशक** antibilious; –**प्रकृति** of bilious temperament, petulant; –**प्रकोप** the bilious humour to be in a disturbed state; ~**हर** antibilious; –**उबलना/खौलना** to be bilious/fretful.

पित्ता pitta: (*nm*) the gall bladder; ~**मार** dry and full of drudgery; **उबलना/खौलना** to be bilious/enraged; –**पानी करना** to drudge; to work very hard; –**मारना** to subside one's wrath.

पित्ताशय pitta:shay (*nm*) the gall bladder.

पित्ती pitti: (*nf*) urticaria, skin rash.

पिदर pidar (*nm*) father; **पिदरं सुल्तान बूद** lit. '(my) father was a monarch'—to harp on one's royal past, to go on talking of glorious heritage.

पिद्दी piddi: (*nf*) a kind of tiny bird —*Thamnobia cambagensis;* an insignificant creature; **क्या पिद्दी क्या पिद्दी का शोरबा** of no consequence whatever, too tiny to be reckoned.

पिधान pidhā:n (*nm*) a lid; cover, covering.

पिनक pinak (*nf*) lethargy reinforced by drowsiness caused by opium intoxication; –में आना to be drowsy due to opium intoxication; –सवार होना to stagger like a drunken man, to behave like an opium intoxicated person.

पिन pin (*nf*) a pin.

पिनकना pinaknā: (*v*) to be drowsily lethargic (owing to opium intoxication); to lament irritatedly.

पिनकी pinki: (*a*) irritative; (*nm*) an opium-addict.

पिनपिन pinpin (*nf*) child-like crying in nasalized tones.

पिनपिना/ना pinpinā:nā: (*v*) to lament like a peevish child in a nasalized manner; hence ~हट (*nf*).

पिनहाँ pinhā: (*a*) latent, inherent.

पिनाक pinā:k (*nm*) the mighty mythological bow of Lord Shiv.

पिनाकी pinā:ki: (*nm*) the wielder of the Pinā:k—an epithet of Lord Shiv.

पिन्नी pinnī: (*mn*) a kind of sweetmeat.

पिन्हाना pinha:nā: (*v*) to clothe, to dress; to cause to wear/put on.

पिपरमिं(में)ट piparmī(e)nṭ (*nm*) peppermint.

पिपासा pipa:sa: (*nf*) thirst; yearning, craving.

पिपासित pipa:sit (*a*) thirsty; a yearning/craving.

पिपासु pipa:su (*a*) thirsty; possessed of an yearning/a craving.

पिपीलिका pipi:lika: (*nf*) an ant.

पिय piy (*nm*) (darling) husband.

पियक्कड़ piyakkaṛ (*nm* and *a*) a drunkard, inebriate, boozy.

पियराई piyarā:i: (*nf*) yellowness; pallour.

पियराना piyara:nā: (*v*) to turn yellow; to get pallid· to lose lustre.

पिया piya: (*nm*) (darling) husband.

पियानो piya:nō (*nm*) a piano; ~वादक a pianist; ~वादन playing on a piano.

पिराना pira:nā: (*v*) to ache, to have pain.

पिरोना pironā: (*v*) to thread; to string; to needle.

पिलना pilnā: (*v*) to make a sudden rush; to make a long-lasting attack; to enter into; to fall upon; to be pressed/crushed; to concentrate with fnll vigour (on a job).

पिलपिल, ~ला pilpil, ~a: (*a*) flaccidly soft; dehardened; flabby, flaccid; softened because of over-riping (as a fruit); ~लाहट flaccid softness; flabbiness, flaccidness; softness through over-riping; ~लाना to render flaccidly soft; to deharden; to get soft through overrip:ng.

पिलाना pila:nā: (*v*) to make to drink, to cause to drink (a liquid etc.); to administer (as डाँट–).

पिल्ला pilla: (*nm*) a pup, puppy; hence पिल्ली (*nf*).

पिशा/च pisha:ch (*nm*) a devil, hell-hound, demon, evil spirit; ~चवाद demonism; ~चविद्या necromancy; hence ~चिका (*nf*); ~ची (*nf*).

पिशुन pishun (*a*) a back-biter; one who speaks ill of others; slanderer; hence ~ता (*nf*);~त्व (*nm*).

पिष्ट pishṭ (*a*) powdered, ground; ~पेषण hackneyed repetition.

पिष्टोक्ति pishṭokti (*nf*) a cliche.

पिसनहारी pisanha:ri: (*nf*) a woman who grinds corn.

पिसना pisnā: (*v*) to be ground/powdered; to be pressed; to labour hard; to be engaged (in arduous work); to be tortured, to be trampled (over); to be afflicted.

पिसाई pisa:i: (*nf*) the work of or

wages/charges for grinding/powdering of a thing; engagement in arduous work.

पिसान pisa:n (*nm*) flour.

पिसौनी pisaunī: (*nf*) see **घिसाई**.

पिस्ता pista: (*nm*) pistachio-nut.

पिस्तौल pistaul (*nf*) a pistol, revol ver.

पिस्सू pissu: (*nm*) a flea.

पिहित pihit (*a*) covered; concealed, hidden, latent.

पींजरा pī:jra: (*nm*) see **पिंजड़ा.**

पी pi. (*nf*) the melodious note of a cuckoo, singing of a cuckoo; (*nm*) husband; **–कहाँ** singing/note of a **पपीहा** (see).

पीक pi:k (*nf*) spittle of chewed betel leaf, salivary secretion mixed with chewed betel; **~दान** a spittoon, cuspidor.

पीकना pi:knā: (*v*) (a cuckoo) to sing, to sing like a cuckoo (esp. used for birds).

पीछा pi:chha: (*nm*) the back/hinder part; rear; pursuit, chase; **–करना** to chase; to track, to hunt; to follow; to run after; **–छुड़ाना** to get rid of; **–छूटना** to be rid of; to get riddance; **–छोड़ना** to leave off, to let go, to abandon.

पीछे pi:chhe (*adv*) behind, on the back side of; after; afterwards; backwards; in the absence of;–, **के** for, for the sake of; **–चलना** to imitate/emulate; to follow; to follow in the footprints of; to accept the lead of; **–छूटना** to be lagging behind, to be outstripped; to be outdone; o**छोड़ना**; to leave behind, to outstrip; o, **किसी के** to deploy somebody for keeping a watch on; **–पड़ना** to dog, to chase, to pursue; to tease, to torment, to harass continuously; **–फिरना** to keep on following, to go behind; **–लगना** to chase; to follow closely; to accompany as an unwanted person; **–लगे फिरना** to hang on; to keep on following; **–हटना** to give ground, to withdraw/retreat; to retrogress; **–होना** to be inferior/lesser; to be at the back of.

पीटना pi:ṭnā: (*v*) to beat, to thrash; to strike; to punish; to defeat; to knock, to dash, to bang; to thump; to finish, to complete somehow; to earn somehow (as **दिन भर में पाँच-छह रुपये पीट ही लेता हूँ**).

पीठ pi:ṭḥ (*nf*) the back; spine; (*nm*) a seat; an institute; **–का/–पर का** born next in succession; **–चारपाई से लगना** to be bedridden; to be confined to bed; to be reduced to skeleton; **–ठोकना** to pat on the back appreciatively; to praise; to give encouragement; **–दिखाना** to show the white feather, to turn tails, to flee from the battlefield; **–देना** to turn tails, to flee, to part company (in a venture); **–पर हाथ फेरना** to part appreciatively, to give encouragement, **–पर हाथ रखना** to support; **–पर होना** to be at the back of; **–पीछे, के** in the absence of; **–फेरना** to turn one's back upon; **–में छुरा घोंपना/भोंकना** to stab in the back, to play (one) foul; **–में धूल/मिट्टी मिलना** to be felled, to suffer defeat; **–मोड़ना** to turn to go, to leave the scene; **–लगना, किसी की** to be defeated (in Indian style wrestling); to be thrown flat on the back; **–सहलाना** to soothe.

पीठिका pi:ṭḥika: (*nf*) background (as **पूर्व~**); stroma; seat, base.

पीठी pi:ṭḥi: (*nf*) ground pulse.

पीड़क pi:ṛak (*nm*) a tormenter, an

oppressor; one who harasses/troubles.

पीड़न pi:ṛān (*nm*) tormentation, oppression; pressing, harassing, troubling.

पीड़ा pi:ṛa: (*nf*) pain, ache, aching; anguish; agony, suffering; ~**कर** painsgiving, tormenting, troublesome; causing agony/anguish; ~**नाशक/हर** pain-relieving, paregoric.

पीड़ित pi:ṛit (*a*) oppressed, tortured; afflicted, distressed.

पीढ़ा pi:ṛha: (*nm*) a low wooden chair-like structure without back-rest; hence **पीढ़ी** (*nf*).

पीढ़ी pi:ṛhi: (*nf*) a generation; see **पीढ़ा**; **-दर-पीढ़ी** from generation to generation; **–,आने वाली** coming generation; **–,उठती हुई** rising generation; **–का अंतराल/की खाई** generation gap; **–, नई** the new generation, the rising generation; **–,वर्तमान** present generation; **–ह्रासमान** decaying/dying generation.

पीत pi:t (*a*) yellow, pallid; drunk; ~**ता** yellowness; pallour; ~**मणि** an emerald; ~**रक्त** yellowish red; ~**हरित** yellowish green.

पीतम pi:tām (*nm*) the most beloved, (darling) husband.

पीतल pi:tal (*nm*) brass; **–युग** the brass age.

पीतांबर pi:tā:mbar (*nm*) yellow silk cloth; yellow silken **धोती** worn by men during worship; Krishnā.

पीताभ pi:ta:bh (*a*) yellowish; having a yellow tinge.

पीतारुण pita:rūn (*a*) reddish yellow, yellowish red.

पीन pī:n (*a*) fat, fatty; corpulent; heavy, hence ~**ता** (*nf*).

पीनक pi:nak (*nf*) see **पिनक**.

पीना pi:nā: (*v*) to drink; to swill, to sip; to smoke (as **सिगरेट––**); to conceal a secret, to absorb, to suppress (as **गुस्सा––**).

पीप pi:p (*nm*) pus.

पीपल pi:pal (*nm*) the pipal tree.

पी/पा pi:pa: (*nm*) a cask, barrel; float, drum; pontoon; buoy, keg, can, canister; tin; ~**पे का पुल** pontoon bridge.

पीब pi:b (*nm*) see **पीप**.

पीयूष pi:yu:sh (*nm*) nectar, ambrosia.

पीर pi:r (*nf*) pain, ache, 'affliction; compassion; (*nm*) a muslim saint; muslim religious preceptor; ~**ज़ादा** son of a **पीर**; **-मुरशिद** a religious preceptor; **–मौला** see **फ़क़ीर**; **–बवर्ची भिश्ती खर** one who can perform a variety of daily chores, numerous roles all rolled into one person.

पील pi:l (*nm*) an elephant; the castle in the game of chess; ~**पाँव** elephantiasis; ~**पाया** abutment; ~**वान** an elephant-driver; hence ~**वानी** (*nf*).

पीला pi:la: (*a*) yellow, pale, pallid; anaemic; ~**पन** yellowness; pallor; etiolation; **–पड़ना/होना** to grow pale/pallid, to become anaemic; to lose (facial/corporeal) lustre.

पीलिमा pi:limā: (*nf*) yellowness, pallor, etiolation.

पीलिया pi:liya: (*nm*) jaundice, chlorosis; icterus.

पीलू pi:lu: (*nm*) a kind of thorny tree; a typical **राग** in classical Indian music.

पीवर pi:var (*a*) fat, fatty, corpulent, fleshy; heavy.

पीस/ना pi:snā: (*v*) to grind, to pound, to powder; to mill; to gnash (the teeth); to cause to labour hard, to exploit; **–कर पी जाना** to swallow, to devour.

पीहर pi:har (*nm*) a woman's parental house/family/kinsfolk.

पुंगव pūṅgav (*a*) great, best, foremost, outstanding amongst (as नरपुंगव).

पुंगीफल pūṅgi:phal (*nm*) a betel-nut.

पुँछल्ला pūchhalla: (*nm*) see पुछल्ला.

पुंज pūṇj (*nm*) a heap, mass; cluster; collection, multitude.

पुंजीभूत pūṅji:bhu:t (*a*) heaped together, massed together; accumulated; clustered; collected.

पुंडरी/क pūṇḍri:k (*nm*) lotus; white lotus; ~काक्ष having lotus-like eyes, an epithet of Lord Vishṇū.

पुंश्चली pūnshchali: (*nf*) lit. 'running after men'—a harlot, an adulteress, a woman of easy virtue.

पुंसवन pūnsawan (*nm*) a ceremony which is performed during the third month of conception.

पुंस्त्व pūnstw (*nm*) manhood, masculineness; virility; ~करण masculinisation; ~हरण emasculation.

पुआ pua: (*nm*) a kind of sweet flour-cake.

पुआल pua:l (*nf*) paddy-straw.

पुकार pukā:r (*nf*) a call; roll;–पड़ना/लगना/होना to be called out by name, to be asked to show up.

पुकारना puk:rnā: (*v*) to call; to cry out; to call for help; to exclaim, to proclaim.

पुखराज pukhra:j (*nm*) a topaz.

पु/ख़्ता pukhta: (*a*) strong; lasting, durable; firm; mature; ~ख़्तगी durability, the quality of being strong/lasting; firmness; maturity.

पुचकार puchka:r (*nf*) fondle, caress.

पुचकारना puchka:rnā: (*v*) to fondle, to caress; to make love.

पुचारा pucha:ra: (*nm*) laying a thin coat, plaster-brush, cloth used for smearing/coating etc; flattery; encouraging words.

पुच्छ puchchh (*nm*) a tail, tail-like structure; rear, hind part.

पुच्छल puchchhal (*a*) tailed, having a tail; –तारा a comet.

पुछल्ला puchhalla: (*nm*) a long tail, tail piece; any tail-like structure; tag; one who always tails after; a stooge, hanger-on, sycophant.

पुछवैया puchhwaiya: (*nm*) one who looks after, helps or cares for; a questioner/interrogator/ enquirer; one who asks/enquires/interrogates.

पुछैया puchhaiya: (*nm*) see पुछवैया.

पुजाई puja:i: (*nf*) (the process or act of) worshipping; the remuneration paid therefor.

पुजापा puja:pa: (*nm*) long-winding worship, articles used in worship; a show of worship; –फैलाना to enact a show of worship.

पुजारी puja:ri: (*nm*) a worshipper, adorer; Hindu priest; hence ~पन (*nm*).

पुजैया pujaiya: (*nm*) a worshipper, adorer; priest.

पुट puṭ (*nm*) seasoning; slight admixture; light touch; a little mixing; a hollow space (as अंजलिपुट), concavity; fold, cavity (as कर्णपुट), ~पाक a typical method of preparing drugs (the various substances being wrapped up in leaves, covered with clay and heated in fire).

पुटास puṭa:s (*nf*) potash.

पुटी puṭi: (*nf*) a vesicle.

पुटीन puṭi:n (*nf*) putty.

पुट्ठा puṭṭha: (*nm*) haunch, hip; spine (of a book).

पुड़ा puṛa: (*nm*) a large paper-packet.

पुड़िया puṛiya: (*nf*) a small paper-packet.

पुण्य puṇṇy (*nm*) good; virtue; right; good deed, righteous action, (*a*) sacred, holy (as —भूमि), virtuous, righteous (as —कार्य); ~कर्म sacred/good deed, virtuous/righteous act; —काल auspicious moment, ~कीर्ति celebrated, bearing a good name; —क्षेत्र a holy/sacred place, a place of pilgrimage: ~तम the purest, the most sacred; ~तर purer, more sacred; —तीर्थ sacred pilgrimage, one whose very sight is as good as a visit to a holy place of pilgrimage; ~दर्शन (of) auspicious/propitious (appearance); —प्रताप celebrity acquired through good deeds, the bounty of good deed, efficacy of virtue or religious merit; ~फल the fruit or reward of virtue or righteous deed; ~बल force acquired through good deeds, strength of virtue; ~भूमि holy land/place; ~म्मन्य thinking oneself to be virtuous/meritorious, ~योग the effect of virtuous actions; ~लोक paradise, virtuous/righteous world; ~श्लोक saintly, pious, celebrated, of good fame or reputation.

पुण्यात्मा puṇṇyā:tmā: (*a*) good, virtuous righteous, saintly, holy, of noble soul.

पुण्यार्थ puṇṇya:rth (*a*) charitable; —औषधालय charitable dispensary.

पुण्योदय puṇṇyoday (*nm*) advent of good fortune (as a result of holy/righteous/good deeds).

पुतला putla: (*nm*) an effigy, a dummy, an image, mannequin, a toy, scarecrow; —जलाना, किसी का to burn the effigy of; —, पाप का an embodiment of sins; —बाँधना, किसी का to defame/slander, to cause infamy.

पुतली putli: (*nf*) a puppet, doll, marionettes, a pupil of the eye; —का तमाशा a puppet show, ~घर cloth-mill; —फिर जाना eyes to be upturned (as in death), the pupils to become still.

पुताई puta:i :(*nf*) the act or process of white-washing/mud-plastering or the remuneration paid therefor, white-wash; whitening, mud-plastering.

पुत्त/लिका, ~ली puttalika; ~ li: (*nf*) see पुतली.

पुत्र puttr (*nm*) a son; ~तुल्य just like a son, -पौत्र sons and grandsons; ~लाभ begetting a son, ~वती a woman blessed with a son or sons; ~वत् just like a son; ~वधू son's wife, daughter-in law; ~हीन sonless, without a son; ~हीना (a woman) without a son, sonless.

पुत्रार्थी puttra:rthi: (*a*) desirous of a son, hankering after a son.

पुत्रिका putrika: (*nf*) a daughter; puppet, doll.

पुत्रिणी puttrīṇī: (*nf*) a woman blessed with a son or sons.

पुत्री puttri: (*nf*) a daughter.

पुत्रेष्टि puttreshṭi (*nm*) a sacrifice (यज्ञ) performed in olden days for the sake of begetting a son; also —यज्ञ.

पुदीना pudi:nā: (*nm*) mint, garden-mint.

पुनः punah (*adv*) again, once more, anew, re—; ~कथन repetition, reutterance, reiteration;–पुनः again and again, time and again; ~प्राप्ति reacquisition, reprocuration; ~समंजन re-adjustment, o करना to re-adjust; ~स्थापन reinstatement, restoration, re-installation, rehabilitation; ~स्थापित reinstated, reinstalled, rehabilitated; o करना to reinstate, to cause restoration, to rehabilitate.

पुनरपि punarapi (*ind*) even so, even then, nevertheless; again and again, time and again.

पुनरवलोकन punaravlokān (*nm*) revision, viewing/seeing/looking at again; reperusal; retrospection.

पुनरस्त्रीकरण punarstri:karān (*nm*) rearmament.

पुनरागत punara:gat (*a*) returned, come back, recurred.

पुनरागमन punara:gamān (*nm*) return, coming again; recurrence.

पुनरावर्ती punara:varti: (*a*) recurrent, returning, coming again.

पुनरा/वृत्ति punara:vritti (*nf*) repetition, recurrence; ~वृत्त repeated; recurred.

पुनरास्था/पन punara:sthā:pān (*nm*) restitution; ~पित restituted.

पुनराह्वान punara:hvā:n (*nm*) resummon/resummoning, call/calling again.

पुनरी/क्षण punari:kshān (*nm*) vetting; revision, reconsideration; ~क्षित vetted; revised, reconsidered.

पुनरुक्त punarukt (*a*) repeated, retold, reiterated.

पुनरुक्ति punarukti (*nf*) repetition, tautology, reiteration.

पुनरुत्तर punaruttar (*nm*) rejoinder, counter-reply.

पुनरुत्थान punaruttha:n (*nm*) resurrection, resuscitation.

पुनरु/त्पादन punarutpa:dān (*nm*) reproduction, regeneration; ~त्पादित/त्पन्न reproduced, regenerated.

पुनर् punar—an allomorph of पुनः used as the first member in numerous compound words.

पुनर्गठन punargaṭhān (*nm*) reorganisation, recasting.

पुनर्जनन punarjanān (*nm*) regeneration, reproduction.

पुनर्जन्म punarjanm (*nm*) rebirth, palingenesis, metempsychosis; ~वाद transmigrationism, the doctrine of rebirth.

पुनर्जागरण punarja:garān (*nm*) renaissance; restoration.

पुनर्जीवन punarji:vān (*nm*) resurrection, resuscitation; resurgence; second birth.

पुनर्निर्माण punarnirmā:n (*nm*) reconstruction, recreation, reproduction.

पुनर्मु/द्रण punarmudrān (*nm*) reprinting/reprint; ~द्रित reprinted.

पुनर्मेल punarmel (*nm*) reconciliation, rapprochement, re-establishment of harmonious relations.

पुनर्वचन punārvachān (*nm*) repetition (of a word, sentence or thing); reiteration.

पुनर्वर्गीकरण punarvargi:karān (*nm*) regrouping; reclassification.

पुनर्वास punarva:s (*nm*) rehabilitation.

पुनर्विचार punarvicha:r (*nm*) revision; re-deliberation, reconsideration.

पुनर्विनियो/ग, ~जन punarviniyog, ~jan (*nm*) reappropriation.

पुनर्विन्यास punarvinnyā:s (*nm*) reorientation; rearrangement.

पुनर्विलोकन punarvilokān (*nm*) review, reperusal; reconsideration.

पुनर्विवाह punarviva:h (*nm*) remarriage; —, विधवा widow remarriage.

पुनश्चर्या punashcharya: (*nm*) refresher course; also—पाठ्यक्रम.

पुनीत puni:t (*a*) holy, pious; sacred;

having a sanctity, hence ~ता (*nf*).

पुरः purah—a Sanskrit prefix used to impart the sense of in front, ahead or before; ~सर a pioneer, leader; accompanied with; foremost, leading.

पुरंजय purāṇjay (*nm*) conqueror of a city.

पुरंदर purāndar (*nm*) one of the numerous names of इंद्र—the chief of gods.

पुर pur (*nm*) a town, city; large leather pot for drawing huge quantity of water out of a well; chamber, room (as अतःपुर); (*a*) filled with, full of; ~जन townfolk; inhabitants of a city/town; ~देवता the protecting deity of a town; ~द्वार main gate of a city/the main entrance to a city/town; ~नारी a prostitute, harlot; ~वधू see ~नारी; ~वासी see ~जन.

पुरअमन pur-amān (*a*) peaceful; quiet.

पुरइन purain (*nf*) a lotus; lotus leaf.

पुरखा purkha: (*nm*) an ancestor; ancestors, forefathers.

पुरज़ा purza: (*nm*) a chit; piece of paper, bill; slip; part (of a machine); –, चलता a cunning/guileful man; पुरजे parts; पुरज़े-पुरज़े करना to break to pieces; to dismantle (a machine etc.); to shatter; पुरज़े-पुरज़े होना/उड़ना to be shattered to pieces.

पुरज़ी purzi: (*nf*) a chit, slip (of a paper); a small letter.

पुरज़ोर purzor (*a*) vigorous; powerful, forceful; hearty, warm, cordial; –अपील a forceful appeal.

पुरजोश purjosh (*a*) full of enthusiasm/zeal. zealous, enthusiastic.

पुरतः purtah (*adv*) in front of, before, ahead.

पुरबिया purbiya: (*a*) eastern; belonging to the east; (*nm*) an inhabitant of the eastern part of the country; one belonging to the eastern part of Uttar Pradesh; hence ~पन (*nm*).

पुरबिहा purbiha: (*a*) see पुरबिया.

पुरवइया purwaiya: (*nm*) see पुरवाई.

पुरवा purwa: (*nm*) a hamlet, small village; a small earthen pot; (*nf*) easterly wind.

पुरवाई purwa:i: (*nf*) east wind, easterly (wind); (*a*) originating/emanating from the east.

पुरवैया purvaiya: (*nf*) see पुरवाई.

पुरश्चरण purasharāṇ (*nm*) performing a हवन or यज्ञ or repeating the name of a deity with a definite aim; also पुरश्चर्या (*nf*).

पुरसाँ (सा) हाल pursā:(sa:)ha:l (*nm*) who is solicitous (of), enquirer after somebody's well-being; one who cares (for) and is concerned (about).

पुरसा pursa: (*nm*) a measure of five cubits (equal to the length of a man with hands stretched overhead), a fathom.

पुरस्कार puraska:r (*nm*) a reward, prize; –वितरण prize distribution.

पुरस्कृत puraskrit (*a*) rewarded, awarded a prize.

पुरस्तात् purasta:t (*ind*) in front of, before, ahead.

पुरस्सर purassar (*a*) forerunning; foremost; (*nm*) a leader, pioneer.

पुरांतक purā:ntak (*nm*) an epithet of Lord Shiv—killer of the demon (त्रि) पुर.

पुरा pura: (*adv*) in the past, in olden times; (*nm*) a small village, hamlet; ~कथा ancient story; old narrative; ~कल्प olden times, ancient age.

पुराण pura:n (*nm*) ancient Hindu mythological scriptures, eighteen in number, viz. विष्णु, पद्म, ब्रह्म, शिव, भागवत, नारद, मार्कंडेय, अग्नि, ब्रह्मवैवर्त, लिंग, वराह, स्कंद, वामन, कूर्म, मत्स्य, गरुड़, ब्रह्मांड, and भविष्य; (*a*) ancient, old.

पुरा/तत्त्व pura:tattv (*nm*) archaeology, antiquity; ~तत्त्वज्ञ an archaeologist, antiquitist; ~तत्त्वविद/वेत्ता an archaeologist; ~तत्त्व-शास्त्र (the science) of archaeology; ~तत्त्व-शास्त्री an archaeologist; ~तात्त्विक archaeological.

पुरातन pura:tan (*a*) ancient, old, age-old, of antiquity, archaic; ~ता archaism; ~तावाद see ~वाद; ~तावादी a lover of archaism; archaic; –प्रयोग archaic usage; archaism; ~वाद antiquarianism; archaism; hence ~वादी (*a* and *mn*).

पुराना pura:nā: (*a*) old, olden, ancient; of the past, of bygone ages; old-fashioned, outdated, antiquated; obsolete; seasoned; experienced; (as –डाक्टर); dilapidated, decrepit; expert; masterly (as –हाथ); ~पन outdatedness, obsoleteness; antiquity; the state of being old/archaic/ancient/decrepit/dilapidated/stale; –खुर्राट/घाघ very cunning/shrewd (person); an old scoundrel; –पापी old Adam; –रोना रोना to chew the red; पुरानी लीक पीटना to tread the oft-trodden path; पुराने चावल a seasoned man; an old hardy man.

पुराभिलेख pura:bhilekh (*nm*) archives/epigraph; ~पाल an archivist; epigraphist; –शास्त्र epigraphy; शास्त्री an epigraphist.

पुरामनोविज्ञान purā:manovigya:n (*nm*) palaeopsychology; ~विद्/वेत्ता palaeopsychologist.

पुरारि pura:ri (*nm*) an epithet of Lord Shiv—the enemy of the demon (त्रि) पुर.

पुरालिपि pura:lipi (*nf*) palaeography; also ~विज्ञान/शास्त्र; ~विद्/शास्त्री a palaeographist.

पुरालेख pura:lekh (*nm*) epigraph; –विज्ञान/शास्त्र epigraphy; ~वैज्ञानिक/शास्त्री an epigraphist.

पुरावशेष pura:vshesh (*nm*) ancient traces, ruins, remnants.

पुरावृत्त pura:vritt (*nm*) chronicle, annals.

पुरावेत्ता pura:vetta: (*nm*) an archaelogist, antiquitist, antiquarian.

पुरी puri: (*nf*) a big city; the city of the deity Jagannā:th (in Orissa).

पुरीष puri:sh (*nm*) excrement, faeces, stool; ordure; dung.

पुरुष purush (*nm*) a man; virile man; person (in Grammar: उत्तम पुरुष first person; मध्यम पुरुष second person; अन्य पुरुष third person); husband; (*a*) male; ~केशरी/केसरी/शार्दूल/सिंह a lion-like man; virile and valorous man; the most valorous amongst man; ~ता/त्व manhood, manliness, virility masculinity, potency; —पुरातन the ancient, old man –Lord Vishnū; –मैथुन sodomy; ~वत् manliness; virile, masculine; ~वाचक personal; oसर्वनाम personal pronoun; –सूक्त a famous सूक्त of the ऋग्वेद.

पुरुषाधम purusha:dhām (*nm*) a mean/lowly/base person.

पुरुषार्थ purusha:rth (*nm*) an object of human pursuit; the four basic aims of human existence (viz. धर्म discharge of duty; अर्थ acquirement of wealth; काम gratification; मोक्ष final emancipation); human effort or exertion; valour; industry; ~हीन efforsless, having no tendency to exert/work hard, in-

valour: hence ~हीनता (*nf*), –थकना one's power of exertion to be exhausted, old age to dissipate one's valour.

पुरुषार्थी purusha:rthi: (*a*) diligent, industrious; valorous, heroic.

पुरुषोत्तम purushottām (*nm*) an epithet of **राम**—the best amongst men.

पुरोगति purogati (*nf*) progress, going ahead; ~**शील** progressive; ~**शीलता** progressivism.

पुरोगा/मी puroga:mī: (*a*) progressive; pioneering; ~**मिता** progressism, progressive quality.

पुरोजन्मा purojanmā: (*a* and *nm*) born earlier; an elder brother.

पुरोडाश puroḍa:sh (*nm*) sacrificial oblation offered to the gods.

पुरोधा purodha: (*nm*) see **पुरोहित**.

पुरोभाग purobha:g (*nm*) frontage; front.

पुरोव/र्ती purovarti: (*a*) precursive, heraldic; (*nm*) a predecessor; herald; forerunner; hence ~**र्तिता** (*nf*).

पुरोहि/त purohit (*nm*) a Hindu priest; priest; patrico; ~**त–तंत्र** priestly hierarchy; ~**ताई/ती** priesthood, priestdom; office and function of a priest; ~**तानी** wife of a **पुरोहित**; a female **पुरोहित**.

पुर्जा purza: (*nm*) see **पुरज़ा**.

पुर्ज़ी purzi: (*nf*) see **पुरज़ी**.

पुल pul (*nm*) a bridge; –,**झूला** hanging bridge; –**बाँधना, किसी की प्रशंसा में** to eulogize no end, to pay tributes in superlatives.

पुल/क pulak (*nm*) thrill, erection or bristling of the hairs of the body (through delight or rapture); ~**कना** to be thrilled, to have the hairs of the body erected or bristling (through delight or rapture); ~**कावली** row of hairs erected or bristling (through delight or rapture); ~**कित** thrilled, in rapture, having the hairs of the body erected or bristled (through rapture or delight).

पुलटिस pulṭis (*nf*) poultice; —**बाँधना** to apply poultice (on a boil etc.).

पुलाक pula:k (*nm*) boiled rice.

पुलाव pula:w (*nm*) a preparation of boiled rice mixed with vegetables (or meat) and seasoned with spices.

पुलिंदा pulīnda: (*nm*) a bundle; sheaf.

पुलिन pulin (*nm*) a bank, sandy bank; alluvium.

पुलिया puliya: (*nf*) a culvert.

पुलिस pulis (*nm*) the police (force); –**कार्यवाही** police action; ~**मैन** a policeman, constable; –**राज** police rule; tyrannous/oppressive rule.

पुश्त pusht (*nf*) the back; back portion; generation; ancestry; –**दर-पुश्त** from generation to generation; hereditarily.

पुश्ता pushta: (*nm*) an embankment; buttress; the back of the binding of a book etc; ~**बंदी** strutting; embankment.

पुश्तैनी pushtainī: (*a*) hereditary, ancestral; –**कारबार** ancestral business; –**जायदाद** ancestral/hereditary property.

पुष्कर pushkar (*nm*) a lake, pond, tank; lotus.

पुष्करिणी pushkariṇī: (*nf*) a lake, pond; pond full of lotus flowers,

पुष्कल pushkal (*a*) plenty, abundant, in abundance; hence ~**ता** (*nf*).

पुष्ट pushṭ (*a*) strong, robust, sturdy; stiff; well-built; shapely, nourished; mature; confirmed (as —**समाचार**); seasoned (with); hence ~**ता** (*nf*)/**त्व** (*nm*).

पुष्टई pushṭai: (*nf*) a nutritious medicine, tonic; an elixir.

ष्टि pushṭi (*nf*) confirmation; nourishment; strengthening; ~कर/कारी confirmatory; nutritious, nourishing, nutrient; invigorating; –मार्ग a mediaval vaishnav sect who believed in identity with God through the acquirement of His grace; hence ~मार्गी (*a*)

ष्प pushp (*nm*) a flower; menses; –काल period of menses; –केसर stamen; ~गर्भ calix, calyx; –पत्र petal of a flower; ~बाण/धन्वा/शर/सायक an epithet of Cupid (कामदेव); ~मय flowery; –माल/–माला a wreath; flower garland; –रज stamen (of flowers); –राग pollen; –रेणु pollen (of flowers); ~वती a woman in menses; -वृष्टि a shower of flowers or flower petals; -वेणी a flower garland; braid studded with flowers; –शैया a bed of flowers; –संबंधी floral; ~हीन devoid of flowers; flowerless; ~हीना a barren woman.

ष्पक pushpak (*nm*) the name of the mythological aircraft of कुबेर (the god of wealth); also –विमान.

ष्पांजलि pushpā:njali (*nf*) a floral tribute, a floral offering; offering of a wreath.

ष्पाकर pushpa:kar (*nm*) the spring season.

ष्पिका pushpika: (*nf*) the colophon.

ष्पित pushpit (*a*) blossomed, flowering; thriving, prospering.

ष्पोद्यान pushpoddya:n (*nm*) a flower garden; ~विद्/वेत्ता a floriculturist; –विद्या floriculture.

ष्य pushy (*nm*) the eighth lunar asterism.

स्त pust (*nf*) see पुश्त; a book; ~कार the writer of a book, author.

स्त/क pustak (*nf*) a book; ~ककार writer/author of a book; ~कीय ज्ञान bookish knowledge.

पुस्तकाकार pustaka:ka:r (*a*) in the form of a book, in book-form.

पुस्तकागार pustaka:ga:r (*nm*) a library, collection of books; a book-depot.

पुस्तकाध्यक्ष pustaka:ddhyaksh (*nm*) a librarian.

पुस्तकालय pustaka:lay (*nm*) a library; –विज्ञान library science.

पुस्तकालयाध्यक्ष pustaka:laya:ddhyaksh (*nm*) a librarian.

पुस्तकीय pustaki:y (*a*) bookish; relating to books; academic; ~ज्ञान bookish knowledge.

पुस्तिका pustika: (*nf*) a booklet; pamphlet.

पुहुप puhup (*nm*) a flower.

पुहुमी puhumī: (*nf*) the earth.

पूँछ pū:chh (*nf*) the tail (of a beast); rear part (of an object); a hanger-on; ~दार howing a tail; –पकड़ कर चलना to follow somebody blindly; to be solely dependent (on); –होना, किसी की to be a hanger-on.

पूँजी pū:ji: (*nf*) capital; investment; –, साझे की joint-stock; –कर capital. levy; ~करण capitalisation, ~कृत capitalised; ~गत परिव्यय capital outlay; ~गत माल capital goods; ~गत लागत capital cost; ~दार having capital or wealth; a capitalist; –निवेश investment; ~पति a capitalist; –परिसंपत्ति capital assets; ~मूलक capitalistic; ~वाद capitalism; ~वादी capitalistic; a capitalist; –संचय capital assets; –साम्राज्यवाद capitalistic imperialism; ~हीनwith no capital; hence ~हीनता (*nf*).

पूगना pu:gnā: (*v*) to be accomplished/attained; to be completed.

पूछ pu:chh (*nf*) (commanding of) respect, enquiry; –गछ, ~ताछ; ~पाछ enquiry; investigation.

पूछना pu:chhnā: (*v*) to enquire, to ask; to investigate; to interrogate, to question; **–ताछना** to make enquiries; to interrogate, to question.

पूछा/ताछी, ~पाछी pu:chha:ta:chhi; ~pa:chhi: (*nf*) enquiring, investigation; interrogation, questioning.

पूजक pu:jak (*nm*) a worshipper, adorer, devotee, votary.

पूजन pu:jān (*nm*) worship, adoring; **-पद्धति/-विधि** liturgy; cult.

पूजना pu:jnā: (*v*) to worship, to adore; to revere, to respect; (a wish etc.) to be fulfilled/gratified.

पूजनीय pujanī:y (*a*) worthy of worship, venerable, adorable.

पूजा pu:ja: (*nf*) worship, adoration; veneration; **–करना** to worship, to adore; to respect; to punish.

पूजार्ह pu:ja:rh (*a*) adorable; venerable, worth being worshipped, reverend.

पूजित pu:jit (*a*) worshipped, adored; revered, venerated, respected.

पूज्य pu:jy (*a*) adorable, reverent, venerable; hence **~ता** (*nf*).

पूज्यमान pu:jymā:n (*a*) one who is being worshipped/adored/revered; see **पूज्य**.

पूड़ा pu:ṛa: (*nm*) a kind of largesized sweet and fried cake; bundle

पूड़ी pu:ṛi: (*nf*) a kind of bread/cake fried in *ghee* or oil.

पूत pu:t (*nm*) a son; (*a*) pious, holy, sacred; cleaned, purified; **–के पाँव/पैर पालने में दिखाई देते हैं/पहचाने जाते हैं** the child is the father to the man.

पूतना pu:tnā: (*nf*) a demonic woman who was commissioned by **कंस**, the king of Mathura:, to kill Lord Krishn by making him suck at her poisoned breasts; **–का दूध** Greek gift, Trojan horse, treacherous gift.

पूतात्मा pu:ta:tmā: (*nm*) a sacred pious soul.

पूति pu:ti (*nf*) purity; sanctity.

पूनी pu:nī: (*nf*) a cotton-roll prepared for spinning on the **चरखा** or **तकली** etc.

पूनो pu:nō (*nf*) see **पूर्णिमा**.

पूय pu:y (*nm*) pus, purulent matter

पूर pu:r (*nm*) stuffing in a sweet delicacy; spate; irrigation by drawing water from a well by a leathern bag; sufficiency, adequacy; **–डालना** to satisfy the requirements/needs; **–पड़ना** to suffice, to be sufficient, to cause to be gratified/satisfied.

पूरक pu:rak (*nm*) a supplement, filler; (*a*) supplementary; reinforcing; hence **~ता** (*nf*).

पूरणीय pu:rani:y (*a*) worth supplementing; worth being filled up; replaceable/repairable (loss etc); hence **~ता** (*nf*).

पूरन pu:rān (*nm*) anything which is to be filled in a cake or pastry etc.; **–की पूड़ी** a kind of stuffed bread or cake.

पूरना pu:rnā: (*v*) to fill; to complete; to supplement; to work a design on the floor with coloured chalk, flour or rice, etc.

पूर/ब pu:rab (*nm*) the east; **~बी** eastern (language, land or people)

पूरबेला pu:rbela: (*nm*) the high tide

पूरयिता pu:rayita: (*nm*) one who fills/satisfies / completes / supplements.

पूरा pu:ra: (*a*) complete; all, whole, entire; full; gross; total; thorough; adequate; (*nm*) sufficiency, adequacy; **–उतरना** to deliver the goods, to come upto the expectations; to pass a test successfully; **–उतरना (कोई काम)** to be duly accomplished; to be fulfilled; –पड़ना, किसी का to be sufficient; not to be wanting; पूरे करना, दिन to mark time; to keep somehow alive; पूरे होना, दिन death to be imminent, to have consumed one's allotted time (of life); to have completed the period of gestation.

पूरित pu:rit (*a*) completed, attained, achieved; fulfilled.

पूरी pu:ri: (*nf*) see पूड़ी; see पूरा.

पूर्ण pu:rṉ (*a*) complete, whole, entire; full; perfect; absolute; sufficient; finished, accomplished; plenary; ~काम fulfilled/gratified; ~कालिक whole-time; ~चंद्र full moon; ~प्रज्ञ perfect in wisdom, having thorough knowledge; –मानदंड absolute standard; –विराम full stop, –विवेक absolute discretion; perfect reason; –शक्तिमत्ता totipotence; –शक्तिमान totipotent; –संख्या integral number.

पूर्णतः pu:rṉātah (*adv*) completely, fully, wholly, entirely.

पूर्ण/ता, ~त्व pu:rṉāta: (*nf*), ~ttv (*nm*) perfection; completeness, wholeness, totality; ~तावाद perfectionism; ~तावादी a perfectionist; perfectionistic.

पूर्णमासी pu:rṉmā:si: (*nf*) full-moon day, fifteenth day of the bright half of a lunar month

पूर्णांक pu:rṉā:ṅk (*nm*) an integer; maximum marks; non-fractional number.

पूर्णायु pu:rṉā:yu (*nf*) fully ripe age; complete age.

पूर्णावतार pu:rṉā:vta:r (*nm*) the perfect incarnation.

पूर्णाश pu:rṉā:sh (*a*) fulfilled, gratified; (one who has) achieved fulfilment of all hopes.

पूर्णाहुति pu:rṉā:huti (*nf*) final oblation/offering; finishing touch; –देना to give the final/concluding touch.

पूर्णिमा pu:rṉīmā: (*nf*) the last day of the bright fortnight of a lunar month, the full-moon day.

पूर्णेंदु pu:rṉēndu (*nm*) the full moon.

पूर्ति pu:rti (*nf*) fulfilment, completion, filling up; satisfaction; supply; ~कारी supplementary; suppletive; that which satisfies/supplies/completes.

पूर्व pu:rv (*nm*) the east; (*a*) former; previous, preceding, prior; anterior; fore—; ~कथन prediction; –कथा tie-in, the earlier story; –कर्म previous deeds/actions; ~कल्पना preconception; ~कल्पित preconceived; anticipated; ~कल्पी anticipative; ~कांस्य युग early bronze age; ~काल past, former times, olden days; ~कालिक past, belonging to former times, ancient; ०क्रिया absolutive verb; ~कालिक कृदंत absolutive participle; ~कालीन past, of the past, of previous times/days/age; ~कृत done or committed previously; ~गत preceding, prior, former; ~गामिता backwardness; ~गामी preceding, prior, former; ~गृहीत presupposed; biassed, prejudiced; ~ग्रह bias, prejudice; ~चिंतन premeditation; prior comprehension; ~चेतन preconscious, preconscious mind; ~ज ancestor(s); ~जन्म previous birth; –जीवन pre-existence; former life; –ज्ञान anticipation; foresight, foreknowledge; inkling; ~ता precedence; priority; ~दत्त given previously; ~दर्शन preview; ~धारणा presumption; concept; notion; ~नियत predestined; appointed earlier; ~नियति destiny; ~निर्णय prejudgment; predetermination;

earlier decision/resolution; ~ निश्चित predecided; predestined; resolved earlier; ~ पक्ष the first objection to an assertion in a discussion; the first statement of the plaintiff; plaint; proposition; the first half of the lunar month; ~ पद the first member of a compound word; ~ पीठिका background; introduction; prolegomenon; ~ पुरुष a progenitor; ancestor(s), forefather(s); ~ प्रत्यय(न) preconception; ~ भूत existing previously; former; late; ~ मीमांसा one of the six systems of Indian philosophy attributed to the savant Jaimini: who, in interpreting the Vedic texts, discusses the eternity of the sound identified with ब्रह्म; ~ मुद्र pre-print; ~ यायी preceding; a predecessor; ~ रंग prologue, prelude of a drama, overture; ~ राग incipient affection; courtship; ~ रूप previous form; prognosis; ~ लेख a protocol; antescript; ~ वत् as before; in tact; ~ वर्तिता precedence; priority; ~ वर्ती previous, prior, preceding, precedent, happening before; a predecessor; ~ वादी a plaintiff; ~ विचारित forethought; preconceived; deliberated upon earlier; ~ विद् one who knows previous things; ~ वृत्त antecedents; anteposition; ~ सूचक premonitory.

पूर्वक pu:rvak—a suffix denoting the sense of with or accompanied by (as सुखपूर्वक, कृपापूर्वक, etc.)

पूर्वाकांक्षित pu:rva:kā:ṅkshit (*a*) prerequisite, pre-desired.

पूर्वानुमान pu:rva:numā:n (*nm*) forecast; estimate.

पूर्वानुराग pu:rva:nura:g (*nm*) previous love/affection, courtship.

पूर्वापर pu:rva:par (*ind*) the previous and the next, the preceding and the following; —क्रम sequence, succession; ~ ता sequence, succession.

पूर्वाभास pu:rva:bha:s (*nm*) premonition, foreboding inkling.

पूर्वाभ्या/स pu:rva:bbhya:s (*nm*) rehearsal; ~ सित rehearsed.

पूर्वार्जित pu:rva:rjit (*a*) pre-earned, acquired earlier.

पूर्वार्द्ध (र्ध) pu:rva:rdh (*a*) the first/former half.

पूर्वावस्था pu:rva:vastha: (*nf*) prephase, pre-stage, earlier stage; initial stage.

पूर्वाह्न pu:rva:nh (*nm*) forenoon, antemeridian; hence ~ ह्निक (*a*).

पूर्वी pu:rvi: (*a*) eastern; also **पूर्वीय**; —द्वीपसमूह the islands of the east—Ja:wa:, Suma:tra:, etc.

पूर्वोक्त pu:rvokt (*a*) aforesaid, mentioned before/above; —कृति op. cit. (opere citato).

पूर्वोत्तर pu:rvottar (*a*) north-east; (*nm*) the north-east quarter.

पूर्वोपाय pu:rvopa:y (*nm*) precaution, precautionary measure(s).

पूला pu:la (*nm*) a bundle of straws, crops, etc.

पूली pu:li: (*nf*) a sheaf.

पूस pu:s (*nm*) the tenth month of the Hindu (lunar) calendar; also **पौष**.

पृक्त prikt (*a*) mixed; touched, contacted (used in Hindi only with prefixes, as संपृक्त).

पृथक् prithak (*a*) separate, isolated; peculiar; different, distinct; (*adv*) aloof, apart; ~ करण separation; ~ क्रिया separation, process of separating; ~ कृत separated; isolated.

पृथिवी prithivi: (*nf*) see **पृथ्वी**.

पृथु prithu (*a*) wide, large; expensive; spacious, copious.

पृथ्वी prithvi: (*nf*) the earth, ground, terrestrial globe; ~नाथ/पति/पाल a king; -पुत्र the Mars; -पूजा geolatory; -संबंधी terrestrial, earthly, tellurian.

पृष्ट prist (*a*) asked; enquired (not in general use).

पृष्ठ prishṭḥ (*nm*) a page; the back; rear, hind part of anything; (*a*) dorsal; ~त: from behind, quietly; dorsally; ~पोषक one who backs, helper, supporter; -फल the area of the upper surface of a solid; -भाग the back or rear portion/part.

पृष्ठास्थि prishṭḥa:sthi (*nf*) the backbone.

पग pēg (*nf*) a swing, oscillation of a swing; -बढ़ाना to take larger strides; to swing farther and farther; -मारना to swing, to toss a swing.

पेंच pēch (*nm*) see पेच.

पेंट pēnṭ (*nm*) paint; ~र a painter.

पेंडल pēnḍal (*nm*) a pendant.

पेंडुकी pēḍuki: (*nf*) a dove.

पेंडुलम pēnḍulām (*nm*) pendulum (of a clock etc.).

पेंडुली pēḍuli: (*nf*) see पिंडली.

पेंदा pēda: (*nm*) the bottom; base; buttocks; पेंदी diminutive and feminine form of पेंदा; पेंदे का लोटा, बिना an unprincipled man, a rolling stone.

पेंशन pēnshān (*nf*) pension; ~भोगी a pensioner; ~याफ़्ता a pensioner; -वाली जगह a pensionable post.

पेंस pēns (*nm*) a British coin of small denomination equivalent to 1/12th of a shilling.

पेंसिल pēnsil (*nf*) a pencil.

पेच pech (*nm*) a screw; complication, intricacy; part of a machine; the entwining of the threads of two flying (paper) kites for a mutual trial of skill; trick; a trick in wrestling, artifice; a kind of ornaments for the head; ~कश/कस a screw-driver; cork-screw; ~दार intricate; complex, tricky; twisted; ~वान the long pipe attached to a hubble bubble (for smoking from a distance); -ओ-ख़म tricks and twists, intricacies and complexities; -डालना to have a bout of (paper) kites; -पड़ना a bout of paper kites to take place; to get complicated, to become more intricate.

पेचक pechak (*nf*) a reel (of thread),

पेचिश pechish (*nf*) dysentery.

पेचीदगी pechi:dgi: (*nf*) intricacy; complication: complexity,

पेची/दा, ~ला pechi:da:, ~la: (*a*) intricate; complicated; complex; ~दापन see पेचीदगी.

पेज pej (*nm*) a page; -प्रूफ़ page-proof.

पेट peṭ (*nm*) the belly, abdomen, stomach; womb; mind; the front side of a thing as opposed to the back (as रोटी का पेट); (*fig.*) livelihood; ~पोंछना the last of a woman's children (as ०बेटा the last and the youngest son); ~वाली a pregnant woman; -ऐंठना to have abdominal convulsions; to have an itch for disclosing a secret; -का born of; -का गहरा one who does not talk out secrets; who can contain secrets; -काटना to save money by imposing self-restraint; -का चक्कर/धंधा business of earning a livelihood; -का पानी न पचना not to be able to keep/contain secrets; -का पानी न हिलना

to have no physical movement whatever, to be absolutely inert and static; –का हलका one who cannot keep/contain secrets; –का हाल, – की बात a secret, secrets stored within; –की आग/ज्वाला the irresistible pangs of hunger; hunger; –की थाह लेना to have an idea of one's inmost feelings; to fathom the depth of one's mind; –की आग बुझाना to satisfy one's hunger; to fill the stomach; –की थाह लेना to probe into one's mind; –की मार मारना to deprive of bread; to deprive of the means of livelihood; –कुलबुलाना to be too hungry, to have abdominal uneasiness through hunger; –खोलना to talk out one's mind; to reveal one's secrets; to give vent to one's grouses/resentments; –गिरना to abort, to commit abortion; –चलना to suffer from diarrhoea; to have loose motions; –छँटना one's paunch to be trimmed; –पर छुरी चलाना/लात मारना to take the bread out of one's mouth, to deprive one of means of livelihood; –पालना to earn one's living somehow; to subsist by effort; –पीठ से लगना, –पीठ एक हो जाना to be emaciated, to be reduced to a skeleton; ~पूजा करना to serve the stomach, to fill the stomach; –फूलना the abdomen to be swollen, the belly to bulge out; to be pregnant; not to be able to keep/contain a secret; –बड़ा होना one's demands to be enormous; –भारी होना the stomach to be heavy (through indigestion); –में घुसना to delve deep into somebody's mind; to develop intimate relations, to get out one's secret; –में चूहे कूदना/दौड़ना to suffer the pangs of hunger; to be very hungry; –में डालना, (कुछ) to have something to eat, to fill the stomach; –में दाढ़ी होना to have an old head over young shoulders; to be very shrewd and cunning, to be seemingly simple but actually shrewd; –रहना to become pregnant; –से होना to be in the family way, to be pregnant.

पेटा peṭa: (*nm*) a sub-entry; abdomen, middle part of a thing; hull (of a ship).

पेटिका peṭika: (*nf*) a small पेटी (see).

पेटी peṭi: (*nf*) a casket; small box, chest, belt; girdle.

पेटीकोट peṭi:koṭ (*nm*) a petticoat; –सरकार petticoat government.

पेटू peṭu: (*a*) gluttonous, voracious; (*nm*) a glutton; gourmand; ~पन/पना gluttony, voraciousness.

पेटेंट peṭēnṭ (*a*) patent.

पेट्रोल peṭṭrol (*nm*) petrol; –पंप a petrol pump.

पेठा peṭha: (*nm*) a species of gourd; a sweetmeat preparation of gourd.

पेड़ peṛ (*nm*) a tree; –पौधे vegetation; trees and plants; –काटना, पत्ते सींचना to water the leaves and cut the root.

पेडल peḍal (*nm*) a pedal (in bicycle etc.).

पेड़ा peṛa: (*nm*) sweetmeat prepared from milk; a globular mass of kneaded flour.

पेड़ू peṛu: (*nm*) the part of the body lying between the naval and the public region.

पेन pēn (*nm*) a pen.

पेनी penī: (*nf*) penny–a British coin

of small denomination.

पेन्हाना penhā:nā (*v*) milk to flow-down into the udders of a cow, buffalo, etc.

पेपर pepar (*nm*) paper; newspaper; question paper; ~**मिल** a paper mill/factory; ~**वेट** a paper weight.

पेय pey (*nm*) a beverage; (*a*) drinkable; potable; hence ~**ता** (*nf*); –**पदार्थ** a beverage,

पेरना pernā: (*v*) to crush (as sugarcane, linseed, etc.); to press hard; to torment; to cause to labour hard; to exploit (a person).

पेलना pelnā: (*v*) to thrust in; to penetrate; to crush; to press; to perform hurriedly; –, **अपनी** to go on blowing one's own trumpet; –,**डंड** to go on labouring without any worthwhile achievement.

पेलव pelav (*a*) soft, delicate; hence ~**ता** (*nf*).

पेवन pevān (*nm*) a patch; –**लगाना** to patch.

पेश pesh (*adv*) in front of, before; ~**कश** an offer; a present, keepsake; memento; presenting; offering; putting forth; introducing; o **करना** to introduce; to offer, to present; to put forth; ~**कार** a court official/clerk; an agent; ~**कारी** the work or office of a **पेशकार**; ~**बंदी** hedging operation; forestalling ; o **करना** to forestall; to take precautionary steps in advance; –**आना** to treat; to behave; to happen; to be confronted with; –**करना** to present, to put forth; to introduce; –**चलना** see **वश चलना**.

पेशगी peshgi: (*nf*) an advance, advance money; –**देना** to advance, to give an advance.

पेशतर peshtar (*ind*) before; prior to.

पेशल peshal (*a*) soft, delicate, tender; ~**ता** softness, delicacy, tenderness.

पेशवा peshwa: (*nm*) the title of the Mara:ṭha: chief minister during the mediaeval period; leader, chief.

पेशवाई peshwa:i: (*nf*) reception (of a guest).

पेशवाज़ peshwa:z (*nm*) the gown or dress worn by a dancing girl during her performance.

पेशा pesha: (*nm*) a profession, vocation, an occupation; –**करना** (said of a woman) to take up prostitution (as a profession); hence –**कराना**; –**बनाना** to turn into a profession; **पेशेवर** professional.

पेशानी pesha:nī: (*nf*) the forehead; lot, fate; –**पर बल आना/पड़ना** lit. wrinkles to appear on the forehead–a sense of anger to be aroused; to have anger writ large on the face, to frown, to scowl.

पेशाब pesha:b (*nf*) urine; –**खाना/घर** urinal; ~**दान** urinal-stall; –**करना** to make water, to pass urine; to urinate; –**करना, (किसी चीज़ पर)** to treat with utter disdain, to damn care; –**से चिराग़/दिया जलाना** to wield overbearing influence.

पेशी peshi: (*nf*) a muscle; presentation, being presented; hearing (of a law-suit.)

पेशीनगोई peshi:ngoi: (*nf*) a forecast.

पेश्तर peshtar (*ind*) see **पेशतर**.

पेषण peshāṇ (*nm*) (the process or work of) crushing/milling/grinding; ~, **पिष्ट** see **पिष्ट**.

पेस्टल pesṭal (*nm*) pastel; –**कलर/रंग** pastel colour; –**ड्राइंग** pastel drawing.

पेहँ/टा pẽhaṭa: (*nm*) a typical edible fruit of a creeper (usually growing in maize fields) which is used for vegetables etc.; also ~टी (*nf*), ~ टुल (*nm*).

पैंग pāig (*nf*) a swing; –बढ़ाना to take bigger swings; to make rapid strides; –मारना to take a swing.

पैंट pāinṭ (*nf*) pants, pantaloon.

पैंठ pāiṭh (*nf*) a temporarily improvised market place; –का दिन a marketing day; –आठवें दिन लगती है, उठी golden chances are but rare; one gets an opportunity only once in a while.

पैंड़ pāiṛ (*nf*) a way, path; system..

पैंड़ा pāiṛa: (*nm*) a piece; fragment.

पैंत/रा pāitra: (*nm*) see पैतरा; ~रेबाज़ी see पैतरेबाज़ी (under पैतरा).

पैंता/न, ~ना pāita:n, ~nā: (*nm*) the lower end of a bedstead/cot.

पैंतालीस pāita:li:s (*a*) forty-five; (*nm*) the number forty-five.

पैंतीस pāiti:s (*a*) thirty-five; (*nm*) the number thirty-five.

पैंसठ pāisaṭh (*a*) sixty-five; (*nm*) the number sixty-five.

पैके(कि)ट paike(i)ṭ (*nm*) a packet.

पैग़म्ब/र paigāmbar (*nm*) a prophet, divine messenger; ~री the function or position of a prophet; of, related with or pertaining to a prophet, prophetic.

पैग़ाम paigā:m (*nm*) a message; –देना to deliver a message; –लाना to bring a message.

पैजनिया paijaniyā: (*nf*) see पैजनी.

पैजनी paijnī: (*nf*) ankle-bells, twinking ankle-ornament.

पैज़ार paiza:r (*nm*) a shoe (used only as the last member in the compound word जूतमपैज़ार).

पैठ paiṭh (*nf*) access to; reach; admission; ingress; penetration; –होना to have an eye for; to have access to; to have a good knowledge of (*e.g.* उसकी रीतिकाव्य में पैठ है).

पैठना paiṭhnā: (*v*) to have access, to enter, to go into; to delve deep; to ingress, to penetrate.

पैड paiḍ (*nm*) a pad, writing pad.

पैडल paiḍal (*nm*) pedal (of a bicycle etc.)

पैड़ी paiṛi: (*nf*) a step, stair; staircase.

पैत/रा paitra: (*nm*) an offensive or defensive move in a wrestling bout; strategic move, countermove, stratagem; ~रेबाज a strategist, dodger; see चालबाज़; ~रेबाज़ी strategy, dodge; see चालबाज़ी; ~रा काटना to make a defensive more; to change one's strategic position; ~रा दिखाना to show one's strategic move, to countermove in defence; to take shrewd steps; ~रा बदलना to play to peep, to change one's strategy; (in wrestling etc.) to change the front posture, to change one's stance; to assume a different posture.

पैताना paita:nā: (*nm*) the lower end of a cot/bedstead.

पैतृक paittrik (*a*) paternal, patronymic; hereditary, ancestral; –गुण paternal/hereditary characteristics or quality; –जायदाद see संपत्ति; –धन patrimony, paternal wealth; –भूमि ancestral land; fatherland; –व्यवसाय hereditary profession; –संपत्ति paternal/ancestral/hereditary property.

पैत्तिक paittik (*a*) bilious, biliary.

पैदल paidal (*a*) pedestrian, walking on foot (as सिपाही); (*nm*) a footman, an infantryman; a pedestrian; a piece in chess; (*adv*) on foot; –सेना infantry; –सैर hiking.

पैदा paida: (*a*) born; created; begotten; produced; earned; (*nf*) income; gain; production; –करना to produce; to earn; to generate; to beget, to reproduce; to manufacture; –होना to be produced/earned/generated/begotten/reproduced/manufactured.

पैदाइ/श paida:ish (*nf*) birth, coming into existence; creation; ~शी natural, innate, inborn, birth; ०हक़ birthright.

पैदावा/र paida:va:r (*nf*) produce, product, production; harvest; yield; also ~री (*nf*).

पैना painā: (*a*) sharp; acute; pointed; (*nm*) the goad of a ploughman; ~पन sharpness; acuteness; pointedness; hence पैनी feminine form.

पैबंद paibānd (*nm*) a patch; –लगाना to patch.

पैबस्त paibast (*a*) see पैवस्त.

पैमाइ/श paimā:ish (*nf*) measurement/surveying (of land); ~शी (*a*).

पैमाना paimā:nā: (*nm*) a scale, meter; any measuring device; a peg (for drinking liquor); –भर जाना/भरना one's cup to be full.

पैर pair (*nm*) a foot, leg; footing, footprint; ~गाड़ी a bicycle; velocipede; –अड़ाना to intermeddle; to interrupt; –उखड़ना to be swept off one's feet, to be routed; –ऊँचे-नीचे पड़ना to go astray; to wobble, to totter; –की जूती utterly contemptuous, of no significance; –की धूल समझना to hold cheap; to treat as unconsequential; –छूना to touch somebody' feet out of respect; to submit; to yield completely; to implore humbly; –जमना to find one's feet, to be well entrenched, to consolidate one's position; –डालना to interfere, to intermeddle (with); –तोड़कर बैठना not to move out at all, to keep indoors; to be absolutely idle; to sit in a leg-twisting posture; –देना to set foot on; –न रखना, धरती पर to assume airs, to think no end of oneself; –पकड़ना to implore humbly, to beseech; –पर पैर रखना to intermeddle, to defy (somebody); –पीछे न रखना not to withdraw in any case; –बढ़ाना to step ahead, to pace ahead; to accelerate one's pace; –भर जाना to be tired out, the feet to be overstrained, to be wearied by walking; –भारी होना (said of a woman) to be pregnant, to be in the family way; –में मेंहदी लगे होना to walk too slow; to avoid walking on some pretext; –में सनीचर होना never to be at rest, to be always on the move; –रखने की जगह न होना to be crowded full, not to have room even to stand; –सोना one's foot/feet to go dead/to be temporarily lost to sensation; पैरों के नीचे से जमीन खिसक जाना to develop cold feet, to be funky, to be dumbfounded; पैरों तले कुचलना/रौंदना to trample over, to crush; पैरों पर खड़े होना to stand on one's own legs; (किसी के) पैरों पर चलना to follow in the footprints of; पैरों में बेड़ियाँ डाल देना to put fetters around one's feet, to put in bondage.

पैरना pairnā: (*v*) to swim; to cross over; पैरा हुआ well-experienced.

पैरवी pairvi: (*nf*) advocacy, pleading, championing; ~कार an advocate, a pleader; champion; –करना, (किसी की) to advocate; to champion (the cause of).

पैरा paira: (*nm*) a paragraph, para.

पैराई paira:i: (*nf*) (the act or process of) swimming,

पैराग्राफ़ paira:gra:f (*nm*) a paragraph.

पैराशूट paira:shu:ṭ (*nm*) a parachute.

पैरोका/र pairoka:r (*nm*) a pleader, an advocate; a champion; hence **~री** (*nf*).

पैरोल pairol (*nm*) parole; **–पर छूटना** to be released on parole.

पैवंद paivānd (*nm*) see **पैबंद**.

पैवस्त paivast (*a*) permeated, informed, infused (by); hence **~गी** (*nf*),

पैशाच paisha:ch (*a*) see **पैशाचिक**.

पैशाचिक paisha:chik (*a*) satanic, demonic(al), in the fashion of or pertaining to a hell-hound, inhuman; horrible; hence **~ता** (*nf*),

पैसना paisnā: (*v*) to enter (into), to penetrate,

पैसा paisa: (*nm*) a pice; wealth, money; **–उगाहना** to recover/procure money; **–उड़ाना/लुटाना** to squander away; to spend (money) extravagantly; **–कमाना मुश्किल नहीं उसे रखना मुश्किल है** he who gets doth much but he who keeps doth more; gear is easier gained than guided; **–खा जाना** to misappropriate; not to repay a debt; to embezzle; to accept monetary gratification, to take bribes; **–चटाना** to give bribe, to entice with monetary gratification; **–ठीकरी कर देना** to get eggs for money. **–डूबना** one's money/capital to be irretrievably lost; **–फूंकना** to squander money; **–बनाना** to mint money, to earn enormous money; **–मारना** to misappropriate other's money; not to repay a debt; **–लगाना** to invest money/capital; **पैसे की गर्मी** vanity/conceitedness born of money, a fat purse, a swollen mind; **पैसे को दाँत से पकड़ना** to be too stingy/niggardly; **पैसे-पैसे को मोहताज होना/को तरसना** to pine for each penny, to be too tight; **पैसे वाला** a wealthy/moneyed (person).

पैसार paisa:r (*nm*) entry, infiltration; admission; entrance, access.

पैसेंजर paisenjar (*nm*) a passenger; **–गाड़ी/ट्रेन** a passenger train.

पों pō (*nf*) the sound of a horn; **-पों** recurrent sound as produced by a horn.

पोंगा pōga: (*a*) nincompoop, stupid; (*nm*) a simpleton; metallic or bamboo pipe; **~पन/~पंथी** stupidity, foolishness.

पोंछन pōchhan (*nf*) wipings, sweepings.

पोंछना pōchhnā: (*v*) to wipe; to clean/cleanse; to rub, to efface; (*nm*) a cloth used for wiping/cleaning etc.

पोंटा pōṭa: (*nm*) mucus (blown out of the nose).

पोआ poa: (*nm*) a young one of a serpent.

पोख/र, ~रा pokh/ar, (*nf*) ~ra: (*nm*) a pond, puddle.

पोखरी pokhri: (*nf*) a small pond, puddle.

पोगंड pogāṇḍ (*nm*) a lad.

पोच poch (*a*) timid, cowardly; meek; **~पन(ा)** timidity, cowardice; meekness.

पोटली poṭli: (*nf*) a small bundle.

पोटाश poṭa:sh (*nm*) potash, potassium permanganate.

पोढ़ poṛh (*a*) mature, seasoned; sound, profound; **–असामी** a sound moneyed man (party).

पोत pot (*nm*) a ship; a tiny artificial pearl; (*nf*) time(s); number of times; rent of land paid by a tenant; young one of an animal; ~दार a treasurer; ~धारी a ship-owner; ~ध्वज flagstaff; ~भंग smashing up of a ship, a ship running aground; ~वाह a sailor, steerer; ~विहार cruise.

पोतक potak (*nm*) young one of an animal.

पोत/ड़ा potṛa: (*nm*) a baby clout; ~ड़ों का अमीर/रईस of blue blood, born with a silver spoon in one's mouth, belonging (by birth) to aristocracy.

पोतना potnā: (*v*) to besmear; to whitewash.

पोतनायक potna:yak (*nm*) the captain of a ship, master of a vessel.

पोता pota: (*nm*) a grandson, a son's son; a testicle; a cleansing clout; –फेरना to whitewash; to spell ruination.

पोताई pota:i: (*nf*) see पुताई.

पोताध्यक्ष pota:dhyaksh (*nm*) see पोतनायक.

पोती poti: (*nf*) a grand-daughter, son's daughter.

पोथा potha: (*nm*) a voluminous book, a big volume.

पोथी pothi: (*nf*) a book.

पोदीना podi:nā: (*nm*) see पुदीना.

पोना ponā: (*v*) to spread doughed flour into bread; to thread, to string together; –, रोटी to spread doughed flour into a bread (in order to bake it); to thread/string/needle/ (pearls/beads etc.).

पोप pop (*nm*) the Pope; –पद papacy; –सम्बन्धी papal; ~लीला hypocrisy, sham religious activity; ~वाद papalism; papal.

पोपला popla: (*a*) toothless; hollow; ~ना (for a person) to become toothless; ~पन hollowness; toothlessness.

पोया poya: (*nm*) see पोआ.

पोर por (*nm*) a knuckle; the space between any two joints of a finger; finger-tip; –पोर में दर्द होना/पिराना every inch/joint of the body to ache.

पोर्टर portar (*nm*) a porter, a coolie.

पोल pol (*nf*) empty/hollow space, hollowness; (*nm*) a gate, an entrance (of a palace etc.); ~दार hollow, empty; ~, ढोल की high-sounding without, hollow within; –खुलना to be exposed; an adverse fact (about somebody) to be revealed; –खोलना to expose, to reveal a secret, to disclose an adverse fact (about somebody).

पोला pola: (*a*) hollow, empty; ~पन hollowness, emptiness.

पोलाव pola:w (*nm*) see पुलाव.

पोलियो poliyo (*nm*) polio (myelitis), infantile paralysis (that incapacitates the legs).

पोलो polo (*nf*) polo; ~स्टिक a polo-stick.

पोश posh—a Persian word used in Hindi compounds as the second member—meaning that which clothes or conceals (as नक़ाबपोश, पलँगपोश).

पोशाक posha:k (*nf*) clothes, dress, attire, raiment; accoutrements.

पोशीदगी poshi:dgi: (*nf*) privity; secrecy; concealment.

पोशीदा poshi:da: (*a*) privy; secret; concealed, hidden.

पोषक poshak (*nm*) fosterer, one who rears/brings up, nourisher;

protector; supporter; hence ~ता (*nf*).

पोषण poshāṇ (*nm*) fostering, rearing, bringing up; nourishment; nutriment, nutrition; protection; support.

पोषाहार posha:ha:r (*nm*) nourishment, nutritious diet.

पोषित poshit (*a*) nourished, reared, nurtured, fostered.

पोष्य poshy (*a*) fit to be nourished/nurtured/fostered; **–पुत्र** a foster child; an adopted son.

पोसना posnā: (*v*) to rear; to bring up; to foster, to nourish; to pet; to domesticate.

पोस्ट posṭ (*nm*) post; **–आफ़िस** a post-office; **–कार्ड** a post-card; **–बॉक्स** post-box; **~मास्टर** a post-master; **~मैन** a postman.

पोस्टमार्टम posṭma:rṭām (*nm*) post-mortem, autopsy.

पोस्टर posṭar (*nm*) a poster; **–युद्ध** poster war.

पोस्टल posṭal (*a*) postal; **–आर्डर** a postal order.

पोस्त post (*nm*) a poppy plant, poppy seed.

पोस्ता posta: (*nm*) a poppy plant.

पोस्ती posti: (*nm*) an opium-addict; a slothful drowsy person.

पोस्तीन posti:n (*nf*) a garment of leather covered with fine wool/hair on it.

पोहना pohnā: (*v*) to string, to thread together; **–, बात** to lodge complaints (against somebody) with distortion of facts.

पौंड pāūnḍ (*nm*) a pound (weight); sterling pound.

पौंड़ा, ~ढ़ा pāūṛa:, ~ṛha: (*nm*) a variety of (juicy) sugarcane.

पौंस/रा, ~ला pāūsra:, ~la: (*nm*) see **पौसरा**.

पौ pau (*nf*) a ray of light; early dawn; one pip (in a dice); **–फटना** the day to break; **~बारह होना** [to be crowned with success (in some enterprise etc.); to have a run of extremely good luck; to come out with bright colours.

पौआ paua: (*nm*) quarter of a seer; a weight equivalent to one-fourth of a seer; a pot which can contain quarter seer of liquid (as milk, oil, etc.); a bottle of liquor; backing, support.

पौढ़ना pauṛhnā: (*v*) to lie, to repose.

पौत्र pauttr (*nm*) a grandson, son's son.

पौत्री pauttri: (*nf*) a grand-daughter, a son's daughter.

पौद paud (*nf*) a seedling, sapling; young plant; (fig.) generation; **–, नयी** new generation, growing generation.

पौदा pauda: (*nm*) a plant, young plant; sapling.

पौध paudh (*nf*) see **पौद**.

पौधा paudha: (*nm*) see **पौदा**.

पौनःपुनिक pāūnāhpunik (*a*) recurrent, repeated again and again.

पौनःपुन्य pāūnāhpunny (*nm*) recurrence, repetition.

पौन pāūn (*nm*) see **पवन**; three-fourth, three quarters.

पौनरुक्त pāūnrukt (*nm*) repeated, reiterated.

पौना pāūnā: (*nm*) a ladle with a long handle; a multiplication table in which the multiples of three-fourth (3/4) are recorded; (*a*) three quarter; three-fourth; **पौने** quarter to (as **पौने चार बजे** at quarter to four); **पौने, औने** – at a discount, at a lower rate.

पौनी pāūnī: (*nf*) people belonging to the servicing class (like the potter, carpenter, washerman, and barber, etc.) who get tips in cash or kind on festive occasions; a small ladle.

पौर paur (*a*) urban, municipal, civic, pertaining to the city; outer verandah in a house: (*nm*) a municipal councillor; ~, महा mayor; –सदन the town hall.

पौरस्त्य paurasty (*a*) eastern.

पौरांगना paurā:ṅgnā: (*nf*) an urban woman.

पौराणिक paurā:ṇik (*a*) mythological; pertaining/belonging to the Pura:ṇas (see); (*nm*) one who is conversant with the Pura:ṇas; –कथा mythological tale, legend; ~ता mythological character.

पौरी pauri: (*nf*) a door; portico.

पौरुष paurush (*nm*) manhood, manliness, masculinity; virility; ~हीन unmanly, impotent; –थकना one's virility to be on the decline, to be no more as much of a vigorous man.

पौरुषेय paurushey (*a*) manly, vigorous; man-made; hence ~ता (*nf*).

पौरोहित्य paurohity (*nm*) priesthood.

पौर्णमासिक paurṇāmā:sik (*a*) pertaining to the full-moon day.

पौर्णमासी paurṇāmā:si: (*nf*) the full-moon day.

पौली pauli: (*nf*) a door, threshold; ~बंद independent (as a house), having a separate entry and exit; ० मकान an independent house.

पौवा pauva: (*nm*) see पौआ.

पौष paush (*nm*) the tenth month of the Hindu (lunar) calendar.

पौष्टिक paushṭik (*a*) nutritive, nutritious; tonic; –आहार nutritive diet, nourishment; hence ~ता (*nf*).

पौस/रा, ~ला pausra:, ~la: (*nm*) a water-kiosk, booth where water is provided free of charge (specially in summers).

पौहारी pauha:ri: (*nm*) one who subsists on milk alone.

प्याऊ pya:u: (*nf*) a water-booth, free water-kiosk; –बैठाना/लगाना to cause a water-kiosk to be run, to set up a water-booth.

प्या/ज़ pya:z (*nm*) onion; ~ज़ी/ज़ू onion-coloured, light pink.

प्यादा pya:da: (*nm*) a footman, an infantryman; pedestrian; a pawn (in chess); –से फरज़ी भयौ टेढ़ो-टेढ़ो जात risen from the ranks, must turn into cranks.

प्यार pya:r (*nm*) love; affection; amour, amorous relationship; –मोहब्बत love and affection; –भरी नज़रों से देखना to give the glad eye, to cast an amorous/festive glance.

प्यारा pya:ra: (*a*) dear, beloved, loved; pleasing, lovely; pretty; (*nm*) a dear one, beloved.

प्याला pya:la: (*nm*) a cup; –भरना/लबरेज़ होना/लबालब होना the cup (*e.g.* of life) to be full.

प्यास pya:s (*nf*) thirst; longing/lust; –बुझाना to quench one's thirst; to satisfy one's lust.

प्यासा pya:sa: (*a*) thirsty.

प्र pra– a Sanskrit prefix imparting the meanings of before; forward; in front; on; forth; away; excessively, eminently, excellently, very much.

प्रकंप prakāmp (*nm*) vibration; quivering; trembling.

प्रकं/पन prakāmpan (*nm*) see प्रकंप; ~पित vibrated; quivered, shivered, trembled.

प्रकट prakat̤ (*a*) manifest; revealed; apparent; obvious, evident, ostensible; overt; ~न manifestation, becoming visible; fade in; -प्रच्छन्न overt and covert; direct and indirect; -करना to manifest; to make apparent/obvious/evident; to reveal; to cause to appear.

प्रकटत: prakat̤tah (*adv*) manifestly; apparently; obviously; evidently.

प्रकटित prakat̤it (*a*) manifested; revealed, disclosed, made apparent/ obvious/evident.

प्रकटीकरण prakat̤i:karān (*nm*) manifestation; revelation, disclosure; (the act or process of) making apparent/obvious/evident.

प्रक/थन prakathān (*nm*) averment; assertion; hence ~थित (*a*).

प्रकर prakar (*nm*) a circle (as of friends, associates, etc.); assembly.

प्रकरण prakarān (*nm*) context; a division of a book–section, topic, chapter; –सापेक्ष contextual.

प्रक/र्ष prakarsh (*nm*) (rising to) eminence/excellence; exaltation, elevation; hence ~र्षी (*a*).

प्रक/ल्पना prakalpanā: (*nf*) presumption taking for granted; ~ल्पित presumptive, presumed.

प्रकांड prakā:nd̤ (*a*) outstanding, eminent; foremost, leading; –विद्वान outstanding / foremost scholar; hence ~ता (*nf*).

प्रकार praka:r (*nm*) kind; quality; mode, manner; way, method; type; pattern; -भेद difference in kind / quality/type; -विद्या typology.

प्रकारांतर praka:rā:ntar (*nm*) a different/another method or manner; –से in another or in a different method/manner/way.

प्रकारात्मक praka:ra:tmāk (*a*) pertaining to type/manner/pattern/ quality; qualitative.

प्रकाश praka:sh (*nm*) light; sunshine; lustre; chapter of a book; ~क्षेपी a reflector; ~मापी lightmeter; -विश्लेषण photolysis; –डालना to throw light on, to elucidate; –में आना to come into lime-light; to come to light; to acquire renown.

प्रकाश/क praka:shak (*nm*) a publisher; one who or that which illuminates, an illuminator; ~कीय of, related with or pertaining to a/the publisher.

प्रकाशन praka:shān (*nm*) a publication; publishing; (the act or process of) bringing to light; release; –अधिकार publication-rights; –संस्था a publishing concern; –उद्‌घाटन (प्रकाशनोद्‌घाटन) release (of a new publication).

प्रकाशमान praka:shmā:n (*a*) glowing, shining; lustrous, resplendent, radiant.

प्रकाशिकी praka:shiki: (*nf*) optics; ~य optical.

प्रकाशित praka:shit (*a*) published; brought to light, manifest, obvious; resplendent

प्रकाशीय praka:shi:y (*n*) optical.

प्रकाश्य praka:shy (*a*) publication-worthy; fit to be brought to light.

प्रकीर्ण praki:rn̤ (*a*) diffused, scattered, dishevelled; miscellaneous; ~क miscellaneous (assembly); ~केश having dishevelled hair; hence ~ता (*nf*).

प्रकुपित prakupit (*a*) infuriated enraged, wrathful; gone into disequilibrium or out of control.

कृत prakrit (*a*) natural; spontaneous; unsophisticated; habitual; genuine; normal; ~वाद naturalism; ~वादी a naturalist; naturalistic.

कृतार्थ prakrita:rth (*nm*) real import, true meaning.

कृति prakriti (*nf*) the nature; temperament, disposition; habit; genius (as of a language); ~ज spontaneous, natural; -भेद difference of nature; temperamental, difference; ~वाद naturalism; naturism; ~वादी a natur(al)ist; natur(al)istic; –विज्ञान natural history; –शास्त्र naturism; ~शास्त्री a naturist; ~शास्त्रीय naturistic; ~सिद्ध natural, spontaneous; ~स्थ composed, cool and composed; poised, sane; ~स्थता composure; sanity.

प्रकृत्या prakrittya: (*ind*) by temperament, by disposition, by nature.

प्रकृष्ट prakrishṭ (*a*) excellent; supreme, best; hence ~ता (*nf*).

प्र/कोप prakop (*nm*) wrath, rage, fury; ~कोपित see प्रकुपित.

प्रकोष्ठ prakoshṭḥ (*nm*) wrist; courtyard; chamber.

प्रक्रम prakkrām (*nm*) a process; sequence; series.

प्रक्रिया prakkriya: (*nf*) a process, procedure; technique, method; ~त्मक procedural; ~विज्ञ/विद् a methodologist; -विज्ञान methodology; hence ~विज्ञानी (*nm*).

प्रक्षा/लन praksha:lān (*nm*) washing, cleansing; ~लित washed, cleansed.

प्रक्षि/प्त prakshipt (*a*) projected; thrown; cast forth; interpolated; ~प्तांश interpolation.

प्रक्षेप prakkshep (*nm*) projection; throw, casting forth; interpolation; ~क a projector; ~ण projection; projecting, throwing.

प्रखर prakhar (*a*) sharp; keen, acute; radical; fierce; ~ता sharpness; keenness, acuteness; radicalism; fierceness.

प्रख्या/त prakkhya:t (*a*) well-known, renowned, reputed; hence ~ति (*nf*).

प्रख्या/पन prakkhya:pān (*nm*) promulgation; ~पित promulgated.

प्रगट pragaṭ (*a*) see प्रकट.

प्रगटना pragaṭnā: (*v*) to become manifest/obvious; to be born/incarnated.

प्रगति pragati (*nf*) progress; development; ~वाद, ~वादिता progressivism; ~वादी progressive; a progressivist; –विरोधी anti-progressive, reactionary; oतत्त्व reactionary elements; ~शील progressive; ~शीलता progressivism; progress.

प्रगल्भ pragalbh (*a*) mature; insolent, impertinent, cheeky; outspoken; venturesome; ~ता maturity; insolence, impertinence, cheekiness; outspokenness; venturesomeness.

प्रगल्भा pragalbha: (*nf*) a matured heroine/woman, according to traditional Indian Poetics a heroine well conversant with the art of love/erotic affairs.

प्रगाढ़ praga:ṛḥ (*a*) profound, deep; dense; exceeding, abundant; hence ~ता (*nf*).

प्रगी/त pragi:t (*nm*) a song; lyric; ~ति a lyric; lyrical; o काव्य lyrical poetry; ~ति- तत्त्व lyrical element.

प्रगु/णन pragūṇān (*nm*) multiplication, raising the prepotence; ~णता prepotency, prepotence;

~णित multiplied; increased in numbers; ~णी prepotent.

प्रघात pragha:t (*nm*) thrust; impact.

प्रचंड prachāṇḍ (*a*) excessively violent, impetuous, furious, fierce; passionate; virulent; terrible, direful; mighty, powerful; ~ता violence; impetuousness, furiousness, fierceness; passionateness; virulence; mightiness; power; –महासागर the Atlantic Ocean.

प्रचलन prachalān (*nm*) currency, prevalence; custom; usage; movement.

प्रचलि/त prachalit (*a*) current, prevalent, in vogue, in usage; common; customary; moved; ~तार्थ current or prevalent meaning/acceptation,

प्रचार pracha:r (*nm*) propaganda; publicity; currency; prevalence; ~क/~कर्त्ता propagator; propagandist; publicist; –जवाबी counter-propaganda; hence ~ण (*nm*); –युग age of publicity/propaganda; –लेख write-up; –संख्या circulation.

प्रचारित pracha:rit (*a*) propagated; publicised; circulated; made current/prevalent, given currency.

प्रचाल/न pracha:lan (*nm*) operation; ~क an operator.

प्रचुर prachur (*a*) plentiful, copious, abundant; ample; ~ता plenty, copiousness, abundance; ampleness.

प्रच्छद prachchhad (*nm*) a lid, cover; covering

प्रच्छन्न prachchhann (*a*) covered; concealed, hidden, latent, stealthy; implicit; secret; indirect; ~चारी secretive; –रूप से secretly/stealthily; indirectly.

प्रच्छन्नता prachchhannāta: (*nf*) concealment; latency; stealthines secrecy,

प्रच्छा/दन prachchha:dan (*nm*) covering; concealment, concealin hiding; a cover, wrapper; hen ~दित (*a*).

प्रज/नन prajanān (*nm*) reproductio (multiplying by) generation, breding; hence ~नित (*a*).

प्रज/ल्पना prajalpanā: (*nf*) tal chatting; talkativeness, gossipin hence ~ल्पित (*a*).

प्रजा praja: (*nf*) subjects; publi ~तंत्र democracy; ~तंत्रात्मक democratic; ~तांत्रिक democrati ~पति the Creator–Lord Brahma a pot-maker; ~पालक protect of the subjects; a benevole king; ~पालन protecting/provi ing subsistence to the subject ~पीड़क a tyrant; tyrannica ~पीड़न tyranny; –सत्ता democrac ~सत्तात्मक democratic; –हित wel being of the subjects/public.

प्रजाति praja:ti (*nf*) species.

प्रजारना praja:rnā: (*v*) to char, burn completely.

प्रज्ञा praggya: (*nf*) prudence, inte lect; ~चक्षु blind; ~वान् pr dent, intelligent; ~हीन stupi nincompoop.

प्र/ज्ञान praggyā:n (*nm*) wisdo noesis; ~ज्ञात well-known; fa ous; reputed; defined; ~ज्ञेय ne mata.

प्रज्ञा/पन pragya:pān (*nm*) notific tion, notice; making know hence ~पित (*a*).

प्रज्व/लन prajjwalān (*nm*) ignitio burning, setting on fire/setti aglow; ~लित ignited, burnt, s on fire; set aglow.

प्रण prāṇ (*nm*) a vow, pledge; –कर

to take a vow, to (take a) pledge; –पालन करना/– पूरा करना/–रखना to keep a pledge, to observe a vow.

प्रणत prāṉat (*a*) bowed (down), bent, obeisant, humble, modest; ~पाल a protector of shelter-seekers.

प्रणति prāṉati (*nf*) (the act or process of) bowing, reverential salutation; obeisance.

प्रणम्य prāṉammy (*a*) reverend, worthy of respect/bowing to with reverence, deserving salutation.

प्रणय prāṉay (*nm*) love; affection, attachment; -कलह amatorial disputation, dispute between lovers.

प्रणयन prāṉayān (*nm*) writing, composition.

प्रण/यी prāṉayi: (*nm*) a lover; (*a*) having affection; amatorial; hence ~यिनी (*nf*).

प्रणव prāṉav (*nm*) the sacred and mystical syllable Om, God Almighty.

प्रणा/म prāṉā:m (*nm*) reverential salutation; bowing with respect; a term used in greeting elders; abandoning, giving up, bidding good-bye to (as ऐसी प्रथा को प्रणाम); ~मी one who bows reverentially; saluting respectfully; ~म करना, दूर से to say good-bye to; to maintain a safe distance.

प्रणाली prāṉa:li: (*nf*) a system; method; ~बद्ध methodical.

प्रणिधान prāṉidhā:n (*nm*) respectful conduct; profound religious meditation; abstract contemplation; prayer.

प्रणिधि prāṉidhi (*nm*) an emissary.

प्रणीत praṉi:t (*a*) written, composed.

प्रणेता praṉēta: (*nm*) a writer, author; composer.

प्रतप्त pratapt (*a*) well-heated; red hot; oppressed; harassed.

प्रता/ड़ना prata:ṛnā: (*nf*) admonition, reproof; affliction; ~ड़ित afflicted.

प्रताप prata:p (*nm*) glorious grace, glory, dignity; glorious renown; overwhelming influence; ~वान see प्रतापी; –से, किसी के through the glorious grace of.

प्रतापी prata:pi: (*a*) glorious, dignified possessing glory and renown/overwhelming influence.

प्रति prati (*nf*) a copy; print; a Sanskrit prefix imparting the meanings of towards, near to; against, in opposition to; back, again, in return; down upon; and also of likeness or comparison; anti; per; ~प्रचार counter-propaganda; –मास per mensem.

प्रतिकर pratikar (*nm*) return; compensation.

प्रतिकरणीय pratikarnī:y (*a*) deserving of return/revenge/retaliation; worth countering, counterable.

प्रतिकर्ष pratikarsh (*nm*) anti-climax; repulsion.

प्रति/कर्षण pratikarshāṉ (*nm*) repulsion; back pull; ~कर्षित repulsed, thrown back; ~कर्षी repulsive; ० शक्ति force of repulsion; ~कृष्ट repulsed, thrust backwards

प्रतिकाय pratika:y (*nm*) a prototype: counterpart.

प्रति/कार pratika:r (*nm*) revenge, retaliation; return; ~कारक antidote, counter; ~कारात्मक retaliatory, born of a sense of revenge; ~कारी retaliator; one who takes revenge; ~कार्यता reactance/counterability/retaliativity.

प्रतिकाष्ठा pratika:shṭha: (*nf*) anti-climax.

प्रतिकूल pratiku:l (*a*) adverse, unfavourable; contrary; opposite; hostile; ~कारी opponent, adversary; ~दर्शन repulsive; ominous, inauspicious; ~वाद contradiction

प्रतिकूलता pratiku:lta: (*nf*) an adversity, unfavourableness; contrariety; opposition; hostility; contravention.

प्रतिकृति pratikkriti (*nf*) a prototype, facsimile, replica; an image.

प्रतिक्रांति pratikkrā:nti (*nf*) counter-revolution; copy, facsimile; ~क/~कारी counter-revolutionary.

प्रति/क्रिया pratikkriya: (*nf*) reaction; ~क्रिया-कलाप retroactivity; ~क्रियात्मक reactionary; ~क्रियावाद reaction(ism); ~क्रियावादी reactionary; a reactionist.

प्रति/क्षेप pratikkshep (*nm*) recoil, rebound; regurgitation; hence ~क्षेपण; ~क्षिप्त recoiled, rebounded; regurgitated.

प्रति/गमन pratigamān (*nm*) return; regression, retrogression; ~गत returned; regressed, retrogressed; ~गामी retrogressive; ~गामी तत्त्व retrogressive elements; ~गामी शक्ति retrogressive force.

प्रति/घात pratigha:t (*nm*) counter-attack, counter-offensive, counter-stroke; hence ~घाती (*nm* and *a*).

प्रतिचय/न pratichay, ~an (*nm*) sampling; ~न-पद्धति/विधि sampling technique.

प्रतिचर pratichar (*nm*) a contra-variant.

प्रतिचार praticha:r (*nm*) make-up.

प्रतिचित्रण pratichitran (*nm*) adumbration, counter-delineation.

प्रतिच्छाया pratichchha:ya: (*nf*) a shadow; image; copy, facsimile; replica.

प्रतिच्छिन्न pratichchhinn (*a*) intersected.

प्रति/च्छेद pratichchhed (*nm*) intersection; hence ~च्छेदन (*nm*).

प्रतिजैविकी pratijaiviki: (*nf*) antibiotics; ~य antibiotic.

प्रतिज्ञा pratiggya: (*nf*) a pledge, vow; promise; enunciation; ~कर्ता a promiser, one who makes a pledge or takes a vow; ~ती a promisee; one to whom a pledge is made; -पत्र a covenant, written pledge; bond; -पालन carrying out of a pledge, implementation of/adherence to a vow; -भंग violation of a pledge, going back on one's vow; breach of a promise.

प्रतिज्ञा/न pratiggyā:n (*nm*) an affirmance; a pledge, vow; hence ~त (*a*).

प्रतिदर्श pratidarsh (*nm*) a specimen; sample; ~न representation; sampling.

प्रतिदान pratidā:n (*nm*) requital, return, recompense; repayment.

प्रतिदिन pratidin (*ind*) every day, daily.

प्रतिदी/प्त pratidi:pt (*a*) fluoresecnt; ~प्ति fluorescence.

प्रतिदेय pratidey (*nm*) that which can be given in return, worth giving in return; requital; (*a*) repayable, refundable; returnable; hence ~ता (*nf*).

प्रतिद्वंद्व pratidvāndv (*nm*) conflict mutual struggle, clash, contest.

प्रतिद्वंद्विता pratidvāndvita: (*nf*) rivalry, mutual conflict, contest.

प्रतिद्वंद्वी pratidvāndvi: (*nm*) a rival contestant; an antagonist.

प्रतिध्वनि pratiddhvanī (*nf*) echo, re-echo, reverberation; resonance

~त echoed, re-echoed, reverberated; resounded.

प्रतिनमस्कार pratināmaska:r (*nm*) responsive salutation, saying 'hello' in response to greetings.

प्रति/नाद pratina:d (*nm*) see प्रतिध्वनि; ~नादित see प्रतिध्वनित.

प्रतिना/यक pratina:yak (*nm*) hero's rival/competitor; a villain; ~यिका a vamp.

प्रतिनिधि pratinidhi (*nm*) a delegate; representative; deputy; ~क representative; ~त्व representation; deputation; delegacy; ~मंडल a delegation, a body of representatives; deputation; -सभा house of representatives.

प्रति/नियुक्त pratiniyukt (*nm*) a deputy; (*a*) deputed; ~नियुक्ति deputation.

प्रतिनिर्देश pratinirdesh (*nm*) cross-reference; cross-referencing; hence ~र्दिष्ट (*a*).

प्रतिनिविष्ट pratinivishṭ (*a*) confirmed, rigid; —मूर्ख a confirmed fool, an incorrigible fool.

प्रतिपक्ष pratipaksh (*nm*) opposition, rival side, hostile camp, contesting party; ~ता opposition, rivalry, contest, hostility.

प्रतिपक्षी pratipakshi: (*nm*) an opponent, rival, contestant; contralateral.

प्रतिपत्ति pratipatti (*nf*) acquisition, acquirement, accomplishment.

प्रतिपत्र pratipattr (*nf*) proxy.

प्रतिपदा pratipada: (*nf*) the first day of the lunar fortnight.

प्रति/पादन pratipa:dān (*nm*) exposition; treatment; enunciation; ~पादक an exponent, interpreter, one who sets forth or enunciates; ~पादित set forth, interpreted; treated; enunciated.

प्रतिपाद्य pratipa:dy (*a* and *nm*) treated of, enunciated; the theme, the subject matter, subject treated of; to be enunciated; hence ~ता (*nf*);—विषय the subject/theme (treated of).

प्रति/पाल pratipa:l (*nm*) a protector, one who sustains, one who provides subsistence; also ~पालक (*nm*).

प्रति/पालन pratipa:lān (*um*) protection, giving sustenance, providing subsistence; maintenance; observance; implementation; ~पाल्य one who is under protection; ~पालन करना to protect, to give sustenance, to provide subsistence; to maintain; to observe; to implement.

प्रतिपालना pratipa:lnā: (*v*) see प्रतिपालन (करना).

प्रतिपालित pratipa:lit (*a*) protected; sustained, given subsistence; maintained; observed; implemented.

प्रतिपुरुष pratipurush (*nm*) an effigy; a substitute; replacement.

प्रतिपूरक pratipu:rak (*a*) complementary; hence ~ता (*nf*).

प्रतिपूर्ति pratipu:rti (*nf*) compensation, recompense; reimbursement.

प्रतिप्रहार pratipraha:r (*nm*) counter-attack, counter-assault, counter-offensive.

प्रतिफल pratiphal (*nm*) requital, consideration; return.

प्रति/फलन pratiphalān (*nm*) culmination, conclusion; reflection; ~फलित culminated (in); concluded; reflected.

प्रति/बंध pratibāndh (*nm*) restriction; ban; proviso; condition; ~बंधित restricted, banned; conditioned; ~बद्ध restricted; banned;

conditioned; committed; ~बद्धता commitment.

प्रतिबल pratibal (*nm*) counter-force; counter-strength; possessing matching strength.

प्रति/बाधा pratiba:dha: (*nf*) reactance; obstruction; harassment; ~बाधित obstructed; harassed.

प्रति/बिंब pratibimb (*nm*) reflection; image, shadow; ~बिंबवाद reflectionism, the philosophical doctrine which asserts that the individual is but the reflection of his Creator; ~बिंबित reflected.

प्रतिबुद्धि/वाद pratibuddhiva:d (*nm*) anti-intellectualism; ~वादी an anti-intellectual; anti-intellectualist; anti-intellectualistic.

प्रति/बोध pratibodh (*nm*) awakening; rousing; also ~बोधक; hence ~बोधन (*nm*).

प्रतिभट pratibhat (*nm*) a rival, rival warrior.

प्रतिभा pratibha: (*nf*) genius; brilliance; ~वान a genius; brilliant; ~शाली genius; brilliant; -संपन्न see ~शाली.

प्रतिभावी pratibha:vi: (*a*) antagonistic.

प्रति/भास pratibha:s (*nm*) illusion; apparent likeness, appearance; ~भासित appeared.

प्रतिभू pratibhu: (*nm*) a surety; guarantee.

प्रतिभूति pratibhu:ti (*nf*) bail; security; guarantee.

प्रतिमंडल pratimāṇḍal (*nm*) a halo.

प्रतिमा pratimā: (*nf*) an image, icon, a statue; effigy; -पूजा idolatory; iconolatory; ~विज्ञान iconoscope; iconography; -भंजन iconoclasm; -भंजक an iconoclast; iconoclastic.

प्रतिमान pratimā:n (*um*) a pattern, specimen; prototype; standard.

प्रतिमूर्ति pratimu:rti (*nf*) an image, icon, idol; prototype.

प्रति/योग pratiyog (*nm*) a competition, rivalry, contest, match; ~योगात्मक competitive; contesting.

प्रतियोगिता pratiyogita: (*nf*) competition, rivalry; match; tournament; contest; -परीक्षा competitive examination.

प्रतियोगी pratiyogi: (*nm* and *a*) a competitor; contestant, rival; matching.

प्रतियोद्धा pratiyoddha: (*nm*) a rival warrior, a contesting fighter/combatant.

प्रति/रक्षा pratiraksha: (*nf*) defence; ~रक्षात्मक defensive; ~रक्षा-सेनाएं defence forces.

प्रति/रूप pratiru:p (*nm*) a pattern; model, prototype; specimen; simulacum; counterpart; (*a*) enantiomorphic; type; ~रूपी typical; counterpart; prototype; specimen; enantiomorphic.

प्रति/रोध pratirodh (*nm*) resistance; contest; obstruction; counteraction; ~रुद्ध resisted: contested; obstructed; ~रोधक resistor; resistant, contestant; antagonistic; causing obstruction; ~रोधित see ~रुद्ध; ~रोधी resistant, obstructive; contesting; counteractive; an antagonist.

प्रतिलाभ pratila:bh (*nm*) return.

प्रति/लिपि pratilipi (*nf*) a copy, duplicate copy; facsimile; ~लिपिक/कार copyist; ~लिप्यधिकार copyright; ~लिप्यधिकारी copyright holder.

प्रतिलेख pratilekh (*nm*) a transcription; anti-graph; ~न transcription; anti-graphing; ~न, सूक्ष्म narrow transcription; ~न, स्थूल

broad transcription.

तिलोम pratilom (*a*) inverse; reverse; resupinate; unwarranted; adverse; vile; –अनुपात inverse proportion; –विवाह the marriage of a man of a lower caste with a woman of a higher caste.

ति/वर्तन prativartān (*nm*) reversion; recurve; obversion; reflex; ~वर्ती reversible; reflexive, reversed; recurved; ~वर्त्य reversible.

तिवाद prativa:d (*nm*) a controversy; refutation, contradiction, counter-statement; responsive argument; –पक्ष the defence (side).

तिवादी prativa:di: (*nm*) a defendant; respondent; –पक्ष defence, respondent's side; hence प्रतिवादिता (*nf*).

तिवासर prativa:sar (*ind*) everyday, daily.

ति/वेदन prativedan (*nm*) report, representation; ~वेदक/वेदी a reporter; one who makes a representation.

ति/वेश prativesh (*nm*) neighbourhood, vicinity; ~वेशी a neighbour.

तिशत pratishat (*ind*) per cent; –अनुपात percentage; –, शत cent percent; ~ता percentage.

प्रतिशब्द partishabd (*nm*) a synonym, equivalent word, synonymous word.

प्रतिशिष्ट pratishishṭ (*nm*) a page; (*a*) deployed, sent on an errand.

प्रति/शोध pratishodh (*nm*) revenge, vendetta, vangeance; reprisal; ~शोधात्मक revengeful, inspired by vendetta; ~ शोधी one who avenges/seeks vendetta.

प्रतिश्रवण pratishshravaṇ (*nm*) playback.

प्रतिश्रुत pratishshrut (*a*) committed, bound, sworn, pledged.

प्रतिश्रुति pratishshruti (*nf*) commitment, binding, swearing, vow, pledge.

प्रति/षेध pratishedh (*nm*) prohibition, forbiddance; taboo; ~ षिद्ध prohibited, forbidden; tabooed.

प्रतिष्ठा pratishṭḥa: (*nf*) prestige, dignity; status; establishment; installation, consecration of an idol in a temple; ~वान enjoying prestige/status, dignified;—करना to instal/establish/consecrate; –का प्रश्न a prestige issue; –भंग होना one's dignity to be violated.

प्रतिष्ठान pratishṭḥā:n (*nm*) an establishment; installation.

प्रतिष्ठा/पन pratishṭḥa:pān (*nm*) establishment; installation; consecration of the image of a deity; hence ~पित (*a*).

प्रतिष्ठित pratishṭḥit (*a*) honourable, respectable; established; installed; consecrated; dignified; enjoying a prestige/status.

प्रतिसं/हरण pratisānharāṇ (*nm*) revocation; hence ~हार (*nm*).

प्रतिस्था/पन pratistha:pān (*nm*) replacement, replacing; substitution; ~पित replaced, substituted.

प्रति/स्पर्धा pratispardha: (*nf*) rivalry, contest; competition; ~स्पर्धी rival, contestant; competitor.

प्रतिस्फीति pratisphi:ti (*nf*) anti-inflation; ~परक anti-inflationary.

प्रतिहत pratihat (*a*) restrained, obstructed, hampered; defeated.

प्रतिहस्त pratihast (*nm*) representative, deputy.

प्रतिहस्ताक्षर pratihasta:kshar (*nm*) counter-signature.

प्रतिहार pratiha:r (*nm*) a gatekeeper; watchman.

प्रतिहारी **pratiha:ri:** (*nm*) see प्रतिहार.

प्रति/हिंसा pratihinsa: (*nf*) vengeance, revenge; retaliation, counter-violence; ~**हिंसक** one who takes revenge, retaliator/retaliatory; violent in reaction; ~**हिंसात्मक** revengeful, retaliatory; inspired by counter-violence/vengeance.

प्रतीक prati:k (*nm*) a symbol; fetish; -**प्रयोग** symbology; symbolism; symbolization; ~**वाद**/~**वादिता** symbolism; ~**वादी** a symbolist; symbolical; -**विद्या** symbolics; symbology; -**विधान** symbology, symbolization.

प्रतीकात्मक prati:ka:tmak (*a*) symbolic, allegorical; ~**ता** symbolism; fetishism.

प्रतीकोपास/ना prati:kopa:snā: (*nf*) symbolatory; ~**क** a symbolater.

प्रती/क्षा prati:ksha: (*nf*) waiting (for); wait; expectation; ~**क्षित** awaited.

प्रतीक्षालय prati:ksha:lay (*nm*) a waiting room,

प्रती/ची prati:chi: (*nf*) the west; ~**चीन**/**च्य** western, pertaining to the west.

प्रतीत prati:t (*a*) appeared; known, acquainted.

प्रतीति prati:ti (*nf*) conviction, assurance, confidence; appearance.

प्रतीप prati:p (*a*) contrary; adverse; repugnant; -**गति**/**गमन** retrogradation, retrogression, going backwards; ~**गामी** retrograde, retrogressive; -**तरण** rowing upstream.

प्रतीयमान prati:yamā:n (*a*) virtual; apparent; hence ~**ता** (*nf*).

प्रत्यं/कन pratyankan (*nm*) transcription; ~**कित** transcribed.

प्रत्यंग pratyāng (*nm*) minor parts (of the body); (*ind*) each and every part.

प्रत्यंचा pratyāncha: (*nf*) a bowstring; -**चढ़ाना** to string the bow; to get ready to fight.

प्रत्यक्ष pratyaksh (*a*) visible, tangible, evident; apparent, obvious; direct; -**ज्ञान** direct comprehension; sensual perception; hence ~**ता** (*nf*); -**दर्शन** witnessing directly (with one's own eyes); first-hand view; ~**दर्शी** an eye-witness; -**दृश्य** tangible, directly perceivable; -**प्रमाण** direct evidence; eye-witness evidence; ~**वाद** direct view; ~**वादिता** positivism; ~**वादी** a positivist; positivistic; -**विहित** explicitly prescribed; -**साक्षी** an eye-witness; bearing direct testimony; -**साक्ष्य** direct testimony; eye-witness evidence; ~**सिद्ध** proved by direct evidence.

प्रत्यक्षीकरण pratyakshi:karān (*nm*) (the act or process) of coming face to face, seeing through one's own eyes; direct perception; -, **बंदी** habeas corpus; **व्याचिका** habeas corpus petition; ~**कृत** come face to face, seen through one's own eyes; directly perceived.

प्रत्यपका/र pratyapka:r (*nm*) reprisal; retaliation; hence ~**री** (*nm*).

प्रत्यभिज्ञा pratyabhigya: (*nf*) recognition, identification; -**दर्शन** a philosophical school which recognises Lord Shiv as the Supreme Power *i.e.* Brahm.

प्रत्यभिज्ञान pratyabhiggyā:n (*nm*) recognition, identification; an identification mark.

प्रत्यभिवादन pratybhiva:dān (*nm*) responsive salutation; saying 'hello' in reply.

प्रत्यय pratyay (*nm*) an idea, concept; credit; assurance, conviction; suffix; ~कारी convincing, reassuring; -पत्र credentials, letter of credence; ~वाद/~वादिता idealism; conceptualism; hence ~वादी (*nm*).

प्रत्ययन pratyayān (*nm*) ideation.

प्रत्या/यन pratya:yān (*nm*) accreditation; ~यक an accreditor; accrediting; ~यित accredited; o दूत accredited envoy; ~यित राजदूत accredited ambassador.

प्रत्यर्थी pratyarthi: (*nm*) a respondent.

प्रत्य/र्पण pratyarpān (*nm*) extradition; return, refund; ~र्पणीय extraditable; returnable/refundable; hence ~र्पित (*a*).

प्रत्यवहार pratyavha:r (*nm*) destruction; annihilation.

प्रत्यवेक्षण pratyavekshān (*nm*) deliberation, consideration of the pros and cons (of a matter).

प्रत्या/ख्यान pratya:kkhyā:n (*nm*) repudiation, refutation, rebuttal; ~ख्यात repudiated, refuted, rebutted.

प्रत्यागत pratyā:gat (*a*) returned, come back.

प्रत्यागमन pratya:gamān (*nm*) return, coming back.

प्रत्याघात pratya:gha:t (*nm*) counter-impact; counter-stroke, counter-blow.

प्रत्या/नयन pratya:nayān (*nm*) restitution; ~नीत restituted.

प्रत्याभूति pratya:bhu:ti (*nf*) a guarantee.

प्रत्या/युक्त pratya:yukt (*nm*) a delegate; ~योग delegation.

प्रत्याव/र्तन pratya:vartān (*nm*) return; reversion; recurrence; restoration; ~र्तित returned; reversed; recurred; restored; ~र्तित्र an alternator; ~र्ती a reversioner; ~र्ती धारा alternating current (A.C.); ~र्तन-नियम alternation law.

प्रत्या/शा pratya:sha: (*nf*) expectation; anticipation.

प्रत्याशित pratya:shit (*a*) expected; anticipated/anticipatory.

प्रत्या/शी pratya:shi: (*nm*) a candidate; ~शिता candidature.

प्रत्या/श्रय pratya:shshray (*nm*) a coverture; refuge, shelter; hence ~श्रित (*a*).

प्रत्या/स्मरण pratya:smarān (*nm*) recall/recalling; ~स्मृत recalled.

प्रत्याहार pratya:ha:r (*nm*) retreat, withdrawal (esp. of the senses from external objects); obstruction; (in Gram.) the comprehension of a series of letters or roots etc. into one syllable.

प्रत्या/ह्वान pratya:hva:n (*nm*) recall, calling back; ~हूत recalled, called back.

प्रत्युक्ति pratyukti (*nf*) reply; counter-plea, counter-argument.

प्रत्युत pratyut (*ind*) on the other hand, contrary to, but.

प्रत्युत्तर pratyuttar (*nm*) reply; replication.

प्रत्युत्पन्न pratyutpānn (*a*) ready; prompt; born/emerged there and then; ~मति witty, quick-witted person, (blessed with) ready wit; ~मतित्व wit, ready wit.

प्रत्युदाहरण pratyuda:harān (*nm*) counter-example, an instance countering the one cited by the opponent.

प्रत्युप/कार pratyupka:r (*nm*) a good turn in return for another; responsive benevolence/beneficence; ~कारी one who returns an obligation; one who does a good turn in return, responsively benevolent/beneficent.

प्रत्युपाय pratyupa:y (*nm*) a counter-measure, counter-step.

प्रत्यूष pratyu:sh (*nm*) the dawn, day-break.

प्रत्येक pratyek (*a*) each, every one, each and every one.

प्रथम prathām (*a*) the first; foremost; prima; **–अक्षर** (**प्रथमाक्षर**) initial letter; **–दर्शन** first sight, first meeting; **–पुरुष** the third person (in Gram.); **–प्रदर्शन** premiere; **–यौवन** the prime of youth; **~क** the first; primary; **~तः** firstly, first of all, in the first place.

प्रथमा prathamā: (*nf*) the nominative case (in Gram.).

प्रथमार्द्ध prathamā:rddh (*nm*) the first half.

प्रथा pratha: (*nf*) custom; practice, usage; **~गत** customary.

प्रदक्षिणा pradakshinā: (*nf*) circumambulation, to go round (a deity's idol) so as to always keep it to the right.

प्रदत्त pradatt (*a*) given. gifted, granted (by), bestowed.

प्रदर pradar (*nm*) moenorrhagia (a disease of women).

प्रदर्श/न pradarshān (*nm*) a show; an exhibition, a display; performance; demonstration; **~क** a performer, showman, one who shows/exhibits/displays/ demonstrates; **~नप्रिय** an exhibitionist; **~नप्रियता** exhibitionism.

प्रदर्शनी pradarshanī: (*nf*) an exhibition.

प्रदर्शित pradarshit (*a*) showed; exhibited, displayed; performed; demonstrated.

प्रदाता prada:ta: (*nm*) a giver; donor.

प्रदान prada:n (*nm*) giving; donating; bestowing, granting; delivery; **–करना** to give; to donate; to bestow, to grant; to deliver.

प्रदाय prada:y (*nm*) supply; present, gift.

प्रदाह prada:h (*nm*) burning, ignition; inflammation; combustion; **~कर** causing burn/inflammation; scorching; igniting.

प्रदीप pradi:p (*nm*) a lamp; an instrument of illumination (as **काव्य-प्रदीप**); one who achieves distinction/reputation for (as **कुल-प्रदीप**); **~न** illumination; causing light/glow, illuminating.

प्रदी/प्त pradi:pt (*a*) illuminated, lit/lighted, glowing; awakened; roused; **~प्ति** light, glow; illumination.

प्रदेश pradesh (*nm*) a region; territory; zone; district; **~गत** regional; **–निष्ठा** regional loyalty; **~परक** regional; **~परकता** regionalism; **~परायण** regional(ist); **~परायणता** regionalism; **–भाषा** regional language.

प्रदेशीय pradeshi:y (*a*) regional; belonging or pertaining to a region.

प्रदोष pradosh (*nm*) (the fast undertaken on) the thirteenth day of each lunar fortnight; also **–व्रत**.

प्रधान pradhā:n (*nm*) the president, chairman; *pradhan*; (*a*) chief, head, principal, main; **~ता/त्व** presidentship; chairmanship dominance, supremacy; pre-eminence; **–कार्यालय** headquarter; **–मंत्री** Prime Minister, Premier.

प्रधानतः pradha:ntah (*adv*) mainly, chiefly; primarily, first of all.

प्रधानांग pradha:nā:ṅg (*nm*) essential part; major portion; chief organ.

प्रधानाचार्य pradha:nā:cha:ry (*nm*) Principal (of a college).

प्रधानाध्यापक pradha:nā:dhya:pak (*nm*) the Headmaster, Principal (of a school).

प्रधानामात्य pradha:nā:mā:tty (*nm*) the Prime Minister, Premier.

प्रधानी pradha:nī: (*nf*) the office or function of a *pradhan*.

प्रनामी pranā:mī: (*nf*) present or offering made to the mentor/preceptor while making a salutation.

प्रपंच prapāṇch (*nm*) illusory creation, manifestation, delusion; mundane affairs; artifice, manipulation; ~बुद्धि manipulating, artful; –रचना to work out a conspiracy, to manipulate.

प्रपंची prapāṇchi: (*nm*) a manipulator, cunning person; one who talks sweet nothings; (*a*) scheming; creating an illusory world by one's talk, too talkative.

प्रपत्ति prapatti (*nf*) exclusive devotion, single-mindedness.

प्रपत्र prapattr (*nm*) a charter; form.

प्रपन्न prapann (*a* and *nm*) admitted under protection, granted patronage; given shelter, seeking protection/shelter.

प्रपलाय/न prapala:yān (*nm*) (the act or process of) absconding; ~क an absconder.

प्रपात prapa:t (*nm*) a fall, waterfall, cataract.

प्रपानक prapa:nāk (*nm*) see पना.

प्रपिताम/ह prapita:mah (*nm*) paternal great-grandfather; ~ही paternal great-grandmother.

प्रपीड़/न prapi:ṛān (*nm*) torture/torturing; oppression/oppressing; harassment/harassing; hence ~क (*nm*).

प्रपौ/त्र prapauttr (*nm*) great-grandson; ~त्री great grand-daughter.

प्रफुल्ल praphull (*a*) blooming, blossomed; cheerful, gay, delighted; hence ~ता (*nf*); ~नयन/नेत्र gleaming/beaming eyes; gay-eyed; ~मुख/वदन gay-looking; cheerful/beaming face.

प्रफुल्लित praphullit (*a*) see प्रफुल्ल.

प्रबंध prabandh (*nm*) management, arrangement; administration; a dissertation; a comprehensive connected narrative; ~क/~कर्ता a manager; organiser; an executive; –कल्पना epic imagination, comprehensive imagination, imagination of vast epic proportions; ~कारिणी समिति executive committee; governing body; ~कारी executive, managing; -काव्य an epic poem; -निदेशक managing director; -व्यवस्था management; –संचालक managing director; -संपादक managing editor; -समिति managing committee.

प्रबंधक prabandhak (*nm*) a manager; an organiser; executive.

प्रबल prabal (*a*) strong, mighty; forceful; powerful; violent, vigorous; predominant, dominant; ~ता strength, force, power; vigorousness, predominance, dominance, loudness.

प्रबुद्ध prabuddh (*a*) awakened, aroused (from slumber); conscious; enlightened; hence ~ता (*nf*).

प्रबोध, ~न prabodh, ~an (*nm*) awakening, rousing (from slumber); consciousness; enlightenment.

प्रबोधक prabodhak (*nm*) one who (or that which) rouses (from slumber), one who (or that which) enlightens; a mentor, preceptor.

प्रभंजन prabhānjan (*nm*) a hurricane.

प्रभव prabhav (*nm*) birth, creation; origin, source.

प्रभविष्णु prabhvishnu (*a*) influential; efficacious, effective; impressive; ~**ता** capacity to influence; efficacy, effectiveness; impressiveness.

प्रभा prabha: (*nf*) lustre, radiance, refulgence; ~**कर** the sun; ~**मंडल** a halo.

प्रभाग prabha:g (*nm*) a division (of an organisation); section.

प्रभात prabha:t (*nm*) the morning; dawn; -**काल/समय** the morning time; **फेरी** singing or slogan-raising groups going round in the morning (to celebrate an important event or for propaganda purposes).

प्रभाती prabha:ti: (*nf*) a typical morning song.

प्रभाव prabha:v (*nm*) influence; effect; impact; impression; ~**कर**/~**कारी** influential; impressive; effective (act, deed, etc.); ~**कार** effectsman; ~**वश्य** susceptible; ~**वश्यता** susceptibility; ~**शालिता** effectiveness, impressiveness; ~**शाली** influential; impressive; effective (person); ~**हीन** unimpressive, devoid of any influence, creating no impact; void; ~**हीनता** unimpressiveness; voidness; the fact or state of having no influence, creating no impression; neutralisation; -**डालना** to impress; to iufluence; -**से ऊपर उठना** to rise above somebody's influence.

प्रभावक prabha:vak (*a*) influential impressive; effective.

प्रभावान्वि/त prabha:va:nvit (*a*) influenced, impressed, having an impact; ~**ति** unity of impact/impression; pointedness of influence/impression.

प्रभावित prabha:vit (*a*) influenced; impressed, receiving an impact.

प्रभा/वी prabha:vi: (*a*) effective, efficacious; dominant. predominant; ~**विता** effectiveness, efficacy; dominance, predominance.

प्रभीत prabhi:t (*a*) terrorized, horrified; panicky.

प्रभु prabhu (*a*) sovereign; hegemonic; all-powerful; (*nm*) a sovereign; the Master; -**भक्त** a loyal devotee; loyal to the Master; –**राज्य** a sovereign state; –**शक्ति** a sovereign power; sovereignty; –**शासन** sovereign rule; –**सत्ता** sovereignty; sovereign authority; ~**सत्तात्मक** sovereign; ~**सत्ता-संपन्न** sovereign; –**को प्यारा होना** to kick the bucket, to leave for one's heavenly abode.

प्रभु/ता, ~**त्व** prabhuta: (*nf*), ~tv (*nm*) sovereignty; hegemony; power; authority, predominance, dominance; Mastery; –**पाइ काहि मद नाहीं** power corrupts and absolute power corrupts absolutely; power begets arrogance.

प्रभूत prabbu:t (*a*) plenty, abundant; ample.

प्रभृति prabhriti (*ind*) etcetera, etc. etc.

प्रभेद prabhed (*nm*) variety; types, kinds,

प्रमत्त pramatt (*a*) intoxicated, dead drunk; hence ~**ता** (*nf*).

प्रमा pramā: (*nf*) understanding; correct notion, accurate perception; ~**त्व** accuracy of perception.

प्रमाण pramā:ṇ (*nm*) evidence, proof; testimony; authority; (in logical jargon) a means of acquiring *prama*: (which are six according to the veda:nt, viz. प्रत्यक्ष (perception by the senses), अनुमान (inference), उपमान (analogy or comparison), शब्द or आप्त वचन (verbal authority), अनुपलब्धि or अभाव-प्रत्यक्ष (non-perception or negative proof), अर्थापत्ति (inference from circumstances); ~कुशल skilful in arguing, skilled in argumentation; ~त्व correctness, authority; -पत्र a certificate; ~पुरुष an arbitrator; mediator; an umpire; ~भूत authoritative; -वचन/वाक्य authoritative statement; authoritative version; ~शास्त्र logic; ~शास्त्री a logician; ~शास्त्रीय logical.

प्रमाणकर्त्ता pramā:ṇkarta: (*nm*) a certifier, one who proves/testifies.

प्रमाणतः pramā:ṇtah (*adv*) according to the evidence/proof, as a proof/an evidence.

प्रमाणित pramā:ṇit (*a*) proved; testified; certified; authenticated; -करना to prove; to testify; to certify; to authenticate.

प्रमाणी/करण pramā:ṇī:karaṇ (*nm*) attestation; act or process of proving/certifying/testifying/authenticating; ~कृत attested; proved; testified; certified; authenticated.

प्रमाता pramā:ta: (*nm*) one who can appreciate, one who understands a subject, one who has correct notion or idea (of something).

प्रमाता/मह pramā:ta:mah (*nm*) maternal great-grandfather; ~मही maternal great-grandmother.

प्रमात्रा pramā:ttra: (*nf*) quantum, amount.

प्रमाद pramā:d (*nm*) negligence; carelessness; ~पूर्ण negligent; careless; ~वश through negligence.

प्रमादी pramā:di: (*a*) negligent: careless (person).

प्रमाप prama:p (*nm*) measurement, scanning, gauge.

प्रमापी prama:pi: (*nm*) a gauge, an instrument for measuring.

प्रमु/क्त pramukt (*a*) unfettered; freed; liberated, delivered; hence ~क्ति (*nf*).

प्रमुख pramukh (*a*) chief; foremost; leading, outstanding, principal; ~ता dominance, eminence, state of being foremost/outstanding, supremacy.

प्रमुदित pramudit (*a*) delighted, pleased, glad, full of joy; ~हृदय full of joy, delighted in heart; glad.

प्रमेय pramey (*nm*) a theorem, probandum.

प्रमे/ह prameh (*nm*) any urinary disease; ~ही suffering from some urinary disease.

प्रमोद pramod (*nm*) entertainment, mirth; joy, delight, gladness.

प्रयत्न prayatn (*nm*) effort, endeavour; attempt; (in Phonetics) manner of articulation; -लाघव economy of effort; ~वान्/शील assiduous, diligent, one who makes efforts; hence ~शीलता (*nf*); -करना to try, to make an effort; to attempt/endeavour.

प्रयाण prayā:ṇ (*nm*) departure, setting out; march; death; -काल/समय departure time; the end.

प्रयास praya:s (*nm*) an effort, endeavour, attempt.

प्रयुक्त prayukt (*a*) used; employed; applied; practical; –**बल** applied force; –**विज्ञान** applied science.

प्रयोक्ता pryokta: (*nm*) user, one who employs/applies; an experimenter.

प्रयोग prayog (*nm*) an experiment; use, employmet; application; exercise; ~**कर्त्ता** an experimenter; one who uses/employs/applies; ~**धर्मा** an experimenter; ~**निपुण** skilled through practice, one who has achieved perfection through experiments/practice; ~**वाद**/~**वादिता** experimentalism; ~**वादी** an experimentalist; experimentalistic; ~**शील** prone to make experiments, ; given to experimenting hence ~**शीलता** (*nf*).

प्रयोगत: prayogtah (*adv*) through experimentation; practically.

प्रयोगशाला prayogsha:la: (*nf*) a laboratory; -**उपकरण** laboratory equipment; -**सुविधाएँ** laboratory facilities.

प्रयोजन prayojān (*nm*) purpose; motive, intention; cause; use; ~**वाद** / ~**वादिता** purposivism; ~**वादी** a purposivist; purposivistic; –**सिद्धि** achievement/fulfilment of a purpose.

प्रयोजनीय prayojanī:y (*a*) usable; applicable; that can be employed/applied/used; hence ~**ता** (*nf*).

प्रयोज्य prayojjy (*a*) to be or worth being used or employed or practised; hence ~**त्व** (*nm*).

प्रलं/ब pralāmb (*a*) pendulous; suspended; prolonged; lengthened; also ~**बित** (*a*).

प्रलयं/कर pralayāṅkar (*a*) catastrophic; devastating, causing destruction or ruin, spelling disaster; hence ~**करी** (*a*).

प्रलय pralay (*nf*) universal destruction, annihilation, destruction of the whole world; catastrophe; ~**कर/कारी** see **प्रलयंकर**; –**काल** the time for universal destruction, the moment of annihilation; ~**वाद** catastrophism; ~**वादी** a catastrophist; catastrophic; –**के बादल छाना/मँडराना** clouds of catastrophe to gather thick; –**मचाना** to work havoc, to raise a tumult.

प्रला/प prala:p (*nm*) logorrhoea; prate, prattle, babble; disjointed/meaningless utterance; hence ~**पी** (*a* and *nm*).

प्रलुब्ध pralubdh (*a*) allured, tempted, induced; seduced.

प्रलेख pralekh (*nm*) a document; ~**न** documentation; ~**बद्ध** documented.

प्रलेप pralep (*nm*) an unguent, ointment, a salve; hence ~**न** (*nm*.)

प्रलोभन pralobhan (*nm*) allurement, temptation, inducement; seduction.

प्रवंचना pravāṇchanā: (*nf*) deprivation; circumvention; deceipt.

प्रवंचित pravāṇchit (*a*) deprived; circumvented; deceived.

प्रवक्ता pravakta: (*nm*) a spokesman.

प्रवचन pravachān (*nm*) a (religious) discourse; sermon.

प्रवण pravāṇ (*a*) inclined or disposed or prone (to); devoted (to); intent (upon); full (of); ~**ता** inclination, disposition, devotedness; propensity, proneness; a gradient.

प्रवर pravar (*a*) senior; superior; select(ed); eminent; as a suffix it means the best, most excellent (as **पंडितप्रवर**); -**समिति** a select committee.

वरता pravarta: (*nf*) seniority; superiority; selectness; eminence; ~नुसार on the basis of/according to seniority or superiority.

वर्त्तक pravartak (*nm*) a pioneer, innovator; one who introduces (something new); one who persuades; an operator.

वर्त्तन pravartān (*nm*) pioneering, introducing something new; operation; persuasion; ~शील pioneering; operative; hence ~शीलता (*nf*).

वर्त्तित pravartit (*a*) pioneered; introduced; put into operation/practice.

वर्त्ती pravarti: (*a*) pioneering; operative.

व/र्धन pravardhān (*nm*) amplification; magnification; development; progress, increase; ~र्धक amplifier, magnifier; hence ~र्धित (*a*).

वहमान pravahmā:n (*a*) flowing; fluent; hence ~ता (*nf*).

वाचक prava:chak (*nm*) a reader; sermonizer, one who delivers religious discourses.

वात prava:t (*nm*) a storm.

वा/द prava:d (*nm*) a rumour; slander, calumny; ~दी a rumour-monger; a slanderer, calumniator.

वारण prava:rān (*nm*) warding off; countering.

वा/स prava:s (*nm*) dwelling abroad; foreign residence; migration; hence ~सन; ~सित sent abroad, exiled.

वासी prava:si: (*nm*) a migrant; one who stays abroad; (*a*) migratory.

वा/ह prava:h (*nm*) flow; fluency; an unbroken sequence; ~हमय fluent, having a flow; ~हित flowed, consigned to a flow of water, etc.

प्रविधि pravidhi (*nf*) a technique; ~ज्ञ a technician; ~ज्ञता technical expertise.

प्रवि/ष्ट pravisht (*a*) entered; admitted; ~ष्टि an entry.

प्रवीण pravi:n (*a*) proficient, adept, expert; ~ता proficiency, expertness.

प्रवृत्त pravritt (*a*) engaged (in); inclined towards; tending to; actively employed (in); active.

प्रवृत्ति pravritti (*nf*) mentality; trend, tendency; (mental) inclination/disposition; instinct; activity; ~गत pertaining to or on the basis of trends/tendencies; –मार्ग (the path of) active association with and interest in mundane affairs; ~वाद the philosophy of active association with mundane existence; hence ~वादी (*a* and *nm*).

प्रवेश pravesh (*nm*) entry, admission, access, inlet; gate, entrance; –द्वार entrance, inlet; gate; threshold; -पत्र a ticket, an admission ticket; visa; -शुल्क admission fee; hence ~क (*nm*); ~न (*nm*).

प्रवेशिका praveshika: (*nf*) a propaedeutic, an elementary study on a subject, introductory study.

प्रवेश्य praveshy (*a*) accessible, where one can get admission/entry; worth entering into; hence; ~ता (*nf*).

प्रव्र/जन pravrajān (*nm*) renunciation; migration; ~जित (one who has) renounced the world; migrated; ~ज्या renunciation, asceticism; migration.

प्रव्राजक pravra:jak (*nm*) an ascetic, a wandering mendicant; a migrant.

प्रव्राजी pravra:ji: (*nm*) an ascetic; a migrant; (*a*) renunciatory, ascetic; migratory.

प्रशंसक prashānsak (*nm*) an admirer, eulogist, one who praises; a fan.

प्रशं/सा prashānsa: (*nf*) praise, admiration; eulogy; ~सनीय praiseworthy, admirable; laudable, commendable; ~सित praised, admired, eulogized; ~स्य see ~सनीय; ~सा करते न थकना to praise no end, to go on singing praises of; ~सा के पुल बाँधना to praise in hyperboles.

प्रश/मन prashamān (*nm*) pacification, soothing, mitigation; subdual; subsidence; hence ~मित (*a*).

प्रशस्त prashast (*a*) vast; wide, broad (as –ललाट); extensive, expansive.

प्रशस्ति prashasti (*nf*) praise, admiration; eulogy; -गाथा eulogical narrative, singing the praise (of).

प्रशांत prashā:nt (*a*) pacific, pacified; tranquil, quiet, calm; ~चित्त tranquil, quiet (person); ~ता calmness, quiet; peace, tranquillity; –महासागर the Pacific Ocean.

प्रशांति prashā:nti (*nf*) peace, tranquillity; quiet, calmness.

प्रशाखा prasha:kha: (*nf*) an offshoot; a twig.

प्रशास/क prasha:sak (*nm*) an administrator; ruler; ~कीय administrative; ~कीय दायित्व administrative responsibility.

प्रशास/न prasha:san (*nm*) administration; rule; ~न–कार्य administrative work/affairs; ~निक administrative.

प्रशासित prasha:sit (*a*) administered; ruled.

प्रशि/क्षण prashikshān (*nm*) training; ~क्षण-क्रम training course; ~क्षण-शिविर a training-camp; ~क्षक an instructor; ~क्षा training, ~क्षार्थी a trainee; ~क्षित trained; ~क्षु a trainee.

प्रश्न prashn (*nm*) a question, query; interrogation; interpellation; problem; ~कर्ता a questioner, an interrogator; interpellant; -पत्र a question-paper; ~माला questionnaire; interrogatives; ~वाचक interrogative; ०चिह्न mark of interrogation; ~वाचक सर्वनाम interrogative pronoun; –उठाना/खड़ा करना to raise/pose a question; –गेहूँ उत्तर जौ the answer to be beside the question; प्रश्नों की झड़ी लगाना to fire a volley of questions.

प्रश्नावली prashnā:vali: (*nf*) a questionnaire; (a set of) exercises.

प्रश्नोत्तर prashnottar (*nm*) question and answer.

प्रश्नोत्तरी prashnottari: (*nf*) a questionnaire; catechism; interrogatories; quiz.

प्रश्रय prashshray (*nm*) patronage, protection; shelter; support; backing; ~दाता a patron, protector, supporter.

प्रश्वास prashshwa:s (*nm*) exhalation.

प्रसंग prasāṅg (*nm*) context; occasion; sexual intercourse, coition; -भेद difference of the context, contextual difference; ~तः incidentally; ~वश/~वशात् incidentally as demanded by the context.

प्रसंवा/दी prasāmva:di: (*a*) harmonic

~दिता harmony.

प्रसंविदा prasāmvida: (nm) a covenant.

प्रसन्न prasann (a) pleased; happy, cheerful, delighted, glad; ~चित्त cheerful, happy, delighted; hence ~चित्तता (nf); –नयन cheerful eyes, beaming/gleaming eyes; ~मुख/वदन cheerful, looking cheerful; –शैली lucid style.

प्रसन्नता prasannāta: (nf) happiness; cheerfulness, delight; pleasure; gladness; ~पूर्वक happily, cheerfully, with pleasure.

प्रस/रण prasaraṇ (nm) (the act or process of) expansion; dispersion; scattering; ~रित expanded; dispersed; scattered.

प्रस/र्पण prasarpaṇ (nm) (the act or process of) creeping; ~र्पित creeping, creepy.

प्रसव prasav (nm) delivery, childbirth, labour; (a) natal; –कक्ष labour room; –काल time of delivery/child-birth; ~गृह see ~शाला; –पीड़ा/वेदना/व्यथा labour pains, pangs of child-birth; ~वती a woman who has delivered a child, a woman in confinement; ~शाला a maternity home.

प्रसविनी prasavinī: (nf) a progenitress, woman who gives birth to a child; (a woman) begetting a child.

प्रसाद prasā:d (nm) blessing, boon; grace; offerings made to an idol (and later distributed amongst the devotees); leavings of food of a pre-eminent religious person; lucidity (of the style of writing etc.); –गुण lucidity (of style); ०संपन्न lucid; –पात्र favourite, one who is in good books.

प्रसादत्व prasā:dattv (nm) lucidity

(of the style of writing).

प्रसादन prasa:dan (nm) cheering up, pleasing; gratification.

प्रसादी prasa:di: (nf) offering made to a deity (and later partaken of by the devotees as leavings).

प्रसाधन prasa:dhān (nm) make-up; make-up aids, beauty aids; cosmetics; adornment; -गृह a beauty saloon; -सामग्री beauty aids, make-up aids; cosmetics.

प्रसामान्य prasa:mā:nny (a) normal; ~क a norm.

प्रसार prasa:r (nm) expansion, dispersion; scattering, extensity; spread; propagation; circulation.

प्रसारण prasa:rāṇ (nm) a broadcast/broadcasting; (the act or process of) expanding/dispersing/scattering/extending/spreading/propagating; -सेवा broadcasting service.

प्रसारित prasa:rit (a) broadcast; expanded; extended; propagated.

प्रसि/द्ध prasiddh (a) famous, reputed, well-known, renowned; ~द्धि fame, repute, renown.

प्रसु/प्त prasupt (a) dormant; asleep; in abeyance; ~प्तावस्था dormant state, in sleep/slumber; abeyance; ~प्ति dormancy, slumber; abeyance.

प्रसू prasu: (nf) a mother, progenitress; one who bears/delivers (a child).

प्रसू/त prasu:t (a) born, brought forth, delivered; ~ता a woman after child-birth/in confinement.

प्रसूति prasu:ti (nf) child-birth, delivery; maternity; labour; offspring; -अवकाश maternity leave; -कक्ष labour-room; -गृह maternity home; ~ज labour pains, pangs of child-birth; -ज्वर post-delivery fever; ~शाला maternity home.

प्रसून prasu:n (*nm*) a flower; -**वर्षा** shower of flowers.

प्रसृत prasrit (*a*) expanded, extended; spread; propagated.

प्रस्तर prastar (*nm*) stone; rock; entablature; -**प्रतिमा** a stone-statue; -**युग** stone age.

प्रस्ताव prasta:v (*nm*) resolution, motion; proposal; –**पारित करना** to pass a resolution.

प्रस्तावना prasta:vnā: (*nf*) a preamble; prologue; preface.

प्रस्तावित prasta:vit (*a*) proposed; projected.

प्रस्तुत prastut (*a*) present(ed); submitted; produced; ready; (subject etc.) under study or discussion; (*nm*) anything that is in sight or of immediate concern; ~**कर्ता** producer, one who presents/ submits; impresario; –**विषय** the subject under consideration/study.

प्रस्तुति prastuti (*nf*) presentation; submission; production; recital; readiness; eulogium, eulogy.

प्रस्तुतीकरण prastuti:karaṉ (*nm*) presentation; production (as of a programme).

प्रस्तोता prastota: (*nm*) one who presents; producer (as of a Radio programme).

प्र/स्थान prastha:n (*nm*) departure, setting out (on a journey); march; articles placed in advance at the auspicious moment in the direction in which one is to journey (in case one's departure is delayed due to some reason); hence ~**स्थित** (*a*).

प्रस्थाप/न, ~ना prastha:pān (*nm*), ~nā: (*nf*) establishment, establishing well; installation.

प्रस्थापित prastha:pit (*a*) well-established, installed.

प्रस्फुट prasphuṭ (*a*) manifest; distinct, clear.

प्रस्फु/टन prasphuṭān (*nm*) efflorescence; manifestation; opening up, blooming; becoming distinct; ~**टित** effloresced; manifested; opened; bloomed; distinct.

प्रस्फु/रण prasphurāṉ (*nm*) emergence, emanation; manifestation; coming up; thrill; hence ~**रित** (*a*).

प्रस्फोट(न) prasphoṭān (*nm*) explosion, bursting up; manifestation.

प्रस्वे/द prasved (*nm*) sweat, perspiration; ~**दी** sweating, perspiring; ~**दित** sweating, perspiring.

प्रहत prahat (*a*) afflicted; beaten; overwhelmed.

प्रहर prahar (*nm*) a measure of time equivalent to three hours; period of three hours.

प्रहरी prahari: (*nm*) a watchman, guard, sentinel.

प्रहर्ष, ~ण praharsh, ~āṉ (*nm*) thrill, merriment, hilarity.

प्रहर्षित praharshit (*a*) thrilled, merry, hilarious.

प्रहस/न prahasān (*nm*) a comedy; ~**नात्मक** comical.

प्रहार praha:r (*nm*) an assault; a blow, stroke; ~**क/कर्त्ता** one who makes an assault or strikes a blow.

प्रहेलिका prahelika: (*nf*) a riddle; an enclave.

प्रांगण pra:ṅgāṉ (*nm*) a courtyard; an enclave.

प्रांजल prā:ṇjal (*a*) lucid, clear; refined; ~**ता** lucidity, clarity; refinement.

प्रांत prā:nt (*nm*) a province; territory; country; district; ~**पति** governor of a province.

प्रांतर prā:ntar (*nm*) a territory; district.

ांतीय pra:nti:y (*a*) provincial; territorial; ~ता provinciality; provincialism.

ाइमरी pra:imari: (*a*) primary (only in the context of a school); –स्कूल a primary school.

ाइवेट pra:ivet (*a*) private, personal; secret; –सेक्रेटरी a private secretary.

ाकट्य pra:katy (*nm*) appearance; advent; manifestation.

ाकार pra:ka:r (*nm*) a parapet; rampart.

ाकाशिक pra:ka:shik (*a*) optical, pertaining to light.

ाकृत pra:kkrit (*a*) natural; unsophisticated, unprocessed; inherent, innate; common; –जन common man; ~वाद/~वादिता naturalism; ~वादी a naturalist; naturalistic.

ाकृतिक pra:kkritik (*a*) natural, nature-made; physical; unsophisticated; unrefined; –अध्ययन a study of nature; –चिकित्सा naturopathy; –भूगोल physical geography; –विज्ञान natural science, physical science.

ाक् pra:k —an allomorph of प्राच् occurring as a prefix in a number of words and imparting the meaning of before, prior to, former, etc.; east; ~काल former times, olden times; ~कालिक/कालीन former; olden; ~कृत performed earlier (as deeds) etc.; ~पक्व premature.

ाक्कथन pra:kkathan (*nm*) a foreword; -लेखक foreword-writer, author of the foreword.

ाक्तन pra:ktān (*a*) former; olden, ancient.

ाक्क/लन pra:kkalān (*nm*) estimate; ~लित estimated; ~लन-सार abstract of estimate.

ाक्क/ल्पना pra:kkalpanā: (*nf*) hypothesis; ~ल्पक, ~ल्पित hypothetical.

प्राक्षेपि/क pra:kshepik (*a*) ballistic, ~की ballistics.

प्रागल्भ्य pra:galbhy (*nm*) see प्रगल्भता under प्रगल्भ.

प्रागैतिहासिक pra:gaitiha:sik (*a*) prehistoric(al); –काल/युग prehistoric times/age; hence ~ता (*nf*).

प्राग् pra:g—an allomorph of प्राच् which occurs in a number of words and imparts the meaning of before, prior to, former etc.; east; ~अनुराग (प्रागनुराग) wooing, courtship; ~अभिहित (प्रागभिहित) afore-mentioned; stated earlier; ~उक्ति (प्रागुक्ति) prediction, forecast; earlier statement; ~उत्तर (प्रागुत्तर) east-northern; ~रूप archetype; ~वृत्त/वृत्तांत antecedents; earlier happenings.

प्राङ् pra:ṅ —an allomorph of प्राच् occurring in a number of words and imparting the meaning of before, prior to, former, etc.; east; ~न्याय res judicata; ~मुख facing the east; east-directed.

प्राचार्य pra:cha:ry (*nm*) principal (of a college); hence ~त्व (*nm*).

प्राची pra:chi: (*nf*) the east; the eastern quarter; the orient; –प्रतीची the orient and the occident.

प्राचीन pra:chī:n (*a*) ancient; old; outdated; antique; –कथा an ancient tale/story; ~तर older; more ancient; earlier; ~तम oldest, most ancient; earliest; ~ता antiquity, ancientness; ०-प्रेम love of antiquity; archaism; primitivism; ~ता-प्रेमी a lover of antiquity; archaist; primitivist.

प्राचीर pra:chi:r (*nf*) a parapet, rampart, surrounding wall (of a city, fort, etc.)

प्राचुर्य pra:chury (*nm*) abundance, plenty.

प्राच्य pra:chy (*a*) east, eastern; oriental; belonging or pertaining to the east; **–भाषा** an oriental language; **~विद्/वेत्ता** an orientalist; **~विद्या** oriental learning, orientology.

प्राज्ञ pra:ggy (*a*) prudent; intelligent, sharp, brilliant; **~म्मन्य** considering oneself to be too prudent; prudence-proud; **~म्मन्यता** thinking oneself to be very prudent; prudence-pride.

प्राण prā:n (*nf*) life; vital breath, vital air; vitality; soul, spirit; sweetheart; (in Gram.) aspiration in the articulation of letters; **-आधार** sweetheart; life-breath; source of sustenance; **~कर** animating, life-giving, that which infuses life or inspires; **-कष्ट** mortal agony; pain of death; **~घात** killing; assassination; murder; **~घातक** fatal; causing destruction of life; killing; **-त्याग** abandonment of life; resigning of life; expiry, death; **-दंड** capital punishment, punishment of death; **~द/दायी** infusing/injecting life, animating, enlivening; **~दाता** life-giver; one who saves somebody's life; **~दान** a gift of life; saving/sparing somebody's life; **~धन** as dear as life; beloved; **~धारी** a living being/organism, a creature; **~नाथ** lord/master of life; husband; **~नाश** destruction of life; killing; **~नाशक** destroyer of life; mortal, deadly; **~पति** see **~नाथ**; **~प्यारा** dear (to soul), beloved, sweetheart; hence **~प्यारी** (*nf*); **~प्रतिष्ठा** infusion/injectment of life; ceremony of consecrating an idol; **~प्रद** life-giving, infusing or imparting life; **~प्रिय** see **~प्यारा**; **-भय** fear of life; risk of life; **~मय** full of vitality; endowed with breath of life; a living being; **०कोश** the vital or organic case; **~ मूलक** vital; essential to or concerned with life; **~मूलकतावाद** vitalism; vital part of the body; **~वायु** vital breath; **~शक्ति** vitality; **-संशय** risk of life, fear of life; **~सम** as dear as life; beloved; **~हर/हारी** mortal, deadly causing the end of life; **~हानि** loss of life; **~हीन** lifeless, inanimate; **–आना** to feel relieved of a scare/fear; **–उड़ जाना** to be mortally scared/frightened; to get terribly panicky; **–ओठों तक आना** see **–मुँह को आना**; **–कंठ में आना** to be mortally afflicted; to be on the verge of death; to be in a frightful suspense; **–का गाहक** a seeker after one's life, destroyer of life mortally oppressive person; **–गले तक आना** to be on the verge of death; death to be imminent; to be in a terrible suspense; **–छूटना/जाना/निकलना** the breath to flit or leave the system; to expire; to die; the life to come to an end; **–छोड़ना/त्यागना** to abandon life; to expire, to die; **–डालना** to infuse/inject life, to animate; **–देना** to die, to give up life; to love more dearly than life; **–निकलना** to die, life to cease to exist; **-पखेरू उड़ जाना** to kick the bucket, to expire; **–फूंकना** to inject life into, to cause to revive; **–बचाना** to save somebody's life; to get rid of, to evade persecution/painful confrontation; **–मुँह**

आना to suffer mortal agony; to be in a frightful suspense; –मुट्ठी में/हथेली पर लिये फिरना to be ever-ready to court death; to face all sorts of risks; –लेना to kill; to tease/persecute to death; –सूखना to be in a frightful suspense; प्राणों से भी प्यारा dearer than one's own life, all in all, very very dear; प्राणों से हाथ धोना to lose life, to be pushed out of existence; प्राणों पर आ बनना to be under a risk of life; to be confronted with mortal agony; प्राणों पर खेलना/खेल जाना to risk/stake one's life.

प्राणवत्ता prā:n̲vatta: (*nf*) vitality; animatedness, spiritedness; the state of being full of life/spirit.

प्राणवान् prā:n̲vā:n (*a*) full of vitality, spirited, animated; strong, powerful, vigorous.

प्राणांत pra:n̲ā:nt (*nm*) the end of life, expiry, death; ~क fatal, mortal, causing the end of life.

प्राणाधार prā:n̲ā:dha:r (*nm*) see प्राण –(आधार).

प्राणाधिक prā:n̲ā:dhik (*a*) dearer than life; all in all, beloved.

प्राणा/याम prā:n̲ā:ya:m (*nm*) exercising control over the process of breathing, restraining or suspending the breath during the mental recitation of the name of a deity or as a religious or *yogic* exercise; ~यामी one who practises प्राणायाम.

प्राणाहुति prā:n̲ā:huti (*nf*) sacrifice of life; martyrdom.

प्राणि prā:n̲ī —an allomorph of प्राणी; ~जगत the animal world/kingdom; the world of living beings; animal life; ~विज्ञान Zoology; ~वैज्ञानिक a zoologist; zoological; –हिंसा killing of or violence towards living beings.

प्राणी prā:n̲ī: (*nm*) a living being, living organism, a creature; an animal.

प्राणे/श prā:n̲ēsh, ~श्वर ~war (*nm*) lord/master of life; beloved, darling.

प्राणोत्सर्ग prā:n̲ōtsarg (*nm*) sacrifice of life; martyrdom.

प्रात: pra:tah (*nm* and *ind*) early (in the) morning, (at) dawn; ~कर्म/~कृत्य morning chores, essential chores performed in the morning; ~काल early (in the) morning; ~कालिक/कालीन pertaining to, or performed in, the morning, of early morning; ~स्मरण remembering, or reciting the name of God in the morning prayer; ~स्मरणीय worthy of being remembered every morning; revered.

प्रातराश pra:tara:sh (*nm*) breakfast.

प्रातिनिधिक pra:tinidhik (*a* and *nm*) representative; –शासन/सरकार representative government.

प्रातिपदिक pra:tipadik (*nm*) the crude form of base of a noun, a noun in its uninflicted state.

प्रातिभ pra:tibh (*a*) intuitive; –ज्ञान intuitive knowledge, intuition.

प्रातिभासिक pra:tibha:sik (*a*) virtual, illusory, existing only in appearance.

प्रातिरूपिक pra:tiru:pik (*a*) counterfeit, spurious, having formal resemblance.

प्रातिवेशिक pra:tiveshik (*nm*) a neighbour.

प्रातीतिक pra:ti:tik (*a*) illusory; imaginary.

प्राथमिक pra:thamik (*a*) primary; elementary; having precedence; –उपचार/चिकित्सा first aid; –शिक्षा primary education.

प्राथमिकता pra:thamikta: (*nf*) priority; precedence; **-क्रम** order of priority; order of precedence.

प्रादर्श pra:darsh (*nm*) a specimen.

प्रादु/र्भाव pra:durbha:v (*nm*) appearance, manifestation; becoming visible, coming into light/existence; **~र्भूत** appeared, manifested; become visible, come into light/existence.

प्रादेश pra:desh (*nm*) a mandate; **-अधीन** mandated; o **क्षेत्र** mandated territory; **प्रादेशात्मक** mandatory.

प्रादेशिक pra:deshik (*a*) regional; territorial; **~ता** regionalism; **-सेना** territorial army.

प्राधान्य pra:dhā:nny (*nm*) predominance, dominance, superiority; supremacy, hegemony.

प्राधि/कार pra:dhika:r (*nm*) authority; **~कारिवर्ग** authorities; **~कारी** (person in) authority; one who wields authority; **~कृत** authorized, authoritative; **~कार देना** to authorize.

प्राध्यापक pra:ddhya:pak (*nm*) a lecturer (in a College/University) **~ता** lecturership.

प्राप्त pra:pt (*a*) got, obtained; procured, acquired; **~काल** appropriate time; **~जीवन** restored to life; **~मनोरथ** fulfilled, gratified; **~यौवन** who has attained puberty or acquired the bloom of youth, youthful.

प्राप्तव्य pra:ptavvy (*nm*) due; to be got/obtained/procured/acquired.

प्रा/प्ति pra:pti (*nf*) receipt; procuration; acquisition; income; profit; **~प्त्याशा** the stage in the action of a drama when the achievement of the desired end seems to be likely.

प्राप्य pra:py (*a*) due; available, attainable, acquirable, procurable.

प्राबल्य pra:baly (*nm*) dominance, predominance; intensity, force.

प्रामाणिक pra:mā:ṇik (*a*) authentic, genuine; authoritative; **~ता** authenticity, genuineness; authoritativeness.

प्रामाण्य pra:mā:ṇṇy (*nm*) authenticity, genuineness; validity; credibility.

प्रायः pra:yah (*adv*) often; usually, generally; almost, more or less, approximately, nearly.

प्राय/द्वीप pra:ydwi:p (*nm*) a peninsula; **~द्वीपीय** peninsular.

प्रायशः pra:yashah (*ind*) most often, mostly; generally, usually.

प्रायश्चित्त pra:yashchitt (*nm*) atonement, penance, expiation; **-करना** to sack cloth and ashes, to atone for.

प्रायिक pra:ik (*a*) probable; **~ता** probability; o **सिद्धांत** probability theory.

प्रायोगिक pra:yogik (*a*) experimental, practical; pilot (scheme, etc.), **~ता** (*nf*).

प्रायोजना pra:yojanā: (*nf*) a project.

प्रायोपवेश, ~न pra:yopvesh, [1]~ān (*nm*) a fast unto death; **~क** one who undertakes a fast unto death.

प्रारंभ pra:rāmbh (*nm*) beginning, commencement; inception; initiation; the starting point.

प्रारंभिक pra:rāmbhik (*a*) starting; preliminary; elementary; original; initial; **-अवस्था** elementary/preliminary stage; **-ज्ञान** elementary knowledge.

प्रारब्ध pra:rabdh (*nm*) destiny, fate, lot; **-लेख** the writ of destiny/

fate.

प्रारूप pra:ru:p (*nm*) a draft; ~कार a draftsman, one who prepares a draft; –बनाना to prepare a draft.

प्रारूपिक pra:ru:pik (*a*) typical; ~तः typically.

प्रार्थना pra:rthanā: (*nf*) a prayer; request, solicitation; petition; ~त्मक precatory, containing a prayer/request; -पत्र an application; a petition; –समाज a socio-religious reformist movement launched in late sixties of the 19th century and influenced by the mediaeval Maharashtrian saints.

प्रार्थनीय pra:rthanī:y (*a*) worth making a request/prayer for, worth petitioning/soliciting for.

प्रार्थित pra:rthit (*a*) prayed/requested/applied / petitioned / solicited (for).

प्रार्थी pra:rthi: (*nm*) an applicant; a petitioner; one who submits a request; one who prays.

प्रावस्था pra:vastha: (*nf*) a phase; ~बद्ध phased.

प्राविधान pra:vidha:n (*nm*) a provision.

प्रावेदन pra:vedān (*nm*) a motion.

प्राशन pra:shān (*nm*) feeding; the first feeding of a child.

प्राश्निक pra:shnik (*nm*) a questioner; an interrogator; (*a*) pertaining to, concerned with or containing a question or questions.

प्रासंगिक pra:sāngik (*a*) relevant; contingent, incidental; contextual; ~ता relevance; contingency, incidental nature or character; contextuality.

प्रासाद pra:sa:d (*nm*) a palace; a palatial mansion.

प्रासूतिक pra:su:tik (*a*) pertaining to or concerned with प्रसूति (see).

प्रास्ताविक pra:sta:vik (*nm*) preliminary matter, prelims; (*a*) introductory; of, pertaining to or related with, a प्रस्ताव; by a motion/resolution/proposal.

प्रिंट print (*nm*) a print; printed design; –आर्डर print order.

प्रिंटिंग printīng (*nf*) printing; –प्रेस a printing press; –मशीन a printing machine.

प्रिंसिप/ल prīnsipal (*nm*) principal (of a school or college); ~ली principalship.

प्रियं/वद priyāmvad (*a*) sweet-spoken; hence ~ वदा (fem. form).

प्रिय priy (*a*) dear, darling, beloved; lovable, lovely; pleasing; pleasant; favourite, liked; (*nm*) a lover; husband; ~जन a beloved one, dear one; near and dear ones; ~तर dearer; ~तम dearest; most beloved; husband; ~दर्शन pleasing, of charming demeanour; ~दर्शी affectionate to all, looking towards all with compassion and kindness; ~भाषी sweet-spoken; ~वचन sweet words; sweet-spoken; ~वादी sweet-spoken; a flatterer; sycophant; –सत्य pleasant truth; –सुहृद dear friend.

प्रिय/ता priyata: (*nf*), ~त्व, ~ttv (*nm*) lovability, the state of being dear/loved, being fond of; used as a suffix to denote fondness or attachment for (e.g. सत्ताप्रियता, कलहप्रियता etc).

प्रिया priya: (*a* and *nf*) beloved, darling; sweetheart; wife.

प्रियाप्रिय priya:priy (*nm*) the pleasant and the unpleasant; the good and the bad; (*a*) good and bad.

प्रीत pri:t (*nf*) see प्रीति.

प्रीतम pri:tam (*nm*) a lover; beloved.

प्रीति pri:ti (nf) love; affection; ~कर/कारक arousing or inspiring love/affection; pleasing, lovely; ~दान gift of love; -पात्र beloved, dear; a toast (for the health of, etc.); ~भोज a love-feast, banquet; -रीति affectionate conduct, amiable behaviour; practice / customs followed in matter of love; -विवाह love-marriage.

प्रूफ pru:f (nm) proof; ~रीडर a proof reader; -शोधन proof-reading, proof-correction.

प्रेक्षक prekshak (nm) an observer; a viewer; spectator; one who sees; -वर्ग/समाज audience, spectators.

प्रे/क्षण prekshaṇ (nm) observing; viewing, seeing; witnessing; ~क्षित observed, viewed, seen.

प्रेक्षणीय prekshaṇī:y (a) worth being seen or to be seen/observed/viewed/witnessed.

प्रेक्षागार preksha:ga:r (nm) an auditorium; a theatre.

प्रेक्षागृह preksha:grih (nm) see प्रेक्षागार.

प्रेत pret (nm) a ghost, goblin, lemures; an evil spirit; a frightful person; -कर्म post-mortem rites performed for the deliverance of the deceased; ~लोक the world of the dead; ~विद्या necromancy; ~सिद्धि necromancy.

प्रेतोन्माद pretonma:d (nm) insanity caused due to obsession (by an evil spirit).

प्रेम prem (nm) love; affection; attachment; -कथा/-कहानी a love story; tale of love; -गीत a love-song; -पगा soaked in love, full of feelings of love; -पत्र a love-letter; -पात्र dear, beloved; -पाश

bond of love; -बंधन bond of love; -भक्ति love-inspired or affection-based devotion; -भाव love, emotion of love; ~मय loving, affectionate; -विहार love-making; -विह्वल love-sick; -व्यापार love-affair; ~शून्य loveless.

प्रेमातुर premā:tur (a) love-lorn; love-sick; hence ~ता (nf).

प्रेमालाप premā:la:p (nm) love-talk; cordial talk.

प्रेमालिंगन premā:liṅgān (nm) a loving embrace; an affectionate hug.

प्रेमाश्रु premā:shshru (nm) love-tears, tears that trickle down when moved by love.

प्रेमिका premika: (nf) a beloved, darling, sweetheart.

प्रेमी premī: (nm) a lover; -प्रेमिका the lover and the beloved.

प्रेय prey (nm) mundane achievement, worldly pleasure /acquirement; ~वाद hedonism; ~वादी a hedonist; hedonistic.

प्रेयसी preyasi: (nf) a beloved; darling, sweetheart.

प्रेरक prerak (a) inductive, that which inspires/ prompts/motivates; (nm) an inspirer; promptor; a motive; hence ~ता; -हेतु a motive.

प्रेर/ण preraṇ (nm) (the act or process of) inspiring / prompting/ motivating; induction; hence ~णीय (a); ~णीयता (nf).

प्रेरणा preraṇa: (nf) inspiration; urge, drive; motive; induction; ~त्मक inspirational; ~प्रद inspiring; ~मय full of inspiration, inspiring. -शक्ति motive force; inspiration; urge; -हेतु motive; inspiration.

प्रेरणार्थक preraṇa:rthak (a) causal; inspiring; causing inspiration;

—क्रिया a causal verb.

प्रेरित prerit (a) inspired; prompted; motivated; induced.

प्रेषक preshak (nm) a despatcher; consigner.

प्रेषण preshān (nm) a despatch; consignment; transmission.

प्रेषित preshit (a) despatched, consigned, transmitted.

प्रेषित्र preshitr (nm) a transmitter; transmission instrument.

प्रेषी preshi: (nm) a transmitter, one who transmits/despatches.

प्रेष्य preshy (a) to be or worth being despatched / consigned/ transmitted.

प्रेस pres (nm) a printing press; the newspapers (in general); —एक्ट the press act; —में होना, किसी चीज का to be under print.

प्रेसिडेंट president (nm) a president.

प्रैक्टिस praikṭis (nf) practice; —करना to practise.

प्रोग्राम progrā:m (nm) a programme.

प्रोत prot (a) permeated (used in Hindi only as the second member in the compound ओत-प्रोत.)

प्रोत्सा/हन protsa:han (nm) encouragement, boosting up; incentive; hence ~हित encouraged, given incentive.

प्रोनोट pronoṭ (nm) a pronote.

प्रोफेसर profesar (nm) a professor.

प्रोषित proshit (a) migrated, gone out; ~पतिका/भर्तृका a woman whose husband is away.

प्रौढ prauṛh (a) mature, full-grown; adult; —मताधिकार adult franchise; —शिक्षा adult education.

प्रौढ/ता, ~त्व prauṛhta: (nf), ~ttv (nm) maturity, full growth; adulthood.

प्रौढि prauṛhi (nf) see प्रौढता.

प्लवन plavan (nm) floating; swimming; ~शील floating; hence ~शीलता (nf).

प्लांचेट pla:ṇchet (nm) a planchet.

प्लांट ploṭ (nm) a plot (of land).

प्लावन pla:vān (nm) inundation, flood; deluge; plunging.

प्लावित pla:vit (a) inundated, flooded, submerged.

प्लास्टर pla:sṭar (nm) plaster; —किया हुआ plastered.

प्लीहा pli:ha: (nm) the spleen; enlargement of the spleen.

प्लुत plut (a) drenched, soaked; protracted sound of a vowel (esp. while calling out somebody by name from afar).

प्लेग pleg (nf) plague.

प्लेट pleṭ (nf) a plate.

प्लेटफार्म pleṭfa:rm (nm) a platform; platform ticket.

प्लेटिनम plaiṭinām (nm) platinum; —तार a platinum wire.

फ

फ pha–the second letter of the fifth pentad (i.e. पवर्ग) of the Devna:gri: alphabet.

फंका phāṅka: (*nm*) the quantity (of powder, etc.) chucked into the mouth in one lot; –लगाना to chuck into the mouth.

फंकी phaṅki: (*nf*) diminutive of फंका (see); the quantity (of medicinal digestive powder etc.) chucked into the mouth in one lot.

फ़ंड faṇḍ (*nm*) a fund; –, प्रोविडेंट the provident fund,

फंद phānd (*nm*) see फंदा.

फंदा phānda: (*nm*) a trap; noose, gin, snare; loop; trick; फंदेदार loopy, having a knot/loop/snare; –छूटना to be relieved of a trap; to get free from a noose; –डालना to ensnare; to form a noose; to knot; –लगाना to knot; to form a loop; फंदे में आना/पड़ना to fall into a trap, to be ensnared; to be caught in a trick.

फँसना phāsnā: (*v*) to be entrapped/ensnared/baited; to be embroiled/implicated/involved; to be caught in a trick; –, किसी से to develop illicit relation with; –,बुरी तरह to be inextricably involved/caught (in a mess); to be in for it.

फँसाना phāsa:nā: (*v*) to trap/entrap, to snare/ensnare; to entangle, to trammel; to involve; to implicate; to ravel; to noose, to bait; to coil.

फँसाव phāsa:v (*nm*) entrapment, entanglement; involvement, embroilment; implication.

फक phak (*a*) pale, anaemic; white; clean, spotless clean; –पड़ना/होना to turn pale, to grow pallid; to lose lustre; to be scared out of wits.

फ़क़त faqat (*a*) only, alone; (*adv*) simply, merely, solely.

फ़कीर faki:r (*nm*) a Muslim mendicant/saint, hermit, recluse; beggar, pauper; hence फ़कीरनी (*nf*); –का घर बड़ा होता है a saint has all that he needs; a saint has room for every shelter-seeker; –की सदा the appeal/call of a फ़कीर.

फ़कीराना faki:ra:nā: (*a*) like a फ़कीर (see), in the fashion of a फ़कीर; (*nm*) land given free to a फ़कीर.

फ़कीरी faki:ri: (*nf*) poverty, indigence; the manner or life of a फ़कीर; mendicity; (*a*) pertaining or belonging to a फ़कीर; फ़कीर-like.

फक्क phakk (*a*) pale, pallid; anaemic; clean; white; hence –पड़ना/होना see फक (–पड़ना/होना).

फक्कड़ phakkaṛ (*a*) carefree; indigent; ~पन/पना carefreeness, carefree manner; indigence; ~मस्ती carefreeness, carefree and unconcerned stance.

फ़ख़्र fakhr (*nm*) pride; –करना to feel proud; –होना to be proud (of).

फगुआ phagua: (*nm*) songs sung at the time of the Holi: festival.

फगुन/हट, ~हटा phagunahaṭ, ~hṭa: (*nf*) the strong dusty wind that blows in the month of फागुन (see).

फ़ज़र fazar (*nm*) morning, dawn.

फ़ज़ल fazal (*nm*) day-break; see फ़ज़्ल.

फ़जीता fazi:ta: (*nm*) see फ़ज़ीहत.

फ़ज़ीहत fazi:hat (*nf*) insult, disgrace; embarrassment; discomfiture; –दीगरे नसीहते, ख़ुद मियाँ embroiled in a mess for oneself, extending advice to others.

फ़ज़ूल fazu:l (*a*) useless, worthless; futile; ~ख़र्च extravagant; dissipating; ~ख़र्ची extravagance; dissipation; o पर कमर बाँधना to burn the candles at both ends.

फ़ज़्ल fazl (*nm*) grace, favour, kindness; –से, ख़ुदा के by the grace of God.

फट phaṭ (*adv*) at once; (*nf*) fluttering sound; see फटना; ~फट an auto-rikshaw; repeated fluttering sounds; –से at once, immediately; there and then.

फटकन phaṭkān (*nf*) chaff; the husks separated from grain by winnowing; unsubstantial stuff.

फटकना phaṭaknā: (*v*) to winnow; to dust; to sift; to shake off, to knock off; to reach, to go near (as किसी के पास न फटकना); to be separated; -पछोरना to examine thoroughly, to sift carefully.

फटकार phaṭka:r (*nf*) a sharp reprimand, scolding; rebuke, chiding; –जमाना/लगाना see फटकारना.

फटकारना phaṭka:rnā: (*v*) to rebuke, to scold, to chide, to reprimand, to give a violent jerk to a cloth (in order to undo its wrinkles.)

फटन phaṭan (*nf*) a rupture, rent, rip; gap, fissure; split.

फटना phaṭnā: (*v*) to be torn, to be split; to burst, to explode, to crack; to tatter; (milk) to become sour (e.g. दूध–); to be put off, to develop a sense of aversion; to be repulsed; फट पड़ना to explode, to shout forth angrily, to burst out into loud invectives/rebuke/reprimand

फटफटाना phaṭphaṭa:nā: (*v*) to make fluttering noise/sound; to flap (wings etc.)

फटफटिया phaṭphaṭiya: (*nf*) a motor-bicycle; an auto-rikshaw.

फटा phaṭa: (*a*) torn; rent; -टूटा worn and torn; -पुराना shabby, old and shattered/tattered, ragged; -फटाया torn and tattered; shabby; फटी आँखों से देखना to cast a blank look, to look aghast; फटी आवाज a hoarse voice, husky voice; फटे बाँस की-सी आवाज hoarse and husky voice; फटे हाल out of elbow, down at heels, in a ragged condition, in a miserable plight, in tatters/rags.

फटिक phaṭik (*nm*) see स्फटिक.

फटीचर phaṭi:char (*a*) shabby, shabbily dressed; putting on tattered/shattered clothes; hence ~पन/–पना (*nm*).

फ/ट्टा,~ट्ठा phaṭṭa:, ~ṭṭhā: (*nm*) a plank, long and wide piece of split plank; ~ट्टी,~ट्ठी thin and small फट्टा/फट्ठा.

फड़ phaṛ (*nm*) a gambling party/spot; a shopkeeper's seat (for transacting business); ~बाज a gambler; ~बाजी gambling; –जमाना to organise a gambling party.

फड़क, ~न phaṛak, ~ān (*nf*) a thrill/throb; throbbing; pulsation, palpitation.

फड़क/ना phaṛaknā: (*v*) to be thrilled, to throb, to palpitate, to pulsate; to flutter; –उठना to be thrilled, to be in extreme exaltation; ~ता हुआ titillating; full of throbs.

फड़फड़ा/ना pharphaṛa:nā: (*v*) to flutter; to flap; to throb; ~हट flutter/fluttering; flapping.

फण phāṇ (*nm*) the hood of a snake; ~**धर** a snake/serpent; cobra.

फणींद्र phaṇi:ndr (*nm*) an epithet of **शेषनाग**–the mythological serpent-king; also **फणीश**, **फणीश्वर**.

फणी phaṇi: (*nm*) a snake, serpent,

फ़तवा fatva: (*nm*) a judgment/decree; a decree by a (muslim) religious judge in accordance with the canons of Islam: –**देना** to pronounce a snap/sweeping judgment.

फ़तह fateh (*nf*) a victory, triumph, conquest; ~**याब** victorious, triumphant, one who has achieved a conquest; ~**याबी** conquest, victory; –**का डंका/नक्कारा** proclamation of victory, drumbeat marking a triumphal expedition.

फतिंगा phatiṅga: (*nm*) an insect, a moth.

फतुही phatuhi: (*nf*) a kind of cotton-stuffed (sleeveless or half-sleeve) waist-coat.

फ़तूर fatu:r (*nm*) see **फ़ितूर**

फ़तह fateh (*nf*) see **फ़तेह**.

फन phān (*nm*) see **फण**.

फ़न fan (*nm*) an art, craft; skill, artifice; ~**कार** an artist; ~**मौला**, **हर** a master of all trades, a versatile person.

फ़ना fanā: (*a*) died, expired; ruined, destructed, devastated; (*nm*) death, expiry; ruin, destruction, devastation.

फन्नी phanni: (*nf*) a fillet, wedge.

फप्फस phapphas (*a*) flabby and flaccid.

फफकना phaphknā: (*v*) to weep bitterly.

फफूं/द, ~**दी** phaphu:d, ~di: (*nf*) fungus.

फफो/ला phaphola: (*nm*) a blister; eruption, scald; ~**ले फोड़ना, दिल के** to pour forth one's accumulated wrath; to talk one's inward grudge out.

फबत phabat (*nf*) befittingness, suitability.

फबती phabti: (*nf*) a banter; befitting remark, sarcastic remark; –**कसना/कहना** to have a fling at, to banter, to make a befitting/sarcastic/satirical remark.

फबना phabnā: (*v*) to befit, to become, to suit, to beseem; the cap to fit (somebody).

फबीला phabi:la: (*a*) becoming, befitting; looking grand/handsome.

फ़रफ़र farfar (*a*) swiftly, quickly; with promptitude; (*nf*) frou-frou; promptitude, swiftness.

फ़रक़ faraq (*nm*) **फ़र्क़**.

फरकना pharakna: (*v*) see **फड़कना**.

फरचा pharcha: (*a*) clean; undefiled, pure; ~**ई** cleanliness; purity.

फ़रज़ंद farzand (*nm*) son.

फ़रज़ faraz (*nm*) see **फ़र्ज़**.

फ़रज़ी farzi: (*nm*) the queen in the game of chess; (*a*) see **फ़र्ज़ी**; –**बनना, प्यादे से** to rise to power from the position of a non-entity; to rise from the ranks to the seat of power.

फ़रमा farmā: (*nm*) a format, forme, (in printing); a (shoe-maker's) frame.

फ़रमाइश farma:ish (*nf*) an imperative request; an order.

फ़रमाइशी farma:ishi: (*a*) made to order; requested; (performed/presented) on specific request.

फ़रमान farmā:n (*nm*) a royal edict/command/decree.

फ़रमाना farmā:nā: (*v*) (a deferential usage) to (be so graceful as to) speak out; to (come out with an) order/command; to make an utterance.

फ़रमाबरदा/र farmā:barda:r (*a*) obedient, submissive; ~री obedience; submissiveness.

फ़रलाँग farlā:g (*nm*) a furlong.

फ़रलो farlo (*nf*) furlough.

फ़रवरी farvari: (*nf*) (the month of) February.

फ़रश farash (*nm*) see फ़र्श.

फ़रशी farshi: (*nf*) a hubble-bubble; (*a*) pertaining to the फ़र्श (see); –सलाम see फ़र्शी सलाम (under फ़र्शी).

फरसा pharsa: (*nm*) see परशु.

फ़रहंग farhāṅg (*nm*) a lexicon; commentary; key.

फरहरा pharehra: (*nm*) a banner, flag; (*a*) soothed, relieved (of fatigue, boredom, etc.); –होना to be soothed/relieved.

फ़रहाद farha:d (*nm*) the legendary hero of the love-lore of Shi:rī: Farha:d; a love-lorn person.

फ़राकत fara:kat (*nf*) see फ़राग़त.

फ़राख़/दिल fara:khdil (*a*) open-hearted, liberal, bounteous;~दिली open-heartedness, liberality, bounteousness.

फ़राग़त fara:gat (*nf*) riddance; carefreeness; discharge of faeces;–जाना to discharge faeces, to ease oneself; –पाना to get rid of; to be eased/relieved.

फ़रामो/श fara:mosh (*a*) forgotten; forgetful, oblivious; ~शी forgetfulness, oblivion.

फरार phara:r (*nm*) see फलाहार.

फ़रार fara:r (*a*) at large, absconding; (*nm*) an outlaw, absconder, a fugitive; –देनदार an absent debtor; –होना to abscond, to run away from the arm of law.

फ़रारी fara:ri: (*a*) absconded; (*nm*) a fugitive; an absconder.

फ़राहम fara:ham (*a*) collected, accumulated; stored.

फ़रासीसी fara:si:si: (*a* and *nm*) see फ्रांसीसी.

फरिया phariya: (*nf*) a kind of short upper covering used by girls.

फ़रियाद fariya:d (*nf*) a petition; complaint: supplication for help or justice; –करना to lodge a complaint; to make a supplication for help or justice.

फ़रियादी fariya:di: (*nm*) a petitioner; suppliant; one who makes an invocation for help or justice.

फ़रि/श्ता farishta: (*nm*) an angel, a divine messenger; ~श्तों को भी ख़बर/पता न होना/लगना none to have the slightest inkling (of).

फ़री/क़ fari:q (*nm*) a party (in a law-suit), a contender; ~क़ैन contending parties (to a lawsuit)

फरुहा pharuha: (*nm*) see फावड़ा; hence diminutive फरुही (*nf*).

फरेंदा pharēda: (*nf*) see फलेंदा.

फ़रेब fareb (*nm*) fraud, duplicity, wiliness, deception; double-dealing.

फ़रेबी farebi: (*a* and *nm*) fraudulent, wily, deceptive (person); a double-dealer.

फरेरा pharera: (*nm*) see फरहरा.

फ़रोख़्त farokht (*a*) sold; (*nf*) sale; –करना to sell, to deal in.

फ़रोश farosh –a Persian suffix used to impart to a word the sense of seller/dealer in/vendor (as दवाफ़रोश, मेवाफ़रोश, वतनफ़रोश, etc.)

फ़र्क़ farq (*nm*) difference; distinction; distance; –करना to distinguish, to make a distinction; to modify.

फ़र्ज़ farz (*nm*) duty; obligation; –अदा करना to do one's duty, to fulfil one's duty/obligation; –करना to imagine, to assume, to suppose; –होना to be a duty.

फ़र्ज़ी farzi: (*a*) imaginary; supposed, assumed; hypothetical; fictitious; see फ़रज़ी; –नाम fictitious name.

फ़र्द fard (*nf*) a list, catalogue; the upper fold of a quilt; –जुर्म a charge-sheet.

फ़र्दन-फ़र्दन fardān-fardān (*adv*) individually, singly.

फ़र्नीचर farnī:char (*nm*) furniture.

फ़र्म farm (*nf*) a firm/business concern.

फ़र्माना farmā:nā: (*v*) see फ़रमाना.

फ़र्रा/टा pharra:ṭa: (*nm*) fluency; promptitude, fastness; haste; ~टे से non-stop, fluently, promptly; hastily, unhesitatingly.

फ़र्रा/श farra:sh (*nm*) a sweeper, a menial worker; ~शी (pertaining to) the work of a फ़र्राश.

फ़र्लांग furlā:g (*nm*) a furlong.

फ़र्श farsh (*nm*) floor (of a room etc.), flooring; carpet, mat; pavement; –से अर्श तक from earth to heaven.

फ़र्शी farshi: (*a*) pertaining to the फ़र्श (see); –सलाम an extra-deferential salutation (by bending the head so low as almost to touch the ground).

फल phal (*nm*) a fruit, reward, return; effect; outcome, result, consequence; product; the point of a cutting or piercing instrument; a ploughshare; ~त: consequently; therefore; accordingly; thus; ~द/दायक/दायी/प्रद fruitful, fructuous; profitable; advantageous; productive; fruit-yielding, efficacious; effective; ~दान the first present made from the bride's side to the bridegroom as a confirmation of the agreement for marriage; ~दार fructiferous, having/bearing fruits; profitable; -प्राप्ति fructification; achievement, accomplishment, acquisition of the result; ~भक्षी frugivorous; ~भागी one who enjoys or suffers the result of a deed; ~भोग suffering or enjoying the result of a deed; ~मूलक pragmatic; ~युक्त bearing fruits, fruitful, fructuous; ~वती fruitful, fructuous; ~वाद pragmatism; ~वादी pragmatic; a pragmatist; ~वान fructuous; fruitful, profitable; with fruits; ~शर्करा fructose, fruit-sugar; ~स्वरूप as a result of; ~हारी see फलाहारी; ~हीन fruitless; –आना to fructify, (a tree) to bear fruits; to bring results; –खाना to enjoy the reward of one's good deeds; to reap the harvest of virtuous deeds; –चखना to suffer/face the consequences of; –देना to yield fruit/result; to fructify; –पाना to be rewarded; to face the result of, to suffer for one's evil deeds; –होना to be the outcome of.

फलक phalak (*nm*) face; blade; a board, plank; canvas; palm (of the hand), a sheet (of paper); slab.

फ़लक falak (*nm*) the sky; heaven; –टूटना the heavens to fall, calamity to befall.

फलन phalān (*nm*) fructification, fruitage, fruition; culmination; reflection; function.

फलना phalnā: (*v*) to bear fruit; to be fruitful/useful; to thrive, to prosper; -फूलना to be prosperous, to thrive.

फ़लसफ़ा falsafa: (*nm*) philosophy.

फ़लसफ़ी falsafi: (*nm*) a philosopher.

फ़लाँ falā: (*a*) so and so, such and such; also—फलाँ; –डिमाक.

फ़लाँगना phalā:gnā: (*v*) to jump over; to cross over.

फला phala: (*nf*) a fluke.

फलागम phala:gām (*nm*) achievement of the result; in Indian dramaturgy, the fourth and penultimate stage of action wherein the hero sees the fructification of his efforts.

फलाढ्य phala:ḍḍhy (*a*) full of fruits, rich in fruits.

फलापेक्षी phala:pekshi: (*nm*) one who awaits or hankers after the results of his deeds/actions.

फलाफल phala:phal (*nm*) good and evil results (of one's deeds/actions); reward and punishment (of one's deeds).

फलार्थी phala:rthi: (*nm*) see फलापेक्षी.

फ़लालैन fala:lain (*nf*) flannel.

फलासक्त phala:sakt (*a*) attached to the results, (one) who hankers after the results.

फलासव phala:sav (*nm*) leavened and preserved fruit-juice (used as a tonic).

फलाहार phala:ha:r (*nm*) fruitarian diet; subsisting on a diet of fruits alone.

फलाहारी phala:ha:ri: (*a*) fruitarian; pertaining to fruitarian diet; (*nm*) a fruitarian, one who subsists on fruits alone.

फलित phalit (*a*) fructified, resulted, fulfilled; fruit-bearing; prospered, thrived; –ज्योतिष astrology.

फलितार्थ phalita:rth (*nm*) essence, essential meaning.

फली phali: (*nf*) a bean, pod of a leguminous plant.

फलीता phali:ta: (*nm*) see पलीता.

फलीभूत phali:bhu:t (*a*) fructified, (that has) borne fruits, resulted in success.

फलेंदा phaleda: (*nm*) a rich variety of जामुन.

फ़व्वारा favva:ra: (*nm*) a fountain.

फलोदय phaloday (*nm*) advent of prosperous times; the time for reward (of past good deeds.)

फ़सल fasal (*nf*) crop, harvest; season, time; ~कट/कट्टा a harvester; reaper (of the crops); –की चीज़ seasonal thing.

फ़सली fasli: (*a*) seasonal; relating to the harvest/crop; (*nf*) cholera; –बटेर a bird of passage, an ever-shifting person; –बुख़ार seasonal fever; –साल agricultural year.

फ़साद fasa:d (*nm*) an altercation, a row, quarrel, disturbance; –का घर/की जड़ the villain of the piece, the root cause of trouble.

फ़सादी fasa:di: (*a* and *nm*) rowdy, one who initiates an altercation/row/quarrel.

फ़साना fasa:nā: (*nm*) a story, a long narrative; see अफ़साना; ~निगार a fictionist, story writer.

फ़साहत fasa:hat (*nf*) (linguistic) lucidity, refined clarity.

फ़सील fasi:l (*nf*) a boundary wall; battlement, parapet.

फ़सीह fasi:h (*a*) pleasant-spoken, (one) who uses lucid and pleasant language.

फ़स्द fasd (*nf*) phlebotomy, opening a vein for excretion of impure blood; –खोलना to split open or operate upon a vein, to cause excretion of impure blood by operation.

फ़हम fehām (*nf*) comprehension, understanding (In Hindi, this word is in use only in the compound आमफ़हम which means commonly understood, of the common man.)

फहराना phehra:nā: (*v*) to hoist; to wave; to flutter in the air, to flap.

फांक phā:k (*nf*) a cut slice (of fruit etc.), fillet, fragment/paring; clove (of a garlic), cleft, slit; –करना to pare, to cut into slices.

फांकना phā:knā: (*v*) to chuk some powdery thing into the mouth (esp. from the palm of the hand); –,धूल to knock about, to be tossed about, to run from pole to post.

फांका phā:ka: (*nm*) the process or act of फांकना (see).

फांट phā:ṭ (*nm*) width, distance between the two banks of a river, pond, lake, etc.

फांद phā:d (*nf*) leaping; jumping, skipping; crossing; –,कूद gambol (ing).

फांदना phā:dnā: (*v*) to jump across, to leap over; to skip; to spring; to cross.

फांस phā:s (*nf*) a noose, snare; knot; trap; tiny thorn-like splinter (of a bamboo, etc.); –निकलना a thorn in one's flesh to be pulled out, to be relieved of a constant source of agony.

फांसना phā:snā: (*v*) to entrap, to trap; to snare, to ensnare, to involve, to embroil.

फांसी phā:si: (*nf*) death by hanging, execution; noose; –चढ़ना, –पर चढ़ना to be hanged, to be executed; –देना, –पर चढ़ाना to hang (by the neck); to execute; –लगाना to commit suicide by hanging; to hang oneself.

फ़ाइन fa:in (*a* and *nm*) fine.

फ़ाइल fa:il (*nm*, also *nf*) a file; –करना to file; to keep in record.

फ़ाउंटेन पेन fa:unṭen pen (*nm*) a fountain pen.

फ़ाक़ा fa:qa: (*nm*) starvation; fast; ~कश starving, starved; ~कशी starvation, starving; फ़ाक़ों का मारा weakened by starvation, starved to emaciation.

फ़ाक़ा(के)/मस्त fa:qa:(e)mast (*a*) cheerful even in extreme poverty/starvation, one whose spirit is not damped even though starved; carefree; ~मस्ती carefreeness even though starved; maintenance of undamped spirit even in deep affliction/crisis.

फ़ाख़/ता fa:ḳhta: (*nf*) a dove; ~तई reddish grey (coloured); ~ते उड़ जाना to be unnerved, to be nonplussed.

फाग pha:g (*nm*) a typical song sung (collectively or individually) during the Holi: festival; Holi: festival and its merry-making; –गाना singing of typical Holi: songs.

फागु/न pha:gūn (*nm*) the twelfth and last month of the year according to the Hindu calendar; ~नी pertaining/belonging to फागुन.

फ़ाज़िल fa:zil (*a*) extra, additional; surplus; learned, scholarly; –बाक़ी amount outstanding, arrears.

फाट pha:ṭ (*nm*) a division (of land etc.).

फाटक pha:ṭak (*nm*) main gate; gate; entrance.

फाट/का pha:ṭka: (*nm*) speculation; ~केबाज a speculationist; ~केबाजी speculation.

फाड़न pha:ṛān (*nm*) a piece (left after tearing or splitting); splinter.

फाड़/ना pha:ṛnā: (*v*) to tear off; to

rend, to rive; to split; to (cause to) crack; to burst open, to lacerate; to cleave, to rip open, to pull apart; –खाना to tear off and devour (as भेड़िए ने फाड़ खाया); –डालना to tear off, to tear asunder.

फ़ातिहा fa:tiha: (*nf*) oblation offered to the manes by Mohammedans, reading the first chapter of the क़ुरान (see); –पढ़ना to be frustrated/dejected, to be hopeless.

फान pha:n (*nm*) a wedge, fillet.

फानना phannā: (*v*) to card (cotton); to commence (a work); to jump over, to cross.

फ़ानी fa:nī: (*a*) transitory, transient, perishable.

फ़ानूस fa:nū:s (*nm*) a chandelier (for burning candles in.)

फ़ाय/दा fa:yda: (*nm*) advantage; gain; profit; benefit; utility, use, good result; ~देमंद advantageous; profitable; beneficial; useful, efficacious; giving good result; ~दा उठाना to make capital out of; ~दे में रहना to emerge as the gainer, to be the ultimate gainer.

फ़ायर fa:yar (*nm*) fire; firing (of guns etc.); -ब्रिगेड fire-brigade; ~मैन a fireman; –करना to fire.

फाया pha:ya: (*nm*) see फ़ाहा.

फ़ारख़ती fa:rḳhati: (*nf*) a deed of separation/riddance / dissolution; quittance.

फ़ारम fa:ram (*nm*) see फ़ार्म.

फ़ारस fa:ras (*nm*) Persia.

फ़ारसी fa:rsi: (*a*) Persian; (*nf*) the Persian language; (*nm*) a Persian, an inhabitant of Persia; ~दाँ one who knows Persian, a Persian scholar; –बघारना/बूँकना to show off one's scholarship/pedantry.

फ़ारिग़ fa:rig (*a*) freed, free (from work); (one who has) fulfilled his obligation; ~ख़ती quittance, a receipt of being quits; –होना to be freed; to ease oneself; to discharge faeces.

फ़ार्नहाइट fa:rnha:iṭ (*nm*) Fahrenheit–the German Scientist who invited the Fahrenheit temperature-scale; –थर्मामीटर the Fahrenheit thermometer.

फ़ार्म fa:rm (*nm*) a form; an agricultural farm.

फाल pha:l (*nm*) a blade, ploughshare; a stride/pace, measure of one pace; betelnut-paring.

फ़ॉल fɔl (*nm*) a fall (in *sa:ri:*, etc.)

फ़ालतू fa:ltu: (*a*) spare; extra, surplus; superfluous (as –बात); useless, worthless; (as –आदमी).

फ़ालसई fa:lsai: (*a*) brownish red (coloured), of the colour of फ़ालसा.

फ़ालसा fa:lsa: (*nm*) a tree and its round tiny fruit–*Grewia asiatica*.

फ़ालिज fa:lij (*nm*) paralysis; palsy; ~ज़दा paralysed, paralysis-stricken; –गिरना/मारना to be attacked by paralysis/paralysed.

फ़ालूदा fa:lu:da: (*nm*) a sweet dish prepared from the starch of wheat, milk, sugar, etc

फाल्गुन pha:lgun (*nm*) the last month of the year according to the Hindu calendar.

फाल्गुनी pha:lgunī: (*nf*) pertaining to फाल्गुन; the name of the eleventh (पूर्वा फाल्गुनी) and twelfth (उत्तरा फाल्गुनी) lunar asterisms (नक्षत्र).

फावड़ा pha:vṛa: (*nm*) a spade, mattock; –चलाना to dig with a फावड़ा; to undertake an assiduous manual work.

फावड़ी pha:vṛi: (*nf*) a badger,

small फावड़ा (see).

फ़ाश fa:sh (*a*) exposed, uncovered, open(ed); disclosed, manifest; –करना to expose; to disclose a secret that undermines somebody's prestige.

फ़ासला fa:sla: (*nm*) a distance; gap; space, spacing; difference.

फ़ासिज़्म fa:sizm (*nm*) fascism.

फ़ासिला fa:sila: (*nm*) see फ़ासला.

फ़ासिस्ट fa:sist (*nm*) a fascist; ~वाद fascism; ~वादी (a) fascist.

फ़ाहा fa:ha: (*nm*) a flock of cotton (used as a lint for dressing a wound); a flock of cotton impregnated with perfume.

फ़ाहिशा fa:hisha: (*nf*) a lewd/morally depraved woman, woman of easy virtue.

फ़िकर fikar (*nf*) see फ़िक्र.

फ़िकरा fikra: (*nm*) a sentence; sarcasm; taunt; –कसना to make a sarcastic remark; to taunt; फ़िकरेबाज़ one who makes sarcastic remarks/taunts; one who uses high-sounding sentences to create effect; hence फ़िकरेबाज़ी (*nf*).

फ़िक्र fikr (*nf*) worry, anxiety; care; concern; ~मंद worried, concerned; anxious, ~मंदी anxiety, worry, concern; –करना to care for, to be anxious/worried/concerned about; –पीती है खूने दिल anxiety is the canker of the heart; –में हाथी भी घुल जाता है care killed the cat; –से कुछ नहीं होता care avails not.

फिचकुर phichkur (*nm*) the foam emitted from the mouth in a swoon or fit of hysteria, etc.

फिटक(कि)री phitka(ki)ri: (*nf*) alum, aluminium sulphate.

फ़िट(टि)न fita(ti)n (*nf*) a phaeton (two-wheeled carriage driven by a horse).

फ़िटर fitar (*nm*) a fitter.

फि/ट्टा phitta: (*a*) showing signs of humiliation, reproved out of countenance; ~ट्टे–मुँह a term of abuse generally used by women –cursed to a humiliated existence.

फ़ितना fitnā: (*a*) crooked, shrewd, full of wiles, wily.

फ़ितरत fitrat (*nf*) disposition, nature; wiliness, cunningness; mischievousness.

फ़ितरती fitarati: (*a*) natural; cunning, mischievous, wily.

फ़ितूर fitu:r (*nm*) craze; unsoundness; infirmity; –समाना, दिमाग में/–सवार होना to go crazy (about something), to be obsessed (by).

फ़िदवी fidvi: (*a*) loyal, devoted; obedient; (*nm*) a devoted servant.

फ़िदा fida: (*a*) infatuated, charmed, attracted; devoted (to); –होना to be infatuated/attracted/devoted.

फ़िनाय(इ)ल fină:ya(i)l (*nm*) naphthaline (liquid).

फ़िरंग firăng (*nm*) syphilis; European; also –रोग (*nm*).

फ़िरंगी firăngi: (*a* and *nm*) (a) European; (an) English; ~गिस्तान England.

फिरंट firănt (*a*) opposed; angry, at cross purposes; –हो जाना to fly in the face of.

फिर phir (*adv*) then; again; afterwards; thereafter; in future; a second time; -फिर again and again, time and again; –जाना to return; to go back (on one's words etc.); –भी notwithstanding, even then, in spite of that; –से anew, afresh.

फ़िर/क़ा firqa: (*nm*) a religious sect, sect; community; ~क़ापरस्त a communalist; sectarian; ~क़ा-परस्ती communalism; sectarianism; ~क़ेवार sectwise, communitywise; ~क़ेवाराना communalistic; sectarian.

फ़िरकी phirki: (*nf*) a spool; reel (of thread); whirligig; –की तरह घूमना/फिरना to go round nonstop; to run about without respite; to know no respite.

फ़िरदौस firdaus (*nm*) the paradise, heaven.

फिरना phirnā: (*v*) to turn; to return; to revolve; to wander; to ramble; to walk about; to go round; to be proclaimed/circulated; to undergo a change (as दिन फिरना); to go back (as बात से फिरना).

फ़िरनी firni: (*nf*) a sweet dish prepared from milk and powdered rice etc.

फिराऊ phira:u: (*a*) (things brought or taken) on approval; returnable, –माल goods/articles (taken) on approval/returnable basis.

फिराक phira:k (*nm*) expectancy (for), looking for, waiting for, keeping a watch for; worry, anxiety; search.

फ़िरा/क़ fira:q (*nm*) separation; ~क़े-यार separation from the beloved; ~क़ में इश्क तड़पता है separation sharpens love.

फ़िरिश्ता firishta: (*nm*) see फ़रिश्ता.

फिरौती phirauti: (*nf*) ransom; –लेकर छोड़ना to release after getting a ransom.

फ़िर्क़ा firqa: (*nm*) see फ़िरक़ा.

फ़िलहक़ीक़त filhaqi:qat (*adv*) in fact, in reality, actually, actually speaking.

फ़िलहाल filha:l (*adv*) for the time being, at present, for the present.

फ़िल्म film (*nm, a*; also *nf*) a film; movie, motion picture; –जगत the film world.

फ़िल्माना filmā:nā: (*v*) to film, to filmise.

फ़िल्मी filmī: (*a*) pertaining to or of the films, cinematographic;–दुनिया the film world; –सितारे film stars.

फिस phis (*a*) unavailing, non-substantial; useless; –हो जाना to be ineffective/useless; to prove of no avail; –, टाँय-टाँय much ado about nothing, ending in a fiasco, proving of no avail after raising high hopes.

फिसड्डी phisaḍḍi: (*a*) tailing behind (in a race); always lagging behind; sluggish, slothful; backward.

फिसलन phislān (*nf*) slipperiness; skid.

फिसलना phisalnā: (*n*) to slip; to slide; to skid; to fall for, to be fascinated.

फ़िहरिश्त fihrisht (*nf*) a list; schedule; inventory.

फ़ी fi: (*ind*) each, every; –आदमी per capita, per head; –सदी per cent, per hundred.

फीका phi:ka: (*a*) tasteless, insipid, vapid; unsweetened, unsweet; faded; dull (coloured); dim, devoid of radiance; ~पन tastelessness, insipidity, vapidity; fadedness; dimness; dullness of colour; state of being without sweet; –पड़ना to lose brilliance/lustre; to grow dull; –लगना to appear insipid/dull/tasteless/unsweet; –स्वर dejected / lifeless / dull voice, a voice devoid of emotion; फीकी बात uniteresting / unimpressive/ lifeless remark/utterance, insipic talk; फीकी मुस्कान an uninspired/insipid smile, a lifeless smile; फीकी हँसी an uninspired laugh.

फ़ीता fi:ta: (*nm*) a lace, ribbon; tape; strap; shoelace; fillet.

फ़ीरनी fi:rnī: (*nf*) see फ़िरनी.

फ़ीरोज़ा fi:roza: (*nm*) an amethyst, a violet-blue gem.

फ़ीरोज़ी fi:rozi: (*a*) violet-blue.

फ़ील fi:l (*nm*) an elephant; a piece in the game of chess; ~खाना a stable for elephants; ~पाँव/पा elephantiasis; ~वान an elephant-driver.

फ़ीस fi:s (*nf*) fee; tuition fee.

फुंकनी fūknī: (*nf*) a blow-tube, blow-pipe (of goldsmith, etc.)

फुँकार phūnka:r (*nf*) hiss (of a snake), hissing.

फुँद/ना fūdnā: (*nm*) a tassel, rosette; ~नेदार having tassels, tasseled.

फुंसी phunsi: (*nf*) a small boil; pimple, whelk.

फुकनी phuknī: (*nf*) see फुँकनी.

फुक्का phukka:; – फाड़कर/मारकर रोना to lament aloud, to bewail loudly.

फ़ुज़ूल fuzu:l (*a*) see फ़ज़ूल.

फुट phuṭ (*a*) alone, separate; without a match or companion.

फ़ुट fuṭ (*nm*) a foot; ~नोट a foot-note; ~पाथ footpath; ~मान foot age.

फुटक/र, ~ल phuṭkar, ~l (*a*) miscellaneous; retail; ~र चीजें odds and ends, miscellaneous articles, sundries; ~र बिक्री/विक्रय retail-sale; ~र बिक्री करना to sell in retail; ~र बेचने वाला, ~र-विक्रेता a retailer.

फुटबा(बॉ)ल futba:(ɔ)l (*nm*) a football; the game of football; –का खिलाड़ी a footballer.

फुड़िया phuṛiya: (*nf*) a tiny boil.

फ़ुतूर futu:r (*nm*) see फ़ितूर.

फुदकना phudaknā: (*v*) to skip (with joy); to caper, to hope, to jump.

फुनगी phungi: (*nf*) the top, tip, upper extremity, summit; cockade; sprout.

फुप्फुस phupphus (*nm*) a lung.

फुफकार phuphka:r (*nf*) kiss, hissing (of a snake etc.); ~ना, –करना to hiss; to make a hissing sound.

फुफिया phuphiya: (*nf*) see बुआ; –ससुर the husband of wife's paternal aunt; –सास sister of father-in-law, paternal aunt-in-law.

फुफेरा phuphera: (*a*) related through or pertaining to फूफा/बुआ; –भाई a son of one's बुआ or paternal aunt; फुफेरी बहन a daughter of one's बुआ (paternal aunt).

फुर phur (*nf*) sound of a bird's wings in flight, flutter; flap; –फुर repeated sounds of फुर (see); –हो जाना to fly away.

फ़ुरक़त furqat (*nf*) parting, separation; –,ग़मे the sorrow of separation.

फुरती phurti: (*nf*) smartness, agility; promptness; –से quickly, with agility; promptly; oकाम करना to go great guns.

फुरतीला phurti:la: (*a*) smart, agile; prompt.

फ़ुरसत fursat (*nf*) see फ़ुर्सत

फुरेरी phureri: (*nf*) a broomstick with cotton wrapped over it and soaked in oil or essence etc. at one end; quivering; a sudden quivering that passes through one's whole being; –आना/लेना to quiver, to feel a sudden sense of quivering.

फुर्ती phurti: (*nf*) see फुरती.

फुर्तीला phurti:la: (*a*) see फुरतीला.

फ़ुर्सत fursat (*nf*) leisure; spare time; respite; —न होना to have one's hands full; —पाना to get a respite; to be free; to get some leisure; to get rid of; —में in leisure, in time(s) of leisure; —से when free, in spare time; in a leisurely fashion.

फुलका phulka: (*nm*) a (thin) bread; also see फुल्का.

फुलकारी phulka:ri: (*nf*) embroidery work, embroidery of flowers.

फुलझड़ी phuljhaṛi: (*nf*) a kind of firework which emits flower-like sparks; a provoking remark uttered in a lighter vein; —छोड़ना to make the fur fly, to let off a squib, to make a provocative remark in a lighter vein.

फुलवा/ड़ी, ~री phulwa:ṛi:, ~ri: (*nf*) a small flower-garden.

फ़ुलस्केप fulskep (*a* and *nm*) foolscap (paper).

फुलाई phula:i (*nf*) the act of puffing up/inflating/swelling; inflation.

फुलाना phula:nā: (*v*) to puff up; to cause to become proud, to inflate; to pump in air; to (cause to) swell; to cause to blossom; —, मुँह to be sulky, to get angry.

फुलाव phula:v (*nm*) puffing up, inflation, swelling.

फुलावट phula:vaṭ (*nf*) puffing up, inflation, swelling.

फुली phuli: (*nf*) see फूली.

फुलेल phulel (*nm*) scented (hair) oil.

फुलौरा phulaura: (*nm*) a big फुलौरी (see).

फुलौरी phulauri: (*nf*) *pakauri*: made of gram-flour.

फुल्का phulka: (*nm*) a thin bread; very light—used in this sense only in the compound हल्का-फुल्का very light and thin.

फुल्ल phull (*a*) see प्रफुल्ल; ~नयन having smiling/cheerful eyes.

फुव्वारा phuwwa:ra: (*nm*) a fountain, shower; —छूटना to gush out like a fountain.

फुस phus (*nf*) a whispering or hissing sound; ~फुस whisper: ०करना see फुसफुसाना; ०करके silently, in a very low tone or hushed voice; in a whisper.

फुसफुसा phusphusa: (*a*) hollow; fragile; not sturdy.

फुसफुसाना phusphusa:nā: (*v*) to whisper, to speak in a hushed up voice or low tone.

फुसफुसाहट phusphusa:haṭ (*nf*) whisper, whispering sound.

फुसला/ना phusla:nā: (*v*) to allure, to entice, to wheedle; to seduce; to coax, to cajole; —कर बात उगलवाना to draw a person out.

फुसलाहट phusla:haṭ (*nf*) allurement, enticement; seduction; coaxing, cajolery.

फुहार phuha:r (*nf*) drizzle/drizzling, fine dense drops of rain; spray; —पड़ना to drizzle,

फुहारा phuha:ra: (*nm*) a fountain; shower.

फुही phuhi: (*nf*) see फुहार.

फूंक phū:k (*nf*) puff; whiff, blow(ing); —निकल जाना the breathing process to come to a stop; to be deflated; sense of pride to be knocked off; to lose breath; —से उड़ जाना to be very lean and thin; to be almost a non-entity.

फूंकना phū:knā: (*v*) to blow; to puff, to whiff; to burn, to ignite, to set on fire; to waste, to squander away, फूंक-ताप डालना to squander away (money or property etc.); फूंक-फूंक कर क़दम/पाँव/पैर रखना to tread as on eggs, to feel one's way, to take every step with utmost caution; to be extra-cautious in one's movements; –मार कर उड़ा देना to destroy without effort.

फूँकनी phū:knī: (*nf*) a blow-pipe; blow tube.

फूँस phūs (*nm*) see फूस.

फूट phu:ṭ (*nf*) disunion/disunity, discord, rift, chasm; a species of large cucumber resembling a musk-melon in appearance that splits up on ripening; see फूटना; used as the second member of the compound टूट-फूट; –के बीज बोना to sow the seeds of disunion/rift/discord; –डालना to set (persons) by the ears/at variance; to cause disunion/rift/discord/chasm; –पड़ना/होना to have a rift/discord, to be divided/disunited.

फूटन phu:ṭān (*nf*) severe cracking pain in the joints of the body; fragments resulting from breaking of something.

फूटना phu:ṭnā: (*v*) to break; to be broken; to crack; to split; to burst; to erupt, to explode; to sprout, to shoot; (a secret) to be revealed, to defect; (eyes) to become blind; फूट-फूट कर रोना to weep bitterly, to try one's heart out.

फूटा phu:ṭa: (*a*) broken; cracked; split up; burst; फूटी आँखों न देख सकना/सुहाना to have extreme repulsion (for), to be put off by the very sight of; फूटी किस्मत see फूटे भाग; फूटी कौड़ी पास न होना to be penniless, to be extremely indigent; फूटे भाग ill luck, damned luck; फूटे मुँह बात न करना / से न बोलना to take absolutely no notice of; not to utter a wo[rd] even by way of courtesy.

फूत्कार phu:tka:r (*nf*) a whizzi[ng] sound, hiss.

फूफा phu:pha: (*nm*) husband of paternal aunt or father's sister.

फूफी phu:phi: (*nf*) father's siste[r] paternal aunt; also बुआ.

फूल phu:l (*nm*) a flower; flower embroidery; post-cremation ashe[s] the burnt part of a wick etc.; very light thing; bronze; ~का embroidery; embroidering flowers; ~गोभी cauliflowe[r] ~दान a flower-vase/flower-po[t] ~दार flowery; embroidere[d] ~माला a flower-garland; –उतारन[ा] लोढ़ना to pluck a flower/flower[s] –चुनना to pluck flowers; to colle[ct] post-cremation ashes (for im[-]mersion in holy rivers); –झड़[ना] to be very sweet in speech; –स[ा] सी very delicate and beautifu[l] very light; –सूँघना to be too ab[s]temious, to eat a very limite[d] quantity; फूलों की सेज a bed [of] roses.

फूलना phu:lnā: (*v*) to flower; [to] bloom, to blossom; to swell; [to] inflate; to be joyous; to be puff[ed] up, to assume airs; to feel prou[d] फूलकर कुप्पा होना to be overjoye[d] to be puffed up with joy; [to] grow too fat; –फलना to prospe[r] to flourish, to thrive; फूलने वा[ला] efflorescent; फूला न समाना to be [in] the seventh heaven, to be t[oo] happy to contain oneself; फूल[ा] फूला फिरना to take airs, to [be] puffed up; फूला हुआ tumid, swo[l]len; bulging out; puffed u[p] happy and joyous; फूले अंग [न] समाना to be overjoyed, to be b[e]side oneself through joy.

फूली phu:li: (*nf*) a hard whitish outgrowth in the pupil of the eye.

फूस phu:s (*nm*) straw, hay.

फूहड़ phu:har (*a*) coarse-grained; sloven(ly); unmannerly; devoid of sense of proportion; (*nm*) a slattern; ~**पन/पना** unmannerliness; slovenliness; ill-manners.

फेंकना phēknā: (*v*) to throw, to cast; to hurl; to fling; to toss; to waste; to emit.

फेंट phēṭ (*nf*) see **फेंटा**.

फेंटना pheṭnā: (*v*) to batter, to beat up into froth; to mix by trituration; to shuffle (as a pack of cards).

फेंटा phēṭā: (*nm*) the part of **धोती** rolled and tucked up round the waist; **–कसना/बाँधना** to roll a portion of the *dhoti*: round the waist; to gird up one's loins, to get ready for any eventuality.

फेंट pheṭ (*nf*) see **फटा**.

फेटा pheṭa: (*nm*) see **फेंटा**.

फेन phēn (*nm*) foam, froth, lather, scum.

फेनिल phenīl (*a*) foamy, frothful; full of lather/scum.

फेनी phenī: (*nf*) a kind of Indian sweetmeat.

फेफड़ा phephṛa: (*nm*) a lung.

फेर pher (*nm*) a detour, circuitous route; turn/turning; curvature; ambiguity; complication; ~**फार/बदल** modification, alteration; **–खाना** to (have to) make a detour; **–देना** to return; **–पड़ना** to get complicated; a complication to arise; to make a difference; **–में पड़ना** to be involved in a complication; to suffer a loss; **–में पड़ना, निन्यानवे के** to be unseemly crazy to amass wealth; to get embroiled in an unseemly activity for material gains; to be involved in a predicament of one's own making.

फेरना phernā: (*v*) to turn; to return; to obvert; to invert; to break a horse (as **घोड़ा–**); to repeat again and again; to proclaim, to announce (as **डौंडी–**); to change the order; to shuffle (as **पान–**).

फेरा phera: (*nm*) going round; round, coming and going back; circumambulation; circuit; a matrimonial rite wherein the bride and bridegroom move together round the sacred fire; **–देना** to make occasional visits/calls; **फेरे पड़ना** the matrimonial rites of going around the sacred fire to be performed; to be bound in wedlock; **फेरे लगाना** to take frequent rounds, to go round again and again; to circumambulate.

फेरी pheri: (*nf*) going round; round; circumambulation; hawking; ~**वाला** a hawker, pedlar; **–देना/लगाना** to go hawking; to circumambulate; to go again and again.

फ़ेल fel (*a*) failed, unsuccessful, plucked; (*nm*) misdeed, deed, doing; action; **–होना** to fail, to be unsuccessful (in an examination).

फ़ेहरिस्त fehrist (*nf*) a list, an inventory,

फ़ैंसी faĩnsi: (*a*) fancy.

फ़ैक्टरी faktri: (*nf*) a factory; **–अधिनियम** the factory act.

फ़ैया/ज़ faiya:z (*a*) liberal, generous, bountiful/bounteous; ~**ज़ी** liberality, generosity, bountifulness/bounteousness.

फ़ैर fair (*nm*) a (gun) fire; **–करना** to fire (a shot etc.).

फैलना phailnā: (*v*) to spread; to be diffused; to expand; to extend; to be stretched; to be radiated (as किरणें–); to be scattered; to spill; to become public (as बात–); to be inflated (as वह तो बहुत फैल गया है); to be on the increase (as कारोबार–); to get uncontrorablle (through anger), to listen to no entreaties, to be angrily cross.

फैलाना phaila:nā: (*v*) to spread; to extend; to expand; to span; to unfold; to outstretch; to stretch; to make calculations, to work out (भाव फैलाना); to propagate; to make public; –, झोली/हाथ to beg for something.

फैलाव phaila:v (*nm*) expanse, expansion; span; spread; stretch; scattering, radiation, space; space-area; roominess.

फैलावट phaila:vaṭ (*nf*) (making of) calculations, working out, process of working out.

फ़ैशन faishan (*nm*) fashion; ~परस्त fashionable; ~परस्ती fashionableness; -माडल a fashion model.

फ़ैशनेबल faishnebal (*a*) fashionable.

फ़ैसला faisla: (*nm*) decision; judgment; settlement; resolution; –करना to decide; to settle, to resolve; –देना to give/announce a verdict, to give one's ruling; –सुनाना to deliver judgment.

फोक phok (*nm*) dejuiced residue, residue left after taking out the essence.

फोकट phokaṭ (*a*) free, free of charge; gratis; –का माल (something) obtained/got free; –में without payment, gratis.

फोकला phokla: (*nm*) the bark, rind.

फ़ोटो foto (*nm*) a photograph; ~ग्राफ़ a photograph; ~ग्राफ़र a photographer; ~ग्राफ़ी photography.

फोड़ना phoṛnā: (*v*) to break; to burst; to split; to successfully induce somebody or to cause to defect (as गवाह–); to break into (as दीवाल–).

फोड़ा phoṛa: (*nm*) a boil; ulcer, tumour.

फ़ोता fota: (*nm*) a testicle; rent (of land); फ़ोतेदार a treasurer, burser; –भरना to pay off the rent of land.

फ़ोनोग्राफ़ fonōgra:f (*nf*) a phonograph.

फ़ोरमैन formaīn (*nm*) a foreman.

फ़ौज fauj (*nf*) an army: a multitude; –फाँटा an army/horde of associates, a large paraphernalia; ~दार a military officer; ~दारी criminal breach of peace; a penal offence; criminal; o क़ानून criminal law; ~दारी, ज़ाब्ता code of criminal procedure, the penal code.

फ़ौजी fauji: (*a*) pertaining to the army; martial; (*nm*) a soldier; -अदालत a military court; –क़ानून martial law; –डिक्टेटर a military dictator; –डिक्टेटरी military dictatorship.

फ़ौत faut (*nf*) death; demise; ~शुदा dead; फ़ौती pertaining to death; o रजिस्टर death record register.

फ़ौरन faurān (*adv*) immediately, instantly, at once, there and then, in an instant; –से पेशतर forthwith, immediately, at once.

फ़ौरी fauri: (*a*) urgent; quick.

फ़ौलाद faula:d (*nm*) steel; ~तन having a steel-like physical frame, very strong and sturdy.

फ़ौलादी faula:di: (*a*) made of or pertaining to steel; strong, stout, sturdy; –आदमी an iron-man.

फ़ौवारा fauwa:ra: (*nm*) see फ़व्वारा.

फ्यास phya:s (*nf*) dandruff.

फ़्रांस fra:ns (*nm*) France.

फ़्रांसबीन fra:nsbī:n (*nf*) a kind of

bean.

फ़ांसीसी fransi:si: (*a*) French; (*nm*) a French; an inhabitant of France; (*nf*) the French language.

फ़ाक, फ़ॉक fra:k, frɔk (*nf*) a frock.

फ़्रेम frem (*nm*) a frame; ~**दार** framed, fitted into a frame.

ब

ब ba–the third letter of the fifth pentad (i.e. **पवर्ग**) of the Devṇa:gri: alphabet; prefix that imparts the meaning of along with, with, for, by, from, upto, to, into, etc., e.g. **बख़ूबी,, बख़ैरियत, बरास्ता**.

बंक bānk (*a*) bent, curved; oblique; crooked; (*nm*) flexure; hence ~**ता** (*nf*) bend, curvature; obliquity; crookedness; ~**नाल** a goldsmith's blow-pipe; ~**साल** a warehouse.

बंकिम bānkim (*a*) bent, curved; oblique; crooked; hence ~**ता** (*nf*).

बंकिमा bānkimā: (*nf*) bend, flexure, curvature; obliquity; crookedness.

बँगला bāgla: (*nm*) a bungalow; (*nf*) the Bengali language; (*a*) of or belonging to Bengal (as –**पान**).

बंगसार bāngsa:r (*nm*) a jetty, pier.

बंगाल bānga:l (*nm*) an Eastern state of pre-partition India which was divided into two during the 1947-partition of the country–the western part being retained in the Indian Union and the eastern part having gone to Pakistan; –, **पश्चिम** West Bengal, an eastern state of the Indian Union.

बंजर bānjar (*a*) barren, unproductive, fallow; (*nf*) fallow/barren land.

बंजारा bānja:ra: (*nm*) a gypsy, nomad; a bird of passage.

बँटना bāṭnā: (*v*) to be divided/distributed/apportioned/partitioned/separated; see **बटना**.

बँटवारा bāṭwa:ra: (*nm*) partition; distribution, division; separation.

बँटाई bāṭa:i: (*nf*) distribution; distribution charges; crop-sharing (basis).

बंटाढा(धा)र bānṭa:ḍḥ(dh)a:r (*nm*) complete ruination, devastation, undoing.

बंडल bānḍal (*nm*) a bundle; (*a*) cunning; damned, condemnable; ~**बाज़ी** cunningness, shrewdness.

बंडा bānḍa: (*a*) tailless, without a tail; (*nm*) a kind of vegetable of the tass-group.

बंडी bānḍi: (*nf*) jacket, waistcoat; (*a*) feminine form of **बंडा**.

बंद bānd (*a*) closed, shut; locked (up); stopped, discontinued; (*nm*) a bandh, closure; bund, bank; knot; a string or strap; body joint; a stanza, verse; as a suffix it means that which ties or binds; –**गली** a blind alley; ~**गोभी** cabbage; -**बंद** each and every joint; ~साल a prison; –करना to close/stop/shut/discontinue; to put behind the bars; -बंद ढीले करना to tire out, to weary.

बंदगी bāndgi: (*nf*) salutation; prayer, worship; –कबूल होना a prayer to be admitted; salutation to be favourably answered.

बंदन bāndan (*nm*) vermilion; –का टीका a vermilion mark.

बंदनवार bāndanwa:r (*nf*) a festoon of flowers and green leaves (hung on festive occasions).

बंदर bāndar (*nm*) a monkey; harbour; –घुड़की/भभकी a hollow threat; mere brow-beating/bluffing; –का घाव an evergreen wound; an ever present affliction; -बाँट a distribution weighted in favour of oneself; –की बला तबेले के सिर mistaken usage—the actual proverb is तबेले की बला बंदर के सिर–transference of the affliction to another head; –क्या जाने अदरक का स्वाद Caviar to the General.

बंदरगाह bāndarga:h (*nf*) a harbour, port.

बंदरिया bādariya: (*nf*) a she-monkey, female monkey.

बंदा bānda: (*nm*) a servant, slave; an individual; humble self (used by a speaker for himself out of modesty); –, खुदा का a man of God, a creation of God; ~निवाज़ kind to one's own men; ~निवाज़ी kindness to one's own men; ~परवर (a deferential form of address) protector of one's own men; hence ~परवरी (*nf*); –जोड़े पली-पली राम उधारें कुप्पा man proposes, God disposes.

बंदिश bāndish (*nf*) a restriction; forestalling; musical pattern; –बाँधना to forestall; to contriv[e] a plan; to impose a restriction[;] to take precautionary measures[;] to work out a musical pattern.

बंदी bāndi: (*nm*) captive, prisoner[;] a bard; ~गृह/घर a prison; ~ज[न] a group of bards; –बनाना t[o] capture, to take a prisoner[;] -प्रत्यक्षीकरण habeas corpus; ० याचिक[ा] habeas corpus petition.

बंदूक bāndu:k (*nf*) a gun; –का घोड़[ा] the hammer of a gun; –की लिबलिब[ी] the trigger of a gun; ~ची a gun[-]ner, gunman; –चलाना/दाग़ना to fir[e] a gun; ~धारी a gunman; equipped with a gun; ~साज़ a gun manufacturer; a gun-repairer[;] hence ~साज़ी (*nf*).

बंदोबस्त bāndobast (*nm*) (land[)] settlement; management; –अफ़स[र] a settlement officer; –, आरिज़[ी] temporary settlement; –, इस्तमरार[ी] permanent settlement.

बंध bāndh (*nm*) a bond; tie; fetters, string; a bund; ligature[;] batch; -पत्र a bond.

बंधक bāndhak (*nm*) pawn; mortgage; surety; mordant; ~कर्त्ता[/] दाता a pledger; mortgager; pawn[-]ner; ~ग्राही a pledgee; mortgagee[;] pawnee; -संपत्ति mortgage pro[-]perty; –रखना to pawn; to mort[-]gage; to pledge.

बंधन bāndhan (*nm*) a bond, tie, th[e] act or process of binding/tying[;] bondage; restriction; a fetter[;] ~कारी binding; ~ग्रस्त in bonds[,] fetters, bound; hence ~ग्रस्तत[ा] (*nf*); –तोड़ना to break the bond[s] of; –में पड़ना to fall into bonds, t[o] be tied down.

बँधना bāndhnā: (*v*) to be tied; t[o] be fastened; to be bound; to b[e] restricted; (*nm*) a string, anythin[g] used for tying; बँधा हुआ tied; still, motionless, static (as पानी); बँधी-बँधाई conventional, traditional; बँधी रक़म definite amount; a lump sum.

बंधनी bāndhanī: (*nf*) a bracket.

बंधानी bāndha:nī: (*nm*) a porter, one who loads and unloads.

बंधारा bāndha:ra: (*nm*) a weir.

बंधु bāndhu (*nm*) a brother; relative; kinsman; ~जन kinsfolk, kinsmen; -बांधव kinsfolk, relatives; –भाव kinship; fraternity, fraternal feeling, fraternalism; -वर्ग see –बांधव; ~हीन desolate, lonely; kinless.

बंधु/ता, ~त्व bāndhuta: (*nf*), ~ttv (*nm*) fraternity, fraternalism, relationship; kinship; affinity; cognation.

बंधेज bāndhej (*nm*) restriction; proviso; stipulation.

बंध्या bāndhya: (*nf* and *a*) (a) barren (woman); sterile; issueless/childless; ~त्व/पन barrenness, sterility; issuelessness / childlessness; –पुत्र an impossible phenomenon.

बंपुलिस bāmpulis (*nf*) public conveniences, public latrine.

बंब bāmb (*nm*) a bomb; the sound of बम-बम.

बंबा bāmba: (*nm*) a hydrant; water-pipe.

बंसी bānsi: (*nf*) a flute; fish gorge, fishing hook; ~धर/वाला an epithet of Krishnā–a flute wizard.

बहँगी bēhāgi: (*nf*) see बँहगी.

बईद bai:d (*ind*) improbable; far off, distant, remote; –नहीं, कुछ भी capable of doing anything, nothing to be beyond.

बक bak (*nm*) a heron; hypocrite, simulator; (*nf*) gabble, jabbering; ~ध्यान feigned meditation designed to create an illusion, simulation; -वृत्ति a heron-like mentality, hypocrisy; simulation; –खुलना to go on talklng idly; to be long-tongued, to go on gabbing endlessly.

बकझक bakjhak (*nf*) babbling, gabble, garrulity; angry prate/outburst; –करना to gab, to gabble, to jabber.

बकतर baktar (*nm*) an armour; ~बंद armoured; oगाड़ी armoured vehicle.

बकना baknā: (*v*) to babble, to gab, to gabble/jabber, to chatter, to make disjointed utterances; to admonish; to rave; -झकना to go on raving; to admonish; to talk angrily.

बकबक bakbak (*nf*) raving, prattle, gabble/jabble; twaddle; –मत करो stop your gab, hold your tongue.

बक़रईद baqari:d (*nf*) an important Muslim festival.

बकरम bakram (*nf*) buckram, a typical stiffened cloth used for stuffing coat-collars and sleeves etc.

बकरा bakra: (*nm*) a he-goat; बकरे की माँ कब तक ख़ैर मनायेगी ? how long shall the mother's prayers secure the kid ?

बकरीद bakri:d (*nf*) see बकरईद.

बक़लम baqlam (*ind*) from the pen of; –ख़ुद from one's own hand.

बकलस baklas (*nf*) a buckle, fibula.

बक/वाद bakva:d (*nf*) twaddle, palaver, tattle, gabble/jabbering; lalorrhoea; ~वादी a twaddler, gabbler/jabber, tattler, idle talker.

बक/वास bakva:s (*nf*) see बकवाद, ~वासी see बकवादी (under बकवाद).

बकस bakas (*nm*) a box.

बकसुआ baksua: (*nm*) a buckle, fibula.

बक़ाया baqa:ya: (*nm*) arrears; balance; (*a*) remaining, outstanding; payable.

बक़िया baqiya: (*a*) remaining, outstanding; payable.

बकुचा bakucha: (*nm*) a bundle, packet.

बकुची bakuchi: (*nf*) diminutive of **बकुचा**; **–मारना** to bundle oneself up, to coil up.

बकोटना bakoṭnā: (*v*) to pinch.

बकोटा bakoṭa: (*nm*) pinching; pinch; a handful.

बक़ौल baqaul (*ind*) according to, as said/stated by.

बक्कल bakkal (*nf*) bark, skin.

बक्काल bakka:l (*nm*) small trader, petty grocer; vegetable dealer; used only as the second member of the compound **बनिया-बक्काल** (it has a derogatory ring).

बक्की bakki: (*a*) chatty, talkative, gabby, voluble, loquacious.

बक्खर bakkhar (*nm*) a cattle-pen.

बखत bakhat (*nm*) see **वक्त**.

बखान bakhā:n (*nm*) description; exposition; eulology, praise.

बखानना bakhā:nanā: (*v*) to describe at length, to dwell in details; to eulogize, to sing the praises (of).

बखार bakha:r (*nm*) a grain-store, granary, barn.

बख़िया bakḥiya: (*nf*) back-stitching, basting; **~गर** one who back-stitches/bastes; **–उधेड़ना** to deseam; to expose thoroughly; to analyse in wearying details.

बख़ियाना bakḥiya:nā: (*a*) to back-stitch, to baste.

बख़ी/ल bakḥi:l (*a*) miserly, parsimonious, niggardly; **~ली** miserliness, parsimony, niggardliness.

बख़ुद bakḥud (*ind*) by oneself, through self, by self.

बख़ुदा bakḥuda: (*ind*) by God; in the name of God.

बख़ूबी bakḥu:bi: (*ind*) very well, excellently; thoroughly; amply.

बखेड़ा bakheṛa: (*nm*) a row, broil; mess; complication; difficulty.

बखेड़िया bakheṛiya: (*a* and *nm*) (a) rowdy, turbulent / quarrelsome (person).

बखेरना bakhernā: (*v*) to spread. to scatter: to diffuse; to dishevel (as **बाल**–).

बख़ैर bakḥair (*ind*) well, safely, safe and sound.

बख़ैरियत bakḥairiyat (*tnd*) well, safely, safe and sound.

बख़्त bakḥt (*nm*) fate, fortune; lot; **~, कम** ill-fated, unfortunate, unlucky; **~, नेक** fortunate, lucky.

बख़्तावर bakḥta:var (*a*) fortunate, lucky, blessed, with a good lot.

बख़्श bakḥsh ––an adjectival suffix imparting the meaning of causing, giving, bestowing, granting, etc. (e.g. **तसल्लीबख़्श**).

बख़्शना bakḥshnā: (*v*) to bestow, to grant; to give; to pardon; to forgive.

बख़्शिश bakḥshish (*nf*) a gift, grant; tip.

बख़्शीश bakḥshi:sh (*nf*) see **बख़्शिश**.

बगटुट bagṭuṭ (*adv*); **–भागना** to run head over heels; to run as fast as one can.

बग़ल bagal (*nf*) a side; flank; an armpit; (*adv*) on one side, by the side (of), close by; **–का फोड़ा** an armpit boil; **–गरम होना** to get warmed up through a woman's intimate company; to sleep with a woman; **~गीर होना** to embrace; **–में** on the flank; close by; in the armpit; in arms; **–में ईमान दबाना**

to ignore honest means, to become unscrupulous, to adopt dishonest means; –में छुरी मुँह में राम-राम to have two faces under one hood, a wolf in lamb's skin; many kiss the hand that they wish cut off; –में छोरा शहर में ढिंढोरा to have a thing in one's pocket yet to look all round for it; –में दबाना to conceal in the armpit; to have in ready possession; बगलें झाँकना to look blank; to be completely cornered; to be non-plussed, to be rendered witless; बगलें बजाना to be exceptionally happy, to be in manifest exaltation/delight.

बगला bagla: (*nm*) a heron; –भगत a hypocrite, dissembler, simulator, sailing under false colours, impostor.

बगली bagli: (*a*) of, belonging or pertaining to the side / flank/ armpit; (*nm*) a tailor's small bag for keeping his needle, thread etc.; a wrestler's trick to dash the opponent down through one's side; –घूँसा a fist-blow through the flank; a blow at the side; an unexpected assault from a supposed friend.

बगलौंहा baglãuhā: (*a*) leaning on one side, aslant; aside.

बग़ावत baga:vat (*nf*) rebellion, revolt; –का झंडा उठाना, –की आवाज़ बुलंद करना to rise in revolt, to raise the voice of revolt; to fly in the face of.

बगिया bagiya: (*nf*) a small garden, backyard garden.

बगी/चा bagi:cha: (*nm*) a small park, garden; ~ची diminutive for बगीचा.

बगुला bagula: (*nm*) see बगला; –भगत see बगला भगत under बगला.

बगूला bagu:la: (*nm*) a whirlwind.

बग़ैर bagair (*ind*) without, excluding, to the exclusion of.

बग्घी bagghi: (*nf*) a four-horse carriage.

बघ bagh–an allomorph of बाघ used as the first member of several compound words; ~छाला tiger's skin (used by devout people to sit on while in meditation); ~नखा a sharp steel-hooked weapon moulded on the pattern of tiger-claw; ~नहाँ see ~नखा.

बघार bagha:r (*nm*) seasoning (of cooked vegetables, pulses, etc.) with boiled *ghee* and spices.

बघारना bagha:rnā: (*v*) to show off; to boast, to talk tall (e.g. शेखी –, पंडिताई –, etc.); to season (with *ghee* etc.).

बघेल/खंड baghelkhāṇḍ (*nm*) parts of the modern Madhya Pradesh state of the Indian Union; ~खंडी the dialect of Baghelkhāṇḍ; belonging or partaining to Baghelkhāṇḍ.

बचकाना bachka:nā: (*a*) puerile, childish; hence बचकानी (feminine form); hence ~पन; –मज़ाक करना to grin through a horse-collar.

बचत bachat (*nf*) saving; saving grace; profit, gain; -योजना a saving scheme.

बचना bachnā: (*v*) to be saved; to remain (unused or unspent); to avoid, to keep away or aloof; to escape; –, बाल-बाल to have a narrow/hair-breadth escape; बच निकलना to fall upon legs, to give the good, to make good one's escape, to flee; –भी बड़ी बहादुरी होती है discretion is the better part of valour.

बच/पन bachpān (*nm*) childhood; ~पना childhood; childishness;

puerility.

बचाना bacha:nā: (*v*) to save; to defend; to protect; to retain (unused or unspent); to (cause to) avoid; to (to cause to) keep away or aloof; to cause to escape; to spare.

बचाव bacha:v (*nm*) safety; protection; defence.

बच्चा bachcha: (*nm*) a child; kid; baby; infant; hence **बच्ची** (*nf*); (*a*) inexperienced; raw, of unripe age; **बच्चेदानी** the uterus; **बच्चे-कच्चे** small children, a host of small children; **बच्चे वाली** a mother, (still) having a nurseling; **–जनना/देना** to give birth to/to beget a child; to reproduce; **–निकलना** to be hatched, a young one to emerge out of an egg; **बच्चों का खेल** an easy job.

बच्छा, बछड़ा bachchha:, bachhaṛa: (*nm*) a he-calf.

बछिया bachhiya: (*nf*) a she-calf; **–का ताऊ** a dunce, blockhead; nitwit.

बछेड़ा bachheṛa: (*nm*) a colt.

बजंतरी bajantari: (*nm*) a bandsman; one who plays on a musical instrument.

बजट bajaṭ (*nm*) a budget; **–, घाटे का** a deficit budget.

बजना bajnā: (*v*) to be played upon; to (produce) sound; to ring; to strike (as a clock etc.), to be struck; fighting to take place; **–, नाम** to be famous.

बजबजाना bajbajā:na: (*v*) to effervesce

बजमारा bajma:ra: (*a*) (a term used by women by way of a curse) (may you be) struck by the bolt!; ill-fated.

बजरंग bajrāṅg (*a*) having a steel-frame, very strong and sturdy; **~बली** an epithet of the monkey-god Hanumā:n.

बजरबट्टू bajarbaṭṭu: (*a* and *nm*) (a) fool, stupid (person); nitwit, blockhead.

बज़रि/या, ~ये bazariya:, ~ye (*ind*) through/through the medium of, through the agency of.

बजवाई bajva:i: (*nf*) charges paid for playing on an instrument.

बजा baja: (*a*) proper, right, suitable.

बज़ाज़ baza:z (*nm*) a cloth merchant/ dealer, clothier, draper.

बज़ाज़ा baza:za: (*nm*) a cloth-market.

बजाना baja:nā: (*a*) to play on (a musical instrument), to ring, to produce a sound; to examine (as a coin); to strike (against); to execute (as **हुकुम**–).

बजाय baja:y (*ind*) instead of, in place of, in lieu of.

बजिंस, ~हू bajins, ~hu: (*ind*) exactly alike, having exact resemblance, similar in every respect; intact.

बजुज़ bajuz (*ind*) except; excepting, excluding; without.

बट baṭ–an allomorph of **'बाट'** (way; weight); a twist (in a string, rope, etc.); **~मार** a highwayman, robber; **~मारी** waylaying, robbing.

बटखरा baṭkhara: (*nm*) a weight.

बटन baṭān (*nf*) a button; switch; twist.

बटना baṭnā: (*v*) to twist (as thread, rope, etc.); to twine; see **बँटना**.

बटलो/ई baṭloi: (*nf*) a round brass vessel used for cooking; also **~ही**.

बटवारा baṭwa:ra: (*nm*) partition; distribution; division; apportionment.

बटाई baṭa:i: (*nf*) crop-sharing, share of (agricultural) yield; **-पत्र** an agreement for crop-sharing.

बटाऊ baṭa:u: (*nm*) a wayfarer, traveller.

बटालियन baṭa:liyān (*nf*) a battalion (in the army).

बटिया baṭiya: (*nf*) a small smooth stone-ball; a small pestle.

बटुआ baṭua: (*nm*) a purse-money, bag.

बटेर baṭer (*nf*) a quail; **~बाज़** one who rears quails; one who organizes quail-fights; **~बाज़ी** rearing of quails; quail-fighting.

बटोरना baṭornā: (*v*) to collect; to accumulate; to gather (together); to amass.

बटोही baṭohi: (*nm*) a wayfarer, traveller.

बट्टा baṭṭa: (*nm*) a discount; brokerage; deficit loss; stone-pestle, round smooth mass of stone; blemish; looking glass; **-खाता** a bad debt account; bad debt, irrecoverable arrear;**-लगना** to suffer a loss; to deal at a discount; (reputation etc.) to be damaged, to be slandered;**-सहना** to suffer a loss/damage.

बट्टी baṭṭi: (*nf*) a cake, small pestle; **–, साबुन की** a soap-cake.

बड़ baṛ–an allomorph of '**बड़ा**' used as the first member in several compound words (e.g. **बड़प्पन, बड़बोला**); (*nm*) a banyan tree; **~दंत** large-toothed, having tusk-like teeth; **~दुमा** long-tailed; **~पेटा** pot-bellied, having a large tummy; **~बोला** a boaster, tall-talker, braggart; **~भाग** fortunate, lucky; **~भागी** fortunate, lucky, blessed with an excellent lot.

बड़प्पन baṛappan (*nm*) greatness; dignity.

बड़बड़ baṛbaṛ (*nf*) grumble/grumbling, mutter/muttering, murmur/murmuring, gabble/jabbering; **–करना** see **बड़बड़ाना**

बड़बड़ाना baṛbaṛa:nā: (*v*) to grumble; to mutter/murmur; to gabble/jabber.

बड़बड़िया baṛbaṛiya: (*a* and *nm*) (a) gabbler/jabberer; grumbler/grumbling, muttering/murmuring.

बड़वाग्नि baṛwa:gni (*nf*) a submarine fire.

बड़वानल baṛwa:nal (*nm*) see **बड़वाग्नि**.

बड़हार baṛha:r (*nm*) the post-marriage feast organised by the bridal party.

बड़ा baṛa: (*a*) big; large; great; huge; important; noble; reputed; commodious; expansive; elder (ly), senior; grown up; rich; (*adv*) very; exceedingly; (*nm*) small fried cakes of ground pulse of **उरद**; **–आदमी** a rich/big/great man, member of an aristocratic family; **–काम** a huge work; an important work; a worthwhile achievement; **–कुल** see **–घराना**; **–घर** a rich man's house, an aristocratic family; a prison; **–घराना** an aristocratic family; a reputed house; **–दिन** the Christmas day; **–दिल** large heart; **–बाबू** head clerk; **-बूढ़ा** elderly; **–बोल** tall talk, boastful statement/utterance; **–साहब** the chief (of an office etc.); **बड़ी-बड़ी बातें करना** to brag, to boast, to talk tall; **बड़ी बात** a far-reaching remark; big talk; a great achievement; **बड़ी बी** a form of address for elderly muslim ladies; **बड़ी माता** small-pox; **बड़े दिल वाला** large-hearted, magnanimous; बड़े घर की हवा खिलाना to lay by the heels; बड़े-बड़े the big guns; high-ups, powerful people; men of reputation; बड़े बरतन की खुरचन leavings of a rich man's dishes; बड़े बाप का बेटा son of a great/reputed man, son of a noble man; बड़े बोल का सिर नीचा pride goeth before a fall; बड़े भाग/भाग्य exceptionally good luck, great fortune; बड़े मियाँ तो/सो बड़े मियाँ छोटे मियाँ सुभान अल्ला the younger is even worse than the elder; the elder was bad, the younger is worse; बड़े लाट the governor-general (in British India of olden days); बड़े लोग aristocratic people; rich/great people; high-ups; बड़ों की बड़ी बातें great men have great views/great ways.

बड़ाई baṛa:i: (nf) praise, eulogy; greatness.

बड़ी baṛi: (a) feminine form of 'बड़ा'; (nf) dried up tiny round cakes of ground pulse.

बढ़ई baṛhai: (nm) a carpenter; a low caste in the Hindu caste-hierarchy; ~गीरी the profession or work of a carpenter, carpentry.

बढ़ती baṛhti: (nf) increase; rise; growth; progress, prosperity; –का पहरा days of prosperity.

बढ़/ना baṛhna: (v) to increase, to multiply; to rise; to grow; to progress, to advance, to prosper; to excel/surpass/exceed/outdo; –कर ahead of; more than; better than; surpassing; –कर चलना to become conceited, to pace ahead out of vanity; –कर बोलना to outbid, to make a higher bid; to talk too tall, to brag; –चढ़/

–बढ़ कर बोलना to brag, to boast, to talk too tall.

बढ़नी baṛhnī: (nf) a broom.

बढ़ा/ना baṛha:na: (v) to increase, to multiply; to extend, to raise; to cause to progress/grow/prosper; to advance; to magnify; to exaggerate; to push ahead; to extinguish (as a दिया–); to close (as दुकान–); -चढ़ाकर कहना to lay it on with a trowel, to draw the long bow, to throw the hatchet.

बढ़ावा baṛha:va: (nm) encouragement, boosting, incentive; instigation.

बढ़िया baṛhiya: (a) fine, excellent, of good quality, choice.

बढ़ोतरी baṛhotri: (nf) increase; increment, addition; progress.

बढ़ौती baṛhauti: (nf) premium.

बणि/क् baṇik (nm) a trader, merchant; ~वृत्ति trading; [a trader's narrow mentality, profit motive.

बत bat–an allomorph of बात used as the first member in several Hindi compound words; ~कही prolonged talk, conversation; discussion; ~बढ़ाव stretching things far more than justified; altercation; carrying an exchange of words too far.

बतख batakh (nf) a duck.

बतर/स batras (nf) an itch for spicy talk; relish of talk/personal conversation; ~सिया one who has itching ears, a lover of relishing conversation.

बतराना batra:na: (v) to talk, to converse.

बताना bata:na: (v) to say/speak, to tell; to inform, to point out; to express; to thrash (मैं तुम्हें अभी बताता हूँ); to instruct.

बतासा bata:sa: (nm) a semi-spherical crisp and spongy sugar-cake; a typical firework; –घुलना to face immediate ruin/destruction; to have a mere momentary existence.

तियाना batiya:nā: (*v*) to talk, to converse.

तौर bataur (*ind*) as; like; just like; in the nature of; on the pattern of.

त्ता batta: (*nm*) a batten.

त्ती batti: (*nf*) a wick; lamp; taper; light; –जलाना to switch on the light; –दिखाना to light one's way; –बुझाना to switch off the light.

त्ती/स batti:s (*a*) thirty-two; (*nm*) the number thirty-two; the denture; ~सी the whole set of thirty-two teeth; oखिलना to laugh heartily, to be very happy; ~सी झड़ना the whole set of teeth to be knocked off; the whole denture to be uprooted; hence ~सी झाड़ना; ~सी दिखाना to laugh; ~सी बजना the teeth to chatter on account of cold.

थुआ bathua: (*nm*) the pot herb *Chenopodium album*.

द bad (*a*) bad; wicked, vile, depraved; ~अख़लाक incivil, uncivilised; ~अमनी disturbance, breach of peace; ~अमली maladministration; disorder, chaos; ~इंतज़ाम maladroit, one who mismanages; bungling; ~इंतज़ामी ill-management, mismanagement, maladroitness; ~कार depraved, debauch; vile, wicked; ~कारी depravity, debauchery; vileness; wickedness; ~क़िस्मत unfortunate, ill-fated; having a bad lot; ~क़िस्मती misfortunate, ill-luck, bad lot; ~ख़त having a bad handwriting; ~ख़ती bad handwriting; ~ख़्वाह ill-intentioned, ill-willed, wishing ill; ~ख़्वाही ill will, rancour, animosity; ~गुमान suspicious, apprehensive; conceited; ~गुमानी suspiciousness, apprehensiveness; conceitedness; ~गोई backbiting; talking ill; ~चलन depraved, of immoral conduct; ~चलनी depravity, immoral conduct; ~ज़बान foul-mouthed, ill-tongued; indecent of speech; ~ज़बानी indecency of speech, intemperance in speech; ~ज़ात wicked, base, vile; ~ज़ायका distasteful, tasteless; insipid; ~तमीज़ unmannerly; uncivilised, rude, of intemperate conduct; ~तमीज़ी unmannerliness; uncivilisedness, rudeness, intemperance of conduct; ~तर worse (than); ~तरीन the worst; ~तहज़ीब uncivilised, unmannerly; rude; ~तहज़ीबी uncivilisedness, unmannerliness; rudeness; ~दयानत dishonest; usurping, having bad faith; ~दयानती dishonesty, usurpation, bad faith; ~दिमाग़ arrogant, conceited; ~दिमाग़ी arrogance, conceitedness; ~दुआ curse, malediction; ~नज़र having an evil/ominous glance; evil-eyed; evil eyes/glance, ominous glance; ~नसीब unfortunate, ill-fated, luckless; ~नसीबी misfortunate, ill-luck, lucklessness; ~नस्ल of ill-breed; wicked, mean; ~नाम disreputed, infamous, of ill fame, notorious; ~नाम हुए तो क्या नाम न होगा notoriety also makes one known; bad name is also a name after all; the notorious are also widely known; ~नामी infamy, ill fame, disrepute; notoriety; slander; ~नामी का टीका a stigma/stain on one's name; ~नीयत (of) bad faith/intention, ill-intentioned, malevolent; avaricious; ~नीयती bad faith, ill intention, malevolence; avariciousness; ~नुमा ugly; unpleasant; ~परहेज़ one who exercises no restraint in diet; one who takes insalubrious food; intemperate in habits (esp. eating habits); ~परहेज़ी intemperate indulgence (in diet), lack of discrimination in eating; ~फ़ेल indulging in evil deeds/sins, licentious; ~फ़ेली indulgence in evil deeds/sins, licentiousness; ~बख़्त unfortunate, unlucky, luckless; ~बख़्ती misfortune, lucklessness; ~बू foul smell, bad odour, stink; ०दार emitting foul smell/bad odour, stinking; ~मज़गी unpleasantness; disagreeableness; a bad taste; ~मज़ा unpleasant, disagreeable, having or leaving a bad taste; ~मस्त intoxicated; licentious, lewd, having no control over oneself; ~मस्ती intoxicatedness; licentiousness, lewdness; absence of self-control; ~मिज़ाज tetchy, ill-tempered, short-tempered; petulant; ~मिज़ाजी ill temper, short temper, petulance, tantrum; ~रंग of a bad colour; discoloured; tarnished; forced out of countenance; grown pallid; of a different colour than the trump (in playing cards); ~राह gone astray, abberrant, (one who has) taken to an evil course; ~रू ugly, grotesque; ~लगाम having no restraint, too outspoken; mischievous (horse); ~वज़ा unmannerly, undignified; ~शक्ल ugly, grotesque; unpleasant; ~शगुन inauspicious; ominous; ~शगुनी inauspiciousness, ominousness, a happening that forbodes evil; ~सलीक़ा mannerless, unmannerly, slovenly; frump; ~सलूकी ill-treatment, maltreatment; ~सूरत ugly; grotesque; ~सूरती ugliness, grotesqueness; ~हज़मी indigestion; ~हवास stunned (out of wits), stupefied, bewildered; ~हवासी the state of being stunned (out of wits), stupefaction, bewilderment; ~हाल in a sorry plight, miserable; –अच्छा बदनाम बुरा a bad man is better than a bad name.

बदन badan (*nm*) the body, physical frame; (*nf*) bet, betting; –जलना to be in high fever, to be running high temperature; –टूटना the joints of the body to be aching/strained; –ढीला करना physical strain to be soothed; –दुहरा होना the body to be completely bent; –बदकर with a bet, deliberately; बदना to bet, to wager; –में आग लगना to be infuriated, to fret and fume; –सनसनाना (the body) to be in a state of tension; to be overwhelmingly excited; –साँचे में ढला होना every part of the body to be symmetrically proportionate, to be cast in a pretty mould; –सूखकर काँटा होना to be too attenuated, to grow very lean and thin, to be emaciated; –हरा होना to be refreshed.

बद/ना badnā: (*v*) to bet, to wager; to settle; ~कर deliberately; with a bet.

बदमाश badmā:sh (*a*) wicked; lewd; mischievous; rowdy; (*nm*) a hooligan, bad character, hoodlum.

बदमाशी badmā:shi: (*nf*) wickedness; lewdness; rowdiness, hooliganism; mischievousness.

बदर badar (*nm*) the jejube tree and its fruit; (*ind*) out, out of the gate.

बदल badal (*nf*) change, alteration (used as the second member of the compound फेर-बदल); replacement.

बदलना badalnā: (*v*) to change, to alter; to convert/to be converted; to replace; to go back (on one's word).

बदला badla: (*nm*) revenge, vengeance; retaliation; recompense; exchange; return; lieu; –चुकाना to be even with, to square accounts with, to take revenge on; –देना to repay, to recompense (with); –लेना to be even with, to put it across a person, to take revenge, to wreak vengeance; बदले में in return for, in lieu of.

बदलाव badla:w (*nm*) change; replacement.

बदली badli: (*nf*) cloudiness; a stray cloud; transfer; substitution.

बदलौअल badlaual (*nm*) exchange; retaliation.

बदस्तूर badastu:r (*adv*) as usual; according to convention, in the customary manner.

बदा bada: (*a*) destined; –होना to be destined, to be the writ of destiny.

बदाबदी bada:badi: (*nf*) competition; spirit of competition; –में in a competitive spirit in a bid to outdo the other party.

बदी badi: (*nf*) the dark half of a lunar month; evil, wickedness.

बदौलत badaulat (*ind*) through the grace of; by means of: by virtue of; for; due to.

बद्ध baddh (*a*) tied; bound; in bond; closed; fixed; ~कोष्ठ suffering from constipation; ~चित्त concentrated, singlemindedly dedicated (to); ~दृष्टि with eyes concentrated on, gazing, staring; resolved; ~निश्चय resolved; determined; ~परिकर girded up; ~प्रतिज्ञ committed; having taken a vow; ~मुष्टि stingy, niggardly, parsimonious; ~मूल deep-rooted; ~मौन see ~वाक्; ~वाक् quiet, speechless; ~वैर with a deep-rooted animosity; ~स्नेह attached (to), bound by love.

बद्धांजलि badhā:ṇjali (*a*) having hands folded together (out of respect).

बध badh (*nm*) see वध.

बधाई badha:i: (*nf*) congratulations, felicitations; –देना to congratulate; to felicitate; –बजना festive music to be played (on the birth of a male child).

बधावा badha:va: (*nm*) festive and auspicious ceremonies (esp, on the birth of a male child).

बधिक badhik (*nm*) a slaughterer; an executioner, a hunter.

बधिया badhiya: (*nf*) a castrated bull/bullock; –करना to castrate; –बैठना a business, project, etc. to crash; to suffer an irreparable loss.

बधियाना badhiya:nā: (*v*) see बधिया करना under 'बधिया'.

बधिर badhir (*a*) deaf; ~ता deafness.

बध्य baddhy (*a*) fit to be or worth being killed/murdered, deserving death; hence ~ता (*nf*).

बन ban (*nm*) a forest, wood; a bun; ~खंड woodland, part of a forest;

~खंडी a dweller of the woods; ~चर a forester; a wild beast; ~चारी treading the woods; ~देवता a forest-god; ~देवी a forest goddess; ~वास dwelling in the woods; ~वासी a dweller of the woods; ~मानस a woodman, forestman; ~राज a lion.

बनजारा bāṇja:ra: (*nm*) a nomad; nomadic grocer

बनना bannā: (*v*) to be made/constructed/built/prepared /composed; to be ready (for use); to be obtained; to become; to feign; to assume airs, to ride the high horse; to be befooled; बन आना to get a rare opportunity, to get a golden chance; –ठनना to prank; to adorn oneself; to make (oneself) up; बनना-सँवरना to prank, to adorn oneself, to make (oneself) up; बन-ठन कर निकलना to be dressed up to the nines; बन पड़ना to be possible/feasible, to be possible to do; to turn out to be; बन बैठना to assume the title/role/status/powers of; to pounce upon; बना-ठना spick and span; बना-बनाया accomplished, achieved; near-completed; oखेल बिगाड़ना to mar a successful effort, to undo an almost accomplished design/scheme; बना रहना to survive; to continue to live/exist/be present.

बन/फ़शा banafsha: (*nm*) a medicinal plant; ~फ़शई violet-coloured.

बनाना bana:nā: (*v*) to make/construct/compose/build/ prepare, to make ready; to form; to pull somebody's leg; to patch up; to develop a good equation with; to befool; –, काम to achieve one's end, to fufil one's purpose; –बिगाड़ना to make or mar, to do or undo; बनाये रखना to keep alive; to cause to live/exist/be present; to maintain; to keep good equation/ relation with.

बनाफर banā:phar (*nm*) a subdivision of the Ra:jpu:ts; chivalrous/adventurous man.

बनाम banā:m (*ind*) versus, as against.

बनाय bana:y (*ind*) extremely, absolutely; excessively; wholly, entirely.

बनाव banā:v (*nm*) composition, make-up; ornamentation; -सिंगार make-up; prank.

बना/वट bana:vaṭ (*nf*) composition; structure; construction; make-up; get-up, show; sham; artificiality; ~वटी artificial, sham; spurious: fictitious; showy; hence ~वटीपन (*nm*).

बनिया banīyā: (*nm*) a subdivision of the Hindu community, the third in the traditional hierarchical set-up–*vaishy*; a trader-grocer; -बक्काल a petty trader/shopkeeper (it conveys a derogatory sense).

बनियाइन baniyā:in (*nf*) an upper under-garment.

बनिस्बत banisbat (*ind*) as compared with, concerning, in regard to.

बनेठी banēṭhi: (*nf*) a long stick with knobs at either end whirled around; ~बाज an adept in the art of wielding a बनेठी.

बनैला banāila: (*a*) wild; of the forest; savage.

बन्ना bannā: (*nm*) a bridegroom; hence बन्नी (*nf*).

बप bap –an allomorph of बाप used as the first member of some compound words; ~मार patricide.

बपतिस्मा baptismā: (*nm*) baptism.

christening; –देना to baptise.

बपौती bapauti: (*nf*) heritage, inheritance; paternal property.

बफारा bapha:ra: (*nm*) medicated steam (inhaled for fomentation purposes).

बबर babar (*nm*) a lion; – शेर a lion.

बबुआ babua: (*nm*) a (plastic) toy; a male child; a word of endearment.

बबूल babu:l (*nm*) the acacia tree; –बोकर/लगाकर आम चाहना he that soweth vice shalt not reap virtue.

बबूला babu:la: (*nm*) a bubble; whirlwind.

बब्बूगोशा babbu:gosha: (*nm*) a softer and sweeter variety of pear.

बम bām (*nm*) a bomb, shell; shreds of paper with relevant hints/notes (one of the unfair means used by students for copying in examinations); an interjection (बमबम or बमबम भोला) meant to propitiate Lord Shiv; the projecting bamboos in a *tonga* or *ekka* between which a horse is harnessed; ~कांड a bomb-explosion; a case of bombing; ~गोला a bombshell; ~बाज़ a bomber; ~बाज़ी bombing, shelling; ~भोला (नाथ) Lord Shiv; ~वर्षा bombardment; ~बम करना to shout बमबम for propitiation of Lord Shiv; –बरसाना to bomb heavily.

बमकना bāmaknā: (*v*) to bombast, to boast aloud.

बमचख़ bāmchaḳẖ (*nf*) an altercation, wordy duel, loud exchanges, brawl.

बमपुलिस bāmpulis (*nm*) see बंपुलिस.

बम/बार, ~मार bāmba:r, ~mā:r (*a* and *nm*) a bomber; bomber aircraft; ~बारी/मारी bombing, shelling; ~बारी/मारी करना to bomb, to shell.

बमुक़ाबला bamuqa:bla: (*ind*) as compared with, in comparison with.

बमुश्किल bamushkil (*ind*) with difficulty; –तमाम with a lot of difficulty.

बमूजिब bamū:jib (*ind*) according to, in accordauce with.

बय bay (*nf*) sale; ~नामा a sale-deed.

बया baya: (*nm*) the weaver-bird.

बयान bayā:n (*nm*) a statement; deposition; an account; –, तहरीरी a written statement; –, ताईदी corroborative/confirmatory statement; –, हलफ़िया a statement on oath; –से बाहर beggaring description; indescribable, that which defies description; बयानात (pl. form of बयान) statements.

बयाना baya:nā: (*nm*) an advance, earnest money.

बयाबान baya:bā:n (*a* and *nm*) see बियाबान.

बयार baya:r (*nf*) breeze; –पीठ तब तैसी दीजे/कीजे, जैसी बहे as the wind blows, you must set your sail.

बया(लि)लीस baya:(li)li:s (*a*) forty-two; (*nm*) the number forty-two.

बयासी baya:si: (*a*) eighty-two; (*nm*) the number eighty-two.

बर bar (*nm*) bridegroom; strength, power; (*a*) best, foremost; carrying, taking away; (*ind*) on the other hand; on, upon; beyond; above, at, in, into, with, forth, back, away, against, based upon, according to, on account of; ~अक्स (on the) contrary, opposed, reverse;

~क़रार intact; effective (as before), maintained (in good form); ~काज marriage; ~ख़िलाफ़ contrary to, opposed (to), adversely disposed (towards); ~ख़ुरदार prosperous, flourishing, thriving; a son; ~ख़्वास्त dismissed, dissolved, discharged; ~ख़्वास्तगी dismissal, dissolution, discharge; ~ज़बान memorised, on the tip of the tongue; ~जस्ता proper, befitting; ~ज़ोर powerful; coercive; exerting pressure; ~ज़ोरी (by) coercion, (under) duress; forcibly; ~तर better, superior, higher; ~तरफ़ removed, discharged, dismissed; ~तरी superiority, excellence; ~वक्त at the appropriate/opportune time; –आना to achieve fulfilment, to culminate in success.

बरक़ंदाज barqānda:z (*nm*) a watchman, sentry.

बरकत barkat (*nf*) prosperity, plenty and prosperity, abundance; auspiciousness; –होना to have prosperity and plenty.

बरकाना barka:nā: (*v*) to evade; to avoid; to ignore (a potential cause for fight).

बरक्षा baraksha: (*nf*) see बरेच्छा.

बरगद bargad (*nm*) a banyan tree.

बरच्छा barachchha: (*nf*) see बरेच्छा.

बरछा barchha: (*nm*) a lance, spear.

बरछी barchhi: (*nf*) a dagger.

बरत barat (*nm*) a very stout rope; see [illegible]

बरतन bartan (*nm*) a utensil, a vessel.

बरतना baratnā: (*v*) to use; to put to use; to deal with.

बरदार barda:r—a Persian suffix meaning one who holds/bears/carries (as नाज़बरदार, फ़रमाबरदार); hence ~बरदारी (*nf*).

बरदाश्त barda:sht (*nf*) tolerance, endurance; forbearance; patience; –करना to endure, to tolerate; –के बाहर होना to be intolerable.

बरनाल barna:l (*nf*) a scupper.

बरपा barpa: (*a*) raised, established. occasioned/produced; –होना to be occasioned/produced; o, तूफ़ान a storm to be raised.

बरबस barbas (*ind*) forcibly, willy-nilly; without any reason; all of a sudden; unexpectedly.

बरबाद barba:d (*a*) ruined, destroyed; wasted; –कर डालना to play the deuce with, to ruin; ~बादी ruination/ruin, destruction; waste/wastage; oसे बचाना to bring off.

बरमा barmā: (*nm*) a drill, auger; Burma.

बरमी barmī: (*nm*) an inhabitant of Burma; a Burmese; (*nf*) the Burmese language; (*a*) Burmese, belonging to Burma.

बरस baras (*nm*) an year; ~गाँठ birthday.

बरसना barasnā: (*v*) to rain, to shower; बरस पड़ना to come down on, to shout forth in anger, to reprimand angrily.

बर/सात barsa:t (*nf*) the rainy season; rain; ~साती (*nf*) a raincoat; portico; an attic; (*a*) rainy; pertaining to the rains or the rainy season.

बरसी barsi: (*nf*) the first death anniversary; the rites performed on the first death anniversary.

बराँडा barā:ḍa: (*nm*) a verandah,

बरात bara:t (*nf*) a marriage party; –करना to join the bridegroom's party as a member.

बराती bara:ti: (*nm*) member of

a marriage party.

बराना bara:nā: (*v*) to evade; to avoid, to keep away; to cause to be jealous, to make jealous.

बराबर bara:bar (*a*) equal; even, level; adjoining; matching; (*adv*) abreast; constantly, continuously, ever, always; –का matching; adjoining (e.g. बराबर के घर में), -बराबर on a basis of parity, in an equal fashion; equally; in close proximity; –करना to make even, to level, to smoothen; to ruin; to squander away; to leave nothing; –छूटना to be drawn (as) a match etc.), to end in a draw.

बराबरी bara:bari: (*nf*) equality, parity; vying, rivalry; –करना to vie with; to imitate; to be insolent/impertinent (by vying with elders/superiors).

बरामद bara:mad (*a*) exposed; recovered; seized; –करना to recover; to seize; –होना to be recovered; to be seized.

बरामदा barā:mda: (*nm*) a verandah.

बराय bara:y (*ind*) for the sake of, in the name of; –खुदा for God's sake; –नाम nominally, only in name; –मेहरबानी be good/kind enough to, please (as –मेहरबानी आप चले आइए be kind enough to leave, please go.)

बरास्ता bara:sta: (*ind*) en route; via.

बराह bara:h (*ind*) see बरास्ता.

बरी bari: (*a*) set free, acquitted; absolved; –करना to set free, to acquit; –होना to be freed, acquitted.

बरेच्छा barechchha: (*nf*) engagement/settlement regarding dowry etc. for marriage.

बरोक barok (*nf*) see फलदान.

बरौनी baraunī: (*nf*) the eyelashes.

बर्क़ barq (*nf*) lightning; ~ज़दा struck by lightning; ~दम very fast-moving.

बर्जना barjanā: (*v*) to forbid; to inhibit; (*nf*) a taboo; an inhibition.

बर्ताव barta:v (*nm*) behaviour, treatment; also बर्तावा (*nm*).

बर्फ़ barf (*nf*) ice; snow; –गिरना to have a snowfall.

बर्फ़ानी barfa:nī: (*a*) icy, snowy; snow-clad; –तूफ़ान snow-storm.

बर्फ़िस्तान barfistā:n (*nm*) an iceland.

बर्फ़ी barfi: (*nf*) a kind of rectangular-shaped sweetmeat prepared from खोया (see).

बर्फ़ीला barfi:la: (*a*) snowy; icy; glacial; hence ~पन (*nm*).

बर्बर barbar (*a*) barbarian, savage; ~ता barbarism, savagery.

बर्र barr (*nf*) a wasp.

बर्राना barra:nā: (*v*) to gab/gabble; to talk disjointedly/incoherently; to talk in sleep.

बल bal (*nm*) strength, power; force; army; potency; vigour, vitality; emphasis; stress; kink; twist, contortion; ~कर/कारक nutritious, vitalising, restorative, potency-raising; ~गति-विज्ञान kinetics; ~दर्प pride of one's strength; -प्रयोग exercise of force, coercion; -बूता strength and vigour, strength; ~मुख्य an army commander; ~वर्धन/वर्धक imparting vitality, nutritious, potency-raising; ~वान powerful, strong, possessing vigour and vitality; ~विज्ञान mechanics; ~शाली powerful, strong, possessing vigour and vitality; ~हीन weak, powerless, having no strength; impotent; –आना to be twisted, to be kinked; –खाना to frown, to get angry; to be twisted; to suffer a loss; to undergo twist, to be bent, to move to and fro flexibly; –खाती हुई coiled; in a zigzag fashion; twisted; –खुलना to be straightened; to be set right; twists/curls to be removed; –देना to reinforce/emphasise; to twist; –निकलना see –खुलना; –पड़ना to curl, to be twisted, to be kinked; to suffer a loss; –पर कूदना, किसी के to be proud on somebody else's strength, to draw one's strength from some extraneous source; to have no inherent strength

बल/ग़म balgām (*nm*) phlegm; ~ग़मी phlegmatic.

बलतोड़ baltoṛ (*nm*) a typical boil said to result from the uprooting of a hair on the limbs.

बलबला/ना balbala:nā: (*v*) to gurgle (as a camel); to simmer; ~हट gurgling; simmering.

बलम balam (*nm*) ree बालम.

बलमीक balmī:k (*nm*) see बाँबी.

बलवंत balwant (*a*) powerful, strong, potent, vigorous.

बलवत्ता balwatta: (*nf*) strength, powerfulness, potency, vigorousness.

बलवा balwa: (*nm*) rebellion; riot, disturbance; ~ई a rebel, rioter; riotous.

बला bala: (*nf*) a calamity, an affliction; misfortune; an evil spirit; -ए-जान an affliction, a trouble that goes on pestering; –उतरना to be rid of an evil spirit; –उतरना, किसी पर to be hit by superhuman wrath; –करे/करने जाये, मेरी my foot ! why on earth shall I do that !; –का of the highest order, of miraculous proportions extremely; –जाने, मेरी why on earth shall I know this !; –टलना to get rid of an affliction, a grave trouble to be avoided; –पीछे लगना to be pestered by an undesirable element, to fall into a trouble; –मोल लेना to deliberately subject oneself to an affliction, to own up a trouble; –सिर (पर) लेना to involve oneself in trouble, to ask for affliction; –से मेरी my foot cares !, I damn care !, damn it !; बलायें लेना to own up somebody else's affliction, to sacrifice oneself on another; to pray for somebody's safe journey in life.

बलात् bala:t (*ind*) forcibly; all of a sudden, suddenly.

बला/त्कार bala:tka:r (*nm*) rape, ravishment, commitment of rape, criminal assault; violence; oppression; ~त्कारी a ravisher, one who commits rape or assaults criminally; ~त्कृत raped, ravished, one who has suffered a criminal assault, one whose chastity has been violated.

बलाध्यक्ष bala:ddhyaksh (*nm*) a commander (of the army).

बलाबल bala:bal (*nm*) strength and weakness; -विचार an assessment of comparative strength and weakness.

बलि bali (*nf*) a sacrifice; an oblation; -कर्म a sacrificial rite/performance; –का बकरा cannon fodder; –चढ़ना to be sacrificed; –चढ़ाना to be sacrifice; to sacrifice oneself on another; see –देना; –जाना to be sacrificed; to be so enamoured as to sacrifice all, to be ready to abandon all; –देना to sacrifice, to make a sacrifice; to make an offering to a deity etc. (by slaughtering the person or animal concerned).

बलिदान balida:n (*nm*) a sacrifice; offering; **–करना** to sacrifice; **–देना** to make a sacrifice.

बलिदानी balidā:nī: (*nm*) one who has made sacrifices, a sacrificer.

बलिष्ठ balishṭḥ (*a*) strongest; very strong, powerful, having tremenuous force/vigour/vitality; hence **~ता** (*nf*).

बलिहारी baliha:ri: (*nf*) sacrifice; **–जाना** to be ready to sacrifice oneself (on somebody); **–लेना** to own up one's afflictions; to pray to steer someone clear of all hazards.

बली bali: (*a*) strong, powerful.

बलीवर्द bali:vard (*nm*) an ox, a bull.

बलुआ balua: (*a*) sandy.

बलैया balaiya: (*nf*) see **बला**; **–उतारना** see **–लेना**; **–लेना** to own up all one's afflictions; to pray for one's well-being.

बल्कि balki (*ind*) on the contrary; on the other hand; nay; but; rather.

बल्ब bulb (*nm*) a bulb.

बल्लम ballam (*nm*) a lance, spear; **~बरदार** a lance-bearer; bodyguard; hence **~बरदारी** (*nf*).

बल्ला balla: (*nm*) a bat; racket; **बल्लेबाज** a batsman; **बल्लेबाजी** batsmanship.

ब/ल्ली balli: (*nf*) a pole, long wooden staff; **~ल्लियों उछलना** to be on high ropes.

बवंडर bavāṇḍar (*nm*) a typhoon, cyclone; **–उठाना/–खड़ा करना/–मचना** to raise a storm; to create hell of a commotion.

बवाल bawa:l (*nm*) see **वबाल**; **–ए-जान** see **वबाल**; **–खड़ा करना** to cause an affliction/a disastrous situation, to create a grave difficulty; **–पालना** to own up an affliction/a difficulty.

बवासीर bava:si:r (*nf*) piles, haemorrhoids.

बशर्ते basharte (*ind*) –, **कि** provided that, with the provision that, only if.

बसं/त basānt (*nm*) see **वसंत**; **~ती** see **वसंती**.

बस bas (*nm*) control; power; (*nf*) a bus; (*ind*) that's all, that'll do; enough; **–का** under control, under sway; **–का न होना** to be beyond control/reach; **– न चलना** to beat the end of one's tether; **–में** under one's complete control; within one's capability; **०करना** to get somebody by the short hairs.

बसना basnā: (*v*) to settle (down); to inhabit; to stay; to live; to be situated/located (as a town, village, etc.); to be imbued with (a scent etc.); (*nm*) see **वसन**; see **बोरिया-बसना**.

बसनी basnī: (*nf*) a long and narrow bag (for carrying cash coins).

बसबब basabab (*ind*) on account of, because of, due to.

बसर basar (*nf*) maintenance; subsistence; **–करना** to spend (days, life); to maintain (oneself), to subsist.

बसाना basa:nā: (*v*) to colonize; to inhabit; to rehabilitate; to build (a city, town, etc.); to (become) stale; to emit bad odour.

बसीला basi:la: (*a*) odorous, stinking, emitting foul smell

बसु(सू)ला basu(u:)la: (*nm*) an adze.

बसूली basu:li: (*nf*) a mason's tool for cutting and setting the bricks; receipt (s); recovery.

बसेरा basera: (*nm*) an abode, a dwelling; nocturnal stay; short stay; –**करना/लेना** to stay for the night; to stay for a while.

बस्त bast (*nf*) used only as the second member of the compound **चीज-बस्त** meaning–things, articles, belongings.

बस्ता basta: (*nm*) a bag, school bag; portfolio; a bundle; (*a*) tied; folded (as **दस्तबस्ता** —with folded hands); –**बाँधना** to make preparations to go; to wind up the day's work.

बस्ती basti: (*nf*) a settlement; satellite town; colony; inhabitation; population.

बहँगी behāgi: (*nf*) a string for carrying things on shoulders.

बहक behak (*nf*) rave, raving, incoherent talking (due to intoxication); going astray, aberration.

बहकना behaknā: (*v*) to rave; to talk incoherently; to be intoxicated; to go astray, to be aberrant; to be misled; to be enticed; to rave, to talk in an incoherent fashion; **बहकी-बहकी बातें करना** to talk incoherently, to rave (in intoxication).

बहकाना behaka:nā: (*v*) to lead astray, to mislead; to entice; to allure; to instigate; to divert one's mind.

बहकावा behka:va: (*nm*) enticement; allurement; instigation.

बहत्तर behattar (*a*) seventy-two; (*nm*) the number seventy-two; –**घाट का पानी पिये होना** to have gone through varied experiences of life; to be very seasoned and cunning.

बह/न behān (*nf*) a sister; ~**नापा** sisterly relation.

बहना behnā: (*v*) to flow, to float; to blow; to drift; to be swept away; to run (as **नाक**); **बहती गंगा में हाथ धोना** to make hay while the sun shines.

बहनापा behanā:pa: (*nm*) see under **बहन**; –**जोड़ना** to establish sisterly relationship, to become as sisters.

बहनेली behneli: (*nf*) adopted sister.

बहनोई behnōi: (*nm*) (younger) sister's husband.

बहनौ/त behnaut (*nm*) a woman's sister's daughter; also ~**ता** (*nm*).

बहबूदी behbu:di: (*nf*) welfare, well-being; betterment.

बहरहाल beharha:l (*ind*) at any rate; however; nevertheless; but for all that.

बहरा behra: (*a*) deaf; hard of hearing; (*fig.*) heedless; ~**पन** deafness; heedlessness; –**पत्थर** stone-deaf; –**बनना** to become/turn deaf; to fein not to hear.

बहलना behalnā: (*v*) to be diverted; to be amused; to be recreated/entertained.

बहलाना behla:nā: (*v*) to divert one's mind; to amuse; to recreate; to entertain; to allure, to entice.

बहलाव behla:v (*nm*) diversion; amusement; recreation; entertainment.

बहलावा behla:va: (*nm*) allurement, enticement; false hope.

बहली behli: (*nf*) a bullock cart fitted with a canopy for cover.

बहस behas (*nf*) a discussion; argumentation; debate; –, **कानूनी** legal debate; -**मुबाहिसा** discussion, debate; –**करना** to break a lance with; to argue (against), to plead (a case).

बहादु/र baha:dur (*a*) bold, brave, valiant; fearless (person); ~**री**

boldness, bravery, valour, fearlessness.

बहादुराना baha:dura:nā: (*a*) bold, brave, gallant, fearless (act); befitting a valiant man.

बहाना baha:nā: (*nm*) a pretext, pretence, an excuse; make believe; (*v*) to cause to flow/blow; to set afloat; to squander (as पैसा बहाना); to ruin, to destroy; बहाने (से) on the pretext of; in the name of; बहानेबाज़ sham, make-believe; a pretender, given to putting forth excuses; बहानेबाज़ी shamming, make belief, pretending, putting forth excuses.

बहार baha:r (*nf*) the spring (season), bloom; merriment, joviality; –आना the spring to cast its magic; –के दिन time of full bloom/youthfulness; –पर आना, –पर होना to be in full bloom; to be ever-prosperous.

बहा/ल baha:l (*ind*) reinstated, restored (to the original status/position); ~ली reinstatement; restoration (to the original status/position).

बहाव baha:v (*nm*) flow; flush, flux; outflow.

बहिः bahih–an allomorph of बहिस् in certain compounds (as बहिःशाला) meaning out, forth, outwards, outside.

बहि/न bahin (*nf*) see बहन; ~नापा see बहनापा (under बहन).

बहिरंग bahirāṅg (*a*) external, outward; extraneous; hence ~ता (*nf*); –रोगी an outdoor patient; –रोगी-विभाग outpatients department (OPD).

बहिरिंद्रिय bahirindriy (*nf*) external senses, outward sense-organ.

बहिर् bahir–an allomorph of बहिस् appearing in certain compound words; see बहिः; ~गत external, outward; gone out; ejected; ~गम an outlet; exit; egress; ~गमन outflow; evagination; going out; egress; ~गामी outflowing; outblowing; outgoing; ~ग्रह a superior planet; ~जगत external world, physical/tangible world; ~द्वार outer gate; main gate; ~मनस्क mentally elsewhere; absent-minded; ~मुख extrovert; ~मुखता extroversion; ~वेशन evagination.

बहिष्–an allomorph of बहिस् appearing in certain compound words; see बहिः; ~करण ex-communication; the act or process of boycotting; ~कार ex-communication; boycot; ~कृत ex-communicated; boycotted.

बही bahi: (*nf*) an account book; a register; ~खाता a ledger, an account book; a record book; –पर चढ़ना/टकना to be recorded in the account book.

बहु bahu (*a*) many; several; plural; ~जनन fecund; prolific; ~जननता fecundity; prolificity; ~जल्प talkative, loquacious; ~ज्ञ well-versed in many things, master of many trades; ~ज्ञता the state of being well-versed in many things; mastery of many trades; ~तंत्र polyarchy; ~त्व plurality; ~त्ववाद pluralism; ~देवपूजन polytheism; ~देववाद polytheism; hence ~देववादी; ~धंधी multipurpose; variously occupied; occupied; busy in multifarious activities; o होना to have too many irons in the fire; ~पक्षी/~पक्षीय multilateral; ~पतिका polyandrous; ~पतित्व polyandry; ~पति-प्रथा polyandry; polyandrous system; ~पत्नीक polygamist;

~पत्नी-प्रथा polygamy; polygamous system; ~पद polynomial; polypod; ~पदी polynomial; ~पाद polypod; ~भाषी polyglot; multilingual; talkative; loquacious; ~भुज polygon; ~भोजी gluttonous; ~मत majority; ० शासन majority rule; ~मान्य universally respected; reputed; ~मुख/मुखी multifarious; ~मुखता multifariousness; ~मूत्र suffering from polyuria; ~मूत्रता polyuria; ~मूल्य precious; invaluable; very costly; ~रंगा/रंगी multicoloured, polychrome; ~रूपिया an expert in disguising oneself through a variety of make-up, one who assumes various forms; multimorphic; ~रूपी multiform; pleomorphic, polymorphous; variegated; ~लिंगी polygamous; ~वर्ण multicoloured; pleochromc; variegated; ~वर्णता multicolouredness; pleochromism; ~वर्णा multicoloured; variegated; ~विध multifarious, varied; polygenous; ~विधता multifariousness; variety; polygenousness; ~विवाह polygamy/polyandry; ~व्रीहि a relative or adjective compound, the last member of which loses its character of a substantive and together with the first member serves to qualify a noun; ~श्रुत well-informed; polymath; ~संख्या majority; ~संख्यक majority; ~स्वर polyphonic; ~स्वरता polyphonic.

बहुक्म, bahukm (*ind*) by the order of, under orders from.

बहुत bahut (*a*) much; many; abundant; good deal, lots of, plenteous, plentiful; too; very, very much; –अच्छा very good, excellent, all right, that will be done!, fine, right!; –करके usually, generally, too often; –कुछ more or less; to a large extent; –ख़ूब very good! well said! well done!; –हो लिया enough of it.

बहुतायत bahuta:yat (*nf*) plenty, abundance; –से in abundance/plenty.

बहुतेरा bahutera: (*a*) much, abundant; (*adv*) in various ways, variously, fully, very much.

बहुतेरे bahutere (*a*) many, numerous.

बहुधा bahudha: (*ind*) usually; in various ways; mostly, generally.

बहुरना bahurnā: (*v*) to return, to come back.

बहुल bahul (*a*) plentiful, plenteous, abundant; plural; frequent; ~क polymer; ~कता polymerism; ~ता plenty, abundance; plurality; ~(ता)वाद pluralism; plurality; hence ~(ता)वादी (*a, nm*).

बहुशः bahushah (*ind*) repeatedly, again and again, many a time, variously.

बहू bahu: (*nf*) wife; daughter-in-law; a newly-wed woman.

बहेड़ा bahera: (*nm*) the medicinal fruit of the tree Belleric myrobalan.

बहेलिया baheliya: (*nm*) a hunter; fowler.

बहैसियत bahaisiyat (*ind*) in the capacity of, as, holding the position of.

बहोरना bahornā: (*v*) to return; to restore.

ब/ह्र bahr (*nm*) an ocean; a sea; (*nf*) measure, metre; ~ह्री marine, oceanic.

बाँ bā: (*nf*) bellowing (of a cow or bull); also –बाँ; ० करना to bellow.

बाँक bā:k (*nf*) curvature; crookedness; a bend; ~**नाल** a goldsmith's narrow blow-pipe; ~**पन/पना** crookedness; dandyism, foppishness, prank; chivalrousness.

बाँका bā:ka: (*a*) dandy; foppish, showy, prankish; chivalrous; gallant (person); –**छैला** a dandy, foppish and prankish; hence ~**पन** (*nm*).

बाँकुरा bā:kura: (*a*) chivalrous, valorous, gallant, adventurous.

बाँग bā:g (*nf*) a prayer call by the *muazzin*; crowing of a cock; loud shout; –**देना** to give a prayer call; to crow; to shout aloud.

बाँगड़ू bā:gṛu: (*nf*) the dialect of Bā:gaṛ region (including the Hisssar, Rohak and Karnal districts of the State of Harya:ṇā: and some parts to the north of Delhi); (*a*) stupid, foolish; rustic.

बाँचना bā:chnā: (*v*) to read, to read aloud.

बाँझ bā:jh (*a*) barren (woman); unfertile, sterile (soil); ~**पन**/~**पना** barrenness; unproductiveness, sterility.

बाँगर bā:gar (*nm*) a meadow.

बाँछ bāchh (*nm*) see **बाछ**.

बाँट bā:ṭ (*nf*) division; partition; distribution; deal (in the game of cards); share; -**बूँट** share, small share; –**में आना** to be allocated, to have as one's share.

बाँटना bā:ṭnā: (*v*) to distribute, to allocate; to apportion; to deal (in the game of cards); to grind (with a pestle).

बांड bā:ṇḍ (*nm*) a bond; –, **बचत** a savings bond; –, **राष्ट्रीय** a national bond.

बाँड़ा bā:ṛa: (*a*) tail-less, whose tail has been cut; helpless; with none to bank upon.

बाँदी bā:di: (*nf*) a slave girl, bondmaid, female serf.

बाँध bā:dh (*nm*) a dam; bund; weir; dike; barrage; an embankment; –**टूटना** a bund to give way; an embankment to be swept away; o, **धैर्य का** one's patience to be exhausted, patience to come to an end; –**बाँधना** to erect a dam, to raise a bund, to construct an embankment.

बाँधना bā:dhnā: (*v*) to tie, to fasten; to bind; to pack; to wrap around (as **पगड़ी**–, **पट्टी**–).

बांधव bā:ndhav (*nm*) brethern, kith and kin, fraternal relation; see **बंधु-बांधव**.

बाँबी bā:bi: (*nf*) an ant hill; a snakehole; –**में हाथ देना** to invite trouble; to risk an avoidable hazard; to confront a danger.

बाँया bā:yā: (*a*) see **बायाँ**.

बाँस bā:s (*nm*) a bamboo; pole; –**पर चढ़ना** to acquire a bad name, to become infamous; to earn disrepute; hence –**पर चढ़ाना**; –**बराबर** tall like a bamboo; **बाँसों उछलना** to be in a state of rapture, to be immensely happy; **बाँसों बढ़ना** to assume very large proportions.

बाँसुरी bā:suri: (*nf*) a flute; ~**वादक** a flutist; ~**वादन** playing a flute.

बाँह bā:h (*nf*) an arm; a sleeve; –**उठाकर प्रतिज्ञा करना** to take a firm vow; –**उतारना** the arm-bone to be dislocated; –**का सहारा**/–**की छाँह लेना** to seek protection/patronage of; –**गहना**/**थामना**/**पकड़ना** to give protection / patronage / support to; –**चढ़ाना** to get ready for a fight; to set right a dislocated arm-bone; to get ready to plunge into work; –**देना** to lend support, to extend help; बाँहों में कसना/भरना to embrace.

बा ba:—a prefix to nouns meaning—having, containing, along with; (*nf*) mother; ~अख़लाक well-mannered, cultured; ~अदब respectfully; respectful; humble; ~असर effective; influential; creating an impact; ~आबरू honourable, respectable; honourably; ~औलाद having a child/children; ~इख़्तियार competent; authorized; ~इज़्ज़त honourably; respectable; ~ईमान honest, scrupulous; ~कमाल working a miracle, miraculous; wonderful; ~क़ायदा regular(ly), formal(ly), orderly, systematic(ally); ~कार employed, gainfully employed; ~ख़ुदा devout, God-fearing; ~गरज़ selfish, having some selfish motive; ~ज़ाब्ता formal (ly); duly; according to rules, regular; ~तहज़ीब civilised; cultured, mannerly; ~मज़ा delicious, tasteful; enjoyable; ~मज़ाक humorous, witty, jovial; ~मुरव्वत/मुरौवत considerate, giving due weight to the factor of personal relationship, obliging; ~वज़ा civilized, dignified; ~वफ़ा faithful, loyal, fidel; ~शऊर mannerly; possessing proper manners; ~सलीक़ा systematic; mannerly; ~हम together, collectively, mutually.

बाइबिल ba:ibil (*nf*) the Bible (Christian scripture).

बाइस ba:is (*nm*) reason, cause; basis.

बाइसिकिल ba:isikil (*nf*) a bicycle.

बाई ba:i: (*nf*) one of the three humours of the body (see बात); gout, rheumatism; delirium; a lady; a prostitute; –जी a prostitute; a respectful form of address for a woman (esp. in Ra:jastha:n); –चढ़ना to be in a state of delirium; –पचना delirious disturbance in one's system to subside.

बाई/स ba:i:s (*a*) twenty-two; (*nm*) the number twenty-two; ~सी a collection of twenty-two (verses, couplets, etc.).

बाएँ ba:ẽ (*ind*) to the left, on the left-hand side; –होना to be adversely disposed, to be hostile.

बाकला ba:kla: (*nm*) a kind of pod-vegetable containing big peas within.

बाकी ba:ki: (*ind*) but if..., but, nevertheless; see बाक़ी; –न उठा रखना, कुछ भी to spare no efforts, to leave no stone unturned.

बाक़ी ba:qi: (*a*) remaining, left over; (*nf*) remainder; balance, arrears; subtraction; ~दार indebted, one who owes.

बाग ba:g (*nf*) the reins; ~डोर the reins, halter; ०हाथ में होना to have control over, to control the reins; ~डोर हाथ से छूटना to lose control over, to lose hold over the reins; –ढीली छोड़ना to give horse the bridle, to lay the bridle on his neck, to abandon control.

बाग़ ba:g̣ (*nm*) a garden, park; -बाग़ extremely delighted, very happy; ~बान a gardener; horticulturist; ~बानी gardening, horticulture.

बागडोर bag:dor (*nf*) see बाग.

बागान ba:ga:n (*nm*) plantation, gardens.

बाग़ी ba:gi: (*a* and *nm*) (a) rebel, revolting; mutineer; –सरदार rebel chief/leader.

बाग़ीचा ba:gi:cha: (*nm*) a small garden.

बाघंबर ba:ghāmbar (*nm*) tiger-skin.

बाघ ba:gh (*nm*) a tiger.

बाचा ba:cha: (*nf*) word; speech; pledge; ~**बद्ध** committed; pledged; ~**हीन** speechless.

बाछ ba:chh (*nf*) extreme tips of the lips; **बाछें खिलना** the lips to be widened (as a manifest sign of happiness); to be very happy, to be manifestly delighted.

बाज़ ba:z (*nm*) a hawk; falcon; a suffix appended to nouns to impart the meaning of one who does/indulges/plays with, or a performer or monger (e.g. **पतंगबाज़, जंगबाज़**); (*a*) desisted; some; –**औक़ात** some times; –**आना** to desist from; to keep aloof; –**रखना** to cause to desist; to keep away (from).

बाजरा ba:jra: (*nm*) millet; pearl millet.

बाजा ba:ja: (*nm*) a musical instrument; band; -**गाजा** band; fanfare; **बाजे-गाजे से** with trumpeting and fanfare.

बाज़ार ba:za:r(*nm*)a market, marketplace; -**भाव** market-rate; –**करना** to go shopping, to go marketing, to make purchases; –**गरम होना** the market to have brisk business, marketing activities to be in full swing; **(किसी चीज़ का) –गरम होना** to be rampant, to be very prevalent; to be the order of the day;–**गिरना** the market to be slack, the prices to go down; the business to be in a state of depression; –**ठहरना** the market to be (come) stable; prices to be stabilised; –**तेज़ होना** prices to shoot up; to be in great demand; –**मंदा होना** the market to be in a state of depression; the business to be slackened; the prices to fall; –**मिलना** to find a market; –**में आग लगना** prices to shoot up, everything to grow costlier; –**में बैठना** to become a marketable commodity, to sell oneself; to take to a prostitute's life; –**में सुर्खी होना** the prices to rocket high, prices to be rising; –**लगना** the market to open, the market to commence business; –**लगाना** to scatter things around; to have a large number of things gathered together.

बाज़ा/री, ~रू ba:za:ri:, ~ru: (*a*) belonging to the market place, commonplace, vulgar (as language); cheap; ~**री/रू औरत** a prostitute, a woman of easy virtue; ~**री/रू गप** an incredible rumour, baseless rumour.

बाजी ba:ji: (*nf*) an elder sister.

बाज़ी ba:zi: (*nf*) a stake; wager, bet; play; performance; turn (as **खेलने की बाज़ी किसकी है ?**); ~**गर** an acrobat; juggler, magician; ~**गरी** acrobatics; jugglery, magical performance; –**आना** to have the turn to play; to have good cards; –**बदना** to take a bet, to wager; –**मारना** to bear the palm, to take the cake, to score a victory; to successfully accomplish a difficult task; –**ले जाना** to carry away the bell, to surpass, to emerge victorious.

बाजीकरण ba:ji:karan (*nm*) imparting immense sexual potency and retentivity; hence -**ओषधि**.

बाज़ू ba:zu: (*nm*) an arm; side; overside; flank; wing; ~**बंद** an armlet; –**टूटना** the arm-bone to be dislocated; to lose a staunch supporter; –, **दायाँ** lit. the right arm, i.e. the most vital/staunchest supporter.

बाट ba:ṭ (*nf*) path, way, course; (*nm*) a weight; used as the second member in the reduplicative compound **ठाठ-बाट** (see); **–का रोड़ा** an impediment, a hindrance; **–जोहना/देखना** to kick one's heels, to wait for, to await anxiously; **–पारना** to waylay.

बाटी ba:ṭi: (*nf*) a small rounded thick dough bread roasted on cowdung or coal-fire.

बाड़ ba:ṛ (*nf*) a fence; hedge; **–लगाना** to erect a hedge.

बाड(ड़)व ba:ḍ(ṛ)av (*nm*) marine-fire.

बाड़ा ba:ṛa: (*nm*) an enclosure, a compound, yard; pen; paddock; corral.

बाडी ba:ḍi: (*nf*) body, physical frame; bodice; **~गार्ड** a body-guard.

बाड़ी ba:ṛi: (*nf*) a small orchard; an enclosure; house.

बाढ़ ba:ṛh (*nf*) a flood, freshet; spate; inundation; salvo, volley; **–आना** to be flooded/inundated with; **–पर चढ़ाना** to instigate, to provoke.

बाण bā:n (*nm*) an arrow; **-वर्षा** a shower of arrows, salvo of arrows, **-विद्या** archery; **~वृष्टि** see **-वर्षा**; **–संधान करना** to place the arrow on the bow.

बाणाभ्यास bā:na:bbhya:s (*nm*) practice of archery.

बाणावली bā:na:vali: (*nf*) a row/succession of arrows.

बात ba:t (*nf*) a thing; matter; fact; point; counsel; talk; discourse; discussion; negotiation; saying; utterance, statement; commitment; word; context; credit; (*pl.*) **बातें** matters; talk, gossip; affairs; sayings; utterances; discourse; **–आई-गई होना** a matter to be lost and gone; to be forgotten and forsaken; **–आना** the topic to have arisen, the context to have presented itself; **–आना, किसी पर** the blame/responsibility to devolve upon; **–आ पड़ना** the context to have presented itself; the topic to have arisen; the responsibility to be cast upon/devolve on; **–उगलना** to speak out the truth, to divulge a secret; **–उछालना** to give a wide publicity to a matter (for slander, defamation, etc.); **–उठाना** to raise a matter; **–उड़ना** a rumour to get afloat, a rumour to go round; **–उड़ाना** to set a rumour afloat, to cause a rumour to go round; **–उलटना** to go back on one's word, to prevaricate; **–करना** to speak/talk/converse; **–कहते** in an instant, in a moment, in no time; **–का ओर-छोर** the logic/rationale behind a thing, the real import of an utterance; **–काटना** to cut one short, to intervene, to interrupt one in one's speech, to break the thread of an utterance; **–का धनी/पक्का/सच्चा** true to one's word, faithful to one's promise; **–कान में पड़ना** to get an inkling of something, to get to know something by chance; **–का बतंगड़** much ado about nothing; making a mountain out of a mole-hill; to exaggerate beyond all limits; **–की तह** the real import of a thing/statement, meaning of an utterance in the ultimate analysis; **–की बात** just a technicality; just a question of prestige; just a contest to preserve one's honour; **–की बात में** in an instant, instantaneously, suddenly; **–खटकना** to feel bad about something; to raise a feeling of suspicion; –ख़ाली जाना an utterance to go waste, one's words to have no effect; –खुलना/फूटना a secret to leak out, a secret to become public; –खोलकर कहना to state in details, to elaborate; –गढ़ना to make up/concoct a story, to fabricate a tale; –गाँठ/गिरह में बाँधना to bear something always in mind, to make a permanent note of something; –गोल करना to evade a topic/statement, to cleverly avoid saying something; not to make a committal statement; –चबा जाना to swallow one's word; –चलाना to initiate a topic, to broach a conversation, to raise a point; –छेड़ना to broach a conversation, to initiate discussion on a topic; to take up or renew a dispute or altercation; –जाना to fail to honour a commitment; a pledge to be dishonoured; a pledge to fall; –टालना to put off, to make excuses, to evade; –टूटना negotiations to break down; –ठहरना an engagement to be fixed; the terms of marriage to be settled; –डालना to reject a request; to turn down a request, to make a request ineffective; –दबाना to hush up a matter;–दुहराना to reiterate a point; to repeat a thing; to harp on a thing,–न करना, सीधे मुँह to be too arrogant to talk, to give no lift; –न निकालना, मुँह से to be dumbfounded, to be rendered speechless; –न पूछना to evince no care/concern/feeling for; to care nothing for; –निकलना a topic to be broached, a point to be raised; –निकलवाना to uncover the truth; to force to speak the truth; –पकना a matter to mature; पक्की करना to make an assurance doubly sure; to confirm an engagement; –पकड़ना to seize censoriously on what is said, to carp or cavil at; to take a statement rather too literally; –पचना a secret to be contained, a secret to be kept; –पर अड़ना to be firm on one's stand, to stick unmovably to one's statement; –पर जाना to go by one's word; to take one's words at their face value; –पर ख़ाक डालना to let bygones be bygones; to forget and forgive; –पलटना to change one's ground, to back out from one's word, to prevaricate; –पाना to get to the bottom of an affair; –पी जाना to suppress one's emotion; to endure quietly; –पूछना to pose a question; to enquire after, to evince care/concern/feeling for; –फूटना see –खुलना; –फेंकना to taunt, to jeer, to mock; –फैलना something to get wide publicity, to become public knowledge; –बढ़ाना to aggravate a dispute, to spin out an altercation, to make a serious affair of; –बदलना to depart from one's word, to shuffle, to change one's ground, to put a new face on; to say one thing and do another; –बनना to successfully attain one's aim, to answer well, things to mould as wished; to gain credit; ~बनाऊ an adept in making excuses; a time server; an expert fabricator of tales; –बनाना to talk much/tall, to make up stories; to talk grandly, to boast; to cause to be accomplished sucessfully; –बाँधना to sophisticate, to prevaricate;

-बात पर बिगड़ जाना to have a chip on one's shoulder, to be quick to take offence; -बात में in each and every word, in every case or instance; in every respect; throughout; in mere talks, in no time; –बिगाड़ना to mar a prospect, to spoil an affair, to thwart/frustrate; to bring disgrace on; –बिलकुल उलटी होना the boot to be on the other leg; –मत करो hold your tongue!, enough of it!; –मन में बसना a point/statement/fact to be borne in mind; something to make a deep impress on the mind; –मानना to comply with one's counsels, to heed somebody's suggestion; –मुँह से ले जाना to take words out of one's mouth, to anticipate and reproduce somebody's intended utterance; –में बात मिलाना to chime in, to concur; –में फ़र्क आना to change one's stand; to lose credit/repute; things to be different from what they were; –में से बात निकालना to drag out or prolong an argument; to carp or cavil at an argument; to read in between the lines; to draw subtle inferences one after the other; –रखना to honour somebody's word; to keep one's credit unimpaired; to maintain somebody's honour unsullied; –रहना to see one's commitment honoured; one's word to be fulfilled or complied with; to get the better in argument; to prevail; –लगना to feel hurt/offended by one's words; –सँभाल लेना to put a good/bold face on (a matter); –सुनना to give due attention to; to follow the advice of; –हल्की पड़ना to lose one's esteem; one's utterance not to produce its expected impact; to be discredited; बातें कम लातें ज्यादा more kicks than half-pence; बातें, चिकनी-चुपड़ी oily words, flattering utterances; बातें छाँटना to talk a bit too much; बातें बघारना to talk grandly, to speak out splendid nothings; to boast; बातें मिलाना/लगाना to tell tales; to back-bite, to calumniate; बातें सुनाना to give a bit of one's mind, to talk harsh things; to revile; to tell one's tale; बातों का चस्का होना to have itching ears; बातों का धनी/बादशाह an empty talker, a gas-bag; बातों की झड़ी an incessant flow of talks, a continuous downpour of talks; बातों की पुड़िया too talkative, loquacious; a chatter-box; बातों-बातों में in the course of a conversation; just in fun; without being serious; in no time; बातों में आना to be taken in; to be cajoled into accepting one's words at their face value; बातों में उड़ाना to talk somebody out, to turn off with a jest; बातों में बहलाना to beguile with words, to talk (somebody) into compliance; बातों में लगाना to engage in conversation, to occupy one's attention; बातों से पेट नहीं भरता fine words butter no parsnips; the tune the old cow died of; to advise instead of giving relief.

बातचीत ba:tchi:t (*nf*) talks, negotiations; conversation; dialogue; –करना to negotiate, to talk over, to converse; to start a dialogue, to be closeted with; –का सिलसिला series of talks/negotiations; course of talks.

बाती ba:ti: (*nf*) the wick of a

lamp.

बातूनी ba:tu:nī: (*a* and *nm*) too talkafive, loquacious, garrulous; a chatter-box, great talker.

बाद ba:d (*nm*) see वाद; (*ind*) after, later, subsequently; (*adj*) subtracted, deducted; (*nf*) air, wind; a suffix used imperatively to mean 'let it be, be it so, may it be, may it continue to be' etc. e.g. ज़िंदाबाद, मुर्दाबाद; –बाक़ी cash in hand; –करना/देना to deduct, to subtract; –का later; subsequent; –में later, subsequently.

बादना ba:dnā: (*v*) to contend, to dispute, to argue, to contest.

बादबान ba:dbā:n (*nm*) a sail (of a boat etc.).

बादल ba:dal (*nm*) a cloud; –उठना/उमड़ना the clouds to gather thick; –खुलना the clouds to be diffused/scattered; –गरजना the clouds to produce a rumbling sound, a thundering sound to be produced; –घिरना the clouds to grow dense, the sky to be overcast; –छँटना/फटना the clouds to be diffused/scattered; –छाना the sky to be overcast with clouds; –में थिगली लगाना lit. to patch up a cleavage in the sky –to accomplish an impossibility, to work wonder, to perform a miracle; बादलों से बातें करना to be very high up in the skies; to establish a rapport with the skies.

बादशाह ba:dsha:h (*nm*) a king, ruler; a piece (the king) in chess; the king in the game of playing cards; a bounteous man; the most outstanding person in a trade, skill, art, craft, etc.; ~शाहज़ादा a prince; ~शाहज़ादी a princess; ~शाहे-वक्त the contemporary ruler, the then ruler.

बादशाहत ba:dsha:hat (*nf*) rule, government; sovereignty; kingdom.

बादशाही ba:dsha:hi: (*a*) kingly, royal, regal, imperial; –खर्च royal expenditure; spending in a royal fashion; –फ़रमान/हुक्म a royal writ, an edict.

बादा/म ba:da:m (*nm*) almond; ~मी almond-coloured; light yellow; prepared from almonds.

बादी ba:di: (*nf*) fat, flatulence; wind; (*a*) fattening; flatulent, windy; ~पन flatulence, windiness; –छाना to get too fat, to become very flatulent; –छाना, आँखों पर to be too arrogant to see reason, to be so arrogant as to heed none; –बढ़ना to grow fat/plump/flatulent.

बाध ba:dh (*nm*) obstruction, impediment; rendering inoperative.

बाधक ba:dhak (*a*) causing hindrance / obstruction / impediment; obstructive, impeding, troublesome; –तत्व an obstructive element; hence ~ता (*nf*).

बाधन ba:dhān (*nm*) proscription; obstruction.

बाधा ba:dha: (*nf*) a hindrance, an obstacle/obstruotion, impediment; bar, handicap; interference, interruption; trouble; disturbance; obsession (of an evil spirit etc.); infestation; ~हर removing or causing to remove an obstacle/impediment/hindrance.

बाधित ba:dhit (*a*) restricted; handicapped; barred; impeded, obstructed; obsessed; rendered inoperative.

बाध्य ba:ddhy (*a*) obliged; compelled, forced; ~**कर** obligatory; ~**ता** duress, coercion; obligation.

बान bā:n (*nm*) an arrow; cord of twisted grass etc. used for bottom of beds (and other purposes); (*nf*) habit, wont, custom; a suffix thatsignifies a possessor, bearer, keeper, man (as **दरबान**).

बानक bā:nak (*nm*) guise; appearance; form; –**बनना** to have things traverse the expected course, to have things proceed smoothly (to a successful conclusion).

बानगी bā:ngi: (*nf*) a specimen, sample; fore-taste.

बानबे bā:nbe (*a*) ninety-two; (*nm*) the number ninety-two.

बाना ba:nā: (*nm*) the woof; dress, fashion or style of dress; guise, appearance, deportment; make-up; (*v*) to open up, to widen (as **मुँह बाना**); to comb(hair); hence –**धारण करना**.

बानि ba:nī (*nf*) wont, habit, custom.

बानी ba:nī: (*nf*) see **वाणी**.

बाप ba:p (*nm*) father; -**दादा** forefathers, ancestors; –**का** paternal; –**का माल/की चीज़ समझना** to take as one's own property, to take as an inheritance; -**दादा का नाम डुबाना** to bring bad name to one's forefathers, to ruin the prestige of the family; –**दादा बखानना** to heap curses on one's ancestors; -**दादा से** from generations; –**बनाना** to flatter, to strike a pose of extreme obedience; –**रे बाप**! an exclamation signifying wonder; fear or agony, gosh !

बापुरा ba:pura: (*a*) poor, indigent, insignificant.

बापू ba:pu: (*nm*) father.

बाबत ba:bat (*ind*) about, pertaining to, in respect of, concerning.

बाबा ba:ba: (*nm*) grandfather; an old man; an ascetic; (in certain areas and communities it is also used to denote) father; –**आदम** the most primitive/earliest man; **०का ज़माना** primitive times, the most ancient times; –**आदम के ज़माने का** absolutely outdated and outmoded, too primitive.

बाबुल ba:bul (*nm*) father.

बाबू ba:bu: (*nm*) an educated man, gentleman; middle class man; a clerk; ~**जी** a word of address for father; a respectable man; –**साहब** a tip-top person, man of fashion.

बाम ba:m (*nm*) the roof; attic; a pain balm.

बायन ba:yān (*nm*) presents (to relatives etc.); an invitation (to participate in a particular celebration); –**देना** to invite; to challenge to have it out.

बायलर ba:ylar (*nm*) a boiler.

बायस्कोप ba:iskop (*nm*) a biscope; movie film.

बायाँ ba:yā: (*a*) left, sinistral; adverse; –**देना** to avoid; to evade; ~**पन** sinistrality; opposition; –**पाँव/पैर पूजना** to concede superiority; to accept as superior in wits; **बायें हाथ का काम/खेल** a child's play, very easy job; too easy to be bothered about; to do it at one's head; **बायें हाथ से गिनवा लेना** to compel to pay; to oblige (somebody) to make payment of one's due.

बायें ba:yẽ (*ind*) to the left; in the opposite camp; adversely disposed;

–होना to be hostile/opposed to, to be adversely disposed (towards).

बारंबार ba:rãmba:r (*ind*) again and again, time and again, repeatedly; –कहना to cram down one's throat; ~ता frequency.

बार ba:r (*nf*) time(s); turn; (*nm*) door (in the compound घर~); burden, weight; a Persian word used as a suffix meaning that which or who scatters or sheds (as अश्कबार); ~बरदार a porter; ~बरदारी porterage; -बार again and again, repeatedly; oकहना to cram down one's throat.

बारजा bā:rja: (*nm*) a balcony.

बारदाना ba:rda:nā: (*nm*) provisions.

बारना ba:rnā: (*v*) to restrain, to check; to forbid; see वारना.

बारह ba:reh (*a*) twelve; (*nm*) the number twelve; ~खड़ी the aggregate of forms a consonant of the Devna:gri: alphabet assumes in combination with the vowels (क, का, कि, की, कु, कू, के, कै, को, कौ, कं, कः); ~दरी see बारादरी; ~बाट scattered all round, cast to winds; at sixes and sevens, at variance and thrown into confusion; ~बानी pure, genuine, perfect; ~मासा a conventional verse composition consisting of twelve stanzas depicting the suffering and agony of separation and the changing moods and characteristics of nature during the twelve months of the year; ~मासी perennial, all-weather, functioning or flowering round the year; oरास्ता all-weather route; ~सिंगा a stag; बारहों all the twelve, the whole twelve; बारहों महीने throughout the year, the whole twelve months; ~बाट करना to scatter all round; to cast to winds; to spell ruination; ~बाट होना to be at sixes and sevens; to be cast to winds; to be thrown into confusion.

बारहवाँ ba:rehvā: (*a*) the twelfth; (*nm*) the twelfth day of post-mortem rites.

बारहा ba:rha: (*ind*) a number of times, time and again, repeatedly.

बारा/त ba:ra:t (*nf*) a wedding party; ~ती member of a wedding party; ~त करना to join a wedding party.

बारादरी ba:ra:dari: (*nf*) lit. having twelve doors—a house or a well-knit locality having twelve in-doors/entrances.

बारिश ba:rish (*nf*) the rain, shower; the rainy season.

बारिस्ट/र ba:ristar (*nm*) a barrister-at-law; ~री practising at the bar, practising law; the work or status of a barrister-at-law.

बारी ba:ri: (*nf*) turn; millet; (*nm*) a low Hindu caste in the traditional caste set-up; बारी से turn by turn.

बारी/क ba:ri:k (*a*) fine; thin; slender; subtle; ~की fineness; subtlety; ~कियों में उतरना/जाना to go into minute details, to delve deep into finer details.

बारू/द ba:ru:d (*nf*) gunpowder; ~दखाना a magazine; ~दघर a magazine; ~दी pertaining to or consisting of ~द; explosive.

बारे ba:re (*ind*); –में about, pertaining/relating to, in respect of.

बारोठा ba:rotha: (*nm*) the door; one of the rites performed during the marriage ceremony.

बाल ba:l (*nm*) a hair; young one,

a child; boy; a crack (in glass etc.); (*nf*) an ear of corn; ~कमानी spring (in a watch); -काल childhood (days); -केलि/-क्रीड़ा infantile fun, childly / childish, frolics; ~गोपाल the children; ~चंद्र the crescent; ~चर a boy-scout; ० संघ a boyscouts' association; ~चरित the fun and frolic of a child or children; infantile/childish / childly gambols; ~तोड़ see बलतोड़; -धन a minor's property; -पक्षाघात infantile paralysis; ~पन childhood; -बच्चे children; family; -बुद्धि puerility; childishness; boyishness; puerile, childish; boyish; -ब्रह्मचारी a celibate all one's life; -भाव childlike; childhood; boyishness; ~मति see ~बुद्धि; ~रवि the early morning sun; ~रोग infantile/children's disease; -वध infanticide; -विधवा childhood widow; -विवाह early marriage, boyhood marriage; ~सफ़ा hair-removing; ~सूर्य see ~रवि; ~हठ childish insistence; -आना/पड़ना to develop a crack; to have a fine crack; to have a hairy growth; -उगना hair to grow; -का कंबल बनाना, -की भेड़ बनाना to exaggerate, to make a mountain out of a mole-hill; -की खाल खींचना/निकालना to split hairs; to indulge in hair-splitting; to be too carping; -खिचड़ी होना to have an abundant sprinkling of grey hair amongst black; -पकाना, धूप में to age without experience; -पकाना, किसी काम में to age with constant experience (in a particular occupation); -बराबर hair-breadth, very narrow; -बाँका न होना to remain unscathed; to emerge from an ordeal without so much as a scratch; -बाल the whole being; from head to foot; hair-breadth, very narrow; -बाल गजमोती पिरोना to be adorned all over, to overornate oneself; -बाल गुनहगार होना to be a sinner through and through; to be every inch a sinner; -बाल बँधा होना the whole being to be under a debt; to be thoroughly bound by obligation; -बाल बचना to have a hair-breadth escape, to have a very narrow escape; -सन होना/सफ़ेद होना the hair to turn grey, to become/get old.

बॉल bɔl (*nf*) a ball; ball-room; -डांस ball-room dance.

बाल/क ba:lak (*nm*) a boy; child; minor; an ignorant person; ~कपन childishness, boyishness; puerility; ~कीय childish; boyish; puerile; ~कोचित childly, child-like.

बालम ba:lām (*nm*) a lover, beloved; husband.

बाला ba:la: (*nm*) an ear-ornament; (*nf*) an adolescent girl; young woman; (*a*) puerile; childly; high, aloft; excellent, best; -ए-ताक set apart, discarded; ~कुप्पी a crane; ~खाना an attic; -जोबन emerging/blooming youth; ~नशीन the best, the finest; ~पन childhood, boyhood/girlhood; -बाला superficially, outwardly.

बालाई ba:la:i: (*a*) superficial; extra; (*nf*) see मलाई; -आमदनी extra income.

बालावस्था ba:la:vastha: (*nf*) childhood; boyhood/girlhood.

बालिका ba:lika: (*nf*) a young girl; -विद्यालय a girls' school.

बालिग़ ba:li:g (*a*) adult; major; ~पन adulthood; majority; -मताधिकार adult franchise, adult suffrage.

बालिश ba:lish (*a*) childish, puerile; infantile; morone; stupid; ~ता childishness, puerility; infantility; moronity, stupidity.

बालिश्त ba:lisht (*nm*) a hand-span; –भर का too young; o छोकरा a young lad; बालिश्तिया midget.

बाली ba:li: (*nf*) an ear-ring; ear of corn; (*a*) tender, young (age); –उमर tender age.

बालुका ba:luka: (*nf*) sand; ~मय sandy, arenaceous.

बालू ba:lu: (*nf*) sand; ~दानी a sandbox; ~शाही a kind of sweetmeat; –का घरौंदा, –की भीत a sandy wall, a structure with an infirm foundation; –से तेल निकालना to wring water from a flint.

बालेय ba:ley (*a*) tender; childish, puerile; hence ~ता (*nf*).

बालोपचार ba:lopcha:r (*nm*) children's treatment.

बाल्टी ba:lṭi: (*nf*) a bucket, pail.

बाल्य ba:ly (*nm*) childhood; ignorance; ~काल childhood.

बावजूद ba:vju:d (*ind*) in spite of, despite.

बावड़ी ba:vṛi: (*nf*) a deep well with a flight of stairs down to the surface of water.

बावन ba:vān (*a*) fifty-two; (*nm*) the number fifty-two; –तोले पाव रत्ती proper and precise, precisely correct, balanced and correct.

बावरची ba:varchi: (*nm*) a cook; ~खाना the kitchen.

बावला ba:vla: (*a*) mad, crazy; insane; ~पन madness, craziness; insanity.

बावली ba:vli: (*nf*) see बावड़ी.

बावेला ba:vela: (*nn*) uproar, tumult, shemozzle; –मचाना to cause an uproar/tumult.

बाशिंदा ba:shinda: (*nm*) a resident, an inhabitant.

बाष्प ba:shp (*nm*) steam, vapour; tear; ~न evaporation; vaporization; ~मय vaporous; ~मापी vaporimeter; ~शील vaporescent.

बाष्पीकरण ba:shpi:karāṇ (*nm*) evaporation; vaporization.

बाष्पाकुल ba:shpa:kul (*a*) tearful, dimmed through tears.

बास ba:s (*nf*) foul smell, bad/disagreeable odour.

बासठ ba:saṭh (*a*) sixty-two; (*nm*) the number sixty-two.

बासन ba:san (*nm*) household utensil.

बासा ba:sa: (*a*) stale, kept overnight; (*nm*) a habitat, dwelling place.

बासी ba:si: (*a*) stale, kept overnight; (*nm*) inhabitant, resident; –ईद the day immediately following Id; -तिबासी (eatables) stale and stinking; kept for days together; –मुँह without having taken anything in the morning; –कढ़ी में उबाल old age, young ways; a lilliputian posing like a giant; –बचे न कुत्ता खाये to polish off all and leave nothing to Paul; –भात में ख़ुदा का क्या साझा ? why invite a guest to share a dish of stale rice ?

बाह/म ba:ham (*a*) mutual, reciprocal; ~मी mutual, riciprocal.

बाहर ba:har (*ind*) out, outside, exterior, without; beyond; away; (*nm*) a foreign land; -बाहर outwardly, externally; superficially; -भीतर within and without; in and out; ~वाला outside, external; an alien; outsider; –करना to expel, to force out; to exclude; –का external, outside; alien, foreign; outsider; –की हवा लगना to be influenced by the surroundings; to go astray; –जाना to go out (of the house); to go abroad; –से externally, outwardly; superficially; from a foreign country; –होना, (आज्ञा, बस, आदि से) to be beyond (the control of, influence of); –बीबी चंगी घर आये माँदी to hang up one's fiddle when one comes home, to be witty abroad and dull at home.

बाहरी ba:hri: (*a*) outward, external, exterior; superficial; alien.

बाहु ba:hu (*nm*) an arm; ~दंड an arm as strong as a staff; ~पाश an arm-embrace; arm-girdle; ~बल strength of one's arms, valour; ~मूल the juncture of the arm; -युद्ध hand to hand fight, close fight; wrestling.

बाहुल्य ba:huly (*nm*) abundance, plenty.

बाह्य ba:hy (*ind*) out, outside; beyond; (*a*) external, outward, exterior; superficial; ostentatious; hence ~ता (*nf*).

बाह्याचार ba:hya:cha:r (*nm*) sham rituals; ritualistic conduct.

बाह्याभ्यंतर ba:hya:bbhyantar (*nm* and *a*) exterior and interior; external and internal; within and without.

बाह्येंद्रिय ba:hyendriy (*nf*) see ज्ञानेंद्रिय.

बिंदी bindi: (*nf*) a point, dot; zero, cipher; a small round mark (of virmilion, sandal, etc.) on the forehead.

बिंदु bindu (*nm*) a point, dot; zero, cipher; spot; (in Indian dramaturgy) a point in drama where a minor episode begins to take shape; see अनुस्वार; a drop; bull's eye (in shooting); –चित्रण/छायांकन stippling.

बिंदुक bīnduk (*nm*) a point; drop.

बिंदुली bīduli: (*nf*) a small round decorative mark (of vermilion etc.) on the forehead.

बिंधना bīdhnā: (*v*) to be pierced; to be inextricably bound.

बिंब bīmb (*nm*) an image; shadow; reflection; the disc of sun or moon; the plant *Memordica mondelpha*; ~फल the bright red ripened fruit of the plant *Memordica mondelpha*; -योजना imagery; ~वाद imagism; hence ~वादी (*a, nm*); -विधान imagery.

बिंबाफल bīmba:phal (*nm*) see बिंबफल under बिंब.

बिंबोष्ठ bīmboshṭh (*a*) having bright red lips; (*nm*) lips as bright red as a 'बिंबफल'.

बिआना bia:nā: (*v*) to reproduce, to give birth (used only for animals).

बिकट bikaṭ (*a*) see विकट.

बिकना biknā: (*v*) to be sold; –, किसी के हाथ to be sold to, to be under somebody's complete control; to be fascinated by.

बिकराल bikra:l (*a*) see विकराल.

बिक/ल bikal (*a*) restless, uneasy; troubled; suffering torture; ~लई/लता/लाई restlessness, uneasiness, torture, troubled state.

बिकसना bikasnā: (*v*) to blossom, to bloom; to be delighted.

बिकाऊ bika:u: (*a*) for sale, saleable,

बिकार bika:r (*nm*) see विकार.

बिकारी bika:ri: (*a*) see विकारी; (*nf*) an arch-like/crescent line signifying rupees or maunds and seers in the Indian accounting system (e.g. १)–one rupee).

बिकास bika:s (*nm*) see विकास.

बिक्रम bikkram (*nm*) see **विक्रम**.

बिक्रमी bikkrāmi: (*a*) see **विक्रमी**.

बिक्री bikkri: (*nf*) sale; circulation; marketing; disposal; **–के योग्य** marketable, saleable.

बिखरना bikharnā: (*v*) to be scattered/strewn; to be dispersed; to be diffused; to be dishevelled.

बिखेरना bikhernā: (*v*) to scatter, to strew, to diffuse; to dishevel.

बिगड़/ना bigaṛnā: (*v*) to be angry/enraged, to lose temper; to be spoilt/damaged; to deteriorate; to be wasted; to follow a wrong path, to go astray, to develop bad habits/character; to be spoilt due to extravagance; to be on bad terms (as **उन दोनों में बिगड़ गई है**); to go out of order (as **मशीन–**); **–जाना** to cut up rough, to show resentment; to go astray; to be corrupted; **बिगड़े दिल** petulant; fastidious; of hot temperament; **बिगड़े नवाब/रईस** an erstwhile aristocrat, a grandee in adversity.

बिगड़ैल bigṛail (*a*) short-tempered, easily provoked; gone astray.

बिगहा bigaha: (*nm*) see **बीघा**.

बिगाड़ biga:ṛ (*nm*) discord, rift, friction; unhappy relations; breakdown; **–करना** to quarrel, to have an altercation; **–के बीज बोना** to sow seeds of discord; **–होना** a discord to be created, a rift to develop, mutual relations to become unhappy.

बिगाड़ना biga:ṛnā: (*v*) to spoil; to destroy, to ruin; to damage; to put out of order; to foil; to cause to go astray.

बिगाड़ू biga:ṛu: (*a*) spoiling, destroying, damaging; (*nm*) a mischief-maker; saboteur; instigator; one who leads astray.

बिगुल bigul (*nm*) bugle; **–बजना** a march to be ordered; an expedition to be commenced.

बिगूचन bigu:chān (*nm*) suspense, perplexity; difficulty.

बिग्रह biggrah (*nm*) see **विग्रह**.

बिघटन bighaṭān (*nm*) see **विघटन**.

बिचकना bichaknā: (*v*) to be startled; (face) to be made wry.

बिचकाना bichka:nā: (*v*) to startle; to make wry (face); **–, मुँह** to make a wry face.

बिचरना bicharnā: (*v*) to go in a leisurely manner; to walk about, to roam, to loiter, to ramble.

बिचला bichla: (*a*) (belonging to the) middle, mid; central.

बिचवई bichwai: (*nm*) a mediator.

बिचार bicha:r (*nm*) see **विचार**.

बिचारना bicha:rnā: (*v*) to think, to ponder over, to consider, to brood over.

बिचारा bicha:ra: (*a*) poor, helpless; **~पन** helplessness.

बिच्छू bichchhu: (*nm*) a scorpion; nettle, prickly plant; **–का डंक** a venomous sting.

बिछलन bichhlān (*nf*) slipperiness.

बिछलना bichhalnā: (*v*) to slip, to skid.

बिछाना bichha:nā: (*v*) to spread out (esp. a bed or mat etc); to strike down; to fell flat.

बिछावन bichha:van (*nm*) bedding, anything spread out.

बिछिया bichhiya: (*nf*) an ornament worn in one of the toes (traditionally, by a married woman whose husband is alive).

बिछु/आ, ~वा bichhua:, **~**wa: (*nm*) see **बिछिया**; see **बिच्छू**.

बिछुड़ना bichhuṛnā: (*v*) to part company, to separate.

बिछोह bichhoh (*nm*) separation (from the beloved).

बिछोही bichhohi: (*a*) separated (from the beloved); suffering the pangs of separation.

बिछौना bichhaunā: (*nm*) see **बिछावन**.

बिजय bijay (*nf*) see **विजय**.

बिजयी bijai: (*a*) see **विजयी**.

बिजली bijli: (*nf*) electricity; lightning; thunderbolt; an ear-ornament, top; ~**घर** a power house; power station; **संबंधी** electro, electrical; –**का कड़का**, –**की कड़क** thunder, thunderclap, thunderpeal; –**की-सी गति** lightning speed; –**कौंधना** lightning to flash; –**गिरना** to be thunder-struck, to be struck by lightning; lightning to strike.

बिजूका biju:ka: (*nm*) a scare-crow.

बिजौरा bijaura: (*nm*) a large-size species of citron.

बिज्जू bijju: (*nm*) a beast resembling the wild cat.

बिटप biṭap (*nm*) see **विटप**.

बिटिया biṭiya: (*nf*) a daughter.

बिट्ठल biṭṭhal (*nm*) one of the names of Lord Vishṇu.

बिठाना biṭha:nā: (*v*) to cause to be seated, to seat; to take (a woman) as a keep.

बिडंबना biḍāmbanā: (*nf*) see **विडंबना**.

बिड़र biṛar (*a*) sparse; diffused, scattered.

बिडा(ड़ा)ल biḍ(ṛ)a:l (*nm*) a he-cat.

बिडालाक्ष biḍa:la:ksh (*a*) cat-eyed.

बिडा/लिका, ~**ली** bida:lika:, ~li: (*nf*) a she-cat.

बिड़ी biṛi: (*nf*) see **बीड़ी**.

बिताना bita:nā: (*v*) to spend, to pass (time).

बित्ता bitta: (*nm*) a hand-span; **बित्ते भर का** too small.

बिदकना bidaknā: (*v*) to be alarmed/startled; to be provoked.

बिदा bida: (*nf*) farewell, departure; adieu; –**करना** to see off, to send off, to bid farewell; –**देना** to give a send-off; to bid farewell; –**लेना** to make one's adieu; to take leave of.

बिदाई bida:i: (*nf*) a send-off, farewell, an adieu; –**देना** to give a send-off, to make one's adieu, to bid farewell.

बिधना bidhnā: (*nm*) Lord Brahmā: —the Creator of the Universe.

बिधवा bidhva: (*nf*) see **विधवा**.

बिधान bidhā:n (*nm*) see **विधान**.

बिधि bidhi (*nf*) see **विधि**—way, method; means; law; affirmation; (*nm*) see **ब्रह्मा**; -**निषेध** affirmation and negation; positive and negative; –**मिलाना** to tally the horoscopes of prospective man and wife; to tally the accounts of income and expenditure.

बिधुर bidhur (*a*) see **विधुर**.

बिन bin (*ind*) see **बिना**.

बिनती binti: (*nf*) an entreaty, a request, supplication.

बिनना binnā: (*v*) to knit, to weave; to be picked up.

बिनय binay (*nf*) see **विनय**.

बिना binā: (*ind*) without; in the absence of; minus; basis; ground; cause; –**तकल्लुफ़ के** free and easy; unceremonious; –**पानी मोजे उतारना** to cry before you are hurt; –**बताए छुट्टी मार लेना** to take French leave; –**बात की बात** for nothing, no rhyme or reason, born out of nothingness; –**बुलाये मेहमान कोई न करता मान** uninvited guests sit on thorns; – **मारे की तोबा** to cry before you are hurt; –**रोये माँ भी दूध नहीं पिलाती** a closed mouth catches no flies; –**लाग-लपेट के** without making any bones about; –संगी-साथी high and dry.

बिनाई binā:i: (*nf*) the work/method/process of knitting/weaving/picking up (unwanted stuff to clean grains etc.); the wages paid therefor.

बिनावट bina:vaṭ (*nf*) see बुनावट.

बिनौला binaula: (*nm*) cotton-seed.

बि/पता, ~पत्ति, ~पदा bipta, ~patti, ~pda: (*nf*) distress, affliction, hardship, trouble; बिपता का कोई न साथी adversity flatters no man.

बिफरना bipharnā: (*v*) to be provoked/displeased, to become unmanageably angry.

बिबाक biba:k (*a*) see बेबाक.

बिबाकी biba:ki: (*nf*) see बेबाकी.

बिभावरी bibha:vri (*nf*) see विभावरी.

बिभीषिका bibhi:shika: (*nf*) see विभीषिका.

बिमोचना bimochnā: (*v*) to set free, to abandon, to release.

बिमोहना bimohnā: (*v*) to fascinate, to charm, to enchant.

बियाबान biya:bā:n (*nm*) a thick forest; a deserted place, wilderness; (*a*) desolate, uninhabited; deserted; –जंगल deserted forest, desolate jungle.

बिरं/ग, ~गा birāṅg, ~ga: (*a*) multicoloured, variegated (used only in the compound रंग-बिरंगा.

बिरंचि birāṇchi (*nm*) see ब्रह्मा.

बिरंजी birāṇji: (*nf*) a small nail.

बिरजिस birjis (*nf*) (a pair of) breeches.

बिरता birta: (*nm*) power, strength; capacity, capability.

बिरमाना birmā:nā: (*v*) to hold back; to fascinate; to lure into wrong ways.

बिर/ला birla: (*a*) rare, scarce; ~ला कोई rarely any; ~ले very few, scarcely any.

बिरवा birwa: (*nm*) a plant, seedling; a small tree; ~ई a clump of plants/seedlings.

बिरस biras (*a*) insipid, indelicious, tasteless.

बिरहा birha: (*nm*) a kind of folksong; separation (from the beloved), pangs of separation.

बिरही birahi: (*a* and *nm*) (one who is) suffering the pangs of separation; separated.

बिराजना bira:jnā: (*v*) to be seated, to grace (by sitting), to grace (an occasion) by one's presence.

बिराद/र bira:dar (*nm*) a brother; ~राना brotherly, fraternal.

बिरादरी bira:dri: (*nf*) fraternity, brotherhood; community; -बाहर होना to be outcasted, to be excommunicated.

बिराना bira:nā: (*a*) alien, not one's own; (*v*) to offend by making wry faces, to jeer, to make mouths at.

बिरियाँ biriyā: (*nf*) time (as चलती बिरियाँ—at the time of departure).

बिरोजा biroja: (*nm*) turpentine; resin.

बिलंब bilāmb (*nm*) delay (see विलंब).

बिलंबित bilāmbit (*a*) delayed; see विलंबित.

बिल bil (*nm*) a burrow; hole; cavity; bill; ~अक्स against, opposite; ~आख़िर at last; ~जब्र forcibly, by force, under compulsion; –करना to burrow; –ढूँढ़ना to seek shelter, to try to find a refuge; –में घुसना to hide back within one's dwelling, to keep indoors.

बिलकुल bilkul (*a* and *adv*) quite, all, complete; wholly, absolutely, completely; utter, sheer; —मुर्दा dead as a door-nail.

बिलखना bilakhnā: (*v*) to wail, to weep bitterly, to lament.

बिलग bilag (*a*) separate, isolated, aloof; bad, ill; –मानना to take ill of, to feel bad; to be displeased.

बिलगाना bilaga:nā: (*v*) to separate/isolate, to keep aloof; to disjoin, to detach.

बिलगाव bilga:w (*nm*) separation; isolation, detachment, aloofness.

बिलटना bilaṭnā: (*v*) to be ruined/spoiled.

बिलटी bilṭi: (*nf*) a railway-receipt; –काटना to despatch, to send away.

बिलनी bilnī: (*nf*) a sty; a kind of black bee.

बिलपना bilapnā: (*v*) to wail, to weep aloud; to lament.

बिलफ़र्ज़ bilfarz (*ind*) supposing, assuming.

बिलबिलाना bilbila:nā: (*v*) to wriggle; to whine; to be restless with pain, to toss about in torment.

बिला bila: (*ind*) without; –तकल्लुफ़ without any formality; –नागा without a gap; regularly; –वजह without any reason; unprovoked; –शक without doubt, undoubtedly; –शुबहा see –शक; –शर्त unconditional (ly); without any condition.

बिलाई bila:i: (*nf*) (a kind of) shutter (for doors), bolt; a cat.

बिलाना bila:nā: (*v*) to disappear; to vanish.

बिलाप bila:p (*nm*) see विलाप.

बिलायत bila:yat (*nm*) see विलायत.

बिला/र bila:r (*nm*) a he-cat; hence ~री (*nf*).

बिलाव bila:w (*nm*) a tom-cat, big cat.

बिलासी bila:si: (*a*) see विलासी.

बिलियर्ड biliyarḍ (*nm*) billiards.

बिलोकना biloknā: (*v*) to see, to look at, to behold.

बिलोड़ना bilorṇā: (*v*) to churn, to stir.

बिलोना bilonā: (*v*) to churn; to stir.

बिलौटा bilauṭa: (*nm*) a kitten.

बिल्ला billa: (*nm*) a tom-cat; badge.

बिल्ली billi: (*nf*) a cat; –का रास्ता काटना, –का रास्ता काट जाना a cat to cross one's way (taken to be an ill omen), to have an ill foreboding; –के गले में घंटी बाँधना to bell the cat; –के भागों छींका टूटना how can the cat help it if the maid be a fool ? ; a windfall to the needy; –के सामने दूध नहीं जमता a watched pot never boils; –को छीछड़ों के ख़्वाब as one's mentality, so one's dreams; its unfulfilled wishes that mould one's dreams; –ने शेर पढ़ाया, बिल्ली को खाने आया my foot, my tutor.

बिल्लौ/र billaur (*nm*) crystal; quartz; ~री crystalline; quartziferous.

बिल्व bilw (*nm*) the wood-apple–*Aegle mormelos*.

बिवाई biwa:i: (*nf*) chilblain(s); –फटना to have chilblain(s).

बिसमिल्ला bismilla: (*nf*) see बिस्मिल्ला.

बिसरना bisarnā: (*v*) to forget.

बिसात bisa:t (*nf*) a chess-board; capacity, capability, power; –के बाहर out of one's depth, beyond (one's) power; –से बाहर काम करना to bite more than one can chew.

बिसातख़ा/ना bisa:tḳha:nā: (*nm*) haberdashery, a general merchandise shop; ~ने का सामान general merchandise.

बिसाती bisa:ti: (*nm*) a haberdasher, general merchant.

बिसायँध bisa:yādh (*nf*) stench;

stinking.

बिसारना bisa:rnā: (*v*) to forget, to force out of mind.

बिसूरना bisu:rnā: (*v*) to wail, to lament; to sob.

बिस्कुट biskuṭ (*nm*) a biscuit.

बिस्त/र ~रा bistar, ~ra: (*nm*) a bedding, bed; ~रबंद, a hold-all; ~र गोल करना to wind up one's bag and baggage

बिस्तुइया bistuiya: (*nf*) a lizard.

बिस्मिल्ला, ~ह bismilla:, ~h (*nf*) beginning, commencement; (*ind*) with the name of God, a word used by Muslims at the commencemet of a work; –करना to commence (an act), to make a beginning; –ही ग़लत होना to misfire at the very outset; to have a wrong beginning.

बिस्वा biswa: (*nm*) a measure of land (equal to one-twentieth of a बीघा).

बिहंग bihāṅg (*nm*) a bird.

बिहँसना bihāsnā: (*v*) to laugh; to be very happy.

बिहग bihag (*nm*) a bird.

बिहरना biharnā: (*v*) to loiter/wander about; to enjoy; to make merry.

बिहाग biha:g (*nm*) a typical राग (see) sung in small hours of the morning.

बिहान bihā:n (*nm*) day-break, dawn.

बिहाना biha:nā: (*v*) to abandon, to leave off.

बिहार biha:r (*nm*) an eastern state of the Indian Union; a Buddhistic monastery.

बिहारी biha:ri: (*a*) belonging or pertaining to बिहार; (*nm*) an inhabitant of बिहार; –होना to run away, to move off.

बिहिश्त bihisht (*nm*) the paradise; –को ठोकर/लात मारना to kick off the greatest attraction, to reject the most covetted aim.

बिही bihi: (*nm*) a quince; guava; ~दाना seed of quince.

बिहीन bihi:n (*a*) see विहीन.

बींधना bī:dhnā: (*v*) to pierce, to bore a hole into.

बी bi: (*nf*) a word of respect for ladies; lady (e.g. बड़ी बी, छोटी बी).

बीघा bi:gha: (*nm*) a measure of land—five-eighth of an acre.

बीच bi:ch (*nm*) the middle (part), centre; –का intermediary, intermediate; central, middle; –, के among(st), between; during; in the midst of; –बाज़ार (में) in public, in a public place; -बिचाव mediation; o करने वाला mediator; -बीच में at intervals; in between; –में in between, meanwhile, during, between, in the meantime, among, amongst, within, amid, in the midst of; o कूदना to intervene, to interrupt; to disturb; to cause obstruction; –में डालना to make a mediator; to cause to mediate; to make a witness; –में पड़ना to mediate, to act as a mediator; to interfere, to cause obstruction; –रखना to maintain a distance, to keep some reservation; ~वाला a mediator.

बीचि bi:chi (*nf*) see वीचि.

बीचों (चो)बीच bi:chō(cho)bi:ch (*adv*) just/exactly in the middle or centre, midway.

बीज bi:j (*nm*) seed; pip; origin; beginning; germ; semen; cause; nucleus; -आवरण seed-coat; ~नाशक germicidal; -पत्र a seed-lobe; ~पुरुष the primal man (of a clan, dynasty, etc.); ~पूर्ण seedy; ~लेख cryptogram; -वपन sowing (of the seed); -संस्कार springization; -डालना to sow the seed; to lay the foundation.

बीजक bi:jak (*nm*) an invoice; a bill (of purchase).

बीजगणि/त bi:jgāṇit (*nm*) (the science of) algebra; ~त-संबंधी algebraical; ~तीय algebraic (al).

बीजमंत्र bi:jmāṇtr (*nm*) the essential मंत्र for propitiating a deity.

बीजांक bi:jā:ṅk (*nm*) cipher; code.

बीजाक्षर bi:ja:kshar (*nm* the first letter of a मंत्र; code characters.

बीजातीत bi:ja:ti:t (*a*) transcendental.

बीजारोपण bi:ja:ropaṇ (*nm*) sowing of the seed; to lay the foundation.

बीजू bi:ju: (*a*) produced from seed or stone (as opposed to grafted tree; e.g. -आम).

बीट bi:ṭ (*nm*) dung of a bird.

बीड़ा bi:ṛa: (*nm*) seasoned and folded betel-leaf;-उठाना to make it one's business to, to undertake an assignment; to accept a challenge.

बीड़ी bi:ṛi: (*nf*) a *bidi* (crude form of cigarette rolled within a leaf.

बीतना bī:tna: (*v*) to pass; to be spent (as time); to elapse; to expire; to befall/happen/occur; बीत गई सो बात गई, बीती ताहि बिसार दे let the past bury its dead, let bygones be bygones; बीता वक्त फिर हाथ नहीं आता time and tide wait for no man, an occasion lost cannot be redeemed; forgive and forget; बीते दिनों की याद सताना to sigh for the flashpots of Egypt, to hanker for the charming past.

बीन bi:n (*nf*) a (snake-charmer's) flute; a classical Indian stringed instrument generally called वीणा; ~कार one who plays on a बीन, a flutist.

बीनना bi:nnā: (*v*) to pick up; to pluck (as flowers); to choose.

बीबी bi:bi: (*nf*) a respected lady; a respectful word used by a woman for her husband's younger sister.

बीभत्स bi:bhats (*a*) abhorrent, disgusting, loathsome; (*nm*) one of the nine *rasas* in poetry—the sentiment of abhorrence or disgust; hence ~ता (*nf*).

बीमा bi:mā: (*nm*) insurance; ~कर्ता an insurer; ~कृत insured;~दार a policy holder; -योग्य insurable; -करना to insure.

बीमार bi:ma:r (*a*) sick, ill; diseased; indisposed, unwell; (*nm*) a patient, valetudinarian.

बीमारी bi:ma:ri: (*nf*) illness, sickness; disease; ailment.

बीर bi:r (*a*) brave; intrepid; (*nm*) brother;~न a brother (often used by a sister).

बीरबल bi:rbal (*nm*) the celebrated minister in the court of the Great Moghul King Akbar (whose name is byword for wit, repartee and sharp intelligence); -की खिचड़ी an assignment that knows no completion, an undertaking that drifts on and on; -के चुटकुले/लतीफ़े the Birbalian anecdotes, anecdotes that reflect sharp wit.

बीरबहूटी bi:rbahuṭi: (*nf*) coecus, lady fly, a red velvety insect.

बीवी bi:vi: (*nf*) wife.

बीस bi:s (*a*) twenty; superior, excelling; (*nm*) the number twenty; -बिसवे in the fullest measure;

certainly; undoubtedly; wholly, absolutely.

बीसी bi:si: (*nf*) a score; group of twenty.

बीहड़ bi:haṛ (*a*) dense, thick (as जंगल); rough and rugged; (*nm*) a dense forest; hence ~पन (*nm*).

बुँदकी būdki: (*nf*) a small round spot/dot; ~दार spotted, dotted.

बुंदा būnda: (*nm*) an ear-top (an ornament); a dot; point.

बुंदीदार būndi:da:r (*a*) dotted, having spots/spotted.

बुंदेलखं/ड būndelkhaṇḍ (*nm*) a district in central India; ~डी see बुंदेली.

बुंदेला būndela: (*nm*) a *kshatriy* caste; an inhabitant of Bundelkhāṇḍ.

बुंदेली būndeli: (*nf*) a dialect of Hindi, spoken mainly in बुन्देलखंड.

बुआ bua: (*nf*) father's sister.

बुकचा bukcha: (*nm*) a bundle (of clothes etc.)

बुकनी buknī: (*nf*) powder; –करना to (reduce to) powder, to levigate.

बुक्का bukka: (*nm*); –फाड़कर रोना to weep bitterly, to lament aloud.

बुख़ार bukḥā:r (*nm*) fever; –आना to have fever, to be running temperature; –उतरना the temperature to go down, fever to subside; excitement to subside, steam to be let off; –उतारना to relieve of excitement / provocation / anger; to cut to size; –टूटना the temperature/fever to normalise.

बुख़ारी bukḥā:ri (*nf*) see बुख़ार.

बुग/चा bugcha: (*nm*) a bundle of clothes etc,); hence बुगची diminutive (*nf*).

बुजदि/ल buzdil (*a*) coward, timid; ~ली cowardice, timidness.

बुजुर्ग buzurg (*a*) elderly, old; venerable, respected; (*nm*) forefathers; elderly people; ~वार elderly; used deferentially for old and respected people.

बुजुर्गाना buzurga:nā: (*a*) elderly; befitting elders/elderly people; –लहजे में बोलन. to talk like a Dutch uncle.

बुजुर्गी buzurgi: (*nf*) elderliness.

बुझना bujhnā: (*v*) to be extinguished; to be quenched; to be put out; to be dejected, to be in low spirits; बुझा-बुझा सा होना to be down in the dumps; बुझे दिल का down in the mouth, dispirited.

बुझाना bujha:nā: (*v*) to extinguish (as आग—); to put out (as दिया—); to quench (as प्यास—); to slake (as चूना—); to temper by dipping into a solution of poison (as जहर में—);—,पहेली to talk in riddles, to speak enigmatically; बुझा हुआ extinguished; dispirited, lifeless, down in the dumps.

बुझौवल bujhauval (*nf*) a riddle, enigma.

बुड़बुड़ाना buṛbuṛa:nā: (*v*) to mutter/murmur, to jabber/gabber.

बुड्ढा buḍḍha: (*a*) old, aged, senile.

बुढ़ाना buṛha:nā: (*v*) to grow old, to age.

बुढ़ा/पा buṛha:pa: (*nf*) old age, senility; ~पे की लकड़ी/लाठी old age support, one who would support when incapacitated by old age.

बुढ़िया buṛhiya: (*nf*) an old woman.

बुत but (*nm*) an idol, a statue, image; (*a*) dumb and lifeless, motionless (like an image); ~ख़ाना a temple (where an idol is installed); ~तराश an idol-maker, a maker of statues; ~परस्त an idolater, idol-worshipper; ~परस्ती

idolatry, idol-worship, iconolatry; —बन जाना, —हो जाना to become still, to be dumbfounded.

बुताना buta:nā: (*v*) see बुझाना.

बुत्ता butta: (*nm*) see झाँसा.

बुदबु/द, ~दा budbud, ~da: (*nm*) a bubble.

बुदबुदा/ना budbuda:nā: (*v*) to mutter; to jabber; to effervesce; ~हट muttering; jabbering; effervescence.

बुद्ध buddh (*nm*) Lord Buddha.

बुद्धि buddhi (*nf*) intellect; intelligence, wisdom; mind; sense; -कौशल, wisdom, sagacity; deftness; ~गम्य/ग्राह्य intelligible, understandable; ~जीवी an intellectual; o वर्ग the intellectuals; -बल intellectual power, wisdom, sagacity; deftness; ~रहित/हत/हीन foolish, stupid, brainless, unintelligent; nincompoop; ~वादिता/वाद intellectualism; ~वादी an intellectualist; -विलास intellectual luxury.

बुद्धिमत्ता buddhimātta: (*nf*) intelligence, wisdom, prudence.

बुद्धिमा/न buddhimā:n (*a*) intelligent; wise, prudent, sensible, sagacious; brilliant; ~नी intelligence; wisdom, sagacity, prudence,

बुद्धिवंत buddhiwānt (*a*) see बुद्धिमान.

बुद्धू buddhu: (*a*) stupid, foolish, dullard, blockheaded nincompoop; a button short; ~पन/पना foolishness, stupidity, dullardness; –समझना to see green in one's eye.

बुद्बुद budbud (*nm*) a bubble.

बुध budh (*nm*) Wednesday; Mercury; (*a*) wise, intelligent; learned; ~जन the wise, prudent people.

बुध/वार budhwa:r (*nm*) Wednesday; also ~वासर.

बुनकर bunkar (*nm*) a weaver.

बुनना bunnā: (*v*) to weave, to knit, to intertwine.

बुनवाई bunwa:i (*nf*) the act or charges for weaving/knitting.

बुनाई buna:i: (*nf*) the act/process or the wages paid for weaving/knitting; texture (of a cloth etc.).

बुनावट buna:waṭ (*nf*) texture (of a knitted/a wove : thing).

बुनिया/द buniya:d (*nf*) foundation, base; basis; ~दी basic; fundamental; o शिक्षा basic education.

बुभु/क्षा bubhuksha: (*nf*) appetite; hunger; ~क्षा-वर्धक appetizing; an appetizer; ~क्षित, ~क्षु hungry; having appetite.

बुर bur (*nf*) the female genital organ, vagina.

बुरकना buraknā: (*v*) to dust; to spray, to sprinkle.

बुर/क़ा burqa: (*nm*) a veil, mantle; ~क़ापोश veiled, mantled, having a veil on; ~क़े में छोछड़े खाना to indulge in debauchery behind the screen, to lead secretly a life of debauchery.

बुरा bura: (*a*) bad; wicked; evil; ill (as –व्यवहार ill-treatment); mis- (as –प्रबंध mismanagement); faulty; defective; –करना to do an ill turn, to do somebody harm; to commit an unpleasant act; –कर बुरा हो do evil and look for like; –चाहना/चीतना to wish (somebody) ill; –बनना to be held responsible for; some adverse act to devolve upon; –भला bad and good, loss and gain; abuse; o कहना to abuse, to chide, to reprimand; to call bad names; –मानना to take a miss, to take ill, to resent, to take offence at; –रास्ता evil course; unhealthy conduct; –लगना to feel bad, to be to somebody's disliking; –हाल होना to be in a miserable plight; to be in an affliction; the condition to worsen; बुरे के साथ भलाई charity towards the uncharitable; बुरे दिन hard days; rainy day (fig); o आना to be down on one's luck; to fall on evil times; o का साथी a friend in need; a friend who stands through thick and thin.

बुराई bura:i: (*nf*) evil, vice; flaw, fault; defect; badness, wickedness; -भलाई evil and good, virtue and vice; –आगे आना to reap the fruits of one's misdeeds, evil to be repaid in actual life; –के बदले भलाई करना to return good for evil; –हाथ लगना to achieve only a bad name.

बुरादा bura:da: (*nm*) saw-dust.

बुरी buri: (*a*) feminine form of बुरा; –आदतें bad habits, morbid ways; o पड़ना आसान है the road to hell is easy; –ख़बर bad news; news of somebody's death; –गत/गति miserable plight, deplorable condition; o करना/बनाना to thrash thoroughly, to reduce to tatters; to push into a miserable plight; –तरह badly; thoroughly; wickedly; o ख़बर लेना/लताड़ना to give one hell; o पेश आना to maltreat, to behave offensively/badly; –नजर evil eye; lustful eye; –संगत से अकेला भला better alone than in a bad company.

ब्रुश burush (*nm*) a brush; –करना/फेरना to clean with a brush; –मारना to brush hurriedly.

बुर्क़ा burqa: (*nm*) see बुरक़ा.

बुर्ज/र्ज burj (*nm*) a tower; turret, pinnacle; also ~र्जी (*nf*).

बुर्जुआ burjua: (*a* and *nm*) bourgeois; bourgeoisie; –वर्ग bourgeoisie.

बुलंद buland (*a*) high, lofty; –आवाज़ loud voice; –इक़बाल lucky, fortunate; –हिम्मत/हौसला high spirits; venturesome, spirited.

बुलंदी bulandi: (*nf*) height, loftiness.

बुलबुल bulbul (*nf*) a nightingale; –हो जाना to feel flattered; to be extremely happy.

बुलबुला bulbula: (*nm*) a bubble; (*a*) transitory, transient.

बुलाक bula:k (*nf*) a nose-pendant, nose-ornament.

बुलाना bula:nā:(*v*) to call, to convene; to summon; to send for; to invite.

बुलावा bula:wa: (*nm*) call, summons; invitation.

बुलाहट bula:haṭ (*nf*) call; summons.

बुवाई buwa:i: (*nf*) sowing.

बुलेटिन buleṭin (*nm*) a bulletin; -, समाचार a news bulletin; -, सूचना a bulletin of information.

बुहारना buha:rnā: (*v*) to sweep, to broom, to sweep clean.

बुहारी buha:ri: (*nf*) a broom.

बूंद bū:d (*nf*) a drop; -बूंद से घट भरे/ -बूंद से भरे तलाब many a pickle make a mickle, many a drop make an ocean, hair by hair you will pull out the horses tail.

बूंदाबांदी bū:da:bā:di: (*nf*) a drizzle, light shower.

बूंदी bū:di: (*nf*) a kind of sweetmeat (in the form of sweetened drops prepared from gram flour).

बू bu: (*nf*) a disagreeable smell/odour, foul smell; –आना to stink, to smell, to give a foul smell; to suspect (presence of); –न जाना (as नवाबी की o) not to get rid of, to continue to entertain feelings of.

बूआ bu:a: (*nf*) see **बुआ**.

बूचड़ bu:chaṛ (*nm*) a butcher; ~**खाना** a slaughter house; butchery.

बूचा bu:cha: (*a*) ear cropped, having one or both ears cropped; dismembered, disfigured due to organic mutilation; **नंगा** disfigured and dismembered.

बूझ bu:jh (*nf*) understanding—used only as the second member in the compound **समझ-बूझ** (see **समझ**).

बूझना bu:jhnā: (*v*) to understand; to make out; to solve; to enquire, to ask.

बूट bu:ṭ (*nm*) a boot shoe; gram pod, green pod of gram.

बूटा bu:ṭa: (*nf*) a large-sized embroidered or printed flower design (on cloth, sa:ri:, etc.)

बूटी bu:ṭi: (*nf*) herb, medicinal plant; small flower or round design embroidered on cloth; a pip (on a playing card); see **भाँग**; –**छानना** to take **भाँग**.

बूढ़ा bu:ṛha: (*a*) old, aged, senile; –**तोता राम-राम नहीं पढ़ता** old dogs will not learn new tricks; **बूढ़े तोते को पढ़ाना** to teach new ways to an old head; **बूढ़े मुंह मुंहासे** symptoms of youth on an old face.

बूढ़ी bu:ṛhi: (*a*) feminine form of **बूढ़ा** (see); –**ईद** the festival that occurs just thirty days after **रमज़ान**.

बूता bu:ta: (*nm*) capacity; capability; power; ~**ते के बाहर** out of one's depth.

बूम bu:m (*nf*) (colloquial use) tall talk; chaotic noise; –**मारना** to talk tall; to talk noisily.

बूरा bu:ra: (*nm*) unrefined powdered sugar.

बृंद brind (*nm*) see **वृंद**.

बृक brik (*nm*) a wolf.

बृह/त् brihat (*a*) large; big; huge; ~**त्तर** larger, bigger.

बृहद् brihad– an allomorph of **बृहत्** (see).

बृहस्पति brihaspati (*nm*) the name of the preceptor of gods according to Hindu mythology; the largest planet of the solar system-Jupiter; thursday; ~**वार** thursday.

बेंच bēṇch (*nf*) a bench.

बेंट bēṭ (*nf*) a handle (of an axe, etc.).

बेंड़ा bēṛa: (*a*) oblique; crooked; difficult, unmanageable (as a man); (*nm*) a draw-bar, log for fastening a door; hence ~**पन** (*nm*).

बेंत bēt (*nm*) a cane; stick; –**की तरह काँपना** the whole being to quiver.

बेंदी bēdi: (*nf*) an ornament worn on the forehead (by women); an ornamental mark (of vermilion etc.) on the forehead.

बे be—a Persian prefix which imparts the meaning of without or devoid of; an interjectional particle signifying indignation and disrespect (**क्यों बे ?**); ~**अन्त** unending, everlasting; infinite; ~**अक़्ल** foolish, stupid; ~**अक़्ली** foolishness, stupidity; ~**अदब** ill-mannered, impolite, rude; impudent; ~**अदबी** ill manners; impoliteness, rudeness; impudence; ~**आब** lustreless, that has lost its glow, devoid of glow; ~**आबरू** insulted, disgraced, humiliated, dishonoured; ~**आबरूई** disgrace, humiliation; dishonour; insult; ~**इंसाफ़** unjust, unfair, inequitable; ~**इंसाफ़ी** injustice, unfairness, inequity; ~**इज्जत** disgraced, humiliated, insulted; ~**इज्जती** disgrace, humiliation, dishonour;

insult; ~इल्म illiterate; uneducated, unlettered; ~ईमान dishonest, unscrupulous, having no integrity; ~ईमानी dishonesty, lack of scruples/integrity; ~क़द्र unappreciated, disgraced, dishonoured; ~क़द्री non-appreciation; disgrace; dishonour, disrespect; ~क़रार restless, uneasy; ~क़रारी restlessness, uneasiness; ~कल perturbed; restless, uneasy; ~कली perturbed state of mind, restlessness, uneasiness; ~कस helpless; humble; ~कसी helplessness; humbleness; ~क़सूर innocent, faultless, not guilty; ~क़ाबू uncontrolled, unrestrained; beyond control; ~काम unserviceable; unemployed; rendered useless; ~क़ायदगी irregularity; unmannerliness; absence of system; ~क़ायदा irregular; illegal; contrary to rule/law; ~कार unemployed; idle; useless; good-for-nothing; ~कार की बातें करना to fiddle-faddle; ~कार से बेगार भली forced labour is better than idleness; ~कारी unemployment; idleness; uselessness; ০ में शैतानी सूझती है an idle brain is a devil's workshop; ~क़ुसूर see ~क़सूर; ~खटके without hitch/apprehension/reserve; unhesitatingly; ~ख़ता see ~क़सूर; ~ख़बर unaware, uninformed; oblivious; senseless; unconscious; ~ख़बरी unawareness; obliviousness; unconsciousness; senselessness; the state of being out of senses/in a swoon; ~ख़ुदी self-forgetfulness; self-oblivion; ~ख़ौफ़ fearless, intrepid; ~ग़रज selfless, having no selfish interest; ~गाना alien; stranger; hence ০ पन; ~गुनाह not guilty, guiltless, innocence; ~गुनाही guittlessness, innocence, the state of being not guilty; ~गुमान unsuspecting, entertaining no doubts/suspicion; undoubtedly; ~ग़ैरत shameless, lost to shame, having no self-respect; hence ~ग़ैरती; ~घर homeless, having no home and hearth; ~चारगी helplessness; ~चारा poor, helpless; ~चिराग़ uninhabited, desolate; ০ होना to be desolated; to lose the only son; ~चैन restless, uneasy, restive; ~चैनी restlessness, uneasiness, restivity; ~जड़ rootless, having no roots; unfounded, baseless; ~ज़बान mute, dumb, not in a position to react (to oppression); ~ज़र poor, indigent; ~जान lifeless, dead, feeble; colourless; ~ज़ाब्तगी irregularity; contrariness to prescribed procedure; ~ज़ाब्ता irregular, contrary to prescribed procedure; ~ज़ार fed up, tired; feeling miserable, afflicted, troubled; ~ज़ारी state of affliction/of being fed up or tired or troubled, troubled state of mind; ~जोड़ matchless, unparalleled, unprecedented; inharmonious, incongruous; ~टिकट without ticket, ticketless; ০ यात्रा ticketless travel; ~ठिकाना unreliable, incredible; uncertain; having no whereabouts; ~ठिकाने untraced/untraceable; unfit, inharmonious; unreliable; ~डौल unsymmetrical; disproportionate; ugly; ~ढंगा unsystematic, disorderly; unsymmetrical; silly, slovenly; ~ढब unmanageable; crooked; outlandish; unsystematic; excessively; thoroughly; ~तकल्लुफ़ informal, observing no formality; unsophisticated, unostentatious; ~तकल्लुफ़ी informality; absence of sophistication/ostentation; ~तकलुल्फ़ी से without ceremony, in an informal way; ~तमीज़ impertinent, impudent, rustic, uncivil; ~तरतीब unsystematic; disorderly; ~तरतीबी absence of a method/system/order, disorderliness; ~तरह improperly, unsuitably; thoroughly, excessively, very much; ~तरीक़ा improper(ly), unsuitable / unsuitably, mannerless, unsystematic; ~तरीक़े unmannerly, unsystematically; ~तहाशा at top speed, very swiftly; wildly; recklessly, indiscreetly; ~ताब see ~चैन; ~ताबी see ~चैनी; ~तार wireless; ~तार का तार wireless; ~ताला unrhythmic, out of tune; ~ताल्लुक़ indifferent; neutral; unrelated; ~ताल्लुक़ी indifference; neutrality; absence of relationship; ~तुका absurd; irrelevant; ridiculous; silly; incongruous, inharmonious; unsymmetrical; grotesque; ~तुकापन absurdity; irrelevance; ridiculousness, silliness; incongruity; inharmoniousness; absence of symmetry; grotesqueness; ~तुकी हाँकना to talk absurd/irrelevant, to go on talking ridiculous things; -ते करना see अबे-तबे करना; ~दख़ल ejected, evicted; ousted; forced out; ~दख़ली ejectment, eviction, dispossession from holding; forcing out; ~दम very weak; lifeless, vigourless; breathless; ~दर्द cruel, heartless, hard-hearted, unsympathetic; ~दर्दी cruel(ty), heartless(ness), hard-hearted(ness), without sympathy; o से in cold blood; ~दाग़ spotless; clean; flawless; blemishless; speckless; unspecked; ~दाना a kind of pomegranate; ~दाम free of charge, without a price, gratis; o का ग़ुलाम an unpaid servant, a servant whom no wages have to be paid, most obedient servant; ~दिल out of sorts, dejected; hence ~दिली; ~दीन irreligious; heretic; ~धड़क unhesitating(ly); dauntless(ly); bold(ly); intrepid-(ly), fearless(ly); ~धरम see ~दीन; ~नकेल unrestrained, out of control; o का ऊँट one on whom none exercises a control, one who roams about without a purpose; ~नज़ीर unprecedented; unparalleled; peerless; matchless; ~नसीब unlucky/luckless, unfortunate; having a wretched lot; ~नाप unmeasured; ~नाम nameless; unnamed; ~नामी कर्ज़ benami loan; ~नामोनिशान untraceable; having no home and hearth, having no whereabouts; ~नियाज़ indifferent; ~नियाज़ी indifference; carefreeness; ~पनाह shelterless; helpless; very much, excessive; ~पर की उड़ाना/हाँकना to draw the long bow, to talk tall, to indulge in baseless gossip, to brag; ~परदगी nakedness; state of being unveiled; encroachment on privacy; exposure; insult; ~परदा naked, unveiled; having no privacy; exposed; ~परवाह careless; carefree; unmindful; indifferent; ~परवाही carelessness, carefreeness; indifference; ~पानी one who has lost grace, disgraced; o कर देना to put to disgrace; to shame; ~पीर cruel, unsympathetic; ~पेंदी boottomless; o का/का लोटा an unprincipled person, unscrupulous; ~फ़सल out of season; untimely; ~फ़ायदा useless(ly), ungainly; fruitless(ly); ~फ़िक्र carefree; careless, unworried; unmindful; ~फ़िक्री carefreeness; carelessness; the state of having no worries/cares; ~बस helpless; ~बसी helplessness; ~बाक forthright; intrepid, dauntless; ~बाक़ paid up, cleared up; o कर देना, हिसाब to square accounts with; ~बाकी dauntlessness; intrepidness; forthrightness; ~बाक़ी being paid up; ~बुनियाद baseless, unfounded; ~भाव unaccounted for; unlimited, boundless; o की पड़ना to be thoroughly beaten up/thrashed; ~मज़गी unpleasantness; tastelessness; ~मज़ा tasteless; dull and drab; insipid; indelicious; ~मन reluctant(ly), unspirited; without any enthusiasm; ~मतलब useless, purposeless, fruitless; ungainly; irrelevant; ~मरम्मत dilapidated; in bad condition; unrepaired; ~मसरफ़ having no utility, useless; that can be put to no purpose; ~मानी useless; meaningless; irrelevant; ridiculous; ~मिसाल unparalleled, unprecedented; unique; ~मुरौवत, (~मुरौवती) inconsiderate(ness); ~मेल incoherent, inharmonious; mismatched; ~मौक़ा, ~मौक़े untimely; inopportune; ~मौसम (फल आदि) out of season; ~रंग colourless, lustreless; lifeless; ~रस see नीरस; ~रहम cruel, merciless; ~रहमी cruelty, mercilessness; ~रुखी inconsiderateness; indifference, disregard; o बरतना/से पेश आना to give/turn cold shoulder to; –रू-रियायत a fair field and no favour; ~रोक-टोक unobstructed, unhampered; smoothly; unhesitatingly, without any hitch; ~रोजगार unemployed; ~रोज़गारी unemployment; ~रौनक़ lustreless; colourless, lifeless; ~लगाम unrestrained, irrepressible; submitting to no pressures; ~लज्ज़त indelicious, tasteless; insipid; ~लाग frank, forthright, straightforward; without any circumlocution; above board; ~लिहाज़ inconsiderate; shameless; ~लुत्फ़ unpleasant; displeasing, disgusting; drab; ~लौस frank, forthright, indulging in no pleasantries, non-indulgent; ~वक्त untimely, inopportune; o की शहनाई untimely step; inopportune merry-making; ~वफ़ा hollow-hearted, infidel; faithless, disloyal; oई infidelity, faithlessness; ~वास्ता for no rhyme or reason; groundless, unprovoked; ~शऊर coarse-grained, mannerless, silly; sloven, slipshod; knowing no etiquette; ~शऊरी mannerlessness; silliness, slovenliness; absence of etiquette; ~शक of course; certainly, undoubtedly; ~शरम/शर्म shameless; ~शरमी/शर्मी shamelessness; ~शुमार innumerable, countless, numberless; ~सबब without cause/reason, groundless, for no rhyme or reason; ~सब्र impatient; restive; fidgety; ~सब्री impatience, restivity, fidgetiness; ~समझी foolishness; stupidity, silliness; ~सलीक़ा unmannerly/mannerless, unsystematic, slipshod; without etiquette; ~साख़्ता all of a sudden, without deliberation; spontaneously; ~सिर-पैर (का) without any rhyme and reason, illogical, nonsensical; ~सिर-पैर की हाँकना to talk through one's hat; ~सिलसिला without any order, disorderly, unsystematic; ~सिलसिले without any order, disorderly, unsystematically; ~सुध senseless; unconscious; careless, carefree; ~सुर/सुरा out of tune, inharmonious; inopportune; ~सूद useless, without any return/reward; limitless, unlimited; ~स्वाद indelicious; tasteless, insipid; stale; ~हद excessive, too (much), limitless/unlimited, unbounded; o पीना to drink like a fish; ~हया shameless; ~हयाई shamelessness; o का जामा पहन लेना, o का बुरक़ा ओढ़ लेना, o का बुरक़ा मुँह पर डाल लेना to be lost to shame, to become thoroughly shameless; ~हाल miserable, in a sad plight, distressed, afflicted; hence ~हाली; ~हिम्मत courageless, timid, coward; ~ हिसाब unlimited, infinite; too much, very much; ~हुनर artless; stupid, silly; ~हुरमत see ~इज्ज़त; ~हुरमती see ~इज्ज़ती; ~होश unconscious, senseless; fainted; in a swoon; ~होशी unconsciousness, senselessness; swoon.

बेग beg (*nm*) a bag; a word deferentially appended to the names of mohammedans of Moghul lineage.

बेगड़ी begaṛi: (*nm*) a jeweller; a diamond-cutter/dresser.

बेगम begām (*nf*) a (Muslim) lady; Mrs.; **बेगमात** plural of **बेगम**; **बेगमी** pertaining to or belonging to a **बेगम**.

बेगार bega:r (*nf*) forced labour; unremunerative work; drudgery; one who is made to work without remuneration/wages;—**टालना** to do a work without due attention/care/interest.

बेगारी bega:ri: (*nf*) forced labour; the act of forcing some one to do unremunerative work.

बेच/ना bechnā: (*v*) to sell, to vend; to dispose of; ~**नेवाला** a vendor; –**खाना** to sell out.

बेचान becha:n (*nm*) endorsement; sale; –**करना** to endorse.

बेजा beja: (*a*) improper, unfair, undue.

बेटा beṭa: (*nm*) a son.

बेटी beṭi: (*nf*) a daughter;—**देना** to give away one's daughter in marriage (to).

बेठन beṭhān (*nm*) a wrapper, covering/wrapping cloth.

बेड़ा beṛa: (*nm*) a fleet; raft; –, **जहाज़ों का** a naval fleet; –**गर्क़ होना**, –**डूबना** one's ship to sink, one's purpose to be lost, to be ruined, to be undone; –**पार करना/लगाना** to cause to reach one's destination, to salvage; to help achieve one's end, to help one cross over; –**पार होना** to reach one's destination, to achieve the end, to cross over.

बेड़ी beṛi: (*nf*) fetters, shackles; –**काटना** to free from bondage; to unfetter, to remove shackles; –**डालना**, –**पहनना** to fetter, to put into shackles.

बेणी beṇī: (*nf*) see **वेणी**.

बेत bet (*nf*) see **बेंत**.

बेदमुश्क bedmushk (*nm*) a variety of cane.

बेध bedh (*nm*) bore; astronomical observation; ~**शाला** an observatory.

बेधक bedhak (*nm*) a piercer; borer (*a*); piercing, heart-rending.

बेधना bedhnā: (*v*) to pierce; to puncture; to bore.

बेधी bedhi: (*a*) piercing, striking (e.g. शब्दबेधी).

बेना benā: (*nm*) a fan.

बेर ber (*nm*) plum, jujube; prune; (*nf*) see बार.

बेरा bera: (*nm*) a bearer.

बेरी beri: (*nf*) a smaller variety of बेर.

बेल bel (*nm*) wood-apple—*Aegle mamelos*; (*nf*) a creeper, flowery decoration-lace; -पत्र leaves of wood-apple; -बूटा foliage, embroidery.

बेलचा belcha: (*nm*) a shovel.

बेलदा/र belda:r (*nm*) a labourer; ~री a labourer's job.

बेलन belān (*nm*) a roller; cylinder.

बेलना belnā: (*nm*) a roller (for rolling kneaded flour into flat round breads/cakes); (*v*) to roll kneaded flour into flat cake/bread.

बेला bela: (*nm*) a variety of jasmine; a kind of violin; a household utensil; (*nf*) time; seashore.

बेवकू/फ़ bewaku:f (*a*) foolish, stupid; ~फ़ी foolishness stupidity; ~फ़/बनाना to befool, to make a fool of; ~फ़ी देना to act foolishly, to be a fool; ~फ़ों के सींग नहीं होते lit. fools do not grow horns over their heads, fools are normal men to look at.

बेवा bewa: (*nf*) a widow.

बेशक़ीम/त, ~ती beshqi:mat, ~ti: (*a*) costly, precious; invaluable.

बेशतर beshtar (*ind*) mostly; generally.

बेशी beshi: (*nf*) excess.

बेस/न besān (*nm*) gram-flour; ~नी of or prepared from gram-flour.

बेहत/र behtar (*a*) better; ~ री betterment; well-being.

बेहबूदी behbu:di: (*nf*) welfare, well-being.

बेहूदगी behu:dgi: (*nf*) nonsense, stupidity, foolishness, vulgarity; irrelevance.

बेहूदा behu:da: (*a*) nonsensical; stupid, foolish; vulgar; irrelevant; hence ~पन (*nm*).

बैंक baiṅk (*nm*) a bank; -बैलेंस bank-balance.

बैंकर bkaiṅar (*nm*) a banker.

बैंगची baiṅgchi: (*nf*) a tadpole.

बैंगन baiṅgān (*nm*) brinjal.

बैंगनी baiṅgnī: (*a*) violet, violet-coloured.

बैंजनी baiṅjnī: (*a*) see बैंगनी.

बैंड baiṅḍ (*nm*) a band; ~ मास्टर a band-master.

बै bai (*nf*) sale (of a farm or plot of land, etc); ~नामा the sale-deed (of a plot of land, farm, etc.).

बैकुंठ baikūnṭh (*nm*) the paradise; ~धाम the paradise; o बासी, ~बासी deceased, late.

बैगन baigān (*a*) see बैंगन.

बैगनी baignī: (*a*) see बैंगनी.

बैजंती, बैजयंती baiṅjantī:, baijyanti: (*nf*) see वैजयंती.

बैज baij (*nm*) a badge.

बैज़ा baiza: (*nm*) an egg; testicles.

बैट baiṭ (*nm*) a bat (in cricket).

बैटरी baiṭri: (*nf*) a battery; torch.

बैठक baiṭhak (*nf*) sitting; meeting; drawing room; a kind of exercise performed by repeated alternation of sitting and standing postures (as डंड-बैठक); a seat; base; a pedestal (of an idol); ~ख़ाना drawing room; ~बाज़ habituated to prolonged sittings (devoted to gossiping, idle talk, etc.); ~बाज़ी prolonged sittings (for gossiping, idle talk. etc).

बैठका baiṭḥka: (*nm*) a drawing room.

बैठकी baiṭḥki: (*nf*) a kind of leg-exercise performed by repeated alternation of sitting and standing postures; plinth.

बैठना baiṭḥnā: (*v*) to sit; to squat, to occupy a seat; to cling, to settle down; to sink; to be adjusted; to be satisfied (as a condition, provision, etc.); to withdraw (as from a contest); to be without occupation/work; to appear (in some examination); to cave in, to crash down; to ride on; to fit in; to live as wife; to become adept (as हाथ–); **बैठ जाना** to crash down; to give way; **बैठा-ठाला** idle, without any occupation/employment; **बैठी मेहराब** drop arch; **बैठे-बिठाए** for no reason, for no fault of (a person); suddenly, unexpectedly; **बैठे से बेगार भली** unremunerative work is better than no work.

बैठाना baiṭḥa:nā: (*v*) to seat; to cause to be seated, to request to take a seat; to press down; to fit in; to readjust; to keep (a woman) as mistress; to instal; to see off; to cause to crash down,

बैठालना baiṭḥa:lnā: (*v*) to seat, to request to take a seat.

बैत bait (*nm*) couplet; verse; ~**बाजी** a verse-reciting competition.

बैताल baita:l (*nm*) a bard; minstrel; ghost.

बैतालिक baita:lik (*nm*) see **वैतालिक**.

बैदूर्य baidu:ry (*nm*) see **वैदूर्य**.

बैन bain (*nm*) saying, speech; utterance.

बैरंग bairāg (*a*) bearing (letter); –**लौटना** to return empty-handed, to draw a blank, to fail in one's mission.

बैर bair (*nm*) enmity, animosity, hostility; -**भाव** (sense of) enmity/hostility; –**काढ़ना/निकालना** to pay tit for tat; to take revenge; –**ठानना** to take up a hostile attitude, to strike a hostile posture, to be resolutely hostile; –**मोल लेना** to knowingly create bad blood, to antagonize somebody deliberately.

बैरक bairak (*nm*) a barrack.

बैरक bairaq (*nm*) a banner, flag.

बै/रन, ~**रिन** bairan, ~rin (*nf*) feminine form of **बैरी**.

बैरा baira: (*nm*) a bearer (in a hotel etc.).

बैरा/ग, ~ **ग्य** baira:g, ~ggy (*nm*) see **वैराग्य**.

बैरागी baira:gi: (*nm*) a recluse; a sect of **वैष्णव** saints.

बैरिस्ट/र bairisṭar (*nm*) a barrister-at-law; ~**री** the position, practice or profession of a barrister-at-law.

बैरी bairi: (*nm* and *a*) an enemy, a foe; hostile.

बैरोजा bairoja: (*nm*) resin.

बैरोमीट/र bairomi:ṭar (*nm*) a barometer; ~**री** barometric; o **ऊँचाई** barometric height.

बैल bail (*nm*) an ox, a bullock; (fig.) a fool; ~**गाड़ी** a bullock-cart; –**की तरह काम करना/पिले रहना** to work like a horse.

बैलून bailu:n (*nm*) a baloon.

बैस bais (*nf*) age; –**चढ़ना** to come of age, to become young.

बैसवाड़ी baiswa:ṛi: (*nm*) a western sub-dialect of **अवधी**.

बैसाख baisa:kh (*nm*) the second month of the year according to the Hindu calendar; ~**नंदन** an ass.

बैसाखी baisa:khi: (*nf*) a Hindu festival celebrated on the full moon-day of the month of **बैसाख**; a crutch (used by a lame person in walking).

बोअनी boani: (*nf*) see **बोआई**.

बोआई boa:i: (*nf*) (the act, process of or wages paid for) sowing.

बोझ bojh (*nm*) a burden; load; **–उठाना** to bear or carry a burden/load; to undertake a responsibility; **–उतरना** to be relieved of a burden; to be relieved of a responsibility; **–उतारना** to unload; to cause to be free; to get rid of a burden/responsibility.

बोझा bojha: (*nm*) see **बोझ**.

बोझिल bojhil (*a*) heavy, weighty, burdensome; hence **~ता** (*nf*), **~पन** (*nm*).

बोटा boṭa: (*nm*) a huge log of wood.

बोटी boṭi: (*nf*) a chop, piece or slice of flesh; **-बोटी करना/काटना** to mince; to cut into small pieces; **-बोटी नोचना** to claw flesh out; **-बोटी फड़कना** to be very fidgety, to be restive; the whole being to be filled with a thrill.

बोड़ा boṛa: (*nm*) a kind of bean used for vegetable.

बोतल botal (*nf*) a bottle; bottle of liquor; **–चढ़ाना** to drink lots of liquor.

बोदा boda: (*a*) timid; meek; lazy; **~पन** timidness; meekness; laziness.

बोध bodh (*nm*) perception; sense; knowledge; understanding; **~गम्य** intelligible; comprehensible, understandable **~गम्यता** intelligibility, comprehensibility.

बोधक bodhak—a Sanskrit prefix meaning that which or one who causes perception/knowledge or informs/indicates (as **विस्मयादि-बोधक**), indicative of; (*nm*) an indicator; one who or that which imparts knowledge/information.

बोधन bodhān (*nm*) indicating/informing; awaking; arousing.

बोधव्य bodhavvy (*a*) knowable, worth knowing/comprehending.

बोधि/तरु, ~वृक्ष bodhitaru, ~vriksh (*nm*) the holy **पीपल** tree in Gaya: whereunder Prince Siddha:rth attained enlightenment and became the Buddha (the Enlightened).

बोधितव्य bodhitavvy (*a*) worth imparting knowledge of; to be communicated.

बोधिसत्व bodhisattw (*nm*) lit. one whose essence is perfect knowledge, one who is on the way to attainment of perfect knowledge or Enlightenment (i.e. a Buddhist saint when he has only one birth to undergo before attaining the state of a Supreme Buddha and then Nirva:ṇ).

बोनस bonas (*nm*) bonus.

बोना bonā: (*v*) to sow; to plant.

बोया boya: (*nm*) a buoy; (*v*) past tense form of **बोना**; **–पेड़ बबूल का आम कहाँ ते होय** to expect flowers in return for thorns; **–हुआ काटना** as you sow so shall you reap.

बोरना bornā: (*v*) to dip; to draw; to sink; to cause the ruination of.

बोरसी borsi: (*nf*) an earthen fire-pot.

बोरा bora: (*nm*) a bag, sack, gunny bag; **-भर** bagful, sackful.

बोरिया boriya: (*nf*) a small sack or gunny bag; **-बँधना/बिस्तर/बुकचा** one's belongings, household effects/goods; o उठाना/समेटना/सँभालना to make preparations for departure; to prepare to leave.

बोरी bori: (*nf*) a small sack/gunnybag.

बोर्ड bord (*nm*) a board.

बोर्डिंग हाउस bordīng ha:us (*nm*) a boarding house, hostel.

बोल bol (*nm*) speech; utterance; opening words of a song; taunt; ~चाल conversation, talk; speaking terms; o का colloquial; ~चाल न रहना/होना not to be on speaking terms, not to talk to each other; –न निकलना/फूटना to be rendered mute, to become speechless; ~पट the talkie; -फूटना words to flow out, an utterance to be made; –मारना to taunt; to slight.

बोलती bolti: (*nf*) speech, utterance; –बंद होना to become speechless, to be turned mute.

बोलना bolnā: (*v*) to speak, to utter; to pronounce; to bid (as बोली–); बोल जाना to die; to crash; to prove a flop; to be exhausted; to be out of use; to become unserviceable; -चालना to converse, to talk.

बोलबाला bolba:la: (*nm*) overbearing influence, sway; –होना to hold complete sway; to exercise overbearing influence; to have a predominant say; to be regarded with awe.

बोलाचाली bola:cha:li: (*nf*) speaking terms; –होना to be on speaking terms.

बोलावा bola:wa: (*nm*) see बुलावा.

बोली boli: (*nf*) a dialect; mode of speaking; bid (in auction); taunt, sarcastic remarks; vulgar remarks; -ठोली sarcastic utterance, sarcasm; vulgar remarks;–बानी speech; –कसना/बोलना/मारना to have a fling/dig at, to taunt; to make slighting remarks; –देना/बोलना/लगाना to bid (in auction); –बोलने/लगाने वाला a bidder.

बोसा bosa: (*nm*) a kiss; ~सेबाज़ी kissing and caressing.

बोहनी bohnī: (*nf*) the first sale of the day; -बट्टा first sales, initiation of sales (on a day).

बोहित bohit (*nm*) a ship; boat.

बौखला/ना baukhla:nā: (*v*) to be furious, to fret and fume, to be terribly enraged; ~हट fury, rage, fretting and fuming.

बौछार bauchha:r (*nf*) a shower, drift of rain; splash.

बौड़म bauṛām (*a* and *nm*) stupid, silly; nincompoop; hence ~पन/पना (*nm*).

बौद्ध bauddh (*a*) Buddhist; pertaining or belonging to Lord Buddha or the religion propounded by him; (*nm*) a Buddhist; follower of Lord Buddha and his religion; –धर्म/मत Buddhism, Buddhist faith; –विहार a Buddhist monastery.

बौद्धिक bauddhik (*a*) intellectual; ~ता intellectualism; intellectuality; –व्यायाम intellectual exercise.

बौना baunā: (*a* and *nm*) dwarfish; dwarf; pigmy.

बौर baur (*nm*) a cluster of blossoms of mango, neem, etc.

बौराना baura:nā: (*v*) to go mad/crazy, to run amuck, to become insane; mango or neem etc. to blossom.

ब्यंग byāng (*nm*) see व्यंग्य.

ब्यंजन byāṇjān (*nm*) see **व्यंजन**.

ब्यथा byatha: (*nf*) see **व्यथा**.

ब्यवहरिया byawhariya: (*nm*) a money-lender.

ब्याज bya:j (*nm*) interest (on money); ~**खोर** a usurer; ~**खोरी** usury; **-दर-ब्याज** compound interest; **-बट्टा** interest etc; interest and discount.

ब्याधि bya:dhi (*nf*) see **व्याधि**.

ब्याना bya:nā: (*v*) to foal, to reproduce, to give birth to (used only in the context of animals).

ब्यापना bya:pnā: (*v*) see **व्यापना**.

ब्यापार bya:pa:r (*nm*) see **व्यापार**.

ब्यापारी bya:pa:ri: (*nm*) see **व्यापारी**.

ब्यालू bya:lu: (*nf*) supper, dinner.

ब्याह bya:h (*nm*) marriage, wedding; **-काज/शादी** wedding, wedding ceremony; **-बरात** wedding ceremony or party.

ब्याहता bya:hta: (*a*) married (woman); (*nf*) wife.

ब्याहना bya:hnā: (*v*) to marry (off); to wed; to get somebody married.

ब्यूरो byu:ro (*nm*) a bureau.

ब्योंचना byōchnā: (*v*) to be sprained, to suffer a sprain.

ब्योंत byōt (*nm*) measurements; cutting of a cloth for tailoring; used as the second member in the compound **कतर-ब्योंत** meaning contriving and manipulating.

ब्योंतना byotnā: (*v*) to cut the cloth according to measurements; to take the measurement (of a person's garment).

ब्यो/रा byora: (*nm*) details; particulars; ~**रेवार** detailed; systematic.

ब्यौंत byaut (*nf*) see **ब्योंत**.

ब्यौंतना byautnā: (*v*) **ब्योंतना** see.

ब्यौ/रा byaura: (*nm*) see **ब्योरा**; ~**रेवार** see **ब्योरेवार**.

ब्यौहार byauha:r (*nm*) dealings, mutual relations.

ब्रज braj (*nm*) see **ब्रजभाषा**; the tract of land around and near Mathura where Lord Krishṇā is supposed to have grown into an adolescent youth amongst all the fun and frolic of his cowherd mates which have found poetic expression in various Indian languages; ~**बुलि** an amalgam of Maithili: and Bengali with a sprinkling of vocabulary from **ब्रजभाषा** used by mediaeval Krishṇā cult poets of Bengal, Assam and Orissa; also ~**भूमि/मंडल**.

ब्रजभाषा brajbha:sha: (*nf*) a dialect of Hindi spoken in the **ब्रज** area.

ब्रजराज brajra:j (*nm*) Lord Krishṇā.

ब्रह्म brahm (*nm*) God; the Eternal Spirit; a Bra:hmāṇ; knowledge; ~**घात** killing a Bra:hmāṇ; ~**घाती** killer of a Bra:hmāṇ; **-जिज्ञासा** quest for the realisation of God; ~**ज्ञ** one who has realised God/the Supreme Spirit; one who has acquired eternal knowledge; **-ज्ञान** divine knowledge; realisation of the Supreme Spirit; ~**ज्ञानी** see ~**ज्ञ**; **–तेज** the radiant glow on the face of an ascetic Bra:hmāṇ; ~**द्रोही** one who is hostile to the Bra:hmāṇs; ~**निष्ठ** one who is dedicated to God/to the quest for Supreme Spirit; ~**पद** salvation, liberation; attainment of identity with the Supreme Spirit; ~**पिशाच** a Bra:hmāṇ condemned to exist as an evil spirit; ~**भोज** collective feeding of the Bra:hmāṇs; ~**मुहूर्त**, see **ब्राह्म(मुहूर्त)**; ~**रंध्र** the suture on the top of the skull; ~**राक्षस**

a Bra:hmāṇ condemned to a demonic existence; ~वादी a follower of the वेदांत system of Hindu Philosophy; ~विद् one who knows God, one who has realized the Supreme Spirit; a theologist; ~विद्या theology; ~शाप a Bra:hmāṇ's curse; ~समाज see ब्राह्म समाज; ~सूत्र the sacred thread worn by caste Hindus; name of a celebrated ancient work; ~हत्या murder/assassination of Bra:hmāṇ; hence ~हत्यारा (nm); –बोलना the Inner Self to speak; –मरना the Inner Self to die/to become inert.

ब्रह्मचर्य brahmchary (nm) the first of the four stages (आश्रम) in a man's life as prescribed by the Hindu scriptures extending till the twenty-fifth year during which one is expected to live strictly as a celibate dedicated to the consummation of his educational effort under the preceptor's direction and guidance.

ब्रह्मचारिणी brahmcha:riṇī: (nf) feminine form of 'ब्रह्मचारी'.

ब्रह्मचारी brahmcha:ri: (nm) a celibate; one who is in the ब्रह्मचर्य आश्रम (see).

ब्रह्मर्षि brahmarshi (nm) a Bra:hmāṇ sage/seer.

ब्रह्मांड brahmā:ṇd (nm) the universe, cosmos; the uppermost point of the skull; –विद्या cosmology; –चटकना/फूटना the skull to crack.

ब्रह्मा brahma: (nm) one of the trinity of mythological Hindu deities; the creator.

ब्रह्मास्त्र brahma:str (nm) In ancient Indian warfare, a missile said to be set in motion by divine force; an unfailing weapon.

ब्राह्म bra:hm (a) pertaining or belonging to ब्रह्म/ब्रह्मा/ब्राह्मण; –मुहूर्त the small hours of the morning; –विवाह marriage solemnized according to the prescribed Hindu traditions wherein the daughter is given away in marriage to a suitable match; –समाज a socio-religious reformist movement founded by Raja Ram Mohan Rai of Bengal in the early nineteenth century.

ब्राह्मण bra:hmāṇ (nm) the first of the four castes in traditional Hindu social hierarchy whose main duty, as prescribed, was to study, to teach, to perform यज्ञ and to subsist through alms; the theological portion of the Vedas; ~त्व brahmanhood; the quality, duty, privilege or dignity of a Bra:hmāṇ; ~वाद Brahmanism; ~वादी Brahmanist; Brahmanistic.

ब्राह्मणी bra:hmāṇī: (nf) the wife of a Bra:hmāṇ.

ब्राह्मी bra:hmi: (nf) a medicinal plant; a widely used ancient Indian script which formed the source of evolution of the देवनागरी and all other indigenous Indian scripts.

ब्रिगेड briged (nm) a brigade (in an army).

ब्रिगेडियर Brigeḍiyar (nm) a brigadier.

ब्रिटिश briṭish (nm and a) the British; English; –राज the British rule;

ब्रेक brek (nm) a brake; –वान the brake van; –मारना/–लगाना to apply the brakes; to bring to a halt.

ब्रैकेट braiket (nm) a bracket.

ब्लाउज bla:uz (nm) a blouse; –पीस a blouse-piece.

ब्लॉक blɔk (*nm*) a block.
ब्लेड bleḍ (*nm*) a blade.
ब्लैक blaik (*a*) black; ~बोर्ड blackboard; ~मार्केट the black market; –का पैसा black money.

भ

भ bh–the fourth letter of the fifth and ultimate pentad (*i.e.* पवर्ग) of the Devna:gri: alphabet.

भंग bhāṅg (*nm*) dissolution; breach; split; disbandment; destruction; fracture; (*nf*) an intoxicating drug made from the leaves of *Cannabis sativa*, hemp; –खाना/चढ़ाना/छानना to be intoxicated, to take भंग.

भंग/ड़, ~ड़ी bhāṅgaṛ, ~ṛi: (*a* and *nm*) (one who is) addicted to the consumption of भंग in large quantities.

भँगड़ा bhāgṛa: (*nm*) a typical popular dance-form of the Punjab involving swift and violent movements.

भँगरा bhāgra: (*nm*) a medicinal plant used in the preparation of hair-darkening oils; also भँगरैया, भृंगराज.

भंगिमा bhāṅgimā: (*nf*) pose, posture; curvature; obliquity; slant.

भंगी bhāṅgi: (*nm*) a sweeper, scavenger; a low caste in the traditional Hindu caste set-up; (*nf*) see भंगिमा.

भंगुर bhāṅgur (*a*) brittle, fragile; transient; perishable; ~ता brittleness, fragility; transience; perishability.

भँगेड़ी bhāgeṛi: (*a* and *nm*) see भंगड़ी.

भंजन bhanjān (*nm*) (the act of) breaking; breach; fracture; destruction, ruination; demolition.

भँजाना bhājā:nā: (*v*) to change (into cash or currency of smaller denominations); to cause to break or twist.

भंड bhānḍ (*nm*) a utensil; sham, hypocrite.

भँड़साल bhārsa:l (*nf*) a barn, utensil-store.

भंडा bhānḍa: (*nm*) a secret; –फूटना a secret to be exposed/revealed/leaked.

भंडाफोड़ bhānḍa:phoṛ (*nm*) exposure/revelation/disclosure / unearthing (of a secret); –होना see भंडा फूटना.

भंडा/र bhānḍa:r (*nm*) a store, storehouse; storage; depository; emporium; also ~रघर (*nm*); ~री a store-manager, incharge of a store-house.

भंडारा bhānḍa:ra: (*nm*) a feast for all, esp. the mendicants; –करना/-लगाना to organise a general feast.

भँडुआ bhāṛua: (*nm*) see भड़ुआ.

भँड़ै/ती bhāṛaiti: (*nf*) the act of a भाँड़; buffoonery, clownish act; also

~तरी (*nf*).

भंभा bhāmbha: (*nm*) a huge hole.

भँवर bhāvar (*nm*) a whirlpool, swirl; eddy; ~जाल the whirlpool of mundane bonds, the net of worldly affairs; –में पड़ना to be caught up in a whirlpool; –से निकलना to get out of a whirlpool.

भँवरा bhāvra: (*nm*) a black-bee.

भइया bhaiya: (*nm*) see भैया.

भकभक bhakbhak (*nf*) the sound of sudden and repeated emergence of jet of smoke; repeated fulguration.

भकभकाना bhakbhaka:nā: (*v*) to fret and fume, to be terribly infuriated.

भकुआ bhakua: (*a*) stupid; foolish, nincompoop.

भकुरना bhakurnā: (*v*) to sulk, to get angry, to be enraged.

भको/सना bhakosnā: (*v*) to raven, to swallow in large quantities; hence ~सू (*a*).

भक्त bhakt (*nm*) a devotee; (*a*) divided; ~राज the foremost of devotees; ~वत्सल affectionately disposed towards devotees, loving the devotees; hence ~वत्सलता (*nf*); ~शिरोमणि the leading-most devotee.

भक्ति bhakti (*nf*) devotion; ~परायण devoted, given to devotion; hence ~परायणता (*nf*); -पात्र deserving devotion; ~पूर्वक devotedly; in a devoted manner; ~प्रवण engrossed in devotion, devout; hence ~प्रवणता (*nf*); -भाजन see -पात्र; –मार्ग the path of devotion (one of the three paths prescribed for the achievement of human salvation; the other two being ज्ञान and योग); hence ~मार्गी (*a* and *nm*); ~योग realisation of the ultimate aim through devotion; –रस intense love towards God (some Indian Poeticians have credited this emotion of भक्ति (devotion) with potentialities of flowering and culminating into a *rasa* (भक्ति रस) over and above the traditionally accepted nine *rasas*).

भक्षक bhakshak (*a* and *nm*) (one) that eats/devours; eater; destroyer.

भक्षण bhakshān (*nm*) eating, feeding (on); -करना to eat, to devour, to feed on; hence भक्षणीय (*a*) (see भक्ष्य).

भक्षी bhakshi:—used as a suffix denoting one who eats, eater (e.g. नरभक्षी man-eater).

भक्ष्य bhakshy (*a*) eatable, edible; (*nm*) diet, food, feed; -अभक्ष्य (भक्ष्याभक्ष्य) eatable and non-eatable, fit for consumption or otherwise; salubrious or otherwise; –वस्तु eatable, something that can be consumed, fit for consumption.

भगंदर bhagandar (*nm*) fistula in the anus.

भग bhag (*nf*) the female genital, vulva.

भग/त bhagat (*a* and *nm*) (a) devotee, one having a religious bent of mind; hence ~तिन (feminine); ~ताई/~ती devotion (used in a derogatory sense) exhibition of devotedness; sense or act of devotion.

भगदड़ bhagdaṛ (*nf*) rout, stampede, running helter-skelter; panic; –मचना a rout/stampede to be caused.

भगना bhagnā: (*v*) see भागना.

भगवती bhagwati: (*nf*) a name of

goddess दुर्गा and लक्ष्मी; a respectable lady.

भगवद्/भक्त bhagwadbhakt (*nm*) (a) devotee of God; ~**भक्ति** devotion to God; ~**विग्रह** the idol of God.

भगवा bhagwa: (*a*) saffron (coloured); –**वस्त्र** saffron-coloured robes; oधारी saffron-robed; an ascetic; a mendicant; –**धारण करना/पहनना** to don saffron robes, to turn into a mendicant/an ascetic.

भगवान् bhagwā:n (*nm*) God, the Lord Almighty; –**के घर जाना/–को प्यारा होना** to go to one's heavenly abode, to pass away, –**भला करे** may God bless you !, God help you ! –**की इच्छा** as God wills !

भगाना bhaga:nā: (*v*) to drive off; to scare away; to cause to run away; to kidnap; to abduct.

भगिनी bhaginī: (*nf*) a sister; ~**पति** brother-in-law, sister's husband.

भगीरथ bhagi:rath (*nm*) an ancient Indian king of the solar dynasty who is supposed to have caused the river Gaṅga: to descend on earth through his unprecedented penance; –**प्रयत्न** a Herculean effort, tremendous effort.

भगोड़ा bhagoṛā: (*a* and *nm*) (a) fugitive, truant; runaway; hence ~**पन** (*nm*).

भगौहाँ bhagaũhā: (*v*) as if ready to flee, on the verge of running away.

भग्गू bhaggu: (*a*) fugitive; coward.

भग्न bhagn (*a*) broken, shattered; demoralised; ~**क्रम** put into disarray, (rendered) disorderly; ~**चित्त** demoralised; disappointed, dejected; ~**मना** see ~**चित्त**; ~**मनोरथ** frustrated; ~**मान** insulted, humiliated; ~**हृदय** broken-hearted, frustrated; hence ~**हृदयता** (*nf*).

भग्नावशेष bhagna:vashesh (*nm*) remains, ruins.

भग्ना/श bhagna:sh (*a*) frustrated; disappointed, dejected; ~**शा** frustration; disappointment, dejection.

भग्नोत्साह bhagnotsa:h (*a*) demoralised; discouraged.

भजन bhajān (*nm*) a devotional song. hymn; repetition of the name of God; -**पूजन** devotion and adoration; -**भाव** devotion and adoration, devotional practices; sense of devotion.

भजना bhajnā: (*v*) to repeat the name of God; to remember God; to be engaged in devotional practices; to enjoy, to derive pleasure; ~**नंदी** concentrated in and enjoying devotional chores.

भजनीक bhajnī:k (*nm*) one who sings devotional songs while delivering religious discourses.

भजनोपदेश bhajanopdesh (*nm*) devotional singing and religious discourses; hence ~**क** (*nm*).

भट bhaṭ (*nm*) a soldier, a warrior.

भटकना bhaṭaknā: (*v*) to lose one's way; to go astray; to gad, to meander, to wander about.

भटियार/ख़ाना bhaṭiya:rḵha:nā: (*nm*) an inn-keeper's abode; a noise-centre, dwelling of lowly vulgur people; ~**पन** the job of an inn-keeper; conduct befitting an inn-keeper; quarrelling and abusing like an inn-keeper.

भटियारा bhaṭiya:ra: (*nm*) an inn-keeper; hence **भटियारी** (*nf*).

भटियारिन bhaṭiya:rin (*nf*) a female

inn-keeper; an inn-keeper's wife; भटियारिनों की तरह लड़ना to indulge in a very low level fight/quarrel.

भटैती bhaṭaiti: (*nf*) the conduct or profession of a भाट (see); speaking of something in hyperboles, panegyric, sycophancy.

भट्ट bhaṭṭ (*nm*) a bard; scholarly Bra:hmāṉ.

भट्टा bhaṭṭa: (*nm*) see भट्ठा.

भट्टारक bhaṭṭa:rak (*a*) (archaic) respectable; honourable.

भट्ठा bhaṭṭha: (*nm*) a kiln; furnace.

भट्ठी bhaṭṭhi: (*nf*) a fireplace; an oven; a distillery.

भड़क bhaṛak (*nf*) gaud; show, pomp, ostentation, tawdry (generally used in this sense as the second member in the compound तड़क-भड़क); flare; blaze; ~दार gaudy, showy; ostentatious.

भड़क/ना bhaṛaknā: (*v*) to flare up; to be provoked/excited/enraged; to burst forth; to go ablaze, to go/blow up into flames; to be startled; –उठना to go (in) off the deep end, to flare up; to burst into flames.

भड़काना bhaṛka:nā: (*v*) to cause to flare up; to provoke/excite/enrage; to set ablaze; to incite/instigate to startle; to scare.

भड़कीला bhaṛki:la: (*a*) gaudy, showy, ostentatious, tawdry; flamboyant; ~पन gaudiness, showiness, ostentatiousness, tawdriness; flamboyance.

भड़कैल bhaṛkail (*a*) skittish; easily alarmed/startled/agitated, panicky.

भड़भड़ bhaṛbhaṛ (*nf*) impetuosity, rashness, thoughtless hastiness; thump.

भड़भड़ाना bharbhara:nā: (*v*) to be impetuous, to be rash, to be thoughtlessly hasty; to thump.

भड़भड़िया bhaṛbhaṛiya: (*a*) impetuous, rash, hasty, fidgety.

भड़भूँजा bhaṛbhū:ja: (*nm*) one whose profession is to parch grain (cereals) and sell the same; a sub-caste amongst the Hindus who subsist by the said profession.

भड़ास bhaṛa:s (*nf*) stored-up spite, accumulated grudge; –निकालना to give free vent to stored-up spite/grudge.

भड़ुआ bhaṛua: (*nm*) a professional procurer, tout; parasite on the earnings of a prostitute, hence ~पन (*nm*).

भणन bhaṇān (*nm*) (the act or process of) saying; a statement.

भणिति bhaṇīti (*nf*) saying; statement.

भती/जा bhati:ja: (*nm*) a nephew; ~जी a niece.

भत्ता bhatta: (*nm*) an allowance.

भदंत bhadant (*a*) honourable, reverend; adored.

भदेस bhades (*a*) rustic; unsophisticated; disproportionate; clumsy; ~पन rusticity; unsophisticatedness; disproportionateness; clumsiness.

भद्द bhadd (*nf*) insult, humiliation, disgrace; –होना to be put to disgrace, to face humiliation.

भद्दड़ bhaddaṛ (*a*) inactive, slothfully corpulent, plump and inert; hence ~पन (*nm*).

भद्दा bhadda: (*a*) ugly; clumsy; ungainly, unseemly, gawky; unsymmetrical, obscence, vulgar; dirty; untoward; ~पन ugliness; clumsiness, ungainliness, unseemliness; absence of symmetry, ob-

परिवार); -भरा rich, full; fleshy, plump; भरी आवाज़ see –गला; भरी गोद ख़ाली होना to lose one's only son; भरी जवानी prime of youth, blooming youth; भरी सभा में in public, in a public gathering.

भराई bhara:i: (*nf*) the act of filling/loading or the charges paid therefor; stopping; filling; packing.

भराव bhara:v (*nm*) filling; fleshiness; stuffing; packing piece; embankment.

भरोसा bharosa: (*nm*) trust, faith; confidence; reliance; भरोसे का reliable, trustworthy; credible.

भर्ता bharta: (*nm*) one who provides maintenance/sustenance; lord; husband.

भर्तार bharta:r (*nm*) husband; Master.

भर्त्सना bhartsanā: (*nf*) admonition, reproach; denunciation.

भर्रा/टा bharra:ṭa: (*nm*) a whizzing sound; ~टे से with a whizzing sound; with top speed.

भर्राना bharra:nā: (*v*) to whizz; (throat) to be choked; (voice) to turn hoarse.

भलमनसाहत bhalmānsa:hat (*nf*) gentlemanliness, nobility.

भलमनसी bhalmānsi: (*nf*) see भलमनसाहत.

भला bhala: (*a*) gentle, noble, good; (*nm*) well-being; good; –आदमी a gentleman; good/noble person; -चंगा hale and hearty, healthy, in good health, sound; reasonably good; -बुरा good and evil, good and bad; virtue and vice, one's own interest; reproach, admonition; ~मानस a gentleman, good/noble person.

भलाई bhala:i: (*nf*) good, welfare, well-being; goodness, gentleness; -बुराई good or bad.

भले bhale (*ind*) well !, good! ;–ही even if, even though.

भव bhav (*nm*) the world; mundane existence; birth; Lord Shiv; ~चक्र the perpetual wheel of birth and death; ~जाल the bond of existence; ~ताप the mundane afflictions; ~पाश-बंधन the mundane bond, the bond of existence, the inevitability of recurrent births and deaths: ~भय the fear of recurrent births and deaths; ~भीति see ~भय; ~मोचन God—who liberates the soul from worldly bonds; -समुद्र सागर/सिंधु the ocean of mundane existence.

भव/दीय bhavdi:y (*ind*) yours; yours sincerely; yours faithfully; ~दीया feminine form of भवदीय.

भवन bhawān (*nm*) a house; building, mansion; an edifice; -निर्माण house-building; ०कला architecture.

भवान bhawā:n (*pron*) your honour, your grace.

भवानी bhavā:nī: (*nf*) goddess Durga: —spouse of Lord Shiv (भव).

भवितव्य bhavitavvy (*a*) destined, fated; (*nm*) the inevitable; ~ता destiny, the inevitable.

भविष्य bhavishy (*nm*) the future; destiny; -काल the future tense; futurity; -कथन prophesy, forecast; -ज्ञान knowledge of the future; ~ दर्शी a seer, one who can see through into the future; ~द्रष्टा see ~दर्शी: -निधि provident fund; ~वक्ता a prophet; an astrologer; ~ वाणी an oracle; prediction,, prophesy; — हाथ में होना to be maker of the destiny (*of*).

भविष्यत् bhavishyat (*a*) future, that is yet to come; (*nm*) the future tense;—**काल** the future tense.

भविष्यद् bhavishyad—an allomorph of **भविष्यत्** used in compound words; ~ **वक्ता** a prophet, an astrologer; ~ **वाणी** see **भविष्यवाणी**.

भवें bhavē (*nf*) plural form of **भौं**; —**तनना** to get enraged/ infuriated.

भव्य bhavvy (*a*) grand; divine; pretty; ~**ता** grandness; divinity; prettiness.

भस्म bhasm (*nf*) ash, cinders, calx; ~**सात्** reduced to ashes, burnt to ashes;—**चढ़ाना/रमाना/लगाना** to turn into an ascetic/a mendicant; –**होना** to be reduced to ashes; to be ruined.

भस्मावशेष bhasmā:vashesh (*nm*) ashes; reduction to ashes; survived only in the form of ashes.

भस्मासुर bhasmā:sur (*nm*) (based on the name of a mythological demonic character) one whose touch reduces everything to ashes; one who digests everything.

भस्मीभूत bhashmī:bhu:t (*a*) burnt to ashes, completely burnt; ruined.

भहराना bhahra:nā: (*v*) to crash down; to tumble down; to give way all of a sudden.

भांग bhā:g (*nf*) the intoxicating hemp—*Cannabis sativa*; –**खाना** to be intoxicated; to talk incoherently; —**छानना** to drink **भाँग**.

भांजना bhā:jnā: (*v*) to fold; to brandish; to twist something.

भांजा bhā:nja: (*nm*) see **भानजा**; hence **भांजी** (*nf*) see **भानजी**.

भांजी bhā:ji: (*nf*) back-biting, censure;—**मारना** to create obstacles (in the way of), to hamper accomplishment of.

भांड bhā:ṇḍ (*nm*) a utensil; wares; ~**शाला** a store-house, warehouse.

भांड़ bhā:ṛ (*nm*) a clown, buffoon, jester.

भांड़ा bhā:ṛā: (*nm*) a utensil;—**फूटना** to be exposed, a secret to become public.

भांडागार bhā:ṇḍa:ga:r: (*nm*) a store-house; warehouse; godown.

भांडार bhā:ṇḍa:r (*nm*) a store-house; also ~**गृह** (*nm*).

भांडारिक/भांडारी bhā:ṇḍa:rik, bhā:ṇḍa:ri: (*nm*) a store-keeper; custodian of a store-house.

भाँति bhā:ti (*nf*) kind; type; manner, mode, method; -**भाँति** varied; variegated; of different types/ kinds.

भाँपना bhā:pnā: (*v*) to guess the (undisclosed) truth, to look through the reality; to make out, to divine.

भाँपू bhā:pu: (*a*) adept in guessing/ looking through the truth; (one) who reaches the bottom of a secret.

भाँय-भाँय bhā:y-bhā:y (*nf*) frou-frou, sound (of rushing wind) produced in a desolate place.

भाँवर bhā:var (*nf*) circumambulation of the sacrificial fire made by both the bride and the bridegroom at the wedding time (seven such rounds are essential to solemnize a wedding according to the Hindu tradition); going round; **भाँवरें पड़ना** the wedding to be solemnized; to be married.

भाँवरी bhā:vri: (*nf*) circumambulation; (see भाँवर); round.

भाई bha:i: (*nm*) a brother; ~चारा fraternity, brotherhood; fraternisation, fraternal understanding; ~दूज the second day of the bright fortnight of the month of कार्तिक; -बंद/बंधु kith and kin, relations, bretheren; -बिरादर kith and kin, bretheren, relations; -भतीजावाद nepotism.

भाग bha:g (*nm*) portion, part, fragment; fraction; share; luck; division; ~फल the quotient; ~वंत/वान् fortunate, lucky; ~हर a co-sharer; ~हारी a co-sharer; successor; –करना/देना to divide; –खुलना/चमकना/जागना to have an advent of good luck, to have a run of good luck; to be graced by the smile of Dame Luck; –फूटना to have a stroke of misfortune; to have a run of ill-luck; adverse times to commence.

भाग-दौड़ bha:g-daur̤ (*nf*) running about; strenuous effort.

भागना bha:gnā: (*v*) to run, to run away; to escape; to flee; to take to heels; to abscond, to give the slip; to make off; to elope (with); भागते भूत की लँगोटी भली salvage what you can of a bad debt.

भागमभाग bha:gambha:g (*nm*) running about, making a desperate bid; (*ind*) through constant running.

भागिनेय bha:giney (*nm*) a sister's son.

भागी bha:gi: (*nm*) a co-sharer, partner (as दोष के भागी); used as a suffix to mean fortunate, lucky (as बड़भागी); ~दार share-holder, partner; ~दारी partnership.

भागीरथी bha:gi:rathi: (*nf*) a name of the river Ganga: (see भगीरथ).

भाग्य bha:ggy (*nm*) fortune, fate, luck; destiny; -क्रम the vicissitudes of fortune; the course of destiny; -दोष drawback of one's luck, fault of one's fortune; ~परायण fatalist; ~परायणता fatalism; –बल the force of luck/fortune; -लक्ष्मी Dame Luck, the goddess of fortune; ~लिपि/लेख the writ of destiny; ~वश/वशात् luckily, fortunately; ~वाद, ~वादिता fatalism; ~वादी a fatalist; fatalistic; –विधाता fortune-maker; controller of the destiny; providence;- विधान providence; -विपर्यय reversal of fortune; ~शालिता the fact or state of being fortunate/lucky, luckiness; ~शाली fortunate, lucky; ~हीन unlucky, unfortunate, ill-fated; hence ~हीनता (*nf*); –का धनी/बली a lucky guy; fortunate; –का रोना रोना/को रोना/को कोसना to blame one's luck; –का साथ देना one's luck to be favourable, to have a run of good luck; –खुलना/चमकना/जागना see under भाग; –खोटा होना one's luck to be adverse; –ठोकना to decry one's luck; ~दशा the state of one's luck; –पलटना/फिरना one's luck to change its course; –फूटना see under भाग; –में लिखा होना to be lotted; –का लिखा मिटता नहीं what is lotted cannot be blotted; ~लक्ष्मी सो जाना Dame Luck to be adversely disposed/to become indifferent; –सो जाना see ~लक्ष्मी सो जाना.

भाग्य/वान् bha:ggyavā:n (*a*) lucky, fortunate; hence ~वती (fem. form).

भाग्योदय bha:ggyoday (*nm*) advent of good luck, commencement of a run of good luck,

भाजक bha:jak (*nm*) divisor; (*a*) dividing.

भाजन bha:jān (*nm*) a utensil, vessel; container; one who deserves; used as a suffix with nouns to mean one who enjoys/suffers/deserves (e.g. कृपाभाजन, कोपभाजन, etc.)

भाजी bha:ji: (*nf*) a vegetable (cooked or otherwise).

भाज्य bha:jjy (*nm*) a dividend; (*a*) divisible; ~फल the quotient.

भाट bha:ṭ (*nm*) a bard, minstrel; sycophant.

भाटक bha:ṭak (*nm*) fare, rent; freight.

भाटा bha:ṭa: (*nm*) the ebb (tide), low tide, falling tide,

भाड़ bha:ṛ (*nm*) a parcher's oven; –झोंकना to do a worthless/low level job; to undertake an unavailing/unrewarding assignment; –भूँजना to manage an oven; to do nothing worthwhile, to have no attainments; –में जाये go to hell !, be damned!; –में झोंकना/डालना to condemn, to damn; to destroy, to ruin.

भाड़ा bha:ṛa: (*nm*) fare; rent; freight; भाड़ेदार a hirer; hence भाड़ेदारी; भाड़े का टट्टू a hireling, hack, mercenary; भाड़े का लेखक hack writer.

भात bha:t (*nm*) boiled rice; presents (on special occasions given to daughters, nieces, etc.); –देना to send presents etc.; to have to arrange feast (as a punishment).

भादों bha:dō (*nm*) the sixth month of the year according to the Hindu calendar.

भाद्रपद bha:ddrpad (*nm*) see भादों.

भान bhā:n (*nm*) change (of smaller denomination) ; awareness; inkling; –होना to have an inkling of.

भानजा bhā:nja: (*nm*) sister's son; hence भानजी (*nf*).

भानमती bhā:nmati: (*nf*) a sorceress; –का कुनबा a weird assortment of heterogeneous elements; –का पिटारा a wonder-casket, container of an amazing variety of things.

भाना bha:nā: (*v*) to be liked; to be agreeable, to be pleasing/appealing.

भानु bha:nū (*nm*) the sun; ~जा the river Yamunā: ; ~दिन, ~वार Sunday; ~सुता see ~जा.

भा/प, ~फ bha:p, ~ph (*nf*) steam; vapour; –लेना to inhale the fumes (of).

भाभी bha:bhi: (*nf*) sister-in-law, brother's wife.

भामिनी bha:minī: (*nf*) a pretty woman; short-tempered woman.

भार bha:r (*nm*) load; weight, burden; encumbrance; onus; obligation; responsibility; -केन्द्र the centre of gravity; -क्षमता capacity; carrying capacity; ~जीवी a porter, carrier; ~वाह/वाहक/वाही a carrier; porter; –उठाना, किसी का to bear the responsibility of, to undertake the responsibility of; –उतरना to be rid of an obligation; to fulfil an obligation; -डालना to put a responsibility, to cause (somebody) to take up a responsibility; –होना to be burdensome.

भारत bha:rat (*nm*) India; ~माता mother India; ~मूलक of Indian origin; ~रत्न the highest national honour awarded by the Govt. of India; ~वर्ष India; the Indian sub-continent; ~वर्षीय Indian; ~वासी an Indian, a native of India; ~विद् an Indologist; ~विद्या Indology; -संतान a son of mother India.

भारती bha:rati: (*nf*) speech; Saraswati:–the goddess of speech; letters; mother India.

भारतीय bha:rati:y (*a* and *nm*) (an) Indian—a native of India; pertaining to India; ~ता Indianness.

भारतीय/करण bha:rati:ykarāṇ (*nm*) Indianisation; ~कृत Indianised.

भाराक्रांत bha:ra:kkrā:nt (*a*) a groaning under a burden/obligation.

भारिक bha:rik (*nm*) a porter.

भारी bha:ri: (*a*) heavy; difficult to digest; weighty, massive; grave; burdensome; ~पन heaviness; weightiness, massiveness; gravity; -भरकम voluminous; heavy; large-sized; of massive structure; profound; –लगना to be burdensome, to appear to be a burden; –होना, (किसी पर) to be more than a match, to be stronger than (e.g. वह अकेला सब पर भारी है).

भार्गव bha:rgav (*nm*) a descendant of the भृगु clan, one of the numerous sub-divisions of Bra:hmāṇs.

भार्या bha:rya: (*nf*) wife, better half; ~त्व wifehood.

भाल bha:l (*nm*) the forehead; used as the second member in the compound देख-भाल meaning looking after, keeping a watch, supervision.

भालना bha:lnā: (*v*) used only as the second member of the compound देखना-भालना meaning—to look after, to keep a watch, to supervise.

भाला bha:la: (*nm*) a spear, lance, javelin; ~धारी a lance-bearer, spearsman.

भालू bha:lu: (*nm*) a bear.

भाव bha:v (*nm*) emotion, sentiment feeling; idea; rate, price(s); quotation; existence, existing state; being; sense, purport; gist; nature, temperament, disposition; –आवेग (भावावेग) passion, intensity of anemotion/feeling; ~गति desire, emotional activity; ~गम्य mentally conceivable, comprehensible; ~ग्राही one who understands or appreciates the sense/emotion; ~ग्राह्य mentally appreciable, that can be appreciated through the heart; -चित्र an ideogram; ~चेष्टित amorous gesture; wanton sport; ~ज that is born of emotion/passion; intellectual creation; ~ज्ञ knowing the heart, one who knows the emotions (of another); –ताव settling the rate, chaffering, bargaining; ~त्व the state of being; the quality of emotion/sentiment; ~प्रकाश (न) expression of one's sentiment; ~प्रधान primarily emotional, dominated by emotion, emotional; ~प्रवण sentimental, emotional; ~प्रवणता sentimentality, emotional disposition; -बंधन emotional/sentimental fetters or bonds; -बल the force of emotion; -बोध the comprehension of a sentiment; emotive content; ~बोधक expressive; -भीना soaked in emotion; emotion-packed; emotion-filled; ~रूप abstract, intangible, existing only on a mental plane, existent; ~वाचक/वाची abstract; ~वाचक संज्ञा abstract noun; ~वाच्य neutral voice; denoting the abstract notion of verb; ~व्यंजक expressive; ~शबलता mixture or union of various emotions; -शांति the allaying or subdual of any transitory emotion; ~शुद्धि purity of mind, emotional purge; ~शून्य devoid of emotion, unattached insensitive; ~शून्यता absence of attachment; the state of being insensitive or devoid of emotions; -संधि the union or co-existence of two emotions; ~समाहित concentrated in mind; ~स्थ existing on the emotional plane; having existence in the mind; ~हीन cold, devoid of emotion, unemotional, unfeeling; ०चेहरा a dead pan, expressionless face; hence ~हीनता (*nf*); -आसमान को छूना the prices to sore sky high; -उतरना the prices to go down; -का भूखा desirous of just good will from the other; -गिरना the prices to fall; -चढ़ना the prices to go up.

भावक bha:vak (*a*) apprecitative; (*nm*) one who is gifted with the faculty of appreciation; hence ~ता (*nf*)

भावज bha:vaj (*nf*) a sister-in-law; brother's wife.

भावन bha:vān (*nm*) conception; comprehension; thinking.

भावना bha:vnā: (*nf*) sentiment, feeling, emotion; ~मय/युक्त sentimental, emotional; भावनाओं को भड़काना to blow the coals, to fan the flames of passion.

भावनात्मक bha:vnā:tmak (*a*) emotional, emotive; sentimental; hence ~ता (*nf*).

भावात्मक bha:va:tmak (*a*) emotional, having an emotive content; -एकता emotional integrity.

भावानयन bha:va:nayan (*nm*) abstraction; ~वाद abstractionism.

भावानुवाद bha:va:nuva:d (*nm*) free translation.

भावाभास bha:va:bha:s (*nm*) affective fallacy.

भावार्थ bha:va:rth (*nm*) sense; purport, substance.

भावित bha:vit (*a*) conceived, comprehended; thought of.

भावी bha:vi: (*a*) future; coming; (*nm*) destiny; future; -पीढ़ी future generation.

भावुक bha:vuk (*a*) sentimental; emotional; ~ता sentimentality/sentimentalism; emotionalism, emotional disposition; hence ~तापूर्ण (*a*).

भावोत्कर्ष bha:votkarsh (*nm*) emotional excellence/elevation.

भावोत्तेज/क bha:vottejak (*a*) agitating (the emotions), provocative, exciting; hence ~कता (*nf*); ~न provocation, causing excitement.

भावोदय bha:voday (*nm*) the emergence/advent of an emotion.

भावोद्दीपक bha:voddi:pak (*a*) helping to excite the emotions, exciting, provocative; hence ~ता (*nf*).

भावोन्मत्त bha:vonmatt (*a*) overwhelmed by emotion, emotion-crazy; hence ~ता (*nf*).

भावोन्मेष bha:vonmesh (*nm*) advent/emergence of an emotion or sentiment.

भाषण bha:shān (*nm*) speech; address; -कला elocution; ~कार a speaker; -प्रतियोगिता elocution competition/contest; -स्वातंत्र्य freedom of speech.

भाषांतर bha:shā:ntar (*nm*) translation, rendering into another language; interpretation; ~कार a translator; interpreter.

भाषा bha:sha: (*nf*) language, speech; -ज्ञान linguistic knowledge, knowledge of a language; ~बद्ध written; -बोध linguistic comprehension / understanding; ~वार linguistic (ally); language-wise; -विज्ञान/शास्त्र linguistics; philology; ~विद्/वेत्ता a linguist, ~वैज्ञानिक/

शास्त्री linguistician; philologist; linguistic; philological; ~वैज्ञानिक/~शास्त्रीय linguistic; philological.

भाषाई bha:sha:i: (*a*) linguistic.

भाषिक bha:shik (*a*) linguistic;–परिशुद्धता linguistic precision; -संरचना linguistic structure.

भाषित bha:shit (*a*) uttered, said; spoken.

भाषी bha:shi:—an adjectival suffix that imparts the meaning of one who speaks(e.g. हिन्दी-भाषी, बँगला-भाषी, तमिल-भाषी, etc.)

भाष्य bha:shy (*nm*) commentary; annotation; ~कार commentator.

भास bha:s (*nm*) brilliance, brightness; appearance; ~मंत brilliant, bright, flashing; ~मान appearing; apparent; –होना to appear.

भासित bha:sit (*a*) bright, brilliant; shining; appeared.

भासुर bha:sur (*a*) bright, brilliant, shining.

भास्कर bha:skar (*nm*) the sun.

भास्वर bha:svar (*a*) bright, brilliant; shining; hence ~ता (*nf*).

भिंडी bhĩndi: (*nf*) (the vegetable called) lady's finger.

भिक्षा bhiksha: (*nf*) alms, charity; begging; ~चर्या occupation of begging; ~जीवी subsisting on alms/charity; -पात्र one who deserves being granted alms; a begging bowl; -भाजन see -पात्र ; -वृत्ति a beggar's occupation, beggary.

भिक्षाटन bhiksha:ṭān (*nm*) going about begging.

भिक्षार्थी bhiksha:rthi: (*nm*) a beggar.

भिक्षु bhikshu (*nm*) a beggar; Buddhist mendicant; hence ~णी (*nf*).

भिक्षुक bhikshuk (*nm*) a beggar.

भिख bhikh—an allomorph of भीख used as the first member of certain compound words; ~मंगा a beggar; hence ~मंगापन (*nm*).

भिखारिणी bhikha:rinī: (*nf*) a begging woman, a female beggar.

भिखारि/न, ~नी bhikha:rin, ~ni: (*nf*) see भिखारिणी.

भिखारी bhikha:ri: (*nm*) a beggar; pauper.

भिगो/ना bhigonā: (*v*) to wet; to drench; to soak, to moisten; -भिगोकर मारना/लगाना to give it hot/right and left.

भिगौना bhigaunā: (*nm*) a typical round household utensil.

भिड़ंत bhiṛānt (*nf*) a clash, skirmish; encounter, confrontation; fighting hand to hand.

भिड़ bhiṛ (*nf*) a wasp; –का छत्ता a hornet's nest, a cluster of wasps; an irritable lot; –के छत्ते को छेड़ना / में हाथ डालना to invite trouble; to disturb an irritable lot, to poke one's hand into a hornet's nest.

भिड़ना bhiṛnā: (*v*) to collide; to clash, to quarrel; see भेड़ना.

भितल्ला bhitalla: (*nm*) the inner side of clothes, quilt, etc.; the lining.

भित्ति bhitti (*nf* and *a*) a wall; mural, parietal; ~चित्र a fresco, mural painting.

भिदना bhidnā: (*v*) to penetrate; to be pierced/permeated, to absorbed, to be assimilated.

भिनकना bhinaknā: (*v*) to hum/buzz; to swarm; to be extremely shabby/dirty (so as to invite humming bees/flies).

भिन-भिन bhin-bhin (*nf*) buzzing/humming of a fly/flies,

भिनभिनाना bhinbhinā:nā: (*v*) to go on buzzing/humming.

भिनसार bhinsa:r (*nm*) dawn, day-break.

भिन्न bhinn (*a*) separate, different, distinct; diverse, dissimilar; (*nf*) a fraction; -भिन्न different; separate, various.

भिन्नता bhinnāta: (*nf*) difference, distinction, dissimilarity.

भिन्नाना bhinnā:nā: (*v*) to feel indignation (e. g. तबियत–); to feel giddy (e. g. सिर–).

भिन्नार्थ bhinna:rth (*a*) having a different/distinct meaning; hence ~ता (*nf*).

भिश्ती bhishti: (*nm*) a water-carrier.

भींगना bhī:gnā: (*v*) see भीगना.

भींचना bhī:chnā: (*v*) to grasp tightly; to tighten, to hold close together (as ओठ भींचना), to bring heavy weight to bear (on); to squeeze.

भीजना bhī:jnā: (*v*) to get wet; to be soaked; to be drenched, to moisten.

भी bhi: (*ind*) also, too, even.

भीख bhi:kh (*nf*) alms; begging; –माँगना to beg, to go abegging.

भीगना bhi:gnā: (*v*) to get wet, to be soaked; to be drenched, to moisten; to be moved (as भीगा स्वर); भीगी बिल्ली बनना to be very meek and quiet; to behave in too submissive a manner;–, रात the night to turn cooler; to be past midnight.

भीड़ bhi:ṛ (*nf*) a crowd; mob, multitude; crisis (e.g भीड़ पड़ना); -भड़क्का/भाड़ hustle and bustle; a jostling crowd; rush; ~भीति ochiophobia; ~तंत्र mobocracy, mob-rule; -छँटना the crowds to be thinned; -जुड़ना crowds to assemble; –पड़ना to be in trouble/in a crisis, to be afflicted.

भीत bhi:t (*a*) afraid; terrified, horrified, scared, fear-stricken; (*nf*) a wall; ~चित्त terrorized, afraid, frightened, scared.

भीतर bhi:tar (*ind*) in, inside, within; –का internal, interior, inner; -बाहर in and out, real and virtual; o एक सा होना to appear what one is in reality, to be the same within and without; –ही भीतर within oneself; in the heart of hearts; in a clandestine fashion, on the quiet.

भीतरी bhi:tari: (*a*) internal; interior, inner, inward; secret; unexpressed.

भीति bhi:ti (*nf*) fear, fright, scare, terror; awe; phobia; ~कर / कारक fearful, frightening, scaring.

भीनी bhi:nī: (*a*) pleasant, sweet (smell); used as a suffix with nouns to mean impregnated/filled/saturated with etc. (as भावभीनी, रसभीनी).

भीम bhi:m (*a*) terrible, awful; gigantic, tremendous; (*nm*) one of the Pa:ṇḍavas; ~पराक्रम awfully/tremendously valorous; hence भीमा (fem, adjectival form).

भीरु bhi:ru (*a*) timid, coward; fearing; shy; ~ता timidness, cowardice, fearing disposition; shyness; ~हृदय same as भीरु.

भील bhi:l (*nm*) a tribe inhabiting the Indian states of Madhya Pradesh, Rajasthan, etc.

भीषण bhi:shaṇ (*a*) fearful, frightening, scaring; awful; tremendous; hence ~ता (*nf*).

भीषणाकार bhi:shaṇā:ka:r (*a*) awe-inspiring, of awful size or form. horrible, terrible.

भीष्म bhi:shm (*a*) terrible, awful,

horrible; name of a patriarch of the Kauravas and Pa:ṇḍavas who fought in the great war of Maha:-Bha:rat and led the armies of the kaurvas. He was known for his determination, wisdom, bravery; -प्रतिज्ञा a difficult but unshakeable vow/pledge.

भुक्क(क्ख)ड़ bhukk(kkh)aṛ (*a*) starving/starved, hungry; voracious, gluttonous; (*nm*) a horse-leech.

भुक्त bhukt (*a*) enjoyed; used; consumed; ~काम (whose wishes are) fulfilled/gratified; ~पूर्व second-hand, enjoyed/used earlier; ~भोगी experienced; one who has enjoyed or suffered (certain experiences).

भुक्ति bhukti (*nf*) enjoyment; use, possession.

भुख bhukh–an allomorph of भूख used as the first member in certain compound words; ~मरा starving/starved, hungry; voracious, gluttonous; ~मरी starvation; famine; hunger.

भुगतना bhugatnā: (*v*) to suffer, to bear; to undergo; to be accomplished/concluded; भुगत लेना to settle score with, to have it out with.

भुगतान bhugtā:n (*nm*) payment; delivery; settlement.

भुगताना bhugta:nā: (*v*) to pay; to deliver; to settle; to conclude, to accomplish.

भुच्चड़ bhuchchaṛ (*a*) stupid, foolish, idiotic.

भुजंग bhujāṅg (*nm*) a snake, serpent; hence भुजंगी (*nf*).

भुजंगम bhujaṅgam (*nm*) see भुजंग.

भुज bhuj (*nm*) an arm; side of a triangle; ~दंड strong arm, a staff-like arm; ~पाश arm-embrace; ~बंद armlet; -बंधन arm-embrace; ~बल strength of the arms, physical strength; ~मूल root / upper extremity of the arms; ~लता tender creeper-like arms.

भुजा bhuja: (*nf*) an arm; side of a triangle; –उठाकर कहना, –उठाना to take a solemn vow, to swear (to do a thing); ~एँ फड़कना one's arms to be restless to fight; ~ओं में बाँध/भर लेना to throw the arms around in embrace.

भुजाली bhuja:li: (*nf*) a small dagger.

भुजिया bhujiya: (*nf*) a cooked green vegetable; a typical dish of snacks.

भुजौना bhujaunā: (*nm*) parched grain.

भुट्टा bhuṭṭa: (*nm*) maize-corn.

भुतहा bhutaha: (*a*) haunted by ghost(s)/evil spirit(s).

भुतनी bhutnī: (*nf*) a female ghost; a woman having utterly dishevelled looks.

भुनगा bhunga: (*nm*) an insect; a maggot; an inconsequential creature; –समझना to treat (a person) with contempt, to regard as of no consequence/as nothing of a match.

भुनभुनाना bhunbhunā:nā: (*v*) gabbeling; inarticulate non-stop expression of indignation/petulance/rage/resentment/protest.

भुनाई bhuna:i: (*nf*) the act of or charges paid for parching.

भुनाना bhuna:nā: (*v*) to get parched; to encash, to cash; to change (into smaller denominational currency).

भुरकुस bhurkus (*nm*) powder; –करना/निकालना to beat black and blue; to beat to a frazzle, to pulverise.

भुरभुरा bhurbhura: (*a*) crisp, friable; dry and powdery; ~पन crispness; friability; ~हट see ~पन.

भुलक्कड़ bhulakkaṛ (*a*) forgetful, temperamentally prone to forget: ~पन/~पना forgetfulness.

भुलावा bhula:va: (*nm*) faint, dodge; an illusion.

भुवन bhuvan (*nm*) the world; earth; -त्रय the three worlds; viz. —this world, the world above and the nether world; ~पति Master, Creator of the world; ~विदित known the world over; भुवनेश/भुवनेश्वर see ~पति.

भुस bhus (*nm*) straw, chaff; ~सौरा/सहुल straw-store; ~स भरना lit. to stuff with straw – to beat to a frazzle; ~स में आग लगाकर तमाशा देखना lit. to join the spectators after causing a fire-break —to be casual after causing a crisis.

भूँकना bhū:knā: (*v*) to bark; to gabble (said indignantly in respect of a human being).

भूँजना bhū:jnā: (*v*) to parch; to blast.

भूँजा bhū:ja: (*nm*) parched grain.

भूँसना bhū:snā: (*v*) to bark, to gabble (said indignantly in respect of a human being).

भू bhu: (*nf*) the earth; the world; ground; soil; land; a suffix denoting born, born of (as स्वयंभू, मनोभू); ~खंड a territory, tract of land, plot; ~गर्भ under-ground, sub-terrain; sub-terranean; ०शास्त्र geology; ~गर्भशास्त्री a geologist; ~गर्भशास्त्रीय geological; ~चित्र a ground plan; ~धर see भूधर; -परिदृश्य a landscape; ~प्रदेश a terrain; territory; ~भाग tract of land; ~मंडल the earth; the globe; -योजना a ground plan; -राजस्व land revenue; ~विज्ञान geology; ~विद् a geologist; ~विद्या geology; ~वैज्ञानिक geological; a geologist; ०काल geological age; ~शायी one who sleeps on the ground; lying on the ground; -सम्पत्ति landed property; ~सुत the Mars; ~सुर a Bra:hmān; ~स्वामी a land-owner; land-holder, master of land.

भूकंप bhu:kāmp (*nm*) an earthquake; seism; -तरंगें seismic waves; ~दर्शी seismoscope; ~नीयता seismicity; -पूर्वेक्षणा seismic prospecting; ~मापी seismometer; -लेख seismogram; -लेखन seismography; ~लेखी a seismograph; ~विज्ञान/शास्त्र seismology; -संबंधी seismic; -सूचक यंत्र seismic detector.

भूख bhu:kh (*nf*) hunger, appetite; desire; -हड़ताल hunger strike; -प्यास न लगना/मर जाना to have neither thirst nor hunger, to be too perturbed to think of food or drink; -मिटाना to satisfy one's hunger/desire; -भली कि पतोहू की जूठ/-में गूलर भी पकवान/-में चने भी मखाने hungry dogs will eat dirty pudding; hunger is the best sauce; भूखों मरना to starve, to famish.

भूखा bhu:kha: (*a*) hungry; esurient; craving; -नंगा poor, pauper, indigent, in a miserable plight; -क्यों रूखा a hungry man is an angry man.

भूगर्भ bhu:garbh (*nm*) underground, the interior of the earth; ~विज्ञान/विद्या/शास्त्र geology; ~वैज्ञानिक/शास्त्री a geologist; ~वैज्ञानिक/शास्त्रीय geological; -सर्वेक्षण geological survey.

भूगोल bhu:gol (*nm*) geography; also ~विज्ञान; ~वेत्ता a geographer.

भूचाल bhu:cha:l (*nm*) see भूकंप.

भूटानी bhu:ṭa:nī: (*a*) pertaining or belonging to Bhu:ṭa:n, situated in the north of असम; (*nf*) Bhu:ṭa:nī: language; (*nm*) a native of Bhu:ṭa:n

भूडोल bhu:ḍol (*nm*) see भूकंप.

भूत bhu:t (*a*) past; bygone; (*nm*) a ghost; an evil spirit; matter; one of the five elements (पृथ्वी–the earth, जल–the water; वायु–the air, पावक–the fire, and आकाश –the ether); any animate or inanimate object of creation; the past tense (also ~काल); a suffix which means 'become' 'turned' or 'rendered' (as घनीभूत, पुंजीभूत); ~काल the past tense; ~कालिक pertaining to the past or past tense; o कृदंत past participle; ~नाथ an epithet of Lord Shiv; -पूजा demonolatry; ~पूर्व ex, former; past; previous; -प्रेत evil spirits, ghosts; ~बाड़ी a haunted house; -बाधा obsession of evil spirits, (under) ghostly influence; ~योनि demonic existence, existence as an evil spirit; ~विद्या ghostology; demonology; –उतारना to exorcise; to drive off an evil spirit; –का डेरा an abode of ghost, a haunted place; –की तरह जुट जाना to work like a demon; –चढ़ना, –सवार होना, –लगना to be possessed by an evil spirit, to be obsessed; –बनकर लगना to obsess; to haunt like a ghost; –सवार होना, किसी बात का to be crazy after; to be thoroughly obsessed by; –सवार होना, सिर पर to be under an obsession, to be possessed by; to be under a terrible emotional pressure.

भूतत्त्व/विज्ञान, ~विद्या bhu:tattvviggya:n (*nm*), ~viddya: (*nf*) geology; ~विज्ञ/विद् a geologist; ~वैज्ञानिक a geologist; geological.

भूतल bhu:tal (*nm*) the surface of earth; the world.

भूताविष्ट bhu:ta:visht (*a*) possessed of an evil spirit, haunted.

भूतिनी bhu:tinī: (*nf*) a female ghost/evil spirit.

भूते/श, ~श्वर bhu:tesh, ~shwar (*nm*) an epithet of Lord Shiv.

भूदान bhu:da:n (*nm*) gift of land; a movement launched by Acharya Vinoba Bhave (in India) for the gifting away of land by big landowners for the betterment of the landless; –आंदोलन Bhu:da:n-movement.

भूदेव bhu:dev (*nm*) a Bra:hmān.

भूधर bhu:dhar (*nm*) a mountain, hill.

भूनना bhu:nnā: (*v*) to parch; to fry; to broil; to roast; to blast; to smash; to reduce to ashes.

भूप, ~ति bhu:p, ~ati (*nm*) a king, an emperor.

भूपाल, भूपेन्द्र bhu:pa:l, bhu:pēndr (*nm*) a king, an emperor.

भू/भल, ~भुर bhu:bhal, ~bhur (*nm*) hot sand/ash.

भूमध्य bhu:maddhy (*nm*) the middle of the earth; ~रेखा the equator; –सागर the mediterranean sea; ~सागरीय mediterranean.

भूमा bhu:mā: (*nm*) God; being; the aggregate of all existing things.

भूमि bhu:mī (*nf*) the earth; land, soil; zone; -उद्धार reclamation; -खंड a territory, tract (of land), plot; ~गत underground; subterranean; ~जीवी a farmer, peasant; ~तत्त्व pedology; ~तल the surface of earth; ~धर a landowner; a mountain; ~धारी a landholder or owner; -भाग a territory, tract of land; region; ~लोक the earth; ~विज्ञान pedology; ~वैज्ञानिक a pedologist; pedological; -शयन sleeping on the ground, the act or practice of sleeping over bare ground; ~शायी one who sleeps over bare ground; ~ष्ठ fallen on the ground; ~सम्भव the planet Mars; ~सुत the planet Mars; ~सुर a Bra:hmāṇ.

भूमिका bhu:mīka: (*nf*) introduction; ground-work; background; role; -बाँधना to prepare the background.

भूय/स् bhu:yas (*a*) abundant, plenty, very much; ~श: abundantly, in plenty.

भूरा bhu:ra: (*a*) brown, grey.

भूरि bhu:ri (*a*) much, very much; -भूरि very much.

भूर्ज bhu:rj (*nm*) the birch, the Bhoj tree, *Betula bhojpatra*; -पत्र the bark of भूर्ज (which was used for writing on).

भूर्लोक bhu:rlok (*nm*) the earth; the present world.

भूल bhu:l (*nf*) a slip, error; mistake; lapse, omission; fault; oversight; -चूक a lapse, error; o लेनी-देनी an accounting slip will be rectified; errors and omissions excepted; -भुलैयाँ a labyrinth, maze; oमें पड़ना to be caught in a labyrinth; -सुधार correction; rectification; errata; -सुधारना to make amends, to rectify; -से by mistake, on account of a slip;

भूलना bhu:lnā: (*v*) to forget; भूलकर by mistake; o नाम न लेना in no case to remember or recall; never to utter the name of; भूलकर भी नहीं in no case, under no circumstances; भूल पड़ना, किधर से/कैसे to make an unexpected appearance (after a long time); भूला-भटका strayed, one who has lost his way; भूला-बिसरा forgotten, faded out of memory: भूले-भटके once in a blue moon, rarely.

भूलोक bhu:lok (*nm*) the earth; the present world.

भूषण bhu:shāṇ (*nm*) an ornament; decoration, anything decorative, embellishment.

भूषा bhu:sha: (*nf*) embellishment, decoration; used as the second member in the compound वेश-भूषा meaning–exterior appearance, get-up.

भूषित bhu:shit (*a*) decorated, adorned, embellished.

भूसा bhu:sa: (*nm*) cut-straw; chaff; –भरना lit. to beat hollow and stuff with straw —to beat blue and black; to thoroughly belabour.

भूसी bhu:si: (*nf*) husk; bran.

भृंग bhrīṅg (*nm*) a kind of large black-bee.

भृंगराज bhriṅgra:j (*nm*) the medicinal shrub *Eclipta prostrata*.

भृंगी bhringi: (*nf*) a female black-bee.

भृकुटि bhrikuṭi (*nf*) eyebrow; frown; ~विलास (playful) movement of the eyebrows; –चढ़ाना/तानना to frown, to scowl, to get into a temper; –टेढ़ी होना/में बल पड़ना to get enraged, to frown, to scowl.

भृत्य bhritty (*nm*) a servant, an attendant.

भेंट bhēṭ (*nf*) present, gift, offering; meeting, interview; –अँकवार embrace; –करने वाला an interviewer; -वार्ता an interview; ~ वार्ताकार

an interviewer.

भेंटना bhēṭnā: (*v*) to embrace; to meet.

भेजना bhejnā: (*v*) to send (forth), to cause to go; to transmit; to remit; to consign.

भेजा bheja: (*nm*) the brain; (*a*) sent; –खाना/चाटना to pester (with persistent queries, doubts, clarifications, etc.);–ख़ाली होना one's brain to be picked/sucked.

भेड़ bheṛ (*nf*) a sheep; timid person; -चाल the tendency of following blindly in others' footsteps; mob-mentality.

भेड़ना bheṛnā: (*v*) to close, to shut (as दरवाजा–); to sell a lame horse to, to hoodwink somebody in to a losing bargain.

भेड़ा bheṛa: (*nm*) a ram.

भेड़िया bheṛiya: (*nm*) a wolf.

भेड़ियाधसान bheṛiya:dhasā:n (*nm*) see भेड़चाल (under भेड़).

भेड़ी bheṛi: (*nf*) a sheep, ewe.

भेद bhed (*nm*) a secret; difference, distinction; discrimination; divergence; division, schism, split; variety, kind, type; ~क/कारक differentiating, distinguishing; one who or that which differentiates/discriminates/distinguishes; -नीति policy of discrimination/differentiation; policy of winning over to one's side by causing dissension; -बुद्धि schism; discrimination, differentiation; perception of a difference or distinction; -भाव discrimination; differentiation; –करना to make a difference; –की बात a secret; –खोलना to let the cat out of the bag; -देना to leak-out a secret; –पाना to know the secret of; –लेना to sound, to try to know the reality the secret.

भेद/न bhedān (*nm*) the act of piercing/boring/disuniting; cleavage; ~नीय fit to be pierced, vulnerable; o ता vulnerability.

भेदिया bhediya: (*nm*) a spy, intelligence agent.

भेदित bhedit (*a*) pierced; disunited; distinguished.

भेदी bhedi: (*nm*) a secret sharer; a confidant; see भेदिया; –लंका ढाए, घर का your conscience-keeper is your worst enemy.

भेद्य bheddy (*a*) vulnerable; pierceable; distinguishable; fit to be divided.

भेरी bheri: (*nf*) a kind of drum, kettledrum; siren;–बजाना battle-drums to be beaten.

भेली bheli: (*nm*) a lump of गुड़–esp. of specified weight (as two and a half seers. five seers, etc).

भेष bhesh (*nm*) appearance, exterior appearance; guise; get-up; —धरना/बनाना to assume the guise of, to look like. —बदलना to (be) disguise(d), to be in a disguise.

भेष/ज bheshaj (*nf*) a drug, medicine; remedy;~जीय medicinal.

भेषजागार bheshaja:ga:r (*nm*) a medico-store.

भेस bhes (*um*) appearance; dress, garb; get-up; guise; –धरना /बनाना to assume the guise (of); to be peculiarly dressed up;-बदलना to(be) disguise (d), to be in a disguise.

भैंगा bhãiga: (*a*) squint-eyed, cross-eyed (person).

भैंस bhãis (*nf*) a she-buffalo; an extra-fat woman; –के आगे बीन बजाना to throw pearls to swines.

भैंसा bhaїsa: (*nm*) a he-buffalo; stout and sturdy man; –दुहना to crush oil out of pebbles, to make a niggard part with some of his money.

भैया bhaiya: (*nm*) a brother, a vocative word for an elder brother as also for youngers or those of equal age; ~दूज a Hindu festival falling on the second day of the bright fortnight of कार्तिक when a sister ties राखी on the wrist of her brother and the brother takes a vow to protect her honour in all circumstances; –बंद see भाई-बंद.

भैरव bhairav (*a*) terrible, awful; (*nm*) Lord Shiv; a typical violent musical mode (राग); hence~ ता (*nf*).

भैरवी bhairvi: (*nf*) a kind of song sung in the small hours of the morning.

भैषजि/क bhaishajik (*nm*) a pharmacist; ~ की pharmacy.

भोंकना bhōknā: (*v*) to poke, to thrust into, to pierce through; to stab (as चाकू–); see भूँकना, भौंकना.

भों/डा, ~ड़ा bhōḍa:, ~ṛa: (*a*) ill-shaped; unsymmetrical; ugly; grotesque, coarse-grained, uncouth; indecent; crude; ~पन grotesqueness; ugliness; indecency; crudity, crudeness.

भोंदू bhodu: (*a*) dullard, booby, simpleton stupid, silly;~ पन/पना dullardness, foolishness, stupidity, silliness.

भोंपा, भोंपू bhōpa:, bhōpu: (*nm*) a siren; horn.

भोक्तव्य bhoktavvy (*a*) enjoyable/to be enjoyed; eatable; to be used/experienced.

भोक्ता bhokta: (*nm* and *a*) (one) who enjoys/eats/uses/experiences.

भोग bhog (*nm*) enjoyment; suffering; sexual pleasure; result of good or evil deeds; experience of pleasure or pain; (residual of the) food offered to a deity; usufruct; -लिप्सा voluptuousness, lewdness; sex-indulgence; hence ~लिप्सु (*a*); ~लोलुप sex-indulgent; lewd; voluptuous; -लोलुपता lewdness; voluptuousness; sex-indulgence; ~वादिता/वाद epicureanism; hedonism; ~ वादी hedonistic, epicurean; an epicureanist; hedonist; –विलास sexual pleasure; enjoyment; luxury; debauchery; –करना to enjoy; to derive sexual pleasure;–लगाना to offer food etc. to the deity.

भोगना bhognā: (*v*) to enjoy; to suffer, to undergo; to derive sexual pleasure; to experience (pleasure or pain).

भोगी bhogi: (*a*) sex-indulgent; sensuous, voluptuous, pleasure-seeking; who enjoys; (*nm*) a snake.

भोग्य bhoggy (*a*) enjoyable, sexually enjoyable; to be used/consumed/enjoyed; hence भोग्या (fem. form).

भोज bhoj (*nm*) a banquet; feast.

भोजन bhojan (*nm*) food, meals; diet; victuals; -काल time for meals; ~गृह/शाला dining room; -नली the food pipe; –भट्ट a glutton; -योग्य eatable/edible, esculent; -व्यवस्था boarding; messing arrangements; -सामग्री eatables, victuals; —पाना (said out of deference) to have food at.

भोजनालय bhojanā:lay (*nm*) a mess; restaurant, eating-house.

भोजनीय bhojnī:y (*a*) eatable, fit to be eaten.

भोज/पत्र bhojpattr (*nm*) the bark of the birch tree (which was used to write on in olden times); ~**वृक्ष** the birch tree.

भोजपुरी bhojpuri: (*nf*) a dialect of Hindi spoken in eastern parts of Uttar Pradesh and western parts of Biha:r; (*a*) pertaining to **भोजपुरी** dialect or its speakers; also **भोजपुरिया** (*a*).

भोजी bhoji: (*a*) an eater (generally used as the second member in compound words — as **शवभोजी, बहुभोजी**.

भोज्य bhojjy (*a*) eatable, fit to be eaten; (*nm*) food; **–पदार्थ** eatable; food.

भोटिया bhoṭia: (*nm*) a Bhutanese; (*nf*) Bhutanese language; (*a*) pertaining to Bhu:ṭa:n (region).

भोथ/र, ~रा bhothar, ~ra: (*a*) blunt, blunt edged.

भोर bhor (*nm*) dawn, day-break; **–का तारा** transient, something that has momentary existence.

भोला bhola: (*a*) innocent, unsophisticated; simple-hearted; ~**नाथ** Lord Shiv; ~**पन** simpleness, simple-heartedness, innocence; **-भाला** innocent, ingenuous, honest and simple.

भौं bhau̅ (*nf*) an eyebrow; **–चढ़ाना/टेढ़ी करना/तानना/सिकोड़ना** lit. to twist the eye-brows—to frown, to scowl; **–में बल/शिकन पड़ना** to frown, to scowl, to be enraged.

भौंकना bhau̅knā: (*v*) to bark; to jabber (said indignantly while referring to a man); to penetrate, to thrust into (as a sword, etc.).

भौंर bhau̅r (*nm*) a whirpool; see **भौंरा**.

भौंरा bhau̅ra: (*nm*) a black-bee, beetle; a top (kind of toy).

भौंरी bhau̅ri: (*nf*) a female black-bee; a whirlpool; circumambulation by the bride and bride-groom round sacred fire in a marriage ceremony (see **भाँवर**).

भौंह bhau̅h (*nf*) see **भौं**.

भौगोलिक bhaugolik (*a*) geographical; ~**ता** geographicality; **–सीमाएँ** geographical boundaries.

भौच/क, ~क्का bhauchak, ~kka: (*a*) aghast; non-plussed, dumb-founded, flabbergasted; ~**क्का रह जाना** to be taken aback, to be flabbergasted, one's breath to be taken away.

भौ/जाई, ~जी bhauja:i:; ~ji: (*nf*) elder brother's wife.

भौतिक bhautik (*a*) material, physical, mundane; corporeal; elemental; **–चिकित्सा** physiotherapy; ~**ता** materialism; materialistic outlook; **–भूगोल** physical geography; ~**वाद** / ~**वादिता** materialism; ~**वादी** a materialist; materialistic; ~**विज्ञान** physics; ~**विद्** a physicist; **–साधन** material resources; **–सुख** physical/material happiness; **–सुख-सुविधाएँ** material amenities.

भौतिकी bhautiki: (*nf*) physics; ~**य** physical; o **विज्ञान** physical science.

भौम bhaum (*a*) pertaining to, born of or concerning the earth; (*nm*) the Mars; ~**वार/वासर** Tuesday.

भौमिक bhaumīk (*a*) pertaining to, born of or concerning the earth; terrestrial, earthly.

भौरी bhauri: (*nf*) a kind of heavy ball-like cake baked on cowdung cakes.

भ्रंश bhrānsh (*nm*) breach, break-down; fall(ing); ruin, destruction,

भ्रंशन bhrānshan (*nm*) breach, break-down; falling; ruination; destruction.

भ्रम bhram (*nm*) misunderstanding, illusion, misconception; confusion; ~जनक illusory, fallacious; ~जन्य resulting from misunderstanding/confusion; -जाल illusion; ~मूलक illusory; caused by misunderstanding/misconception; -टूटना to be disillusioned; -में होना to be under an illusion.

भ्रमण bhramaṇ (*nm*) walk; going round; excursion; travel, roaming; -वृत्तांत a travelogue; ~शील wandering / roaming / rambling/ roving.

भ्रम/र bhramar (*nm*) a large blackbee; beetle; ~रावली a row of blackbees; ~री a female blackbee.

भ्रमात्मक bhramā:tmak (*a*) illusive, illusory.

भ्रमित bhramīt (*a*) under an illusion; confused; strayed; misled.

भ्रमोत्पादक bhramotpa:dak (*a*) illusory, that which misleads/confuses/causes illusion; hence ~ता (*nf*).

भ्रष्ट bhrashṭ (*a*) corrupt(ed); spoilt; fallen; depraved; ruined; wanton; hence भ्रष्टा feminine form; ~ता corruption, depravity, state of being spoilt/fallen/ ruined; wantonness.

भ्रष्टाचार bhrashṭa:cha:r (*nm*) corruption; depravity; wantonness; -उन्मूलन abolition of corruption; ~ग्रस्त corrupt; deprave, wanton.

भ्रष्टाचा/री bhrashṭa:cha:ri: (*a* and *nm*) (one who is) corrupt/depraved/wanton; hence ~रिता (*nf*).

भ्रांत bhrā:nt (*a*) misled, mistaken; aberrated, strayed (as -व्यक्ति); wrong, incorrect (as -धारणा).

भ्रांति bhrā:nti (*nf*) error, mistake; illusion: ~जनक causing illusion, confusing; ~जन्य resulting from an illusion / confusion/misunderstanding; ~मूलक illusory; caused by an illusion, misconceived.

भ्राता bhra:ta: (*nm*) a brother.

भ्रातृ bhra:ttri (*nm*) a brother; ~त्व brotherhood; fraternity; -भाव brotherly feeling/affection, brotherhood; ~हत्या fratricide; ~हत्यारा a fratricide; ~स्नेह brotherly affection, fraternal love.

भ्रामक bhra:māk (*a*) illusory, confusing; hence ~ता (*nf*).

भ्रू bhru: (*nm*) an eyebrow; ~भंग/ भंगिमा attractive movement or contraction of eyebrows, a twist of the eyebrows; frown; ~मध्य middle of the eyebrows; -विक्षेप frowning; scowling; -विलास amorous movement of the eyebrows; frowning, scowling.

भ्रूण bhrū:ṇ (*um*) foetus, embryo; ~विज्ञान embryology; ~हत्या foeticide.

भ्रूणीय bhru:ṇī:y (*a*) embryological.

भ्रौणिकी bhrāuṇīki: (*nf*) embryology; ~य embryological.

म

म mā –the fifth and final letter of the fifth pentad (i.e. पवर्ग) of the Devna:gri: alphabet.

मँगता māgta: (*nm*) a beggar; ~पन beggary.

ंगनी māgnī: (*nf*) betrothal, engagement; loan, a borrowed thing; –की चीज a borrowed thing; –देना to lend; –लेना to borrow; –होना to be engaged/betrothed.

गल māṅgal (*nm*) (the planet) Mars; Tuesday; auspiciousness; well-being, welfare; (*a*) auspicious; –कलश see –घट; –कामना good wishes, benediction; ~कारक/कारी good, auspicious; benedictory; -कार्य a festive occasion, an auspicious ceremony/function; -गान/गीत auspicious song/singing; –ग्रह the Mars; lucky star; -घट the water-filled itcher placed in front of the deity n auspicious occasions; -देवता tutelary deity; -ध्वनि the tumulous sound of auspicious songs tc.; marriage-music or singing; ~प्रद good, bestowing welfare, uspicious; benedictory; ~मय ood, happy, auspicious; ~वार/सर Tuesday; -शब्द auspicious/enedictory utterance or word; समाचार good news, happy news; ~सूचक auguring good luck, uspicious; ~सूत्र lit. the lucky read—the sacred marriage thread orn by a woman as long as her usband lives; the thread wrapped round the wrist on auspicious occasions; –गाना to sing auspicious songs on festive occasions.

मंगलाचरण māṅgala:charāṇ (*nm*) benediction, benedictory verse(s) recited on auspicious occasions; pronouncing a blessing; the initial verse in a book meant to invoke divine blessing.

मंगलाचार māṅgala:cha:r (*nm*) initial benedictory recitations or songs etc. marking the commencement of a ceremony/festive occasion.

मंगलामुखी māṅgala:mukhi: (*nf*) a prostitute.

मंगली maṅgali: (*a*) a boy or girl whose horoscope has Mars in the fourth, eighth or the twelfth place.

मंगलेच्छु māṅgalechchhu (*a*) wishing well/prosperity, desirous of (somebody's) well-being.

मंगलोत्सव māṅgalotsav (*nm*) celebration, festivity; benedictory function.

मँगाना māga:nā: (*v*) to cause to bring; to order.

मँगेतर māgetar (*nm* and *nf*) fiance or fiancee; (*a*) betrothed.

मंगो/ल māṅgol (*nm*) a central Asian tribe; ~ ली Mangolian.

मंच māṇch (*nm*) a dais, stage; platform; forum; -उपस्थापन presentation on the stage; ~न staging; presentation on the stage; -प्रस्तुति stage presentation; -भीति

stage consciouness/nervousness.

मंचीय mānchi:y (*a*) pertaining to or concerned with the stage, theatrical; **–रूप** theatrical/stage representation.

मंजन mānjān (*nm*) tooth powder, dentifrice.

मँजना mājnā: (*v*) see **माँजना**; **मँजा हुआ** seasoned, skilled; refined.

मंज़र mānzar (*nm*) a scene, spectacle.

मंजरित mānjarit (*a*) having clusters of flowers, blossomed, flowered.

मंजरी mānjari: (*nf*) a sprout, new shoot/cluster of flowers; an ear of corn.

मँजाई māja:i: (*nf*) (process or act of) cleansing/polishing or the remuneration paid therefor; refinement, polishing.

मंज़िल mānzil (*nf*) destination, stage; storey; **–ए-मकसूद** the appointed destination; **-दर-मंज़िल चलते जाना** to go on crossing one destination after another; to go on marching non-stop; **–भारी होना** a journey to be very assiduous/hard; **–मारना** to cut a gordian knot; to complete a journey, to reach one's destination.

मंजिष्ठ mānjishṭh (*nm*) madder.

मंजीर mānji:r (*nm*) cymbal(s).

मँजीरा māji:ra: (*nm*) cymbal(s)

मंजु mānju (*a*) beautiful, pretty, comely, lovely; **~केशी** having beautiful/lovely hair; hence **~ता** (*nf*).

मंजुल mānjul (*a*) see **मंजु**; hence **~ता** (*nf*).

मंज़ूर mānzu:r (*a*) approved; sanctioned; granted; accepted; **~शुदा** approved, sanctioned; okayed.

मंज़ूरी mānzu:ri: (*nf*) approval; sanction; acceptance; **–देना** to approve, to sanction, to okay; **–मिलना** to get approval/sanction, to be okayed; **–लेना** to obtain the approval of.

मंजा mānja: (*nm*) see **मंझा**.

मंजूषा mānju:sha: ((*nf*) a casket, box, chest.

मँझधार mājhdha:r (*nf*) see **मझधार**.

मँझला mājhla: (*a*) see **मझला**.

मंझा mānjha: (*nm*) the kite-flying thread made sharper and stiffer by being treated with powdered glass; a cot; see **माँझा**.

मँझोला mājhola: (*a*) see **मझोला**.

मंड mānḍ (*nm*) starch.

मंडन mānḍān (*nm*) corroboration support through argumentation decoration, ornamentation, embellishment; **~कर्त्ता** one who corroborates/supports.

मंडप mānḍap (*nm*) a pavilion.

मँडराना māḍra:nā: (*v*) to hover, to hang around; to gather thick.

मंडल mānḍal (*nm*) a circle; ring; zone, territory; board; orbit; the path or orbit of a heavenly body; halo; multitude, collection; each of the ten divisions of the Rigved.

मंडलाकार mānḍala:ka:r (*a*) circular, round (ed).

मंडली mānḍali: (*nf*) a party; team; ring, gang, band; circle.

मंडलीय mānḍali:y (*a*) zonal, pertaining to a district or territory.

मँड़वा māṛwa: (*nf*) a pavilion, canopy.

मंडित mānḍit (*a*) corroborated, supported; decorated, adorned, embellished, ornamented.

मंडी mānḍi: (*nf*) a wholesale m

ket, market; market place.

मंड़ुआ māṛua: (*nm*) a kind of coarse grain.

मंडूक mānḍu:k (*nm*) a frog; –गति hopping like a frog.

मंडूर mānḍu:r (*nm*) red incrustation on iron (used as medicine).

मंतर māntar (*nm*) spell; incantation; –मारना to cast a spell/charm on.

मंतव्य māntavvy (*nm*) intention; design; opinion, view.

मंत्र māntr (*nm*) an incantation, charm, spell; a vedic hymn; sacred formula; mystical verse or magical formula; ~कार one who composes *mantras*; -तंत्र hoccus-poccus, voodooism, spell and incantation; ~दाता a preceptor; adviser; ~द्रष्टा the *rishis* who were composers of vedic hymns, a seer; ~पाठ recitation of a मंत्र in the traditional way; -बल the amazing power of मंत्र: o से through the power of मंत्र; ~बीज the initial portion/line/morph of a मंत्र; ~भेद revelation of a secret; ~मुग्ध spellbound, charmed; hence ~मुग्धता (*nf*); ~विद् well-versed in *mantras*; ~विद्या the science of spell or *mantras*; -शक्ति the power of मंत्र; ~सिद्धि successful culmination of the endeavour to wield a मंत्र effectively; –चलाना to cast a spell/charm on; –देना to initiate (into a sect etc.); to give secret advice; –पढ़ाना to tutor, to misguide; –लगना a spell to become effective, a charm to show results.

मंत्रणा māntraṇā: (*nf*) advice, counsel; ~कार/दाता an adviser, a counsel.

मंत्रालय māntra:lay (*nm*) ministry, the offices headed by a minister.

मंत्रित māntrit (*a*) consecrated by a मंत्र or spell.

मंत्रित्व māntrittv (*nm*) ministership; the office or work of a minister.

मंत्रिमंड/ल māntrimānḍal (*nm*) cabinet, ministry; ~लीय ministerial, cabinet.

मंत्री māntri: (*nm*) a minister; secretary (of an organisation etc.); ~,उप Deputy Minister; –,प्रधान Prime Minister; –,मुख्य Chief Minister; -,राज्य Minister of state.

मंत्रोदक māntrodak (*nm*) water consecrated by a मंत्र.

मंथन mānthān (*nm*) churning; stirring, agitating; deep pondering over something (for acquisition of knowledge etc.).

मँथनी māthnī: (*nf*) a churning pot; churning stick.

मंथर mānthar (*a*) slow, slow-moving; sluggish, tardy; –गति slow speed.

मंद mānd (*a*) slow, tardy; mild; dull (as बुद्धि); inert; low (as स्वर); faint, weak, feeble; a Persian suffix meaning having or possessing (as ज़रूरतमंद, ग़ैरतमंद); ~क a moderator; ~गति slow, tardy, slow-moving; ~चारी slow, sluggish, tardy; ~चेता/धी/बुद्धि/मति blockheaded, dull, blunt; a dunce; ~ता slowness, tardiness; dullardness; ~बुद्धिता feeble mindedness, dullardness; ~भाग/भागी unlucky, ill-fated, unfortunate; ~वीर्य feeble, weak.

मंदड़िया māndaṛiya: (*nm*) a bear, speculator for a fall.

मंदन māndan (*nm*) retardation, diminishing of speed; fading.

मंदा mānda: (*a*) slow; tardy, slack; cheap; (*nm*) depression.

मंदाकिनी mānda:kinī: (*nf*) the Ganges; celestial Ganges.

मंदाग्नि mānda:gnī (*nf*) indigestion, dyspepsia.

मंदार mānda:r (*nm*) a celestial tree; coral tree.

मंदिर māndir (*nm*) a temple.

मंदी māndi: (*nf*) depression in price; slump (in the market); (*a*) feminine form of **मंदा**; a compound persian suffix composed of **मंद** meaning having, possessing and **ई** used for formation of an abstract noun – e.g. **अक्लमंदी** (wisdom).

मंद्र māndr (*nm*) a deep note; the first note in the diatonic scale; (*a*) deep; delightful; hence **~ता** (*nf*).

मंशा mānsha: (*nm, nf*) intention, purpose, motive.

मंसब mansab (*nm*) see **मनसब**; **~दार** see **मनसबदार**; **~दारी** see **मनसबदारी**.

मंसू/ख़ mansu:ḳḥ (*a*) cancelled, rescinded; **~ख़ करना** to cancel to rescind; **~ख़ी** cancellation; rescission.

मंसूबा mansu:ba: (*nm*) see **मनसूबा**.

मँहगा mẽhga: (*a*) see **मँहगा**; **~ई** see **मंहगाई**.

मई mai: (*nf*) the month of May; **–दिवस** May Day.

मकई makai: (*nf*) maize.

मकड़ा makṛa: (*nm*) a large spider.

मकड़ी makṛi: (*nf*) a spider; **–का जाला** spider's web.

मकतब maktab (*nm*) a (primary) school (esp. where Arabic and Persian are taught).

मकतबा maktaba: (*nm*) a book-shop; library.

मक़ता maqta: (*nm*) the colophon, the last couplet of a **ग़ज़ल** which bears the poet's name, identity, etc.

मक़बरा maqbara: (*nm*) a tomb, mausoleum.

मक़बू/ल maqbu:l (*a*) accepted, approved; favourite; **~लियत** popularity, state of being a favourite.

मकरंद makrānd (*nm*) the juice of a flower.

मकर makar (*nm*) the Capricornus–tenth sign of the zodiac; a crocodile; one of the nine *nidhis* of Kuber–the god of wealth; hence **मकरी** (*nf*); **~केतन/केतु/ध्वज** Cupid–the god of love; **~रेखा** tropic of the Capricorn; **–संक्रांति** the day of transition in the month of **माघ** when the sun enters the mansion Capricornus.

मक़सद maqsad (*nm*) aim, object motive, intention.

मक़सूद maqsu:d (*a*) desired, aimed at, intended.

मकान maka:n (*nm*) a house, residence, abode; **~दार** a house owner, landlord; **मकानात** plural form of **मकान**; **-मालिक** house owner, landlord.

मक़ा/म maqā:m (*nm*) see **मुक़ाम** **~मी** see **मुक़ामी**.

मकुना makunā: (*nm*) a male elephant with small tusks or with no tusks at all; a clean-shaven man.

मकुनी makunī: (*nf*) a kind of stuffed bread.

मकोड़ा makoṛa: (*nf*) a small insect (used only in the compound **कीड़ा मकोड़ा**).

मकोय makoy (*nm*) a kind of prickly plant and its fruits.

मक्का makka: (*nf*) maize, corn.

मक्का/र makka:r (*a*) cunning, deceitful, crafty; hypocrite; ~री cunningness, craftiness, hypocrisy.

मक्की makki: (*nf*) maize, corn.

मक्खन makkhan (*nm*) butter; ~बाज़ a flatterer, sycophant; ~बाज़ी flattery, sycophancy; –लगाना to butter up, to flatter; -सा मुलायम as soft as butter.

मक्खी makkhi: (*nf*) a fly: ~मार a fly-killer; flykilling; idle, slothful; –निगलना, जीती to connive at a wrong; to deliberately perpetuate a wrong; –की तरह निकाल फेंकना to throw out as of absolutely no consequence, to reject somebody outright; ~मार fly-killer; o काग़ज़ fly paper; –पर मक्खी मारना to imitate blindly, to be foolishly letter-bound; –मारना to idle away time, to sit idly.

मक्खीचूस makkhi:chu:s (*a*) cheese-paring, stingy, terribly parsimonious, niggardly.

मक्षिका makshika: (*nf*) a fly;– स्थाने मक्षिका copying blindly, stupidly letter-bound.

मख makh (*nm*) a sacrifice, sacrificial performance (see यज्ञ).

मख़तूल maḳhtu:l (*nm*) black silken thread.

मखनिया makhanīya: (*nm*) a butter man; (*a*) separated (milk).

मख़मल maḳhmal (*nm*) velvet, plush; –, सूती velveteen; –में गाढ़े/टाट का पैबंद a hessian patch in velvet.

मख़मली maḳhmali: (*a*) velvety, velutinous, plushy; pertaining to मख़मल; soft and tender/delicate.

मखाना makha:nā: (*nm*) a kind of dry fruit (prepared by parching lotus seeds).

मख़ौल maḳhaul (*nm*) joke, jest; mockery, derision; –उड़ाना to subject to mockery, to ridicule, to deride; –समझना to take (something) to be too easy, to treat as a joke/ mockery; –बनाना to deride; to ridicule, to make a fool (of).

मग mag (*nm*) way, path, path-way; a mug.

मग़ज़ magaz (*nm*) brain; kernel; pith; marrow; ~चट pestilent, too much of a gabby, one who perpetually pesters by talking; ~पच्ची too much of brain-taxing, mental over-exertion, assiduous concentration on or constant pondering over something; see मग्ज़; –खाना/ख़ाली करना/चाटना to talk a person's head off; –मारना to tax one's brain; to do intensive mental exercise, to make an intensive mental effort; –लड़ाना to try to find a solution; to make an intensive mental effort, to tax one's brain; to ponder constantly.

मग़ज़ी magzi: (*nf*) edging, border; hem.

मग/द, ~ल magad, ~al (*nm*) a kind of sweetmeat (prepared from wheat flour or the flour of मूँग/उड़द, sugar and घी); –का लड्डू round balls of मगद.

मगन magān (*a*) see मग्न.

मगर magar (*nm*) a crocodile; (*conj*) but; ~मच्छ a crocodile; –के आँसू crocodile tears; –से बैर करके पानी में रहना it is hard to sit in Rome and strive against the Pope.

मग़रि/ब magrib (*nm*) west; western direction; ~बी western; o तहज़ीब western civilisation/culture.

मग़रूर magru:r (*a*) proud; arrogant.

मगसर magsar (*nm*) see अगहन.

मगही maghi: (*nf*) a dialect of Hindi spoken in parts of Biha:r province; (*a*) belonging to or produced in **मगध** (southern part of Biha:r); **—पान** a celebrated variety of betels (**पान**).

मग़्ज़ magz (*nm*) see **मगज** ; **~चट** see **मगज़चट** (under **मगज़**); **~पच्ची** see **मगज़पच्ची** (under **मगज़**); **-खाना/ ख़ाली करना/चाटना** to gabble, to pester by perpetual gabbling; see **मगज़** .

मग्न magn (*a*) absorbed, engrossed; engaged, busy; immersed, drowned; glad, happy, delighted.

मघवा maghwa: (*nm*) **इन्द्र** —the chief of gods; **-भाषा बिडौजा टीका** the commentary to be more abstruse than the text.

मघा magha: (*nm*) the tenth **नक्षत्र** in Indian astronomy.

मचक machak (*nf*) creaking or bending under pressure (or on being heavily laden); tramping; **-मचक कर चलना** to walk slowly and heavily, to tramp.

मचकना machaknā: (*v*) to tramp; to creak or to be bent under pressure (as a bedstead).

मचना machnā: (*v*) to be occasioned, to happen, to be caused, to be raised up, to be committed, to be perpetrated.

मचमचा/ना maehmacha:nā: (*v*) to creak (under pressure or on being heavily laden–as a bedstead); to be or become excited; to be in a heat; hence **~ हट** (*nf*).

मचलना machalnā: (*v*) to be wayward/perverse/obstinate, to go on insisting (upon); to be cross, to sulk, to pant (as a wayward child).

मचलाना machla:nā: (*v*) to nauseate, to feel like vomitting, to feel sick (used generally as **जी–**).

मचली machli: (*nf*) nausea; **-आना** to nauseate, to feel like vomitting.

मचान machā:n (*nm*) a raised platform (for shooting wild animals from or for scaring beasts away from farms); hence **-बनाना/बाँधना.**

मचिया machiya: (*nf*) a small wicker stool.

मच्छ/ड़, ~र machchhaṛ, ~ar (*nm*) a mosquito; gnat; **~ड़/रदानी** a mosquito curtain/net **~ड़/र पर तोप लगाना** small kill, big bill.

मच्छी machchhi: (*nf*) see **मछली; ~मार** a fisherman.

मछली machhli: (*nf*) fish; pisces; **-खाने वाला** piscivorous; **–पकड़ने वाला** an angler; **–सारे/पूरे तालाब को गन्दा करती है, एक** one dirty fish infects the whole water.

म/छवा, ~छुआ, ~छुवा, machhwa:, ~chhua:, ~chhuwa: (*nm*) a fisherman; **-नाव** a fishing boat; **मछेरिन** a fisherwoman.

मज़कूर mazku:r (*a*) said, mentioned; referred to; **-ए-बाला** above-mentioned.

मज़दूर mazdu:r (*nm*) a labourer, worker; **-एकता** solidarity/unity of labour; **–दल** the labour party; workers' team; **-वर्ग** the working class; the labour class; **-संघ** labour union.

मजदूरी mazdu:ri: (*nf*) wage(s); labour charges; act or process of labouring; work of a labourer.

मजनूँ majnū: (*nm*) the celebrated lover of Laila:; a mad or insane man, a love-lorn person; an emaciated man.

मज़बूत mazbu:t (*a*) strong, sturdy; lasting, durable; firm; **–दिल का**

strong-willed; bold, courageous.

मजबूती mazbu:ti: (*nf*) strength; durability; firmness.

मजबूर majbu:r (*a*) helpless; obliged, compelled; forced, constrained; –होना with one's back to the wall.

मजबूरी majbu:ri: (*nf*) helplessness; compulsion, obligation; –का नाम महात्मा गांधी patience is the poor man's virtue.

मजबूरन majbu:rān (*ind*) under pressure, being compelled/forced/obliged; having no alternative.

मज/मा majmā: (*nm*) a gathering; hotch-potch assembly; ~मेबाज (one who is) adept in attracting crowds; hence ~मेबाज़ी (*nf*).

मजमूआ majmu:a: (*nm*) a collection; gathering; crowd; hotch-potch assembly.

मज़मून mazmū:n (*nm*) a topic; subject; text; essay.

मजलि/स majlis (*nf*) assembly, meeting, congregation; ~सी pertaining to an assembly / meeting; fond of assembling people together; ~स जोड़ना to assemble people together.

मज़ह/ब mazhab (*nm*) religion; creed; ~बपरस्त religious-minded, devoted to one's religion; bigot; ~बपरस्ती religious-mindedness, devotion to religion; bigotry; ~बी religious; ~बी आज़ादी religious freedom; ~बी कट्टरता religious fanaticism; ~बी लड़ाई a crusade; religious bickering/struggle.

मज़ा maza: (*nm*) pleasure, relish; savour, taste, flavour; fun, jollity; –उड़ाना/लूटना to enjoy, to relish, to revel; to make fun; –किरकिरा करना to mar the pleasure/taste/flavour (of); –किरकिरा होना pleasure/relish / taste / flavour to be marred; –चखाना to punish for; to teach a lesson; to settle score (with); मज़े का enjoyable, worth-relishing; agreeable; useful, serviceable; humoursome; मज़े की बात an interesting thing/feature; मज़े में with (perfect) ease, to be at home (in); ० होना to be hale and hearty; to be enjoying; मज़े-मज़े में without an effort, with ease; मज़े से happily, comfortably; with ease, easily.

मज़ाक़ maza:q (*nm*) a joke, jest; prank, waggery; humour; fun, buffoonery; ridicule; ~पसंद humorous, fun-loving, pranky, waggish; –उड़ाना to make a fun of; to ridicule; –करना to (cut a) joke; –बनाना to make a fool of, to ridicule; –में in joke, as a matter of joke; non-seriously; –समझना to treat/take as a fun/joke.

मज़ाक़न maza:qān (*ind*) in joke/jest, out of fun, in a humorous vein.

मज़ाक़िया maza:qiya: (*a*) witty, humorous, waggish, pranky, fun-loving; (*nm*) a wag, jester, witty/humorous man.

मजाज़ी maja:zi: (*a*) mundane, earthly, worldly (as इश्क-ए-); unreal, imaginative.

मज़ार maza:r (*nm*) a tomb; grave.

मजाल maja:l (*nf*) cheek, audacity; strength, power; –होना to have the cheek (to).

मजिस्ट्रे/ट majistreṭ (*nm*) a magistrate; ~टी magistrateship.

मज़ेदार mazeda:r (*a*) delicious, savoury, tasty, full of relish, enjoyable; packed with fun and frolic; humoursome.

मजीरा maji:ra: (*mn*) small cymbals.

मजूर maju:r (*nm*) see मज़दूर.

मजूरी maju:ri: (*nf*) see **मज़दूरी**; **–चोखा काम, खरी** good wages, good work.

मज्जका majjaka: (*nf*) medulla.

मज्जन majjān (*nm*) dip, dipping; bath, bathing.

मज्जा majja: (*nf*) marrow, bone-marrow; pith.

मझधार majhḍa:r (*nm*) mid-stream, mid-current; **–में छोड़ना** to leave in a lurch, to desert midway; **–में होना** to be midway, to be neither here nor there.

मझला majhla: (*a*) middle, mid; medium.

मझोला majhola: (*a*) medium-sized, neither big nor small, of average size.

मटक maṭak (*nf*) coquetry, strut: coquettish gestures; affected gracefulness.

मटकना maṭaknā: (*v*) to affect coquettish gestures, to strut, to swagger; to show off with affected gracefulness.

मटका maṭka: (*nm*) a large earthen pitcher/pot; a special kind of silken cloth; a kind of speculation.

मटकाना maṭka:nā: (*v*) to move in a coquettish manner (as **आँख/हाथ–**); to show off with affected gracefulness; to gesticulate in a frivolous manner.

मटकी maṭki: (*nf*) a small earthen pot / pitcher.

मटमैला maṭmaila: (*a*) dusty, dust-coloured; hence **~पन** (*nm*).

मटर maṭar (*nf*) pea.

मटरग/श्त maṭargasht (*a*) vagrant; roving, wandering, rambling; **~श्ती** vagrancy; roving, wandering, ramble/rambling.

मटियाना maṭiya:nā: (*v*) to cleanse or cover with soil/dust/ash.

मटियामेट maṭiya:meṭ (*a*) undone, ruined, destroyed; razed (to the ground); hence **–करना/होना**.

मटियाला maṭiya:la: (*a*) dust-coloured; dusty; hence **~पन** (*nm*).

मट्ठ maṭṭḥ (*a*) slow, sluggish, dull; blunt; also **~र**.

मट्ठा maṭṭḥa: (*nm*) butter-milk.

मठ maṭḥ (*nm*) a monastery; **~धारी** an abbot; chief of a monastery.

मठ/री, ~ली maṭḥri:, **~**li: (*nm*) a small fried saltish cake.

मठा maṭḥa: (*nm*) butter-milk.

मठाधीश maṭḥa:dhi:sh (*nm*) an abbot, head of a monastery.

मड़ई maṛai: (*nf*) a small hut/ cottage.

मड़राना maṛra:nā: (*a*) see **मँडराना**.

मड़वा maṛwa: (*nm*) a canopy, pavilion.

मड़ैया maṛaiya: (*nf*) a small hut.

मढ़ना maṛḥnā: (*v*) to frame, to mount; to gild, to cover (with); to impose; to impute; **–, जिल्द** to bind; **–सिर** to impose on, to compel to accept.

मणि māṇī (*nf*) a jewel, gem; **~कांचन योग** a rare harmonious and beautiful combination; **~कार** a jeweller; **~दीप** a be-jewelled or gem-studded lamp; **~धर** a snake; **~बंध** the wrist; **~भ** crystal; **~मंडित** studded with jewels; **~राज** a diamond; **–फेंककर काँच बटोरना** to throw away gems and collect glass pieces.

मतंग matāṅg (*nm*) an elephant.

मत mat (*nm*) an opinion, view; belief, tenet, doctrine; sect; creed, faith; vote; **~गणना** counting of votes; **~दान** poll, polling, casting of votes; **०केन्द्र** polling station/ booth; **~दाता** a voter, an elector; **० सूची** electoral roll; **~पत्र** ballot,

ballot paper; ~ पेटिका/पेटी a ballot-box; -पर्ची ballot paper; -परिवर्तन change of creed/doctrine/view; -प्रचार propaganda; ~प्रचारक a propagandist; -मतांतर divergent and diverse views, different views; -संग्रह plebiscite; referendum; -स्वातंत्र्य freedom of vote; freedom of opinion.

मतभेद matbhed (*nm*) disagreement, difference of opinion; dissension.

मत/वाद matva:d (*nm*) dogma; doctrine; ~वादी dogmatic; doctrinaire; hence ~वादिता (*nf*).

मतल/ब matlab (*nm*) meaning; purpose; concern; aim, motive, self-interest; ~ब की बात करना to get down to brass tacks; ~बी selfish, self-concerned; o यार fair-weather friends; oयार किसके, दम लगाई खिसके the selfish serves only his own ends; ~ब का बंदा/यार selfish, concerned only about one's own ends; –की बात कहना/पर आना to touch ground, to come to brass tacks; –गाँठना/निकालना/साधना to fulfil one's own ends, to achieve one's own objective; –समझ लेना to get the hang/knack of.

मतलाना matla:nā: (*v*) to nauseate, to feel like vomiting, to feel sick; –, जी to nauseate, to feel like vomiting, to feel sick.

मतली matli: (*nf*) nausea, a feeling like vomiting.

मतवाला matwa:la: (*a*) intoxicated, drunken; wayward; tipsy; (*nm*) a kind of toy; ~पन intoxicatedness, drunkenness; waywardness; tipsiness.

मतांकन matā:nkān (*nm*) poll-assessment.

मतांतर matā:ntar (*nm*) other/different opinion, divergent view.

मतांध matā:ndh (*a* and *nf*) a fanatic; dogmatic; bigot; ~ता fanaticism; dogmatism; bigotry.

मता mata: (*nm*) assets, wealth (used only in the compound माल-मता).

मता/ग्रह mata:ggrah (*a*) dogma; dogmatism; fanaticism; ~ग्रही dogmatic; fanatic.

मताधिकार mata:dhika:r (*nm*) franchise, suffrage, eligibility to vote; –, बालिग़/वयस्क adult franchise.

मताधिकारी mata:dhika:ri: (*nm*) an eligible voter, one who is authorised to vote.

मतानुयायी mata:nuya:i: (*a* and *nm*) (a) follower (of a creed, sect, etc.).

मतावलंबी mata:wlāmbi: (*a* and *nm*) see मतानुयायी.

मति mati (*nf*) intellect; understanding; thought; opinion, view; ~भ्रंश psychosis, derangement; ~भ्रम/भ्रांति hallucination; confusion; ~भ्रष्ट deranged, mentally derailed; ~मंद idiot, low-witted, nincompoop; ~हीन stupid, foolish; –फिरना one's view/stand to undergo a change; one's thought/view to be degenerated; –मारी जाना to lose wits, to be stupefied, to be stunned; -हर लेना to render thoughtless/incapable of thinking.

मतिमान matimā:n (*a*) intelligent, wise, prudent.

मतैक्य mataikky (*nm*) unanimity, agreement, unison, unity of view.

मत्कुण matkūn (*nm*) a bug.

मत्त matt (*a*) drunken, intoxicated; wayward; vagrant; ~ता drunkenness; waywardness.

मत्था mattha: (*nm*) the forehead; head; –टेकना to bow in reverence; मत्थे on one's head/responsibility; o मढ़ना to throw (responsibility, blame, etc.) over somebody else; to shift (to); to impose on.

मत्स/र matsar (*nm*) jealousy; jealousness; envy; ~रयुक्त jealous, envious.

मत्स्य matsy (*nm*) a fish; -उद्योग fishery; fishing industry; -क्षत्र fishery; ~जीवी one who lives on fishing, fisherman; ~पालन pisc culture; ~भक्षी/भोजी fish-eater, piscivorous; -विज्ञान/शास्त्र ichthyology.

मत्स्यावतार matsya:vta:r (*nm*) the first of the ten incarnations of Lord Vishnū (in the form of a big fish).

मथन mathān (*nm*) churning; stirring.

मथना mathnā: (*v*) to churn; to stir deeply; to batter; to agitate; to probe profoundly, to make an in-depth study.

मथनी, मथानी mathnī:, matha:nī: (*nf*) a dolly; churning stick/pot.

मथित mathit (*a*) churned; deeply stirred; profoundly probed.

मद mad (*nm*) intoxication; passion; arrogance, pride; a fluid substance which oozes out from the temple of a passionate male elephant; (*nf*) item; head; category; ~कर/प्रद intoxicating; provoking; -भंग करना to knock out pride/arrogance; -भंग होना passion to be shed out; to be deflated; -भरा intoxicated; intoxicative; arrogant; full of passion; ~मत्त passionate; intoxicated; full of passion; in a fit of passion; -चूर करना/झाड़ना to deflate a swollen head, to knock out one's arrogance, to fix in one's proper place.

मदक madak (*nm*) a preparation of opium which causes deep intoxication; ~ची a मदक-addict.

मदद madad (*nf*) help, assistance, aid; support; relief; reinforcement; ~गार helper; supporter; assistant.

मदन madān (*nm*) see कामदेव; ~दहन/रिपु an epithet of Lord Shiv; ~मोहन Lord Krishnā.

मदनोत्सव madnotsav (*nm*) see होली.

मदरसा madarsa: (*nm*) a school.

मदरासी madra:si: (*nm*) a native of Madra:s (capital of the South Indian State of Tamilna:ḍu); (*a*) belonging or pertaining to Madra:s.

मदहो/श madhosh (*a*) dead drunk, intoxicated out of senses; rendered senseless; ~शी drunkenness, intoxicatedness.

मदांध madā:ndh (*a*) passion-blind, drunken, deeply intoxicated; hence ~ता (*nf*).

मदार mada:r (*nm*) *Calotrapis gigantea*—the plant swallow wort.

मदारी mada:ri: (*nm*) a juggler; conjurer, trickster; hence ~पन/पना (*nm*).

मदिर madir (*a*) intoxicating, intoxicative; hence ~ता (*nf*).

मदिरा madira: (*nf*) liquor, wine, spirit; ~गृह/लय a bar.

मदोद्धत madoddhat (*a*) deeply arrogant, passionately proud; arrogantly insolent; hence ~ता (*nf*).

मदोन्मत्त madonmātt (*a*) arrogant; intoxicated; hence ~ता (*nf*).

मद्द madd (*nf*) item.

मद्दा madda: (*a*) cheap; in depression, slumped.

मद्दे madde; ~नजर in view; ०रखते हुए keeping in view.

मद्ध(द्धि)म maddhā(ddhī)m (*a*) slow; dim; moderate.

मद्धे maddhe (*ind*) in the account of; about; concerning.

मद्य maddy (*nm*) wine, liquor, spirit; -निर्माणशाला a distillery; ~प/पायी one who consumes liquor/drinks; -पान drinking, consuming liquor; intoxication.

मद्योन्माद maddyonmā:d (*nm*) alcoholomania; intoxication.

मधु madhu (*nm*) honey; wine, liquor; juice of flowers; the spring; -ऋतु the spring (season); ~कंठ having a melodious voice; a cuckoo; ~कर a large black bee; ~करी female black bee; cooked food gathered in alms from different sources; ~कोश bee-hive; ~प a large black bee; ~पर्क a beverage prepared in olden times by mixing curd, honey, sugar and water; ~पायी a large black bee; a liquor-addict, one who consumes liquor; ~मक्खी/मक्षिका honey-bee, bee; ०पालन apiculture; bee-keeping; ~मत्त intoxicated, deep drunk; ~मय sweet; attractive, beautiful; ~मास the month of चैत heralding the spring; ~मेह diabetes; ~मेही a diabetic; diabetes patient; ~यामिनी the first night of a couple's union; ~रस honey-dew; ~राज/लोलुप a large black bee; one who goes in quest of sweetness; ~शर्करा sugar prepared from honey; ~शाला a bar; ~सूदन an epithet of Lord Krishnā.

मधुमती madhumāti: (*nm*) the final stage of trance where all mundane conflicts are automatically resolved.

मधुर madhur (*a*) sweet; melodious, pleasant; mellifluous; ~ता/त्व sweetness; melodiousness; mellifluence; softness; ~भाषी honey-tongued, sweet-spoken; मधुराई see ~ता.

मधुरित madhurit (*a*) sweetened.

मधुरिमा madhurimā: (*nf*) sweetness, harmoniousness, melodiousness, mellifluousness.

मधूक madhu:k (*nm*) the tree *Bassia Latifolia* or its flower (from the blossoms and seeds of this tree arrack is distilled and oil extracted).

मध्य maddhy (*a*) middle, central, mid–; (*nm*) middle; centre; the middle part or religion; ~काल mediaeval period; ~कालीन mediaeval; ~कालीनता mediaevalism; ~ता the middle position of a thing; ~देश an ancient nomenclature for the mid-region of the country lying between the Vindhya:chal, Kurukshetra and Allahabad; midland; –पंक्ति middle row; ~पद means; the term situated in between; ~पूर्व middle-east; pre-middle; ~प्रदेश one of the Hindi speaking Indian states situated in the middle parts of the country adjoining Uttar Pradesh, Ra:jastha:n and Maha:rashtra; midland; –भाग centre; core; mid-region; ~मान mean; ~मार्ग middle course, moderate course; ~मार्गी centrist, steering the middle course; ~युग the middle ages; ०संबंधी mediaeval; ~युगी (person etc.) belonging to or characteristic of the mediaeval times; mediaeval; ~युगीन mediaeval; belonging to or characteristic of mediaeval times; ~युगीनता mediaevalism; ~रात्रि midnight, dead of night; ~लोक the earth, this world; ~वय of middle age; ~वर्ग middle class; ~वर्गीय belonging to or characteristic of the middle class, bourgeois;~वर्गीयता

characteristics of the middle class/bourgeoisie; ~वर्ती central; intermediary, medial, intermediate; ~वित्त bourgeois.

मध्यम maddhyam (*a*) medium; middle, intermediate; fourth note of the Indian gamut; slow; dim; –पुरुष second person (in Grammar); ~मार्ग moderate course; ~मार्गी centrist; moderate; ~वर्ग the middle class; hence ~वर्गीय (*a*); ~वर्गीयता (*nf*).

मध्यमा maddhyamā: (*nf*) the middle finger; (*a*) lying in the middle, medial, intermediary.

मध्यस्थ maddhyasth (*a*) intermediate, situated in the middle, intermediary, medial; (*nm*) a mediator; middleman; ~ता mediation.

मध्यांतर maddhyā:ntar (*nm*) interval, intermission.

मध्यावकाश maddhya:vka:sh (*nm*) an interval; space.

मध्याह्न maddhya:nh (*nm*) noon, midday; –रेखा the meridian.

मध्याह्नोत्तर maddhya:nhottar (*nm*) the afternoon.

मन:कल्पित manahkalpit (*a*) imaginary/imagined, fancied, fabricated.

मन:प्रसूत manahprasu:t (*a*) imaginary/imagined, fancied, fabricated.

मन:शक्ति manahshakti (*nf*) mental faculty; moral strength, morale.

मन:श्रांति manahshrā:nti (*nf*) neurasthenia.

मन:स्थिति manahsthiti (*nf*) mood, state of mind.

मन mān (*nm*) mind; heart; desire, wish; disposition; maund–a weight equal to forty seers; ~कामना see मनोकामना; ~गढ़ंत/घड़ंत fabricated; concocted; imaginary/imagined; ~चला Don Quixote, fidgety; frivolous, easy prey to female brandishments; ~चाहा/चीता favourite, desired, wished or longed for; ever desired; ~पसंद after one's own heart, favourite, to one's liking; oचीज one's cup of tea; ~बहलाव amusement, entertainment, recreation; ~भाया favourite; pleasing; loved; ~भावन favourite, liked, beloved; charming, attractive; ~माना arbitrary; licentious; self-willed; ~मानी feminine form of ~माना; o घर जानी arbitrary conduct with no restraint; ~मुटाव bad blood, ill-feeling, estrangement; rift; antagonism; ~मोदक castles in the air, day-dreaming, illusory delight; o फोड़ना to build castles in the air, to day-dream; ~मोहन one who casts a spell of charm; an epithet of Lord Krishnā; ~मौजी whimsical, self-willed; capricious; hence o पन (*nm*); ~हर/हरण see मनोहर; –अटकना/आना, किसी पर to take a fancy for, to fall for;– आधा होना to be disheartened/discouraged; –उछलना to be exalted;– उड़ना to be unsteady, to be in a state of lack of concentration; –उलझना, किसी से to fall for, to have an infatuation for, to be attracted towards; –कच्चा करना to lose courage, to be worried; to discourage; –कड़ा करना to harden one's heart, to keep up one's nerves; –का उजला जीभ का कड़ुवा his bark is worse than his bite; –का कच्चा weak-minded; –का काला/मैला vicious; evil-hearted; –का मैल धोना to circumcise the heart; –की आँखें mind's eye, inner vision; –की गाँठ reservations.

complex; –की थाह लेना to probe into the depth of somebody's heart; –की बात मन में रहना one's wish not to be fulfilled; –के लड्डू खाना/फोड़ना to build castles in the air; to be delighted by mere imagination; to day-dream; –खट्टा होना to develop a sense of bitterness, to be estranged; –खिंचना to feel a sense of repulsion; (–, किसी की ओर) to be attracted; –खोलना to reveal oneself; –चलना to be captivated / attracted; to wish/desire; –छूना to touch, to move; –छोटा करना to feel disheartened / dejected; –जमना to feel reassured/convinced; –जीतना to win over one's heart; –टटोलना to probe into one's heart, to throw a feeler; –टूटना to lose courage; to be disheartened; to be distracted; –ठहरना to feel steady; –ठुकना to feel assured; –डाँवाडोल होना/डिगना to be swept off; to be unsteady; –डोलना to be moved; to be attracted; to lose self-restraint; –देना to disclose one's secrets; to do something with full heart; –नाचना to be in exaltation, to be in a state of extreme delight; –पढ़ना to read somebody's feelings; –पाना to get the backing of; to know the mind of; –फटना/फिर जाना to be disillusioned; to be estranged; –बढ़ना to gain confidence, to be heartened; –बहलाना to amuse, to recreate; –बूढ़ा होना to become mentally old, to lose youthful feelings; –भरना to be fed up, to be satiated/satisfied; –भारी होना to have a heavy heart; –मन भावै मुँडी हलावै "No, thank you", has lost many a good butter cake; –मसोस कर रह जाना to keep one's feelings under suppression, to be agonisingly helpless; –मारना to suppress one's feelings; –मारे (हुए) dejected; in pensive mood; sadly; –मिलना to be of one / similar taste, inclination or ideas; to feel one with; to love each other; –में आना to occur in one's mind; –में कहना to speak within; –में गाँठ पड़ना to develop a complex/reservation for; –में घर करना/जगह करना/बसना to make a place in one's heart, to become somebody's beloved; –में बैठना to strike deep root in the heart, to become permanently embedded in; –में मैल आना ill-will to be aroused within; a sense of dishonesty to prevail within; –में रखना always to remember, to keep in view, to keep concealed to oneself; not to divulge; –मैला करना to feel dejected, to be disheartened; –मैला होना to be in the grip of evil; to have a sense of estrangement; –रखना to comply with someone's wish; to do as one wishes (so as not to let him/her feel bad); –रमना to feel engrossed/absorbed; to identify with; –लगना to feel at home; to feel easy; to like; to be one with; –लेना to probe into one's heart, to find one's inner feeling; –साफ़ होना to be clear, to have no grudge against, to have no reservations; –से उतरना to be liked no more, to lose appeal; –हटना to be distracted, to be repelled; –हरा होना to feel happy; to be delighted; –हल्का होना to feel relieved, to feel easy, to feel better; –हाथ में होना to have self-control, to have control over one's feelings; –ही

मन within one's heart, secretly; –ही मन कुढ़ना to eat one's heart out; –होना to wish, to desire.

मनई manai: (*nm*) a man.

मनका mānka: (*nm*) a bead.

मनकूला mānku:la: (*a*) movable; –जायदाद movable property.

मनन manān (*nm*) meditation, contemplation; brooding, pondering/thinking deeply over something; ~शील meditative/contemplative; thoughtful; hence ~शीलता (*nf*); मननीय contemplatable; –करना to brood/ponder over/think deeply; to contemplate, to meditate.

मनवांछित manva:ṇchhit (*a*) see मनोवांछित.

मनवाना manwa:nā: (*v*) to cause someone to accept/agree to.

मनश्चक्षु mānashchakshu (*nm*) the mental eye.

मनश्चिकि/त्सा mānashchikitsa: (*nf*) psychotherapy, psychological treatment; ~त्सक an alienist, a psychotherapist.

मनसब mānsab (*nm*) an office; status in official hierarchy; ~दार an officer.

मनसबी mānsabi: (*a*) official, pertaining to or related with one's office.

मनसा mānasa: (*a*) mental, born of the mind; (*adv*) mentally, through the mind; ~ना to be inspired/motivated; -वाचा-कर्मणा through the mind; speech and deed.

मनसिज mānsij (*nm*) born in the mind / emotion—Cupid (god of love).

मनसू/ख mānsu:kḥ (*a*) cancelled; ~खी cancellation.

मनसूबा mānsu:ba: (*nm*) intention; plan; design; ~बाज a schemist, a scheming person; –बाँधना to formulate a plan; to design.

मनस् mānās (*nm*) the psyche, psychic element, mind.

मनस्काम mānaskā:m (*nm*) a desire, wish.

मनस्तत्त्व mānastattv (*nm*) the psyche, psychic element.

मनस्ताप mānasta:p (*nm*) afflic ion, sorrow, mental agony.

मनस्तुष्टि mānastushṭi (*nf*) mental gratification, inner satisfaction.

मनस्तृप्ति mānastripti (*nf*) mental contentment, inner satisfaction.

मन/स्वी mānasvi: (*a*) cerebrotonic, single-minded; thoughtful, contemplative; hence ~स्विता (*nf*).

मनहू/स mānhū:s (*a*) ominous, inauspicious; ill-fated; gloomy, sombre; ~सियत ominousness, inauspiciousness; gloominess; ~स शक्ल न दिखाना not to darken one's door.

मनहूसी mānhu:si: (*nf*) gloominess, sombreness.

मना mānā: (*a*) forbidden, prohibited; ~ई see मनाही.

मनादी māna:di: (*nf*) see मुनादी.

मनाना māna:nā: (*v*) to persuade; to appease, to bring round by persuasion (to one's point of view); (*nm*) the act or process of bringing round by persuasion; appeasement.

मनावन māna:van (*nm*) persuasion, the act or process of bringing round by persuasion, appeasement.

मनाही māna:hi: (*nf*) forbiddance; prohibition.

मनिया mānīya: (*nf*) a bead.

मनि/हार māniha:r (*nm*) a bangle-dealer; also ~हारा; hence ~हारिन/हारी feminine form of मनिहार.

मनीआर्डर mānī:a:rḍar (*nm*) a money order.

मनीज/र māni:jar (*nm*) a manager; ~री manager's function or office.

मनीषा manī:sha: (*nf*) intellect, intellectual faculty, wisdom.

मनीषी mānī:shi: (*a* and *nm*) (the) wise; thinker/thoughtful.

मनु mānū (*nm*) the primogenitor of human race; ~ज/जात the offspring of मनु, man; ~जता/जत्व humanity, humaneness, human quality.

मनुष्य mānushy (*nm*) a man, human being; ~कृत man-made; artificial; -गणना census; -जाति the human race, mankind; -लोक the earth, this world.

मनुष्य/ता, ~त्व mānushyata: (*nf*), ~ttv (*nm*) humanity, humaneness; the aggregate of human qualities.

मनुहार mānuha:r (*nf*) persuasion; appeasement; persuasive effort to restore (somebody) to normal mental disposition; -नीति policy of appeasement.

मनुहारना mānuha:rnā: (*v*) to persuade; to appease.

मनोकामना mānoka:mnā: (*nf*) a desire, wish;—पूजना a desire to be fulfilled.

मनो/गत mānogat (*a*) mental, interior; ~गति mental disposition/activity; desire, wish.

मनो/ग्राही mānogra:hi: (*a*) lovely, attractive, charming, appealing; hence ~ग्राहिता (*nf*).

मनोज mānoj (*nm*) Cupid—the god of love.

मनोजात mānoja:t (*a*) psychogenic, mentally created; see **मनोज**.

मनोज्ञ mānoggy (*a*) lovely, charming, attractive, appealing; ~ता loveliness, charm, attractiveness, appealing quality.

मनोदशा manodasha: (*nf*) mood, state of mind,

मनोनिग्रह mānonigrah (*nm*) mental restraint, self-control.

मनोनिवेश mānonivesh (*nm*) concentration; insight.

मनोनीत mānonī:t (*a*) nominated; designated/designate.

मनोबंध mānobāndh (*nm*) scheme.

मनोबल mānobal (*nm*) morale, moral strength; —टूटना to be demoralised.

मनोभंग mānobhaṅg (*nm*) gloominess, depression, out of sorts.

मनोभाव mānobha:v (*nm*) emotion, feeling, sentiment; hence ~ना (*nf*).

मनोभ्रंश mānobhrānsh (*nm*) dementia.

मनोमय mānomay (*a*) psychic, mental; abstract,

मनोमालिन्य mānoma:linny (*nm*) estrangement, ill will; alienation.

मनोमिति mānomīti (*nf*) psychometrics.

मनोयोग manoyog (*nm*) concentration, single-mindedness.

मनो/रंजक mānorāṇjak (*a*) interesting; amusing; entertaining; recreative; hence ~रंजकता (*nf*).

मनोरंजन manoraṇjān (*nm*) amusement, entertainment, recreation; -कर entertainment tax.

मनोरचना manorachanā: (*nf*) mental make-up; fabrication.

मनोरथ mānorath (*nm*) desire, wish; longing; -सिद्धि gratification, fulfilment of a desire.

मनोरम mānoram (*a*) lovely, pretty, charming, attractive; hence ~ता (*nf*).

मनोराग mānora:g (*nm*) affection; feeling.

मनोराज्य mānora:jjy (*nm*) mental

world; fancy.

मनो/रोग mānorog (*nm*) psychosis, psychopathy, mental ailment; ~रोगी a psychopath.

मनो/वांछा mānovā:ṇchha: (*nf*) a desire, wish.

मनो/वांछित mānova:ṇcḥhit (*a*) desired, wished.

मनो/वाद mānova:d (*nm*) mentalism; ~वादी a mentalist; mentalistic.

मनोविकार mānovika:r (*nm*) emotion, feeling, passion; mental derangement, psychopathy.

मनोविच्छेद mānovichchhed (*nm*) dissociation.

मनो/विज्ञान mānoviggya:n (*nm*) psychology; ~विज्ञानवाद psychologism.

मनोविनोद mānovinod (*nm*) amusement, pastime; hobby.

मनो/विलास mānovila:s (*nm*) reverie, musing, fancy; ~विलासी fanciful, musing.

मनोविश्ले/षण mānovishleshān (*nm*) psycho-analysis; ~षक a psycho-analyst; ~षिक psycho-analytic.

मनोवृत्ति mānovritti (*nf*) mentality; mental disposition/attitude.

मनोवेग mānoveg (*nm*) a passion; impulse; -प्रेरित impulsive.

मनोवैकल्य mānovaikally (*nm*) mental deficiency/handicap.

मनोवैज्ञानिक mānovaigya:nīk (*a* and *nm*) psychological; a psychologist; ~ता psychologism, psychologicality; —सुखवाद psychological hedonism.

मनोव्यथा mānovyatha: (*nf*) affliction; mental agony.

मनोव्याधि mānovya:dhi (*nf*) psychosis; mental ailment; affliction.

मनोहत mānohat (*a*) frustrated; disappointed/dejected.

मनो/हर mānohar (*a*) lovely, comely; charming; alluring, captivating; ~हरता loveliness; comeliness, charm; allurement, captivation.

मनोहारी mānoha:ri: (*a*) see मनोहर.

मनौती mānauti: (*nf*) offerings pledged to a deity on fulfilment of some desire, a vow of offering; —मानना see मन्नत मानना.

मन्नत mānnat (*nf*) see मनौती; —मानना to vow to make an offering to a deity (on fulfilment of a wish).

मन्मथ mānmath (*nm*) Cupid—the god of love.

मन्वंतर mānvantar (*nm*) the commencement of the tenure of a मनु.

मम/ता~त्व māmta: (*nf*), ~ttv (*nm*) affection, attachment, the sense of owning or being one with something or somebody.

ममिया māmīyā: (*a*) related through or pertaining to maternal uncle; —ससुर meternal uncle-in-law; —सास maternal aunt-in-law.

ममी mami: (*nf*) a mummy (a dead body kept for long in a preservative); mother.

ममेरा māmera: (*a*) see ममिया.

मयंक māyāṅk (*nm*) the moon.

मय may—a sanskrit suffix imparting the meanings of abounding in, full of, comprised/composed of, etc. to the nouns they are appended to; along with; (*nf*) wine, liquor: ~कदा/खाना a bar; ~परस्त a drunkard; ~परस्ती drinking; ~फ़रोश a wine merchant.

मयस्सर mayassar (*a*) available; —होना to be available, to be able to get.

मयूख mayu:kh (*nm*) a ray.

मयूर mayu:r (*nm*) a peacock; hence मयूरी (*nf*); -नृत्य a peacock-dance.

मरकज़ markaz (*nm*) centre, headquarter.

मरकत markat (*nm*) an emerald.

मरकहा markaha: (*a*) see मरखना.

मरखना markhanā: (*a*) prone to hit (esp. with horns—as a cow, bull, bufalo, etc.).

मरखोर markhor (*a*) prone to hit (with horns) or beat.

मरघट marghaṭ (*nm*) cremation ground; **–की शांति** the quiet spell of death.

मरजिया marjiya: (*nm*) a pearl-diver.

मरजीवा marji:va: (*nm*) see **मरजिया.**

मरण marāṇ (*nm*) death, demise, expiration; mortality; **-दर** rate of mortality; **~धर्मा / शील** mortal; **–भय/भीति** thanatophobia; **–शैया** death bed.

मरणांतक marṇā:ntak (*a*) fatal, killing, culminating in death.

मरणासन्न maraṇā:sann(*a*) on the verge of death, confronted with-imminent death.

मरणोन्माद marṇōnma:d (*nm*) thanatomania.

मरणोन्मुख marṇōnmukh (*a*) dying, decaying, heading towards the end, facing imminent death; hence **~ता** (*nf*).

मरतबा martaba: (*nm*) rank, order; turn; time.

मरतबान maratbā:n (*nm*) a jar.

मरता marta: (*a*) dying, on the verge of death; **–क्या न करता** a desperate man leaves nothing to chance; **मरते को मारना** to flog the dead; to harass the already afflicted; **मरते-जीते** somehow; with immense difficulty; **मरते दम तक** to the bitter end, till the last breath; **मरते-मरते** at the last moment; till the end.

मरदुआ mardua: (*nm*) (used by woman in contempt for a man) a wretch, damned fellow, contemptible man.

मरदूद mardu:d (*a*) damned, condemned; contemptible.

मरना marnā: (*v*) to die, to pass away; to wither away; to become ineffective; to vanish, to disappear; to discontinue; to be absorbed (as **पानी**–); to be out (as in a game); to fall for (somebody); (*nm*) death; post-death rites; **मरकर जीना** to have a lease of life; **मर-खप कर** somehow, after going through lots of ordeals, with great difficulty; **मर-खप जाना** to be dead and gone; **–जीना** life and death; the wheel of birth and death; festive and tragic occasions; **मरने तक की फ़ुर्सत न होना** to be terribly rushed, not to have a moment's respite; **-पचना** to work very assiduously. to pass through terrible ordeals; **मर-मर कर** by tremendous toil; **मर-मिटकर** with immense difficulty; **मर मिटना** to be ruined, to be under a spell of disaster; to be infatuated; **मरे को मारना** to hit a man when he is down; **मरे शेर से जीती बिल्ली भली** a living dog is better than a dead lion.

मरभुक्खा marbhukkha: (*a*) famished; voracious, ravenous; greedy; hence **~पन** (*nm*).

मरमर marmar (*nm*) marble.

मरम्मत marammāt (*nf*) repair, mending; **~तलब** needing repairs; reparable; **–करना** to give it hot/right and left: to dust one's coat, to dress down; to repair.

मरसिया marsiya: (*nm*) a long elegiac poem (eulogizing the valour of a hero, esp. the martyrs of Karbala:).

मरहम marhām (*nf*) an ointment; **-पट्टी** dressing/bandage.

मरहूम marhū:m (*a*) late, deceased.

मराठा mara:ṭḥa: (*nm*) an inhabitant of Maharashtra.

मराठी mara:ṭḥi: (*nf*) the language spoken in Maharashtra.

मराल mara:l (*nm*) a goose, swan.

मरियम mariyām (*nf*) (virgin) Mary –Christ's mother.

मरियल mariyal (*a*) sickly, feeble, rickety; –टट्टू a feeble/sickly man.

मरीचिका mari:chika: (*nf*) a mirage; illusion; ~ग्रस्त under an illusion.

मरीज़ mari:z (*a* and *nm*) a patient, diseased; hence मरीज़ा (*nf*).

मरु maru (*nm*) a desert; ~देश/भूमि-स्थल desert land.

मरुत marut (*nm*) air; the airgod.

मरोड़ maroṛ (*nf*) twist; torsion; contortion, spasm, grip; wrench.

मरोड़ना maroṛnā: (*v*) to twist; to contort; to wring.

मरोड़ा maroṛa: (*nm*) contortion, torsion, abdominal wrench.

मरोरी marori: (*nf*) prickly-heat.

मर्कट markaṭ (*nm*) a monkey.

मर्ज़ marz (*nm*) a disease, malady, ailment; –लाइलाज होना the disease ailment/malady to be incurable.

मर्ज़ी marzi: (*nf*) desire, will; inclination; pleasure; –से wilfully; deliberately.

मर्तबा martaba: (*nm*) see मरतबा.

मर्तबान martba:n (*nm*) see मरतबान.

मर्त्य marty (*a*) mortal; ~धर्मा mortal, who is destined to pass away; ~लोक the mortal world, the earth.

मर्द mard (*nm*) a man; potent male; brave/fearless person; husband; (*a*) manly, dauntless; –आदमी a valorous/dauntless man; masculine man, he-man; –(का) बच्चा valorous, brave, dauntless.

मर्दन mardan (*nm*) massage; rubbing; crushing down, trampling.

मर्दानगी mardā:ngi: (*nf*) bravery, valour; masculinity.

मर्दाना marda:nā: (*a*) male; masculine; potent, valorous; ~पन (*nm*).

मर्दित mardit (*a*) massaged; rubbed; crushed down/trampled over.

मर्दुआ mardua: (*nm*) see मरदुआ.

मर्दुम mardūm (*nm*) a man, common man; ~ख़ोर man-eater; ~शुमारी census.

मर्म marm (*nm*) vulnerable / vital part (of the body); essence; core; secret; real meaning; ~घाती one who strikes at the most vulnerable point, who makes a fatal stroke; ~ज्ञ one who knows the inner meaning; having decp penetration into the secret; ~पीड़ा/वेदना/व्यथा intense mental agony; -प्रहार fatal stroke, vital stroke; -भेद revelation of a secret; see -प्रहार; ~भेदी moving, touching; poignant; heart-rending; –वचन touching words; subtle words; –वाक्य secret/real utterance; ~बेधी see ~भेदी; ~स्थल a vulnerable point; vital spot; –जानना to know the inner secret; –छूना to touch one's inner being, to move deeply; –पाना to get at the depth of, to know profoundly; –लेना to try to know the essence of.

मर्मर marmar (*nm*) marble; rustling: –ध्वनि rustling noise; मर्मरी made of marble.

मर्मरित marmarit (*a*) rustled; making rustling noise.

मर्मस्पर्शिता marmasparshita: (*nf*) the quality of being touching/heart-rending/moving, poignance.

मर्मस्पर्शी marmasparshi: (*a*) touching, moving, poignant, heart-rending.

मर्मांतक marmā:ntak (*a*) heart-rending, mortal; poignant; –पीड़ा/वेदना heart-rending agony.

मर्माघात marmā:gha:t (*nm*) a stroke on a vulnerable point, vital stroke.

मर्मान्वे/षण marmā:nveshān (*nm*) probe into the essentials; investigation into the secret; hence ~षी (*a*).

मर्माहत marma:hat (*a*) vitally struck, heart-rent; stunned.

मर्मी marmī: (*a*) knowing the secret/inner meaning.

मर्मोद्घाटन marmodgha:ṭān (*nm*) exposition/revelation/uncovering of the secret or the inner meaning.

मर्यादा marya:da: (*nf*) dignity, decorum, propriety of conduct; ethical self-restriction; rank, ambit; limit, moderation; ~हीन wanton, without propriety of conduct, having no restraint/moderation; hence ~हीनता (*nf*).

मर्यादित marya:dit (*a*) ethically restrained, bound by propriety; limited; dignified.

मर्सिया marsiya: (*nm*) see मरसिया.

मलंग malāṅg (*nm*) a class of Muslim recluses; (*a*) carefree and self-contained (person).

मल mal (*nm*) faeces, stool, excrement; sewage; rubbish, filth, dirt; ~कूप a sink; ~त्याग excretion of faeces; ~द्वार the anus; –परीक्षा stool test; ~पात्र a commode; –मास an intercalary month; -मूत्र urine and faeces, excrement; रोधक constipative; -विसर्जन excretion of faeces; ~शुद्धि purgation.

मलकूत malku:t (*nm*) the world of angels (according to Islam).

मलखंभ malkhambh (*nm*) a typical Indian acrobatic exercise.

मलिका malika: (*nf*) a queen.

मलना malnā: (*v*) to rub; to press hard; to anoint, to smear; to massage.

मलबा malba: (*nm*) debris, wreckage.

मलमल malmal (*nf*) muslin.

मलय malay (*nm*) a south Indian mountain abounding in sandal trees wherefrom cool and fragrant air-currents are said to emanante; the part of Western Ghats lying South of Mysore and east of Travancore; ~गिरि the Malay mountain; –समीर air-current emanating from the Malay-mountain.

मलयाचल malaya:chal (*nm*) see मलयगिरि (under मलय).

मलयानिल malaya:nil (*nm*) see मलय-समीर under मलय.

मलयालम malaya:lām (*nf*) one of the four major Dravidian languages spoken in the extreme south Indian state of Kerala.

मलयाली malya:li: (*a*) of or pertaining to Malaya:lam; Malaya:lam.

मलाई mala:i: (*nf*) cream; –उतारना to defend flatteringly, to cover the drawbacks of (as an effort to flatter).

मलाबा/र mala:ba:r (*nm*) a part of the South Indian state of Kerala situated on the Arabian sea-coast; ~री an inhabitant of Mala:ba:r; of or pertaining to Mala:ba:r.

मलामत mala:māt (*nf*) used only as the second member of the compound लानत-मलामत meaning –reproach and reproof, condemnation, rebuke and rebuff.

मलाल mala:l (*nm*) remorse, compunction; regret; —आना/होना, मन

में to have a sense of remorse; to feel heavy within; hence–करना.

मलावरोध mala:vrodh (*nm*) constipation.

मलाशय mala:shay (*nm*) the rectum.

मलिक malik (*nm*) a king, ruler; an honourable title for muslims; hence **मलिका** see.

मलिन malīn (*a*) dirty, filthy, tarnished; shabby; gloomy; ~ता dirtiness, filthiness; shabbiness; tarnish; gloominess; ~प्रभ lustreless, who has lost brilliance; tarnished; ~मुख sad; melancholy, gloomy.

मलियामेट maliya:meṭ (*a*) completely ruined, devastated, destructed; razed to the ground.

मलीदा mali:da: (*nm*) a sweet preparation of baked bread, butter or ghee and sugar thoroughly mashed.

मलीन malī:n (*a*) see मलिन; ~ता see मलिनता (under मलिन).

मलेच्छ malechchh (*nf*) see म्लेच्छ,

मलेरिया maleriya: (*nm*) malaria; –बुखार malarial fever.

मलोत्सर्ग malotsarg (*nm*) excretion of faeces.

मल्ल mall (*nm*) a wrestler; ~क्रीड़ा wrestling, wrestling sport; –भूमि/शाला the arena; –युद्ध wrestling, hand to hand fight; –विद्या the art of wrestling.

मल्ला/ह malla:h (*nm*) a sailor, boatman, mariner; ~ही pertaining to or related with a sailor/boatman; the job of a sailor/boatman/mariner, boatmanship.

मल्लिका mallika: (*nf*) a fragrant flower resembling the jasmine.

मल्हराना, मल्हारना malhara:nā:, malha:rnā: (*v*) to fondle, to caress; to hug.

मल्हार malha:r (*nm*) a राग (musica mode) in Indian music sung esp in the rainy season.

मवाद mava:d (*nm*) pus, puruler matter.

मवाली mava:li: (*nm*) a barbari south-Indian tribe; (*a*) boorish barbaric; uncouth.

मवेशी maveshi: (*nm*) cattle; ~खान a cattle pond.

मशक mashak (*nm*) a mosquito (*nf*) a large leathern water-ba (used for sprinkling water on th roads etc.).

मशकूर mashku:r (*a*) obliged grateful, thankful.

मशक़्क़/त mashqqat (*nf*) toil, har labour; ~ती one who toils labours hard, hard-working involving toil/hard labour; ~त की कमाई hard-earned income.

मशग़ूल mashgu:l (*a*) busy, occupi ed with, engaged in.

मशरि/क़ mashriq (*nm*) the east ~क़ी eastern.

मशविरा mashvira: (*nm*) advise counsel.

मशहूर mashhu:r (*a*) famous, well known, reputed; मशहूरी fame -ओ-मारूफ़ having name and fame enjoying a vast repute; करना t make known; to proclaim.

मशाल masha:l (*nf*) a torch: ~ची torch-bearer; –लेकर ढूंढना to mak a thorough search all over.

मशीन mashi:n (*nf*) a machine ~गन a machine-gun; ~मैन machineman; ~री machinery.

मश्क mashk (*nf*) a large leather water-bag (used for sprinklin water on the roads, etc.).

मश्क़ mashq (*nf*) practice; exercise

मस mas (*nf*) soft hair appearin

above the upper lip of a lad heralding the imminent advent of youth; (*nf*) a mosquito; मसें भींजना/भीगना to be on the threshold of youth.

सक masak (*nm*) a mosquito.

सकना masaknā: (*v*) to press, to press hard; to split, to burst, to tear asunder.

सका maska: (*nm*) butter; –लगाना to butter up, to flatter; मसकेबाज़ a flatterer, sycophant; मसकेबाज़ी flattery, sycophancy.

सख़रा maskhara: (*a*) funny; humoursome, waggish; (*nm*) a jester, funny man, wag; buffoon; ~पन waggery/ wagging, buffoonery, jesting, fun/funniness.

सख़री maskhari: (*nf*) waggery/wagging; buffoonery jesting.

सजिद masjid (*nf*) a mosque; –में चिराग़ जलाना to light lamps in a mosque (as a mark of gratefulness for a wish fulfilled).

सनद masnad (*nf*) a bolster, large round pillow (to recline on); –का गधा a moneyed fool.

सन्वी masnavi: (*nf*) a typical poetic genre, in Urdu and Persian, epical in dimension.

सनूई masnu:i: (*a*) artificial; contrived; hence ~पन (*nm*).

सरफ़ masraf (*nm*) utility, usefulness; purpose.

सरू/फ़ masru:f (*a*) busy, occupied; ~फ़ियत the state of being busy, heavy occupation.

सल masal (*nf*) a saying, proverb; illustration; –मशहूर है as the proverb goes, as is the well--known saying.

सलन maslān (*nf*) rubbing, pressing; pressing hard, crushing; (*ind*) for example, for instance, to cite an example.

मसलना masalnā: (*v*) to rub; to press; to press hard; to crush.

मसलहत maslehat (*nf*) expediency; ~अंदेश expedient; suitability ~न for the sake of expediency, expediently.

मसला masla: (*nm*) an issue, question, problem; –हल होना a problem to be solved, solution of an issue to be achieved.

मसविदा masvida: (*nm*) a draft; ~कार a draftsman.

मसहरी mashari: (*nf*) a mosquito net/curtain.

मसा masa: (*nm*) see मस्सा.

मसान masā:n (*nm*) cremation ground; –जगाना to undertake difficult and frightful rituals in a cremation ground for the purpose of taming evil spirits.

मसाना masā:nā: (*nm*) the urinary bladder; –कमज़ोर होना to piss a bit too often; to be meek, to lack courage.

मसाला masa:la: (*nm*) spices; condiments; मसालेवार spiced, pungent, treated with condiments.

मसि masi (*nf*) ink; ~जीवी a writer, professional writer; ~धानी an inkpot; ~पात्र an inkpot; ~मुख black-faced, with a tarnished image, infamous.

मसी/ह masi:h (*nm*) Jesus Christ—the founder of Christianity; ~ही (*a*) Christian; ०धर्म Christianity.

मसीहा masi:ha: (*nm*) a messiah, one endowed with powers to revive the dead; ~ई messianic.

मसू/ड़ा, ~ढ़ा masu:ṛa:, ~ṛha: (*nm*) the gums.

मसूर masu:r (*nf*) lentil, a kind of pulses.

मसूरिका masu:rika: (*nf*) measles.

मसृण masrīn (*a*) soft, smooth, soft and smooth; hence ~**ता** (*nf*).

मसोसना masosnā: (*v*) to press, to repress; to restrain, to subdue; to grieve within; —, **मन** to subdue one's emotional upsurge, to confine one's grief to oneself.

मसौदा masauda: (*nm*) a draft; ~**कार** a draftsman.

मस्जिद masjid (*nm*) see **मसजिद**.

मस्त mast (*a*) intoxicated; intoxicated by passion; carefree, wanton; sexually excited; radiant with joy, in a lively frolic; ~**मौला** a lively and carefree person; ~**राम** see ~**मौला**.

मस्तक mastak (*nm*) head; forehead; **–ऊँचा होना** to feel proud of, to raise one's head high; **–झुकाना** to bow in reverence; to lower the head out of shame.

मस्ताना masta:nā: (*v*) to be in an intoxicated state; to get intoxicated with passion; to be sexually excited; to be in a wanton mood, to be radiant with joy, to be in a lively frolic; (*a*) intoxicated; wanton; sexually excited; frolicsome, carefree.

मस्तिष्क mastishk (*nm*) the brain, cerebrum, mind.

मस्ती masti: (*nf*) (state of) intoxication, joi de vivre; passionateness, sexual excitement; carefreeness, wantonness, joyous radiance, frolicsomeness; **–झाड़ना/निकालना** to knock off one's passion/pride; **–पर आना** to acquire youthful radiance; to be sexually excited.

मस्तूल mastu:l (*nm*) the mast (of a boat); hounding.

मस्सा massa: (*nm*) a wart; **मस्सेदार** warty.

महँगा mehānga: (*a*) dear; expensiv costly; ~**ई** dearness; expensiv ness, costliness; o **भत्ता** dearne allowance; **–रोये एक बार सस्ता रो बार-बार** the cheaper buyer tak no meat.

महँगी mehāgi: (*nf*) high cost, costl ness, expensiveness; (*a*) see **महँग**

महं/त mehant (*nm*) head priest of temple, a monk; self-wille leader; ~**ताई/ती** the function job of a **महंत**; ~**ती** office status of a **महंत**.

महक mehak (*nf*) fragrance, arom perfume, scent; ~**दार** fragran aromatic, perfumed, scented.

महकना mehaknā: (*v*) to emit fr grance/perfume.

महकमा mahakmā: (*nm*) a depar ment.

महकीला mehki:la: (*a*) fragrant, ar matic, perfumed, scented.

महज़ mehaz (*a*) merely, only; abs lutely; simply.

महता/ब mehta:b (*nm*) the moo ~**बी** a kind of fireworks; a raise central platform in a garde etc.

महतारी mehta:ri: (*nf*) mother.

महती mehti: (*a*) see **महत्**.

महतो mehto (*nm*) a title of wel to-do peasant families; a leadin peasant.

महत् mehat (*a*) great; big; exce lent; hence **महती** feminine form.

महत्तम mehttam (*a*) greatest, bi gest; best, most excellent; **–समाप वर्त्तक** G.C.M. (greatest commo measure).

महत्तर mehttar (*a*) greater, bigge better,

महत्ता mehatta: (*nf*) importanc significance; greatness; magnitud

महत्त्व mehattv (*nm*) importanc

significance; greatness; magnitude.

महत्त्वपूर्ण mehattvpu:rṇ (*a*) important, significant, urgent; superb.

महत्त्वाकां/क्षा mehattva:ka:ṅksha: (*nf*) ambition; ~**क्षी** ambitious.

महदूद mehdu:d (*a*) limited, restricted; defined/confined.

महद् mehad–an allomorph of **महत्** as it appears in a modified form in certain compounds; ~**आशय** (**महदाशय**) noble, noble-minded; ~**गुण** having the characteristics of a great man.

महनीय mehnī:y (*a*) adorable; respectable, honourable, glorious; dignified.

महफ़िल mehfil (*nf*) a private assembly / congregation, recreational assembly; –**जमाना/जोड़ना/लगाना** to organise a recreational assembly.

महफ़ूज़ mehfu:z (*a*) safe secure; protected.

महबूब mehbu:b (*a*) beloved, dear; hence **महबूबा** (feminine form).

महमहाना mehmaha:nā: (*v*) to emit fragrance, to pervade with aromatic air, to be full of scent.

महर mehar (*nm*) wedding gift in cash or kind given by the husband to the wife amongst the Mohammedans.

महरा mehra: (*nm*) one who cleans household utensils; hence **महरी** (*nf*).

महरूम mehru:m (*a*) deprived.

महर्षि mehrshi (*nm*) a great sage (seer),

महल mehal (*nm*) a palace, palatial mansion; ~**सरा** a thalamus, female apartment in a palace.

महला mehla: (*nm*) a storey.

महल्ला mehalla: (*nm*) a street, ward (in a town or city).

महसू/ल mehsu:l (*nm*) duty, custom, levy; ~**ली** dutiable, taxable; custom to be paid.

महसूस mehsu:s (*a*) experienced; felt; perceived; –**करना/होना** to experience; to feel; to perceive.

महा maha:—an allomorph of **महत्** as it appears in numerous compounds; ~**कवि** a great poet; an epic poet; ~**काय** mammoth, a colossus; ~**काल** the Annihilator; the Time Indefinite; ~**काव्य** an epic; ~**कुष्ठ** leprosy; ~**ग्रंथ** a voluminous book; a significant work; ~**जाल** a drag-net; ~**देव** an epithet of Lord Shiv; ~**देवी** an epithet of goddess Pa:rvati: –Shiv's spouse; queen consort; ~**देश** sub-continent; ~**नगर/नगरी** a metropolis; cosmopolitan city; ~**धमनी** the aorta; ~**धिकार-पत्र** magna charta; ~**निद्रा** death; ~**न्यायवादी** attorney general; ~**पथ** a highway; ~**पराध** high crime; ~**पातक** a great sin (five such sins have been enumerated by the Hindu scriptures–killing a Bra:hmāṇ, consuming liquor, theft, committing incest with the preceptor's wife and associating with one who has committed any of these sins); ~**पातकी** a great sinner; ~**पाप** see) ~**पातक**; ~**पापी** see ~**पातकी**; ~**पुरुष** a great man; ~**पुरुषोचित** befitting a great man; ~**प्रयाण** see ~**प्रस्थान**; ~**प्रलय** the great deluge; ~**प्रस्थान** death; the final journey; ~**प्राज्ञ** a great scholar endowed with great wisdom; ~**प्राण** an aspirate; possessing tremendous vitality; ~**बलाधिकृत** Commander-in-Chief, Supreme Commander; ~**बली** very powerful, a great warrior; an epithet of Lord Hanumā:n; ~बाहु large-armed, valiant, valorous; ~ब्राह्मण a Brah:mān who performs cremation rituals and accepts payment therefor in cash or kind; ~भाग fortunate, lucky; also used as a form of address; ~मात्य prime minister, premier; ~मति talented, very wise; noble; ~मना noble; liberal; ~महिम Your/His Majesty; ~मात्र prime minister; ~मान्य most Honourable, most revered, His Highness; ~माया female personification of worldly illusions; ~मुनि a great sage; ~मूर्ख a blithering idiot; ~यात्रा the geat journey–death; ~यान one of the three main sects of Buddhism; ~रथी a great warrior; a leading luminary in any field of activity; ~रात्रि the unending night–the great deluge; ~लेखाकार accountant-general; ~वाक्य a sentence impregnated with an expression of essential truth (as अहं ब्रह्मास्मि – I am Brahma); ~व्रती one who undertakes great pledges; ~शिरा ducus venosus; ~शून्य the vast sky; ~सती a very chaste woman; ~समुद्र/सागर an ocean.

महाज/न maha:jan (*nm*) a private banker, money-lender; ~नी banking; money-lending (business).

महात्मा maha:tmā: (*a* and *nm*) a saint, sage, saintly (person), noble / enlightened soul; hence ~पन (*nm*).

महान maha:n (*a*) great; big; eminent; ~ता greatness; eminence, nobility.

महानुभाव maha:nubha:v (*nm*) a great noble / liberal-minded person; also used as a respectable form of address.

महामारी maha:ma:ri: (*nf*) an epidemic; plague.

महायुद्ध maha:yuddh (*nm*) a war, world war.

महारत maha:rat (*nm*) practice, expertise; skill.

महा/राज maha:ra:j (*nm*) a king; a term of respect; a cook; ~राजा a king, ruler; ~राजाधिराज a king of kings, an emperor; ~राज्ञी queen consort; ~राणा a title held by some rulers of former Indian princely states; ~रानी a queen.

महा/राष्ट्र maha:ra:shṭr (*nm*) the south-western Indian state comprising the mara:ṭhi:-speaking areas of the country; ~राष्ट्रीय belonging, pertaining or relating to Maharashtra.

महार्घ maha:rgh (*a*) costly; precious; ~ता costliness; preciousness.

महावट maha:vaṭ (*nf*) winter-rains.

महावत maha:vat (*nm*) a mahaut, elephant-driver.

महावर maha:var (*nm*) the red lac-solution used by woman to adorn their feet.

महाविद्यालय maha:viddya:lay (*nm*) a college.

महावीर maha:vi:r (*a*) having tremendous valour, extremely valorous/gallant; (*nm*) Lord Mahavir; Lord Hanuman.

महाशय maha:shay (*a* and *nm*) noble, liberal (person); a form of address meaning– Mr.

महासभा maha:sabha: (*nf*) a congress; ~सभाई member of a महासभा.

महि mahi (*nf*) the earth; ~धर a

mountain, hill.

महिमा mahimā: (*nf*) exaltation, greatness, dignity; majesty; importance; ~**मंडित** exalted; dignified; majestic; bearing the stamp of greatness/importance; ~**मय/वान** dignified, exalted, great, majestic; important.

महिला mahila: (*nf*) a lady.

महिष mahish (*nm*) a he-buffalo.

महिषी mahishi: (*nf*) a she-buffalo; queen consort.

मही mahi: (*nf*) the earth; soil; buttermilk; ~**धर** a mountain; hill; ~**प/पति** a king.

महीन mahi:n (*a*) thin; soft.

महीना mahi:nā: (*nm*) a month; menses; **महीने से** in menses.

महुअर mahuar (*nf*) the snake-charmer's flute.

महुआ mahua: (*nm*) *Bassia latifolia*–a tree bearing sweet flowers that are used for preparing liquor.

महे/श mahesh (*nm*) Lord Shiv; ~**श्वर** see **महेश**.

महोगनी mahoganī: (*nm*) the mahogani tree.

महोत्सव mahotsav (*nm*) a great celebration, festival.

महोदधि mahodadhi (*nm*) an ocean.

महोदय mahoday (*a*) Sir; an honorofic used as a form of address or otherwise; hence **महोदया** madam.

महोर्मि mahormī (*nf*) a huge surge.

महौषध mahaushadh (*nf*) a panacea.

माँ mā: (*nf*) mother; ~**जाया** a real brother; **-बाप** parents, mother and father; all in all; **–का दूध लजाना** to bring shame to one's mother, to slander one's mother's milk (by an act of cowardice).

मांग mā:g (*nf*) demand; requirement, requisition; indent; the line of demarcation in parting and setting the locks of hair on the head; **–और पूर्ति** demand and supply; **-चोटी/पट्टी** (a woman's) parting and brading the locks of hair; make-up; o **करना** to make (oneself) up, to prank; ~**जली** a widow (an abusive term used by a woman for another); **–टीका** an ornament for the forehead; **-पत्र** an indent; charter of demands; **-उजड़ना/लुटना** to be widowed, to be deprived of the protection of the husband; **–भरना** to fill the **माँग** of a woman with vermilion (esp. done by the husband. The process signifies the status of a **सुहागिन** amongst Hindu women).

मांगना mā:gnā: (*v*) to demand; to ask/call for; to claim; to invite (as tender); to solicit.

मांगलिक mā:ngalik (*a*) auspicious, propitious; benedictory; hence ~**ता** (*nf*).

मांगल्य mā:ṇgally (*nm*) well-being; **-कामना** prayer for (one's) well-being.

मांजना mā:jnā: (*v*) to cleanse, to scour; to polish; to refine; to practise.

मांझा mā:jha: (*nm*) **मंझा**; **-ढीला होना** to feel weak and deficient, to be vigourless; **-ढीला, भरी जवानी** to be in the prime of youth and yet devoid of youthful vigour; young age, old ways.

मांझी mā:jhi: (*nm*) a boatman; steersman, sailor.

मांड़ mā:ṛ (*nm*) rice-starch, boiled rice-water.

मांड़ना mā:ṛnā: (*v*) to knead (flour); to separate grain from the ears of corn; to wage (as **रार**–).

माँ/डी, ~ड़ी ma:ḍi:, ~ṛi: (*nf*) starch.

माँतना mā:tnā: (*v*) see **मातना; माँता** see **माता**.

मांत्रिक mā:ntrik (*a*) pertaining or relating to a **मंत्र**; (*nm*) a scholar of *mantras*.

माँथ mā:th (*nm*) see **माथ**.

माँद mā:d (*nf*) a lair, den (of a beast etc.)

माँदगी mā:dgi: (*nf*) fatigue, tiredness; illnesss.

माँदा mā:da: (*a*) fatigued; tired; ill, sick, diseased; used as the second member in the compound word **थका-माँदा** meaning—tired and worn out.

मांस mā:ns (*nm*) meat; flesh;–, **गाय का** beef;–, **बकरी का** meat;–, **बछड़े का** veal; –**सुअर का** pork;–, **हिरन का** venison –**ग्रंथि** a gland; ~**पिंड** a tumour, lump of flesh; the physical frame; ~**पेशी** a muscle; –**भक्षण** meat-eating; ~**भक्षी/भोजी** a meat-eater; carnivorous/carnivore; –**रस** meat soup; ~**ल** fleshy, corpulent, plump; carnal; tangible, concrete; ~**लता** fleshiness, corpulence, plumpiness; carnality; tangibility; concreteness; ~**वृद्धि** a tumour; fleshy outgrowth; growth of fat, fattiness; –**सार** fat.

मांसाहा/र mā:nsa:ha:r (*nm*) non-vegetarianiasm; meat-eating; ~**री** non-vegetarian; meat-eating; carnivorous.

मांसोपजीवी mā:nsopji:vi: (*nm*) a butcher, meat-seller.

माइल ma:il—see **मायल**.

माईं mā:ī: (*nf*) maternal aunt.

माई ma:ī: (*nf*) mother; a maid-servant; an old woman; –**का लाल** courageous / brave/valorous/generous person (this expression has challenging overtones, as **है कोई माई का लाल** !); –**बाप** all in all, the only source of help; o **समझना** to regard as the only protector/source of help.

माक़ू/ल ma:qu:l (*a*) proper, appropriate, fair; reasonable; fit, suitable; hence ~**लियत** propriety, appropriateness; fitness, suitability; fairness.

माक्षिक mā:kshik (*a*) pertaining to a fly or flies.

माखन mā:khan (*nm*) butter; ~**चोर** an epithet of Lord Krishṇā.

मागधी ma:gdhi: (*nf*) a Pra:krit dialect spoken in eastern parts of India during mediaeval times.

मा/घ ma:gh (*nm*) the eleventh month of the year according to the Hindu calendar; ~**घी** pertaining to or falling in **माघ**; the full-moon day in the month of **माघ** (also called **माघी पूर्णिमा**).

माचिस mā:chis (*nf*) safety matches, a match-box; match-stick; –**दिखाना** to burn down.

माजरा ma:jra: (*nm*) matter; affair incident, occurrence.

माजून ma:ju:n (*nf*) a medicine in the form of sweetmeat; an intoxicating sweetmeat prepared with **भाँग** as an ingredient.

माजूफल ma:ju:phal (*nm*) gall-nut; medicinal gum of a tree.

माट mā:ṭ (*nm*) a large earthen pitcher/pot.

माटा mā:ṭa: (*nm*) a kind of yellow ant found on trees.

माटी mā:ṭi: (*nf*) see **मिट्टी**; –**की मूरत** a nincompoop, stupid fellow; ineffective person.

मॉडल moḍal (*nm*) a model; –**बनाना** to (prepare a) model.

माणि/क, ~क्य mā:ṇik, ~ky (*nm*)

a ruby.

मातंग ma:tāng (*nm*) an elephant.

मात mā:t (*a*) defeated, vanquished; outdone; outwitted; (*nf*) defeat; –खाना to kick the beam; to be defeated/vanquished, to be outdone/outwitted; –देना to defeat/vanquish, to outdo/outwit; –न दे सकना to get no change out of a person.

मातदिल mā:tdil (*a*) moderate, temperate (as आबहवा).

मातना mā:tnā: (*v*) to be intoxicated; to be pride-ridden.

मातब/र mā:tbar (*a*) trustworthy; reliable; credible; ~री trustworthiness; reliability; credibility.

मातम mā:tam (*nm*) mourning, bereavement; grief; ~पुरसी expression of condolence(s); ०करना to express condolences, to mourn; to lament; –मनाना to mourn.

मातमी mā:tmī: (*a*) mournful, indicative of a state of mourning; ० धुन mournful tune; मातमी पोशाक/लिबास mourning dress.

मातह/त mā:tahat (*a*) subordinate, subservient, under; ~ती subordination, subservience.

माता mā:ta: (*nf*) mother; small pox; (*a*) intoxicated; pride-ridden; –निकलना to have an attack of small pox; -पिता parents; mother and father.

माताम/ह mā:ta:mah (*nm*) maternal grandfather, mother's father; ~ही maternal grandmother, mother's mother.

मातु mā:tu (*nf*) mother.

मातु/ल mā:tul (*nm*) maternal uncle, mother's brother; ~लानी/ली wife of maternal uncle, maternal aunt; ~लेय son of मातुल.

मातृ mā:tri (*nf*) mother (used in this form only in compound words); ~क maternal, related to the mother; ~गामी one who commits incest with one's mother; ~घातक/घाती a matricide; ~तंत्र matriarchy; ~त्व maternity, motherhood; ~पक्ष maternal side; ~पितृहीन an orphan; ~पूजन mother-worship; ~पूजक mother-worshipper; ~पूजा mother-worship; ~भक्त devotee of one's mother; ~भाषा mother-tongue; ~भूमि mother-land; ~वत् motherly, mother-like; ~श्री respected mother; ~सत्ता matriarchy; ~सत्तात्मक matriarchical; ~स्तन्य mother's milk; ~हंता matricide; ~हत्या matricide; ~हीन motherless.

मात्र mā:ttr (*ind*) only; merely, barely; mere, bare, sheer.

मात्रक mā:ttrak (*nm*) a unit.

मात्रा mā:ttra: (*nf*) quantity; scale; a dose; degree; a vowel-mark in the Devna:gri: and other allied scripts; length of time taken in pronouncing a vowel or consonant; ~त्मक/मूलक quantitative; based on मात्रा.

मात्रिक mā:ttrik (*a*) pertaining to or belonging to a vowel-mark; based on the number of *ma:tra:s* (as छंद).

मात्सर mā:tsar (*a*) jealous, envious; malicious.

मात्सर्य mā:tsary (*nm*) jealousy, envy; malice.

मात्स्यकी mā:tsyaki: (*nf*) fishery; -क्षेत्र fisheries.

माथ mā:th (*nm*) the forehead; head.

माथा mā:tha: (*nm*) the forehead; forepart; –कूटना to lament, to wail; -गरम होना to be enraged, to get angry; –घिसना to make repeated entreaties and requests, to implore in all humility; –झुकाना –टेकना/नवाना to make deferential salutation; to bow low; to yield; –ठनकना to have an inkling of imminent danger, to have a foreboding of the coming affliction/catastrophe; –ठोकना to lament for one's luck, to curse one's luck; –धुनना see –पीटना; –पकड़कर बैठ जाना to be helpless through frustration, to be hard hit by affliction; ~पच्ची करना to tax one's brain; to take pains in elucidating something; to over-exert mentally (to bring home a point to somebody); –पीटना to lament: to wail; –मारना see ~पच्ची करना; –रगड़ना to implore in deep humility.

माथुर ma:thur (*a*) belonging to or related with the ancient cultural city of Mathura: (Uttar Pradesh).

माथे māthe (*adv*) on the head/forehead; depending / banking on; with the backing of; –का लिखा/की लिखावट/की रेखा the writ of destiny/fate, what is lotted; –चढ़ाना to accept with humility and reverence, to welcome humbly; –पर बल/सिलवट पड़ना to express anger (through deep wrinkles on the forehead), to scowl; to frown; –पर शिकन पड़ना to get into a temper; to feel perturbed; –मढ़ना to impute, to ascribe.

मादक ma:dak (*a*) intoxicating; bewitching, fascinating; ~ता intoxication, drunkenness; fascinating power/charm.

मादर ma:dar (*nf*) mother; –ए-वतन the mother land; ~जाद born of the same mother; ~जाद नंगा stark naked; मादरी maternal; ० जबान mother tongue.

मादा ma:da: (*a*) female; of female sex (used only with animals as–चीता).

माद्दा ma:dda: (*nm*) ingredient; element; essence; pith; root (in Grammar); capability.

माधव ma:dhav (*nm*) an epithet of Lord Krishnā; the spring (season).

माध/विका, ~वी ma:dhavika, ~vi: (*nf*) a creeper which yields fragrant flowers–*Gaertnera racemosa*; also–लता.

माधुरी ma:dhuri: (*nf*) sweetness; pleasantness.

माधुर्य ma:dhury (*nm*) sweetness; pleasantness; one of the poetic qualities which is marked by the exclusive usage of soft or liquid sounds and sound-combinations; -प्रधान abounding in (the quality of) माधुर्य.

माध्यंदिन ma:ddhyāndin (*a*) middle, central, intermediate.

माध्य ma:ddhy (*a*) mean; medium; intermediate, middle; (*nm*) mean value; ~मान mean value.

माध्यमिक ma:ddhyamik (*a*) secondary; middle; intermediary; –पाषाण युग middle stone age; –शिक्षा secondary education; –पाठशाला secondary school.

मान mā:n (*nm*) esteem, respect; prestige, dignity; value; measure, scale; conceit, arrogance; amorous sulking; ~गृह an exclusive retreat chamber for the beloved when in anger; ~चित्र a map; ~चित्रण mapping; -चित्रावली an atlas; ~दंड a standard; criterion; ~पत्र an address (of welcome); ~भंग disillusionment/discomfiture (of the heroine) in a love-affair; ~भरी (said of the beloved) full of sham arrogance, coquettish; resorting to sulkiness to express displeasure; -मन्दिर see ~गृह; -मनौती entreaties and persuasion (esp. amongst lover and beloved) to abandon angry posture; -मर्दन knocking off somebody's arrogance, to fix somebody in his proper place; -मोचन bringing round an angry lover or beloved; –करना to express displeasure by refusing to talk; –निकालना to evaluate; –रखना to honour, to act in deference (to); –रहना one's honour to be maintained/not to be. undermined.

मान/क mā:nāk (*a* and *nm*) standard, norm; ~कीकरण standardization; ~कीकृत standardized; –क भाषा standard language; ~क समय standard time.

मानता mā:nta: (*nf*) importance; recognition, reckoning (as great, powerful, etc.); see मनौती.

मानदेय mā:ndey (*nm*) honorarium.

मानना mā:nnā: (*v*) to agree, to accept; to admit, to confess; to regard, to respect; to presume, to suppose; to assume, to imagine; to take for granted; to accede to; to yield; माना हुआ imaginary, hypothetical; outstanding, recognized (as माने हुए विद्वान).

माननीय mā:nanī:y (*a*) honourable; revered; respectable; (*int*) your honour.

मानव mā:nav (*nm*) a man; human being; mankind; –जाति the human race; mankind; –भूगोल human geography; -मनोविज्ञान ethno-psychology; ~जाति-विज्ञान/शास्त्र ethnology; ethnography; ~त्व humanity, humaneness, -प्रेम philanthropy; love towards humanity: ~मिति anthropometry –वध homicide; ~वधोन्माद homicidal mania; -मनोविज्ञान human psychology; ~वाद humanism; ~वादी a humanist; humanistic; –विज्ञान/शास्त्र anthropology; ~वैज्ञानिक anthropological; an anthropologist; ~शास्त्री an anthropologist; ~शास्त्रीय anthropological.

मानवता mā:navta: (*nf*) humanity; humaneness; mankind; ~वाद humanism; ~वादी a humanist; humanistic.

मानवती mā:nvati: (*a* and *nf*) (a) beloved who amorously assumes a sulking posture (for some lapse on the part of the lover).

मानविकी ma:naviki: (*nf*) the Humanities; ~य pertaining or belonging to the Humanities.

मानवी mā:navi: (*a*) see मानवीय; (*nf*) a woman.

मानवी/करण ma:navi:karan (*nm*, personification; humanization: ~कृत personified; humanized.

मानवीय mā:navi:y (*a*) human/humane, humanitarian pertaining to man/human beings; hence ~ता (*nf*); –संवेदना human sensibilities.

मानवेंद्र mā:navēndr (*nm*) a king; great man.

मानवोचित mā:navochit (*a*) humane, befitting a man/makind.

मानस mā:nas (*nm*) the psyche, mind; heart; a famous lake–मानसरोवर (in the Himalayas); (*a*) mental; psychical; –पुत्र psychic progeny; ~रोग -चिकित्सा psychiatry; ~रोग -चिकित्सक

psychiatrist; ~विज्ञान/शास्त्र psychology.

मानसरोवर mā:nsarovar (*nm*) a famous lake in the Himalayas.

मानसिक mā:nasik (*a*) psychic, mental; ~ता psyche, psychological make-up; –रोग mental disease, psychological ailment.

मानसी mā:nasi: (*a*) mental, psychic.

मानसून mā:nsū:n (*nm*) the monsoon.

मानहानि mā:nha:nī (*nf*) defamation; –का दावा defamation suit; –संबंधी defamatory.

मानाभिषेक māna:bhishek (*nm*) investiture; -समारोह nvestiture ceremony.

मानार्थ mā:na:rth (*a*) complimentary; –प्रति complimetary copy; –सूची complimentary list, free list.

मानिंद mā:nīnd (*a*) like, similar, resembling.

मानिक mā:nik (*nm*) see माणिक.

मानिनी mā:ninī: (*a*) arrogant; arroggantly sulking (woman); (*nf*) a woman who sulks on account of her lover's lapse.

मानी mā:nī: (*nm*) meaning, purport, import; (*a*) proud, haughty.

मानीटर mā:niṭar (*nm*) a monitor.

मानुषिक mā:nushik (*a*) human, pertaining to or befitting mankind/a human being; hence ~ता (*nf*).

मानुषी mā:nushi: (*a*) human, pertaining or befitting a human being; (*nf*) a woman.

माने mā:ne (*nm*) meaning, purport, import.

मानो mā:nō (*ind*) as if, as though; supposing.

मान्य mā:nny (*a*) respectable, respected; honourable; having a privileged position in relationship —e.g. sister's son, son-in-law, etc.; valid; tenable; recognised; ~करण validation; ~ता recognition; validity; accredition; ०प्राप्त recognised (as मान्यता-प्राप्त स्कूल); accredited; मान्या feminine form of मान्य.

माप mā:p (*nm*) measurement/measure; size; dimension; ~क meter; measurer; ~क्रम a scale; ~चित्र plan; -तोल complete assessment, full investigation; weights and measures; ~दंड touchstone; standard; ~न measuring.

मापना mā:pnā: (*v*) to measure, to scale; to assess.

मापनी mā:pnī: (*nf*) a scale, ruler.

मापांक ma:pa:ṅk (*nm*) modulus.

मापी mā:pī: (*nm* and *a*) a meter; measuring.

माफ़ mā:f (*a*) excused, pardoned, forgiven; –करना to excuse, to pardon; –करो leave me alone; excuse me; I beg your pardon; –कीजियेगा (I am) sorry ! I beg your pardon.

माफ़िक़ mā:fiq (*a*) agreeable, suitable, favourable; fit, befitting; –आना to suit; to befit.

माफ़िक़त māfiqat (*nf*) agreeability, agreeableness; fitness; suitability, favourability.

माफ़ी mā:fi: (*nf*) forgiveness, pardon; condonation; remission; exemption; rent-free grant, freehold/rent-free land; ~दार one who holds a rent-exempted land, a rent-free grantee; hence ~दारी (*nf*).

मामला mā:mla: (*nm*) a case; an affair, matter, business, cause; hence मामलात (plural form); –गाँठना to fulfill one's objective; to bring things round to a favourable and; –ढीला पड़ना

things to slacken; –तूल पकड़ना things to be aggravated.

ा/मा mā:mā: (*nm*) maternal uncle; also मामूँ (generally used by Muslims); ~मी maternal aunt.

ामूली ma:mu:li: (*a*) ordinary, so-so; common, commonplace, usual; moderate.

ायका ma:yka: (*nm*) mother's home, maternal house/village/city/place (of a married woman); मायके का कुत्ता भी प्यारा होता है every damn thing belonging to a woman's paternal home is dear to her.

ायल ma:yal—An Arabic adjective used as a suffix in Hindi meaning tinged, having a tinge, mixed, slightly intermixed (as सुर्खीमायल); tending towards, inclined, bent.

ाया ma:ya: (*nf*) illusion, delusion, unreality; trick; riches; earthly ignorance; phantasm; phantam; attachment; ~जाल phantasmagoria, the web of worldly illusion; ~पटु delusive, illusive; ~मय phantasmal, full of illusion, illusory; -मृग the illusive golden deer that misled Ra:m and helped thereby the abduction of Si:ta: in the Ra:mā:yan; any illlusive object; मोह illusion and attachment; ~वाद the philosophical doctrine propounded by the great philosopher Shankara:cha:rya that the world is nothing but unreal and illusory, illusionism; ~वादी one who believes in the doctrine of मायावाद, an illusionist; illusionistic; –जोड़ना to accumulate wealth; -काटना to undo the bonds of mundane attachments; –में फँसना to be overwhelmed by worldly attachments.

मायावी ma:ya:vi: (*a*) illusive, delusive; phantasmal; deceitful; hence मायाविनी (feminine form).

मायिक ma:ik (*a*) illusory, delusory; phantasmal; deceptive.

मायू/स ma:yu:s (*a*) frustrated, dejected, disappointed; ~सी frustration, dejection, disappointment.

मार ma:r (*nm*) beating, thrashing, belabouring; striking range; see कामदेव; (*ind*) abundantly, a lot of, in plenty (e.g. मार आफ़त मचा रखी है); -काट bloody encounter, mutual killing/fight; -धाड़ fighting and killing; noisy encounter; -पिटाई/-पीट scuffle, exchange of blows; beating; battery; –के आगे/से भूत भागता है the rule of the rod frightens one and all; –खाना to be beaten/thrashed, to receive a thrashing.

मारक ma:rak (*a*) killing, deadly, causing death.

मार/का marka: (*nm*) mark, trademark; sign; ~के का remarkable (as मारके की बात).

मारकीन marki:n (*nf*) a kind of coarse unbleached cloth.

मारण ma:rāṉ (*nm*) slaughter, killing; a *ta:ntrik* process of killing an adversary through the influence of relevant *mantras*; –मंत्र a *mantra* for killing an adversary.

मारतौल ma:rtaul (*nm*) a kind of big hammer, slegde hammer.

मारना ma:rnā: (*v*) to kill; to beat, to belabour; to hit, to strike; to punish; to subdue (as गुस्सा–); to misappropriate, not to repay (as पैसा–); to chop off (as गर्दन–); to win (as मैदान–); to turn ineffective (as जहर–); to reduce to ashes (as धातु–); मार डालना to kill, to slay, to murder; –, गोली to shoot; to leave; –, मन to exercise self-restraint, to subdue one's desires; मार-मार कर अधमरा कर देना to flog a person within an inch of his life; मार-मार कर कचूमर निकालना/मलीदा बनाना to beat black and blue, to beat into pulp; मार-मार कर वैद्य/हकीम बनाना, मार-मार कर गधे को घोड़ा बनाना to beat an ass into a horse; मारा-मारा फिरना to wander aimlessly, to knock about from door to door; मारामारी mutual killing/fight, bloody encounter.

मारफ़त ma:rfat (*ind*) through, through the agency of, through the medium of; by; care of (c/o).

मारवाड़ी ma:rwa:ṛi: (*nf*) the dialect spoken in Ma:rwa:ṛ (in Ra:jastha:n); (*nm*) a resident of Ma:rwa:ṛ; (*a*) pertaining to Ma:rwa:ṛ.

मारी ma:ri: (*nf*) see महामारी.

मारुत ma:rut (*nm*) the air-god; air, wind.

मारू ma:ru: (*nm*) a kind of large war kettle-drum; war-time musical mode; also –बाजा; (*a*) killing, deadly; devastative; arousing martial enthusiasm.

मारूफ़ ma:ru:f (*a*) see मशहूर-ओ-मारूफ़.

मारे ma:re (*ind*) due to, because of; on account of, for (e.g. मारे शर्म के); for the sake of.

मार्का ma:rka: (*nm*) see मारका.

मार्कि(के)ट ma:rki(ke)ṭ (*nm*, also *nf*) a market.

मार्क्स/वाद ma:rksva:d (*nm*) Marxism, Marxist ideology; ~वादी (a) Marxist.

मार्ग ma:rg (*nm*) way, path, route, course; road; track; passage, outlet; -कर toll, toll-tax; -(प्र)दर्शक a guide; pioneer; -प्रदर्शन guidance; –खोलना/प्रशस्त करना to open the way, to open an avenue; –बनाना to pave the way; –में रोड़े अटकाना/बिछाना to create impediments in the way of; –रोकना to block the way; –से via; –से भटकना/हटना to deviate from one's course, to stray.

मार्गशिर, मार्गशीर्ष ma:rgashir, ma:rgashi:rsh (*nm*) see अगहन.

मार्गी ma:rgi:—a suffix denoting (one) following/traversing a course (as वाममार्गी); (*nm*) a traveller.

मार्च ma:rch (*nm*) the month of March; (*nf*) march / marching, pacing ahead (as of troops).

मार्जन ma:rjan (*nm*) cleansing, cleaning; purifying/purification; refinement; clearing (a debt); rectifying; wiping.

मार्जनी ma:rjanī: (*nf*) a broom.

मार्जनीय ma:rjanī:y (*a*) which can be or is to be cleansed/cleaned/rectified/purified/refined.

मार्जा/र ma:rja:r (*nm*) a he-cat; ~री a she-cat.

मार्जित ma:rjit (*a*) cleansed, cleaned, rectified; refined; purified.

मार्तंड ma:rtāṇḍ (*nm*) the sun.

मार्दंगिक ma:rdāṅgik (*nm*) one who plays on the percussion-instrument called मृदंग (see).

मार्दव ma:rdav (*nm*) softness; gentleness; compassionateness; leniency, mildness.

मार्फ़त ma:rfat (*ind*) (see) मारफ़त.

मार्मिक ma:rmik (*a*) poignant, touching, moving; vital, affecting the vital parts; ~ता poignancy, power to move, touching/moving quality.

मार्शल ma:rshal (*nm*) a marshal

a house of parliament); (*a*) martial; –लॉ martial law.

माल ma:l (*nm*) goods; commodity; things, articles; effects; stuff; merchandise; cargo; produce; stock; wealth, riches; property; public revenue; dainties; (slang) a youthful and good-looking woman; (*nf*) a wide highway; garland; series; –अदालत a revenue court; ~ख़ाना warehouse, storehouse; ~गाड़ी a goods train; ~गुज़ार a tenant, one who pays land revenue; ~गुज़ारी land revenue, rent; ~गोदाम a godown, warehouse; store-house; -टाल wealth, riches, money; assets; ~दार wealthy, rich; opulent; ~पुआ a kind of sweet cake fried in *ghee*; -मंत्री revenue minister; -मता assets, riches, wealth; effects; ~मस्त money-proud, arrogant on account of opulence; ~मस्ती money-pride, arrogance inspired by opulence; -महकमा the department of revenue; -सूची the stock list; goods inventory; –उगलवाना/निकलवाना to recover (stolen) things; –उड़ाना to consume dainties, to take rich meals; to misappropriate; to spend lavishly; –ए-मुफ़्त दिले बेरहम freely got is lavishly spent; –काटना to eat dainties, to take rich meals; to earn large amounts through dubious means; to be amassing wealth; –बरामद होना (stolen) things to be recovered; –मारना to embezzle, to misappropriate, to usurp somebody's money.

माल्टा ma:lṭa: (*nm*) a kind of large-sized round citrous fruit—*malta*.

मालती ma:lti: (*nf*) a kind of creeper that yields very sweet-smelling flowers.

मालदह ma:ldah (*nm*) a variety of mango.

मालवी ma:lwi: (*nf*) a dialect of Hindi spoken in Ma:lwa:.

मालवीय ma:lvi:y (*nm*) a sub-caste of the Bra:hmāṇs.

माला ma:la: (*nf*) a garland; wreath; rosary, string of beads; series; chain, row, line; ~कार a garland-maker; circular; –जपना/फेरना to tell beads, to remember God by feeling the beads of a rosary one by one; –पहनाना to garland.

मालामाल ma:la:ma:l (*a*) opulent, very prosperous, immensely rich; –होना to make a fortune.

मालिक ma:lik (*nm*) a master, employer; owner, lord (as landlord); proprietor; husband; -नौकर the employer and the employee; -मजदूर the employer and the worker; -मजदूरों का झगड़ा labour dispute; मालिकान plural form of मालिक.

मालिका ma:lika: (*nf*) a row, line; series.

मालिकाना ma:lika:nā: (*nm*) proprietorship, ownership; (*a*) proprietary; masterly, in the fashion or style of an employer/landlord/proprietor/master.

मालिकी ma:liki: (*nf*) ownership, proprietorship.

मालिन ma:līn (*nf*) a maid gardener; wife of a gardener (feminine form of माली).

मालिन्य ma:linny (*nm*) sullenness; rancour, estrangement; impurity, dirtiness.

मालियत ma:liyat (*nf*) value, worth; wealth.

मालिश ma:lish (*nf*) massage; –करना to massage; to flatter, to try to appease.

माली ma:li: (*nm*) a gardener; garlander; (*a*) economic; –**मामले** economic affairs/matters; –**हालत** economic state/position.

मालुम ma:lum (*a*) known; –**होना** to be known, to be in the know.

मालू/म ma:lu:m (*a*) see **मालुम**; ~**मात** knowledge.

माल्टा ma:lṭa: (*nm*) see **मालटा**.

मा/ल्य ma:ly (*nm*) a garland; ~**ल्यार्पण** offering a garland.

मावा ma:wa: (*nm*) see **खोया**; essence, pith.

माश mā:sh (*nm*) black gram.

माशा mā:sha: (*nm*) a weight equivalent to eight ratti:s or one-twelfth of a tola:; -**तोला होना** to be fidgety, to be ever-wavering.

माशाअल्लाह ma:sha:alla:h (*inf*) Good God!, O Gosh!, Excellent; What a wonder !

माशू/क़ ma:shu:q (*nm*) a beloved; hence ~**क़ा** (*nf*).

माशूक़ाना ma:shu:qa:nā: (*a*) in the fashion or style of a **माशूक़** or **माशूक़ा**, like a lover or beloved; –**अंदाज** alluring or fascinating ways, seductive techniques.

माशूक़ी ma:shu:qi: (*nf*) belovedness, coquetry; alluring/fascinating disposition.

माष mā:sh (*nm*) see **माश**.

मास mā:s (*nm*) a month; ~**कालिक** monthly; ~**देय** monthly payable; ~**फल** astrological predictions for a (particular) month.

मासांत mā:sa:nt (*nm*) the end of a month.

मासिक mā:sik (*a*) monthly; per mensem; (*nm*) menstruation; a monthly magazine;–**धर्म** menstruation, monthly course: –**पत्र/पत्रिका** monthly journal/magazine.

मासू/म mā:su:m (*a*) innocent; harmless; guileless; ~**मियत** innocence; harmlessness; guilelessness.

मास्ट/र mā:sṭar (*nm*) a teacher, master; ~**राना** befitting or like a school-teacher.

मास्टरी mā:sṭari: (*nm*) teaching (profession/job); work of a school-teacher; –**करना** to teach, to work as a teacher.

माह ma:h (*nm*) a month; see **माघ**; ~**ताब** the moon; ~**नामा** monthly paper/magazine; -**ब-माह** month by month, monthly; ~**रुख़** beautiful like the moon; ~**वार** monthly, per mensem; ~**वारा** monthly salary, ~**वाराना** monthly, on a monthly basis; ~**वारी** monthly; menstruation.

माहली ma:hli: (*nm*) a harem-attendant, valet.

माहात्म्य ma:ha:tmy (*nm*) greatness, glory; efficacy of a deity or god.

माहाना ma:ha:nā: (*a*) monthly.

माहिर ma:hir (*a* and *nm*) (an) expert; a specialist; adept; a dead hand.

माही ma:hi: (*nf*) a fish.

माहेश्वर mā:heshwar (*a*) pertaining to **महेश्वर** (Lord Shiv).

मिंगी mīgi: (*nf*) the kernel of a fruit; kernel of boiled water-chestnut.

मिंड़ाई mīṛa:i: (*nf*) the act of rubbing, crushing or twisting also; the charges therefor.

मिकदार mikda:r (*nf*) quantity; measure.

मिकनाती/स miknā:ti:s (*nm*) a magnet; loadstone; ~**सी** magnetic.

मिक्सचर mikschar (*nm*) a (medicinal) mixture.

मिचकाना mīchka:nā: (*v*) to wink, to blink; (**पलकें**—the eyelashes; **आँखें** —the eyes).

मिचना michnā: (*v*) to be shut, to be closed (per force).

मिचलाना mīchla:nā: (*v*) –, **जी** to nauseate, to feel like vomiting, to feel sick.

मिचली mīchli: (*nf*) feeling like vomiting, nausea; **–आना** see **मिचलाना**, **जी**.

मिचोली mīcholi: (*nf*) used only as the second member in the compound **आँख-मिचोली** lit. covering the eyes (of another)—(the game of) hide and seek.

मिचौनी michaunī: (*nf*) see **मिचोली**.

मिज़राब mizra:b (*nf*) a plectrum, metal ring worn on the forefinger (for playing on a stringed instrument etc.).

मिज़ाज miza:j (*nm*) temperament; nature; disposition; temper, mood; conceit; fastidiousness; **~दार** conceited, fastidious; **~पुरसी** enquiring after one's well-being; **~वाला** conceited; fastidious; **–आसमान पर होना** see–**सातवें आसमान पर होना**; **–ख़राब होना** to be in a temper; to be bad-tempered; **–गरम होना** to be infuriated, to be in a fury; **–दिखाना** to show a short temper to show one's fastidiousness/conceitedness; **–न मिलना** to think no end of oneself; to be ever cross; **–पहचानना** to know one's nature; to know one's likes and dislikes; **–पूछना** to enquire after one's well-being; **–मुबारक/–शरीफ़** how do you do?; **–सातवें आसमान पर होना** to be too hot-headed, to be too conceited; to think no end of oneself; **–होना** to be fastidious, to be conceited.

मिज़ाजी miza:ji: (*a*) conceited; arrogant; fastidious.

मिज़ोराम mizora:m (*nm*) an eastern state of the Union of India.

मिटना miṭnā: (*v*) to be effaced; to be erased; to be ruined, to be undone, to be destructed.

मिटाना miṭa:nā: (*v*) to efface; to erase; to blot out; to obliterate; to ruin, to undo, to destroy.

मिट्टी miṭṭi: (*nf*) earth, soil; clay: dirt, dust; mortal remains;**–का तेल** kerosene oil; **–उठना** one's mortal remains to be carried away (for last rites); to be carried away for funeral rites; **–करना** to ruin, to destroy; **–का पुतला** man —made up of mortal stuff; **–का लोंदा** a pile of clay, an absolutely inert fellow; **–का शेर** a clay tiger; **–की मूरत** human physique; see **–के माधो**; **–के माधो** a stupid fellow, a nitwit; **–के मोल** damn cheap; as cheap as dirt; **–ख़राब होना / बिगड़ना / बरबाद होना** the last rites to be mismanaged; the last rites not to be duly performed; **–छुए तो सोना हो जाए** all he touches turns to gold; **–ठिकाने लगाना** to duly perform the last rites; **–डालना** to cover up an evil; **–देना** to bury the dead body; to collectively lay the dead body to rest; **–पकड़ना** to take deep roots; **–पलीद होना** to be in a miserable plight; to be humiliated/insulted/embarrassed; the last rites not to be duly performed; **–में मिलना** to be razed to the ground; to be ruined/wasted.

मिट्ठी miṭṭhi: (*nf*) a kiss (esp. when implanted on a child's cheek).

मिट्ठू miṭṭhu: (*nm*) a parrot.

मिठ miṭh—an allomorph of '**मीठा**' used as the first member in certain compound words; **~बोला** sweet-spoken.

मिठाई miṭha:i: (*nf*) sweetmeat; confectionery; –चढ़ाना to make an offering of sweetmeat to a deity; –बाँटना to distribute sweetmeat (to celebrate some happy occasion).

मिठास mitha:s (*nf*) sweetness.

मिडिल midil (*a*) middle; ~ची (said indignantly) one who has studied only upto the middle standard; –स्कूल a middle school.

मित mit (*a*) moderate, temperate; restricted; frugal; ~भाषण temperance in speech; reticence; ~भाषी temperate in speech; reticent; ~पान temperance in drink; ~भोजन temperance in food; ~भोजी eating a small quantity; ~मति a nit-wit, stupid; ~व्यय thrift, frugality; ~व्ययिता thriftiness, frugality, ~व्ययी thrifty, frugal.

मिताई mita:i: (*nf*) friendship, alliance.

मिता/चार mita:cha:r (*nm*) temperance, moderateness; ~चारी temperate, moderate.

मिता/हार mita:ha:r (*nm*) temperance in food, abstinence; ~हारी temperate in eating, abstinent.

मिति miti (*nf*) measure/measurement; limit.

मिती miti: (*nf*) a date according to the lunar month; ~काटा discount; –डालना to date (a document).

मित्र mittr (*nm*) a friend; an ally; ~घात killing a friend; ~घाती killer of a friend; ~ता/त्व friendship, intimacy; alliance; –देश a friendly country; an ally; ~द्रोह disloyalty to a friend; acting faithlessly towards a friend; ~द्रोही disloyal to a friend; -भाव friendship, friendliness, alliance; ~मंडली a circle of friends; ~राष्ट्र (the) allies; an ally; ~वत् like a friend.

मिथ mith (*nm*) a myth; ~क a myth, mythus.

मिथु/न mithun (*nm*) a couple, pair; mating, (sexual) union; the third sign of the zodiac–Gemini; ~नीकरण mating.

मिथेन mithen (*nm*) fire-damp.

मिथ्या mitthya: (*a*) untrue, false, pseudo-; sham, spurious; delusory (*nm*) untruth; falsehood; illusion; –कोप sham anger; ~चर्या hypocrisy, sham conduct; ~चार see मिथ्याचार; –ज्ञान illusion, illusory knowledge; –दृष्टि false view; ~प्रतिज्ञ one who does not keep one's pledge; ~भाषी a liar, mendacious; ~मति ignorant; misunderstanding; erroneous; –वचन, वाद mendacity, false utterance falsehood; ~वादी mendacious untruthful, false.

मिथ्याचार mitthya:cha:r (*nm*) hypocrisy, sham conduct.

मिथ्यात्व mitthya:ttv (*nm*) falsehood untruthfulness.

मिथ्यापवाद mitthya:pva:d (*nm*) slander, false accusation.

मिथ्याभिमान mitthya:bhimā:n (*nm*) vanity, false sense of dignity pride.

मिनकना minākn़ā: (*v*) to speak inarticulately, to speak through the nose.

मिनजानिब minja:nib (*ind*) on behalf of.

मिनट minaṭ (*nm*) a minute.

मिनमिन mīnmīn (*nf*) inarticulate speech; speech through the nose.

मिनमिनाना mīnmīnā:nā: (*v*) to speak in an articulate fashion; to speak through the nose.

मिनहा mīnha: (*nm*) deducted; ~ deduction; –करना to deduct; –होना

to be deducted.

मिनिस्ट/र ministar (*nm*) a minister, ~**री** ministership; ministry.

मिन्नत mīnnat (*nf*) entreaty, request; supplication.

मिमियाना mīmīya:nā: (*v*) to bleat (as a goat); to speak through the nose.

मियाँ mīyā: (*nm*) a respectful address for a Mohammedan; husband; -**बीवी** husband and wife; -**मिट्ठू** a sweet-spoken person; a parrot; -**की जूती मियाँ की चाँद**, -**की जूती मियाँ के सिर** to beat somebody with his own stick; -**बीवी राज़ी तो क्या करेगा काज़ी** while two are locked in embrace, the third becomes an intruder; -**मिट्ठू बनना, अपने मुँह** to indulge in self-praise, self-praise is no recommendation.

मिया/द miya:d (*nf*) duration; time limit, term, tenure; period; ~**दी** extending over a certain period; timed, time-bound; ०**बम** time bomb; ~**दी बुख़ार** typhoid.

मियान miyā:n (*nf*) a sheath, scabbard; -**में से निकले पड़ना** to be ever-ready to quarrel, to be too hot-headed.

मियाना miyā:nā: (*a*) medium, medial, mediate; (*nm*) a type of palanquin open on the sides; -**क़द** medium size.

मियानी miyā:nī: (*nf*) the gusset of the trousers; a mezzanine room.

मिर/गी mirgi: (*nf*) epilepsy; ~**गिया** epileptic; ~**गी आना** to have an attack of epilepsy; to be epileptic.

मिरजई mirzai: (*nf*) a typical indigenous jacket.

मिरज़ा mirza: (*nm*) a title of the princes of the Timur dynasty or the moghuls; son of a nobleman.

मिरा/क़ mira:q (*nm*) craze, craziness, madness; ~**क़ी** crazy, mad.

मिर्गी mirgi: (*nf*) see **मिरगी**.

मिर्च mirch (*nf*) chillies; pepper; **मिर्चें लगना** to be provoked, to be suddenly worked-up.

मिल mil (*nf*) a mill; -**मज़दूर** a mill-worker; -**मालिक** a mill-owner.

मिलता-जुलता milta:-julta: (*a*) resembling, having resemblance, like, identical.

मिलन milan (*nm*) a meeting; union; contact; ~**सार** sociable; affable; ~**सारी** sociability, affability.

मिलना milnā: (*v*) to meet; to encounter; to be mixed, to be mingled; to unite; to merge; to tally; to conform; to obtain, to get; to acquire / to be acquired; to beget; to embrace; to form an alliance (with); **मिल-जुलकर** jointly, collectively; together; in a concerted manner; -**जुलना** to meet (people), to have social intercourse; **मिल-बाँटकर खाना** to accommodate all in the gains/profits, to share duly with all; **मिलने वाला** a visitor; **मिला-जुला** coalition; (as-—**शासन**); mingled, mixed; combined, linked; joined, connected.

मिलनी milni: (*nf*) one of the various ceremonies involved in a wedding (a meeting and mutual embracing by the people on the two sides).

मिलवाई milwa:i: (*nf*) meeting; money paid for effecting a meeting.

मिलाई mila:i: (*nf*) meeting (with), visit (esp. paid to a prisoner or a patient); see **मिलवाई**.

मिलान milā:n (*nm*) comparison; reconciliation; collation; tallying (of accounts etc.); ~**कर्त्ता** a tally-man; collator.

मिलाना mila:nā: (*v*) to unite; to compare; to reconcile; to mix, to mingle, to blend; to join, to connect; to harmonize; to tune; to cause to meet, to bring together.

मिलाप mila:p (*nm*) meeting; reconciliation; union, unity; **–होना** to come together; to have a reconciliation.

मिलावट mila:vaṭ (*nf*) adulteration/adulterant; blend, mixing; alloy.

मिलिंद milind (*nm*) see **भौंरा**.

मिलिटरी militari: (*a* and *nf*) (the) military.

मिलित milit (*a*) met, come together, joined.

मिलीभगत mili:bhagat (*nf*) sinister alliance alliance in a conspiracy.

मिल्कियत milkiyat (*nf*) property; estate, landed property.

मिल्लत millat (*nf*) friendship; fraternity; sect.

मिशन mishān (*nm*) (*a*) mission; **~री** a missionary.

मिश्र mishr (*a*) mixed; complex; blended, combined; **–वाक्य** a complex sentence.

मिश्रण mishshrāṇ (*nm*) a mixture; blend; combination; **मिश्रित** mixed; blended; combinded; complex.

मिष mish (*nm*) pretext, pretence, pretension, excuse.

मिष्ट mishṭ (*a*) sweet; **~भाषी** sweet-spoken.

मिष्टान्न mishṭa:nn (*nm*) sweetmeat, confectionery; **-प्रेमी** a lover of sweets.

मिस mis (*nm*) a pretext, pretence, excuse.

मिसका(कॉ)ट miska:(ɔ)ṭ (*nf*) a conspiracy, conspirational consultations.

मिसरा misra: (*nm*) one-half of a couplet.

मिसरी misri: (*nf*) sugarcandy; **–की डली** a sweet thing; **–घोलना** to give rise to sweet feelings; to talk sweet.

मिसाल misa:l (*nf*) precedent; example; **–के तौर पर/~न** for example, to cite an example.

मिसिल misil (*nf*) a case-file; file; **-मिलान** collating.

मिसकी/न miski:n (*a*) indigent, poor; helpless; hence **~नी** (*nf*).

मिस्टर misṭar (*nm*) Mister.

मिस्त्री mistri: (*nm*) a mechanic, mistry; technician; artisan, craftsman; **~गीरी** the job, assignment or profession of a mechanic/artisan/craftsman/technician.

मिस्मिरेजम mismirejam (*nm*) mesmerism.

मिस्री misri: (*nm*) see **मिसरी**; an Egyptian; (*a*) Egyptian, belonging to or of **मिस्र** (Egypt).

मिस्ल misl (*a*) like, just like, resembling, similar to.

मिस्सी missi: (*nf*) a black powder (that was) used by women for tinging their teeth; (*a*) mixed; made of a mixture of wheat and gram flour; **-काजल/सुरमा** make-up, face-lift.

मिहिर mihir (*nm*) the sun; the moon; a cloud.

मींगी mī:gi: (*nf*) see **मिंगी**.

मींचना mī:chnā: (*v*) to shut, to close (as eyes etc.).

मींजना mi:jnā: (*v*) to rub/to crush/to press (with the hands or fingers).

मींड़ना mī:ṛnā: (*v*) see **मींजना**.

मीज़ान mi:zā:n (*nm*) sum, total; **–मिलना** the total to tally.

मीटर mi:ṭar (*nm*) a meter.

मीटिंग mi:ṭing (*nf*) a meeting.

मीठा mi:ṭha: (*a*) sweet, pleasant; (*nm*)

sweetmeat; gur; –ज़हर sugar-coated poison; –ठग a sham friend, treacherous person, sweet-spoken cheat; –तेल oil of sesame; –पानी fresh water; –बोल/वचन sweet words; –बोलना to be sweet-spoken; to speak sweet; –मीठा sweet; pleasantly mild; gentle; –मीठा गप-गप कड़ुवा-कड़ुवा थू-थू to own up all that is sweet and to reject all that is bitter; –विष see ज़हर; –मुँह कराना to offer sweetmeat (to celebrate a good news or a happy occasion).

मीठी mi:ṭhi: (*a*) feminine form of मीठा (see); –गाली pleasant vituperation, agreeable abuses (often showered through songs by women in conventional marriages); –चुटकी a pleasant pinch, sweet joke; –छुरी a sweet-spoken traitor, a cheat in friend's garb; –नज़र tender looks, affectionate or amorous glances; –नींद carefree and restful sleep, sound and comfortable sleep; –बात a sweet remark; –बोली sweet speech; –मार slow torture; –आँच पर पकाना to cause internal agony; to give slow fire; –छुरी चलाना to pretend as a friend and hit hard;–दवा देना to gild the pin, to soften the blow; –नज़रों से देखना to give the glad eye.

मीड़ mi:ṛ (*nf*) a glide.

मीत mī:t (*nm*) a friend.

मीन mī:n (*nf*) a fish, Pisces—the twelfth sign of the zodiac; ~केतन/~केतु/~ध्वज Cupid—the god of love; -मेख करना/निकालना to fiddle-faddle, to find faults, to pick holes in.

मीना mī:nā: (*nm*) blue colour; a false gem of blue colour; enamel; ~कार an enameller; ~कारी enamelling; –बाज़ार a fancy fair.

मीनार mī:nā:r (*nf*) a minaret; tower.

मीमां/सा mī:mā:nsa: (*nf*) one of the six systems of Indian philosophy (~सा, पूर्व the philosophy of Jaimini, also termed कर्ममीमांसा; ~सा, उत्तर the Vedantic philosophy of बादरायण, also termed ब्रह्ममीमांसा); profound thought or reflection, deep deliberation, thorough investigation; ~सक a follower of the मीमांसा system of philosophy; an investigator, one who has given profound thought or reflection (to a subject); ~सित well thought over/reflected upon, duly investigated/examined; ~स्य to be thought over or reflected upon, to be examined or investigated.

मीर mī:r (*nm*) an allomorph of अमीर—a nobleman; chieftain; leader; winner in a competition; –मजलिस chairman/president of an assembly/meeting; –मुहल्ला leader of a locality or ward.

मीरास mi:ra:s (*nf*) hereditary property, patrimony.

मीरासी mi:ra:si: (*nm*) a muslim sect that lives by singing and dancing; a singer and dancer (in a derogatory sense).

मीरी mi:ri: (*nm*) the winner in competition, one who stands first; leadership.

मील mi:l (*nf*) a mile; –का पत्थर a milestone.

मीलन mi:lan (*nm*) closing, shutting; contraction.

मीलित mi:lit (*a*) closed, shut; contracted.

मुँग/रा mūgra: (*nm*) mallet, wooden

hammer; ~री a small sized मुँगरा.

मुँगौरी mūgauri: (*nf*) a small dried up ball of mashed green lentil etc.

मुंड muṇḍ (*nm*) the head; head severed from the trunk; ~माल(ा) a garland of (severed) heads/skulls; ~माली an epithet of Lord Shiv (supposed to wear a मुंडमाल).

मुंडन muṇḍān (*nm*) shaving of the head, the tonsure ceremony, a Hindu संस्कार involving the first-ever shaving of the hair on a child's head.

मुँड़ना mūṛanā: (*v*) to have the head shaven; to be fleeced, to be relieved of one's money or belongings.

मुंडा mūṇḍa: (*a*) hornless (as बैल); bald-headed; shaven-headed; (*nf*) a language spoken by some aboriginals in Biha:r; (*nm*) a lad; boy-servant; boots.

मुँड़ाई mūṛa:i: (*nf*) the process or work of, or the wages paid for, shaving the hair on the head; fleecing.

मुँड़ाना mūṛa:nā: (*v*) to get shaved; to cause to be fleeced/cheated.

मुँड़िया mūṛiya: (*nf*) a script used in indigenous accountancy and book-keeping (being without headline for economy of effort).

मुंडी mūṇḍi: (*nf*) a shaven-headed woman; the medicinal plant—*Spluranthus indicus*; head (*a*) shaven-headed.

मुँडे(ड़े)/र mūḍ(ṛ)er (*nf*) a demarcation wall; parapet; battlement; also ~री a small ~र.

मुंतख़ब muntḳhab (*a*) selected, chosen.

मुंतज़िम muntzim (*nm*) a manager; organiser; one entrusted with arrangements; (*a*) having organising capability, good at making arrangements.

मुंतज़िर muntzir (*a*) waiting, expecting; (*nm*) one who waits/expects.

मुँदना mūdnā: (*v*) to be closed/shut; to be covered/hidden

मुँदरी mūdri: (*nf*) a ring; finger-ring.

मुंशियाना munshiya:nā: (*a*) befitting a मुंशी, in the nature or fashion of a मुंशी; (*nm*) the remuneration due or paid to a मुंशी.

मुंशी munshi: (*nm*) a scribe, clerk (esp. of a pleader or an advocate) munshi; a (Urdu or Persian) teacher; ~गीरी the work or profession of a scribe/clerk.

मुंसरिम munsarim (*nm*) the head clerk of a court entrusted with files etc; manager.

मुंसिफ़ munsif (*nm*) a munsif—judge of a subordinate civil court; –की अदालत the court of a munsif; मुंसिफ़ी the work, post, profession or court of a मुंसिफ़.

मुँह mūh (*nm*) the mouth; face; the forepart (of anything); an opening, orifice, hole, aperture; inlet; outlet; source; courage, strength; fitness; –अँधेरे/उजाले very early in the morning, before day-break; ~चढ़ा see ~लगा; ~चोर bashful, shy, sheepish, shamefaced; ~चोरी bashfulness, sheepishness, shamefacedness; ~छिपाऊ bashful, skulking/skulker; ~छुआई extension of a mere formal invitation, to ask or enquire just casually; ~छुट see ~फट; ~ज़बानी verbal, oral; ~ज़ोर insolent, impertinent, impudent; high-spirited, hard-mouthed (as a घोड़ा); ~ज़ोरी insolence, impudence; high-spiritedness, hard-mouthedness; ~झौंसा (an abuse used by womenfolk) one with a charred face; charred-faced; ~तोड़ apt, befitting; crushing; incontrovertible; retaliatory (as मुँहतोड़ जवाब); –जवाब देना to give a crushing/befitting reply; -दर-मुँह face-to-face; ~दिखाई present (in cash or kind) offered to a newly-wed bride (on seeing her for the first time by womenfolk of the bridegroom's household); ~देखी superficial; involving sham regard; just for appeasement; ~फट loose-tongued, outspoken, intemperate in speech; ~बंद closed-mouthed; reticent; unblossomed; ~बोला adopted; ~माँगा as explicitly demanded or asked for; fully answering one's wish; ~माँगी मुराद heart-felt wish, any object or thing obtained in fulfilment of expressed wish; ~लगा insolent. impudent, given too much/allowed too much liberty;–आँसुओं से धोना to weep bitterly; –आना to suffer from mouth-sore, to have one's mouth filled with pilules; mouth to be salivated; –इतना-सा निकल आना to be reduced to gaunt; to grow very much emaciated and pallid; to be too much ashamed; to lose one's facial lustre; –उजला होना to come out unscathed from an accusation; to be exonerated; to be spared humiliation and disgrace; to have one's face saved; to come out with flying colours; –उठे on rising (from bed);–उतरना the face to grow lustreless; to be dismal-looking; to have the face withered due to shame/disease/exhaustion/tiredness; the face to become shrunken/reduced/drawn; –करना (a boil etc.) to develop an opening; –करना, किसी की ओर to to turn the face towards; –का कड़ा/सख्त harsh-spoken, insolent; hard mouthed –का कड़ुवा bitter-spoken; –का कौर/निवाला to be damn easy, as easy as the swallowing of a morsel;–का कौर/टुकड़ा/निवाला छीनना to take the bread out of one's mouth, to deprive someone of livelihood/subsistence; to deprive somebody of his acquirement; –का कौर समझना/होना to take as easy; –का मीठा superficially sweet, soft-spoken; sweet without but malicious within; –काला करना lit. to blacken one's face – to be disgraced, to disgrace; to go about wenching; to get out of sight; to damn (it); –काला हो be damned; be disgraced; –काला होना to be disgraced, one's face to be blackened; to have gone out of sight; to have been damned; ~की खाना to lick/kiss the dust, to have one's gruel, to eat an humble pie; to suffer a humiliating defeat; to receive a blow on the face, to be brow-beaten; –की बात छीनना/–से बात छीनना to snatch words out of somebody's mouth; –की लाली रखना to maintain one's grace/dignity; –की लोई उतरना to lose the sense of shame; to be lost to shame, to become brazen; –के बल गिरना to fall facelong; to stoop to a very low level; to go all out in pursuit of; –के लायक़ होना to conform to somebody's status; to befit/to become under a particular set of circumstances;

–ख़राब करना to spoil one's taste; to utter indecent/vituperative words; –खिलना to be delighted, to be full of joy; –खुलना to speak out; to speak out unrestrictedly; –खुलवाना to cause somebody to speak out; to incite to be impertinently frank; –ख़ुश्क होना see–सूखना; –खोलकर रह जाना to be wonder-struck/astounded; to gape in amazement; –खोलना to speak out; to ask for something; to be vituperatively outspoken; –चाटना to caress; to toady, to make much of; –चिढ़ाना to make faces at, to mock, to ridicule; –चुराना to hide one's face, to avoid, not to face; –चूम लेना to plant a kiss on the face of; to concede superiority, to compliment for working wonders; –छिपाना/छुपाना to evade (somebody), to skulk, to be bashful, to hide ones' face; –छूना to extend a mere formal invitation (without meaning it); to talk insincerely; –ज़रा-सा निकल आना see –इतना-सा निकल आना; –टेढ़ा करना to make wry faces; to be displeased; to show aversion/displeasure; –डालना to interfere, to poke one's nose into, to muzzle into; –तकना/ताकना to gaze/stare at the face (of); to be astonished; to look blank/foolish, to expect something of (as उनका मुँह मत ताको); ~तोड़ जवाब देना to jump down a person's throat; –दिखाना to make an appearance; –दिखाने लायक़ न रहना to lose face, to be thoroughly disgraced; –देखकर बात कहना to flatter, to appease through agreeable words, to be superficially sweet, to say pleasant things (to); –देखते रह जाना to be lost in astonishment; to look aghast, to be taken aback; –देखी बात करना see –देखकर बात कहना; –देखे का superficial, not cordial; –धो रखो have no hopes !, have no illusions !; –न लगाना not to touch one with a barge pole; –पकड़ना to hold somebody's tongue, not to allow to speak out; –पर on one's face, in the presence of; openly;–पर कालिख पोतना/लगाना to bring disgrace/slander to; –पर झाड़ू मारना to damn !; –पर झूठ नहीं बोला जाता face to face the teeth come out; –पर ताला लग जाना to be tongue-tied; to be rendered mute; not to utter a word; –पर थूकना to spit at/upon, to express ignominious indignation; –पर नाक न होना to be shameless, to be brazen-faced;–पर फ़ाख़्ता उड़ना to change colour, to look blank/confounded/astounded; –पर मारना to fling in one's teeth; –पर मुहर लगना to be tongue-tied; the lips to be sealed, not to be able to speak out; –पर लाना to utter, to speak out, to bring to the lips; –पर हवाइयाँ उड़ना see–पर फ़ाख़्ता उड़ना; –पसारना to gape in wonder, to look aghast; to ask for ever more; –पाना to get tacit instigation; to find one favourably disposed; to get into the good graces (of); to presume on the favour (of);–पीला पड़ना to turn pale or pallid (from fear etc.), to lose lustre; –पेट चलना to have an attack of cholera, to have both motions and vomits; –फ़क हो जाना to turn pale; see–पर फ़ाख़्ता उड़ना; ~फट होना to wear one's heart upon one's sleeve; to lack reserve, to be outspoken; –फिरना to be satiated/cloyed/ disgusted / displeased (with); –फुलाना/सुजाना to sulk, to be sulkily reticent to be displeased, to make a wry face, to distend the cheeks; –फेरना to abstain (from); to avoid, to turn the face away from; –फैलाना see –बाना; –बंद करना to hold one's tongue; to bribe, to give hush-money (to); to cut the ground from under one's feet; –बनाना to make a wry face; to look displeased/ sour; to frown or scowl; to mock; –बाँधकर बैठना to sit quiet, not to utter a word; –बाना to expire; to yawn; to desire too much; –बिगाड़ना to leave a bad taste in the mouth; see–बनाना; –बिचकाना to make a wry face; –भर आना the mouth to water/to salivate; –भर कोसना to heap curses on; –भरना to give hush money, to bribe; –मीठा करना to give one a treat; to offer sweets to celebrate a happy occasion or a good news; –में कालिख पुतना/लगना to be disgraced, to face ignominy; –में/को ख़ून/लहू लगना to get a taste for impropriety, to get accustomed to depravity; –में गुड़-घी/–में घी-शक्कर may what you say turn out to be true!; –में ज़बान न रखना to be tongue-tied, not to speak at all; to be very meek; –में ज़बान रखना/होना to be able to speak out; to be reactive; –में दही जमना to speak just nothing, not to be able to speak; –में दाँत न पेट में आँत to be very old; –में पानी भर आना to lick one's chaps/chops; the mouth to water/salivate; to have an intense desire to enjoy/ possess something; –में राम बगल में छुरी beads about the neck and devil in the heart, many kiss the hand that they wish cut off; –में लगाम न होना to be absolutely intemperate in speech; to have no restraint whatever over one's utterance, to be in the habit of saying any and everything; –मोड़ना to turn one's back upon; to turn away the face from, to disregard; to be averse to; to abstain from; –रखना to keep a good countenance; –लगना to suit the palate of; to be agreeable to the taste of; to become used to; to bandy words (with); –लगाना to give undue lift to (an inferior or junior person); to allow someone to take undue liberties; –लटकाना, –लटका होना to pull/wear/draw a long face, to be down in the mouth; to be expressly displeased; to sulk; –लाल करना to make one's face red by slapping; –लाल होना to flush with anger, to be red with anger; to be blushed red; –लेकर रह जाना, अपना-सा to face severe discomfiture; to be thoroughly chagrined; –सँभाल कर बोलना to have one's tongue in one's cheek, to talk sensibly; –सीना to seal the lips (of), not to allow to speak; to silence (a person); to give hush-money; –सूखना the face to become thin/emaciated / withered / dried up; to be thirsty; –से निकल जाना to utter per chance; to make an unguarded utterance; to say something that should not have been said; –से फूल झड़ना soft words to flow out, to be very gentle in speech; (ironical) to condemn in round terms, to reproach or abuse; –से बात न निकलना to be tongue-tied; not to be able to speak out; –से

बात छीन लेना see –की बात छीन लेना; –ही मुँह में in an inarticulate fashion, within oneself, to oneself.

मुँहामुँह mūhā:mūh (*a*) upto the brim, brimful; (*adv*) face to face; –भरना to fill to the brim; to overstock.

मुँहासा mūhā:sa: (*nm*) (a) pimple (on the face supposedly signifying the advent of youth).

मुअज्जम muazzām (*a*) great; respectted; elderly.

मुअत्त(त्ति)/ल muatta(tti)l (*a*) suspended; ~ली suspension; o का हुक्म suspension order.

मुअल्लिम muallim (*nm*) a teacher, preceptor.

मुआ mua: (*a*) dead; good-for-nothing (an abuse often used by womenfolk).

मुआइ(य)ना mua:i(ya)nā: (*nm*) inspection; visit; –फ़रमाना to be kind to inspect/pay a visit.

मुआफ़ mua:f (*a*) see माफ़.

मुआफ़िक़ mua:fiq (*a*) see माफ़िक़.

मुआमला mua:mla: (*nm*) see मामला.

मुआवज़ा mua:wza: (*nm*) compensation, recompense; indemnity; remuneration.

मुआहिदा mua:hida: (*nm*) an agreement.

मुक़दमा muqadmā: (*nm*) a case; suit, law-suit; –करना / –ठोकना / –दायर करना to file a law-suit; to launch legal proceedings; –खड़ा करना to litigate, to institute a legal suit; –लड़ना to fight a case, to pursue a law-suit.

मुक़दमेबा/ज muqadmēba:z (*a* and *nm*) (a) litigant; ~जी litigation.

मुक़द्दर muqaddar (*nm*) fate, luck, destiny.

मुक़द्दस muqaddas (*a*) holy, pious, sacred.

मुकम्मल mukammal (*a*) complete/completed, finished, perfected; also मुकम्मिल.

मुकरना mukarnā: (*v*) to deny, to refuse; to back out; to go back upon one's word; to belie.

मुकरनी, मुकरी mukarni:, mukri: (*nf*) an enigmatic poem, a poetic riddle, short verse-riddle which controverts numerous suggested replies and ultimately puts forth something new.

मुक़र्र/र muqarrar (*a*) fixed, appointed; posted; employed, deployed; ~र करना to fix, to appoint; to employ / deploy; ~री posting, appointment; employment, deployment.

मुकलावा mukla:wa: (*nm*) see गौना.

मुक़ाब(बि)ला muqa:b(bi)la: (*nm*) encounter; opposition; comparison, competition; equality; ~ला करना to oppose, to encounter; to compare/to compete; to contend; ~ला होना to have an opposition, to have a competition (between); ~ले का match, matching; ~ले की टक्कर a Greek meeting Greek, a matching opponent, a match; ~ले पर आना to come face to face for a showdown; to contend, to oppose.

मुक़ाबिल muqa:bil (*adv*) in front of.

मुक़ाम muqā:m (*nm*) a place, site; quarter, halting place, halt; –करना to halt; –बोलना to order a halt.

मुक़ामी muqa:mī: (*a*) local, colloquial.

मुकियाना mukiya:nā: (*v*) to give fistblows.

मुकुंद mukund (*nm*) Lord Krishṇā, Lord Vishṇū.

मुकुट mukuṭ (*nm*) a crown; diadem,

crest, coronet; ~धर / ~धारी crowned, wearing a crown.

मुकुर mukur (*nm*) a mirror, looking glass.

मुकुल mukul (*nm*) a bud, blossom.

मुकुलित mukulit (*a*) semi-blossomed, budded; blinking.

मु/क्का mukka: (*nm*) a fist-blow, punch; boxing; ~क्केबाज़ a boxer, pugilist; ~क्केबाज़ी boxing, pugilism.

मुक्की mukki: (*nf*) a light fist-blow.

मुक्त mukt (*a*) free/freed, independent, released; unfettered; liberated, delivered, emancipated; ~कंठ से freely, without any reserve/reservation; enjoying liberty of speech; ० प्रशंसा करना to shower unreserved praises (upon); ~केश having uncombed / unbraided/dishevelled hair; ~चक्षु open-eyed ~चेता a free/non-committed thinker; –छंद free verse; –जल free water; ~ता salvation; liberation, freedom; deliverance; ~द्वार having doors thrown open, ever-ready to welcome; –पत्तन free port; –व्यापार free trade; ~हस्त liberal, bounteous; –करना to liberate, to free, to cause salvation.

मुक्तक muktak (*a* and *nm*) stray, independent, not forming a connected whole; independent poems or couplets; –काव्य independent poetic verses; poetry that is not epical in character.

मुक्ता mukta: (*nf*) a pearl; ~फल a pearl; ~वली a string of pearls.

मुक्ति mukti (*nf*) salvation, emancipation, deliverance; liberation; release; freedom; exemption, riddance; ~दाता/प्रद a saviour, deliverer, one who brings salvation/emancipation, rescuer; –धाम an abode of salvation; -पथ the path of salvation; -पत्र a release order, release warrant; -मार्ग see -पथ; -लाभ (achievement of) salvation, deliverance, emancipation; -सेना liberation army.

मुख mukh (*nm*) the mouth; face; forepart; front; brim; opening; exit or entrance; principal; -कमल lotus-like face, lovely/beautiful face; -कांति facial lustre; -चित्र the frontice piece; cover-design; -पट a veil; -पत्र an organ; ~पृष्ठ the cover page; -प्रक्षालन washing the face; ~मंडल the face, countenance; ~बंध the preface, introduction; ~शुद्धि cleansing or purifying the mouth after meals; chewing a betel etc. after meals; ~श्री facial glow, face-lustre; –सुख economy of effort (in pronunciation); (causing) ease of pronunciation; ~स्राव the saliva.

मुखड़ा mukhṛa: (*nm*) face; pretty face; intro.

मुख़तार mukḥta:r (*nm*) an agent, attorney; ~नामा power of attorney; मुख़तारी attorneyship.

मुख़न्नस mukḥannās (*a*) impotent.

मुख़फ़्फ़फ़ mukḥaffaf (*a*) abridged/shortened, short (as 'घुड़' for घोड़ा in घुड़दौड़).

मुख़बि/र mukḥbir (*nm*) an approver, informer; the act of an approver/informer; hence ~री (*nf*).

मुखर mukhar (*a*) explicit; outspoken; loud; talkative, garrulous.

मुखरित mukharit (*a*) explicit; outspoken; loud; voiced.

मुखाकृति mukha:kkriti (*nf*) countenance; facial features.

मुखाग्र mukha:ggr (*a*) committed to memory, on the tip of the tongue; (*nm*) the frontage; forepart.

मुख़ातिब mukḥa:tib (*a*);—होना, किसी

की ओर/से to address (somebody), to talk to, to turn towards (for speaking to).

मुखापे/क्षी mukha:pekshi: (*a*) dependent/subsisting on somebody else; hence ~क्षिता (*nf*).

मुख़ाल(लि)फ़त mukha:l(li)fat (*nf*) opposition; antagonism.

मुख़ालिफ़ mukha:lif (*a*) an opponent, adversary; antagonist.

मुखिया mukhiya: (*nm*) a chief, head, leader; the headman (of a village or clan etc.).

मुखौटा mukhauṭa: (*nm*) a mask.

मुख़्तलिफ़ mukhtalif (*a*) different; distinct; various, varied.

मुख़्तसर mukhtasar (*a*) brief, short, concise, abridged; –में in short, briefly speaking.

मुख्य mukkhy (*a*) principal, chief; main; salient; staple; leading; capital, cardinal; pre-eminent; predominant; –गायक the precentor; ~त/~तया primarily; chiefly, mainly; ~ता leading status, pre-eminence; predominance; –पात्र the protagonist, the leading character; –मंत्री chief minister; –स्वर cardinal vowel; predominant voice.

मुख्यार्थ mukkhya:rth (*nm*) main/principal meaning; –बाध होना the principal meaning to be rendered inoperative.

मुख्यालय mukkhya:lay (*nm*) headquarters.

मुगदर mugdar (*nm*) a mace/club used in physical exercise.

मुग़ल mugal (*nm*) a Moghul; famous race whose native land is Mangolia; ~ई pertaining/belonging to a Moghul or to the Moghul race or dynasty.

मुग़लिया mugliya: (*a*) see मुग़लई (under मुग़ल); –ख़ानदान the Moghul dynasty.

मुग़ालता muga:lta: (*nm*) illusion; mistake; misconception.

मुग्ध mugdh (*a*) infatuated; charmed, under a spell; attracted (towards); ~कर/कारी charming, that which casts a spell or causes infatuation, attractive.

मुग्धा mugdha: (*a* and *nf*) according to traditional Indian Poetics, a simple, innocent and artless heroine within whose person youth has just been ushered.

मुचल/का muchalka: (*nm*) a personal bond; recognizance; ~के लेना to get a personal bond executed.

मुछंदर muchhāndar (*a*) having long and clustered moustaches, whiskered.

मुछड़िया muchha:ṛiya: (*a*) see मुछंदर.

मुछमुंडा muchhmūṇḍa: (*a*) clean shaven.

मुछैल muchhail (*a*) see मुछंदर.

मुज़क्कर muzakkar (*a*) male; masculine (gender–in Grammar).

मुजरा mujra: (*nm*) deduction; salutation; a singing session (by a prostitute); –करना to deduct; to salute deferentially.

मुजरिम mujrim (*nm*) a criminal.

मुजस्सम mujassām (*a*) in person; personified; incarnate.

मुजस्समा mujassamā: (*nm*) an idol, a statue.

मुज़ायका muza:yka: (*nm*) obstruction; worry, anxiety; –नहीं, कोई does not matter, don't bother/worry.

मुजाहिद muja:hid (*nm*) a crusader.

मुज़िर muzir (*a*) harmful, having adverse effect.

मुझ mujh (*pro*) oblique form of मैं; ~को to me; –पर unto/on me; ~में (with) in me; ~से from me;

with me; out of myself.

मुझे mujhe (*pro*) to me.

मुटरी mutri: (*nf*) see गठरी.

मुटाई muṭa:i: (*nf*) thickness; sturdiness; pride; –चढ़ना to become arrogant/proud.

मुटाना muṭa:nā: (*v*) to grow fat/plump/wealthy, to fatten.

मुटापा muṭa:pa: (*nm*) fatness, fleshiness, plumpness.

मुटिया muṭiya: (*nm*) a porter, coolie.

मुट्ठा muṭṭha: (*nm*) a bundle (of straw etc. which can be held in one's grip); handle.

मुट्ठी muṭṭhi: (*nf*) a fist; grip; clutch(es); the breadth of a closed palm; handful; –गरम करना to grease one's palm; to bribe; to accept bribe; to buy over; –गरम होना to be bribed; –ढीली होना to shell out some money; –भर handful; –में under one's control/sway/clutches; –में हवा बंद करना to try to achieve an impossibility; –में होना to get somebody by the short hairs, to be under one's control, to be under the sway of.

मुठभेड़ muṭhbheṛ (*nf*) an encounter, a confrontation, clash.

मुठिया muṭhiya: (*nf*) a handle, haft; the mallet of a (cotton) carder.

मुड़ना muṛnā: (*v*) to turn; to be twisted; to bend/to be bent; to return; मुड़ा हुआ bent; turned; twisted.

मुड़िया muṛiya: (*nf*) see मुँड़िया.

मुड़ेर muṛer (*nf*) see मुँडेर.

मुड्ढा muḍḍha: (*nm*) the shoulders; the joints of shoulders and arms.

मुतअल्लिक़ mutalliq, मुतल्लिक़ mutalliq (*a*) concerning; –, के about, concerning, regarding, as regards.

मुतना mutnā: (*nm*) a piss-a-bed; (*a*) who pisses much, over-pissing, over-urinating.

मुतफ़न्नी mutfannī: (*a*) guileful, cunning, crafty, wily.

मुतफ़र्रि/क़ mutfarriq (*a*) miscellaneous, different, of different kinds/sorts; ~क़ात miscellaneous (things), sundries; ~क़ खर्च miscellaneous expenditure.

मुतबन्ना mutbannā: (*a* and *nm*) adopted (son).

मुतबर्रिक mutbarrik (*a*) holy, pious, sacred.

मुतलक़ mutlaq (*adv*) absolutely, extremely, in the extreme.

मुतवल्ली mutwalli: (*nm*) a guardian (of a minor boy); trustee.

मुतसद्दी mutsaddi: (*nm*) a scribe, clerk; an accountant.

मुताबिक़ muta:biq (*ind*) in accordance with, according to; –, के in accordance with, according to.

मुतालबा muta:lba: (*nm*) arrears; dues.

मुतास muta:s (*nf*) an inclination to piss/urinate, feeling like making water.

मुताह muta:h (*nm*) a kind of temporary marriage valid amongst the Shia muslim community.

मुत्तला muttala: (*a*) informed, apprised.

मुद mud (*nm*) joy, pleasure, delight.

मुदर्रि/स mudarris (*nm*) a teacher; ~सी the teaching profession, teachership.

मुदा muda: (*ind*) but, the purport being, I mean to say.

मुदाख़लत muda:khalat (*nf*) interference; intervention.

मुदित mudit (*a*) pleased, happy, delighted.

मद्ग mudg (*nm*) a kind of bean, horse-bean.

मुद्गर mudgar (*nm*) see मुगदर.

मुद्दई muddai: (*nm*) a plaintiff; complainant;–सुस्त गवाह चुस्त the bridegroom's men to be more keen on marriage than the groom himself.

मुद्दत muddat (*nf*) period, length of time, limit; duration; a long time; –का antiquated, time-worn.

मुद्दती muddati: (*a*) old, antiquated, time-worn; of fixed duration.

मुद्दा mudda: (*nm*) issue; theme, intention,

मुद्दालेह mudda:leh (*nm*) defendant; respondent.

मुद्रक muddrak (*nm*) a printer; -पंक्ति print line.

मुद्रण muddrān (*nm*) printing; -आदेश print order; -कला art of printing.

मुद्रणालय muddranā:lay (*nm*) a printing press.

मुद्रां/क muddrā:nk (*nm*) a stamp; ~कन stamping; ~कित stamped.

मुद्रा muddra: (*nm*) a seal; stamp; money, coin; countenance, demeanour; mien, pose, posture; ~क्षर type; ~लेख legend; ~विज्ञान/शास्त्र numismatics; ~स्फीति inflation.

मुद्रिका muddrika: (*nf*) a finger-ring.

मुद्रि/त muddrit (*v*) printed; stamped; sealed; ~तालभ्य out of print.

मुनक्का munaqqa: (*nm*) a large-size dried grape, big currant.

मुनशी mūnshi: (*nm*) see मुंशी.

मुनहस(सि)र munehsa(si)r (*a*) depended; based; –होना to depend upon, to be based on.

मुनादी munā:di: (*nf*) proclamation (esp. by beat of drum); –करना to proclaim; to proclaim by beat of drum.

मुनाफ़ा muna:fa: (*nm*) profit; gain; ~ख़ोर a profiteer;~ख़ोरी profiteering.

मुनासिब munā:sib (*a*) reasonable, appropriate, proper, fit.

मुनि munī: (*nm*) an ascetic, a hermit; -कन्या/सुता daughter of a मुनि; ~वर the best/foremost of *munis*.

मुनियां muniyā: (*nf*) a kind of red-coloured small female bird; a small girl.

मुनी/म munī:m (*nm*) an indigenous system accountant; ~मी the work or profession of a मुनीम.

मुनी/श, ~श्वर muni:sh, ~shvar (*nm*) a great ascetic/hermit/saint.

मु/न्ना munnā: (*nm*) a term of endearment for a child, small one, a dear child; ~न्ने की माँ (usual form of address for one's) wife.

मुफ़लि/स muflis (*a*) poor, indigent; pauper; ~सी poverty, indigence; pauperdom; ~सी में आटा गीला yet another misery for an already miserable man.

मुफ़स्स(स्सि)ल mufassa(ssi)l (*a*) mofussil; detailed; (*nm*) a suburb of a town/city/centre.

मुफ़ीद mufi:d (*a*) useful, beneficial.

मुफ़्त muft (*a*) free of charge, without price, gratis; ~ख़ोर/ख़ोरा a social parasite, one who lives on others' earnings; ~ख़ोरी having a parasitic existence, living on others' earnings; –का free, gratis, procured without payment or exertion; –में uselessly; for no rhyme or reason; without paying any price; gratis; without being due, without any effort.

मुफ़्ती mufti: (*nm*) a (muslim) law-giver/legislator.

मुबलिग़ mublig (*a*) in all, numbering, totalling; (*nm*) the amount (e.g. –पाँच रुपये the amount of five rupees).

मुबारक muba:rak (*a*) auspicious; blessed, fortunate; ~बाद congratulations, felicitations; ०कहना/देना to congratulate, to felicitate; ~बादी

felicitations, congratulations, blessing; –हो may be auspicious to you (as ईद मुबारक हो); मुबारकी see ~बादी.

मुबाहिसा muba:hisa: (*nm*) discussion (used only in the compound बहस-मुबाहिसा).

मुब्तला mubtala: (*a*) involved (in), occupied (with); –, में involved in, busy with, occupied; –होना to be involved in, to be busy with.

मुमकिन mumkin (*a*) possible, feasible.

मुमानि/अत, ~यत mumā:nīat, ~yat (*nf*) prohibition, forbiddance.

मुमु/क्षा mumuksha: (*nf*) desire for the attainment of salvation; ~क्षु desirous of attaining salvation.

मुमू/र्षा mumu:rsha: (*nf*) the death-instinct, desire to die; ~र्षु desirous of death; on the verge of death.

मुरकी murki: (*nf*) a small ear-ring, ear-top; a kind of musical ornamentation around a note.

मुरग़ा murga: (*nm*) see मुर्ग़ा.

मुरग़ाबी murga:bi: (*nf*) see मुर्ग़ाबी.

मुरग़ी murgi: (*nf*) see मुर्ग़ी (under मुर्ग़ा); –के (a term of abuse) You offspring of a hen! You Chicken!

मुरचंग murchang (*nm*) a jew's harp.

मुरछल murchhal (*nm*) a whisk/flapper made of peacock feathers.

मुरछा murchha: (*nf*) see मूर्च्छा.

मुरछाना murchha:nā: (*v*) to faint, to become unconscious/senseless.

मुरझाना murjha:nā: (*v*) to wither, to fade; to lose lustre; to become dejected/gloomy.

मुरत्तब murattab (*a*) duly arranged, systematically arranged.

मुरदा murda: (*nm*) a corpse, dead body; (*a*) dead, lifeless; devoid of verve; ~ख़ोर a corpse-eater; ~घर mortuary; ~दिल lifeless, devoid of verve, melancholy; ~दिली lifelessness; melancholia; dead, lifeless; devoid of vigour, verve or vitality; ~संख yellow orpiment; –उठाना to carry a corpse for cremation/burial; –कर देना to render lifeless (as मार-मार कर मुरदा कर देना to beat to death); –निकले may you die! (a term of abuse generally used by women); –होना to be lifeless; मुरदे की नींद सोना or मुरदे से शर्त बाँध/लगाकर सोना to go into a sleep as if never to awake, to go into a deep carefree sleep; मुरदे को जिंदा करना/जिलाना, मुरदे में जान डाल देना to infuse life in the dead, to fill a lifeless person with enthusiasm.

मुरब्बा murabba: (*nm*) jam; conserve; a square; ~फ़रोश a jam-dealer.

मुरमुरा murmura: (*nm*) parched and puffed rice.

मुरलिका muralika: (*nf*) see मुरली.

मुरली murli: (*nf*) flute, pipe; ~धर a flute-player, piper; an epithet of Lord Krishnā; ~ मनोहर Lord Krishnā.

मुरव्व/त muravvat (*nf*) considerateness; gentility; obligingness; benevolent politeness; affability; ~ती considerate, obliging, gentle; benevolently polite; affable.

मुरशिद murshid (*nm*) a spiritual guide, preceptor.

मुराद mura:d (*nf*) desire, wish; longing, craving; –पाना/बर आना a longing to be fulfilled; मुरादों के दिन youthful days.

मुरारि mura:ri (*nm*) an epithet of Lord Krishnā; also मुरारी.

मुरीद muri:d (*nm*) a follower, disciple.

मुरेठा muretha: (*nm*) a turban.

मुरौव/त murauwwat (*nf*) see मुरव्वत; ~ती see मुरव्वती (under मुरव्वत).

मुर्ग़ murg (*nm*) a cock; –**मुसल्लम** the whole roasted hen/chicken (for a dish).

मुर्ग़ा murga: (*nm*) a cock; fowl; rooster; – **छोटा** cockerel; –, **पालतू** a leghorn; – **बधिया** capon; hence **मुर्ग़ी**–a hen.

मुर्ग़ाबी murga:bi: (*nf*) a guinea-hen.

मुर्चा murcha: (*nm*) rust; –**लगना** to rust.

मुर्दनी murdanī: (*nf*) deathly stillness; mournfulness, melancholy; –**छाना** a melancholy heaviness to dawn on (the atmosphere, face, etc.), to be overwhelmed by melancholia.

मुर्दा murda: (*nm*) see **मुरदा**.

मुर्दार murda:r (*a*) near-dead, lifeless.

मुर्री murri: (*nf*) the rolled portion of a *dhoti*: on the waist; twisted ends of threads to be joined together.

मुर्शिद murshid (*nm*) see **मुरशिद**.

मुलज़िम mulzim (*nm*) an accused.

मुलतवी multawi: (*a*) see **मुल्तवी**.

मुलतानी multa:nī: (*a*) of or belonging to Multan (a West Punjab town now in Pakistan); (*nm*) an inhabitant of Multan; (*nf*) a dialect of Western Punjabi:; –**मिट्टी** a kind of soft clay.

मुलम्मा mulammā: (*nm*) gilding, plating; coating; external show, ostentation;~**कार** a gilder;~**कारी** gilding; ~**गर/साज** a gilder; plater; –**उतारना** to take the gilt off the ginger-bread; –**चढ़ाना** to gild, to plate; to make showy.

मुलहठी mulehṭhi: (*nf*) liquorice.

मुलाक़ा/त mula:qa:t (*nf*) meeting, visit; interview; acquaintance; ~**ती** a visitor; an acquaintance.

मुलाज़मत mula:zmāt (*nf*) employment, service.

मुलाज़िम mula:zim (*nm*) an employee; servant.

मुलाय/म mula:yam (*a*) soft, tender; gentle;~**म करना** to soften;~**मियत** softness; tenderness; gentleness.

मुलाह(हि)ज़ा mula:ha(hi)za: (*nm*) seeing, having a look; regard, consideration; –**करना** to be so good as to see/have a look at; to be considerate, to be soft;–**फ़रमाना** to be so gracious as to see/view/look at.

मुलेठी mulethi: (*nf*) see **मुलहठी**.

मु/ल्क mulk (*nm*) a country;~**ल्की** belonging or pertaining to the/a country.

मुल्तवी multawi: (*a*) postponed; adjourned.

मुल्ला mulla: (*nm*) a Muslim priest; a Muslim teacher of the Qora:n; –**की दौड़ मस्जिद तक** a priest goes no farther than the Church.

मुवक्क(क्कि)ल muwakka(kki)l (*nm*) client (of a pleader).

मुशायरा musha:yra: (*nm*) a poetic symposium.

मुश्क mushk (*nm*) musk; (*nf*) the arm; **मुश्कें बाँधना** to pinion, to tie up one's arm(s) on the back.

मुश्किल mushkil (*a*) difficult, hard; intricate; (*nf*) difficulty, hardship; –**में पड़ना** to get into a difficulty; **मुश्किलों में होना** to be hard put to it.

मुश्की mushki: (*a*) musky, black..

मुश्त musht (*nm*) a fist; ~, **एक** in a lump sum; in one lot.

मुश्तर/क mushtarak (*a*) undivided; joint, combined; ~**का** see **मुश्तरक**; ~**ख़ानदान** joint family; ~**का जायदाद** joint property.

मुष्टि mushti (*nf*) a fist; fist-blow; also ~**का**; -**प्रहार** a fist-blow; -**युद्ध**

boxing, pugilism,

मुसक(कु)रा/ना muska(ku)ra:nā: (*v*) to smile; ~हट a smile.

मुसकान muska:n (*nf*) a smile.

मुसकाना muska:nā: (*a*) see **मुसकराना**.

मुसन्ना musannā: (*nm*) a counterfoil; duplicate; copy.

मुसन्निफ़ musannif (*nm*) a writer; an author (of a book).

मुसब्बर musabbar (*nm*) aloes.

मुसम्मात musammā:t (*nf*) a woman; widow; (*a*) an honorofic affixed to the name of a woman; named (used for women only).

मुसलमा/न musalmā:n (*nm* and *a*) a Mohammedan; Muslim; ~नी Muslim; a Muslim woman.

मुसलिम muslim (*nm* and *a*) see **मुसलमान**.

मुसल्लम musallam (*a*) whole, complete, entire.

मुसलसल musalsal (*a*) continuously, without break.

मुसव्वि/र musavvir (*nm*) a painter, an artist; ~री the profession of a **मुसव्विर**, painting.

मुसाफ़िर musa:fir (*nm*) a traveller, wayfarer; passenger; ~ख़ाना a waiting room (at a railway station or bus station); –गाड़ी a passenger train.

मुसाहि/ब musa:hib (*nm*) one meant chiefly to provide a company; flunkey, sycophant; ~बी flunkeyism; sycophancy.

मुसीबत musi:bat (*nf*) difficulty, disaster, affliction; misfortune, calamity; ~ज़दा, –का मारा afflicted, struck by misfortune/calamity; –का सामना करना to take the bull by the horns; –के दिन hard days, calamitous days; –खड़ी करना to cause a difficulty; –झलना to bite on the bridles; –झेलना, हँसते-हँसते to make the best of a bad bargain; –में होना to be in hot waters; –मोल लेना to burn one's finger, to ride for a fall; मुसीबतों का पहाड़ टूट पड़ना a series of calamitics to befall; मुसीबतों से जूझते रहना to pull the devil by the tail.

मुस्क(कु)रा/ना muska(ku)ra:nā: (*v*) see **मुसकराना**.

मुस्कान muska:n (*nf*) see **मुसकान**.

मुस्टंडा mustaṇḍa: (*a*) stout-bodied, robust; rough and robust; hence ~पन (*nm*).

मुस्तक़बिल mustaqbil (*nm* and *a*) future.

मुस्तक़िल mustaqil (*a*) permanent; confirmed; fixed; settled; –जगह permanent job; –मिज़ाज poised, composed; unwavering.

मुस्तनद mustanad (*a*) authoritative; standard; trustworthy.

मुस्तै/द mustaid (*a*) agile, vigilant; ready, active;~दी agility, vigilance, readiness; ०से promptly, with agility.

मुहतर/म muhtaram (*a*) honourable, respectful, respected; hence ~मा feminine form.

मुहताज muhta:j (*a*) dependent on, needy, necessitous, poor; मुहताजी poverty, indigence; –करना to impoverish, to render indigent; –होना to be in utter poverty, to be indigent.

मुहब्ब/त muhabbat (*nf*) love; affection; fondness; ~ती loving, affectionate.

मुहय्या muhayya: (*a*) see **मुहैया**.

मुहर muhar (*nf*) seal; stamp; a gold coin; ~बंद sealed; –लगाना to stamp; to seal.

मुहरा muhra: (*nm*) the front-part; face, countenance; a pawn or piece of chess; vanguard.

मुहरी muhri: (*nf*) see **मोहरी.**

मुहर्र/म muharram (*nm*) the day of Imam Hussain's martyrdom which is held sacred by Mohammedans and celebrated as a day of mourning; ~**मी** melancholy, gloomy, dismal; o **सूरत** gloomy look, melancholy countenance; a face as long as fiddle.

मुहर्रि/र muharrir (*nm*) a scribe; clerk; ~**री** work or profession of a मुहर्रिर.

मुहलत muhlat (*nf*) period of grace; span of extra time (to do a thing or to get ready); **–के दिन** period of grace.

मुह/ल्ला muhalla: (*nm*) a locality/ward/street (in a city or town); ~**ल्ला-टोला** locality; ~**ल्लेदारी** mutual good relations (as between people of the same locality).

मुहाना muha:nā: (*nm*) estuary, source or mouth of a river.

मुहाफ़िज़ muha:fiz (*nm*) protector; guardian.

मुहार muha:r (*nf*) facade.

मुहाल muha:l (*a*) difficult; impossible; (*nf*) facade.

मुहाव/रा muha:vra: (*nm*) idiom; expression; practice, habit; ~**रेदार** idiomatic; o **भाषा** idiomatic language.

मुहिम muhim (*nf*) an expedition, campaign; an arduous task; **–पर जाना** to undertake an expedition; to take up an arduous task; **–सर करना** to accomplish a difficult job; to successfully complete an expedition, to score a victory.

मुहूर्त muhu:rt (*nm*) an auspicious moment (to commence or undertake a work); a moment of future possibilities; **–निकलना** see **–बीतना**; **–निकालना** to calculate and find out an auspicious/lucky moment (for undertaking any work); **–बीतना** the auspicious moment to pass.

मुहैया muhaiyya: (*a*) available; procured; **–करना** to make available; **–होना** to be available.

मुह्यमान muhyamā:n (*a*) heading towards unconsciousness, growing senseless.

मूँग mū:g (*nf*) green lentil; **–की दाल** pulse of green lentil; **–खाने वाला** a weakling, a timid man.

मूँगफली mū:gphali: (*nf*) ground-nut.

मूँगा mū:ga: (*nm*) coral.

मूँगिया mū:giya: (*a*) of dark-green colour.

मूँछ mū:chh (*nf*) moustaches; whiskers; **–उखाड़ना** to humiliate, to knock off one's pride; to outmanoeuvre; **–ऊँची होना** the head to be raised high, to feel proud of; **–ऐंठना** see **–पर ताव देना**; **–टेना** see **–पर ताव देना**; **–नीची होना** to suffer humiliation, to be disgraced; **–पर ताव देना** to be on the top of the world; to twist one's moustaches out of haughtiness/pride; to be safe and secure; to care for nothing in the world; **–मुँडाना** to concede victory, to concede superiority to the other party; to get the moustaches shaven as a confession of defeat; **मूँछें तानकर** proudly, arrogantly, with an air of arrogance; **मूँछों की लाज रखना** to vindicate the honour of one's manhood.

मूँछी mū:chhi: (*nf*) a kind of gruel.

मूँज mū:j (*nf*) a kind of long reed used for making ropes etc.

मूँड़ mū:ṛ (*nm*) head; **–मारना** to tax one's brain; to exert; to try to explain something to a nitwit;

–मुंड़ाना to get the head shaven (esp. as a mark of adoption of ascetic life).

मूंड़न mū:ṛān (*nm*) see **मुंडन**.

मूंड(ड़)ना mū:d(ṛ)nā: (*v*). to shave; to shave the hair of the head; to fleece, to cheat; to initiate somebody into an ascetic life.

मूंदना mū:dnā: (*v*) to close, to shut; to cover/to hide.

मूक mū:k (*a*) dumb; mute, speechless; **–अभिनय** pantomime; **~ता** aphonia, dumbness; muteness, speechlessness; **–समर्थन** silent backing; **–स्वीकृति** tacit approval.

मूगरी mu:gri: (*nf*) see **मुंगरी**.

मूजिब mu:jib (*nm*) cause, reason; through; see **बमूजिब**.

मूजी mu:zi: (*a*) crudely stingy, miser, niggardly, close-fisted; **–का माल** a miser's money.

मूठ mū:ṭh (*nf*) a hilt; handle, haft; grip; knob; application of a sorcerer's spell; **–चलाना** to commit an act of sorcery, to practise sorcery; **–लगाना** to haft, to fix a handle.

मूढ़ mu:ṛh (*a*) stupid, foolish, imbecile, silly; infatuated; hence **~बुद्धि/मति** (*a*).

मूढ़ता mu:ṛhta: (*nf*) stupidity, foolishness, silliness, imbecility; infatuation; also **मूढ़त्व** (*nm*).

मूत mu:t (*nm*) urine, piss.

मूतना mu:tnā: (*v*) to piss, to make water, to pass urine.

मूत्र mu:ttr (*nm*) urine, piss; **-कृच्छ** painful discharge of urine–strangury; **-दोष** uranaemia; urinary trouble; **-धानी** urinal stall; **-नली** urinary duct; **-निरोध/रोध** ischuria; **-परीक्षा** urine test; **-मार्ग** urethra, ureter; **-विषयक** urinary; **-शूल** see **-कृच्छ**.

मूत्राशय/य mu:ttra:shay (*nm*) urinary bladder, vesica; **~यी** vesical.

मूरख mu:rakh (*a*) see **मूर्ख**.

मूरत mu:rat (*nf*) see **मूर्ति**.

मूर्ख mu:rkh (*a*) foolish, stupid, idiot, dullard, silly, dolt, booby; **~मंडली** an assembly of fools, a group of idiots; **–बनाना** to befool.

मूर्खता mu:rkhta: (*nf*), **मूर्खत्व** mu:rkhattv (*nm*) folly, foolishness, stupidity, idiocity, silliness; **~पूर्ण** foolish, silly, idiotic.

मूर्च्छन mu:rchhān (*nm*) fainting, swooning.

मूर्च्छना mu:rchhanā: (*nf*) cadence, modulation (in music); the scale obtained by a module shift within a gamut.

मूर्च्छा mu:rchha: (*nf*) fainting, swoon, fit state of unconsciousness, syncope; **–टूटना** to recover from unconsciousness, to come back to senses.

मूर्च्छित mu:rchhit (*a*) fainted, swooned; unconscious; **–अवस्था** swoon, state of unconsciousness.

मूर्त mu:rt (*a*) concrete; corporeal, tangible; solid; formal; **-अमूर्त** concrete and abstract; **~ता** concreteness, tangibility; **-विधान** objective correlative.

मूर्ति mu:rti (*nf*) an idol, statue; image; **-कला** sculpture; statuary; **~कार** sculptor; statuary; **~पूजक** an idolater; **-पूजन/पूजा** idolatry; **~भंजक** an iconoclast; **-भंजन** iconoclasm; **~विज्ञान** iconography; **-संग्रह** statuary; **–, लघु** statuette; **–तोड़ना** to indulge in iconoclasm; to shatter a statue/an image.

मूर्तिमान mu:rtimā:n (*a*) personified, incarnate.

मूर्द्धन्य mu:rdhanny (*a*) top-ranking, leading, pre-eminent (as **विद्वान**);

cerebral; –ध्वनि cerebral sound; मूर्धन्यीकरण cerebralisation; मूर्धन्यीकृत cerebralised.

मूर्द्धा mu:rdha: (*nm*) cerebrum, uppermost part of hard palate; head; the uppermost point.

मूल mu:l (*nm*) root; an edible tuber/root; principal (sum); origin, source; the nineteenth नक्षत्र; the original text (of a book etc.); (*a*) radical; original; essential, fundamental; basic; principal, chief; parent; –अर्थ the principal/chief meaning; –कारण the root cause; o होना to be at the bottom of, to be the root cause of; –ग्रंथ original book/work; source book/work; –ग्रह primary planet; ~च्छेद uprooting, eradication; hence ~च्छेदन; ~त: basically, fundamentally, primarily; essentially; –तत्त्व the essential / basic / main element; –त्वचा epiblema; –द्रव्य the principal; ~धन the principal; –पत्रक master sheet; master copy; –पाठ text, original text; –पुरुष the progenitor (of a race/family); –प्रकृति essential/fundamental/basic nature; ~भूत fundamental, essential, basic; original; –मंत्र the key-note; essence, essential element; –रूप prototype, archetype; –वंश racial origin; –व्याधि the real malady; –सिद्धांत fundamental/essential/basic principle; –स्थान the key-point; source point; original home/abode; –स्रोत main source, original source; –गँवाना to lose even the capital; –से ब्याज प्यारा होता है the lure of interest is more compelling than that of the principal itself.

मूलक mu:lak—a suffix which means based or depending on, growing or emanating/originating from (as ध्वनिमूलक, जातिमूलक).

मूलांग mu:lā:ṅg (*nm*) rhizoid.

मूलाधार mu:la:dha:r (*nm*) one of the six ganglions in the human body (according to हठयोग); also called मूलाधार चक्र.

मूली mu:li: (*nf*) radish; -गाजर समझना to consider (somebody) as of no consequence, to treat with contemptuous indignation.

मूल्य mu:ly (*nm*) the cost, price; worth; value; -तारतम्य hierarchy/system of values; -निर्धारण evaluation; assessment; ~रहित without cost; useless, worthless; of no value; ~वत्ता valuability; preciousness; ~वान valuable, costly, precious; -वृद्धि appreciation, rising of the price; -सूचक price-indicator; -सूचकांक price-index; -सूची price list; -स्तर price level; ~हीन worthless. useless; of no value/avail; hence ~हीनता (*nf*); -ह्रास depreciation; o निधि depreciation fund; –घटना/घटाना to devalue, to depreciate; –निर्धारित करना to assess the price/value.

मूल्यन mu:lyan (*nm*) valuation, evaluation, assessment,

मूल्यांकन mu:lyā:ṅkan (*nm*) assessment; evaluation/valuation.

मूल्यानुसार mu:lya:nusa:r (*a*) ad valorem.

मू/षक mū:shak (*nm*) a rat; hence ~षिका (*nf*).

मूस mu:s (*nm*) a rat: ~दानी a rat-trap.

मूसना mu:snā: (*v*) to steal; to fleece; to squeeze out; to wrinkle.

मूस/ल mu:sal (*nm*) a spigot; pounder; pestle; ~लचंद stout, sturdy (person); ~लों ढोल बजाना to be extremely happy; ~लचंद, दाल

भात में a wrong man in a wrong place, an intruder.

मूसलाधार mu:sla:dha:r (*a*) heavy (rain), torrential; –वर्षा heavy rain, heavy downpour.

मूसली mu:sli: (*nf*) a small pestle; a medicinal plant, its root.

मूसा mu:sa: (*nm*) a rat; the founder of Jewish religion; ~ई a jew.

मूसी/क़ी mu:si:qi: (*nf*) music, art/science of music; ~क़ार a musician.

मृग mrig (*nm*) a deer; ~चर्म/छाला deer-skin; ~छौना/शावक a fawn, young one of a deer; ~जल/-तृष्णा/-मरीचिका mirage; delusion; Jack o'lantern; ~धर the moon; ~नयनी/लोचनी deer-eyed; having beautiful eyes like those of a deer; ~नाभ/नाभि musk; ~राज a lion; ~शिरा one of the twenty-seven नक्षत्रs—orion.

मृगया mrigaya: (*nf*) hunting.

मृगांक mrigā:nk (*nm*) the moon.

मृगाक्षी mriga:kshi: (*a*) deer-eyed (woman).

मृगी mrigi: (*nf*) a hind.

मृगेंद्र mrigendr (*nm*) a lion.

मृणाल mrina:l (*nm*) the root of a lotus plant; lotus-stalk.

मृणालिनी mrinā:linī: (*nf*) a lotus-plant; lotus.

मृण्मय mrīnmay (*a*) earthly, clayey; hence ~ता (*nf*).

मण्मूर्ति mrīnmu:rti (*nf*) a clayey idol, clay model.

मृत mrit (*a*) dead; extinct; ~जात still-born; ~संजीवनी (बूटी) the mythological herb that restores the dead to life; anything that infuses new life.

मृतक mritak (*nm*) a dead body, corpse; –कर्म death rituals, last rites.

मृतोत्थान mritotthā:n (*nm*) resurrection.

मृतोपजी/विता mritopji:vita: (*nf*) saprophytism; ~वी saprophagous.

मृत्तिका mrittika: (*nf*) earth; clay; –उद्योग ceramic industry.

मृत्युंज/य mrittyūnjay (*nm*) one who has conquered death; (*a*) immortal, deathless; an epithet of Lord Shiv; hence ~यी (*a*).

मृत्यु mrittyu (*nf*) death, demise; mortality/fatality; the end; ~कर deadly, fatal; -कर death-duty; -काल time of death; -गीत an epicedium; -दंड capital punishment; -दर death-rate, rate of mortality; -भय/भीति death-scare; ~भीत scared of death; -मुख the jaws of death; o में in the jaws of death; -लोक the mortal world; the earth, this world; ~शय्या death-bed; o पर पड़ा होना to be on the death-bed; -शोक bereavement, mourning; -संख्या mortality, fatality; -समाचार obituary.

मृदं/ग mridāng (*nf*) a drum-like Indian musical percussion instrument; ~गिया one who plays on a मृदंग.

मृदु mridu (*a*) soft; sweet; tender; gentle, mellow, mild; slow (as गति); ~कर that which softens/mellows; ~करण tempering, softening; ~ता softness; sweetness; mildness, gentleness; tenderness; mellowness; ~भाषी soft-spoken; –रेचक laxative; –वात slow and mild breeze.

मृदुल mridul (*a*) soft; sweet; tender; gentle, mild; ~ता softness; sweetness; mildness; ~हृदय tender-hearted, gentle.

मृषा mrisha: (*a*) false, untrue; (*adv*) falsely; uselessly; in vain; –ज्ञान illusion, false knowledge; ~त्व

falseness; untruth; ~भाषी/वादी a liar.

में mē (*ind*) in; into; among; between; at; on, of; –से out of; from.

मेंगनी mēgnī: (*nf*) orbicular dung balls of sheep/goat/camel etc.

मेंड, ~ड़ mēḍ, ~ṛ (*nf*) see मेड़.

मेंढक mēḍhak (*nm*) a frog; toad; hence मेंढकी (*nf*); o को जुकाम होना to take to queer ways; an improbable phenomenon to take place.

मेंब/र mēmbar (*nm*) a member; ~री membership.

में-में mēmē (*nf*) bleating (of sheep/goat); –करना to bleat; not to speak distinctly; to speak meekly.

मेंह mēh (*nm*) rain; –बरसना to rain.

मेंहदी mēhdi: (*nf*) myrtle (the leaves of this shrub are powdered and the powder when soaked in water over a period leaves red stain on application on the palms, feet etc. and is used as such by Indian women); –रचाना to decorate the palms and feet with myrtle powder; to walk too slow (like a woman).

मेख mekh(*nm*) a ram; the first sign of the zodiac—Aries.

मेख़ mekḥ (*nf*) a nail, peg.

मेखला mekhla: (*nf*) a girdle; zone, range.

मेघ megh (*nm*) a cloud; a typical musical mode associated with rains; -गर्जन/गर्जना/घोष/नाद/निर्घोष/रव thunder; -घटा dark black clouds; -जाल formation of clouds; -धनुष a rainbow; ~मंडल the sky; ~माला an accumulation of clouds; ~राज an epithet of Lord Indra; ~वर्ण cloud-coloured; also ~वर्णी (*a*).

मेघा megha: (*nm*) a cloud; frog.

मेघाच्छन्न megha:chhann (*a*) cloudy, covered/overcast with clouds.

मेघाडंबर meghaḍāmbar (*nm*) thunder of the clouds.

मेघालय megha:lay (*nm*) an eastern state of the Union of India.

मेज़ mez (*nf*) a table; ~पोश a table cloth, table cover.

मेज़/बान mezbā:n (*nm*) a host; ~बानी playing the host, acting as the host.

मेजर mejar (*nm*) a major (in the army); –जनरल a major-general.

मेट meṭ (*nm*) a foreman (of labourers).

मेटा meṭa: (*nm*) an earthen pot.

मेटिया meṭiya: (*nf*) a small earthen pot.

मेठ meṭḥ (*nm*) see मेट.

मेड़ meṛ (*nf*) a list; boundary-wall between two fields or beds; field-ridge; ~बंदी listing; hedging.

मेडल medal (*nm*) a medal.

मेढ़ा meṛha: (*nm*) a ram, tud; ~सिंगी a medicinal creeper.

मेथी methi: (*nf*) (the plant) finugreek.

मेदा meda: (*nm*) the stomach.

मेदिनी medinī: (*nf*) the earth.

मेध medh (*nm*) a sacrifice; killing.

मेधा medha: (*nf*) intellect, brilliance, mental sharpness.

मेधा/वान, ~वी medha:vā:n, ~vi: (*a*) intelligent, brilliant, sharp-witted.

मेम mēm (*nf*) madam; European lady; –साहब/साहिबा lady, madam.

मेमना mēmnā: (*nm*) a lamb; lambkin.

मेमार mēma:r (*nm*) mason; one who constructs.

मेय mey (*a*) measurable; ~ता measurability.

मेयर meyar (*nm*) a mayor.

मे/रा mera: (*pro*) my, mine; hence

~री (feminine form); मेरे मन कछु और है कर्त्ता के कछु और man proposes, God disposes.

मेरु meru (*nm*) a mythological mountain supposed to be of gold; also called सुमेरु.

मेरुदंड merudāṇḍ (*nm*) spine, backbone; spinal column; ~हीन without backbone; wavering (man).

मेल mel (*nm*) concord; consonance, agreement; match; mixture, combination; unity; conciliation; connection; mail train; –का matching; -जोल/मिलाप intimacy; reconciliation, rapprochement; union; –गाड़ी a mail train; -मुलाक़ात approach; association, friendly relationship; -मोहब्बत mutual goodwill / affection; –खाना to match; to be in agreement.

मेला mela: (*nm*) a fair; festival crowd; -ठेला fanfare, hustle and bustle, crowd and confusion; –उठना festivities to come to an end; –, चार दिन का a short-lived attraction.

मेली meli: (*nm*) a friend, an associate; -मुलाक़ाती friends and comrades, companions.

मेवा mewa: (*nm*) dry fruit; ~फ़रोश dry fruit-dealer.

मेवाड़ी mewa:ṛi: (*nf*) a dialect of Hindi spoken in Mewa:ṛ (Ra:jastha:n).

मेवाती mewa:ti: (*nf*) a dialect of Hindi spoken in Mewa:t (Ra:jastha:n).

मेष mesh (*nm*) Aries—the first sign of the zodiac; a ram; –संक्रांति the day when the sun crosses into the mansion of Aries.

मेस mes (*nm*) a mess.

मेह meh (*nm*) rain; rainfall; diabetes (in मधुमेह).

मेहत/र mehtar (*nm*) a sweeper, scavenger; ~रानी sweepress; wife of a sweeper.

मेहनत mehnāt (*nf*) labour, industry, hard work, toil; exercise; ~कश a labourer; -मजदूरी toil and labour; –की रोटी hard-earned bread; –ठिकाने लगना hard work to bear fruit.

मेहनताना mehanta:nā: (*nm*) remuneration (as to a lawyer); wages.

मेहनती mehnāti: (*a*) laborious, industrious, hard working, diligent.

मेहमान mehmā:n (*nm*) a guest; ~खाना a guest house; ~दार a host; ~दारी playing as the host; hospitality; ~नवाज़ hospitable; ~नवाज़ी hospitality.

मेहमानी mehmā:nī: (*nf*) staying as guest, enjoying hospitality (of).

मेहर mehar (*nf*) kindness, compassion; (*nm*) security money in cash or kind customarily paid by the husband to the wife in Muslim marriages; ~बान kind, compassionate; ~बानी (act of) kindness; favour.

मेहरा mehra: (*nm*) an effeminate man; a household utensil cleaner.

मेहराब mehra:b (*nf*) an arch; vault; ~दार/मेहराबी arched, vaulted; ० छत an arched roof, vault.

मेहरारू mehra:ru: (*nf*) a woman; wife.

मेहरी mehri: (*nf*) a woman who works as household utensil cleaner.

मैं maī (*pro*) I; –खुद/स्वयं I myself.

मैका maika: (*nm*) see मायका.

मैगज़ीन maigzi:n (*nf*) a magazine.

मैच maich (*nm*) a match.

मैजिक maijik (*nm*) magic.

मैत्री maittri: (*nf*) friendship, cordiality.

मैथिली maithili: (*nf*) a dialect of Hindi spoken in Mithila: (Biha:r).

मैथुन maithun (*nm*) coitus, cohabitation, sexual/carnal intercourse, copulation; (*a*) pertaining to a couple; **–विषयक/संबंधी** sexual, copulatory.

मैदा maida: (*nm*) very fine wheat-flour.

मैदान maidā:n (*nm*) a field; battle-field; plains; **मैदाने-जंग** a battle-field; **–खाली करना** to leave the battlefield; **–छोड़ देना** to throw up one's cards, to chuck/throw up the sponge, to show the white feather; **–जाना** to go to ease, to go to answer the call of nature; **–जीतना/मारना/सर करना/हाथ रहना** to score a victory, to carry the day, to hold the field; **–बदना** to fix an encounter, to settle a date and time for trial of strength; **–में आना/उतरना** to enter into the battlefield/arena, to be ready for a fight; to throw one's hat into the ring, to take the field; **–में डटे रहना** to keep the field, to continue the campaign; **–साफ़ कर देना** to clear all obstacles; to kill or rout all the adversaries.

मैदानी maida:nī: (*a*) pertaining to plains; even.

मैनफल maīnphal (*nm*) the fruit of the prickly plant *Vangeoria spinosa*.

मैनसिल maīnsil (*nf*) red arsenic, realgar.

मैना maīnā: (*nf*) a black Indian bird famous for its melodious notes.

मैनेजर maīnejar (*nm*) a manager.

मैयत maiyat (*nf*) dead body, corpse; last rites; **–उठना** the dead body to be removed (for last rites).

मैया maiya: (*nf*) mother.

मैल mail (*nf*) dirt, filth; scum; **~खोर/खोरा** dust-absorbing (as रंग, कपड़ा); **–काटना** to clean, to counter (as साबुन मैल काटता है).

मैला maila: (*a*) dirty, filthy; unclean; foul; (*nm*) excrement, faeces; **-कुचैला** dirty and defiled, dirty and filthy; very dirty; **~पन** filthiness, dirtiness.

मोंगरा mōgra: (*nm*) see **मुँगरा**.

मोढ़ा mōṛha: (*nm*) a stool made of reeds.

मोक्ष moksh (*nm*) salvation, deliverance, final liberation; **~दात्री/दायिनी** she who brings or grants salvation/deliverance/final liberation; **-साधन** means of salvation/deliverance/ final liberation.

मोखा mokha: (*nm*) a scuttle, an aperture/opening.

मोगरा mogra: (*nm*) maul; see **मुँगरा**.

मोघ mogh (*a*) infructuous; ineffective.

मोच mōch (*nf*) sprain; twist;**–आना/खाना** to be sprained.

मोचन mochan (*nm*) riddance; liberation, salvation, deliverance; release; as a suffix it means one who causes riddance/liberation (from)–as **संकटमोचन, भवमोचन** etc.

मोची mochi: (*nm*) a shoe-maker cobbler.

मोजा moza: (*nm*) socks; stocking.

मोट moṭ (*nf*) a bundle; large leathern bucket for drawing huge quantities of water out of a well

मोटर moṭar (*nf*) a motor-car

motor; ~कार a motor-car; ~खाना a motor-garrage; -ड्राइवर a motor-car driver; chauffeur; ~बोट a motor-boat; -साइकिल a motor-bicycle.

मोटरी motri: (*nf*) a bundle.

मोटा moṭa: (*a*) fat, plump; corpulent; thick; coarse, rough; gross; —अंदाज़ rough estimate; —अनाज millets; -आसामी a moneyed man; ~ई fatness, plumpness, corpulence; thickness; coarseness, roughness; grossness; —काम manual work, mechanical work, a work that does not require much intelligence; -झोटा rough, coarse; gross, inferior; -ताज़ा chubby, fleshy; robust; मोटी अकल/बुद्धि/समझ blunt head, dull brain; ०का a nitwit, stupid; मोटी आवाज़ hoarse and heavy voice; मोटी आमदनी fat/handsome income; मोटी तनख्वाह fat/handsome/salary; मोटी बात plain talk, an utterance that has no subtlety; मोटी-मोटी बातें main features; मोटी रक़म a substantial amount; मोटे तौर पर roughly speaking; मोटेमल a a corpulent/plump person; मोटे हिसाब से roughly, approximately, according to rough estimates; —खाना/पहनना to have a low standard of living.

मोटाई moṭa:i: (*nf*) see under मोटा.

मोटाना moṭa:nā:(*v*)to fatten, to grow fat/plump/fleshy; to grow wealthy.

मोटापा moṭa:pa: (*nm*) fatness, plumpness, fleshiness, corpulence.

मोठ moṭh (*nf*) a kind of grain in lentils.

मोड़ moṛ (*nm*) a turn; turning point; folds; bend; twist; orientation; -तोड़ turn and twist, distortion.

मोड़ना moṛnā: (*v*) to turn; to turn back or in another direction; to bend; to fold; to reorientate.

मोतदिल motdil (*a*) moderate, temperate (as आबहवा).

मोतबर motbar (*a*) reliable, credible, trustworthy.

मोतिया motiya: (*nm*) a kind of jasmine flower; (*a*) pearl-coloured.

मोतियाबिंद motiya:bīnd (*nm*) cataract (formed in the eye).

मोती moti: (*nm*) pearl; —की सी आब pearly lustre; ~चूर very tiny sweetened balls of gram flour from which लड्डू is prepared; ~झरा typhoid; —पिरोना to string pearls together; to write distinctly and beautifully; —भरना to embellish a woman's head with stringed pearls; to amass a fortune without toil; to give a rich and auspicious make-up; —से मुँह भरना to bestow infinite riches on one who brings good news.

मोथरा mothra: (*a*) blunt, blunt-edged, dull; hence ~पन (*nm*).

मोद mod (*nm*) delight, happiness.

मोदक modak (*nm*) a typical indigenous sweetmeat;–see लड्डू.

मोदी modi: (*nm*) a grocer; ~खाना a provision store.

मोना monā: (*a*) clean-shaven (person).

मोनोग्राम monōgra:m (*nm*) a monogram.

मोनो/मशीन monōmashī:n (*nf*) a monotype printing machine;–टाइप monotype.

मोम mōm (*nf*) wax; ~जामा oil-cloth, oil-skins; tarpaulin; ~दिल soft-hearted, compassionate; ~बत्ती a candle-stick; —की नाक a rolling stone, fidgety or fickle-minded person; ~की मरियम very tender woman; —होना to soften, to be moved by compassion.

मोमिया mōmiyā: (*nf*) a mummy; preserving mixture; (*a*) wax, made of wax, wax-like; **–काग़ज़** tracing paper.

मोमी mōmī: (*a*) made of wax; wax; **–काग़ज़** tracing paper; **–मोती** an artificial pearl.

मोयन moyan (*nm*) (the mixing of) *ghee* in kneaded flour to impart extra-softness to the ultimate preparation; **~दार** containing **मोयन**.

मोर mor (*nm*) a peacock; **~चंद्रिका** moon-like figure at the end of a peacock feather; **~छल** a whisk made of peacock feather; **~नी** a peahen; **~पंख** a peacock-feather; **~पंखी** of the colour of peacock-feather; **~मुकुट** a crown made of peacock feathers; pleasure-boat shaped on the pattern of peacock feathers.

मोरचा morcha: (*nm*) a battle-front, front; rust (also **मुर्चा**); **~बंदी** stratagem, battle-array, taking up strategic positions; **–खाना** to be rusted; **–थामना** to keep the front; **–बाँधना** to array, to take up strategic positions; **–मारना/लेना** to achieve victory on a front.

मोरनी mornī: (*nf*) see under **मोर**.

मोरी mori: (*nf*) a culvert; drain, sewer, conduit; drain-hole; **–के रास्ते जाना** to go down the drain.

मोर्चा morcha: (*nm*) see **मोरचा**.

मोल mol (*nm*) cost, price; **-तोल/भाव** higgling, chaffering; bargaining; **–करना** to higgle, to chaffer; to bargain; **–का** bought, purchased; **–बढ़ाना** to raise the price; **–लेना** to buy, to purchase.

मोह moh (*nm*) illusion; ignorance; affection; infatuation; fascination; spell; **-निद्रा** a slumber steeped in ignorance; **~पाश** the snare of worldly illusion; **~भंग** disillusionment; **-ममता** affection and attachment.

मोहक mohak (*a*) charming, fascinating, casting a spell, causing illusion; hence **~ता** (*nf*).

मोहताज mohta:j (*a*) see **मुहताज**; **~ख़ाना** a work-house.

मोहन mohan (*a*) charming, attractive; tempting; (*nm*) enchantment; charm, *mantra* employed for purposes of sorcery; an epithet of Lord Krishnā; **~भोग** a special type of **हलवा**; **~माला** a garland made of beads.

मोहना mohnā: (*v*) to cast a spell, to charm, to attract; to tempt; to infatuate.

मोहनी mohnī: (*nf*) a spell, enchantment; delusion; **–डालना** to cast a spell, to bewitch.

मोहब्ब/त mohabbat (*nf*) see **मुहब्बत**; **~ती** see **मुहब्बती** under **मुहब्बत**.

मोहर mohar (*nf*) a stamp, seal; a guinea, gold coin; **–लगाना** to stamp, to put a seal.

मोहरा mohra: (*nm*) the mouth (of a pot, etc.), opening, facing; fascia; fore-end, stock; a pawn in chess, chessman

मोहरी mohri: (*nf*) the circumference of each of the lower openings of a trousers or pants.

मोहर्रिर moharrir (*nm*) see **मुहर्रिर**

मोहलत mohlat (*nf*) see **मुहलत**.

मोहल्ला mohalla: (*nm*) a locality, ward, street.

मोहित mohit (*a*) charmed, attracted, enchanted, spell-bound; fallen in love.

मोहिनी mohinī: (*a*) who tempts/charms / attracts / casts a spell (feminine adjectival form); (*nf*) see मोहनी.

मौक़ा mauqa: (*nm*) chance; occasion; location; situation: site, work-site, site of occurrence; **मौक़े-बेमौक़े** any and every time; without considering whether the time is appropriate or not; in times of crisis/need; **–गँवा बठना** to miss the bus; **–तकना/देखना** to wait for a proper occasion/opportunity, to lie in ambush; **–देना** to give a chance; to give a handle to; **–शर्त है** if there is a chance..., if the situation permits...; **–हाथ लगना** to have the ball at one's feet, to have an opportunity; **मौक़े की ताक में रहना** to play a waiting game, to lie in ambush; **मौक़े पर** at the appropriate time, on the spot; **मौक़े से** duly, just in time.

मौखिक maukhik (*a*) verbal, oral; **–परीक्षा** viva-voce (test); **–रूप से** verbally; **– साक्ष्य** testimony.

मौखिकी maukhiki: (*nf*) viva-voce, oral examination.

मौज mauj (*nf*) a whim, caprice; delight; luxury; a wave; **-मजा** enjoyment; **–मारना** to live in luxury or luxurious comfort; to have it easy; **–में** in full high feather, in good spirits; **–में आना** to be swayed off by a caprice, to be in an impulsive/mirthful mood.

मौजा mauza: (*nm*) a village.

मौजी mauji: (*a*) capricious, whimsical; merry, mirthful; **–जीव** a mirthful and whimsical person, capricious person.

मौजूं mauzū: (*a*) reasonable; befitting, suitable.

मौजूद mauju:d (*a*) present; existing; **~गी** presence; existence.

मौजूदा mauju:da: (*a*) current, present; **–जमाना** current times.

मौत maut (*nf*) death, demise; mortality; **–आना** the end to come; a mortal calamity to befall; **–का घर देख जाना/लेना** death to have known the road that leads to one's threshold; **–का शिकार होना** to fall a prey to death, to die; **–का सामना** face to face with death, being in the grip of a mortal crisis; **–का सिर पर खेलना** death to hover around the corner, **–की घड़ी** the moment of death, the end; **–के घाट उतारना** to put to death; **–के मुँह में कूदना/जाना** to risk one's life; to be in the cruel clutches of death; **–के मुँह से बचना** a close call; **–सिर पर खेलना/नाचना/मँडराना** death to stare in the face.

मौन maun (*a*) mum, quiet, quiescent, silent, speechless, mute; tacit; (*nm*) silence, quiescence; **-भंग** breaking the spell of silence; speaking out; **-मुद्रा** quiescence, adoption of silence; **-व्रत** a vow to keep quiet, to adopt silence; **~व्रती/व्रतधारी** one who has taken a vow for silence; **–सम्मति** tacit concurrence; **मौनं सम्मति लक्षणम्** quiescence reflects tacit concurrence, silence is half-consent; **–तोड़ना** to break a (prolonged) spell of silence, to break one's silence; **-लेना / –साधना** to observe silence, to take a vow to keep silence.

मौनी maunī: (*a*) under a vow not to speak, pledged to quiescence.

मौर maur (*nm*) a pyramid-like wickerwork crown worn by the bridegroom in traditional Indian marriage ceremonies, a crown; diadem; as an adjectival suffix it imparts the meaning of one that stands out as pre-eminent (as सिरमौर).

मौरूसी mauru:si: (*a*) hereditary, patrimonial; **–काश्तकार** hereditary cultivator/tenant.

मौर्ख्य maurkhy (*nm*) see **मूर्खता** (under **मूर्ख**).

मौलवी maulvi: (*nm*) a scholar of Islamic law, Arabic and Persian; an Arabic/Persian teacher; **~गिरी** the work or profession of a **मौलवी**.

मौलसिरी maulsiri: (*nf*) a perennially blooming tree yielding very fragrant small flowers – *Ninsops dengi*.

मौला maula: (*nm*) the Master; a typical carefree man with no encumbrances whatever; used as the second member in the compound **मस्त-मौला** meaning–a carefree man recognising no obligations.

मौलाना maula:nā: (*nm*) a title given to a great muslim scholar; a scholar of Arabic.

मौलि mauli (*nm*) the crown of the head, diadem; summit; (*a*) best, foremost, most outstanding.

मौलिक maulik (*a*) original; primordial; fundamental; essential; radical; **~ता** originality; **–लेखन** original writing; **–विज्ञान** fundamental science.

मौसंबी mausambi: (*nf*) a big-sized sweet variety of the citrus family.

मौसम mausam (*nm*) season; weather; opportune time; **–, बहार का** the spring season; **–विज्ञान/शास्त्र** meteorology; **~वैज्ञानिक** meteorological; a metereologist: **मौसमी** seasonal; see **मौसंबी**; **मौसमीपन** seasonability.

मौ/सा mausa: (*nm*) the husband of mother's sister; **~सी** mother's sister.

मौसेरा mausera: (*a*) related through or connected/concerned with or born of **मौसी**, (as **–भाई**); hence **मौसेरी**–feminine form.

म्याऊँ myā:ū: (*nf*) mewing (of a cat); **–का मुँह, –की ठौर** the cat's mouth; **० पकड़ना** to bell the cat, to face the real hazard; **–म्याऊँ करना** to speak in inarticulately hushed up tones (out of fear).

म्यान myā:n (*nf*) a sheath; **–में दो तलवारें नहीं रहतीं, एक** two bigs will not go in one bag; **–में रहना** to keep within bounds.

म्याना myā:nā: (*a* and *nm*) see **मियाना**.

म्यानी myā:nī: (*nf*) see **मियानी**.

म्युनिसिपल myunicipal (*a*) municipal; **–कमेटी** municipal committee; **–बोर्ड** municipal board.

म्यूज़ियम myu:ziyām (*nm*) a museum.

म्रियमाण mriyamā:n (*a*) moribund, on the verge of death, near dead, almost dead.

म्लान mlā:n (*a*) wilt, withered, faded; languid; **~ता** wilting, witheredness, fadedness; languor; **~मना** melancholy, gloomy, out of sorts.

म्लेच्छ mlechchh (*nm*) an alien (invader); a non-Aryan; (*a*) lowly; unclean, shabby; un-Indian (in a contemptuous sense); **–जाति** an alien race; **–भाषा** an alien language/speech; hence **~ता** (*nf*).

य

य ya—the first of the य, र, ल, व series of the Devna:gri: alphabet, traditionally called अंतःस्थ (semi-vowels). Modern Phoneticians, however, regard only य and व as semi-vowels.

यंत्र yāntr (*nm*) a machine; an instrument; amulet, talisman; mystical diagram; ~कार a machine-maker; ~चालित mechanized; machine-operated; ~निर्मित machine-made, mechanical; -मंत्र conjuring, witchcraft; ~मानव a robot; -युग machine age; ~वत् like a machine; ~वाद mechanistic theory; mechanism; ~वादी mechanistic; ~विद् a mechanician; machinist; -विद्या the art of manufacturing or handling/working machines; -विधान mechanism; ~शाला machine-room; -सज्जित mechanized.

यंत्रणा yāntranā: (*nf*) torture, torment.

यंत्रालय yāntra:lay (*nm*) a printing press; machine-room.

यंत्रित yāntrit (*a*) mechanized.

यंत्रीकरण yāntri:karān (*nm*) mechanization.

यक yak (*a*) one; alone; for other compound words like ~जान, ~तरफ़ा, -ब-यक, ~बारगी, ~मंज़िला, ~रंगा, ~सर, ~सार see 'एक' [and subsequent entries].

यकलख़्त yaklak̲h̲t (*adv*) suddenly, all of a sudden; quite.

यका/र yaka:r (*nm*) the letter य and its sound; ~रांत (word) ending in य्.

यक़ीन yaqī:n (*nm*) trust, faith, confidence; certainty; assurance; ~न certainly, surely; without fail; -आना to feel assured/confident, to have trust (in); -करना to trust/believe; -दिलाना to assure; -लाना to believe, to trust, to have faith in; -होना to be or feel confident, to have faith (in).

यक़ीनी yaqi:nī: (*a*) see यक़ीनन; -तौर पर surely, certainly, undoubtedly.

यकृत yakkrit (*nm*) the liver; -विषयक/संबंधी hepatic; -शोथ/-की सूजन hepatitis; यकृतीय hepatic.

यक्ष yaksh (*nm*) a class of mythological demi-gods; ~नायक/पति Kuber—the chief of yakshas and the god of wealth.

यक्षिणी yakshinī: (*nf*) fem. form of यक्ष (see); -सिद्ध करना to tame a यक्षिणी to acquire supernatural powers.

यक्ष्मा yakshmā: (*nm*) tuberculosis; ~ग्रस्त tubercular; suffering from tuberculosis.

यख़नी yak̲h̲nī: (*nf*) gravy, the strew extracted from meat.

यजन yajan (*nm*) the act or process of performing a sacrifice (यज्ञ).

यजमान yajmā:n (*nm*) one who performs a यज्ञ; client of a priest or of attendants (who do their chores on auspicious occasions or rituals. They are offered gratification, in cash or kind, for performance of rituals, sacrifice etc.).

यजमानी yajmā:nī: (*nf*) the work,

function or position of a यजमान; the habitat of a यजमान or of यजमानs collectively; the conventional right of a priest and others (like a washerman, barber, etc.) to perform their respective chores in rituals.

यजुर्वे/द yajurved (*nm*) the third of the four Vedas; ~दी an adherent/scholar of the यजुर्वेद.

यज्ञ yaggy (*nm*) sacrifice, an ancient Hindu institution of religious sacrifice and oblation; -कुंड fire pit for performance of a यज्ञ; -क्रिया the process of performing a यज्ञ; -दक्षिणा the gratification—in cash or kind—for the priest who performs a 'यज्ञ'; -पशु the animal to be sacrificed in a 'यज्ञ'; -भूमि the place of performance of a 'यज्ञ'; -मंडप the pavilion wherein a यज्ञ is performed; -वेदिका/वेदी the altar on which a 'यज्ञ' is performed; ~शाला the enclosure within which a 'यज्ञ' is performed; ~सूत्र see यज्ञोपवीत; -स्थाणु the pillar with which the 'यज्ञ'-पशु is tethered.

यज्ञीय yaggi:y (*a*) pertaining or belonging to or related with a 'यज्ञ'.

यज्ञोपवीत yaggyopavi:t (*nm*) the sacred thread traditionally worn by caste Hindus; one of the sixteen major संस्कारs (also called यज्ञोपवीत संस्कार) wherein a young lad is given a sacred thread to wear for the first time.

यति yati (*nf*) a pause, check, caesura (in metre); (*nm*) an ascetic, anchoret (who has subdued his passions); -गति (in metrical writing) pausing and pacing; -धर्म asceticism; renunciation; -भंग a metric flaw when caesura does not appear at its proper position; -भ्रष्ट (a metre) having -भंग (pausal defect).

यतीम yati:m (*nm* and *a*) (an) orphan; ~खाना an orphange.

यतीमी yati:mi: (*nf*) orphanage, the state of being an orphan.

यत्किंचित yatkiṇchit (*adv*) somewhat, a little, to a slight degree.

यत्न yatn (*nm*) effort, endeavour; attempt; care; ~पूर्वक with effort/attempt; with care; ~वती feminine form of ~वान; ~वान/शील making effort, effortive.

यत्र yatr (*adv*) where; -यत्र wherever; in whatever place; -तत्र here and there, hither and thither; ० सर्वत्र here, there and everywhere.

यथांश yathā:nsh (*a*) according to one's portion/quota; (*nm*) quota.

यथा yatha: (*adv*) as per; thus; for example, for instance; in whatever manner; ~कथित as mentioned before; ~कर्त्तव्य according to one's duty, as one's duty demands; ~कर्म according to one's deeds; ~काम as one likes/wishes; ~क्रम in order, systematically; successively, respectively; methodical, systematic, regular; ~तथ्य as it is, intact; exact, accurate; hence ~तथ्यता (*nf*); ~दृष्ट as seen; ~नियम as per rule; ~निर्दिष्ट as mentioned; as directed; ~नुक्रम in order, according to the order laid down; ~नुपान prorata; ~नुपूर्व according to tradition, conventional; ~पूर्व as before, status quo; ~पूर्व स्थिति status quo ante; ~पेक्ष adequately; as expected; ~प्रयोग as per usage/experiment; ~बुद्धि/मति according to (one's) understanding; ~भिप्रेत

as desired, as intended; ~भिमत as per one's liking/opinion; ~मूल्य ad valorem; ~योग्य suitably, properly; according as one deserves; ~रीति as per tradition, as usual; ~रुचि according to one's liking/taste; ~लाभ according to the profit, based on profit; ~वत् in situ, intact, as before; stet; ~वसर according to opportunity/time, as the occasion demands; ~विधि according to law/rule; systematic(ally); ~विहित as directed/prescribed; according as enjoined; ~शक्ति/शक्य as far as possible, according to one's power/capacity; ~शास्त्र according to the prescription of the शास्त्रs; as ordained/directed by the scriptures; ~शीघ्र as early/promptly as possible; ~संभव as far as possible; ~साध्य as far as practicable; according to one's power/capacity; ~समय in due course, at the proper time, when an opportunity comes; –सुविधा as convenient, according to convenience; ~स्थान at the proper place; ~स्थिति as the case may be, as the situation warrants; –राजा तथा प्रजा a good master makes a good servant, like ruler like ruled.

यथार्थ yatha:rth (*a*) real, actual; accurate; ~तः de facto, really, actually; factually; ~ता reality; accuracy; ~वाद realism; ~वादिता realism; reality; ~वादी a realist; realistic.

यथेच्छ yathechchh (*a* and *adv*) as one likes, according to one's wish/desire; arbitrary; –क्षेत्र arbitrary area.

यथेच्छाचा/र yathechchha:cha:r (*nm*) licentious/arbitrary conduct; licentiousness; absolutism; ~री licentious; one who acts or behaves as he pleases/in an arbitrary fashion.

यथेष्ट yatheshṭ (*a*) sufficient, enough; adequate; ~ता sufficiency; adequacy.

यथोक्त yathokt (*a*) as stated, as mentioned, as said earlier.

यथोचित yathochit (*a*) due; proper, appropriate, reasonable; rightful; (*adv*) duly; properly, reasonably; rightfully.

यथोपरि yathopari (*ind*) ditto, as above.

यदा yada: (*ind*) when; where; -कदा occasionally, sometimes.

यदि yadi (*ind*) if, in case, provided that.

यदु/नंदन, ~नाथ, ~पति, ~राज yadunāndan, ~na:th, ~pati, ~ra:j (*nm*) Lord Krishnā—the leading luminary of the Yadu clan.

यदृच्छ yadrichchh (*a*) arbitrary; random; ~या arbitrarily; at random.

यदृच्छा yaddrichchha: (*nf*) arbitrariness; randomness.

यद्यपि yaddyapi (*ind*) though, although, even though.

यम yam (*nm*) the god of death; restraint of passions; two; ~ज/जात twins; ~जित् one who conquers death, immortal; ~दंड the punishment inflicted by यम—the god of death (for evil deeds); ~दुतिया/द्वितीया the second day of the bright half of the month of कार्तिक (same as भैयादूज); ~दूत a messenger of the god of death; ~पुर/पुरी/लोक afterworld; the world of the god of death; the infernal world, the world where sinners are supposed to be lodged after death; o पहुँचाना to put to death; -यातना the pangs of death; ~ल twin; ~वाहन a he-buffalo.

यमक yamāk (*nm*) a particular word-based figure of speech, a kind of pun.

यमुना yamunā: (*nf*) one of the most important Indian rivers (considered to be sacred by the Hindus).

यव yav (*nm*) barley; ~क्षार nitrate of potash.

यवन yavan (*nm*) a Greek; a Mohammedan; hence यवनी (*nf*).

यवनिका yavanika: (*nf*) a curtain; drop-scene; -पतन drop curtain.

यशःकाय yashahka:y (*a*) who lives through his glory, living through glorious deeds.

यशःशरीर yashahshari:r (*a*) see यशःकाय.

यशःशेष yashahshesh (*a*) dead; one who is survived by his name and fame.

यश yash (*nm*) fame, reputation, renown, glory; -कमाना to earn name and fame; -गाना to sing the praises of; to eulogize, to extol; -लूटना to usurp fame, to acquire glory.

यश/स्वी yashassvi: (*a*) celebrated; reputed, renowned; glorious; hence ~स्विनी feminine form.

यशोगाथा yashoga:tha: (*nf*) a tale/narrative of glory or great deeds.

यशोगान yashoga:n (*nm*) encomium, eulogy, singing the praises (of).

यष्टि yashṭi (*nf*) a stick; rod.

यष्टिका yashṭika: (*nf*) see यष्टि.

यह yeh (*pro*) this; it;- मुँह और मसूर की दाल like lip, like lettuce.

यहाँ yaḥā: (*adv*) here, hither, in/at this place.

यहीं yahī: (*adv*) at this very place, here itself.

यही yahi: (*a*) this very.

यहू/दी yahu:di: (*nm*) a Jew; ~दिन (*nf*) a Jewish woman.

यांचा yā:ṇcha: (*nf*) a prayer, solicitation.

यांत्रि/क ya:ntrik (*a*) mechanical; (*nm*) a mechanist; ~क अवतारणा deus ex machina; ~कता mechanism, mechanicality; ~की mechanics; mechanism; ~कीकरण mechanization; ~कीकृत mechanized.

या ya: (*conj*) or, either;—इलाही/ख़ुदा Oh God!; My God!;—क़िस्मत what a luck/lot!

याचक ya:chak (*nm*) a beggar; suppliant; ~ता begging, the job of a beggar.

याचन ya:chan (*nm*) begging.

याचना ya:chanā: (*nf*) begging, entreaty; asking for something.

याचिका ya:chika: (*nf*) a petition; feminine form of याचक.

याचित ya:chit (*a*) begged (for), solicited, asked for, prayed for.

याजक ya:jak (*nm*) one who performs a 'यज्ञ'.

याज्ञिक yaggik (*nm*) one who performs a 'यज्ञ'; (*a*) pertaining to a sacrifice.

यातना ya:tnā: (*nf*) torture, torment.

यातायात ya:ta:ya:t (*nm*) traffic, coming and going;—जाम होना traffic to be jammed.

यात्रा ya:ttra: (*nf*) a journey, travel; wayfaring; trip; tour; pilgrimage; march; a kind of popular play prevalent in Bengal; -चित्र travelogue film; -वृत्त a travelogue.

यात्रिक ya:ttrik (*nm*) a traveller, wayfarer; passenger; pilgrim.

यात्री ya:ttri: (*nm*) a traveller, wayfarer; passenger; pilgrim.

याथातथ्य ya:tha:tatthy (*nm*) exactness, accuracy.

याद ya:d (*nf*) memory, recollection, remembrance; –आना to be haunted by the memory (of), to remember; –करना to memorise; to recall/remember; –दिलाना to remind; –फ़रमाना to (be gracious to) remember.

यादगा/र ya:dga:r (*nf*) a monument; memorial; memento; also ~री (*nf*).

याददाश्त ya:dda:sht (*nf*) memory.

याददेहानी ya:ddeha:nī: (*nf*) recollection, remembrance; reminding.

यादी ya:di: (*nf*) a memo.

यादृच्छि/क ya:ddrichchhik (*a*) random; arbitrary; ~कता arbitrariness; randomness; ~कीकरण randomization; making arbitrary.

यान yā:n (*nm*) a van; vehicle.

या/नी,~ने yā:nī:; ~ने (*ind*) that is, that is to say.

यापन ya:pan (*nm*) spending, passing away (it generally appears as the second member in compound words, as जीवनयापन).

याफ़्ता ya:fta:—a suffix used to denote one who has been awarded/given (as सजायाफ़्ता; सनदयाफ़्ता),

याम ya:m (*nm*) three hours' time.

यामिनी ya:mīnī: (*nf*) the night.

याम्योत्तर ya:myottar (*a*) meridian; –रेखा meridian line; equatorial line.

यायाव/र ya:ya:var (*nm*) a nomad; wanderer; ~री-वृत्ति wandering spirit, instinct to go round.

यार ya:r (*nm*) a friend, companion; paramour, lover; ~बाश a friend of friends, good companion; hence ~बाशी (*nf*).

याराना ya:ra:nā: (*a*) friendly; (*nm*) friendship; illicit relationship/intimacy; alliance; –गाँठना to develop friendship, to have an alliance.

यारी ya:ri: (*nf*) friendship; romantic intimacy; illicit love; alliance.

यावत् ya:vat (*a*) as much; (*adv*) until, as long as, as far as.

यीशु i:shu (*nm*) Jesus Christ; ~मसीह Jesus Christ.

युक्त yukt (*a*) united, combined; joined with; fitted with; befitting, suitable; proper, right; ~क jointer; ~तम optimum; ~ता fittingness, suitable; propriety.

युक्ति yukti (*nf*) device; means; tactics, artifice, manoeuvre; skill; argument, plea; ~करण rationalisation; ~पूर्ण rational; tactful; sound; ~निपुण tactician, having manoeuvring skill; advancing sound arguments; ~युक्त befitting; rational, reasonable; proper, suitable; ~संगत reasonable, rational; ~hence ~संगतता/संगति (*nf*); ~संगतन rationalisation; ~हीन tactless; hence ~हीनता (*nf*).

युग yug (*nm*) an age, epoch; era; period; times; one of the four ages–viz. सतयुग, त्रेता, द्वापर, कलियुग- of the world according to Indian tradition; a pair, couple; -चेतना contemporary consciousness; ०संपन्न conscious of the times; ~धर्म contemporaniety, conformation to the times; ~पत् simultaneous(ly); ~पुरुष man of the age; –युग (for) ages, (for) all times; ~ल a pair, couple; both, the two; ~ल-गान/~ल-गीत/~लबंदी duet; –बीत जाना ages to be past, a long time to roll by.

युगांत yuga:nt (*nm*) the end of an age, cosmic destruction.

युगांतर yuga:ntar (*nm*) another/new era, advent of a new epoch; ~कारी revolutionary, epoch-making; –उपस्थित करना to bring in a new era.

युगावतार yuga:wata:r (*nm*) representative of the age, man of the age.

युग्म yugm (*nm*) pair; couple; (*a*) two; ~क pair, couple; ~ज twins.

युत yut—a suffix denoting the sense: endowed with, possessed of or possessing (as श्रीयुत).

युति yuti (*nf*) conjunction; fusion, merger.

युद्ध yuddh (*nm*) war/warfare; battle; fight/fighting; combat, hostilities; ~कारी fighting/fighter; combating/combatant; -काल wartime; period of fighting; -क्षेत्र battle-field, theatre of war; -नीति strategy; -पोत warship, man of war; ~प्रवण bellicose, pugnacious, martial, militant; ~प्रवणता bellicosity, pugnacity; ~प्रवीण expert/skilled in warfare; ~प्रिय a warmonger; bellicose, pugnacious, militant, martial; ०ता war-mongering; bellicosity, pugnaciousness; ~बंदी a prisoner of war; cesssation of hostilities; -भूमि the battle-field; -मंत्री minister for war; ~रत belligerant; -विज्ञान/शास्त्र science of warfare; military science; -विद्या art of warfare; -विराम cease-fire; ०संधि cease-fire pact, cease-fire agreement; -शक्ति fighting potential, power/capacity to wage a war; -संबंधी military; pertaining to war/battle/fighting; -स्थगन cessation of hostilities.

युद्धोन्मत्त yuddhonmatt (*a*) war-crazy; war-mongering; hence ~ता (*nf*).

युद्धोन्मा/द yuddhonma:d (*nm*) war-craze; war-hysteria; hence ~दी (*a*).

युद्धोपकरण yuddhopkarāṇ (*nm*) armament; fighting apparatus.

युयुत्सा yuyutsa: (*nf*) pugnacity, bellicosity, belligerence.

युयुत्सु yuyutsu (*a*) pugnacious, bellicose, belligerent.

युरोप yurop (*nm*) Europe.

युरोपियन yuropiyan (*a*) European.

युरोपीय yuropi:y (*a*) European.

युवक yuwak (*nm*) a youth; young-man; -युवती young men and women.

युवती yuwati: (*nf*) a young woman, youthful woman.

युवराज yuwra:j (*nm*) a prince.

युवराज्ञी yuwraggi: (*nf*) a princess.

युवा yuwa: (*a*) youthful; (*nm*) youth.

यूँ yū: (*adv*) in this way, in this manner; like this, thus; —तो while, whereas; although; —ही exactly in this way; for nothing; casually; accidentally, by chance.

यूक yu:k (*nm*) a louse.

यूथ yu:th (*nm*) a group, company, band; ~चारी gregarious, moving in groups; -वृत्ति gregarious instinct; ~पति leader of a herd/group; ~भ्रष्ट gone astray (from the group).

यूनानी yu:na:nī: (*a*) of or belonging to यूनान (Greece); (*nm*) a Greek; —चिकित्सा-पद्धति Yunani system of medicine.

यूनिफ़ार्म yu:nīfa:rm (*nf*) uniform (dress).

यूनियन yu:niyān (*nf*) a union.

यूनिवर्सिटी yu:nīwarsiṭi: (*nf*) a university.

यू/प yu:p (*nm*) the post with which the sacrificial animal in a 'यज्ञ' is tied; ~पिका a toggle.

यूरेनियम yu:renīyām (*nm*) uranium.

यूरो/प yu:rop (*nm*) Europe; ~पियन European; ~पीय European.

ये ye (*pro*) these.

येन-केन-प्रकारेण yēnkēnpraka:rēn (*ind*) catch as catch can, somehow, somehow or the other, by fair or foul means: by hook or crook.

यों yō (*adv*) like this; in this way/manner; –तो while, whereas, though, although; –ही exactly in this way; for nothing; casually; accidentally, by chance.

योग yog (*nm*) total, sum total; recipe; combination; addition; joining together; conjugation; mixture; contribution; a system of concentration and meditation, concentrational exercise; means of salvation, union with the Universal Soul by means of contemplation; one of the six schools of Indian philosophy; an auspicious or opportune moment; opportunity; device; -क्षेम welfare, well-being; -दर्शन Yogic philosophy; ~दान contribution; -निद्रा Lord Vishnū's long-lasting sleep after the annihilation of the world; ~फल total, the sum total, sum; -बल power of योग, moral power derived through continuous meditation, concentration and contemplation; ~भ्रष्ट one who has aberrated/astrayed/deviated from योग; ~रूढ़ि a compound word used in a much more restricted sense as compared with the direct meaning of its components; ~विद् well-versed in योग (meditative contemplation, etc.); -शक्ति see -बल; ~शास्त्र the famous treatise on योग by the sage Patāṇjali; one of the six schools of Indian philosophy; ~शास्त्री well-versed in ~शास्त्र; ~सूत्र the collection of *Su:tras* on योग composed by the sage Patāṇjali; ~स्थ absorbed in योग or meditative contemplation.

योगाचार yoga:cha:r (*nm*) yoga practices.

योगाभ्या/स yoga:bbhya:s (*nm*) the practice of योग; ~सी one who practises योग; ~स करना to practise योग.

योगासन yoga:sān (*nm*) the योग-posture; the posture adopted in contemplative meditation.

योगिराज yogira:j (*nm*) an ascetic or योगी of the highest order.

योगी yogi: (*nm*) one who practises योग, an ascetic; hence योगिनी feminine form.

योगी/श, ~श्वर yogi:sh, ~shwar (*nm*) an epithet of Lord Krishnā —the most outstanding of the Yogi:s.

योग्य yoggy (*a*) qualified; able; deserving; capable; competent; worthy; eligible; suitable; meritorious; no flies on him; ~ता ability; qualification; capability; competence; worthiness; eligibility; suitability, fitness; merit; ~ता-प्राप्त qualified.

योजक yojak (*a*) uniting, joining; (*nm*) one who or that which unites/joins; -चिह्न a hyphen.

योजन yojan (*nm*) joining, uniting; union; junction, a measure of distance (roughly equal to eight miles).

योजना yojnā: (*nf*) a plan/planning, scheme; disposition. arrangement (as शब्द-योजना); –आयोग Planning Commission; ~कार a planner; -चित्र a plan.

योजित yojit (*a*) planned; arranged; joined, united.

योद्धा yoddha: (*nm*) a warrior, fighter, combatant.

योधन yodhan (*nm*) fighting, combating; -शक्ति fighting potential; -संभार armament; fighting equipment.

योनि yonī (*nf*) vagina, female organ of generation; the form of existence or station fixed by birth (according to Hindu traditional belief these forms number eighty four lacs); ~**द्वार/मुख** the orifice of the womb; ~**भ्रंश** a disease in which uterus is displaced–*prolapsus uteri*; -**मार्ग** vagina; -**विषयक/संबंधी** vaginal, sexual.

योरोप yorop (*nm*) see **यूरोप**.

योरोपियन yoropiyān (*a*) see under **यूरोप**.

योषा yosha: (*nf*) a woman.

यौं yaū (*adv*) see **यों**.

यौगिक yaugik (*a*) pertaining to **योग**; compound; conjunctive, derivative; –**शब्द** a compound word.

यौतुक yautuk (*nm*) dowry, nuptial gift.

यौद्धिक yauddhik (*a*) combative, of or pertaining to war/battle/fighting.

यौन yaun (*a*) sexual; vaginal; –**ग्रंथि** sex complex; –**तृप्ति** sexual gratification; –**मनोविज्ञान** sex psychology; ~**रोग** venereal disease; –**वर्जना** sexual inhibition; –**विकृति** sexual perversion; –**विज्ञान** sexology; ~**वैज्ञानिक** sexologist; sexological; –**संबंध** sexual relations.

यौम yaum (*nm*) day; -**ए-आज़ादी** independence day.

यौवन yauwan (*nm*) youth, youthfulness; -**काल** period of youth; -**दर्प** pride of youth; -**प्राप्त** one who has attained puberty/youth.

र

र ra—the second amongst the series **य, र, ल, व** of the Devna:gri: alphabet, (traditionally) designated as semi-vowels–**अंत:स्थ**; see **य**.

रंक rāṅk (*a*) poor, indigent, pauper: (*nm*) a beggar, penniless person.

रंग rāng (*nm*) colour; dye; complexion; paint; a suit, trump (in playing cards); grandeur; beauty; ways; influence; whim; kind, category; gaiety; stage; -**आमेज़** a painter; one who applies colour; -**आमेज़ी** painting; colouring; ~**कर्म** stagecraft; ~**कर्मी** a stage-man; (one) applying colour; ~**कार** a painter; -**क्षेत्र** a stage; -**गृह** a theatrical pavilion, theatre; -**ढंग** ways, manners, demeanour, conduct; ~**दार** coloured; ~**पीठ** a theatre; -**बिरंगा** variegated, multi-coloured; -**भवन** see ~**महल**; ~**भूमि** theatre, stage; arena; ~**मंच** stage; ~**मंडप** theatre, theatrical pavilion; ~**महल** the apartment meant for amorous sport, private apartment; -**मेल** matching of colours; -**रँगीला** variegated, colourful; ~**रली** see **रंगरेली**; -**रूप** physical appearance, looks; ~**वर्धक** mordant; ~**वाट** an amphitheatre; ~**शाला** theatrum, theatre; ~**साज़** a painter; ~**साज़ी** painting; ~**स्थापक** a mordant; ~**हीन** colourless; –**आना** to assume fullness; to assume true colours; to become colourful; to achieve youthful grace and grandeur; to enjoy thoroughly; –**उखड़ना** to lose influence; to lose charm; to fall into adversity; the tide of enjoyment to ebb away; –उड़ना/उतरना to fade; to lose facial lustre; to lose wits; to turn pale/pallid; –खुलना colour/complexion to be brightened up; to become clearer; –खेलना/डालना/फेंकना to drench with coloured water (during the Holi festival); –चढ़ना to be in high spirits; to be coloured; to be influenced; to be colourfully youthful; to be in full bloom; –चूना/टपकना to be in the fullest bloom; youthful charm to be manifest all over; youth to attain its fullness and charm; –छोड़ना to give up colour, to be decoloured; –जमना to have attained influential position, to establish supremacy; to be held in esteem; to be in full swing (as महफ़िल में रंग जमना); to be enjoying thoroughly; –जमाना to hold under a spell/sway, to attain influential position; to establish one's supremacy; to impart fullness; –देखना to watch the ways of; –न जमना to fall flat, not to win applause; –निखरना the colour to be brightened up; to become fairer; one's essential self to emerge; –पकड़ना to acquire/attain fullness; to be in full bloom; to acquire the colour/ways of; –पर आना to assume true colours; to be in full swing to attain fullness, to be in full bloom; –फीका पड़ना/होना to fade out; to lose brightness/lustre; one's influence to be on the wane; –बदलना to change colours; to undergo a radical change; to assume a different stance; –बिगड़ना one's influence to be on the wane, one's spell to be broken; adversity to set in; –भरना to fill in colours; to impart fullness/completeness (to a picture); –में in good spirits, in full/high feather; –में ढलना to be moulded according to some influence, to be under somebody's sway; –में भंग a skeleton at the feast, a fly in the ointment; –में भंग करना to mar a happy occasion, a melancholic to appear in a gay gathering; –में भंग करने वाला a wet blanket, a spoil-sport; a kill-joy; –में रँगना to mould after one's image; to exercise overwhelming influence; –रचाना to go gay; to celebrate with gay abandon; –लाना to have an effect; to manifest the real effect; to present/emerge in true colours.

रंगत rāngat (*nf*) colour; complexion; plight, condition; relish; delight; –आना to be enjoying to the full, to relish; to be in a delightful state; –उड़ना to lose lustre; to lose countenance; to get pallid.

रँगना rāgnā: (*v*) to colour; to dye; to paint.

रँगरूट rāgru:ṭ (*nm*) a recruit; novice.

रँगरे/ज rāgrez (*nm*) a dyer; hence ~ज़िन (*nf*); ~जी the act, process or job of dyeing.

रँगरे/ली rāgreli: (*nf*) usually used in plural form; ~लियाँ rejoicing; merry-making / merriment, dalliance; o मनाना to live fast, to go gay, to have full rejoicing, to make merry, to enjoy with a gay abandon.

रँगा rāga: (*a*) coloured; –सियार a wolf in lamb's guise, a hoax, sham gentleman; रँगे हाथों पकड़ना to catch red-handed, to catch flat-footed.

रँगाई rāga:i: (*nf*) dyeing; dyeing charges.

रंगजीवी rāṅgji:vi: (*nm*) a painter; dyer; a stage-artist.

रंगामेज़ी rāṅga:mezi: (*nf*) applying colour, colouration.

रँगारँग, रंगारंग rāga:rāg, raṅga:raṅg (*a*) full of colours, of many colours, colourful; having a variety; –कार्यक्रम variety programme.

रँगावट rāga:vaṭ (*nf*) dyeing (pattern).

रंगीन rāṅgi:n (*a*) coloured; colourful, gay, luxury-loving; jovial; ~तबियत see ~मिज़ाज; ~मिज़ाज gay, colourful, sportive; mirthful; luxury-loving; ~मिज़ाजी see रंगीनी.

रंगीनी rāṅgi:nī: (*nf*) colourfulness; gaiety, sportiveness, mirthfulness.

रँगीला rāgi:la: (*a*) colourful, gay, sportive, mirthful; ~पन colourfulness, gaiety, sportiveness, mirthfulness.

रंच, ~क rāṇch, ~ak (*a*) slight, somewhat, a little.

रंज rāṇj (*nm*) sorrow, grief, sadness, gloominess; -ओ–ग़म sorrows and sufferings.

रंजक rāṇjak (*nm*) a pigment; dyestuff, dye; dyer; (*a*) recreative, entertaining; hence ~ता (*nf*).

रंजन rāṇjān (*nm*) dyeing; entertainment, recreation.

रंजित rāṇjit (*a*) coloured, dyed; delighted.

रंजिश rāṇjish (*nf*) animus, animosity, ill-feeling; estrangement.

रंजी/दा rāṇji:da: (*a*) grieved, sorry, sad, gloomy; ~दगी state of being grieved/sorry, sadness, gloominess.

रँडा(ड़ा)पा rāḍa:(ṛa:)pa: (*nm*) widowhood.

रंडी rāṇḍi: (*nf*) a prostitute, harlot, woman of easy virtue; ~बाज़ one who wenches with prostitutes; ~बाज़ी wenching with prostitutes.

रँडु(ड़ु)आ rāḍu(ṛu)a: (*nm*) a widower; -भँडुआ cheap and worthless person, riff-raff.

रंदा rāṇda: (*nm*) a carpenter's plane, planer.

रं/ध्र rāndhr (*nm*) foramen, hole, an orifice, aperture; stomata; pore; ~ध्रक foramen; ~ध्रिल faveolate, foraminate, stomate, having holes; porous; ~ध्री stomatal, foramenal, pertaining to a hole/orifice/aperture.

रँभाना rābha:nā: (*v*) to bellow (said of a cow).

रअय्यत raayyat (*nf*) see रैयत.

रका/र raka:r (*nm*) the letter 'र' (ra) and its sound; ~रांत (a word) ending in र्.

रई rai: (*nf*) a churn-staff.

रईस rai:s (*nm*) a nobleman; rich man, grandee; (*a*) rich, wealthy; ~ज़ादा son of a रईस; hence ~ज़ादी (*nf*).

रईसी raī:sī: (*nf*) nobility; grandiosity; wealthiness, richness.

रक़बा raqba: (*nm*) area.

रक़म raqam (*nf*) a sum, an amount; cunning, crafty (person); –उड़ाना to squander away a big amount; –खाना/डकारना/मारना to misappropriate;–, चलती mischievous/scheming person.

रकाब raka:b (*nm*) a stirrup; ~दार an attendant to help a groom ride the horse; –में पाँव रखना to ride a horse; –में पाँव रहना to be always on the move, to be ever on horse-back.

रक़ाबत raqa:bat (*nf*) rivalry (in love).

रक़ाबी raka:bi: (*nf*) a plate, dish; –चेहरा flat face; ~मज़हब a sycophant, flunkey.

रक़ीब raqi:b (*nm*) a rival (in love).

रकेबी rakebi: (*nf*) see रकाबी.

रक़्क़ासा raqqa:sa: (*nf*) a dancing-girl, a danseuse.

रक्त rakt (*nm*) blood; (*a*) red; saffron; attached; ~क्षीणता anaemia; ~चाप blood pressure; ~ज born of blood; ~ता redness; ruddiness; -निर्माण sanguification; ~पात bloodshed; shedding of blood; o पूर्ण sanguinary; accompanied with blood-shed; ~पायी blood-sucker; blood-sucking; -पिपासा blood-thirst; -पिपासु blood-thirsty, sanguinary; ~पूर्ण full of blood, bloody; ~रंजित bloody; sanguinary; causing blood-shed; ~वर्ण red; ~वसन saffron-robed; an ascetic; -संबंध consanguinity; blood relation; ~स्राव haemorrhage, flow of blood; –की नदी बहाना to shed a stream of blood; –में होना to be in the blood.

रक्तांबर raktā:mbar (*a*) red-robed, donning red robes; (*nm*) an ascetic.

रक्ताभ rakta:bh (*a*) having a red tinge, red-tinged, sanguine, ruddy.

रक्तिम raktīm (*a*) red-tinged, sanguine, ruddy; hence ~ता (*nf*).

रक्तोत्पल raktotpal (*nm*) red lotus.

रक्षक rakshak (*a* and *nm*) protectant/protector; saviour/defender; guard; keeper; custodian; -दल guard.

रक्षण rakshān (*nm*) protection, guarding; reservation, custody; maintaining/safe-keeping; ~कर्त्ता see रक्षक; hence रक्षणीय (*a*).

रक्षा raksha: (*nf*) defence; protection; guarding; safe-keeping; custody; -कवच an armlet reinforced by a charm/spell and meant to defend somebody against likely affliction/calamity; -कार्य defence work; –गृह a defence-post; ~बंधन a festival (also called सलूनो) held on the full-moon day of the month of श्रावण when sisters tie a sacramental thread on the wrist of their brothers and are guaranteed life-long protection; -पंक्ति line of defence; -मंत्रालय the ministry of defence; -मंत्री Defence Minister; -सेना defence force.

रक्षात्मक raksha:tmāk (*a*) defensive; safeguarding; ensuring protection/custody; –नीति defensive policy.

रक्षित rakshit (*a*) defended; protected; maintained; safeguarded; (*nm*) a protege; –राज्य a protectorate; hence रक्षिता feminine form.

रक्षी rakshi: (*nm*) a guard; –दल guard, guarding force.

रक्ष्य rakkshy (*a*) protectable, defendable; to be defended.

रक़्स raqs (*nm*) dance, dancing; dance performance.

रखना rakhnā: (*v*) to put; to place; to keep; to possess; to have; to employ, to appoint; to keep as wife/husband; रख-रखाव maintenance/safe keeping/upkeep.

रखवाला rakhwa:la: (*nm*) a guard, watchman.

रखवाली rakhwa:li: (*nf*) guarding, watch/watchmanship, safe-keeping, safeguarding, care

रखाई rakha:i: (*nf*) the process of guarding / maintaining/ safe-keeping or upkeep or the charges paid therefor.

रखाना rakha:nā: (*v*) to guard, to watch; to care; to maintain.

रखैया rakhaiya: (*nm*) a protector, guard; custodian.

रखैल rakhail (*nf*) a concubine, mistress, woman who lives with a man without being his wife.

रखौना rakhaunā: (*nm*) a pasture land, pasturage.

रग rag (*nf*) a vein; a fibre; ~**दार** fibrous; veinous; -**पट्ठा** veins and muscles; o **पहचानना** to be thoroughly familiar, to know through and through; -**रेशा** veins and fibres, structural details; every particle; —**उतरना** to have a rupture; to recover from a fit of obstinacy; —**दबना** to be under somebody's sway; to be under subjugation; —**पहचानना** to know thoroughly well; to know the inner secret; —**पाना** to know the truth/secret; —**फड़कना** a nerve to vibrate/throb; to have an ill foreboding; —**फूलना** a nerve to be swollen; —**में दौड़ जाना** to have a profound effect, to infuse each and every nerve; -**रग फड़कना** each and every nerve to throb in excitement, to be exhilarated, to be enthused all over; -**रग में** all over, in each and every nerve; -**रग से वाकिफ़ होना** to know through and through; **रगें निकल आना** to be emaciated; to be anaemic; **रगें ढीली पड़ना/मरना** to lose virility and vitality; to become impotent; **रगों में ख़ून/बिजली दौड़ना** to be in high spirits; to be excited.

रगड़ ragaṛ (*nf*) rub, friction; bruise; abrasion; —**खाना** to be bruised, to get rough rubbing; —**देना** to bruise; to crush thoroughly; to harass; —**लगना** to get a bruise; to face rough treatment.

रगड़ना ragaṛnā: (*v*) to rub, to scrub to grate; to bruise; to cause harassment; to toil without progress.

रगड़ा ragṛa: (*nm*) a rub, rubbing friction; bruise; toil; -**झगड़ा** quarrel, disputation; wrangling; —**देना** to rub, to give a rub/bruise.

रगेदना ragednā: (*v*) to rout, to chase away.

रघुकुल raghukul (*nm*) the solar dynasty of ancient India, one of whose great rulers was **रघु**; ~**गौरव**/**चन्द्र**/**तिलक**/**नाथ** / **पति**/**मणि** / **राज** / ... Rā:m—the greatest of the rulers of the solar dynasty.

रचना rachnā: (*nf*) composition artistic creation; structure; (*v*) to create, to compose; to make; to form, to construct; ~**कार** author writer, creator; -**तंत्र** structure set-up; system.

रचयिता rachaita: (*nm*) creator composer; author.

रचाना racha:nā: (*v*) to organise (as **रास**–); to stain (as **मेंहदी** –)

रचित rachit (*a*) constructed; created composed; stained (with).

रज raj (*nf*) menstruation; dust (*nm*) the second of the three **गुण** characterising human nature (see **रजोगुण**); an allomorph of **राज** (i.e. **रजवाड़ा**); ~**कण** dust particle.

रजत rajat (*nm*) silver; (*a*) silvery white; bright; —**जयंती** silver jubilee; ~**पट** silver screen, cinema screen; -**पात्र** a utensil; ~**मय** silvery, made of silver.

रजनी rajnī: (*nm*) night; ~**कर**/**पति** the moon; ~**चर** a demon, nocturnal being.

रजनीश rajnī:sh (*nf*) the moon.

पूती rajpu:ti: (*nf*) the characteristic attributes of a Ra:jpu:t—chivalry, valour; (*a*) characteristic of or like a राजपूत (as रजपूती शान).

जवहा rajvaha: (*nf*) a distributory.

जवाड़ा rajva:ṛa: (*nm*) native state, a former princely state of India.

जस्वला rajaswala: (*a*) menstruous, in menstruation; —होना to menstruate.

रजा raza: (*nf*) will, wish; consent, permission.

रज़ामं/द raza:mānd (*a*) willing; consenting, agreeing; ~दी will; consent, agreement.

रज़ाई raza:i (*nf*) a quilt.

रजिस्टर rajisṭar (*nm*) a register.

रजिस्ट्रार rajisṭra:r (*nm*) registrar.

रजिस्ट्री rajisṭri: (*nf*) registration; registered post; ~शुदा registered.

रजोगुण rajogūn (*nm*) one of the three attributes of nature which manifests itself in luxuriousness, merry-making, exhibitionism and such other attitudes.

रजो/दर्शन, ~धर्म rajodarshān, ~dharm (*nm*) monthly course, menstruation.

रज्जु rajju (*nf*) a rope, cord; -मार्ग ropeway.

रटंत raṭānt (*nf*) cramming, memorizing, commission to memory.

रट raṭ (*nf*) constant reception/reiteration.

र/टना raṭnā: (*v*) to repeat/reiterate constantly; to cram, to commit to memory, to memorize; ~ट्टू a crammer; o पीर an adept in cramming, a master crammer.

रण rān (*nm*) war, battle, fighting, combat; ~कर्म fighting; combating; ~कामी war-mongering; bellicose; ~कारी fighting, combating belligerent; -कोष war-fund; ~क्षेत्र the battlefield, theatre of war; ~चंडी Bellona; the war-goddess; ~तूर्य/भेरी bugles of war, war-trumpets; -नीति strategy; -बाँकुरा valorous; a great fighter; ~भूमि the battlefield; -रंग the battlefield, theatre of war; fighting spirit; -शिक्षा training in the art of fighting; -संकुल fierce fighting; -सज्जा war-preparation; battle equipment; armament; ~सिंहा see ~तूर्य; ~स्थल the battlefield.

रणांगण rānā:ṅgān (*nm*) the battlefield, battle zone.

रत rat (*a*) attached, loving; used as a suffix to mean engaged in, occupied with (as कार्यरत); (*nm*) an allomorph of 'रात' used as the first member in certain compound words; ~जगा keeping awake the whole night (to celebrate a happy occasion through singing devotional songs or otherwise).

रतना/रा ratnā:ra: (*a*) reddish, ruddy; hence ~री feminine form.

रतालू rata:lu: (*nm*) yam.

रति rati (*nf*) love, enjoyment of love; sexual passion; oestrus; copulation; name of the wife of कामदेव (Cupid) — hence, a very pretty woman; —उन्माद erotomania; ~क्रिया copulation, sexual intercourse; ~जन्य venereal; born of sexual intercourse; ~दान sexual intercourse, copulation; ~नाथ Cupid—the god of love; ~प्रिय sexy; erotic; ~बंध copulatory postures; ~बाँकुरा chivalrous; -भाव amorous sentiment, sentiment of love; -रस the sexual relish; -रोग a venereal disease; ~शास्त्र science of love-making; erotic; sexology,

रतुआ ratua: (*nm*) rust.

रतौंधी ratāudhi: (*nf*) nyctalopia, night-blindness; **–आना** to suffer from nyctalopia

रत्ती ratti: (*nf*) seed of *Abrus precatorius*; weight approximately equivalent to $2\frac{1}{4}$ grains; **–भर उम्मीद न होना** not a dog's chance; **-भर परवाह न करना** not to care a brass farthing.

रत्न ratn (*nm*) a gem, precious stone; the most outstanding individual of a class; **~कार** a jeweller; **~गर्भा** the earth; **-पारखी** a connoisseur of precious stones; valuer of gems; **~माला** a necklace of gems.

रत्ना/कर ratnā:kar (*nm*) the sea, ocean; **~भूषण** begemmed ornaments; gems and ornaments

रत्यात्मक ratya:tmāk (*a*) erotic; amatorial, amorous; **~ता** eroticism; amorousness.

रथ rath (*nm*) a chariot; **~कार** chariot-maker; **-यात्रा** a celebration organized on the second day of the bright fortnight of **आषाढ़** when the devotees take out the idols of the deities in a huge procession; **~वान्** a charioteer, one who rides a chariot.

रथी rathi: (*a*) riding a chariot; (*nm*) a fighter, warrior.

रथोत्सव rathotsav (*nm*) see **रथ-यात्रा**.

रथ्या ratthya: (*nf*) course of a chariot; a highway.

रद rad (*nm*) a tooth; **~च्छद** the lips; **-छद** teeth-marks (esp. on the cheeks, left in amatorial sport); **~न** a tooth.

रद्द radd (*a*) rejected; cancelled; annulled; **~गी** rejection, cancellation; annulment; **–करना** to reject; to cancel; to annul; **– होना** to be rejected; to be cancelled; to be annulled.

रद्दा radda: (*nm*) stratum; a layer (of bricks or mud etc.); **–चढ़ाना/जमाना** to instigate; to provoke; to utter (another) instigatory remark; to accuse, to cast another aspersion; **–रखना** to fix another layer; to level another accusation.

रद्दी raddi: (*a*) worthless; inferior, of inferior quality; rough; (*nf*) waste paper; spoilage; **–माल** waste, dead metal.

रद्दोबदल raddo-badal (*nf*) change, alteration; modification.

रन ran (*nm*) a run (in cricket); a reclaimed part of the sea (e.g. **कच्छ का रन**).

रनिवास raniva:s (*nm*) the seraglio, the female apartment (in a palace).

रपट rapaṭ (*nf*) a report; slipping, sliding/slipperiness; **–करना/दर्ज करना/लिखाना** to lodge a report.

रपट/ना rapaṭnā: (*v*) to slip; to slide; to skid; (*a*) slippery; **~वाँ** slippery; sliding; **०दरवाज़ा** sliding door.

रपटीला rapṭi:la: (*a*) slippery.

रपट्टा rapaṭṭa: (*nm*) slipping; pounce, swoop.

रफ़ raf (*a*) rough; **–काम** rough work.

रफल raphal (*nf*) a woollen wrapper, shawl.

रफ़ा rafa: (*a*) settled; finished; **-दफ़ा** settled finished; **–करना, -दफ़ा करना, झगड़ा** to settle; to bring about a rapprochement; to dispose off.

रफ़ू rafu: (*nm*) darning; **~गर** a darner; **~गरी** darning.

रफ़ूचक्कर rafu:chakkar; **–होना** to do a guy, to show a clean pair of heels, to turn tails, to make good one's escape.

रफ़्तार rafta:r (*nf*) speed, pace; -ए-जमाना ways of the world; whirligig of the times; –पकड़ना to gain speed.

रफ़्ता-रफ़्ता rafta:-rafta: (*adv*) slowly, gradually, by degrees.

रब rab (*nm*) God, Master; –, या oh, God !

रब/ड़ rabaṛ (*nf*) rubber; an eraser; ~ड़ की चीजें rubber goods; ~ड़-छंद elastic metre.

रबड़ी rabṛi: (*nf*) a typical sweetmeat prepared from boiled milk and sugar.

रबर rabar (*nf*) see रबड़.

रबी rabi: (*nm*) spring; crop reaped in the spring season; –की फ़सल the rabi crop.

रब्त rabt (*nm*) practice; association, intercourse, mixing; -जब्त association, social intercourse; relations; –छूटना to be out of practice; –डालना to gain practice.

रम/क ramak (*nf*) whim, caprice; swing; ~की whimsical, capricious.

रमकना ramaknā: (*v*) to take a swing; to be in a caprice.

रमज़ा/न ramzā:n (*nm*) Ramadan—the ninth month of the muslim year which is traditionally a month of day-long fasts; ~नी pertaining to *ramzan*.

रमण ramāṇ (*nm*) sporting, amorous dalliance, erotic playfulness, merriment; (*a*) sportive, playful; as an adjectival suffix it means dear (to), as 'उमारमण'.

रमणी ramaṇī: (*nf*) a pretty woman, young woman.

रमणीक ramaṇi:k (*a*) beautiful, pretty, charming, winsome; attractive; hence ~ता (*nf*).

रमणीय ramaṇi:y (*a*) beautiful, pretty, charming, winsome, attractive; enjoyable; ~ता beauty, prettiness, charm, winsomeness, attraction; enjoyability.

रमता ramta: (*a*) wandering, vagrant; roving, roaming, going about; –जोगी a wandering mendicant; –जोगी, बहता पानी a wandering mendicant and flowing water do not stay at one place.

रमना ramnā: (*v*) to enjoy, to make merry; to roam/rove, to wander about,

रमल ramal (*nm*) a mode of fortune-telling (borrowed from the Arabs) with the help of dice; –लगाना to speculate.

रमा ramā: (*nf*) Lakshmī: — the goddess of wealth; ~कांत/रमण Lord Vishṇū.

रमी ramī: (*nf*) rummy—a game of playing cards.

रमे/श, ~श्वर ramesh, ~shwar (*nm*) Lord Vishṇū.

रमैया ramaiya: (*nm*) Ram —the Lord Almighty.

रम्माल rammạ:l (*nm*) a fortune-teller (who casts a dice for the purpose).

रम्य rammy (*a*) beautiful, pretty, winsome; charming, attractive; hence ~ता (*nf*).

रर(ड़)क rar(ṛ)ak (*nf*) smarting, painful sensation (as when an alien matter falls into the eye).

रर(ड़)कना rar(ṛ)aknā: (*v*) to smart, to produce painful sensation (as by a coal particle falling into the eye).

रलना ralnā: (*v*) to get mixed/mingled up, to be intermixed/intermingled; -मिलना to get mixed/

mingled up, to be intermixed/intermingled.

रव rav (*nm*) noise, tumult.

रवन्ना ravannā: (*nm*) an invoice; a paper containing the details of goods despatched; passage permit.

रवाँ ravā: (*a*) trained; practised; well-versed; fluent.

रवा rava: (*nm*) a particle, grain; crystal; filings; semolina; ~**दार** granular; crystalline; considerate; ~**दारी** granularity; considerateness; –**भर** a very small quantity; equal to a grain.

रवानगी ravā:ngi: (*nf*) departure; setting out.

रवाना rava:nā: (*a*) departed, set out; despatched; –**करना** to despatch; to cause to depart; –**होना** to depart, to set out.

रवानी rava:nī: (*nf*) flow; fluency.

रवि ravi (*nm*) the sun; ~**कर** a sunray; ~**दिन** sunday; ~**मंडल** the halo round the sun; ~**वार/वासर** sunday.

रविश ravish (*nf*) walking passage between flower beds; movement, speed; ways, conduct.

रवैया ravaiya: (*nm*) attitude; behaviour; practice.

रश्क rashk (*nm*) envy.

रश्मि rashmī (*nf*) a ray; ~**माली** the sun.

रस ras (*nm*) juice; (aesthetic) relish; sentiment; pleasure, enjoyment; taste, flavour; ~**गुल्ला** a typical round and spongy Bengali sweet; ~**दार** juicy, luscious; tasty, relishing; ~**ग्रहण** appreciation; ~**ज्ञ** one who has capability to relish, blessed with aesthetic sense; who has profound understanding of poetic sentiments; a connoisseur; hence **ज्ञाता** (*nf*); -**भंग** interruption/interception of aesthetic relish; ~**भरी** raspberry; ~**भीना** full of flavour, well-steeped in sentiment; **राज** the king of all sentiments; the erotic sentiment; ~**वाद** pleasant/erotic talk; wrangle; taking interest in erotic talks; talkativeness; ~**वादी** one who takes interest in erotic talks/quarrels; talkative; -**विरोध** discordance of **रस**; ~**शास्त्र** alchemy; ~**सिद्ध** an expert in manifestation of **रस**; –**आना** to enjoy, to relish; –**बरसाना** to cause a constant flow of (aesthetic) pleasure; –**लुटना** all relish to be gone, source of pleasure to be exhausted; –**लेना** to enjoy, to relish.

रसद rasad (*nf*) supply/ supplies, provision(s).

रसना rasnā: (*nf*) the tongue; –**खोलना** to speak out; –**तालू से लगना** to become mute, to be quiet.

रसनीय rasnī:y (*a*) delicious, tasty, worth relishing.

रसनेंद्रिय rasanendriy (*nf*) the tongue.

रसरी rasri: (*nf*) a rope, cord.

रसवं/त rasvānt (*a*) full of relish; juicy; having aesthetic sense; (*nm*) one who has enjoyed love-making/aesthetic relish; hence ~**ती** (fem. form).

रसवती rasvati: (*a*) full of **रस** i.e. aesthetic relish; juicy.

रसवत्ता rasvatta: (*nf*) juiciness, relish, enjoyability.

रसवान rasvā:n (*a*) filled with or possessing **रस**.

रसाँ rasā: (*a*) an adjectival suffix meaning one who reaches/goes far away (as **चिट्ठीरसाँ**).

र/सा rasa: (*nf*) the earth; soup, broth; juice; ~सेदार soupy, having broth; juicy.

साई rasa:i: (*nf*) approach; association, contacts.

सातल rasa:tal (*nm*) the netherworld; hell; –को पहुँचना to go to the bottom; to be devastated/ruined; –को पहुँचाना to destroy, to devastate, to ruin completely.

सात्मक rasa:tmak (*a*) full of रस; juicy; aesthetic, beautiful; hence ~ता (*nf*).

साभास rasa:bha:s (*nm*) a mere semblance of रस.

सायन rasa:yan (*nm*) Chemistry; (*a*) chemical; ~ज्ञ well-versed in Chemistry; -विज्ञान/शास्त्र Chemistry; ~वेत्ता a chemist, a scholar of Chemistry.

सायनिक rasa:yanīk (*nm*) an alchemist; (*a*) see रासायनिक.

साल rasa:l (*a*) juicy; delicious, tasty; (*nm*) a mango.

सास्वा/द rasa:sva:d (*nm*) aesthetic relish, emotive relish; ~दन the act or process of aesthetic enjoyment/relish; ~दी one who relishes रस.

सिआउर rasia:ur (*nf*) a typical preparation of rice in sugarcane juice.

सिक rasik (*a* and *nm*) a man of taste, one having aesthetic sense, one who appreciates beauty or excellence; an amorist; dilettante; hence ~ता (*nf*).

रसिया rasiya: (*nm*) having aesthetic relish; liking juicy talks; frivolous; a class of typical folk songs sung during the month of फागुन in parts of U.P.

रसीद rasi:d (*nf*) a receipt; –करना to give, to implant (as थप्पड़, घूंसा); –काटना to issue a receipt.

रसीदी rasi:di: (*a*) regarding or pertaining to a receipt; fixed on a receipt; –टिकट a revenue stamp.

रसीला rasi:la: (*a*) juicy; tasteful, delicious; loving juicy talks; amorous; frivolous; hence रसीली –feminine form; ~पन (*nm*).

रसूल rasu:l (*nm*) a prophet, divine messenger.

रसे-रसे rase-rase (*adv*) slowly, gradually, by degrees.

रसोइया rasoiya: (*nm*) a cook.

रसोई rasoi: (*nf*) cooked food; kitchen; ~ख़ाना/घर a kitchen; ~दार a cook; ~दारी cooking.

रसौली rasauli: (*nf*) a tumour; a disease attended with tumour-formation over the eyebrows.

रस्म rasm (*nf*) a ceremony, ritual; formality; custom; practice; -ओ-रिवाज customs and practices; ~न as a matter of custom/convention/formality.

रस्मी rasmī: (*a*) formal, ceremonial; related with or conforming to a ritual; –ताल्लुक़ात formal relations; -तौर पर formally, formally speaking.

रस्सा rassa: (*nm*) a stout thick rope; ~कशी a tug-of-war.

रस्सी rassi: (*nf*) a rope, cord; –जल गई पर बल न गया to be full of airs though vanquished; –हाथ में रखना to exercise control over.

रहँट rehāṭ (*nf*) a Persian wheel (for drawing water out of a well).

रह reh—an allomorph of राह used in several compound words; ~गुज़र a highway; ~ज़न a highwayman, brigand; ~ज़नी waylaying, brigandage; ~नुमा a guide;

~नुमाई guidance; ~बर a guide; ~बरी guidance.

रहन rehān (*nm*) a pawn, pledge, mortgage; (mode of) living; -सहन living; ways; ०का स्तर standard of living.

रहना rehnā: (*v*) to live; to stay; to reside; to remain; to continue; रह-रहकर intermittently, spasmodically.

रहम rehām (*nm*) pity, mercy, compassion; ~ दिल compassionate, kind, merciful; ~दिली compassionateness, kindness, mercifulness; –पर छोड़ देना, किसी के to leave at the mercy of.

रहमत rehmāt (*nf*) kindness, mercy, compassion.

रहस्य rahasy (*nm*) a secret; mystery; secrecy; ~पूर्ण/मय mysterious; secretive; ~मयता mysteriousness; ~वाद a poetic movement of the third and fourth decades in Hindi that stressed the identity of the Universal and the Individual and addressed itself to the Non-Manifest; ~वादिता mysteriousness, the attribute or approach of a रहस्यवादी; ~वादी an adherent of रहस्यवाद; pertaining to रहस्यवाद.

रहस्योद्घाटन rahasyodgha:ṭān (*nm*) revelation.

रहा raha: (*a*) past tense of 'रहना'; -सहा remaining, residual, left over.

रहित rahit (*a*) without, devoid of, bereft of.

रहीम rahi:m (*a* and *nm*) kindly, kind-hearted, compassionate; the Lord.

राँग, ~गा rā:g, ~a: (*nm*) tin; solder.

राँचना rā:chnā: (*v*) to be in love, to be attracted; to be coloured.

राँड़ rā:ṛ (*nf*) a widow; a term of abuse.

राँधना rā:dhnā: (*v*) to cook (food).

राँभना rā:bhnā: (*v*) to bellow (as a cow).

रा ra:—a genitive suffix used in the first and second person pronouns (as तुम्हारा, हमारा).

राइफ़ल ra:ifal (*nf*) a rifle.

राई ra:i: (*nf*) mustard; black mustard; -काई करना to shatter to pieces; to split into pieces; -का पर्वत/पहाड़ करना/बनाना to make a mountain of a mole hill; -नोन उतारना countering the effect of an evil glance (by moving mustard and salt round one's head and consigning it to flames); –भर very small particle; very small quantity; -रत्ती करके in the minutest details; -रत्ती जानना to know each and every thing, to know the minutest details, to know every detail.

राका ra:ka: (*nf*) the night of the full moon; ~पति the moon.

राकेट ra:keṭ (*nm*) a rocket; -युद्ध rocket warfare; -विद्या rocketry.

राकेश ra:kesh (*nm*) the moon.

राक्षस ra:kshas (*nm*) a demon, monster; (*a*) ruthless, demonic; ~राज the king of demons; -विवाह one of the various types of marriages, referred to in ancient Indian literature, wherein the groom fought his way to the bride's hand.

राक्षसी ra:kshasi: (*nf*) an ogress; monstress; (*a*) monstrous, demonic; –माया demonic conjuration.

राख ra:kh (*nf*) ash(es); ~दान ashpan; ~दानी ash-tray; –डालना to hush up, to try to conceal; –में मिला देना to devastate, to reduce to ashes; –होना to be turned to ashes; to be ruined.

राखी ra:khi: (*nf*) a sacred thread tied by a sister on the wrist of her brother as a mark of affection that binds the brother to protect her in times of crisis; ~बंद on whose hand a राखी has been tied; o भाई adopted (by a woman) as a brother (by tying a राखी around his wrist).

राग ra:g (*nm*) a melodic mode or structure with a fixed sequence of notes, melody; tune; attraction, attachment; passion, emotion, love; -द्वेष attachment and malevolence; love and hatred/rancour; -रागिनी musical modes and notes; -विराग attraction and repulsion, attachment and detachment; -अलापना to go on harping one's own tune

रागान्वित ra:ga:nvit (*a*) filled with emotion/affection; fallen in love.

रागाभाव ra:ga:bha:v (*nm*) acatheris, absence of attachment/affection/love.

रागिनी ra:gini: (*nf*) a musical mode or a variation/modification thereof

रागी ra:gi: (*a* and *nm*) filled with or full of love, a lover; finger millet.

राघव ra:ghav (*nm*) Ra:m (see)—an outstanding personage of the Raghu or Solar dynasty of ancient India.

राज ra:j (*nm*) a kingdom, realm; state; reign; an allomorph of 'राजा' which when prefixed or suffixed to numerous other words denotes of the king/state or excellence, supremacy, etc.; a builder, mason; ~कथा the tale of a king's exploits; ~कन्या a princess; -कर statetax; ~काज public affairs, affairs of the state; governance; ~कार्य see ~काज; ~कुमार a prince; ~कुमारी a princess; ~कुल a dynasty, regal family; ~कोष fisc; public/state exchequer; treasury; ~कोषीय fiscal; ~क्षमा amnesty; ~गद्दी royal throne; ~गीर a mason; ~गीरी masonry; ~गृह a palace, regal mansion; ~चिह्न regalia, royal insignia; state emblem; ~तंत्र monarchy, monarchical system of government; ~तंत्रवादी royalist(ic); ~तंत्रीय monarchical; ~तिलक coronation; annointing at the time of coronation; ~दंड regal command; royal sceptre; punishment prescribed by law; ~दूत an ambassador; ~दूत, असाधारण ambassador extraordinary; ~दूतावास an embassy; ~द्रोह lese-majesty, sedition, treason; ~द्रोह, घोर high treason; ~द्रोहपूर्ण seditious; ~द्रोहात्मक seditious; ~द्रोही a seditionist; ~धर्म state religion; royal duty; ~पथ a highway; -पद्धति royal system; polity; royal policy; ~पाट reign, royal throne; o सौंपना to hand over the reins of kingdom/governance; ~पाल a governor; ~पुत्र a prince; ~पुत्री a princess; ~पुरुष a state employee/official; ~पूत a class of *kshatriyas* known for their valour and bravery; ~पूताना the land of the Ra:jpu:ts, Ra:jastha:n; ~प्रासाद a palace; ~बाहा a big canal; ~भक्त a loyalist; loyal to the ruler/state; ~भक्ति loyalism, loyalty or allegiance to the ruler/state; ~भत्ता privy purse; ~मंडल satellite states; chamber of princes; -मंत्री a minister of a king; ~मर्मज्ञ a statesman; ~मर्मज्ञता statesmanship; ~महल a palace; ~महिषी a queen;

~मुद्रा signet, royal seal; ~यक्ष्मा tuberculosis; ~योग an auspicious combination of planets (in one's horoscope) that forebodes elevation to royalty; -योग्य befitting a king; -रोग an incurable or long-lasting disease; tuberculosis; ~लक्ष्मी regal majesty, royal grandeur, kingly prosperity and splendour; state goddess of prosperity; ~वंश a dynasty; ~वित्तीय fiscal; ~विद्या see राजनीति; -विद्रोह revolt, rebellion, insurrection; ~विद्रोही a rebel, an insurgent; -विप्लव anarchy, revolt; ~वृत्ति privy purse; ~वैद्य physician of a king; an eminent physician; -व्यवस्था polity; ~श्री royal grandeur / majesty, regal splendour and prosperity; see ~लक्ष्मी; -संस्करण de luxe edition; ~सत्ता royal authority; monarchy; ~सत्तात्मक monarchical, pertaining to a system of government where authority is wielded by a ruler; ~सभा a royal court; ~समाज an assembly of princes, princely assembly; royal court; ~सूय a typical sacrifice in olden times which, when successfully performed by a king, entitled him to the designation of an Emperor (सम्राट); ~सिंहासन the royal throne; ~हंस a kind of swan or goose (with red legs and bill, sometimes compared to a flamingo); -उलटना to bring about a coup, to overthrow the established administration; -करना to rule; to enjoy royal privileges/luxury; -देना to hand over the reins of kingdom; -पर बैठना to ascend the throne, to be installed as the ruler; -रजना to live in princely splendour, to live like a prince.

राज़ ra:z (*nm*) a secret; ~दाँ/दार one who knows the secret; one who shares (somebody's) secret, confidant; -खोल देना/-फ़ाश करना to let the cat out of the bag, to blow the gaff.

राजकीय ra;jki:y (*a*) royal; public, official; pertaining to the state.

राजधानी ra:jdha:nī: (*nf*) a capital, metropolis; -परिषद् metropolitan council.

राजन/य ra:jnāy (*nm*) diplomacy; ~यज्ञ a diplomatist; ~यिक a diplomat; diplomatic; ० प्रतिनिधि diplomatic representative.

राजनीति ra:jnī:ti (*nf*) politics; ~क political; ० सत्ता political authority / power; ~ज्ञ a politician; -विज्ञान/शास्त्र politics; political science.

राजन्य ra:janny (*nm*) a king, prince; -वर्ग princely class.

राजप ra:jap (*nm*) a regent; ~ता regency.

राजप/त्र ra:jpattr (*nm*) gazette; ~त्रित gazetted; ० अधिकारी a gazetted officer.

राजभवन ra:jbhawān (*nm*) governor's house; palace.

राजभाषा ra:jbha:sha: (*nf*) official language; -आयोग official language commission.

राजर्षि ra:jarshi (*nm*) a princely sage, seer born in a *kshatriya* family.

राजवि/त्त ra:jvitt (*nm*) fisc, public finance; ~त्तीय fiscal.

राजशाही ra:jsha:hi: (*a*) royal, regal, kingly.

राजस ra:jas (*a*) born of or appropriate to रजोगुण; passionate; see राजसी; (*nm*) arrogance; rage; excitement.

राजसात्करण ra:jsa:tkarān (*nm*) confiscation/requisition by the state.

राजसिक ra:jsik (*a*) born of or appropriate to **रजोगुण**; see **राजसी**.

राजसी ra:jsi: (*a*) royal, regal, kingly, princely, befitting or becoming a king or prince; **-ठाट-बाट** royal prank, regal grandeur and splendour.

राजस्था/न ra:jastha:n (*nm*) one of the many Hindi-speaking states of the Indian Union, traditionally known for its chivalry and valour; **~नी** a sub-language of Hindi comprised of many dialects spoken in Ra:jastha:n; pertaining or belonging to Ra:jastha:n.

राजस्व ra:jassv (*nm*) revenue; **-अधिकारी** a revenue officer; **-लेखा** revenue account.

राजा ra:ja: (*nm*) a king, monarch, prince; darling; **-बेटा** good boy; **-के घर मोतियों का क्या काल ?** there is as good fish in the sea as ever came out of it.

राजाज्ञा ra:ja:ggya: (*nf*) royal command, imperial decree.

राजाधिराज ra:ja:dhira:j (*nm*) a king of kings, an emperor.

राजाधिष्ठान ra:ja:dhishṭha:n (*nm*) royal headquarter; seat of a king.

राजाभिषेक ra:ja:bhishek (*nm*) coronation, a king's installation on the throne.

राजासन ra:ja:sān (*nm*) royal throne/seat.

राजि ra:ji (*nf*) a row, line.

राजित ra:jit (*a*) to be resplendent, to shine, to be illuminated; to be (present) in all glory.

राज़ी ra:zi: (*a*) willing, agreeable; (*nf*) willingness; well-being; **-खुशी** welfare, well-being; **~नामा** an agreement; compromise.

राजीव ra:ji:v (*nm*) a lotus flower; **~नयन/लोचन** lotus-eyed.

राजेश्वर ra:jeshshwar (*nm*) a monarch, an emperor.

राज्ञी ra:gyi: (*nf*) a queen.

राज्य ra:jjy (*nm*) the state; kingdom; polity, rule, reign; **~कर्त्ता** a ruler; **-काल** reign; rule; **-क्षमा** clemency; amnesty; **क्षेत्र** (state) territory; expanse of the state; **~च्युत** dethroned, deposed; **~च्युति** dethronement, deposition; **-तंत्र** polity; **-त्याग** abdication; **~त्व** statehood; **-द्रोह** sedition; **~द्रोही** a seditionist; **-पद** statehood; **~पाल** a governor; **-प्रमुख** head of a/the state; **-भंग** breakdown of law, anarchy; **-विप्लव** coup d'etat; **-व्यवस्था** polity, state system; **-सभा** Upper House of the Indian Parliament, council of states.

राज्याधिकार ra:jjya:dhika:r (*nm*) jura regia; power of the state.

राज्याध्यक्ष ra:jjya:ddhyaksh (*nm*) head of a/the state.

राज्याभि/षेक ra:jjya:bhishek (*nm*) coronation, installation or accession to the throne; **~षिक्त** installed on/acceded to the throne.

राज्यारोहण ra:jjya:rohaṇ (*nm*) accession to the throne.

राणा rā:ṇā: (*nm*) a title of Ra:jpu:t kings of certain Ra:jpu:ta:nā: states and Nepal.

रात ra:t (*nf*) (the) night; **-का राजा** an owl; **-दिन** day and night; ever, always, at all times; **~रानी** a typical fragrant flower that blooms during the night, also called rajani:gandha:; **-आँखों में काटना** to keep wide awake the whole night, not to have a wink through the night; **-को रात दिन को दिन न समझना** lit. to make no distinction between day and night, to work day and night; **-गहराना**

the night to advance; –ढलना a substantial part of the night to pass; –दिन का अंतर lit. difference of day and night—vast difference; –भर काम में जुटे रहना to burn the midnight oil; –भर रोए एक न मरा to run round in circles, be fussily busy with little results.

रातिब ra:tib (*nm*) food for cattle, concentrates.

रात्रि ra:ttri (*nf*) (the) night; ~कर the moon; ~चर/चारी a demon; noctural; -जागरण keeping awake through the night; -पाठशाला a night school.

रा/धा ra:dha: (*nf*) the legendary favourite beloved of Lord Krishnā; ~धिका see राधा.

रान ra:n (*nf*) thigh; –में जोर होना to have virility/masculine vitality.

रानी ra:nī: (*nf*) a queen; beloved; –बिटिया good daughter; –रूठेंगी अपना सुहाग लेंगी the worst one could do is to do what one can.

राब ra:b (*nf*) molasses, treacle.

राम rā:m (*nm*) *Ramchandra*–the greatest of the ancient Indian kings of Solar dynasty and the hero of the great Indian epic—Ra:ma:yāṉ; God, an incarnation of Vishnu; ~कहानी a tale of woe; long narration of events of one's own life; ~धाम the abode of Ra:m—Ayodhya:; the paradise; ~नवमी the birthday of Ra:m–the ninth day of the bright fortnight of चैत; ~नामी an overall cover cloth with the name of Ra:m written all over; ~बाण a panacea, an unfailing remedy, sure cure; ~रज yellow ochre; ~रस salt; ~राज्य the rule of Ra:m—golden rule; just, equitable and ideal rule; Utopia; -राम a form of mutual salutation; Good God!, an interjectional utterance expressive of hate, surprise, indignation, etc.; ०करके/०कहकर somehow, with great difficulty; ~लीला a celebration involving enactment of the exploits and adventures of Ra:m; –का नाम लो Think of Heavens ! What do you talk ! It's just absurd; –जाने God (alone) knows; –नाम सत्य है lit. the name of God alone is true—a saying repeatedly chanted during a Hindu funeral procession; –भरोसे छोड़ना to let things go as they may, a hostage to fortune; –भरोसे जो रहे मार सके ना कोय what God will, no frost can kill; –राम जपना पराया माल अपना a robber in a saint's garb.

राय ra:y (*nf*) opinion, view; advice; (*nm*) a king; –क़ायम करना to form an opinion; –माँगना to seek the advice of; –मिलना to see eye to eye; –मिलाना to compare notes, to exchange views.

रायता ra:yta: (*nm*) a dish prepared by mixing minced vegetable etc. in salted curd.

रार ra:r (*nf*) a quarrel, wrangling, dispute, alteration; –बढ़ाना to aggravate a quarrel; –मचाना to raise one quarrel after another; to kick up a row; –मोल लेना to seek/ask for a quarrel.

राल ra:l (*nf*) resin; ~दार resinous; –टपकना to be greedy of, to want something forthwith.

राव ra:v (*nm*) a prince, title of the princes of certain former states of India.

रावटी ra:vṭi: (*nf*) a tented apartment.

रावण ra:vāṉ (*nm*) the **king of**

ancient Ceylon who kidnapped Ra:m's queen consort Si:ta: and later fought him and was killed, villain of the great epic Ra:ma:-yān; a demonic person.

रावल ra:val (*nm*) a title of certain Indian princes.

राशन ra:shān (*nm*) ration/rationing.

राशि ra:shi (*nf*) a sum, amount; quantity; heap; sign of the zodiac; ~**चक्र** zodiac; ~**नाम** the name given according to the relevant sign of the zodiac; -**आना** to prove favourable, to be beneficial; -**मिलना** to be agreeably inclined to each other by temperament; to be born in mutually concordant signs of the zodiac.

राष्ट्र ra:shṭr (*nm*) a nation; -**कवि** a poet of the nation; -**गान/गीत** the national anthem; -**चिह्न** the national emblem; -**तंत्र** polity, system of governance; ~**त्व** nationhood; ~**ध्वज** the national flag; -**नीति** national policy, -**पताका** see ~**ध्वज**; ~**पति** President (of a country/nation); ~**भाषा** the national language; ~**मंडल** the Commonwealth; ~**मंडलीय** of or belonging to the Commonwealth; ~**वाद/वादिता** nationalism; ~**वादी** a nationalist; nationalistic; ~**वासी** a national; -**विप्लव** insurrection, revolt against the nation; -**संघ** the League of Nations; -**समाज** comity of nations; ~**हीन** stateless; ~**हीनता** statelessness, the state of being stateless.

राष्ट्रिक ra:shṭrik (*a* and *nm*) (*a*) national; ~**ता** nationality; ~**ता-अर्जन** acquisition of nationality.

राष्ट्रीय ra:shṭri:y (*a*) national; ~**करण** nationalisation; ~**कृत** nationalised.

राष्ट्रीयता ra:shṭri:yata: (*a*) nationality; nationalism.

रास ra:s (*nm*) a circular dance performance associated with the legend of Krishnā and the gopi:s; reins (of a horse etc.); (*a*) favourable, befitting; ~**धारी** a performer who enacts the exploits of Krishnā and represents episodes from his life on the stage; ~**मंडली** the ring of performers of **रास**; ~**लीला** the sport of Krishnā and gopi:s, the enactment on the stage of the exploits of Krishnā and episodes from his life; -**आना** to prove favourable/good/beneficial; -**रचाना** to organise a **रास**; to have a posse of damsels around, to enjoy in the company of pretty women; -**लेना** to adopt (a child).

रासायनिक ra:sa:ynīk (*a*) chemical; -**खाद** chemical fertiliser.

रासो ra:so (*nm*) a class of early Hindi poetic compositions which were written in **डिंगल** and abounded in accounts of amorous exploits of, and battles waged by, kings.

रास्त ra:st (*a*) proper, befitting; -, **राहे** proper course.

रास्ता ra:sta: (*nm*) way, path; route, course; passage; an approach; -**कटना** distance (to the destination) to be covered; -**काटना** to intercept one's course (considered an ill foreboding); -**खुलना** an avenue to open up; hurdles in the way to be cleared; -**चलता** wayfaring; a stranger; -**देखना** to wait (for); -**देना** to allow to pass, to give passage to; -**नापना** to go one's own way, not to meddle with others' affairs;

−निकालना to find a way out;−पकड़ना/लेना to take to one's course, to go one's way; −बताना to evade; to get rid; −बदलना to change one's course; −बनाना to chalk out one's course; −भूलना; to make a chance appearance; to come after a long gap; −साफ़ करना to clear the way, to remove obstacles; −रास्ते का काँटा/रोड़ा an obstacle/impediment; a thorn in the flesh of; रास्ते पर लाना to bring-round, to lead on to the proper course; to win over; रास्ते लगना to follow one's own path/course.

रास्ती ra:sti: (nf) patience; straightforwardness; −से काम लो have patience.

राह ra:h (nf) a way, path; route, course; passage; -खर्च travel expences; ∼गीर a traveller; wayfarer; pedestrian; ∼दारी a passport; octroi, toll; −चलता wayfaring; a stranger; hence oआदमी; -चाह manners, ways; -जन a highwayman; brigand; -जनी waylaying; brigandage; −देखना, अपनी to mind one's own business, to go one's way; ∼बर a guide; ∼बरी guidance; -रस्म/रीति mutual relations, give and take; contacts; −में, खुदा की in the name of God, for God's sake; −ताकना/देखना to wait, to keep waiting (for); −पर लाना to bring round; to win over; −पूछना to seek information regarding the way; to seek guidance; −लगना to go one's way; to mind one's own business; see also रास्ता.

राहत ra:hat (nf) comfort; relief; -कार्य relief operations; −देना to give comfort; to relieve; −मिलना to get comfort; to get relief.

राहित्य ra:hitty (nm) want; absenc the state or condition of bei devoid/bereft of.

राही ra:hi: (nm) a traveller, wa farer; pedestrian.

राहु ra:hu (nm) one of the ni principal planets; the ascendi node of moon; -केतु tradition foes; लगना to fall into adversit to be in a crisis. to be surrou ded by sworn enemies.

रिंग rīṅg (nf) a ring; -मास्टर a rin master.

रिंग/ण, ∼न rīṅgāṇ, ∼n (nm) t act or process of crawling.

रिंच riṅch (nm) a wrench.

रिंद rīnd (nm) a libertine, one wl does not believe in religious tie

रिआय/त ria:yat (nf) concessio favour; ∼ती on concessio concessional; oदर concession rate.

रिआया ria:ya: (nf) subjects.

रिकवँछ rikwāchh (nf) an eatab prepared with बेसन and aru leaves.

रिकशा riksha: (nm) see रिक्शा.

रिकाब rika:b (nf) see रकाब.

रिकाबी rika:bi: (nf) रकाबी.

रिकार्ड rika:rḍ (nm) a record; g mophone record;-रूम record-roo −कायम करना to establish a recor −तोड़ना to break a record; −रख to maintain a record.

रिक्त rikt (a) empty, void; evacu ted; ∼क vacuum; ∼ता vacanc vacuum, void; emptiness; ∼ह penniless, destitute, indige empty-handed; hence ∼हस्त (nf); −करना to evacuate; to empt

रिक्ति rikti (nf) a vacancy; vacuu void.

रिक्थ rikth (nm) legacy; ∼ग्राही/भ a legatee; -पत्र will, testamen

~दान करना to legate.

रिक्शा riksha: (*nm*) a rickshaw; ~वाला a rickshav-puller.

रिज़र्व rizarv (*a*) reserve(d); –पुलिस reserve police; –करना to reserve.

रिज़र्वेशन rizarveshān (*nm*) reservation; –करना to get reserved, to reserve.

रिझाना rijha:nā: (*v*) to captivate, to fascinate, to charm.

रिटायर riṭa:yar (*a*) retired; –होना to be retired.

रिपु ripu (*nm*) an enemy, a foe; ~घाती/घ्न/दमन/सूदन a destroyer of the enemy; ~ता enmity, hostility.

रिपोर्ट riporṭ (*nf*) a report; ~र a reporter; –करना to lodge a report; –देना to (submit a) report.

रिबन riban (*nm*) a ribbon.

रिमझिम rimjhīm (*nf*) drizzling (of rain); –बरसना/होना to drizzle.

रिमार्क rima:rk (*nm*) a remark; –कसना to pass a remark.

रियाज़ riya:z (*nm*) practice; exercise; –करना to practise; to practise for long hours; to keep one's hand in; –टूटना to be out of practice.

रियाज़ी riya:zi: (*a*) industrious; who undertakes long practice, in constant practice.

रियाय/त riya:yat (*nf*) see रिआयत; ~ती see रिआयती (under रिआयत).

रियास/त riya:sat (*nf*) a state; a former princely state of India; an estate; ~ती pertaining/belonging to a ~त; princely; stately.

रिरिया/ना ririya:nā: (*v*) to beslaver, to supplicate meekly, to talk in a very submissive manner; hence ~हट (*nf*).

रिवाज riwa:j (*nm*) custom; vogue, practice.

रिवायत riva:yat (*nf*) tradition, custom; ~न traditionally, as a matter of custom.

रिवाल्वर riva:lvar (*nm*) a revolver.

रिश्ता rishta: (*nm*) relation, relationship; affinity; connection; रिश्ते-नाते relations and connections.

रिश्ते/दार rishteda:r (*nm*) a relative, relation; kinsman; kith and kin; ~दारी relationship, kinsmanship; kinsfolk, body of relations.

रिश्वत rishwat (*nf*) a bribe, illegal gratification; ~ख़ोर a bribee, one who takes bribe; ~ख़ोरी bribery; –खाना/लेना to accept/take bribe; –देना to bribe; –देने वाला a briber; –का बाज़ार गर्म/का बोलबाला होना bribery to be too rampant.

रिस ris (*nf*) anger, wrath; –करना to be angry/enraged; –मारना to subdue anger.

रिसना risnā: (*v*) to leak; to ooze; to percolate.

रिसाना risa:nā: (*v*) to get angry/infuriated/enraged.

रिसालदा/र risa:lda:r (*nm*) a Risaldar—a non-commissioned officer of the cavalry; hence ~री (*nf*).

रिसाला risa:la: (*nm*) cavalry; a journal, magazine.

रिस्टवाच ristwa:ch (*nf*) a wrist-watch.

रिहर्सल riharsal (*nm*) rehearsal; –करना to rehearse.

रिहल rihal (*nm*) a satchel, wooden stand to place an open book upon while reading.

रिहा riha: (*a*) released, set free; discharged; ~ई release; setting free; discharge.

रिहाइ(य)/श riha:i(ya)sh (*nf*) lodging; residence; ~शी residential; इलाक़ा residential area.

रींधना rī:dhnā: (*v*) to cook; to boil.

री ri: (*ind*) a non-honorofic vocative particle used in addressing a female (as **क्यों री!**); a genetive feminine suffix (see **रा**).

रीछ ri:chh (*nm*) a bear.

रीझना rijhnā: (*v*) to be fascinated/charmed/infatuated/attracted.

री/ठा ri:ṭha: (*nm*) soapnut, soap-wart; also **~ठी** (*nf*).

रीडर ri:ḍar (*nm*) a reader.

रीढ़ ri:ṛh (*nf*) back-bone, spine; also **–की हड्डी**; **~दार** spiny; **~हीन** spineless; unsteady, wavering (person); **–टूटना** to become incapacitated, to lose all one's strength.

रीत ri:t (*nf*) see **रीति**.

रीतना ri:tnā: (*v*) to become empty, to be emptied; a vacuum/void to be created.

रीता ri:ta: (*a*) empty; vacant, void; **~पन** emptiness, vacancy, voidness.

रीति ri:ti (*nf*) method, manner, mode; custom, way, practice, vogue; tradition; style; **-ग्रंथ** one of a class of books defining various classifications of heroes, heroines, figures of speech, etc. and setting forth illustrations thereof; **~बद्ध** stylised; traditionalised; **~मुक्त** de-stylised, free from traditionality; **-रिवाज** customs; traditions; **~विधान** methodology.

रीम rī:m (*nm*) ream (of paper); rim (as of a wheel).

रील ri:l (*nf*) a reel (of thread, film, etc).

रुंड rūṇḍ (*nm*) atorso; (headless) trunk; **-मुंड** torso and head.

रुँधना rūdhnā: (*v*) to be choked; to be obstructed; –, **गला** the throat to be choked (with emotion).

रुआँ rūā: (*nm*) fuzz; wool; **~(ए)दार/वाला** fuzzy.

रुआब rua:b (*nm*) see) **रोब**.

रुई rui: (*nf*) cotton; **~दार** cotton-stuffed; **–का गाला** flake of cotton; **–की तरह धुनना** to card like cotton; **-सा** soft, soft and white.

रुकना ruknā: (*v*) to stop; to halt; to stay; to stagnate; to stand; **रुक-रुक कर** haltingly, by fits and starts, spasmodically.

रुकावट ruka:vaṭ (*nf*) hurdle, obstacle, hindrance; barricade; blockade; bar; resistance; **–डालना** to create a hurdle, to obstruct; to barricade, to blockade; to resist.

रुक्क़ा ruqqa: (*nm*) a chit, slip; note; promissory note; a briefly scribbled letter.

रुक्ष ruksh (*a*) arid, hard; harsh, curt, blunt; dry; uneven; rough, rugged; **~ता** aridity; curtness; bluntness; dryness.

रुख़ rukḥ (*nm*) attitude, direction; trend; aspect; the castle (in chess); forepart, face; favourable eye; (*a*) in the direction; **–करना, की ओर** to turn towards; **–देखना** to watch the attitude of; **–पाना** to find favourable attitude of, getting the connivance of; **–बदलना** to change one's attitude; to turn one's face from one direction to another; to change the direction; **–मिलना** to see eye to eye; **–मिलाना** to turn towards, to look into the eyes of.

रुख़सत rukḥsat (*nf*) permission; departure; leave; leisure; **–करना** to give a farewell; **–होना** to take leave.

रुख़सती rukḥsati: (*nf*) farewell, departure (esp. of bride); (*a*) concerning leave/departure.

रुख़सार rukḥsa:r (*nm*) cheek.

रुखाई rukha:i: (*nf*) curtness; harshness, roughness; bluntness.

रुखानी rukha:ni: (*nf*) a chisel.

रुग्ण rugṇ (*a*) ill, sick; unwell, indisposed; diseased, morbid; ~ता illness, sickness; indisposition, morbidity; –मनोवृत्ति morbid mentality; –मिल a sick mill.

रुचना ruchnā: (*a*) to be agreeable; to be of interest, to be interesting; to be to one's liking/taste; to be liked.

रुचि ruchi (*nf*) interest; liking; taste; relish; fancy; ~कर interesting, to one's liking/taste/relish, tasteful, relishing; ~कर्म a hobby; ~कारक/कारी see ~कर.

रुचिर ruchir (*a*) winsome; pleasing, agreeable, beautiful, sweet; hence ~ता (*nf*).

रुझान rujhā:n (*nm*) inclination; aptitude, proclivity, propensity; trend, flair; tendency; bias.

रुत/बा rutba: (*nm*) status; rank; position; overwhelming influence; ~बेदार/~बे वाला of high rank, occupying high position.

रुदंती rudānti: (*nf*) a medicinal plant.

रुदन rudan (*nm*) weeping crying, lamentation; hence रुदित (*a*).

रुद्ध ruddh (*a*) hindered, obstructed, stopped; choked; ~कंठ having a choked throat.

रुद्र ruddr (*nm*) an epithet of Lord Shiv and inferior manifestations of the Lord; hence रुद्राणी—Pa:rvati: —the spouse of Lord Shiv

रुद्राक्ष ruddra:ksh (*nm*) the seeds of the tree *Eleocarpus ganitrus* used for making rosaries.

रुधिर rudhir (*nm*) blood; ~न्यूनता anaemia; ~पायी blood-sucker/blood-sucking; ~मय bloody, full of blood; -विकार impurity of blood; -विज्ञान haematology; ~वैज्ञानिक haematologist; haematological; ~स्राव haemorrhage.

रुधिराक्त rudhira:kt (*a*) blood-stained, blood-soaked.

रुनझुन runjhūn (*nf*) tinkling (of small bells); –करना to tinkle.

रुपया rupya: (*nm*) a rupee; money, wealth; -पैसा money; wealth; रुपयेवाला opulent, rich, wealthy, moneyed; –उड़ाना to squander, to spend extravagantly; –ऐंठना to fleece/extort money; –खरा होना to have earned a sum, money to be as good as in hand; –जोड़ना to accumulate money/wealth; –ठीकरी करना to squander away one's wealth, –डूबना money to become irrecoverable, money to be lost; –तुड़वाना/तोड़वाना to change (into smaller coins); —पानी की तरह बहाना/–पानी में फेंकना to squander away one's money; to make the money fly; –बनाना to make money like hay, to mint money, to earn a fortune; –भुनाना to change (into smaller coins); –मारना to embezzle; to misappropriate; not to repay one's money; रुपये की गर्मी होना to be purse proud, to have a swollen head on account of fat purse; रुपये के पाँव होना money is round and roll away; your money burns a hole in your pocket.

रुपहला rupehla: (*a*) silvery; –पर्दा silver screen.

रुबाई ruba:i: (*nf*) a quatrain, four-foot persian metre used in Urdu (and also Hindi) poetry; ~यात plural form of रुबाई.

रुमाल ruma:l (*nm*) see रूमाल.

रुलाई rula:i: (*nf*) a feeling like crying; weeping, crying, wailing.

रुलाना rula:nā: (*v*) to cause to weep/

cry/lament; to harass, to trouble.

रुष्ट rushṭ (*a*) displeased, angry; **~ता** anger, displeasure.

रुसवा rusva: (*a*) infamous; disgraced, dishonoured; **~ई** infamy; disgrace.

रुस्तम rustām (*nm*) a famous Persian warrior and wrestler; (hence) a very strong man; –, **छिपा** a dark horse, a man of unexpected traits; **-ए-ज़माँ** world champion wrestler; **-ए-हिंद** champion wrestler of India.

रुहेला ruhela: (*nm*) a sub-class of Paṭhā:ns.

रूँ/क, ~गा rū:k, ~ga: (*nm*) a small quantity of a thing given as a consideration over and above that purchased; **–में देना** to give extra quantity as a matter of grace along with the purchase.

रूँधना rū:dhnā: (*v*) to obstruct; to block; to surround.

रू ru: (*nm*) face, countenance, frontage; **~पोश** veiled; an absconder; **~पोशी** veiling one's face; absconding; **-ब-रू** face to face; in the presence of; **-रियायत** consideration; concession; leniency.

रूई ru:i: (*nf*) see **रुई**.

रूक्ष ru:ksh (*a*) see **रुक्ष**; **~ता** see **रुक्षता**.

रूखा ru:kha: (*a*) dry; rough; harsh, curt, blunt; unsympathetic, inconsiderate; without *ghee*, to which *ghee* has not been added (as **रूखा खाना**); dry as a chip, flavourless; uninteresting; **~पन** dryness; roughness; curtness, bluntness; absence of sympathy, inconsiderateness; **-सूखा** plain and simple (esp. used for food); without *ghee*; dry; **-जवाब देना** to give a curt/blunt reply; **–पड़ना** to become curt; to get rough/dry/hard **रूखी हँसी** a superficial laugh.

रूज ru:j (*nm*) rouge.

रूठना ru:ṭhnā: (*v*) to sulk/to b[e] sulky, to be displeased.

रूढ़ ru:ṛh (*a*) established; curren[t] popular; traditional, conventiona[l] stereotyped; indivisible (as [a] number); hence **~ता** (*nf*); **–शब[्द]** conventional/popular word, [a] word that has acquired a meanin[g] not directly connected with i[ts] eltymology.

रूढ़ाचा/र ru:ṛha:cha:r (*nm*) conve[n]tion, custom, traditional conduc[t] hence **~री** (*a*).

रूढ़ार्थ ru:ṛha:rth (*nm*) acceptatio[n] conventional/established/ popu[lar] meaning, meaning establish[ed] through usage.

रूढ़ि ru:ṛhi (*nf*) convention/conve[n]tionalism; usage; **~गत** conve[n]tional, stereotyped; **~ग्रस्त** co[n]vention-bound, conventionalist conservative; hence **~ग्रस्तता** (*n*[*f*]) **~बद्ध** conventionalised; co[n]servative; **~वाद** conventionalis[m] conservatism; **~वादिता** conve[n]tionality; conservatism; **~वादी** conventionalist; conventionalist conservative; o, **अति ~** ultrac[on]servative; too conventional.

रूप ru:p (*nm*) form, shape, appe[ar]ance; beauty; (good) looks, aspe[ct] image; mould; type; **~कार** make[r] man; **~गत** formal; **~ गर्विता** (a m[ai]en) proud of (her) beauty; **~**[...] a portrait; **-तत्त्व** formal eleme[nt] **~धारी** see **बहुरूपिया**; **~परक** m[or]phological; formal; **~मय** bea[uti]ful; hence **~मयी** (feminine for[m]) **~वाद/~वादिता** formalism; **~**[...] a formalist; formalistic; **~वि**[...] morphology; **-विधान** form, for[...]

structure; ~वैज्ञानिक a morphologist; morphological; ~शाली beautiful, handsome, good-looking; -सज्जा make-up.

पक ru:pak (*nm*) a metaphor; an allegory; a play, feature; –अलंकार a metaphor; –विषयक/संबंधी metaphorical; allegorical; –, सांग sustained metaphor; रूपकात्मक allegorical; metaphorical; hence रूपकात्मकता (*nf*).

रूपरेखा ru:prekha: (*nm*) an outline, a synopsis; blueprint; contour.

रूपलेख ru:plekh (*nm*) a feature.

रूपवंत ru:pwānt (*a*) beautiful, handsome, good-looking.

रूप/वान ru:pwa:n (*a*) handsome, good-looking; hence ~वती feminine form.

रूपसी ru:psi: (*nf*) a beautiful damsel, a beauty.

रूपांतर ru:pā:ntar (*nm*) metamorphosis, transformation; variation; adaptation; modification; ~कार adaptor, one who adopts; ~ण undergoing a metamorphosis, transforming; adaptation; modification; ० व्याकरण transformational grammar.

रूपा ru:pa: (*nm*) silver; ~जीवा a prostitute.

रूपात्मक ru:pa:tmak (*a*) formal, characteristic of or belonging to the form; hence ~ता (*nf*).

रूपादर्श ru:pa:darsh (*nm*) a type, specimen; model.

रूपा/यन ru:pa:yan (*nm*) act or process of casting into a form, giving a form, formation; hence ~यित (*a*).

रूपी ru:pi: (*a*) a suffix used in the sense of having the form of, or of the shape of; similar to (as समुद्ररूपी संसार).

रूबरू ru:baru: (*a*) see under रू.

रूमा/नी ru:mā:nī: (*a*) romantic; ~नियत romantic temperament/spirit, romanticism; ~नी रंग चढ़ाना to romanticize.

रूमाल ru:ma:l (*nm*) handkerchief; –पर रूमाल भिगोना to shed a stream of tears, to go on weeping.

रूमाली ru:ma:li: (*nf*) a triangular privy cover.

रूल ru:l (*nm*) a scale; ruler; line; rule; –खींचना to draw a line.

रूलना ru:lnā: (*v*) to draw lines (with the help of a scale).

रूसना ru:sna: (*v*) to get displeased/angry; to sulk.

रूसी ru:si: (*a*) Russian; (*nm*) a Russian; (*nf*) Russian language; dandruff.

रूह ru:h (*nf*) soul; spirit; essence; ~अफ़ज़ा refreshing; –कब्ज़ होना to be frightened out of wits; –काँपना to shudder, to be mortally scared; –फ़ना होना to be mortally scared, to shudder.

रूहा/नी ru:ha:nī: (*a*) spiritual; ~नियत spiritualism.

रेंकना rēknā: (*v*) to bray; to sing/shout hoarsely.

रेंगटा rēgṭa: (*nm*) young one of an ass.

रेंगना rēgnā: (*v*) to creep; to crawl.

रेंड़ rēṛ (*nm*) see) एरंड; see रेढ़; –करना/मारना see रेढ़ करना/मारना.

रें/डी, ~ड़ी reḍi: ~ṛi: (*nf*) castor seed; –का तेल castor oil.

रे re (*ind*) a vocative particle used out of indifference, contempt or disrespect (क्यों रे !); (*nm*) the second note in the Indian musical scale; a genetive suffix (see रा).

रेख rekh (*nf*) a line; mark; just-grown whiskers in early youth; –पत्थर की bound to be true/

happen, a certain eventuality; –आना/भींजना/भीगना/फूटना whiskers to make their first appearance; –खींचना to delimit; to aver; –में मेख मारना to accomplish a very diffiult task, to accomplish an impossibility.

रेखनी rekhnī: (*nf*) a ruler.

रेखां/कन rekhā:ṅkān (*nm*) lining, lineation, underlining; demarcation; ~कित lined, underlined; striated; demarcated; ~कित करना to underline; to demarcate.

रेखांश rekhā:nsh (*nm*) terrestrial longitude.

रेखा rekha: (*nf*) a line; lineament; mark; furrow; (~एँ–pl.) lines on the palm of the hand—fate; destiny; ~कार one who draws a line or demarcates; linear; ~कृति a plan; sketch; liniature line-drawing; ~गणित geometry; ~गणितीय geometrical; ~चित्र a sketch; figure; line-drawing; ~चित्रण sketching; drawing a figure: ~च्छादन hachure; ~लेख a diagram.

रेखित rekhit (*a*) lined, lineate, line-marked; demarcated.

रेखीय rekhi:y (*a*) linear.

रे/ख़्ता rekhta: (*nf*) an earlier form of Urdu with a characteristic mixed vocabulary; ~ख़्ती a typical form of रेख़्ता used by muslim women in particular (hence the nomenclature).

रेगमाल, ~र regma:l, ~r (*nm*) sand-paper, emery paper.

रेगिस्ता/न regista:n (*nm*) a desert; ~नी sandy; of, pertaining or belonging to a desert; ०जहाज a camel.

रे/चक rechak (*a*) purgative; (*nm*) a purgative, jalap; a stage in प्राणायाम when deeply inhaled air is expelled through the nose; ~चन the evacuation of the bowels expulsion of deeply inhaled air through the nose in प्राणायाम ~चित evacuated; purged out (inhaled air) expelled (through the nose).

रेज़/गारी, ~कारी rezga:ri:, ~ka:ri: (*nf*) change (of currency), smaller coins.

रेज़गी rezgi: (*nf*) see रेज़गारी.

रेज़ा reza: (*nm*) a fragment; a small piece.

रेज़र rezar (*nm*) a razor.

रेजिमेंट rejimeṇṭ (*nm*) a regiment.

रेट reṭ (*nf*) rate.

रेडार reḍa:r (*nm*) a radar.

रेडियम reḍiām (*nm*) radium.

रेडियो reḍio (*nm*) radio; ~धर्मिता radioactivity.

रेढ़ reṛh (*nf*) ruination, destruction, devastation; रेढ़ी one who ruins/destructs/devastates; –करना/पीटना/मारना to ruin, to destroy, to davastate.

रेणु renu (*nf*) dust, soil; sand; a small particle, an atom.

रेणुका renuka: (*nf*) see रेणु.

रेत ret (*nf*) sand; –,मोटी gritty sand; –की दीवार house of cards; –पर नाव चलाना to ply a vehicle on water; –से तेल निकालना to milk the bull.

रेतन retan (*nf*) filings.

रेतना retnā: (*v*) to file, to rasp; to polish by filing/rasping.

रेता reta: (*nm*) sand.

रेताई reta:i: (*nf*) work/process of filing or the remuneration paid therefor.

रेती reti: (*nf*) a file; sand.

रेतीला reti:la: (*a*) sandy; gritty; ~पन sandiness; grittiness; –मैदान sandy plain.

रेफ reph (*nm*) the letter र or its

allographs as in क्र, र्क, ट्र.

रेफ़री refri: (*nm*) a referee.

रेल rel (*nf*) rail, railway; railway line; railway train; a flow; current; abundance; -कामगार railwayman; –की पटरी the railway; ~गाड़ी a railway train; -दुर्घटना a railway accident; -पुल a railway bridge; -बिल्टी a railway receipt; –मंत्री Railway Minister; -मार्ग the railways; -लाइन railway (line).

रेलना relnā: (*v*) to rush; to thrust; to push forward.

रेलपेल relpel (*nf*) abundance; plenty; overcrowding; immense influx; rush, throng, jostle; –करना to throng, to overcrowd; to cause or create immense influx/abundance.

रेलवे relwe (*nf*) railway; -पुल railway bridge; -लाइन railway line.

रेला rela: (*nm*) a rush, push; thrust; a huge wave, influx, flood.

रेलिंग reliṅg (*nf*) railing.

रेवड़ rewaṛ (*nm*) a flock (of sheep or goats etc.), herd.

रेवड़ा rewṛa; (*nm*) large-sized रेवड़ी (see).

रेवड़ी rewṛi: (*nf*) a kind of crisp sweetmeat (prepared from solidified sugar covered with sesamum seeds).

रेशम reshām (*nm*) silk; –का कीड़ा a silk-worm; –का कोया a cocoon; –की गाँठ a gordian knot; knot in a silk-thread which is difficult to unknot; arduous task; –ग्रंथि silk-gland; –की लच्छी a ball of silk-thread; -सा as soft as silk.

रेशमी reshmī: (*a*) silken; silk; soft like silk; –कपड़ा/वस्त्र silken cloth, silk fibre; –धागा silk thread.

रेशा resha: (*nm*) a fibre, crude fibre; grain; staple; –, महीन fibrill; **रेशेदार** fibrous.

रेस्टोरेंट, रेस्ट्राँ, रेस्तोराँ, रेस्त्राँ restoreṇṭ, restrā:, restorā:, restrā: (*nm*) a restaurant: –का मालिक, ~वाला a restaurant owner.

रेह reh (*nf*) saline or brackish soil, fossil alkali, fuller's earth (that abounds in certain soils as an efflorescence and renders them barren).

रेहन rehān (*nm*) mortgage, pawn; ~दार mortgagee; ~नामा mortgage-deed.

रेहल rehal (*nf*) see रिहल.

रैअत raiat (*nf*) रैयत.

रैके(कि)ट raike(ki)ṭ (*nm*) a racket.

रैड़ी raiṛi; (*nf*) a handcart; ~वाला a handcart-owner.

रैन rain (*nf*) the night; ~बसेरा nightshelter, a roost.

रैयत raiyat (*nf*) subject; tenant; ~दारी tenancy.

रैयाराव raiya:ra:w (*nm*) a feudal lord.

रैय्यत raiyyat (*nf*) see रैयत.

रोंग/टा rōgṭa: (*nm*) small and soft hairs on the body; ~टे खड़े होना to give one the creeps, to make one's flesh creep, to make one's hair stand on end, to horripitate, to be horrified.

रोंवाँ rowā: (*nm*) see रोआँ.

रो/आँ roā: (*nm*) small and soft hair on the body; ~आँ-रोआँ कर्ज़ में बिंधा होना one's whole being to be under debt, to be under very heavy debts; see also रोयाँ; ~एँ-रोएँ से आशीर्वाद देना to spell out whole-hearted blessings, to bless from the core of the heart.

रोएँदार rōeda:r (*a*) hairy, woolly.

रोक rok (*nf*) a ban, restriction, check; prevention; stay; scotch, hedge; hindrance; barrier; -टोक

restriction, obstruction; opposition; -थाम prevention; check, temporary remedy; –लगाना to impose a ban/restriction.

रोकड़ rokaṛ (*nf*) cash, ready money; cash book; –जमा opening balance; –बही a cash-book; –बाक़ी cash balance in hand; –मिलाना to tally the balance.

रोकड़ा rokṛa: (*a*) cash; –बाक़ी cash balance in hand; –बिक्री cash sale.

रोकड़िया rokaṛiya: (*nm*) a cashier, treasurer.

रोकना roknā: (*v*) to stop; to detain; to prevent, to check; to ban; to withhold; to cease; to stay; to discontinue; to forbid; to impede; to suppress, to repress, to curb; (*nm*) engagement, a ceremony for confirmation of engagement; रोकने वाला preventive/restrictive; checker; one who checks/prevents etc.; रोके रखना to hold at bay.

रोग rog (*nm*) a disease; illness, ailment, sickness; malady; affliction; ~कर/कारक/कारी infectious, causing illness, sickening; ~ग्रस्त ailing; diseased, ill, sick; ~नाशक/हर/हारी curative; cure; -निदान diagnosis, pathogenesis; ~निरोधी prophylactic; ~भ्रम hypochondria; ~भ्रमी hypochondriac; ~मुक्ति cure; -लक्षण symptom (of disease); ~वाहक disease-carrier; –की जड़ खाँसी लड़ाई की जड़ हाँसी jokes lie at the root of all conflicts as cough at the root of all physical ailments; –पालना to knowingly own a malady; to develop an unhealthy habit.

रोग़न rogān (*nm*) varnish, paint; polish; grease; ~दार varnished; polished; greasy.

रोग़नी rognī: (*a*) oily, smeared with varnish or oil.

रोगार्त्त roga:rt (*a*) diseased, sick, ailing.

रोगिल rogil (*a*) diseased, ailing.

रोगी rogi: (*nm*) a patient, diseased; valetudinarian; (*a*) ailing; -कक्ष a ward; hence रोगिणी (*nf*).

रोचक rochak (*a*) interesting, pleasing, entertaining; hence ~ता (*nf*).

रोज़ roz (*nm*) day; (*adv*) everyday, daily; -ब-रोज़ everyday; daily; day-by-day; ~मर्रा everyday, daily; -रोज़ everyday, daily; –का चक्कर/धंधा the daily grind; –कुआँ खोदना रोज़ पानी पीना to labour for the day's two meals; –के टपके पत्थर भी घिघल जाता है constant dropping wears the stone away.

रोज़गार rozga:r (*nm*) a business, trade; employment; profession, occupation: –का दफ़्तर, -कार्यालय employment exchange; –चमकना business to brighten up, to have a run of good luck in business.

रोज़नदा/र rozanda:r (*nm*) a labourer (working) on daily wage, daily wage labour; ~री daily wages; ~री पर on daily wages.

रोज़नामचा roznā:mcha: (*nm*) a dairy; daily account book; daily report book.

रोज़नामा rozna:mā: (*nm*) daily paper.

रोज़ा roza: (*nm*) a fast (observed by muslims during the month of Ramja:n); ~दार fasting, observing fast; –खोलना to break one's रोज़ा (fast); –तोड़ना to violate a रोज़ा (fast); –रखना to observe a रोज़ा (fast); –बख़्शाते नमाज़ गले पड़ना to work for deliverance, to add to the bonds.

रोज़ाना roza:nā: (*adv*) daily, everyday; –का काम daily chore; routine duty.

रोज़ी rozi: (*nf*) livelihood; living, means of subsistence; -रोटी livelihood, means of subsistence; o कमाना to earn one's livelihood; –लेना to deprive somebody of his means of livelihood.

रोज़ीना rozi:nā: (*adv*) daily, everyday; ~दार, रोज़नदार; see रोज़नदारी.

रोट roṭ (*nm*) a large and thick bread; sweet thick loaf.

रोटी roṭi: (*nf*) a bread; meals; food; lunch; livelihood; -कपड़ा food and clothing, means of subsistence; –कमाना to earn one's livelihood; –का पेट the front of a bread (which is baked first); –का सवाल a matter of daily bread; –की पीठ the back of bread; -दाल lit. bread and pulse—plain and simple food, the barest minimum in respect of diet; -दाल चलाना to make two ends meet, to manage one's livelihood somehow or other; -दाल समझना (a job assignment, work, etc.) to take as a routine, to take as usual, to take as simple and straight; ~वाला a baker; bread-seller; -बेटी का संबंध (said of different groups) mutual relation through socially sanctioned collective eating and marriages amongst one another, collective messing and mutual marrying relations; रोटियों के मोहताज होना/लाले पड़ना to be too tight even for two square meals; रोटियाँ तोड़ना to eat the bread of idleness.

रोडवेज roḍwez (*nm*) roadways.

रोड़ा roṛa: (*nm*) pebbles, fragments of stones or bricks; obstruction, hindrance; impediment; –होना to be an impediment/obstruction/ a hindrance; रोड़े अटकाना/डालना to obstruct, to create an obstacle/ impediment; to pave the way with obstructions.

रोड़ी roṛi: (*nf*) rubble.

रोदन rodan (*nm*) weeping, crying.

रोध rodh (*nm*) a bar; obstruction, hindrance.

रोना ronā: (*v*) to weep, to cry: to bewail, to lament; (*nm*) weeping, crying; bewailing, lamenting; tale of woe (as अपना रोना ले बैठना); –,फूट-फूटकर to weep bitterly, to bewail; रोते गये मरे की ख़बर लाये he that asks faintly begets a denial; –आना to feel like crying; -गाना to express sorrow or joy; to weep and wail; sorrows and joys; -धोना/पीटना to weep and wail; weeping and wailing; to lament/lamenting; रोनी सूरत gloomy/ sad countenance, sombre appearance/ face; oबनाना to pull/wear/ draw a long face; रोने वाला न रहना, कोई to have none to mourn one's end.

रोप rop (*nf*) seedling.

रोपण ropan (*nm*) (the act or process of) planting, plantation, implanting; sowing.

रोपना ropnā: (*v*) to plant; to implant; to establish firmly; to transplant; to sow; –, पाँव to entrench oneself firmly; to stay determinedly in one's position; to intermeddle.

रोपनी ropnī: (*nf*) transplantation of a seedling (esp. of paddy).

रोपित ropit (*a*) transplanted/implanted, planted.

रोब rob (*nm*) overbearing influence, sway; commanding/imposing quality; -दाब awe, overbearing influence, sway; ~दार commanding; awe-inspiring, imposing; —गाँठना/ग़ालिब करना/जमाना to overwhelm, to overawe; to try to cow down; —में आना to be overawed/cowed down.

रोबीला robi:la: (*a*) see रोबदार (under रोब); hence ~पन (*nm*).

रोमंथ romanth (*nm*) rumination; ~न rumination.

रोम rom (*nm*) (small and soft) hair (on the body); ~कूप the pores on the surface of the skin; ~गुच्छ cirri; ~पूर्ण hairy, lanate; ~राजी see रोमाली; ~हर्षक thrilling; awful, dreadful, terrible; ~हर्षण horripilation; -रोम में in the whole being, throughout the body: o बसना to pervade through the whole being; -रोम से with heart and soul, with one's whole being.

रोमक romak (*nm*) cilia.

रोमां/च romā:nch (*nm*) horripilation, titillation, thrill, standing of the hairs on end; ~चित thrilled, in rapture; horripilated/horripilant, titillated; o करना to horripilate, to titillate; to thrill; रोमांचित होना to be thrilled; to be horripilated; to be in a rapture.

रोमांतिका romā:ntika: (*nf*) measles.

रोमा/नी romā:ni: (*a*) romantic; ~नियत romanticism, romantic character.

रोमा/ली ~वलि, ~वली roma:li:, ~wali, ~wali: (*nf*) the line of hairs over the body (esp. extending above the navel).

रोमिका romika: (*nf*) cilia.

रोमिल romil (*a*) hairy, lanate; pubescent; ~ता hairiness.

रोयाँ royā: (*nm*) see रोम; रोयेंदार hairy, woolly; रोयें खड़े होना to horripilate; to be thrilled; —टेढ़ा न होना to be put to no harm whatever, to emerge unscathed; —पसीजना to be moved by compassion; -रोयाँ आशीर्वाद देना see रोएं-रोएं का आशीर्वाद देना under रोआँ.

रोर ror (*nm*) noise, clamour, outcry.

रोरी rori: (*nf*) see रोली.

रोलर rolar (*nm*) a roller; —फेरना to level (with the ground); to devastate.

रोला rola: (*nm*) an important Hindi poetic metre consisting of 24 *ma:tra:s* in one line; see रौला.

रोली roli: (*nf*) a mixture of turmeric and lime powder (used for applying तिलक on the forehead on auspicious occasions),

रोवनहार rowanha:r (*nm*) a mourner, one who laments.

रोवाँ rowā: (*nm*) see रोआँ, रोयाँ.

रोशन roshan (*a*) lighted, lit; shining, bright; famous; manifest; ~दान a ventilator; —करना to bring to light; to make known; hence —होना.

रोशनाई roshnā:i: (*nf*) ink.

रोशनी roshnī: (*nf*) light, illumination; eye-sight; —डालना to throw light on.

रोष rosh (*nm*) anger, rage, wrath, resentment; —प्रकट करना to express anger/resentment; —में आना to fly into a rage, to be in a temper.

रोहण rohān (*nm*) climbing, ascending, mounting.

रोहा roha: (*nm*) see रोहे.

रोही rohi: —a suffix used in the sense of one who climbs/mounts.

रोहू rohu: (*nf*) a kind of large fish.

रोहे rohe (*nm*) trachoma.

रौंद raund (*nm*) trampling (over), crushing under the feet; round; —पर जाना to go on a round.

रौंदना rāūdnā: (*v*) to trample down, to tread over, to crush down.

रौ rau (*nf*) motion, flow; impulsive mood; **–में होना** to be under an impulse, to be on the crest of a wave of impulse.

रौग़न raugān (*nm*) see **रोग़न**.

रौग़नी raugnī: (*a*) see **रोग़नी**.

रौज़ा rauza: (*nm*) a tomb.

रौद्र rauddr (*a*) terrible, fearful, furious; **–रस** the sentiment of wrath or furiousness in Indian poetics; **–रूप धारण करना** to show one's furious form, to be in a fierce rage.

रौनक़ raunāq (*nf*) gaiety, splendour, brightness and brilliance; **~अफ़्ज़ा/अफ़्रोज होना** to grace an occasion; **~अफ़्ज़ाई/अफ़्रोज़ी** gracing of an occasion; **~दार** gay, splendid, bright and brilliant.

रौप्य rauppy (*a*) silvery, made of silver; (*nm*) silver.

रौरव raurav (*nm*) the name of the worst of hells according to Hindu mythology.

रौला raula: (*nm*) noise, clamour; **–डालना** to create a noise.

रौशन raushān (*a*) see **रोशन**.

रौशनी raushnī: (*nf*) see **रोशनी**.

ल

ल la—traditionally, the third of the semi-vowel series **य, र, ल, व** of the Devna:gri: alphabet. Modern phoneticians do not, however, recognise the letter as a semi-vowel in Hindi but as a consonant.

लंक lāṅk (*nf*) the waist, loins; see **लंका**.

लंका lāṅka: (*nf*) Ceylon—the island in the Indian ocean where Ra:wāṉ, the demon king and villain of the ancient epic Ra:mā:yāṉ, ruled; **~नाथ/पति** the ruler of **लंका** —an epithet of Ra:wāṉ; **~कांड** arson, a burning episode; **–में सब बावन गज/हाथ के** where every hand fleeceth, the sheep go naked; all as black as the devil.

लंकिनी lāṅkinī: (*nf*) a witch.

लंके/श, ~श्वर lāṅkesh, ~shwar (*nm*) see **लंकानाथ** (under **लंका**).

लंग lāṅg (*nf*) lameness, limp/limping; **–करना/खाना** to limp (said of a horse etc.)

लंगड़ lāngaṛ (*a*) see **लँगड़ा**; (*nm*) a piece of stone/pebble tied to kite-flying thread (used by children for catching hold of kites etc.); **~दीन** a limping fellow.

लँगड़ा lāgṛa: (*a*) lame, limp; (*nm*) a lame person; **~पन** lameness, limpness; **–बुख़ार** dengue (fever); **-लूला** cripple/crippled; **~हट** see **~पन**.

लँगड़ाना lāgṛa:nā: (*v*) to limp.

लँगड़ी lāgṛi: (*nf*) a leg-trick; (*a*) see **लँगड़ा**; **–मारना/–लगाना** to apply a leg-trick, to fell somebody through the application of leg-trick.

लंगर lāṅgar (*nm*) an anchor; a public kitchen, an alms-house; a heavy wooden piece/block tied to a cattle's neck (to check it from running far); pendulum; tentative stitches made at long distances in a cloth; a privy cover worn by wrestlers; a piece of stone tied at the end of a long thread; (*a*) mischievous, naughty; vile; ~**खाना** a public kitchen, an alms-house; –**उठाना** to set sail, to take off anchor, –**करना/डालना** to come to an anchor, to cast anchor; –**खोलना** to start a public kitchen.

लंगूर, लँगूर lāṅgu:r, lāgu:r (*nm*) a kind of black-faced monkey with a stiff long tail, an ape; ~**मुँहा** having an ape-like face, ape-faced.

लंगो/ट, ~टा lāgoṭ, ~ṭa: (*nm*) a strip of cloth tucked round the waist to cover privities; ~**ट का कच्चा/ढीला** lewd, lustful, of loose character; one who has a weakness for sex indulgence; ~**ट का सच्चा** sexually righteous, one who has no sex-weakness, incorruptible on the sexual plane; ~**ट फाड़ डालना** to give up wrestling; ~**टबंद** a celibate; sexually righteous/incorruptible; ~**टिया यार** a chum, bosom friend; ~**टी** a comparatively smaller **लँगोट**; ~**टी बँधवाना** to render penniless/indigent; ~**टी बिकवाना** to cause to be deprived of the barest minimum, to render absolutely indigent; ~**टी में मस्त** happy and carefree in utmost adversity; ~**टी लगाये घूमना** to be extremely indigent, to have nothing even to clothe onese[lf] decently.

लंघन laṅghan (*nm*) going withou[t] meals, forcible or imposed fas[t] fasting; transgressing, crossing.

लंघनीय laṅghnī:y (*a*) transgress[a]ble, fit to be crossed; also **लंघ[्य]** hence ~**ता** (*nf*).

लंच lanch (*nm*) lunch.

लंठ lanṭh (*a*) stupid; boorish, unc[i]vil; ~**राज** an extremely stupi[d] and boorish fellow, the greate[st] of fools.

लंड lanḍ (*nm*) penis.

लंतरानी lantara:nī: (*nf*) braggadoci[o] boasting; self-praise.

लंप lamp (*nm*) a lamp.

लंपट lampaṭ (*a*) lewd, wanto[n] lascivious (person); unchast[e] ~**ता** lewdness, wantonness, lasc[i]viousness.

लंब lamb (*nm*) a perpendicular; (*a*) long; an allomorph of **लंबा**; ~**क[र्ण]** having long ears; ~**केश** ha[v]ing long hair; ~**त:** perpend[i]cularly; -**तड़ंग** strapping, tall a[nd] tough; ~**ता** perpendicularity; ~[...] lengthening; prolonging, pendin[g] ~**मान** prolonged; perpendicula[r] pendent.

लंबर/दार lambarda:r (*nm*) hea[d]man (of a community, villag[e] etc.); ~**दारी** headmanship.

लंबलेट lambleṭ (*a*) fallen flat: –**हो[ना]** to fall flat.

लंबा lamba: (*a*) long, lengthy; ta[ll] -**चौड़ा** vast, spacious, extensi[ve] tall and well-built; -**तड़ंगा** strap[p]ing, tall and tough; –**करना** tell off, to compel to move o[ff] –**बनना/होना** to slip away, to sh[ow] a clean pair of heels; –**हाथ मा[रना]** to grab a sizable fortune, to ha[ve] a big windfall; **लंबे डग भरना**

take long strides; लंबे हाथ resourcefulness; (person etc.) having a long reach/range.

लंबाई lamba:i: (*nf*) length; height; **-चौड़ाई** length and breadth/width; dimensions.

लंबान lambā:n (*nm*) see लंबाई;-/चौड़ान see लंबाई-चौड़ाई (under लंबाई).

लंबायमान lamba:ymā:n (*a*) lengthened, lying flat; prolonged, pendent.

लंबित lambit (*a*) penduline; prolonged; lengthened; pending.

लंबी lambi: (*a*) long; tall; **-चौड़ी हाँकना** to boast/brag, to talk tall; to talk through one's hat; **–तनख़्वाह** fat salary; **–तानकर सोना** to enjoy a carefree sleep; **–तानना** to sleep carefreely; **–साँस खींचना/भरना/लेना** to heave a sigh, to draw a deep sigh; to be remorseful; **–साँस छोड़ना** to heave a sigh of helplessness/despair.

लंबू lambu: (*nm*) a lankey; (*a*) tall (and thin man); **~दास** a lanky fellow.

लंबोतरा lambotra: (*a*) longish, somewhat long.

लंबोदर lambodar (*a*) pot-bellied; long-bellied, paunchy; gluttunous; (*nm*) an epithet of Ganēsh; a glutton.

लंबोष्ठ lamboshṭḥ (*a*) long-lipped.

लकड़ lakaṛ—an allomorph of लकड़ी used as the first member in many compound words, e.g. लकड़हारा, लकड़फोड़ा, etc.; used to convey vertical relationship with one's forefathers/great great-grand (as लकड़दादा great great grandfather),

लकड़फोड़ा lakaṛphoṛa: (*nm*) a woodpecker.

लकड़बग्घा lakaṛbaggha: (*nm*) a hyena.

लकड़हारा lakaṛha:ra: (*nm*) a woodcutter, woodman.

लकड़ाना lakaṛa:nā: (*v*) to become wooden/lifeless; to be lanky.

लकड़ी lakṛi: (*nf*) wood; fuel, firewood; timber; a stick; a support (as अंधे की लकड़ी); **-का** wooden; **–की मेख** dowel; **-सा** lean and thin; **–होना** to be very lean and thin, to be lanky; **–के बल बंदर नाचे** lit. the rod makes the monkey dance, it is some sort of support/instigation that makes one venture beyond one's tether.

लक़दक़ laqdaq (*a*) shining, brilliant, spotlessly white, neat and clean.

लक़ब laqab (*nm*) a title; designation.

लक़लक़ laqlaq (*a*) lanky, lean and thin (man).

लक़वा laqwa: (*nm*) paralysis, palsy; **–मारना/लगना** to be paralysed/palsied, to suffer an attack of paralysis.

लका/र laka:r (*nm*) the letter ल and its sound; **~रांत** word ending in ल्.

लकीर laki:r (*nf*) a line; trail, streak; track; stride; **–का फ़कीर** a conventionalist/traditionalist, one wedded irrevocably to convention/tradition; **–पर चलना** to follow one's conventions/traditions, to tread a beaten track; **–पीटना** to follow the traditions; to repent, to be remorseful.

लकुटी lakuṭi: (*nf*) a small stick.

लक्कड़ lakkaṛ (*nm*) a log; wood.

लक्का कबूतर lakka: kabu:tar (*nm*) a fan-tailed species of pigeon.

लक्ष laksh (*a* and *nm*) a lac; the number one hundred thousand; a mark, target; **~पति** a millionaire, a wealthy person; ~बेधी hitting the target/mark·

लक्षण lakshāṇ (nm) a symptom; indication; trait, characteristic feature, characteristic mark; ~विज्ञान semiology; ~विज्ञानी semiologist; ~वैज्ञानिक semiological; –दिखाई पड़ना to be on the horizon.

लक्षणा lakshaṇā: (nf) indirect, implied or figurative sense of a word; ~मूलक arising out of लक्षणा; hence ~मूलकता (nf); –शक्ति the word-power of indirect or implied or figurative expression·

लक्षणात्मक lakshaṇā:tmak (a) symptomatic; indicative of; characteristic; figurative; indirect; implied; ~ता the state of being implied/figurative/indirect; indicativeness, figurative/symptomatic quality.

लक्षणी lakshaṇī: (a) having some typical लक्षण (feminine form).

लक्षित lakshit (a) implied, hinted, indicated; marked; observed; reflected.

लक्षितार्थ lakshita:rth (nm) a meaning based on लक्षणा, indirect/implied or figurative meaning of a word.

लक्ष्मण lakshmāṇ (nm) a younger brother of Ra:m in the ancient Indian epic of Ra:mā:yāṇ; ·रेखा in the epic Ra:ma:yāṇ, the line drawn by Lakshmāṇ bidding Si:ta: not to cross it for her own security·

लक्ष्मी lakshmī: (nf) the goddess of wealth and spouse of Lord Vishṇū; prosperity, fortune; used deferentially for a woman as symbolising prosperity; ~कांत/नाथ/पति/रमण/वल्लभ an epithet of

Lord Vishṇū; ~पूजा the worship of लक्ष्मी on the day of दीपावली; ~वान wealthy; prosperous; –का वाहन lit. vehicle of Lakhsmi, viz. the owl—in India a symbol of foolishness, a fool.

लक्ष्य lakkshy (nm) the aim, object/objective, target, goal; (a) indicated, implied; -पूर्ति fulfilment of the target, -बेध hitting the target; -सिद्धि attainment of one's aim/object/goal·

लक्ष्यार्थ lakkshya:rth (nm) indicated, implied or figurative meaning (of a word).

लखप/ती lakhpati: (nm) a millionaire, very wealthy person; ~तराश derisively said of a man who makes a show of wealthiness·

लखरांव lakhrā:w (nm) a vista.

लखलखा lakhlakha: (nm) a strongly scented medicine used to restore consciousness·

लगन lagān (nf) devotion; perseverence; inclination; attachment; an auspicious moment (for performing a ceremony); ·पत्र/-पत्री a letter intimating fixation of marriage (sent by bride's side to that of the bridegroom's); –धरना to fix the date of marriage; —सोधना to calculate astrologically an auspicious moment (for performing a marriage ritual)·

लगना lagnā: (v) to seem, to appear; to be engaged (in); to be employed; to be united/attached/connected; to strike roots (as पौदा–); to be grafted; to be related (as वह मेरा साला लगता है); to be applied (as मलहम–); to have a painful sensation, to cause pain (as आंखों में दवा लग रही है); to be affixed to; to be struck, to be hit (as डंडा–);

to be burnt (as दूध–, दाल–); to cost (as इस पर चार रुपये लगे); to devote oneself to (कल से उस काम में लगूँगा); to continue; to be wounded by (as गोली–); to follow (as पीछे–); to be levied (as टैक्स–); to feel bad, to pinch (as बात–); to smart; to be rubbed; to scratch; to pierce (as काँटा–); to have an affect (as पानी–); to be caused (as भीड़–); to have a quarrel (उनकी आपस में लगती है); to fall in love with (दोनों ओर लगी हुई है); to bear (as फल–) to have sexual intrecourse; लगकर with concentration; in a determined/concentrated/resolute manner (as ०काम करना, ०इलाज करना); लगती बात an utterance that pinches: लगी-लगाई fixed; settled; लगे तो तीर नहीं तो तुक्का if it hits it's a sure shot, if it doesn't an awry missile; लगे लग्गे में/हाथ while still in it, in continuity; along with other things, in the same effort.

लगभग lagbhag (*ind*) approximately, almost, about; roughly, nearly.

लगलग laglag (*a*) weak, lanky, lean and thin.

लगाऊ laga:u: (*a* and *nm*) back-biting; a back-biter; having rift-creating designs; an instigator; also -बुझाऊ (see लगाना-बुझाना).

लगातार laga:ta:r (*adv*) continuously; incessantly, constantly; (*a*) continuous, continual, sustained.

लगान lagā:n (*nm*) land revenue/rent.

लगाना laga:nā: (*v*) to engage; to employ; to attach, to join, to connect; to plant (as पौदा–); to apply (as मलहम–); to affix (as टिकट–); to make someone hang around (as पीछे–); to levy (as टैक्स–); to touch (as हाथ–); to invest (as पैसा–); to paste, to stick (as इश्तहार–); to set, to fix; to shut, to close (as दरवाजा–); to keep; to backbite; to inflame; to add; –बुझाना to backbite, to distort facts so as to instigate, to indulge in instigatory talks.

लगाम lagā:m (*nf*) reins, bridle, hackmore; –कड़ी करना/कसना to restrain; to be strict; to keep in check: –चढ़ाना to bridle; –ढीली करना to give one his head, to give free rein; to give/allow latitude/free play; to withdraw restraint; to allow to go as one wishes;–देना to keep under restraint; to withhold; –हाथ में लेना to take the reins in one's hand, to undertake the control of.

लगालगी laga:lagi: (*nf*) involvement, attachment, love; intimate contact.

लगाव laga:w (*nm*) attachment, love, affection; –होना to be attached (to/with).

लगी lagi: (*nf*) longing, ardent desire, what has been taken to heart; –बुझना one's longing to be fulfilled; –बुरी होती है the flame of love once ignited must have its toll, love leaves none unscathed; –छूटती नहीं the inefection of love persists; the heart once lost can never be retrieved.

लगुन lagun (*nf*) see लग्न-पत्र (under लग्न).

लग्गा lagga: (*nm*) a thick long pole; commencement, start; –लगाना to start/commence; लग्गे से पानी पिलाना to render only nominal help.

लग्गी laggi: (*nf*) a thin long pole; a large pole (used to propel a boat); a fishing rod.

लग्गू laggu: (*a* and *nm*) who sticks to a man/work; who dogs/follows; a hanger-on; a paramour; -बज्झू/भग्गू a hanger-on, riff-raff.

लग्न lagn (*nf*) an auspicious moment for performance of a ceremony or commencement of a work; an appointed day/time of marriage etc.; (*a*) attached, connected; ~पत्र/पत्रिका a formal letter or document in which the date and time etc. of the marriage ceremony are formally intimated; see लगन.

लग्नक lagnak (*nm*) a surety, guarantor.

लघिमा laghimā: (*nf*) smallness, littleness; lightness; one of the eight *siddhis* which enables a man to assume as tiny a form as he likes.

लघु laghu (*a*) tiny, small, little, short; light; acute (as कोण); insignificant; low, mean; reduced; ~करण reduction; abridgement; ~काय tiny, of tiny form; ~कोण acute angle; ~गणक logarithm; ~चित्र miniature; ~चेता low-minded, mean, parochial; -तंत्रिका nervule; ~तम minimum, lowest; smallest; o समापवर्त्य least common multiple (l.c.m.); ~तर smaller; lower; ~ता/त्व insignificance; smallness; meanness; humiliation; o की भावना inferiority complex; ~पेशी a follicle; ~मति fool, foolish; blockheaded; ~रूप/रूपी, ~रूपचित्र miniature; –रूपक a skit; ~शंका urine; making water, urinating; o करना to piss, to urinate; –संस्करण abridged edition, miniform; –सप्तर्षि ursa minor.

लघ्वाहार lagghwa:ha:r (*nm*) light refreshment.

लच lach (*nf*) see लचक.

लचक lachak (*nf*) elasticity, flexibility, resilience; springiness; ~दार flexible, elastic, resilient/resiling; ~न see लचक; ~ना to resile, to spring; to bend.

लचकीला lachki:la: (*a*) see लचीला.

लचना lachnā: (*v*) to bend; to mellow down; to assume flexibility.

लचर lachar (*a*) untenable; weak; ineffective; unstable; –दलील an untenable argument; hence ~पन (*nm*).

लचलचा lachlacha: (*a*) see लचीला; ~पन see लचीलापन (under लचीला).

लचीला lachi:la: (*a*) flexible, elastic, resilient, pliable; springy, willowy; ~पन flexibility, resilience, elasticity, pliability.

लच्छा lachchha: (*nm*) skein (of thread/yarn etc.), hank; circular silver ornament for the feet; a kind of sweetmeat.

लच्छी lachchhi: (*nf*) skein (of thread/yarn), hank.

लच्छेदार lachchheda:r (*a*) having fine shreds; interesting, fascinating; –बात fascinating talk, pleasant/amusing nothings; –भाषा fascinating language; –शैली fascinating style.

लजाना laja:nā: (*v*) to blush, to feel shy; to be ashamed.

लजीज़ lazi:z (*a*) tasteful, tasty, delicious.

लजीला laji:la: (*a*) shy, bashful; hence ~पन (*nm*).

लजौहाँ lajauhā: (*a*) feeling somewhat shy/blushed, reflecting some shyness.

लज़्ज़त lazzat (*nf*) taste, relish; deliciousness; tastefulness; ~दार tasty, delicious, tasteful.

लज्जा lajja: (*nf*) shame; modesty; shyness, bashfulness; ~कर/कारी/जनक/प्रद shameful; ~लु bashful, shy; hence ~लता (*nf*); ~वती bashful/shy (woman); ~वान bashful/shy (man); –घोलकर पी जाना to be absolutely brazen/shameless, to be completely lost to shame; see लाज.

लज्जावंती lajja:wānti: (*nf*) a typical sensitive plant; (*a*) bashful/shy/blushing (woman).

लज्जित lajjit (*a*) ashamed; blushed; –करना to put to the blush, to put to shame.

लट laṭ (*nf*) a tress, lock of hair, tangled hair; ringlet; –छिटकाना to scatter tresses/tangled or locked hair, to have dishevelled locks of hair.

लटक laṭak (*nf*) a bend, coquetry, blandishment; affected movement.

लटकन laṭkān (*nm*) a hanging pendant, pendulum; nose-drop; anything hanging.

लटकना laṭaknā: (*v*) to hang, to overhang; to hang in the balance; to swing, to lop; to suspend; to be in a suspense, to keep in a state of indecision; to be delayed.

लट/का laṭka: (*nm*) a formula, tip; nostrum; device, trick; affected movement; ways; mannerism; ~केबाज one who shows off typical mannerism, one who tries to impress through typical devices; ~केबाजी display of typical mannerism, an effort to impress through typical devices.

लटकाना laṭka:nā: (*v*) to hang, to overhang; to suspend, to keep waiting, to keep in suspense; to delay.

लटकौआ laṭkaua: (*a*) hanging.

लटना laṭnā: (*a*) to thin, to become lean and thin.

लटपटा laṭpaṭa: (*a*) loose; faltering, stumbling.

लटपटाना laṭpaṭa:nā: (*v*) to stumble, to stagger, to falter; –, जीभ to mispronounce, the tongue to slip/falter.

लटा laṭa: (*a*) lean and thin, weakened; also -दुबला.

लटापोट laṭa:poṭ (*a*) bursting with laughter; fascinated, bewitched.

लटियाना laṭiya:nā: (*a*) to form into tresses, hair to be tangled in locks.

लट्टू laṭṭu: (*nm*) a (spinning) top; bulb; knob; ~दार fitted with a bulb/knob; –होना to be fascinated/enamoured/bewitched; to fall in love.

लट्ठ laṭṭh (*nm*) a cudgel; long heavy staff; (*a*) blockhead, stupid; –गँवार stupid and boorish; ~बंद equipped with a लट्ठ; a cudgel-wielder; one who is equipped with a लट्ठ; ~बाज skilled in wielding or brandishing a लट्ठ; ~बाज़ी cudgel fighting; skill in wielding a लट्ठ; ~मार uncivil; harshly forthright; –लिए फिरना to be always out to fight, inclined to pick up a fight; to be hostile to; –लिए फिरना, अक़्ल के पीछे to go out demanding tribute of the dead.

लट्ठा laṭṭhā: (*nm*) a log, raft; a five and half hand-span long bamboo used for land-measurement; long cloth, a kind of white cloth.

लठियल laṭhiyal (*v*) see लठैत.

लठैत laṭhait (*a* and *nm*) skilled in wielding/brandishing लाठी, an expert in brandishing a cudgel, cudgel fighter.

लड़ laṛ (*nf*) a string; row.

लड़क laṛak—an allomorph of लड़का

used as the first member in certain compounds (as लड़कपन); ~बुद्धि puerility/puerile; childishness/childish.

लड़क/पन, ~पना laṛakpan, ~panā: (*nm*) childhood; boyhood; childishness, puerility.

लड़का laṛka: (*nm*) a boy, lad; male child; son; bridegroom; an inexperienced person; लड़केवाला the bridegroom's father/guardian; लड़के-वाले progeny; members of bridegoom's party/side; लड़कों का खेल child's play, non-serious affair; an easy job.

लड़की laṛki: (*nf*) a girl; daughter; bride; ~वाला the bride's father/guardian; ~वाले members of the bride's side/party.

लड़खड़ा/ना laṛkhaṛa:nā: (*v*) to stagger, to stumble; to falter, to totter, to wobble, to titubate; ~हट stagger/staggering, titubation; totter/tottering; stumbling.

लड़ना laṛnā: (*v*) to quarrel; to fight; to struggle; to collide, to clash; to contend; to wrestle; to combat; -झगड़ना/भिड़ना to pick up quarrels; to have altercation; quarrelling/altercation; लड़ मरना to fight like kilkenny cats, to fight to mutual destruction; लड़ते-झगड़ते/भिड़ते रहना to lead cat and dog life; लड़ने-वाला a fighter, wrestler; combatant; quarrelsome.

लड़ाई laṛa:i: (*nf*) fight; war, battle; quarrel; encounter, clash; enmity; -झगड़ा/लड़ाई broil, altercation, quarrel; —के बीज बोना to sow dragon's teeth; —में लिहाज कैसा all is fair in love and war; —मोल लेना to get embroiled in a fight, to own up a fight.

लड़ा/का, ~कू laṛa:ka:, ~ku: (*a*) quarrelsome; pugnacious; warlike, militant, bellicose; ~कापन/~कूपन quarrelsomeness, pugnacity; militant spirit, bellicosity.

लड़ाना laṛa:na: (*v*) see लड़ना; to caress, to fondle (as लाड़–).

लड़ी laṛi: (*nf*) a string; chain; row; —बाँधना/लगाना to cause a row to be constituted, to have a continuous series.

लड़ुआ laṛua: (*nm*) see लड्डू.

लड़ैत laṛait (*a* and *nm*) a fighter, combatant; skilled in fighting.

लड़ैता laṛaita: (*a*) darling, beloved.

लड्डू laḍḍu: (*nm*) a typical ball-like Indian sweetmeat; —खाना, मन के to build castles in the air; ~फोड़ना, मन ही मन to revel within, to be very happy at heart; —बँटना to have festivities; to have an easy gain.

लढ़ा laṛha: (*nm*) a bullock-cart.

लढ़िया laṛhiya: (*nf*) a small bullock-cart.

लत lat (*nf*) an addiction, a bad habit; an allomorph of लात used as the first member in some compound words; ~खोर/खोरा who is used to kicks; an object of contempt, self-debased: ~मर्दन trampling under foot; ~हा (said of a horse, bullock, etc.) in the habit of kicking.

लतर latar (*nf*) a creeper.

लतरा latra: (*nm*) a kind of bean used as a vegetable.

लतरी latri: (*nf*) a kind of vetchling.

लता lata: (*nf*) a creeper; vine; ~कुंज/गृह/भवन/मंडप a bower, arbour; ~वेष्टित covered with creepers, enveloped by creepers.

लताड़ lata:ṛ (*nf*) scolding, rebuke; —पिलाना/—बताना to rebuke/scold roundly.

लताड़ना lata:ṛnā: (*v*) to scold roundly, to rebuke.

लताफ़त lata:fat (*nf*) delicacy, tenderness, grace.

लतिका latika: (*nf*) a creeper, vine.

लतियल latiyal (*a*) used to kicking (as a cow etc)

लतियाना latiya:nā: (*v*) to kick, to spurn; to humiliate, to insult.

लती/फ़ा lati:fa: (*nm*) an anecdote, a witticism; ~फ़ागो/~फ़ेबाज an anecdotist, a witticist; one whose talk is replete with anecdotes; ~फ़ागोही/~फ़ेबाजी anecdotage, witticism, abundance of anecdotes in talk.

लत्ता latta: (*nm*) a rag, tatter, a tattered piece of cloth; लत्ते उड़ जाना to be shattered to pieces, to be tattered; लत्ते ले डालना to rebuke/reprove sharply, to scold roundly.

लथपथ lathpath (*a*) soaked, drenched (in), besmeared (with).

लथेड़ना latheṛnā: (*v*) to drag, to draggle; to cause to trail behind on the ground; to rebuke roundly.

लदना ladnā: (*v*) to be loaded/laden/burdened; to be apprehended; gone/past (as वे दिन लद गये gone/past are the days when...); लदा-फँदा over-laden, too burdened.

लदाऊ lada:u: (*a*) (meant) for loading.

लदाव lada:w (*nm*) loading; load, cargo.

ल/दुआ, ~द्दू ladua:, ~ddu: (*nm* and *a*) (a) beast of burden; pack-horse; used to carrying loads.

लद्धड़ laddhaṛ (*a*) lethargic, slothful, slow (moving); ~पन slothfulness; lethargy, slowness.

लप lap (*nf*) elasicity; a sound produced by moving a stick forcefully in the air or by a dog etc. while drinking water; palmful of anything; ~झप unsteady, fidgety; agility; ~लप करना to produce लप-लप sound by moving a stick forcefully in the air or by a dog etc. while drinking water; –से at once, quickly.

लपक lapak (*nf*) addiction (to grab advantage); flash, flame; gusto, swiftness; –पड़ना to get addicted (to group advantages).

लपकना lapaknā: (*v*) to catch (as गेंद–); to rush forth; to pounce upon, to go out with a gusto.

लपट lapaṭ (*nf*) a flame; blaze; heat wave; a blast of fragrance.

लपना lapnā: (*v*) to be bent, to resile; to bend and resile in quick succession (as a cane).

लपलपा/ना laplapa:nā: (*v*) to be resiliently flexible (as a cane); to be bent repeatedly; to brandish (as a sword); to show out the tongue (as in quick breathing); hence ~हट (*nf*).

लपसी lapsi: (*nf*) a glutinous substance; porridge, a kind of हलुआ comparatively less thickened and containing lesser amount of *ghee*.

लपेट lapeṭ (*nf*) a fold, twist; winding, turn; ambiguity; involvement, embroilment; striking range; ~दार ambiguous; involved; folded, twisted, having windings/turns.

लपेटन lapeṭān (*nf*) folding, winding; a wrapper, cover.

लपेट/ना lapeṭnā: (*v*) to roll up, to fold; to reel; to wind; to cover; to unfurl; to involve; to entangle/implicate/embroil; ~वाँ folding; wrapping.

लपेटा lapeṭa: (*nm*) fold, twist; winding, turn.

लप्पड़ lappaṛ (*nm*) a slap, blow of the palm.

लफ़ं/गा lafāṅga: (*nm* and *a*) a loafer/rogue; roguish, of loose character; hence ~गापन; ~गेबाज़ी roguery, swindling.

ल/फ़्ज़ lafz (*nm*) a word; -ब-लफ़्ज़ word by word; ~फ़्ज़ी wordy, of words; ० मानी word meaning, direct meaning.

लफ़्फ़ा/ज़ laffa:z (*a*) verbose; using high-sounding phraseology; talkative; ~ज़ी verbosity, talkativeness; use of high-sounding phraseology.

लब lab (*nm*) lip; brim; rim; edge; bank (of a river etc.); ~रेज full to the brim; -ए-दरिया on the bank of a river; -ए-सड़क by/beside the road, on the road-side; -ओ-लहजा delivery, manner of speaking, –ख़ुश्क होना the lips to get dried up; to be scared mute; –खोलना to speak out; –पर आना to find expression; to be on the verge of being expressed; –सीना to be tongue-tied, to keep quiet; लबों पर दम आना to be on the verge of death.

लबड़धोंधों labaṛdhōdhō (*nf*) clamour and confusion, row, mess; mismanagement; (*a*) slothful and stupid, inefficient.

लबदा labda:(*nm*)a small heavy stick.

लबाड़िया laba:ṛiya: (*a*) liar; tattler, babbler; hence ~पन (*nm*).

लबादा laba:da: (*nm*) a cloak, gown; a heavy overall; –पहनना to don a heavy overall.

लबाब laba:b (*nm*) gist, essence.

लबार laba:r (*a*) see लबाड़िया.

लबालब laba:lab (*adv* and *a*) full to the brim; brimful;–भरा होना to be full to the brim.

लबेद labed (*nm*) a custom, convention.

लब्ध labdh (*a*) obtained, got, acquired; (*nm*) a quotient: ~काम fulfilled, gratified, one whose wish has been fulfilled; ~कीर्ति/नाम/प्रतिष्ठ renowned, who has acquired fame; ~चेत/संज्ञ restored to consciousness.

लब्धांक labdhā:ṅk (*nm*) a quotient.

लब्धि labdhi (*nf*) acquirement, achievement; quotient.

लभ्य labbhy (*a*) available, attainable, accessible, within reach.

लम/गोड़ा, ~छड़, ~टंगा lamgoṛa:; ~chhaṛ, ~ṭāṅga: (*a*) gangling, gangly.

लम/हा lamha: (*nm*) a moment: ~हे भर में in a moment.

लय lay, lai (*nf*) rhythm; concord; cadence, melody, tune; fusion, merging; disappearance; destruction, annihilation (of the world); ~बद्ध rhythmic, attuned; –में in a rhythmic fashion; measured in tune; ~हीन rhythmless; ० करना to attune; to mould in a rhythm; –होना to be merged; to disappear; to be annihilated.

लयकारी layka:ri: (*nf*) attunement; moulding into a rhythm; (*a*) that which attunes/moulds into a rhythm.

लयात्मक laya:tmak (*a*) rhythmic(al), attuned.

लरज laraj (*nf*) vibration, quivering, shuddering.

लरजना larajnā: (*v*) to vibrate; to quiver; to shudder.

लरज़िश larzish (*nf*) vibration, quivering, shuddering.

ललक lalak (*nf*) craving, yearning, longing.

ललकना lalaknā: (*v*) to crave, to have a longing.

ललकार lalka:r (*nf*) a challenge, gage.

ललकारना lalka:rnā: (*v*) to (issue/hold out) a challenge, to halloo, to throw/fling down the gauntlet/glove.

ललचना lalachnā: (*v*) to be tempted, to be allured, to feel greedy.

ललचाना lalcha:nā: (*v*) to tempt, to allure, to wheedle, to entice; to covet; –,**जी** to feel tempted, to be allured; to covet.

ललचौहाँ lalchāuhā: (*a*) wistful, full of greed.

ललछौहाँ lalchhāuhā: (*a*) reddish; having a reddish tinge.

ललना lalnā: (*nf*) a woman; ~**प्रिय** a women's man; one who loves women.

लला lala: (*nm*) a word of address or a vocative word for a child/boy.

ललाई lala:i: (*nf*) redness, ruddiness.

ललाट lala:ṭ (*nm*) forehead; destiny, fortune; -**रेखा**, –**का लिखा** writ of (individual) destiny; o **अमिट है** what is lotted cannot be blotted; –**में होना** to be the writ of destiny, to be one's fate.

ललाम lalā:m (*a*) beautiful, lovely, handsome.

ललित lalit (*a*) pretty, comely, sweet; elegant, graceful; –**कला** fine arts; o **अकादेमी** academy of fine arts; –**शैली** elegant style; –**साहित्य** belles lettres.

ललौहाँ lalāuhā: (*a*) reddish, slightly red.

लल्ला lalla: (*nm*) an affectionate term (of address) for a child/boy; –**जानना, दद्दा न जानना** to have learnt only taking, not giving; to believe in only one way traffic of intake.

लल्लो-चप्पो, लल्लो-पत्तो lallo chappo, lallo patto (*nf*) huggery, wheedling, adulation; –**करना** to curry favour, to ingratiate oneself by officiousness.

लवंग lawāṅg (*nm*) a clove; -**पुष्प** clove flower; ~**लता** clove-creeper; a kind of sweetment.

लव lav (*nm*) a very small division of time; whit, particle; see **लौ**; ~**लीन** absorbed, engrossed (as in thought).

लवण lavāṇ (*nm*) salt; -**कच्छ** salt marsh; -**काच** salt glaze; -**क्षार** a kind of salt; -**जल** saline water, sea water; ~**ता** salinity; beauty; -**पटल** salt-pan; -**भास्कर** a kind of medicinal powder (mixture of many kinds of salts and other things) used for curing stomach disorders; -**समुद्र** sea of salt.

लवणित lavāṇīt (*a*) salted.

लवणिमा lavāṇimā: (*nf*) saltness, beauty.

लवणीय lavāṇi:y (*a*) saline.

लवणोदक lavaṇōdak (*nm*) saline water, sea (of salt water).

लवन lavān (*nm*) reaping, harvesting.

लवनी lavnī: (*nf*) butter.

लवनीय lavnī:y (*a*) reapable, harvestable.

लवलेश lavlesh (*nm*) a whit, very small quantity.

लवा lava: (*nm*) a kind of bird, lark; parched rice.

लवाज़(ज़ि)मा lawa:z(zi)mā: (*nm*) accoutrement, paraphernalia; necessities; hence ~**त** (plural).

लशक(श्क)/र laṣhkar (*nm*) cantonment, encampment (of army); host, irregular army; ~**री** pertaining to army; ० बोली the hotch-potch language of soldiers.

लस las (*nm*) pastiness, stickiness, adhesiveness; ~दार glutinous, sticky, adhesive.

लसलसा laslasa: (*a*) glutinous, sticky, adhesive; ~ना to be viscous; to be sicky; to stick; ~हट adhesiveness, stickiness.

लसित lasit (*a*) adorned.

लसीका lasi:ka: (*nm*) lymph.

लसीला lasi:la: (*a*) glutinous, sticky, adhesive; ~पन glutinousness, adhesiveness, stickiness.

लसो/ड़ा, ~ढ़ा lasoṛa:, ~ṛha: (*nm*) *Cordia myxa*—a tree and its fruit (used as vegetable etc.)

लस्टम-पस्टम lasṭām-pasṭām (*ind*) somehow or the other; slowly and slothfully, in a disorderly or ill-arranged manner.

लस्त last (*a*) exhausted, weary, worn out; –पस्त wearied, exhausted.

लस्तगा lastaga: (*nm*) start, beginning; relation; series.

लस्सी lassi: (*nf*) a typical cold beverage (made of churned curd or milk mixed with sugar, ice and sometimes scent or essence etc.).

लहँगा lẽhga: (*nm*) a long loose skirt worn round the loins flowing down to the ankles.

लहक lehak (*nf*) flame, flash; blaze, glitter, glare.

लहकना lehaknā: (*v*) to rise up into flames, to blaze; to glitter, to glare.

लहकाना lehka:nā: (*a*) to cause to get excited; to incite to violence; to instigate (as a dog) to attack.

लहकारना lehka:rnā: (*v*) to excite; to incite to violence, to instigate to make an attack.

लहजा lehja: (*nm*) tone, accent; intonation; manner of speech.

लहना lehnā: (*nm*) due amount; outstanding debt; -पावना credit and debit, dues payable and amount recoverable.

लहर lehar (*nf*) a wave, ripple; surge; undulation; caprice, whim; a wavy pattern; vertigo caused by the poisonous effect of snake-bite; impulse; ~दार wavy; undulatory, sinuous/sinuate; –आ जाना to be under an impulse; to be in a capricious mood; लहरें लेना to undulate, waves to surge (in the sea/river); लहरें गिनना to do a worthless job; to undertake an unproductive assignment.

लहराना lehra:nā: (*v*) to undulate, to wave; to shimmy; to fluctuate; to waver.

लहरिया lehriya: (*nm*) the total effect of wavy lines, wavy design or pattern of lines; ~दार wavy, meandering, zigzag; having a wavy or zigzag design/pattern.

लहरी lehri: (*nf*) a ripple, small wave; (*a*) capricious, whimsical.

लहरीला lehri:la: (*a*) see लहरदार (under लहर); ~पन sinuosity.

लहलह lehleh, lahlah (*a*) verdant, green; flourishing; blooming.

लहलहा lehleha: (*a*) verdant, green; flourishing, delighted, rapturous.

लहलहाना lehlaha:nā: (*v*) to flourish, to bloom; to be green; to be verdant; to wave.

लहसुन lehsun (*nm*) garlic.

लहसुनिया lehsuniyā: (*nm*) cat's eye, a precious grey-coloured stone.

लहालह laha:lah (*a*) verdant, green; delighted, blooming.

लहालोट laha:loṭ (*a*) bursting with laughter, extremely delighted;

enamoured.

लहीम lahi:m (*a*) flabby; -शहीम huge and tall.

लहुरा lahura: (*a*) younger, junior.

लहू lahu: (*nm*) blood; ~लु(लो)हान blood-smeared, drenched in blood; blood-stained; –उबलना/खौलना blood to boil through rage; to simmer; to be red-hot in rage; –औंटना to simmer, the blood to boil; –का घूँट पीकर रह जाना to suppress one's rage; to endure somebody's excesses; –का प्यासा bloodthirsty, after one's blood; –खुश्क कर देना to be terribly scared; to be stunned still; –चूसना to suck the blood (of), to exploit thoroughly; –पिलाकर पालना to feed with blood; to rear with great difficulty; –पीना to harass/pester no end, to trouble constantly; –बोलना the secret of murder to manifest itself, the murder mystery to be out; –में नहाना to be smeared with blood; to be drenched in blood all over; –में हाथ रँगना to stain one's hands with the blood of; –लगाकर शहीद होना to be a sham martyr, to pose as a martyr; –सफ़ेद हो जाना to be lost to human emotions, to become inhumane.

लाँग lā:g (*nf*) the part of धोती that is tucked up at the rear; –खुलना to become nervous, to yield tamely.

लाँघना lā:ghnā: (*v*) to cross, to jump over; to transgress.

लांछन lā:ṇchhān (*nm*) a stigma, blemish; slander.

लांछना lā:ṇchhanā: (*nf*) stigma; blame, slander.

लांछित lā:ṇchhit (*a*) stigmatised, blamed; slandered.

लांपट्य lā:mpaṭṭy (*nm*) see लंपटता (under लंपट).

ला la:—an Arabic prefix used to express negation, or the sense of being without and beyond etc. (as लाइलाज, लावारिस); (*v*) imperative second person singular form of the verb लाना.

लाइट la:iṭ (*nf*) light; ~हाउस a light-house.

लाइन la:in (*nf*) a line; ~क्लीयर line-clear (a signal given on railway stations); –साफ़ होना to have no obstruction/obstacle, the line to be clear.

लाइफ़ la:if (*nf*) life; ~बॉय lifebuoy; ~बेल्ट a life-belt; ~बोट a lifeboat.

लाइब्रेरियन la:ibrarian (*nm*) a librarian.

लाइब्रेरी la:ibreri: (*nf*) a library.

लाइलाज la:ila:j (*a*) incurable, irremediable.

लाइल्म la:ilm (*a*) illiterate, uneducated.

लाइसेंस la:isēns (*nm*) a licence; ~दार licensed; a licensee.

लाई la:i: (*nf*) parched rice; backbiting; -लुतरी back-biting; –लगाना to back-bite.

लाक़लाम la:qala:m (*a*) speechless, silent.

लाकि(के)ट la:ki(ke)ṭ (*nm*) a locket.

लाक्षण la:kshāṇ (*a*) pertaining to or related with a लक्षण.

लाक्षणिक la:kshāṇīk (*a*) metaphorical; symbolic; allegorical; pertaining or belonging to the meaning conveyed through लक्षणा; hence ~ता (*nf*).

लाक्षा la:ksha: (*nf*) lac; shellac; ~गृह/भवन a house made of lac; an inflammable house; ~वृक्ष see पलाश.

लाख la:kh (*nf*) lac; sealing lac; shellac; (*nm*) the number one lac;

(*a*) a hundred thousand, lac; a large number; ~पति/पती a millionaire, a very rich man; –कहना to say a million times, to impress (upon somebody) again and again; –टके/रुपये की बात a very remarkable utterance, invaluable remark; –से लीख होना to lose all one's wealth, to fall from plenty into pauperdom; लाखों में खेलना to have tons of money, to have millions to spend and squander.

लाखा la:kha: (*nm*) colour made from lac; ~गृह a house made of lac; an inflammable house; –रंग lac-colour.

लाखी la:khi: (*a*) of the colour of lac, lac-coloured.

लाग la:g (*nf*) hostility, rancour; competition; skill in performing a job; something tagged/embroiled / involved; -डाट rancour, rivalry; competition; -लपेट की बात something said in a round about manner; -लपेट न रखना to call a spade a spade.

लागत la:gat (*nf*) cost, cost price, expenditure; outlay; –, कुल total outlay; total expenditure; –के दाम cost price.

लाग/र la:gar (*a*) lean and thin, weak, feeble; ~री weakness, feebleness.

लागू la:gu: (*a*) applicable; enforceable; in force; –करना to apply; to enforce; to implement; –होना to be applicable/enforceable; to be implemented.

लाघव la:ghav (*nm*) skill, dexterity, smartness; littleness; minuteness.

लाचार la:cha:r (*a*) helpless; compelled; obliged, constrained; (*adv*) being helpless/constrained; –करना to compel, to force; –होना to be obliged, to be constrained.

लाचारी la:cha:ri: (*nf*) helplessness; compulsion.

लाज la:j (*nf*) shame; shyness, bashfulness; modesty; honour; ~वंत shamefaced; modest; shy, bashful; ~वंती/वती a very sensitive plant called touch-me-not; feminine form of ~वंत; –के मारे due to shame/shyness; out of modesty; –रखना to save one's face, protect (one's) honour; –से गड़ जाना to be very much embarrassed, to hang the head through shame.

लाज़मी la:zmī: (*a*) essential, inevitable, obligatory, compulsory; incumbent (on).

लाजवर्द la:jward (*nm*) an amethyst –a kind of precious stone; ultramarine.

लाजवाब la:jawa:b (*a*) unique, matchless, peerless; speechless, unable to reply back.

लाजा la:ja: (*nm*) puffed paddy, parched rice.

लाज़िम la:zim (*a*) see लाज़िमी.

लाज़िमी la:zimī: (*a*) essential, inevitable, obligatory, compulsory; incumbent (on); –तौर पर essentially; compulsorily.

लाट la:ṭ (*nm*) a lord; governor; pillar, lofty pillar; –, बड़ा governor-general, Viceroy (in pre-independence India); –साहब a lordly person; a big gun/guy; V.I.P.; ० समझना to take as a V.I.P., to regard a big gun.

लाटरी la:ṭri: (*nf*) lottery; –निकलना to win a lottery.

लाठालाठी la:ṭha:la:ṭhi: (*nf*) hitting one another with *lathis*; exchanging cudgel blows.

लाठी la:ṭhi: (*nf*) a big staff; cudgel; *lathi*; ~चार्ज lathi-charge; ~चलना

fighting with *lathis* to take place; –चलाना to fight with/brandish/ wield a *lathi*; –के ज़ोर से by brute force; –बाँधना to be equipped with a *lathi*; –उसकी भैंस, जिसकी might is right.

लाड़ la:ṛ (*nm*) affection, fondness, endearment; caressing; -चाव/प्यार see लाड़; –करना/लड़ाना to fondle, to caress; -लड़ंता fonded, dear/ darling.

लाड़ला la:ṛla: (*a*) dear, darling (child, baby, son, etc.).

लात la:t (*nf*) a leg; kick; –के देवता/ भूत बात से नहीं मानते rod is the logic of fools; a nod for the wise and a rod for the fool; well ! well! honey is not for the ass's mouth; –खाना to be kicked, to endure kicks; –चलाना to kick; –मारना to kick; to spurn, to abandon with contempt.

लातादाद la:ta:da:d (*a*) innumerable, numberless.

लातीनी la:ti:nī: (*a* and *nf*) Latin.

लाद la:d (*nf*) belly; entails, bowels; burden, loading; –निकलना tummy to bulge out.

लादना la:dnā: (*v*) to load, to burden; to cumber; to heap one upon the other.

लादवा la:dawa: (*a*) see लाइलाज.

लादिया la:diya: (*nm*) a porter, one whose profession is loading.

लादी ladi: (*nf*) the load placed on the back (of a beast of burden); a bundle of dirty clothes meant for washing; –की लादी धोना to wash a large number of clothes.

लॉन lɔn (*nm*) a lawn; –टेनिस lawn-tennis; ० प्रतियोगिता lawn-tennis championship.

लानत la:nāt (*nf*) condemnation, reproach, reproof; rebuke, censure; -मलामत reproach, reproof; curse; ० करना to curse, to reprove, to reproach. –का तौक़ गले में पड़ना to be condemned, to be infamized; –भेजना to damn (it), to let go to hell.

लानती la:nati: (*a*) reproachable; cursable, damned; reproached, cursed.

लाना la:nā: (*v*) to bring, to bring along, to fetch; to introduce.

लापता la:pata: (*a*) missing; disappeared, gone underground; untraceable; –होना to be missing; to go underground, to disappear; to be untraceable.

लापरवाह la:parwa:h (*a*) careless, negligent; heedless, inattentive.

लापरवाही la:parwa:hi: (*nf*) carelessness, inattention.

लापिका la:pika: (*nf*) a riddle.

लाभ la:bh (*nm*) profit; gain; advantage; benefit; dividend; ~कर/कारक/ कारी/दायक/दायी profitable; gainful; advantageous; beneficial; ०होना to bring grist to the mill; ~हीन unprofitable; inadvantageous; thankless; hence ~हीनता (*nf*).

लाभांश la:bhā:nsh (*nm*) dividend; bonus.

लाभालाभ la:bha:la:bh (*nm*) profit and loss; advantage and disadvantage.

लामं la:m (*nm*) war-front; army; -काफ़ कहना to reproach and reprove; –तोड़ना to demobilise; –पर जाना to go to the war-front; ~बंदी mobilisation; ० करना/–बाँधना to mobilise.

लामकान la:makā:n (*a*) homeless, destitute.

लामजह/ब, ~बी la:mazhab, ~bi: (*a*) having no religion, one who does not believe in any religior religionless.

लामा la:mā: (*nm*) a Buddhist monk.

लामिसाल la:misa:l (*a*) unparalleled, peerless, matchless; unique.

लामुहाला la:muha:la: (*ind*) being constrained/forced/obliged, having no other way out.

लाय/क़ la:yaq (*a*) able, capable, competent; worthy, fit; proper; ~**क़ियत**, ~**क़ी** ability, capability; competence; worthiness.

लार la:r (*nf*) drivel, saliva; ~**पूर्ण/-भरा** slobbery; -**विषयक/संबंधी** salivary; –**आना, मुँह में** to drivel, the mouth to water, to have eager desire to eat/obtain a thing; –**टपकना, मुँह से** to lick one's chaps/chops, to beslobber, to drivel, one's mouth to be salivated, to have an intense desire to obtain/eat a thing.

लारी la:ri: (*nf*) a lorry.

लार्ड la:rḍ (*nm*) a lord.

लाल la:l (*a*) red, ruddy; angry, infuriated; communist (as –**चीन**); (*nm*) beloved/dear child/boy/son; beloved person; a kind of small bird; ruby; –**अंगारा/भभूका** extremely red, red hot; red hot due to anger, terribly infuriated; –**चंदन** red sandalwood; –**पगड़ी** the police (man); –**परी** wine, liquor; –**पानी** wine, liquor; ~**फ़ीता** red tape; o**शाही** red-tapism; –**बुझक्कड़** village wisecare, an ignorant fool who thinks very highly of himself and feels competent to answer any question; o**बूझिहै और न बूझै कोय** the ass waggeth his ears; –**मिर्च** chilly; –**शक्कर** unrefined/crude sugar; –**सागर** red sea; –**सेना** communist army; –**आँखें दिखाना / निकालना** to look angrily, to frown; -**पीला होना** to be black in the face, to be purple with passion; to fret and fume, to be red hot with rage.

लाल/च la:lach (*nm*) greed/greediness, covetousness, avarice; allurement, temptation; ~**ची** greedy; covetous; avaricious; ~**च बुरी बला है** no vice like avarice.

लालटेन la:lṭen (*nf*) a lantern.

लालन la:lān (*nm*) caressing, fondling; -**पालन** rearing; nurturing; o**करना** to rear; to nurture, to nourish.

लालसा la:lsa: (*nf*) craving, longing, yearning.

लाला la:la: (*nm*) a word of respect prefixed to the names of certain Hindu castes like **बनिया** and **कायस्थ** etc. (as –**लाजपतराय**); a term of address used for both elders and youngers; a kind of flower or its plant.

लालायित la:la:it (*a*) eager; tempted, enamoured.

लालित la:lit (*a*) reared, nourished, cherished; also -**पालित**.

लालित्य la:litty (*nm*) grace, gracefulness, delicacy.

लालिमा la:limā: (*nf*) redness, reddishness, ruddiness.

लाली la:li: (*nf*) redness, ruddiness; lipstick; rouge.

लाले la:le; –**पड़ना** to become rare/inaccessible/beyond reach;–**पड़ना, जान के** life to be in danger; to become difficult to protect life; –**पड़ना, दाने-दाने के** to have to look eagerly for each grain, each and every grain to be difficult to get.

लाव la:w (*nm*); -**लश्कर** an array of followers/companions, large paraphernalia, goods and chattels.

लावण्य la:vānny (*nm*) charm, beauty, loveliness, comeliness.

लावनी la:wnī: (*nf*) a kind of popular folk-song; ~**बाज** an adept in singing लावनी.

लावल्द la:vald (*a*) issueless, childless.

लावा la:va: (*nm*) lava; puffed paddy, parched rice.

लावारसी la:va:rsi: (*a*) see लावारिसी (under लावारिस).

लावारि/स la:va:ris (*a*) (used both for men and things) unclaimed, unowned; heirless; also ~सी (used only for things): ~स बच्चे gutter snipes/children; ~स/~सी माल unclaimed property.

लाश la:sh (*nf*) corpse, dead boby; carcass; ~घर mortuary; –गलियों में खिंचवाना to cause to be dragged in streets to insult after death; –पर लाश गिरना fighting men to fall one after another, a heap of corpses to be piled up; लाशों से पट जाना to be strewn all over with corpses.

लासा la:sa: (*nm*) a glutinous/adhesive substance; bird-line; a bait; lure; –देना to lure, to bait; –लगाकर चिड़िया फँसाना to lure a bird into captivity; –लगाना to involve into a trap; to cause a quarrel.

लासानी la:sa:nī: (*a*) matchess, peerless, incomparable; unique.

लास्य la:ssy (*nm*) a kind of graceful female dance.

लाह la:h (*nf*) lac, sealing lac; shellac.

लाही la:hi: (*nf*) a typical insect that destroys (wheat and barley) crops; parched rice.

लाहूत la:hu:t (*nm*) this world, mortal world; the state of identity with God.

लाहौल वला कूवत la:haul vala:ku:vat—an Arabic phrase used to express disgust, indignation, hatred, regret, etc; be it damned!, damn it!

लिंग lïṅg (*nm*) male genital organ, penis, phallus; the phallus deity representing Lord Shiv; gender (in Grammar); sex; -उपासना phallus worship; phallicism; –और वचन gender and number (in Grammar); -देह/शरीर the ethereal form of corporeal body (that is supposed to accompany the soul to face the consequences of one's worldly deeds); ~पूजक a phallus-worshipper; phallicist; ~पूजा phallus-worship, phallicism; -दोष a mistake of gender; –प्रतिष्ठा installation of the phallus-deity.

लिंगायत lïṅga:yat (*nm*) a sect of Shaivites.

लिंगिता lïṅgita: (*nf*) sexuality.

लिंगेंद्रिय lïṅgēndriy (*nm*) phallus, penis.

लिंगोपास/ना lïṅgopa:snā: (*nf*) phallus-worship, phallicism; ~क phallus-worshipper.

लिंटर lïnṭar (*nm*) a lintel.

लिए lie (*ind*) for, with a view to, for the sake of, on account of; (*a*) taking, carrying, bearing; (*v*) past participle masculine plural form of लेना.

लिक्खाड़ likkha:ṛ (*nm*) a prolific writer (used sarcastically).

लिखत likhat (*nf*) writing; document; -पढ़त document, documentation; written deed; ० करना to reduce (an agreement etc.) to writing.

लिखना likhnā: (*v*) to write, to note down, to record, to inscribe; to enter (in a book); -पढ़ना to study; writing and reading, studying; –, किसी के नाम to debit to the account of; to address (a letter etc.) to·

लिखनी likhni: (*nf*) the process/act of writing; fate, lot; —टलती नहीं what is lotted cannot be blotted.

लिखवाई likhwa:i: (*nf*) remuneration for writing.

लिखा likha: (*a*) written, what is written; lotted, destined; —न मेट सकना what is lotted cannot be blotted.

लिखाई likha:i: (*nf*) writing, the act/process of writing or the remuneration paid therefor; -पढ़ाई study, education.

लिखापढ़ी likha:parhi: (*nf*) written agreement; correspondence; documentation (of conditions etc.)

लिखावट likha:waṭ (*nf*) hand, handwriting; writing.

लिखित likhit (*a*) written, recorded, reduced to black and white.

लिखितव्य likhitavvy (*a*) to be written; writable, worth writing·

लिजलिजा lijlija: (*a*) abominable, physically loathsome, repulsive; spineless, lifeless; impotent; hence ~पन (*nm*).

लिटाना liṭa:na: (*v*) to make somebody lie down; to (cause to) lay·

लिटर liṭar (*nm*) a litre·

लिट्ट liṭṭ (*nm*) a thick and large bread, pancake·

लिट्टी liṭṭi: (*nf*) a small-sized लिट्ट.

लिपटना lipaṭna: (*v*) to embrace; to cling, to coil around; to be smeared; to concentrate on a work.

लिपाई lipa:i: (*nf*) the process of or wages paid for pargetting/plastering; —पुताई plastering and whitewashing; cleaning and tidying; giving a face lift·

लिपा-पुता lipa:puta: (*a*) clean and tidy; pargetted and whitewashed (used for mud houses)·

लिपि lipi (*nf*) a script; writing; ~कर/कार a scribe; clerk; copy; —काल the date of copying/scribing; ~ग्राम grapheme; o विज्ञान graphemics; ~बद्ध recorded, written, reduced to black and white; hence ~बद्धता; ~विज्ञान/शास्त्र science of writing.

लिपिक lipik (*nm*) a clerk, scribe.

लिप्त lipt (*a*) engrossed, absorbed; deeply attached, involved; hence ~ता (*nf*).

लिप्यंतरण lippyāntaraṇ (*nm*) transcription; transliteration·

लिप्सा lipsa: (*nf*) lure, greed, ardent desire·

लिप्सु lipsu (*a*) greedy, overpowered by lure, ardently desirous·

लिफ़ाफ़ा lifa:fa: (*nm*) an envelope; wrapper, cover; —खुल जाना the secret to be out; to be exposed; —बदलना to be dressed anew; to have a fresh make-up.

लिफ़ाफ़िया lifa:fiya: (*a*) showy; delicate, weak, feeble; not durable; —पहलवान a weak and delicate person.

लिबड़ना libarna: (*v*) to be smeared.

लिबरी libri: (*nf*) liveries; -बारदाना ration and clothes, household effects.

लिबलिबा libliba: (*a*) gummy; tame, spineless, unassertive (man).

लिबलिबी liblibi: (*nf*) trigger; -दबाना to fire·

लिबास liba:s (*nm*) dress, attire; -ए रस्मी formal dress·

लिया liya: (*v*) masculine singular past participle form of the verb लेना; -बेची purchase and sale, buying and selling.

लियाक़त liya:qat (*nf*) ability, merit; qualification.

लिलार lila:r (*nm*) see ललाट.

लिली lili: (*nf*) lily.

लिवर livar (*nm*) liver; –बढ़ना; the liver to be enlarged.

लिसलिसा lislisa: (*a*) gummy, sticky; adhesive; hence ~पन (*nm*).

लिसोड़ा lisoṛa: (*nm*) see लसोड़ा.

लिस्ट list (*nf*) a list; –बनाना to draw up a list.

लिहाज liha:z (*nm*) considerateness; deference, respect; point of view; –करना to be considerate (to), to be deferential; –से, इस from this point of view, in this respect.

लिहाज़ा liha:za: (*ind*) thus, therefore; on this account, accordingly.

लिहाफ़ liha:f (*nm*) a quilt.

लीं lī: (*v*) past participle feminine plural form of the verb लेना (मैंने किताबें लीं).

ली li: (*v*) past participle feminine singular form of the verb लेना.

लीक li:k (*uf*) track, trackway; rut; trace; -चाल tracking; following established track; to go by tradition; –खींचना to resolve; to announce a resolution; –पकड़ना to follow the track; –पर चलना to follow a trodden path/the tradition; –पीटना to follow the tradition; to blindly, follow the beaten path; to stick to worn-out traditions; -लीक चलना to follow an established course; to follow the tradition; –से बेलीक होना to go astray, to violate the traditional course.

लीख li:kh (*nf*) a tiny louse.

लीग li:g (*nf*) a league; ~गी a leaguer, member of a league.

लीचड़, ~र li:chaṛ, ~r (*a*) lethargic, sluggish, slow; stingy, clumsy in one's dealings; ~पन/पना sluggishness, lethargy; stinginess; clumsiness in dealings.

लीची li:chi: (*nf*) *lichi* (a kind of fruit).

लीजिए li:jie (*v*) deferential imperative form of the verb लेना (signifying immediate future).

लीजिएगा li:jiyega: (*v*) deferential imperative form of the verb लेना signifying immediate or distant future (*cf.* लीजिए) as also deferential interrogation conveying the sense 'would you like to take it ?' (क्या लीजिएगा ? what would you like to have ?).

लीडर li:ḍar (*nm*) a leader; ~री leadership; ०करना to be a professional leader; ~री जमाना to establish oneself as a leader, to establish one's leadership.

लीडराना li:ḍra:nā: (*a*) befitting a leader, leader-like, in the nature of a leader;–अंदाज़ (the) fashion/manner of a leader.

लीथो li:tho (*nm*) lithograph.

लीद li:d (*nf*) dung (of a horse/ass/elephant etc.); –करना to yield tamely; to be scared.

लीन lī:n (*a*) absorbed, engrossed; merged; vanished, disappeared; hence ~ता (*nf*).

लीपना li:pnā: (*v*) to plaster; to coat; to smear; -पोतना to clean and tidy up; to whitewash and plaster; लीप-पोतकर बराबर करना to mar irreparably, to ruin completely; लीपा-पोती plastering and whitewashing; patching up; marring/impairing/spoiling completely.

लीलना li:lnā: (*v*) to swallow, to gulp.

लीला li:la: (*nf*) sport, play;

amorous sport; fun and frolic; stage representation [of the deeds of divine incarnations, *e.g*, रामलीला, रास-लीला]; -कलह love strife; ~प्रिय frolicsome; ~पुरुष an epithet of Lord Krishnā who revelled in his divine sport; ~मय sportive; playful; ~स्थल site of amorous sport/play.

लीवर li:var (*nm*) lever (of a lock).

लुंगी lūṅgi: (*nf*) a sarong, a strip of cloth tucked round the waist.

लुंचन lūṇchan (*nm*) plucking (hair etc.).

लुंचित lūṇchit (*a*) plucked; ~केश one whose hair has been plucked, a Jain ascetic.

लुं/ज, ~जा lūṇj, ~ja: (*a*) crippled; fleshy and flaccid; -पुंज flaccid, and feeble/fleshy, having no muscles.

लुंठन lūṇṭhān (*nm*) rolling.

लुंठित lūṇṭhit (*a*) rolled; -व्यंजन rolled consonant.

लुंड lūṇḍ (*nm*) a torso; round rolled packet; -मुंड crippled; bundled up.

लुं/डा lūṇḍa: (*nm*) a round ball of thread; (*a*) tailless (as -बैल); hence ~डी feminine form.

लुआ/ठ lua:ṭḥ (*nm*) burning wood; also ~ठी (diminutive).

लुआब lua:b (*nm*) slime; pith; essence, gist; ~दार slimy, sticky.

लुकना luknā: (*v*) to hide, to be concealed; to go underground; लुक-छिपकर clandestinely, stealthily.

लुक़मा luqmā: (*nm*) a morsel.

लुक़मान luqmā:n (*nm*) a famous Arab physician known for his curing powers; -के पास भी दवा नहीं, , वहम की तो none can ever cure a hypochondriac; -को हिक़मत सिखाना to retail tips of the trade to an expert.

लुकाछिपी luka:chhipi: (*nf*) hide and seek; clandestine existence/goings.

लुकाट luka:ṭ (*nm*) a tree and its fruit.

लुकाठ luka:ṭḥ (*nm*) see लुआठ; a tree and its fruit.

लुग़त lugat (*nm*) a dictionary.

लुगदी lugdi: (*nf*) pulp; ~दार pulpy.

लुगरी lugri: (*nf*) old and tattered; -धोती tattered cloth.

लुग़वी lugwi: (*a*) of dictionary; -मानी dictionary meaning.

लुगाई luga:i: (*nf*) a woman; wife; ~बाज़ a womanizer; ~बाज़ी womanizing.

लुग़ात luga:t (*nm*) plural of लुग़त a dictionary.

लुग्गा lugga: (*nm*) cloth.

लु/चई, ~चुई luchai:, ~chui: (*nf*) soft and very thin पूरी (prepared of मैदा).

लुच्चा luchcha: (*a* and *nm*) vile, wanton (person), abject, depraved; a scoundrel, black sheep, a bad egg/hat; ~पन vileness, wantonness, scoundrelism, depravity.

लुटना luṭnā: (*v*) to be robbed/plundered/marauded.

लुटाऊ luṭa:u: (*a*) squandering.

लुटाना luṭa:nā: (*v*) to squander; to allow to be plundered, to blow the expense.

लुटिया luṭiya: (*nf*) a small लोटा; -डुबोना to bring ruin, to cause undoing (of); to bring disgrace.

लुटेरा luṭera: (*nm*) robber, plunderer, marauder, bandit; hence ~पन (*nm*).

लुढ़कना luṛḥaknā: (*v*) to roll down, to be toppled, to tumble down

लुतरा lutra: (*a*) backbiter; ~पन backbiting.

लुत्फ़ lutf (*nm*) fun; pleasure, enjoyment; -ए-ज़िंदगी pleasure of life; –उठाना/लेना to have fun; to enjoy.

लुनना lunnā: (*v*) to reap a harvest.

लुनाई luna:i: (*nf*) the process or act of reaping a harvest or the wages paid for it; prettiness; beauty.

लुप्त lupt (*a*) disappeared, vanished; hidden; extinct, obsolete; missing, omitted; –अर्थ obsolete meaning; hence ~ता (*nf*); -पद an omitted term; where a term has elided; ~/–प्रयोग obsolete (usage).

लुप्तावशेष lupta:vashesh (*nm*) vestige; traces.

लुप्ति lupti (*nf*) elision; omission.

लुब्ध lubdh (*a*) charmed, attracted, allured.

लुब्बे-लु(ल)बाब lubbe-lu(la)ba:b (*nm*) essence, gist.

लुभाना lubha:nā: (*v*) to lure; to to charm, to attract, to tantalise; to entice; to captivate; to be lured/charmed/ attracted/tantalised/ lured/enticed.

लुहार luha:r (*nm*) a blacksmith; ~ख़ाना a blacksmith's workshop.

लुहारी luha:ri: (*nf*) the profession or work of a blacksmith.

लू lu: (*nf*) warm air; heat wave; sunstroke; –मारना to suffer a sunstroke; –लगना to have a sunstroke.

लूक lu:k (*nm*) a meteor, falling or shooting star.

लूका lu:ka: (*nm*) flash, flare, blaze; burning wood.

लूट lu:ṭ (*nf*) plunder; booty; spoil; –का माल booty; spoils; -खसोट plunder, pillage, maraudery; -पाट/मार plundering and killing; pillage, marauding; –मचाना to plunder at will, to cause a havoc through plunder.

लूटना lu:ṭnā: (*v*) to plunder, to maraud, to pillage, to loot; -खसोटना/–खाना to maraud, to live by plunder; to misappropriate others' money; -पाटना see लूटना.

लूण lū:ṇ (*nm*) salt.

लूता lu:ta: (*nf*) a spider; -तंतु spider's web.

लूनना lūnanā: (*v*) to reap a harvest.

लूम lu:m (*nm*) tail; a (hand) loom; –, पावर a power loom.

लूला lu:la: (*a*) handless, with a dismembered hand; maimed; -लँगड़ा crippled, disabled.

लूलू lu:lu: (*a* and *nm*) (an) idiot, nincompoop; a nitwit; –बनाना to befool, to make fun of.

लें/ड,~ड़ lẽḍ, ~ṛ (*nm*) hard excrement; ~ड़ा timid, coward.

लेंड़ी lẽṛi: (*nf*) small round dung (of goat, sheep, etc.).

लेंस lēns (*nm*) a lens; ~दार fitted with a lens.

लेंह/ड़ lẽhāṛ (*nm*) herd, flock (of beasts); also ~ड़ा (*nm*), ~ड़ी (*nf*).

लेई lei: (*nf*) (adhesive) paste (prepared from flour or arrowroot etc.); due; -पूँजी all one's assets, total effects.

लेकिन lekin (*ind*) but; on the other hand; however.

लेक्चर lekchar (*nm*) a lecture; ~र a lecturer; ~बाज़ी too much of lecturing; –झाड़ना (said in a satirical vein) to deliver a discourse, to start lecturing; –देना to lecture; –पिलाना to administer a good dose of lecturing.

लेख lekh (*nm*) an article; paper; writing, handwriting; writ; ~बद्ध written; reduced to black and white.

लेख/क lekhak (*nm*) a writer, an author; ~**की** the job or work of or as a writer; ~**कीय** of or pertaining to an author.

लेखन lekhān (*nm*) writing, scribing, writing work; -**कला** art of writing, calligraphy; chirography; -**पद्धति** system/method of writing; ~**शास्त्र** graphology; -**शैली** hand-writing; style of writing; -**सामग्री** stationery, writing material; ~**सामग्री-विक्रेता** a stationer.

लेखनी lekhnī: (*nf*) a pen; -**का धनी** who wields the pen effectively.

लेखनीय lekhnī:y (*a*) worth writing, fit to be written; hence ~**ता** (*nf*).

लेखपाल lekhpa:l (*nm*) a lekhpal—person who maintains (village) land-records.

लेखांश lekhā:nsh (*nm*) a portion of a **लेख**.

लेखा lekha: (*nm*) account(s); record; ~**कार** an accountant; -**जोखा** calculation; estimate; account; -**परीक्षक** an auditor; -**परीक्षण** / -**परीक्षा** audit (ing); ~**पाल** an accountant; ~**बद्ध** accounted for, entered into the accounts; o **करना** to account for, to enter into the accounts; -**बही** an account book, a cash-book; ledger; -**विधि** accounting (system); -**शास्त्र** accountancy, accounting.

लेखिका lekhika: (*nf*) feminine form of **लेखक** an authoress.

लेखी lekhi:—a suffix used in the sense of who or that which records (as **तापलेखा**).

लेखे lekhe (*ind*); –, **के** for, as far as ...is concerned, to (so and so); (*nm*) accounts.

लेख्य lekkhy (*a*) worth writing/recording; accountable; –**पत्र** a document; an instrument.

लेज(जि)म lezā(zi)m (*nf*) a kind of bow fitted with iron chain (used for exercise).

लेट leṭ (*a*) late; –**फ़ीस** late fee.

लेटना leṭnā: (*v*) to lie; to lie down; to repose, to recline.

लेटरबा(बॉ)क्स leṭarba:(bɔ)ks (*nm*) a letter-box.

लेड leḍ (*nm*) lead (metal), also the metal strip for widening space between the lines in printing.

लेडी leḍi: (*nf*) a lady; –**डाक्टर** a lady doctor.

लेन len (*nm*) taking, receiving; ~**दार** a creditor; -**देन** transaction, exchange; dealings; o **न होना** to have no dealings at all; ~**हार** a borrower.

लेना lenā: (*v*) to take; to accept; to borrow; to buy; to hold; to receive –, **आड़े हाथों** to put to shame by sarcastic remarks; to rebuke and reprove; **ले उड़ना** to cut off from the context and misrepresent; to pinch something and make good one's escape; to run away with; **ले डालना** to ruin, to destroy; **ले डूबना** to be drowned along with, to involve others in one's fall; **ले-देकर** on the whole, somehow, with great difficulty; **ले-दे करना** to wrangle, to clamour, to dispute; **ले-दे मचना** to have too much of clamouring/wrangling; -**देना** see **लेन-देन** (under **लेन**); –**एक न देना दो** to have no concern whatsoever; for nothing, for no purpose at all; **लेने के देने पड़ना** to have the tables turned upon oneself; to sustain a blow while trying to hit; to lose while expecting to profit; **ले बैठना** to crash along with, to perish along with; **ले मरना** to perish along with; to cause ruination to others along with oneself; ले रखना to keep in reserve.

लेप lep (*nm*) ointment; smearing; –करना to anoint; to coat; to smear (with).

लेपन lepan (*nm*) anointing; coating; smearing.

लेपना lepnā: (*v*) to anoint; to coat; to smear.

लेपनीय lepnī:y (*a*) worth anointing/coating/smearing.

लेप्य leppy (*a*) लेपनीय.

लेफ़्टिनेंट lefṭineṇṭ (*nm*) lieutenant; -कर्नल lieutenant colonel; -जनरल lieutenant general.

लेब(बि/बु)ल leba(bi/bu)l (*nm*) a label; –लगाना to label.

लेबोरेटरी leboreṭari: (*nm*) a laboratory; -असिस्टेंट a laboratory assistant.

लेमन/चूस, ~जूस lemānchu:s, ~ju:s (*nm*) lemon-juice.

लेमनेड lemāneḍ (*nm*) a lemonade.

लेव lew (*nm*) see लेप; accumulation of adequate quantity of water in the field for planting paddy.

लेवा lewa: (*nm*) a thin mattress of (shattered) cloth; one who takes (e.g. नामलेवा).

लेश lesh (*a*) very little; (*nm*) modicum, iota, trace; whit; –मात्र a trace of, an iota of, modicum of.

लेस les (*nm*) stickiness; adhesiveness; ~दार sticky, gummy.

लेहना lehnā: (*nm*) fodder, provender (for cattle).

लेहाजा leha:za: (*ind*) see लिहाज़ा.

लेहाफ़ leha:f (*nm*) लिहाफ़.

लैंगिक laiṅgik (*a*) sexual; phallic.

लैंप laimp (*nm*) lamp.

लैटिन laiṭin (*nf*) Latin.

लैला laila: (*nf*) the heroine of the celebrated love-tale of लैला-मजनूँ; -मजनूँ crazy lovers.

लैवेंडर laiveṇḍar (*nm*) levendar.

लैसंस laisāns (*nm*) licence; ~दार a licensee; licensed.

लैस lais (*a*) equipped/fitted (with); ready.

लोंदा lōda: (*nm*) a ball of any wet powder (as मिट्टी का–); –, मिट्टी का absolutely inert (person), inactive and slothful.

लो lo (*ind*) a term for expressing surprise or attracting somebody's attention; now see this one !

लोइया loiya: (*nf*) a small ball of kneaded flour to be spread into a bread.

लोई loi: (*nf*) a kind of thin woollen wrapper or blanket; see लोइया.

लोक lok (*nm*) the world; one of the three worlds – स्वर्ग, पृथ्वी, पाताल; one of the fourteen worlds (of which seven are above and seven below); people, folk; public; (*a*) popular, public; -आख्यान a folk myth; -कथा a folk tale, folk lore; -कल्याण public welfare; -कहानी folk tale; -गाथा a ballad; -गीत a folk song; -चित्र folk mind, popular mind; -जीवन public life; ~तंत्र democracy; ~तंत्रीय democratic; ~तांत्रिक democratic; a democrat; ~त्रय/त्रयी the three worlds–आकाश, पाताल and मृत्युलोक; ~द्वय the two worlds—earth and heaven; -निंदा public slander; -नीति folk ethics, folk morals; -नृत्य folk dance; -पद्धति popular method/way; -पाल the protector of the world; ~परक secular; ० ता secularism; -प्रवाद hearsay; rumour; ~प्रसिद्ध renowned, world-famous; ~ प्रिय popular; ०ता popularity; ~बाह्‌य ousted from the society; -बुद्धि popular wisdom;

-भाषा popular language; ~मत public opinion/view; -मन popular mind; -मर्यादा popular observance, bounds of decency, established usage or custom; -मानस the popular mind; ~रंजक that entertains/satisfies people at large, he who or that which serves popular interest or results in public welfare; -रंजन popular entertainment/satisfaction / welfare; serving popular interest; -राज popular rule; -रिवाज a folk custom; -रीति popular custom / method/ ways; -लाज loss of shame amongst people, safeguarding of honour, avoidance of public slander; -लीक popular course, popular tradition; -वाद rumour; -वार्ता folk lore; ~विख्यात world famous/ renowned; -विज्ञान popular science; -विरुद्ध anti-public, anti-social; opposed to the people; ~विश्रुत see ~विख्यात; -विश्वास popular belief; -व्यवहार popular dealings, dealings with others; -शासन popular government; -संगीत folk music; -संग्रह public welfare; experience gained through intercourse with men; -संस्कृति folk culture; -सत्ता public authority/power; ~सभा House of the People (the lower house of the Indian Parliament); -समाज community at large; ~सम्मत enjoying popular support, having the backing of the people; ~सिद्ध established or current among the people; ~सेवक public servant; ~सेवा public service; o आयोग public service commission; -स्वास्थ्य public health; ~हित public welfare; philanthropy; o भावना public spirit; ~हितैषी a philanthropist; public-spirited.

लोकना loknā: (*v*) to catch (a thing falling down).

लोकल lokal (*a*) local; ~ट्रेन a local train.

लोकान्तर lokā:ntar (*nm*) the other world; ~गमन to die; death.

लोकाचा/र loka:cha:r (*nm*) ethos, mores; convention, popular custom/tradition; ~री worldly-wise, practical.

लोकाट loka:ṭ (*nm*) see लुकाट.

लोकापवाद loka:pwa:d (*nm*) public slander.

लोकायतन loka:yatān (*nm*) an atheist, a materialist.

लोकैषणा lokaishṇā: (*nf*) desire for worldly prosperity.

लोकोक्ति lokokti (*nf*) a proverb; popular saying.

लोकोत्तर lokottar (*a*) supernatural, transcendental; extra-worldly; extraordinary; hence ~ता (*nf*).

लोकोपका/र lokopka:r (*nm*) philanthropy; ~रक a philanthropist/ philanthrope; ~री philanthropic.

लोग log (*nm*) a man; people, public; -बाग people; men in general; -लुगाई man and woman.

लोच loch (*nf*) flexibility, elasticity; tenderness; ~दार flexible, elastic; tender.

लोचन lochan (*nm*) eye (s).

लोट loṭ (*nf*) rolling; lying; (*nm*) a (currency) note; -पोट rolling; resting; bursting with laugh, rolling around in laughter; o होना to roll around in laughter; to burst with laugh.

लोटन loṭan (*a*) weltering, rolling; tumbling; -कबूतर a kind of pigeon.

लोटना loṭnā: (*v*) to roll, to wallow, to welter; to toss; लोट जाना to fall down; to fall senseless on the ground; to die.

लोटा loṭa: (*nm*) a small round metal utensil for the household.

लोढ़ना loṛhnā: (*v*) to pluck (flowers).

लोढ़ा loṛha: (*nm*) a stone pestle, muller.

लोथ loth (*nf*) corpse, carcass; –गिरना to fall dead, to be killed.

लोथड़ा lothṛa: (*nm*) a lump of flesh.

लोदी lodi: (*nf*) a sub-division of the Paṭhā:ns.

लो/ध lodh (*nm*) the tree *Symploco racemoze* (its bark and twigs are used for medicinal purposes); also ~ध्र.

लोना lonā: (*a*) salty; pretty, pretty-looking; hence ~पन (*nm*).

लोनी lonī: (*nf*) a kind of green vegetable; unprocessed butter.

लोप lop (*nm*) disappearance; elimination; elision; obsolescence; hence ~न (*nm*).

लोबान loba:n (*nm*) (gum) benzoin, oil creosote.

लोबिया lobiya: (*nm*) a kind of bean used for vegetable, cow pea.

लोभ lobh (*nm*) greed, avarice; covetousness; temptation, lure; –से कुछ नहीं मिलता all covet, all lost.

लोभी lobhi: (*a*) greedy, avaricious, covetous; ~पन/पना greediness, avariciousness; –का पेट सदा ख़ाली a covetous man is ever in want, the more you covet the more you need.

लोम lom (*nm*) hair; soft hair on the body; wool; ~नाशक depilatory; ~हर्ष see रोमांच; ~हर्षक, ~हर्षण see रोमांचकारी.

लोमक lomāk (*nm*) cilium (cilia—pl.)

लोमड़ी lomṛi: (*nf*) a fox.

लोरी lori: (*nf*) a lullaby.

लोलक lolak (*nm*) a pendant; pendulum.

लोलित lolit (*a*) oscillated; flickered.

लोलुप lolup (*a*) see लोभी; ~ता see लोभीपन.

लोशन loshān (*nm*) a lotion.

लोष्ट losht (*nm*) a lump of clay/earth.

लोह loh (*a*) see लौह.

लोहबान lohbān (*nm*) see लोबान.

लोहस lohas (*a*) ferrous.

लोहा loha: (*nm*) iron; (*a*) very hard; very strong; –, कच्चा pig-iron; –,पक्का steel; –करना/फेरना to iron (a cloth); –बजना a battle/war to be waged, fighting with swords to ensue; –मानना, किसी का to acknowledge/confess supremacy; to concede somebody's superiority/superior skill; –लेना, किसी से to cross swords (with), to wage war; –होना to turn into steel, to become as hard as steel; लोहे का दिल strong heart; unfeeling/ruthless heart; लोहे की छाती strong heart; unfeeling heart; लोहे के चने an assiduous job; a hard nut to crack; o चबाना to undertake an assiduous task; लोहे को लोहा काटता है diamond cuts diamond, cunning outwits cunning.

लोहाना loha:nā: (*v*) (food or drink) to have a touch of iron in taste (by prolonged storing or boiling in an iron utensil).

लोहार loha:r (*nm*) a blacksmith; forgeman; ~ख़ाना blacksmith's workshop; लोहारी blacksmith's profession or work.

लोहासव loha:sav (*nm*) see लौहासव.

लोहित lohit (*a*) red, reddened; ~नयन red-eyed, one whose eyes are red (with anger etc).

लोहिया lohiya: (*nm*) an iron-dealer; a Hindu sub-caste (amongst *vaishyas*) whose original profession was iron-mongering.

लोहू lohu: (*nf*) blood.

लौंग laũg (*nf*) a clove; nose-stud.

लौंड laũḍ—an allomorph of **लौंडा** used as the first member of certain compound words; ~**पन** boyishness, brattishness.

लौंडा laũḍa: (*nm*) a boy, lad, brat; a passive participant in sodomy, one with whom sodomy is committed; ~**पन** brattishness, boyishness; **लौंडेबाज़** a sodomite, bugger; **लौंडेबाज़ी** sodomy, buggery.

लौंडिया laũḍiya: (*nf*) (derogatory usage) a lass, girl.

लौंडी laũḍi: (*nf*) a servant girl, slave girl, bond-maid.

लौ lau (*nf*) flame, glow; unwavering deep concentration; attachment; **–लगाना** to concentrate on; to be deeply attached to; **–लगाये** engrossed in, identified with, deeply concentrated on.

लौका lauka: (*nm*) huge bottle gourd.

लौकिक laukik (*a*) secular; earthly; worldly, mundane; ~**ता** secularity; earthliness; worldliness; mundaneness; **–व्युत्पत्ति** folk/popular etymology; **–संस्कृत** Classical Sanskrit (as opposed to Vedic); **–साहित्य** secular literature.

लौकी lauki: (*nf*) bottle gourd.

लौज lauz (*nf*) almond; a special type of **बर्फ़ी** prepared by the admixture of almond, *khoya*: and sugar.

लौट lauṭ (*nf*) returning; **-पौट** topsy-turvy/topsyturvied; **-फेर** substantial change (of order etc.); modification.

लौटना lauṭnā: (*v*) to return, to come back: to retreat, to withdraw; to topsyturvy/to be topsyturvied; to be upturned.

लौटाना lauṭa:nā: (*v*) to return, to give back; to send back; to refund; to topsyturvy; to upturn.

लौटानी lauṭa:nī: (*ind*) while returning or coming back, in return trip.

लौना launā: (*nm*) fuel.

लौनी launī: (*nf*) unprocessed butter.

लौह lauh (*nm*) iron; (*a*) made of iron; ferrous; ~**कार** a blacksmith; ~**किट्ट** rust of iron; ~**चूर्ण** iron filings; **–पट** iron curtain; **–पात्र** ironware; **–पुरुष** an iron man; ~**मय** ferric, ferrate; abounding in iron; **–युग** iron age; ~**सार** steel.

लौहासव lauha:sav (*nm*) a medicinal tonic, a beverage prepared from processed iron and other ingredients.

व

व va—the last of the traditional semi-vowel set **य, र, ल, व**. Modern phoneticians, however, regard only **य** and **व** as semi-vowels and not **र** and **ल** which, according to them, are pure consonants; a conjunctive particle meaning 'and' (as भारत व पाकिस्तान).

वंक vāṅk (*a*) bent, curved; hence ~ता (*nf*); ~नाल a nerve of the body; ~नाली the nerve *Sushumna*:.

वंकट vāṅkaṭ (*a*) curved; intricate, difficult.

वंकिम vaṅkim (*a*) slightly curved/bent; hence ~ता (*nf*).

वंग vāṅg (*nm*) the eastern Indian state of Bengal; tin or tin-ash; ~ज vermilion; brass; born in Bengal; a Bengali; ~भंग the partition of Bengal in pre-Independence India which sparked off an unprecedented stir; -देश the state of Bengal; -संस्कृति the Bengali culture; वंगीय of, pertaining or belonging to, Bengal.

वंच/क vāṇchak (*a* and *nm*) fraudulent, deceitful; a humbug, an impostor; hence ~कता (*nf*); ~न (*nm*).

वंच/ना vāṇchanā: (*nf*) deprivation; deception, imposture, humbug; hence ~नीय (*a*).

वंचित vāṇchit (*a*) deprived; cheated, deceived, tricked.

वं/टन vaṇṭan (*nm*) (the act or process of) allotting, allotment; hence ~टित (*a*).

वंदन vāndan (*nm*) adoration, obeisance; vermilion.

वंदनवार vandanva:r (*nf*) bunting of green leaves (that are hung up on auspicious occasions).

वंदना vāndanā: (*nf*) deferential salutation; obeisance, worship.

वंदनीय vāndnī:y (*a*) adorable, worthy of worship.

वंदित vandit(*a*)worshipped; revered.

वंदीजन vandi:jan (*nm*) a bard; a Hindu sub-caste (professionally employed in the olden times for singing the eulogies of royal patrons).

वंध्य vandhy (*a*) unproductive, sterile; ~करण sterilization.

वंध्या vandhya: (*a*) (fem. form) barren, unfertile, unproductive; ~त्व barrenness; unfertility, unproductivity; -सुत an imaginary/impossible phenomenon.

वंश vansh (*nm*) lineage; family; clan; stock; dynasty; a bamboo; -उन्नति-शास्त्र eugenics; -कीर्ति fame/reputation of a family; -क्षय family decay; ~गत pertaining to a family/lineage; ~चरित genealogy; family history; ~ज a descendant, progeny; -तालिका genealogy or genealogical table; ~धर a descendant, progeny; -नाश the end or extermination of a family; -परंपरा lineage; family tradition; -लक्ष्मी family goddess; prosperity of a family; ~लोचन a whitish earthy formation in the hollow of a bamboo used for medicinal purposes; ~वृक्ष a genealogical tree; genealogy; bamboo tree; ~वृद्धि family prosperity, family development.

वंशाग/त vansha:gat (*a*) inherited, obtained by inheritance; ~ति inheritance.

वंशानुक्र/म, ~मण vansha:nukkram, ~ān (*nm*) family succession, genealogy; ~मिक hereditary, inherited.

वंशानुगत vansha:nugat (*nm*) hereditary, obtained through lineal inheritance.

वंशावली vansha:vali: (*nf*) genealogy, genealogical tree.

वंशी vanshi: (*nf*) a pipe, flute; fife; fishing hook; an adjectival suffix conveying the sense—belonging to the lineage/dynasty/clan of; also वंशीय; ~धर an epithet of Lord Krishnā.

वक़त vaqat (*nf*) value, worth.

वका/र vaka:r (*nm*) the letter व and its sound; ~रांत (word) ending in व् (*v*).

वक़ार vaqa:r (*nm*) prestige, honour, dignity; gravity.

वकालत vaka:lat (*nf*) advocacy, pleadership/pleading; practising law; ~नामा power of attorney; ~पेशा practising law, lawyer; –करना to plead for; to practise law; to hold brief for; to argue in favour of.

वकील vaki:l (*nf*) a lawyer, pleader, an advocate; –, सरकारी prosecution counsel, public prosecutor; counsel for the state.

वक़्त vaqt (*nm*) time; opportunity; –का पाबंद punctual; –आ जाना the destined time to arrive; the hour of death to come; –गुज़ारना to lead a tight life, to mark time; to be in straits; –पड़ना to be in a crisis; to be in trouble; -बेवक़्त at all times; in times of difficulty/crisis; -वक़्त पर at times; periodically; वक़्ती temporary, momentary; timely.

वक़्तन-फ़-वक़्तन vaqtān-fa-vaqtān (*ind*) occasionally, now and then, from time to time.

वक्तव्य vaktavvy (*nm*) a statement; (*a*) worth stating.

वक्ता vakta: (*nm*) a talker; spokesman; speaker.

वक्तृ/ता, ~त्व vaktrita: (*nf*), ~ttv (*nm*) eloquence, art of speaking, oratory; speech; ~त्व-कला art of speaking, rhetorics, oratory.

वक़्फ़ vaqf (*nm*) a wakf, charitable endowment; ~नामा the waqf-deed.

वक़्फ़ा vaqfa: (*nm*) (time) interval, intermission; recess.

वक्र vakkr (*a*) curved; oblique; cunning; –गति zigzag motion; crooked, unpredictable; cunning move; ~बुद्धि dishonest; crooked; –दृष्टि oblique glance, an angry look, frown; scowl.

वक्रता vakkrta: (*nf*) curvature/curvedness; crookedness; obliquity.

वक्री vakkri: (*a*) crooked; moving in an adverse direction (planets etc.).

वक्रोक्ति vakkrokti (*nf*) innuendo; an oblique utterance.

वक्ष vakksh (*nm*) chest, thorax; ~स्थल chest, chest region.

वक्षश्छद vakkshashchhad (*nm*) an armour.

वक्षोज vakkshoj (*nm*) breast of a woman.

वग़ै/रह, ~रा vagairah, ~ra: (*ind*) etcetera (etc.).

वचन vachan (*nm*) utterance, speech; talk; a quotation of a treatise or scripture; number (in Grammar); commitment, promise, pledge; ~ग्राही obedient; ~बंध an engagement; –मात्र empty words, mere words;–तोड़ना to break a promise/one's word; –देना to make a promise, to give word to; to commit, to vow; –निभाना see –पालन करना; ~बद्ध होना to promise, to commit; to make a contract; ~बद्ध करना to bind by promise or commitment; –पालन करना to adhere to one's word, to implement one's promise;–भंग करना to break a promise; to break one's word; –हारना to be pledged; to be committed.

वज़न vazān (*nm*) weight; importance, value; the measure of an alphabet or metre in Urdu or Persian language; ~दार weighty, heavy; important.

वज़नी vazanī: (*a*) heavy, weighty; important.

वजह vajeh (*nf*) cause, reason.

वज़ारत vaza:rat (*nf*) ministership; ministry.

वज़ीफ़ा vazi:fa: (*nm*) a scholarship, stipend; –मिलना to be awarded a scholarship.

वज़ी/र vazi:r (*nm*) a minister; the queen (in chess); ~रे-आज़म the Prime/Chief Minister.

वज़ू vaju: (*nm*) washing of hands and feet (by a Mohammedan) before prayers; –करना to wash one's hands and feet.

वजूद vaju:d (*nm*) existence; presence.

वजूहात vaju:ha:t (*nm*) plural of 'वजह'.

वज्र vajjr (*nm*) thunderbolt, lightning; a fatal weapon; (*a*) very hard, impenetrable; -घोष a thunder, thunderpeal; ~देह very hardy and sturdy; ~हृदय a cruel/unfeeling man; hard-hearted; –गिरना a calamity to befall.

वज्रपात vajjrpa:t (*nm*) the stroke of lightning/thunderbolt; a terrible calamity.

वज्रया/न vajjrya:n (*nm*) a degenerate offshoot of later Buddhist belief; ~नी a follower of the ~न sect; pertaining to ~न.

वज्रा/घात vajjra:gh:t (*nm*) a thunder-stroke, stroke of lightning; terrible calamity; ~हत thunder-struck, struck by lightning; struck by a calamity/calamitous blow.

वट vaṭ (*nm*) a banyan tree; also ~वृक्ष.

वटिका vaṭika: (*nf*) a pill, tablet; ball, small lump or round mass.

वटी vaṭi: (*nf*) a pill. a tablet.

वटु vaṭu (*nm*) a bachelor

वटुक vaṭuk (*nm*) see वटु.

वडा vaḍa: (*nm*) round balls of ground pulse fried in *ghee* or oil.

वणिक vānik (*nm*) a trader, business-man, merchant; a member of the *Vaishya* community; -कर्म (क्रिया) work of a trader, trading.

वणिग्वृत्ति vānigvritti (*nf*) the outlook/mentality of a trader; a trader's profession.

वणिज vānij (*nm*) a merchant, trader, tradesman.

वतन vatān (*nm*) homeland, native country; ~परस्त a patriot; ~परस्ती patriotism, patriotic feelings; ~फ़रोश who sells his country, a traitor; hence ~फ़रोशी (*nf*).

वतनी vatnī: (*nm*) a compatriot; (*a*) pertaining or belonging to a certain country, native.

वत् vat—a suffix to nouns or adjectives meaning similar to, akin to, like, resembling, etc. (as विधिवत्, पुत्रवत्).

वत्स vats (*nm*) offspring, progeny; used as a vocative word for son, nephew and younger relatives or near ones in general.

वत्सर vatsar (*nm*) an year.

वत्सल vatsal (*a*) affectionate, tender; ~ता affection, fondness, tenderness; –भाव affectionate feeling, tenderness.

वदन vadan (*nm*) the face, features.

वदान्य vada:nny (*a*) munificent, bounteous, generous; eloquent; hence ~ता (*nf*)

वदि vadi (*nf*) appended to the name of a lunar month to mean its dark half (as सावन वदि/बदी) etc.

वध vadh (*nm*) killing, murder; ~जीवी a slaughterer; ~स्थल/स्थली

a place of slaughter.

वधिक vadhik (*nm*) a murderer, an executioner; a hunter, fowler.

वधू vadhu: (*nf*) a bride, wife; **-पक्ष** the bridal party.

वध्य vaddhy (*a*) fit to be killed or murdered; who is to be killed or slaughtered; hence **~ता** (*nf*).

वन van (*nm*) wood, forest, jungle; water; **~खंड** forest; land; forestry; woodland; **~गमन** going to the forest; taking to asceticism; **–, गहन** dense forest; **~चर/चारी** a forester, woodman, forest-farer; **~ज/जात** wild, born in the jungle; a lotus flower; **~द** a cloud; **~देवता** a satyr, sylvanus; **–देवी** a dryad; **~धान्य** wild foodgrain; **~प्रांत** forest; forestry; woodland; **~पाल** a forester; forest ranger; **-महोत्सव** an Indian movement for augmentation of the forest wealth; **~माला** a wreath of wild flowers; **~राज** a lion; **-रक्षण** forest preservation; **~रोपण** afforestation; **~लक्ष्मी** a forest-beauty; forest-godness; **~वास** dwelling in a forest; exile, banishment; **o देना** to command to dwell in the forest, exiled, banished; **~वासी** inhabitant of a forest; an ascetic; **~विद्या** forestry; **·संवर्धन** forestation; **-संस्कृति** forest culture; **~स्थली** woodland, forest land.

वनस्पति vanaspati (*nf*) vegetation; vegetable; hydrogenated oil of groundnut etc; **–घी** vegetable oil, hydrogenated oil of groundnut etc; **~ज्ञ** a Botanist; **-विज्ञान/शास्त्र** Botany; **~वैज्ञानिक** botanical; a Botanist; **·शास्त्री** a Botanist; **~शास्त्रीय** botanical.

वनस्पतिज्ञ vanaspatiggy (*nm*) a Botanist, botanical expert.

वनिता vanita: (*nf*) a woman; beloved.

वनी vani: (*nf*) a small forest.

वनौषधि vanaushadhi (*nf*) a wild medicinal shrub.

वन्य vanny (*a*) wild, born in a forest; savage; **–पक्षी** a wild bird; **–पशु** a wild beast.

वपु vapu (*nm*) the body, physique; **~मान** good-looking; tangible.

वफ़ा vafa: (*nf*) fidelity, loyalty; **~दार** faithful, loyal; **~दारी** loyalty, fidelity, faithfulness.

वफ़ात vafa:t (*nf*) death, demise; **–पाना** to die.

वफ़ारा vafa:ra: (*nm*) moist fumigation.

वबा vaba: (*nf*) an epidemic, pestilence.

वबाल vaba:l (*nm*) a curse, calamity, affliction; **-ए-जान** a calamitous proposition, calamity.

वमन vamān (*nm*) vomiting, puke; **–करना** to vomit, to puke; **–करने की इच्छा** nausea, qualm.

वय:क्रम vayahkram (*nm*) age; stage of development in time.

वय:संधि vayahsāndhi (*nf*) age of adolescence, the age of confluence of childhood and youth.

वय vay (*nf*) age.

वयस्क vayask (*a*) adult; major; **-मताधिकार** adult franchise.

वयस्कता vayaskata: (*nf*) adulthood; majority; **–की आयु** age of majority.

वयोवृद्ध vayovriddh (*a*) aged, old; veteran.

वर var (*nm*) bridegroom; a boon; (*a*) good, excellent, beautiful; a Persian suffix meaning having, possessing, endowed with (as **नामवर, ताक़तवर** etc.); hence **~वरी** (as **नामवरी**); **~द** boon-giving, gratifying one's desire (as ~द हस्त); ~दाता/ दानी/दायक one who confers a boon; -पक्ष the bridegroom's party/side.

वरक़ varaq (nm) thin and fine leaves of silver or gold; page of a book; the petals of a flower; ~साज a manufacturer of thin and fine silver or gold leaves; hence ~साज़ी (nf); –उलटना to turn a page, to open up a new page.

वरज़ि/स varzis (nf) exercise, physical exercise; hence~सी (a).

वरण varaṇ (nm) selection, choice; marriage by choice; –करना to select, to choose/select a husband.

वरणीय varaṇī:y (a) worth selection/ choice.

वरदान varda:n (nm) a boon.

वरदी vardi: (nf) uniform; ~धारी in uniform.

वरना varnā: (v) to select or choose; (ind) otherwise, or else.

वरन् varān (ind) but, on the other hand.

वरम varam (nm) swelling, inflammation.

वरांगना vara:ṅgnā: (nf) a beautiful woman.

वराकांक्षी vara:kā:ṅkshi: (a) who prays for the fulfilment of a desire; desirous of a husband/ bridegroom.

वरासत vara:sat (nf) see विरासत.

वरासन vara:sān (nm) seat of the bridegroom.

वराह vara:h (nm) a boar, pig; –अवतार one of the ten incarnations of Lord Vishṇu.

वरिष्ठ varishṭh (a) senior; best, most preferable; ~ता seniority;~ता-क्रम order of seniority; –विद्वान a senior scholar; –सदस्य a senior member.

वरीय vari:y (a) senior, having precedence; preferable; ~ता seniority, precedence; ~ता-क्रम order of seniority / precedence / preference.

वरुण varūṇ (nm) the presiding deity of waters according to the Hindu mythology; waters; -लोक the kingdom of Varūṇ, waters.

वरुणालय varūṇa:lay (nm) the ocean.

वरे vare (ind) near, this side.

वरेण्य varenṇy (a) choice; classical; -ग्रंथ a classical work, classic; hence ~ता (nf).

वर्ग varg (nm) a class, category, group; group of letters pronounced from the same part of the vocal organ (as कवर्ग, चवर्ग, etc.); a square; square number; –, उच्च the upper class; –और जाति/वर्ण class and caste; ~गत pertaining to a class, characteristic of a class; o विशेषताएँ class characteristics; -द्वंद्व class struggle, class conflict; –, निम्न the lower class; –, निम्न मध्य lower middle class; -पहेली crossword puzzle; ~फल square; -भेद class distinction/discrimination; ~मुक्त classless;~मूल square root; ~वार classwise; -संघर्ष class struggle, class conflict; -समाज class society; –स्वार्थ class interest; –हित class interest;~हीन classless; o समाज classless society.

वर्गाकार varga:ka:r (a) square, square-shaped.

वर्गीकरण vargi:karaṇ (nm) classification, categorization; taxonomy.

वर्गीकृत vargi:krit (a) classified, categorized; –विज्ञापन classified advertisement.

वर्गीय vargi:y (a) class, pertaining to a particular brand/class/category or group.

वर्गोत्तम vargottam (*nm*) the last letter of each of the five pentads of the Indian alphabet.

वर्ग्य varggy (*a*) belonging to a certain class or group; (*nm*) a colleague.

वर्च/स्व varchassv (*nm*) vitality, energy; vigour; lustre, shine; hence ~**स्विता** (*nf*); ~**स्वी** full of vitality, vigorous, energetic; lustrous, shining.

व/र्जन varjān (*nm*) inhibition, taboo, prohibition; ~**र्जनीय** worth being or to be inhibited/tabooed/prohibited; ~**र्जित** inhibited, tabooed, prohibited; ~**र्ज्य** see **वर्जनीय**.

वर्जना varjanā: (*nf*) an inhibition, a taboo; prohibition; (*v*) to inhibit, to taboo, to prohibit; ~**ग्रस्त** inhibitive, characterised/marked by taboos.

वर्ण varn (*nm*) a caste; colour; dye (used for colouring or writing); a letter of the alphabet; -**क्रम** colour scheme, spectrum; classification; alphabetical order; ~**क्रममापी** spectrometer; ~**क्रमलेखी** spectrograph; ~**क्रम-विज्ञान** spectroscopy; ~**क्रमानुसार** in alphabetical order; ~**क्रमिकी** spectroscopy; -**दूषण** tarnish; -**धर्म** the duty or profession of a particular caste; -**भेद** caste/colour discrimination/distinction; ~**मंडल** chromosphere; ~**माला** the alphabet; ~**रेखा** streak; -**विकार** the transformation of one alphabet or sound into another; -**विचार** orthography; -**विन्यास** spelling; -**विपर्यय** metathesis, transposition of letters; -**विभाग/विभाजन** division of the Hindu community into four classes; -**व्यवस्था** the caste system; ~**संकर** cross-breed, hybrid; ~**संकरता** panmixia; hybridism; -**संसर्ग** intercaste union; ~**हीन** casteless; colourless; etiolated; ~**हीनता** castelessness; colourlessness; etiolation.

वर्णक varṇāk (*nm*) pigment; a painter.

वर्णन varṇān (*nm*) description, narration; commentary; hence **वर्णना** (*nf*); ~**कर्त्ता** a narrator.

वर्णनातीत varṇanā:ti:t (*a*) indescribable, defying description.

वर्णनीय varṇanī:y (*a*) describable, fit to be described or narrated; hence ~**ता** (*nf*).

वर्णांध varṇā:ndh (*a*) colour-blind; ~**ता** colourblindness.

वर्णागम varṇa:gam (*nm*) augment; addition or insertion of a letter (to a word).

वर्णानुक्र/म varṇā:nukkram (*nm*) alphabetical order; ~**मिक** alphabetical; ~**मणिका/मणी** alphabetical index.

वर्णानुप्रास varṇa:nuppra:s (*nm*) a kind of alliteration.

वर्णाश्रम varṇa:shshram (*nm*) the caste and the stage of life i.e. **आश्रम**; -**धर्म** duties related to the caste and the stage of life (**आश्रम**).

वर्णित varṇit (*a*) described, related, narrated.

वर्ण्य varṇy (*a*) fit to be described/narrated; -**विषय** the theme; topic of description/treatment.

वर्तन vartān (*nm*) refraction; turning; (*a*) revolution, grinding.

वर्तनांक vartanā:ṅk (*nm*) refractive index.

वर्तनी vartanī: (*nf*) spelling; -**व्यवस्था** spelling system; -**सुधार** reform of spelling.

वर्तमान vartamā:n (*a*) present, existing; current; (*nm*) the present; hence ~**ता** (*nf*); -**काल** the present tense (in Grammar); **–समय** the present.

वर्तिका vartika: (*nf*) a vick.

वर्तित vartit (*a*) set in rotation or motion; done; past.

वर्तु/ल vartul (*a*) rotund, round, spherical, circular; **~लता** roundness, rotundity; **~लाकार** rotundus, spherical, circular; **~लन** rounding.

वर्दी vardi: (*nf*) see **वरदी**.

वर्ध/न vardhān (*nm*) thriving; developing, increasing, growing; **~क** which causes development / increase/growth; hence **वर्धित** (*a*).

वर्धमान vardhamā:n (*a*) developing, growing, increasing.

व/र्म varm (*nm*) an armour; **~र्मित** armoured.

वर्ष varsh (*nm*) a year; vast tract of land (as **भारतवर्ष**); **~गाँठ** birthday, birth anniversary; **-प्रवेश** the beginning of a new year; **~बोध** an yearbook; **~फल** astrological predictions for a (particular) year.

वर्षा varsha: (*nf*) rain; rainfall; **-काल** rainy season; **-जल** rain water.

वर्षागम varsha:gam (*nm*) the coming of rains; advent of a new year.

वर्षानुवर्षी varsha:nuvarshi: (*a*) perennial, following year after year.

वर्षीय varshi:y (*a*) aged, of a certain number of years; ...year old; annual.

वलन valan (*nm*) fold; revolution, rotation.

वलय valay (*nm*) a ring, circle; fold.

वलयाकार valaya:ka:r (*a*) ring-shaped.

वलयित valayit (*a*) encircled; revolved.

वलित valit (*a*) folded, bent, enveloped.

वली vali: (*nm*) guardian, master; successor, heir; **~अहद** heir-apparent, heir-designate, **-वारिस** guardian or heir, near relative, kith.

वल्कल valkal (*nm*) the bark of a tree; **–वस्त्र** cloth made from **वल्कल**.

वल्गा valga: (*nf*) rein, bridle.

व/ल्द vald (*ind*) son of; **~ल्दियत** father's name; parentage.

वल्मीक valmi:k (*nf*) white ant; an anthill.

वल्लभ vallabh (*a* and *nm*) dear one; beloved; lover.

वल्लरी vallari: (*nf*) a creeper, creeping plant.

वल्लाह valla:h (*ind*) Good God !, oh !, oh God !

वल्ली valli: (*nf*) a creeper, creeping plant.

वशंवद vashāmvad (*a*) obedient; subordinate(d).

वश vash (*nm*) power; control; subjugation; used as a suffix to mean obliged by, compelled by (as **कार्यवश, स्नेहवश**); **~वर्ती** under control / sway, subjugated; **–का** under control, under the authority (of); **–चलना** to exercise control/sway (over); to have a say; **–में करना** to tame, to bring under control/subjugation; **–में होना** to be under the control/authority (of).

वशानुग vasha:nug (*a*) obedient, under control, subordinate(d).

वशि/ता, ~त्व vashita: (*nf*), **~ttv**; (*nm*) subjection; subjugation; fascination.

वशी/करण vashi:karān (*nm*) fascinating or enchanting into submission/control; **~कृत** fascinated/enchanted into submission; **~करण-मंत्र** a conjuration to bring (someone) under complete sway.

वशीभूत vashi:bhu:t (*a*) overpowered; tamed. brought under control;

fascinated.

वश्य vashshy (*a*) worth controlling; to be tamed/overpowered; ~**ता** subjection, subjugation.

वसंत vasānt (*nm*) the spring (season); a kind of *ra:g* in Indian classical music sung during the spring; -**काल** the time of spring; -**पंचमी** an important Hindu festival celebrated on the fifth day of the moonlit fortnight of the month of **माघ**; the fifth day of moonlit fortnight of the month of **माघ**.

वसंती vasānti: (*a*) pertaining to '**वसंत**' (spring); light yellow; (*nm*) light yellow colour.

वसंतोत्सव vasāntotsav (*nm*) the festival and merry-making of **होली**.

वसन vasān (*nm*) clothing, clothes, raiment.

वसा vasa: (*nf*) fat, fats and oils.

वसी vasi: (*nm*) a testamentary, one in whose favour a will is executed.

वसीक़ा vasi:qa: (*nm*) a document, deed; a stipend.

वसीय/त vasi:yat (*nf*) a will, testament; legacy; ~**तकर्त्ता** a testator; ~**तनामा** a will, testament; ~**ती** testamentary, pertaining to a testament; testate.

वसीला vasi:la: (*nm*) source, means, support.

वसुंधरा vasūndhara: (*nf*) the earth.

वसूल vasu:l (*a*) realised; collected; -**करना** to realise, to collect; ~**ना** see – **करना**.

वसूली vasu:li: (*nf*) realisation (of dues etc.), recovery.

वस्तु vastu (*nf*) an article, thing; object; substance, material; action/plot of a drama; content; -**जगत** substantial world, phenomenal world; -**ज्ञान** knowledge of the essentials; -**निर्देश** an inkling of the plot; ~**निष्ठ** objective; ~**निष्ठता** objectivity; ~**निष्ठतावाद**, ~**निष्ठावाद** objectivism; positivism; -**रचना** plot structure; ~**वाद** objectivism; objectivity; ~**वादी** an objectivist; objectivistic; -**विनिमय** barter, exchange; o **व्यवस्था** barter system; ~**स्थिति** reality, real position, actual state of things.

वस्तुत: vastutah (*ind*) de facto; actually, in reality.

वस्त्र vastr (*nm*) cloth(es), textile, fibre, raiment; –**विन्यास** drapery.

वस्त्रागार vastra:ga:r (*nm*) a cloth-house, textile shop.

वस्त्राभूषण vastra:bhu:shān (*nm*) dress and ornaments, overall prank.

वस्ल vasl (*nm*) union; lovers' union cohabitation.

वह ve(a)h (*pron*) he; she; it; that as a suffix '**वह**' imparts the sense of one who or that which bear or carries (e.g. **गंधवह, भारवह**).

वह/न vehān (*nm*) conveying, carrying, bearing; transportation; hence ~**नीय** (*a*).

वहम vehām (*nm*) doubt, suspicion false notion; superstition;–**का पुतला** a very suspicious man.

वहमी vehamī: (*a*) suspicious; superstitious.

वहशत vehshat (*nf*) embarrassment savagery; madness.

वहशियाना vehashiya:nā: (*a*) wild fierce, (like or resembling a savage.

वहशी vehashi: (*a*) savage, barbarous; mad; ~**पन** savagery, barbarousness; madness.

वहाँ vahā: (*adv*) there.

वहिर् vahir—see **बहिर्** and co

pounds under that entry.

वहीं vahī: (*ind*) there itself, at that very place/point, on the spot; ibid; –के वहीं there itself, there and then; on the spot.

वही vahi: (*pron*) the same, the very, the very same.

वह्नि vanhī (*nf*) fire.

वांछनीय vā:ṇchhanī:y (*a*) desirable, worth wishing for; ~ता desirability; –व्यक्ति persona grata.

वांछा vā:ṇchha: (*nf*) desire, wish.

वांछित vā:ṇchhit (*a*) desired, wished for.

वा va: (*ind*) or, or else; either—or, whether—or; (*int*) oh! ah! alas!

वाइदा va:ida: (*nm*) see **वायदा**.

वाइसराय va:isara:y (*nm*) a viceroy.

वाउचर va:uchar (*nm*) a voucher.

वाक़ई va:qai: (*ind*) in fact, actually, really.

वाक़फ़ियत va:qfiyat (*nf*) acquaintance; conversance.

वाकिफ़ va:qif (*a*) acquainted; conversant; (*nm*) acquaintance; ~कार an acquaintance; acquainted; having the know-how (for a job); ~कारी conversance, acquaintance; –होना to be acquainted/conversant with.

वाक़िया va:qiya: (*nm*) incident, event happening; ~त chain of events/incidents.

वाक़े va:qe (*a*) happening, taking place; actual; –होना to happen, to take place.

वाक् va:k (*nf*) speech, voice; utterance; goddess of speech; ~कलह altercation, quarrel; ~केलि jesting, witty conversation; ~छल quibble/quibbling, prevarication; equivocation; ~तंतु vocal cord; ~पटु eloquent, skilled in speech; ~पटुता / पाटव eloquence, skill in speech; ~पीठ a forum.

वाक्य va:kky (*nm*) a sentence; ~खंड a clause; -पद्धति method of sentence formation; -भेद syntactical difference; -रचना syntax, construction of a sentence; -विज्ञान syntax; -विन्यास amphibology, the order of a sentence; –विशेष a particular sentence; -विश्लेषण sentence-analysis; -संयोग grammatical construction.

वाक्यांश va:kyā:nsh (*nm*) a phrase.

वाक्याडंबर va:kya:ḍāmbar (*nm*) verbosity, bombastic language, turgidity.

वागाडंबर va:ga:dāmbar (*nm*) boastful language, grandiloquence; ~पूर्ण declamatory, grandiloquent.

वागिंद्रिय va:gīndriy (*nf*) vocal organ, organ of speech.

वागी/श, ~श्वर va:gi:sh, ~shshvar (*nm*) master of speech, an eloquent person, a great orator; a poet, an author.

वाग्जाल va:gja:l (*nm*) confused mass or multitude of words, grandiloquence; prevarication.

वाग्द/त्त va:gdatt (*a*) betrothed, engaged; hence ~त्ता feminine form.

वाग्दान va:gdā:n (*nm*) betrothal, engagement.

वाग्देवी va:gdevi: (*nf*) Saraswati:—the goddess of speech.

वाग्बद्ध va:gbaddh (*a*) tongue-tied, speechless, mute; hence ~ता (*nf*).

वाग्मिता va:gmīta: (*nf*) eloquence, apt and forceful use of words.

वाग्मी va:gmī: (*a* and *nm*) eloquent; an orator.

वाग्/युद्ध va:gyuddh (*nm*) an altercation, wordy quarrel; hence ~योद्धा (*nm*).

वाग्विकार va:gvika:r (*nm*) lilopathy;

also वाग्विकृति.

वाग्विदग्ध va:gvidagdh (*a*) eloquent, skilled in speech; witty; hence ~ता (*nf*).

वाग्विला/स va:gvila:s (*nm*) play of words, grandiloquence; elegance of speech; ~सी playing on words, grandiloquent.

वाग्विश्वास va:gvishshwa:s (*nm*) parole.

वाग्वीर va:gvi:r (*nm* and *a*) a tall-talker; talkative (person).

वाग्वैदग्ध्य va:gwaidagdhy (*nm*) eloquence, skill in speech, wittiness.

वाग्वैभव va:gvaibhav (*nm*) richness of language, glory of speech.

वाङ्मय vā:ṅmay (*nm*) literature (in a wider sense).

वाचक va:chak (*nm*) a narrator; reader; an announcer; (*a*) denoting; signifying; ~ता/त्व significance; expression; –पद significant/meaningful word.

वाचन va:chan (*nm*) reading; narration; citation; -पत्र citation.

वाचनालय va:chanā:lay (*nm*) a reading room.

वाचनिक va:chnik (*a*) verbal, oral.

वाचस्पति va:chaspati (*nm*) master of speech–Brihaspati : mythologically, the preceptor of gods.

वाचा va:cha: (*ind*) through speech; (*nf*) speech, word; ~बंध pledge, commitment; ~बंधन taking of a pledge, making of a commitment; ~बद्ध pledged, committed; -विरुद्ध not fit to be uttered; unworthy of speech.

वाचाल va:cha:l (*a* and *nm*) outspoken; talkative, chattering, gabby; ~ता outspokenness, talkativeness, gabbiness.

वाचिक va:chik (*a*) vocal, verbal, oral; (*nm*) acting through speech; –पत्र a written agreement, contract.

वाच्य va:chchy (*a*) predicable, expressible through words; (*nm*) denoted/literal meaning; voice (as कर्तृवाच्य—active voice, कर्मवाच्य—passive voice, भाववाच्य—neutral voice); ~ता/त्व literality, denotement.

वाच्यार्थ va:chchya:rth (*nm*) literal/primary meaning (of a word).

वाज va:j (*nm*) a fin; wing; ~युक्त winged; having fins.

वाज़ va:z (*nm*) a sermon, instruction.

वाजि/ब va:jib (*a*) reasonable, proper, incumbent; ~बी reasonable, proper, incumbent; ~बुल -अदा due.

वाज़िह, वाज़ेह va:zih, va:zeh (*a*) explicit, clear; –रहे/हो be it known/clear/explicitly understood.

वाजी va:ji: (*nm*) a horse; (*a*) winged; strong; ~कर aphrodisiac; ~करण sex-stimulation, excitement of sexual passion or enhancement of sexual potency through aphrodisiacs or stimulant drugs.

वाट va:ṭ (*nf*) see–बाट; (*nm*) watt.

वाटर va:ṭar (*nm*); -कलर water-colour; -पेंटिंग water painting; ~प्रूफ़ water-proof; -मार्क water-mark; ~मेन the watermain; ~वर्क्स waterworks.

वाटिका va:ṭika: (*nf*) a small garden.

वाडव va:ḍav (*nm*) submarine fire; also वाडवाग्नि, वाडवानल.

वाणिज्य va:ṇijjy (*nm*) commerce; trade; ~क a trader; -दूत a trade-consul; -दूतावास consulate; -मंडल chamber of commerce; ~वाद mercantilism; –विषयक/संबंधी mercantile, commercial.

वाणिज्यिक va:ṇijjik (*a*) commercial, mercantile; –हित commercial interest.

वाणी va:ṇi: (*nf*) speech, voice; Saraswati:—the goddess of speech; ~रहित/शून्य/हीन speechless, mute.

वात va:t (*nm*) air; wind–one of the three humours of the body (the other two being पित्त and कफ़); gout, rheumatism; ~कर/कारी producing wind; ~चक्र a whirlwind; ~ज caused or generated by wind; ~जीवी aerobic; -प्रकृति dominated by the wind humour; -प्रकोप disorder caused by the excess of wind within the system; ~युक्त aerated; -रंध्र lentical; -रोग/दोष/विकार ailment caused by disorder of the wind within the system, rheumatic ailment; ~हत hysteric.

वातानुकू/लन va:ta:nuku:lān (*nm*) air-conditioning; ~लित air-conditioned; also ~ल (*a*).

वातापेक्षी va:ta:pekshi: (*a*) aerobic.

वातायन va:ta:yān (*nm*) a ventilator; -व्यवस्था ventilation.

वातावरण va:ta:varān (*nm*) atmosphere; ~गत atmospheric; o अव्यवस्था atmospheric disturbance.

वातास va:ta:s (*nf*) air; breeze.

वातित va:tit (*a*) aerated, air-inflated.

वातीय va:ti:y (*a*) pertaining to air.

वातुल va:tul (*a*) rheumatic; delirious; crazy; hence ~ता (*nf*).

वातोन्माद va:tonma:d (*nm*) delirium.

वात्या va:ttya: (*nf*) a whirlwind; ~चक्र a whirlwind.

वात्सल्य va:tsally (*nm*) affection, affectionate love, fond/tender feeling (esp. towards the offspring); -भाजन an object of affection, who is loved; the loved one; -भाव affectionate feeling, sentiment of affection; ~मय affectionate, having fond attachment; –रस manifestation or relish of the sentiment of affection.

वाद va:d (*nm*) a suit, law-suit; cause; discussion; dispute; controversy; theory; –ism; -कला polemics; ~कारी a litigant; ~ग्रस्त controversial; -पत्र a plaint; –प्रतिवाद discussion, disputation, controversy; ~रत engaged in dispute/controversy/discussion; -विवाद dispute, discussion, controversy; debate; o प्रतियोगिता debating competition.

वादक va:dak (*nm*) an instrumentalist, one who plays on a musical instrument; -वृंद orchestra.

वादन va:dān (*nm*) playing on an instrument; hence वादित (*a*).

वादा va:da: (*nm*) see वायदा.

वादी va:di: (*nm*) a suitor, plaintiff; complainant; the dominant or the most important note in a *ra:g*; (*nf*) a valley; -पक्ष the plaintiff's side; -प्रतिवादी the plaintiff and the defendant; –स्वर the dominant or most important note in a melody.

वाद्य va:ddy (*nm*) a musical instrument; (*a*) (musical instrument) that can be played upon; (fit) to be played upon; ~वृंद the orchestra; -संगीत instrumental music.

वान va:n – a sanskrit suffix (वान्) adopted in Hindi—meaning वाला.

वानप्रस्थ va:nprasth (*nm*) the third of the four stages (आश्रम) of life prescribed by tradition for a caste Hindu—the stage of abandoning worldly things; hence –आश्रम; वानप्रस्थी (*nm* and *a*).

वानप्रस्थ्य va:nprasthy (*a*) pertaining to वानप्रस्थ.

वान/र va:nar (*nm*) a monkey, an ape; hence ~री (*nf*); (*a*) monkeyish, like a monkey; o सेना an army of monkeys.

वानस्पत्य va:nāspatty (*a*) vegetal; (*nm*) vegetation; arboriculture.

वापस va:pas (*a*) returned, given

back; come back; reverted; refunded, reimbursed; –आना to revert; to return, to come back; –करना to return/refund/reimburse/ give back; –बुलाना to recall, to summon back.

वापसी va:psi: (*nf*) coming back, return; refund, reimbursement; giving back; –किराया return fare; –टिकट a return ticket; –मुलाक़ात return call; –सफ़र return journey.

वापी va:pi: (*nf*) a deep well-like reservoir of water.

वाब/स्तगी va:bastagi: (*nf*) attachment; relationship; ~स्ता attached; related.

वाम vā:m (*a*) left, sinistral; reverse, contrary; adverse, perverse; vile, base; ~ता perversity; leftism, sinistrality; –पार्श्व left flank; sinistral; –पार्श्वता sinistrality; ~पार्श्विक sinistral; ~मार्ग the *Ta:ntrik* cult (which prescribes wine, woman, etc. as essentials); ~मार्गी a follower of ~मार्ग; pertaining to the ~मार्ग.

वामन va:mān (*nm*) a dwarf, dwarfish/short-statured person; a pigmy; the name of the fifth incarnation of Vishnu wherein he assumed the form of a dwarf; (*a*) dwarfish, short-statured.

वामा va:mā: (*nf*) a woman.

वामाचा/र va:mā:cha:r(*nm*)a *Ta:ntrik* cult; ~री an adherent of **वामाचार**.

वामाव/र्त va:mā:vart (*a*) anti-clockwise, counter-clockwise, laevorotatory; ~र्तन anti/counter-clockwise movement, laevorotation; ~र्ती anti-clockwise, counter-clockwise, laevorotatory; sinistral.

वायदा va:i(y)da: (*nm*) a promise; commitment; ~ख़िलाफ़ who breaks a promise or violates commitments; ~ख़िलाफ़ी breach of a promise, violation of a commitment; -बाज़ार future-market; **वायदे के सौदे** futures.

वायना va:ynā: (*nm*) presents of sweetmeats (to relatives on the occasion of a marriage, etc.).

वायलिन va:ylin (*nm*) a violin; ~वादक a violinist; hence ~वादन (*nm*).

वायव va:yav (*a*) aerial, relating or pertaining to air or wind.

वायवी va:yavi: (*nf*) north-western quarter; (*a*) north-western; see **वायवीय**.

वायवीय va:yavi:y (*a*) aerial; windy, airy, ethereal, impalpable; ~ता impalpability.

वायव्य vayavvy (*a*) pertaining or belonging to the air, aerial; having **वायु** as its presiding deity.

वायस va:yas (*nm*) a crow.

वायु va:yu (*nf*) air, wind; windy humour; wind formation within the system; mythologically, the air-god; -आशय air bladder; -कोष्ठ air chamber; ~गति as swift as wind, fleet; ~गतिक aerodynamic; ~गतिकी aerodynamics; ~ग्रस्त flatulent, affected by wind; ~दाब air-pressure; ० मापी a barometer; -निवृत्ति cure of windy disorder; -पंप an air pump; -बंध an airlock; ~बल the air force; -भार air pressure; ~भारमापी (यंत्र) the barometer; ~मंडल atmosphere; ~मापी an aerometer; -मार्ग airways; air-route; ~रुद्ध airtight; air-proof; ~वाहित airborne; ~विज्ञान aerology; ~वेग having the velocity of wind; ~वैज्ञानिक an aerologist; aerological; ~श्वासी air-breather; -सेना air force; -सेवा air-service; ~सैनिक an airman; ~हीन destitute of wind, windless.

वायुयान va:yuyā:n (*nm*) an aeroplane, aircraft; ~**वाहक** an aircraft-carrier; -**सेवा** air-service.

वारंट va:rānṭ (*nm*) a warrant; -**गिरफ़्तारी** warrant of arrest; -**तलाशी** a search warrant; -**रिहाई** a release warrant.

वारंवार va:rāmva:r (*ind*) again and again; frequently; ~**ता** frequency.

वार va:r (*nm*) an assault; a stroke, blow; a day of the week; the nearer side (as against **पार**—the farther side); (*nf*) (not in common use) a harlot, courtesan (as **वारवधू**); as a suffix it means 'wise' on the basis of (as **भाषावार** languagewise, **ब्यौरेवार** detailed; **राज्यवार** statewise), and also **वाला** (as **सोमवार**); -**पार** full expanse; this side and the other; across, from this side to the other; o **करना** to pierce through; -**पार होना** to be run through; to traverse the whole expanse; ~**वधू/वनिता/विलासिनी/सुन्दरी** a prostitute; -**करना** to strike; -**ख़ाली जाना/चूकना** a stroke to go amiss, to miss the target, to fan the air.

वार/ण va:rāṇ (*nm*) warding off; restraining, resisting; opposing; prevention; hence ~**क** (*nm*); ~**णीय** (*a*); and **वारित** (*a*).

वारदात va:rda:t (*nf*) a mishap, unfortunate/untoward event; an affray.

वारना va:rnā: (*v*) to sacrifice (on someone); to dedicate; to make an offering of.

वारनिश va:rnish (*nf*) varnish.

वारांगना va:rā:ṅganā: (*nf*) a prostitute.

वाराण/सी va:rā:ṇasi: (*nf*) the holy city of Benares; ~**सेय** belonging to or related with **वाराणसी**.

वाराना va:ra:nā:—a Persian compound suffix meaning 'wise', on the basis of (as **माहवाराना** monthly/monthwise; **फ़िरकेवाराना** communalistic; communitywise).

वारा-न्यारा va:ra:-nya:ra: (*nm*) settlement, decisive culmination; outcome; **वारे-न्यारे करना** to decide once for all; to have immense returns/acquirements; **वारे-न्यारे होना** to be decided once for all; to have immense returns/acquirements.

वाराह va:ra:h (*a*) of or related with a boar.

वारि va:ri (*nm*) water; ~**गर्भ** a cloud; ~**चर/चारी** aquatic; ~**ज/जात** a lotus; ~**द/धर** a cloud; ~**धि/निधि** an ocean, a sea; ~**बंध** a dam; ~**वाहन** a cloud; ~**विहार** aquatics, aquatic sport.

वारिस va:ris (*nm*) an heir, successor.

वारुणी va:rūṇī: (*nf*) wine, liquor.

वार्ड va:rḍ (*nm*) a ward; ~**र** a warder.

वार्डन va:rḍān (*nm*) a warden.

वार्तमानिक va:rtamā:nīk (*a*) pertaining to or related with the present.

वार्ता va:rta: (*nf*) a talk; talks, negotiation; ~**कार** a talker; negotiator; ~**वह/हर** a messenger, courier; ~**रंभ** commencement of talks/negotiation.

वार्तालाप va:rta:la:p (*nm*) conversation, talks; negotiation.

वार्तिक va:rtik (*nm*) a gloss, commentary; ~**कार** a commentator.

वार्द्धक्य va:rdhakky (*nm*) senility, old age.

वार्षि/क va:rshik (*a*) annual, yearly; per annum; ~**की** annuity; o **ग्राही** annuitant.

वालंटिय/र va:lānṭiyar (*nm*) a volunteer; ~**री** the job or function of a volunteer, volunteerism.

बाला va:la:—a suffix denoting an agent, doer, owner, possessor, keeper or inhabitant; hence **बाली** feminine form.

वालिद va:lid (*nm*) father; –**बुज़ुर्गवार** respected father; hence **वालिदा** mother.

वालिदैन va:lidain (*nm*) parents.

वालुका va:luka: (*nf*) sand; ~**मय** sandy.

वावैला va:vaila: (*nm*) uproar, tumult; turmoil, row; outcry; weeping and wailing; –**करना/मचाना** to kick up a row, to cause a tumult, to raise an outcry, to create a havoc.

वाशर va:shar (*nm*) a washer.

वाष्प va:shp (*nm*) vapour; ~**मय** vaporous; ~**मापी** vaporimeter; ~**शील** vaporescent; -**स्नान** vapour/steam bath.

वाष्प/न va:shpan (*nm*) vaporization; ~**नीय** vaporable, vaporizable.

वाष्पाकुल va:shpa:kul (*a*) tearful.

वाष्पी/करण va:shpi:karān (*nm*) vaporization; ~**कृत** vaporized; ~**य** vaporific, vapoury.

वासंती va:santi: (*a*) of or pertaining to **वसंत** (spring); (*nf*) a kind of sweet smelling creeper.

वास va:s (*nm*) habitation, dwelling, residence; fragrance, aroma; ~**भूमि** homestead.

वासना va:snā: (*nf*) passion, intense sexual desire; the impression(s) in the unconscious; knowledge derived from memory; hence ~**त्मक** (*a*); ~**परक** (*a*).

वासर va:sar (*nm*) a day.

वासा va:sa: (*nm*) lodging.

वासी va:si: (*nm*) a dweller, an inhabitant.

वासुदेव va:sudev (*nm*) an epithet of Lord Krishnā—the son of king **वसुदेव**.

वास्कट va:skaṭ (*nf*) a waistcoat.

वास्तव va:stav (*a*) real, actual, factual; genuine; substantial; –**में** really, actually, in reality, in fact.

वास्तविक va:stavik (*a*) real, actual, factual; genuine, bonafide; substantial; true, ex-post; ~**ता** reality, truth.

वास्ता va:sta: (*nm*) concern; connection; relation; –**देना** to invoke (in) the name of; –**पड़ना** to be concerned with; to have to deal with; –**होना** to be concerned with; to be related with, to have dealings with.

वास्तु va:stu (*nm*) building; -**कर्म** building work; -**कला** architecture; –**ज्ञान** architecture, architectural know-how; -**विद्या/शास्त्र** the science of architecture; -**शिल्प** architecture.

वास्ते va:ste (*ind*) for, for the sake of; in the name of.

वाह va:h (*int*) an exclamatory word denoting admiration, appreciation, contempt, opposition, surprise, etc. well done ! bravo ! excellent ! how can that be ! that can't be so, a suffix denoting one who or that which carries or bears; -**वाह** hurrah ! very good ! excellent ! -**वाह करना** to applaud; ~**वाही** tumultuous applause; applause; cheer; ~**वाही की धूम मच जाना** to bring down the house, to elicit tumultuous applause; ~**वाही लूटना** to appropriate applause/cheer.

वा/हक va:hak (*nm*) a carrier; vehicle; bearer; porter; hence ~**हिका** (*nf*).

वाहन va:hān (*nm*) a vehicle, conveyance; an animal used to ride upon.

बाहि/त va:hit (*a*) carried, borne; ~त्र a carrier.

बाहिनी va:hinī: (*nf*) an army; ~पति an army commander.

बाहियात vahiya:t (*a*) nonsense; useless; ridiculous.

बाही va:hi:—a suffix meaning he who or that which carries, bears, causes to flow; -तबाही irrelevant nonsense; ० बकना to talk irrelevant nonsense.

बाह्य va:hy (*a*) worth being or to be carried/borne; see बाह्य; hence ~ता (*nf*).

बाह्येंद्रिय va:hyendriy (*nf*) external sense or organ.

विंदु vindu (*nm*) a dot; drop; point; speck.

विंध्य vīndhy (*nm*) the mountain range in Central India dividing north India from the South and extending to the northern end of Eastern and Western Ghats.

विंध्याचल vindhya:chal (*nm*) see विंध्य.

वि vi—a prefix (generally to verb and nouns and other parts of speech derived from verbs) to express division, distinction, distribution, arrangement, opposition or deliberation as also through, between; sometimes it gives a meaning opposite to the idea contained in the simple root or also intensifies the idea.

विकंप, ~न vikāmp, ~ān (*nm*) trembling, quivering, wavering.

विकं/पित vikāmpit (*a*) trembling/trembled, quivering/quivered; unsteady, wavering; hence ~पी (*a*).

विक/च vikach (*a*) blooming; opened up; also ~चित (*a*)

विकट vikaṭ (*a*) horrible, dreadful, frightful; monstrous; formidable; hence ~ता (*nf*).

विकराल vikara:l (*a*) horrible, dreadful, frightful; hideous, monstrous; formidable; hence ~ता (*nf*).

विकर्ण vikarn (*nm*) a diagonal; ~तः diagonally.

विक/र्षण vikarshān (*nm*) repulsion; aversion, distate; ~र्षिता repulsiveness; aversion, distastefulness; ~र्षी repulsive; causing aversion, distasteful.

विक/ल vikal (*a*) restless, agitated; dismembered, mutilated, crippled; ~लांग crippled, disabled; ~लित restless; agitated.

विकल/क vikalak (*nm*) disintegrator; ~न disintegration.

विकलाना vikla:nā: (*v*) to be restless, to be agitated.

विकलेंद्रिय viklēndriy (*a*) crippled, having impaired or defective organs (of sense).

विकल्प vikalp (*nm*) an option, alternative; uncertainty; -जाल a web of uncertainties.

विकसना vikasnā: (*v*) to bloom; to open up; to grow.

विकसित vikasit (*a*) bloomed; opened; grown, developed; -देश a developed country.

विकार vika:r (*nm*) deformation, defilement; change or variation (for the worse); deviation from a natural state; perversion; disorder.

विकारी vika:ri: (*a*) variable, changeable (for the worse); perverse; oblique; -रूप oblique form.

विकार्य vika:ry (*a*) variable; deformable, changeable (for the worse); perversible; hence ~ता (*nf*).

विकाश vika:sh (*nm*) display, manifestation; splendour; expansion.

विकास vika:s (*nm*) evolution; development, growth; bloom; ~वाद theory of evolution; evolutionism; ~वादी an evolutionist; evolutionistic; ~शील developing; evolving.

विकासमान vika:smā:n (*a*) developing, in the process of development; hence ~ता (*nf*).

विकिरण vikirān (*nm*) radiation/radiance; diffusion; ~मापी radiometer; ~मिति radiometry; -विज्ञान radiology; ~वैज्ञानिक radiologist.

विकीर्ण viki:rn (*a*) diffused, scattered; disseminated; ~न diffusion, scattering; dissemination.

विकुंचित vikūṇchit (*a*) contracted; curled; knitted (as the eyebrows).

विकृत vikkrit (*a*) deformed, defiled; mutilated; changed (for the worse); deviated from the natural course, perverted; distorted; disordered; strained; oblique; ~दर्शन deformed, (turned) ugly; -रूप oblique form; ~स्वर (having) a hoarse voice.

विकृति vikkriti (*nf*) deformation; defilement, mutilation; defect; change or variation (for the worse); morbidity; deviation from the natural course, perversion; disorderliness; strain; caricature; -विज्ञान pathology; ~वैज्ञानिक pathologist; pathological.

विकृती/करण vikkriti:karān (*nm*) denaturalization; mutilation; perversion; defilement.

विकृष्ट vikkrisht (*a*) repulsed, thrown back.

विकेंद्रण vikendrān (*nm*) see विकेंद्रीकरण.

विकेंद्रित vikendrit (*a*) decentralised.

विकेंद्री/करण vikendri:karān (*nm*) decentralisation; ~कृत decentralised.

विकेट viket (*nm*) a wicket (in cricket); ~कीपर a wicket-keeper; -गिरना a wicket to fall; -लेना to take/capture a wicket.

विक्रम vikkram (*nm*) heroism, valiance, valour; name of an ancient great king of Ujjain, founder of an era which commenced earlier than the Christian era (also known as विक्रमादित्य).

विक्रमाब्द vikkrama:bd (*nm*) the *Vikram*-era.

विक्रमी vikkramī: (*a*) heroic, valiant, valorous; pertaining to विक्रम or his era.

विक्र/य vikkray (*nm*) sale, selling; ~य कर sales tax; ~य-पत्र sale deed; cash memo; ~यी a seller, vendor.

विक्रांत vikkrā:nt (*a*) radiant; mighty.

विक्री vikkri: (*nf*) see बिक्री.

विक्रीत vikkri:t (*a*) sold.

विक्रेता vikkreta: (*nm*) a seller, vendor; salesman.

विक्रेय vikkrey (*a*) marketable, saleable; ~ता marketability, saleability.

विक्षत vikkshat (*a*) wounded, injured.

विक्षिप्त vikkshipt (*a*) mad, crazy; bewildered; perplexed; ~ता madness, craziness; bewilderment; perplexity.

विक्षुब्ध vikkshubdh (*a*) agitated, perturbed/disturbed, turbulent; hence ~ता (*nf*).

विक्षेप vikkshep (*nm*) deflection; madness; perplexity; bewilderment; ~क deflector; -करना to deflect.

विक्षेपण vikkshepān (*nm*) deflection.

विक्षोभ vikkshobh (*nm*) agitation, perturbation, disturbance; turbulence.

विखं/डन vikhāṇḍān (*nm*) fission, fragmentation; breaking/splitting up; ademption; ~डनज fissiparous; ~डनात्मक fissiparous; ~डनीय fissionable; ~डित broken/split up, divided into fragments.

विख्यात vikkhya:t (*a*) renowned well-known, famous, reputed, celebrated.

विख्याति vikkhya:ti (*nf*) fame, name, renown, repute.

विगठ/न vigaṭhān (*nm*) disorganisation, disintegration; ~नात्मक disintegrating, fissiparous.

विगत vigat (*a* and *nm*) (the) past; used as a suffix it means deprived/divested of, minus, one who or that which has lost (as ~बल rendered or turned powerless); ~ज्ञान rendered/turned senseless; ~राग lost to attachment, having no attachments any more.

विगति vigati (*nf*) past; sad plight.

विगर्ह/ण vigarhāṇ (*nm*), ~णा, ~ṇā: (*nf*) censure, condemnation; ~णीय censurable, to be condemned; hence विगर्हित (*a*).

विग/लन vigalān (*nm*) fusion, melting away; moving; ~लित fused; melted away; moved.

विग्र/ह viggrah (*nm*) a strife, quarrel; form, idol (e.g. देवविग्रह); (in Grammar) resolution (of a compound word) into constituent parts, separation or analysis of a compound word; ~ही bellicose; pugnacious, quarrelsome.

विघट/न vighaṭan (*nm*) disintegration; disorganisation; disruption; decomposition; disbandment; dismemberment (e.g. of a state); dismantlement; ~नात्मक disintegrating, disruptive; ० प्रवृत्ति disruptive trend/tendency.

विघटित vighaṭit (*a*) disintegrated, disorganised, disrupted; decomposed; disbanded; dismembered; dismantled.

विघ्न vighn (*nm*) an interruption; interference, meddling; obstacle; disturbance; ~कर/कर्त्ता/कारी one who or that which interrupts/interferes/obstructs/disturbs; meddlesome; -विनाशक one who removes/counters all obstructions; an epithet of the deity Ganesh (whose worship is supposed to counter all obstacles).

विचकित vichakit (*a*) stunned, amazed, flabbergasted.

विचक्षण vichakshāṇ (*a*) extremely sagacious, far-sighted.

विचर vichar (*a*) strayed, wandered or swerved from; (*nm*) a variable; ~ण wandering, strolling; movement; variation; ०करना to wander/move about; to variate; hence विचरित (*a*).

विचल vichal (*a*) moving about; unsteady; ~न departure; deviation; moving about; yaw; unsteadiness; ~ना to yaw; to aberrate/deviate.

विचलता vichalata: (*nf*) deviation; unsteadiness; nervousness.

विचलित vichalit (*a*) restless; demoralised, nervous; fickle, unsteady; deviated; gone astray; hence ~ता (*nf*).

विचार vicha:r (*nm*) thought, thinking; idea; view, observation(s); pondering, deliberation, reflection; contemplation, reasoning; consideration; trial; ~क a thinker; one who deliberates/contemplates; ~कर्त्ता one who sits in judgment; thinker, one who deliberates/contemplates; -गोष्ठी a seminar; ~मूढ़

devoid of thinking power, stupid; ~वाद idealism; ~वादी an idealist; idealistic; ~वान see ~शील; –विमर्श discussion, exchange of views; ~शक्ति reasoning faculty, thinking power; ~शील thoughtful; reflective, contemplative/reasoning; ~शीलता thoughtfulness, contemplative character; -स्वातंत्र्य freedom of thought.

विचारण vicha:rāṇ (*nm*) thinking, reflecting, contemplating, reasoning, considering; ideation.

विचारणा vicha:raṇā: (*nf*) thought/thinking, contemplation, reasoning.

विचारणीय vicha:rṇī:y (*a*) to be deliberated about, worth/needing consideration, fit to be given thought to; dubious, questionable; hence ~ता (*nf*).

विचारधारा vicha:rdha:ra: (*nf*) ideology; ~परक ideological.

विचारना vicha:rnā: (*a*) to think, to deliberate on, to consider.

विचाराधीन vicha:ra:dhi:n (*a*) under consideration; under trial, subjudice.

विचारित vicha:rit (*a*) thought of, considered, deliberated on.

विचार्य vicha:ry (*a*) see **विचारणीय**.

विचिकित्सा vichikitsa: (*nf*) scepticism, doubt.

विचित्र vichittr (*a*) strange; surprising. amazing, wonderful; queer, curious; peculiar; ~ता strangeness; singularity; peculiarity.

विच्छित्ति vichchhitti (*nf*) cutting asunder or off, dissection; caesura, pause in a verse.

विच्छिन्न vichchhinn (*a*) isolated, cut off; discontinued; disjointed, disconnected; ~ता isolatedness; discontinuance; disjointedness; disconnectedness.

विच्छेद vichchhed (*nm*) dissection; division; difference; disintegration, separation; discontinuance; breach; breaking up; hence ~क (*nm*); ~न (*nm*); ~नीय (*a*); विच्छेद्य (*a*).

विच्छेदी vichchhedi: (*nm* and *a*) a disintegrator; secessionist(ic).

विछो/ह vichhoh (*nm*) separation (from the beloved); ~ही one who is separated, suffering the pangs of separation.

विजड़ित vijaṛit (*a*) stunned, stilled, rendered motionless; inlaid, inset; hence ~ता (*nf*).

विजन vijan (*a*) solitary, lovely; (*nm*) a lonely place, solitude; ~ता loneliness, solitude.

विजय vijay (*nf*) victory, conquest, triumph; ~कर victorious, triumphant, conquering; -दुंदुभि triumphal drum-beating; –देवी the goddess of victory; -ध्वज/पताका the banner of victory, triumphal flag; -यात्रा victorious/triumphal tour, conquering expedition; -लक्ष्मी/श्री the goddess of victory; ~शील ever victorious/triumphant, conquering; -सिद्धि accomplishment of victory, conquest.

विजया vijaya: (*nf*) see **भाँग**; ~दशमी see **दशहरा**.

विजयोत्सव vijayotsav (*nm*) a festival to celebrate victory.

विजाति vija:ti (*nf*) another/different caste, class or genre.

विजातीय vija:ti:y (*a*) of different caste, class or genre; heterogeneous; hence ~ता (*nf*).

विज़िटिंग कार्ड viziṭīng ka:rḍ (*nm*) a visiting card.

विजित vijit (*a*) conquered, won (over).

विजेता vijeta: (*nm*) a conqueror,

victor, one who has achieved victory.

विज्जु vijju (*nf*) lightning; ~लता forked lightning.

विज्ञ viggy (*a* and *nm*) knowledgeable; learned, wise (person); ~जन the learned; ~ता knowledgeability; learning, wisdom; -मंडल Brains Trust.

विज्ञप्ति viggyapti (*nf*) a communique; -, प्रेस a press communique.

विज्ञात viggya:t (*a*) well-known, famous, reputed.

विज्ञान viggyā:n (*nm*) science; ~मय scientific; consisting of knowledge or intelligence; o कोश the intelligence sheath (of the soul, according to the वेदांत); ~वाद Idealism—the doctrine that only intelligence has reality (and not the objects exterior to us); ~वादी an Idealist, a believer in the doctrine of विज्ञानवाद; idealistic; ~वेत्ता a Scientist, man of Science.

विज्ञानी viggya:nī: (*nm*) a Scientist.

विज्ञा/पन viggya:pan (*nm*) an advertisement; announcement; a poster; -दर advertising rate; ~दाता advertiser; ~पन-निर्देशिका advertising directory; ~पन-माध्यम advertising medium; ~पन -विभाग advertisement department; ~पन-विशेषज्ञ advertising expert; ~पन-सलाहकार advertising consultant; ~पनीय worth being advertised/notified; ~पित advertised; notified.

विज्ञापक viggya:pak (*nm*) an advertiser.

विज्ञेय viggyey (*a*) worth knowing/comprehending; comprehensible; hence ~ता (*nf*).

विटप viṭap (*nm*) a tree.

विटामिन viṭa:min (*nf*) vitamin.

विडंबन viḍāmban (*nm*) mimicry; -काव्य a parody.

विडंबना viḍāmbanā: (*nf*) anomaly; mockery; hence **विडंबनीय** (*a*); **विडंबित** (*a*).

विडा/ल viḍa:l (*nm*) a he-cat; hence ~ली (*nf*); ~लाक्ष/लाक्षी cat-eyed.

वितंडा vitāṇḍa: (*nm*) perverse argumentation, ungainly controversy; ~वाद arguing for the sake of argument, perverse argumentation, ungainly controversy; hence ~वादी (*a, nm*); –खड़ा करना to raise an ungainly controversy.

वितत vitat (*a*) spread out, extended; drawn (as a bow-string); hence **वितति** (*nf*).

वितथ vitath (*a*) false, untrue.

वित/रण vitarāṇ (*nm*) distribution; disbursement; delivery, service; ~रण-व्यवस्था distribution system; ~रक a distributor; ~रिका distributory; ~रित distributed; disbursed; delivered.

वित/र्क vitark (*nm*) discussion, reasoning; ~र्कित discussed; thought over, reasoned; ~र्क्य to be or worth being discussed/reasoned.

वितल vital (*nm*) an abyss; traditionally, one of the seven nether worlds.

वितस्ति vitasti (*nf*) a hand-span.

विताड़/न, ~ना vita:ṛān (*nm*) ~nā:(*nf*) rebuke, reproach, scolding.

वितान vita:n (*nf*) a canopy; extension.

वित्तीर्ण viti:rṇ (*a*) remote, distant.

वितुंड vituṇḍ (*nm*) an elephant.

वितृप्त vitript (*a*) well-satisfied, gratified, fulfilled.

वितृष्णा vitrishṇā: (*nf*) repulsion, repugnance; ~जनक repulsive, repugnant.

वित्त vitt (*nm*) finance; wealth; -कार्य

financial affairs;~ **दाता** a financer; ** o बैंक** a financing bank; **-प्रबंध** financing; **-मंत्रालय** Finance Ministry; **-मंत्री** Finance Minister; **-वर्ष** financial year; **-विधेयक** finance bill; **-विभाग** finance department; **-विशेषज्ञ** financial expert; **-व्यवस्था** financial set-up; **-संचय** accumulation of wealth; **-सचिव** Finance Secretary; **-साधन** financial resources; ~**हीन** indigent, poor; hence ~**हीनता** (nf).

वित्तीय vitti:y (a) financial; **–मामले** financial matters.

वित्तीयन vitti:yan (nm) financing.

वित्तेषणा vittaishṇā: (nf) craving for money, greed for wealth.

विथकित vithakit (a) fatigued, exhausted, tired.

विथराना vithra:nā: (v) to scatter, to diffuse; to dishevel.

विदग्ध vidagdh (a) witty; ingenious; skilful; ~**ता** wittiness; ingenuity; skilfulness; hence **विदग्धा** (feminine form).

विद/रण vidarāṇ(nm) splitting, bursting, cleavage, cracking; hence ~**रित** (a).

विदर्भ vidarbh (nm) ancient name for modern Berar (now revived).

विदलन vidalān (nm) tearing; shattering; crushing.

विद/लना vidalnā: (v) to tear; to shatter; to crush; ~**लित** torn; shattered; crushed.

विदा vida: (nf) taking leave, farewell, adieu; a woman's departure from her mother's or from her in-law's house; **–करना** to send off, to bid farewell; **–लेना** to take leave, to make one's adieu; **–होना** to bid farewell; to depart.

विदाई vida:i: (nf) farewell, sending off; departure; present made at the time of departure.

विदा/रण vida:rāṇ (nm) laceration, rending, tearing, ripping open, splitting; hence ~**रक** (nm); ~**रित** (a).

विदारना vida:rnā: (v) to rend, to tear, to split.

विदित vidit (a) known.

विदीर्ण vidi:rṇ (a) lacerate, rent asunder, torn, ripped open, split up; hence ~**ता** (nf); **हृदय** heart-rent, broken-hearted.

विदुषी vidushi: (nf) a learned/wise woman.

विदूषक vidu:shak (nm) a jester, buffoon; the jocose companion and confidential friend of the hero in traditional Sanskrit drama.

विदूषित vidu:shit (a) vitiated, polluted, contaminated; corrupted.

विदेश videsh (nm) a foreign land/country; ~**गमन** migration; ~**ज** exotic; alien; foreign; **-नीति** foreign policy; **-मंत्रालय** Ministry of External Affairs; **-मंत्री** Foreign Minister; **-वास** foreign sojourn; **-विभाग** department of Foreign/External Affairs; **-व्यापार** foreign trade; **-संबंध** foreign relations; **-सचिव** foreign secretary; **-सेवा** foreign service.

विदेशी videshi: (a) foreign; alien; exotic; (nm) a foreigner; foreign national; **–मुद्रा** foreign exchange; **–विनिमय** foreign exchange.

विदेशीय videshi:y (a) foreign; alien; exotic; hence ~**ता** (nf)/**त्व** (nm) foreignism.

विदेह videh (a) incorporeal; beyond physical bonds; ~**त्व** bodilessness; the state of being beyond physical bonds.

विद्ध viddh (a) pierced, penetrated;

hence ~ता (*nf*).

विद्यमान vidyamā:n (*a*) present, existent; extant; ~ता presence, existence.

विद्या viddya: (*nf*) learning, knowledge; education; science; discipline; skill; -कर्म the study of science; -दान teaching, imparting knowledge; -देवी Saraswati:—the goddess of learning; -परिषद् academic council; ~पीठ a school, seat/centre of learning; -मंदिर temple of learning; -युग educational age; -लाभ acquisition of learning/education; ~विहीन illiterate; stupid; hence ~विहीनता (*nf*); -व्यवसाय pursuit of knowledge; scholarly profession; -व्यसनी addicted to learning/education; ~हीन illiterate, stupid; hence ~हीनता (*nf*); -झूठी पड़ना learning/skill to prove of no avail; -फलना learning/skill to bear fruit.

विद्याभिमा/न viddya:bhimā:n (*nm*) pride of learning/scholarship; ~नी learning-proud.

विद्याभ्या/स viddya:bbhya:s (*nm*) pursuit of learning, study; ~सी studious.

विद्यारंभ viddya:rāmbh (*nm*) commencement of education.

विद्यार्जन viddya:rjan (*nm*) acquisition of education, study.

विद्यार्थी viddya:rthi: (*nm*) a student; scholar.

विद्यालय viddya:lay (*nm*) a school, educational institution.

विद्यु/त् viddyut (*nm*) electricity, electro-, power; lightning; ~त्-अपघटन electrolysis; ~त्-अपघटनी electrolytic; ~त्-अपघट्य electrolyte; ~त्-चुंबक electro-magnet; ~तन, ~तीकरण electrification; ~त्-विशेषज्ञ an electrician; ~त्-विश्लेषण electrolysis; ~त्-शक्ति power; ~त्-सक्रिय electro-active; ~दग्र electrode; ~दणु an electron; ~द्घात electocution; ~द्वाहक electromotive; ~न्मय electrified; ~न्मापी electrometer; ~न्मिति electrometry.

विद्योचित viddyochit (*a*) academic.

विद्योपार्जन viddyopa:rjan (*nm*) acquisition of education, study.

विद्रुम viddrum (*nm*) coral; the coral tree.

विद्रूप viddru:p (*a*) distorted, ugly, hideous; monstrous; (*nm*) ludicrousness; monstrosity; irony; a parody; -काव्य a parody.

विद्रो/ह viddroh (*nm*) uprising, revolt, rebellion, mutiny, insurrection; ~ही revolting, a rebel/rebellious; mutineer/mutineering; ~ह करना to revolt, to rebel (against), to mutiny; ~ह का झंडा उठाना to rise in revolt.

विद्वज्जन viddwajjan (*nm*) learned/scholarly people, the wise.

विद्वत्ता viddwatta: (*nf*) learning, scholarship.

विद्वान् viddwa:n (*a* and *nm*) learned (man), a scholar.

विद्वे/ष viddwesh (*nm*) rancour. malice, spitefulness; antipathy; ~षी rancorous, malicious, spiteful, antipathetic.

विधना vidhnā: (*nm*) Providence, Brahmā:—the Creator; -का लेख destiny, writ of destiny.

विध vidh (*nf*) see विधि; as a suffix it means—of a type/form or types/forms (as बहुविध, एकविध).

विध/र्म vidharm (*nm*) heresy; a religion other than one's own, nonconformist religion; (*a*) unjust, inequitable; ~र्मी a heretic/heretical; follower of another religion;

unjust, inequitable.

विधवा vidhwa: (*nf*) a widow; ~पन widowhood; -विवाह widow-remarriage; ~श्रम a house for the maintenance of widows.

विधा vidha: (*nf*) genre; form, type; device.

विधाता vidha:ta: (*nm*) the Creator—Brahmā:, Destiny personified; a legislator, law-maker; —का वरदान a divine gift.

विधान vidhā:n (*nm*) legislation, rule, regulation; disposition; manner/method; ~ज्ञ legislative expert; -परिषद् legislative council; ~पालिका legislature; ~मंडल legislature; -शक्ति legislative power; -सभा legislative assembly; —बनाना to legislate.

विधानांग vidha:nā:ṅg (*nm*) legislature.

विधायक vidha:yak (*a* and *nm*) legislative; creative; a legislator; creator.

विधायन vidha:yan (*a*) law-making, legislative.

विधायिका vidha:ika (*nf*) legislature; (*a*) legislative.

विधायी vidha:i: (*a*) legislative; creative; —कार्य legislative function; —शक्ति legislative/creative power.

विधि vidhi (*nf*) law; method, manner; system; direction; rule; a prescribed act or rite or ceremony, prescription; imperative; destiny; providence; (*nm*) the Creator—Lord Brahmā:; —और व्यवस्था law and order; ~क legal, in accordance with law; ~कर्त्ता a legislator; law giver; ~ज्ञ a legist; lawyer, legal expert; an adept in any technical field; ~त: de jure; -निषेध dos and don'ts; prescription and negation; ~पूर्वक duly, methodically, systematically; ~मान्य valid; ~मान्यता validity; ~लिंग the potential mood (in Grammar); ~वक्ता a barrister-at-law; ~वत् duly, methodically, systematically; in conformity with rules, as prescribed by law; -वर्ग the bar; ~वश/वशात् by providence; -विधान method and manner; writ of providence; ०पूर्वक/से methodically following elaborate prescription; —विपर्यय providential adversity; -विरुद्ध unlawful, lawless; ~विहित valid; prescribed by law, ordained by law; ~वेत्ता legist; a jurist; juris consultant; -शास्त्र jurisprudence; ~शास्त्री a jurisprudent, jurist; ~संगत/सम्मत legitimate; ~हीन lawless; violating the law; without a system/method, irregular; hence ~हीनता (*nf*); —का लेख, —का विधान the writ of destiny; —की विडंबना irony of fate; —बैठना to be harmonised, to conform; to have things move as one wishes; —मिलना the horoscopes (of a boy and a girl) to conform; —वाम, विपरीत होना one's destiny to be adversely disposed, to be ill-fated.

विधु vidhu (*nm*) the moon; ~मुखी, वदनी blessed with a moon-like face, pretty-faced.

विधुर vidhur (*nm*) a widower; (*a*) widowed.

विधूम vidhu:m (*a*) smokeless.

विधेय vidhey (*a*) that can be legislated; to be performed or practised; to be enjoined (as a rule etc.); (*nm*) the predicate; hence ~ (*adv*); ~ता (*nf*); ~त्व (*nm*); -विशेषण predicative adjective.

विधेयक vidheyak (*nm*) a bill (in a legislature).

विध्यात्मक viddhya:tmak (*a*) positive

~ता positivity, positivism; -निषेधात्मक positive and negative.

विध्वंस viddhwans (*nm*) destruction, devastation; subversion; demolition; ~क a destroyer; destructive, one who or that which spells devastation; ~कर्ता destroyer; —के बीज बोना to sow the seeds of devastation/destruction.

विध्वंसी viddhwānsi: (*nm*) a destroyer; one who or that which destroys.

विध्वस्त viddhwast (*a*) destroyed, devastated.

विनत vināt (*a*) bowing/bowed; modest, humble.

विनती vinti: (*nf*) prayer; request, entreaty.

विनम्र vinammr (*a*) humble, meek, submissive; respectful; courteous; ~ता humbleness, meekness, submissiveness; courtesy, humility.

विनय vinay (*nf*) modesty, politeness, humbleness, humility; ~शील humble, modest, polite; ~शीलता humbleness, modesty, politeness, humility.

विनयावनत vinaya:vanāt (*a*) see विनम्र.

विनयी vinayi: (*a*) modest, polite, humble.

विनश्वर vinasshvar (*a*) perishable, transient, transitory; ~ता perishability, transience, transitoriness.

विनष्ट vinashṭ (*a*) perished, destroyed, devastated; wrecked; ruined; ~दृष्टि who has lost his sight, turned blind; ~धर्म fallen from religion/duty.

विना vinā: (*ind*) without, in the absence of; –शर्त unconditional (ly), without any conditon.

विनायक vinā:yak (*nm*) the god Ganesh.

विनाश vinā:sh (*nm*) destruction, devastation; disaster, ruin, wreck; ~क destroyer/destructive, devastating/one who devastates or ruins; ~धर्मी perishable, transient, transitory; -हेतु the cause for destruction/devastation; ~काले विपरीत बुद्धि whom God would destory, He first makes mad.

विना/शी vinā:shi: (*a*) destructive, spelling disaster/destruction, disastrous; hence ~शिता (*nf*).

विनाशोन्मुख vinā:shonmukh (*a*) heading towards disaster/destruction, decaying; hence ~ता (*nf*).

विनिधान vinidha:n (*nm*) allocation; –करना to allocate.

विनिबंध vinībāndh (*nm*) a monograph.

विनि/मय vinimay (*nm*) exchange; ~मय-दर rate of exchange; ~मय-पत्र a letter of exchange; ~मेय exchangeable; ~मेयता exchangeability.

विनियं/त्रण viniyantran (*nm*) decontrol; ~त्रित decontrolled.

विनियम viniyam (*nm*) a regulation; ~न (the act or process of) regulation.

विनियुक्त viniyukt (*a*) appropriated.

विनियो/ग viniyog (*nm*) appropriation; ~जन (the act or process of) appropriation; ~जित appropriated; ~ग/जन करना to appropriate.

विनिर्णय vinirnay (*nm*) adjudgement; –करना to adjudge.

विनिर्णायक vinirnā:yak (*nm*) an adjudicator.

विनिर्णीत vinirni:t (*a*) adjudged.

विनि/र्देश vinirdesh (*nm*) specification; ~र्दिष्ट specified.

विनिर्मा/ण vinirmā:n (*nm*) manufacture/manufacturing; ~ण-संस्था manufacturing concern; ~ता a manufacturer, manufacturing concern.

विनिर्मि/त vinirmit(*a*) manufactured; ~**ति** a manufacture, product.

विनिहित vinihit (*a*) allocated.

विनीत vinī:t (*a*) humble, modest; submissive, meek; ~**ता** humbleness, modesty; submissiveness, meekness.

विनोद vinod (*nm*) wit; humour, amusement, recreation; skit; ~**प्रिय** humorous, witty, jovial, jocose; jocular; hence ~**प्रियता** (*nf*); -**वृत्ति** sense of humour; ~**शील** witty, humorous, jolly, jovial; ~**शीलता** wittiness, humorousness, jollity, joviality.

विनोदी vinodi: (*a*) witty, humorous, jocular, jolly, jovial;-**स्वभाव** witty/jolly/jovial/humorous nature.

विन्यस्त vinnyast (*a*) arranged, set in order, planned, laid out; marshalled; hence ~**ता** (*nm*).

विन्यास vinnya:s (*nm*) structure, disposition, arrangement; setting, plan, lay-out; marshalling; ~**दर्शी** a stereoscope.

विपंची vipāṇchi: (*nf*) a typical lyre.

विपक्ष vipaksh (*nm*) the opposition (party/side); adversary; -**भाव/वृत्ति** opposition, hostility.

विपक्षी vipakshi: (*a*) opposition, rival, hostile; (*nm*) an opponent, a rival; an enemy; -**दल** opposition party; -**दल का नेता** leader of the opposition; -**नेता** rival leader, opposition leader.

विपण vipan (*nm*) a market, small market.

विपणन vipanān (*nm*) marketing.

विपणि vipanī (*nf*) a shop; market; commodity.

विपण्य vipanny (*a*) marketable; (*nm*) commodity; ~**ता** marketability.

विपत् vipat—an allomorph of **विपद्** used as the first member in certain compound words; ~**कर** troublesome, causing affliction/distress/hardship; ~**काल** times/days of distress, rainy days/season, hard days.

विपत्ति vipatti (*nf*) distress; affliction; calamity; hardship; ~**कर** causing affliction/hardship/distress, calamitous; -**काल** rainy season, times of distress/affliction; bad/hard days; ~**ग्रस्त** afflicted, distressed, fallen into calamity; ~**वाद** catastrophism; -**उठाना/झेलना** to bear/face/endure hardship or calamity; -**काटना** to mark/endure calamitous times, to go through times of distress; -**भोगना** to suffer hardships, to endure a calamity; -**में पड़ना** to be afflicted, to be in distress; -**मोल लेना,** -**सिर पर लेना** to own up avoidable distress/calamity, to get oneself (foolishly) embroiled in a calamitous/troublous affair.

विपत्र vipattr (*nm*) a bill; (*a*) leafless, without leaves.

विपथ vipath (*nm*) a wrong course path; ~**गामी** aberrant, (one) going astray; ~**न** aberration, going astray.

विपद् vipad (*nf*) distress, affliction; hardship; calamity; crisis; ~**ग्रस्त** in a crisis, in distress, afflicted; struck by a calamity.

विपन्न vipann (*a*) distressed, afflicted; fallen into a calamity, in a critical state; hence ~**ता** (*nf*).

विपरीत vipari:t (*a*) opposite/opposed; contrary, reverse; ~**गति** (going in) the opposite direction; ~**ता/त्व** contrariety; antithesis; ~**बुद्धि/मति** mentally aberrant, wayward; -**रति** a typical copulative posture where the woman assumes an active role; –लक्षणा antiphrasis.

विपरीतार्थ vipari:ta:rth (*a*) antonym, antonymous word; also ~क.

विपर्यय viparyay (*nm*) metathesis, transposition; reversal; -, स्थिति reversal of the situation, peripeteia.

विपर्यस्त viparyast (*a*) disturbed, disarranged, topsyturvied, inter-reversed; hence ~ता (*nf*).

विपर्याय viparya:y (*nm*) an antonym, antonymous word; ~वाचक/वाची antonymous.

विपर्यास viparya:s (*nm*) upsetting, disarray; contrariety; interchange; peripeteia/reversal (of the situation).

विपल vipal (*nm*) one-sixtieth part of a पल.

विपाक vipa:k (*nm*) result, consequence (of actions etc.); ripening; maturing.

विपा/टन vipa:ṭan (*nm*) the act or process of tearing/uprooting/breaking; ~टित torn, uprooted; broken.

विपिन vipin (*nm*) a forest, jungle; ~चर forest-faring, living in/treading the forest; ~विहारी an epithet of Lord Krishnā.

विपुत्र viputtr (*a*) having no male child, without a son.

विपुल vipul(*a*) large, big; abundant, copious; extensive; mammoth, colossal; ~ता largeness; bulk; abundance; copiousness, extensiveness; hence विपुला–feminine form.

विप्र vippr (*nm*) a Bra:hmāṇ.

विप्रतिक्षेप vippratikshep (*nm*) cross-reflex; ~ण cross-reflection.

विप्रति/पत्ति vippratipatti (*nf*) divergence; contradiction; incompatibility (of two views or rules etc.); hence ~पन्न (*a*).

विप्रतीप vipprati:p (*a*) perverse; opposite; ~ता perversity.

विप्र/योग vipprayog (*nm*) separation (esp. from the beloved); disagreement; hence ~युक्त (*a*).

विप्रलंभ vippralambh(*nm*) separation (of lovers); –शृंगार according to Indian poetics, one of the two types of शृंगार wherein the lovers suffer separation from each other.

विप्रल/ब्ध vippralabdh (*a*) separated (from the beloved), suffering the pangs of separation; frustrated; hence ~ब्धा (feminine form).

विप्ल/व viplav (*nm*) insurrection, insurgency, revolt; ~वकारी/वी revolting; an insurgent; insurrectional/insurrectionary.

विफल viphal (*a*) failed, unsuccessful; vain, inefficacious; fruitless, futile; ~ता failure; inefficacy, fruitlessness, futility.

विबुध vibudh (*nm*) a god, deity.

विबो/ध vibodh (*nm*) awakening, consciousness; ~धन awakening; arousing consciousness; ~धित awakened, (made) conscious.

विभंग vibhāṅg (*a*) fractured; ruptured; broken, split.

विभंजन vibhāṇjān (*nm*) fracture; rupture; breaking, splitting.

विभक्त vibhakt (*a*) divided; partitioned; separated; hence ~ता (*nf*).

विभक्ति vibhakti (*nf*) a case ending/termination, inflection, case; division; ~ग्राही (Grammar) flexible; ~परक कोटि/संवर्ग inflectional category; ~प्रधान inflectional; -रूप declension(s); -ह्रास deflexion; विभक्त्यात्मक flectional.

विभग्न vibhagn (*a*) shattered; split;

broken.

विभव vibhav (*a*) potential; (*nm*) omnipresence; wealth, riches, affluence, prosperity; luxury; -क्षय fall from prosperity, loss of affluence; ~युक्त affluent, prosperous; luxurious, glorious; ~वान/शाली prosperous, affluent, glorious.

विभा vibha: (*nf*) shine, glow, brilliance, lustre; ~कर the Sun.

विभाग vibha:g (*nm*) a department; division; portion, part; ~तः/शः departmentwise; divisionwise.

विभागीय vibha:gi:y (*a*) departmental; –तारघर departmental telegraph office; –पदोन्नति departmental promotion; –परीक्षा departmental examination.

विभाजक vibha:jak (*a*) dividing, parting; (*nm*); a divisor; hence ~ता (*nf*).

विभाजन vibha:jan (*nm*) division, partition.

विभाजित vibha:jit (*a*) divided, partitioned.

विभाज्य vibha:jjy (*a*) divisible; ~ता divisibility.

विभाव vibha:w (*nm*) any condition which excites or develops a particular state of mind or body, any cause (persons–आलंबन विभाव; or circumstances and surroundings –उद्दीपन विभाव) that rouses an emotion.

विभावरी vibha:vari: (*nf*) the night.

विभाषा vibha:sha: (*nf*) a sub-language; dialect.

विभिन्न vibhinn (*a*) different, various, diverse; ~ता variety, diversity.

विभीषण vibhi:shān (*nm*) the youngest brother of रावण and a devotee of राम in the epic story of Ra:ma:yān; a traitor, renegade.

विभीषिका vibhi:shika: (*nf*) horror, terror; the act or means of terrifying.

विभु vibhu (*nm*) God–the all-pervading, omnipresent; mighty; powerful, omnipotent.

विभुता vibhuta: (*nf*) omnipresence; omnipotence; power, supremacy.

विभूति vibhu:ti (*nf*) ash; majesty/magnificence; an outstanding personality, personage.

विभूषित vibhu:shit (*a*) adorned, ornamented, decorated, embellished.

विभेद vibhed (*nm*) variety, kind; subdivision, distinction, difference, discrimination; ~क/कारी differentiating, discriminating; ~न differentiation / differentiating; penetration, piercing, splitting; hence विभेदी.

विभेद्य vibheddy (*a*) differentiable, distinguishable; separable; pierceable, fit to be penetrated; hence ~ता (*nf*).

विभो vibho (*int*) vocative form of विभु—O, God Almighty !

विभोर vibhor (*a*) fully overwhelmed/engrossed/absorbed.

विभ्रम vibbhram (*nm*) delusion, confusion, flurry; restlessness, unsteadiness; amorous gestures or action of any kind.

विभ्रां/त vibbhra:nt (*a*) confused, mistaken; perturbed, restless, in a flurry; ~ति confusion, perturbation; mistake, error.

विभ्राट vibbhra:ṭ (*nm*) confusion, turmoil; disaster.

विमंडित vimāndit (*a*) adorned, decorated; embellished.

विम/त vimat (*nm*) contrary/dissenting opinion; counter principle; (*a*) having contrary opinion/principle; dissenting; ~ति dissent, disagreement, discord.

विमन vimān (*a*) downcast, dejected, out of sorts.

विमनस्क vimānask (*a*) absent-minded; downcast, dejected; ~ता absent-mindedness; sadness, dejection.

विम/र्दन vimardan (*nm*) trampling, crushing, pounding; ~र्दित trampled, crushed, pounded.

विमर्श vimarsh (*nm*) consultation; consideration, examination; reflection, deliberation.

विमल vimal (*a*) clear, clean; dirtless, spotless, flawless; pure; hence ~ता (*nf*).

वि/मा vimā: (*nf*) a dimension; ~मीय dimensional.

विमा/ता vimā:ta: (*nf*) a step-mother; ~तृज a step-brother; ~त्रीय novercal.

विमान vimā:n (*nm*) an aeroplane, aircraft, airliner; -क्षेत्र airfield; aerodrome; -चालन aviation; -चालक a pilot; ~न aviation; -पत्तन airport; -परिचारिका air-hostess; ~वाहक aircraft-carrier; ~वाहित airborne; -विज्ञान aeronautics; ~वैज्ञानिक aeronautical.

विमार्ग vima:rg (*nm*) a wrong path/course.

विमिति vimiti (*nf*) dimension.

विमिश्रित vimishshrit (*a*) mixed/mingled, intermixed/intermingled.

विमु/क्त vimukt (*a*) acquitted, released; exempted; emancipated, delivered, liberated; ~क्ति acquittal, release; exemption; emancipation, deliverance, liberation; ०वादी a liberationist.

विमुख vimukh (*a*) indifferent, indifferently disposed, disinclined, having a sense of aversion; ~ता indifference, disinclination, aversion.

विमुग्ध vimugdh (*a*) infatuated; fascinated, attracted, charmed; ~कारी infatuating, fascinating; attractive, charming; hence ~ता (*nf*).

विमूढ़ vimu:ṛh (*a*) see मूढ़; ~चेता/धी a stupid fellow, nitwit; silly; ~ता stupidity, silliness.

विमूर्च्छित vimu:rchhit (*a*) see मूर्च्छित.

विमू/लन vimu:lan (*nm*) abolition, uprooting; extermination; devastation; hence ~लित (*a*).

विमो/चन vimochan (*nm*) acquittal, liberation, release; ~चित acquitted, liberated, released; ~च्य/चनीय acquittable; to be released/liberated.

विमो/हक vimohak (*a*) fascinating, attractive, charming; alluring, enticing; ~हन (*nm*) fascination, allurement, attraction; ~हित fascinated, attracted, charmed; enticed, allured.

वियत viyat (*nm*) the sky.

वियु/क्त viyukt (*a*) separated; deserted, abandoned; isolated; ~क्तता/~क्ति separation; isolation.

वियोग viyog (*nm*) separation, disunion; bereavement; -श्रृंगार see विप्रलंभ श्रृंगार.

वियोगांत viyogā:nt (*a*) (a story or plot) ending in separation; tragic.

वियोगिनी viyoginī: (*a* and *nf*) (a beloved/wife) separated from her lover/husband.

वियोगी viyogi: (*a* and *nm*) a lover/husband separated from his beloved/wife.

वियोजक viyojak (*a* and *nm*) a separator, (one) who or (that) which separates.

वियो/जन viyojān (*nm*) separation;

disintegration; disjoining; abscission; ~जनीय/~ज्य to be separated/disunited/disjoined; ~जित separated; disunited, disintegrated, disjoined.

विरंग virang (*a*) discoloured; faded.

विरं/च, ~चि viranch, ~chi (*nm*) Brahmā:—the Creator of the universe.

विरंज/क virānjak (*nm*) a bleaching agent; (*a*) bleaching; ~कता bleaching capacity; ~न (act or process of) bleaching; ~नीय bleachable.

विर/क्त virakt (*a*) detached (from the world); disaffected, averse; indifferent; (*nm*) a recluse; ~क्तता/क्ति detachment, indifference; disaffection; aversion, disgust.

विरच/न virachān (*nm*) composition, writing; ~यिता an author, one who composes/writes.

विरचित virachit (*a*) composed, written.

विर/त virat(*a*)detached, disaffected; desisted, disengaged; indifferent; ~ति detachment; disaffection, indifference, disengagement.

विर/द virad (*nm*) see विरुद; ~दावली see विरुदावली.

विरल viral (*a*) thin; sparse; rare, scarce; ~ता rarefaction, sparseness, thinness, scarcity; ~न rarefaction; thinning, becoming sparse.

विरलित viralit (*a*) rarefied; rendered thin/sparse.

विरस viras (*a*) tasteless; insipid; juiceless; boring; ~ता insipidity, tastelessness; rancidity.

विरह vireh (*nm*) separation (from loved one);~जनित/जन्य caused by separation; –ज्वर the anguish of separation; –वेदना/व्यथा pangs of separation, agony of separation; –की आंच agony of separation; –में जलना to suffer the agony of separation (from the loved one).

विरहाग्नि viraha:gnī (*nf*) the anguish/agony of separation.

विरहानल virha:nal (*nm*) see विरहाग्नि.

विरहिणी virahinī: (*a* and *nf*) (one) separated from her lover/husband, grass widow.

विरही virahi: (*a* and *nm*) (one) separated from his beloved/wife.

विरा/ग vira:g (*nm*) renunciation; detachment; aversion, dislike, indifference; ~गी detached, one who has renounced or is averse to mundane affairs, an ascetic.

विराजना vira:jnā: (*v*) to grace (an occasion, place, etc.); to take seat, to be seated (used in a deferential context), to look splendid/glorious; hence विराजित (*a*).

विराजमान vira:jmā:n (*a*) (graciously) seated; sitting (used deferentially), gracing (an occasion) by one's presence; looking splendid/glorious.

विराट vira:ṭ (*a*) colossal, gigantic, enormous, huge; hence ~ता (*nf*).

विराम vira:m (*nm*) pause; pause in or at the end of a sentence; (full) stop; stoppage; repose, rest; halt; respite; interval/intermission; -चिह्न full-stop—a punctuation mark; ० लगाना to punctuate; to put a full-stop; -संधि an armistice.

विरामावस्था vira:mā:wastha: (*nf*) interkinesis, position of rest.

विरामी vira:mī: (*a*) intermittent.

विरासत vira:sat (*nf*) legacy, inheritance.

विरुज viruj (*a*) healthy, free from disease, hale and hearty.

विरुद virud (*nm*) laudatory attributes (of an eminent personage); a laudatory poem, panegyric.

विरुदावली viruda:wali: (*nf*) (totality of) laudatory attributes; a panegyric.

विरुद्ध viruddh (*a*) against, opposed; opposite; contrary, adverse, hostile; ~**ता** hostility; opposition; contrariety.

विरूप viru:p (*a*) misshapen, defaced, deformed; monstrous, grotesque; ~**क** obliterator; that which defaces/deforms; ~**ता** deformity; grotesqueness, ugliness; monstrosity; ~**न** disfigurement, defacing; –**करना** to deface, to deform; to disfigure.

विरूपाक्ष viru:pa:ksh (*a*) lit. having deformed eyes—an epithet of Lord Shiv.

विरेचक virechak(*a*) cathartic, purgative; (*nm*) a purgative.

विरेचन virechān (*nm*) catharsis, purgation; –**सिद्धांत** the theory of catharsis (in Poetics).

विरेचित virechit (*a*) purged; cleaned up.

विरेच्य virechchy (*a*) to be purged/cleaned; fit to undergo a catharsis.

विरोध virodh (*nm*) opposition, antagonism; hostility; resistance, objection; antimony, contrariety; protest; contradiction; –**करना** to oppose; to resist; to object; to protest; to contradict; to contest; to strike a blow against; to set one's face against.

विरोधाभा/स virodha:bha:s (*nm*) a paradox; ~**सी** paradoxical.

विरोधित virodhit (*a*) opposed, objected to; protested; contradicted, resisted.

विरोधिनी virodhinī: (*nf* and *a*) feminine form of **विरोधी**.

विरोधी virodhi: (*nm* and *a*) an adversary, rival, opponent; objector; hostile, opposing, antagonistic; contradictory, contrary; –**दल** opposition party; o **का नेता** leader of the opposition –**पक्ष** opposition (party/side).

विलं/ब vilamb (*nm*) delay, procrastination; lag; tardiness; ~**बकारी** procrastinating/procrastinator, delaying; ~**बन** delay/delaying, procrastination; ~**ब-शुल्क** late fee, demurrage; ~**बित** delayed, late, tardy, procrastinated; slow tempo (in music); ~**बी** delaying; a procrastinator.

विलक्षण vilakshān (*a*) queer, strange, peculiar, wonderful; remarkable, exceptional, extra-ordinary; fantastic; prodigious; precocious; ~**ता** strangeness, queerness, peculiarity; remarkability; precocity, uncommonness.

विलग vilag (*a*) separate, detached, disunited/disjointed; ~**न** separation; insulation.

विल/य vilay (*nm*) annihilation/destruction (of the world); dissolution/dissolving; merger/merging; ~**यन** a solution; dissolution, merger; absorption; ~**यशील** soluble, solute; ~**यशीलता** solubility; ~**यी** soluble, that which dissolves.

विलसना vilasnā: (*v*) to look pretty/splendid; to enjoy; to make merry.

विलसित vilasit (*a*) looking pretty/splendid; making merry, enjoying.

विलाप vila:p (*nm*) lamentation, crying, weeping, wailing; ~**ना** to lament, to cry, to weep, to wail.

विलाय/त vila:yat (*nf*) a foreign land/country; Europe; England; ~**ती** foreign; English; European; ~**ती-पन** foreignism, Englishism, Europeanism; ~ती माल foreign goods.

विलास vila:s (*nm*) enjoyment; luxury; amorous playfulness; wantonness; lust; -गृह/भवन/मंदिर a pleasure house; ~पूर्वक in a lustful/luxurious fashion, enjoyingly; wantonly; amorously; -करना to enjoy, to make merry; to have fun/good time (esp. with women).

विलासिनी vila:sinī: (*nf*) a lustful/luxury loving woman; (*a*) lustful, wanton; luxury-loving, pleasure-seeking.

विला/सी vila:si: (*a*) lustful, debauch, pleasure-seeking, wanton; luxury-loving; ~सिता debauchery, wantonness, amorous playfulness; luxuriousness.

विलीन vili:n (*a*) vanished, disappeared; merged; absorbed, engrossed.

विलीयन vili:yan (*nm*) absorption, disappearance.

विलु/प्त vilupt (*a*) extinct; obsolete; vanished, disappeared; ~प्ति extinction; obsoleteness; disappearance.

विलेख vilekh (*nm*) a deed, a legal instrument.

विलेप vilep (*nm*) anointing; ointment; anything that is anointed; ~न applying ointment, anointing; smearing.

विलेय viley (*a*) soluble; ~ता solubility; ~शील solute; hence ~शीलता (*nf*).

विलोकनीय viloknī:y (*a*) worth seeing/beholding.

विलोकित vilokit (*a*) seen, beholden, viewed.

विलो/ड़न viloṛan (*nm*) thorough investigation/study; stirring up, churning; whirling; ~ड़ित thoroughly investigated/studied: stirred; whirled.

विलो/प vilop (*nm*) extinction; disappearance; obsolescence; also ~पन; ~पित extinct; disappeared; obsolete.

विलोम vilom (*a* and *nm*) reverse; converse; contrary; antonym; -क्रिया inverse operation; ~जात born in the reverse order (i.e. born feet-long); ~तः conversely; ~ता reversion; contrariety; converseness; antonymousness; -शब्द an antonym; a word having opposite meaning; विलोमित reversed; conversed.

विलो/ल vilol (*a*) fickle; quivering, unsteady; hence ~लन (*nm*), ~लित (*a*).

विल्व vilv (*nm*) wood-apple tree and its fruit —*Aegle marmelos*; ~पत्र leaves of the wood apple tree.

विव/क्षा vivaksha: (*nf*) implication; meaning, purport; desire; ~क्षित implied; intended; desired; ०अर्थ implied/intended meaning.

विवर vivar (*nm*) a cavity, cavitation, cave; hole, sinus; -, नासिका nasal cavity; -, मुख oral cavity.

विवर/ण vivarāṇ (*nm*) an account, description; commentary; particulars, details; minutes; briefing; report, statement; account; ~णकार commentator; ~णिका a brochure; prospectus; ~णी report, return.

विव/र्जन vivarjan (*nm*) see वर्जन; ~र्जित see वर्जित.

विवर्ण vivarṇ (*a*) faded, dimmed; (rendered) colourless; pallid; of a low caste (as opposed to सवर्ण); ~न discolouration.

विवर्त vivart (*nm*) a whirlpool; illusion, falsity; ~न going round; shifting; crisis; ~वाद/~वादिता the Vedantic theory which propounds the unreality of the world and opines that it is a mere illusion; ~वादी a believer in the doctrine named ~वाद; pertaining to ~वाद; hence विवर्तित (*a*).

विव/र्धन vivardhan (*nm*) magnification/magnifying; growing; ~र्धित magnified; grown.

विवश vivash (*a*) helpless; compelled, under compulsion; forced, obliged; disabled; ~ता helplessness, disability, compulsion; –करना to compel, to force, to oblige.

विवसन vivasan (*a*) nude, naked, unclothed.

विवस्त्र vivastr (*a*) see विवसन.

विवाच/क viva:chak (*nm*) an arbiter/arbitrator; ~न arbitration; ०करना to arbitrate.

विवा/द viva:d (*nm*) a dispute; altercation, quarrel; discussion; contention, controversy; ~दास्पद controversial; ०दावा controversial claim; ~दी a disputant, disputing/contending; a discordant note of a राग (sometimes used for effect); ~द उठाना to raise a controversy/dispute/discussion; ~द करना to dispute, to altercate, to debate, to wrangle.

विवाह viva:h (*nm*) marriage, wedding, matrimony; -उत्सव nuptials, marriage celebrations; –करना to marry, to wed; –के गीत epithalamium, wedding songs; -द्वेष misogamy; -बंधन wedlock; -योग्य marriageable; a match; ०आयु marriageable age; -विच्छेद breaking of marriage; -संबंध matrimonial relation; ०तोड़ना to divorce; to break the wedlock; -संबंधी/विषयक matrimonial, nuptial; विवाहोत्सव nuptials, marriage celebrations.

विवाहि/त viva:hit (*a*) married; ~ता (fem. form) married (woman).

विवि/क्त vivikt (*a*) isolated; separated; aloof; ~क्तता/~क्ति isolation; separation; aloofness; ~क्तिवाद isolationism; ~क्तिवादी an isolationist; isolationistic.

विविध vividh (*a*) different; diverse, various, miscellaneous; ~ता diversity, variety variation; –प्रकार का diverse, miscellaneous, manifold.

विविधा vividha: (*nf*) a miscellany.

विवृत vivrit (*a*) open, exposed, uncovered; unravelled; expanded; hence ~ता (*nf*); –स्वर open vowel.

विवृति vivriti (*nf*) openness; commentary, explanation, exposition, interpretation; unravelling.

विवृ/त्त vivritt (*a*) going/whirling round; opened, uncovered; ~त्ति whirling, revolution; expansion; opening.

विवे/क vivek (*nm*) reason, discretion; judgment; wisdom; ~क-बुद्धि reason; discretion; wisdom; ~क-भ्रष्ट/शून्य/हीन irrational, illogical; ~कवान ~कशील see ~की; ~काधीन discretionary; at the discretion of; ०शक्तियाँ discretionary powers; ~की prudent, wise, discreet.

विवेचक vivechak (*nm*) a critic, one who judiciously assesses good and bad aspects.

विवेच/न vivechan (*nm*), ~ना na: (*nf*) critical appreciation; evaluation, investigation; argument, discussion, discrimination; ~नीय worth critical appreciation/investigation/evaluating/interpretation/discussion.

विवेचित vivechit (*a*) critically appreciated; discussed; evaluated, investigated.

विवेच्य vivechy (*a*) under discussion/

study/evaluation/critical appreciation; worth being discussed/studied/evaluated; –विषय the subject under discussion/study.

विशद vishad (*a*) elaborate, detailed; clear-cut; hence ~ता (*nf*).

विशारद visha:rad (*a*) expert, learned.

विशाल visha:l (*a*) huge, large, big, spacious; grand, extensive, vast; great, gigantic, colossal; ~ता hugeness, largeness, vastness; ~हृदय magnanimous, liberal, bounteous; hence ~हृदयता (*nf*).

विशालाक्षी visha:la:kshi: (*a* and *nf*) large-eyed; a woman having large eyes.

विशिख vishikh (*nm*) an arrow, a pointless arrow.

विशि/ष्ट vishisht (*a*) special, specialized, specific; particular; prominent; characteristic. typical; ~ष्टता speciality, specificity; singularity; characteristic; ~ष्टि specification; ~ष्टीकरण specialization; ~ष्टीकृत specialized.

विशिष्टाद्वैत vishishta:dwait (*nm*) 'qualified non-duality'—a philosophical doctrine that human spirit has a qualified identity with the Supreme Spirit; also ~वाद; ~वादी one who asserts or believes in the doctrine of विशिष्टाद्वैत.

विशुद्ध vishuddh (*a*) pure/purified; chaste, virtuous; genuine; unmixed/unadulterated; ~चरित्र chaste, virtuous; ~ता genuineness; purity; chastity; –भाव pure sentiment; genuineness; –विज्ञान pure science.

विशुद्धात्मा vishuddha:tmā: (*a*) virtuous, pure at heart.

विशुद्धि vishuddhi (*nf*) purity; chastity; virtuosity; ~वाद puritanism; ~वादी a purist/puristic, puritan/puritanic.

विश्रृंखल vishshriṅkhal (*a*) disintegrated, disorderly, disarrayed; hence ~ता (*nf*).

विशेष vishesh (*a*) special, specific; particular; distinctive, characteristic; typical; much; ~क qualifying, characteristic; ~ज्ञ an expert, a specialist; ~ज्ञता specialization; ~ताएं characteristics; –नाम an epithet; –संस्करण special edition.

विशेषता visheshta: (*nf*) speciality, peculiarity, singularity; quality, attribute, characteristic.

विशेषण visheshaṇ (*nm*) an adjective; attribute, epithet; –पद attributive; -विपर्यय transferred epithet.

विशेषांक vishesha:ṅk (*nm*) a special issue/number (of a newspaper, journal or magazine etc.).

विशेषाधि/कार vishesha:dhika:r (*nm*) privilege; ~कारी a special officer; privileged person; ~कार-प्राप्त privileged.

विशेषित visheshit (*a*) specialised; qualified.

विशेषी/करण visheshi:karaṇ (*nm*) specialization; ~कृत specialised.

विशेष्य visheshy (*nm*) that which is qualified; a noun with an adjective qualifying it, substantive.

विशोक vishok (*a*) free of sorrow/care.

विश्रांत vishshrā:nt (*a*) reposed, one who has taken rest, calm, at ease; hence ~ता (*nf*).

विश्रांति vishshrā:nti (*nf*) rest, repose; ease; interval/intermission; -काल recess, interval.

विश्राम vishshra:m (*nm*) rest, repose, relaxation; -कक्ष a lounge; -काल period of rest; interval, recess; vacation; -गृह rest house; -स्थान place of rest or relaxation.

विश्रामालय vishshra:mā:lay (*nm*) a

retiring room; rest house.

विश्रु/त vishshrut (*a*) renowned, reputed, famous, well-known; hence ~ति (*nf*).

विश्लिष्ट vishshlisht (*a*) analysed.

विश्ले/ष vishshlesh (*nm*) analysis; separation; disintegration; ~षात्मक analytical; hence ~षात्मकता (*nf*).

विश्लेषण vishleshān (*nm*) analysis; –और संश्लेषण analysis and synthesis; ~परक analytical; -बुद्धि analytical sense/faculty; -, वाक्य- sentence analysis.

विश्लेषणात्मक vishleshnā:tmak (*a*) analytical; hence ~ता (*nf*).

विश्लेषणीय vishleshani:y (*a*) analysable, worth being or to be analysed.

विश्लेषित vishshleshit (*a*) analysed.

विश्वंभर vishshvāmbhar (*nm*) God—the all-supporting, all-nourishing.

विश्वंभरा vishshvāmbhara: (*nf*) the earth.

विश्व vishshv (*nm*) the world, universe; ~कोश an encyclopaedia; ~कोशीय encyclopaedic; -गणराज्य world republic; ~जनीन/जनीय universal; ~जयी/जित् conqueror of the universe/world; ~नाथ an epithet of Lord Shiv; ०नगरी/पुरी a name of the city of Va:ra:nāsi:; ~पूजित universally adorned, worshipped/respected by the whole world or by all; ~पूज्य all-venerable, worshippable/venerable for all or the world; ~प्रसिद्ध world-renowned, known all over the world; -भ्रातृत्व world fraternity; -राज्य world-state; ~वाद universalism; ~वादी universalist; universalistic; ~विख्यात world-known, renowned throughout the whole world; ~विजयी a world-conqueror, conqueror of the world; ~विद all-knowing, omniscient; ~विश्रुत see ~विख्यात: ~व्यापक/व्यापी all pervading, omnipresent, pervading the whole universe/world; -शांति world peace; -संगठन/संस्था world organisation; -संहार annihilation of the world; -साम्राज्य world-kingdom; -सृष्टि creation of the universe; ~स्रष्टा creator of the universe, ~हर्ता an epithet of Lord Shiv; –हेतु the cause of the universe.

विश्वविद्यालय vishshwavidya:lay (*nm*) a university; -परिसर university campus; -अनुदान-आयोग University Grants Commission; -शिक्षा university education; विश्वविद्यालयीय pertaining or belonging to or of a/the university.

विश्वसन vishshvasan (*nm*) believing, trusting, relying.

विश्वसनीय vishshvasnī:y (*a*) reliable, dependable, trustworthy; believable, credible; ~ता reliability, dependability, trustworthiness; credibility.

विश्वस्त vishshvast (*a*) see विश्वसनीय; confidential; confidant; –अनुचर a reliable follower/attendant; ~ता see विश्वसनीयता (under विश्वसनीय); –सूत्र a reliable source.

विश्वात्मा vishshva:tmā: (*nm*) God—the Universal Spirit.

विश्वाधार vishshva:dha:r (*nm*) God—the support and basis of the universe.

विश्वास vishshva:s (*nm*) belief, trust, faith; reliance, confidence; assurance; ~घात betrayal, treachery, violation of trust; infidelity; ०करना to blow the gaff; to betray, to betray one's trust; ~घाती treacherous, one who betrays, a traitor, ~पात्र/भाजन a reliable/trustworthy/dependable (person), confidant; ~प्रद arousing or raising trust/reliance/belief; -भंग breach of trust/faith; betrayal; ~हंता a traitor, (one) who betrays; -उठना to lose faith/confidence (in); -उपजना confidence to be created; to begin to have trust (in); -करना to trust, to rely, to believe;-जमाना to arouse confidence/trust, to earn somebody's confidence; -दिलाना to assure, to arouse confidence; -हिल उठना faith/confidence to be shaken.

विश्वासी vishshva:si: (*a* and *nm*) one who believes/trusts, trustful; a believer.

विश्वेश, ~श्वर vishshvesh, ~shwar (*nm*) God—the Master of the Universe.

विष vish (*nm*) poison, venom; ~कंठ an epithet of Lord Shiv; ~कन्या a girl/woman so impregnated with poison that a man copulating with, or even kissing, her dies; ~कृत treated with poison, poisoned; ~घातक/घाती/घ्न anti-venom, antidote to poison; ~दंत a fang; ~दाता/दायक one who administers poison; ~धर a snake, poisonous snake; ~नाशी poison-destroying, anti-poison; -बेल see-वृक्ष; -भक्षण taking poison; -मंत्र a मंत्र for curing snake-bite; ० विद a snake-bite curer through मंत्र; -मात्रा toxicity; ~वत् poisonous, venomous; ~वमन vituperative/virulent utterance; ०करना to make virulent utterances, to say vituperative words; ~विद्या science of curing snake-bite etc; cure of poisons by drugs or charms; -वृक्ष a poison-tree—a beginning that causes ever greater harm; -विज्ञान toxicology; hence ~वैज्ञानिक (*nm*) ~वैद्य a physician who cures snake-bite or other poisonous stings (either by charms or by drugs); ~हर see ~घाती; ~हीन poisonless, non-venomous; hence ~हीनता (*nf*); ~हृदय vituperative, full of venom; -उगलना to disgorge venom; to make vituperative utterances/remarks; -की गाँठ the root of all evils, the villain of piece; -के दाँत तोड़ना to render poisonless/incapable of causing harm; -के बीज बोना to sow the seeds of evil/disharmony; -घोलना to put venom in (words); to cause disharmony/quarrel; -चढ़ना poison (to begin) to have effect (said only in the context of snake-bite, scorpion-bite, etc.); -पीना to assimilate virulence/bitter experiences.

विषण्ण vishann (*a*) melancholic, gloomy, sombre; downcast; ~ता melancholy, gloominess, sombreness; downcast state; ~मानस/मना melancholic, gloomy, sombre, in low spirits; ~मुख/वदन melancholic, dejected, downcast.

विषपायी vishpa:yi: (*a*) lit. a drinker of poison–one who assimilates all sorts of virulence.

विषम visham (*a*) odd; heterogeneous, incongruous; uneven, rough; adverse, dissimilar; difficult (to traverse); disagreeable; ~कोण an oblique angle; ~ता contrast; dissimilarity; inequity, oddity; difficulty; disproportion, incongruity, heterogeneousness; ruggedness; -रूप heterogeneous; incongruous; dissimilar.

विषमांग vishamā:ng (*a*) heterogeneous; incongruous; dissimilar.

विषय vishay (*nm*) a subject; topic; matter; content; sexual/sensual pleasure/enjoyment; an affair; object; ~गत/परक subjective; sexual, pertaining to sexual affairs; ~निष्ठ subjective; ~निष्ठता subjectivity; ~परकता subjectivity; ~भोगवाद sensualism; ~रत sexy, engrossed in sexual pleasure; hence ~रति (*nf*); ~लोलुप voluptuous, lustful, sexy, sensual; hence ~लोलुपता; (*nf*) -वासना sexuality and lust; sensuality, sensualism; ~वस्तु theme; -संबंधी sensual, sensuous; concerning a topic/subject; -समिति subjects committee; -सुख sensual pleasure, sexual pleasure; -सूची a list of contents, table of contents.

विषयक vishayak (*ind*) concerning/ pertaining to or related with (used as a suffix as शिक्षा-विषयक, स्वास्थ्य-विषयक).

विषयांतर vishaya:ntar (*nm*) digression, another topic.

विषयात्मक vishaya:tmak (*a*) sensual, sexual; pertaining to/or related with the subject/topic.

विषयानुक्रम/णिका, ~णी vishaya:nukkramaṇika:, ~nī: (*nf*) subject-index; list of contents.

विषयास/क्त vishaya:sakt (*a*) sensual, lustful, given to sexual indulgence, debauch, lewd; (*nm*) debauchee; ~क्ति sensuality, sensualism, lustfulness, sexual indulgence.

विषयी vishayi:(*a*)voluptuous, lustful; sensual; a subject (as opposed to odject i.e. विषय); (*nm*)a sensualist.

विषाक्त visha:kt (*a*) toxic, poisonous, venomous; vituperative; ~ता toxicity, poisonousness, venomousness, vituperation

विषाण visha:ṇ (*nm*) a horn (of a beast); tusk (of a boar etc.).

विषाणु visha:ṇū (*nf*) virus; –रोग disease caused by virus infection; -संक्रमण virus infection.

विषाद visha:d (*nm*) gloom, sombreness, melancholy, despondency; ~जनक resulting in or causing gloom/ melancholy/ despondency; ~पूर्ण/मय melancholic, sombre, gloomy; –रोग melancholia.

विषादित visha:dit (*a*) dejected, gloomy, melancholy.

विषान्न visha:nn (*nm*) poisoned or poisonous food/meal.

विषुव/त् vishuwat (*a*) equatorial; ~तीय equatorial; ~द्रेखा the equator; ~द्वृत्त the equator.

विषूचिका vishu:chika: (*nf*) cholera; ~ग्रस्त suffering from cholera.

विषैला vishaila: (*a*) poisonous; venomous, toxic, vituperative, virose; ~पन poisonousness, venomousness, vituperativeness, toxicity: –पौधा the upas (plant).

विष्कंभक vishkāmbhak (*nm*) in interlude (in a drama).

विष्ठा vishṭha: (*nf*) faeces, excrement, night soil.

विष्णु vishṇu (*nm*) one of the Hindu mythological divine trinity—ब्रह्मा, विष्णु and महेश, the preserver of the world, God Almighty; ~पत्नी goddess लक्ष्मी—the spouse of विष्णु.

विसंग/त visangat (*a*) irrelevant, illogical; incoherent; ~ति irrelevance/irrelevancy; illogicality; incoherence.

विसंज्ञ/क visangyak (*nm* and *a*) an anaesthetist; anaesthetic; ~न anaesthetization.

विसं/पर्क visāmpark (*nm*) isolation; segregation; ~पृक्त isolated; segregated; aloof.

विसम्मत visammāt (*a*) dissenting, disagreeing,

विसम्मति visammāti (*nf*) disagreement; dissent; -टिप्पणी note of dissent.

विसरण visarāṉ (*nm*) diffusion; dissemination; ~ता diffusity; ~शील diffusive; ०ता diffusiveness.

विसर्ग visarg (*nm*) a colon-like sign (:) used in the Devna:gri: script, characteristic of Sanskrit word-formations and resembling 'h' in pronunciation (as in दुःख).

विस/र्जन visarjān (*nm*) dispersal; abandonment; ~र्जन करना to disperse; to abandon; ~र्जित dispersed; abandoned.

विसार visa:r (*nm*) diffusion.

विसाल visa:l (*nm*) union (of lover and beloved).

विसूचिका visu:chika:(*nf*) see विषूचिका.

विसृति vissriti (*nf*) diffusion; diffusedness.

विसैन्यी/करण visainyi:karāṉ (*nm*) demilitarization; ~कृत demilitarized.

विस्तरण vistarāṉ (*nm*) span; extension, enlargement; spreading.

विस्तार vista:r (*nm*) expanse, span, spread; extent; extension, elaboration; enlargement; details; volume; ~ण amplification, extension, elaboration; ~पूर्वक/-से extensively; in details, elaborately.

विस्तारित vista:rit (*a*) expanded; enlarged; elaborately explained; spread; detailed.

विस्तीर्ण visti:rṉ (*a*) expanded, spread out; spacious; elaborate, copious; hence ~ता (*nf*).

विस्तृ/त vistrit (*a*) expanded; commodious; voluminous; elaborate, detailed; lengthy; ~ति voluminousness; elaboration; expandedness, expansion; extent.

विस्था/पन vistha:pan (*nm*) displacement; ~पित displaced; ० व्यक्ति a displaced person.

विस्फारित vispha:rit (*a*) opened wide; spread.

विस्फोट visphoṭ (*nm*) explosion, blast; burst; crack (ing); ~क/~कारी explosive; a cracker; ~क पदार्थ explosive substance; ~न explosion; –होना to explode, to crack; to blast, to burst.

विस्मय vismay(*nm*) wonder, surprise, astonishment, amazement; ~कर/कारी/जनक wonderful, surprising, amazing; sensational.

विस्मयाकुल vismaya:kul (*a*) stunned aghast, non-plussed, wonder-struck.

विस्मयी vismayi: (*a*) see विस्मयकारी (under विस्मय).

विस्मरण vismarāṉ (*nm*) forgetting, oblivion; ~शील forgetful, oblivious; ~शीलता forgetfulness, obliviousness.

विस्मित vismit (*a*) wonder-struck, amazed, surprised, astonished; –करना to amaze, to astonish, to surprise.

विस्मृ/त vismrit (*a*) forgotten, gone into oblivion; ~ति forgetfulness, oblivion.

विस्वर vissvar (*a*) discordant, disharmonious; (*nm*) a discordant note; ~ता disharmony, discord.

विस्वाद vissva:d (*a*) tasteless; insipid.

विहंग vihāṅg (*nm*) a bird; ~राज Garuṛ—the mythological king of birds.

विहंगम vihāṅgam (*nm*) a bird; –दृष्टि a bird's eye-view.

विहंगावलोकन vihaṅga:vlokān (*nm*) a bird's eye-view.

विहग vihag (*nm*) a bird; ~पति/राज see विहंगराज (under विहंग).

विह/सन vihasān (*nm*) laughter, laughing; ~सित laughing, laughed,

विहाग viha:g (*nm*) a typical Indian musical mood (राग).

विहान viha:n (*nm*) day-break.

विहार viha:r (*nm*) merry-making, having good time, pastime; wandering, roaming; sexual enjoyment; a (Buddhistic) monastery; -गृह a pleasure-house; -स्थल/स्थली a pleasure-resort; hence विहारी (*a* and *nm*); विहारिणी (*a* and *nf*).

विहित vihit (*a*) prescribed, ordained, enjoined (by); in order, valid.

विहीन vihi:n—a suffix used to impart a negative sense—without/deprived of/divested of/bereft of; hence ~ता (*nf*).

विह्वल vihval (*a*) overwhelmed; perturbed, agitated; ~ता state of being overwhelmed; perturbation, agitation; ~हृदय overwhelmed; perturbed, mentally agitated; hence ~हृदयता (*nf*).

वीक्ष/ण vi:kshāṇ (*nm*) observance/observing, seeing; ~णीय worth observance/seeing.

वी/चि, ~ची vi:chi, ~chi: (*nf*) a ripple, wave; ~चिमाली the sea.

वीटो vi:ṭo (*nm*) veto; -अधिकार veto-power; –का प्रयोग use of the veto; –करना to veto, to use veto against.

वीणा vī:ṇā: (*nf*) a typical Indian lute (with a large gourd at either end); ~दंड body of the वीणा between the two end-gourds; ~पाणि an epithet of सरस्वती – the goddess of learning; ~रव melodious notes of a वीणा; ~वादक a lute-player, one who plays on a वीणा; ~वादन playing on a वीणा; ~वादिनी see ~पाणि.

वीत vi:t—an adjectival prefix used to impart the sense of past/finished/left off /beyond/ended/freed from/without etc.; ~कल्मष freed from sin; ~काम who has no longing/desire, calm, tranquil; ~चिंत having no worries, freed from anxieties; ~जन्म not subject to birth; ~जरा not subject to senility, ever-young; ~दंभ beyond conceit, who has no vanity left; ~भय/भीति fearless; dauntless; intrepid; ~मोह freed from illusion/worldly attachments; ~राग freed from passions or affections; dispassionate; hence ~रागता (*nf*); ~शोक freed from sorrow/gloom; ~स्पृह freed from wish or desire, having no longing,

वी/थि, ~थी vi:thi; ~thi: (*nf*) an alley, avenue; gallery.

वीथिका vi:thika: (*nf*) an alley, avenue; gallery.

वीभत्स vi:bhats(*a*) see बीभत्स.

वीर vi:r (*a*) heroic; brave, valiant, valorous, gallant; (*nm*) a hero; brother; ~कर्म a heroic deed, deed of bravery; gallant act; ~कर्मा brave, valorous, valiant; one who performs courageous deeds; ~काव्य heroic poetry, poetry eulogizing heroic deeds; ~केशरी the bravest of the braves, a hero of heroes; ~गति heroic end, the attainment of heaven which is supposed to be the happy lot of a warrior killed in action; ०को प्राप्त होना, ०मिलना to go to glory, to achieve a heroic end, to be killed in action, to attain access to heaven through martyrdom; ~गाथा saga of heroic deeds/heroism; ~जननी/प्रसवा/प्रसू/माता mother of a hero/warrior, a mother who begets a brave/warrior child; -पूजा hero-worship;

~भोग्यावसुंधरा fortune favours the brave; -युग heroic age; –रस the sentiment of heroism (in Indian Poetics); ~रस-प्रधान heroic; ~ललित brave yet tender-hearted; ~शय्या the battlefield; ~श्रेष्ठ the best amongst heroes, the greatest of heroes; ~हृदय brave, stout-hearted.

वीरता vi:rta: (*nf*) heroism; bravery, valour, daring, gallantry; ~पूर्ण heroic, brave, valorous, gallant; ~पूर्वक bravely, heroically, valiantly, gallantly.

वीरत्व vi:rattv (*nm*) heroism, bravery, valour, daring, gallantry.

वीरांगना vi:rā:ṅgnā: (*nf*) a heroine; brave woman.

वीरा/न vi:rā:n (*a* and *nm*) deserted, devastated, desolate; uninhabited (place); ~नी desolateness, desertedness.

वीराना vi:ra:nā: (*nm*) a deserted/desolated place.

वीरासन vi:ra:san (*nm*) a heroic posture, particular sitting posture.

वीरोचित vi:rochit (*a*) heroic, befitting a hero, gallant, valorous, valiant.

वीरोत्तम vi:rottām (*nm*) the bravest of braves.

वीर्य vi:ry (*nm*) semen; potency, manly vigour, virility; heroism, valour; ~कर strength-giving, raising virility, marrow; -कीटाणु spermatozoon; ~पात discharge of semen; -पारमिता (with Buddhists) the highest degree of fortitude or energy (one of the six perfections); ~वान/शाली virile, potent, manly; powerful; -संबंधी seminal, spermatic; -हानि loss of virility, impotency; ~हीन impotent; weak, feeble; hence ~हीनता (*nf*).

वीर्याधान vi:rya:dha:n (*nm*) impregnation.

वीही vi:hi: (*nf*) quince.

वुज़ू vuzu: (*nm*) the act of washing the face, hands and feet by a (Mohammedan) devotee before offering his prayers.

वुजूद vuju:d (*nm*) existence, being.

वृंत vrīnt (*nm*) a stalk, stem or main axis (of a plant etc.).

वृंद vrīnd (*nm*) multitude, assembly; ~गान chorus; ~गायक the chorus, collective singers; ~गायन collective/choral singing; ~वादन orchestration; ~वादनकार orchestrator.

वृक vrik (*nm*) a wolf.

वृक्काकार vrikka:ka:r (*a*) reniform.

वृक्ष vriksh (*nm*) a tree; ~कोटर cavity of a tree; ~च्छाया shadow of a tree; -देवी a hamadryad; ~मूल the root of a tree; -रोपण tree-plantation; ~वत् arborescent; -वाटिका a garden; ~वासी arboreal; ~विज्ञान/शास्त्र dendrology; -संकुल arboreous; -संवर्धन arboriculture; -सेचन watering the trees; ~हीन treeless.

वृक्षाकार vriksha:kar (*a*) dendriform.

वृक्षाभ vriksha:bh (*nm*) dendroid.

वृक्षायुर्वेद vriksha:yurved (*nm*) dendrology, the science of arboreal diseases and their cure.

वृत्त vritt (*nm*) circle; ring; account, record; news; verse, meter; ~खंड an arc; a sector; segment of a circle; –, छोटा circlet; -चित्र a documentary (film); ~मुखी rounded, circular; ०स्वर rounded vowel; ~रूपक documentary feature; ~सार final act.

वृत्तांत vrittā:nt (*nm*) news; a report, narrative, account.

वृत्ताकार vritta:ka:r (*a*) circular,

round; hence ~ता (*nf*).

वृत्ति vritti (*nf*) instinct; mentality; profession, vocation; (conventional) function; stipend (as छात्रवृत्ति); commentary (esp. on a *su:tra*); ~का stipend; -कर profession tax; ~कार a commentator; ~दाता one who provides livelihood; supporter, affording maintenance; ~भोगी stipendiary.

वृत्तीय vritti:y (*a*) circular; professional/vocational; stipendiary.

वृथा vritha: (*a*) useless, fruitless; ineffective; (*adv*) in vain, vainly, to no effect; ~त्व uselessness, futility, fruitlessness; ~मति foolish, blockheaded; ~वृद्ध aged without experience, grown old but not wise; —करना to render fruitless/ineffective; to cause to be in vain; to nullify, to stultify.

वृथोक्त vrithokt (*a*) said/uttered in vain.

वृथोत्पन्न vrithotpann (*a*) born in vain.

वृद्ध/द्ध vriddh (*a*) old, elderly, aged; (*nm*) an aged man, old man; ~द्धत्व old age, senility; hence ~द्धा (*a* and *nf*).

वृद्धावस्था vriddha:vastha: (*nf*) old age, senility.

वृद्धि vriddhi (*nf*) increase/increment, rise, growth; progress; enlargement, augmentation; enhancement; magnification; ~कारी promoting growth, augmentative, magnifying; -दर growth rate, rate of increase.

वृश्चिक vrishchik (*nm*) a scorpion; -राशि Scorpio—the eighth sign of zodiac.

वृष vrish (*nm*) a bull, bullock; -राशि the zodiacal sign—Taurus.

वृषभ vrishabh (*nm*) a bull, bullock; -राशि the zodiacal sign—Taurus.

वृष्टि vrishṭi (*nf*) rain; ~कारी causing rains; -काल rainy season.

वृह/त् vrihat (*a*) large, big; great; ~द् an allomorph of वृहत् appearing as the first member in compound words.

वृहस्पति vrihaspati (*nm*) see बृहस्पति; ~वार see बृहस्पतिवार.

वेंकटेश्वर veṅkaṭeshshwar (*nm*) an epithet cf Lord Vishnū.

वे ve (*pro*) they, those; —लोग those (people); —खुद/स्वयं they themselves.

वेग veg (*nm*) speed, velocity; momentum; ~मापी velocimeter; ~वती feminine form of ~वान; ~वान speedy, swift; —धारण करना to acquire speed.

वेणिका veṇika: (*nf*) see वेणी.

वेणिबंध veṇībandh (*nf*) (a woman's) braided hair-locks.

वेणी veṇī (*nf*) a braid of hair or braided hair.

वेणु veṇū (*nf*) a flute; bamboo; ~कार a flute-maker; ~वादक a flute-player; ~वादन flute-playing.

वेतन vetan (*nm*) pay, salary; wages; ~जीवी salaried(person), subsisting by wages; ~दाता paymaster, employer; ~भोगी salaried, receiving wages; stipendiary; -वृद्धि increment; -वृद्धि, वार्षिक annual increment.

वेतस् vetas (*nm*) a cane.

वेताल veta:l (*nm*) a goblin, evil spirit, ghost.

वेत्ता vetta: (*nm*) one who knows, a Sanskrit word used as a suffix to impart the sense of one who knows or who is an expert in, as तत्त्ववेत्ता, विधिवेत्ता, etc.

वेत्र vettr (*nm*) a cane, stick.

वेद ved (*nm*) the most ancient and

sacred scriptures of the Hindus, four in number, viz, ऋग्वेद, यजुर्वेद, सामवेद, अथर्ववेद; knowledge, divine knowledge;~कर्ता/कार composer of the वेद; -कुशल a Vedic scholar; ~ज्ञ conversant with the Vedas, Vedic scholar; -तत्त्व the truth or essence of the Vedas;~त्रय/त्रयी the three comparatively earlier Vedas, viz. the ऋग्वेद, यजुर्वेद and सामवेद; ~दर्शी one who discerns the truth of the Vedas; -निंदक an unbeliever, one who denies the authority of the Vedas; an atheist; ~पाठ recitation of the Vedas; -पाठक/~पाठी a reciter of the Vedas; -मंत्र a Vedic verse/hymn; -वचन Vedic text or statement; -वाक्य a Vedic quotation; an irrefutable statement/truth;~विद see~ज्ञ;~विहित prescribed by or enjoined in the Vedas; ~व्यास name of an ancient Hindu sage; -सम्मत conforming to or ordained by the Vedas.

वेदना vednā: (*nf*) ache, pain; agony; ~ग्रस्त in agony, suffering from pain, afflicted.

वेदांग vedā:ṅg (*nm*) the six subordinate branches of the Vedas; viz. **शिक्षा** (the rules of correct pronunciation of Vedic *mantras*); **कल्प** (details of religious ceremonies); **निरुक्त** (etymology and explanation of Vedic words); **छंद** (prosody); **ज्योतिष** (astronomy); and **व्याकरण** (grammar).

वेदांत veda:nt (*nm*) one of the six systems of Hindu philosophy (so called either as teaching the ultimate scope of the Veda or simply as explained in the Upanishads, which come at the end of the Vedas);~ज्ञ/विद् conversant with the Vedanta system of philosophy; ~वादी one who believes in the वेदांत philosophy; -सूत्र the aphorism of Vedanta, compiled by the sage-philosopher Vya:s or Ba:dra:yān.

वेदांती veda:nti: (*a* and *nm*) (one) conversant with or adhering to the Vedanta system of philosophy.

वेदाध्ययन veda:ddhyayan (*nm*) study of the Vedas.

वेदाध्यायी veda:ddhya:i: (*nm* and *a*) a student of the Vedas; studying the Vedas.

वेदाभ्या/स veda:bbhya:s(*nm*) study of the Vedas; ~सी student of the Vedas.

वेदिका vedika: (*nf*) an altar; a platform, terrace.

वेदी vedi: (*nf*) an altar, a platform; terrace; a suffix used in the sense of a knower or scholar of the Vedas (as चतुर्वेदी, त्रिवेदी).

वेदोक्त vedokt (*a*) ordained by or enjoined in the Vedas.

वेध vedh (*nm*) perforation; penetrating/piercing; (planetary) observation; ~क perforator; he who or that which penetrates/pierces/observes; ~न perforation; penetration/piercing; observation; hence ~नीय, वेध्य (*a*).

वेधशाला vedhsha:la: (*nf*) an observatory (of stars and planets etc.)

वेधी vedhi: (*a*) one who or that which perforates/pierces/hits a target.

वेला vela: (*nf*) time; an hour; coast shore.

वेल्लन vellan (*nm*) rolling

वेश vesh (*nm*) guise; external appearance; dress, costume; ~धारी assuming the guise or appearance of; -भूषा apparel; get-up, appearance

-धारण करना to apparel; to guise (as), to assume the appearance of.

वेश्या veshshya: (*nf*) a prostitute; ~गमन (act of)prostitution; ~गामी one who indulges in prostitution; -गृह a brothel; -पुत्र son of a prostitute; -वृत्ति (profession or institution of) prostitution.

वेश्यालय veshshya:lay (*nm*) a brothel.

वेष vesh (*nm*) see **वेश**.

वेष्टन veshṭan(*nm*) a package; wrapping/wrapper; enclosure.

वेष्टित veshṭit (*a*) enclosed, surrounded; wrapped.

वैकल्पिक vaikalpik (*a*) optional, alternative; ~ता/त्व optionality.

वैकुंठ vaikunṭh (*nm*) the heaven, paradise; ~पुरी/लोक the city of Lord Vishnū—heaven; **वैकुंठीय** pertaining to **वैकुंठ**.

वैखरी vaikhari: (*nf*) articulate speech.

वैखानस vaikha:nās (*nm*) a Bra:hmān in the third stage of his life—an anchorite.

वैचारिक vaicha:rik (*a*) ideological; pertaining to thought/thinking/deliberation/reflection; hence ~ता (*nf*).

वैचारिकी vaicha:riki: (*nf*) ideology; ~य ideological.

वैचित्र्य vaichittry (*nm*) peculiarity, typicalness; characteristic quality; strangeness.

वैजयंती vaijayanti: (*nf*) a shield; banner; mythological garland of Lord Vishnū.

वैज्ञानिक vaigya:nīk (*nm*) a scientist; (*a*) scientific; ~ता scientism; scientific outlook; -वृत्ति scientific attitude/profession.

वैतनिक vaitnīk (*a*) salaried, on payment or salary basis.

वैतरणी vaitarnī: (*nf*) styx, a mythological river in the hell.

वैतालिक vaiṭa:lik (*nm*) a minstrel, bard.

वैदग्ध्य vaidagdhy (*nm*) wits, intelligence; sharpness, acuteness.

वैदिक vaidik (*a*) pertaining or belonging to or related with the Vedas; of the Vedas, Vedic; -युग the Vedic age; -संस्कृत the Sanskrit used in Vedic literature as distinct from that used in later times (and known as **लौकिक संस्कृत** or just **संस्कृत**); also called **वैदिकी**.

वैदुष्य vaidushy (*nm*) scholarship, learning.

वैदूर्य vaidu:ry (*nm*) baryl, a cat's eye (gem); also -मणि.

वैदेशिक vaideshik (*a*) foreign, external; pertaining to a foreign country; -कार्य foreign/external affairs; ० मंत्रालय Ministry of External Affairs; -मंत्री Minister for External Affairs; -नीति foreign policy; -व्यापार foreign trade.

वैदेही vaidehi: (*nf*) daughter of **विदेह** —an epithet of **सीता**.

वैद्य vaiddy (*nm*) an Ayurvedic physician; ~राज most outstanding of *vaidyas*, a pre-eminent *vaidya*; -विद्या/शास्त्र the Indian medicinal system.

वैद्यक vaiddyak (*nm*) the Indian medicinal system; the science or practice of medicine.

वैध vaidh (*a*) valid; legal, legitimate; tenable; ~ता validity; legitimacy, legality; tenability; ० वादी a legitimist.

वैधर्म्य vaidharmmy (*nm*) heresy; heterogeneity (as साधर्म्य-वैधर्म्य).

वैधव्य vaidhavvy (*nm*) widowhood; -अभिशाप the curse of widowhood.

वैधिक vaidhik (*a*) see **वैध**.

वैधीकरण vaidhi:karān (*nm*) legal-i

sation, legitimatization; validation.

वैपरीत्य vaippari:tty (*nm*) nominal formation from विपरीत (see).

वैपुल्य vaipully (*nm*) nominal formation from विपुल (see).

वैभव vaibhav (*nm*) grandeur, glory, magnificence; wealth, prosperity, riches; ~शालिता the state of being ~शाली; ~शाली grand, glorious; magnificent, full of grandeur / glory / magnificence; wealthy, prosperous, rich.

वैभिन्न्य vaibhinny (*nm*) see विभिन्नता.

वैमनस्य vaimanassy (*nm*) rancour, malice; hostility, enmity.

वैमा/त्र, ~त्रेय vaimā:ttr, ~ttrey (*a*) born of step-mother, step-motherly, novercal.

वैमानि/क vaimā:nīk (*a*) aeronautical, pertaining or related with aviation/aircraft; ~की aeronautics; ~कीय aeronautical, aviational.

वैयक्तिक vaiyaktik (*a*) individual, personal; private; subjective; ~ता individuality; subjectivity; –बंध personal bond; –विधि personal law.

वैयाकरण vaiya:karāṉ (*nm*) a grammarian; (*a*) grammatical; –कोटि grammatical category.

वैर vair (*nm*) enmity, animosity, hostility; ~कर/कारक/कारी arousing or instigating hostility/animosity; -प्रतिकार/प्रतिशोध revenge; -भाव animosity, hostility, bad blood.

वैरस्य vairassy (*nm*) see विरसता.

वैरागी vaira:gi: (*a* and *nm*) detached; a recluse, one who is not attached to worldly affairs.

वैराग्य vaira:ggy (*nm*) (attitude of) renunciation, detachment (from worldly affairs); -भाव(ना) spirit of renunciation/detachment.

वैरी vairi: (*nm*) an enemy, a foe hostile person.

वैरूप्य vairu:ppy (*nm*) see विरूपता.

वैवाहिक vaiva:hik (*a*) matrimonial nuptial, married; –जीवन married matrimonial life; –संबं matrimonial/married relations.

वैशा/ख vaisha:kh (*nm*) the secon month of the Hindu calendar ~खी a major Indian festiva observed on the full moon-day in the month of वैशाख; ~खनंद an ass, a donkey.

वैशिष्ट्य vaishishṭy (*nm*) speciality characteristic (quality); peculiarity.

वैशेषिक vaisheshik (*nm*) one of the six major systems of Indian Philosophy.

वैश्य vaishshy (*nm*) the third वर्ण (caste) in the traditional Hindu hierarchical caste set-up with trade as its main profession; a trader; -कर्म trade, business.

वैश्वानर vaishshva:nar (*nm*) an epithet of the god of fire; fire.

वैषम्य vaishammy (*nm*) see विषमता.

वैषयिक vaishaik (*a*) subjective, pertaining to a / the subject; disciplinary; pertaining to sex or sexual enjoyment, sensual.

वैष्णव vaishṉāv (*nm*) a devotee of विष्णु; (*a*) pertaining to or belonging to विष्णु; hence वैष्णवी (*nf*).

वैसा vaisa: (*a*) of that kind/nature, like that, such as that; –ही exactly like that, of that very type/manner.

वैसे vaise (*ind*) that way, in that manner; in the same manner; –ही just like that; casually, without any specific purpose.

वो vo (*pro*) a variant of वह (in

pronunciation only).

वोट voṭ (*nm*) vote; –देना to vote, to cast one's vote; –माँगना to ask for/seek votes.

वोटर voṭar (*nm*) a voter; -सूची voter-list.

व्यंग्य vyāṅgy (*nm*) suggestion; irony, sarcasm, innuendo; caricature; -कवि satyric poet; ~कार satirist; -काव्य satyrical verse/poetry; -चित्र a cartoon; ०कार a cartoonist; ~पूर्ण sarcastic, ironical; -बाण sarcastic utterance/remark; -मिश्रित with a touch of sarcasm/irony; -रूपक a skit; –लेख satirical article; ~लेखक satirist; –लेखन satirical writing; -वचन sarcastic/ironical remarks; –कसना to pass sarcastic remarks.

व्यंग्यार्थ vyāṅgya:rth (*nm*) suggested meaning, suggestion.

व्यंग्योक्ति vyāṅgyokti (*nf*) a sarcastic/ironical utterance or remark, sarcasm.

व्यंजक vyāṇjak (*a*) expressive; suggestive; ~ता expressiveness; suggestivity.

व्यंजन vyāṇjān (*nm*) a consonant; rich (cooked) food, dainties.

व्यंजना vyāṇjanā: (*nf*) suggestion, suggested meaning; -शक्ति suggestive power (of a word).

व्यंजित vyāṇjit (*a*) suggested, conveyed through suggestion.

व्यक्त vyakt (*a*) expressed; manifest(ed); articulate; hence ~ता (*nf*).

व्यक्ति vyakti (*nm*) an individual, a person; subject; ~क individual, personal; ~गत subjective; individual, personal; ~निष्ठ subjective; -पद singular term; ~वाचक proper; ●संज्ञा proper noun; ~वाद individualism; ~वादिता individualism; individualistic outlook; ~वादी an individualist; individualistic; ~वैचित्र्यवाद (in literature) the theory of subjective/personal typicality/identity; hence ~वैचित्र्यवादी (*a, nf*).

व्यक्तित्व vyaktittv (*nm*) personality; individuality; ~हीन devoid of a personality, having no personality; hence ~हीनता (*nf*).

व्यक्ती/करण vyakti:karāṉ (*nm*) individualisation; personalisation; imparting a personal/individual character; ~कृत individualised; personalised; given a personal/individual character.

व्यक्तोच्चार vyaktochcha:r (*nm*) articulation, articulate pronunciation.

व्यग्र vyaggr (*a*) restless, perturbed, concerned; impatient; ~ता restlessness, perturbation; concern, anxiousness; impatience; ~मना restless, perturbed; concerned; impatient.

व्यजन vyajān (*nm*) a fan.

व्यतिकर vyatikar (*nm*) interference, interruption.

व्यतिक्रम vyatikkrām(*nm*) metathesis; violation of established order; default, infraction; hence ~ण (*nm*).

व्यतिक्रांत vyatikkrā:nt (*a*) transgressed; rendered disorderly; defaulted.

व्यतिरे/क vyatirek (*nm*) difference; contrast; discontinuance; ~की contrastive; ~की भाषाविज्ञान contrastive linguistics; ~की विश्लेषण contrastive analysis; ~की व्याकरण contrastive grammar.

व्यतिहा/र vyatiha:r (*nm*) interchange, reciprocity; ~री reciprocal.

व्यतीत vyati:t (*a*) passed, past; –काल bygone days, past.

व्यत्यय vyattyay (*nm*) reversal; transposition, metathesis; -, **वर्ण** metathesis.

व्यथा vyatha: (*nf*) pain, agony, anguish; ~**कर** agonising; ~**कुल** see **व्यथित**; ~**क्रांत** see **व्यथित**; ~**तुर** see **व्यथित**; ~**रहित/शून्य** free from pain/agony/anguish.

व्यथित vyathit (*a*) in agony/anguish, pained, afflicted.

व्यभिचा/र vyabhicha:r (*nm*) fornication, wenching; lewdness, debauchery; adultery; ~**रिणी** fast/lewd (woman), wanton woman; ~**रिता** debauchery, lewdness; adultery; ~**री** a debauchee; an adulterer; lewd, libertine; ०**भाव** a transitory mental (also, in some cases physical) state (such states number thirty-four according to Indian poeticians).

व्यय vyay (*nm*) expense, expenditure; cost, outlay; consumption; ~**साध्य** expensive, costly.

व्यर्थ vyarth (*a*) useless, fruitless; futile; ineffective; unprofitable; ~**ता** uselessness, fruitlessness, futility; ineffectiveness; -**का काम करना** to beat the air; to bite/gnaw file: -**समय गँवाना** to shoe the goose.

व्यवक/लन vyavkalan (*nm*) subtraction; ~**लित** subtracted.

व्यवच्छिन्न vyavachchhinn (*a*)separated; divided; interrupted.

व्यवच्छेद vyavachchhed (*nm*) separation; division; interrupted; also ~**न** (*nm*).

व्यव/धान vyavdhā:n (*nm*) hindrance; intervention, interruption; ~**हित** hindred; intervened, interrupted.

व्यवसा/य vyavsa:y (*nm*) profession, vocation, calling, occupation; practice; ~**य संबंधी** professional; vocational, occupational; ~**यिक** see **व्यावसायिक**; ~**यिकी** occupationology; ~**यी** professional; a practitioner.

व्यवस्था vyavastha: (*nf*) order, system; management, arrangement; organisation; provision; ruling; scouting; ~**बद्ध** systematized, organised, orderly; hence ~**बद्धता** (*nf*); -**करना** to organise, to systematize; to provide; to put in order; to arrange, to manage; -**देना** to impart a system; to give a ruling.

व्यवस्था/पक vyavastha:pak (*nm*) an organiser, a manager, one who directs/systematizes;~**पन** organising, systematizing, imparting an order; ~**पिका सभा** a legislature, legislative assembly.

व्यवस्थि/त vyavasthit (*a*) systematic, in order, methodical; settled, provided (for); ~**ति** systematisation; system, method.

व्यवहर्त्ता vyavharta: (*nm*) a practitioner.

व्यवहार vyavha:r (*nm*) behaviour; dealings, treatment; transaction; practice; usage, use; application; -**और सिद्धांत** practice and theory; -**कला** art of behaviour; ~**कुशल** tactful in one's dealings, worldly wise, knowing the ways of the world; -**कुशलता** tactfulness, worldly wisdom; knowledge of the ways of the world; ~**त:** in practice, as a matter of practice; -**में** in practice; ~**वाद** positivism; ~**वादी** a positivist; positivistic; -**करना** to behave; to treat; to use; to act; to deal; to apply.

व्यवहारिक vyavha:rik (*a*) see **व्यावहारिक**.

व्यवहार्य vyavha:ry (*a*) practicable, feasible; ~**ता** practicability, feasibility.

व्यवहित vyavhit (*a*) see under व्यवधान.

व्यवहृत vyavhrit (*a*) used; applied; practised;–कला applied art.

व्यष्टि vyashṭi (*nm*) an individual; –और समष्टि the individual and the community/society: ~तः individually; one by one; ~प्रेयवाद individualistic hedonism; -मानव individual man; ~वादिता, ~वाद individualism; ~वादी individualistic; an individualist; ~सुखवाद individualistic hedonism.

व्यसन vyasan (*nm*) addiction (esp. to a vice); besetting sin; –पड़ना to be/get addicted.

व्यसनी vyasnī: (*a* and *nm*) addicted (esp. to a vice); an addict.

व्यस्त vyast (*a*) busy, occupied, engaged; ~ता busyness, the state or quality of being busy/occupied.

व्याकरण vya:karaṇ (*nm*) Grammar; –, ऐतिहासिक historical Grammar; –, तुलनात्मक comparative Grammar; –, रूपांतरण transformational Grammar; –, वर्णनात्मक descriptive Grammar; –विषयक/संबंधी grammatical; –, व्यवस्थापक systematic Grammar; -सम्मत/~सिद्ध grammatically correct.

व्याकरणिक vya:karṇik (*a*) grammatical; –कोटि grammatical category.

व्याकुल vya:kul (*a*) perturbed, (mentally) upset, restless; impatient; ~चित्त/मना/हृदय perturbed, restless, mentally upset; ~ता perturbation, restlessness, impatience.

व्याकृ/त vya:kkrit (*a*) composed; ~ति composition.

व्या/कोच vya:koch (*nm*) lengthening; expansion; ~कुचित lengthened; expanded.

व्याख्या vya:kkhya: (*nf*) interpretation; explanation, elaboration, commentary, annotation; exposition; ~कार a commentator; an annotator; ~त interpreted, elaborated, explained, commented on; ~ता a commentator; an interpreter; lecturer; ~त्मक explanatory; interpretative; oटिप्पणी explanatory/ interpretative note; –करना to explain; to interpret; to elaborate.

व्याख्यान vya:kkhya:n (*nm*) speech, lecture, oration; exposition, interpretation, elaboration; ~दाता an orator; a lecturer; –विषयक/संबंधी oratorical; –झाड़ना (said in a satirical vein) to deliver a discourse (to an unwilling listener), to dump a discourse on.

व्याख्येय vya:kkhyey (*a*) worth being or to be explained/interpreted/ annotated/elaborated.

व्याघा/त vya:gha:t (*nm*) interruption; hindrance, obstruction; contradiction; ~तक/ती contradictory; causing interruption/obstruction.

व्याघ्र vya:gghr (*nm*) a tiger; -चर्म tiger skin; ~नख claw of a tiger; ~मुख/मुखी having a tiger-like face; terrible.

व्याज vya:j (*nm*) pretext, pretence; see ब्याज (and entries thereunder); ~निंदा artful or ironical censure; ~स्तुति indirect eulogy, ironical commendation.

व्याजोक्ति vya:jokti (*nf*) a dissimulating statement.

व्या/ध vya:dh (*nm*) a hunter, fowler; also ~धा.

व्याधि vya:dhi(*nf*)a malady, disease, an ailment; ~कर/जनक causing an ailment/a malady; ~ग्रस्त/पीड़ित ill, afflicted by a malady, ailing, diseased; ~नाशक/हर countering or removing an ailment/malady;

-मंदिर the physical frame (full of diseases); ~मुक्त/रहित/शून्य free from maladies/ailments; healthy; ~युक्त afflicted by a malady, ill, ailing.

व्यापक vya:pak (*a*) comprehensive; extensive, wide(spread); pervasive; ~ता/त्व comprehensiveness; extensiveness, pervasiveness.

व्यापना vya:pnā: (*v*) to be afflicted (by); to spread, permeate or pervade through.

व्यापार vya:pa:r (*nm*) trade, business; traffic; function; action; phenomenon; -चिह्न trade-mark: -विषयक/संबंधी mercantile; pertaining to trade/business; -संघ mercantile association; -गुट trade block; -निदेशिका trade directory; -वर्गीकरण trade classification; -शेष balance of trade; -संघ trade association; व्यापारे वसति लक्ष्मा trade is the mother of money.

व्यापारिक vya:pa:rik (*a*) pertaining to or related with a trade/business, mercantile; ~ता mercantilism; commercialism; -हित business interest(s).

व्यापारी vya:pa:ri: (*nm*) a businessman, trader, merchant; (*a*) engaged in trade/business; -संघ mercantile/trade association; -समाज/समुदाय business community.

व्यापी vya:pi:—a suffix used to give the sense of pervasive/permeating/comprehensive/spread or spreading (as सर्वव्यापी, विश्वव्यापी, दूरव्यापी).

व्याप्त vya:pt (*a*) pervaded, permeated; spread, extended.

व्याप्ति vya:pti (*nf*) permeability/permeation, pervasiveness; extensity/extensiveness.

व्याप्य vya:ppy (*a*) pervasive, permeable.

व्यामो/ह vya:moh (*nm*) illusion, mental confusion; bewilderment; ~हित under an illusion, mentally confused, bewildered.

व्यायाम vya:ya:m (*nm*) physical exercise, exercise; gymnastics; ~शाला a gymnasium.

व्यायामी vya:ya:mī: (*a* and *nm*) (an) athlete, (a) gymnast; pertaining to athletics/gymnastics.

व्या/ल vya:l (*nm*) a snake, serpent; hence ~ली (*nf*).

व्यावर्तक vya:varttak (*a*) differentiating, distinctive, distinguishing; –धर्म differentiating/distinctive feature, characteristic.

व्यावर्तन vya:varttan (*nm*) differentiation, distinction.

व्यावसायिक vya:vsa:ik (*a*) professional, vocational; occupational; –खिलाड़ी professional player; –पाठ्यक्रम professional courses; –रंगमंच professional stage; –शिक्षा professional education.

व्यावहारिक vya:vha:rik (*a*) practical; customary; ~ता practicalness/practicality; customariness.

व्यास vya:s (*nm*) diameter, calibre; diffusion; a celebrated ancient Indian sage and savant; ~पीठ dais; -शैली diffused style.

व्याहत vya:hat (*a*) injured, afflicted.

व्युत्क्रम vyutkram (*nm*) anastrophe; reversal, cross order; reciprocal; ~ण reversal; reciprocation.

व्युत्पत्ति vyutpatti (*nf*) etymology (of a word), derivation; origin; ~क etymological; derivative; –, भ्रामक false etymology; –, लौकिक popular etymology; -विज्ञान/शास्त्र (science of) etymology; ~वैज्ञानिक an etymologist; etymological.

व्युत्पन्न vyutpann (*a*) derived, originated; learned; accomplished; ~**मति** witty; accomplished; –**शब्द** derived word, derivative.

व्युत्पा/दन vyutpa:dan (*nm*) etymological explanation, derivation (from); hence ~**दक** (*nm*).

व्युत्पाद्य vyutpa:ddy (*a*) derivable, capable of being traced back to the root; to be explained or discussed.

व्यूह vyu:h (*nm*) a military array; strategic disposition/placement; ~**न** forming an array; strategic placement; -**निपुण** a strategist; ~**बद्ध** strategically arranged/arrayed;–**रचना** array, tactical placement or strategic disposition of forces.

व्योम vyom (*nm*) the sky; -**गंगा/सरिता** the milky way (in the sky); ~**गामी/चर/चारी/विहारी** sky-faring.

व्रजन vrajan (*nm*) going; roaming; wandering.

व्रण vraṇ (*nm*) a boil; ulcer, wound.

व्रत vrat (*nm*) a fast; vow, pledge; -**भंग** violation of a fast/vow/pledge; -**समापन** conclusion of a fast/vow/pledge.

व्रती vrati: (*a* and *nm*) (one who is) observing a fast/vow, one who takes a pledge; engaged in religious observance.

व्रात्य vra:tty (*nm*) a pagan, a non-Aryan; ~**वाद** paganism.

व्री/डा, ~**ड़ा** vri:ḍa:, ~ṛa: (*nf*) bashfulness; modesty.

श

श sha–the first of the conventional sibilant-trio (**श, ष, स**) of the Devna:gri: alphabet. In current Hindi sound-pattern, however, the cerebral (**ष**) has merged its identity into the palatal sibilant (**श**).

शंकर shaṅkar (*nm*) Lord Shiv–the annihilator of the universe; a great Indian philosopher who flourished during the last quarter of the eighth and first quarter of the ninth century and who fought successfully against Buddhism for the revival of Brahmāṇism.

शंका shāṅka: (*nf*) doubt; suspicion; mistrust; ~**कुल** perturbed by doubt/mistrust, suspicious, mistrustful; ~**जनक** creating or raising suspicion/doubt/mistrust; suspicious; -**निवारण/निवृत्ति** allaying of suspicion, clearing or removing a doubt; ~**न्वित/मय** filled with doubt/mistrust/suspicion; ~**शील** suspicious (by nature), of suspicious disposition; ~**शीलता** suspiciousness, suspicious disposition; -**समाधान** setting a doubt at rest, allaying suspicion/mistrust; ~**स्पद** doubtful, questionable, fit to be doubted/spected/distrusted.

शंकालु shaṅka:lu (*a*) (of) suspicious (nature), mistrustful: ~**ता** suspiciousness mistrustfulness.

शंकित shańkit (*a*) alarmed; filled with mistrust/doubt/suspicion; ~मन mistrustful, apprehensive.

शंकु shańku (*nm*) a cone; -कोण conical angle; –, खोखला hollow cone; –, ठोस solid cone; ~फल a cone; -बिंदु conical point; -रूप conical; –, वृत्तीय circular cone.

शं/ख shańkh (*nm*) a conch, conch-shell; a number equal to a thousand billion or 10,00,000 crores; ~खमय conchiferous; ~खाकार conchate; ~खाभ conchoid; ~ख-ध्वनि/नाद blowing of a conch-shell signifying commencement of battle; ~ख बजाना to rejoice; to go about announcing one's achievements; ~ख फूँकना to make a declaration of war; to arouse/awaken.

शंखिनी shańkhini: (*nf*) one of the four major categories of women according to ancient Indian sexologists.

शंबु shambu, ~क k (*nm*) a bivalve shell; snail.

शंभु shambhu (*nm*) Lord Shiv.

शऊर shau:r (*nm*) mannerliness, decency; discretion, sense; ~दार mannerly; sensible; discreet.

शक shak (*nm*) doubt, suspicion; —संवत् an era introduced by Emperor Sha:liva:han of India (in78A.D.) and revived by the post-Independence government of the country.

शकट shakaṭ (*nm*) a cart.

शकर shakar (*nf*) sugar; ~कंद sweet potato; ~खोर who has a taste for or is addicted to sweets; ~जबान sweet-spoken; ~दानी a sugar pot; ~पारा a kind of sweet (or saltish) preparation of fried flour.

शकल shakal (*nf*) same as शक्ल; -सूरत see शक्ल-सूरत.

शकाब्द shaka:bd (*nm*) see शक संवत् (under शक).

शका/र shaka:r (*nm*) the consonant श and its sound; ~रांत (word) ending in 'श्'.

शकील shaki:l (*a*) charming, beautiful/handsome.

शकुन shakun (*nm*) an omen, augury; -विचार/विद्या augury; -शास्त्र the science of omens; —आना/जाना receiving/sending of auspicious articles on happy occasions (like marriage etc.); -करना to commence (a work etc.) at an auspicious moment; to perform an engagement-ritual; —देखना/निकालना/विचारना to look for a good omen; to look for an auspicious conjunction of planets; to practise augury.

शकुनिया shakunīyā: (*nm*) see शकुनी.

शकुनी shakunī: (*nm*) an augur, a soothsayer.

शक्कर shakkar (*nf*) see शकर.

शक्की shakki: (*a*) suspicious (by nature), sceptic; ~मिजाज sceptic, suspicious by disposition.

शक्ति shakti (*nf*) power, strength, potency, energy; name of the goddess personifying divine power; -कुंठन powerlessness; de-energising; ~पूजक a worshipper of *shakti*; -पूजा worship of *shakti*; ~मान strong, powerful; forceful; potent; ~युक्त forceful; powerful, strong; ~वर्धक invigorating; nutritive; ~वाद energism; ~वादी a worshipper of *shakti*; ~हीन powerless, impotent, enervated; —लगाना to apply force/energy.

शक्तिमत्ता shaktimatta: (*nf*) powerfulness/forcefulness, potentiality.

शक्तिमान shaktimā:n (*a*) powerful/forceful, having potential.

शक्य shakky (*a*) feasible, possible, capable of being effected or done; ~ता feasibility, possibility.

शक्र shakkr (*nm*) Lord Indra—the king of gods.

शक्ल shakl (*nf*) shape, form; looks, appearance, countenance; -सूरत looks, appearance; –तक न पहचानना not to know from Adam; –तो देखो (ironically) look at the cheek! what a man and what a mind!; —दिखाना to turn up, to show up, to make an appearance; —देखते रह जाना to gaze in astonishment; to be wonderstruck at the sight of; —न दिखाना not to turn up/show up, to shun a meeting; –पहचानना to recognise by face; to identify by (the very) looks; –बनाना to wear a strange look; to be out of countenance; —बिगाड़ना to develop ugly looks, to wear an outlandish look; to be deformed/defaced.

शख्स shaḳhs (*nm*) a human being; person, an individual.

शख्सियत shaḳhsiyat (*nf*) personality.

शख्सी shaḳhsi: (*a*) individual; personal; –तौर पर personally, pesonally speaking.

शग़ल shagal (*nm*) a pastime, recreation; hobby; –करना to recreate, to do a thing for recreation.

शगुन shagun (*nm*) see शकुन.

शगुनिया shagunīa: (*nm*) see शकुनिया.

शगूफ़ा shagu:fa: (*nm*) see शिगूफ़ा.

शजरा shajara: (*nm*) a genealogical tree; a versified eulogical presentation of the genealogy; a patwari's map of fields; –पढ़ना to read out the details of the genealogical tree.

शठ shaṭh (*a*) wicked, knave, crafty, cunning; ~ता wickedness, knavery, craftiness, cunningness; शठे शाठ्यं समाचरेत deal with the devil in his own way, tit for tat.

शत shat (*nm*) one hundred; ~धा in a hundred ways; ~पत्र the lotus (flower); –प्रतिशत cent per cent; ~वार्षिकी centenary; ०समारोह centenary celebration.

शतक shatak (*nm*) a century, one hundred; -बनाना to score a century.

शतदल shatdal (*nm*) a lotus flower.

शतपद shatpad (*nm*) a centipede.

शतरं/ज shatrāṇj (*nf*) the game of chess; a chess-board; ~जी a chess-board; a good chess-player; a bed cover with chess-board design printed over it; ~ज का मोहरा cat to paw, person used as a tool.

शतश: shatshah (*ind*) in a hundred ways.

शतांश shata:nsh (*nm*) a hundredth part.

शताधिक shata:dhik (*a*) over a hundred, more than a hundred.

शताब्/द, ~ब्दी shata:bd (*nm*); ~bdi: (*nf*) a century, span of hundred years; ~ब्दी-समारोह centenary celebration.

शतायु shata:yu (*a*) of hundred years (of age), centenarian; -हो! may you live for a hundred years!

शतायुध shata:yudh (*a,nm*) (a warrior) wielding a hundred weapons.

शती shati: (*nf*) a collection of hundred; century.

शत्रुंजय shattrūṇjay (*a* and *nm*) (*a*) conqueror of the enemy.

शत्रु shattru (*nm*) an enemy, a foe; ~घ्न/घाती destroyer/killer of the enemy; ~जित conqueror of the enemy; -पक्ष enemy side; hostile camp; ~साल causing agony/woe to the enemy.

शत्रुता shattruta: (*nf*) enmity, animosity, hostility.

शनाख्त shana:ḳhṭ (*nf*) identification; —करना to indentify.

शनि shanī (*nm*) Saturn—the seventh of the nine planets; Saturday; ~वार Saturday; ~वासर Saturday; —की दृष्टि to be under the influence of evil stars, to be badly afflicted.

शनिश्चर, शनीचर shanishchar, shanī:char (*nm*);—see शनि.

शनैः shanaih (*ind*) gradually, slowly; -शनैः by degrees, little by little, gradually.

शपथ shapath (*nf*) an oath, swearing; —ग्रहण करना to take an oath, —, गोपनीयता की oath of secrecy; —दिलाना to administer an oath; -पत्र an affidavit; —भंग करना to commit a breach of oath; —लेना to take an oath.

शफ़ताल्‍ू shafta:lu: (*nm*) nectarine.

शफ़री shafri: (*nf*) a kind of fish.

शफ़ा shafa: (*nf*) (restoration to) health, recovery; curative power; ~खाना a clinic, dispensary.

श/ब shab (*nf*) night; ~बेबारात the fifteenth night of the month of *sha:ba:n*; ~बे-महताब moonlit night; ~बे-वसाल/वस्ल night of amorous dalliance.

शबनम shabnam (*nf*) dew; a very fine quality of muslin.

शबनमी shabnamī: (*nf*) a mosquito net (which also serves as a protection from dew).

शबल shabal (*a*) variegated, diverse; ~ता variegatedness, diverseness.

शबाब shaba:b (*nm*) youth, prime of life; —फूटना, —फट पड़ना to be in full bloom, to be a picture of youthfulness.

शबीह shabi:h (*nf*) a picture, portrait; resemblance.

शब्द shabd (*nm*) a word, term; sound; ~कार producing sound; creator of words; ~कोष/कोश a dictionary; ~गत pertaining to or related with a/the word; ~ग्राम totality of sounds; -चयन choice of words; diction; -चित्र a word-sketch; -जाल jugglery of words, verbosity; -पहेली crossword puzzle; -बोध comprehension of words; -प्रमाण testimony; -ब्रह्म the Veda considered as revealed sound and word; word (sound) identified with the Supreme Being; -भेद part of speech; ~भेदी see ~वेधी; -रचना word-construction, word-formation; -रूप the (grammatical) form of a word; -विरोध mere vocal opposition; -विशेष a particular word/sound; ~वीर/~शूर (blessed) with a gift of the gab, a past master in mere talks; ~वेधी hitting at the sound(as an arrow), hitting at an object perceived only through the ear; -व्युत्पत्ति word-etymology; -शक्ति the force or signification of a word; -शासन the Scienc of words; grammar; -शास्त्र lexicography; grammar; -संक्षेप abbreviation; -संग्रह a glossary; -सौंदर्य see -सौष्ठव; -सौकर्य facility of expression; -सौष्ठव elegance of words; grace of style; ~हीन speechless, mute; hence ~हीनता (*nf*); शब्दों का गोरखधंधा a cloud of words; शब्दों में बाँधना to express in words.

शब्दशः shabdshah (*ind*) verbatim, word by word; -अनुवाद word by word translation.

शब्दाडंबर shabda:ḍambar (*nm*) ampullosity bombast, verbiage/verbosity; hence ~पूर्ण (*a*).

शब्दातीत shabda:ti:t (*a*) indescribable, defying description.

शब्दानुकरण shabda:nukarān (*nm*) imitatian of words, going word for word.

शब्दानुवाद shabda:nuva:d (*nm*) a literal translation.

शब्दानुशासन shabda:nūsha:sān (*nm*) grammar, grammatical instruction.

शब्दानुसार shabda:nusa:r (*a* and *adv*) literal; literally.

शब्दार्थ shabda:rth (*nm*) the literal meaning; -विज्ञान/शास्त्र semasiology, semantics.

शब्दालंकार shabda:lāṅka:r (*nm*) a word-based figure of speech.

शब्दावली shabda:vali: (*nf*) vocabulary; terminology.

शब्दावृत्ति shabda:vritti (*nf*) word-frequency; word-repetition.

शब्देंद्रिय shabdēndriy (*nf*) the organ of hearing, ear.

शब्दोच्चार shabdochcha:r (*nm*) articulation; phonation.

शम sham (*nm*) calmness; tranquillity of mind.

शमन shamān (*nm*) (the act or process of) pacification, allaying; quenching; suppression; -करना to pacify, to allay; to quench; to supppress.

शमशीर shamshi:r (*nf*) a sword; -के जौहर wonders in wielding a sword.

शमांतक shamā:ntak a (*a*) disturbing, perturbing; causing disquiet.

शमा shamā: (*nf*) a candle, lamp; ~दान a candle-base, sconce; -परवाना the lamp and the moth.

शमित shamit (*a*) pacified; tranquillized; quietened, suppressed; quenched.

शयन shayan (*nm*) sleep, (the act of) sleeping, lying down; -कक्ष/गृह/शाला a bed-chamber, bed-room.

शयनागार shaynā:ga:r (*nm*) a bed-chamber, bed-room.

शय्या shayya: (*nm*) a bed, bedstead; ~गत gone to bed, confined to bed; ~गृह a bed-chamber, bed-room; ~सक्त bed-ridden,

शर shar (*nm*) an arrow; -वृष्टि a shower of arrows; ~वेग swift as an arrow; -शैया bep (made) of arrows; -संधान taking aim with an arrow.

शरअ sharaa (*nf*) custom, convention.

शरच्चं/द्र sharachchandr (*nm*) the moon; ~द्रिका the autumnal moonshine/moonlight.

शरज्ज्योत्स्ना sharajjyotsnā: (*nm*) see शरच्चंद्रिका.

शरण sharāṉ (*nf*) shelter, refuge; recourse; protection; ~दाता one who affords a protection; ~प्रद sheltering; -स्थान a sanctuary, refuge, an asylum, a haven; -देना to afford refuge, to grant shelter, to harbour.

शरणाग/त sharaṉa:gat (*a* and *nm*) (one who has) come for shelter/protection; a refugee; ~गति approachlen for protection/shelter.

शरणा/र्थी sharaṉā:rthi: (*nm*) a refugee,shelter-seeker; ~र्थिन feminine form of ~र्थी.

शरण्य sharāṉny (*a*) seeking/needing or deserving shelter.

शरत sharat (*nf*) the autumn; ~**काल** the autumn season.

शरद sharad (*nf*) the autumn; -**पूनो**/-**पूर्णिमा** the full moon night in the month of **क्वार**.

शरब/त sharbat (*nm*) a sweet beverage (of different kinds); syrup; ~**ती** of the colour of ~**त**; sweet; syrupy.

शरम sharām (*nm*) see **शर्म**.

शरमाना sharmā:nā: (*v*) to feel shy, to be abashed/ashamed, to blush; to put to shame.

शरमाशरमी sharmā:sharmī: (*adv*) through shame; out of bashfulness/shyness.

शर्मिंदगी sharamīndagi: (*nf*) see **शर्मिंदगी** under '**शर्मिंदा**'.

शरमीला sharmi:la: (*a*) see **शर्मीला**; ~**पन** see **शर्मीला** (~**पन**).

शरह shareh (*nf*) rate; detailed account; see **शरअ**; ~**बंदी** list; -**लगान** rate of rent; -**सूद** rate of interest.

शराकत shara:kat (*nf*) partnership; participation; ~**नामा** partnership deed/agreement.

शरापना shara:pnā: (*v*) to curse, to imprecate.

शराफ़त shara:fat (*nf*) gentlemanliness, civility; -**का पुतला** an embodiment of gentlemanliness, a thorough gentleman; -**घोलकर पी जाना** to have no sense of gentlemanliness.

शराब shara:b (*nf*) wine, spirit, liquor; ~ **ख़ाना** a bar, wine shop; ~**ख़ोर** a drunkard, boozy; ~**ख़ोरी** addiction to liquor, habitual drinking;-**का दौर चलना** to booze, to have a bout of drinking; -**बनाना** to brew.

शराबी shara:bi: (*nm* and *a*) a drunkard; boozy; -**कबाबी** exercising no temperance in food and drinks.

शराबोर shara:bor (*a*) thoroughly drenched/soaked.

शरार/त shara:rat (*nf*) mischief/mischievousness; wickedness;~**तन** mischievously, out of mischief, with a mischievous intention; ~**ती** naughty, playful; mischievous; wicked; o**पन** naughtiness; playfulness; mischievousness.

शरीअत shari:at (*nf*) divine law, religious law; justice.

शरीक shari:k (*d*) participating/associating; partnering/ co-sharing, included; -**होना** to participate; to co-share; **शरीके-जुर्म** an accomplice; **शरीके-राय** in agreement.

शरीफ़ shari:f (*a*) gentlemanly; noble, virtuous, -**ख़ानदान** a noble family; ~**ज़ादा** son of a gentlman, belonging to a noble family, of noble descent; hence ~**ज़ादी** (fem. form).

शरीफ़ा shari:fa: (*nm*) the custard apple.

शरीर shari:r (*nm*) body, physique; (*a*) mischievous; -**और आत्मा** body and soul; -**क्रिया** physiology; ~**क्रियात्मक** physiological; ~**क्रिया-विज्ञान** physiology; ~**क्रिया-वैज्ञानिक** a physiologist; physiological; -**गठन** physique, body-build, physical frame; -**त्याग** death; -**दंड** physical punishment; -**पतन/पात/निपात** death, demise; -**रक्षक** a bodyguard, escort; -**रचना** anatomy, physical structure; o **विज्ञान/शास्त्र** anatomy; ~**रचना-वैज्ञानिक** an anatomist; anatomical; ~**विज्ञान/शास्त्र** physiology; ~**वैज्ञानिक** a physiologist; physiological; -**शास्त्री** a physiologist; ~**शास्त्रीय** physiological; -**संबंध** physical relationship, sexual relationship;

-संबंधी corporeal, pertaining to the body/physical frame; -संस्कार sixteen rituals or consecrations of physical purification prescribed by the Vedas; ~स्थ located or concentrated in the body; confined to the physical element; –गलना/घुलना to be on the wane, to be decrying, to decay; –छूटना to pass away, to die; –छोड़ना/–त्यागना to die, to pass away; –जलना to be running very high temperature;–भर जाना to acquire fullness of bloom; to acquire healthy flesh; –में बिजली दौड़ जाना to be thrilled with excitement.

शरीरांत shari:rā:nt (*nm*) death, demise.

शरीरार्पण shari:ra:rpāṇ (*nm*) surrender of the body, physical surrender.

शरीरी shari:ri: (*a*) physical, corporeal; concrete; (*nm*) an organism.

शर्क/रा sharkara: (*nf*) sugar, saccharose; ~रामय sacchariferous; ~रामापी saccharimeter; ~रीय saccharine.

शर्त shart (*nf*) a condition, precondition, term; provision; bet, wager; ~बंद bound, committed; –बदना/लगाना to bet, to wager; –यह है कि provided that; –होना, किसी बात की to be a pre-condition for.

शर्तिया shartiya: (*a* and *adv*) sure; unfailing (as — इलाज); positively, definitely, without fail.

शर्ती sharti: (*a*) conditional, qualified.

शर्ब/त sharbat (*nm*) see 'शरबत'; ~ती see 'शरबती'.

शर्म sharm (*nf*) shame; bashfulness, shyness; ~नाक shameful, disgraceful; ~सार ashamed; shy; hence ~सारी (*nf*); शर्माहुज़ूरी through modesty/personal consideration; -हया shame and modesty; shame; –आना to feel shy; to be ashamed; –करना to be ashamed; to be shy/bashful; –की बात something to be ashamed of, disgraceful thing;–के मारे मुँह न दिखाना to hide one's head; –खाना to be ashamed; to feel shy/bashful; –से गड़ जाना/–से पानी-पानी होना to die through shame, to feel thoroughly ashamed; –से गर्दन झुकना to hang the head down through shame.

शर्माना sharma:nā: (*v*) see शरमाना.

शर्मि/दा sharmīnda: (*a*) ashamed; ~दगी shame; shamefulness.

शर्मीला sharmi:la: (*a*) shy, bashful; ~पन shyness, bashfulness.

शर्वरी sharvari: (*nf*) night; ~श the moon.

शलग़म shalgam (*nf*) turnip.

शलज/म shaljam (*nf*) see 'शलग़म'; ~मी turnipy, resembling ~म.

शलभ shalabh (*nm*) a moth.

शलाका shala:ka: (*nf*) a rod; spoke; bar; (archaic usage) ballot; –पुरुष a divine personage.

शल्य shally (*nm*) a surgical instrument; a thorn; ~कर्म/क्रिया surgery, a surgical operation; -चिकित्सक a surgeon; -चिकित्सा surgical operation; surgery; -विद्या/शास्त्र surgery.

शल्ल shall (*a*) exhausted, wearied, fatigued;–हो जाना to be extremely exhausted/wearied/fatigued.

शव shav (*nm*) a corpse, dead body; ~दाह cremation; ० स्थान a crematorium; -परीक्षा autopsy, postmortem; ~शाला mortuary; -संस्कार last funeral rites.

शव/ल shaval (*nm*) see शबल; ~लित see शबलित.

शश shash (*nm*) a rabbit, hare; the number six; (*a*) six; ~माही six-monthly, half-yearly.

शशक shashak (*nm*) a rabbit, hare.

शशांक shasha:ṅk (*nm*) the moon; ~शेखर Lord Shiv.

शशि shashi (*nm*) the moon; -कला a digit of the moon; ~मंडल the disc of the moon; ~मुख having a moon-like/pretty face, beautiful; hence ~मुखी (*a*).

शस्त्र shastr (*nm*) an arm, weapon; instrument, tool; ~कार an armourer; ~जीवी a professional soldier, serviceman; -त्याग renouncing (the use of) arms, abandonment of the arms; ~धारी a warrior; armed; -प्रहार blow of a weapon; -विद्या the science of arms, military science; ~शाला armoury, arsenal; ~सज्जित equipped with arms; armed; -समर्पण surrender of arms; -डाल देना to surrender arms.

शस्त्रागार shastra:ga:r (*nm*) an armoury, arsenal.

शस्त्राभ्यास shashtra:bbhya:s (*nm*) practice of arms, military exercise.

शस्त्रास्त्र shastra:str (*nm*) arms (both used as missiles and for throwing); -की होड़ race of arms.

शस्त्रीकरण shastri:karaṉ (*nm*) armament, (the act or process of) equipping with arms.

शस्त्रोपजी/वी shastropji:vi: (*nm*) a professional warrior/soldier; hence ~विता (*nf*).

शस्य shassy (*nm*) see सस्य.

शहंशा/ह shehansha:h (*nm*) an emperor, a king of kings; ~हियत regality, royal splendour, majestic ways; ~ही majestic, regal, kingly; royalty, regality, regal ways.

शह sheh—an allomorph of शाह; (*nf*) instigation, incitement; a check (in chess); ~जादा a prince; ~जादी a princess; ~जोर powerful; strong; ~जोरी powerfulness, strength; ~तूत the mulberry tree and its fruit; caneapple; ~बाला the younger boy (esp. brother) who accompanies the bridegroom in various wedding functions; ~मात the conclusive check (in chess); o करना to render helpless; ~सवार an adept horseman/rider; ~सवारी horsemanship; -देना to incite; to apply a check.

शहतीर shehti:r (*nm*) a beam, girder.

शहद shehad (*nm*) honey; (*a*) very sweet; -की छुरी a honey-tongued crook; -की मक्खी a bee; -घुलना, ज़बान में to be honey-tongued/sweet-spoken; -लगाकर चाटना to bother overmuch for a vain thing; to be of no avail whatsoever, to bring no returns.

शहनाई shehna:i: (*nf*) a clarionet; -बजना marriage celebrations to commence, marriage to be solemnized/performed.

शहर shehar (*nm*) a city, town; ~गश्त city patrol; ~पनाह city walls; -बाहर exiled/expelled from the city; -ब-शहर from one city to another; ~बाश a citizen, city-dweller; -की दाई a hear-all tell-all woman; -की हवा लगना (in a derogatory sense) to become urbanised, to be affected by urbanity/urban sophistication/urban selfishness.

शहरी shehri: (*a*) urban, belonging/pertaining to the city/town; sophisticated; (*nm*) resident of a city (as opposed to rural folk); ~करण urbanization; ~कृत urbanized.

शहवत shehvat (*nf*) sexual lust; ~परस्त sexy, lustful; ~परस्ती sexuality, lustfulness; -होना to be hot with lust.

शहादत shaha:dat (*nf*) evidence; martyrdom; –**देना** to tender/give evidence.

शहाना shaha:nā: (*a*) princely, regal, majestic.

शहीद shahi:d (*a* and *nm*) (a) martyr; -**दिवस** a martyr's day; –**होना** to be martyred, to die as a martyr.

शहीदी shahi:di: (*a*) ready to be martyred, pertaining to a martyr.

शांकव shā:nkav (*a*) conic(al).

शांत sha:nt (*a*) peaceful/pacific; still; silent, quiet, quiescent, tranquil, unperturbed; ~**चित्त** unperturbed, having tranquillity of mind; of peaceful disposition; hence ~**चित्तता** (*nf*); ~**चेता** calm, resolute, quiescent; ~**मना** see ~**चित्त**; –**करना** to pacify, to quiet down; –**होना** to be quiet/tranquil; to die; –**रहना** to keep one's head; to keep quiet, to be silent.

शांति sha:nti (*nf*) peace; calmness, quiet, tranquillity, quietude; silence; –**और व्यवस्था** law and order; ~**कर/कारी** pacificatory/pacifying; affording peace/tranquillity; tranquillizing; ~**काम** peace-loving, pacific; ~**काल** peace time; ~**दाता** pacifier; affording peace; ~**दायक/दायी** pacifying, tranquillizing; -**पाठ** recitation of Vedic peace-hymns; scriptural recitation for general and individual peace; ~**प्रद** same as **शांति-दायक**; ~**प्रिय** peace-loving, peaceable; hence ~**प्रियता** (*nf*); -**भंग** breach of peace, eruption of disturbances; ~**मय** peaceful, peaceable; ~**रक्षक** soldiers or defenders of peace; -**रक्षा** maintenance of peace, defence of peace; ~**वादिता** /~**वाद** pacifism; ~**वादी** a pacifist; pacific; -**वार्ता** peace negotiation; -**संधि** peace treaty; -**सम्मेलन** peace conference; -**स्थापना** establishment/restoration of peace, pacification.

शाइस्तगी sha:istagi: (*nf*) civility; gentility, modesty.

शाइस्ता sha:ista: (*a*) civil, modest; polite, gentle.

शाक sha:k (*nm*) vegetable.

शाकाहा/र sha:ka:ha:r (*nm*) vegetarian diet/food; ~**री** a vegetarian.

शाक्त sha:kt (*a* and *nm*) pertaining to **शक्ति**; a worshipper of **शक्ति**.

शाख़ sha:kḥ (*nf*) a branch, twig, bough; an offshoot; lineage; –**निकलना** emergence of an offshoot/something novel; faults to appear; –**निकालना** to find faults; growing of an offshoot; to produce something novel; –**लगाना** growing of a branch; developing of a fault.

शाखा sha:kha: (*nf*) a branch; offshoot; sect; –**कार्यालय** branch office; –**नगर** a satellite town, suburban town; –**नदी** a distributory.

शाख़ा sha:kḥa: (*nf*) a twig, branch.

शाखोच्चार sha:khochcha:r (*nm*) citation of the genealogies of the bride and the groom at the time of wedding by their respective priests.

शागि/र्द sha:gird (*nf*) pupil, disciple; an apprentice; ~**र्दी** pupilage, discipleship; apprenticeship.

शाज़ोनादिर sha:zonā:dir (*ind*) sometimes, once in a while.

शातिर sha:tir (*a*) cunning, crooked, guileful, vile.

शाद sha:d (*a*) delighted, full of joy, happy; ~**मान** happy, delighted, pleased.

शादी sha:di: (*nf*) marriage, wedding; -**ब्याह** wedding and other important rituals, wedding etc. –रचाना to get married (with fanfare).

शान sha:n (*nf*) magnificence, splendour, grandeur; pomp; a touchstone; whetting; ~ची boastful; a brag, braggadocio; ~दार magnificent; pompous, splendid, grand; -शौक़त pomp and show, grandeur and splendour; –चढ़ाना to whet, to give pointedness/intensity; –दिखाना to do the grand; –धरना to whet, to sharpen; –बघारना/मारना to give oneself airs, to ride the high horse; to boast, to brag; –बरसना to look grand or grandly impressive, to be a picture of grandeur; -बान grandeur, magnificence; pomp and show; –में, किसी की undermining the honour/prestige of (as उनकी शान में ऐसी बात नहीं कहनी चाहिए थी); –में फ़र्क आना one's honour/prestige to be undermined/jeopardised; –में बट्टा लगना a fair name to be tarnished.

शानियल sha:niyal (*a*) see शान(~ची).

शाप sha:p (*nm*) a curse, an imprecation; ~ग्रस्त accursed, afflicted through a curse; hence ~ग्रस्तता (*nf*); -निवृत्ति/मोक्ष liberated from the effect of a curse; –देना to curse, to imprecate.

शापित sha:pit (*a*) cursed, accursed, imprecated.

शाबाश sha:ba:sh (*int*) bravo! well done! excellent; attaboy.

शाबाशी sha:ba:shi: (*nf*) applause, praise; –देना to applaud.

शा/ब्द, ~ब्दी sha:bd, ~bdi: (*a*) pertaining to a word/sound; literal, verbal; vocal.

शाब्दिक sha:bdik (*a*) verbal, vocal; superficial; literal/literalistic; –अनुवाद literal translation; –अर्थ literal meaning.

शाब्दिकता sha:bdikta: (*nf*) verbatism; literalism, literality.

शाम sha:m (*nf*) evening, dusk; –की सुबह करना to keep awake the whole night; -सुबह करना to evade, to shirk, to dilly-dally.

शामत sha:mat (*nf*) misfortune, ill-luck, affliction; ~ज़दा ill-fated; unfortunate, unlucky; –आना/–सिर पर सवार होना to be in for an affliction, to be in the grip of misfortune; –का मारा ill-fated, unlucky, afflicted.

शामती sha:mati: (*a*) ill-fated, unlucky, unfortunate.

शामियाना sha:miya:na: (*nm*) a canopy.

शामिल sha:mil (*a*) included, associated, connected; annexed, united; –करना to include, to associate; to annex; to unite; –होना to join, to participate, to be included/associated.

शामिलात sha:mila:t (*nf*) joint property; partnership.

शामिलाती sha:mila:ti: (*a*) joint, held jointly in partnership.

शायक sha:yak (*nm*) an arrow.

शायद sha:yad (*ind*) perhaps, probably, possibly.

शाय/र sha:yar (*nm*) a poet; ~राना poetic, befitting a poet; ~री poetry, poetic composition.

शाया sha:ya: (*a*) published, brought to light; –करना to publish, to bring to light.

शायिका sha:ika: (*nf*) a sleeper berth.

शायित sha:it (*a*) sleeping, lying.

शारद sha:rad (*a*) autumnal; born, produced in or pertaining to autumn; also शारदी, शारदीय (*a*).

शारदा sha:rda: (*nf*) Saraswati:–the goddess of learning; an ancient Indian script prevalent in the tenth century A.D. in the Punjab and Kashmir areas.

शारदीया sha:radi:ya: (*a*) autumnal, pertaining or belonging to the autumn.

शारीर sha:ri:r (*nm*) Anatomy; (*a*) anatomical, corporeal; **-तत्त्व** physical/corporeal/anatomical element; **-विद्या/शास्त्र** (the science of) Anatomy; **~शास्त्रीय** anatomical.

शारीरिक sha:ri:rik (*a*) physical, bodily, corporeal; concrete; **-अभ्यास/व्यायाम** physical exercise; **-शिक्षा** physical education.

शार्दूल sha:rdu:l (*nm*) a tiger.

शाल sha:l (*nf*) a shawl; the sal tree; **~ग्राम** sacred stone worshipped by the Vaishnavas and supposed to be pervaded by the presence of Vishnu (it is black stone containing fossil ammonite).

शाला sha:la: (*nf*) a house, residence; school; suffixed as the second member in compound words to denote a place dedicated to or meant for a particular purpose (as **पाठशाला, धर्मशाला**).

शाली sha:li:—used as an adjectival suffix to mean one who or that which has or possesses (e.g. **बलशाली, संपत्तिशाली**, etc.).

शालीन sha:li:n (*a*) modest, gentle, well-behaved, cultured; **~ता** modesty, gentleness, politeness,

शावक sha:vak (*nm*) young one of an animal.

शाश्वत sha:shvat (*a*) eternal, immortal, perpetual; permanent; **~ता** eternity, perpetuality, immortality; permanence.

शासक sha:sak (*nm*) a ruler; king; master; **-वर्ग** ruling group; **-समाज** the ruling society.

शासकीय sha:saki:y (*a*) governmental, administrative, public; **-क्षेत्र** public sector.

शासन sha:san (*nm*) government, administration; rule; command; **~कर्त्ता** a ruler, administrator; **-तंत्र** polity, system of government; government, regime; **-पत्र** governmental decree; white paper; **-पद्धति/प्रणाली** polity, system of government; **-व्यवस्था** government, system of government.

शासनांतर्गत sha:sanā:ntargat (*a*) under the government/administration.

शासनाधीन sha:sanā:dhi:n (*a*) see **शासनांतर्गत**.

शासनिक sha:sanik (*a*) governmental, administrative.

शासित sha:sit (*a*) governed, ruled; administered.

शासी sha:si: (*a*) governing; **~मंडल** governing body.

शास्ति sha:sti (*nf*) a sanction, consideration operating to enforce obedience to any rule of conduct.

शास्त्र sha:str (*nm*) scripture(s), a religious or scientific treatise, a composition of divine or secular authority; science; a discipline; literature of knowledge; **~कार** the author of a *shastra*; **-चर्चा** study and discussion on *shastras*; **-चिंतक** a learned man, one who reflects and deliberates on *shastras*; **~ज्ञ** one who is well-versed in *shastras*; **-ज्ञान** knowledge of a *shastra* or the *shastras*; **~दर्शी** see **~ज्ञ**; **-दृष्टि** scriptural point of view; viewpoint peculiar to a discipline; **-प्रवक्ता** a spokesman of the scriptures (shastras) or a discipline; **~वर्जित** forbidden by the scriptures (**शास्त्र**); **-विधान** a precept or prescription of the scriptures (*shastras*); -विधि permission of the scriptures (शास्त्र); ~विमुख profane, opposed to or negligent of the scriptures (शास्त्र); ~विरुद्ध opposed to the scriptures; profane, heretic; ~विहित approved of or ordained by the scriptures, provided for in the scriptures (*shastras*); ~संगत/सम्मत see ~विहित; ~सिद्ध proved by the scriptures, in accordance with the scriptures (शास्त्र).

शास्त्रानुमोदित sha:stra:numodit (*a*) approved of or commended by the scriptures.

शास्त्रानुशीलन sha:stra:nushi:lan (*nm*) deliberation upon or study of the scriptures (शास्त्र).

शास्त्रार्थ sha:stra:rth (*nm*) discussion, contention or debate on the scriptures (शास्त्र); the purport or meaning of the scriptures (शास्त्र).

शास्त्री sha:stri: (*a*) see शास्त्रज्ञ; (*nm*) a scholar of or authority on the scriptures (or shastras).

शास्त्रीय sha:stri:y (*a*) scriptural; academic; scientific, disciplinary; classical; –ज्ञान academic knowledge; bookish knowledge; –संगीत classical music.

शास्त्रोक्त sha:strokt (*a*) as ordained by the *shastras*/scriptures; as laid down in a discipline.

शाहंशा/ह shahānsha:h (*nm*) an emperor, a monarch; (*a*) very liberal; ~हियत royal grandeur; majestic conduct; ~ही monarchical, royal; royalty; the royal throne or the duties thereof.

शाह sha:h (*nm*) a king; the king in playing cards or in chess; master; title of Mohammedan fakirs; -ए-वक्त the contemporary ruler; ~कार a masterpiece; ~ख़र्च a spendthrift, extravagant; ~ख़र्ची extravagance, spending with an open hand; ~जादा a prince; ~जादी a princess; –जी a title of Mohammedan fakirs; now a common mode of address in north India, more particularly amongst the Panja:bi:s; ~बलूत the oak (tree); ~बाला see शह(~बाला); ~राह a highway; ~सवार see शह(~सवार).

शाहाना sha:ha:nā: (*a*) kingly, royal, regal, magnificent; –जोड़ा the nuptial suit worn by the bridegroom; –मिजाज lordly/regal temperament.

शाही sha:hi: (*a*) royal, regal, majestic; used as a suffix to denote a system (as नौकरशाही दफ़्तरशाही); liberal.

शिंजिनी shinjinī: (*nf*) the bow-string.

शिकं/जा shikanja: (*nm*) a clamp pressing appliance; clasp, grasp clutches; ~जा कसना to tighten the grasp; ~जे में खींचना to torture; ~जे में जकड़ना to hold tight in one's grasp; ~जे में फँसना to fall into the clutches (of).

शिकन shikan (*nf*) wrinkle, shrivel crease; –न पड़ना to show no grouse whatever.

शिकमी shikmī: (*a*) inherent, instinctive; (*nm*) sub-tenant (of a holding. –काश्तकार a sub-tenant (of a lease), sub-lessee.

शिकवा shikva: (*nm*) a grudge grouse, grievance; -शिकायत grudges grievances and complaints.

शिकस्त shikast (*nf*) defeat; –खाना to suffer defeat; –देना to (inflict a defeat.

शिकस्ता shikasta: (*a*) broken, deva

stated; ~हाल afflicted, broken.

शिकायत shika:it, ~yat (*nf*) a complaint, grievance; accusation, backbiting; –की किताब complaint book; ailment; ~न by way of complaint, as a complaint; –करना to complain; to backbite.

शिकायती shika:iti: (*a*) containing a complaint or grievance; (*nm*) a complainant.

शिकार shika:r (*nm*) a victim, prey; ~गाह hunting ground/resort; –की टट्टी small camouflage of a hunter; –करना to hunt, to prey; to trap; –खेलना to go hunting; –हाथ से जाता रहना/निकल जाना a bird to fly away; –होना to fall a victim/prey (to).

शिकारा shika:ra: (*nm*) a long (partly covered) boat, house-boat.

शिकारी shika:ri: (*a* and *nm*) hunting; a hunter, huntsman; –कुत्ता a hound; –जानवर an animal that kills others for food; -पक्षी a bird of prey.

शिक्ष/क shikshak (*nm*) a teacher; ~कवर्ग/समाज teaching class/community; ~कीय of or pertaining to a teacher/the teacher-community.

शिक्षण shikshaṇ (*nm*) teaching, instruction, education; (*a*) academic, educational;-कला the art of teaching -वृत्ति/व्यवसाय teaching profession; -संस्था educational institution; hence शिक्षणीय (*a*).

शिक्षा shiksha: (*nf*) education, instruction; teaching; moral; -दीक्षा education and initiation; education in general; -पद्धति system of education; -परिषद् academic council; -प्रणाली see -पद्धति; ~प्रद educative; instructive, imparting a moral; hence ~प्रदता (*nf*); -मंत्रालय Ministry of Education; -मंत्री Minister for Education; -विधि method of teaching; -विभाग department of Education; -वृत्ति fellowship; -व्यवस्था academic set-up, educational system; -शास्त्र the science of Education; Pedagogy; ~शास्त्रीय pedagogical.

शिक्षार्थी shiksha:rthi: (*nm*) a student; pupil.

शिक्षालय shiksha:lay (*nm*) a school, educational institution.

शिक्षित shikshit (*a*) educated.

शिक्षु shikshu (*nm*) an apprentice; ~ता apprenticeship.

शिखंडी shikhaṇḍi: (*nm*) a typical fighter in the Maha:bha:rat who was supposed to be a woman in his previous birth and who had vowed to wreak vangeance on the great old warrior–Bhi:shm Pita:-mah; an impotent man, eunuch.

शिखर shikhar (*nm*) a peak, top, summit, pinnacle; vortex, apex; -सम्मेलन a summit conference.

शिखा shikha: (*nf*) a tuft or distinctive lock of hair on the crown of the head, traditionally worn by the Hindus, a top-knot; a pointed flame; the crown of a cock or peacock; apex.

शिखी shikhi: (*nm*) a peacock.

शिगु/फ़्ता shigufta: (*a*) blooming, happy, delighted; ~फ़्तगी bloom; happiness, delightedness.

शिगूफ़ा shigu:fa: (*nm*) a bud, blossom; a titbit, an anecdote; queer utterance; –खिलाना to cause a scene; to make a queer utterance; to let off a squib; -छोड़ना to let off squib.

शिताबी shita:bi: (*a*) hasty, making hurry, rash; ~पन hastiness, rashness.

शिथिल shithil (*a*) loose, lax; slow, tardy, languid; slack; weary; not hard or compact, flaccid; ~प्रयत्न whose effort has been slackened; a spent-up force.

शिथिलता shithilata: (*nf*) looseness, laxity, lassitude; weariness, tardiness, slackness; flaccidity.

शिथिलित shithilit (*a*) loosened, lax; slowed, slackened, wearied, fatigued, exhausted.

शिथिली/करण shithili:karān (*nm*) the act or process of becoming or rendering loose/wearied/exhausted/slack/flaccid/tardy; hence ~कृत (*a*).

शिद्दत shiddat (*nf*) difficulty; severity; intensity; vehemence; –से with difficulty.

शिना/ख़्त shina:ḳht (*nf*) identification; hence ~ख़्ती (*a*).

शिफ़ा shifa: (*nf*) see शफ़ा; ~ख़ाना see शफ़ाख़ाना under 'शफ़ा'.

शिफ़्ट shifṭ (*nm*) a shift; ~वार by shifts.

शिया shiya: (*nm*) one of the two major sects of the Muslims.

शिर:पीड़ा shirahpī:ṛa: (*nf*) headache.

शिर:शूल shirahshu:l (*nm*) see शिर:-पीड़ा.

शिर shir (*nm*) the head; -व्यवच्छेद -व्यवच्छेदन beheading, chopping off the head; ~स्त्राण headwear, head-dress.

शिरकत shirkat (*nf*) partnership; participation; ~नामा partnership deed; –करना to participate.

शिरकती shirkati: (*a*) joint, combined; (in) partnership.

शिरस्थ shirasth (*a*) top, leading, outstanding.

शिरा shira: (*nf*) a vein; -जाल veinous system.

शिरोधार्य shirodha:ry (*a*) worthy of respect or to be respected, to be greatly honoured.

शिरोबिंदु shirobindu (*nm*) zenith; acme, pinnacle.

शिरोमणि shiromāni (*nm*) the most outstanding person; the chief (of) (as कवि-शिरोमणि); a jewel worn in a diadem or crown.

शिरोरेखा shirorekha: (*nf*) headline of the alphabet (as in Devna:gri:).

शिरोवर्ती shirovarti: (*a*) head, chief.

शिला shila: (*nf*) a rock, large piece of stone; foundation stone; cliff; ~मुद्रक lithographer; ~मुद्रण lithograph; ~लिपि/लेख (rock) inscription, petrograph.

शिलान्यास shila:nnya:s (*nm*) laying the foundation/foundation stone.

शिलिंग shiliṅg (*nm*) a shilling (British currency).

शिल्प shilp (*nm*) craft; architecture; -कला technology; craft; ~कार/~ज्ञ a craftsman; an architect; ~कारिता/कारी/-कौशल craftsmanship; ~जीवी a craftsman, an artisan; -विद्या technology; craft; architecture; -विद्यालय a school for crafts; -विधि technique; ~विधिज्ञ technician; ~वैज्ञानिक a technologist; technological; ~शाला a workshop; school for teaching crafts/technology; -संघ craft union.

शिल्पी shilpi: (*nm*) a craftsman; an artist; a sculptor.

शिव shiv (*nm*) one of the divine trio (ब्रह्मा, विष्णु and महेश) of the Hindus; the good; well-being, welfare; (*a*) happy; auspicious; ~भक्त a devotee of Lord Shiv; ~भक्ति devotion to Lord Shiv; ~रात्रि a Hindu festival observed on the fourteenth day of the dark half of the month of Ma:gh; ~लिंग phallus—worshipped as the symbol of Shiv; ~लोक *kaila:sh*—the abode of Shiv; ~वाहन bull—the vehicle of Lord Shiv.

शिव/ता, ~त्व shivata: (*nf*), ~ttv (*nm*) the good; well-being.

शिवालय shiva:lay (*nm*) a temple of Shiv.

शिवाला shiva:la: (*nm*) see शिवालय.

शिविका shivika: (*nf*) a palanquin.

शिविर shivir (*nm*) a camp, tent.

शिशि/र shishir (*nm*) the winter; ~रांत the end of winter.

शिशु shishu (*nm*) an infant; a baby; child; -कल्याण child welfare; -कल्याण केन्द्र child welfare centre; ~गृह a nursery; ~घात/ ~घातक infanticide; -पक्षाघात infantile paralysis; ~पालन rearing of children; ~पालन-गृह a nursery; -बलि child sacrifice; ~हत्या infanticide; -हत्यारा infanticide.

शिशु/ता shishuta: (*nf*), ~त्व ~ttv (*nm*) childhood, infantilism.

शिश्न shishn (*nm*) penis, phallus, male genital organ; ~देव worshippers of the phallus deity.

शिष्ट shishṭ (*a*) civilised, courteous, gentle, decent, well-behaved; ~मंडल a delegation; deputation; -सभा civil council; -समाज civilised society.

शिष्टता shisṭata: (*nf*) civility, courteousness, gentleness, good behaviour, decency: –के नाते out of courtesy/decency.

शिष्टाचार shisṭa:cha:r(*nm*) etiquette; courtesy, decency; –के नाते out of courtesy/etiquette.

शिष्टाचा/री shishṭa:cha:ri: (*a*) courteous, well-behaved, decent in manners, cultured and refined; hence ~रिता (*nf*).

शिष्य shishy (*nm*) a pupil, disciple; student; ~ता/त्व pupilage, discipleship; studentship; -परंपरा discipular lineage/tradition; hence शिष्या (*nf*).

शिस्त shist (*nf*) alignment; a fingertip; –बाँधना to align.

शीआ shi:a: (*nm*) see शिया.

शीघ्र shi:gghr (*adv*) immediately, soon, urgently; promptly, quickly, rapidly, sharp(ly), hurriedly, speedily; ~गामी/गति speedy, fast (moving); ~पात quick ejaculation (in sexual intercourse).

शीघ्रता shi:gghrata: (*nf*) quickness, rapidity, promptitude; hurry, haste/hastiness;–करना to expedite, to hasten, to make haste.

शीत shi:t (*a*) cold, frigid, chilly; (*nm*) the winter; –कटिबंध frigid zone; ~कर/कारी cooling or causing coolness; the moon; ~काल the winter season; ~कालीन winter; pertaining to the winter season; hence ~ता (*nf*); -प्रधान cold; –युद्ध cold war; –लहर a cold wave.

शीतक shi:tak (*a*) causing coolness; freezing.

शीतल shi:tal (*a*) cool; cold, frigid; ~ता coolness; coldness, frigidity; ~पाटी a thin smooth mat prepared from cane.

शीतला shi:tala: (*nf*) small-pox.

शीतोष्ण shitoshn (*a*) temperate, moderate; -जलवायु moderate climate; ~ता temperateness, moderateness.

शीत्कार shi:tka:r (*nf*) the sound of shi:shi: (supposed to indicate the thrill of intense pleasure or agony of severe pain).

शीन shi:n (*a*) frozen, congealed; a letter of the Arbic script; -काफ़ दुरुस्त न होना not to have a flawless pronuciation.

शी/र shi:r (*nm*) a python; milk; ~र-शकर milk and sugar; ० हो जाना to get inseparably intermixed (like milk and sugar), to develop extreme intimacy, to become one with each other.

शीरा shi:ra: (*nm*) syrup; molasses.

शीराज़ा shi:ra:za: (*nm*) the stitching of the back of a book; organisation, integration; ~बंदी stitching of the printed forms of a book; –बिखरना to get disintegrated, to be diffused.

शीरीं shi:rī: (*a*) sweet; lovely; (*nf*) the celebrated beloved of Farha:d; ~कलाम/ज़बान sweet-spoken; ~बयान sweet-spoken; ~बयानी sweet speech.

शीर्ण shi:rṇ (*a*) broken; worn out; crushed, shattered; decayed; ~ता broken or shattered condition, decay; wearing out.

शीर्ष shi:rsh (*nm*) the head; top, summit; apex; line; headline; deck; ~च्छेद/च्छेदन beheading, chopping off the head; ~त्राण headwear, head-dress; –बिंदु the top, the apex; –समाचार headline (news); ~स्थ top; leading, supreme; head, chief; –स्थान top (position); head; ~स्थानीय top; leading, supreme.

शीर्षक shi:rshak (*nm*) a title, heading.

शीर्षासन shi:rsha:san (*nm*) a yogic posture wherein one stands upright on one's head.

शील shi:l (*nm*) modesty; piety, virtue, moral conduct; chastity; (mental) disposition; used as a suffix to denote natural or acquired disposition of aptitude (as प्रगतिशील, क्रोधशील, etc.); -त्याग abandonment of modesty; ~धारी well-behaved, modest; -भंग outrage of modesty; ~वर्जित devoid of modesty/moral conduct; –तोड़ना to become harsh, to be blunt; to outrage the modesty (of); –न होना to have no modesty; –निभाना to stick to one's own disposition; to be good inspite of provocation; to retain one's modesty.

शील/वान shi:lvā:n (*a*) modest; well-behaved, urbane, of good moral character, pious, virtuous; hence ~वती feminine form.

शीश shi:sh (*nm*) the head; an allomorph of शीशा used as the first member in compound words; -ए-दिल heart—as brittle as glass; ~फूल a head ornament; ~महल a palace fitted with mirrors all round; ० में बंदर a bull in China shop; –झुकाना/नवाना to bow (in reverence/deference/obeisance).

शीशम shishām (*nf*) the Indian rosewood tree—*Dalbergia sisso*.

शी/शा shi:sha: (*nf*) glass, a mirror, looking glass; ~शे में उतारना to confine (a ghost etc.) into a glass bottle; to bring under control; ~शे में मुंह तो देखो lit. have a look at yourself in the looking glass—Damn it ! You don't deserve it; what nonsense !

शीशी shi:shi: (*nf*) a small bottle, a phial, a vial; –सुंघाना to render senseless.

शुंड shuṇḍ (*nm*) the trunk of an elephant.

शुक shuk (*nm*) a parrot; ~नास/नासिका having a parrot-like nose.

शुक्ति shukti (*nf*) an oyster, a pearl oyster; -तट oyster-bank, oyster-bed.

शुक्र shukkr (*nm*) semen; (the planet)

Venus; Friday; thanks, (an expression of gratitude); see शुक्राचार्य; ~गुज़ार grateful, thankful; thanksgiver; ~गुज़ारी gratefulness, thanks-giving; ~वार Friday; –करना to thank God; –है thanks, it is God's kindness, thank God !

शुक्राचार्य Shukkra:cha:ry (*nm*) mythologically, the preceptor of the Asuras (demons)—opposite number of बृहस्पति in the demonic camp; one-eyed person.

शुक्राणु shukkrā:ṉū (*nm*) a spermatozoon.

शुक्राना shukra:nā: (*nm*) thanks-offering—money paid by a client to one's legal counsel (and his clerks) over and above the usual remuneration (for winning a case).

शुक्राशय shukkra:shay (*nm*) the vesicular seminalis.

शुक्रिया shukriya: (*nm*) thanks (giving), (expression of) gratitude; (*int*) thanks !, thank you !; –अदा करना to thank.

शुक्ल shukl (*a*) white, clean; (*nm*) a sub-division of Bra:hmans; –पक्ष the moonlit half of a lunar month.

शुग़ल shugal (*nm*) hobby; fun; avocation; –करना to have fun.

शुचि shuchi (*a*) pure, sacred, virtuous; clean; ~ता/त्व purity, sanctity; virtuousness; clean(li)-ness.

शुतुरमुर्ग़ shuturmurg (*nm*) an ostrich.

शुदा shuda:—used as an adjectival suffix to impart the meaning of 'that which has been (performed) or is accompanied by' (as रजिस्ट्रीशुदा, शादीशुदा).

शुदि shudi (*ind*) see सुदी.

शुद्दा shudda: (*nm*) hardened faeces (on account of lack of lubrication in the bowels).

शुद्ध shuddh (*a*) pure; unadulterated; sacred; uncorrupt; correct; rectified, amended; clean; natural (note—in music); net (as—लाभ); ~गतिविज्ञान kinematics; ~मति honest, scrupulous, straightforward; ~हृदय clean, clean-hearted; hence ~हृदयता (*nf*).

शुद्ध/ता, ~त्व shuddhata: (*nf*), ~ttv (*nm*) purity; sacredness; state of being unadulterated/uncorrupted; correctness; rectification; cleanliness; naturality of a note (in music).

शुद्धाचार/वाद shuddha:cha:rva:d (*nm*) puritanism; ~वादी a puritan; puritanic.

शुद्धात्मा shuddha:tmā: (*a*) virtuous, noble, clean at heart.

शुद्धाद्वैत/वाद shuddha:dvaitva:d (*nm*) philosophical doctrine propounded by the mediaeval saint-philosoper Vallabha:cha:ry who believed in the माया-free (शुद्ध) non-dualistic element as the Ultimate Reality; hence ~वादी (*a, nm*).

शुद्धि shuddhi (*nf*) purity; correction; correctness; rectification; purification; -पत्र corrigendum; errata; -संस्कार purificatory rite.

शुद्धी/करण shuddhikarāṉ (*nm*) purification; purgation; rectification; hence ~कृत (*a*).

शुभ shubh (*a*) auspicious; good; (*nm*) the good, well-being; –कर्म a good deed; ~कामनाएँ good wishes; –ग्रह an auspicious/favourable star; ~चिंतक a well-wisher; ~दर्शन good-looking; of auspicious aspect; –मुहूर्त auspicious moment/instant; –शकुन a good omen; –संदेश good news;

~सूचक portending good; –सूचना good news; ~स्य शीघ्रं well done, soon done; the sooner done, the better.

शुभाकांक्षी shubha:kā:ṅkshi: (*nm* and *a*) (a) well-wisher; well-wishing.

शुभागमन shubha:gāmān (*nm*) welcome, welcome arrival.

शुभाशीर्वाद shubha:shi:rva:d (*nm*) blessings, benediction.

शुभाशीष shubha:shi:sh (*nm*) see शुभाशीर्वाद.

शुभाशुभ shubha:shubh (*a*) good and evil; pleasant and unpleasant; agreeable and disagreeable; –फल good and evil result.

शुभेच्छु shubhechchu (*a* and *nm*) well-wishing, well-wisher, one who wishes well.

शुभैषी shubhaishi: (*a* and *nm*) well-wishing; well-wisher, one who wishes well.

शुभ्र shubbhr (*a*) radiant, shining; clear, spotless (as कीर्ति); bright-coloured; white; ~ता radiance; spotlessness; whiteness, brightness.

शुमार shuma:r (*nm*) counting accounting; computing; calculation; numbering; –करना to count; to take into account; –में न रहना, –में न होना to be countless; to be unaccountable; –में न लाना to ignore, not to take into account; hence शुमारी (as in मर्दुमशुमारी census).

शुमा/ल shuma:l (*nm*) left hand; the north; ~ली northern.

शुरू shuru: (*nm*) beginning, commencement; –करना to begin, to commence, to initiate; –होना to be commenced, to be initiated.

शुरूआत shuru:a:t (*nf*) beginning, commencement; initiation; –करना to make a beginning, to initiate; –होना to be commenced, to be initiated.

शुल्क shulk (*nm*) fee; subscription; duty; -दर tariff; -पद्धति tariff (system); ~मुक्त duty-free; –, वार्षिक annual subscription.

शुश्रूषा shushru:sha: (*nf*) attendance, nursing.

शुष्क shushk (*a*) dry/dried; withered, parched; arid; emaciated; tedious (as–कार्य); prosaic; unfeeling; hard; ~ता dryness; parched condition; aridity; witheredness; emaciatedness/emaciation; tedium, prosaicness; unfeeling temperament; hardness; –व्यवहार unfeeling dry behaviour.

शूक shu:k (*nm*) a bristle.

शूकर shu:kar (*nm*) a boar, hog, pig.

शूटिंग shu:ṭiṅg (*nf*) shooting (of a movie film etc.).

शू/द्र shu:ddr (*nm*) a member of the fourth of the four original classes or castes in the traditional hierarchical set-up of the Hindu society; hence ~द्रा, ~द्राणी (*nf*).

शून्य shu:nny (*a*) empty, void; vacant (as—दृष्टि); hollow; desolate; absent-minded; non-existent; (*nm*) a cipher, zero; void, voidance; vacunm, blank; emptiness; space; non-entity; absolute non-existence; ~क vacuum, void; ~चित्त absent-minded, vacant-minded; ~ता/त्व emptiness; desolateness; absent-mindedness; nothingness; non-existence; illusory nature (of all worldly phenomena); –बिन्दु the mark of a cipher, zero mark; –भाव emptiness, state of being empty; absent-mindedness; ~मनस्क/मना absent-minded, vacant-minded; hence ~मनस्कता (*nf*); ~वाद

nihilism; the Buddhist doctrine of non-existence (of any spirit–either Supreme or human); ~वादी a nihilist; a believer in or affirmer of the ~वाद; nihilistic; ~हस्त empty-handed, indigent.

शून्यीकरण shu:nni:karān (*nm*) evacuation; causing a void/vacuum; rendering blank.

शूर shu:r (*a* and *nm*) valiant, brave, heroic, gallant, mighty, valorous (man); a hero; warrior; ~ता/त्व heroism, valour, bravery, gallantry; ~म्मन्य one who thinks himself a hero; -वीर brave and valorous, hero, valiant; ~सेन mediaeval name of the territory lying in and around Mathura:.

शूर्पणखा shu:rpanakha: (*nf*) the notorious sister of demon king Ra:van in the Rama:ya:n whose nose was chopped off by Lakshman at the instance of Ra:m to punish her for her brazen sexual overtures; an ugly snub-nosed woman.

शूल shu:l (*nm*) sharp or acute pain (esp. in the stomach); grief, sorrow; any sharp and pointed instrument: a spear prong; ~धारी/पाणि wielding a spear; an epithet of Lord Shiv; ~हर removing or relieving pain; –उठना to suffer from sharp/acute pain; –देना to inflict sorrow, to torment/torture.

शूलना shu:lnā: (*v*) to inflict pain/sorrow, to torture/torment.

शृंखला shrinkhala: (*nf*) a chain, fetters; series, order; range; connection;belt; ~बद्ध systematic, orderly; bound by a chain or fetters; hence ~बद्धता (*nf*).

शृंखलित shrinkhalit (*a*) systematic, orderly; bound by chain or fetters; strunged together.

शृंग/ग shring (*nm*) top/summit (esp. of a mountain), peak; pinnacle, acme; horn (of an animal); ~गी horned,

शृंगार shringa:r (*nm*) love, the erotic sentiment, sexual passion or desire; elegant, make-up; adornment; गीत amorous/amatory song-a song conveying erotic/amorous feelings; -चेष्टा love/amorous gesture, indication of love through gestures; –रस one of the nine *rasas* – according to Indian Poetics, this one is the most comprehensive and extensive and is known as रसराज (the king of *rasas*); शृंगारात्मक amatory / amorous, erotic.

शृंगारी shringa:ri: (*a*) inspired by amorous passion/erotic feeling/love; disposed to prank/make-up.

शृगा/ल shriga:l (*nm*) a jackal; hence ~ली (*nf*).

शेख़ shekḥ (*nm*) one of the four major sub-castes amongst muslims.

शेख़चिल्ली shekḥchilli: (*nm*) a conventional fool who builds castles in the air, a typical nitwit ever living in a fool's paradise; –के मनसूबे fantastic schemes.

शेखर shekhar (*nm*) the top or crown of the head.

शेख़ी shekḥi: (*nf*) boast, brag; ~ख़ोर/ख़ोरा/~बाज़ boastful; a braggadocio, braggart, boaster; ~बाज़ी boastfulness;–किरकरी होना -झड़ना to be humiliated, all sense of boastfulness to be knocked off; –बघारना / -मारना / –हाँकना to blow one's own horn, to boast, to brag.

शेड shed (*nm*) a shade; shed.

शेफाली shepha:li: (*nf*) *Vitex negunda.*

शेयर shear (*nm*) a share; –**बाज़ार** share market; ~**होल्डर** a shareholder.

शेर sher (*nm*) a lion; couplet (in Urdu poetry); ~**दहाँ** lion-mouthed, (a house) having the front shaped like a lion's mouth; ~**दिल** with the heart of an oak, lion-hearted—brave, intrepid, fearless; ~**नुमा** formed like a lion, lion shaped; ~**बच्चा** young one of a lion; fearless, intrepid; ~**बबर** a lion; –**मर्द** a masculine man, he-man, lion-like man;–**करना** to cause to become fearless; to encourage too far; **की खाल में गधा** an ass in lion's skin; –**की माँद में घुसना/हाथ डालना** to do a risky job, to do a job involving pretty risk to life; –**के मुँह में जाना** to undertake a risk of life; to face a hazard to life; –**के मुँह से शिकार छीन लेना** to salvage somebody from the jaws of death; **चहों का शिकार नहीं करता** the eagle doesn't hawk at flies; –**बकरीका एक घाट पानी पीना** to have rule of perfect equity; to have the same treatment meted out to high and low; –**होना** to become too cheeky; to be encouraged too far.

शेरवानी sherwa:nī: (*nf*) a typical long-tight coat.

शेवाल sheva:l (*nm*) algae.

शेष shesh (*a* and *nm*) rest, remaining; outstanding; residue; balance, remainder; ~**काल** the moment/time of death; ~**नाग** name of the celebrated mythological thousand-headed serpent (regarded as an emblem of eternity); ~**शायी** Lord Vishnū (who is supposed to sleep over the **शेषनाग** during intervals of creation).

शेषांश sheshā:nsh (*nm*) the remaining portion, remainder, residue.

शै shai (*nf*) a thing, article, object.

शैक्षणिक shaikshanik (*a*) of or pertaining to **शिक्षण** (teaching); academic; –**दृष्टि से** academically.

शैक्षिक shaikshik (*a*) academic, educational; scholastic; –**जगत** academic world; –**व्यवस्था** academic set-up.

शैतान shaita:n (*nm*) the Satan, devil; a mischief monger; (*a*) naughty; mischievous, guileful, wicked; ~**वाद** satanism; –**का बच्चा** mischievous through and through, extremely guileful; –**का लश्कर** a horde of mischief-mongers;–**की आँत** a tale that knows no end, any long-winding thing; –**की आरती उतारना** to hold a candle to the devil; –**की ख़ाला** a quarrelsome woman; –**उतरना** to be liberated from a devilish obsession; to be pacified; –**के कान काटना** to outdo a devil in devilism; –(**सिर पर**) **चढ़ना /सवार होना** to be obsessed by a devilish passion; to be too enraged.

शैतानी shaita:nī: (*nf*) naughtiness; mischievousness, wickedness; –**लश्कर** a horde of mischief-mongers; –**हरक़त** a devilish deed, mischief.

शैथिल्य shaithily (*nm*) looseness, laxity; lethargy ;flaccidity, relaxation;unsteadiness; laches; negligence, inattention.

शैदा shaida: (*a*) love crazy, erotomaniac; ~**ई** lover, love-crazy.

शैल shail (*nm*) a rock; hill, mountain; ~**राज** the Himalayas; -**संधि** a valley; pass.

शैलि/की shailiki: (*nf*) petrology; ~**कीय** petrological.
शैली shai:li: (*nf*) style; diction; manner, method; ~**कार** a stylist; ~**बद्ध** stylised; ~**विज्ञान** stylistics.
शैलेंद्र shailēndr (*nm*) the Himalayas.
शैलेय shailey (*a*) rocky, craggy; hilly, mountainous.
शैव shaiv (*nm*) a worshipper/devotee of Lord Shiv; (*a*) pertaining or belonging to Lord Shiv.
शैवाल shaiva:l (*nm*) see **शेवाल**.
शैशव shaishav (*nm*) childhood; infancy; infantilism.
शोक shok (*nm*) sorrow, grief; condolence; -**गीत** an elegy; dirge; ~**ग्रस्त** sorrowful, grieved, afflicted by sorrow; bereaved; ~**मय** sorrowful, full of grief/sorrow; ~**विकल** overwhelmed by sorrow; ~**विह्वल** afflicted with sorrow; ~**संतप्त** consumed by sorrow, grief-stricken; -**संदेश** a condolence message; -**सभा** a condolence meeting.
शोकाकुल shoka:kul (*a*) overwhelmed by sorrow.
शोकातुर shoka:tur (*a*) see **शोकाकुल**.
शोकाभिभूत shoka:bhibhu:t (*a*) see **शोकाकुल**.
शोकार्त्त shoka:rtt (*a*) grieved, overwhelmed/overpowered/afflicted by grief/sorrow.
शोकावेग shoka:veg (*nm*) intensity of grief; fit or paroxysm of sorrow.
शोख़ shokḥ (*a*) insolent; playful, sportive; coquettish; bright, loud (as–**रंग**).
शोख़ी shokḥi: (*nf*) insolence; playfulness, sportiveness; coquetry; brightness, loudness (as of **रंग**).
शोच shoch (*nm*) see **सोच**.
शोचनीय shochanī:y (*a*) critical; causing concern/anxiety; hence ~**ता** (*nf*).
शोच्य shochchy (*a*) see **शोचनीय**.
शोणित shōnit (*nm*) blood; (*a*) red, bloody; -**शर्करा** blood sugar.
शोथ shoth (*nm*) swelling, morbid intumescence.
शोध shodh (*nf*) research; purification; cleansing, refinement; rectification, correction; setting right; (re-)payment; calculation regarding hour of marriage; ~**कर्त्ता** a researcher; rectifier; -**क्षमता** solvency; -**पत्र/पत्रिका** research gournal; -**प्रबंध** reseach thesis, dissertation; –**लेख** research article,
शोधन shodhan (*nm*) purification; cleansing, refinement; rectification, correction, setttng right; (re-) payment; treatment; hence **शोधक** (*nm*); **शोधनीय, शोधित, शोध्य** (*a*).
शोधना shodhnā:(*v*) to purify/cleanse/refine/ correct; to work out an auspicious moment (for marriage etc.) by astrological calculation.
शोधार्थी shodha:rthi: (*nm*) a researcher, research scholar.
शोबा shoba: (*nm*) part, branch.
शोभ/न shobhan (*a*) befitting, becoming; graceful; hence ~**नीय** (*a*).
शोभा shobha: (*nf*) grace, elegance, beauty; glamour, splendour, brilliance, lustre; ~**मय** splendid, brilliant, lustrous, radiant; beautiful; ~**यात्रा** pageant; ~**शून्य/हीन** devoid of glamour/grace/beauty; ugly.
शोभान्वित shobha:nnvit (*a*) full of lustre or beauty, glamorous, graceful.
शोभायमान shobha:ymā:n (*a*) looking graceful/pretty/splendid/brilliant, beautiful, lustruous.
शोभित shobit (*a*) splendid, radiant, beautiful, adorned or embellish-

ed.

शोर shor (*nm*) noise; tumult, din, hue and cry; **-गुल/शराबा** noise, tumult, din; hue and cry; **०मचाना** to blow great guns, to be too boisterous.

शोरबा shorba: (*nm*) soup, broth.

शोरा shora: (*nm*) soda, nitre (sodium nitrate); **~पुश्त** insolent, unruly.

शोला shola: (*nm*) a flame of fire; **–भड़कना** a flame to burst suddenly; **शोलों को हवा देना** to fan the flame.

शोशा shosha: (*nm*) a projecting point (as in some Arabic letters); queer thing; feeler; **–छोड़ना** to let off a squib, to give a feeler.

शोषक shoshak (*nm*) an exploiter, one who exploits; an absorber, that which absorbs; hence **~ता** (*nf*); **-वर्ग** exploiting class.

शोष/ण shoshāṇ (*nm*) exploitation; soaking; hence **~णीय** (*a*).

शोषित shoshit (*a*) exploited.

शोहदा shohda: (*nm*) a rogue, knave, scoundrel; libertine; a bad egg/hat; **~पन** roguery, scoundrelism, knavery.

शोहरत shohrat (*nf*) fame; renown, celebrity.

शौक़ shauq (*nm*) fondness; fancy; hobby; **-करना/फ़रमाना** to enjoy; to be fond of; to have a fancy for; **–चर्राना** to be extremely fond (of); to manifest fondness for; **–से** with great pleasure.

शौक़िया shauqiya: (*a* and *adv*) amateurish; as a hobby; fondly, fashionably; (*nm*) an amateur.

शौक़ीन shauqi:n (*a*) fashionable; fond of fine things; foppish, dandy; **~मिज़ाज** fashionable; foppish, dandy; hence **~मिज़ाजी** (*nf*).

शौक़ीनी shauqi:nī: (*nf*) fashionableness, fondness; foppishness, dandyism.

शौच shauch (*nm*) evacuation of excrement, toilet, ablution; cleanliness; purification (esp. from defilement caused by the death of a relation); **–कर्म** act of purification; evacuation of excrement; **~गृह** see **शौचालय**.

शौचालय shaucha:lay (*nm*) a latrine, lavatory.

शौरसेनी shaursenī: (*a*) a regional variation of the Pra:krit (**–प्राकृत**) and the Apabhransh (**–अपभ्रंश**) languages.

शौर्य shaury (*nm*) chivalry, gallantry, valour, heroism.

शौहर shauhar (*nm*) husband; **-बीवी** husband and wife.

श्मशान shmasha:n (*nm*) the cremation ground, crematorium, nacropolis; **-वैराग्य** momentary detachment from mundane affairs aroused in the cremation ground; **-साधन** magical or *tantric* rites performed by sitting over the chest of a corpse in the cremation ground; **–जगाना** to undertake *tàntric* rites in the **श्मशान**; to keep the **श्मशान** fire burning.

श्मश्रु shmashshru (*nm*) beard and moustache.

श्यान shyā:n (*a*) viscous; **~ता** viscosity.

श्याम shya:m (*a*) black, dark-coloured; dark blue; (*nm*) Lord Krishṇā; **~पट्ट** a black-board; **~सुंदर** Lord Krishṇā; hence **श्यामा** (*nf*).

श्यामता shya:mta: (*nf*) blackness, dark colour/complexion.

श्याम/ल shya:mal (*a*) dark-complexioned, dark-coloured, black; hence **~लता**, **~लिमा** (*nf*).

श्यालक shya:lak (*nm*) a brother-in-law—wife's brother.

श्येन shyen (*nm*) a hawk, falcon.

श्रद्धांजलि shraddhā:ṇjali (*nf*) tribute, homage; -**अर्पित करना** to pay homage/tribute.

श्रद्धा shraddha: (*nf*) faith, veneration; reverence; ~**मय/युक्त** see ~**वान**; ~**रहित/शून्य/हीन** faithless, infidel; ~**हीनता** infidelity, faithlessness.

श्रद्धालु shraddha:lu (*a*) having faith/veneration, trustful; ~**ता** the state of having faith/belief, trustfulness.

श्रद्धावान shraddha:vā:n (*a*) having faith, trustful, believing.

श्रद्धास्पद shraddha:spad (*a*) venerable, worthy of or deserving faith/reverence.

श्रद्धेय shraddhey (*a*) venerable, reverend; worthy of faith.

श्रम shram (*nm*) labour, toil, exertion; -**अधिकरण** labour tribunal; -**कण** perspiration (caused by hard work); ~**कर/कारी** causing fatigue; -**कल्याण** labour welfare; ०**अधिकारी** labour welfare officer; ~**क्लांत** fatigued, tired by toil; ~**जल** see ~**कण**; ~**जीवी** a worker, labourer, one who lives by one's sweat; -**तंत्र** labour machinery; ~**दान** voluntary contribution of labour for a public cause; -**मंत्रालय** Ministry of Labour; -**मंत्री** Labour Minister; ~**बिंदु** see ~**कण**; ~**वाद** labourism; -**विधि** labour law; -**विभाग** labour department; -**विवाद** labour dispute; ~**शील** laborious, assiduous, hard-working; hence ~**शीलता** (*nf*); -**संघ** a labour union; ~**साध्य** arduous, strenuous; hence ~**साध्यता** (*nf*).

श्रमण shramān (*nm*) a Buddhist monk/mendicant.

श्रमिक shramik (*nm* and *a*) a labourer; labour; -**आंदोलन** labour movement; -**नेता** labour leader; -**वर्ग** labour class; -**विवाचन** labour arbitration; -**संघ** a labour union.

श्रमी shramī: (*a* and *nm*) assiduous, hard-working, laborious (person).

श्रवण shravān (*nm*) an ear, organ of hearing; audition; -**गुण** acoustics (of a room etc.); ~**गोचर** audible, perceptible through the ear; -**पथ** the ears; -**विषय** object of hearing; -**योग्य** audible.

श्रवणीय shravanī:y (*a*) audible, perceptible through the ear; worth hearing; auditory; hence ~**ता** (*nf*).

श्रवणेंद्रिय shravanēndriy (*nf*) ear—the organ of hearing.

श्रव्य shravvy (*a*) audible; worth hearing; -**काव्य** one of the two main divisions of literature in Sanskrit Poetics—literature that can be read and heard (the other being **दृश्य काव्य**—literature that is to be presented on the stage); ~**ता** audibility; range of audibility.

श्रांत shra:nt (*a*) tired, wearied, fatigued, exhausted; ~**चित्त/मना** wearied or exhausted.

श्रांति shrā:nti (*nf*) tiredness, weariness, fatigue, exhaustion; ~**कर** tiring, arduous, wearying.

श्राव/ण shra:van (*nm*) the fifth month of the year according to the Hindu calendar (one of the rainy months); ~**णी** a festival celebrated on the full moon-day of **श्रावण** (see **सावन**).

श्री shri: (*a*) an honorific adjective prefixed to male names; Mr.; (*nf*) Lakshmi—the goddess of wealth;

wealth, treasure, prosperity; lustre, brilliance, radiance, splendour; ~गणेश commencement (of an auspicious work, rite, etc.); ०करना to break ground; to commence a work/process; ~मंत having or possessing श्री; prosperous, rich; aristocrat; ~मान् an honorific title prefixed to male names, Mr ; Sir (also used in an address); ~मुख (used in deference) radiant/graceful face/mouth; ~युत an honorific title prefixed to male names, Mr.; ~हीन lack-lustre; hence ~हीनता (*nf*).

श्रुत shrut (*a*) heard, received through the ear.

श्रुति shruti (*nf*) the Vedas; ear; ~कटु disagreeable to the ear; harsh (sound, words, etc.); -मधुर agreeable, sweet, melodious; ~सम्मत ordained by the Vedas.

श्रेणी shreṇī: (*nf*) class; category, rank, order; range; series; ~करण categorization; hence ~कृत (*a*); ~बद्ध categorized; hence ~बद्धता (*nf*).

श्रेय shrey (*nm*) credit; the good; summum bonum, bliss; the highest coveted other-worldly achievement; -और प्रेय achievements for the other world and in this world; hence ~वाद (*nm*); ~वादी (*a, nm*).

श्रेयस् shreyas (*nm*) see श्रेय; ~कर good, salutary, conducive to happiness.

श्रेष्ठ shreshṭḥ (*a*) the best; good; excellent, superior; hence ~तर (*a*); ~तम (*a*); ~त्व (*nm*), ~ता (*nf*).

श्रेष्ठि shreshṭḥi (*nm*) a distinguished wealthy man.

श्रोणि shrōṇi (*nf*) the waist; hip, buttocks; ~देश the region of hips.

श्रोतव्य shrotavvy (*a*) worth hearing; audible.

श्रोता shrota: (*nm*) a listener; audience; ~गण audience; -वर्ग audience.

श्लथ shlath (*a*) languid, slothful; flaccid; feeble; diffused; hence ~ता (*nf*).

श्लाघनीय shla:ghni:y (*a*) praiseworthy, laudable, admirable, commendable; hence ~ता (*nf*).

श्लाघा shla:gha: (*nf*) praise, admiration, commendation.

श्लिष्ट shlishṭ (*a*) punned; equivocal, susceptible of double interpretation; clasped, joined together; hence ~ता (*nf*).

श्लीपद shli:pad (*nm*) elephantiasis.

श्लील shli:l (*a*) clean, not vulgar.

श्लेष shlesh (*nm*) pun, paranomasia; agnomination.

श्लेष्म shleshm—an allomorph of श्लेष्मा as it appears in compound words; ~क phlegm, phlegmatic humour; ~ल phlegmatic.

श्लेष्मा shleshmā: (*nm*) phlegm, mucus.

श्लोक shlok (*nm*) a (Sanskrit) couplet; hymn of praise; praise, glory; ~बद्ध composed into a श्लोक, versified.

श्वसन shvasan (*nm*) (the act or process of) respiration, breathing; -रंध्र nostril(s).

श्वान shwa:n (*nm*) a dog; -निद्रा lit. dog's sleep—light slumber, sleeping with one eye open.

श्वास shwa:s (*nm*) breath, respiration; -कष्ट hard breathing; -क्रिया the act of breathing; -नली bronchital tube; -प्रश्वास breathing in and out; -रोध obstruction of breath, suffocation.

श्वासोच्छ्वास shwa:sochchhwa:s (*nf*) deep inspiration and expiration, respiration.

श्वेत shwet (*a*) white; bright; blemishless; spotless; fair-complexioned; ~कुष्ठ leucoderma; –केश grey hair; –पत्र a white paper; ~प्रदर leucorrhoea.

श्वेतांबर shweta:mbar (*nm*) one who dons white; one of the two chief sects of Jainism (the other being दिगंबर).

ष

ष sha—the second of the sibilant-trio (श, ष, स) of the Devna:gri: alphabet. In Modern Hindi sound pattern, however, this has lost its identity and is invariably pronounced as palatal sibilant (श) rather than as cerebral (as it originally was).

षंड shanḍ (*nm*) a bull; bullock.

षका/र shaka:r (*nm*) the letter ष and its sound; ~रांत (a word) ending in ष्.

षट् shaṭ (*a*) six; (*nm*) the number six; ~कर्ण heard by six ears, heard by a third person (besides the speaker and listener); having six ears; very alert, attentive; ~कोण a hexagon; six angled; ~खंड having six parts/divisions; ~चक्र the six mysterious *chakras* (viz. मूलाधार, अधिष्ठान, मणिपुर, अनाहत, विशुद्ध and आज्ञा of the body according to हठयोग); ~पद/पाद six-footed; big male black-bee; ~शास्त्र the six schools of Indian philosophy (viz. न्याय, सांख्य, योग, वैशेषिक, पूर्वमीमांसा and उत्तरमीमांसा); ~शास्त्री well-versed in all the six *shastras*.

षड् shaḍ—an allomorph of षट् (six) appearing as the first member in some compound words; ~अंग (षडंग) the six principal parts of the body (viz. the head, the waist, two hands and two feet); ~आनन/मुख six-faced, having six faces—(कार्तिकेय –the god of war); ~ऋतु the six seasons of the year (viz. ग्रीष्म, वर्षा, शरत, हेमन्त, शिशिर, वसंत); ~ज the first of the primary notes of Indian music; –दर्शन see षट्शास्त्र (under षट्); ~धा in six ways; ~भुज a hexagon; ~रस the six main tastes or flavours of food (viz. मीठा, नमकीन, कड़वा, तीता, कसैला, खट्टा); ~राग the six main strains in Indian music (viz. भैरवी, मल्हार, श्री, हिंडोल, मालकोस and दीपक); see झंझट; ~रिपु the six internal enemies of man according to Indian tradition (viz. काम, क्रोध, मद, लोभ, मोह, मत्सर); ~विध of six kinds/varieties, in six ways.

षड्यंत्र shaḍyāntr (*nm*) a conspiracy, plot, an intrigue; ~कारी a conspirator, an intriguer; –रचना to hatch a conspiracy/plot, to conspire.

षण् shaṇ—an allomorph of षट् (six) appearing as the first member in some compound words; ~मासिक six-monthly; ~मुख six-faced (viz. कार्तिकेय—the god of war).

षष्टि shashṭi (*a*) sixty; (*nm*) the number sixty; ~पूर्ति (observation or celebration of) the sixtieth birthday; ~वर्षी of sixty years.

षष्ठ shashṭḥ (*a*) sixth.

षष्ठांश shashṭḥa:nsh (*nm*) the sixth part.

षष्ठी shashṭḥi: (*nf*) the sixth day of a fortnight; the sixth day from the day of child-birth; possessive case; -पूजन/पूजा the worship of goddess दुर्गा on the sixth day after child-birth; -विभक्ति the genitive case-ending.

षाण्मासिक sha:ṇm:āsik (*a*) six monthly, half-yearly.

षोडश shoḍash (*a*) sixteen; (*nm*) the number sixteen; -श्रृंगार see सोलह सिंगार.

षोडशी shoḍashi: (*nf*) a girl of sixteen years of age, a girl in the prime of youth.

स

स sa—the last of the sibilant-trio (श, ष, स) of the Devna:gri: alphabet. In Hindi sound-pattern, this one happens to be the most dominant of the three; used as a prefix to mean accompanied by, along with, with (as सपत्नीक accompanied by one's wife); belonging to the same, alike; having affinity (as सगोत्र); good (as सपूत).

संकट sāṅkaṭ (*nm*) a crisis, emergency; danger, hazard; -की घड़ी hour of crisis, critical moment; -की स्थिति emergency, crisis; -के बादल मँडराना a crisis to hover around; -के साथी a friend in need; ~पूर्ण/मय dangerous, hazardous; ~स्थ in distress, in the grip of a crisis.

संकटापन्न sāṅkaṭa:pann (*a*) in distress, in difficulty, afflicted.

संकर sāṅkar (*a*) hybrid, cross; intergrade; ~ज cross-breed; ~ता hybridism; -शब्द a hybrid word.

संकरण sāṅkaran (*nm*) heterodyne; cross-breeding; hybridization.

सँक/रा sākra: (*a*) narrow; strait; ~रे में पड़ना to be in difficulty, to be in distress.

संकरी/करण sāṅkari:karaṇ (*nm*) hybridization, cross-breeding; hence ~कृत (*a*).

संकल/न sāṅkalan (*nm*) compilation; collection; assemblage; summation; ~क/नकर्त्ता a compiler, assembler.

संकलप sāṅkalap (*nm*) see संकल्प.

संकलपना sāṅkalpanā: (*v*) see संकल्पना.

संकलित saṅkalit (*a*) compiled, collected; amassed, assembled.

संकल्प sāṅkalp (*nm*) determination, resolve; resolution, will; animus; -शक्ति will power; -करना to resolve; to gift away; -पारित करना to pass a resolution.

संकल्पना sāṅkalpnā: (*nf*) concept; (*v*) to make a resolve; to conceive (of); ~वाची conceptual; ~वाची शब्द a conceptual word.

संकल्प/वाद sāṅkalpva:d (*nm*) voluntarism; ~वादी a voluntarist; voluntaristic.

संकल्पनात्मक sāṅkalpana:tmāk (*a*) conceptual; pertaining to resolution/determination.

संकल्पित sāṅkalpit (*a*) imaginary, fancied; conceptual.

संका/य saṅka:y (*nm*) a faculty (in a University); ~याध्यक्ष Dean (of a faculty).

संकीर्ण sāṅki:rṉ (*a*) parochial, narrow; ~ता parochialism, narrowness.

संकीर्तन saṅki:rtan (*nm*) (collective) singing of hymns/devotional songs.

संकुचित sāṅkuchit (*a*) parochial, narrow; mean; contracted; –दृष्टि narrow/parochial outlook.

संकुल sāṅkul (*a*) crowded; congested; confused, chaotic; ~ता crowdedness, congestion.

संकेत sāṅket (*nm*) a sign; signal; indication, hint; tip; token; rendezvous; -चिह्न abbreviations; -शब्द a keyword; -स्थल rendezvous; -वाक्य logogram.

संकेतक sāṅketak (*nm* and *a*) a pointer; indicative (of).

संकें/द्रण sāṅkendrāṉ (*nm*) concentration; ~द्रित concentrated.

संकेतित sanketit (*a*) indicated, hinted, pointed.

संकोच sāṅkoch (*nm*) hitch, hesitation; shyness; contraction ~शील shy, bashful; reserved; hesitant; hence ~शीलता (*nf*).

संकोची sāṅkochi: (*a*) hesitant; reserved; shy, bashful.

संक्रमण sāṅkrāmāṉ (*nm*) infection; contagion; transition; transgression; -काल transitional period; ~नाशक disinfectant; ~शील infectious, infective; hence ~शीलता (*nf*); संक्रमित (*a*).

संक्रामक sāṅkra:mak (*a*) infectious; contagious; –रोग an infectious/contagious disease.

संक्रामण sāṅkra:māṉ (*nm*) causing to be infected; causing contagion; transference/transfer.

संक्रिया sāṅkriya: (*nf*) operation; ~त्मक operational.

संक्षिप्त sāṅkshipt (*a*) brief, short, summary; abridged; –टिप्पणी a brief note; ~ता brevity; abridgement: –संस्करण abridged edition.

संक्षिप्तावृत्ति sāṅkshipta:vritti (*nf*) recapitulation.

संक्षिप्ति sāṅkshipti (*nf*) abridgement; brevity.

संक्षिप्तीकरण sāṅkshipti:karāṉ (*nm*) summarization; abridgement.

संक्षुब्ध sāṅkshubdh (*a*) turbulent; agitated.

संक्षेप sāṅkshep (*nm*) a compendium; summary, brief; abbreviation; abridgement; ~त: in brief/short; –में in short, in brief; summarily.

संक्षेपण sāṅkshepāṉ (*nm*) abridgement; summarization; precis.

संक्षेपाक्षर sāṅkshepa:kshar (*nm*) initials; abbreviation.

संखिया sāṅkhiya: (*nf*) arsenic, white arsenic; –देना to poison; to administer arsenic.

संख्यक sāṅkhyak–used as an adjectival suffix denoting number, numbering (as अल्पसंख्यक forming a minority in numbers).

संख्यांकन sāṅkhya:ṅkan (*nm*) numbering.

संख्या sāṅkhya: (*nf*) a number; numeral; figure; strength; degree; ~तीत innumerable; ~त्मक numerical; ०दृष्टि से numerically (speaking).

संग sāṅg (*nm*) company, association, contact; attachment; stone; (*ind*) with, along with; ~ज born through contact; ~दिल stone-hearted, cruel; ~दिली stone heartedness, cruelty; ~मरमर marble; ~मरमरी white and gracious like marble; ~रोध quarantine; –सोना to go to bed (with).

संगठन sāṅgaṭhan (*nm*) (the act or process of) organization (or an organised body or system or society); union, unity; consolidation; –में शक्ति है union is strength.

संगठित sāṅgaṭhit (*a*) organised.

संगण/न, ~ना sāṅgaṇān (*nm*), ~nā: (*nf*) computation; reckoning; –करना to compute/reckon.

संगत sāṅgat (*nf*) company; accompaniment; (*a*) relevant; logical, rational; compatible; –करना to accompany; ~कार an accompanist; ~ता rationality; logicality; relevance; compatibility.

संगतरा/श sāṅgtara:sh (*nm*) a stone-cutter/carver/dresser; ~शी stone cutting/carving/dressing.

संगति sāṅgati (*nm*) company, association; consistency/consistence; compatibility; rationality; coherence, harmony; relevance; –देना to rationalise; –बैठना to be harmonised; to become coherent/cogent; to tally.

संगतिया sāṅgatiya: (*nm*) an accompanyist.

संगम sāṅgam (*nm*) a confluence; union; junction, juncture; federation; ~न meeting, coming together.

संगर sāṅgar (*nm*) a battle, fighting, hedge.

संग/लन sāṅgalan (*nm*) fusion; ~लक fuse; ~लित fused.

सँगाती sāga:ti: (*nm*) a companion; an associate.

संगिनी sāṅginī: (*nf*) a female companion.

संगी sāṅgi: (*nm*) a companion; an associate; -साथी friends and companions.

संगीत sāṅgi:t (*nm*) music; -, कंठ vocal music; ~कार a composer; -नाटक an opera; -निदेशक music director; –, वाद्य instrumental music; -विभाग department of music; –, शास्त्रीय classical music; -संकाय faculty of music.

संगीतज्ञ sāṅgi:taggy (*nm*) a musician, one well-versed in music; hence ~ता (*nf*).

संगीताचार्य sāṅgi:ta:cha:ry (*nm*) master of musical art; a great musical composer.

संगीतात्मक sāṅgi:ta:tmak (*a*) musical; melodious; ~ता musicality; element of music, musical quality, melodiousness.

संगीन sāṅgi:n (*nf*) bayonet; (*a*) serious; critical; –जुर्म serious crime; –हालत critical condition; –की नोक पर at the point of the bayonet.

संगृहीत sāṅgrihi:t (*a*) collected; gathered, amassed; compiled.

संग्रह sāṅgreh (*nm*) collection; compilation; compendium; repository, deposit, storage; reserve; ~कर्त्ता compiler, one who collects/stores/compiles.

संग्रहण sāṅgrahān (*nm*) collection; reception; ~शील receptive; ~शीलता receptivity.

संग्रहणी sāṅgrahnī: (*nf*) an acute form of chronic diarrhoea.

संग्रहणीय sāṅgraha:nī:y (*a*) fit to be collected/preserved, fit to be acquired; hence ~ता (*nf*).

संग्रहालय sāṅgraha:lay (*nm*) a museum; -अध्यक्ष curator.

संग्रही sāngrahi: (*a*) given to collection/accumulation, of accumulative disposition.

संग्राम sāngra:m (*nm*) war, battle; fight, combat.

संग्राहक sangra:hak (*a*) receptive; ~ता receptivity.

संघ saṅgh (*nm*) a federation; union; league, organisation, association; ~चारी gregarian, moving in groups: -न्यायालय Union court; -भाव/भावना/वृत्ति esprit de corps, team spirit; ~वाद federalism; ~वादी a federalist; federalistic.

संघटक saṅghaṭak (*a*) component, constituent; (*nm*) component/constituent part, ingredient; -तत्व constituent factor; component, ingredient.

संघटन saṅghaṭan (*nm*) organisation; formation; constitution, composition.

संघट्ट saṅghaṭṭ (*nm*) impact, collision; multitude; hence ~न (*nm*).

संघर्ष saṅgharsh (*nm*) struggle; conflict, strife, friction; ~शील prone to struggle; hence ~ शीलता (*nf*).

संघर्षण saṅgharshaṇ (*nm*) struggle/struggling; conflict/conflicting, friction, strife.

संघर्षी saṅgharshi: (*a*) fricative; struggling, conflicting.

संघात saṅgha:t (*nm*) stroke, blow; heap, multitude.

संघाधिपत्य/वाद saṅgha:dhipattyva:d (*nm*) syndicalism; ~वादी a syndicalist; syndicalistic.

संघाराम saṅgha:ra:m (*nm*) a Buddhist monastery.

संघी saṅghi: (*nm*) member of a *sangh*; (*a*) belonging or pertaining to a *sangh*; federal.

संघीय saṅghi:y (*a*) federal; pertaining to union, union.

संचय sāṇchay (*nm*) accumulation, collection: reserve, deposit; hoard; hence ~न (*nm*); ~शील (*a*); ~शीलता (*nf*).

संचयी sāṇchai: (*a*) who accumulates/collects/saves.

संचरण sāṇcharaṇ (*nm*) transmission; movement (of a body etc.); hence ~शील (*a*); ~शीलता (*nf*).

संचलन sāṇchalaṇ (*nm*) movement; locomotion.

संचायक saṇcha:yak (*nm*) one who accumulates, accumulator.

संचार sāṇcha:r (*nm*) communication; transmission; movement; -मंत्रालय Ministry of Communications; -मंत्री Minister for Communications; -साधन means of communication; -व्यवस्था communication system.

संचारण sāṇcha:raṇ (*nm*) (the act or process of) communication, transmission: movement.

संचारी sāṇcha:ri: (*a*) communicable; mobile, moving; an auxiliary sentiment in Poetics which strengthens the main sentiment (also called–भाव); –रोग a communicable disease.

संचारेक्षण sāṇcha:rekshaṇ (*nm*) monitoring; -व्यवस्था monitoring system.

संचालक sāṇcha:lak (*nm*) a director; conductor: hence ~ता (*nf*).

संचालन sāṇcha:lan (*nm*) direction; conduction (as of a meeting etc.).

संचालित saṇcha:lit (*a*) directed, conducted.

संचित sāṇchit (*a*) accumulated; collected, gathered; reserved; hoarded; –कर्म accumulated past deeds (held in reserve for retribution); hence संचिति (*nf*).

संजाफ़ sāṇja:f (*nf*) a border cloth: border (in a quilt-cover etc.).

संजीदगी sāṇji:dgi: (*nf*) solemnity: seriousness/gravity, sobriety; **–के साथ/–से** solemnly, seriously/gravely; in a sober manner.

संजीदा sāṇji:da: (*a*) solemn, serious, grave; sober; hence **~पन** (*nm*).

संजीवनी sāṇji:vanī: (*nf*) an elixir; a kind of plant with powers to reanimate/revive or restore the dead to life; also **–बूटी**.

संजोग sanjog (*nm*) see **संयोग**.

सँजोना sājonā: (*v*) to put things systematically/in order; to arrange, to arrange in a presentable manner; to keep in good shape.

संज्ञक saṅgyak—an adjectival suffix meaning–'named'.

संज्ञा sāṅgya: (*nf*) (in Gram.) a noun; denomination, name; appellation; consciousness; **-उपवाक्य** nominal clause; **–, जातिवाचक** a common noun; **·पदबंध** noun/nominal phrase; **~प्रधान** nominal; **–, भाववाचक** an abstract noun; **~वान** in senses. conscious; having a name; **–, व्यक्तिवाचक** a proper noun; **~हीन** unconscious: hence **~हीनता** (*nf*).

संज्ञापन sāṅgya:pān (*nm*) an advice; notification.

सँझला sājhla: (*a*) younger than the middle (brother).

सँझवाती/संझावाती sājhva:ti:/sāṇjha:-va:ti: (*nf*) an evening song sung at the time of lighting the lamps.

सँझोखा sājhokha: (*nm*) dusk, twilight.

संड sāṇḍ (*nm*) a bull: **·मुसंड** stout/robust fellow (said contemptuously).

संड़सी sārsi: (*nf*) pincers, household iron forceps.

संडा sāṇḍā: (*a*) stout/robust (fellow ––said of a man in a contemptuous vein).

संडास sāṇḍa:s (*nm*) a lavatory, latrine.

सँड़ासी sāṛa:si: (*nf*) see **सँड़सी**.

संत sānt (*a* and *nm*) saintly; a saint; **~पन (पना)** saintly stance; hypocritic behaviour; **·समागम** association with saints; a congregation of saintly people.

संतत sāntat (*a*) continuous.

संतति sāntati (*nf*) offspring, progeny; **-निग्रह/निरोध** family planning.

संतप्त sāntapt (*a*) grieved, distressed, tormented, troubled.

संतरण sāntarāṇ (*nm*) crossing over.

संतरा sāntara: (*nm*) an orange.

संतरी sāntari: (*nm*) a sentry.

संतान sānta:n (*nf*) issue, progeny; **–निग्रह/निरोध** see **संतति-निग्रह/निरोध**.

संताप sānta:p (*nm*) grief, distress, woe, sorrow, contrition, compunction.

संतुलन sāntulan (*nm*) balance, equilibrium, equipoise.

संतुलित sāntulit (*a*) balanced, equipoised, in equilibrium

संतु/ष्ट sāntushṭ (*a*) satisfied, gratified; content; hence **~ष्टि** (*nf*).

संतृ/प्त sāntript (*a*) saturated; satiated, gratified; **~प्ति** saturation; satiety, gratification.

संतोल sāntol (*nm*) balance, equilibrium, equipoise; hence **~न** (*nm*).

संतोष sāntosh (*nm*) satisfaction, gratification; contentment; **~जनक/प्रद** satisfactory; **–कड़ुआ है पर फल मीठा** patience is bitter but its fruit sweet; **–परम धन है** a contented mind is a contented feast, contentment is more than a kingdom.

संतोषी sāntoshi: (*a* and *nm*) (*a*)

contented (person); –परम/सदा सुखी content is happiness.

संत्रस्त sāntrast (*a*) terrorised, horrified, frightened, alarmed.

संत्रास sāntra:s (*nm*) terror, horror, fright, alarm.

संदंश sāndānsh (*nm*) forceps; sting.

संदर्भ sāndarbh (*nm*) reference, context; allusion; -ग्रंथ a reference book/work; bibliography; –ग्रंथसूची bibliography; ~गत contextual; ~गर्भित allusive; ~छिन्न torn from the context; -सहित with reference to the context; –साहित्य reference literature.

संदर्शिका sāndārshika: (*nf*) a guide (book).

संदल sāndal (*nm*) sandal (wood).

संदि/ग्ध sāndigdh (*a*) doubtful, uncertain; ambiguous, equivocal, amphibological; suspicious; ~ग्धता ambiguity, equivocation, amphibology; ~ग्धार्थ ambiguous, equivocal, amphibological; ~ग्धार्थक see ~ग्धार्थ; ~ग्धार्थकता ambiguity, equivocation, amphibology.

संदूक sāndu:k (*nm*) a box; hence ~ड़ी (*nf*).

संदूक/चा sāndu:kcha: (*nm*) a box; hence ~ची fem. (dim.) form.

संदेश sāndesh (*nm*) a message; –काव्य a poetic form wherein a lover sends his message of love and yearning to the beloved through clouds, aves, etc.; ~वाहक/~हर a messenger.

संदेशा sādesha: (*nm*) see संदेश.

संदेह sāndeh (*nm*) a doubt, suspicion; ~जनक doubtful, arousing suspicion; hence ~जनकता (*nf*); ~शील suspicious, of suspicious disposition; hence शीलता (*nf*).

संधान sāndhā:n (*nm*) searching; aiming at; joining together, uniting, union; fixing (as an arrow on the bow).

संधारण sāndha:rān (*nm*) maintenance; -व्यय maintenance cost.

संधि sāndhi (*nf*) a treaty; conjunction, union; (in Grammar) morphophonemic change—euphonic junction of final and initial sounds (as राम+आज्ञा=रामाज्ञा, देव+इन्द्र=देवेन्द्र); liaison; a juncture or division of a drama (reckoned to be five, viz. मुख, प्रतिमुख, गर्भ, विमर्श and निर्वहण); joint; articulation; ~कर्त्ता a treaty-maker, peacemaker; -काल a period of conjunction of two stages or states; -पत्र a treaty; -, मैत्री an alliance; -भंग to break or violate a treaty; -विच्छेद separation of the constituents in a conjunct word; -, विराम armistice; -, शांति peace treaty.

संध्या sāndhya: (*nf*) evening, twilight; select Vedic hymns recited in the morning or evening prayers; -काल evening (time); ~कालीन pertaining to the evening; ~लोक twilight; -वंदन (evening) prayers.

संध्योपासना sāndhyopa:snā: (*nf*) evening prayers/meditation/adoration.

संना/द sānna:d (*nm*) consonance; ~दी harmonic.

संन्यास sānnya:s (*nm*) renunciation, asceticism; abandonment of worldly ties or mundane interests; the fourth stage of life according to Hindu tradition (when one is supposed to renounce all worldly considerations)—see आश्रम; —लेना to renounce the world.

संन्यासी sannya:si: (*nm*) an anchorite; an ascetic, a monk; one who has renounced the world; hence ~सिन fem. form.

संपत्ति sāmpatti (*nf*) property; estate, wealth; affluence, prosperity; -कर property-tax; ~वान/शाली opulent, wealthy.

संपदा sāmpada: (*nf*) wealth; opulence, prosperity.

संपन्न sāmpann (*a*) prosperous, rich; well-off; completed, accomplished; ~ता prosperity, wealthiness.

संपर्क sāmpark (*nm*) contact; liaison; -अधिकारी liaison officer; -स्थापित करना to establish contact.

संपा/त sāmpa:t (*nm*) coincidence; ~ती coincident.

संपादक sāmpa:dak (*nm*) an editor; ~त्व editorship; मंडल board of editors; hence संपादिका feminine form (of संपादक).

संपादकीय sampa:dki:y (*nm* and *a*) (an) editorial; ~, उप sub-editor; -दायित्व editorial responsibility; -विभाग editorial department; -, सह co-editor; -, सहायक assistant editor.

संपादन sāmpa:dān (*nm*) editing; accomplishment.

संपादित sampa:dit (*a*) edited; accomplished.

संपीड़न sampi:ṛān (*nm*) compression, pressing, squeezing; affliction; harassing.

संपीड़ित sāmpi:ṛit (*a*) compressed, squeezed; afflicted, harassed.

संपुट sāmpuṭ (*nm*) a hemispherical bowl or any thing so shaped (as when the two palms are joined together leaving hollow space in between); a posture of coitus.

संपुटक sāmpuṭak (*nm*) a matrix.

संपूरक sāmpu:rak (*nm* and *a*) a supplement; supplementary; hence ~ता (*nf*).

संपूर्ण sāmpu:rṇ (*a*) whole; entire; complete; perfect; finished; total; ~तः/तया wholly, entirely; completely; totally; perfectly; ~ता entirety, completeness, perfection; -होना to be completed/finished; to be perfect.

संपूर्ति sāmpu:rti (*nf*) compensation; fulfilment; completion.

सँपेरा sāpera: (*nm*) a snake-charmer.

सँपोला sāpola: (*nm*) young one of a snake; a water-snake.

संप्रति sāmprati (*ind*) at present, now.

संप्रतिपत्ति sāmpratipatti (*nf*) consensus.

संप्रदान sāmpradā:n (*nm*) the act of giving or bestowing, handing over, the dative case (in Grammar); -कारक the dative case.

संप्रदाय sāmprada:y (*nm*) a community; sect; ~गत/परक communal; sectarian; ~वाद communalism; sectarianism; ~वादी (*a*) communalist; sectarian; ०दृष्टिकोण communal/sectarain outlook.

संप्रवाह sāmprava:h (*nm*) a flux, flow.

संप्रश्न sāmprashn (*nm*) an interpellation.

संप्राप्ति sampra:pti (*nf*) acquisition; attainment.

संप्रेषण sampreshan (*nm*) communication; despatch; ~णीय communicable; to be communicated; ~णीयता communicability.

संप्रेषक sampreshak (*nm*) sender, one who despatches/communicates.

संप्रेष्य sāmpreshshy (*nm*) content (to be communicated); communicable; (*a*) see संप्रेषणीय; ~ता see संप्रेषणीयता.

संबंध sāmbāndh (*nm*) relation/relationship; connection; association; affinity, ~वाचक genitive, possessive (case); –जोड़ना to establish relations with; –टूटना relations to be cut off/broken.

संबंधन sāmbāndhān (*nm*) affiliation; connection.

संबंधित sāmbāndhit (*a*) related, connected, affiliated.

संबंधी sāmbāndhi: (*nm*) a relative/relation: used as a suffix to mean related with or pertaining to.

संबद्ध sāmbaddh (*a*) joined, connected, attached to; bound; affiliated; related; relevant; ~ता relevance; -होना to be affiliated/connected.

संबल sāmbal (*nm*) support, backing.

संबलित sāmbalit (*a*) reinforced.

संबोध/न sāmbodhān (*nm*) address; calling aloud; the vocative case (in Grammar); ·गीति an ode; ~नकारक the vocative case.

संबोधित sambodhit (*a*) addressed; –करना to address.

संभरक sāmbharak (*nm*) a supplier.

संभरण sāmbharāṉ (*nm*) supply; ~कर्त्ता a supplier; -विभाग department of supply.

संभलना sābhalnā: (*v*) to pull (oneself) together; to be alert; to be supported; to save from a fall; to upstay, to be cautious.

संभव sāmbhav (*a*) possible; hence ~ता (*nf*).

संभवत sāmbhavtah (*adv*) possibly, probably; perhaps.

संभार sāmbha:r (*nm*) equipment; accumulation/collection.

सँभार Sābha:r (*nf*) maintenance upkeep.

सँभाल sābha:l (*nf*) care-taking, upkeeping, maintenance; being in senses.

सँभालना sābha:lnā: (*v*) to take care of; to support; to hold; to keep in careful custody; to manage; to supervise.

संभावना sāmbha:vnā: (*nf*) possibility, probability, likelihood.

संभावित sāmbha:vit (*a*) probable, likely (to happen).

संभाविता sāmbha:vita: (*nf*) probability; likelihood; chance.

संभाव्य sambha:vy (*a*) probable; ~ता probability.

संभाषण sāmbha:shāṉ (*nm*) dialogue, talks.

संभोग sāmbhog (*nm*) coition, carnal intercourse, sexual enjoyment; delight, pleasure; -शृंगार see संयोग-शृंगार (under संयोग).

संभोग्य sāmbhoggy (*a*) enjoyable, fit to be consumed/used/enjoyed; fit for coition.

संभ्रम sāmbhram (*nm*) confusion; awe; ~कारी confusing; awe-inspiring.

संभ्रांत sāmbhrā:nt (*a*) respectable, well-to-do; confused; hence ~ता (*nf*); –परिवार a well-to-do family; ~मना confused; awe-struck.

संभ्रांति sāmbhrā:nti (*nf*) respectability; confusion/perplexity.

संयंत्र sānyāntr (*nm*) a plant (fixtures, machinery, etc. used in industrial process); –स्थापित करना to erect a plant.

संय/त sānyat (*a*) controlled, restrained, guarded; sober; ~तता state of being under control, restraint; sobriety; ~ति control, restraint; sobriety.

संय/म sānyām (*nm*) (self) restraint, control, check; moderation, temperance; sobriety; ~मी who exercises control over self, moderate, temperate, abstemious; sober.

संयुक्त sānyukt (*a*) united; joint; mixed, blended; (two or more consonants) combined; –कुटुंब/परिवार joint family; –खाता joint account; hence ~ता (*nf*); –मंत्रिमंडल coalition cabinet; –राष्ट्र संघ United Nations Organisation; –वाक्य compound sentence; –सम्पत्ति joint property.

संयुक्ताक्षर sanyukta:kshar (*nm*) consonant cluster.

संयोग sānyog (*nm*) coincidence, chance; accident; mixture; coalition, combination; conjunct consonant; communion, union; carnal contact; –शृंगार in Poetics, one of the two kinds of शृंगार रस wherein the lover and the beloved are united; –से by chance; –से पा जाना to blunder upon, to find by fluke.

संयोजक sānyojak (*nm*) a convenor; conjunction (in Grammar); -चिह्न a hyphen; ~ता convenorship; valence/valency.

संयोजन sānyojan (*nm*) the act of joining or uniting, conjugation; composition; assemblage/assembly; attachment.

संयोजी sānyoji: (*nm*) a matrix; that which binds together.

संरक्षक sānrakshak (*nm*) a guardian; patron; protector; conservator; custodian; ~ता guardianship custodianship.

संर/क्षण sānrakshān (*nm*) guardianship; patronage, protection; conservation; tutelage; ~क्षण-काल protectorate; ~क्षण-शुल्क protective duty; ~क्षा protection; guardianship, custody; ~क्षित guarded, protected; preserved; conserved; a ward; hence ~क्षी (*a*); ~क्षित राज/प्रदेश a protectorate.

संरचना sānrachnā: (*nf*) structure; composition; anatomy; ~गत/~त्मक/परक structural; ~त्मक भाषाविज्ञान structural linguistics.

संरेखण sānrekhān (*nm*) the act or process of aligning; alignment.

संलग्न sānlagn (*a*) attached, enclosed, appended; adjacent; engaged; associated; –पत्र enclosure, enclosed letter: hence ~ता (*nf*).

संलाग sānla:g (*nm*) an attachment.

संलेख sānlekh (*nm*) a protocol.

संवक्ता sāmvakta: (*nm*) a rapporteur.

संवत् sāmvat (*nm*) a contraction of **संवत्सर** (see), a year; era (as *shak* or *Vikrami*:) year.

संवत्स/र sāmvatsar (*nm*) a year; ~रीय annual, yearly.

संवरण sāmvarān (*nm*) selection, liking; subjugation of passions; complication (in a dramatic plot).

संवरणी sāmvarāni: (*nf*) a sphincter.

सँवरना sānarnā: (*v*) to be mended/amended/rectified; to be arranged, to be put in order; to be made up; to be decorated, to be pranked; to be tip-top.

सँवरिया sāvariya: (*nm*) an epithet of Lord Krishnā; a lover, hero.

संवर्ग sāmvarg (*nm*) a cadre.

संवर्धक sāmvardhak (*nm* and *a*) a magnifier; culturist; magnifying, providing nourishment, helping in growth or causing to grow.

संवर्धन sāmvardhān (*nm*) magnification; enrichment; culture; promotion; increase, growth.

संवर्धित sāmvardhit (*a*) magnified; grown, increased; promoted; enriched.

संवहन sāmvahān (*nm*) (the act or process of) conduction; carrying/

bearing.

संवातन sāmva:tān (*nm*) ventilation; -व्यवस्था ventilation.

संवाद sāmva:d (*nm*) a dialogue; conversation, discussion; news; information, message; ~दाता a correspondent, pressman; ~हर a messenger.

संवा/दी sāmva:di: (*a*) concordant (as a note–संवादी स्वर in music); agreeing or harmonising with; ~दिता likeness, concordance; harmoniousness.

सँवार sānwa:r (*nf*) maintenance/maintaining, upkeep; -सुधार repairs, maintenance, upkeep.

सँवारना sāva:rnā: (*v*) to make up; to dress up neatly; to prank; to decorate; to arrange; to mend/amend/rectify; to channelize along successful lines.

संवा/हन samva:hān (*nm*) conduction; ~ही a conductor, that which conducts.

संविदा sāmvida: (*nm*) a contract; compact; –करना to enter into a contract; ~कारी contracting; ०पक्ष contracting party.

संविधा/न sāmvidhā:n (*nm*) constitution; ~न, अनम्य rigid constitution; ~न, नम्य flexible constitution; ~नवाद constitutionalism; ~न-विशेषज्ञ constitutional expert; ~न-सभा constituent assembly; ~निक constitutional; ~निक सभा a constituent assembly; ~नी constitutional(ist).

संविहित sāmvihit (*a*) constitutional; valid, tenable; prescribed, enjoined.

संविरचना sāmvirachnā: (*nf*) composition.

संवृत samvrit (*a*) closed; wound up; subjugated (as passions); –स्वर closed vowel.

संवृद्धि sāmvriddhi (*nf*) enrichment; growth; increase.

संवेग sāmveg (*nm*) momentum; impetus; emotion, passion; ~वाद emotive theory; -सिद्धांत emotive theory,

संवेगात्मक sāmvega:tmak (*a*) emotional, passionate; hence ~ता (*nf*).

संवेदन sāmvedan (*nm*) sensation, feeling; sensitizing; the act or process of experiencing; ~कारी sensitizer; causing sensitiveness; ~वाद sensationalism; sensitivism; -शक्ति sensitivity; ~हारी anaesthetic.

संवेदनशील sāmvedanshi:l (*a*) sensitive, sensible; feeling; ~ता sensitivity, sensitiveness; feeling.

संवेदना sāmvednā: (*nf*) sensitivity, sensation; sensibility, feeling; ~त्मक sensitive; sensory; ~कारी anaesthetaising.

संवेदनीय sāmvedani:y (*a*) sensible, perceptible (through senses); worth experiencing.

संवेदिक sāmvedik (*a*) sensory.

संवेदिता sāmvedita: (*nf*) sensitivity, sensitiveness.

संवेदी sāmvedi: (*a*) sensitive; sensory.

संवेद्य sāmveddy (*a*) sensible: perceptible (through senses); worth experiencing; ~ता sensibility, perceptibility (through) the senses; worthiness of experience.

संवैधानिक samvaidha:nīk (*a*) constitutional; ~ता constitutionality; constitutionalism.

संशय sānshay (*nm*) suspicion, doubt; uncertainty; ~वाद scepticism; ~वादी sceptic, scepticist.

संशयात्मक sānshaya:tmāk (*a*) doubtful; uncertain; hence ~ता (*nf*).

संशयात्मा sanshaya:tma: (*a*) sceptic, unbelieving, of suspicious nature.

संशयालु sānshaya:lu (*a*) sceptic; suspicious; **~ता** scepticism suspiciousness.

संशयी sānshai: (*a* and *nm*) a sceptic, suspicious (person),

संशोधक sānshodhak (*nm* and *a*) a mendor/rectifier / purifier; who amends or corrects.

संशोधन sānshodhān (*nm*) amendment; correction, rectification; revision; purification; **~वाद** revisionism; **~वादी** a revisionist; revisionistic.

संशोधित sānshodhit (*a*) corrected; amended, revised; improved; purified.

संश्रय sānshray (*a*) alliance; coverture.

संश्लिष्ट sānshlisht (*a*) synthetic; synthesised; mixed up.

संश्ले/ष, ~षण sānshlesh, ~shan (*nm*) synthesis; synthesism; **~षणीय** worth synthesising; fit to be synthesized, **~षात्मक** (**~षणात्मक**) synthetic (al); hence **~षात्मकता, ~षणात्मकता** (*nf*); **~षित** synthesised, mixed up.

संस/द sānsad (*nf*) parliament; **~दसदस्य** member of parliament; **~दीय** parliamentary; **०व्यवस्था** parliamentary system; **~दीय सरकार** parliamentary government.

संसर्ग sānsarg (*nm*) intercourse; association, commingling; contact; contagion; connection; conjunction; **~ज, ~जात** contagious, born through contact/contagion; **-दोष** evil consequence of association (with evil); misophobia; **-रोध** quarantine.

संसाधन sānsa:dhān (*nm*) resource; **-सम्पन्न** resourceful.

संसार sānsa:r (*nm*) the world; **-चक्र** circuit of worldly existence; **-बंधन** the worldly fetters; **-सागर** the ocean of the world; **-छोड़ना/त्यागना** to renounce the world; to depart for the other world; **-से उठ जाना/चले जाना/विदा होना** to expire.

संसारी sānsa:ri: (*nm* and *a*) a mortal being; belonging to the world, mundane.

संसिक्त sānsikt (*a*) drenched; fertilized.

संसृति sānsriti (*nf*) the world, course of mundane existence.

संस्करण sānskarān (*nm*) an edition, issue (of a journal etc); correction; curing; **-, लघु** pocket edition; **-, राज** de-luxe edition; **-, संक्षिप्त** abridged edition.

संस्कार sānska:r (*nm*) mental impression(s) (forming the mind); sacrament; rite/ritual, ceremony; purification; improvement, refinement; **~वान, ~शील** cultured, well-reared, of refined taste; hence **~शीलता** (*nf*); **~हीन** uncultured, ill-bred/ill-reared, unrefined.

संस्कारी sanska:ri: (*a*) cultured, well-reared, having refined taste.

संस्कृत sanskrit (*a*) cultured, refined; Sanskrit (language); **~मूलक** derived from or born of the Sanskrit language; **-, लौकिक** classical Sanskrit; **-, वैदिक** vedic Sanskrit; **संस्कृतीकरण** sanskritisation.

संस्कृति sanskriti (*nf*) culture; **~हीन** uncultured, having no culture.

संस्तु/ति sānstuti (*nf*) recommendation; **~त** recommended.

संस्था sānstha: (*nf*) an institution; organisation, concern; **~गत** institutional; **~बद्ध** formed into an institution; institutionalised.

संस्थान sānsthā:n (*nm*) an institute.

संस्थापक sānstha:pak (*nm*) a founder; -सदस्य a founder-member.

संस्था/पन sānstha:pan (*nm*) establishment/establishing, founding; ~पना establishment, founding; ~पित founded, established.

संस्थि/ति sansthiti (*nf*) collection; ~त collected.

संस्पंदन sānspāndān (*nm*) resonance, resonation.

संस्पर्श sānsparsh (*nm*) contact; touch.

संस्मरण sānsmarāṉ (*nm*) memories, reminiscences; ~शील reminiscent.

संस्मारक sānsma:rak (*a*) memorial.

संस्मृति sansmriti (*nf*) reminiscence; mneme; -विज्ञान mnemonics, mnemotechny; -विषयक mnemonic, mnemotechnic.

संहत sānhat (*a*) compact; assembled, collected, gathered; –भाषा compact language; –शैली compact style.

संहति sānhati (*nf*) a mass; system; compactness; ~वाद syncrotism.

संहार sānha:r (*nm*) annihilation; massacre; -करना to annihilate; to massacre; ~कारी see संहारक.

संहारक sānha:rak (*a*) an annihilator; destroyer, slaughterer.

संहारी sānha:ri: (*nm* and *a*) annihilator/annihilating; destroyer/destructive.

संहृति sānhit (*a*) gathered, accumulated; heaped up; mixed; uninterrupted; ~ति accumulation; mixing; uninterruptedness.

संहिता sānhita: (*nf*) a code; -,आचार code of conduct; ~करण codification; ~कार a codifier; ~बद्ध codified.

सआदत saa:dat (*nf*) the good, virtue; ~मंद good, virtuous; obedient; ~मंदी goodness, virtuousness; obedience.

सइन sain (*nf*) an ulcer.

सइयाँ sāīyā: (*nm*) lover; husband.

सई sai: (*nm*) prosperity; increase; effort; just (सही); –साँझ just evening, as soon as it is evening; -सिफ़ारिश manipulation, wire-pulling.

सई/स sai:s (*nm*) a groom; ~सी the work or function of a groom.

सकंटक sakāṉṭak (*a*) thorny, hazardous, full of obstructions.

सकंप, ~न sakāmp, ~an (*a*) shivering, tremulous, vibrating.

सकट sakaṭ (*nm*) a cart.

सकत sakat (*nf*) strength, power; –भर as far as possible.

सक/ता sakta: (*nm*) state of being confounded/flabbergasted, awe; ~ते की हालत में in a stunned state; ~ते में आना to be flabbergasted/stunned.

सकना saknā: (*v*) can; may; to be capable/competent; to be able to handle/deal with (तुम उससे सकोगे नहीं).

सकपका/ना sakpaka:nā: (*v*) to be startled/amazed, to be confounded out of wits; to be overawed; hence ~हट (*nf*).

सकर sakar (*nf*) sugar; ~कंद/कंदी sweet potato; ~पारा/पाला a kind of lozenge-shaped sweet (or saltish) fried preparation.

सकरा sakara: (*a*) see सखरा.

सकरुण sakaruṉ (*a*) pitiful, compassionate.

सकर्मक sakarmāk (*a*) transitive; –क्रिया a transitive verb; ~ता transitiveness.

सकल sakal (*a*) whole, all, entire; total.

सकाम saka:m (*a*) desirous, inspired by a desire; lustful; ~**ता** state of being desirous or inspired by desire; lustfulness; –**भक्ति** devotion with an ulterior motive.

सका/र saka:r (*nm*) the letter **स** and its sound; acceptance; ~**रना** to accept; ~**रांत** (a word) ending in **स**; ~**रात्मक** positive, affirmative; ० **और नकारात्मक** affirmative positive and negative; hence ~**ता** (*nf*).

सकारे saka:re (*adv*) early in the morning, at day-break.

सक़ील saqi:l (*a*) difficult, abstruse (e.g.—**ज़बान**).

सकु/चना, ~**चाना** sakuchnā: ~cha:nā: (*v*) to hesitate: to be abashed/ashamed: to wither (as a flower); to shrink; ~**चाहट** hesitation/hitch; shyness; bashfulness; shame; ~**चीला** ~**चौहाँ** hesitant; shy, bashful.

सकुन sakun (*nm*) see **शकुन**.

सकुल sakul (*a*) with family, with kith and kin.

सकूनत saku:nāt (*nf*) (place of) residence.

सकृत sakkrit (*ind*) once.

सकेलना sakelnā: (*v*) to push; to gather up, to collect.

सकोच sakoch (*nm*) see **संकोच**.

सकोड़ना sakoṛnā: (*v*) see **सिकोड़ना**.

सकोरा sakora: (*nm*) an earthen cup.

सक़्क़ा saqqa: (*nm*) a water-bearer, one who carries water in a large leathern bag; **सक़्क़े की बादशाही** short-lived spell of authority/reign.

सक्तु, ~**क** saktu, ~k (*nm*) a meal of parched and powdered grain.

सक्रिय sakkriy (*a*) active; ~**ता** activity.

सक्षम sakshām (*a*) competent; capable; –**अधिकारी** competent authority; ~**ता** competence; capability.

सखर/च, ~**ज** sakharach, ~j (*a*) lavish, unsparing, open handed.

सख/रा, ~**री** sakhra: (*nm*); ~ri : (*nf*) food cooked in water (as opposed to **निखरा** i.e. cooked in or with ghee).

सखा sakha: (*nm*) a friend, companion; -**भाव** friendship; friendly feeling; -**समाज** circle/company of friends.

सख़ावत sakḥa:wat (*nf*) bounteousness, generosity, openhandedness.

सखी sakhi: (*nf*) a (female) friend, (female) companion; –**संप्रदाय** a sect of Vaishnāvas wherein the devotee considers himself to be his deity's spouse; hence –**भाव** this type of devotion.

सख़ी sakḥi: (*a*) bounteous, generous, open-handed; –**से सूम भला जो तुरंत दे जवाब** he gives twice who gives in a trice.

सख़ुन sakḥun (*nm*) poetry, verse; conversation; ~**तकिया** a pop-word, an expletive, a habitual or favourite word or phrase used by a speaker every now and then without meaning anything.

सख़्त sakḥt (*a*) hard; harsh (as —**अल्फ़ाज़**); strong, stiff; strict; rigorous; serious (as–**बीमार**); dire (as—**ज़रूरत**); –**आदमी** a hard nut to crack; –**क़ैद** rigorous imprisonment; –**ज़बान** harsh speech; harsh-spoken; ~**ज़बानी** harsh-wordedness; harshness of speech; ~**जान** thick-skinned; strict; hard-bitten, tough; ~**जान होना** to die hard; ~**दिल** hard-hearted, cruel; hence ~**दिली** (*nf*); –**मिज़ाज** hot-headed, short tempered; ~**लगाम** see **मुँहज़ोर** (esp. said of a horse; -ग़लती करना to put one's foot in it; -सुस्त कहना to chide, to rebuke.

सख़्ती sakhti: (*nf*) hardness; strictness; harshness; stiffness; rigorousness; सख़्तियाँ उठाना to face rigours, to stand excesses; to put up with harshness/strictness; –करना to deal with strictly, to be strict; –से strictly, harshly; with a heavy hand; ० पेश आना to deal with strictly; to be harsh.

सख्य shakkhy (*nm*) friendship; friendliness; -भाव friendly feeling/emotion; -भक्ति devotion inspired by friendly feeling and emotion.

सगंध sagandh (*a*) fragrant, aromatic; having a smell.

सगनौती sagnauti: (*nf*) see सगुनौती.

सगर्भा sagarbha: (*a*) pregnant.

सगा saga: (*a*) real, born of the same parents; kin; ~पन kinship, near-relationship; –भाई real brother; hence सगी—femine form of सगा.

सगाई saga:i: (*nf*) betrothal; engagement; –होना to be engaged/betrothed.

सगु/ण sagun (*a*) possessed of attributes (as –ब्रह्म); endowed with qualities; ~णी endowed with qualities; ~णोपासना worship of God possessed of attributes.

सगुन sagun (*nm*) an omen, good omen; augury; see सगुण.

सगुनिया saguniyā: (*nm*) an augury, a soothsayer.

सगुनौती sagunauti: (*nf*) augury.

सगुरा sagura: (*a*) who has been initiated; having a preceptor (गुरु).

सगोती sagoti: (*a*) see सगोत्र.

सगोत्र sagottr (*a*) belonging to or of the same गोत्र (clan); allied by blood; hence ~ता (*nf*).

सग्गड़ saggar (*nm*) a hand-cart.

सघन saghan (*a*) dense, thick; intensive; overcast with clouds, cloudy; –खेती intensive cultivation; ~ता denseness/intensity; cloudiness; ~तामापी densimeter.

सच such (*a*) true; right; (*nm*) the truth; (*int*) really !

सचकित sachakit (*a*) amazed, astonished, wonder-struck.

सचमुच sachmuch (*adv*) actually, truly, really, surely, in fact; –का real; genuine.

सचराचर sachara:char (*a*) with animates and inanimates; all; (*nm*) the whole world; –जगत the entire world.

सचाई sacha:i: (*nf*) truth; truthfulness; reality; fact; integrity.

सचान sacha:n (*nm*) a falcon, hawk.

सचित्र sachittr (*a*) pictorial; illustrated (with pictures); –पत्रिका a pictorial/an illustrated magazine.

सचिव sachiv (*nm*) secretary; –, निजी private secretary.

सचिवाल/य sachiva:lay (*nm*) secretariat; ~यी secretarial.

सचेत sachet (*a*) conscious; careful, alert; attentive; –होना to be conscious/careful/attentive.

सचेतक sachetak (*nm*) a whip;–, मुख्य chief whip.

सचेतन sachetan (*a*) conscious; -कलाकार a conscious artist; ~ता consciousness; diligence.

सचेष्ट sachesht (*a*) alert, active; attemptive; hence ~ता (*nf*).

सच्चरि/त, ~त्र sachcharit, ~ttr (*a*) virtuous, of good moral character or integrity; hence ~त्रता (*nf*).

सच्चा sachcha: (*a*) true; truthful; genuine; sincere; loyal: faithful; real; ~पन truth, truthfulness; reality.

सच्चाई sachcha:i: (*nf*) truth, truthfulness; reality; fact, integrity; -से आँखें मूँदना to blink the fact.

सच्चिदानंद sachchida:nānd (*nm*) an epithet of the Supreme Soul (as the Ultimate resort of Truth, Consciousness and Happiness).

सज saj (*nf*) adoration/adorning, ornamentation; -धज/बज prank; ornamentation.

सजग sajag (*a*) alert, cautious, vigilant, careful; ~ता alertness, cautiousness, vigilance, carefulness.

सजन sajan (*nm*) husband; lover.

सजना sajnā: (*v*) to be adorned/decorated/embellished/beautified; to prank; to be made-up; to be neatly arranged; (*nm*) see सजन; -धजना/-सँवरना to dress up to the nines, to groom, to make-up, to prank.

सजनी sajnī: (*nf*) beloved, sweetheart; wife.

सजल sajal (*a*) full of water; tearful; hydrous, aquous; ~नयन/नेत्र having tearful eyes; (on the verge of) weeping, shedding tears.

सजा saza:(*nf*) punishment; penalty; -ए-मौत capital punishment; ~याफ़्ता convicted, punished; -का मजा मिलना to reap the harvest of one's evil deeds.

सजा/ति saja:ti (*a*) of one and the same caste/class; homogeneous; ~तीय see सजाति; ~तीयता homo geneity, affinity, homology; ~तीय विवाह endogamy.

सजाना saja:nā: (*v*) to decorate, to adorn, to embellish, to beautify; to furnish; to arrange; to dress neatly; सजा-धजा made-up; well-adorned, decorated.

सजाव saja:v (*nm*) see सजावट; –दही curd of good quality prepared from well-boiled and thickened milk.

सजाव/ट saja:vaṭ (*nf*) decoration, ornamentation; make-up; display, array; ~टी decorative; pranked.

सज़ाव/ल saza:val (*nm*) a tax or rent collector; ~ली the office or function of a ~ल.

सजिल्द sajild (*a*) bound (book etc.).

सजीला saji:la: (*a*) decorated; foppish, grand, graceful; ~पन decoratedness; foppishness, grandeur, gracefulness.

सजीव saji:v (*a*) living, alive, lively; vivacious; hence ~ता (*nf*).

सज्जन sajjan (*nm* and *a*) a gentleman; noble, gentle; ~ता gentility, nobility.

सज्जा sajja: (*nf*) embellishment, decoration, adorning; dressing-up; equipment; lay out.

सज्जित sajjit (*a*) decorated, adorned, embellished, beautified; dressed-up; equipped.

सज्जी sajji: (*nf*) saltpetre; also –खार.

सज्ञान saggya:n (*a*) learned, wise, knowing; ~ता learnedness, wisdom, the state of being in know.

सझिया sajhiya: (*nm*) see साझेदार; ~ई see साझेदारी.

सटकना saṭaknā: (*v*) to slip away; to turn tails, to make good one's escape.

सटना saṭnā: (*v*) to be in close proximity, to be in physical contact; to stick; to adhere to; to be adjacent.

सटपटाना saṭpaṭa:nā: (*v*) to be flabbergasted/stunned; to be nonplussed, to be embarassed out of wits.

सटर-पटर saṭar-paṭar (*nf*) noisy/chaotic/clamorous activity; (*a*) petty, trifle (e.g. –सामान petty belongings.

सटा saṭa: (*nf*) mane; thickened locks of hair; (*a*) see **सटना**.

सटाक saṭa:k (*nm*) the cracking of a whip or thin stick; **~से** with a cracking noise; instantly.

सटाकी saṭa:ki: (*nf*) a thin stick.

सटीक saṭi:k (*a*) apt, befitting, correct and accurate; with commentary/annotation; **—बैठना, कोई बात** to be very apt and appropriate.

सटोरिया saṭoriya: (*nm*) a speculator.

स/ट्टा saṭṭa: (*nm*) speculation; **~ट्टेबाज़** a speculator; **~ट्टेबाज़ी** speculation.

सट्टी saṭṭi: (*nf*) market-place.

सठिया/ना saṭhiya:nā: (*v*) to suffer senile decay, to be in dotage; to be decrepit, to come to one's autumn; also **सठिया जाना**.

सड़क saṛak (*nf*) a road, street; **–के नियम** rules of the road.

सड़न saṛan (*nf*) decay, decomposition; putrefaction, rot, rottenness.

सड़ना saṛnā: (*v*) to decay, to decompose; to rot, to ferment, to putrefy; to be or fall in misery.

सड़सठ saṛsaṭh (*a*) sixty-seven; (*nm*) the number sixty-seven.

सड़सी saṛsi: (*nf*) tongs.

सड़ांध saṛā:dh (*nf*) stench, putrefaction, putrescence, putridity; mustiness; **·भरा** putrid, stenching, stinking.

सड़ा saṛa: (*a*) rotten, decayed, putrid, putriscent; **-गला** rotten and decayed; hence **सड़ी** (fem. form); **०गर्मी** humidly hot weather.

सड़ाक saṛa:k (*nf*) (sound produced by) cracking of a whip; **—से** with a cracking noise; instantly.

सड़ान saṛa:n (*nf*) decay/decaying, rot/rotting, putrefaction/putridity.

सड़ाना saṛa:nā: (*v*) to (cause to) decay, to rot, to decompose, to cause to putrefy.

सड़ायँध saṛa:yādh (*nf*) stench, putrescence, putridity; **~युक्त** putrid, stenching.

सड़ासड़ saṛa:saṛ (*adv*) with repeated sounds of cracking (of a whip); in quick succession.

सड़ियल saṛiyal (*a*) rotten; putrid, putrescent; worthless.

सत sat (*nm*) essence, juice; strength vitality; truth, truthfulness; an allomorph of **सात** used as the first member in certain compound words; **~गुना** seven times; **~गुरु** true/good preceptor; God; **~जुग** one and the first of the four *yugas* (the other being **द्वापर, त्रेता** and **कलि**) of the universe according to Indian mythology. The **सतयुग** is said to be the best or golden period/age of creation; **~युगी** belonging to the **~युग**; **~नजा** a mixture of seven corns; **~रंग/रंगा** seven-coloured; multicoloured; **~मासा** of seven months; a ceremony performed about the seventh month of pregnancy; (a child) born in the seventh month of pregnancy; **~लड़ा** seven-stringed (necklace, etc.); **~वंती** (a) chaste (woman); **~वाँसा** see **~मासा**; **~सई** a collection of seven hundred (and odd) couplets (generally **दोहा** and **सोरठा**); see **सत्**; **–डिगा जहान डिगा** when character is lost all is lost; **–पर (जमे) रहना** to hold on to the righteous path; to maintain one's chastity.

सतत satat (*adv* and *a*) incessantly; continuous; ever; always.

सतथ्य satatthy (*a*) factual, with facts.

सतर satar (*nf*) a line; row; (*a*)

erect; upright

सतरह satrah (*a*) seventeen; (*nm*) the number seventeen.

सतर्क satark (*a* and *adv*) cautious, vigilant, alert, careful; argumentative; ~ता alertness, vigilance; carefulness; with argument.

सत/ह sateh (*nf*) surface; level; ~ही superficial; ~हीपन superficiality.

सतहत्तर satahattar (*a*) seventy-seven; (*nm*) the number seventy-seven.

सताना sata:nā: (*v*) to trouble; to harass, to torment, to oppress; to victimise.

सतावर sata:var (*nf*) asparagus.

सती sati: (*nf*) a chaste and faithful/loyal woman devoted to her husband; a woman who burns herself willingly on the funeral pyre (चिता) of her husband out of devotion; (*a*) chaste, virtuous (said of a married woman); ~त्व/पन chastity, virtuousness; o भंग/हरण rape (of a woman); outraging a woman's modesty; -साध्वी/सावित्री a woman extremely devoted to her husband; –होना (for a woman) to burn oneself on the funeral pyre of her husband.

सतीर्थ sati:rth (*nm*) a co-student.

सतुआ satua: (*nm*) see सत्तू; -संक्रांति see मकर संक्रांति.

सतून satu:n (*nm*) a pillar.

सतोगु/ण satogun (*nm*) virtue, the quality of purity and goodness; one of the three *guṇas* (see सत्त्व, रजस् and तमस्); ~णी having the qualities of goodness and purity, virtuous.

सत् sat (*a*) good; pious, virtuous; present; true; -डिगा जहान डिगा when character is lost all is lost.

सत्क/र्म satkarm (*nm*) virtuous action/deed; piety; ~र्मी virtuous in action/deed.

सत्कवि satkavi (*nm*) a good poet.

सत्कार satka:r (*nm*) hospitality; welcome; ~शील hospitable;–करना to extend all hospitality; to greet/welcome.

सत्कार्य satka:ry (*nm*) see सत्कर्म.

सत्काव्य satka:vy (*nm*) good poetry.

सत्कीर्ति stki:rti (*nf*) good name, fame, reputation.

सत्कृत satkrit (*a*) welcomed, who has enjoyed hospitality: done well.

सत्त satt (*nm*) essence, extract; truth; integrity, chastity; –डिगना to lose integrity, one's integrity to be in danger; chastity to be in danger or jeopardy.

सत्तर sattar (*a*) seventy; (*nm*) the number seventy; –चूहे खाये होना to have gathered/acquired varied (immoral) experiences.

सत्तरह sattarah (*a*) seventeen; (*nm*) the number seventeen.

सत्ता satta: (*nm*) being, existence, entity; power, sway, authority; reality; playing card with seven pips; ~धारी ruling, (in) authority; a man of authority/power; ~रूढ़ ruling; wielding power; potentiate; ~रोह(ण) ascendancy; ~वाद authoritarianism; ~वादी authoritarian; an authoritarianist.

सत्ताई(इ)स sattai:(i)s (*a*) twenty-seven; (*nm*) the number twenty-seven.

सत्तानवे satta:nve (*a*) ninety-seven; (*nm*) the number ninety-seven.

सत्तावन satta:van (*a*) fifty-seven; (*nm*) the number fifty-seven.

सत्तासी satta:si: (*a*) eighty-seven; (*nm*) the number eighty-seven.

सत्तू sattu: (*nm*) powder of parched gram, barley or other grains; –बाँधकर पीछे पड़ना to hound somebody doggedly; to pursue with single-minded devotion.

सत्त्व sattv (*nm*) being, existence; entity; reality; substance; spiritual essence, quintessence; strength, vitality; quality of purity and goodness; –गुण the quality of purity and goodness; ~हीन devoid of सत्त्व.

सत्पथ satpath (*nm*) the path of virtue/good.

सत्पात्र satpa:ttr (*nm*) a deserving/worthy/befitting person.

सत्फल satphal (*nm*) good result.

सत्य satty (*a*) true, veritable; (*nm*) veracity, truth, verity; ~काम truth-loving; ~त: truly, in fact/reality, really; ~ता truth; verity, veracity; ~दर्शी discerning, seeing through the truth; ~निष्ठ veridical, dedicated to truth; solemn; ~पर/परायण thoroughly honest, ~भाषी veridicious, speaking the truth; ~युग see सतयुग under सत; ~युगी see सतयुगी; ~वाचक/वाची/वादी see ~भाषी; ~व्रत strictly truthful, who has taken a vow to be truthful; ~शील disposed to truth, temperamentally truthful; ~शीलता disposition towards truth, temperamental truthfulness.

सत्यनारायण sattyna:ra:yāṇ (*nm*) name of a particular divinity representing a form of Lord Vishṇū; –का व्रत fast in honour of सत्यनारायण; –की कथा a story recounting the acts of kindness of सत्यनारायण read out during the fast observed in honour of the deity.

सत्यनिष्ठा sattynishṭḥa: (*nf*) truthfulness; integrity.

सत्यभावी sattybha:vi: (*a*) veridical.

सत्यवा/दिता, ~दित्व sattyva:dita: (*nf*), ~dittv (*nm*) truthfulness, veracity; ~दी truthful, veracious.

सत्यां/कन sattya:ṅkān (*nm*) ratification; ~कित ratified.

सत्याग्र/ह sattya:ggrah (*nm*) insistence on truth—passive resistance offered to uphold truth (a weapon made popular by Gandhiji during the Indian freedom movement); ~ही one who offers *satya:ggrah*.

सत्यानाश sattya:na:sh (*nm*) complete ruin, total destruction, devastation; –करना to destroy/ruin/devastate; –होना to go to the devil, to go to dogs.

सत्यानाशी sattya:na:shi: (*a*) ruining, devastating; destructive; (*nm*); *Argemone mexicana*.

सत्या/पक sattya:pak (*nm*) verifier; ~पन verification; ~पनीय verifiable; ~पन करना to verify; ~पित verified.

स/त्र sattr (*nm*) a session; ~त्रांत conclusion of a session; ~त्रांश a term (in an academic institution); ~त्रावसान prorogation (of an assembly etc.); conclusion of a session.

सत्रह sattreh (*a*) seventeen; (*nm*) the number seventeen.

सत्व sattv (*nm*) see सत्त्व; ~हीन see सत्त्वहीन under सत्त्व.

सत्वर sattvar (*adv*) expeditiously, quickly; ~ता expeditiousness, quickness.

सत्सं/ग satsāṅg (*nm*) intercourse or association with good/pious men; also ~गत (*nf*); ~गी one who lives in good/noble company.

सद/क़ा sadqa: (*nm*) propitiatory offering; sacrifice; graciousness; gracious favour; ~**क़े उतारना** to make a propitiatory offering in honour of (somebody); ~**क़े जाना** to be proud of, to be ready to be sacrificed (for somebody); ~**क़े में** by the graciousness/gracious favour of.

सदन sadan (*nm*) a house; house of legislature, chamber; –, **उच्च** upper house; –**का नेता** leader of the house; -**त्याग** walk out (from the house); –, **निचला** lower house; ~**सदनी**, **एक** unicameral; ~**सदनी**, **द्वि** bicameral.

सदमा sadmā: (*nm*) a blow, emotional stroke, shock; –**उठाना** to stand a blow; –**पहुँचना**/**लगना** to suffer a blow; to suffer a terrible shock.

सदय saday (*a*) kind, compassionate; ~**ता** kindness, compassionateness; ~**हृदय** kind, compassionate.

सदर sadar (*a*) head, main; (*nm*) chief, chairman; president; –**आला** a sub-judge; –**बाज़ार** main market; –**मजलिस** president/chairman of an assembly; –**मुकाम** headquarters.

सदरी sadri: (*nf*) a kind of sleeveless jacket.

सदस/त् sadasat (*a*) true and false, good and evil; ~**द्विवेक** discretion/discretionary faculty, discriminating the good from evil.

सदस्य sadassy (*nm*) a member; ~**ता** membership; o**शुल्क** membership fee.

सदा sada: (*adv*) always, ever; (*nf*) call; echo; ~**नीरा** perennial stream; ~**बहार** perennial, evergreen; a plant having pink or white flowers; ~**वर्त** pledge to distribute free food daily; free food so distributed; o**बाँटना** to distribute free food; ~**वर्ती** one who distributes free food; ~**सुहागिन** a woman ever enjoying the protection of her her husband; a prostitute; –**सुहागिन रहो** a benediction addressed to women, meaning—'May you always enjoy the coverture of your husband; –**देना**/**लगाना** to make a cell (as a faqir).

सदाक़त sada:qat (*nf*) truthfulness, forthrightness.

सदाचरण sada:charān (*nm*) good/moral conduct.

सदाचा/र sada:cha:r (*nm*) morality, virtuous/moral conduct, rectitude; ~**रिता** morality, moral conduct; virtuousness, rectitude; ~**री** righteous, moral; virtuous man, moralist; hence ~**रिणी** (feminine form).

सदारत sada:rat (*nf*) presidentship; chairmanship; –**करना** to preside over.

सदाशय sada:shay (*a*) genuine, of good faith; noble, magnanimous; (*nm*) good faith; ~**ता** bonafides, genuineness; nobility, magnanimity; **सदाशयी** bonafide, well-meaning.

सदिश sadish (*nm*) a vector.

सदी sadi: (*nf*) a century.

सदुक्ति sadukti (*nf*) an excellent/remarkable saying.

सदुपदेश sadupdesh (*nm*) good advice; moral teaching.

सदुपयोग sadupayog (*nm*) good or proper use/usage.

सदृश saddrish (*a*) like, similar, alike, resembling; ~**ता** similarity, resemblance.

सदेह sadeh (*a* and *adv*) with the

body, in a physical form, corporeal; bodily, physically.

सदैव sadaiv (*adv*) always, ever.

सदोष sadosh (*a*) faulty; wrong; ~ता culpability.

सद् sad—an allomorph of सत् as it appears in numerous compounds; ~गति salvation, assignment to a better abode in the post-death existence; ~गुण virtue; merits, qualities; ~गुणी virtuous; meritorious; ~गुरु worthy preceptor/teacher; God; ~ग्रंथ a good book; an ethically sound book; ~भाव goodwill; kindly feeling; presence; ~भावना goodwill, kindly feeling; ~भावना-मिशन a goodwill mission; ~भावना-संदेश a message of goodwill; ~युक्ति sound logic/argument; ~वंश high/noble family; ०जात born in a high/noble family; –वृत्त righteous, good, morally disposed; ~वृत्ति (the) good; righteousness, moral disposition.

सद्म sadm (*nm*) a house, abode.

सद्यः saddyah (*adv*) at once, immediately; just, recently; ~कृत just performed/done; ~प्रसूत just born; newly born; ~स्नात just-bathed; ~स्नाता (a lady who has) just-bathed.

सद्योजा/त saddyoja:t (*a*) new born, just born; hence ~ता feminine form.

सद्र sadr (*nm*) see सदर.

सधना sadhnā: (*v*) to be tamed; to be accomplished/completed; to get habituated/accustomed; target to be hit; to be aligned (as निशाना).

सध/र्म, ~र्मा, ~र्मी sadharm, ~rmā:, ~rmī: (*nm* and *a*) (a) co-religionist; who follows the same religion.

सधवा sadhva: (*a* and *nf*) (a woman) whose husband is living.

सधाना sadha:nā: (*v*) to break in, to tame, to cause to get used/habituated; to habituate.

सधाव sadha:v (*nm*) state or fact of being trained; stability, equilibrium.

सधूम sadhu:m (*a*) smoky, fuming.

सन san (*nm*) a year; an era; a kind of jute, hemp; (*nf*) whizzing sound; (*a*) stupefied; –की रस्सी a hemp-rope; ~सन whizzing sound; –से निकल जाना to pass with a whizzing sound; to pass with extra-ordinary speed.

सनई sanai: (*nf*) *sunhemp*—a kind of hemp.

सनक sanak (*nf*) whim, caprice, eccentricity; craze, mania, frenzy; –आना, –चढ़ना, –सवार होना to have something on the brain, to go crazy, to be overwhelmed by a whim/craze, to be in a caprice.

सनकना sanaknā: (*v*) to go crazy, to be in a frenzy.

सनकी sanki: (*a* and *nm*) eccentric, capricious, crazy, crank, whimsical (person); hence ~पन (*nm*); –होना to have bats in the belfry.

सन/द sanad (*nf*) a certificate, testimonial; deed; ~दयाफ़्ता certified; holding a certificate; ~दी see ~दयाफ़्ता authentic.

सनना sannā: (*v*) to be kneaded/besmeared/stained/soiled, to be drowned (as पाप में–).

सनम sanām (*nm*) dear, beloved one; a statue; ~क़दा/ख़ाना a temple; abode of the beloved.

सनमान sanmā:n (*nm*) see सम्मान.

सनसनाना sansanā:nā: (*v*) to produce a whizzing sound; to have a thrilling sensation.

सनसनाहट sansana:haṭ (*nf*) whizzing

sound; thrilling sensation.

सनसनी sansanī: (*nf*) thrilling sensation; excitement; ~**खेज/दार** sensational; o**खबर** sensational news.

सनातन sana:tan (*a*) eternal; ancient; orthodox; time-honoured; –**धर्म** the orthodox Hindu religion; –**पुरुष** the Eternal Lord —Vishnū; **सनातनी** a follower of the –**धर्म**; ancient, traditional, orthodox, conservative; time-honoured.

सनाथ sanā:th (*a*) having a patron/protector/guardian/husband; gratified/fulfilled; –**करना** to provide protection; to fulfil, to gratify.

सनाभि sana:bhi (*a*) concentric; nuclear, with nucleus.

सनाय sana:y (*nf*) senna, a plant the leaves of which are used as a purgative; such a pvrgative.

सनासन sanā:san (*adv*) with/producing a whizzing sound.

सनाह sana:h (*nm*) helmet, head-armour.

सनियम sanīyam (*a*) regular, with rules.

सनीचर sani:char (*nm*) Saturn; Saturday; an ominous person; –**लगना** to be under the influence of ominous stars; to be poverty-stricken.

सनोबर sanobar (*nm*) a pine-tree (tall and beautiful).

सन् sān (*nm*) an era, a year; –, **ईस्वी** the Christian era; –, **हिजरी** Mohammedan era.

सन्न sann (*a*) stunned, stupefied, dumb-founded, flabbergasted; (*nm*) swollen-headedness, hot-headedness, arrogance, hubris; –**रह/हो जाना** to be stunned/stupefied/dumb-founded/flabbergasted.

सन्नद्ध sannaddh (*a*) ready, equipped.

सन्नाटा sannā:ṭa: (*nm*) still; silence, quietude; –**खींचना/मारना** to keep still/mum; –**होना** to have no activity whatever; to be still; **सन्नाटे में आना** to be stunned/dumb-founded/stupefied.

सन्निकट sannikaṭ (*ind*) close, proximal, at hand, near by; imminent, approximate; hence ~**ता**; ~**न** approximation.

सन्निकर्ष sannikarsh (*nm*) nearness, proximity.

सन्निधान sannīdha:n (*nm*) juxtaposition, proximity.

सन्निधि sannīdhi (*nf*) juxtaposition.

सन्निविष्ट sannivishṭ (*a*) entered; included; proximated.

सन्निवे/श sannivesh (*nm*) entry/entrance (into); inclusion; insertion; ~**शन** act or process of causing entry into; inclusion; insertion; ~**शित** included; inserted.

सन्निहित sannihit (*a*) implied; vested; lying within.

सन्मान sanmā:n (*nm*) see **सम्मान**.

सन्मार्ग sanma:rg (*nm*) path of virtue, moral/good course.

सन्मुख sanmukh (*ind*) see **सम्मुख**.

सन्यास (*nm*) see **'संन्यास'**.

सपक्ष sapaksh (*a*) winged, having wings; belonging to the same side/party; hence ~**ता** (*nf*).

सपटल sapaṭal (*a*) tamellar.

सपत्नी sapatnī: (*nf*) a co-wife; ~**क** along with one's wife.

सपदि sapadi (*adv*) at once; quickly.

सपना sapnā: (*nm*) a dream; –**देखना** to dream; –**सा होना** to be very short-lived, to have disappeared too soon; –**होना** to have a mere mental existence; to be just an object of dream, to be beyond reach in reality; **सपने में भी नहीं** not even in dreams, never, under no circumstances.

सपरदा saparda: (*nm*) an accompanyist of a dancing girl.

सपरना saparnā: (*v*) to be accomplished; to be completed; to be wound up.

सपरिकर saparikar (*a* and *adv*) with paraphernalia, along with attendants.

सपरिवार sapariva:r (*a* and *adv*) with family.

सपरेटा sapreṭa: (*a* and *nm*) separated/skimmed (milk); –**दूध** separated/ skimmed milk.

सपर्ण saparn (*a*) with/having leaves; hence ~**ता** (*nf*).

सपाट sapa:ṭ (*a*) flat; plain, smooth, level, even; unfeeling; ~**पन** flatness; ~**बयानी** flat description/ expression.

सपा/टा sapa:ṭa: (*nm*) speed; expeditiousness; run; ~**टे से** quickly, expeditiously, with speed.

सपूत sapu:t (*nm*) a worthy or dutiful son.

सपेरा sapera: (*nm*) a snake-charmer.

सपोला sapola: (*nm*) see **सँपोला**.

सप्त sapt (*a*) seven; (*nm*) the number seven; ~**क** octave; the seven notes in music; an aggregate of seven; ~**दश** seventeen; the number seventeen; ~**पदी** the ceremony of seven circumambulations of the sacred sacrificial fire as an integral part of the Hindu wedding process; ~**भुवन** see ~**लोक**; ~**म** seventh; ~**मी** the seventh day of each half of a lunar month; the locative case (in Grammar); ~**र्षि** Ursa Major; the seven sages (**मरीचि, अत्रि, अंगिरा, पुलह, क्रतु, पुलस्त्य, वसिष्ठ**); ~**लोक** the seven worlds (**भूलोक, भुवर्लोक, स्वर्लोक, महर्लोक, जनलोक, तपोलोक, सत्यलोक**); ~**स्वर** the seven notes of music (**स रे ग म प ध नी**).

सप्ता/ह sapta:h (*nm*) a week; ~**हांत** week-end.

सप्रमाण sappramā:ṇ (*a*) with proof; substantiated.

सफ़ saf (*nf*) a line, row.

सफ़तालू safta:lu: (*nm*) a typical fruit-bearing tree.

सफ़र safar (*nm*) travel, journey; -**ख़र्च** travel expenses; ~**नामा** a travelogue, travel account.

सफ़रमैना safarmaīna: (*nm*) sappers and miners.

सफ़री safri: (*a*) pertaining to travel; travel; convenient during a journey.

सफल saphal (*a*) successful; effective; fruitful; ~**ता** success; achievement; o **की कुंजी** key to success; –**होना** to succeed.

सफलीभूत saphali:bhu:t (*a*) successful, succeeded.

सफ़ा safa: (*nm*) a page; clean, white; ~**चट** blank; perfectly clean.

सफ़ाई safa:i: (*nf*) cleanliness; purity; conservancy; defence (in a law suit); clarification; –**पक्ष** the defence (side); –**देना** to justify; to clarify; –**से** with exquisiteness; in a clean manner, cleanly; in a forthright manner.

सफ़ाया safa:ya: (*nm*) clean sweep; end, ruination, destruction; o**करना** to sweep clean; to destroy.

सफ़ीना safi:nā: (*nf*) subpoena.

सफ़ीर safi:r (*nm*) an ambassador, envoy.

सफ़ूफ़ safu:f (*nm*) a powder.

सफ़ेद safed (*a*) white; clean; blank; –**झूठ** blatant lie; total lie; –**दाग़** leucoderma; ~**पोश** white-collared; dressed in white; o**वर्ग** white-collar class; hence ~**पोशी** (*nf*);

–बाल grey hair; ०होना to be richly experienced/seasoned; -सियाह/स्याह good and/or bad, right and/or wrong; doing and/or undoing; ०करना to make or mar;–हाथी a white elephant; an expensive do-nothing brand (of man); –करना to whiten; to cleanse; –पड़ जाना to be rendered pallid, to be anaemic; –होना, ख़ून to lose all sense of self-respect, to be lost to shame, to be timidly passionless; to be inhumane.

सफ़ेदा safeda: (*nm*) white lead.

सफ़ेदी safedi: (*nf*) whiteness; white-wash; –आना to grow grey, to age; –छाना to be turned anaemic/pallid; to age, to grow grey.

सफ़्तालू safta:lu: (*nm*) see सफ़तालू

सब sab (*a*) all; entire, whole; (prefix) sub–; -इंस्पेक्टर a sub-inspector; –ओर all round, in all directions; -कुछ all; all in all; –जज a sub-judge; –डिप्टी इंस्पेक्टर a sub-deputy inspector; –डिविजन a sub-division, –रजिस्ट्रार a sub-registrar; -कुछ दाँव पर लगाना to bet one's bottom dollar; –को अपना मतलब प्यारा everybody knows his own interest best; –को एक आँख से देखना not to make flesh of one and fish of the other; –तरफ़ से पड़ना/पिटना to run the gauntlet; to be attacked on all sides; –तरीक़े आजमाना to ring the changes, to work it for all its worth; –धान बाईस पसेरी to treat good and bad alike; –मिलाकर all told; –से भला चुप silence is gold; सबै सहायक सबल के God sides with the strongest.

सबक़ sabaq (*nm*) a lesson; moral; –देना/पढ़ाना/सिखाना to teach a lesson; –मिलना to learn a lesson.

सबब sabab (*nm*) a reason; cause.

सबरी sabri: (*nf*) (a house-breaker's) jemmy (used for breaking through a wall).

सबल sabal (*a*) strong, forceful/powerful; valid; ~ता strength, forcefulness/powerfulness.

सबा saba: (*nf*) easterly wind.

सबूत sabu:t (*nm*) a proof, an evidence; –देना to give proof.

सबे/रा sabera: (*nm*) (the) morning; dawn, day-break; ~रे in the morning; ~रे-सबेरे early in the morning.

सब्ज़ sabz (*a*) green; –बाग़ दिखलाना to lead the person up the garden, to arouse high hopes in vain.

सब्ज़ी sabzi: (*nf*) vegetable; herbage; -मंडी a vegetable market; ~वाला a vegetable-seller.

सब्बल sabbal (*nm*) a crowbar.

सब्र sabbr (*nm*) patience; contentment; –का फल मीठा होता है patience pays, bear and forbear is good; –बड़ा धन है contentment is more than a kingdom.

सभय sabhay (*a*) with fear, fearing.

सभा sabha: (*nf*) an assembly, association; a meeting; society; -कक्ष meeting room, committee room; ~गार/गृह an assembly hall, chamber; -त्याग walkout; ~पति chairman; ~पतित्व chairmanship; ०में under the chairmanship (of); -भवन auditorium, assembly hall; ~मंडप a pavilion; -मंच platform, dais; ~सद member of an assembly; –जोड़ना (derisively) to gather a crowd.

सभार sabha:r (*a*) onerous; with gratitude.

सभीति sabhi:ti (*a*) with fear, fearing.

सभोचित sabhochit (*a*) appropriate in a सभा (see).

सभ्य sabbhy (*a*) civilised/civil, courteous; –जाति civilised race; –राष्ट्र a civilised nation.

सभ्यता sabbhyata: (*nf*) civilization; courtesy, decency.

सभ्याचार sabbhya:cha:r (*nm*) good manners, mannerly conduct.

समंजन samānjan (*nm*) adjustment, coordination; –करना to adjust, to coordinate.

समंदर samandar (*nm*) see समुद्र.

सम sam (*a*) even; equal; homogeneous; regular pro-; (*nm*) even number; first accented beat in a rhythmic cycle; ~करण equalisation; ~कुलपति Pro-Vice-Chancellor (of a University); ~कुलाधिपति Pro-Chancellor; ~नाम homonym; homonymous; ~नामता homonymy; ~पक्षीय homolateral; ~प्ररूपी homotypical; ~प्रसार relay; ~रेखण alignment; ~लिंगरति homosexuality; ~शब्द analogue; ~सामाजिकता homosociability; ~स्वन homophone.

समकक्ष samkaksh (*a*) equal/equivalent; matching; of the same stature; hance ~ता (*nf*).

समकालिक samka:lik (*a*) synchronizing/synchronous; ~ता synchronism.

समकालीन samka:li:n (*a*) contemporary / contemporaneous; ~ता contemporaneity.

समकोण samkon (*nm*) a right angle; (*a*) having equal angles; ~क a set square; –चतुर्भुज a square; –त्रिभुज right-angled triangle.

समको/णिक, ~णीय samkōnik, ~nī:y (*a*) right-angle(d).

समक्रमिक samkramik(*a*)synchronous/synchronizing; ~ता synchronism.

समक्ष samaksh (*adv*) before, in front of, faee to face with.

समग्र samaggr (*a*) total; whole, entire; ~ता totality; –रूप से at all points, on the whole, in entirety.

समचित्त samchitt (*a*) equanimous; ~ता equanimity.

समचिह्न samchinh (*a*) isotropic; ~ता isotropy.

समजात samja:t (*a*) homologous; ~ता homology.

समजातीय samja:ti:y (*a*) homologous; homogeneous; of equal or same caste/species/class; ~ता homology, homogeneity.

समझ samajh (*nf*) understanding, intellect, sense; comprehension, grasp; discretion; ~दार keen; intelligent; sensible; wise; ~दार को इशारा काफ़ी a word to the wise is enough; ~दारी wisdom; intelligence; (sense of) understanding, sense; -बूझ discretion; (keenness of) understanding; –के बाहर होना, (किसी की) to be Greek (to); to be out of one's ken; –पर पत्थर पड़ना to be out of one's head, to be bereft of senses, to lose one's wits; –में आना to understand, to comprehend.

समझना samajhnā: (*v*) to understand, to grasp, to comprehend; to catch, to follow; to assume airs (वह अपने आपको बहुत/कुछ समझता है); to have it out (समझ लूँगा !); समझ-बूझकर deliberately; knowingly, wittingly.

समझाना samjha:nā: (*v*) to persuade; to explain; -बुझाना to persuade; to cajole; to calm down.

समझौता samjhauta: (*nm*) a compromise, understanding; pact, agreement, settlement; –करना to patch up the difference, to come to a compromise.

समतल samtal (*a* and *nm*) level,

plain; flat; ~न levelling; slabbing; –भूमि the plain.

समता samta: (*nf*) equality, parity; equity,. equanimity; similarity. likeness, resemblance; evenness; ~वाद equalitarianism; ~वादी equalitarianist(ic).

समतापी samta:pi: (*a*) isothermal.

समतुलित samtulit (*a*) of equal weight.

समतुल्य samtully (*a*) equivalent; similar; ~ता equivalence; similarity.

समतोल samtol (*nm*) equilibrium.

समत्रिभुज samtribhuj (*nm*) an equilateral triangle.

समत्व samattv (*nm*) see समता.

समद/र्शी samdarshi: (*a*) equanimous; impartial; ~र्शिता equanimity; impartiality.

समदिक्ता samdikta: (*nf*) isotropy.

समदूरस्थ samdu:rasth (*a*) equidistant; hence ~ता (*nf*).

समदृष्टि samdrishṭi (*nf*) equanimity; impartiality.

समधिक samadhik (*a*) very much, much; hence ~ता (*nf*).

समधिन samdhin (*nf*) mother-in-law (or aunt-in-law, etc.) of son or daughter.

समधिया/न, ~ना samdhiyā:n, ~nā: (*nm*) place/abode of समधी.

समधी samdhi: (*nf*) father-in-law (or uncle-in-law, etc.) of son/daughter.

समन samān (*nm*) summons; –तामील करना to serve summons (on).

समनाम samnā:m (*a*) namesake.

समन्व/य samānnvay (*nm*) coordination; harmony; ~यकारी coordinating; ~यी a coordinator/coordinating; one who harmonizes, harmonizing.

समन्वि/त samannvit (*a*) coordinated; harmonized; hence ~ति (*nf*).

समन्वेषण samannveshāṇ (*nm*) thorough exploration/investigation.

समपृष्ठ sampristḥ (*a*) level, even, of level/even surface.

समबाहु samba:hu (*a*) equilateral.

समबुद्धि sambuddhi (*a* and *nm*) equanimous; equanimity.

समभार sambha:r (*a*) having equal weight.

सममि/त samamit (*a*) symmetrical; ~ति symmetry.

समय samay (*nm*) time; period; times; timings; occasion; leisure; a convention; –का पक्का/~निष्ठ punctual; ~निष्ठता punctuality; ~मान timely, on time; timings; –रहते while there is time, in time; -संकेत time signal; -सारणी a time-table; –से in time; –से पहले prematurely; before time; –आ जाना/निकट होना the end to come, the end to be imminent; –का पलटा खाना, –फिरना the times to take a turn; -कुसमय in times of need; –को दुर्लभ जानो make hay while the sun shines; –पर टाँका नौ का काम देता है a stich in time saves nine;–बदलना the times to change.

समयांतर samayā:ntar (*nm*) time-interval, time-gap.

समयु/ग्मक samyugmāk (*a* and *nm*) isogamete; ~ग्मी isogamous.

समयोचित samayochit (*a*) opportune, timely; expedient; –उपदेश/बात timely advice, a word in season; ~ता expediency, the fact or state of being timely/opportune.

समयोपरि samayopari (*nm*) overtime; –कार्य overtime work.

समर samar (*nm*) a war; battle; -तंत्र strategy, tactics, war-tactics; ~तंत्री tactician, strategist;~तंत्रीय tactical, strategic; -नीति strategy; ~बंध a cartel; -भूमि battlefield;

~पोत a warship; -विजयी a conqueror; -शूर a brave fighter.

समरस samras (*a*) equanimous; harmonious; ~ता equanimity; harmony.

समरांगण samrā:ngān (*nm*) a battlefield.

समरू/प samru:p (*a*) pari passu, homogeneous; identical; similar; homomorph; ~पता similarity; constancy, homogeneity; homomorphism; ~पादर्श isotype.

समरोचित samarochit (*a*) fit for war/battle, appropriate in times of war.

समरोद्यत samaroddyat (*a*) ready to fight; equipped for war/battle; hence; ~ता (*nf*).

समर्थ samarth (*a*) capable, competent; ~ता capability, competence.

सम/र्थक samarthak (*nm*) a supporter; vindicator; ~र्थन support; vindication; corroboration; o करना to support, to second; ~र्थनीय worth supporting; vindicatable; ~र्थित supported, vindicated.

सम/र्पण samarpān (*nm*) dedication; surrender; ~र्पणकर्त्ता one who dedicates/surrenders; ~र्पित dedicated; surrendered.

समर्या/द, ~दा samarya:d, ~da: (*a*) with limit(s)/bounds.

समलंकृत samalānkrit (*a*) well-decorated, fully adorned, embellished.

समवयस्क samvayask (*a*) of the same age, equal in age; hence ~ता (*nf*).

समव/र्ती samvarti: (*a*) concurrent; adjacent, contiguous; hence ~र्तिता (*nf*).

समवर्ण samvarn (*a*) of the same caste/colour; hence ~ता (*nf*).

समवाय samva:y (*nm*) collection, company; concourse; concomitance; –संबंध inseparable relation, intimate and constant connection.

समवायी samava:yi: (*a*) inseparable; concomitant; substantial; o कारण material or substantial cause.

समवृत्ति samvritti (*a*) analogous; co-professional, of the same calling; ~ता analogy; co-professionalism.

समवेत samvet (*a* and *adv*) collective (ly); –गान chorus, collective singing.

समवेदना samavednā: (*nf*) condolence; –संदेश message of condolence; -सभा a condolence meeting.

समशीतोष्ण samshi:toshn (*a*) moderate, temperate; –कटिबंध tropics.

समष्टि samashṭi (*nf*) collectiveness, totality, aggregate; –और व्यष्टि the collective/society and the individual; –मन/मानस collective mind; –मानव the collective man; ~वाद collectivism; ~वादी a collectivist; collectivistic.

समसामयिक samsa:maik (*a*) contemporary, contemporaneous; –चेतना contemporary consciousness; ~ता contemporaneity.

समस्त samast (*a*) all; whole, complete, entire; compound(ed); hence ~ता (*nf*); –पद compound word.

समस्थिति samasthiti (*nf*) constancy; equanimity.

समस्या samassya: (*nf*) a problem; the last portion or line of a metrical composition which is meant for completion in the same metre by a competitor; –नाटक a problem play; -पूर्ति completing a metrical composition posed as a 'समस्या'; ~मूलक problematic; –का समाधान solution of a/the problem.

समस्वरण samasvarān (*nm*) tuning.

समहित samhit (*nm*) entente.

समाँ samā: (*nm*) occasion; weather; gaiety; finery; spectacle, –**बँधना** to be bound by a spell, a spell-binding performance to be occasioned; –**बदल जाना** things to undergo a change; –**बाँधना** to spell-bind, to occasion a fascinating spectacle or performance; –**वाला** spell-binding.

समांग samā:ṅg (*a*) homogeneous; sound; ~**ता** homogeneity; soundness.

समांतर samā:ntar (*a*) parallel; ~**ता**/~**वाद** parallelism.

समाई sama:i: (*nf*) capacity; capability; patience.

समाकार sama:ka:r (*a*) homomorphous, of the same form/shape; hence ~**ता** (*nf*).

समाकुल sama:kul (*a*) very eager; restless; hence ~**ता** (*nf*).

समागत sama:gat (*a*) arrived; returned.

समागम sama:gām (*nm*) arrival; intercourse.

समाचार samā:cha:r (*nm*) news; information; -**एजेंट** a news agent; ~**दाता** a news, reporter; ~**पत्र** a newspaper; -**प्रसार (ण)** news relay, dissemination of news; -**फ़िल्म** a newsreel; –**साप्ताहिक** a news weekly; –**देना** to break news, to convey a news.

समाज sama:j (*nm*) society; community; -**निरपेक्ष** non-social; -**निरपेक्षता** the state or fact of being non-social, independent of the society; ~**वाद** socialism; ~**वादी** a socialist; socialistic; o**राज्य** socialistic state; ~**वादी व्यवस्था** socialistic order; -**विषयक/सम्बन्धी** social; -**व्यवस्था** social order; ~**शास्त्र** Sociology; ~**शास्त्रज्ञ/शास्त्री** a sociologist; ~**शास्त्रीय** sociological; -**सुधार** social reform/uplift; -**सुधारक** social reformer; –**सेवक** a social worker; –**सेवा** social service; -**सेविका** a female social worker; -**सेवी** rendering social service, social worker.

समाजी sama:ji: (*nm*) an instrumental musician who accompanies a singing and dancing girl; member of a **समाज** (as **आर्यसमाजी**, **ब्रह्मसमाजी**); (*a*) social.

समाजी/करण samā:ji:karāṉ (*nm*) socialization ~**करण, अहंकार का**; socialization of ego; ~**कृत** socialized.

समादर sama:dar (*nm*) reverence, honour, respect, veneration; ~**णीय** respectable, venerable.

समादिष्ट samā:dishṭ (*a*) commanded; commissioned.

समादृत sama:ddrit (*a*) respected, honoured.

समादेश sama:desh (*nm*) command; commission.

समा/धान sama:dhā:n (*nm*) solution (of a problem, etc.); ~**धेय** solvable; ~**धेयता** solvability.

समाधि sama:dhi (*nf*) trance; intense meditation; a tomb; ~**निष्ठ** devoted to intense meditation; -**भंग** interruption in the process of meditation; ~**स्थ** in a trance, in intense meditation; -**लेख** an epitaph; –**टूटना** process of meditation to be broken/disturbed; to be disturbed in one's meditation; –**लगाना** to go into a trance; to concentrate one's mind; to meditate; –**लेना** to go into eternal trance; o(**जल में**) to go to one's watery grave.

समान samā:n (*a*) equal, equivalent; similar, alike, identical; tantamount; ~**ता** equality, equivalence; parity, similarity, likeness.

समानांतर samā:nā:ntar (*a*) parallel; ~ता parallelism.

समाना samā:nā: (*v*) to be contained (in); to enter; to fit (in); to permeate.

समानाधिकरण samā:nā:dhikaran (*nm*) see समानाधिकार; apposition, coordination.

समानाधिका/र samā:nā:dhika:r (*nm*) equal rights; ~री possessing equal rights; joint heir.

समानार्थक samā:na:rthak (*a*) synonymous; ~ता synonymity.

समापन samā:pan (*nm*) conclusion; completion; -समारोह closing/concluding function.

समापवर्तक samā:pavartak (*nm*) common factor/measure; –, महत्तम greatest common measure (G. C. M.).

समापवर्त्य samā:pvarty (*nm*) common multiple; –, लघुतम least common multiple (L.C.M.).

समापिका samā:pika: (*a*) that which ends; (*nf*) after-piece; –क्रिया finite verb.

समापित samā:pit (*a*) concluded; completed.

समाप्त samā:pt (*a*) finished, ended, concluded, terminated; completed; ~प्राय almost finished/ended/concluded/completed/terminated.

समाप्ति samā:pti (*nf*) the end, conclusion, termination; completion.

समाप्य samā:ppy (*a*) to be or worth being concluded/finished/terminated/completed.

समाभिनंदन samā:bhināndān (*nm*) acclamation.

समामेलन samā:melan (*nm*) annexation; amalgamation.

समाम्नाय samā:mnā:y (*nm*) traditional collection (of sacred texts); handing down by tradition or memory.

समायो/जन samā:yojan (*nm*) compering; adjustment; ~जक one who adjusts; a compere; hence ~जित (*a*).

समारंभ samā:rambh (*nm*) inauguration, commencement, beginning.

समाराधन samā:ra:dhan (*nm*) appeasement; propitiation, gratification.

समारोह samā:roh (*nm*) celebration, festivity, function.

समार्थ samā:rth (*a*) synonymous; ~क a synonym; synonymous.

समालाप samā:la:p (*nm*) an interview; conversation.

समालोच/क samā:lochak (*nm*) a critic; ~न see समालोचना.

समालोचना samā:lochnā: (*nf*) criticism; critical appreciation; critique; ~त्मक critical; –शास्त्र criticism; -शिल्प craft of criticism.

समावर्तन samā:vartan (*nm*) returning home (esp. after completion of studies); -संस्कार/समारोह a convocation; समावर्तनीय pertaining to or fit for समावर्तन.

समाविष्ट samā:vishṭ (*a*) included, entered, incorporated; pervaded, permeated.

समावृत sama:vrit (*a*) covered; enveloped.

समावृत्त samā:vritt (*a*) returned after completion of studies.

समावे/श samā:vesh (*nm*) inclusion, entry, incorporation; pervasion, permeation; hence ~शित (*a*).

समा/श्वस्त samā:shshvast (*nm*) a warrantee; (*a*) assured; ~श्वासक a warrantor; ~श्वासन warranty; ० देना to warrant.

समास samā:s (*nm*) a compound (word); abridgement; concision, terseness; ~बहुल abounding in compound words; -शैली terse style.

समासीन samā:si:n (*a*) seated well/comfortably.

समासोक्ति samā:sokti (*nf*) a figure of speech in Indian Rhetorics which is a varity of allegory, brevity of speech.

समा/हरण samā:harān (*nm*) concentration, collection, accumulation; procuration; ~हर्ता one who collects/accumulates/causes concentration; a procurator; ~हार collection, accumulation, concentration; procuration; sum, totality, aggregate; conjunction or connection of words or sentences; compounding of words.

समाहित samā:hit (*a*) collected, concentrated; merged (into); ~मना with the mind concentrated on.

समिति samīti (*nf*) a committee; -कक्ष committee room; -कार्य committee work.

समिधा samīdha: (*nf*) sacrificial firewood; an oblation to fuel or firewood.

समीकरण samī:karān (*nm*) equation; –, अवकल differential equation; –, एकघात linear equation; –, समाकल integral equation.

समीकृत samī:krit (*a*) equated.

समीक्ष/क samī:kshak (*nm*) a reviewer; ~ण reviewing/criticizing/commenting.

समीक्षा sami:ksha: (*nf*) a review; criticism; commentary; ~कार see समीक्षक.

समीक्षित samī:kshit (*a*) reviewed/criticised/commented upon.

समीक्ष्य sami:kshy (*a*) under review; worth reviewing/criticising/commenting (on).

समीचीन samī:chi:n (*a*) proper, fit, right; equitable; ~ता propriety, fitness, right; equitability.

समीप samī:p (*a*) near (in place or time), beside, proximate, close by, at hand; hence ~ता (*nf*); ~वर्ती neighbouring, proximate; ~स्थ situated near/close by, proximate.

समीर samī:r (*nf*) air, breeze; ~ण air, breeze.

समुंदर samūndar (*nm*) see समुद्र.

समुचित samuchit (*a*) proper, right, fit, appropriate; hence ~ता (*nf*).

समुच्चय samuchchay (*nm*) set; collection, aggregate/aggregation, totality, assemblage; conjunction of words or sentences; ~बोधक conjunction.

समुच्छ्वास samuchchva:s (*nm*) deep sigh.

समुज्ज्वल samujjval (*a*) shining brightly, bright; hence ~ता (*nf*).

समुत्कंठा samutkānṭha: (*nf*) deep longing, craving.

समुत्कर्ष samutkarsh (*nm*) self-elevation; eminence, prominence.

समु/त्थान samuttha:n (*nm*) rise, elevation; uplift; hence ~त्थित (*a*).

समुत्सुक samutsuk (*a*) anxiously desirous, yearning, craving, longing; hence ~ता (*nf*).

समुदाय samuda:y (*nm*) community; aggregate, collection; ~गत collective.

समुद्यत samuddyat (*a*) ready, in readiness.

समुद्र samuddr (*nm*) an ocean, a sea; ~कंप sea-quake; ~गामी seafaring; -तट/तीर sea shore; ~तटवर्ती coastal; ~तटीय व्यापार coastal trade; -मंथन churning of the ocean (In Indian mythology, the ocean was churned by the gods and the demons taking शेषनाग as the churn-string and the मंदराचल

(mountain) as the churn staff. It is supposed to have yielded, among other things, goddess Lakshmi:, nectar and poison; -यात्रा voyage, travel by ship; ~वर्ती maritime; -पर पुल बाँधना to set the Thames on fire.

समुद्री samuddri: (*a*) oceanic, marine; sea-borne; -डाकू a pirate; -तार a cable; -यात्रा a voyage.

समुद्रीय samuddri:y (*a*) oceanic, pertaining to the sea.

समुन्न/त samūnnat (*a*) risen, elevated; progressed, developed; ~ति progress, development; elevation, rise; hence ~यन (*nm*).

समुपस्थि/त samupasthit (*a*) present; come, turned up; hence ~ति (*nf*).

समुल्लास samulla:s (*nm*) exhiliration; chapter (of a book).

समूचा samū:cha: (*a*) all, whole, entire.

समूल samu:l (*a*) having root(s); well-founded; (*adv*) from the root; root and branch; -नाश complete ruination/destruction, extermination; ०करना to destroy root and branch.

समूल्य samu:ly (*a*) priced.

समूह samu:h (*nm*) a group; collection; aggregate, assemblage, multitude; community; ~त: en bloc, en masse; ~न aggregation, collection; ~वाचक indicative of community/aggregate; collective; ०संज्ञा collective noun.

समृद्ध samriddh (*a*) prosperous, flourishing; affluent, rich.

समृद्धि samriddhi (*nf*) prosperity, flourish; affluence, richness.

समेक/न samekan (*nm*) (the act or process of) integration; consolidation; ~ता integration; consolidation, solidarity; ~तावाद solidarism.

समेटना samēṭnā: (*v*) to wrap up, to roll up; to wind up; to gather/collect; to rally; to amass.

समेत samet (*a* and *adv*) with, together with, along with; accompanied by.

समैक्य samaiky (*nm*) solidarity, integration.

समोना samonā: (*v*) to (cause to) permeate, to pervade; to infuse (with).

समोवार samova:r (*nm*) a samovar.

समोसा samōsa: (*nm*) a kind of stuffed pie of a triangular shape.

सम्मत sammāt (*a*) supported (by), approved of (by), authenticated (by).

सम्मति sammāti (*nf*) opinion; consent; advice.

सम्मन sammān (*nm*) summons.

सम्मर्द sammard (*nm*) crowd; trampling.

सम्मान sammā:n (*nm*) respect, honour; prestige; ~पूर्ण respectable, honourable; ~पूर्वक respectfully, honourably.

सम्माननीय sammā:nnī:y (*a*) honourable, respectable; hence ~ता (*nf*).

सम्मानित sammā:nīt (*a*) honoured, respected.

सम्मान्य sammā:ny (*a*) see सम्माननीय.

सम्मिलन sammilan (*a*) coming together, union; coalescence.

सम्मिलित sammilit (*a*) united; mixed; included.

सम्मि/श्र sammishr (*a*) intermixed, commingled; combined; compound(ed); also ~श्रित (*a*).

सम्मिश्रण sammishrāṇ (*nm*) the act or process of intermixing/commingling; combining.

सम्मुख sammukh (*a*) before, in front of; opposite; facing, confronting, being face to face; propitious.

सम्मेलन sammelan (*nm*) a conference; meeting; assembly.

सम्मो/ह sammoh (*nm*) hypnosis; fascination; stupefaction; beguilement; ~**हक** hypnotic/hypnotising; a hypnotis; ~**हन** hypnosis, hypnotising; fascinating; stupefying; ~**हन-अस्त्र** a missile that stupefies; ~**हन-विद्या** hypnotism; ~**हनी** hypnotic spell; ~**हित** hypnotised; fascinated; stupefied,

सम्यक् sammyak (*adv* and *a*) thoroughly, completely, wholly; duly, well; due.

सम्यग् samyag—an allomorph of **सम्यक्** as it appears in some compound words; ~**ज्ञान/बोध** precise knowledge, thorough knowledge; ~**वाक्** precise in speech.

सम्राज्ञी samra:ggi: (*nf*) an Empress.

सम्राज्य samra:jjy (*nm*) see **साम्राज्य**.

सम्राट् samra:ṭ (*nm*) an Emperor.

सम्हलना samhalnā: (*v*) see **सँभलना**.

सयानपन saya:npān (*nm*) cleverness; cunningness.

सयाना saya:nā: (*a*) grown up; clever; cunning; ~**पन** grown up state; cleverness, cunningness; —**कौवा गू खाता है, कूड़े पर** every fox must pay his skin to the furrier; positive men are often in error.

सरंजाम sarāṇja:m (*nm*) preparations; arrangements; accomplishment; —**करना/बांधना** to make arrangements/preparations; —**होना** preparations/arrangements to be made.

सर sar (*nm*) see **सिर**; a pond, pool; an arrow; one of the four top-valued playing cards; (*a*) conquered, subdued; ~**अंजाम** see **सरंजाम**; ~**कश** mischief monger; impudent, rebellious; ~**कशी** mischief-mongering; impudence, rebelliousness; ~**खत** stamped agreement/document, etc; ~**गना** leader (of a gang), ring-leader; ~**गर्मी** hectic activity; passionate effort; enthusiasm; ~**गुज़श्त** description, narration; happening, event; ~**गोशी** whispers, whispering campaign/complaints (against); ~**ज़मीन** country; territory; ~**ज़ोर** impudent, insolent; hence ~**ज़ोरी** (*nf*); ~**ताज** see **सिरताज**; ~**दर्द** headache; botheration; ~**दर्दी** botheration; source of anxiety/concern; ~**दार** a chieftain; leader; boss; a sikh; ~**दारी** the office, function or status of a **सरदार**; ~**नाम** well-known, renowned, famous; ~**नामा** form of address and superscriptional formalities in a letter etc.; ~**पंच** the head **पंच**; ~**परस्त** a patron; supporter; ~**परस्ती** patronage; support; ~**पेच** an ornament worn over the turban, a diadem; ~**फ़राज़** honoured; arrogant; hence ~**फ़राज़ी** (*nf*); ~**फ़रोश** ready to sacrifice one's life; intrepid; ~**फ़रोशी** readiness to sacrifice life; intrepidness; ~**शार** full to the brim; bubbling; buoyant; -**व-समान** bag and baggage; ~**शुमारी** census; ~**सब्ज़** green, verdant; prosperous; **सरे-इजलास** in the court, while the court is in session; **सरे-दरबार** openly; **सरे-नौ** afresh, anew; **सरे-बाज़ार** openly, publicly; **सरे-शाम** early in the evening, as soon as the evening sets in; –**करना** to conquer; to subdue; to vanquish; –**होना** to be conquered; to be subdued; to be vanquished; –**मँढ़ना** to impose on; –**मुंडाते ही ओले पड़े** ill-luck overtaking at the very outset.

सरकंडा sarkāṇḍa: (*nm*) (a kind of) reed.

सरकना saraknā: (*v*) to slip; to slide; to creep.

सरकस sarkas (*nm*) a circus.

सरकार sarka:r (*nf*) government; administration.

सरकारी sarka:ri: (*a*) governmental; public; official; administrative; **–आमदनी** public revenue; **–इमारत** a public building; **–कागज़** an official paper; **–काम** an official work; **–गवाह** prosecution witness; **–तंत्र** governmental machinery; **–नौकर** government/public servant; **–नौकरी** government/public service; **–मुलाज़िम** a government/public servant; **–वकील** prosecution counsel; government pleader.

सरकारीकरण sarka:ri:karāṉ (*nm*) governmentalisation, taking over by the government, bringing under government control/administration.

सरगम sargam (*nf*) the gamut; a syllabic form of musical composition.

सरणि saranī (*nf*) a channel; **~बद्ध** channelized.

सरता-बरता sarta:barta: (*nm*) mutual division of share; **–करना** to carry on with mutual aid.

सरथ sarath (*nm*) a charioteer; (*a*) riding a chariot.

सरना sarnā: (*v*) to be accomplished; to be seen through; **–, काज/काम** a work to be accomplished.

सरपट sarpaṭ (*a* and *adv*) galloping; apace; **–चाल** galloping speed, gallop.

सरफोंका sarphōka: (*nm*) see **सरकंडा**; a medicinal plant.

सरमा/या sarma:ya: (*nm*) capital; **~येदार** a capitalist; **~येदारी** capitalism.

सरल saral (*a*) easy; simple; straight; direct; straight-forward; ingenuous; light; **~ता** easiness; simplicity; straightness; directness; straightforwardness; ingenuity; **–ब्याज** simple interest; **–रेखा** a straight line; **–संगीत** light music; **~हृदय** simple-hearted, straight, ingenuous; **~हृदयता** simple-heartedness, straightness, ingenuity.

सरली/करण sarali:karāṉ (*nm*) simplification; **~कृत** simplified.

सरवर sarvar (*nm*) a pond, pool.

सरस saras (*a*) juicy; sweet; delicious, tasteful; relishable; hence **~ता** (*nf*).

सरसठ sarsaṭh (*a*) sixty-seven; (*nm*) the number sixty-seven.

सरसना sarasnā: (*v*) to flourish, to prosper; to acquire fullness; to be in full bloom; to be full of relish/charm.

सरसर sarsar (*nf*) rustling noise, frou-frou.

सरसरा/ना sarsara:nā: (*v*) to produce a rustling noise, to cause a frou-frou; **~हट** frou-frou, rustle.

सरसरी sarsari: (*a*) cursory; hurried; **–जाँच** hurried check-up; brief examination; **–तौर पर** cursorily, summarily; roughly; **–नज़र/निगाह** cursory glance; **०डालना** to throw a cursory glance.

सरसाना sarsa:nā: (*v*) to cause to flourish/prosper/acquire fullness; to be full of relish/charm, to be in full bloom.

सरसिज sarsij (*nm*) a lotus-flower.

सरसी sarsi: (*uf*) a small pond/pool.

सरसों sarsō (*nf*) mustard seed or plant; **–का तेल** mustard oil; **–फूलना, आँखों में** to be elated.

सरस्वती saraswati: (*nf*) the goddess

of learning/speech; speech; name of a river.

सरहज sarhaj (*nf*) brother-in-law's (साले की) wife.

सरह/द sarhad (*nf*) boundary, frontier; ~दबंदी demarcation; ~दी pertaining to/related with or belonging to ~द.

सरापना sara:pnā: (*v*) to curse; to condemn, to imprecate.

सरापा sara:pa: (*adv*) from head to foot; all over.

सरा/फ़ sara:f (*nm*) a dealer in gold and silver (jewellery); ~फ़ा gold and silver exchange market.

सराफ़ी sara:fi: (*nf*) the business of a सराफ़; the script used by Indian style accountants which is just an expedient variation of Devna:gri:.

सराबोर sara:bor (*a*) completely drenched; soaked.

सराय sara:y (*nf*) an inn, a tavern.

सरासर sara:sar (*adv*) downright, sheer; altogether, entirely; –ज्यादती downright/sheer excess.

सराह/ना sara:hnā: (*v*) to praise, to applaud, to commend; to eulogize, to appreciate; (*nf*) praise, appreciation, applause; eulogy.

सराहनीय sara:hnī:y (*a*) praise-worthy, laudable, commendable.

सरिता sarita: (*nf*) a river, stream.

सरिया sariya: (*nm*) an iron-bar.

सरि/श्ता sarishta: (*nm*) a department; court; ~श्तेदार a court-official; ~श्तेदारी job or office of a सरिश्तेदार.

सरिस saris (*a*) equal; like, identical.

सरीखा sari:kha: (*a*) like, resembling, identical.

सरीसृप sari:srip (*a* and *nm*) (the) reptile(s).

सरीहन sari:han (*adv*) openly, publicly.

सरूप saru:p (*a*) having a form/shape; hence ~ता (*nf*).

सरूर saru:r (*nm*) see सुरूर.

सरेदस्त saredast (*adv*) now, this very time.

सरेबाज़ार sareba:za:r (*adv*) openly, publicly.

सरे/श, ~स saresh, ~s (*nf*) glue.

सरो saro (*nm*) a cypress tree.

सरोकार saroka:r (*nm*) concern, business.

सरोज saroj (*nm*) a lotus-flower.

सरोद sarod (*nf*) *sarod*—a stringed musical instrument.

सरोरुह saroruh (*nm*) a lotus-flower.

सरोवर sarovar (*nm*) a pond, pool.

सरोष sarosh (*a* and *adv*) with rage, enraged, furious(ly); wrathful(ly).

सरौता sarauta: (*nm*) a nut-cracker.

सर्कस sarkas (*nm*) a circus.

सर्किल sarkil (*nm*) a circle.

सर्कुलर sarkular (*nm*) a circular (letter, etc).

सर्ग sarg (*nm*) a canto; world; ~बद्ध divided into cantos.

सर्चलाइट sarchla:iṭ (*nf*) a search-light.

सर्जन sarjan (*nm*) creation; a surgeon; ~हार a creator.

सर्जना sarjanā: (*nf*) creation.

सर्जरी sarjari: (*nf*) surgery.

सर्टीफ़िकेट sarṭi:fikeṭ (*nm*) a certificate.

सर्द sard (*a*) cold; cool; frigid; lifeless; -गर्म ups and downs whirligigs (of life); o देखे हुए होना to have faced ups and downs, to have stood the whirligigs of life; ~बाज़ारी slump in the market market-depression; ~मिज़ाज cold unresponsive; –हो जाना to become still/lifeless; to die; to lose warmth.

सर्दा sarda: (*nm*) a sweeter and

tastier species of melon.

सर्दी sardi: (*nf*) cold; winter; -गरमी winter and summer; vicissitudes of life; -खाना to be struck by cold.

सर्प sarp (*nm*) a serpent, snake; ~दंश snake-bite; -निर्मोक the slough (of a snake); -फण the hood of a snake; ~राज Va:suki —the mythological serpent king; a huge snake; -विद्या the art of snake-charming; hence सर्पिणी (*nf*).

सर्पण sarpān (*nm*) creeping, crawling.

सर्पिल sarpil (*nm* and *a*) a spiral; zigzag.

सर्फ़ sarf (*a*) spent, expended; -करना to spend; -होना to be spent/expended.

सर्रा/फ़ sarra:f (*nm*) see सराफ़; ~फ़ा see सराफ़ा.

सर्व sarv (*a*) all; whole, entire, complete; ~काम्य universally popular; coveted/desired by all; ~काल for or at all times, always; ~कालीन belonging to all times, perpetual; ~क्षमा amnesty; ~गति omnipresent; ~जन everybody; all; ~जनीन universal; applying to or concerned with all and sundry; ~जित all-conquering; ~ज्ञ a know-all, omniscient; ~ज्ञता omniscience; ~दर्शी all-seeing; ~दलीय all-party, consisting of representatives of all parties; ~दान gift of one's all; ~देशीय cosmopolitan, universal; ~देशीयता cosmopolitanism; universality; ~नाम a pronoun; ~नाश holocaust, complete ruin, utter destruction/devastation; o होना to go to the devil; ~नाशी all-destroying, causing complete ruin; ~नियंता all-controlling, Master of all; ~पालक all-preserving, all-protecting; ~प्रिय all-loving; loved by all, universally popular; hence ~प्रियता (*nf*); ~भक्षी omnivorous, all consuming; ~मंगल good of all, universal good; ~राष्ट्रवाद cosmopolitanism; ~विद omniscient; ~व्यापक omnipresent; universal; ~व्यापकता omnipresence; universality; ~व्यापी omnipresent; universal; ~शक्तिमान omnipotent; ~शुभवाद optimism; ~शुभवादी an optimist; optimistic; ~श्री Messrs; ~श्रेष्ठ the best, best of the lot, pick of the basket; hence ~श्रेष्ठता (*nf*); ~सम्मत unanimous; ~सम्मति unanimity; o से स्वीकृत होना, प्रस्ताव आदि to be adopted/passed unanimously; ~सह all enduring; ~साधारण the common man; people at large; ~सामान्य common, commonplace; ~सुलभ easily accessible to all; ~हर appropriating everything, all-usurping; ~हारी all appropriating; all-usurping; ~हित general welfare, common good.

सर्वतः sarvatah (*ind*) all round, everywhere, from all sides/directions.

सर्वतो sarvato—an allomorph of सर्वतः as it appears in a number of compound words; ~गामी going all round, going in all directions; ~भद्र auspicious, good for all; clean-shaven all over; ~भाव omnipresence; ~भावेन in every way, fully, thoroughly; ~मुख facing all directions; ~मुखी in all directions; versatile; oप्रतिभा versatile genius.

सर्वत्र sarvattr (*in*) everywhere; allways, in every case.

सर्वथा sarvatha: (*ind*) entirely, thoroughly, in all respects, in every way.

सर्वदा sarvada: (*ind*) always, at all times.

सर्वशः sarvashah (*ind*) all-round, in all respects, completely.

सर्वश्रेष्ठ sarvashreshṭḥ (*a*) see under 'सर्व'; hence ~ता (*nf*).

सर्वस्व sarvassv (*nm*) one's all, all one's belongings/possessions.

सर्वहारा sarvaha:ra: (*nm*) the proletariat; –वर्ग the proletariat class; ०की तानाशाही dictatorship of the proletariat.

सर्वांग sarva:ṅg (*nm*) the whole person; all over; ~पूर्ण complete in all respects; ~सम congruent; ~समता congruence; ~सुन्दर pretty in all respects, shapely all over.

सर्वांगीण sarvā:ṅgī:ṇ (*a*) permeating all parts, all-sided, all round, in all respects; hence ~ता (*nf*).

सर्वांतर्यामी sarvā:ntarya:mī: (*a*) All-Pervasive; (*nm*) God.

सर्वा/त्मा sarva:tmā: (*nm*) the Universal Soul; the All-Pervading; ~त्म(त्मक)वाद animism; ~त्म(त्मक)वादी an animist; animistic.

सर्वाधिक sarva:dhik (*a*) most; ahead of all.

सर्वाधिकार sarva:dhika:r (*nm*) all rights; ०सुरक्षित all rights reserved.

सर्वाधिकारी sarva:dhika:ri: (*a*) plenipotentiary, wielding or vested with all rights.

सर्वाधिपत्य sarva:dhipatty (*nm*) exercise of hegemony over all, autocracy; ~वाद autocracy; ~वादी autocratic; an autocrat.

सर्वार्थ sarva:rth (*nm*) universal good, good of all; ~वाद universalism; ~वादी a universalist; universalistic.

सर्वास्ति/वाद sarva:stiva:d (*nm*) the doctrine that all existence is real; ~वादी an adherent or follower of ~वाद.

सर्वाहारी sarva:ha:ri: (*a*) omnivorous.

सर्वीय sarvi:y (*a*) relating/pertaining to all.

सर्वेक्ष/ण sarvekshāṇ (*nm*) survey; ~क a surveyor; ~णकर्ता a surveyor, one who surveys; –, भाषा linguistic survey.

सर्वे/श, ~श्वर sarvesh, ~shshvar (*nm*) Master of all, God.

सर्वेसर्वा sarvesarva: (*a*) all-in-all, all-powerful.

सर्वोच्च sarvochch (*a*) paramount, supreme, above all, best, uppermost; hence ~ता (*nf*); –न्यायालय Supreme Court; –सत्ता supreme authority; –सम्मान the blue ribbon; –सेनापति Supreme Commander.

सर्वोत्तम sarvottam (*a*) the best, most excellent; optimum.

सर्वोत्कृष्ट sarvotkrishṭ (*a*) best, superior-most, above all; hence ~ता (*nf*).

सर्वोदय sarvoday (*nm*) uplift of all; (–आन्दोलन) a non-violent movement in India meant for the uplift of all men without distinction of caste, creed, sex or status (and led by Acharya Vinoba Bhave and Jaya Prakash Narayan).

सर्वोपरि sarvopari (*a*) supreme; paramount; above all, ahead of all; ~ता supremacy, paramountcy.

सलज्ज salajj (*a*) shy, bashful; modest; hence ~ता (*nf*).

सलमा salmā: (*nm*) a band of embroidery; -सितारा a kind of embroidery consisting of small shining stars between embroidered bands.

सलवट salvaṭ (*nf*) see सिलवट.

सलवार salva:r (*nf*) a kind of trousers.

सलहज salhaj (*nf*) see सरहज.

सलाई sala:i: (*nf*) a knitting needle, needle; thin wire; stick.

सलाख़ sala:ḳḥ (*nf*) a thin iron rod, bar.

सलाद sala:d (*nm*) salad.

सलाम sala:m (*nm*) salutation; adieu, good-bye; –अलैकुम good morning to you, greetings/salutation to you; –करना to salute, to greet; to desist or refrain (from); to acknowledge the superiority of; –देना to bid adieu; to present compliments; to request the presence of; –लेना to accept and return the salutation (of); सलामोपयाम salutations and kind messages.

सलामत sala:mat (*a*) safe, sound, secure, well; –रहना to be safe and sound, to be secure.

सलामती sala:mati: (*nf*) safety; well-being, welfare; –का जाम पीना to drink to the health (of); –चाहना to wish well; –से safely, well.

सलामी sala:mī: (*nf*) salutation; salute (in honour of a guest, esp. by booming of guns); guard of honour; –देना to present a guard of honour, to salute (esp. with the booming of guns): –लेना to inspect a guard of honour.

सलाह sala:h (*nf*) advice, counsel; opinion; cordial relations; reconciliation; –सदा अच्छी counsel is never out of date.

सलाहका/र sala:hka:r (*nm*) an adviser; counsellor; (*a*) advisory; hence ~रिता (*nf*).

सलाहियत sala:hiyat (*nf*) goodness; mannerliness; ability, capability.

सलिल salil (*nm*) water.

सली/क़ा sali:qā: (*nm*) manners, etiquette; ~क़ेदार mannerly; ~क़ेमंद mannerly.

सलीपर sali:par (*nm*) slippers.

सली/ब sali:b (*nf*) cross; ~बी pertaining to the cross; Christian.

सलीमशाही sali:msha:hi: (*nf*) a typical light and soft shoe.

सलीस sali:s (*a*) simple, easy; current (as–ज़बान).

सलूक salu:k (*nm*) treatment, behaviour.

सलूका salu:ka: (*nm*) a full-sleeve jacket.

सलूनो salu:nō (*nf*) see रक्षा-बंधन (under रक्षा).

सलोतरी salotari: (*nm*) a veterinary doctor.

सलो(लौ)ना salo(au)nā: (*a*) charming, winsome; saltish; ~पन charm, winsomeness; saltishness.

सल्तनत saltanat (*nf*) sultanate; kingdom; –जमना/बैठना authority to be established.

सवयस्क savayask (*a*) of the same age, equal in age.

सवर्ण savarṇ (*a*) of the same colour/caste; caste; belonging to the three upper castes (of the Hindu social set-up); hence ~ता (*nf*); –हिंदू a caste Hindu.

सवा sawa: (*a* and *nm*) (the number) one and a quarter; –सोलह आने ठीक/सच होना to be true to the core, to be absolutely true.

सवाक् sava:k (*a*) talking, gifted with speech; –चित्र talkie.

सवाब sava:b (*nm*) reward/recompense/return (for good deeds and obedience to God); –कमाना to earn reward (for good deeds).

सवाया sava:ya: (*a*) one and a quarter times; more (than), ahead (of).

सवार sava:r (*nm*) a rider, horseman; person sitting in or on a carriage/vehicle; (*a*) mounted, riding.

सवारी sava:ri: (*nf*) a conveyance, vehicle; passenger; a procession; –गाड़ी a passenger train; –आना a graceful personality to make an appearance; tableau to pass; –कसना/गांठना to ride (roughly) over; to sit over the head of; –देना to act as a vehicle, to carry; –लेना to ride.

सवाल sava:l (*nm*) a question, query; an exercise/problem (in Mathematics); demand; -जवाब question and answer; ~नामा questionnaire; –करना to (put a) question; to put forth a demand; –कुछ जवाब कुछ, –दीगर जवाब दीगर the answer to be beside the question; सवालों की झड़ी लगाना to put one question after another in quick succession.

सवालात sava:la:t (*nm*) plural form of सवाल.

सवालिया sava:liya: (*a*) interrogatory; interrogative; –निशान mark of interrogation; –फ़िकरा an interrogative sentence.

सवाली sava:li: (*nm*) a questioner, petitioner; beggar.

सवास sawa:s (*a*) aromatic, perfumed; having a dwelling (place).

सविकल्प; ~क savikalp, ~ak, (*a*) possessing variation or admitting of distinctions or alternatives/ options, differentiated.

सविकार savika:r (*a*) undergoing modification or decomposition, variable.

सविता savita: (*nm*) the sun.

सविनय savinay (*a* and *adv*) courteous(ly), modest(ly), polite(ly); civil; –अवज्ञा civil disobedience; ०आंदोलन civil disobedience movement (launched by Gandhiji during the Indian freedom movement).

सविलास savila:s (*a*) wanton, amorous; playful, sporting.

सविशेष savishesh (*a*) peculiar, singular, characteristic.

सविस्तर savistar (*a*) detailed, elaborate; also सविस्तार.

सविस्मय savismay (*a* and *adv*) amazed, astonished; with amazement.

सवेग saveg (*a* and *adv*) speedy/ speedily; expeditious / expeditiously.

सवे/रा savera: (*nm*) morning, daybreak; ~रे in the morning, at day-break); ~रे-सवेरे early in the morning.

सवैया savaīya: (*nm*) a popular metric composition in Hindi (during the mediaeval ages).

सव्याज savya:j (*a*) guileful, cunning.

सशंक sashānk (*a*) suspicious, sceptic; hence ~ता (*nf*).

सशक्त sashakt (*a*) potential, powerful, strong, forceful; ~ता potentiality, force(fulness), power (-fulness), strength.

सशब्द sashabd (*a*) noisy; wordy.

सशरीर sashari:r (*adv* and *a*) bodily, physically; embodied.

सशर्त sashart (*a*) qualified, conditional.

सशस्त्र sashastr (*a*) armed, equipped with arms; –पुलिस armed police; –सेना armed force; –सैनिक armed troops; –हस्तक्षेप armed intervention.

सश्रम sashshram (*a*) tired, fatigued, wearied, exhausted; rigorous; –कारावास rigorous imprisonment.

ससंभ्रम sasāmbhram (*a*) confused, perplexed.

ससि sasi (*nm*) the moon.

ससुर sasur (*nm*) father-in-law; a term of abuse generally used by menfolk.

ससुरा sasura: (*nm*) see ससुर—generally used in the latter sense i.e. as a term of abuse.

ससुराल sasura:l (*nf*) father-in-law's house, house/place of (one's) in-laws.

ससैन्य sasainny (*a*) with the army, backed by armed forces.

सस्ता sasta: (*a*) cheap; trash, inferior; (सस्ती) जगह inexpensive place; –जमाना cheap/inexpensive times; ~पन cheapness; –माल cheap stuff; –समय see –जमाना; –साहित्य cheap literature, trash; –छूटना to go cheap; be let off at a discount; to have to spend less than usual; –रोये बार बार महँगा रोये एक बार strike a cheap bargain and be ill at ease ever after; सस्ते (में) without much price/difficulty/botheration.

सस्ती sasti: (*nf*) cheapness; depression; (*a*) see सस्ता.

सस्त्रीक sastri:k (*a*) with one's wife.

सस्नेह sasneh (*adv* and *a*) with love; loving, affectionate.

सस्पृह sasprih (*a*) desirous, having a desire/craving/longing.

सस्मित sasmit (*a*) smiling.

सस्य sassy (*nm*) crop; -क्रांति green revolution; ~पाल a field-guard; ~शाली full of corn; –श्यामला lush green and cropwise rich.

सह sah (*ind*) with, along with, simultaneously; co–; (*a*) enduring, bearing; proof (as जलसह waterproof); -अपराधिता complicity; -अपराधी an accomplice; -अभियुक्त co-accused; -अस्तित्व co-existence; ~कर्त्ता a colleague; collaborator; ~कार cooperation, cooperative enterprise; collaboration; ~कारिता cooperation; collaboration; oआंदोलन cooperative movement; ~कारी cooperative; collaborative; a colleague, junior colleague; assistant; oसमाज cooperative society; ~क्रिया synergy; ~क्रियात्मक synergic; ~गमन self-immolation of a widow with her deceased husband; hence ~गामिनी; (*nf*); ~चर an associate; a companion, friend; a co-variant; hence ~चरी (feminine form of सहचर); ~चारी an associate, a companion, friend; associate element; gregarious, going together; ~जन्मा a twin brother; ~जात congenital; twins; innate, natural; ~जीवन symbiosis; co-existence; ~जीविता symbiosis; co-existence; ~जीवी co-existent; symbiotic; ~धर्म common duty/law/religion; ~धर्मिणी one's wife; ~धर्मी co-religionist; charged with the same duties; ~नर्तन/नृत्य dancing together, collective dancing; enclosure; ~पाठी a class fellow, classmate; ~भागिता partnership; complicity; ~भागी a partner; an accomplice; existing together; coexistence; ~भोज collective feasting/eating; ~भोजी a mess-mate; ~मरण see ~गमन; ~यात्री a co-traveller, fellow passenger; companion; ~राज्य condominium; associate state; ~राष्ट्रिक co-national; ~लेखक co-author; collaborator; hence ~लेखकत्व (*nm*); ~लेखन

co-authorship; collaboration; ~वर्तिता concomitance, concurrence; ~वर्ती concomitant, concurrent; ~शिक्षा co-education; ~शिक्षात्मक/शैक्षिक co-educational; -संपादक co-editor; ~संबंध correlation; ~स्वर harmonious; ~स्वरता harmony.

सहज sahaj (*a*) easy, simple; spontaneous; straight-forward; ingenuous: innate, natural; congenital; -ज्ञान intuitive knowledge; ~ता easiness, simplicity; spontaneity; straightforwardness; ingenuity; innateness, naturality; -बुद्धि common sense; ~यान a sect of the Buuddhist faith; hence ~यानी (*a* and *nm*); ~वृत्ति instinct; ~सिद्ध spontaneous; innate, natural; hence ~सिद्धि (*nf*).

सहत्व sahatv (*nm*) co-existence, being together.

सहन sahan (*nm*) patient endurance, forbearance; tolerance; a courtyard; ~दार having a courtyard (as ~दार मकान); -शक्ति endurance, forbearance, tolerance; ~शील enduring, forbearing, tolerant; ~शीलता endurance, tolerance, forbearance; -करना to endure, to forbear, to tolerate.

सह/ना sahnā: (*v*) to endure, to forbear, to tolerate, to stand; ~नीय tolerable.

सहम/त sahmāt (*a*) agreed; consented/concurred; ~ति agreement; concurrence, consent.

सहमना sahamnā: (*v*) to be panicked, to be struck with terror, to be nervous.

सहयो/ग sahyog (*nm*) cooperation; collaboration; ~गात्मक cooperative; collaborative; ~गिता synergism; cooperation; collaboration; ~गी a colleague; supporter, one who extends cooperation.

सहर sahar (*nm*) dawn, day-break; ~दम very early in the morning.

सहरा sahra: (*nm*) a desert.

सहल sahal (*a*) easy, simple.

सहलाना sahla:nā: (*v*) to rub gently; to tickle; to titillate.

सहवास sahva:s (*nm*) cohabitation; -करना, के साथ to cohabit (with).

सहसा sahsa: (*ind*) suddenly, all of a sudden; unexpectedly; -विप्लव coup de main; -शासन-परिवर्तन coup d'etat.

सहस्र sahasr (*a*) one thousand; (*nm*) the number one thousand; ~कर the sun; ~गुण/गुणा one thousand times; ~धा in a thousand ways; thousand times; ~श: thousand times; सहस्रों thousands.

सहस्रा/ब्द, ~ब्दी sahasra:bd (*nm*), ~bdi: (*nf*) a millennium.

सहाई saha:i: (*nm*) a helper; an assistant; (*nf*) help; assistance.

सहाध्यायी saha:ddhya:i: (*nm*) a class-fellow, co-student.

सहानुभूति saha:nūbhu:ti (*nf*) sympathy; ~प्रवण/शील sympathetic; ~पूर्ण sympathetic; ~पूर्वक sympathetically.

सहापरा/धी saha:para:dhi: (*nm*) an accomplice; ~धिता complicity.

सहाय saha:y (*nm*) a helper, supporter.

सहायक saha:yak (*nm*) a helper; an assistant; (*a*) auxiliary; assistant; -नदी a tributary.

सहायता saha:yta: (*nf*) help, support; assistance; aid, relief; -करना to strike a blow for, to help/assist.

सहार saha:r (*nm*) tolerance, endurance.

सहारना saha:rnā: (*v*) to tolerate, to endure.

सहारा saha:ra: (*nm*) support; backing; aid, succour; a strut; –देना to give a knee to, to (lend) support.

सहालग saha:lag (*nm*) auspicious period for solemnization of marriages.

सहित sahit (*ind*) with, together with, along with, accompanied by.

सहिदानी sahida:nī: (*nf*) a memento.

सहिष्णु sahishnū (*a*) tolerant, enduring; ~ता tolerance, endurance.

सही sahi: (*a*) correct, right; true; accurate; authentic; hence ~पन; -सलामत safe and sound, hale and hearty; secure; -सही correct, accurate; true; –करना to sign; to endorse.

सहूलियत sahu:liat (*nf*) convenience; facility.

सहृदय sahriday (*a*) humane, compassionate, tender-hearted; considerate; ~ता humaneness, compassion, tender-heartedness, considerateness.

सहेजना sahejnā: (*v*) to keep securely, to keep with care; to entrust.

सहेट saheṭ (*nf*) a rendezvous.

सहेतु, ~क sahetu, ~k (*a*) logical; having a reason/cause.

सहेली saheli: (*nf*) a female companion.

सहोदर sahodar (*nm*) a real brother; (*a*) real, born of the same mother.

सह्य sahy (*a*) tolerable, endurable; hence ~ता (*nf*).

साँईं sā:ī: (*nm*) God, Lord; master; husband; a title used for Mohammedan faqirs.

साँकल sā:kal (*nf*) a chain.

सांकेतिक sa:ṅketik (*a*) token; nominal; symbolic; indicative; –शब्द a password,

सांक्षेपिक sā:ṅkshepik (*a*) concise; abbreviated, abridged.

सांख्य sa:ṅkkhy (*nm*) one of the six major Indian Philosophical systems; ~वादी an adherent of सांख्य doctrine.

सांख्यिकी sa:ṅkhiki: (*nf*) (the science of) Statistics; ~य statistic(al); ~विद्/वेत्ता a statistician.

साँग sa:g (*nf*) a heavy iron implement for digging up a well.

सांग sā:ṅg (*a*) having limbs or body, together with the body; complete, entire; organic; –रूपक sustained metaphor.

सांगोपांग sā:ṅgopā:ṅg (*a*) complete (with limbs and parts), entire.

सांग्रामिक sā:ṅgra:mīk (*a*) strategic, pertaining to battle/warfare.

सांघातिक sā:ngha:tik (*a*) fatal, mortal.

साँच sā:ch (*a*) true, correct; (*nm*) truth; –को आंच नहीं/कहाँ truth knows no fear.

साँचा sā:cha: (*nm*) a modelling tool; model; die, mould, moulding pattern; ~चे में ढला cast in a pretty mould, well-shaped, shapely.

साँझ sā:jh (*nf*) evening, dusk; –का झुटपुटा/धुँधलका twilight.

साँझा sā:jha: (*nm*) see साझा.

साँट sā:ṭ (*nm*) a cane.

साँठ-गाँठ sā:ṭḥ-gā:ṭḥ (*nf*) a plunder-bond, conspiratorial alliance; secret relationship; intrigue.

साँड़ sā:ṛ (*nm*) a bull; –, कमेटी का a wandering bull; a sturdy man with no moorings; –की तरह घूमना to roam about in a carefree manner; –की तरह डकारना to bellow.

साँड़नी sā:ṛnī: (*nf*) a fast-moving she-camel; -सवार one who rides a साँड़नी, a messenger.

साँड़ा sā:ṛa: (*nm*) a species of sand-lizard.

सांत sā:nt (*a*) finite, having an end.
सांततिक sā:ntatik (*a*) continuous; contributing to the continuity of a lineage.
सांतत्यक sā:ntattyak (*nm*) continuum.
सांत्वना sā:ntvanā: (*nf*) consolation, solace; –देना to console, to soothe.
सांद्र sā:ndr (*a*) concentrated, thick; strong; solid; stereo; ~ता concentration, thickness; strength; solidity.
सांध्य sā:ndhy (*a*) pertaining to the evening; ~काल evening; ~कालीन (pertaining to or functioning in the) evening; ~वेला evening (time).
साँप sā:p (*nm*) a snake, serpent, viper; (fig) a venomous person; –उतारना to counter the effect of snake-bite; –कलेजे या छाती पर लोटना to burn within on account of jealousy; –का काटा रस्सी से डरे a burnt child dreads the fire; –का पांव देखना to try to see what does not exist; –का बच्चा a venomous being; –की तरह फन मारकर रह जाना to make desperate bids in vain; –कीलना to render a snake ineffective through charm; –की लहर snake-bite convulsions; –की-सी केंचुली झाड़ना to undergo a metamorphosis; –के बिल में हाथ डालना to risk an avoidable hazard, to invite danger; –के मुँह में to be faced with risk of life; –के सँपोले ही होंगे as the crow is, so the egg shall be; –को दूध पिलाना to nourish a potential killer; –छछूंदर की सी गति होना to be on the horns of a dilemma; –निकल जाने पर लकीर पीटना to kiss the hare's foot, to be a day after the fair; –पालना to rear a snake, to put a viper in bosom; –भी मर जाये लाठी भी न टूटे (–मरे न लाठी टूटे) to kill a snake without a stake; –सूंघ जाना to cast a chill over, to be rendered still; –से खेलना to be in a dangerous company.
सांपत्तिक sā:mpattik (*a*) pertaining to or related with property, property.
साँपिन sā:pin (*nf*) a female snake/serpent.
सांप्रतिक sā:mpratik (*a*) modern, pertaining to present times.
सांप्रदायिक sā:mprada:ik (*a*) communal; sectarian; –कट्टरता communal bigotry; –दंगा a communal riot; –भावना communal feeling; –रहस्य sectarian secrets.
सांप्रदायिकता sā:mprada:ikta: (*nf*) communalism; sectarianism.
साँभर sā:bhar (*nm*) a kind of Indian antelope.
सांयोगिक sā:nyogik (*a*) chance, accidental, fortuitous; ~ता accidentalism, fortuitism.
सांवत्सरिक sā:mvatsarik (*a*) annual, pertaining to a संवत्सर.
साँवला sā:vla: (*a*) slightly dark-complexioned; ~पन slight darkness of complexion.
साँवलिया sā:valiya: (*nm*) a lover; husband.
साँवाँ sā:vā: (*nm*) little millet—a coarse foodgrain
सांविधिक sā:mvidhik (*a*) statutory; ~ता conformation to statutory provisions, accordance with the statute(s); –व्यवस्था statutory provision; –स्थिति statutory status/position.
सांश्लेषिक sā:nshleshik (*a*) synthetic; ~ता synthetism.
साँस sā:s (*nf*) breath/breathing; –यंत्र respirator, respiratory apparatus; –अंदर की अंदर बाहर की बाहर रह जाना

to be stunned breathless; –उखड़ना to be out of breath; –उल्टी चलना death to be hovering around; –का रोग asthma; –खींचना to hold in the breath; –गिनना to count the breaths; death to be imminent; –घुटना to be suffocated; –चढ़ना to be short of breath; –चढ़ाना to pretend to be dead; to hold in one's breath, to stop the breathing process for a while; –चलना to be breathing; –छोड़ना to expire; to breathe out; –टूटना to pant; to be out of breath; –तब तक आस, जब तक while there is life, there is hope; –तक न लेना just to be still; –देखना to examine the state of breathing (of an ailing person); –निकलना to breath one's last; -फूलना to gasp; to be out of breath; –भरना to draw a deep breath, to heave a sigh; to be out of breath; to be fatigued; –रहते as long as living, till the last breath; –रुकना breathing process to be obstructed; to be suffocated; –लेना to take breath, to breathe; –लेना, लंबी to heave a sigh; –लिने की जगह न होना not to have even breathing space, to be too crowded; –लेने की फ़ुर्सत breathing interval/respite; –लेने की फ़ुर्सत न होना not to have even a breathing respite.

सांसत sā:sat (*nf*) distress, affliction, trouble; –में होना, जान to be in deep distress, to be afflicted.

सांसद sa:nsad (*a*) parliamentary, pertaining or belonging to the parliament.

सांसदिक sa:nsadik (*a*) parliamentary; (*nm*) a parliamentarian.

सांसर्गिक sa:nsargik (*a*) born of contact, contagious.

सांसारिक sā:nsa:rik (*a*) worldly, mundane, mortal, earthly; secular; ~ता worldliness; secularity; –बुद्धि worldly wisdom.

सांस्कारिक sā:nska:rik (*a*) ritualistic; pertaining to or related with संस्कार, connected with one's mental impressions.

सांस्कृतिक sā:nskritik (*a*) cultural; –कार्य cultural affairs; –कार्यक्रम cultural programme; –मामले cultural affairs; –संबंध cultural relations.

सांस्थानिक sā:nstha:nīk (*a*) institutional.

साइंस sā:ins (*nf*) science; ~दाँ a scientist.

सा sa: (*ind*) like, similar to, resembling, following; (*nm*) a basic note of the musical gamut.

साइज sa:iz (*nm*) size.

साइकिल sa:ikil (*nf*) a bicycle.

साइत sa:it (*nf*) moment, hour, time; auspicious moment.

साइनबोर्ड sa:inborḍ (*nm*) a signboard.

साई sa:i: (*nf*) earnest money, security; advance (money to fix a deal).

साई/स sa:i:s (*nm*) a horse-keeper, groom; ~सी horse-tending, grooming.

साक sa:k (*nm*) see साग.

साकल्य sa:kally (*nm*) entirety, completeness.

साकांक्ष sa:kā:ṅksh (*a*) desirous, tending a wish/desire.

साका sa:ka: (*nm*) an era; overwhelming influence, eminence; –चलना to have an era named after; to be a historical figure; to be very important and influential.

साकार sa:ka:r (*a*) formal, having a form; concrete; ~ता the state of having a form; concreteness.

साकारोपासना sa:ka:ropa:snā: (*nf*) worshipping a formal deity, idol worship.

साकिन sa:kin (*nm*) resident (of); –हाल presently residing (at).

साक़ी sa:qi: (*nm*) a cup-bearer, one who serves a drink (liquor).

साक्षर sa:kshar (*a*) literate; ~ता literacy; oआंदोलन literacy campaign.

साक्षात् sa:ksha:t (*adv*) in the presence of, in person, visibly; (*a*) manifest, tangible, visible; ~कार an interview; ~कारी an interviewer; ~कृत interviewed.

साक्षी sa:kshi: (*nm*) a witness, deponent; (*nf*) evidence, testimony; -परीक्षा cross examination of a witness; ~भूत who has witnessed.

साक्षेप sa:kshep (*a*) taunting, containing an objection/insinuation/irony/reproach/reflection.

साक्ष्यं/कन sa:kshyāṅkan (*nm*) attestation; ~कित attested.

साक्ष्य sa:kshy (*nm*) evidence, testimony; vouchment; ~,अंत: internal evidence; ~,बहि: external evidence.

साख sa:kh (*nf*) credit; goodwill; reputation; trust; –पत्र letter of credit, credit note; –उठ जाना/डूबना/में बट्टा लगना one's credit/goodwill to be gone/liquidated, goodwill to be lost; –ऊँची उठना one's credit/goodwill to be enhanced/to go up; –जमना one's credit/goodwill to be firmly established.

साखी sa:khi: (*nm*) a witness.

साग sa:g (*nm*) vegetable; greens; -पात vegetables and herbs; -सब्ज़ी vegetables; -पात समझना to treat with contempt.

सागर sa:gar (*nm*) the ocean, sea; ~गामी sea-faring; -संगम estuary.

साग़र sa:gar (*nm*) a peg, (wine) cup.

सागवान sa:gwā:n (*nf*) teak (wood).

सागौन sa:gaun (*nf*) see सागवान.

साज sa;j (*nm*) accoutrements, embellishment; appurtenance; see साज़; -गृह green room; -सँवार upkeep, maintenance; –सजाना to organise a spectacle; to present in a particular manner.

साज़ sa:z (*nm*) a musical instrument; implement, equipment; harness; used as a suffix to mean –a mendor or manufacturer of (as ज़ीनसाज़); ~गार favourable, suitable; -बाज़ intrigue, conspiracy; paraphernalia; -संगीत instrumental music; -सामान furnishings, appurtenance, equipment; necessaries; –छेड़ना to commence playing of a musical instrument; to prepare the ground for.

साजन sa:jan (*nm*) lover; husband.

साज़िंदा sa:zīnda: (*nm*) an instrumentalist, accompanyist.

साज़ि/श sa:zish (*nf*) a conspiracy, plot, intrigue; hence ~शी (*a*).

सा/झा sa:jha: (*nm*) partnership; share; (*a*) common; ~झेदार a partner, shareholder; ~झेदारी partnership; ~झे की खेती a work in partnership, a common concern; ~झे की हँडिया चौराहे पर फूटती है a common horse is worst shod.

साझी sa:jhi: (*nm*) a partner; ~दार see साझेदार (under साझा); ~दारी see साझेदारी (under साझा).

साटन sa:ṭān (*nf*) satin (cloth).

साठ sa:ṭh (*a*) sixty; (*nm*) the number sixty.

साठा sa:ṭha: (*a*) of sixty years of age; –सो पाठा youth sets in as one reaches sixty.

साड़ी sa:ṛi: (*nf*) a *sari*.

साढ़ू sa:ṛhu: (*nm*) the husband of wife's sister.

साढ़े sa:ṛhe (*a*) plus half; ~**साती** (seven and a half years') Saturnian position foreboding evil; ०**लगना** to be in for a prolonged ominous period.

सात sa:t (*a*) seven; (*nm*) the number seven; –**जनम में भी नहीं** never, never—in this or even afterlife; –**घर भीख माँगना** to go abegging; -**पाँच** guiles, cunningness; ०**न जानना** to be guileless, to be extremely credulous; -**पाँच लगाना** to higgle, to raise numerous objections; –**परदों में रखना** to keep away from all eyes, to keep well in-doors; –**समुंदर पार** across the seven seas, very very far.

सातत्य sa:tatty (*nm*) continuity, uninterruptedness.

सात/वाँ sa:twā: (*a*) seventh; occupying the seventh position; ~**वें आसमान पर होना, दिमाग़** to be too swollen-headed.

सात्विक sa:ttvik (*a*) endowed with the quality of **सत्त्व** (purity and goodness), virtuous, righteous; hence ~**ता** (*nf*); –**तेज** glow of virtue/righteousness.

साथ sa:th (*adv*) with, together, along with, withal; by; (*nm*) company, association; support; -**साथ** together; ०**रहना** to associate with, to live in the company of; –**का खेला** chum; -**खोना** to be deprived of the company of; -**घसीटना** to oblige to accompany; –**छूटना** to be cut off; –**देना** to make common cause with; to keep company with; to stand by; –**निबाहना** to continue to be a loyal companion; to steadfastly stand by; –**रहना** to live together; –**लग लेना** to thrust oneself on; to join a reluctant person; –**लगा रहना** to be ever on somebody's heels, to constantly hover around; –**लेकर डूबना** to involve someone in a sure tragedy; –**सोना** to share bed with; –**ही** besides, apart from this; along with this; –**ही साथ** together; –**होना** to be one with; to stand by, to participate.

साथी sa:thi: (*nm*) a companion, comrade; mate, associate; fellow; hence **साथिन** (*nf*).

सादगी sa:dgi: (*nf*) simplicity, plainness.

सादर sa:dar (*adv* respectfully, with regards.

सादा sa:da: (*a*) simple; plain; flat; blank; unadorned; artless; –**कपड़ा** plain cloth; –**काग़ज** plain paper; ~**पन** simplicity; plainness; artlessness; ~ **मिजाज** plain and frank; artless; ~ **मिजाजी** artlessness; hence **सादी** feminine form of **सादा**.

सादृश्य sa:ddrishshy (*nm*) resemblance, likeness, analogy; affinity; ~**मूलक** based on likeness, analogical; hence ~**मूलकता** (*nf*); ~**वाचक**, ~**वाची** analogical.

साद्यंत sa:ddyānt (*a*) whole, entire; from beginning to end.

साध sa:dh (*nf*) an ambition, a craving, longing; –**न रहना** to have no wishes unfulfilled, to be gratified on all fronts.

साधक sa:dhak (*nm*) one engaged in or devoted to spiritual achievement/accomplishment; (*a*) effective, instrumental, conducive; engaged in or devoted to spiri-

tual achievement/accomplish-
ment; ~ता engagement or devotion to spiritual achievement/
accomplishment; effectiveness,
instrumentality, conduciveness.

साधन sa:dhan (nm) medium. means;
equipment; device, an implement; processing; solution; resources; realization; –, जन-संचार
mass media; -संपन्न resourceful;
hence -संपन्नता (nf).

साधना sa:dhnā: (nf) devotion;
practice, mental training; spiritual endeavour or performance
(esp. aspiring for an end); (v) to
tame; to aim; to train; to practise; ~परक relating to mental
training; hence ~परकता (nf).

साधनीय sa:dhnī:y (a) fit to be
achieved / accomplished/proved;
worth achieving/accomplishing/
proving.

साधर्म्य sa:dharmmy (nm) homogene-
ousness; parallelism; the state of
having some duties/characteris-
tics; ~मूलक based on homogene-
ousness/affinity of duties or
characteristics; hence ~मूलकता
(nf).

साधार sa:dha:r (a) having a basis/
ground.

साधारण sa:dha:rāṇ (a) ordinary;
simple; common, commonplace;
usual, moderate; –कारावास/कैद
simple imprisonment; –धर्म common characteristic; universal
duty; hence ~ता (nf); –वाक्य a
simple sentence.

साधारणतः sa:dha:rāṇtah (ind) ordi-
narily; usually.

साधारणतया sa:dha:rāṇtaya: (ind) see
साधारणतः.

साधारणी/करण sa:dha:rāṇī:karāṇ (nm)
generalisation; impersonalisation;

objectivisation; hence ~कृत (a).

साधित sa:dhit (a) trained, tamed;
solved; achieved, accomplished.

साधु sa:dhu (nm) a saint, saintly
person; hermit; a religious mendicant; (a) good, noble, virtuous;
~वृत्त moral, saintly; ~शील
pious, virtuous; ~सम्मत backed
by virtuous men; -साधु good !
excellent ! well done !

साधुता sa:dhuta: (nf) saintliness;
nobility, goodness, virtuousness,
rectitude.

साधुवाद sa:dhuva:d (nm) acclamation, applause.

साधू sa:dhu: (nm) a hermit, a religious mendicant.

साध्य sa:ddhy (nm) the end; that
which is to be proved; (a) practi-
cable/feasible; (fit) to be achie-
ved/accomplished; curable; ~ता
practicability/feasibility; fitness
or worthiness for achievement/
accomplishment; curability;
~वाद teleology.

साध्यवसान sa:ddhyavasā:n (nm) an
allegory; (a) allegorical.

साध्वी sa:ddhvi: (a) chaste (woman),
virtuous.

सानंद sa:nānd (a and adv) happy/
happily; pleased/with pleasure.

सान sā:n (nf) whetting; sharpness;
a whetstone; -गुमान a clue, hint.

सानना sa:nnā: (v) to make into a
paste; to besmear; to implicate/
involve.

सानी sā:nī: (nf) cattle-food (consisting of chaff and oilcake mixed
together); (nm) a match, an
equal.

सानुकंप sa:nukāmp (a) kindly disposed, compassionate.

सानुकूल sa:nuku:l (a) favourably
disposed (towards).

सानुनय sa:nunāy (*a*) humble, obedient; (*adv*) humbly, obediently.

सानुनासिक sa:nunā:sik (*a*) nasalised; ~ता nasalisation.

सानुप्रास sa:nuppra:s (*a*) alliterative.

सानुबंध sa:nubāndh (*a*) systematic; uninterrupted, having a contract.

सान्निध्य sa:nniddhy (*nm*) proximity, nearness

सापेक्ष sa:peksh (*a*) qualified, conditional; relative; ~ता relativity; ~वाद relativism; theory of relativity; hence ~वादी (*a* and *nm*)

साप्ताहिक sa:pta:hik (*a*) weekly; (*nm*) a weekly journal; –पत्र a weekly.

साफ़ sa:f (*a*) clean, clear; slick; plain, frank; categorical, forthright, straight-forward; processed; refined; undefiled; distinct; unscathed; (*adv*) openly, frankly, plainly; fully; clearly; cleverly; –इनकार frank refusal; a straight 'no'; ~गो frank; ~गोई frankness; –जवाब a frank reply, forthright reply; ~दिल clean at heart; ~दिली cleanness (of heart), straight-forwardness; –बात a frank statement/word; -साफ़ openly, clearly, frankly, plainly; ०कहना/बताना/मानना to come clean, to own up everything; –करना to clean(se); to sweep clean; to process, to refine; to clear (as बाधाएँ); to clear off (as हिसाब—); to claim life after life; to practise; –कहना to say plainly/frankly; –छूटना to go unscathed; to go scot free; –बचना/बच निकलना to get away with it, to escape retribution, to pass unhurt, to go unscathed; –बोलना to have a distinct delivery; to speak frankly; –मैदान पाना to be faced with no obstacles whatever, to have a smooth go; –होना to be swept clean; to be clear; –जगह पर मैल और भी बुरा लगता है dirt looks dirtiest on a snow-white surface.

साफल्य sa:phally (*nm*) success.

साफ़ा sa:fa: (*nm*) a turban.

साफ़ी sa:fi: (*nf*) a filtering cloth.

साबिक़ा sa:biqa: (*nm*) concern, contending; –पड़ना to be concerned with, to have to contend with.

साबित sa:bit (*a*) entire, complete, unbroken; unwavering, steady; proved; ~क़दम steady; ~क़दमी steadiness.

साबुत sa:but (*a*) entire, complete; unbroken.

साबु/न sa:bun (*nm*) a soap; ~न की टिकिया a soap cake; ०नदानी a soap-case; ~नीकरण saponification; ~नसाज soap manufacturer; hence ~नसाज़ी (*nf*).

साबूदाना sa:bu:da:nā: (*nm*) sago.

साभार sa:bha:r (*adv*) gratefully, with gratitude.

साभिप्राय sa:bhippra:y (*a* and *adv*) intentional(ly), deliberate(ly).

साभिमान sa:bhimā:n (*a*) proudly, arrogantly, with a sense of pride.

सामंजस्य sa:mānjassy (*nm*) harmony; consistence/consistency; ~पूर्ण harmonious; consistent.

सामंत sa:mānt (*nm*) a feudal lord, feudatory, landlord; –राज्य a principality; ~वाद feudalism; ~वादी a feudalist; feudalistic; ~शाही feudal(ism).

सामंती sa:mānti: (*a*) feudal; –तंत्र feudal system; –युग feudal age; –वैभव feudal grandeur/splendour.

साम sa:m (*nm*) one of the four Vedas; tranquillizing, calming; gentle words intended to win over an adversary; conciliation;

~कारी tranquillizing, calming; conciliatory; -दाम-दंड-भेद the four methods of dealing with people in general and enemies in particular as specified in the Indian diplomatic tradition; -नीति policy of conciliation (one of the four traditionally prescribed means used against an enemy).

सामवेद sa:mved (*nm*) the second of the four Vedas, after the ऋग्वेद.

सामग्री sa:maggri: (*nf*) matter; material, things, stuff; data.

सामना sa:mnā: (*nm*) confrontation, encounter, meeting; opposition; frontage.

सामने sa:mnē (*ind*) face to face; before, in front of; as compared with; against; in opposition to; –आना to confront, to come face to face; –करना to present, to bring in the presence of; –का in one's presence; witnessed; frontal; –की चोट frontal attack; –की बात as seen by one; –पड़ना to happen to come face to face; to block the course (of); –होना to come face to face; to confront.

सामयिक sa:mayik (*a*) opportune, timely; current; topical, periodic(al); casual; (*nm*) a periodical; ~ता timeliness; periodicity; topicality; the state or fact of being opportune; –चर्चा current/topical affairs; –पत्र a periodical; –वार्ता topical talk; –विषय current affairs.

सामरस्य sa:marassy (*nm*) harmony; equipoise.

सामरिक sa:marik (*a*) strategic(al); military; ~ता militarism; –महत्त्व strategic importance.

सामर्थ्य sa:marthy (*nf*) competence; capacity; power, strength; ~वान competent, capable; powerful, strong; ~हीन incompetent, incapable; powerless, weak.

सामवायिक sa:mva:ik (*a*) collective; concomitant.

सामाजिक sa:ma:jik (*a*) social; (*nm*) member of an assembly; viewer/reader (of a work of art); –चेतना social consciousness; –तत्त्व social element; social sense; ~ता sociality; conformation to social values; –विज्ञान social science(s); –व्यवस्था social order; –संगठन social organisation; –संघटन social integration.

सामान sa:mā:n (*nm*) goods; luggage, bag and baggage; material, stuff; stock; ~घर luggage office; –करना to make preparations; to prepare the ground (for).

सामा/न्य sa:ma:nny (*a*) general; common; usual; normal; routine; ~न्य ज्ञान general knowledge; ~न्यता generality; commonness; usualness; normality; routine state or condition; ~न्य भविष्यत् future indefinite; ~न्य भूत past indefinite; generalised; ~न्य लक्षण common characteristic; ~न्य वर्तमान present indefinite; ~न्यीकरण generalisation; normalisation; ~न्यीकृत generalised; normalised.

सामान्यत: sa:ma:nnytah (*ind*) generally, usually; normally; as a matter of routine.

सामासिक sa:mā:sik (*a*) composite; collective; pertaining to a compound; terse; –शैली terse style; –संस्कृति composite culture.

सामिष sa:mīsh (*a*) non-vegetarian; –भोजन non-vegetarian food.

सामी sa:mī: (*a*) semitic; –भाषा semitic language.

सामीप्य sa:mī:ppy (*nm*) proximity, nearness; vicinity.

सामुदायिक sa:muda:ik (*a*) collective; (pertaining to) community; ~ता collectivity / collectivism; -विकास community development.

सामुद्रिक sa:muddrik (*nm*) chiromancy; (*a*) oceanic.

सामूहिक sa:mu:hik (*a*) collective; community; -खेती collective farming; ~ता collectivity/collectivism; the state of being community-based.

सामोपचार sa:mopcha:r (*nm*) conciliatory method.

सामोपाय sa:mopa:y (*nm*) see **सामोपचार**.

साम्य sa:mmy (*nm*) community; equality; resemblance, similarity; equilibrium; -तंत्र communism; ~वाद communism; ~वादी a communist; communistic.

साम्यावस्था sa:mmyā:vastha: (*nf*) (state of) equilibrium.

साम्यिक sa:myik (*a*) equitable.

साम्राज्य sa:mra:jjy (*nm*) an empire; ~वाद imperialism; ~वादी an imperialist; imperialistic.

साम्राज्यिक sa:mra:jjyik (*a*) imperial.

सायं sa:yām (*nf*) see **सायंकाल**; -प्रात: morning and evening.

सायंका/ल sa:yāṅka:l (*nm*) the evening, dusk; ~लिक/लीन of or pertaining to the evening, evening.

सायक sa:yak (*nm*) an arrow.

सायत sa:yat (*nf*) an auspicious moment (for marriage etc.).

सायबान sa:yba:n (*nm*) an awning; a shed.

सा/या sa:ya: (*nm*) shade; shadow; influence; shelter, protection; a petticoat; ~येदार shady; ~या उठना to be deprived of a protective hand, a benevolent person to be no more; ~या उतरना shadows to be cast; ~या पड़ना to be influenced by (a bad company), an association to have its ill effect; ~ये की तरह साथ-साथ रहना to always hang around like a shadow; to shadow somebody; ~ये में रहना to live under the protection/patronage of; ~ये से बचना never to come near; to maintain a distance, to keep oneself at a safe distance (from); ~ये से भागना to avoid an encounter with, to keep at a safe distance (from).

सायुज्य sa:yujjy (*nm*) complete union, a kind of मुक्ति (beatitude) wherein the individual soul becomes one with the Supreme Soul.

सारंग sa:raṅg (*nm*) a kind of antelope, deer; the bow of Lord Vishnū; (*a*) variegated; ~पाणि an epithet of Lord Vishnū.

सारंगी sa:raṅgi: (*nf*) a typical stringed Indian musical instrument.

सार sa:r (*nm*) substance, gist, purport, abstract; essence, extract; epitome; iron; ~कथन recapitulation; ~गर्भित substantial; meaningful; full of pith/marrow; ~ग्राहिता capability to understand the essentials/substance, a connoisseur's faculty; ~ग्राही a connoisseur; ~तत्त्व extract; substance; ~भूत essential; substantial; ~लेख abstract; condensed article; ~वान substantial, significant, meaningful; precious; useful; ~वृत्त resume; -संग्रह compendium, digest.

सारणिक sa:rṇik (*a*) tabular.

सारणी sa:rṇi: (*nf*) a table; schedule; ~करण tabulation; ~कार a tabulator; ~कृत tabulised; -, समय time table; ~बद्ध tabular; ~यन

tabulation.

सार/थि ~थी sa:rathi, ~thi: (*nm*) a charioteer; ~थ्य chariot-driving, manning a warrior's chariot.

सारल्य sa:raly (*nm*) simplicity, easiness.

सारस sa:ras (*nm*) a species of heron, a crane.

सारस्य sa:rassy (*nm*) juiciness; melodiousness, sweetness, charm.

सारस्वत sa:rasswat (*a*) pertaining to Saraswati:—the goddess of learning / the invisible river (so-named); (*nm*) ancient name for the tract of land lying on the bank of river Saraswati:.

सारांश sa:ra:nsh (*nm*) abstract, summary, gist, purport.

सारा sa:ra: (*a*) entire, whole; all; –का सारा all; –जाता देखिए आधा लीजे बाँट better give the wool than the whole sheep.

सारालेख sa:ra:lekh (*nm*) precis; ~न precis-writing, preparing a precis.

सारिका sa:rika: (*nf*) a kind of Indian bird —*Turdus Salica* (also called मैना) famous for its melodious notes.

सारिणी sa:rinī: (*nf*) see सारणी.

सारी sa:ri: (*a*) feminine form of सारा; (*nf*) see साड़ी.

सारूप्य sa:ru:ppy (*nm*) similarity of form, identity of appearance; a kind of मुक्ति (beatitude) wherein the individual soul achieves formal identity with God.

सार्जेंट sa:rjenṭ (*nm*) a sergeant.

सार्थ sa:rth (*a*) with a meaning, meaningful, significant; (*nm*) a convoy; ~पति chief of a convoy; ~वाह a convoy; chief of a convoy.

सार्थक sa:rthak (*a*) articulate, meaningful, significant; effective useful; ~ता articulation, significance, meaningfulness; usefulness; importance.

सार्वकालिक sa:rvaka:lik (*a*) universal, pertaining/belonging to all times; perennial, everlasting; hence ~ता (*nf*).

सार्वज/निक, ~नीन, ~न्य sa:rvajanik, ~nī:n, ~nny (*a*) universal; common; public, relating to public in general; ~निकता/~नीनता/~न्यता universality; the state of belonging to the people/public; generality.

सार्वत्रिक sa:rvattrik (*a*) universal, pertaining to any and every place; hence ~ता (*nf*).

सर्वदेशिक sa:rvadeshic (*a*) universal, pertaining/belonging to all lands or territories; hence ~ता (*nf*).

सार्वनामिक sa:rvanā:mīk (*a*) pronominal.

सार्वभौम sa:rvabhaum (*a*) universal; ~ता universality.

सार्वभौमिक sa:rvabhāumīk (*a*) universal, pertaining or belonging to all beings/all places; ~ता universality.

सार्वराष्ट्रीय sa:rvara:shṭri:y (*a*) universal, international, pertaining or belonging to all nations or the whole nation; hence ~ता (*nf*).

सार्वलौकिक sa:rvalaukik (*a*) universal, cosmopolitan, hence ~ता (*nf*).

सालंकार sa:lāṅka:r (*a*) ornamented, decorated.

सालंब sa:lāmb (*a*) having support/help/assistance.

साल sa:l (*nm*) an year; pain; the Sal tree; -ब-साल every year, year by year; ~गिरह birthday; -हा-साल for years; –पलटना the new year to commence; the year to be changed; –भारी होना an year to be troublous/inauspicious.

सालन sa:lan (*nm*) meat or fish or vegetable curry.

सालना sa:lnā: (*v*) to torment, to torture; to fit a tenon in a mortise.

सालम मिस्री sa:lam missri: (*nf*) an esculent tuber used as tonic.

सालसा sa:lsa: (*nm*) a blood-purifying medicine.

साला sa:la: (*nm*) a brother-in-law—wife's brother; a term of abuse (directed to men).

सालाना sa:la:nā: (*a*) yearly, annual.

सालारजंग sa:la:rjāṅg (*nm*) commander-in-chief.

सालिम sa:lim (*a*) complete, whole, entire; unbroken.

सालियाना sa:liya:nā: (*nm*) yearly gratuity; (*a*) yearly, annual.

सालिस sa:lis (*nm*) a middle-man.

साली sa:li: (*nf*) a sister-in-law—wife's sister; a term of abuse (addressed to women).

सालोक्य sa:lokky (*nm*) a grade of मुक्ति (beatitude) which enables the soul to dwell in the company of God in the same लोक.

सावकाश sa:waka:sh (*a*) having leisure, free.

सावधा/न sa:vdhā:n (*a*) careful, alert, cautious; attentive; (in) attention! (in drill etc.); ~न करना to warn; to alert, to caution; ~न होना to be on one's guard, to be alert/cautious; ~नता/नी precaution; carefulness, alertness, cautiousness/caution; attention; ~नी बरतना to take precaution; to be cautious/alert/attentive.

सावधि sa:vadhi (*a*) timed, with a time-limit.

साव/न sa:van (*nm*) the fifth month of the Hindu calendar; ~नी pertaining to the month of सावन; of सावन; –के अन्धे को हरा ही हरा दिखता/सूझता है see through coloured glasses and all you see will be coloured.

सावरण sa:varāṇ (*a*) covered, unexposed, closed; enveloped.

सावशेष sa:vshesh (*a*) incomplete.

सावाँ sa:wā: (*nm*) a kind of coarse grain, little millet.

साशय sa:shay (*a* and *adv*) intentional(ly), deliberate(ly); meaningful(ly).

साश्चर्य sa:shchary (*adv*) with astonishment/amazement.

साष्टांग sa:shṭā:ṅg (*a*) with the whole body or with all its members; –प्रणाम reverential prostration of the whole body.

सास sa:s (*nf*) mother-in-law, mother of wife or husband; –मेरी घर नहीं मुझे किसी का डर नहीं when the cat is away, the mice will play.

साह sa:h (*nm*) a good man or gentleman (as opposed to a thief –चोर); a trader, merchant; –जी a form of address esp. prevalent amongst the Panja:bi:-speaking people.

साहचर्य sa:hchary (*nm*) association, company; synergy/synergism; -दोष fault resulting from (bad) company/association; -भाव feeling of association.

साह(हि)/ब sa:ha(hi)b (*nm*) the Master, Lord; a whiteman, European; boss; gentleman, white-collared person; a title of courtesy; (vocative) word of respect; ~बजादा son of a साहब; son; ~बजादी daughter of a साहब; daughter; ~ब-बहादुर a (vocative) word of respect; ~ब-सलामत a nodding acquaintance; ~बान plural of साहब; ~बाना lordly; ~बाना अंदाज़ lordly ways/mannerism; o से in a lordly fashion/manner; ~बियत lordliness, lordly conduct; ~बी lordliness; oकरना to live in a lordly manner; ~बी दिखाना to show off as a lord; ~बे-जायदाद owning property, propertied (man).

साह/स sa:has (*nm*) courage, nerve, guts; boldness, daring; enterprise; ~सिक daring, bold, courageous; oकार्य adventure, daring deed; ~सी courageous; enterprising, adventurous; ~स छूटना one's courage to give way; –स दिखाना to put up a bold face, to act boldly; ~स बटोरना to muster/pluck up courage, to take heart of grace.

साहाय्य sa:ha:yy (*nm*) see सहायता.

साहि/त्य sa:hitty (*nm*) literature; ~त्यकार a litterateur, writer; ~त्य-शास्त्र Poetics; ~त्य-शास्त्री a Poetician; ~त्यिक literary; ~त्यिक चोरी plagiarism; ~त्यिक भाषा literary language; ~त्यिकता literariness.

साहि/ब sa:hib (*nm*) see साहब; ~बी see साहबी (under साहब).

साहिल sa:hil (*nm*) a shore, bank.

साही sa:hi: (*nf*) a porcupine; –का काँटा lit. porcupine's thorn--supposedly causing internecine quarrels in homes where it is planted or thrown.

साहु sa:hu (*nm*) see साह: a respectful vocative word used for a member of the *Vaishya* community.

साहुल sa:hul (*nm*) a plumbline.

साहूका/र sa:hu:ka:r (*nm*) a money-lender, private banker, rich man, man of means; ~रा/री money-lending business, banking.

साहेब sa:heb (*nm*) see साहब.

सिंकना sīknā: (*v*) to be roasted; to be fomented/heated.

सिंगरफ़ sīgaraf (*nm*) see इंगुर.

सिंगार sīga:r, singa:r (*nm*) make-up, prank; ornamentation, embellishment; ~दान a dressing case; -मेज़ a dressing table; –, सोलह see सोलह सिंगार.

सिंगारना sīga:rnā: (*v*) to make-up, to prank; to decorate, to embellish.

सिंगासन singa:sān (*nm*) see सिंहासन.

सिंगी sīngi: (*nf*) see सींगी; –लगाना see सींगी लगाना under सींगी.

सिंघाड़ा sīgha:ṛa: (*nm*) a waternut, water chestnut; a kind of firework.

सिंचाई sīcha:i: (*nf*) irrigation; wages paid for irrigation.

सिंचित sīnchit (*a*) irrigated; drenched.

सिंचौनी sīchaunī: (*nf*) सिंचाई.

सिंडिकेट sīndiket (*nm*) a syndicate.

सिंदूर sīndu:r (*nm*) vermilion; symbol of an Indian woman's happy state of enjoying coverture (husband's protection); ~दान a case for storing vermilion; putting vermilion mark on the head of a bride for the first time (at the time of wedding); –उजड़ना/लुटना (said in respect of a woman) to lose coverture, to be deprived of husband's protection; husband to pass away.

सिंदू/रिया, ~री sīndūriya:, ~ri: (*a*) vermilion-coloured, of the colour of vermilion.

सिंदौरा sīdaura: (*nm*) a vermilion case.

सिंधी sīndhi: (*a*) belonging or pertaining to Sindh; (*nm*) a person belonging to the Province of Sindh; (*nf*) the Sindhi language.

सिंधु sīndhu (*nm*) ocean, sea; the province of Sindh.

सिंधुर sīndhur (*nm*) an elephant; ~**वदन** Ganesh—the elephant-faced Hindu god.

सिवान sīw:an (*nm*) see **सिवान**.

सिंह sīngh (*nm*) a lion; leo—the fifth sign of the zodiac (also **सिंह राशि**); a caste title amongst the *kshatriyas*; ~**द्वार/पौर** main gate; portal, propylaea, propylon; ~**ध्वनि/नाद/रव** roar(ing) of a lion; war cry, challenging cry; ~**नी** see **सिंहिनी**; ~**मुखी** having the face of a lion, lion-faced; ~**वाहिनी** an epithet of goddess Durga:; ~**गति/गामी** with a majestic lion-like gait; -**सटा** mane; ~**स्कंध** having shoulders like those of a lion; -**के मुँह में उँगली देना** to knowingly hazard a risk to life, to indulge in a misadventure.

सिंहल sīnghal (*nm*) an ancient name for Çeylon; also ~**द्वीप**.

सिंहली sīnghali: (*nf*) the Sinha:li: language; (*nm*) an inhabitant of Ceylon; (*a*) belonging or pertaining to Ceylon.

सिंहावलोकन sīngha:vlokān (*nm*) a round-up; retrospection; a conspectus.

सिंहासन sīngha:sān (*nm*) a throne; -**पर बैठना** to ascend the throne; -**से उतारना** to dethrone.

सिंहिनी sīnghinī: (*nf*) a lioness.

सिंहोदरी sīnghodari: (*a*) having a lion-like waist, tenuous-waisted (woman).

सिकंजबीन sikāṇjabi:n (*nm*) a typical sweet beverage prepared with fresh lemon-juice, water and sugar as ingredients.

सिकंदर sikāndar (*nm*) Alexander; -, **तकदीर का** exceptionally fortunate, a man of unusually good luck; **सिकंदरी** of, pertaining or belonging to, Alexander; **सिकंदरे-आज़म** Alexander the Great.

सिकड़ी sikṛi: (*nf*) a chain.

सिकता sikta: (*nf*) sand, sandy soil; ~**मय** sandy, full of sand.

सिकत्तर sikattar (*nm*) a secretary.

सिकली sikli: (*nf*) act of cleansing and polishing (rusty instruments—as lance, sword, etc.); ~**गर** a burnisher.

सिकहर sikahar (*nm*) a hanging pot-rest.

सिकुड़न sikuṛān (*nf*) shrinkage; contraction; a wrinkle, pucker; winder welt.

सिकुड़ना sikuṛnā: (*v*) to contract; to shrink; to pucker, to wrinkle; to cower.

सिकोड़ना sikoṛnā: (*v*) to contract, to pucker; to cause to shrink.

सिक्कड़ sikkaṛ (*nm*) a (big and heavy) chain.

सिक्का sikka: (*nm*) a coin, coinage; lead; ~**बंद** sealed; standard; -**जमना/बैठना** to acquire sway, to come to wield tremendous influence (over); -**मानना** to concede the superiority/supremacy/tremendous influence of.

सिक्ख sikkh (*nm*) a Sikh (follower of Guru Nā:nak); -**धर्म/पंथ** the Sikh religion, Sikhism.

सिक्त sikt (*a*) drenched, soaked, wet; irrigated; hence ~**ता** (*nf*).

सिख sikh (*nm*) see **सिक्ख**.

सिखनौटा sikhnāūṭa: (*nm*) an apprentice; a novice.

सिखरन sikhran (*nm*) a sweet beverage prepared with milk, curd, sugar, etc. as ingredients.

सिखलाई sikhla:i: (*nf*) training; also

सिखाई.

सिखाना sikha:nā: (*v*) to train; to teach, to instruct, to school; -पढ़ाना to tutor.

सिखावन sikha:van (*nf*) counsel, advice, instructioned.

सिगनल signal (*nm*) a signal; -होना the signal to be down(ed).

सिगरेट sigreṭ (*nf*) a cigarette.

सिगार siga:r (*nm*) a cigar; ~दान a cigar case.

सिजदा sijda: (*nm*) prostration, salutation, a process of Muslim prayers wherein the head, nose, knee, etc. of the worshipper touch the ground; ~गाह a place of worship (esp. of Muslims).

सिझना sijhnā: (*v*) to be cooked/boiled.

सिटकिनी siṭkinī: (*nf*) latch (of a door, window, etc.); -लगाना to latch.

सिटपिटाना siṭpiṭa:nā: (*v*) to be stupefied; to be embarrassed; to be in a fix.

सिट्टी siṭṭi: (*nf*) bragging; -गुम हो जाना, -पिट्टी गुम हो जाना, -पिट्टी भूल जाना, -भूल जाना to be in blue funk, to be struck all of a heap, to be nervous, to be in a panic, to be stunned/stupefied.

सि/ड़ siṛ (*nf*) eccentricity, craziness, crankiness, whim; ~ड़ी eccentric, crazy, cranky, whimsical; ०पन/पन see ~ड़; ~ड़ सवार होना to be under the sway of a whim/eccentricity/craziness, to run crazy.

सितंबर sitāmbar (*nm*) the month of September.

सित sit (*a*) white; clear; ~कंठ white-throated—an epithet of Lord Shiv; ~ता whiteness.

सितम sitām (*nm*) tyranny, oppression; ~गर tyrannical; an oppressor; ~गरी tyranny, oppressiveness; ~ज़दा oppressed, tyrannized; -ढाना/तोड़ना to oppress, to do grave injustice, to tyrannize.

सितार sita:r (*nm*) a typical stringed Indian musical instrument; ~वादक one who plays on a सितार; ~वादन playing on a सितार.

सितारा sita:ra: (*nm*) a star, planet; fate; a popular screen or stage artist; small shining tablets of metal or mica which are studded on a sa:ri:, cap, shoe, etc; -चमकना/-बुलंद होना one's star to be in the ascendance, to have an advent/run of good fortune; -डूबना to be in the grip of adversity, adverse times to commence.

सितारिया sita:riya: (*nm*) one who plays on a सितार.

सितासित sita:sit (*nm*) white and black; good and evil.

सितोत्पल sitotpal (*nm*) white lotus.

सिद्ध siddh (*a*) proved; accomplished, perfected/perfect; endowed with supernatural powers; (*nm*) a saint; name of a special cult of saints; one who has acquired supernatural powers; -करना to prove/achieve; ~काम a person whose desires are all fulfilled; ~कार्य successful; -गुटिका a mysterious pill or tablet which kept in the mouth, is supposed to make a man invisible to others; ~ता/त्व perfection; the state of having achieved supernatural powers; accomplishment; ~नाथ an epithet of Lord Shiv; ~पीठ/क्षेत्र/भूमि a holy place where devotion is said to bring about the desired end in a quick fashion; ~प्राय almost accomplished/fulfilled/achieved/proved; ~रस mer cury, quick silver; ~रसायन an elixir; ~ह'त proficient, perfect; skilful, expert; ~हस्तता expertness, perfection; exquisite skill.

सिद्धांजन siddhā:ṇjān *(nm)* a (magical) collyrium (said to make a man see things buried underground).

सिद्धांत siddhā:nt *(nm)* a principle; theory; doctrine; ~त: theoretically; as a matter of principle; -पक्ष theoretical aspect; ~वाद theoreticalism, wedding to theory/doctrine / principles; ~वादी doctrinaire; a theoretician; man of principles; -शैथिल्य latitudinarianism; -स्थापन theorization.

सिद्धांती siddhā:nti: *(a* and *nm)* (a) theoretician/theorist; dogmatic; a man of principles; ~करण theorization.

सिद्धांतीय siddhā:nti:y *(a)* doctrinal; theoretical; pertaining to a principle/principles.

सिद्धान्न siddhā:nn *(nm)* cooked cereals.

सिद्धार्थ siddha:rth *(a)* whose wishes have been fulfilled; *(nm)* pre-enlightenment name of Lord Buddha.

सिद्धासन siddha:san *(nm)* a typical sitting posture.

सिद्धि siddhi *(nf)* acquisition, accomplishment; proof; fulfilment, success; supernatural powers supposed to be acquired through Yogic practices (see अष्ट-सिद्धि); ~कर/कारक/प्रद causing to achieve or helping in the achievement of a सिद्धि; ~गुटिका see ~सिद्धगुटिका (under सिद्ध).

सिद्धेश्वर siddheshshwar *(nm)* an epithet of Lord Shiv.

सिधाई sidha:i: *(nf)* see सीधापन (under सीधा); alignment.

सिधाना sidha:nā: *(v)* to tame; to domesticate; to help acquire practice

सिधारना sidha:rnā: *(v)* to go, to depart; to expire.

सिनकना sinaknā: *(v)* to snort, to force mucus out of the nostrils with a jet of air from within.

सिनेट sinēṭ *(nf)* a senate; -सदस्य a member of a senate.

सिनेमा sinemā: *(nm)* a cinema; ~ई cinematic; ~घर a cinema hall.

सिपह sipah—an allomorph of सिपाही used in some compound words; ~गरी the work or profession of a soldier; ~सालार commander of an army.

सिपाह sipa:h *(nm)* an army; ~गरी see सिपहगरी (under सिपह).

सिपाहियाना sipa:hiya:nā: *(a)* soldierly, of or befitting a soldier/policeman.

सिपाही sipa:hi: *(nm)* a soldier; sepoy, constable; policeman; ~गीरी the work or profession of a policeman/soldier.

सिपुर्द sipurd *(a)* see सुपुर्द.

सिप्पा sippa: *(nm)* influence; approach; device; chance; –जमना/बैठना/भिड़ना/लगना/लड़ना to get/procure/obtain by a chance, to be a chance attainment; –जमाना/बैठाना/भिड़ाना/लगाना/लड़ाना to make an approach; to manoeuvre; to see a scheme through.

सिफ़त sifat *(nf)* a characteristic (quality); attribute.

सिफ़र sifar *(nm)* a cipher, zero; blank; –होना to be just blank.

सिफ़ारत sifa:rat *(nf)* the post or profession of an ambassador; ~खाना an embassy.

सिफ़ारि/श sifa:rish *(nf)* recommendation; ~शी recommendatory; ~शी टट्टू one whose achievements are a tribute to his recommendations; ~शी चिट्ठी/पत्र recommendatory letter.

सिब्बंदी sibbandi: (*nf*) an establishment.

सिमटना simāṭnā: (*v*) to contract; to shrink.

सिमा/न,~ना simā:n, ~nā: (*nm*) see सिवान.

सिम्त simt (*nf*) direction.

सियराना siyra:nā: (*v*) to cool, to get cool/cold; to subside.

सियापा siya:pa: (*nm*) mourning, weeping and wailing over a death; –करना to mourn, to weep and wail for the dead.

सियार siya:r (*nm*) a jackal; cunning fellow; –बोलना to be deserted.

सियासत siya:sat (*nf*) politics; ~दाँ a politician.

सियासी siya:si: (*a*) political; –मामले political affairs.

सियाह siya:h (*a*) see स्याह.

सियाही siya:hi: (*nf*) see स्याही.

सिर sir (*nm*) head; top, apex; highest part or point; ~कटा beheaded, headless, decapitated; ~खपाई (the process of) taxing one's brain over-much; too much of mental exertion; ~चढ़ा cheeky, given too much of lift; ~ताज (lit. and fig.) crown, the best (amongst); diadem; chief; master, husband; ~त्राण a headwear; ~नामा form of address (in a letter etc.); ~पेंच a typical turban; an ornament fixed on the turban; ~मुंडा having a clean-shaven head; ~मौर see ~ताज; ~हाना head rest; the upper end of a bedstead; –अलग करना to behead, to chop off the head; –आना, के to possess, to obsess; to be charged with; -आँखों पर with one's heart and soul; most willingly, most cordially; -आँखों पर बिठाना/रखना to give a most cordial and affectionate treatment; –आँखों पर होना to be deferentially welcome; to be obeyed with reverence; –उठाकर चलना to hold one's head high, to have nothing to be ashamed of, to walk proudly/conceitedly, to look big; to strut; –उठाते ही कुचल डालना/देना to nip in the bud, to crush in the egg; –उठाना to rise in revolt, to rebel; –उठाने की फ़ुरसत न होना not to have a moment's respite; –उड़ जाना to be beheaded, the head to be chopped off; –उड़ा देना to behead, to chop off the head; –उतारना to behead; –ऊँचा करना to hold one's head high, to be proud (of), to feel a sense of pride; –क़दमों पर रखना to bow in obeisance; to make a complete surrender; –क़लम करना to behead, to chop off the head; –कहाँ फोड़ूँ ? where to seek ?, where to find ?, where to go ?; –का न पाँव का having neither beginning nor end, absurd; –का पसीना पाँव को आना to work assiduously; to perspire profusely; –का बोझ उतरना to be freed of a burden; to fulfil an obligation; –का बोझ टालना to finish with an assignment, to see a thing through somehow or the other; –का बवाल होना to be a headache, to be a source of botheration; –की आफ़त टलना to be rid of a headache/botheration; –की क़सम lit. by the head—I swear by my life !; –की टली जान पर आई spared by one calamity, attacked by another; –की सुध न पाँव की बुध to be out of senses, to be conscious neither of self nor of surroundings; –के बल headlong; with due deference; –के साथ होना to be with one's life, to last as long as life lasts; –कोरे उस्तरे/छुरे से मूँडना to fleece ruthlessy; –खपाना to beat one's brains, to tax one's brain, to exert; –खाना to pester, to plague, to go on bothering; –खाली करना to over-tax one's brain; to chatter somebody's brain out; –खुजलाना to be in for a beating/thrashing; –खुजलाने/खुजाने की फ़ुरसत/मुहलत न होना to be up to the elbows, to be up to the eyes in the work, to have one's hands full, to have not even breathing respite; –खोलना to break somebody's skull; –गंजा कर देना, मार मारकर to thrash someone bald; to give a sound beating; –गिराना to behead; –घुटनों में देना to be gloomy/glum; to bow the head in shame; –घूमना to feel giddy, to suffer from vertigo; –चकराना see –घूमना; –चढ़ना to take too much liberty; to take much lift; –चढ़कर बोलना the cat to jump out of the bag, the secret to be exposed by itself; to gab through obsession; –चढ़कर बोले, जादू वह जो a spell must somehow procure a tangible expression; –चढ़ना to become too cheeky, to take too much liberty; –चढ़ाना to spoil (as a child/servant etc.) by indulgence; to make too much of; –चाटना to go on pestering, to tax one's brain, to plague; –जाना to lose one's life; (a responsibility etc.) to devolve on; –झुकना to feel ashamed, to hang the head (in shame); –झुकाकर सजा भोगना to kiss the rod; –झुकाना to bow the head (in salutation); to look down through shame; to acquiesce; –टकराकर मर जाना to make desperate bids in vain; to meet a sad end in frustration; –टकराना to dash the head against; to suffer too much of mental exertion; –डालना to impose upon, to cause (a responsibility etc.) to devolve (on); –तराशना to behead; to chop off the head; ~तोड़ कोशिश करना to make a frantic/desperate bid; –थाम कर बैठ जाना lit. to sit with the head resting on the hands—to suffer a stroke of ill-luck; –थाम लेना to hold the head (as expressive of having suffered a tragic blow); –थोपना to impose (upon); to accuse; –दुखना to suffer from headache; –देना to stake one's life, to die (for); –धड़ की बाजी लगाना to burn one's boats; –धुनना to beat the head as a mark of mourning; to weep and wail aloud; –न उठाने देना to allow no respite, to keep thoroughly engaged; to give no lift/quarter; to give no opportunity to rise against; –न पांव/पैर groundless, having no logic whatever, absolute absurdity; –नवाना to bow one's head (in obeisance); –नहीं उठा सकना too burdened with somebody's acts of grace to claim equal footing; to be too busy; –नीचा करना to inflict a defeat; to cause embarrassment; to hang one's head in shame; –नीचा होना to suffer a defeat; to feel embarrassed/ashamed; –पकड़कर बैठना see –थाम कर बैठ जाना; –पकड़ कर रह जाना to be stunned still by grief; –पकड़ कर रोना to bemoan, to weep and wail; –पटकना to make frantic efforts; to mourn, to weep and wail; –पड़ना to be obliged to shoulder (a responsibility etc.); to be imposed on; to have (an obligation etc.) devolved on; –पड़ी बला झेलना to hold the baby; –पड़े का सौदा a matter with no alternative; to have to undertake per force, to be obliged to take up; –पर on the head, close at hand; –पर अहसान रखना to make someone grateful, to impose a burden of gratitude; –पर आँखें न होना to be mentally blind, to be unheeding; –पर आ जाना to approach very near; to be imminent; to be face to face with; to devolve on; –पर (आसमान/घर) उठाना to create a havoc; to cause an uproar; to kick up a row; –पर आसमान टूटना to be in the grip of a terrible affliction, a calamity to befall; –पर कफ़न बाँधना to risk one's life, to hold one's life in one's hand; –पर क़यामत टूटना a great calamity to befall, to be in the grip of a terrible affliction; –पर क़यामत बरपा करना to cause a calamity to befall, to create a havoc; to cause an uproar; –पर काली हँडिया रखना to feel ashamed; –पर क़ुरान उठाना to swear by the Qoran; –पर क़ुरान रखना to bind by an oath of the Qoran; –पर कोई न होना to have none to guide or to provide protection; –पर कोदों दलना to deliberately offend somebody, to do a thing merely to arouse jealousy; –पर खड़ा होना to hang or hover around; to pester by persistent presence; –पर ख़ाक उड़ना/डालना to mourn; –पर ख़ून चढ़ना या सवार होना to be overwhelmed by murder-mania; to see things bloodshot; –पर घर उठा लेना to cause a tremendous uproar; to kick up a row; –पर चढ़ना to behave with extreme rudeness (said of children or inferiors); –पर चढ़ाना to spoil (as a child) through indulgence; to pamper a bit too much; to encourage into insolence; –पर छत उठा लेना see –पर घर उठा लेना; –पर जुनून चढ़ना to go crazy; to stick crazily to an obstinate resolve; –पर जिन चढ़ना see –पर भूत सवार होना; –पर डालना to shift a botheration; to put a responsibility over; –पर ढोल बजाना to cause a tumultuous scene, to create too much of noise; –पर पड़ना (a responsibility etc.) to devolve upon/to have to be shouldered; –पर पाँव रखकर भागना या उड़ जाना to take to one's heels, to show a clean pair of heels; –पर बनना to be in hot waters, to be in trouble, to be confronted with an affliction; –पर बिठाना/बैठाना to extend respectful welcome, to receive with deference; –पर बोझ लेना to take up/shoulder a responsibility; –पर भूत सवार होना to be under an obsession, to turn into a maniac; to go crazy through an obstinate resolve; – पर मौत खेलना death to hover around, to face a hazard to life; to be in close proximity with death; –पर रखना to treat with great respect, to revere; –पर लादकर ले जाना to carry along (to the next world); –पर लादना to carry over the head; to entrust a burden (to), to cause (an obligation etc.) to devolve upon; –पर लिए फिरना

to carry around ov , the head, to run about with a burden; –पर ले जाना to carry over one's head; to cause to be transported on one's responsibility; –पर लेना to accept the responsibility, to own a responsibility; –पर वारना to sacrifice on (somebody), to revolve (a coin etc.) round a dear one's head and then gift it away; –पर शैतान चढ़ना/सवार होना to be overwhelmed by sinful mentality/evil; to be obsessed by a sense of anger/obstinacy; –पर स(श)नीचर सवार होना to be in adversity, to be under the sway of ominous stars; –पर सफ़ेदी आना to go grey; –पर सवार रहना to ever hover around; to keep under constant watch; to behave in an insolent manner, to keep on bullying; to keep under obsession; –पर सवार होना to bully, to behave insolently; –पर साया रखना to provide constant protection to; –पर साया रहना/होना to enjoy the shadow of a protective hand, to be under the protection of; –पर सींग होना to have some abnormal characteristic, to have a distinctive feature; –पर सेहरा बाँधना to earn a distinction; to be plumed; –पर हाथ धर कर रोना to lament, to bewail; –पर हाथ धरना to take under one's protection/patronage; –पर हाथ फेरना to fondle; to console; –पर होना to be imminent, to be near at hand; to be over and above, to be on the back; -पाँव न होना or -पैर न होना to make no head or tail, to make no sense; to be absurd, to be ridiculously illogical/incoherent; –पाँव पर धरना to yield completely, to be submissive in the extreme; –पीटना to lament with a violent beating of the head, to be full of remorse; –पीट कर रोना to lament violently, to weep and wail; -पैर होना to be rational/logical, to make some sense; –फटा जाना/पड़ना the head to crack with pain, to have severe headache; –फिरना to go crazy, to run amuck; to be out of senses; to go to one's head; ~ फिरा crazy, eccentric; ०होना to have bats in the belfry; –बाँधना to tie up the hair, to plait or braid the hair; –बीतना, किसी के to suffer, to undergo an ordeal; –बेचना to own up a hazard to life; –भन्नाना see –भिन्नाना; –भारी होना to have headache; to have a heaviness in the head; –भिन्नाना to feel giddy, to suffer from vertigo; to have a fit of anger; –मटकाना to nod the head ironically; –मँढ़ना to pass the buck to, to make a dupe of a person, to lay at the door of, to thrust on, to impose on (an obligation, accusation, etc.); –मारना to tax one's brain, to try to explain something to a nitwit, to make strenuous efforts, to try no end, to take great pains; –मुँड़वा देना to get the head shaven; –मुँड़ाते ही ओले पड़ना to be confronted with obstacles at the very first step, ill-luck to overtake at the very outset; –मुँड़ाना lit. to have the head shaven—to adopt the life of a mendicant, to turn an ascetic; –रँगना to make one's head bleed, to break somebody's head; –लगना to be accused, to be faced with an accusation; –लेना to own up, to undertake a responsibility; –से कफ़न बाँधना to be ready to face death, to stake one's life; –से (बला)टालना to get rid of a botheration; to be done with; –से तिनका उतारने का अहसान मानना to be grateful even for the semblance of a good turn; –सेहरा बँधना to get the credit for (a success etc.), to get applause for an achievement; –सहलाए भेजा खाए to cause a jam and apply the balm; –सिरहाने या पैताने कमर वहीं रहेगी as broad as it is long, one way or the other would bring about the same result; –से पैर तक chin deep, up to the chin; –से पैर/पाँव तक from head to foot; ० आग लगना to be furious with rage; –से पानी ऊपर होना/गुजरना all bounds to be crossed, to become just intolerable; –से पैर तक (लैस) cap-a-pie; –से बला टालना to get rid of an unpleasant context, to be done with somehow; –से बोझ उतारना to rid oneself of a burden; –से बोझ बाँधना to own up an obligation; –से साया उठना to be deprived of a benevolent hand, a patron/protector to be no more; –हथेली पर धरना/रखना to be ever-ready to face death, to be never scared of death; –हाजिर है to be ready to risk life with pleasure, to be ready to take up a risk; –हिलाना to nod the head (to express approval or disapproval); –होना to go on pestering; –होना, किसी के (responsibility, accusation, etc.) to devolve on, to be shouldered by.

सिरका sirka: (*nm*) vinegar.

सिरकी sirki: (*nf*) a kind of reed or reed-mat used to keep off rain.

सिरजन sirjan (*nm*) creation; ~हार the Creator; maker.

सिरजना sirjanā: (*v*) to create, to give birth to, to make.

सिरताज sirta:j (*nm*) see under सिर.

सिरत्राण sirtrā:ṇ (*nm*) see under सिर.

सिरना/म sirna:m (*a*) see सर (~नाम); ~मा (*nf*) see सिर (~नामा).

सिरमौर sirmaur (*nm*) see सिर (~मौर).

सिरहाना sirha:nā: (*nm*) see सिर (~हाना).

सि/रा sira: (*nm*) an edge; end; head, top; ~रे extremities, ends; ~रे से, (नये) anew, afresh, de novo.

सिराना sira:nā: (*v*) to cool; to subside; to consign to river water.

सिरिस siris (*nm*) a typical Indian tree which grows very soft flowers.

सिरोपा, ~व, siropa:, ~v (*nm*) a long robe (flowing from head to foot) that was given by kings as a token of honour in olden times.

सिर्फ़ sirf (*a* and *adv*) only, mere(ly).

सिल sil (*nf*) a stone-slab on which spices etc. are ground; ~खरी/खड़ी chalk; -बट्टा a stone-slab and mill-stone.

सिलना silnā: (*v*) to sew/stitch; to be sewn/stitched.

सिलवट silvaṭ (*nf*) a wrinkle/cockle; pucker; ~दार puckered; wrinkled/cockled.

सिलवाई silva:i: (*nf*) the act or process of sewing/stitching; stitching charges.

सिलसि/ला silsila: (*nm*) a chain; series; line; arrangement; system; ~लेवार serial(ly); consecutive(ly); systematic(ally); ~ला निकालना to find out an access or approach.

सिलह sileh (*nm*) a weapon; ~खाना an armoury, arsenal.

सिला sila: (*nm*) return, reward, consideration.

सिलाई sila:i: (*nf*) (the act or process of) sewing/stitching; stitching charges.

सिलौ/टा silauṭa: (*nm*) see **सिल बट्टा** (under **सिल**); ~**टी** a small stone-slab for grinding (**भाँग** etc.).

सिल्क silk (*nf*) silk; –**का** silken.

सिल्ली silli: (*nf*) a slab (of stone, ice or wood etc.); whetstone, hone; –**पर तेज़ करना** to hone, to whet.

सिव/इयाँ, ~**ईं** sivaīyā:, ~ī: (*uf*) vermicelli.

सिवा, ~**य** siva:, ~y (*ind*) except, but.

सिवान siwa:n (*nm*) boundary, frontier (of a village, town, etc.).

सिवाला siva:la: (*nm*) a temple dedicated to Lord Shiv.

सिविल sivil (*a*) civil; –**विमानन** civil aviation; –**सर्जन** a civil surgeon; –**सेवा** civil service.

सिवैयाँ sivaīyā: (*nf*) see **सिवइयाँ**.

सिसकना sisaknā: (*v*) to sob.

सिसका/रना siska:rnā: (*v*) to hiss, to produce a hissing sound; to sob; ~**री** hissing (sound); sobbing.

सिसकी siski: (*nf*) a sob; sobbing; –**भरना** to sob.

सिहरन siharān (*nf*) a thrill; shiver.

सिहरना siharnā: (*v*) to be thrilled; to shiver.

सींक sī:k (*nf*) wicker of a broom; a spit; skewer;–**खड़ी होना** to establish dominating position, to acquire a unique status/unusual sucess.

सींकचा sī:kcha: (*nm*) window-bars.

सींका sī:ka: (*nm*) a hanging pot-rest.

सींकिया sī:kiya: (*a*) lanky, thin as wicker; –**पहलवान** (said ironically) a lanky.

सींग sī:g (*nm*) a horn; –**कटाकर बछड़ो में मिलना** to be a bull and feign a calf, ripe age raw ways; –**जमना**, –**निकलना** lit. to grow horns –to take to abnormally queer ways; –**मारना** to strike with the horns; –**समाना** to find accommodation/refuge; –**होना, सिर पर/सिर में** lit. to have horns over the head–to have a rare characteristic,

सींगी sī:gi: (*nf*) a small trumpet made of stag horn; a hollow pipe for drawing out impure blood; –**लगाना** to draw out impure blood (in a crude fashion) through a hollowed horn-pipe.

सींचना sī:chnā: (*v*) to irrigate, to water.

सींव sī:v (*nf*) boundary.

सींवन sī:vān (*nf*) seam; –**उधड़ना** seam to give way.

सी si: (*ind*) feminine form of **सा** meaning–like, similar, resembling, identical with, etc; (*nf*) sibilance, muffled spirant sound expressive of intense joy or excessive pain; -**सी** repeated sounds of **सी-सी**; o **करना** to express intense joy or pain through muffled spirant sounds.

सी० आई० डी० si: a:i: ḍi: (*nf*) a spy, an intelligence man; (member of the criminal investigation department, –now the CBI).

सीकर si:kar (*nm*) a tiny drop (of water etc.).

सीकाकाई si:ka:ka;i (*nf*) a particular tree the pods of which are used for preparing hair shampoo.

सीख si:kh (*nf*) teaching, advice; moral; –**देना** to advise, to impart a teaching; –**लेना** to draw a moral;

to learn a lesson.

सीख़ si:ḳḥ (*nf*) a spit, skewer.

सीखना si:khnā: (*v*) to learn; **सीखा-पढ़ा** well-conversant; clever; **सीखा-सिखाया** skilled, clever, well-up.

सीट si:ṭ (*nf*) a seat; braggadocio; **–मारना** to brag, to boast.

सीटी si:ṭi: (*nf*) a whistle; **~बाज़** habituated to whistling; hence **~बाज़ी** (*nf*); **–देना** to whistle (as an engine etc.).

सीठा si:ṭha: (*a*) insipid; **~पन** insipidity.

सीठी si:ṭhi: (*nf*) dregs.

सीढ़ी si:ṛhi: (*nf*) a ladder; stairs, staircase; escalator: stile; stepping stone; **~नुमा** resembling or similar to a staircase; **–का डंडा** a stair; **–चढ़ना** to go up a staircase; to rise step by step.

सीतलपाटी si:talpa:ṭi: (*nf*) a typical mat.

सीता si:ta: (*nf*) the celebrated daughter of king Janak (of Mithila:) who was married to Ra:m, the hero of the renowned Indian epic of Ra:mā:yāṉ; **-स्वयंवर** the episode of the **स्वयंवर** of **सीता** (in the Ra:mā:yāṉ); **~हरण** the episode of the kidnapping of **सीता** by the demon-king **रावण** (in the Ra:ma:yaṉ).

सीताफल si:ta:phal (*nm*) see **कद्दू**; a custard apple.

सीत्कार si:tka:r (*nf*) sibilance, a muffled spirant sound expressive of intense joy or excessive pain.

सीध si:dh (*nf*) alignment; straightness; **–बाँधना** to align; to take an aim; to dig marks symbolising commencement of a construction work; **–में** in a straight line, aligned; **–लेना** to make an alignment, to take an aim

सीधा si:dha: (*a* and *adv*) straight; simple; right; erect, upright; direct; gentle; naive; good; forthrightly; through; (*nm*) victuals earmarked for a Bra:hmāṉ as alms; **~पन** simplicity; straightness; uprightness; gentleness; naivete; **-सादा/साधा** simple, innocent; gentle; naive; good; docile; **–हाथ** right hand; **–आना** to come straight, to come without a halt or detour; **–करना** to put straight; to knock out one's haughtiness/conceit, to fix in one's proper place; to align; **–तीर-सा** direct; as fast and straight as an arrow; **–होना** to be put straight; to have one's haughtiness/conceit knocked out; to be fixed in one's proper place; to be aligned.

सीधी si:dhi: (*a* and *adv*) feminine form of **सीधा**; **-सादी** see **सीधा-सादा**; **–आँख** favourable glance; **–तरफ़** right side, right hand side; **–तरह** in a gentlemanly manner; without a quarrel; quietly; **–नज़र/निगाह** favourable glance; **–बात** straight/forthright talk; an easy point; an expression without reservations; **–राह** a straight path; moral course; **–लकीर** a straight line; **–उँगली से घी नहीं निकलता** softness does not evoke compliance; **–सुनाना** to rebuke right and left.

सीधे si:dhe (*adv*) straight; without a halt or detour; without protest; quietly; in a gentlemanly fashion; **–मुँह** with due courtesy/in an appropriate manner; **०बात न करना** not to talk in an appropriate manner/with due courtesy; **-सीधे** without further delay, with out ifs and buts, without any resistance/protest; –से quietly, without protest, in a gentlemanly fashion; –हाथ को to the right hand.

सीन si:n (*nm*) a scene.

सीनरी si:nari: (*nf*) scenery.

सीना si:nā: (*v*) to sew; to stitch; (*nm*) chest; ~चाक shattered heart; gloomy; ~ज़ोर exercising coercion, over-assertive, unashamedly aggressive; ~ज़ोरी obstinate show of strength, over-assertiveness, unashamed aggressiveness; -पिरोना stitching and needle-work; stitching etc.; ~ज़ोरी से काम निकालना to brazen out, to carry off impudently; –तानना to stand upright, to stand undaunted, to brave all that comes; –ताने सहना to brave it out; –धड़कना see दिल धड़कना; सीने का उभार bulge of the breasts, contours of the breasts; सीने पर पत्थर रखना to endure patiently, to suppress agony in a quiet manner.

सीप si:p (*nf*) oyster shell, mother pearl.

सीपी si:pi: (*nf*) see सीप.

सीमंत si:mānt (*nm*) the parting line of the locks of hair on the head in combing; –संस्कार a ritual performed in the seventh or eighth month of a pregnant woman.

सीमंतोन्नयन si:māntonnayan (*nm*) see सीमंत संस्कार.

सीम si:m (*nf*) silver; see सीमा; ~तन silver-coloured, fair-complexioned; –चाँपना to usurp or capture another's territory.

सीमां/कन si:mā:ṅkan (*nm*) demarcation; ~कित demarcated.

सीमांत si:mā:nt (*a* and *nm*) frontier; limit; margin/marginal; extreme; -द्वार threshold; -प्रदेश frontier territory; –लाभ marginal profit; ~वाद extremism; -समन्वय marginal adjustment.

सीमा si:mā: (*nf*) a border, boundary/bounds; frontier; range; limit, extent; verge; -कर terminal tax; -चिह्न a landmark; -चौकी terminal post; -निर्धारण demarcation; delimitation of the boundary; -रेखा border-line; line of demarcation; -विवाद a boundary dispute; –में रहना to be confined within limits; –से बाहर जाना to cross the limit.

सीमातिक्रमण si:mā:tikkramāṇ (*nm*) violation of a territory or territorial integrity.

सीमावरोध si:mā:varodh (*nm*) territorial barriers.

सीमित si:mīt (*a*) restricted, limited, bounded; qualified; ~ता limitation.

सीमेंट si:menṭ (*nm*) cement; –कंक्रीट cement concrete.

सीमोल्लंघन si:mollaṅghān (*nm*) violation of territory or territorial integrity.

सीयन si:yan (*nf*) seam; stitching, sewing.

सीर si:r (*nf*) self cultivated land; (*nm*) a plough; –करना to self-cultivate; –में होना to be under cultivation.

सीरत si:rat (*nf*) disposition; nature.

सीरा si:ra: (*nm*) molasses.

सीरी si:ri: (*nm*) a cropper.

सील si:l (*nm*) see शील; (*nf*) damp/dampness, moisture; a seal; kinds of carnivorous amphibious marine mammal; ~बंद sealed; -मुहर होना to be sealed; –लगाना to put a seal.

सीलन si:lān (*nf*) dampness, moisture; -भरा damp.

सीलना si:lnā: (*v*) to dampen, to be/get damp(ed).

सीवँ sī:vā (*nf*) see **सिवान**.

सीवन si:vān (*nf*) see **सीयन**.

सीस si:s (*nm*) the head; ~फूल an ornament worn on the head.

सीसम si:sam (*nm*) a particular tree (that yields a rich variety of timber for furniture etc.).

सीसा si:sa: (*nm*) lead.

सीसी si:si: (*nf*) see **सी-सी**; see **शीशी**.

सुँघनी sūghnī: (*nf*) a snuff; sneezewort.

सुँघाना sūgha:nā: (*v*) to cause to smell.

सुंदर sundar (*a*) beautiful, handsome, pretty; fine; good; ~ता beauty, prettiness; goodness; hence **सुंदरी** feminine form of **सुंदर**.

सुंबी sumbi: (*nf*) punch, punching instrument.

सु su—a prefix imparting the meanings of good, beautiful, pretty, excellent, thorough, well, easy, etc.

सुअर suar (*nm*) a boar, pig.

सुअवसर suavasar (*nm*) an opportunity, a good chance.

सुआ sua: (*nm*) a big needle; marking pin.

सुई sui: (*nf*) a needle; hand of a watch; pointer.

सुकंठ sukanṭh (*a*) having a melodious voice, sweet-voiced.

सुकर sukar (*a*) easy; ~ता easiness.

सुक/र्म sukarm (*nf*) a good deed; ~र्मा performing good deeds, righteous, virtuous; ~र्मी see ~र्मा.

सुकवि sukavi (*nm*) a good poet.

सुकाज suka:j (*nm*) a good/righteous deed.

सुकान suka:n (*nm*) a rudder; -खंभा rudder post; -दंड rudder stock.

सुकाल suka:l (*nm*) good time, time of prosperity and plenty.

सुकीर्ति suki:rti (*nf*) reputation, renown; (*a*) reputed, renowned, celebrated.

सुकुमा/र sukuma:r (*a*) delicate, tender; ~रता delicacy, tenderness; hence ~री feminine adjectival form of ~र.

सुकून suku:n (*nm*) peace, comfort; consolation.

सुकून/त suku:nāt (*nf*) residence; ~ती residential.

सुकृत sukkrit (*nm*) a good deed; (*a*) well-done; righteous.

सुकृती sukriti: (*a*) good, righteous, virtuous.

सुकृत्य sukrity (*nm*) good deed, virtuous act.

सुकेशी sukeshi: (*a*) (a woman) having beautiful hair.

सुकोमल sukomal (*a*) extremely soft, very delicate; ~ता extreme softness/delicacy.

सुख sukh (*nm*) happiness, pleasure; comfort; felicity; contentment; ~कर happy, pleasant, comfortable/comforting; ~कारी causing happiness, pleasant, comfortable/comforting; -चैन happiness and comfort; ~जनक causing happiness/pleasure; comforting; ~जीविता the state or qualtiy of taking things easy; ~जीवी easygoing; ~द happy; pleasant, pleasurable, comfortable; hence ~दता (*nf*); ~दाता pleasuregiving, one who imparts happiness/pleasure; ~दायिनी feminine form of ~दायी; ~दायी see ~द; -दुःख happiness and sorrow; pleasure and pain; ~पूर्वक happily; comfortably; ~प्रद see ~द; -भोग luxurious living, enjoyment; ~मृत्यु euthanasia; ~राशि in whom happiness vests; ever-happy; -लिप्सा longing for happiness; ~लिप्सु one who longs for happiness; ~वाद/वादिता hedonism; ~वादी a hedonist; hedonistic; -शांति comfort/joy and peace, happiness and peace, felicity; -संपत्ति pleasure and plenty, happiness and prosperity; -साधन amenities; -साधना quest for happiness; ~साध्य easy; –सुविधा amenities; -सौभाग्य pleasure and plenty, physical and mental happiness; -स्वच्छंदता happiness and freedom; –की नींद carefree sleep; –देखना to live a happy/comfortable life; –मानना to feel happy/gratified; –लूटना to enjoy, to make merry.

सुख़न sukḥan (*nm*) verse, poetry; ~तक़िया a prop word, an expletive; ~फ़हम a connoisseur of poetry; ~फ़हमी appreciation of poetry.

सुखांत sukhā:nt (*a*) with a happy ending, ending happily; also ~क; hence ~ता (*nf*); –नाटक a comedy; –नाटककार a comedy-writer.

सुखांतिकी sukhā:ntiki: (*nf*) a comedy; ~कार a comedy-writer.

सुखात्मक sukha:tmāk (*a*) happy, imparting happiness; hedonic; hence ~ता (*nf*).

सुखाना sukha:nā: (*v*) to dry, to desiccate; to torrefy; to cause to wither away; to emaciate.

सुखी sukhi: (*a*) happy; contented.

सुखोदय sukhoday (*nm*) advent of a happy period.

सुख्या/त sukkhya:t (*a*) well-known, reputed, renowned; hence ~ति (*nf*).

सुगंध sugandh (*nf*) scent, fragrance, perfume, aroma; ~युक्त scented, fragrant, perfumed, aromatic.

सुगंधि sugandhi (*nf*) see सुगंध; ~युक्त see सुगंधयुक्त (under सुगंध).

सुगंधित sugandhit (*a*) scented, fragrant, perfumed, aromatic.

सुगठित sugaṭhit (*a*) shapely, well-built; muscular; well-organised.

सुगति sugati (*nf*) happy state; salvation, beatitude.

सुगम sugam (*a*) easy; approachable, accessible; light; intelligible; ~ता easiness; approachability, accessibility; intelligibility; –संगीत light music.

सुगम्य sugammy (*a*) see सुगम.

सुग्गा sugga: (*nm*) a parrot.

सुग्राहिता suggra:hita: (*nf*) susceptibility; sensitivity.

सुग्राही suggra:hi: (*a*) susceptible; sensitive.

सुग्राह्य suggra:hy (*a*) acceptable, tenable; intelligible, easy; hence ~ता (*nf*).

सुघट sughaṭ (*a*) shapely, well-built; well-organised; quite probable, easy to happen; hence ~ता (*nf*).

सुघटित sughaṭit (*a*) see सुघट.

सुघट्य sughaṭṭy (*a*) plastic; ~ता plasticity.

सुघड़ sughaṛ (*a*) shapely, well-built; elegant; dexterous; ~ता see सुघड़ाई; ~पन see सुघड़ाई.

सुघड़ाई sughaṛa:i: (*nf*) concinnity; shapeliness, elegance; dexterousness.

सुघड़ी sughaṛi: (*nf*) auspicious moment/instant.

सुघ/र sughar (*a*) see सुघड़; ~राई see सुघड़ाई.

सुचारु sucha:ru (*a*) charming, pretty, comely; hence ~ता (*nf*); –रूप से well; duly.

सुचिंतित suchintit (*a*) well-considered, deliberated upon; –मत well-considered opinion/view.

सुचित्त suchitt (*a*) equipoised, well-poised; hence ~ता (*nf*).

सुजन sujan (*nm*) a gentleman; ~ता gentlemanliness.

सुजन/न sujanān (*nm*) eugenics; ~न-विज्ञान eugenics; ~निक eugenic; ~निकी eugenics.

सुजनी sujanī: (*nf*) a thick (multi-coloured or single-coloured) bed-sheet.

सुजला sujala: (*a*) having plenty of rivers/water.

सुजात suja:t (*a*) well-born, born in a noble/prosperous family; hence ~ता (*nf*).

सुजान suja:n (*a*) wise, learned; hence ~ता (*nf*).

सुझाना sujha:nā: (*v*) to suggest; to propose; to indicate.

सुझाव sujha:v (*nm*) a suggestion, proposal.

सुठि suṭhi (*a*) good; pretty, beautiful.

सुड़कना suṛaknā: (*v*) to sniff up, to inhale with the breath; to drink noisily.

सुडौल suḍaul (*a*) shapely, comely, well-built; hence ~ता (*nf*)/~पन (*nm*).

सुढर suḍhar (*a*) favourably inclined, kindly disposed.

सु/त sut (*nm*) a son; hence ~ता (*nf*).

सुतनु sutanū (*a*) shapely, comely; tenuous, of delicate build.

सुतरां sutara:m (*ind*) moreover; thus, therefore; what more.

सुतली sutli: (*nf*) twine, thin rope.

सुतार suta:r (*nm*) smooth harmonious state of things; -कुतार harmony and disharmony (of state of things), the state of being in gear and out of gear.

सुतीक्ष्ण suti:kshn (*a*) very sharp/pointed; hence ~ता (*nf*).

सुथना suthnā: (*nm*) loose pyjamas.

सुथरा suthra: (*a*) clean, neat and tidy; refined; ~ई/पन cleanliness, neatness and tidiness; refinement.

सुदर्शन sudarshan (*a*) good-looking, winsome, elegant; (*nm*) the name of the mythological discus wielded by Lord Vishnū; –चक्र see सुदर्शन (*nm*).

सुदामा suda:mā: (*nm*) a very poor friend and class-fellow of Lord Krishnā at the school of their preceptor संदीपन मुनि; very helpless and indigent fellow; –के तंदुल present of rice by Suda:mā: to Krishnā at their legendary meeting; a poor man's present.

सुदि sudi (*nf*) the moonlit fortnight of a lunar month.

सुदिन sudin (*nm*) fine/happy day; happy times.

सुदी sudi: (*nf*) see सुदि.

सुदीर्घ sudi:rgh (*a*) very long, long-winding; detailed.

सुदूर sudu:r (*a*) very far, remote; ~पूर्व far east; ~वर्ती remote, far-flung.

सुदृढ़ suddriḍh (*a*) very strong; very firm; very rigid; hence ~ता (*nf*).

सुदौसी sudausi: (*ind*) early.

सुद्दा sudda: (*nm*) dry faeces.

सुध sudh (*nf*) memory; consciousness, senses; -बुध memory; consciousness, senses; ०खोना/०न रहना see –न रहना; –दिलाना to remind; –न रहना to forget; to lose or be out of senses; –बिसरना to forget; to lose or be out of senses; –लेना to remember; to enquire after.

सुधरना sudharnā: (*v*) to be reformed; to be improved; to be amended/corrected; to be repaired.

सुध/र्म sudharm (*nm*) virtuous duty, piety; hence ~र्मा (*a*); ~र्मी (*a*).

सुधवाना sudhva:nā: (*v*) to cause to be or to get calculated (as an auspicious moment); to get purified.

सुधांशु sudhā:nshu (*nm*) the moon.

सुधा sudha: (*nf*) nectar; ~कर/धर/निधि the moon; ~रस nectar; ~वृष्टि rain of nectar—plenty and prosperity.

सुधाना sudha:nā: (*v*) to get (an auspicious moment) calculated; to get purified.

सुधार sudha:r (*nm*) reform/reformation; uplift; repair, amendment; modification; improvement; correction; ~क a reformer; ameliorant; ~वाद reformism; meliorism; ~वादी a reformist; reformatory.

सुधारना sudha:rnā: (*v*) to reform; to repair, to mend/amend; to improve; to uplift; to correct.

सुधारालय sudha:ra:lay (*nm*) a reformatory.

सुधि sudhi (*nf*) see सुध.

सुधी sudhi: (*a* and *nm*) (a) wise/learned (man); the wise; ~जन learned people, the wise.

सुनना sunnā: (*v*) to hear, to listen; to pay heed; (*nm*) hearing, audition; सुना-सुनाया hearsay, based on hearsay; सुनी-अनसुनी करना to pay no heed, to ignore.

सुनम्य sunammy (*a*) plastic; flexible; ~ता plasticity; flexibility.

सुनयना sunaynā: (*a*) (a woman)having beautiful eyes, pretty-eyed.

सुनवाई sunwa:i: (*nf*) hearing (of a case etc.)

सुनवैया sunwaiya: (*nm*) a hearer; listener (of woes).

सुनसान sunsa:n (*a*) desolate, deserted; lonely; (*nm*) loneliness; stillness.

सुनह/रा, ~ला sunehra:, ~la: (*a*) golden; ~पन goldenness; ~रा मौक़ा golden chance.

सुनाना sunā:nā: (*v*) to cause to hear; to relate; to read out; to recite; to pronounce.

सुनाम sunā:m (*nm*) repute, celebrity, fame; goodwill.

सुना/र suna:r (*nm*) a goldsmith; ~री the profession or work of a goldsmith; a goldsmith's wife; a good woman; hence ~रिन (*nf*).

सुनावनी sunā:wani: (*nf*) news of a death (from a distant place).

सुनिश्चय sunishchay (*nm*) assurance; definiteness.

सुनिश्चित sunishchit (*a*) assured; definite; hence ~ता (*nf*).

सुनीति suni:ti (*nf*) equity; -संगत equitable.

सुन्न sunn (*a*) still(ed); insensitive, benumbed, etherised; stupefied; -पड़ना to be benumbed/rendered insensitive; to be stupefied.

सुन्नत sunnat (*nf*) circumcision; -करना to circumcise; to convert into a Mohammedan.

सुन्ना sunnā: (*nm*) a zero cipher.

सुन्नी sunnī: (*nm*) one of the two major sub-divisions of Mohammedans (the other being शिया).

सुपंथ supanth (*nm*) the course of morality/equity/justice.

सुपक्व supakkw (*a*) well-ripe, well-ripened; hence ~ता (*nf*).

सुपच supach (*a*) easily digestible.

सुपथ supath (*nm*) see सुपंथ.

सुपथ्य supatthy (*a*) salubrious; (*nm*) salubrious diet.

सुपरवाइज़/र suparva:izar (*nm*) a supervisor; ~री supervisory; position or post of a supervisor.

सुपरिंटडेंट suparinṭenḍēnṭ (*nm*) a superintendent.

सुपाच्य supa:chchy (*a*) easily digestible; hence ~ता (*nf*).

सुपाठ्य supa:ṭṭhy (*a*) legible; readable; worth reading; hence ~ता (*nf*).

सुपात्र supa:ttr (*nm*) a deserving (person), one who deserves; (*a*) deserving; hence ~ता (*nf*).

सुपारी supa:ri: (*nf*) betel-nut; areca-nut.

सुपुर्द supurd (*a*) entrusted, committed; charged (with); ~गी trust; charge, care; delivery; –करना to entrust, to hand over, to place under the charge/care (of); to deliver.

सुप्त supt (*a*) asleep, dormant; (rendered) senseless; –चेतना dormant consciousness.

सुप्ति supti (*nf*) sleep, slumber.

सुप्रतिष्ठित suppratishṭhit (*a*) well-established; reputed, celebrated.

सुप्रभात supprabha:t (*nm*) good/auspicious/happy morning.

सुप्रभाव supprabha:v (*nm*) good/welcome effect.

सुप्रयुक्त supprayukt (*a*) well-applied; properly utilised.

सुप्रयोग supprayog (*nm*) good usage/application; proper utilisation.

सुप्रसन्न supprasann (*a*) very happy.

सुप्रसिद्ध supprasiddh (*a*) reputed, renowned, famous, celebrated.

सुफ/ल suphal (*nm*) good/welcome result; hence ~ला (fem. form).

सुबह subeh (*nf*) morning; dawn; -सुबह early (in the) morning; -सवेरे early (in the) morning; –का तारा short-lived, certain to disappear soon; –कर देना to spend the night without sleep; –का भूला शाम को आए veering round to the proper course at long last; –की पूछो शाम की कहना the reply to be much beside the question; -शाम करना to dilly-dally, to go on evading; –से शाम तक from morning till evening, from dawn to dusk; –से ही मिज़ाज बिगड़ा होना to get out of bed on wrong side.

सुबास suba:s (*nf*) see सुवास.

सुबुक subuk (*a*) light, delicate; quick, nimble-handed; ~दस्त quick at work; ~दोश rid of a burden; –होना to feel small, to be humiliated; to feel lighter.

सुबुद्धि subuddhi (*nf*) good/moral sense, wisdom; (*a*) wise, intelligent.

सुबोध subodh (*a*) intelligible, easy; ~ता intelligibility, easiness.

सुभ/ग subhag (*a*) beautiful; lucky; ~गा feminine form of ~ग; ~गे! vocative word for a beautiful woman; hence ~ता (*nf*).

सुभानअल्ला subha:n alla: (*int*) Thou art Great/Holy !; what wonder !; how wonderful !

सुभाषित subha:shit (*a*) well-said; (*nm*) a maxim; pithy/quotable saying; –संग्रह analects.

सुभी/ता subhi:ta: (*nm*) convenience; comfort; ~ते से conveniently; comfortably.

सुमति sumati (*nf*) unity/union; see सुबुद्धि (*nf* and *a*).

सुमधुर sumadhur (*a*) very sweet, melodious.

सुमन sumān (*nm*) a flower; (*a*) favourably disposed; happy; ~स्क happy, pleased.

सुमा/र्ग suma:rg (*nm*) good/moral course, just course; ~**र्गी/र्गगामी** traversing the righteous course/path.

सुमिरनी sumirnī: (*nf*) a rosary (of beads).

सुमुखी sumukhi: (*a* and *nm*) (a) pretty-faced (woman), beautiful.

सुमेरु sumeru (*nm*) the mythological mountain of gold.

सुमेल sumel (*nm*) harmony.

सुम्मा summā: (*nm*) a drift bolt.

सुम्मी summī: (*nf*) a dowel.

सुयश suyash (*nm*) reputation, renown.

सुयोग suyog (*nm*) a happy chance/coincidence; –**से** by a happy coincidence.

सुयोग्य suyoggy (*a*) very able, worthy.

सुरंग surāṅg (*nf*) a tunnel; mine; (*a*) having a good/pleasant/pretty colour; –**बिछाना** to lay a mine.

सुर sur (*nm*) tone; a note in music; vowel; a god; ~**गण** gods, the whole body of gods; -**तान** tone and tune; o**में करना** to attune; ~**त्व** godhood; ~**दार** melodious, harmonious; ~**धाम** the abode of gods; o**सिधारना** to leave for one's heavenly abode—to die; -**भंग** see **स्वरभंग**; ~**राज** king of gods—Indra; ~**लहरी** musical wave, melody; ~**सरिता** the river Gaṅga:; –**मिलाना** to attune, to harmonise; –**में सुर मिलाना** to chime in.

सुरक्षण surakshāṇ (*nm*) (the act or process of) protection, security; reservation.

सुर/क्षा suraksha: (*nf*) protection, security; ~**क्षित** safe, secure, protected; reserved.

सुरति surati (*nf*) memory, recollection; amorous dalliance, sexual enjoyment.

सुरभि surabhi (*nf*) fragrance, aroma; perfume, scent; ~**त** fragrant, aromatic; perfumed, scented.

सुरभी surabhi: (*nf*) see **सुरभि**; a cow.

सुरमई surmai: (*a*) dark grey, of the colour of **सुरमा**.

सुरमा surmā: (*nm*) collyrium, antimony ground into fine powder; ~**दानी** collyrium phial or receptacle; –**करना/बनाना** to grind into fine powder.

सुरम्य surammy (*a*) charming, attractive, beautiful; hence ~**ता** (*nf*).

सुरलहर surlahar (*nf*) intonation.

सुरस suras (*a*) flavoury, juicy; sweet.

सुरसा surasa: (*nf*) mythologically, a monstrous figure said to be the mother of snakes, who blocked Hanumā:n's expedition to **लंका** trying to devour him by opening her mouth wider than Hanumā:n's increasing size.

सुरसुरा/ना sursura:nā: (*v*) to rustle; to creep or crawl like an insect; to itch; ~**हट** rustling; creeping or crawling; itching.

सुरसुरी sursuri: (*nf*) see **सुरसुराहट** (under **सुरसुराना**); thrill.

सुरा sura: (*nf*) wine, liquor; –**और सुंदरी** wine and women; ~**कर्म** brewing; ~**कर्मशाला** a brewery; ~**गृह** a wine shop, bar; -**पात्र** a peg, wine glass; ~**पान** drinking of wine; ~**सार** spirit, alcohol.

सुराख sura:ḳḥ (*nm*) a hole, cavity, an aperture.

सुराग sura:g (*nm*) a clue; trace; –**पाना/मिलना/लगना** to get a clue.

सुरागाय sura:ga:y (*nf*) a yak.

सुरा/ज sura:j (*nm*) good rule; independence; ~जी a fighter for independence.

सुराज्य sura:jjy (*nm*) good rule; worthy state.

सुरासुर sura:sur (*nm*) the gods and demons; -युद्ध/संग्राम mythological battle of the gods and demons.

सुराही sura:hi: (*nf*) a flagon, long-necked earthen water-pot; ~दार shaped like a *sura:hi:*; o गर्दन long and slender neck; ~नुमा shaped like a *sura:hi:*.

सुरीला suri:la: (*a*) sweet, melodious; -कंठ/गला melodious voice; ~पन sweetness, melodiousness; symphony.

सुरुचि suruchi (*nf*) refined taste, good taste; ~पूर्ण refined, tasteful; ~वान (a man) of refined taste; -संपन्न gifted with a good taste.

सुरूप suru:p (*a*) good looking, beautiful, shapely; hence ~ता (*nf*).

सुरूर suru:r (*nm*) mild/slight intoxication; pleasant after-effects of mild/slight intoxication; -आना to be under the influence of the first mild wave of intoxication; -जमना to be in the pleasant state of mild/slight intoxication.

सुरेंद्र surendr (*nm*) Indra—the chief of gods.

सुरेख surekh (*a*) beautiful, shapely; with symmetrical lines.

सुर्ख़ surḳh (*a*) red, ruddy; ~पोश dressed in red; hence ~पोशी (*nf*); ~रू reputed, having reputation; honourable; oहोना to be vindicated; -होना to be ruddy, to be in the pink of health.

सुर्ख़ाब surḳha:b (*nm*) a ruddy goose—*Anas casarca*; -का पर an unusual feature; —के पर लगे होना to be blessed with an unusual feature, to have any remarkable characteristic; to be privileged.

सुर्ख़ी surḳhi: (*nf*) redness, ruddiness; a headline; brickdust; lipstick; upward trend (in price); ~मायल with a red tinge, reddish; -छाना to be ruddy; to be in the pink of health.

सुलक्ष/ण sulakshān (*a*) gifted with laudable ways; having auspicious features / characteristics / marks; fortunate, lucky; hence ~णा, ~णी feminine forms of ~ण.

सुलगना sulagnā: (*v*) to smoulder; to burn (esp. inwardly); to begin to burn, to be ignited.

सुलगाना sulga:nā: (*v*) to kindle; to ignite, to (cause) to burn.

सुलझन suljhan (*nf*) disentanglement; resolution; unravelling.

सुलझना sulajhnā: (*v*) to be disentangled; to be unravelled; to be solved.

सुलझाना suljha:nā: (*v*) to disentangle; to unravel; to solve; to set right.

सुलझाव suljha:v (*nm*) disentanglement; solution.

सुलटा sulṭa: (*a*) straight, direct (generally used in the compound उलटा-सुलटा).

सुलता/न sulta:n (*nm*) a Sultan; ~नी pertaining/belonging to or position of a Sultan, regal, majestic.

सुलफ़ sulaf (*nm*) refreshment, breakfast; used in Hindi only as second member of the compound सौदा-सुलफ़ (see).

सुल/फ़ा sulfa: (*nm*) an intoxicating drug; crude tobacco smoked without using filter; ~फ़ेबाज addicted to सुलफ़ा; hence ~फ़ेबाजी (*nf*).

सुलभ sulabh (*a*) easy; accessible, available, handy; ~ता easiness; accessibility, availability.

सुलभ्य sulabbhy (*a*) easily accessible/available; hence ~ता (*nf*).

सुललित sulalit (*a*) charming, graceful, elegant.

सुलह suleh (*nf*) an agreement; reconciliation, rapproachement; ~कार a peace-maker; ~कुल friendly with all; ~नामा (a written) agreement; compromise deed; peace-treaty.

सुलाना sula:nā: (*v*) to cause to sleep; to lull to sleep.

सुलाभ sula:bh (*nm*) (good) advantage.

सुलूक sulu:k (*nm*) treatment, behaviour.

सुलेख sulekh (*nm*) calligraphy; ~क see ~कार; -कला (the art of) calligraphy; ~कार a calligraphist; ~न calligraphy.

सुलोचना sulochnā: (*a*) beautiful-eyed (woman), having charming eyes.

सुवक्ता suvakta: (*nm*) an orator, a good speaker.

सुवचन suvachan (*nm*) good/pleasant words.

सुवर्ण suvarn (*nm*) gold; good colour; higher caste.

सुवश्य suvashshy (*a*) docile, submissive; hence ~ता (*nf*).

सुवाच्य suva:chchy (*a*) readable, ~ता readability.

सुवार्ता suva:rta: (*nf*) good news.

सुवा/स suva:s (*nf*) fragrance, aroma; perfume, scent; ~सित fragrant, aromatic; perfumed, scented.

सुविख्यात suvikkhya:t (*a*) renowned, reputed.

सुविचार suvicha:r (*nm*) good/subtle idea.

सुविचारित suvicha:rit (*a*) well-considered; -मत well-considered view.

सुविदित suvidit (*a*) well-known.

सुविधा suvidha: (*nf*) facility; convenience; -का सौदा agreement/marriage of convenience; ~जीवी easy-going; ~पूर्वक conveniently.

सुवृ/त्त suvritt (*a*) virtuous, righteous; hence ~त्ति (*nf*).

सुवेश suvesh (*a*) well-dressed; good looking.

सुव्यक्त suvvyakt (*a*) well-expressed, distinctly expressed; distinct; manifest; articulated; hence ~ता (*nf*).

सुव्यवस्था suvvyavastha: (*nf*) order/orderliness; good organisation/administration.

सुव्यवस्थित suvvyavasthit (*a*) orderly; regular; well-organised; well-administered.

सुशा/सन susha:san (*nm*) good government/rule / administration; ~सित well-governed, well-ruled, well-administered.

सुशिक्षित sushikshit (*a*) well-educated, highly educated.

सुशीतल sushi:tal (*a*) very cool.

सुशी/ल sushi:l (*a*) courteous, suave; modest; ~लता courteousness, suavity; modesty; hence ~ला feminine form of ~ल.

सुशोभित sushobhit (*a*) (well) adorned; graceful: -करना to adorn; to grace; -होना to be adorned; to be graced; to look splendid.

सुश्राव्य sushshra:vvy (*a*) sonorous, melodious; well-audible.

सुश्री sushshri: (*a*) an honorofic prefixed to the name of a woman – married or unmarried.

सुश्रूषा sushshru:sha: (*nf*) see शुश्रूषा.

सुषमा sushmā: (*nf*) beauty, exceptional prettiness, charm; ~युक्त beautiful, pretty, charming.

सुषु/प्त sushupt (*a*) asleep, in deep slumber; dormant; ~प्तावस्था the state of deep sleep; dormancy.

~प्ति deep sleep.

सुषुम्ना sushumnā: (*nf*) one of the three principal or major nerves, according to the *haṭhyogi:s*, that plays an important role in the achievement of Supreme Bliss.

सुष्ठु sushṭḥu (*a*) elegant; appropriate; ~ता elegance; appropriateness.

सुसंगत susāṅgat (*a*) very appropriate/logical, valid/tenable/reasonable; concordant; relevant; hence ~ता (*nf*).

सुसंगति susāṅgati (*nf*) good association, commendable company, validity; relevance; concord (ance); rationality.

सुसंपन्न susāmpann (*a*) prosperous, affluent; well-to-do; hence ~ता (*nf*).

सुसंस्कृत susānskrit (*a*) well cultured; refined,

सुसंह/त susanghat (*a*) compact; ~ति compactness.

सुसज्जित susajjit (*a*) well-adorned; well-equipped.

सुसाध्य susa:ddhy (*a*) easily achievable; curable without difficulty; hence ~ता (*nf*).

सुस्त sust (*a*) slow, languid; indolent; lazy, idle; in low spirit; spiritless, depressed.

सुस्ताना susta:nā: (*v*) to relax, to rest; to have a respite.

सुस्ती susti: (*nf*) languor, indolence; laziness, idleness; spiritlessness, depression.

सुस्थ susth (*a*) normal, in a normal state; composed, equipoised, well-composed; hence ~ता (*nf*).

सुस्थित susthit (*a*) well-situated, well-located; well-poised; hence ~ता (*nf*).

सुस्थिर susthir (*a*) well-poised, steady, stable; firm; well-established; hence ~ता (*nf*).

सुस्वनिक susswanīk (*a*) sonorous.

सुस्वर susswar (*a* and *nm*) melodious voice/tune; hence ~ता (*nf*).

सुस्वादु susswa:du (*a*) delicious, tasty; ~ता deliciousness, tastiness.

सुहबत suhbat (*nf*) company, association; cohabitation, coition; **–करना, किसी से** to have sexual intercourse; **–का असर** imprint/influence of the company; **–बिगड़ना** to fall into bad company.

सुहबती suhbati: (*a*) sociable, affable.

सुहाग suha:g (*nm*) coverture, the happy state of a woman when her husband is alive; husband; good fortune; **-पिटारी** an auspicious chest carrying a woman's ornaments and make-up stuff symbolising her **सुहाग**; **-भरी** happy and prosperous, blessed with good fortune; ~रात the first night of a couple's union; **–अचल होना** to be ever blessed with coverture; **–उजड़ना/लुटना** (said of a woman) to be widowed, to lose coverture/protection of the husband; **–मनाना** to pray for the husband's longevity, well-being.

सुहागन suha:gan (*a* and *nf*) (a woman) whose husband is alive, who is ever-blessed with coverture/the protective presence of the husband.

सुहागा suha:ga: (*nm*) borax, plank.

सुहागि/न, ~नी, ~ल suha:gin, ~nī:, ~l (*a* and *nm*) see **सुहागन**.

सुहाता suha:ta: (*a*) pleasant; pleasantly warm (water etc.).

सुहाना suha:nā: (*v*) to be pleasing; to look charming; to be liked; (*a*) pleasing, charming; likeable.

सुहावना suha:vnā: (*a*) pleasing; charming; likeable.

सुहृद suhrid (*a*) friendly, loving; (*nm*) a friend.

सूँघना sū:ghnā: (*v*) to smell, to scent; to sniff; to eat very little.

सूँड़ sū:ṛ (*nf*) the trunk (of an elephant), proboscis.

सूँड़ी sū:ṛi: (*nf*) a grub.

सूँस sū:s (*nf*) a porpoise.

सूअर su:ar (*nm*) a boar, pig; a word of abuse—swine; very dirty/thick-skinned person; –**का बच्चा** a term of abuse meaning a pig; –, **वनैला** a wild boar.

सूआ su:a (*nm*) a big needle.

सूई su:ī: (*nf*) a needle; the hands of a watch/clock; –**का काम** needle-work; –**का नाका** eye of a needle; –**का भाला/फावड़ा बना देना** to make a mountain of a molehill, to exaggerate no end; –**के नाके में से ऊँट/हाथी निकालना** to perform a miracle/an impossible feat.

सूक/र su:kar (*nm*) see **सूअर**; hence ~**री** (*nf*).

सूक्त su:kt (*nm*) a *mantra* of the V*edas*; ~**द्रष्टा** a composer/seer of a **सूक्त**.

सूक्ति su:kti (*nf*) a maxim, an epigram, a pithy pointed saying; -**संग्रह** analects.

सूक्ष्म sukshm (*a*) subtle, minute; fine; thin; –**अर्थ** subtle meaning; ~**ता** subtlety, minuteness, fineness, thinness; precision; ~**दर्शक यंत्र** a microscope; ~**दर्शिकी** microscopy; ~**दर्शी** a microscope; keen observer; keen-eyed; ~**दृष्टि** keen-sighted; keen sight; o**ता** keen-sightedness; –**देह/शरीर** the subtle body.

सूक्ष्माणु sukshmā:ṇū (*nm*) a microbe.

सूख/ना su:khnā: (*v*) to dry up, to wither; to dwindle; to be attenuated; to evaporate; –**कर काँटा हो जाना** to become too tenuous, to be reduced to a skeletion; –**जाना, मारे डर के** to be terrorized out of wits, to be horror-stricken.

सूखा su:kha: (*a*) dry, sapless; blunt; flat (as **जवाब**); all-told, with nothing extra; (*nm*) drought; (in children) cramp (also called –**रोग**); –**जवाब देना** to refuse flatly; –**टालना** to say a flat 'no'; **सूखी खुजली** a kind of dry itch (disease); **सूखी तनख्वाह** only cash pay (with nothing extra in kind); **सूखे धानों पर पानी पड़ना** to achieve one's fulfilment when in utter despair.

सूचक su:chak (*nm*) an informant/informer; a pointer; (*a*) suggestive, symptomatic; indicative.

सूचकांक su:chakā:ṅk (*nm*) an index.

सूचना su:chnā: (*nf*) information, intimation; notice, notification; announcement; -**पट्ट** a notice-board; -**अधिकारी** information officer; -**केंद्र** information centre; -**ब्यूरो** information bureau; -**पत्र** a notification, circular; -**माध्यम** medium of information; ~**र्थ** for information; –**देना** to inform, to intimate; to report; to notify; –**देने वाला** an informer/

informant, a reporter.

सूचनीय su:chnī:y (*a*) reportable or to be reported; informable or to be informed.

सूचिका su:chika: (*nf*) a needle; feminine form of सूचक.

सूचित su:chit (*a*) informed, intimated; –करना to inform/intimate; –होना to be informed/intimated.

सूची su:chi: (*nf*) a list, catalogue; -पत्र a catalogue; ० बनाना to (prepare a) catalogue; ~भेद्य to be pierced only by a needle, very dense; palpable; ० अंधकार palpable darkness, thick envelope of darkness; –बनाना to (prepare a) list.

सूजन su:jan (*nf*) swelling, inflammation.

सूजना su:jnā: (*v*) to swell; सूजा हुआ swollen.

सूजा su:ja: (*nm*) a big needle, an awl; distaff; (*a*) swollen.

सूज़ाक su:za:k (*nm*) gonorrhoea.

सूजी su:ji: (*nf*) semola, semolina.

सूझ su:jh (*nf*) insight, vision, imagination; perception; -बूझ imagination; understanding, intelligence; ० से काम लेना to use one's imagination/intelligence.

सूझना su:jhnā: (*v*) to be visible, to be seen; to occur to one's mind.

सूट su:ṭ (*nm*) a suit (of clothes); ~केस a suit-case.

सूत su:t (*nm*) yarn, thread; length equal to one-eighth of an inch; a charioteer; one who relates ancient legends; –कातना to spin; –न कपास जुलाहे से लट्ठम-लट्ठा to count one's chickens before they are hatched, first catch your hare then cook him; to contend without a bone of contention.

सूतक su:tak (*nm*) impurity or defilement which, according to the Hindu tradition, is caused by a death/birth in the family; –लगना an impurity or defilement caused due to a death/birth.

सूता su:ta: (*nm*) thread.

सूति(का)गृह su:ti(ka:)grih (*nm*) a confinement chamber.

सूती su:ti: (*a*) cotton–, made of cotton; –कपड़ा cotton cloth.

सूत्र su:ttr (*nm*) a thread, yarn, fibre; source; aphorism; formula; sacred thread (जनेऊ); ~कर्ता a composer of aphorism (of philosophy, grammar, etc.); ~धार the stage manager (in a dramatic performance); ~पात beginning, commencement: ~बद्ध formulated; integrated; -शैली terse style, condensed style.

सूत्राकार su:ttra:ka:r (*a*) filiform.

सूत्रात्मक su:ttra:tmak (*a*) in the nature of a formula, terse, pithy; hence ~ता (*nf*).

सूत्रालेख su:ttra:lekh (*nm*) a monograph.

सूत्रित su:ttrit (*a*) formulated.

सूत्रीकरण su:ttri:karaṇ (*nm*) formulation.

सूथ/न, ~नी suthān (*nm*), ~nī: (*nf*) trousers.

सूद su:d (*nm*) interest; ~ख़ोर usurer; usurious; ~ख़ोरी usury; -दर-सूद compound interest.

सूदन su:dan—a Sanskrit suffix used to denote a killer/destroyer/conqueror of (as रिपुसूदन, मधुसूदन, etc.).

सूना sū:nā: (*a*) lonely, desolate; empty; ~पन loneliness, desolation; emptiness; सूना लगना to appear desolated.

सूप su:p (*nm*) a winnowing basket; soup, broth; ~**कार** a cook; ~**शास्त्र** the science of cookery; –**बोले सो बोले छलनी क्या बोले (जिसमें बहत्तर छेद)** the pot calling the kettle black.

सूफ़ियाना su:fiya:nā: (*a*) befitting a Su:fi:; plain and simple; –**अंदाज़** in the manner of a Su:fi:.

सूफ़ी su:fi: (*nm*) a sect of Muslim saints (whose characteristic quality is their plain and simple ways).

सू/बा su:ba: (*nm*) a province; ~**बेवार** provincewise.

सूबेदा/र su:beda:r (*nm*) a governor, head of a province; a non commissioned army rank; ~**र-मेजर** a Subedar-Major—non-commissioned army rank; ~**री** post/office or work of a ~**र**.

सूम sū:m (*a*) penurious, miser, niggardly; (*nm*) a miser; ~**पन/पना** penury, miserliness, niggardliness.

सूर su:r (*a*) brave; blind; (*nm*) the sun; ~**दास** (euphemistically) a blind person; o **कारी कामरि पै चढ़ै न दूजो रंग** can the Ethiopian change his colour!, black will take no other hue.

सूरज su:raj (*nm*) the sun; see **सूर्य**; ~**मुखी** see **सूर्यमुखी**; ~**सुता** an epithet of the river Yamunā:, –**को चिराग़/दीपक दिखाना** (to be stupid enough) to light the course of the sun, to try to instruct the Omniscient Himself, to introduce the well-known; –**छिपना/डूबना/ढलना** the sun to set; –, **उगता** the rising sun; –, **डूबता** the setting sun; –**पर थूकना**, –**पर धूल फेंकना** to accuse the infallible and be self-debased.

सूरत su:rat (*nf*) countenance, face; appearance, looks; form; case; condition, state; ~**परस्त** a beauty-worshipper, a hanker after looks; ~**वाला** beautiful, good-looking; -**शक्ल** appearance; looks; -**सीरत** beauty and quality; looks and merits; ~**हराम** of deceptive looks; **सूरत(ए)हाल** present state/condition; –**दिखाना** to show up, to turn up; –**नज़र आना** to find a way out, to think of a solution (to a problem); –**निकल आना** to grow prettier; a solution (to a problem) to emerge; –**बदलना** to disguise; things to change; –**बिगाड़ना** to deface; to make wry faces; to express displeasure; –**में, इस** in this case; –**से बेज़ार होना** not to be able to stand the sight of; to be absolutely fed up of; –**से सीरत का अंदाज नहीं होता** beauty is but skin deep, all that glitters is not gold.

सूरन su:ran (*nm*) elephant's foot; an edible root/tuber.

सूरमा su:rmā: (*a* and *nm*) brave; a hero; warrior; ~**ई/पन** bravery, heroism.

सूराख़ su:ra:ḳḥ (*nm*) a hole, an aperture, orifice; a puncture; eyelet; ~**दार** having a hole or holes; –**करना** to drill, to bore a hole.

सूर्य su:ry (*nm*) the sun; ~**कर/रश्मि** rays (of the sun); ~**कांत** the jasper; ~**केंद्रीय** heliocentric; ~**ग्रहण** solar eclipse; –**घड़ी** a sun-dial; ~**चित्रिक** heliograph; ~**चित्रीय** heliographic; ~**तनया/नंदिनी/पुत्री** an epithet of the river Yamunā:, -**परिमंडल** corona of the sun; ~**पूजा** heliolatry; -**प्रभा** sunlight; -**बिंब/**

मंडल the orb or disc of the sun; ~मणि the jasper; ~मुखी the sunflower—*Helianthus annus*; having the colour of the skin rendered white (through disease); ~वंश a celebrated ancient Indian dynasty of *Kshatriya* kings; ~वंशी one belonging to the solar dynasty (सूर्यवंश).

सूर्यानुव/र्त्तन su:rya:nuvartan (*nm*) heliotropism; ~र्ती heliotropic.

सूर्यास्त su:rya:st (*nm*) sunset.

सूर्योदय su:ryoday (*nm*) sunrise; –से सूर्यास्त तक from sunrise to sunset, whole day, throughout the day.

सूर्योपास/क su:ryopa:sak (*nm*) a sun-worshipper, heliolater; ~ना sun-worship, heliolatry.

सूली su:li: (*nm*) gallows, gibbet; –देना, –पर चढ़ाना to hang to death, to execute by hanging.

सृजन srijan (*nm*) creation; -शक्ति/~शीलता creativity, creative power; ~शील creative; ~हार creator (of the world).

सृष्ट srishṭ (*a*) created.

सृष्टि srishṭi (*nf*) creation; the world; ~कर्ता Creator (of the world); -विज्ञान/शास्त्र cosmology; ~वैज्ञानिक a cosmologist; cosmological; ~शास्त्रीय cosmological.

सेंकना sẽknā: (*v*) to foment; to bake; to roast; to warm; –, आँख see under आँख; –, धूप to bask.

सेंगरा sẽgra: (*nm*) a stick for carrying heavy things (like a log or stone etc.).

सें/ड़ा sẽṛa: (*a* and *nm*) a nitwit; stupid (fellow); ~ड़पन stupidity.

सेंट sẽnṭ (*nm*) scent; a cent.

सेंटर sẽnṭar (*nm*) a centre.

सेंट्रल sẽnṭral (*a*) central.

सेंठा sẽṭha: (*nm*) the lower end of a reed.

सेंत sẽt (*a*) gratis, free of charge/cost; –कर रखना to keep in safe custody; –में gratis; -मेंत see सेंत; ०में gratis; without any charge.

सेंध sẽdh (*nf*) a hole (made) in a wall (by a burglar); burglary, house-breaking; –मारना/लगाना to burgle, to break through a wall, to break into a house.

सेंधा sẽdha: (*nm*) rock salt; –नमक rock salt.

सेंधिया sẽdhiya: (*nm*) a burglar.

सेंवई sẽvaī: (*nf*) vermicelli; –पूरना to prepare vermicelli (with hands).

सेंसर sẽnsar (*nm*) censor; -बोर्ड censor board; -व्यवस्था censor system; censorship.

सेंसरी sẽnsari: (*nf*) censorship.

सेंहुआ sẽhuā: (*nm*) a kind of skin disease (causing white blots).

सेंहुड़ sẽhūṛ (*nm*) a kind of cactus.

से se (*ind*) from; with; by; than; since; (*a*) similar, equal.

सेइया seiya: (*nf*) porcupine; –का काँटा porcupine quill; dragon's teeth; ०डाल देना, किसी के घर में to sow dragon's teeth.

सेकना seknā: (*v*) see सेंकना.

सेकें(कं)ड sekẽ(kā)nḍ (*nm*) a second (one-sixtieth of a minute).

सेक्रेटरियट sekreṭariaṭ (*nm*) secretariat.

सेक्रेटरी sekreṭari: (*nm*) secretary.

सेक्शन sekshan (*nm*) section; -अफ़सर a section officer.

से/चन sechan (*nm*) irrigation, watering; ~चक an irrigator; ~चनीय to be irrigated; worth irrigating; ~चित irrigated.

सेज sej (*nf*) a bed, richly decorated bed; –, फूलों की easy and luxurious living.

सेट seṭ (*nm*) a set (of things).

सेटना seṭnā: (*v*) to regard; to

accept.

सेठ seṭh (*nm*) a wealthy merchant, moneyed man; hence **सेठानी** (*nf*).

सेठा seṭha: (*nm*) see **सेंठा**.

सेतु setu (*nm*) a bridge; causeway; ~**पथ** the span or extent of a bridge; ~**बंध** (constructing) a bridge.

सेनांग senā:ṅg (*nm*) the arms (of a defence force viz. the army, navy and air force).

सेना senā: (*nf*) army, military; horde; (*v*) to hatch; (arch.) to serve; –**की शाखाएँ** arms; ~**प्र/मुख** vanguard; ~**जीवी** a soldier; ~**दार**/~**धिप** /~**धिपति** /~**धीश** /~**ध्यक्ष**/~**नायक**/~**नी** /~**पति** /~**पाल** commander, general (of an army); ~**पत्य** commandership; -**व्यूह** a battle-array, strategic deployment of the forces; –, **खटिया/चारपाई** to lie idly; to keep confined to bed for long.

सेफ़ sef (*nf*) an iron safe.

सेब seb (*nm*) see **सेव**.

सेम sem (*nf*) bean, kidney-bean (name of a particular vegetable).

सेम/र, ~ल semar, ~l (*nm*) silk cotton (tree or its flower).

सेमा semā: (*nm*) a large variety of **सेम**.

सेमिकोलन semikolān (*nm*) a semicolon.

सेमिटिक semiṭik (*a*) semitic.

सेर ser (*nm*) a seer—weight equivalent to 16 chhaṭa:ks or a little over 2 lbs; –**को सवा सेर मिलना** to catch a tartar, to come across one who is more than a match.

सेलखड़ी selkhaṛi: (*nf*) soap-stone, silica, chalk, talc.

सेला sela: (*nm*) a kind of rice.

सेली seli: (*nf*) a garment of hermits.

सेल्हा selha: (*nm*) see **सेला**.

सेवँई sevāi: (*nf*) vermicelli.

सेव sev (*nm*) an apple; a saltish/sweet vermicelli-like preparation of gram flour.

सेवक sevak (*nm*) a servant, an attendant; ~**गण** totality of servants, suite (of servants); hence **सेविका** (*nf*).

सेवकाई sevka:i: (*nf*) service; attendance.

सेवड़ा sevṛa: (*nm*) a saltish good preparation.

सेवती sevti: (*nf*) a kind of plant and its white flower.

सेवन sevan (*nm*) taking (as medicine, etc.), consuming; using, use; serving.

सेवनीय sevnī:y (*a*) usable; worth taking/consuming; worth serving.

सेवर sevar (*a*) not fully baked (said of pottery).

सेवा seva: (*nf*) service; attendance; -**काल** tenure of service; -**टहल** servitude, service; ~**दार** attendant; ~**दारी** attendance; ~**निवृत्त** retired; ~**निवृत्ति** retirement; -**वृत्ति** service; –**करना** to serve; to attend on.

सेविंग बैंक seviṅg baiṅk (*nm*) savings bank.

सेविका sevika: (*nf*) see under **सेवक**.

सेवित sevit (*a*) served; used; taken, consumed.

सेवितव्य sevitavvy (*a*) fit to be or worthy of being served.

सेवी sevi:—a suffix used to impart the sense of using or doing service for, etc. (as **स्वयंसेवी**).

सेव्य sevvy (*a*) fit or deserving to be served; (*nm*) one to whom service is rendered; master; -**सेवक** the served and server; o**भाव** the relationship of the server and the served.

सेशन seshan (*nm*) sessions; –कोर्ट sessions court; –जज a sessions judge; –सुपुर्द करना to commit to sessions; –सुपुर्द होना to be committed to sessions.

सेहत sehat (*nf*) health; ~गाह a sanitorium, health resort; ~मंद healthy.

सेहरा sehra: (*nm*) a nuptial headwear, a head-dress worn by the bridegroom at the time of marriage; eulogical verses read at a wedding; auspicious song sung at the time of wedding; ~बंदी the ceremony/process of tying the nuptial headwear; –बँधना to be married; to get the credit for; –बाँधना to tie/don a nuptial headwear, to get married; –होना, सिर to get the credit for, to be responsible for.

सेंहुड़ sẽhuṛ (*nm*) a kind of cactus.

सैंतालीस saĩta:li:s (*a*) forty-seven; (*nm*) the number forty-seven.

सैंतीस saĩti:s (*a*) thirty-seven; (*nm*) the number thirty-seven.

सैंपल saĩmpal (*nm*) a sample.

सैयाँ saĩyā: (*nm*) husband; lover.

सैक/ड़ा saikṛa: (*nm*) one hundred; a group of one hundred; ~ड़े percent, per hundred.

सैकत saikat (*nm*) sand; (*a*) sandy.

सैद्धांतिक saiddha:ntik (*a*) theoretical, pertaining to some theory or doctrine; –चर्चा/विवाद theoretical discussion; ~ता theoreticality.

सैनापत्य sainā:patty (*a*) pertaining to the commander of an army; (*nm*) commandership.

सैनिक sainik (*nm*) a soldier; (*a*) military, pertaining to the army; soldier-like; –क्रांति military revolution; –तानाशाह military dictator; –तानाशाही military dictatorship; –निरंकुशता military autocracy; –न्यायालय military court; –बल/शक्ति armed might; armament; –राज military rule; ~वाद militarism; ~वादी a militarist; militaristic; –विद्रोह military revolt; –व्यवस्था military set-up/system; –शासन military rule; –सत्ता military authority.

सैन्य sainny (*a*) military, pertaining to army; ~नायक/पति/पाल a commander; –बल/शक्ति armament, military might; ~मुख a vanguard; ~वाद militarism; ~वादी a militarist; militaristic; –सज्जा armed equipment; war-preparation.

सैन्या/धिपति, ~ध्यक्ष sainnya:dhipati, ~dhyaksh (*nm*) the commander-in-chief (of an army).

सैन्यी/करण sainyi:karan (*nm*) militarization; ~कृत militarized.

सैयद saiyad (*nm*) a particular subdivision of the Muslim community; any man/woman born in this sub-division.

सैयाँ saiyā: (*nm*) husband; lover.

सैयाद saiya:d (*nm*) a fowler, hunter.

सैर sair (*nf*) walking/walk; ramble; excursion; outing; stroll; ~गाह a place of excursion/walking/strolling; -सप टा see सैर.

सैलानी saila:nī: (*nm*) a tourist; wanderer; holiday-maker; ~पन tourism; mentality of a tourist; holiday-making.

सैला/ब saila:b (*nm*) flood; ~बी pertaining to or in the nature of a flood.

सैलून sailu:n (*nm*) a saloon (barber's shop or a railway carriage meant for high officials etc.).

सोंटा sõṭa: (*nm*) a cudgel; wand-stick; ~बरदार a cudgel-beeare, staff-bearer; —जमाना/लगाना to beat with a cudgel.

सौंठ sōṭḥ (*nf*) dry ginger.

सोंधा sōdha: (*a*) aromatic, sweet-smelling; having the pleasant smell of just-wetted soil; ~पन fragrance, sweet smell; pleasant smell of just-wetted soil.

सो so (*ind*) therefore; thus; (*pro.*) that, he.

सोऽहम् soham—I am the Supreme Soul (the basic maxim of the *Védanta* Philosophy identifying the individual with the Supreme Soul).

सोखना sokhnā: (*v*) to dry up; to absorb.

सोख़्ता sokḥta: (*nm*) a blotting paper; blotter.

सोग sog (*nm*) mourning, bereavement; ~वार mourner, bereaved; —मनाना to mourn.

सोगी sogi: (*nm*) a mourner, bereaved.

सोच soch (*nf*) anxiety; brooding, musing; consideration, reflection; -विचार reflection, thinking, pondering, consideration; hesitation; —समझ कर deliberately, after considering all aspects/pros and cons; ० क़दम उठाना to count the cost.

सोचना sochnā: (*v*) to think/to reflect, to ponder, over, to consider; -विचारना to think; to hesitate; -समझना to deliberate upon, to think from all angles.

सोच्छ्वास sochchhwa:s (*a* and *adv*) with or accompanied by a sigh, heaving a sigh.

सोजिश sozish (*nf*) swelling, inflammation.

सोझा sojha: (*a*) simple; straight, direct.

सोटा soṭa: (*nm*) see सोंटा.

सोडा soḍa: (*nm*) soda; -वाटर soda-water.

सोता sota: (*a*) sleeping; (*nm*) a stream, spring, brook; source; सोते-जागते always, every moment; -फूटना/बहना a stream (of water etc.) to originate/emerge.

सोत्कंठ sotkānṭḥ (*a* and *adv*) anxious(ly), worked-up by anxiety.

सोत्कर्ष sotkarsh (*a* and *adv*) with excellence/distinction; causing or achieving an elevation/excellence.

सोथ soth (*nm*) swelling, inflammation.

सोदाहरण soda:harāṇ (*a*) illustrated, exemplified, with example; -वार्ता an illustrated talk.

सोद्यम soddyam (*a* and *adv*) with उद्यम (see).

सोद्योग soddyog (*a* and *adv*) with उद्योग (see).

सोद्वेग soddveg (*a* and *adv*) restless(ly), with uneasiness.

सोन son (*nm*) soanes; an allomorph of सोना (gold) used as the first member in several compound words (as सोनचिरैया, सोनजुही).

सोनजुही sonjuhi: (*nf*) a kind of yellow jasmine.

सोनहा sonha: (*nm*) a dog-like small carnivorous beast.

सो/ना sonā: (*nm*) gold; an excellent thing; (*v*) to sleep; ~ना-चाँदी gold and silver; wealth; ~नापाठा a typical lofty tree the bark and fruits of which are used in medicine; ~नामक्खी/नामाखी pyrites; ~ना उगलना to yield large quantities of gold, to yield riches; ~ना कसना to test gold (on a touch-stone) for purity; ~ना चढ़ाना to gild; ~ना बरसना to rain gold—to be minting money; ~ने का घर मिट्टी कर देना to turn riches into ruins, to spell ruin on a prosperous household; ~ने का पानी thin layer of gold; ~ने का अंडा देने वाली मुर्गी the hen that lays golden eggs; ~ने का वरक़ gold leaf; ~ने का संसार a richly happy home; ~ने का होना to be good as gold; ~ने की कटार lit. a gold dagger—a charming though fatal thing; ~ने की चिड़िया El dorado; an extremely rich victim; ०उड़ / हाथ से जाना to miss an extremely rich victim; ~ने की चिड़िया मिलना to lay hands on an extremely rich victim; ~ने के दिन happy prosperous days; ~ने के मोल very costly; ~ने में सुगंध added excellence/richness; ~ने में सुहागा added excellence/richness, one excellence superimposed over another; ~ने से लदा to be covered with gold, to have too many ornaments on one's person.

सोपाधि, ~क sopa:dhi, ~k (*a*) qualified, conditional.

सोपा/न sopa:n (*nm*) a stair, staircase; ~नक्रम hierarchy; ~नक्रमिक hierarchical; ~नवत् scalariform; ~निक hierarchical; ~नित fitted with stairs.

सोफ़ा sofa: (*nm*) a sofa; ~सेट a sofa-set.

सोफ़ियाना sofiya:nā: (*a*) elegant; simple but attractive; sophisticated; hence ~पन (*nm*).

सोभना sobhnā: (*v*) to appear impressive, to befit; to suit.

सोम som (*nm*) the moon; Monday; the moon-creeper yielding an intoxicating juice which was drunk at sacrifices (यज्ञ) in ancient times; ~कर moon-rays; -पात्र a peg, wine glass; ~पान drinking of सोमरस; ~पायी one who drinks ~रस; ~यज्ञ the यज्ञ which was performed with सोम juice; ~रस the intoxicating juice of the सोम creeper; ~लता / लतिका / वल्लरी / वल्लिका/वल्ली a creeper from which an intoxicating juice was extracted for यज्ञ and drinking; ~वंश the lunar dynasty of *kshatriyas* in ancient India; ~वंशीय of the lunar race; ~वती/वारी अमावस्या the अमावस्या i e. last day of the dark half of a month falling on a Monday.

सोमवार somva:r (*nm*) Monday.

सोयम soyam (*a*) third.

सोया soya: (*nm*) a sweet smelling plant used for preparing a vegetable; (*a*) slept; सोये शेर को शिकार नहीं मिलता a closed mouth catches no flies.

सोयाबीन soya:bi:n (*nm*) soyabean.

सोरठा sorṭha: (*nm*) a popular metre (couplet) in mediaeval Hindi poetry.

सोरही sorahi: (*nf*) a game in which sixteen *kauṛi:s* (or pebbles etc.) are used.

सोलह soleh (*a*) sixteen; (*nm*) the number sixteen; -सिंगार made up in all the possible sixteen (traditional) ways; सोलहों आने completely, totally, fully.

सोल्लास solla:s (*a* and *adv*) with great pleasure/happiness.

सोविय/त, ~ट soviyat, ~ṭ; -संघ the Soviet Union.

सोशलि/ज्म soshalizm (*nm*) socialism; ~स्ट a socialist.

सोसाइ(य)टी sosa:i(ya)ṭi: (*nf*) society.

सोहं sohām—see सोऽहम्.

सोहनप(पा)पड़ी sohānpa(a:)pṛi: (*nf*) a kind of crisp sweetmeat preparation.

सोहनहलवा sohanhalwa: (*nm*) a typical Indian sweetmeat.

सोहना sohnā: (*v*) to look attractive/

beautiful / pleasing; to befit, to suit.

सोहबत sohbat (*nf*) company, association; copulation, sexual intercourse; see सुहबत.

सोहर sohar (*nm*) a typical song sung by women to celebrate the birth of a male child.

सोहाग soha:g (*nm*) see सुहाग.

सोहागा soha:ga: (*nm*) see सुहागा.

सोहागिन soha:gin (*nf*) see सुहागिन.

सोहारी soha:ri: (*nf*) a bread fried in *ghee* or oil.

सौंदर्य sa̱undary (*nm*) beauty, charm, prettiness; ~बोध aesthetic sense; oशक्ति aesthetic faculty; ~बोधी aesthetic; ~वाद aestheticism; ~वादी aestheticist; ~शास्त्र aesthetics; ~शास्त्री an aesthetician; ~शास्त्रीय aesthetic; ~संवेदी aesthete, gifted with an aesthetic sense; सौंदर्यानुभव aesthetic experience; सौंदर्यानुभूति aesthetic experience/sensibility.

सौंध sa̱udh (*nf*) fragrance, sweet smell; also सौंधाइंध (*nf*).

सौंपना sa̱upnā: (*v*) to hand over, to give, to entrust; to surrender; to delegate (as powers); to assign.

सौंफ़ sa̱uf (*nf*) anise, aniseed; fennel.

सौ sau (*a*) hundred; many, numerous (as तुम्हारे झूठ की सौ मिसालें हैं); (*nm*) the number hundred; ~गुना hundred times; ~वाँ hundredth; –काम छोड़कर leaving all else, at the cost of all other things; –की एक बात see –बात की एक बात; –कोस (दूर) भागना to keep miles away from, to run away from; –घड़े पानी पड़ना to be thoroughly ashamed, to die of shame; –जतन करना to try in a hundred ways; to try through all possible ways; –जान से wholeheartedly; (with) heart and soul; o आशिक़ / क़ुर्बान / फ़िदा होना to be terribly infatuated, to love with (one's) heart and soul; –तरह का of different ways/types/varieties; -दो सौ में one in hundreds; –बात की एक बात the long and short of a matter, the essence; –बात सुनाना to scold roundly, to utter forth a whole series of invectives; –सुनार की एक लुहार की hundred times more furious counter-blast; –हाथ की ज़बान होना to be cheekily talkative.

सौकर्य saukary (*nm*) easiness; convenience.

सौकुमार्य saukuma:ry (*nm*) tenderness, delicacy.

सौगं/द, ~ध saugānd, ~dh (*nf*) an oath, vow, swearing; ~ध खाना to take an oath/vow, to swear; ~ध टूटना a vow to be broken.

सौगंधिक saugāndhik (*nm*) a perfumer.

सौगम्य saugammy (*nf*) easiness; accessibility.

सौग़ा/त sauga:t (*nf*) a present, gift; ~ती by way of a present, given to somebody as a ~त; worth giving as a present.

सौजन्य saujanny (*nm*) goodness; courtesy; –से by courtesy (of).

सौड़ saur̤ (*nm*) a quilt, sheet for covering oneself up while sleeping.

सौत saut (*nf*) a co-wife.

सौतिया डाह sautia: d̤a:h (*nm*) extreme jealousy, malice/jealousy as between co wives.

सौतेला sautela: (*a*) pertaining to or related with or born of सौत; half-blood; –पुत्र/बेटा step-son; –भाई step brother; –व्यवहार step motherly treatment; सौतेली बहन half-sister; सौतेली माँ step-mother.

सौदा sauda: (*nm*) a bargain, transaction; negotiation; goods, commodity; –**करने वाला** a bargainer; ~**कारी** bargain(ing); ~**गर** a trader, merchant; ~**गरी** business, trade, commerce; o **माल** business goods; -**सुलफ़/सुलुफ़** commodity, goods; **सौदेबाज़** haggler; **सौदेबाज़ी** haggling; –**करना** to bargain; to negotiate; –**पटना** a bargain to be settled/struck; -**होना** a bargain to be struck/to be entered into.

सौदाई sauda:i: (*a* and *nm*) mad, insane (person).

सौदामिनी sauda:mini: (*nf*) lightning.

सौपानिक saupa:nik (*a*) hierarchical; pertaining to or resembling a staircase.

सौप्तिक sauptik (*a*) pertaining to sleep/slumber.

सौफ़ियाना saufia:nā (*a*) see **सोफ़ियाना**.

सौभागिनी saubha:ginī: (*nf*) a woman whose husband is alive, a woman of good luck.

सौभाग्य saubha:ggy (*nm*) good luck, fortune; -**चिह्न** sign of a woman whose husband is alive (as **सिंदूर, महावर,** etc.); ~**वती** see **सौभागिनी**; ~**वान्** fortunate; ~**शालिनी** see **सौभागिनी**, fortunate (fem.);~**शाली** fortunate.

सौमनस्य saumānassy (*nm*) goodwill; happiness, pleasure.

सौमित्र saumittr (*nm*) an epithet of **लक्ष्मण** —(son of Sumitra:) brother of Ra:m.

सौम्य saummy (*a*) amiable, gentle; ~**ता/त्व** amiability, gentility.

सौर saur (*a*) solar; (*nm*) a (cotton) wrapper; –**दिन/दिवस** day; from sun-rise to sun-set, a solar day; –**परिवार** solar system; –**मास** a solar month; –**वर्णक्रम** solar spectrum; –**वर्ष/संवत्सर** a solar year; –**विकिरण** solar radiation.

सौर/भ saurabh (*nm*) fragrance, aroma; ~**भयुक्त** fragrant, aromatic ~**भित**, ~**भीला** fragrant, aromatic.

सौरी sauri: (*nf*) a lying-in/confinement chamber.

सौर्य saury (*a*) solar.

सौलभ्य saulabbhy (*nm*) availability; abundance.

सौष्ठव saushṭhav (*nm*) grace, elegance, charm.

सौहार्द sauha:rd (*nm*) amity, friendship, love; good relations.

सौहृद sauhrid (*nm*) a friend; (*a*) friendly.

स्कंध skandh (*nm*) the shoulder; stem or trunk of a tree; division of an army; stock.

स्कंधावार skandha:va:r (*nm*) royal camp/pavilion.

स्काउ/ट ska:uṭ (*nm*) a scout: ~**टिंग** scouting.

स्कूल sku:l (*nm*) a school; –, **प्राइमरी** a primary school; –, **मिडिल** a middle school; –, **हाई** a high school; –, **हायर सैकंड्री** a higher secondary school -**टीचर/मास्टर** a school-teacher, school-master; **स्कूली** school, of or pertaining to a school; o **शिक्षा** school education.

स्क्रू, स्क्र्यू skru:, skryu: (*nm*) a screw.

स्क्वाड्रन skva:ḍran (*nm*) a squadron; –**लीडर** a squadron-leader.

स्ख/लन skhalan (*nm*) a lapse, slip; discharge; ~**लन, वीर्य**-discharge of the semen; ~**लित** lapsed, slipped; discharged; o **वीर्य** whose heroism has been frustrated, who has lost his heroic qualities.

स्टांप sṭa:mp (*nm*) a stamp; -पेपर a stamp paper.

स्टॉ/क sṭok (*nm*) stock; ~क रजिस्टर a stock register; ~किस्ट a stockist.

स्टाफ़ sṭa:f (*nm*) staff; -रूम staff room.

स्टॉल sṭol (*nm*) a stall; –, टी a tea-stall.

स्टीमर sṭi:mar (*nm*) a steamer.

स्टूल sṭu:l (*nm*) a stool.

स्टेंसिल sṭẽnsil (*nm*) a stencil; –किया हुआ stencilled.

स्टेज sṭej (*nf*) a stage; –करना to stage, to enact on the stage.

स्टेट sṭeṭ (*nf*) a state.

स्टेशन sṭeshān (*nm*) a station; –मास्टर station master.

स्टैंड sṭaind (*nm*) a stand; -, बस a bus-stand; -, साइकिल a cycle-stand.

स्टोर sṭor (*nm*) a store; -कीपर a store-keeper.

स्टोव sṭov (*nm*) a stove.

स्ट्राइक sṭra:ik (*nf*) a strike.

स्ट्रीट sṭri:ṭ (*nf*) a street.

स्तंभ stambh (*nm*) a column; pillar; stem; stupefaction, torpor; see ~न; -लेखक a columnist, column-writer.

स्तंभक stambhak (*nm*) a retentive drug; astringent; ~ता retentivity; astringency.

स्तंभन stambhan (*nm*) retention; astringency; restraining, stopping, arresting.

स्तंभित stambhit (*a*) stupefied, benumbed; wonder-struck, flabbergasted.

स्तन stan (*nm*) the female breast; udder; -चचुक/मुख teat, nipple; ~धार a mammal; ~पान sucking of the (female) breast; ~पायी a mammal, sucking (babe or otherwise); ~युक्त mammiferous; –वाले प्राणी the mammals.

स्तनी stanī: (*nm* and *a*) mammals; having breasts/udders.

स्तन्य stanny (*nm*) milk (of the breast); (*a*) contained in the breast; -त्याग weaning; ~प/पायी a mammal; sucking (child); -पान sucking (the female breast).

स्तबक stabak (*nm*) see स्तवक.

स्तब्ध stabdh (*a*) stupefied; stilled; stunned, flabbergasted; spastic; ~ता/त्व spasticity; stupefaction; stillness; ~मति stupid, dullard.

स्तर star (*nm*) standard, level; layer, stratum/strata; fold; grade; ~ण levelling; grading; stratifying; ~णीय fit to be levelled/graded/stratified; स्तरिक stratified; levelled; स्तरित/स्तरीकृत stratified; graded; levelled; स्तरीकरण levellizing; stratification; स्तरीय level/levelled; stratified; standard; –का (of a certain) standard.

स्तव stav (*nm*) praise, eulogy, panegyric.

स्तवक stavak (*nm*) a bunch of flowers, bouquet; chapter of a book.

स्तव/न stavān (*nm*) praising/praise, eulogy, panegyric; ~नीय praiseworthy, fit to be eulogized.

स्तुति stuti (*nf*) prayer, invocation; eulogy, praise.

स्तुत्य stutty (*a*) laudable, praiseworthy, admirable.

स्तूप stu:p (*nm*) a (Buddhistic) monument (generally of a pyramidal or dome-like form and erected over the sacred relics of the Buddha or on spots consecrated as the scenes of his acts).

स्तूपिका stu:pika: (*nf*) a finial.

स्तेय stey (*nm*) theft.

स्तोता stota: (*nm*) a hymn-reciter; panegyrist.

स्तो/त्र stotr (*nm*) a hymn (of praise); eulogism, doxology; ~त्रिय pertaining to a ~त्र.

स्त्रियोपयोगी striyopayogi: (*a*) (incorrect word-formation) see स्त्री (-उपयोगी).

स्त्री stri: (*nf*) a woman, female; wife; -उपयोगी befitting women, useful suitable for women; ~करण feminization; ~गमन cohabitation, sexual intercourse; -चरित्र nature/character of a woman; -जाति womenfolk; -तंत्र gynarchy; -तुल्य effeminate, womanly, womanish; ~त्व womanhood, femineity/feminality; -द्वेषी a woman-hater; -धन/वित्त dowry; a woman's wealth; -धर्म duty of a woman; menstruation; -पूजा gyniolatry, adoration of women; ~प्रज्ञ/बुद्धि womanish brain; -प्रसंग/भोग/संभोग/समागम/सेवन sexual intercourse; ~प्रिय woman loving, lover of women; a ladies' man; -भक्ति gyniolatry, devotion to women-folk; -भीति gynephobia; -रत्न a gem amongst women, a woman of outstanding merits; -राज्य gynarchy, petticoat government; -रोग a female disease; ०विज्ञान gynaecology; ०विशेषज्ञ a gynaecologist; ~लिंग feminine (gender); ~वश henpecked, under a woman's domination; ~वश्य see ~वश; ~व्रत devotion to one's own wife; ~व्रती devoted to one's own wife; -संयोग union with a woman/the wife; -सुख sexual enjoyment; -हरण kidnapping/abduction of a woman; ~हर्ता a kidnapper, abductor of a woman.

स्त्रैण strain (*a*) effeminate; feminine, womanish/womanly; henpecked; hence ~ता (*nf*).

स्थ stha—a Sanskrit suffix used in the sense of situated, residing, fixed, present or engaged, etc. (as तटस्थ, शीर्षस्थ, स्वस्थ etc.); hence ~स्थता (*nf*) (as तटस्थता).

स्थकित sthakit (*a*) tired, fatigued, wearied.

स्थगन sthagan (*nm*) postponement; adjournment; -प्रस्ताव adjournment motion.

स्थगित sthagit (*a*) postponed; adjourned.

स्थल sthal (*nm*) land; place; site, location, venue; field (as युद्धस्थल battlefield); -कमल/पद्म a kind of plant and its flowers; ~चर/चारी terrestrial; living on land; ~डमरूमध्य neck of land, isthmus; ~मार्ग roadway; ०से by road, by land; -सेना land forces, army.

स्थलाकृति sthala:kkriti (*nf*) topography; -विवरण topography, topographical account.

स्थली sthali: (*nf*) land; place; spot, site; field (as युद्ध~); ~य terrestrial, pertaining to land.

स्थविर sthavir (*nm*) a Buddhist monk.

स्थाणु stha:nu (*nm*) a pillar; trunk of a tree; an epithet of Lord Shiv.

स्थान stha:n (*nm*) place, spot; site; space, room; accommodation; post; position, station; premises, venue; residence; locality; ~च्युत displaced, removed or fallen from a place or position; -प्राप्ति

acquisition or acquirement of a place or position; ~भ्रष्ट see ~च्युत; -विज्ञान topology; ~वैज्ञानिक a topologist; topological.

स्थानांत/र stha:nā:ntar (*nm*) transfer; another or different place/position/post; transposition; displacement; ~रण transfer; displacement; translation, translocation; transposition; ~रित transferred, displaced; translocated; transposed, removed from one place/post/position to another.

स्थानापन्न stha:nā:pann (*a* and *nm*) acting, officiating; a sit-in man, substitute; locum tenens; alternate; hence ~ता (*nf*).

स्थानिक stha:nīk (*a*) local/localised; resident; endemic; –घटना spot event.

स्थानीकृत stha:nī:krit (*a*) localised.

स्थानीय stha:nī:y (*a*) local, endemic; colloquial; hence ~ता (*nf*).

स्थापक stha:pak (*nm*) a founder; erector, fixer; –, रंग a mordant.

स्थापत्य stha:patty (*nm*) architecture; -कला architecture.

स्थापन stha:pan (*nm*) foundation, erection, fixation; propounding; establishment, setting up.

स्थापना stha:panā: (*nf*) propounding; founding, establishing; installing (an idol); see स्थापन; –करना to propound; to found, to establish; to institute; to fix; to instal an idol (in a temple).

स्थापनीय stha:panī:y (*a*) worth being propounded/established/installed/founded; hence ~ता (*nf*).

स्थापित stha:pit (*a*) propounded; founded; established; instituted, set up; fixed, placed; erected; installed; –करना to propound; to set up; to found/establish/institute/erect.

स्थायित्व stha:ittv (*nm*) permanency; stability; durability; ~कारी stabiliser.

स्थायिकल्प stha:ikalp (*a*) quasi-permanent, almost permanent.

स्थायिता stha:yita: (*nf*) stability; durability.

स्थायिवत् stha:ivat (*a*) quasi-permanent, as good as permanent,

स्थायिवत्ता stha:ivatta: (*nf*) quasi-permanency.

स्थायी stha:i: (*a*) permanent; stable, lasting, durable; regular, steady; (*nm*) refrain; the first part/line of a song usually confined to the lower and middle octavo and repeated again and again; ~करण confirmation; making permanent/stable, stabilisation; ~कृत confirmed; made permanent, stabilised; –नियुक्ति permanent appointment; –बंदोबस्त permanent settlement; –भाव enduring emotion, lasting state of mind [in Indian Poetics, the emotions that are enduring are called स्थायी भाव, as compared with संचारी भाव which are fleeting].

स्थाली stha:li: (*nf*) a big metallic plate; ~पुलाक (न्याय) random sampling; the rule of boiled rice in a cooking vessel (i.e. inferring of the condition of a whole from that of a part, as of the good cooking of rice from tasting a single grain); ~पुलाक - परीक्षा random sampling.

स्थावर stha:var (*a*) immovable; stable, stationary; -जंगम immovable and movable; –संपत्ति immovable property, immovables.

स्थित sthit (*a*) situated, located,

placed; circumstanced; ~प्रज्ञ firm in judgment, gifted with unshakable mental equilibrium; hence ~प्रज्ञता (*nf*).

स्थिति sthiti (*nf*) position; situation, location; place, site; state, condition, stage; phase; status, set-up; attitude; ~ग्राही a statoreceptor; ~ज potential; –पटल tote; -विषयक pertaining to a position/situation/condition, etc.

स्थिर sthir (*a*) stable, firm; steady; still, unmoved, motionless, immobile; constant; stationary; quiescent, calm, pacific; inflexible; ~चित्त/चेता/बुद्धि/मति/मना of steady mind, firm, unwavering; resolved/resolute; ~ता/त्व steadiness; stability; quiescence; poise.

स्थिरीकरण sthiri:karān (*nm*) stabilization, making steady/firm/calm.

स्थूण sthu:n (*nm*) a pillar, post.

स्थूल sthu:l (*a*) plump, fat, bulky, corpulent; thick; massive; rough, crude; gross; ~ता/त्व fatness, bulkiness, corpulence; thickness; crudeness; grossness; ~धी/बुद्धि/मति a nitwit; crude; –रूप से roughly: crudely; –शरीर the gross body (as opposed to सूक्ष्म शरीर).

स्थूलांग sthu:lāṅg (*a*) fat, corpulent, bulky; hence ~ता (*nf*).

स्थूलोदर sthu:lodar (*a*) pot-bellied, paunchy.

स्थैति/क sthaitik (*a*) static; ~की Statics.

स्थैर्य sthairy (*nm*) steadiness; firmness; stability.

स्नात sna:t (*a*) bathed (in).

स्नात/क sna:tak (*nm*) a graduate; bachelor (as कला-); ~कोत्तर postgraduate.

स्नान snā:n (*nm*) bath, ablution; ~गृह a bath, bathroom; -ध्यान bathing and meditating, the routine morning chores.

स्नानागार snā:nā:ga:r (*nm*) see स्नानगृह (under स्नान).

स्नायविक sna:ywik (*a*) nervous, pertaining to sinews/nerves, ligamentary.

स्नायु sna:yu (*nm*) nerves, sinews, ligament; –विषयक/संबंधी see स्नायविक.

स्निग्ध snigdh (*a*) affectionate; smooth, glossy; oily, greasy; ~ता affectionateness; smoothness, glossiness; oiliness, greasiness.

स्नुषा snusha: (*nf*) daughter-in-law, son's wife.

स्नेह sneh (*nm*) love, affection; oil, oily substance; ~क a lubricant; ~न lubrication; massaging oil; ~नीय see -योग्य; ~बद्ध attached, bounded by love/affection; -पात्र object of love, beloved; -योग्य lovable; -जोड़ना to establish bonds of affection/love; –तोड़ना to break bonds of love.

स्नेहाकुल sneha:kul (*a*) moved by love/affection; hence ~ता (*nf*).

स्नेहित snehit (*a*) loved.

स्नेहिल snehil (*a*) loving, of loving nature/disposition.

स्नेही snehi: (*nm*) a lover; (*a*) loving, affectionate.

स्नैग्ध्य snaigdhy (*nm*) see स्निग्धता.

स्पं/ज spāṇj (*nm*) a sponge; ~जी spongy.

स्पंद spānd (*nm*) vibration, pulsation; throbbing.

स्पं/दन spāndan (*nm*) vibration, pulsation, throb(bing); ~दनविहीन/~दनहीन stilled, rendered still/quiet/motionless; hence ~दनविहीनता/~दनहीनता (*nf*); ~दित vibrated, throbbed, pulsated.

स्पर्धनीय spardhani:y (*a*) enviable.

स्पर्धा spardha: (*nf*) rivalry, envy.

स्पर्धी spardhi: (*a*) rival, competing.

स्पर्श sparsh (*nm*) touch, contact, feel; stop (as –व्यंजन stop consonant); ~क feeler; ~गोचर palpable, perceptible through touch; ~ज/जन्य contagious, caused by touch/contagion; ~ज्या a tangent; -ज्ञान feeling; perception through touch; ~न touching, contacting; ~नीय tangible; oता tangibility; -रेखा a tangent; -संघर्षी affricate; -संबंधी pertaining to touch/contact; tactile, imparted through touch/contact.

स्पर्शित sparshit (*a*) touched.

स्पर्शेंद्रिय sparshēndriy (*nf*) sense of touch, the skin.

स्पष्ट spasht̤ (*a*) clear; vivid, lucid; evident, apparent; obvious; articulate, distinct; positive, unambiguous, conspicuous; intelligible; express; explicit, blunt, categorical, point-blank, plain; ~तः clearly; vividly, lucidly; plainly; obviously; apparently; distinctly; expressly, explicitly; bluntly; ~तया plainly, clearly, lucidly; obviously; ~ता clarity, clearness, vividness, lucidity; obviousness; openness; oपूर्वक/से clearly; lucidly, obviously, vividly; expressly; ~भाषी/वक्ता/वादी outspoken, straight-forward, plain-speaking; –रूप से distinctly, clearly, ostensibly, obviously.

स्पष्टार्थ spasht̤a:rth (*nm*) distinct/unequivocal meaning; categorical expression; hence ~ता (*nf*).

स्पष्टीकरण spasht̤i:karān (*nm*) clarification; explanation.

स्पष्टीकृत spasht̤i:krit (*a*) clarified, explained.

स्पिरिट spirit̤ (*nf*) spirit.

स्पीच spi:ch (*nf*) a speech.

स्पृश्य sprishy (*a*) touchable, perceptible through touch.

स्पृष्ट sprisht̤ (*a*) touched.

स्पृष्टि sprisht̤i (*nf*) touch; see स्पर्श.

स्पृहणीय sprihani̤:y (*a*) covetable, worth craving for; ~ता covetability.

स्पृहा spriha: (*nf*) covetousness, craving; hence स्पृह्य see स्पृहणीय.

स्पृही sprihi: (*a*) covetous, craving; wistful.

स्पृह्य sprihy (*a*) see स्पृहणीय.

स्पेशल speshal (*a*) special.

स्प्रिंग spriṅg (*nf*) a spring; ~दार springed, fitted with spring; ~वाला a spring-maker.

स्फटिक sphat̤ik (*nm*) crystal, quartz.

स्फटित sphat̤it (*a*) torn, split open, cleft.

स्फा/र, ~रित spha:r, ~rit (*a*) expanded, opened wide; widely diffused.

स्फीत sphi:t (*a*) inflated; swollen.

स्फीति sphi:ti (*nf*) inflation; swelling.

स्फुट sphut̤ (*a*) miscellaneous; distinct; manifest; apparent; hence ~ता (*nf*).

स्फु/टन sphut̤ān (*nm*) shooting forth, blossoming; becoming distinct/manifest/apparent; hence ~टित (*a*).

स्फुटीकरण sphut̤i:karān (*nm*) manifestation, the act or process of becoming distinct/apparent or of blossoming.

स्फु/रण sphurān (*nm*) spurt; throbbing, pulsation; scintillation; twitch; hence ~रित (*a*).

स्फुलिंग sphuliṅg (*nm*) a spark.

स्फूर्ति sphu:rti (*nf*) agility, smartness, quickness; tone; freshness; ~कारक/कारी/दायी imparting agility/smartness; refreshing.

स्फोट sphoṭ (*nm*) explosion, burst; the eternal and imperceptible element of sounds and words and the real vehicle of the idea which bursts or flashes on the mind when a sound is uttered; ~वाद the philosophical doctrine of स्फोट; hence ~वादी (*a, nm*).

स्फोटक sphoṭak (*a* and *nm*) (an) explosive; –पदार्थ an explosive substance; ~ता explosiveness.

स्फोटन sphoṭān (*nm*) explosion, sudden bursting or splitting asunder.

स्फोटित sphoṭit (*a*) exploded, burst, split or torn asunder.

स्मर smar (*nm*) Cupid—the god of love.

स्मरण smarān (*nm*) memory; remembrance, recollection; -पत्र/पत्रक a reminder; -शक्ति memory.

स्मरणीय smarani:y (*a*) memorable, worth remembering; hence ~ता (*nf*).

स्मारक sma:rak (*nm*) a monument, memorial.

स्मारिका sma:rika: (*nf*) a souvenir.

स्मार्त sma:rt (*a*) pertaining/belonging to स्मृति (code of traditional Hindu law); (*nm*) one who believes in the *Smriti*.

स्मित smit (*nf*) a smile; (*a*) smiling.

स्मिति smiti (*nf*) a smile.

स्मृत smrit (*a*) recollected, brought to memory, memorised.

स्मृति smriti (*nf*) memory, remembrance; books of traditional code of Hindu law (as मनुस्मृति, याज्ञवल्क्य-स्मृति, etc.) said to be 18 in number; ~कार author of *Smriti* (as मनु, याज्ञवल्क्य etc.); –चिह्न a souvenir; -पत्र a reminder; ~भ्रंश/लोप amnesia, loss of memory; ~विद् well-versed in the code of law defined in the *Smritis*; -शास्त्र the science of Hindu code of law as given in the *Smritis*; ~शास्त्रज्ञ well-versed in the *Smritis*; ~शेष living only in memory, late; ~सम्मत approved by or enjoined in the *Smritis*; ~हीन oblivious, forgetful; ~हीनता amnesia; obliviousness, forgetfulness.

स्यंदन syandan (*nm*) a chariot.

स्यंदनारूढ़ syandanā:ru:ṛḥ (*a* and *nm*) riding a chariot; a charioteer.

स्यात् sya:t (*ind*) perhaps.

स्याद्वाद sya:dva:d (*nm*) the sceptical or agnostic doctrine of the Jains.

स्याना sya:na: (*a*) see सयाना.

स्यापा sya:pa: (*nm*) mourning, bewailing on a (relative's) death.

स्यार sya:r (*nm*) a jackal; ~पन cowardice.

स्याह sya:h (*a*) black, dark; -सफ़ेद dark or bright; good or bad; ०करना to make or mar.

स्याही sya:hi: (*nf*) ink; darkness, blackness; ~दान an inkpot; ~सोख a blotting paper.

स्यूत syu:t (*a*) interwoven.

स्रष्टा srashṭa: (*nm*) a creator, maker; the Creator (of the universe).

स्राव sra:v (*nm*) flow, oozing; miscarriage.

स्रोत srot (*nm*) source, resource; a stream, current; ~स्विनी a river/stream.

स्लीपर sli:par (*nm*) slippers.

स्लेज slej (*nf*) a sledge.

स्लेट sleṭ (*nf*) a slate (for writing purposes).

स्व swa (*pro*) one's own, personal; self; ~त्व (one's) due; ~शासन

self-rule.

स्वकीय swaki:y (*a*) own, one's own, personal.

स्वकीया swaki:ya: (*nm*) (in Indian Poetics) a loyal heroine; wife.

स्वगत swagat (*a*) aside, speaking to oneself; ~**कथन/भाषण** aside, soliloquy; ०**करना** to soliloquize.

स्वचल swachal (*a*) automatic; ~**ता** automaticity.

स्वचालित swacha:lit (*a*) automatic; –**क्रिया** automatic action.

स्वच्छंद swachchhãnd (*a*) self-willed; unrestrained; ~**चर/चारी** moving at will, arbitrary; ~**चारिता** arbitrariness, movement at will; ~**ता** arbitrariness; absence of restraint, liberum arbitrium; ~**तावाद/~तावादिता** Romanticism; ~**तावादी** Romanticist; romantic.

स्वच्छ swachchh (*a*) clean, clear, neat; pure; transparent; ~**ता** cleanliness, neatness; purity; transparence; -**करना** to clean, to cleanse, to rinse, to clarify, to filter.

स्वजन swajān (*nm*) kith and kin, kinsfolk.

स्वजात swaja:t (*a*) self-born.

स्वजातीय swaja:ti:y (*a*) co-racial, belonging to one's own caste/race/kind.

स्वजित swajit (*a*) self-conquered.

स्वतंत्र swatantr (*a*) independent, free, sui juris, autonomous; unrestrained, uncontrolled; separate; ~**ता** independence, freedom, liberty; ~**ता-आंदोलन** freedom movement; ~**ता-संघर्ष** struggle for independence; ~**ता-सेनानी** freedom fighter; –**लेखन** free lance writing; –**करना** to free, to liberate.

स्वत: swatah (*adv*) of one's own accord, voluntarily; spontaneously, ipso facto; self; ~**क्रिया** self-activity; –**विरोधी** self contradictory; ~**प्रमाण** an axiom; ~**सिद्ध** self evident.

स्व/त्व swattv (*nm*) one's due, right; copyright; ~**त्वधारी** proprietor; copyright-holder; ~**त्वाधिकारी** owner, master; copyright-holder.

स्वदर्शी swadarshi: (*a*) autoscope.

स्वदेश swadesh (*nm*) one's own country, motherland, homeland, native land; -**त्याग** emigration; ~**त्यागी** an emigrant; ~**प्रियता** patriotism; -**प्रेम** patriotism; -**प्रेमी** a patriot; -**भक्त** a patriot; -**भक्ति** patriotism.

स्वदेशी, ~**य** swadeshi, ~y (*a*) native, indigenous, belonging to one's own country.

स्वधर्म swadharm (*nm*) one's own duty/religion; ~**च्युत** who has neglected his duty/religion, fallen from duty or religion; -**च्युति** falling from duty or religion; -**त्याग** apostasy; ~**त्यागी** a renegade; apostate; negligent of duty/religion.

स्व/न swan (*nm*) sound, phone; ~**नन** phonation; ~**न-विज्ञान** phonetics/phonology; ~**निक** phonetic/phonological; ~**निम** phoneme; ~**निम-विज्ञान** phonemics.

स्वनाम swanā:m (*nm*) one's own name; having a reputation through one's own self; ~**धन्य** celebrated (through one's own self).

स्वप/क्ष swapaksh (*nm*) one's own side/party; ~**क्षीय** of or pertaining to one's own side/party; friendly.

स्वप्न swapn (*nm*) a dream; ~**कर** causing dreams; ~**दर्शी** a dreamer, dreamy; a dream-visionary; ~, **दिवा** day-dreaming; ~**दर्शी**, **दिवा**

a day-dreamer; ~दोष emission, pollution nocturna; ~द्रष्टा see ~दर्शी; ~पूर्ण full of dreams; ~मय dreamy; -लोक dreamland, dream-world; ~वत् like a dream; unreal; ~शील visionary; dreamy; –देखना to dream; to visualize; to imagine; –में नहीं not even in dream, never, under no circumstances.

स्वप्नावस्था swapnā:wastha: (*nf*) state of dreaming.

स्वप्निल swapnīl (*a*) dreamy.

स्वभाव swabha:v (*nm*) nature; temperament, disposition; habit; ~ज/~जनित natural, innate; ~तः naturally, by nature; ~सिद्ध natural, innate.

स्वयं swayam (*adv*) by oneself, of one's own accord; personally; automatically; ~कृत done by self, self-committed; ~तथ्य an axiom; ~पाकी (one) who cooks one's own meals; ~प्रकाश/प्रकाशमान self-manifesting; self-illumined/self-lit; ~प्रमाण/प्रमाणित self-evident; self-proved; ~भू absolute; ingenerate, self-born; self begotten, self-existent; an epithet of Lord Vishnu/Shiv; ~मृत who has died a natural death or a self-willed death; ~वर lit. self-choice—an ancient custom wherein a bride chose her husband of her own accord, selection by a bride of her husband from amongst a galaxy of suitors; ०सभा the assembly where a स्वयंवर takes place; ~वरण selection/choice by a bride of her husband from amongst numerous suitors; ~वरा the bride who selects her husband from amongst a number of suitors; ~सिद्ध a truism, an axiom; axiomatic; self-evident; ~सिद्धि a postulate, an axiom; ~सेवक a volunteer; ०संघ a volunteer corps; ~सेवा self-service; ~सेविका a female volunteer.

स्वयमर्जित swayamarjit (*a*) self-earned; self-acquired.

स्वयमेव swayamev (*adv*) by oneself; of one's own accord; in person.

स्वयम् swayam (*adv*) see स्वयं.

स्वर swar (*nm*) a vowel; sound, voice; tone; gamut; note; -कंप tremolo; trembling of the voice; –, गदगद् emotion-charged voice; -गुण vowel-quality; quality of the voice; ~ग्राम musical scale; ~दर्शी tonoscope; -पेशी vocalis; ~प्रधान a राग in which the स्वर dominates and not the ताल; ~बद्ध rhythmic, moulded in a rhythm; -भंग soreness/hoarseness (of throat); loss of voice; -माधुर्य melody; ~मान pitch; -मेल unison; –, मूल pure vowel; -यंत्र larynx; -लहरी melody; -लिपि musical notation; -लोप loss/elision of a vowel; -विकार vocal disorder; -विरोध cacophony; –, विवृत open vowel, -व्यवस्था vowel system; tonal set-up; -संगति harmony of musical notes; vowel-harmony; –, संवृत close vowel; -संधि (in Grammar) fusion of adjacent vowels into one; –संपन्न having a sweet/melodious voice; -सप्तक the gamut, seven notes of music; –ऊँचा होना to speak in a high pitch; –चढ़ाना to raise the voice or the musical note; –भरना to elongate the same note; –भीगना one's voice to be charged with emotion; –मिलाना/–में स्वर मिलाना to chime in; –साधना to practise mastery over musical notes.

स्वरति swarati (*nf*) autoeroticism.

स्वरस swaras (*nm*) pure (unadulterated) juice.

स्वरांत swara:nt (*a*) ending in a vowel; -अक्षर an open syllable.

स्वरांश swara:nsh (*nm*) vocalic element.

स्वराघात swara:gha:t (*nm*) pitch; accent.

स्वराज्य swara:jjy (*nm*) independence; autonomy; home-rule, self-government.

स्वरात्मक swara:tmak (*a*) vocalic; pertaining to or having a vowel.

स्वराष्ट्र swara:shtr (*nm*) homeland; one's own country; -मंत्रालय the Home Ministry; -मंत्री the Home Minister; स्वराष्ट्रीय domestic, pertaining to one's own country.

स्वरित swarit (*nm*) accentuated, having circumflex accent.

स्वरुचि swaruchi (*nf*) one's own taste, individual taste.

स्वरूप swaru:p (*nm*) shape, form; appearance; character; nature; ~गत/परक natural; characteristic; formal; ~वान beautiful, handsome.

स्वरैक्य swaraiky (*nm*) unison.

स्वर्गंगा swarganga: (*nm*) the Ganges of paradise, the milky way, galaxy.

स्वर्ग swarg (*nm*) paradise, heaven, abode of gods; ~गत dead, expired, late; ~गमन dying, death; ~च्युत fallen from heaven; ~जित् one who has conquered the heaven/paradise; –तरु the celestial tree—generally called कल्पवृक्ष; ~धाम/पुरी/लोक see स्वर्ग; ~नदी see स्वर्गंगा; -लाभ acquiring a place in the heaven; death, dying, passing away; ०करना to pass away, to die; ~वधू a nymph; fairy; ~वाणी an oracle; ~वास heavenly abode–death; ०होना to die, to pass away; ~वासी late; ~स्थ/स्थित dead, late; –की गुलामी से नरक का राज भला it is better to rule in hell than to serve in heaven, better be the head of an ass than tail of a horse; –सिधारना to die; to pass away.

स्वर्गारोहण swarga:rohān (*nm*) ascendance into the heaven/paradise; death.

स्वर्गिक swargik (*a*) divine, transcendental; late.

स्वर्गी/य swargi:y (*a*) late, dead; hence ~या (fem. form).

स्वर्ण swarn (*nm*) gold; ~कण/कणिका a gold-particle; ~कार a goldsmith; ~कारी goldsmithy; –जयंती golden jubilee: ~जुही yellow jasmine; -तस्कर a gold smuggler; –तस्करी gold-smuggling; -पत्र golden leaf; -मुद्रा a gold coin; -युग the golden age; ~वर्ण (of) golden (colour); ~वर्णा (a woman) of golden colour.

स्वर्णाक्ष/र swarnā:kshar (*nm*) a golden letter; ~रों में लिखना to write in letters of gold.

स्वर्णिम swarnīm (*a*) golden.

स्व/र्धुनी, ~र्नदी swardhunī:; ~rnadi: (*nf*) see स्वर्गंगा.

स्वर्लोक swarlok (*nm*) see स्वर्ग.

स्व/ल्प swalp (*a*) little, very little; very small; ~ल्पाहार light refreshment; ~ल्पाहारी one who eats a very limited quantity.

स्वल्पेच्छ swalpechchh (*a*) having few longings/wishes; contented.

स्ववश swavash (*a*) under one's own control, in self-control.

स्वशासन swasha:san (*nm*) self-rule, home-rule, self-government.

स्वसंगति swasangati (*nf*) self-consistency.

स्वसा swasa: (*nf*) a sister.

स्वसुख swasukh (*nm*) one's own happiness, egoistic hedonism; ~**वाद** egoistic hedonism; hence ~**वादी** (*a* and *nm*).

स्वस्तार swasta:r (*nm*) vocal cord.

स्वस्ति swasti (*int*) (a word of benediction) May you be happy !; (*nf*) well-being, prosperity; ~**पाठ**/chanting of benedictory *mantra*; ~ **वाचन** bendictory words.

स्वस्तिक swastik (*nm*) a benedictory or auspicious mark (卐).

स्वस्थ swasth (*a*) healthy, hale; robust; ~**चित्त** sane, mentally healthy; ~**चित्तता** sanity, mental healthiness; ~**ता** health; healthiness.

स्वहित swahit (*nm*) self-interest.

स्वांग swā:g (*nm*) mimicry; farce, sham; –**बनाना** to mimic; –**भरना, का** to impersonate for, to guise as, to mimic—.

स्वांगी swā:gi: (*a* and *nm*) (a) mimic.

स्वांगी/करण swa:ngi:karān (*nm*) assimilation; ~**कृत** assimilated.

स्वांत:सुखाय swa:ntahsukha:y (*adv*) for one's own happiness.

स्वाक्षर swa:kshar (*nm*) autograph.

स्वागत swa:gat (*nm*) welcome, reception; -**अभिभाषण** welcome address; -**कक्ष** reception room; -**समिति** reception committee; -**समारोह** a reception; **स्वागती** a receptionist; -**करना** to welcome, to receive.

स्वाग्र/ह swa:ggrah (*nm*) self-assertion; ~ **हिता** assertiveness.

स्वातंत्र्य swa:tantry (*nm*) freedom, independence, liberty; ~ **प्रिय** freedom-loving; -**संघर्ष/समर** freedom fight, independence struggle; -**सेनानी** a freedom fighter.

स्वा/ति, ~ती swa:ti, ~ti: (*nf*) the fifteenth of the twenty-seven traditional *nakshatras*; ~**बिंदु** a rain drop in the **स्वाति नक्षत्र**.

स्वाद swa:d (*nm*) taste; flavour, relish; –**खोना** to lose taste; taste to be lost; –**चखना** to taste; –**लेना** to taste; to relish.

स्वादिष्ट swa:disht (*a*) tasteful, delicious, dainty, palatable, relishable; ~**ता** tastefulness, palatability, deliciousness; -**भोजन** dainties; delicious food.

स्वादु swa:du (*a*) see **स्वादिष्ट**; ~**ता** tastefulness, deliciousness.

स्वाधिकार swa:dhika:r (*nm*) one's own right.

स्वाधीन swa:dhi:n (*a*) free, independent, sui juris; ~**ता** freedom, independence, liberty; ~**पतिका** absolute mistress; –**करना** to liberate, to make free.

स्वाध्या/य swa:ddhya:y (*nm*) study; ~**यी** studious.

स्वानुभव swa:nubhav (*nm*) self-experience, personal/individual experience.

स्वानुभूति swa:nubhu:ti (*nf*) self-experience, personal/individual sensibilities.

स्वापक swa:pak (*a*) narcotic.

स्वाभाविक swa:bha:vik (*a*) natural; innate, inherent, inborn; ~**ता** naturality, inartificiality.

स्वाभिमा/न swa:bhimā:n (*nm*) self-respect; ~**नी** self-respecting.

स्वामित्व swa:mittv (*nm*) ownership, proprietorship; -**अधिकार** proprietory/ownership rights.

स्वामिनी swa:minī: (*nf*) mistress; female proprietor, proprietress; patroness; ~, **गृह** wife; housewife.

स्वा/मी swa:mī: (*nm*) master, lord; proprietor, owner; husband; a title used with the name of saints and ascetics (as स्वामी दयानंद); ~मिभक्त loyal, faithful; ~मि-भक्ति loyalty, faithfulness.

स्वाम्य swa:mmy (*nm*) proprietorship, ownership.

स्वायत्त swa:yatt (*a*) autonomous; ~ता autonomy; -शासन autonomous government; ~शासी autonomous; o निकाय autonomous body.

स्वार्थ swa:rth (*nm*) selfishness; self-interest; ~ता selfishness; -त्याग self-denial; ~त्यागी selfless; ~पर/परायण selfish, self-seeking; ~परक selfish, self-seeking; ~परता/परायणता selfishness; egoism; -परमार्थ/परार्थ personal good and universal good; -लिप्सा self-interestedness; ~लिप्सु self-seeking; self-interested; selfish; ~वाद egoism; ~वादी an egoist; egoistic; -साधक a self-seeker; -साधन(ना) self-seeking; ~सिद्धि accomplishment of self-interest; ~हीन selfless; unselfish; ~हीनता selflessness.

स्वार्थांध swa:rtha:ndh (*a*) blinded by selfishness; ~ता utter selfishness, blindness caused by selfishness.

स्वार्थाचार swa:rtha:cha:r (*nm*) jobbery; selfish conduct.

स्वार्थी swa:rthi: (*a* and *nm*) selfish, self-seeking; an egoist.

स्वावलं/बन swa:vlamban (*nm*) self-reliance; self-sufficiency; voluntarism; ~बिता self-reliance; self-sufficiency; ~बी self-relying; self-sufficient.

स्वास्थ्य swa:sthy (*nm*) health; healthiness; ~कर/प्रद wholesome; congenial to health, healthy; sanitary; -मंत्रालय Health Ministry; -मंत्री Health Minister; -रक्षा security of health, maintenance of one's health, -विज्ञान hygiene; -विभाग Health department; -संबंधी sanitary; pertaining to health; -गिरना/बिगड़ना (one's) health to go down; -बनाना to be physically strong, to be growing healthier; to grow stronger.

स्वाहा swa:ha: (*ind*) a word uttered while offering oblation to sacrificial fire; burnt; -करना to ruin/destory, to burn to ashes, -होना to be burnt to ashes, to be ruined/destroyed.

स्विच swich (*nf*) a switch; -बोर्ड a switchboard.

स्वी/करण swi:karan̄ (*nm*) acceptance/accepting; granting; sanctioning; ~कर्ता one who accepts/admits/agrees to grants; ~कार्य acceptable, admissible; sanctionable; ~कार्यता acceptability, admissibility; sanctionability.

स्वीकार swi:ka:r (*a*) accepted; confessed; granted; (*nm*) acceptance; confession; -करना/~ना to accept; to confess; to recognise; to grant; to sanction; to assent, to consent; to acknowledge.

स्वीकारोक्ति swi:ka:rokti (*nf*) confession.

स्वीकृत swi:kkrit (*a*) accepted, approved; granted; sanctioned; -करना see स्वीकार करना.

स्वीकृति swi:kkriti (*nf*) acceptance, sanction, approbation; acknowledgement; consent.

स्वेच्छ swechchh (*a*) arbitrary; voluntary; ~या arbitrarily; voluntarily.

स्वेच्छा swechchha: (*nf*) one's own will, free will, ~चारिता arbitrariness; autocracy; ~चारी self-willed, autocratic; arbitrary; ~तंत्रवाद libertarianism; ~नुसार

according to one's free will; ~पूर्वक, -से voluntarily, of one's own free will; -मृत्यु death according to one's own will.

स्वेद swed (*nm*) sweat, perspiration; -कण/बिंदु a drop of sweat; ~ज sweat-born; -जल sweat; ~न sweating, perspiration.

स्वेदित swedit (*a*) sweated, perspired.

स्वैच्छिक swaichchhik (*a*) voluntary; arbitrary; ~ता voluntarism; arbitrariness.

स्वैर swair (*a*) licentious, self-willed; -कल्पना fantasy; ~चारिता licentiousness, self-willedness; ~चारिणी licentious (woman); ~चारी licentious (man); ~ता licentiousness, self-willedness; -वृत्ति liberum arbitrium, self-willedness.

स्वैराचा/र swaira:cha:r (*nm*) licentious/self-willed conduct, licentiousness; hence ~री (*a* and *nm*).

ह

ह ha—the last and the thirty-third letter of the Devna:gri: alphabet, aspirated in sound.

हँकवा hãkwa: (*nm*) in lion-hunt, the process of driving the lion towards the hunter's station by uproarious beating of drums, cans, etc.

हँकार hãka:r (*nf*) a halloo, calling aloud; hence ~ना (*v*).

हंगामा hanga:mā: (*nm*) uproar, tumult; upheaval, affray, riotous scene; ~पसंद one who likes tumultuousness / riotousness / upheaval; hence ~पसंदी (*nf*).

हंगामी hanga:mi: (*a*) tumultuous, uproarious, boisterous, noisy; emergent (as हंगामी इजलास).

हंटर hanṭar (*nm*) a whip, flog, lash; -जमाना/लगाना to flog, to lash.

हँडना hãḍnā: (*v*) to ramble, to wander, to roam about aimlessly.

हंडा hanḍa: (*nm*) a huge brass pot (for storing water etc.), cauldron; a big gas lantern.

हँड़ि(डि)या haṛi(ḍi)ya: (*nf*) a small earthen pot.

हंत hant (*int*) an interjectional word for expressing sorrow, regret, grief, etc.

हंतव्य hantavy (*a*) worth killing/slaying, fit to be killed.

हंता hanta: (*nm*) a slayer, murderer.

हंस hans (*nm*) a swan, goose; noble/liberated soul; the sun; ~गति gifted with a swan-like gait, walking gracefully; ~गमन graceful gait as that of a swan; ~गामिनी (a woman) blessed with a graceful (swan-like) gait; ~पंक्ति see ~माला; ~पद a script-mark to denote interposition of a word, letter or a symbol in intervening space; ~माला a row of swans; ~यान/वाहन the god Brahmā: (supposed to have a swan for his vehicle); ~वाहिनी the goddess Saraswati; –श्रेणी see ~माला; –उड़ जाना the soul to leave the body. the soul to be liberated of earthly bonds.

हँसना hāsnā: (*v*) to laugh; to deride, to ridicule; to joke; हँसता चेहरा happy face; हँसकर चुप कर देना to laugh down; हँसकर टाल देना/बात उड़ाना to laugh away; हँसते-बोलते while joking, in jokes; हँसते-हँसते while laughing; happily; laughing non-stop; with perfect ease, without any difficulty, ०झेलना to grin and bear it, to take (pain etc.) stoically; ० दोहरा हो जाना/पेट में बल पड़ जाना to laugh into cramps; ० लोट-पोट हो जाना to burst sides with laughing, to burst into an uncontrollable fit of laughter; हँस देना just to laugh; to begin laughing; हँसना-बोलना to exchange pleasantries; to exchange jokes; to talk happily; हँसने लायक worth laughing at, fit to be derided/ridiculed; laughable, amusing; हँस पड़ना to laugh, just to laugh, to begin laughing; हँस-बोलकर बसर कर देना to pass time/live happily.

हँसमुख hāsmukh (*a*) gay, cheerful, having a smiling face.

हँसली hāsli: (*nf*) the collar-bone; an ornament worn around the neck.

हँसाई hāsa:i: (*nf*) derision, ridicule; –कराना to cause derision/ridicule.

हँसाना hāsa:nā: (*v*) to cause to laugh, to amuse.

हंसिनी hansinī: (*nf*) a female swan/goose.

हँसिया hāsiya: (*nm*) a sickle.

हँसी hāsi: (*nf*) laughter; joke; derision, ridicule; -खुशी happily; happiness; -खेल an easy job; fun, fun and frolic; ० समझना to take lightly/as a fun; to think to be easy; -ठट्ठा an easy job; joking and jesting; -ठिठोली joking and jesting; –उड़ना to be made fun of, to be ridiculed/derided; –उड़ाना to make fun of, to ridicule/deride; –छूटना to burst into laughter; –जब्त कर लेना to suppress/restrain laughter; –की बात a laughing matter; –में उड़ाना/उड़ा देना to laugh away/off; –में टालना to laugh away; –में फूल झड़ना to laugh charmingly; –में ले जाना to take as a joke/fun; to take a serious matter as a joke; –समझना to treat as an easy job/as a joke; –सूझना to feel like joking.

हँसुली hāsuli: (*nf*) see हँसली.

हँसोड़ hāsoṛ (*a*) jolly, humorous; (*nm*) jester; hence ~पन (*nm*).

हक hak (*a*) stunned, still; (*nm*) palpitation; –होना to be stunned; to become still; to die.

हक़ haq (*nm*) right; entitlement; due; return (as नमक का हक़ अदा करना); truth, reality; ~तलफ़ी usurpation, depriving somebody of his right; ~दार rightful, entitled; one who has a right; ~दारी right, entitlement; -नाहक़ right and wrong, rightful and wrongful; wrongfully; ~परस्त righteous; ~परस्ती righteousness; –, मौरूसी ancestral right; ~शफ़ा (शुफ़ा) pre-emption; –अदा करना to perform one's duty; –के लिए/–पर लड़ना to fight for one's right; –मारना to deprive of one's due; to usurp one's right; –में in respect of; for; ०कांटे बोना to do an evil turn to; to create obstacles (for).

हकबकाना hakbaka:nā: (*v*) to be

stunned, to be non-plussed.

हकला hakla: (*a* and *nm*) stammering; one who stammers, a stammerer; ~पन stammer/stammering; ~हट stammer/stammering.

हकलाना hakla:nā: (*v*) to stammer.

हका/र haka:r (*nm*) the letter 'ह' and its sound; ~रांत (a word) ending in ह्.

हक़ारत ḥaqa:rat (*nf*) contempt; –की नज़र/निगाह से देखना to treat with contempt/disdain.

हक़ीक़त haqi:qat (*nf*) reality, fact; truth; ~बयानी statement of truth; –खुल जाना the truth to be revealed, to be exposed; –में in reality, really speaking.

हक़ीक़तन haqi:qatan (*ind*) in fact, in reality.

हक़ीक़ी haqi:qi: (*a*) real (as –भाई); true; denotative (as –अर्थ).

हकीम haki:m (*nm*) a physician (trained in the *Unani* system); –खतर-ए-जान, नीम a little knowledge is a dangerous thing.

हकीमी haki:mī: (*nf*) medical practice (through the *Unani* system); the Unani System of medicine.

हक़ीर haqi:r (*a*) contemptuous; small.

हक्का-बक्का hakka:bakka: (*a*) stunned, stupefied; ०रह जाना to be taken aback, to be discomfited.

हगना hagnā: (*v*) to discharge faeces.

हगाना haga:nā: (*v*) to cause to discharge faeces; to weary out.

हगास haga:s (*nf*) a feeling like discharging faeces, inclination to evacuate the bowels; –लगना to feel like discharging faeces.

हज haj (*nm*) a pilgrimage to Mecca; –करना to go on a pilgrimage to Mecca.

हजम hazam (*a*) digested; usurped; –करना to digest; to usurp, to misappropriate; –करके डकार तक न लेना to usurp without leaving a trace; –होना to be assimilated; to be usurped/misappropriated.

हज़रत hazrat (*int*) a vocative term of honour, Sir; (*nm*) a title for eminent men; prophet Mohammed; (*a*) mischievous, cunning; हज़रते दाग़ a capricious man.

हजामत haja:mat (*nf*) shaving; hair-cutting; –बनना to be shaven; to be fleeced; –बनाना to shave; to fleece.

हज़ार haza:r (*a*) one thousand; innumerable; (*nm*) the number one thousand; ~हा thousands; innumerable; –जान से whole-heartedly.

हज़ारा haza:ra: (*nm*) a water-sprinkler, watering can.

हज़ारी haza:ri: (*a*) of, pertaining to or related with a thousand; controlling a thousand (troops etc.).

हज़ारों haza:rō (*a*) thousands; –घड़े पानी पड़ जाना to be immensely ashamed; –में publicly; in a multitude, amongst thousands; ०एक one in a thousand, of incomparable excellence.

हजूम haju:m (*nm*) a crowd, multitude.

हजूर haju:r (*ind*) see हुज़ूर.

हज्जाम hajja:m (*nm*) a barber.

हटकना haṭaknā: (*v*) to restrain, to forbid; to keep under control.

हटना haṭnā: (*v*) to move/go away; to recede; to withdraw; hence हटाना.

हटरी haṭari: (*nf*) an earthen temple-like structure for lighting lamps in (on the occasion of *Diwali*).

हटाव haṭa:v (*nm*) shift, extent of change of position.

हट्टा-कट्टा haṭṭa:-kaṭṭa: (*a*) strong and sturdy, well-built; hale and hearty; hence ०पन (*nm*).

हठ haṭh (*nm*) obstinacy, stubbornness; ~धर्मी intransigence; ~योग a type of Yoga; ~योगी one who practices हठयोग; ~शील obstinate, stubborn; hence ~शीलता (*nf*); –करना/ठानना/पकड़ना to stubbornly stick to some resolve; to become obstinate; –रखना to yield or submit to one's obstinate demand.

हठात् haṭha:t (*ind*) forcibly; suddenly, all of a sudden.

हठी haṭhi: (*a*) obstinate, stubborn.

हठीला haṭhi:la: (*a*) refractory; of obstinate disposition, temperamentally stubborn; ~पन refractoriness; hence हठीली feminine form of हठीला.

हड़ haṛ (*nf*) myrobalan;—an allomorph of हाड़ used as the first member of certain compound words; ~कंप turmoil, panic; terror; ०मचना a great turmoil to occur, reign of terror to ensue; ~फूटन see हड़कन.

हड़क haṛak (*nf*) hydrophobia, rabies; longing, yearning.

हड़कन haṛkan (*nf*) pain in the joints (of the body), lingering ache.

हड़कना haṛaknā: (*v*) to yearn, to long.

हड़का/ना haṛka:nā: (*v*) to turn rabid; ~या rabid; ०कुत्ता a rabid dog.

हड़ता/ल haṛta:l (*nf*) strike; ~ल करना to strike; ~ली a striker.

हड़ना haṛnā: (*v*) to cause aversion, to repel, to be repugnant; to become torturous; to be troublesome.

हड़पना haṛapnā: (*v*) to swallow, to gulp; to purloin; to usurp.

हड़बड़ haṛbaṛ (*nf*) see हड़बड़ी.

हड़बड़ाना haṛbaṛa:nā: (*v*) to be impetuous; to act hastily/in a hurry; to be non-plussed/confused/perplexed.

हड़बड़िया haṛbaṛia: (*a*) impetuous, hasty, rash.

हड़बड़ी haṛbaṛi: (*nf*) impetuosity, hastiness, rashness; –पड़ना to be impetuous/hasty/rash; –सवार होना to be obsessed by haste, to act rashly.

हड्डी haḍḍi: (*nf*) a bone; ~तोड़ परिश्रम rigorous/hard labour; –उतरना a bone to be dislocated; –खुजाना to feel like being thrashed, a beating to be imminent; हड्डियाँ लोहे की होना to have bones of steel, to be very strong; हड्डियाँ तोड़ना to thrash thoroughly; हड्डियाँ दिखाई देना या निकल आना to be reduced to a network of mere bones, to be too much reduced; -पसली एक करना/तोड़ना to thrash thoroughly.

हत hat (*a*) killed; struck; ~चेत rendered unconscious, senseless; ~ज्ञान see ~चेत; ~दैव ill-fated, unlucky; ~बुद्धि rendered senseless/witless, stupid; ~प्रभ out of wits; non-plussed; ~प्राय almost killed; ~बल that has lost its vitality/vigour; ~भाग्य/भागा/भागी unfortunate, luckless; ~मान humiliated, insulted; ~वीर्य bereft of gallantry/bravery; ~संज्ञ unconscious, rendered senseless; ~हृदय dejected, frustrated.

हतक hatak (*nf*) insult; defamation; –इज्जत defamation.

हता/श hata:sh (*a*) despondent, hopeless; ~शा despondency, dejection.

हताहत haṭa:hat (*a*) casualties, killed and wounded.

हतोत्साह hatotsa:h (*a*) demoralised, disheartened.

हत्था hattha: (*nm*) a handle; hand; butt, batten; arm (of a chair).

हत्थमहत्था hatthamhattha: (*nf*) hand to hand fight(ing).

हत्थी hatthi: (*nf*) a handle; palm (of the hand); **–टेकना** to yield, to submit; to lend support.

ह/त्थे hatthe (*ind*) in hand; **~त्थेदार** fitted with/having a handle; **~त्थे चढ़ना/पड़ना** to fall into the clutches (of); **~त्थे पर से कटना** to be swept off completely, to lose every inch of one's ground, to be left with no footing at all; **~त्थे लगना** to obtain; to acquire.

हत्या hatya: (*nf*) murder, assassination; **~कांड** a case of murder/assassination; **–टलना** a botheration/affliction to be put off; a bully to be got rid of; **–पल्ले बाँधना** to involve oneself in a broil/quarrel; to own up a botheration/an affliction; **–मोल लेना** see **–पल्ले बाँधना**; **–पड़ना/–लगना** to earn the sin of a murder; **–सवार होना** to be roused to the point of readiness to kill; to be violently enraged; **–सिर मढ़ना** to level an accusation; to impose an affliction/botheration; **–सिर लेना** see **–पल्ले बाँधना**; to commit a sin.

हत्या/रा hatya:ra: (*nm*) a murderer, an assassin; hence **~रिन**, **~री** (*nf*).

हथ hath—an allomorph of **हाथ** (as in **हथकड़ी**) and **हाथी** (as in **हथसार**) as it appears in many compound words; **~उधार** unrecorded short-term cash loan; **~कंडा** sleight; trick, tactics; intrigue; **~कंडे दिखाना** to show one's tricks; to give evidence of tactical capabilities; **~कटा** having a hand dismembered; **~कड़ी** handcuffs; **~कड़ी डालना** to handcuff; to arrest; **~कड़ी पड़ना** to be handcuffed; to be arrested; **~कल** a spanner; **~गोला** a hand-grenade; **~चल** an adept in pinching things, a swindler; **~छुट** in the habit of striking forthwith out of provocation; **~फेर** see **~उधार**; **~बना** hand made; **~बुना** hand-spun; **~लपक** one who pinches things, a swindler; **~लिखाई** hand-writing; hand lettered.

हथनाल hathnā:l (*nf*) a light cannon.

हथसार hathsa:r (*nf*) a stable for elephants.

हथिनी hathinī: (*nf*) (fem. form of **हाथी**) a she-elephant.

हथियाना hathiya:na: (*v*) to usurp, to grab, to seize, to acquire by force.

हथियार hathiya:r (*nm*) a weapon, arms; **~घर** an arsenal, armoury; **~बंद** armed, equipped with arms; **~बंदी** armament; **–उठाना** to take up arms; **–डालना** to strike one's colours/flags, to surrender; **–बाँधना** to equip oneself with arms, to be armed.

हथेली hatheli: (*nf*) palm of the hand; **–खुजाना/खुजलाना** lit. palm to itch—a happy augury for an income; an inkling for inflicting a beating; **–देना/लगाना** to lend support; **–पर जान/सिर रखना या लिये फिरना** to risk one's life; **–पर जान होना** to be exposed to risk of life; **–पर दही जमाना** to strive for instant accomplishment of a job; **–पर सिर रखना** to undertake a risk of life, to expose one's life to danger; **–पर सरसों जमाना** to accomplish a task within an impossible span of time; –पर सरसों नहीं जमती Rome was not built in a day; –पीटना/बजाना to laud/to revel by clapping; –में छेद होता है money burns hole in (one's) pocket.

हथौटी hathauṭi: (*nf*) manual dexterity/skill; imprint of a skilful hand;–जमना/सधना to acquire skill in a manual work.

हथौड़ा hathauṛa: (*nm*) a hammer, malleus; –चलाना to strike with a hammer; hence हथौड़ी—a hand/small hammer.

हद had (*nf*) limit/limitation, boundary; extent; ~बंदी delimitation; demarcation; –कर देना/करना to commit an excess; to reach the farthest limit; –पार करना to cross the limit; –बाँधना to draw the line at, to set a definite limit; –से गुज़रना to cross the limit; –से ज़्यादा beyond the limit; too much; to a fault; ०खुल जाना to take liberties/freedom with.

हदीस• hadi:s (*nf*) traditional sayings of prophet Mohammed.

हनन hanān (*nm*) slaughter, killing, assassination, murder.

हन/ना hananā: (*v*) to kill, to slay, to slaughter, to assassinate; hence ~नीय (*a*).

हनु hanu (*nf*) the chin, jaw-bone, ~मान/मंत the monkey god who was one of the mightiest generals in the army of Ra:m that invaded Ra:vāṇ's Lanka: (as narrated in the great epic Ra:ma:yāṇ).

हप hap (*nf*) the sound produced in striking the two lips together; –कर जाना/करना to gulp/swallow the whole thing.

ह/फ़्ता hafta: (*nm*) a week; ~फ़्तेवार/~फ़्तेवारी weekly.

ह/ब्शी habshi: (*nm*) a negro; hence ~ब्शिन (*nf*).

हबीब habi:b (*a*) dear, darling.

हम ham (*pro*) we—plural form of the first person pronoun मैं; (*a*) similar; equal; together; ~उम्र contemporary; of equal age; ~ख़्याल having similar views/ideas; ~जिंस co-professional; ~ज़ुल्फ़ married to sisters; husband of wife's sisters; ~जोली associate or companion, of the same age-group; ~दम a friend; ~दर्द sympathetic; a sympathizer; ~दर्दी sympathy; ~नाम namesake; ~पेशा co-professional; ~बिस्तर sharing bed (with); sexually related; ~बिस्तरी going to bed together, having sexual intercourse; ~मज़हब a co-religionist; ~राज़ a confidant; ~राह travelling together; ~राही a co-traveller; ~वतन a compatriot; ~वार even; ~शक्ल having similar looks/appearance, exactly resembling (each other); ~सफ़र a co-traveller, travelling together; ~सर equal; ~सरी equality; ~साया a neighbour; ~सिन see ~उम्र.

हमल hamal (*nm*) conception, pregnancy; –गिराना to cause an abortion; –रहना to conceive, to become pregnant.

हमला hamla: (*nm*) attack, assault; ~वर an invader, an assailant, aggressor; –बोलना to launch an attack.

हमारा hama:ra: (*pro*) possessive form of हम—our, ours.

हमाहमी hamā:hamī: (*nf*) manipulation for selfish ends, mad race for self-gratification; –करना to manipulate for selfish ends, to indulge in a mad race for self-gratification.

हमें hamē (*pro*) the objective and dative form of the first person plural pronoun हम—to us.

हमेल hamel (*nf*) a typical necklace of gold and silver coins.

हमेशा hamesha: (*ind*) always, ever,

हम्माम hammā:m (*nm*) a warm-bath, bagnio.

हम्माल hamma:l (*nm*) a porter, coolie.

हयंद hayand (*nm*) horse (of a good breed).

हय hay (*nm*) a horse; ~शाला a stable.

हया haya: (*nf*) shame, sense of shame; modesty; ~दार modest; ~दारी modesty.

हयात haya:t (*nf*) life.

हर har (*a*) each, every; (*nm*) a denominator; Lord Shiv; a suffix imparting the meaning of one who or that which takes away/deprives/seizes; –एक everyone, each and every; –कहीं everywhere; –कोई every one all and sundry; ~चंद however much; ~जाई flirt, disloyal (woman); –तरह in every way/manner; –तरह से down to the ground, in all respects, thoroughly; ~दम always, ever; ~दिल अज़ीज़ liked/loved by all, popular; ~फ़नमौला a jack of all trades; ~फ़नमौला हर फ़न अधूरा jack of all trades master of none; –मर्ज़ की दवा heal-all, a panacea; –रोज every day, daily.

हरकत harkat (*nf*) movement, activity; mischief; –करना to (make a) move; –में लाना to make things hum, to activate things.

हरकारा harka:ra: (*nm*) a courier; dak-runner.

हरगिज़ hargiz (*ind*) ever, under any circumstances; –नहीं never, under no circumstances.

हरचंद harchand (*ind*) all possible, in every way; to the farthest extent.

हरज haraj (*nm*) see हर्ज (हर्ज)

हरजा harja: (*nm*) see हर्जा.

हरजाना harja:nā: (*nm*) see हर्जाना.

हरड़ harar̤ (*nf*) myrobalan.

हर/ण harān (*nm*) kidnapping, abduction, forcible carrying away, seizing; as a suffix it imparts the meaning of one who or that which carries away, seizes or takes by force, rids, etc.; ~णीय fit to be kidnapped/abducted/taken away by force.

हरताल harta:l (*nf*) yellow orpiment; –फेरना to undo, to efface.

हरदा harda: (*nm*) yellow rust.

हरना harnā: (*v*) to kidnap, to abduct, to carry away by force, to seize.

हरबा harba: (*nm*) arms, tools; -हथियार arms and ammunition; ०से लैस होना to be equipped with arms and ammunition.

हरम haram (*nm*) a harem, female apartment; ~सरा a harem.

हरमज़दगी haramzadgi; (*nf*) bastardy, rascality, scoundrelism.

हरसाना harsa:nā: (*v*) to be happy/pleased/amused.

हरसिंगार harsinga:r (*nm*) a particular sweet-smelling flower and its plant.

हरहा harha: (*nm*) a plough-bull; (*a*) troublous (animal).

हरा hara: (*a*) green, verdant; fresh; gay, delighted; ~पन greenness; verdancy; hence हरी (fem. form); ०खाद green manure; -भरा verdant; prosperous, flourishing; gay; –करना, (मन) to delight; –होना,

(मन) to be delighted, to be gay.

हराना hara:nā: (*v*) to defeat, to vanquish.

हराम hara:m (*a*) ill-begotten; unlawful, forbidden; improper; ~कार lewd, debauch; hence ~कारी (*nf*); ~खोर subsisting on ill-begotten resources or on others' earnings; slothful, basely indolent; ~खोरी subsistence on ill-begotten resources; slothfulness, base indolence; ~जादा ill-begotten; bastard; rascal, scoundrel; hence ~जादी; ~जादापन see हरमजदगी; –कर देना to make (things) difficult/impossible; –का ill begotten; –का खाना to subsist on ill-begotten resources or on others' earnings; –का पेट ill-begotten pregnancy; –का माल illegitimate earnings; –की कमाई ill-begotten earnings/money; –होना to be difficult/impossible.

हरामी hara:mī: (*a*) ill-begotten, illegitimate; unscrupulous; doing just nothing, utterly indolent; (*nm*) a bastard, rascal, scoundrel; ~पन/पना illegitimacy; unscrupulousness; utter indolence; –का पिल्ला/बच्चा son of a bastard/scoundrel.

हरारत hara:rat (*nf*) temperature; feverishness; –होना to be feverish, to have slight temperature.

हरावल hara:wal (*nm*) vanguard; –दस्ता vanguard.

हरि hari (*nm*) Lord Vishnū/Krishnā; –इच्छा the will of God; ०बलवान inevitable is the will of God; -कथा the tales of God's incarnations and activities; -कीर्तन individual or collective singing of the eulogies of हरि; ~तालिका the third day of the bright fortnight of the month of भादों when women observe fast; ~धाम the heaven—abode of हरि; ~नाम name(s) of हरि; ०स्मरण remembering the names of हरि; -भक्ति devotion to हरि; -मंदिर a temple of हरि; ~लीला the playful sport of हरि; -स्मरण remembering हरि; -हर Lords Vishnū and Shiv.

हरिजन harijan (*nm*) an untouchable; –उद्धार uplift of the *harijans*.

हरि/ण harin (*nm*) a deer; hence ~णी (*nf*).

हरित harit (*a*) green, verdant; delighted, gay.

हरिद्रा haridra: (*nf*) turmeric, curcuma.

हरियल hariyal (*a*) greenish; unripe (as a fruit).

हरियाना hariya:nā: (*v*) to turn green, to be full of verdure; to be delighted; (*nm*) one of the northern Hindi-speaking states of the Union of India.

हरियाली hariya:li: (*nf*) greenery, verdure; vegetation; –तीज the third day of the latter half in the month of भादों; –छाना to be verdant all round; –ही हरियाली दीखना to sense happiness all round.

हरीतिमा hari:timā: (*nf*) greenery, verdure, verdancy.

हरीरा hari:ra: (*nm*) a kind of sweet potage prepared from milk and other ingredients.

हरूफ़ haru:f (*nm*) a letter (of the alphabet).

हरे hare (*int*) O God!; –कृष्ण O Krishnā, ! O God!; –राम O Ra:m, O God!

हरेक harek (*a*) everyone, everybody.

हर्ज, ~र्जा harz, ~za: (*nm*) harm; loss, damage; –करना to cause harm/loss/damage; –होना to be put to harm/loss/damage.

हर्जाना harza:nā: (*nm*) damages, compensation, indemnity; –देना/-भरना to pay damages.

हर्ता harta: (*nm*) a kidnapper, abductor, one who carries away forcibly, usurper.

हर्फ़ harf (*nm*) a letter (of the alphabet); -ब-हर्फ़ literal; letter by letter; –आना to be accused/blamed; –लाना to cause an accusation to be levelled or a blame to devolve on.

हर्म्य harmmy (*nm*) a palace, a palatial mansion.

हर्र harr (*nf*) myrobalan; –लगे न फिटकरी रंग चोखा आये to invest nothing, to gain everything.

हर्ष harsh (*nm*) joy, jubilation, mirth, delight, happiness; ~कर/~कारक exhilirating, causing happiness/delight; ~गद्गद् overwhelmed by joy, (with) voice choked with joy; ~ध्वनि/नाद/स्वन cry of joy/jubilation; ~विह्वल overwhelmed by joy.

हर्षातिरेक harsha:tirek (*nm*) ecstasy, rapture, excessive joy.

हर्षातिशय harsha:tishay (*nm*) see हर्षातिरेक.

हर्षाना harsha:nā: (*v*) to be full of joy, to be delighted.

हर्षित harshit (*a*) joyous, delighted, cheerful.

हर्षोत्फुल्ल harshotphull (*a*) full of joy, in a rapture.

हर्षोन्माद harshonmā:d (*nm*) ecstasy, rapture.

हलंत halant (*a*) (a word) ending in a consonant (and not a vowel).

हल hal (*nm*) a plough; solution; ~जीवी a farmer/peasant; –करना to solve.

हलक़ halaq (*nm*) the throat; windpipe; –तक भरना to be full to the throat; –पर छुरी फेरना to cut somebody's throat; to cause immense loss; –से नीचे उतरना to be comprehensible (as बात); to appear reasonable.

हलका halka: (*a*) light; cheap (as हलका आदमी; हलकी बात); thin (as कपड़ा); faint; (*nm*) a circle, area; -अफ़सर a circle officer; ~पन lightness; cheapness; thinness; –करना to insult, to cause humiliation; –पड़ना to prove lesser; –बनना/होना to be cheap; to be disgraced; –बांधना to envelope/encircle; to fix an area (for work etc.).

हलकान halka:n (*a*) troubled, bothered; tired, fatigued.

हलकोर halkor (*nf*) a massive billow.

हलचल halchal (*nf*) commotion, hustle; agitation, movement; –मचना a commotion to be created; –होना movement to take place; commotion to be caused.

हलदिया haldia: (*a*) yellow; (*nm*) jaundice; a variety of big yellowish frog.

हलदी haldi: (*nf*) turmeric, curcuma; –के हाथ होना marriage to take place; –लगाकर बैठना to sit idle.

हलफ़ halaf (*nm*) an oath; ~दरोग़ी self-contradiction; ~नामा an affidavit; –उठाना to swear, to take an oath; –देना to give an oath; –लेना to take an oath.

हलफ़न halfan (*adv*) on oath.

हलफ़िया halfia: (*a*) see हलफ़ी.

हलफ़ी halfi: (*a*) (statement etc.) given on oath.

हलराना halra:nā: (*v*) to fondle, to

caress, to dandle.

हलवा halwa: (*nm*) a typical Indian pudding; ~सोहन a celebrated Indian sweetmeat; (अपने) -मांडे से काम होना to be worried only about one's own bread and butter.

हलवाई halwa:i: (*nm*) a sweetmeat manufacturer/seller, confectioner.

हलवाहा halwa:ha: (*nm*) a farmer, peasant.

हलहलाना halhala:nā: (*v*) to shake violently.

हलाक hala:k (*a*) slaughtered, slain; –करना to slaughter, to slay; –होना to be slaughtered, to be slain.

हलाल hala:l (*a*) legitimate; hard-earned, well-begotten; (*nm*) an animal slaughtered in accordance with conventional prescription; ~ख़ोर subsisting on scrupulous earnings/well-begotten earnings; a sweeper; ~ख़ोरी subsistence on scrupulous earnings/well-begotten earnings; –करके खाना to subsist on hard-earned money; –करना to slaughter in the conventionally prescribed manner; to do slowly to death; –का legitimate; scrupulous, well-begotten; –की कमाई hard-earned income.

हलाहल hala:hal (*nm*) deadly poison.

हलुआ, हलुवा halua:, haluwa: (*nm*) see हलवा.

हलोर halor (*nf*) a heave; billow.

हलोरना halornā: (*v*) to cause turmoil/agitation (within a liquid by hand etc.); to winnow.

हल् hal (*nm*) a pure consonant; a symbol appended at the foot of a letter to denote devowelized consonant (्).

हल्का halka: (*a* and *nm*) see हलका.

हल्दी haldi: (*nf*) see हलदी.

हल्ला halla: (*nm*) noise, uproar, tumult, tumultuous activity; -गुल्ला uproarious scene, tumult and uproar; –बोलना to raid; –मचाना to create a noise/uproar; to cause a tumultuous scene.

हवन hawan (*nm*) a fire sacrifice; ~कुंड a sacrificial pit.

हवलदा/र hawalda:r (*nm*) a havildar; ~री the job or office of a havildar.

हवस hawas (*nf*) lust, passion, passionate longing; –निकालना to have it out; a longing to be fulfilled; –बुझना a passion to subside, longing to die out; –होना to have passion (for), to be lustful.

हवा hawa: (*nf*) air, wind, breeze; ~ख़ोरी a stroll, walk; ~चक्की a wind-mill; ~दार airy; well-ventilated; ~दारी ventilation; -पानी climate; ~बाज़ an airman; a tall-talker, braggadocio; ~बाज़ी airmanship; tall talk, bragging; ~मार anti-aircraft; ~मार तोप an anti-aircraft gun; ~सह wind-proof; -सा very slight, flimsy; –उखड़ना to suffer a set-back to one's reputation; –उड़ना a rumour to be afloat; news to go round; –उड़ाना to give currency to a rumour; to make a false propaganda; –का गुज़र न होना to be inaccessible/impossible (for anyone or anybody) to pass through; –का रुख़ जानना to know which way the wind is blowing; –का रुख़ देखना to see which way the cat jumps, the cult of jumping cat; to have/keep an ear to the ground; to fly a kite; to wait and watch; to move according to the whirligig of time; –का रुख़ बताना to forecast the shape of things to come; –के घोड़े पर सवार होना to be in a terrible hurry; –के रुख जाना to flow downstream; to move in the direction of the wind; to move according to the times; –खाना to go for a walk, to enjoy fresh air; to fail to achieve; (कहीं की) –खाना to go/pay a visit (to a particular place); –खिलाना to cause to fail; to inflict failure; (कहीं की)–खिलाना to cause to go (to a particular place); –गरम होना the air to have a touch of warmth; to be in great demand; –गिरना to have a slump/depression; –छोड़ना to dismiss foul air; –देखकर पीठ देना to take a turn after assessing the turn of events, to judge things and act accordingly; –देखना to watch which way the wind blows; –देना to instigate, to provoke; –न लगने देना to allow none to have an inkling of; –पलटना the shape of things to undergo a change; the direction of the wind to change; –पीकर/फाँक कर रहना to go without meals (said ironically); –फेंकना to discharge a jet/blast of air; –निकालना to deflate; ~बंद airtight; –बदलना things to change; –बँधना the air to become still; a reputation/name to be earned; –बताना to try to tell off; to dilly-dally; –बाँधना to earn a reputation/name; to boast, to brag; –बिगड़ना the atmosphere to be polluted/poisoned; to be in a tight corner; –भर जाना to be inflated; to be puffed up, to be full of pride; –लगना to feel the touch of air; to be possessed (by an evil spirit); to be puffed up; to be influenced by; –लगना, किसी की to have an adverse effect of somebody's company; –से बातें करना to be moving at a terrible speed; to talk in the air; –से लड़ना to be out to pick up a quarrel; to fight without any provocation/without the existence of a second party; to be too truculent; –हो जाना to disappear; to flee, to run away.

हवाई hawa:i: (*a*) aerial; false, imaginary; –अड्डा an aerodrome, airport; –करतब aerobatics; –क़िला/महल imaginary things, castle that exists in the air; –क़िले बनाना to build castles in the air; –ख़बर/बात a rumour; –छतरी a parachute, an air umbrella; –जहाज़ an aeroplane, aircraft; –डाक airmail; –धावा an air attack; –फ़ायर fire in the air; –मार्ग/रास्ता airways, air-passage; –मुठभेड़ aerial encounter; –यात्रा air journey; –युद्ध/लड़ाई air warfare; –संरक्षण air umbrella; –हमला an air raid/attack; हवाइयाँ उड़ना, चेहरे/मुँह पर the face to lose all lustre, to appear non-plussed.

हवाल hawa:l (*nm*) conditions; news.

हवा/ला hawa:la: (*nm*) a reference; trust, custody; ~ला देना to cite a reference; ~ले करना to entrust, to hand over (to).

हवाला/त hawa:la:t (*nf*) lock-up, (police) custody; ~ती under (police) custody, in (police) lock-up; ~त की हवा खाना to be sent behind the bars.

हवाली-मवाली hawa:li:mawa:li: (*nm*) (in a derogatory sense) comrades and companions, rag-tag.

हवास hawa:s (*nm*) senses (used only as the second number in the compound होश-हवास).

हवि havi (*nm*) see हविष्य.

हविष्य havishy (*a* and *nm*) (oblations) offered to gods or to the sacrificial fire.

हवेली haweli: (*nf*) a (palatial) mansion.

हव्य havvy (*a* and *nm*) (fit to be offered as) oblation (to the sacrificial fire).

हशमत hashmat (*nf*) glory and grandeur; huge paraphernalia.

हशीश hashi:sh (*nf*) hashish (see भंग).

हश्र hashshr (*nm*) consequence, result; ultimate end.

हसद hasad (*nm*) jealousy, malice.

हसरत hasrat (*nf*) wistfulness, longing, craving; desire; **~मंद** having a longing/craving, desirous; **-भरा** wistful, full of longings; **–करना** to long/crave for; **–टपकना** longing/craving to be manifest/apparent; **–निकलना/पूरी होना** a longing/craving to find its fulfilment; **–निकालना** to have it out; to see one's longing/craving materialised; **–बाक़ी रहना** a longing/craving to remain unfulfilled.

हसीन hasi:n (*a*) beautiful, pretty; charming.

हस्त hast (*nm*) a hand; trunk of an elephant; **-कला** handicraft; **-कार्य** manual work; **-कौशल** manual skill; **~गत** in hand, obtained, received; **~मैथुन** masturbation; **-रेखा** the lines of one's palm (supposed to signify one's destiny); **-लाघव** manual skill; **~लिखित** hand-written, in manuscript form; **~लिपि/लेख** hand. handwriting; manuscript.

हस्तक hastak (*nm*) a handle

हस्तक्षेप hastakshep (*nm*) interference; **–करना** to interfere.

हस्तांत/रण hastā:ntarāṇ (*nm*) transfer/transference; **~रित** transferred (to another hand); **~रणीय** transferable; **~रणीयता** transferability.

हस्ताक्ष/र hasta:kshar (*nm*) signature; hand-writing; **~रकर्त्ता** signatory; **~रित** signed.

हस्तामलक hasta:malak (*nm*) lit. 'the fruit or seed of the emblic myrobalan' in the hand'—absolutely clear and readily comprehensible; **~वत्** like –, clear and readily comprehensible/understood.

हस्ती hasti: (*nf*) existence, being; worth; personage; (*nm*) an elephant; **–खोना** to lose existence; **–मिटना** to be ruined, to be forced out of existence; **–होना** to be existent; to be worth reckoning.

हस्ते haste (*ind*) through, through the agency of.

ह/स्ब hasb (*ind*) according to, in accordance with; **~स्बे-जाबता** according to law; **~स्बे-जैल** as per details below; **~स्बे-मामूल** as usual.

हहा haha: (*nf*) sound produced while laughing; humble entreaty; **–करना** to make humble entreaties.

हाँ hā: (*nf*) yes, yea; (*ind*) a word-denoting agreement, fulfilment, affirmation, etc ; **हाँ-हाँ** yes, yes; a word expressing negation/affirmation that would depend on its intonation); **~जी-हाँजी करना** to chime in; to keep on flattering; **–में हाँ मिलाना** to keep on flattering, to say 'yes' to everything, to chime in; **–हाँ करना** to affirm, to say 'yes'.

हाँक hā:k (*nf*) bawling; calling aloud; **–देना/मारना/लगाना** to call aloud, to bawl.

हाँकना hā:knā: (*v*) to drive (an animal or an animal-driven vehicle);

to goad, to urge on; to call aloud.

हाँका ha:ka: (*nm*) in hunting, an uproar (through beating of drums, cans, etc) to drive the prey towards the spot where the hunter is seated.

हाँड़ना hā:ṛnā: (*v*) to roam about, to loiter.

हाँड़ी hā:ṛi: (*nf*) a small earthen pot; –**पकना** things in a pot to boil; a plot to be hatched.

हाँफना hā:phnā: (*v*) to pant, to breathe heavily.

हाँफनी hā:phnī: (*nf*) panting; –**छूटना** to start panting, to be breathing heavily.

हा ha: (*int*) oh !, Gosh !, a particle expressive of pleasure, pain, regret, contempt, amazement, etc.; a Persian suffix which imparts plurality (as **बारहा, हज़ारहा,** etc.).

हाइफ़न ha:ifan (*nm*) a hyphen.

हाई ha:i: (*a*) high; –**कोर्ट** a high court; –**स्कूल** a high school.

हाकि/म ha:kim (*nm*) a ruler; boss; ~**माना** befitting a ruler/officer/boss; ~**मी** rule, ruling; work as an officer; ~**म से बैर कैसा,** ~**म से बैर तो कहाँ की खैर** kings have long hands.

हा(हॉ)की ha:(ɔ)ki: (*nf*) hockey.

हाजत ha:jat (*nf*) need, requirement; pressure in the bowels; ~**मंद** needy; hence ~**मंदी** (*nf*); –**रफ़ा करना** to satisfy one's needs; to discharge faeces.

हाजती ha:jti: (*nf*) a urine-pot; (*a*) desirous.

हाज़मा ha:zma: (*nm*) digestion; –**खराब होना** digestive system to be upset, the stomach to be upset.

हाज़िम ha:zim (*a*) digestive.

हाज़िर ha:zir (*a*) present; ready; ~**जवाब** quick-witted, witty; ~**जवाबी** quick-wittedness, ready wit; -**नाज़िर** present and watching; **हाज़िरीन** pl. form of **हाज़िर**—those present (as **हाज़िरीन-ए-जलसा** those present in the meeting); –**में हुज्जत नहीं** to be in my hands, is to be at your disposal.

हाज़िरी ha:ziri: (*nf*) presence; attendance, roll call; breakfast; –**देना** to notify/intimate one's presence; –**बजाना** to dance attendance upon; –**लेना** to have the roll call, to mark attendance.

हाजी ha:ji: (*nm*) a Mohammedan who has been to the haj pilgrimage.

हाट ha:ṭ (*nf*) a temporary and periodic market; (improvised) market-place, bazar, mart; –**उठना** the market to be wound up; things to come to an end; –**करना** to go marketing; -**बाज़ार करना** to go out making purchases, to go out marketing; –**लगना** marketing activity to commence; a bazar to come up.

हाटक ha:ṭak (*nm*) gold.

हाड़ ha:ṛ (*nm*) a bone; –**पेलना** to work assiduously/very hard.

हाता ha:ta: (*nm*) see **अहाता**.

हाथ ha:th (*nm*) a hand; manual skill; the skill to strike; turn (in a game of cards); handle; arm (of a chair); –**आँखों से लगाना** to give immense respect (in admiring an artistic masterpiece); –**आगे करना** to stretch out the hand (to give or take something); –**आज़माना** to have a fling at; to try one's hand; -**आना** to have in hand, to come under control; to gain; –**उठाकर कहना** to take a vow, to pledge; –**उठाना, किसी पर** to lay hands on, to beat, to inflict a beating; –उठा बैठना to strike all of a sudden; –उठा लेना to throw up one's hands; –उतरना the arm-bone to be dislocated; –ऊँचा करना to be bounteous; to be a spendthrift; to pray for; to bless; –ऊंचा रहना to have an upper hand; to be in a position to oblige; –ओछा पड़ना a stroke not to be full-blooded; –कंगन को आरसी क्या the obvious needs no evidence; –कट जाना to be helpless; to be helpless on account of a commitment; –कटा देना/लेना to be rendered helpless through a commitment; –कलम करना to dismember a hand; –का काम the work in hand; handiwork; –का खिलौना a puppet, a tool in the hands (of); –का झूठा dishonest in dealings; in the habit of pinching things; unreliable in money matters, –का दिया gifted away; –कानों पर रखना to vow not to repeat; to vow never to do again; to swear incompetence to do; –का मैल (money) to be of no consequence, to be too trivial an object; –का सच्चा honest in one's dealings, reliable in money matters; –की कठपुतली see –का खिलौना; –की बात, (किसी के) something that one can do, something within one's capability; –की लकड़ी a support; –की सफ़ाई manual skill; nimbleness of the hand; finnesse in one's stroke; –के तोते उड़ जाना to be stunned, to be extremely nervous; –के नीचे आना to fall into one's clutches, to be under the control (of); –को हाथ नजर न आना/सूझना to be pitch dark; –को हाथ पहचानता है an empty hand is no lure for a hawk; ~खर्च pocket-money, personal expenses; –खाना to be slapped/struck; –खाली जाना a stroke/chance to be missed; a trick/device not to work; –खाली न होना to be busy; to have no time; –खाली होना to be penniless/in utter penury; to be free, to have no work in hand; –खींचना/खींच लेना to withdraw support/active association; to refrain from financial aid/support; to wash one's hands off; to draw/pull in one's horns; –खुजलाना to be a good augury for incoming money; to feel like slapping/beating; –खुलना to be bounteous; to be a spendthrift; to have money in hand; to be in the habit of striking readily; –ख़ून से रंगे होना hands to be stained in blood, to have committed murder; –गलना to be benumbed by cold; –गले में डालना to throw an arm embrace round the neck; to caress, to fondle; –चढ़ना to fall into the clutches of, to come under the control (of); –चलना to be nimble-fingered, to be quick at work; to be in the habit of beating/striking (others); –चूमना lit. to kiss one's hand—to be all praise for somebody's handiwork; –छोड़ना to (begin to) strike; –जड़ना to implant a slap, to strike; –जमना a slap to be implanted, a stroke to be given; to have one's hand firmly (in); finnesse/perfection in a handiwork to be acquired; –जमाना to slap, to strike; to acquire finnesse/perfection in a handiwork; –जोड़कर with cap/hat in hand, humbly; –जोड़ देना to fold hands (—as symbolic of acceptance of defeat); to beg pardon; –जोड़ना to salute by folded hands; to present one's compliments; to entreat, to make an entreaty; to request forgiveness; (ironically) to have nothing to do any more; –झाड़ना to give a slap; to go on striking; to show that one has no money on his person, to show one's pennilessness; –झूठा पड़ना to miss a stroke; an expert hand to lose its efficaciousness; to be rendered incapable for manual work; –डालना (किसी काम में) to take in hand, to undertake a work; –डालना, किसी पर to have a fling at, to launch an attack on; to strike; –डालते हिचकिचाना to shiver on the brink, to hesitate to plunge; –तंग होना to be tight, to be in a financial stringency; –तक न हिलना not to do a hand's turn, not to make the slightest effort; –थामना to provide support, to intercept (beating); –दबना to be in a crisis/in hot waters; to be in a tight corner; –दबाकर खर्च करना to spend discreetly/with proper restriction; –दिखाना to give a proof of one's efficacy; to get one's palm read (by a palmist); –देखना to witness one's efficacy/mettle; to read somebody's palm; –देना to lend a hand; –धोकर पीछे पड़ना to go heart and soul after; to concentrate all efforts to inflict harm on; –धोना, धो बैठना to lose, to write off; –धोना, बहती गंगा में to make capital out of; to turn to personal advantage; –न उठाना to hold one's hand, to refrain from punishing (or other action); –न धरने देना to yield to no persuasion/entreaties/arguments; to allow no quarter whatever; –नब्ज/नाड़ी पर होना to feel the pulse of, to know in and out; –न सूझना, (हाथ को) to be pitch dark; –पकड़ते पहुँचा पकड़ना to try to turn small concession into big liberties; to strive for ever bigger benefits out of someone; –पकड़ना see –थामना; –पकड़े की लाज रखना to stand by a commitment for protection till the end; –पड़ जाना/–पड़ना to fall into the hands (of), to come one's way; to obtain without effort; to be slapped; –पर क़ुरान/पर गंगाजल रखना to swear by the Qoran/by the holy water of the Ganges; –पर तोता पालना to ever nurse a wound etc; to allow a wound/boil etc. to persist; –पर धरा रहना/होना to be kept in readiness; –पर हाथ धरकर बैठ जाना to be complacent; to be frustrated; –पर हाथ धरे बैठे रहना to be utterly complacent, to sit idly; –पर हाथ मारना to make a commitment, to enter into a mutual agreement; –पसारना to beg; to make an entreaty for help; –पसारे जाना to go empty-handed (to the other world); -पाँव का जवाब देना to be incapacitated, to be rendered incapable (through disease or old age); -पाँव चलना to be industrious; to be capable to work; -पाँव जोड़ना to make humble entreaties; -पाँव ठंडे होना to be on the verge of death; to pass away; to be stupefied/stunned; -पाँव ढीले होना to be rendered muscleless/languid, to be wearied; -पाँव पीटना to make futile efforts; -पाँव फूलना to look blue, to be in a flutter, to be nervous; to lose one's wits; -पाँव फैलाना to extend one's scope/sphere of influence, to gather more and more power; to grow; -पाँव बचाना to keep oneself secure, to keep out of risk; –पाँव मारना to make (frantic) efforts; to try one's level best; -पाँव रह जाना the limbs to be benumbed/to be incapacitated; -पाँव सीधे करना to relax the limbs; -पाँव हारना to be incapacitated; to be demoralised; -पाँव हिलाना to work, to do something; –पीले करना to give away in marriage; –फेर देना to pinch, to pilfer; –फेरना to fondle, to caress; –फैलाना to beg, to extend a needy hand for help; –बँटाना to lend a hand, to cooperate, to help/extend cooperation; –बचाना to defend oneself against a stroke; –बढ़ाना to extend a hand; –बाँधे खड़े रहना to serve somebody hand and foot, to be at somebody's beck and call; to be always in attendance, to be at the service of; –बिकना/बिकाना to be a slave to, to be in utter subservience; –बेचना to sell out to; –बैठना to acquire finnesse in/practice of/expertise in; to be hit with full vigour; –भर का कलेजा होना to have immense courage; to be in raptures; –भर की जबान होना to be too intemperate in speech, to be insolently outspoken; –भरना the hands to be wearied; –भेजना, (के) to send through; –मँजना to acquire a finnesse (in doing a thing); –मजबूत करना to strengthen the hands of; –मलना to be remorseful; –मारना to pinch; to take a bet; to acquire control over/possession of; –मिलना to shake hands (with); –में in hand; –में खुजली होना to feel like beating (somebody); (an omen which bids fair for a monetary gain) to anticipate a monetary gain; –में पड़ना see –आना; –में लाना see में करना; –में नकेल होना to be under the control of, to move at the behest of; –में बागडोर होना to have control over, to hold the reins of; –में मेंहदी लगी होना to be absolutely idle; –में लेना to take up; –में सनीचर होना to be prone to lose everything; –में हाथ hand in hand; –में हाथ देना to give away in marriage; –में हाथ होना to be with; to be under the protection of; –में हुनर होना to be skilled in (a handiwork); –में होना, (के) to be under the sway of; –रँगना to stain one's hands with a sin/misdeed; to take a bribe; –रखना, सिर पर to give protection; –रवाँ करना होना to get one's hand in to become at home in; –रवाँ रखना to keep one's hand in; –रह जाना the hand(s) to be benumbed; -रोकना to cause hindrance; to slacken the pace of work; to restrain from striking; –लगना to blunder upon; to find by fluke; to be touched by hand; (a work) to be initiated; –लगाना to touch; to commence a work; to lay hands on, to slap; –लगाये कुम्हलाना to be as tender as touch-me not; –लगा मैला होना to be as shining as to be rendered untidy by mere touch; –समेटना see –खींचना; –साधना see –आजमाना; –साफ़ करना to polish off, to consume; to misappropriate; to put to death; –साफ़ होना to have clean hands; to have finnesse (in work); to be misappropriated; –सिर पर रख कर रोना to be full of remorse, to weep and wail; –सिर पर रखना to swear by; –से जाना/निकलना to slip/get out of hand, to lose; –से दिल जाना

to lose heart to, to fall for; –से बे हाथ होना to get out of hand/control; –हिलाते आना to come empty-handed; –होना to have in; हाथों में खेलना to play somebody's game, to play in the hands of; (दोनों) हाथों समेटना to amass huge wealth; हाथोंहाथ from hand to hand, in no time; –उठा लेना to give a rousing welcome, to receive with utmost readiness; ० बिक जाना to sell like hot cakes, to have a hot sale; ० लेना to receive with great warmth; to extend a very cordial reception.

हाथा ha:tha: (*nm*) see हत्था.

हाथा/पाई, ~बाँही ha:tha:pa:i:, bā:hī: (*nf*) a scuffle, skirmish, tussle; ~पाई पर उतर आना to come to blows, to sfart a scuffle.

हाथी ha:thi: (*nm*) an elephant; a jumbo; castle/rook (in the gamc of chess); (*a*) too fat; huge; ~खाना a stable for elephants; ~दाँत ivory; tusk ०का सामान ivory goods; ~पाँव elephantiasis; ~वान see महावत; –की टक्कर हाथी ही सँभाले only an elephant can bear the elephant's load; –के दाँत खाने के और दिखाने के और what is obvious is not always the ultimate truth; -घूमे गाँव-गाँव जिसका हाँथी उसका नाँव an elephant will be known by the name of his owner wherever he may be; –निकल गया मगर दुम रह गई eaten a horse and tail hangs out; –पर चढ़ना to be very rich; to go high up; to earn tremendous reputation; –बाँधना to maintain an elephant; –हो जाना to become very corpulent/ plump.

हादसा ha:dsa: (*nm*) an accident, a mishap; –गुजरना an accident/mishap to occur.

हानि ha:nī (*nf*) loss; damage; detriment; harm; ~कर/~कारक/~कारी damaging: harmful; detrimental; –उठाना to sustain a loss/damage; –पहुँचाना to harm, to cause damage to.

हाफ़िज ha:fiz (*nm*) a protector; a Mohammedan who remembers the whole of the Qoran by heart.

हामिला ha:mila: (*a*) pregnant (woman).

हामी ha:mī: (*nf*) assent, acceptance; (*nm*) a supporter; champion (of); ~दार an underwriter; ~दारी underwriting; –भरना to say 'yes', to give assent (for).

हाय hay (*int*) oh ! ah me !, alas!; also a particle expressive of mental or physical agony; (*nf*) curse (as किसी की हाय न लो); -तोबा loud protestation; havoc, uproar, bewailing, –दैया O, God ! Gos h!; -हाय see हाय; affiction; rush (of work etc.—as हर वक्त हाय-हाय पड़ी रहती है); panic and confusion; –हाय करना to be rushed; to be afflicted; -हाय पड़ना utter panic and confusion to prevail; –करके रह जाना to be obliged to suffer mental or physical agony; –पड़ना a curse to come true; –होना to be jealous (of somebody's prosperity, progress, etc.).

हार ha:r (*nf*) defeat; loss; a garland, necklace; a suffix meaning one who or that which carries away per force or usurps, charms, etc; or denotes a doer (as सिरजनहार);-जीत defeat and victory; –खाना to suffer a defeat; –देना to inflict a defeat; –न मानना never say die, not to give in; –मानना

to cry enough, to acknowledge defeat, to concede supremacy.

हारक ha:rak (*a*) who carries away per force, usurps or charms.

हारना ha:rnā: (*v*) to be defeated, to lose; to be wearied; हारा-थका worn and wearied.

हारमोनियम ha:rmonīam (*nm*) a harmonium.

हारा ha:ra:—a suffix carrying the sense of a doer (as सिरजनहारा); (*a* and *v*) defeated; –हुआ जुआरी lit. a defeated gambler – a man in a completely reticent unresponsive state of mind, frustrated and lost (man).

हारिल ha:ril (*nm*) a typical green-coloured bird; –की लकड़ी a constant companion.

हार्दिक ha:rdik (*a*) cordial, hearty; ~ता cordiality; heartiness.

हाल ha:l (*nm*) state; condition; account; news; a hoop, metallic tyre over a wooden wheel; turmoil; violent vibration/agitation; a hall; (*a*) present, current; -चाल general condition, state of affairs; news; –का recent; fresh; –में for the time being; in the near past/ future; recently; –पतला होना to be in a terrible affliction.

हाल/त ha:lat (*nf*) state, condition; ~त पतली होना to be in a miserable plight; ~त संगीन होना to be in a critical state; हालात conditions, circumstances.

हालाँकि ha:lā:ki (*ind*) though, although.

हाला ha:la: (*nf*) wine, liquor.

हाली ha:li: (*a*) current, contemporary.

हाव ha:w (*nm*); -भाव gestures, blandishments; amorous dalliance (of a woman).

हावी ha:vi: (*a*) dominant; –होना to dominate.

हाशि/या ha:shiya: (*nm*) margin; border; fringe; ~ये पर on the margin/fringe.

हास ha:s (*nm*) laughter/laughing, derisive laughter, fun, joke; the abiding emotion of हास्य रस; ~कर inspiring laughter; -परिहास fun and humour.

हासिल ha:sil (*a*) acquired, obtained; what is carried forward; –जमा total; –करना to acquire, to obtain; –होना to be acquired, to be obtained.

हास्य ha:ssy (*nm*) humour; ridicule, fun; –कथा a humorous tale; ~कर/ कारक/जनक humorous; provoking laughter; -कौतुक fun and humour; -चित्र a cartoon; ~चित्रकार a cartoonist; –भाव sense of humour; –रस the final and successful culmination of the sense of humour (हास्य) into a *rasa*; ~रसात्मक full of or abounding in हास्यरस; –रूपलेख humorous feature; -व्यंग्य humour and satire/wit.

हास्यास्पद ha:ssya:spad (*a*) ludicrous, ridiculous, funny; ~ता ludicrousness, funniness.

हास्योत्पादक ha:ssyotpa:dak (*a*) ludicrous, ridiculous, funny; hence ~ता (*nf*).

हाहा ha:ha: (*nf*) (sound produced by) loud laughter; entreaties, humble supplication; (*int*) a particle expressive of amazement, grief, etc; –ठोठी joke and jest, fun and humour; –हीही see –ठीठी; ० करना to have humour and hilarity; ० मचाना/० होना to have a bout of jokes and jests; –हूह loud laughter and hilarity; –करना/खाना to make humble entreaties/supplication; –मचना/होना to have fun and hilarity.

हाहाकार ha:ha:ka:r (*nm*) loud lamentation, distressful commotion, tumult, uproar.

हिंगु hingu (*nm*) asafoetida—a tree or the poignant-smelling ooze from its root.

हिंडो/रा, ~ला hiḍora:, ~la: (*nm*) a swing, sway.

हिंद hīnd (*nm*) India.

हिंदवी hīndvi: (*nf*) a name used for the Hindi language by mediaeval writers.

हिंदसा hindsa: (*nm*) a digit, number.

हिंदी hīndi: (*nf*) the Hindi language; (*a*) Indian; –न फ़ारसी मियाँ जी बनारसी the ass waggeth his ears.

हिंदुत्व hīndutt v (*nm*) Hinduism; the state of being, or characteristics of, a Hindu; –की भावना the spirit of Hinduism.

हिंदुस्ता/न hīndusta:n (*nm*) India; ~नियत Indian-ness.

हिंदुस्तानी hīndusta:nī: (*a*) Indian; belonging to central parts of India—esp. Uttar Pradesh; (*nm*) an Indian, native of India; a native of Uttar Pradesh; (*nf*) a theoretically existent style of the Hindi language which is supposed to consist of current and simple words of any sources whatever and is neither too much biassed in favour of Perso-Arabic elements nor has any place for too much high-flown Sanskritized vocabulary; –संगीत Hindustani classical music (as distinct from Carnatic).

हिंदुस्था/न hīndustha:n (*nm*) India; ~नी (an) Indian.

हिंदू hīndu: (*nm* and *a*) (a) Hindu; ~पन/~पना Hinduism; the state of being, or characteristics of, a Hindu.

हिंदो/ल, ~ला hindol, ~la: (*nm*) a sway.

हिंदोस्तान hīndosta:n (*nm*) see हिंदुस्तान.

हिंदोस्तानी hīndosta:nī: (*nm* and *a*) see हिंदुस्तानी.

हिंसक hinsak (*a*) violent (person); ferocious, fierce; (*nm*) a murderer, killer; –जंतु/पशु ferocious beast/animal; hence ~ता (*nf*).

हिंसा hīnsa: (*nf*) violence; ~त्मक violent (act, etc.); hence ~त्मकता (*nf*); ~रत violent, committing violence; ~लु/शील violent, fierce; ~लुता/शीलता violence, fierceness.

हिंस्र hīnsr (*a*) violent, fierce, ferocious; –जंतु/पशु ferocious beast/animal; ~ता violence; fierceness.

हिकम/त hikmat (*nf*) medical practice under the Unani system; a contrivance; manoeuvring; ~ती manoeuvring, pastmaster at manipulation.

हिक़ारत hiqa:rat (*nf*) contempt; –की नज़र contemptuous look; –से देखना to cast a contemptuous look, to look down upon.

हिचक hichak (*nf*) hitch, hesitation; shilly-shally.

हिचकना hichaknā: (*v*) to hesitate, to hitch; to shrink; to shilly-shally.

हिचकिचा/ना hichkicha:nā: (*v*) see हिचकना; to make two bites of a cherry; ~हट hesitation, hitch; shilly-shally.

हिचकी hichki: (*nf*) hiccup; –बँध जाना/हिचकियाँ बँध जाना/हिचकियाँ लेना to have a fit of hiccup; to have non-stop hiccuping; to sob bitterly.

हिचको/ला hichkola: (*nm*) a jerk; jolt; ~ले लगना to receive jolts, to be jolted again and again.

हिज/ड़ा hijṛa: (*nm*) eunuch; (*a*) impotent; ~ड़ा बनाना to emasculate, to castrate; ~ड़े के घर बेटा goat's wool.

हिजरी hijri: (*nf*) the Mohammedan era (which commences from the day of Prophet Mohammed's flight from Mecca to Medina on the 15th July, 622 A. D.).

हिज्जे hijje (*nm*) spelling; -करना to spell.

हिज्र hijjr (*nm*) separation.

हित hit (*nm*) welfare, well-being; interest; gain, benefit; ~कर beneficial, useful, advantageous; ~कारक see ~कर; ~कारी see ~कर; a benefactor; ~चिंतक a well-wisher, benefactor; ~चिंतन well wishing, being concerned about somebody's welfare.

हिताकां/क्षी hita:ka:ṅkshi: (*a* and *nm*) well-wishing; (a) well-wisher; hence ~क्षिता (*nf*).

हितार्थी hita:rthi: (*a* and *nm*) well-wishing; (a) well-wisher.

हिताहित hita:hit (*nm*) good and bad.

हितू hitu: (*a*) see हितैषी

हिते/च्छा hitechchha: (*nf*) well-wishing; ~च्छु see हितैषी.

हितै/षी hitaishi: (*a* and *nm*) well-wishing; a well-wisher; ~षणा see हितेच्छा; ~षिता well-wishing.

हिदायत hida:yat (*nf*) instruction; ~नामा a manual of instructions, series of instructions.

हिनहिना/ना hinhinā:nā: (*v*) to neigh, to whinny; ~हट neighing, whinnying.

हिना hina: (*nf*) myrtle.

हिफ़ाज़त hifa:zat (*nf*) protection, security, safety; -करना to guard, to safeguard, to defend/protect/secure.

हिफ़ाज़ती hifa:zati: (*a*) protective; -कार्यवाही protective measures.

हिफ़्ज़ hifz (*a*) memorised, committed to memory; -करना to memorize, to commit to memory.

हिब्बा hibba: (*nm*) a gift, present; ~नामा a gift deed.

हिम him (*nm*) snow, ice; frost; ~कंदुक a snow-ball; ~कण a snow-particle; ~कर the moon; ~काल ice age; ~क्षेत्र snowfield, ~गिरि the Himalayas; -चादर an ice-sheet; ~च्छद an ice-cap; -झंझावात a snow-storm; ~नद an esker; ~नदी a glacier, an ice-river; ~पुंज an ice-pack; ~पात/प्रपात ice/snow-fall; ~बद्ध ice-bound, snow bound; ~बाधित ice/snow-bound; -मानव snow-man; ~युग the ice-age; ~लव snow flakes; -रेखा snow-line; ~लंब icicle; ~वर्तिका icicle; ~वर्षा freezing rain; snow-fall; ~वृष्टि snow-fall; ~शिखर ice-cap; ~शैल an iceberg; ~श्वेत snowhite; -संचय/संघात a snow-heap; ~सागर an ice-sea; -स्फटिक ice-crystal.

हिमवान himwa:n (*nm*) the Himalayas.

हिमांध himā:ndh (*a*) snow-blind; ~ता snow-blindness.

हिमांशु himā:nshu (*nm*) (an epithet of) the moon.

हिमाक़त hima:qat (*nf*) stupidity, foolishness, idiocy.

हिमाचल hima:chal (*nm*) the Himalayas; -प्रदेश a centrally-administered northern state of the Union of India.

हिमाच्छन्न hima:chhann (*a*) snow-clad, snow covered.

हिमाद्रि hima:ddri (*nm*) see हिमालय.

हिमानी himā:nī: (*nf*) a glacier; an avalanche.

हिमाभ himā:bh (*a*) snowy, appearing like snow.

हिमाय/त hima:yat (*nf*) support, backing; defence, protection; **~ती** a supporter; defender, protector, patron.

हिमालय hima:lay (*nm*) the Himalayas.

हिमावृत hima:vrit (*a*) snow-capped, snow-clad.

हिम्मत himmat (*nf*) courage, boldness; **-अफ़ज़ाई** encouraging/encouragement; **~वर** courageous; hence **~वरी** (*nf*); **–छूटना/जवाब देना/टूटना/पस्त होना** (one's) courage to be exhausted; to yield; **–न हारना** to hold up one's head; **–पड़ना** to have the cheek; to feel upto; to muster courage (to); **–बढ़ाना** to encourage; to allow liberty, to cause to be cheeky; **–बाँधना** to screw/pluck up courage; to gather resolution; **–से काम लेना** to put a good/bold face on; **–हारना** to lose courage, to be demoralised; **हिम्मते मर्दां मददे ख़ुदा** God helps those who help themselves.

हिम्मती himmati: (*a*) courageous, bold.

हिय; ~रा hiy, ~ra: (*nm*) the heart, bosom.

हिया hiya: (*nm*) the heart, bosom; courage; **–काँपना** to be terribly fear-stricken, to be struck with extreme terror; **–जलना** to be angry; to be full of jealousy; to suffer extreme agony; **–ठंडा होना** to be gratified, to feel assuaged (on account of an adversary's distress); **–फटना** to have the heart rent by deep sorrow; **–भर आना** to be moved by emotion; **हिये का अंधा** having no mental vision; block-headed, foolish; **हिये की फूटना** to lose one's senses/wits, to become absolutely witless; **हिये लगाना** to embrace.

हिरण hirāṇ (*nm*) a deer, an antelope.

हिरण्मय hirāṇmay (*a*) golden; (made) of gold.

हिरण्य hiraṇny (*nm*) gold; **~गर्भ** an epithet of Brahmā:, mythologically born of a gold egg.

हिरन hiran (*nm*) a deer, an antelope; **–हो जाना** to take to heels, to flee; to disappear.

हिरनौटा hirnāuṭa: (*nm*) a young deer.

हिर फिर hir phir; **–कर** to turn up again like a bad half-penny.

हिरमजी hirmaji: (*nf*) a kind of red clay.

हिराना hira:nā: (*v*) to be lost; to vanish.

हिरासत hira:sat (*nf*) custody; **–में करना/लेना** to take into custody; **हिरासती** under custody.

हि/र्स hirs (*nf*) (spirit of) competition, envy; greed; **~र्सी** having a spirit of competition, envious; greedy.

हिलको/र, ~रा hilkor (*nf*), ~ra: (*nm*) a surge, billow.

हिलना hilnā: (*v*) to move; to shake; to swing; to get very familiar; **-डोलना** to move; to be physically active; **-मिलना** to have intimacy with, to associate with; **हिल-मिलकर** with a friendly/cooperative spirit.

हिलाना hila:nā: (*v*) to move; to shake; to jolt; to swing; to cause to get very intimate.

हिला-मिला hila:mila: (*a*) on intimate terms.

हिलोर, ~रा hilor (*nf*), ~ra: (*nm*) a surge, billow; **–उठना** to surge;

हिलोरें लेना to surge.

हिल्लोल hillol (*nf*) a surge, billow.

हिसाब hisa:b (*nm*) arithmetic; account; calculation; rate; manner, custom, ·किताब account(s); ०करना to account for, to settle or work out the accounts; ०बैठना things to be adjusted, things to veer round; –, टेढ़ा difficult affair; ·बही an account-book, a ledger; –करना, पाक/बेबाक to pay off, to clear the account; –चुकता करना/चुकाना to square accounts with; to clear off all the accounts or dues; –तलब करना to call for accounts; to ask for an explanation; –देना to render accounts; to explain; —में चढ़ना to be entered into the account book/ledger; –बैठना the account to tally; things to veer round; –बैठाना to tally the accounts; to make necessary coordination; –लेना to ask to render the account; to ask for an explanation; –साफ़ करना to clear off the account (of); –से properly, proportionately; considering all the pros and cons.

हिसाबी hisa:bi: (*a*) calculative; well-versed in arithmetic/calculations.

हिस्टीरिया histi:riya: (*nm*) hysteria; ~ग्रस्त hysteric.

हिस्सा hissa: (*nm*) part, portion; share; division; -बखरा portion; share.

हिस्सेदा/र hisseda:r (*nm*) a co-sharer, partner; shareholder; ~री partnership, co-sharing.

हींग hī:g (*nf*) asafoetida.

हीं-हीं hī:-hī: (*nf*) grinning, sound of subdued laughter.

ही hi: (*ind*) only, solely, alone; none but.

हीक hi:k (*nf*) stench; –मारना to stench.

हीजड़ा hi:jṛa: (*nm*) see हिजड़ा.

हीन hi:n (*a*) inferior, worthless, deficient; used as the second member in compound words to mean devoid or divested of; ~कर्म/~कर्मा one involved in low deeds, vicious; ~कुल low-born; –ग्रन्थि inferiority complex; ~चरित vicious, wicked, immoral; ~ता/~त्व inferiority; deficiency; ०ग्रन्थि see –ग्रंथि; –पक्ष weak side; weak aspect; ~बल/वीर्य emasculated, impotent; feeble; ~बुद्धि/मति a stupid, nitwit; –भावना inferiority complex, feeling of inferiority.

हीनहया/त hi:nhaya:t (*nf* and *adv*) (during the) life-time; ~ती for the whole life.

हीनांग hi:nā:ṅg (*a*) cripple/crippled.

हीर hi:r (*nm*) pith, essence, quintessence; see हीरा.

हीरक hi:rak (*nm*) a diamond; –जयंती diamond jubilee.

हीरा hi:ra: (*nm*) a diamond; –आदमी a good egg, a gem amongst men; –चाटना, हीरे की कनी चाटना to commit suicide (by licking a diamond or diamond particle).

हीरो hi:ro (*nm*) a hero.

हीरोइन hi:roin (*nf*) a heroine.

हीला hi:la: (*nm*) evasion; pretext; pretence/pretension; ·हवाला dilly-dally, shilly-shally, evasion; pretence; ०करना to dilly-dally/shilly-shally; to feign, to pretend; –गरान बहाना बिसियार he who has a mind to beat his dog will easily find a stick, if you want to throw a stone every lane will furnish one.

हीलेबाज hi:leba:z (*a* and *nm*) pretending; a pretender.

हो-ही hi:-hi: (*nf*) grinning, sound of subdued laughter.

हुं hū (*int*) a particle denoting assent, yes.

हुंकार hūṅka:r (*nm*) roaring, bellowing; loud sound produced by a man to express menacing disposition or readiness to fight/strike; –भरना to roar, to bellow; to express resolution to fight; to give a call for a fight.

हुंकारी hūṅka:ri: (*nf*) to show assent by uttering 'हुं'; –भरना to utter 'हुं' for expressing assent.

हुंकृति hunkkriti (*nf*) see हुंकार.

हुंड़ार hūṛa:r (*nm*) a wolf.

हुंडी hūṇḍi: (*nf*) a bill of exchange, draft; –सकारना to honour/accept (a bill of exchange).

हुक huk (*nm*) a hook.

हुकुम hukum (*nm*) see हुक्म.

हुक़ूक huqu:k (*nm*) plural of हक़—rights.

हुकूमत huku:mat (*nf*) government; rule; jurisdiction;–करना to govern, to rule; –चलाना to run a government; to order about; –जताना to show one's authority/eminence; to try to order about.

हुक़्क़ा huqqa: (*nm*) a hubble-bubble; -पानी social intercourse; ०बन्द करना to freeze out, to completely boycott, to excommunicate, to cease to have social intercourse; ~बरदार an attendant who carries a (refill for the) hubble-bubble; ~बरदारी to fill a hubble-bubble; to render menial service; –भरना to render (menial) service to; to flatter.

हुक्काम hukka:m (*nm*) plural form of हाकिम—officers; rulers.

हुक्म hukm (*nm*) order, command; one of the suits in playing cards—the spade; ~उदूली disobedience, defying orders; –, जो as you command !; ~नामा an edict, a written order; ~बरदार an obedient servant; loyal; ~बरदारी carrying out of orders; loyalty; ~रान rulers; commanding authority; ~रानी rule, government; –तामील करना to obey or carry out one's order; –चलाना to issue an order; to order about; to rule/govern; –तोड़ना to disobey an order, to violate one's authority; –बजाना to carry out one's order; –मानना to obey one's order; –में होना to be obedient/subservient to.

हुक्मी hukmī: (*a*) imperative, mandatory; pertaining to an order; –बंदा obedient servant.

हुजूम huju:m (*nm*) a crowd, multitude; –खड़ा करना to raise a crowd.

हुज़ूर huzu:r (*int*) your honour, your majesty, your lordship !; Sir !; (*nm*) gracious presence; ·ए-वाला your lordship, your honour !; –में in the court (of); in the gracious presence of.

हुज़ूरी huzu:ri: (*nf*); ~, जो sycophancy, servile attitude.

हुज्ज/त hujjat (*nf*) altercation, wrangling; pugnacity; fuss; ~ती altercating, wrangling; pugnacious; a fuss-pot.

हुड़क huṛak (*nf*) pining, longing.

हुड़कना huṛaknā: (*v*) to pine, to fret

हुड़का huṛka: (*nm*) pining, fretting.

हुड़दं/ग huṛdaṅg (*nm*) commotion, uproar, tumult; ~गी uproarious, riotous, commotive; ~ग मचाना to cause an uproar/tumult.

हुत hut (*a*) thrown into fire (as an oblation); sacrified.

हुताग्नि huta:gnī (*nf*) oblation fire.
हुतात्मता huta:tmata: (*nf*) martyrdom.
हुतात्मा huta:tmā: (*nm*) a martyr.
हुनर hunar (*nf*) art, craft; skill; ~मंद an artist; skilful, skilled; ~मंदी artistry; skilfulness.
हुब्बुलवतनी hubbulwatanī: (*nf*) patriotism, love of the motherland.
हुमकना humaknā: (*v*) to thrust; to dance about with joy, to be hilarious.
हुमा humā: (*nf*) an imaginary bird of paradise.
हुमेल humel (*nf*) a kind of necklace.
हुरमत hurmat (*nf*) honour, dignity.
हुरहुर hurhur (*nm*) a kind of medicinal plant.
हुर्रा hurra: (*int*) hurrah !
हुलसना hulasnā: (*v*) to be hilarious; to be full of joy/aspirations; to look pretty.
हुलास hula:s (*nm*) hilarity; joy; aspiration.
हुलिया huliya: (*nf*) physical features; description; –बताना to describe the physical features (of a missing, absconding person etc.); –टाइट/तंग होना to be in very hot waters; to be terribly afflicted; –बिगाड़ना to knock into a cocked hat, to harass no end; to put into very hot waters.
हुल्लड़ hullaṛ (*nm*) shemozzle, tumult, uproar; ~बाज one who causes uproar/tumult; ~बाजी causing tumultuous scenes/shemozzle; –करना/मचाना to raise a tumult, to kick up a row.
हुश hush (*int*) hush !; keep silent !; don't do !.
हुस्न husn (*nm*) beauty, prettiness; ~परस्त a lover of beauty; ~परस्ती love of beauty; –का आलम age of superb beauty; times or world of superb beauty.
हूँ hū: (*ind*) yes; (*v*) am.
हूँठा hū:ṭha: (*nm*) three and a half.
हूँसना hū:snā: (*v*) to curse.
हूक hu:k (*nf*) haunting agony, smarting pain/affliction.
हूकना hu:knā: (*v*) to have smarting pain; to suffer from a haunting agony.
हूबहू hu:bahu: (*a*) exactly alike, similar in all respects, on all fours on.
हूर hu:r (*nf*) a fairy; beauty, very beautiful woman; –की परी a superb beauty.
हूश hu:sh (*a*) rustic, rude, uncivil; ~पन/~पना rusticity, rudeness, incivility.
हृत hrit (*a*) taken away, stolen, pilfered; ~ज्ञान out of wits, stupefied; ~सर्वस्व rendered penniless, who has lost his all.
हृत्कंप hritkamp (*nm*) palpitation.
हृदयंगम hridayaṅgam (*a*) taken to heart; mentally assimilated.
हृदय hriday (*nm*) the heart; core, best part; darling (person); ~कंप palpitation, heart-throb; ~गत/स्थ taken to heart, mentally assimilated; ~ग्राही captivating, charming; ~ज्ञ who knows the heart, penetrating into the mind; -दौर्बल्य weakness of heart, faint-heartedness; ~विदारक heart-rending; ~वेधी heart-piercing, causing extreme anguish or mental agony; ~शून्य/हीन dry, hard-hearted, unfeeling; ~स्पर्शी pathetic, touching, moving; ~हारी charming, attractive, gripping; –को छूना to touch one's heart, to move; –फटना/विदीर्ण होना the heart to

rend, to be anguished; –से लगाना to embrace; to give a warm welcome.

हृदयाकाश hridaya:ka:sh (*nm*) lit. the sky of the heart—the mental canvas.

हृदये/श, ~श्वर hridayesh, ~shwar (*nm*) lit. the lord of one's heart–dear one; dear husband/lover; hence ~श्वरी (*nf*).

हृदयोन्मादिनी hridayonma:dinī: (*a*) causing erotomania; captivating the heart.

हृद्गत hridgat (*a*) gone into the heart, well-comprehended, assimilated.

हृद्रोग hridrog (*nm*) heart-disease.

हृद्व्यथा hridvyatha: (*nf*) mental anguish, agony.

हृषीकेश hrishi:kesh (*nm*) an epithet of Lord Vishṇū or Krishṇā.

हृष्ट hrisṭ (*a*) glad, delighted, pleased; -पुष्ट stout, robust.

हेंगा hẽga: (*nf*) a (field) leveller.

हें-हें hẽhẽ (*nf*) grinning sound (of laughter); making humble entreaties, imploring; –करना to laugh in subdued tones; to beseech/implore in an humble manner.

हे he (*ind*) a vocative particle.

हेकड़ hekaṛ (*a*) hubristic; unyielding, stubborn; exercising force.

हेकड़ी hekṛi: (*nf*) hubris, arrogance; stubbornness; exercise of coercion, show of force/strength; -जताना/दिखाना to show arrogance, to be hubristic; to apply coercion; –भूल जाना hubristic attitude to be shed away; to lose all one's wits.

हेच hech (*a*) worthless, trifling.

हेठा heṭha: (*a*) inferior, low, mean; ~पन inferiority, meanness, lowness.

हेठी heṭhi: (*nf*) humiliation, insult, indignity; –करना to humiliate/insult, to heap indignity on;–होना to suffer humiliation/insult/indignity.

हेड heḍ (*a*) head; –ऑफ़िस head office; ~क्वार्टर headquarter; ~मास्टर headmaster; ~मास्टरी headmastership.

हेतु hetu (*nm*) reason, cause; motive; -कथा etiological tale; ~ता/त्व causation, causativeness, existence of cause or motive; ~वाद a statement of reasons or arguments, assigning of cause; ~विज्ञान/विद्या/शास्त्र teleology, science of logic; ~वैज्ञानिक teleologist; teleologistic; ~शास्त्री a teleologist; ~सिद्ध telesis.

हेत्वाभास hettva:bha:s (*nm*) a fallacy; sophism.

हेमंत hemānt (*nm*) the winter season.

हेम hem (*nm*) gold; ~कांति glittering like gold.

हेमाभ hemā:bh (*a*) having the lustre of gold.

हेरना hernā: (*v*) to search; to see; -फेरना to change the order.

हेर-फेर her-pher (*nm*) interchange; change; rotation; manipulation, unscrupulousness; –करना to vary, to make alterations/amendments; to make unscrupulous changes.

हेराफेरी hera:pheri: (*nf*) manipulation, unscrupulous activity.

हेलमेल helmel (*nm*) intimacy, close relationship.

हेलीमेली heli:meli: (*nm*) a friend, an intimate person.

हैं haĩ (*v*) are; (*ind*) no, what is this; a particle showing astonishment, negation or non-acceptance.

हैंडबैग haĩṇḍbaig (*nm*) a handbag.

हैंडिल haĩṇḍil (*nm*) a handle.

है hai (*v*) is.

हैगा haiga: (*v*) see है.

हैज़ा haiza: (*nm*) cholera; –होना to have an attack of cholera.

हैट haiṭ (*nm*) a hat.

हैतुक haituk (*a*) having a cause or reason, founded on some motive; also हैतुकी; (*nm*) a rationalist.

हैरत hairat (*nf*) amazement, astonishment; ~अंगेज़ amazing, astonishing; ~ज़दा amazed, astonished.

हैरान haira:n (*a*) tired, wearied; perplexed, confounded; amazed, astonished; –करना to harass.

हैरानी haira:nī: (*nf*) surprise, amazement; botheration, trouble; weariness; harassment.

हैवा/न haiva:n (*nm*) an animal; savage, brute, beast; ~नात plural of हैवान; ~नियत beastliness, brutality, savagery; हैवानी beastly, savage, brutal.

हैसियत haisiyat (*nf*) status; capacity; –के अनुसार according to status; –से, की/ ~, ब in the capacity of; ~दार/मंद having a status.

होंठ hoṭh (*nm*) see ओठ; –काटना/चबाना to be full of wrath; –सी जाना to be dumbfounded, to be speechless; –फड़कना lips to tremble (through intense emotional strain); –बिचकाना to show contempt/dislike (by movement of lips); –हिलाना to move the lips; to commence speech.

हो/टल, ~टेल hoṭal, ~ṭel (*nm*) a hotel.

होठ hoṭh (*nm*) see ओठ.

होड़ hoṛ (*nf*) competition, race; bet; –लगाना to enter into a competition, to have a race/rivalry.

होड़ा-होड़ी hoṛa:hoṛi: (*nf*) competition; (*adv*) by way of or through competition/rivalry.

होतव्य hotavvy (*a* and *nm*) destined to happen, the inevitable, predestined; ~ता inevitability, destiny.

होता hota: (*nm*) one who offers oblation (to the sacrificial fire).

होतृ hottri (*nm*) see होता.

होनहार honha:r (*a*) promising; (*nm*) the inevitable, destiny; –बिरवान के होत चीकने पात coming events cast their shadows before.

होना honā: (*v*) to be; to occur, to happen; to exist; to be born; –, एक समय में to synchronize, to be synchronous; हो न हो probably, perhaps, in all likelihood, may be; हो चलना to be well on the way; हो चुकना to be finished; होना-हवाना to be done, to happen; हो रहना, किसी का to belong to somebody; हो लेना, किसी के साथ to accompany somebody.

होनी honī: (*nf*) destiny, predestination; the inevitable; –के बस में, तीन लोक the entire universe is bound by destiny.

होम hom (*nm*) a sacrifice; an oblation fire; ~कुंड a pit for oblation fire; -सामग्री the articles for putting into the oblation fire; –करते हाथ जलना to do a good turn and earn a bad name; –करना to perform a sacrifice, to offer oblation to fire.

होमियोपै/थ homīyopaith (*nm*) a homoeopath; ~थिक homoeopathic; ~थी (the science of) homoeopathy; practising medicine through the homoeopathic system.

होरसा horsa: (*nm*) a flat and round piece of stone used for rubbing sandalwood or for rolling breads.

होला hola: (*nm*) green gram.

होलिका holika: (*nf*) the **होली** festival; ~**दहन** burning of the pile of fuel on the occasion of **होली**.

होली holi: (*nf*) a Hindu festival celebrated on the last day of the month of **फागुन** when coloured water is thrown on one another; **-खेलना** to throw coloured water (on); **-जलाना** to make a bonfire (of).

होल्ड-ऑल/होल्डाल holḍɔl, holḍa:l (*nm*) a hold-all.

होल्डर holḍar (*nm*) a holder.

होश hosh (*nm*) sense, consciousness; **-हवास** see **होश**; **-आना** to come to senses; to regain consciousness; **-उड़ना/उड़ जाना/काफ़ूर या गुम होना/जाते रहना/फ़ाख़्ता होना/हवा होना/हिरन होना** to be frightened out of one's senses, to be at one's wit's end, to lose wits, to be thoroughly confounded; **-करना** to recollect; to be alert; **-की दवा करो** sell your ass; get your head shaved !; come to senses !; talk sense !; **-खोना** to lose one's wits/senses, to become senseless; **-ठिकाने आना/होना** to come to senses; to be fixed in one's proper place, to learn a lesson; **-न रहना** to be unconscious, to lose senses; **-में आना** to come to senses; to gain consciousness; **-में लाना** to bring round; to restore to consciousness; **-रखना** to be careful, to retain wits; **-रहना** to continue to be in senses; to be conscious; **-सँभालना** to gain consciousness; to come of age; **-से बाहर होना** to lose senses; to be unconscious; to lose one's wits through anger; **-होना** to be in senses.

होशियार hoshiya:r (*a*) clever, wise, intelligent; careful; **-रहना** to be careful/alert.

होशियारी hoshiya:ri: (*nf*) cleverness, wisdom, intelligence; carefulness.

होस्टल hosṭal (*nm*) a hostel.

हौंस haũs (*nf*) craving, longing; deep aspiration.

हौआ haua: (*nm*) see **हौवा**.

हौज़ hauz (*nm*) a tank, reservoir (of water etc.); sink.

हौद haud (*nm*) see **हौज़**.

हौदा hauda: (*nm*) an open or covered seat placed over an elephant; a pond; see **हौज़**.

हौदी haudi: (*nf*) a small tank, reservoir; sink.

हौल haul (*nm*) fear, dread; a hall; ~**दिल** stunned, terrified; ~**दिली** a stunned state, state of utter nervousness; ~**नाक** stunning, fearful, dreadful.

हौली hauli: (*nf*) a liquor shop, tavern.

हौले-हौले haule-haule (*adv*) slowly; gently; quietly.

हौवा hauwa: (*nm*) a bogey, bugbear; scare-crow; a scare—word used for frightening children.

हौसला hausla: (*nm*) courage; morale; **हौसलेमंद** courageous; ~**अफ़ज़ाई** encouragement; **-करना** to take courage, to pluck courage; **-तोड़ना** to throw cold water on, to demoralise, to discourage; **हौसले निकालना** to have it out; to gratify all one's longings; **-पस्त होना** to be demoralised.

ह्रस्व hrassv (*a*) short, small; **-स्वर** a short vowel.

ह्रास hra:s (*nm*) decay; fall, downfall; diminution; ~**मान** decaying, falling, suffering a downfall.

ह्रासोन्मुख hra:sonmukh (*a*) decaying, diminishing, decadent; **–अवस्था** decadent state; **–संस्कृति** decadent culture; **~ता** decadence; **–राष्ट्र** a decadent nation; **–सभ्यता** a decadent civilization.

ह्विस्की wiski: (*nf*) whisky.

ह्वेल wel (*nf*) a whale.